# Lecture Notes in Computer Science 16000

The series Lecture Notes in Computer Science (LNCS), including its subseries Lecture Notes in Artificial Intelligence (LNAI) and Lecture Notes in Bioinformatics (LNBI), has established itself as a medium for the publication of new developments in computer science and information technology research, teaching, and education.

LNCS enjoys close cooperation with the computer science R & D community, the series counts many renowned academics among its volume editors and paper authors, and collaborates with prestigious societies. Its mission is to serve this international community by providing an invaluable service, mainly focused on the publication of conference and workshop proceedings and postproceedings. LNCS commenced publication in 1973.

Yael Tauman Kalai · Seny F. Kamara
Editors

# Advances in Cryptology – CRYPTO 2025

## 45th Annual International Cryptology Conference
Santa Barbara, CA, USA, August 17–21, 2025
Proceedings, Part I

Springer

*Editors*
Yael Tauman Kalai
Massachusetts Institute of Technology
Cambridge, MA, USA

Seny F. Kamara
MongoDB
New York, NY, USA

ISSN 0302-9743 ISSN 1611-3349 (electronic)
Lecture Notes in Computer Science
ISBN 978-3-032-01854-0 ISBN 978-3-032-01855-7 (eBook)
https://doi.org/10.1007/978-3-032-01855-7



This Springer imprint is published by the registered company Springer Nature Switzerland AG
The registered company address is: Gewerbestrasse 11, 6330 Cham, Switzerland

# Preface

The papers in this volume were presented at the International Cryptology Conference (CRYPTO 2025), which is an annual conference organized by the International Association for Cryptologic Research (IACR). It was held at the University of California, Santa Barbara, California, USA, from August 17th to August 21st, 2025.

CRYPTO welcomes papers on any cryptographic topic, including foundational and theoretic topics, the design and analysis of cryptographic primitives and protocols, secure implementations and optimization in hardware or software, and applied cryptography.

We received a record of 643 submissions (the prior record was 528 submissions at CRYPTO 2024). Of these, a record of 156 fantastic papers were accepted. Four pairs among the accepted papers were softly merged, which means that they were given one speaking slot while remaining separate in the proceedings. To accommodate the record high number of presentations, CRYPTO had three tracks (similar to the past two years), and each talk was 20 minutes long, including questions and answers.

The review process was handled by a fabulous program committee (PC), consisting of 108 outstanding cryptographers (excluding the chairs), who are all listed below. The PC members worked diligently to produce a fantastic program, and we are extremely grateful to each and every one of them. Of this committee, the following 11 members were given the leadership role of being area chairs: Shweta Agrawal, Sonia Belaïd, Zvika Brakerski, Craig Costello, Yuval Ishai, Dakshita Khurana, Gaëtan Leurent, Rafael Pass, Mike Rosulek, Elaine Shi and Daniel Wichs. Each area chair was in charge of handling roughly 60 papers in the area of their expertise. The area chairs were invaluable to us, they handled the submissions with great expertise, and we could not have done this without them!

Each paper was assigned to three program committee members who reviewed it either by themselves or with the help of a sub-reviewer. We benefited from a total of 667 sub-reviewers, all of whom are named below. We are grateful to the sub-reviewers for their peer reviews, which was paramount in the creation of a successful program.

The review process was double-blind. It proceeded in two phases. In the first phase, which consisted of roughly seven weeks, the PC chose 418 submissions to continue to consider; 224 submissions were rejected and one was withdrawn. The submissions that remained under consideration were given comments and invited to submit a response (rebuttal) with clarifications. Each and every one of the submissions, whether rejected (early or not) or accepted, received at least 3 reviews.

During the entire review process, we encouraged the PC to send to the authors (through us) as many clarification emails as needed to ensure that they understood the submissions. Many emails were sent to the authors during the review process asking for clarifications, and we believe that this interaction was very helpful.

We deeply thank all the authors who submitted their papers to CRYPTO 2025, and engaged with us during the review process. The majority of the submissions, including those that were ultimately not selected, were of high quality, and we are very honored that CRYPTO was the venue that the authors chose for their work. We are additionally grateful to the authors of the accepted papers for the extra work of incorporating the reviewers' feedback and presenting their papers at the conference.

This year three Best Paper Awards were given to the following submissions:

- Compact Lattice Signatures via Iterative Rejection Sampling, authored by Joel Gärtner. We would like to emphasize that Joel is a PhD student, and thus this paper received both the Best Paper Award and the Best Young Researcher Award! This is an incredible achievement, congratulations Joel!
- $\mathrm{KLPT}^2$: Algebraic Pathfinding in Dimension Two and Applications, authored by Wouter Castryck, Thomas Decru, Péter Kutas, Abel Laval, Christophe Petit, and Yan Bo Ti.
- On One-Shot Signatures, Quantum vs Classical Binding, and Obfuscating Permutations, authored by Omri Shmueli and Mark Zhandry.

We are grateful to the IACR Board of Directors and especially to Kevin McCurley and Kay McKelly for their help with many technical aspects. A deep thanks to Leonid Reyzin and Douglas Stebila, the PC chairs of CRYPTO 2024, for their invaluable resources, advice, and patience. Most importantly, we thank Francisco Rodríguez-Henríquez for serving as our General Chair and for all his amazing work on getting sponsors, helping attendees with visas, and making sure the conference went smoothly and that we all had a great time.

We would also like to thank our amazing industry sponsors: A huge thanks to our platinum sponsors, AWS and Google, for their extremely generous contribution! Also a special thanks to our gold sponsors: MongoDB and Apple; to our silver sponsors: Technology Innovation Institute, Meta, a16zcrypto, JP Morgan, and Input Output Hong Kong; and to our bronze sponsors: NTT Research, PQ Shield and IBM. The conference could not have happened without this extremely valuable financial support! Finally, we thank UC Santa Barbara for allowing us to use their amazing space for the conference and Prabhanjan Ananth for his help finding the student volunteers who helped with all the arrangements during the conference.

August 2025

Yael Tauman Kalai
Seny F. Kamara

# Organization

## General Chair

| | |
|---|---|
| Francisco Rodríguez-Henríquez | Technology Innovation Institute, UAE |

## Program Committee Chairs

| | |
|---|---|
| Yael Kalai | MIT, USA |
| Seny Kamara | MongoDB, USA |

## Area Chairs

| | |
|---|---|
| Shweta Agrawal | Indian Institute of Technology Madras, India |
| Sonia Belaid | CryptoExperts, France |
| Zvika Brakerski | Weizmann Institute of Science, Israel |
| Craig Costello | Queensland University of Technology, Australia |
| Yuval Ishai | Technion and AWS, USA |
| Dakshita Khurana | UIUC, NTT Research, USA |
| Gaëtan Leurent | Inria, France |
| Rafael Pass | Cornell, USA |
| Mike Rosulek | Oregon State University, USA |
| Elaine Shi | Carnegie Mellon University, USA |
| Daniel Wichs | Northeastern University, USA |

## Program Committee

| | |
|---|---|
| Martin R. Albrecht | King's College London, UK |
| Marshall Ball | New York University, USA |
| Zhenzhen Bao | Tsinghua University, China |
| James Bartusek | NYU, USA |
| Christof Beierle | Ruhr University Bochum, Germany |
| Fabrice Benhamouda | Amazon Web Services, USA |
| Tim Beyne | KU Leuven, Belgium |
| Andrej Bogdanov | University of Ottawa, Canada |
| Alexandra Boldyreva | Georgia Tech, USA |

| | |
|---|---|
| Jonathan Bootle | IBM Research Europe, Switzerland |
| Christina Boura | IRIF, Université Paris Cité, France |
| Pierre Briaud | Simula UiB, Norway |
| Christian Cachin | University of Bern, Switzerland |
| Anne Canteaut | Inria, France |
| David Cash | University of Chicago, USA |
| Nishanth Chandran | Microsoft Research India, India |
| Yilei Chen | Tsinghua University, China |
| Kai-Min Chung | Academia Sinica, Taiwan |
| Aloni Cohen | University of Chicago, USA |
| Thomas Debris-Alazard | Inria Saclay and Laboratoire d'Informatique de l'École Polytechnique, France |
| Itai Dinur | Ben-Gurion University, Israel and Georgetown University, USA |
| Maria Eichlseder | Graz University of Technology, Austria |
| Diego F. Aranha | Aarhus University, Denmark |
| Ben Fisch | Yale University, USA |
| Steven Galbraith | University of Auckland, New Zealand |
| Chaya Ganesh | Indian Institute of Science, India |
| Gayathri Garimella | Brown University, USA |
| Pierrick Gaudry | CNRS - Nancy, France |
| Ashrujit Ghoshal | Carnegie Mellon University, USA |
| Niv Gilboa | Ben-Gurion University, Israel |
| Aarushi Goel | Purdue University, USA |
| Vipul Goyal | NTT Research, USA |
| Lorenzo Grassi | Eindhoven University of Technology, Netherlands |
| Jiaxin Guan | New York University, USA |
| Jian Guo | Nanyang Technological University, Singapore |
| David Heath | University of Illinois Urbana-Champaign, USA |
| Nadia Heninger | UC San Diego, USA |
| Tetsu Iwata | Nagoya University, Japan |
| Stanislaw Jarecki | UC Irvine, USA |
| Zhengzhong Jin | Northeastern University, USA |
| Antoine Joux | CISPA, Helmholtz Center for Information Security, Germany |
| Bhavana Kanukurthi | Indian Institute of Science, India |
| Nathan Keller | Bar-Ilan University, Israel |
| Dmitry Khovratovich | Ethereum Foundation, Luxembourg |
| Lisa Kohl | CWI Amsterdam, Netherlands |
| Ilan Komargodski | Hebrew University of Jerusalem, Israel |
| Venkata Koppula | Indian Institute of Technology Delhi, India |
| Abhiram Kothapalli | University of California, Berkeley, USA |

| | |
|---|---|
| Akshayaram Srinivasan | University of Toronto, Canada |
| François-Xavier Standaert | UCLouvain, Belgium |
| Akira Takahashi | J.P. Morgan, USA |
| Ni Trieu | Arizona State University, USA |
| Eran Tromer | Boston University, USA |
| Nirvan Tyagi | University of Washington, USA |
| Prashant Nalini Vasudevan | National University of Singapore, Singapore |
| Xiao Wang | Northwestern University, USA |
| Mor Weiss | Bar-Ilan University, Israel |
| Benjamin Wesolowski | CNRS, ENS Lyon, France |
| Kevin Yeo | Google and Columbia University, USA |
| Eylon Yogev | Bar-Ilan University, Israel |
| Yupeng Zhang | University of Illinois Urbana Champaign, USA |

## Additional Reviewers

Michel Abdalla
Ittai Abraham
Damiano Abram
Ojaswi Acharya
Anasuya Acharya
Siddharth Agarwal
Amit Agarwal
Divesh Aggarwal
Rashmi Agrawal
Adi Akavia
Daniel Alabi
Navid Alamati
Eden Aldema Tshuva
Nouri Alnahawi
Joël Alwen
Ghous Amjad
Ignacio Amores-Sesar
Hari Krishnan P. Anilkumar
Daniel Apon
Ananya Appan
Gal Arnon
Daniel Augot
Karen Azari
Paco Azevedo Oliveira
Kaartik Bhushan
Florian Bourse
Renas Bacho
Ruben Baecker
Chen Bai
Shi Bai
Jenish Bajracharya
Henry Bambury
Akhil Bandarupalli
Fabio Banfi
Manuel Barbosa
Mohammed Barhoush
Augustin Bariant
Cruz Barnum
Paulo Barreto
Christopher Battarbee
Balthazar Bauer
Carsten Baum
Anubhav Baweja
Amit Behera
Amos Beimel
Mihir Bellare
Shany Ben-David
Huck Bennett
Benjamin Benčina
Jordan Beraud
Thiago Bergamaschi
Sebastian Berndt
Daniel J. Bernstein
Tyler Besselman

Ward Beullens
Adithya Bhat
Deepak Bhati
Ritam Bhaumik
Beatrice Biasioli
Alexander Bienstock
Alex Biryukov
Alex Block
Jan Bobolz
Aurélien Boeuf
Madalina Bolboceanu
Maxime Bombar
Xavier Bonnetain
Cecilia Boschini
John Bostanci
Katharina Boudgoust
Anas Boudi
Alexandre Bouez
Charles Bouillaguet
Clemence Bouvier
Pedro Branco
Nicholas Brandt
Gianluca Brian
Dung Bui
Paul Bunn
Julien Béguinot
Alper Cakan
Matteo Campanelli
Pedro Capitão
Kévin Carrier
Gaëtan Cassiers
Guilhem Castagnos
Wouter Castryck
Sofía Celi
André Chailloux
Rutchathon Chairattana-Apirom
Bishwajit Chakraborty
Suvradip Chakraborty
Jeffrey Champion
Benjamin Chan
Anirudh Chandramouli
Sylvain Chatel
Rohit Chatterjee
Megan Chen
Shan Chen
Shiyao Chen
Yu Long Chen
Long Chen
Liyan Chen
Boyang Chen
Siyuan Chen
Jie Chen
Binyi Chen
Yanbo Chen
Jiaqi Cheng
Jung Hee Cheon
Céline Chevalier
Clémence Chevignard
Nai-Hui Chia
James Chiang
Sohto Chiku
Wonseok Choi
Kevin Choi
Wutichai Chongchitmate
Arka Rai Choudhuri
Miranda Christ
Hao Chung
Hao Chung
Michele Ciampi
Christian Cianfarani
Carlos Cid
Valerio Cini
Pierre Civit
Benoît Cogliati
Daniel Collins
Sandro Coretti
Anamaria Costache
Jolijn Cottaar
Alain Couvreur
Daniele Cozzo
Hongrui Cui
Hila Dahari-Garbian
Marcel Dall'Agnol
Quang Dao
Sourav Das
Pratish Datta
Hannah David
Alex Davidson
Leo de Castro
Bor de Kock

Paola de Perthuis
Alexandre Debant
Thomas Decru
Giovanni Deligios
Amit Deo
Patrick Derbez
Rathin Desai
Lalita Devadas
Julien Devevey
Youlong Ding
Sam Dittmer
Fangqi Dong
Xiaoyang Dong
Nico Dottling
Benjamin Dowling
Nir Drucker
Léo Ducas
Clément Ducros
Jesko Dujmovic
François Dupressoir
Stefan Dziembowski
Martin Ekerå
Youssef El Housni
Fatima Elsheimy
Saroja Erabelli
Daniel Escudero
Zachary Espiritu
Thomas Espitau
Pouria Fallahpour
Sebastian Faller
Sebastian Faust
Joël Felderhoff
Patrick Felke
Weiqi Feng
Giacomo Fenzi
Dario Fiore
Denis Firsov
Pouyan Forghani
Danilo Francati
Cody Freitag
Daniele Friolo
Ariel Gabizon
Philippe Gaborit
Pierre Galissant
Jiahui Gao
Rachit Garg
Romain Gay
Konstantin Gegier
Marilyn George
David Gerault
Simon Gerhalter
Satrajit Ghosh
Soumik Ghosh
Valerie Gilchrist
Eli Goldin
Junqing Gong
Louis Goubin
Rishab Goyal
Matthew Gray
Scott Griffy
Yanqi Gu
Ziyi Guan
Morgane Guerreau
Antonio Guimarães
Aditya Gulati
Sam Gunn
Yue Guo
Chun Guo
Kanav Gupta
Debayan Gupta
Aparna Gupte
Kamil Doruk Gur
Julia Guskind
Felix Günther
Hossein Hadipour
Mohammad Hajiabadi
Shai Halevi
Peter Hall
Mathias Hall-Andersen
Miro Haller
Matan Hamilis
Shuai Han
Guillaume Hanrot
Lucjan Hanzlik
Keisuke Hara
Keitaro Hashimoto
Valérian Hatey
Aditya Hegde
Rachelle Heim
Julius Hermelink

Julia Hesse
Laura Hetz
Hans Heum
Minki Hhan
Taiga Hiroka
Charlotte Hoffmann
Clément Hoffmann
Alexander Hoover
Akinori Hosoyamada
Marc Houben
Patrick Hough
Wyatt Howe
Yao-Ching Hsieh
Yuncong Hu
Miryam Huang
Tairong Huang
Loïs Huguenin-Dumittan
Janik Huth
Rahul Ilango
Deep Inder
Akiko Inoue
Takanori Isobe
Ryoma Ito
Håkon Jacobsen
Joseph Jaeger
Eli Jaffe
Aayush Jain
Abhishek Jain
Jonas Janneck
Sam Jaques
Ashwin Jha
Xinting Ji
Liheng Ji
Yanxue Jia
Dingding Jia
Ziyang Jin
Haoxiang Jin
Daniel Jost
Eliran Kachlon
Anders Kallesøe
Chethan Kamath
Simon Holmgaard Kamp
Harish Karthikeyan
Julia Kastner
Shuichi Katsumata
Mustafa Khairallah
Nakul Khambhati
Hamidreza Khoshakhlagh
Jaehyung Kim
Susumu Kiyoshima
Christian Knabenhans
Markulf Kohlweiss
Sebastian Kolby
Vladimir Kolesnikov
Dimitris Kolonelos
Jovan Komatovic
Yashvanth Kondi
Alexis Korb
Katharina Koschatko
Hugo Krawczyk
William Kretschmer
Christiane Kuhn
Rajendra Kumar
Naman Kumar
Rajendra Kumar
Ranjit Kumaresan
Eyal Kushilevitz
Lukas Kölsch
Haoxing Lin
Thijs Laarhoven
Yi-Fu Lai
Russell W. F. Lai
Kim Laine
Roman Langrehr
Oleksandra Lapiha
Arthur Lazzaretti
Duc Le
Gregor Leander
Guirec Lebrun
Jooyoung Lee
Keewoo Lee
Eysa Lee
Byeonghak Lee
Charlotte Lefevre
Jason Legrow
Julia Len
Tancrede Lepoint
Jonathan Levin
Yunqi Li
Hanjun Li

Baiyu Li
Wenjie Li
Zhe Li
Xiao Liang
Damien Ligier
Wei-Kai Lin
Yao-Ting Lin
Yehuda Lindell
Song Ling
Eik List
Haolin Liu
Xiangyu Liu
Tianyi Liu
Hanlin Liu
Tianyi Liu
Zeyu Liu
Yanyi Liu
Qipeng Liu
Yinchen Liu
Fukang Liu
Tianren Liu
Chen-Da Liu-Zhang
Pierre Loidreau
Patrick Longa
Julian Loss
Paul Lou
Johanna Loyer
George Lu
Mingqi Lu
Jinyu Lu
Stefan Lucks
Ji Luo
Hengyi Luo
Han Luo
Hanyu Luo
Yiping Ma
Fermi Ma
Shihe Ma
Varun Madathil
Lorenzo Magliocco
Rasoul Akhavan Mahdavi
Mohammad Mahmoody
Luciano Maino
Subhamoy Maitra
Christian Majenz
Eleftheria Makri
Giulio Malavolta
Mohamed Malhou
Mary Maller
Harjasleen Malvai
Mark Manulis
Xinyu Mao
Varun Maram
Mario Marhuenda Beltrán
Elisa Masserova
Loïc Masure
Surya Mathialagan
Ian McQuoid
Jonas Meers
Willi Meier
Nikolas Melissaris
Kelsey Melissaris
Silvia Mella
Florian Mendel
Rebekah Mercer
Antonio Merino-Gallardo
Elena Micheli
Francesco Migliaro
Ankit Kumar Misra
Anuja Modi
Ameer Mohammed
Arup Mondal
Hart Montgomery
Ethan Mook
Thorben Moos
Tushar Mopuri
River Moreira-Ferreira
Fabrice Mouhartem
Changrui Mu
Marta Mularczyk
Saachi Mutreja
Anne Müller
Marcel Nageler
Wenjie Nan
Mridul Nandi
Jade Nardi
Anand Natarajan
María Naya-Plasencia
Phillip Nazarian
Barak Nehoran

Patrick Neumann
Son Nguyen
Jerome Nguyen
Phuong-Hoa Nguyen
Ngoc Khanh Nguyen
Ky Nguyen
Wilson Nguyen
Quyen Nguyen
Phong Nguyen
Kent Nielsen
Guilhem Niot
Ryo Nishimaki
Martha Norberg Hovd
Maciej Obremski
Miyako Ohkubo
Claudio Orlandi
Maximilian Orlt
Morten Øygarden
Alex Ozdemir
Tapas Pal
Giorgos Panagiotakos
Mahak Pancholi
Sunoo Park
Andrew Park
Aditi Partap
Alain Passelègue
Valerio Pastro
Sikhar Patranabis
Subhasre Patro
Chris Peikert
Angelos Pelecanos
Alice Pellet-Mary
Yevhen Perehuda
Léo Perrin
Edoardo Persichetti
Kabir Peshawaria
Naty Peter
Thomas Peters
Christiane Peters
George Petrides
Xuanrong Piao
Rafael del Pino
Supartha Podder
Bertram Poettering
Simon Pohmann
Guru Vamsi Policharla
Eamonn W. Postlethwaite
Thomas Prest
Sihang Pu
Kirthivaasan Puniamurthy
Willy Quach
Rashmi Raghu
Rahul Rachuri
Rajeev Raghunath
Srinivasan Raghuraman
Mostafizar Rahman
Apurva Rai
Justin Raizes
Mahesh Rajasree
Sebastian Ramacher
Rishabh Ranjan
Shahram Rasoolzadeh
Deevashwer Rathee
Christian Rechberger
Michael Reichle
Joost Renes
Mahshid Riahinia
Thomas Ricosset
Doreen Riepel
Guilherme Rito
Silvia Ritsch
Damien Robert
Léo Robert
Bhaskar Roberts
Maxime Roméas
Leah Rosenbloom
Joachim Rosenthal
Melissa Rossi
Lior Rotem
Joe Rowell
Lawrence Roy
Arnab Roy
Luigi Russo
Keegan Ryan
Caroline Sandsbraten
Giacomo Santato
Paolo Santini
Maria Corte-Real Santos
Santanu Sarkar
Yu Sasaki

Rahul Satish
Or Sattath
Guillaume Scerri
Sarah Scheffler
Gabe Schoenbach
Peter Scholl
André Schrottenloher
Marek Sefranek
Gregor Seiler
Sruthi Sekar
Nicolas Sendrier
Joon Young Seo
Karn Seth
Yannick Seurin
Jonathan Shafer
Avital Shafran
Akash Shah
Harshal Bhadreshkumar Shah
Girisha Shankar
Laura Shea
Kaiyan Shi
Sina Shiehian
Omri Shmueli
Dan Shumow
Ferdinand Sibleyras
Janno Siim
Thom Sijpestijn
Daniel Slamanig
Christopher Smith
Tomer Solomon
Yifan Song
Yongsoo Song
Pratik Soni
Eduardo Soria-Vazquez
Julien Soumier
Pierre-Jean Spaenlehauer
Jannik Spiessens
Nicholas Spooner
Mahesh Sreekumar Rajasree
Srivatsan Sridhar
Sriram Sridhar
Shravan Srinivasan
Kate Stange
James Stearn
Douglas Stebila
Damien Stehlé
Matthias Steiner
Ron Steinfeld
Igors Stepanovs
Gilad Stern
Roy Stracovsky
Christoph Striecks
Thorsten Strufe
Adam Suhl
Nuozhou Sun
Siwei Sun
Erkan Tairi
Yuhao Tang
Ilan Tennenhouse
Stefano Tessaro
Lea Thiemt
Julian Thomas
Tyge Tiessen
Jean-Pierre Tillich
Yosuke Todo
Kabir Tomer
Junichi Tomida
Patrick Towa
Monika Trimoska
Max Tromanhauser
Eliad Tsfadia
Ida Tucker
LaKyah Tyner
Elad Tzalik
Aleksei Udovenko
Rei Ueno
Akin Ünal
Dominique Unruh
Neekon Vafa
Gilles Van Assche
Wessel van Woerden
Nikhil Vanjani
Akhil Vanukuri
Michiel Verbauwhede
Frederik Vercauteren
Damien Vergnaud
Psi Vesely
Juan Villacis
Fernando Virdia
Madars Virza

Turan Vural
Yuejun Wang
Benedikt Wagner
Alexandre Wallet
Yuyu Wang
William Wang
Haoyang Wang
Weijie Wang
Ruida Wang
Linya Wang
Mingyuan Wang
Ding Wang
Shichang Wang
Gaven Watson
Fiona J. Weber
Daniel Weber
Hoeteck Wee
Yu Wei
Weiqiang Wen
Chenkai Weng
Francois-Xavier Wicht
Ivy K. Y. Woo
David J. Wu
Zhili Wu
Ke Wu
Keita Xagawa
Jiayu Xu
Haiyang Xue
Anshu Yadav
Sophia Yacoubov
Saikumar Yadugiri
Sophia Yakoubov
Shota Yamada
Hailun Yan
Luhan Yan
Kang Yang
Guangxu Yang
Yibin Yang
Yiran Yao
Xiaxi Ye
Kazuki Yoneyama
Victor Youdom Kemmoe
Yu Yu
Quan Yuan
Gabriel Zaid
Arantxa Zapico
Greg Zaverucha
Runzhi Zeng
Mark Zhandry
Liu Zhang
Yinuo Zhang
Wenhao Zhang
Tina Zhang
Shiduo Zhang
Jiaheng Zhang
Tianyu Zhang
Zhelei Zhou
Yunxiao Zhou
Chenzhi Zhu

# Contents – Part I


**Mathematical Foundations and Isogeny-Based Cryptography**

Computing Asymptotic Bounds for Small Roots in Coppersmith's Method via Sumset Theory ..... 3
*Yansong Feng, Hengyi Luo, Qiyuan Chen, Abderrahmane Nitaj, and Yanbin Pan*

New Results on the $\phi$-Hiding Assumption and Factoring Related RSA Moduli ..... 33
*Jun Xu, Jun Song, and Lei Hu*

PEGASIS: Practical Effective Class Group Action using 4-Dimensional Isogenies ..... 67
*Pierrick Dartois, Jonathan Komada Eriksen, Tako Boris Fouotsa, Arthur Herlédan Le Merdy, Riccardo Invernizzi, Damien Robert, Ryan Rueger, Frederik Vercauteren, and Benjamin Wesolowski*

Deterministic Algorithms for Class Group Actions ..... 100
*Marc Houben*

More Efficient Isogeny Proofs of Knowledge via Canonical Modular Polynomials ..... 131
*Thomas den Hollander, Sören Kleine, Marzio Mula, Daniel Slamanig, and Sebastian A. Spindler*

KLPT$^2$: Algebraic Pathfinding in Dimension Two and Applications ..... 167
*Wouter Castryck, Thomas Decru, Péter Kutas, Abel Laval, Christophe Petit, and Yan Bo Ti*

**Code-Based Cryptography**

Sample Efficient Search to Decision for $k$LIN ..... 203
*Andrej Bogdanov, Alon Rosen, and Kel Zin Tan*

Error Floor Prediction with Markov Models for QC-MDPC Codes ..... 221
*Sarah Arpin, Jun Bo Lau, Antoine Mesnard, Ray Perlner, Angela Robinson, Jean-Pierre Tillich, and Valentin Vasseur*

Highway to Hull: An Algorithm for Solving the General Matrix Code Equivalence Problem ........ 253
*Alain Couvreur and Christophe Levrat*

Stationary Syndrome Decoding for Improved PCGs ........ 284
*Vladimir Kolesnikov, Stanislav Peceny, Srinivasan Raghuraman, and Peter Rindal*

**Lattice-Based Cryptography**

On Gaussian Sampling for $q$-ary Lattices and Linear Codes with Lee Weight ... 321
*Maiara F. Bollauf, Maja Lie, and Cong Ling*

Wagner's Algorithm Provably Runs in Subexponential Time for $\mathrm{SIS}^{\infty}$ ........ 353
*Léo Ducas, Lynn Engelberts, and Johanna Loyer*

Refined Attack on LWE with Hints: Constructing Lattice via Gaussian Elimination ........ 385
*Jinzheng Cao, Haodong Jiang, and Qingfeng Cheng*

Uncompressing Dilithium's Public Key ........ 417
*Paco Azevedo-Oliveira, Andersson Calle Viera, Benoît Cogliati, and Louis Goubin*

Assessing the Impact of a Variant of MATZOV's Dual Attack on Kyber ....... 444
*Kevin Carrier, Charles Meyer-Hilfiger, Yixin Shen, and Jean-Pierre Tillich*

Improved Lattice Blind Signatures from Recycled Entropy ........ 477
*Corentin Jeudy and Olivier Sanders*

Compact Lattice Signatures via Iterative Rejection Sampling ........ 514
*Joel Gärtner*

The Algebraic One-More MISIS Problem and Applications to Threshold Signatures ........ 548
*Chenzhi Zhu and Stefano Tessaro*

**Complexity-Theoretic Foundations**

Uniform Black-Box Separations via Non-malleable Extractors ........ 585
*Marshall Ball and Dana Dachman-Soled*

Hardness Along the Boundary: Towards One-Way Functions from the Worst-Case Hardness of Time-Bounded Kolmogorov Complexity .... 617
*Yanyi Liu and Rafael Pass*

Pseudorandomness Properties of Random Reversible Circuits ................ 651
*William Gay, William He, Nicholas Kocurek, and Ryan O'Donnell*

Efficient Randomized Strong 2-Source Non-malleable Extractor for Any Linear Min-Entropy ........................................................ 679
*Divesh Aggarwal, Pranjal Dutta, Saswata Mukherjee, Satyajeet Nagargoje, and Maciej Obremski*

**Author Index** ........................................................ 715

# Mathematical Foundations and Isogeny-Based Cryptography

# Computing Asymptotic Bounds for Small Roots in Coppersmith's Method via Sumset Theory

Yansong Feng[1,2], Hengyi Luo[1,2], Qiyuan Chen[1,2], Abderrahmane Nitaj[3], and Yanbin Pan[1,2(✉)]

[1] State Key Laboratory of Mathematical Sciences, Academy of Mathematics and Systems Science, Chinese Academy of Sciences, Beijing, China
{fengyansong,luohengyi,chenqiyuan,panyanbin}@amss.ac.cn
[2] School of Mathematical Sciences, University of Chinese Academy of Sciences, Beijing, China
[3] LMNO, Normandie Univ, UNICAEN, CNRS, Caen 14000, France
abderrahmane.nitaj@unicaen.fr

**Abstract.** Coppersmith's method is a well-known and practical method for solving polynomial modular equations involved in some cryptosystems such as RSA. An important and tedious task in this method consists in computing the asymptotic bounds. In this work, we address the challenge of computing such asymptotic bounds by introducing the Sumsets theory from Additive Combinatorics as a new analytical tool, which significantly streamlines manual calculations. More precisely, we develop the first provable algorithm for determining these asymptotic bounds, whereas the recent methods based on simple Lagrange interpolation are heuristic. Moreover, the experiments showed that our method is much more efficient than the previous method in practice. We also employ our method to improve the cryptanalytic results for the Commutative Isogeny Hidden Number Problem. Our approach may deepen the understanding of Coppersmith's method and inspire more security analysis methodologies.

**Keywords:** Additive combinatorics · Coppersmith's method · automated cryptanalysis · lattice-based cryptanalysis · asymptotic bounds

## 1 Introduction

In 1996, Coppersmith [12] introduced methods for finding small roots of a single univariate modular polynomial, which were later extended to multivariate polynomials, integer polynomials, and modular polynomials by works such as [6,13–15,27,28,33]. These methods have since found wide applications in cryptanalysis [8,9,17,24,32,34,40]. The core paradigm of Coppersmith's method begins with constructing a set of polynomials sharing roots with the target polynomial.


Y. Tauman Kalai and S. F. Kamara (Eds.): CRYPTO 2025, LNCS 16000, pp. 3–32, 2025.
https://doi.org/10.1007/978-3-032-01855-7_1

The coefficients of these polynomials form a lattice to be reduced. Crucially, the construction of polynomials determines all aspects of the method's performance - including root bounds and time complexity - making polynomial set construction the key optimization lever.

To find small integer roots of a single polynomial equation $f(x_1,\ldots,x_k) \equiv 0 \mod M$ in modular arithmetic, the Jochemsz-May Strategy [28] remains the state-of-the-art approach for general single polynomial equations. The method systematically constructs polynomial families $G_m$ for a specific integer $m$, where each polynomial $g \in G_m$ satisfies $g(x_1,\ldots,x_k) \equiv 0 \mod M^m$. This generalizes Blömer-May's bivariate optimization [6] to multivariate cases. Recent work by Meers–Nowakowski [35] extended this to polynomial systems, with subsequent variants [38,39].

**The Bound Determination Challenge.** The bound of Coppersmith's method, $\mathbf{X} = (X_1,\ldots,X_k)$, determines the maximal solution size $|x_i| < X_i$ that is recoverable via Coppersmith's method. The goal to improve Coppersmith's method is obviously to enlarge the bound, since a better bound leads to better attack in cryptanalysis. However, determining the bound usually has to be performed manually each time when a specific polynomial family $G_m$ is considered. It is typically very time-consuming and tedious. Hence, fast automated computation of the bound allows us to efficiently determine in advance whether a specific polynomial family $G_m$ can improve the previous results and makes the automated selection of better polynomial families in Coppersmith's method possible. Note that in Coppersmith's method, the bound arises from an inequality of the form

$$\det(\mathcal{L}) = X_1^{p_1(m)} \cdots X_k^{p_k(m)} M^{p_{\mathcal{F}}(m)} < M^{m \dim(\mathcal{L})},$$

where $\mathcal{L}$ is a lattice, $\det(\mathcal{L})$ is its determinant, $\dim(\mathcal{L})$ is its dimension, and $p_1(m), p_2(m), \ldots, p_k(m)$, and $p_{\mathcal{F}}(m)$ are functions in $m$. To optimize the solution, we need to analyze the asymptotic bound as $m \to \infty$.

**Flawed Automation Attempts.** At Asiacrypt '23, Meers and Nowakowski [35] proposed a heuristic approach to compute the asymptotic bounds, where they assumed $p_{\mathcal{F}}$ is a degree-$(k+1)$ polynomial in $m$ and employed Lagrange interpolation at $k+2$ points. Below, we expose critical flaws and limitations in their method:

- **A counterexample of heuristic in** [35]: For $k$-variable polynomials, the claim that $p_{\mathcal{F}}(m)$ is a polynomial in $m$ of degree-$(k+1)$ fails for $f(x) = x^5+x+1$: the sequence $\{p_{\mathcal{F}}(m)\}_{m=1}^{\infty} = \{2, 8, 20, 40, 65, 95, \ldots\}$ satisfies $\frac{5}{2}m^2+\frac{5}{2}m-10$ only when $m \geq 3$. We establish a corrected version of the heuristic: For any $k$-variable polynomial $f$, there exists $N \in \mathbb{N}$ such that for any $m > N$, $p_{\mathcal{F}}$ is a degree-$(k+1)$ polynomial in $m$. The proof can be found in Sect. 4. Moreover, their assertion that $m \dim(\mathcal{L})$ and the exponents $p_1,\ldots,p_k$ are degree-$(k+1)$ polynomials in $m$ suffers from the same fundamental flaw.

- **Infeasible Computation**: While our corrected heuristic suggests Lagrange interpolation to recover $p_{\mathcal{F}}$ when $m > N$, state-of-the-art additive combinatorics results [22] reveal fundamental limitations: For some 4-variable polynomials, the required threshold becomes $N > 2^{300}$. This implies we must compute the number of monomials in $f^m$ for huge $m > 2^{300}$ to ensure correctness, which is computationally infeasible in practice. Furthermore, the local convergence phenomenon in Lagrange interpolation may yield incorrect results, which means that the output of their methods is unreliable.

As a consequence, the following natural question arises:

*Can we compute* $\dim(\mathcal{L})$ *and* $\det(\mathcal{L})$ *more efficiently?*

### 1.1 Our Contribution

We provide a positive answer to the above question and present a novel approach that avoids the tedious computation of asymptotic bounds in Coppersmith's method. This enables us to handle more complicated polynomial equations and achieve better results. We list our contributions as follows:

**New Tools from Additive Combinatorics.** We introduce fruitful results from additive combinatorics—including sumset theory and integer point counting in convex hull—into Coppersmith's method. These tools offer new perspectives for analyzing lattices in Coppersmith's method.

Beyond providing an efficient methodology for computing $\dim(\mathcal{L})$ and $\det(\mathcal{L})$, we re-examine prior heuristics through an additive combinatorial lens. While Meers *et al.* [35] and Sarkar [39] assumed that $m \dim(\mathcal{L})$, $p_1, \dots, p_k$, and $p_{\mathcal{F}}$ are degree-$(k+1)$ polynomials in $m$ (or jointly in $m$ and $t$), our counterexample demonstrates that these heuristics require the critical precondition that $m$ (or $m$ and $t$ jointly) must exceed a sufficient threshold. After establishing the necessary conditions, we formally prove that:

- Meers *et al.*'s heuristic holds for sufficiently large $m$.
- Sarkar's heuristic holds when both $m$ and $t$ are sufficiently large.

We believe these tools from additive combinatorics not only strengthen our theoretical understanding but also have the potential to inspire novel cryptanalytic techniques.

**Formulas for Asymptotic Bounds in Coppersmith's Method.** As $m \to \infty$, we derive elegant formulas for the bounds computation in Coppersmith's method. Taking the Jochemsz–May Basic Strategy as an example, we present the following formulas, for any arbitrarily small constant $\varepsilon > 0$:

$$\prod_{i=1}^{k} X_i^{\int_{N(f)} x_i \, dV} \cdot M^{\frac{k}{k+1} \int_{N(f)} 1 \, dV} < M^{\int_{N(f)} 1 \, dV - \varepsilon},$$

where $N(f)$ denotes the Newton polytope of $f$ – the convex hull of exponent vectors $A(f) = \{(i_1, \ldots, i_k) \mid x_1^{i_1} \cdots x_k^{i_k}$ is a monomial of $f\}$.

The Jochemsz–May Extended Strategy generalizes the Jochemsz–May Basic Strategy by introducing additional shift polynomials and guarantees results at least as strong as those of the latter. We also provide related formulas for the Jochemsz–May Extended Strategy. Recently, the Jochemsz–May Basic Strategy was generalized from a single polynomial equation to a system of polynomial equations [35,39]. By adding additional shift polynomials, we further generalize these variants and derive the corresponding formulas. Since the approaches of Meers–Nowakowski [35] and Sarkar [39] can be regarded as special cases of our generalization, our formulas naturally encompass their results.

Moreover, we point out that we also provide methods for computing the integrals $\int_{N(f)} x_i dV$ and $\int_{N(f)} 1 dV$ in the formulas or equivalently the bounds. Taking the formulas of the Jochemsz–May Basic strategy as an example, the computation of $\dim(\mathcal{L})$ is based on calculating the volume of the convex hull of the subset $A(f) \subset \mathbb{Z}^k$. For the integrals used in the computation of $p_1, \ldots, p_k$ and $p_{\mathcal{F}}$, we construct $(k+1)$-dimensional subsets of $\mathbb{Z}^{k+1}$. The integral is equivalent to the volume of the convex hull of the subset, and the number of points in these subsets is bounded by at most twice that of $A(f)$. This approach makes our formulas more computer-friendly, as they can be computed directly from the input $A(f)$. For other generalized strategies, we apply a similar treatment. We have implemented our algorithms, and most of them completed within one second; our approach offers significant advantages over both manual computation and heuristic methods in [35,39]. Further details can be found in Sect. 5.1.

We provide an efficient open source implementation of our algorithm for computing asymptotic bounds in SageMath. The source code is available at:

https://github.com/fffmath/AsymptoticBounds.

Our formulas enable *efficient* and *provable* computation of asymptotic root bounds $X_i$, advancing toward fully automated implementations of Coppersmith's method.

**Cryptanalytic Advances for CI-HNP.** Building on the Commutative Isogeny Hidden Number Problem (CI-HNP) introduced at Asiacrypt '23 [35], we achieve new *state-of-the-art* bounds for CI-HNP over CSURF (CSIDH on the surface [11]).

We compare our results with previous work in Table 1, where "Heuristic?" in this context means that a heuristic approach is adopted to compute the bound. We still need the Assumption 1 in Sect. 2 for Coppersmith's method. Our framework enables precise security parameter selection for isogeny-based protocols by eliminating heuristic assumptions in bound computation and providing the first non-heuristic improvement over previous work.

**Table 1.** Comparison of CI-HNP Results (Required MSBs)

| Work | Required MSBs (%) | Heuristic? |
|---|---|---|
| [35] | 75.61 | Yes |
| [38] | 74.72[a] | Yes |
| [39] | 74.03 | Yes |
| **This work** | **74.01** | **No** |

[a] An March, 2025 revision of Ryan's work [38] achieves 73.91% but still heuristic.

## 1.2 Technical Overview

Here we focus on the Jochemsz-May Basic Strategy to present our key ideas. Related formulas for the other cases are provided in Sect. 3 and 4.

**Starting Point: the Jochemsz-May Basic Strategy.** Let $f \in \mathbb{Z}[x_1, \ldots, x_k]$ be a monic polynomial with small root $\mathbf{u} = (u_1, \ldots, u_k)$ satisfying $|u_i| < X_i$ for known bounds $X_i$, and modulus $M$. For a fixed integer $m$, the Jochemsz-May Basic Strategy defines the set:

$$J_\ell = \left\{ \lambda \,\middle|\, \lambda \text{ is a monomial of } f^m \text{ and } \frac{\lambda}{\mathrm{LM}(f)^\ell} \text{ is a monomial of } f^{m-\ell} \right\}, \quad (1)$$

for $0 \le \ell \le m$ and $J_{m+1} = \emptyset$, where $\mathrm{LM}(f)$ denotes $f$'s leading monomial. The strategy constructs basis polynomials for every monomial $\lambda \in J_\ell \setminus J_{\ell+1}$:

$$g_\lambda(x_1, \ldots, x_k) = \frac{\lambda}{\mathrm{LM}(f)^\ell} f^\ell M^{m-\ell}, \quad \lambda \in J_\ell \setminus J_{\ell+1}. \quad (2)$$

All $g_\lambda(x_1, \ldots, x_k)$'s form the set $G_m$. The lattice $\mathcal{L}$ is constructed by taking the coefficient vectors of the polynomials $g_\lambda(x_1 X_1, \ldots, x_k X_k)$ as a basis. Then the lattice $\mathcal{L}$ constructed via Equation (1) and Equation (2) satisfies:

$$\dim(\mathcal{L}) = |\bigcup_{0 \le \ell \le m} J_\ell|, \quad (3)$$

$$\det(\mathcal{L}) = \prod_{g_\lambda(x_1, \ldots, x_k) \in G_m} \mathrm{LC}(g_\lambda(x_1 X_1, \ldots, x_k X_k)) = \prod_{j=1}^{k} X_j^{p_j} M^{p_{\mathcal{F}}}, \quad (4)$$

where $|\cdot|$ denotes the cardinality of a set and $\mathrm{LC}(\cdot)$ denotes leading coefficient.

*Example 1 (Univariate Case).* For $m = 2$, $k = 1$, and $f(x_1) = x_1 + 1$, the lattice basis matrix constructed by the Jochemsz-May Basic Strategy is:

$$\begin{pmatrix} M^2 & 0 & 0 \\ M & MX_1 & 0 \\ 1 & 2X_1 & X_1^2 \end{pmatrix},$$

and we know that $\dim(\mathcal{L}) = 3$ and $\det(\mathcal{L}) = X_1^3 M^3$.

However, in the Jochemsz-May Basic Strategy paper [28], they assume that the monomials of $f, f^1, \ldots, f^{m-1}$ are all contained in the monomials of $f^m$. If this doesn't hold, the definition of $J_\ell$ in Equation (1) can be slightly changed such that $J_\ell$ contains all monomial $\lambda$ of $f^j$ for $j = 1, \ldots, m$ for which $\lambda/\mathrm{LM}(f)^\ell$ is a monomial of $f^i$ for some $i = 0, \ldots, m$.

To ensure the above assumption holds and to align with the sumset theory, we also modify Eq. (1). Recall that for two sets $A$ and $B$, their Minkowski sum is defined as $A + B = \{a + b \mid a \in A, b \in B\}$, and $mA$ denotes the Minkowski sum of $m$ copies of $A$.

For the leading monomial $x_1^{\alpha^{(1)}} \cdots x_k^{\alpha^{(k)}}$ of $f$, let $\alpha = (\alpha^{(1)}, \ldots, \alpha^{(k)}) \in \mathbb{Z}^k$ and define $A(f) = \{(i_1, \ldots, i_k) \mid x_1^{i_1} \cdots x_k^{i_k}$ is a monomial of $f\}$. We replace $J_\ell$ in Equation (1) as follows:

$$\begin{aligned} J_\ell &= \{x_1^{i_1} \cdots x_k^{i_k} \mid (i_1, \ldots, i_k) \in mA(f) \text{ and } (i_1, \ldots, i_k) \in (m-\ell)A(f) + \ell\alpha\} \\ &= \{x_1^{i_1} \cdots x_k^{i_k} \mid (i_1, \ldots, i_k) \in (m-\ell)A(f) + \ell\alpha\}, \end{aligned}$$

ensuring that the monomials of $f, f^1, \ldots, f^{m-1}$ are all contained among the monomials of $f^m$.

**Our Formulas.** In this section, we require $f \in \mathbb{Z}[x_1, \ldots, x_k]$ to be a *well-defined k-variate* polynomial, that is, it satisfies the following conditions:

1. $f(0, \ldots, 0) \neq 0$.
2. The lattice generated by $A(f)$ has finite index as a sublattice of $\mathbb{Z}^k$.

For simplicity, in this section, we assume that the index of the lattice generated by $A(f)$ is 1. For the general case, see Sect. 3.

For any *well-defined k-variate* polynomial $f$, our formulas show that the inequality $\det(L) < M^{m \dim(L)}$ can be asymptotically written as, for any arbitrarily small constant $\varepsilon > 0$:

$$\prod_{i=1}^{k} X_i^{\int_{N(f)} x_i \, dV} \cdot M^{\frac{k}{k+1} \int_{N(f)} 1 \, dV} < M^{\int_{N(f)} 1 \, dV - \varepsilon},$$

where $N(f)$ is the Newton polytope of $f$, that is the convex hull of $A(f)$. Below we will show how to prove these formulas.

**Computing Dimension via Additive Combinatorics.** We first need to rewrite $\dim(\mathcal{L})$ to match the sumset theory. As $J_\ell = \{x_1^{i_1} \cdots x_k^{i_k} \mid (i_1, \ldots, i_k) \in (m-\ell)A(f) + \ell\alpha\}$, we have

$$J_{m+1} \subset \cdots \subset J_0,$$

which allows us to rewrite Equation (3) as follows:

$$\dim(\mathcal{L}) = |\bigcup_{0 \leq \ell \leq m} J_\ell| = |J_0| = |mA(f)|. \tag{5}$$

The equivalence between Equation (3) and Equation (5) is powerful and makes the computation of $\dim(\mathcal{L})$ match well with additive combinations.

Taking $G = \mathbb{Z}^k$ and $B = \emptyset$ in Theorem 1 and Corollary 1 in [29], we have the following result, which is also a special case of Lemma 5 with $\operatorname{ind} A = 1$:

**Lemma 1.** *For any finite subset $A \subset \mathbb{Z}^k$ satisfying $\mathbb{Z}^k(A)$ (generated by $\{\sum n_i a_i \mid a_i \in A, n_i \in \mathbb{Z}, \sum n_i = 0\}$) is $\mathbb{Z}^k$, the cardinality of $mA$, i.e., $|mA|$, becomes polynomial in $m$ for sufficiently large $m$, with leading coefficient equal to the volume of the convex hull of $A$.*

Direct application of this lemma completes the computation of $\dim(\mathcal{L})$.

*Example 2.* Taking the modular polynomial equation $f(x_1, x_2) = a_1x_1x_2 + a_2x_1 + a_3 \equiv 0 \mod M$ as an example. By manual calculation, the Jochemsz-May Basic Strategy yields a lattice $\mathcal{L}$ and the corresponding $\dim(\mathcal{L})$ is

$$|\{\lambda|\lambda \text{ is a monomial of } f^m\}| = \sum_{i_1=0}^{m}\sum_{i_2=0}^{m-i_1} 1 = \frac{1}{2}m^2 + \frac{3}{2}m + 1 = \frac{1}{2}m^2 + o(m^2).$$

Using our formulas, we can compute the leading coefficient of $\dim(\mathcal{L})(m)$ by calculating the volume of the triangle with vertices $\{(0,0),(1,0),(1,1)\}$, which has an area of 1/2. See Fig. 1.

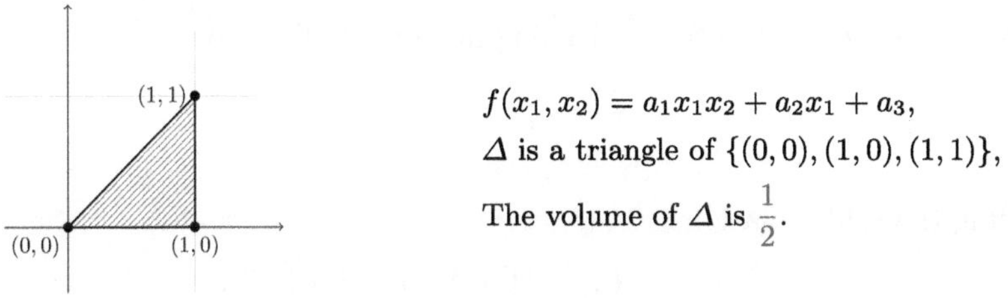


**Fig. 1.** Newton polytope corresponding to $f(x_1, x_2) = a_1x_1x_2 + a_2x_1 + a_3$.

**Computing Determinant via Additive Combinatorics.** The determinant of the lattice $\mathcal{L}$ satisfies:

$$\det(\mathcal{L}) = X_1^{p_1} \cdots X_k^{p_k} \cdot M^{p_{\mathcal{F}}}.$$

Thus, computing $\det(\mathcal{L})$ reduces to determining $p_j$ for $j = 1, \ldots, k$ and $p_{\mathcal{F}}$, where a key challenge lies in expressing $p_{\mathcal{F}}$ through sumsets.

Computation of $p_j$: From Equation (2), each monomial $\lambda$ induces a polynomial $g_\lambda(x_1, \ldots, x_k)$ whose leading monomial is indeed $\lambda$. Hence, the exponent of $X_j$ in $\mathrm{LC}(g_\lambda(x_1X_1, \ldots, x_kX_k))$ is equal to the exponent of $x_j$ in monomial $\lambda$.

This enables us to formally express $p_j(m)$ using $A(f)$:

$$p_j(m) = \sum_{(i_1,\ldots,i_k)\in mA(f)} i_j. \tag{6}$$

Considering the set $\mathcal{H}_j(A)$:

$$\mathcal{H}_j(A) = \bigcup_{(i_1,\ldots,i_k)\in A} \{(i_1,\ldots,i_k,0),(i_1,\ldots,i_k,1),\ldots,(i_1,\ldots,i_k,i_j)\},$$

it enables the following identity:

$$\sum_{(i_1,\ldots,i_k)\in mA(f)} i_j = |\mathcal{H}_j(mA(f))| - |mA(f)| = |m\mathcal{H}_j(A(f))| - |mA(f)|.$$

By Lemma 1, $p_j$ is a polynomial with degree $k+1$ in $m$ when $m$ is large enough. Similar to above, the leading coefficient of $p_j$ is exactly the volume of the convex hull of $\mathcal{H}_j(A(f))$, which also equals the integral of $x_j$ over $N(f)$ (see Lemma 10).

Computation of $p_{\mathcal{F}}$: The central challenge is how to express $p_{\mathcal{F}}$ through sumsets. Applying Abel's summation formula yields:

$$p_{\mathcal{F}}(m) = \sum_{\ell=0}^{m}(m-\ell)|J_\ell \setminus J_{\ell+1}| = \sum_{\ell=0}^{m}(m-\ell)(|J_\ell|-|J_{\ell+1}|) = (m+1)|J_0| - \sum_{\ell=0}^{m}|J_\ell|.$$

To compute $\sum_{\ell=0}^{m}|J_\ell|$, we construct $(k+1)$-dimensional polytopes:

$$\widetilde{A}(f) = \{(i_1,\ldots,i_k,1) \mid (i_1,\ldots,i_k)\in A(f)\} \cup \{(\alpha^{(1)},\ldots,\alpha^{(k)},0)\},$$

where $x_1^{\alpha^{(1)}}\cdots x_k^{\alpha^{(k)}}$ denotes $f$'s leading monomial. This gives:

$$\sum_{\ell=0}^{m}|J_\ell| = |m\widetilde{A}(f)|,$$

enabling the reformulation:

$$p_{\mathcal{F}}(m) = (m+1)|mA(f)| - |m\widetilde{A}(f)|.$$

Both $|mA(f)|$ and $|m\widetilde{A}(f)|$ become polynomials in $m$ asymptotically. Crucially, $\widetilde{A}(f)$ forms a conical extension of $A(f)$ with volume scaling factor $\frac{1}{k+1}$, establishing the leading coefficient's fractional relationship.

**Roadmap.** Sect. 2 establishes foundational concepts including polynomial notation, lattice definitions, sumset theory, and Coppersmith's method. In Sect. 3 we present the formulas for a single polynomial equation with Jochemsz-May Extended Strategy. In Sect. 4, we systematically generalize the Jochemsz-May Extended Strategy from a single polynomial equation to a system of polynomial equations while deriving related formulas. Section 5 presents how to compute the asymptotic upper bounds and our improvements to the CI-HNP over CSURF. Moreover, in order to fully demonstrate the efficiency of computing asymptotic upper bounds, we have conducted sufficient experiments, which also can be found in Sect. 5. Finally, Sect. 6 states our conclusions.

## 2 Preliminaries

We use $\mathbb{N}$, $\mathbb{Z}$, $\mathbb{Q}$ and $\mathbb{R}$ to denote the set of all non-negative integers, the ring of integers, the field of rational numbers and the field of real numbers, respectively. We use little-o notation $o(\cdot)$ or big-O notation $O(\cdot)$ to represent the loose or tight upper bound for a function. For the vector $\mathbf{u} = (u_1, \ldots, u_k)$, we use $\|\cdot\|$ to represent the Euclidean norm, defined as $\|\mathbf{u}\| = \left(\sum_{i=1}^{k} u_i^2\right)^{1/2}$. We also use $\|\cdot\|_\infty$ to denote the infinity norm. We denote by $|\cdot|$ the cardinality of a set.

### 2.1 Polynomials

For a $k$-variable polynomial $f \in \mathbb{Z}[x_1, \ldots, x_k]$, it can be written as

$$f(x_1, \ldots, x_k) = \sum_{i_1, \ldots, i_k \in \mathbb{N}} \alpha_{i_1, \ldots, i_k} \cdot x_1^{i_1} \cdot \ldots \cdot x_k^{i_k},$$

where $\alpha_{i_1, \ldots, i_k} \in \mathbb{Z}$.

A term $x_1^{i_1} \cdot \ldots \cdot x_k^{i_k}$ is called a *monomial* of $f$ if its coefficient $\alpha_{i_1, \ldots, i_k} \neq 0$. The set of all monomials in $f$ is denoted by $\mathrm{supp}(f)$. The *total degree* $\deg(f)$ of $f$ is defined as

$$\deg(f) = \max_{\alpha_{i_1, \ldots, i_k} \neq 0} (i_1 + \cdots + i_k).$$

**Definition 1 (Monomial Order).** *Let $\mathcal{M}$ be a set of monomials. A* monomial order *on $\mathcal{M}$ is a total order $\prec$ that satisfies the following properties:*

1. *For every $\lambda \in \mathcal{M}$, it holds that $1 \prec \lambda$.*
2. *If $\lambda_1 \prec \lambda_2$, then $\lambda \cdot \lambda_1 \prec \lambda \cdot \lambda_2$ for every monomial $\lambda \in \mathcal{M}$.*

Using the lexicographic monomial order ($\prec_{\text{lex}}$) with $x_1 \prec_{\text{lex}} x_2 \prec_{\text{lex}} x_3$ as an example, this order first compares the exponents of $x_3$ in the monomials; if those are equal, it then compares the exponents of $x_2$, and so on. Then we have $x_2^2 \prec_{\text{lex}} x_3$ and $x_1 \prec_{\text{lex}} x_2 \prec_{\text{lex}} x_2^2$.

If $\prec$ is a monomial order, the *leading monomial* of a polynomial $f$ is the unique monomial $\lambda$ in $f$ that satisfies $\lambda' \prec \lambda$ for every other monomial $\lambda'$ in $f$. The *leading coefficient* is the coefficient of the leading monomial. We denote the leading monomial and the leading coefficient of $f$ by $\mathrm{LM}(f)$ and $\mathrm{LC}(f)$, respectively. The *leading term* of $f$ is given by

$$\mathrm{LT}(f) = \mathrm{LC}(f) \times \mathrm{LM}(f).$$

A polynomial is *monic* if $\mathrm{LC}(f) = 1$.

## 2.2 Lattices

A *lattice* is a discrete additive subgroup of $\mathbb{R}^m$ where $m \in \mathbb{N}$. Another equivalent definition is presented as follows.

**Definition 2 (Lattice).** *Let* $\mathbf{v_1}, \mathbf{v_2}, \ldots, \mathbf{v_n} \in \mathbb{R}^m$ *be* $n$ *linearly independent vectors with* $n \leq m$. *The* lattice $\mathcal{L}$ *spanned by* $\{\mathbf{v_1}, \mathbf{v_2}, \ldots, \mathbf{v_n}\}$ *is the set of all integer linear combinations of these vectors, i.e.,*

$$\mathcal{L} = \left\{ \mathbf{v} \in \mathbb{R}^m \mid \mathbf{v} = \sum_{i=1}^{n} a_i \mathbf{v_i},\ a_i \in \mathbb{Z} \right\}.$$

The integer $n$ is called the *rank* of the lattice $\mathcal{L}$, while $m$ is referred to its *dimension.* The lattice $\mathcal{L}$ is said to be *full-rank* if $n = m$.

A lattice can be represented using a basis matrix $\mathbf{B} \in \mathbb{R}^{n \times m}$, where each row corresponds to a basis vector $\mathbf{v_i}$. The *determinant* of $\mathcal{L}$ is defined as

$$\det(\mathcal{L}) = \sqrt{\det\left(\mathbf{B}\mathbf{B}^t\right)},$$

where $\mathbf{B}^t$ denotes the transpose of $\mathbf{B}$. If $\mathcal{L}$ is full-rank, this simplifies to $\det(\mathcal{L}) = |\det(\mathbf{B})|$. In this paper, we consider full-rank lattices.

**Definition 3 (Fundamental Parallelepiped).** *For any full-rank* $n$*-dimensional lattice* $\mathcal{L}$ *with basis matrix* $\mathbf{B}$, *we define*

$$\mathcal{P}(\mathbf{B}) = \{\mathbf{B}x \mid x \in \mathbb{R}^n, \forall i : 0 \leq x_i < 1\},$$

*called the* fundamental parallelepiped *of* $\mathcal{L}$. *The* index *of* $\mathcal{L}$ *as a sublattice of* $\mathbb{Z}^n$ *is defined as the volume of* $\mathcal{P}(\mathbf{B})$.

**Definition 4 (Index of Sublattice of $\mathbb{Z}^n$ ).** *For any full-rank* $n$*-dimensional lattice* $\mathcal{L} \subseteq \mathbb{Z}^n$ *with basis matrix* $\mathbf{B}$, *the* index *of* $\mathcal{L}$ *as a sublattice of* $\mathbb{Z}^n$ *is defined as the volume of* $\mathcal{P}(\mathbf{B})$, *or equivalently, the determinant of* $\mathcal{L}$.

**Definition 5 (Shortest Vector Problem (SVP)).** *Given a lattice* $\mathcal{L}$, *the Shortest Vector Problem (SVP) asks to find a non-zero lattice vector* $\mathbf{v} \in \mathcal{L}$ *of minimum Euclidean norm, i.e., find* $\mathbf{v} \in \mathcal{L} \backslash \{\mathbf{0}\}$ *such that* $\|\mathbf{v}\| \leq \|\mathbf{w}\|$ *for all non-zero* $\mathbf{w} \in \mathcal{L}$.

The Shortest Vector Problem (SVP) has been proven to be NP-hard under randomized reductions [1]. However, using the well-known LLL algorithm [30], it is possible to efficiently compute a relatively short vector in polynomial time.

**Lemma 2 (LLL Basis Reduction).** *Let* $\mathcal{L} \in \mathbb{Z}^n$ *be a lattice. The LLL algorithm finds, in polynomial time, a basis* $(\mathbf{v}_1, \ldots, \mathbf{v}_n)$ *of* $\mathcal{L}$ *satisfying*

$$\|\mathbf{v}_i\| \leq 2^{\frac{n(n-1)}{4(n+1-i)}} \det(\mathcal{L})^{\frac{1}{n+1-i}},$$

*for all* $i = 1, \ldots, n$.

### 2.3 Sumset Theory for Polynomials

This section presents some results from additive combinatorics (sumset theory) and demonstrates their application to polynomials in $\mathbb{Z}[x_1, \ldots, x_k]$. We also introduce some results concerning the problem of counting the number of lattice points contained within a convex bounded polyhedron, commonly referred to as a polytope.

**Newton Polytope.** For any polynomial $f \in \mathbb{Z}[x_1, \ldots, x_k]$, define its monomial exponent set as:

$$A(f) = \{(i_1, \ldots, i_k) \mid x_1^{i_1} \cdots x_k^{i_k} \text{ is a monomial of } f\}.$$

**Definition 6 (Convex Hull).** *The convex hull of a set $S \subset \mathbb{R}^n$ is denoted as $N(S)$ and is defined as the smallest convex set containing $S$. Formally, it is given by:*

$$N(S) = \left\{ \sum_{i=1}^{m} \lambda_i x_i \mid x_i \in S, \, \lambda_i \geq 0, \, \sum_{i=1}^{m} \lambda_i = 1 \right\}$$

*where the sum is over some finite set of points $\{x_1, x_2, \ldots, x_m\}$ from $S$, and $\lambda_i$ are the convex coefficients.*

**Definition 7 (Newton Polytope).** *The* Newton polytope *of $f \in \mathbb{Z}[x_1, \ldots, x_k]$, denoted by $N(f)$, is the convex hull of $A(f)$ in $\mathbb{R}^k$.*

*Example 3.* For $f$ with $\operatorname{supp}(f) = \{1, x_1, x_1^2, x_2\}$, we have:

- $A(f) = \{(0,0), (1,0), (2,0), (0,1)\}$
- Newton polytope: Triangle with vertices $(0,0)$, $(2,0)$, and $(0,1)$

**Definition 8 (Minkowski Sum).** *For sets $A, B \subset \mathbb{Z}^k$, their* Minkowski sum *is:*

$$A + B = \{a + b \mid a \in A, \, b \in B\}.$$

For $m \in \mathbb{N}$, denote by $mA$ the sum of $m$ identical sets $A$.

*Property 1.* For all nonzero $f_1, f_2 \in \mathbb{Z}[x_1, \ldots, x_k]$:

$$N(f_1 \cdot f_2) = N(f_1) + N(f_2).$$

**Well-Defined $k$-Variate Polynomials.** To avoid cases like $f_1 = x_1x_2 + 1$ reducible to $f_2 = z_1 + 1$ via substitution $z_1 = x_1x_2$, where $f_1^m$ exhibits univariate-like monomial growth despite its bivariate form, we need some requirements on $f$.

**Definition 9 (Well-Defined $k$-Variate Polynomials).** *A polynomial $f \in \mathbb{Z}[x_1, \ldots, x_k]$ is called* well-defined $k$-variate *if:*

1. $f(0,\ldots,0) \neq 0$.
2. *The lattice generated by* $A(f)$ *has finite index in* $\mathbb{Z}^k$, *denoted by* $\operatorname{ind} A(f)$.

We consider two types of summations. The first is the number of elements in $mA(f)$: $\sum_{\lambda\in mA(f)} 1$. The second is a weighted version: for homogeneous $\phi$, $\sum_{\lambda\in mA(f)} \phi(\lambda)$. We also consider cases with multiple subsets like $m_1A(f_1) + m_2A(f_2)$.

**Summation of** $\sum_{\lambda\in mA(f)} 1$. For any finite subset $A \subset \mathbb{Z}^k$, Khovanskii [29] first established polynomial growth of $\sum_{\lambda\in mA} 1$. We adapt Theorem 1 ($G = \mathbb{Z}^k$, $B = \emptyset$) and Corollary 2 from [29]:

**Lemma 3 ([29], Theorem 1).** *Let $A$ be any finite subset of $\mathbb{Z}^k$. For all sufficiently large $m \in \mathbb{N}$, $|mA|$ is a polynomial in $m$ with degree $< |A|$.*

**Lemma 4 ([29], Corollary 2).** *For finite $A \subset \mathbb{Z}^k$ where $\mathbb{Z}^k(A)$ (generated by $\{\sum n_ia_i \mid a_i \in A, n_i \in \mathbb{Z}, \sum n_i = 0\}$) has finite index* $\operatorname{ind} A$ *in $\mathbb{Z}^k$:*

$$\lim_{m\to\infty} \frac{|mA|}{m^k} = (\operatorname{ind} A)^{-1}V(A),$$

*where $V(A)$ denotes the volume of the convex hull of $A$.*

Using Lemma 3 and Lemma 4, we have the following result:

**Lemma 5 (Summation of $\sum_{\lambda\in mA(f)} 1$).** *For any well-defined $k$-variate $f$, the number of points in $mA(f)$ is polynomial in $m$ with degree $k$ when $m$ is large enough. Specifically, the leading coefficient is the volume of the Newton polytope corresponding to $f$ divided by* $\operatorname{ind} A(f)$. *That is,*

$$|mA(f)| = \frac{\int_{N(f)} 1\, dV}{\operatorname{ind} A(f)} m^k + o(m^k).$$

*Proof.* From Definition 9, $\mathbf{0} \in A(f)$ ensures, for any $v$ in the lattice generated by $A(f)$:

$$\exists n_i \in \mathbb{Z},\ a_i \in A(f):\ v = \sum n_ia_i + (-\sum n_i)\mathbf{0},$$

with $\sum n_i + (-\sum n_i) = 0$. Thus the lattice generated by $A(f)$ is $\mathbb{Z}^k(A(f))$ with index $\operatorname{ind} A(f)$. Lemma 4 then applies directly. □

Granville et al. [22] bounded the polynomialization threshold:

**Lemma 6 ([22], Theorem 1.1).** *For finite $A \subset \mathbb{Z}^k$, $\exists p \in \mathbb{Q}[x]$ with $\deg p \leq k$ such that:*

$$|mA| = p(m) \quad \forall m \geq (2\,A| \cdot w(A))^{(k+4)|A|}$$

*where* $w(A) = \max_{a,b\in A} \|a - b\|_\infty$.

For $f = x_1^3 + x_1x_2 + x_1x_3 + x_2 + x_3^2x_4^2 + x_4^5 + 1$, this requires:

$$m > (2 \cdot 7 \cdot 5)^{8\cdot 7} \approx 2^{343}.$$

Lemma 3 was generalized to the multiple subsets setting by [23,36,37].

**Lemma 7 ([37], Theorem 2).** *For finite sets $A_1, ..., A_r$ in abelian semigroup $S$, there exists a polynomial $p(t_1, \ldots, t_r)$, such that*

$$|h_1 A_1 + \cdots + h_r A_r| = p(h_1, ..., h_r)$$

*for all sufficiently large integers $h_1, \ldots, h_r$.*

Ehrhart's theorem [19] establishes that for any integral polytope $N \subset \mathbb{R}^k$, the lattice point count

$$|mN \cap \mathbb{Z}^k|$$

is a polynomial in $m$. The leading coefficient of this polynomial is equal to the volume of $N$, as stated in Theorem 1 of [16].

**Lemma 8.** *Suppose $N \in \mathbb{R}^k$ is an integral polytope whose vertices have integral coordinates, then $|mN \cap \mathbb{Z}^k|$ is a polynomial in $m$ with degree $k$ and its leading coefficient is the volume of $N$.*

It is straightforward to derive the following result:

**Lemma 9 (Summation of $\sum_{\lambda \in mN(f)} 1$).** *For any well-defined $k$-variate $f$, the number of points in $mN(f)$ is polynomial in $m$ with degree $k$. Specifically, the leading coefficient is the volume of the Newton polytope corresponding to $f$. That is,*

$$|mN(f) \cap \mathbb{Z}^k| = \int_{N(f)} 1 \, dV \, m^k + o(m^k).$$

*Proof.* Instantiate Lemma 8 with $N = N(f)$. □

**Summation of $\sum_{\lambda \in mA(f)} \phi(\lambda)$.** Initial work by [10] analyzed

$$\sum_{\lambda \in mN \cap \mathbb{Z}^k} \phi(\lambda)$$

for integral polytopes $N$ and homogeneous polynomials $\phi$. Recently, further progress has been reported in this area [2]. It is shown that this summation forms a polynomial in $m$ of degree $k + \deg(\phi)$, with the leading coefficient given by $\int_{N(f)} \phi \, dV$. These integrals have been studied in [3–5]. We specialize to $\phi = x_j$, the homogeneous coordinate function:

**Lemma 10.** *For any well-defined $k$-variate polynomial $f$, the sum $\sum_{(i_1,\ldots,i_k) \in mA(f)} i_j$ is polynomial in $m$ with degree $k+1$ when $m$ is large enough. Specifically, the leading coefficient is $\int_{N(f)} x_j \, dV$ divided by $\operatorname{ind} A(f)$. That is,*

$$\sum_{(i_1,\ldots,i_k) \in mA(f)} i_j = \frac{\int_{N(f)} x_j \, dV}{\operatorname{ind} A(f)} m^{k+1} + o(m^{k+1}),$$

*where $x_j : \mathbb{R}^k \to \mathbb{R}$ acts as $x_j((i_1, \ldots, i_k)) = i_j$.*

Next, we consider the setting with shift $E = \{(0,\ldots,0),(1,0,\ldots,0)\} \subset \mathbb{Z}^k$:

**Lemma 11.** *For any well-defined $k$-variate polynomials $f$, the summation*

$$\sum_{(i_1,\ldots,i_k)\in m_1 A(f)+m_2 E} i_j$$

*is a polynomial in $m_1$ and $m_2$ of degree $k+1$ when $m_1$ and $m_2$ are sufficiently large. That is,*

$$\sum_{\lambda\in m_1 A(f)+m_2 E} x_j(\lambda) = \underbrace{b_0^{(j)} m_1^{k+1} + b_1^{(j)} m_1^k m_2 + \ldots + b_{k+1}^{(j)} m_2^{k+1}}_{\textit{all monomials with degree } k+1} + \ldots.$$

*Besides, for all $\delta \in \mathbb{N}$, $b_i^{(j)}$ satisfy*

$$\sum_{i=0}^{k+1} b_i^{(j)} \delta^i = \frac{\int_{N(A(f)+\delta E)} x_j \, dV}{\operatorname{ind} A(f) + \delta E}$$

*where $x_j : \mathbb{R}^k \to \mathbb{R}$ acts as $x_j((i_1,\ldots,i_k)) = i_j$.*

Detailed proofs for both Lemma 10 and 11 can be found in Appendix in our full version [20].

*Remark 1.* Using an analogous proof, this result can be extended to multiple subsets.

## 2.4 Coppersmith's Method

Suppose $f \in \mathbb{Z}[x_1,\ldots,x_k]$ has a small root $\mathbf{u} = (u_1,\ldots,u_k) \in \mathbb{Z}^k$ modulo some integer $M$. Here, a small root means that $|u_i| < X_i$ for known bounds $X_i$, for $i = 1,\ldots,k$.

In Coppersmith's method [12,13,33], one initially fixes an integer $m$ and then constructs a set of polynomials that share a common root with the target polynomial modulo $M^m$. Subsequently, the coefficient vectors of these polynomials are used to construct a lattice $\mathcal{L}$ serving as the lattice basis. Then, one searches for short vectors $v_j$ ($j = 1,\ldots,k$) in the lattice, such that the corresponding polynomials $h_j(x_1,\ldots,x_k)$ satisfies the conditions of Lemma 12 [26].

**Lemma 12.** *Let $h(x_1,\ldots,x_k) \in \mathbb{Z}[x_1,\ldots,x_k]$ be a polynomial with at most $\omega$ monomials, and let $M$ be a positive integer. If there exist integers $(u_1,\ldots,u_k)$ satisfying the following two conditions:*

1. *$h(u_1,\ldots,u_k) \equiv 0 \mod M$,*
2. *there exist positive integers $X_1,\ldots,X_k$ such that $|u_i| < X_i$ for $i = 1,\ldots,k$, and*

$$\|h(x_1X_1,\ldots,x_kX_k)\| < \frac{M}{\sqrt{\omega}},$$

*then* $h(u_1,\ldots,u_k)=0$ *holds over* $\mathbb{Z}$.

Hence, for each $h_j$, both

$$h_j(\mathbf{u})\equiv 0 \mod M^m \quad \text{and} \quad h_j(\mathbf{u})=0 \quad \text{over } \mathbb{Z}$$

hold. Then the roots can be found by solving the equations $h_j(\mathbf{u})=0$.

Note that we aim to find short vectors that satisfy condition 2 of Lemma 12 in polynomial time. Using the LLL algorithm, one can efficiently approximate relatively short vectors. Combining Lemma 12 and Lemma 2, we require the lattice $\mathcal{L}$ to satisfy

$$\det(\mathcal{L}) < M^{m\cdot\dim(\mathcal{L})}. \tag{7}$$

Since both $\det(\mathcal{L})$ and $\dim(\mathcal{L})$ depend on $m, X_1,\ldots,X_k$, Equation (7) can be used to bound $X_j$ for $j=1,\ldots,k$.

After constructing the lattice $\mathcal{L}$ and applying the LLL algorithm, Coppersmith's method further requires the following assumption commonly required for the multivariate case [7,21,25], and this heuristic holds for most instances encountered in practice:

**Assumption 1.** The polynomials obtained from the LLL-reduced basis in Coppersmith's method generate an ideal corresponding to a zero-dimensional variety.

# 3 Solving a Single Polynomial Equation

In this section, we review the Jochemsz-May Extended Strategy and present its corresponding formulas for the asymptotic bounds. Since the Jochemsz-May Basic Strategy can be seen as a special case of the Jochemsz-May Extended Strategy, all our results for the extended strategy works for the basic strategy.

## 3.1 The Jochemsz-May Extended Strategy

Let $f\in\mathbb{Z}[x_1,\ldots,x_k]$ be monic with small root $\mathbf{u}=(u_1,\ldots,u_k)$ satisfying $|u_i|<X_i$ for bounds $X_i$ and the modulus is $M$. For integers $m$ and $t$, the Jochemsz-May Extended Strategy introduces additional shifts in $x_1$ compared to the Jochemsz-May Basic Strategy. For the leading monomial $x_1^{\alpha^{(1)}}\cdots x_k^{\alpha^{(k)}}$ of $f$, let $\alpha=(\alpha^{(1)},\ldots,\alpha^{(k)})\in\mathbb{Z}^k$ and define $A(f)=\{(i_1,\ldots,i_k)\mid x_1^{i_1}\cdots x_k^{i_k}$ is a monomial of $f\}$. The only difference lies in the definition of $J_\ell$, which is defined as:

$$J_\ell=\bigcup_{0\le j\le t}\left\{x_1^j\cdot\lambda \mid \lambda\in(m-\ell)A(f)+\ell\alpha\right\}. \tag{8}$$

The lattice $\mathcal{L}$ constructed via the Jochemsz-May Extended Strategy satisfies:

$$\dim(\mathcal{L})=\Big|\bigcup_{0\le\ell\le m} J_\ell\Big|, \tag{9}$$

$$\det(\mathcal{L})=\prod_{g_\lambda(x_1,\ldots,x_k)\in G_{m,t}} \mathrm{LC}(g_\lambda(x_1X_1,\ldots,x_kX_k)). \tag{10}$$

*Remark 2.* Typically, $t$ is chosen to be a constant multiple of $m$. Thus, in our asymptotic analysis, for convenience, we will abbreviate $\sum_{i+j<k} m^i t^j$ as $o(m^k)$. When $t$ is set to 0, the approach reduces to the Jochemsz-May Basic Strategy.

*Remark 3.* To ensure that the assumption in the Jochemsz-May Extended Strategy—that the monomials of $f, f^1, \ldots, f^{m-1}$ are all contained among the monomials of $f^m$—holds, we modify the original definition of $J_\ell$. Specifically, we replace

$$J_\ell = \bigcup_{0\leq j\leq t} \left\{ x_1^j \cdot \lambda \;\middle|\; \lambda \in \text{supp}(f^m) \text{ and } \frac{\lambda}{\text{LM}(f)^\ell} \in \text{supp}(f^{m-\ell}) \right\}$$

with

$$J_\ell = \bigcup_{0\leq j\leq t} \left\{ x_1^j \cdot \lambda \mid \lambda \in (m-\ell)A(f) + \ell\alpha \right\}.$$

### 3.2 Our Formulas.

For the leading monomial $x_1^{a^{(1)}} \cdot \ldots \cdot x_k^{a^{(k)}}$ of $f$, denote $\alpha = (\alpha^{(1)}, \ldots, \alpha^{(k)}) \in \mathbb{Z}^k$. Define $A(f)$ and $\widetilde{A}(f)$ as follows

$$A(f) = \{(i_1, \ldots, i_k) \mid x_1^{i_1} \cdots x_k^{i_k} \in \text{supp}(f)\},$$
$$\widetilde{A}(f) = \{(i_1, \ldots, i_k, 1) \mid (i_1, \ldots, i_k) \in A(f)\} \cup \{(\alpha^{(1)}, \ldots, \alpha^{(k)}, 0)\},$$

We also denote $E$ and $\widetilde{E}$ as follows:

$$E = \{(0, \ldots, 0), \quad \underbrace{(1, 0, \ldots, 0)}_{\text{Only the 1-th position is 1}} \quad\} \subset \mathbb{Z}^k,$$
$$\widetilde{E} = \{(0, \ldots, 0, 0), \quad \underbrace{(1, 0, \ldots, 0, 0)}_{\text{Only the 1-th position is 1}} \quad\} \subset \mathbb{Z}^{k+1}.$$

Now we focus on the following inequality which derives the bound directly:

$$\det(\mathcal{L}) < M^{m \dim(\mathcal{L})}. \tag{11}$$

**Computing** $\dim(\mathcal{L})$ **via Additive Combinatorics.** For dimension, we obtain the following theorem:

**Theorem 1.** *For any well-defined $k$-variate $f$, the* $\dim(\mathcal{L})$ *obtained by the Jochemsz-May Extended Strategy is polynomial in $t$ and $m$ when $t$ and $m$ are large enough. More precisely,*

$$\dim(\mathcal{L})(m,t) = a_0 m^k + a_1 t m^{k-1} + \ldots + a_k t^k + o(m^k),$$

*when $t = O(m)$. Besides, denote $A(1 + x_1)$ as $E$. For all $\delta \in \mathbb{N}$, the coefficients $a_i$ satisfy*

$$\sum_{i=0}^{k} a_i \delta^i = \frac{\int_{N(A(f)+\delta E)} 1\, dV}{\text{ind}\, A(f) + \delta E}$$

*from which we can compute all $a_i$ for $i = 0, \ldots, k$.*

*Proof.* We observe that

$$|\bigcup_{0\le \ell\le m} J_\ell| = |mA(f)+tE|,$$

so we can rewrite Equation (9) as follows:

$$\dim(\mathcal{L}) = |mA(f)+tE|. \tag{12}$$

The equivalence between Equation (9) and Equation (12) is powerful and makes the computation of $\dim(\mathcal{L})$ match well with additive combinations.

From Lemma 7, we know $\dim(\mathcal{L})$ is a polynomial in $m$ and $t$ for large enough $m$ and $t$. Substituting $t = m$, using Lemma 5, $\dim(\mathcal{L}) = |m(E + A(f))|$ is a polynomial of degree $k$ in $m$ for large enough $m$, implying that the total degree of $\dim(\mathcal{L})(m,t)$ is $k$, that is, there exists $\{a_i\}_{0\le i\le k}$,

$$\dim(\mathcal{L})(m,t) = a_0 m^k + a_1 t m^{k-1} + \ldots + a_k t^k + o(m^k).$$

When substituting $t = \delta m$ for $\delta = 0,\ldots,k$, we have $\dim(\mathcal{L}) = |m(A(f)+\delta E)| = (\sum_{i=0}^k a_i\delta^i)m^k + o(m^k)$. Comparing the coefficients of $m^k$ on both sides, we obtain

$$\sum_{i=0}^{k} a_i\delta^i = \frac{\int_{N(A(f)+\delta E)} 1\,dV}{\operatorname{ind} A(f)+\delta E}$$

from which can compute all $a_i$ for $i = 0,\ldots,k$. □

**Computing** $\det(\mathcal{L})$ **via Additive Combinatorics.** The determinant of the lattice $\mathcal{L}$ satisfies:

$$\det(\mathcal{L}) = X_1^{p_1}\cdots X_k^{p_k}\cdot M^{p_{\mathcal{F}}}.$$

Thus, computing $\det(\mathcal{L})$ reduces to determining $p_j$ for $j = 1,\ldots,k$ and $p_{\mathcal{F}}$. Detailed proof can be found in our full version [20].

**Our Final Formulas.** For any *well-defined k-variate* polynomial $f$, we can now provide formulas for the bound yielded by the Jochemsz-May Extended Strategy for Coppersmith's method, i.e., there exist $\{a_i\}_{0\le i\le k}$, $\{b_i^{(j)}\}_{0\le i\le k+1}$, and $\{c_i\}_{0\le i\le k+1}$, such that $\det(\mathcal{L}) < M^{m\dim(\mathcal{L})}$ can be rewritten as follows, for any arbitrarily small constant $\varepsilon > 0$:

$$\prod_{j=1}^{k} X_j^{\sum_{i=0}^{k+1} b_i^{(j)} m^{k+1-i} t^i}\cdot M^{\sum_{i=0}^{k+1} c_i m^{k+1-i} t^i} < M^{\sum_{i=0}^{k} a_i m^{k+1-i} t^i - \varepsilon} \tag{13}$$

These coefficients satisfy the following system of equations, which can be determined by solving the linear equation system for $\delta = 0, \dots, k+1$:

$$\begin{cases} \sum_{i=0}^{k} a_i \delta^i = \dfrac{\int_{N(A(f)+\delta E)} 1\, dV}{\operatorname{ind} A(f) + \delta E}, \\ \sum_{i=0}^{k+1} b_i^{(j)} \delta^i = \dfrac{\int_{N(A(f)+\delta E)} x_j\, dV}{\operatorname{ind} A(f) + \delta E}, \\ \sum_{i=0}^{k+1} c_i \delta^i = \dfrac{\int_{N(A(f)+\delta E)} 1\, dV}{\operatorname{ind} A(f) + \delta E} - \dfrac{\int_{N(\widetilde{A}(f)+\delta \widetilde{E})} 1\, dV}{\operatorname{ind} \widetilde{A}(f) + \delta \widetilde{E}}. \end{cases}$$

*Remark 4.* The Jochemsz-May Extended Strategy serves as a general framework. However, in cryptanalysis, certain problems demand specialized techniques to achieve stronger results, as seen in the case of the Small Private Exponent RSA Problem [7,25]. In our full version [20], we further investigate the use of Newton polytopes to compute the dimension and determinant of these lattices involved with special techniques.

## 4 Solving a System of Polynomial Equations

In this section, we first generalize the Jochemsz-May Extended Strategy for a single polynomial equation to a system of polynomial equations, and then derive related formulas for the generalized case in Sect. 4.2. Furthermore, by introducing additional shift polynomials to the strategies proposed by Meers–Nowakowski [35] and Sarkar [39] for solving systems of polynomial equations, we extend their methods to a more generalized framework and derive the corresponding formulas. Since the approaches of Meers–Nowakowski and Sarkar can be regarded as special cases of our generalization, our formulas naturally encompass their results.

**Notations.** In this section, we use the following notations. Suppose $\mathcal{F} = \{f_1, \dots, f_n\} \subseteq \mathbb{Z}[x_1, \dots, x_k]$ is a set of polynomials with a common small root $\mathbf{u} = (u_1, \dots, u_k) \in \mathbb{Z}^k$ modulo some integer $M$. Here, a small root means $|u_i| < X_i$ for known bound $X_i$, for $i = 1, \dots, k$. Let $\alpha_j \in \mathbb{Z}^k$ represent the integer points corresponding to the leading monomial of $f_j$ for $j = 1, \dots, n$. That is, for $\alpha_j = (\alpha_j^{(1)}, \dots, \alpha_j^{(k)})$, we have $\mathrm{LM}(f_j) = x_1^{\alpha_j^{(1)}} \cdot \dots \cdot x_k^{\alpha_j^{(k)}}$. We denote $B$ as $\{\alpha_1, \dots, \alpha_n\}$. And we define $\widetilde{A}(f)$ as follows

$$\widetilde{A}(f) = \{(i_1, \dots, i_k, 1) \mid (i_1, \dots, i_k) \in A(f)\} \cup \{(\alpha^{(1)}, \dots, \alpha^{(k)}, 0)\},$$

where $x_1^{\alpha^{(1)}} \cdot \dots \cdot x_k^{\alpha^{(k)}}$ is the leading monomial of $f$.

### 4.1 Generalized Jochemsz-May Extended Strategy with Shift $x_1$

We first generalize the Jochemsz-May Extended Strategy to solve a system of polynomial equations with shift $x_1$ and then provide the corresponding formulas for $\dim(\mathcal{L})$ and $\det(\mathcal{L})$ later.

We denote $A(\mathcal{F})$ as follows:

$$A(\mathcal{F}) = \bigcup_{j=1}^{n} A(f_j). \tag{14}$$

Fix integers $m$ and $t$. We define the sets

$$\begin{aligned} S_\ell &= \{x_1^{i_1} \cdot \ldots \cdot x_k^{i_k} \mid (i_1, \ldots, i_k) \in tE + (m-\ell)A(\mathcal{F}) + \bigcup_{\substack{\ell_1+\cdots+\ell_n=\ell \\ 0\le \ell_j \le m}} \sum_{j=1}^{n} \ell_j \alpha_j\} \\ &= \{x_1^{i_1} \cdot \ldots \cdot x_k^{i_k} \mid (i_1, \ldots, i_k) \in tE + (m-\ell)A(\mathcal{F}) + \ell B\}, \end{aligned} \tag{15}$$

for $0 \le \ell \le m$ and $S_{m+1} = \emptyset$, so that $S_m \subset \ldots \subset S_0$. The strategy constructs basis polynomials for every monomial $\lambda = x_1^{i_1} \cdot \ldots \cdot x_k^{i_k} \in S_\ell \setminus S_{\ell+1}$:

**Step 1**: Compute $\ell_1, \ldots, \ell_n$ with $\sum_{j=1}^{n} \ell_j = \ell$, such that

$$(i_1, \ldots, i_n) \in tE + (m-\ell)A(\mathcal{F}) + \sum_{j=1}^{n} \ell_j \alpha_j.$$

**Step 2**: Construct $g_\lambda(x_1, \ldots, x_k)$ as follows:

$$g_\lambda(x_1, \ldots, x_k) = \frac{\lambda}{\prod_{j=1}^{n} \mathrm{LM}(f_j)^{\ell_j}} \prod_{j=1}^{n} f_j^{\ell_j} M^{m-\ell}. \tag{16}$$

Then we use the coefficient vectors of all $g_\lambda(x_1X_1, \ldots, x_kX_k)$ to form the basis of lattice $\mathcal{L}$.

### 4.2 Our Formulas for $\dim(\mathcal{L})$ and $\det(\mathcal{L})$

Next, we provide related formulas for computing the dimension and determinant for our Generalized Jochemsz-May Extended Strategy with shift $x_1$.

**Our Formulas.** We can now compute the relevant formulas for the bounds obtained using our strategy in Coppersmith's method. There exist $\{a_i\}_{0\le i\le k}$, $\{b_i^{(j)}\}_{0\le i\le k+1}$, and $\{c_i\}_{0\le i\le k+1}$, such that $\det(\mathcal{L}) < M^{m\dim(\mathcal{L})}$ can be rewritten as follows, for any arbitrarily small constant $\varepsilon > 0$:

$$\prod_{j=1}^{k} X_j^{\sum_{i=0}^{k+1} b_i^{(j)} m^{k+1-i} t^i} \cdot M^{\sum_{i=0}^{k+1} c_i m^{k+1-i} t^i} < M^{\sum_{i=0}^{k} a_i m^{k+1-i} t^i - \varepsilon} \tag{17}$$

These coefficients satisfied the following equations, which can be determined by solving the linear equation system for $\delta = 0, \ldots, k+1$:

$$\begin{cases} \sum_{i=0}^{k} a_i \delta^i = \dfrac{\int_{N(A(\mathcal{F})+\delta E)} 1\, dV}{\operatorname{ind} A(\mathcal{F}) + \delta E}, \\ \sum_{i=0}^{k+1} b_i^{(j)} \delta^i = \dfrac{\int_{N(A(\mathcal{F})+\delta E)} x_j\, dV}{\operatorname{ind} A(\mathcal{F}) + \delta E}, \\ \sum_{i=0}^{k+1} c_i \delta^i = \dfrac{\int_{N(A(\mathcal{F})+\delta E)} 1\, dV}{\operatorname{ind} A(\mathcal{F}) + \delta E} - \dfrac{\int_{N(\widetilde{A}(\mathcal{F})+\delta \widetilde{E})} 1\, dV}{\operatorname{ind} \widetilde{A}(\mathcal{F}) + \delta \widetilde{E}}. \end{cases}$$

*Remark 5.* The proof can be found in our full version [20].

*Remark 6.* When considering multiple shifts, i.e., using $\sum_{j=1}^{k} t_j E_j$ instead of $tE$ in Equation (15), the dimension of the lattice is given by $|mA(\mathcal{F}) + \sum_{j=1}^{k} t_j E_j|$, which is a polynomial in $m, t_1, \ldots, t_k$ for sufficiently large $m, t_1, \ldots, t_k$. The formulas for $\dim(\mathcal{L})$ and $\det(\mathcal{L})$ are analogous to those presented in Sect. 4.2.

### 4.3 Some Variants

By incorporating additional shift polynomials, we further generalize the approaches of Meers–Nowakowski [35] and Sarkar [39], referred to as Variant I and Variant II, respectively, and derive the corresponding formulas. Proofs for the related formulas are analogous to those presented in Sect. 4.2.

**Variant I.** We first define the sets of vertices as follows:

$$V_{\ell_1,\ldots,\ell_n} = \sum_{j=1}^{n} (\frac{m}{n} - \ell_j) A(f_j) + \ell_j \alpha_j,$$

and

$$V_\ell = \bigcup_{\substack{\ell_1+\cdots+\ell_n=\ell \\ 0 \le \ell_j \le \frac{m}{n}}} V_{\ell_1,\ldots,\ell_n}.$$

Now we can define the following monomial sets as

$$S_\ell = \left\{ x_1^{i_1} \cdot \ldots \cdot x_k^{i_k} \mid (i_1, \ldots, i_k) \in tE + \bigcup_{\substack{\ell_1+\ldots+\ell_n=\ell \\ 0 \le \ell_j \le \frac{m}{n}}} \sum_{j=1}^{n} (\frac{m}{n} - \ell_j) A(f_j) + \ell_j \alpha_j \right\}.$$

for $0 \le \ell \le m$ and $S_{m+1} = \emptyset$, so that $S_m \subset \ldots \subset S_0$. Variant I constructs basis polynomials for every monomial $\lambda = x_1^{i_1} \cdot \ldots \cdot x_k^{i_k} \in S_\ell \setminus S_{\ell+1}$:

**Step 1**: Compute $\ell_1, \ldots, \ell_n$ with $\sum_{j=1}^{n} \ell_j = \ell$ and $0 \le \ell_j \le \frac{m}{n}$, such that

$$(i_1, \ldots, i_n) \in tE + V_{\ell_1,\ldots,\ell_n}.$$

**Step 2**: Construct $g_\lambda(x_1, \ldots, x_k)$ as follows:

$$g_\lambda(x_1, \ldots, x_k) = \frac{\lambda}{\prod_{j=1}^{n} \mathrm{LM}(f_j)^{\ell_j}} \prod_{j=1}^{n} f_j^{\ell_j} M^{m-\ell}.$$

We use the coefficient vectors of all $g_\lambda(x_1X_1, \ldots, x_kX_k)$ to form the basis of the lattice $\mathcal{L}$.

We define $A(\mathcal{F}) = \frac{1}{n}\sum_{j=1}^{n} A(f_j)$ and $\widetilde{A}(\mathcal{F}) = \frac{1}{n}\sum_{j=1}^{n} \widetilde{A}(f_j)$. The formulas yielded by Variant I are the same as those presented in Sect. 4.2 with the newly defined $A(\mathcal{F})$ and $\widetilde{A}(\mathcal{F})$.

*Remark 7.* Here, we require $0 \le \ell_j \le \frac{m}{n}$ to simplify the calculations. However, when $f_j$ has special structures, special structures, such as $f_1 = x_1 + 1$ and $f_2 = (x_1 + 1)(x_2 + 1)(x_3 + 1)$ where $f_1$ divides $f_2$, allowing $\ell_j > \frac{m}{n}$ can lead to a better bound. In this case, it does not affect $p_M$ and $p_j$ for $j = 1, \ldots, k$, but the computation of $p_{\mathcal{F}}$ requires additional manual computations based on our formulas.

*Remark 8.* The Meer–Nowakowski Strategy is a special case of Variant I with $t = 0$, so our proof can be viewed as a proof of their new heuristic.

**Variant II.** Fix integers $t_1$, $t_2$ and $m$. Define $A^{(1)}(\mathcal{F}) = \bigcup_{j=1}^{n} A(f_j)$ and $A^{(2)}(\mathcal{F}) = \sum_{j=1}^{n} A(f_j)$. We define the sets

$$\begin{aligned} S_\ell = \bigcup_{\substack{\ell_1+\ell_2=\ell \\ \ell_1,\ell_2\ge 0}} \{x_1^{i_1} \cdot \ldots \cdot x_k^{i_k} \mid (i_1, \ldots, i_k) \in (m-\ell_1)A^{(1)}(\mathcal{F}) + \ell_1 B \\ + \bigcup_{\substack{\ell_2^{(1)}+\ldots+\ell_2^{(n)}=\ell_2 \\ 0\le \ell_2^{(j)} \le t_1}} \sum_{j=1}^{n} (t_1 - \ell_2^{(j)})A(f_j) + \ell_2^{(j)}\alpha_j + t_2 E\} \end{aligned} \tag{18}$$

for $0 \le \ell \le m$ and $S_{m+1} = \emptyset$, so that $S_m \subset \ldots \subset S_0$. Variant I constructs basis polynomials for every monomial $\lambda = x_1^{i_1} \cdot \ldots \cdot x_k^{i_k} \in S_\ell \setminus S_{\ell+1}$:

**Step 1**: Compute $\ell_1, \ldots, \ell_n$ with $\sum_{j=1}^{n} \ell_j = \ell$, such that

$$(i_1, \ldots, i_n) \in (m-\ell)A^{(1)}(\mathcal{F}) + \ell B + t_1 A^{(2)}(\mathcal{F}) + t_2 E.$$

**Step 2**: Construct $g_\lambda(x_1, \ldots, x_k)$ as follows:

$$g_\lambda(x_1, \ldots, x_k) = \frac{\lambda}{\prod_{j=1}^{n} \mathrm{LM}(f_j)^{\ell_j}} \prod_{j=1}^{n} f_j^{\ell_j} M^{m-\ell}.$$

We use the coefficient vectors of all $g_\lambda(x_1X_1,\ldots,x_kX_k)$ to form the basis of the lattice $\mathcal{L}$, and define $\widetilde{A}^{(1)}(\mathcal{F})=\bigcup_{j=1}^n \widetilde{A}(f_j)$ and $\widetilde{A}^{(2)}(\mathcal{F})=\sum_{j=1}^n \widetilde{A}(f_j)$. The formulas for the bound obtained by Variant II of Coppersmith's method are as follows:

There exist polynomials $g_M$, $g_1,\ldots,g_k$ and $g_{\mathcal{F}}\in\mathbb{Q}[x_1,x_2]$ with total degree $k+1$, such that $\det(\mathcal{L})<M^{m\dim(\mathcal{L})}$ can be rewritten as follows, for any arbitrarily small constant $\varepsilon>0$:

$$\prod_{j=1}^{k} X_j^{m^{k+1}g_j(\frac{t_1}{m},\frac{t_2}{m})}\cdot M^{m^{k+1}g_{\mathcal{F}}(\frac{t_1}{m},\frac{t_2}{m})}<M^{m^{k+1}g_M(\frac{t_1}{m},\frac{t_2}{m})-\varepsilon}.$$

These coefficients of polynomials $g_M$, $g_1,\ldots,g_k$ and $g_{\mathcal{F}}$ satisfied the following equations, which can be determined by solving the linear equation system for different values of $\delta_1$ and $\delta_2$:

$$\begin{cases} g_M(\delta_1,\delta_2)=\dfrac{\int_{N(A^{(1)}(\mathcal{F})+\delta_1A^{(2)}(\mathcal{F})+\delta_2E)}1\,dV}{\operatorname{ind}A^{(1)}(\mathcal{F})+\delta_1A^{(2)}(\mathcal{F})+\delta_2E},\\ g_j(\delta_1,\delta_2)=\dfrac{\int_{N(A^{(1)}(\mathcal{F})+\delta_1A^{(2)}(\mathcal{F})+\delta_2E)}x_j\,dV}{\operatorname{ind}A^{(1)}(\mathcal{F})+\delta_1A^{(2)}(\mathcal{F})+\delta_2E},\\ g_{\mathcal{F}}(\delta_1,\delta_2)=\dfrac{\int_{N(A^{(1)}(\mathcal{F})+\delta_1A^{(2)}(\mathcal{F})+\delta_2E)}1\,dV}{\operatorname{ind}A^{(1)}(\mathcal{F})+\delta_1A^{(2)}(\mathcal{F})+\delta_2E}-\dfrac{\int_{N(\widetilde{A}^{(1)}(\mathcal{F})+\delta_1\widetilde{A}^{(2)}(\mathcal{F})+\delta_2\widetilde{E})}1\,dV}{\operatorname{ind}\widetilde{A}^{(1)}(\mathcal{F})+\delta_1\widetilde{A}^{(2)}(\mathcal{F})+\delta_2\widetilde{E}}.\end{cases}$$

*Remark 9.* Sarkar's strategy [39] is a special case of Variant II with $t_2=0$, so our proof can be viewed as a proof of the new heuristic. Moreover, our strategy in Sect. 4.1 is also a special case of Variant II with $t_1=0$.

**Variant III.** We also analyze how to improve the lattice without using additional shift polynomials and propose Variant III as follows.

Fix integers $m$ and $t$. Consider $A(\mathcal{F})=\bigcup_{j=1}^n A(f_j)$, we define the sets

$$S_\ell=\{x_1^{i_1}\cdot\ldots\cdot x_k^{i_k}\mid(i_1,\ldots,i_k)\in(m-\ell)A(\mathcal{F})+\ell B\}.$$

for $0\le\ell\le m$ and $S_{m+1}=\emptyset$, so that $S_m\subset\ldots\subset S_0$. The strategy constructs basis polynomials $g_\lambda(x_1,\ldots,x_K)$ for every monomial $\lambda=x_1^{i_1}\cdot\ldots\cdot x_k^{i_k}\in S_\ell\backslash S_{\ell+1}$, satisfying $g_\lambda(\mathbf{u})\equiv 0 \mod b^t$:

**Step 1**: Compute $\ell_1,\ldots,\ell_n$ with $\sum_{j=1}^n\ell_j=\ell$, such that

$$(i_1,\ldots,i_n)\in tE+(m-\ell)A(\mathcal{F})+\sum_{j=1}^n\ell_j\alpha_j.$$

**Step 2**: Construct $g_\lambda(x_1,\ldots,x_k)$ as follows:

$$g_\lambda(x_1,\ldots,x_k)=\frac{\lambda}{\prod_{j=1}^n\mathrm{LM}(f_j)^{\ell_j}}\prod_{j=1}^n f_j^{\ell_j}M^{\max(t-\ell,0)}.$$

Use the coefficient vectors of all $g_\lambda(x_1X_1,\ldots,x_kX_k)$ to form the basis of the lattice $\mathcal{L}$.

**Our Formulas.** Define $\widetilde{A}(\mathcal{F}) = \bigcup_{j=1}^{n} \widetilde{A}(f_j)$ and $A'(\mathcal{F}) = \{(i_1, \ldots, i_k, 1) \mid (i_1, \ldots, i_k) \in A(\mathcal{F})\}$. The formulas for the bound obtained by Variant III of Coppersmith's method are as follows:

$$\begin{cases} \dim(\mathcal{L}) = \dfrac{\int_{N(A(\mathcal{F}))} 1\, dV}{\operatorname{ind} A(\mathcal{F})} m^k + o(m^k), \\ p_j = \dfrac{\int_{N(A(\mathcal{F}))} x_j\, dV}{\operatorname{ind} A(\mathcal{F})} m^{k+1} + o(m^{k+1}), \\ p_{\mathcal{F}} = \sum_{i=0}^{k+1} c_i m^{k+1-i} t^i + o(m^{k+1}), \end{cases}$$

where $c_i$ satisfied the following equations, which can be determined through interpolation at $\delta = 0, 1, \frac{1}{2}, \ldots, \frac{1}{k+1}$:

$$\sum_{i=0}^{k+1} c_i \delta^i = \frac{\int_{N(A(\mathcal{F}))} 1\, dV}{\operatorname{ind} A(\mathcal{F})} - \frac{\int_{N(\delta \widetilde{A}(\mathcal{F}) + (1-\delta) A'(\mathcal{F}))} 1\, dV}{\operatorname{ind} \delta \widetilde{A}(\mathcal{F}) + (1-\delta) A'(\mathcal{F})}.$$

One may ask if introducing $t$ is meaningful, i.e., leads to a better result. We also prove that it works if and only when the modulus is an unknown divisor of a known integer.

**Corollary 1.** *Let $M$ be an unknown factorization integer with a divisor $b \geq M^\beta$. Furthermore, let $f(x)$ be a monic polynomial. Then when we use the above strategy to find solutions of the equation $f(x) \equiv 0 \mod b$, the extremum point of $t$ is not $\frac{t}{m} = 1$, which means the introduction of $t$ is useful.*

*Proof.* Suppose $b = M^\beta$ is an unknown divisor of $M$, now we consider the following inequality

$$X_1^{p_1} \cdot \ldots \cdot X_k^{p_k} \cdot M^{p_{\mathcal{F}}} < b^{t \dim(\mathcal{L})}.$$

Only focus on terms that contain $t$, we have

$$m^k t - \frac{m^{k+1} - (m-t)^{k+1}}{k+1} < \beta t m^k.$$

Suppose $\frac{t}{m} = \delta$, the above inequality can be rewritten as

$$(k+1)\delta - (1 - (1-\delta)^{k+1}) - (k+1)\beta\delta < 0.$$

The optimal value for $\delta$ is $\delta_0 = 1 - (1-\beta)^{\frac{1}{k}}$. Hence, when $\beta \neq 1$, we have $\delta_0 \neq 1$. □

## 5 Applications

We first provide methods for computing these integrals in our formulas, which yield the asymptotic bounds directly. Then, we use these formulas to present our improvements to the CI-HNP over CSURF.

### 5.1 How to Compute the Integral?

Since the Jochemsz–May Basic/Extended Strategy is a special case of our strategy in Sect. 4.1, we focus on this strategy in this section. For our formulas in Sect. 4.2, we first demonstrate that these integrals are, in fact, the volumes of the convex hulls of specific subsets and that the number of points in these subsets is bounded by $d = 2(k+2)|\sum_{j=1}^{n} A(f_j)|$. Consequently, the computation of the integrals is reduced to computing the volume of the convex hull for a subset containing a given number $d$ of points. Next, we present existing results on computing the volume of the convex hull for a subset of $d$ points and conduct experiments to show its efficiency.

**Computing Dimension.** We need to compute the integral $\int_{N(A(\mathcal{F})+\delta E)} 1\, dV$ for $\delta = 0, \ldots, k$. This integral is the volume of the convex hull for $A(\mathcal{F}) + \delta E$, and the number of points in this subset is bounded by $(\delta+1)|A(\mathcal{F})|$.

**Computing Determinant.** Computing $\det(\mathcal{L})$ reduces to computing $p_j$ for $j = 1, \ldots, k$ and $p_{\mathcal{F}}$.

Computation of $p_j$: We need to compute the integral $\int_{N(A(\mathcal{F})+\delta E)} x_j\, dV$ for $\delta = 0, \ldots, k$. Denote $\mathcal{H}_j$ as

$$\mathcal{H}_j(A) = \bigcup_{(i_1,\ldots,i_k)\in A} \{(i_1,\ldots,i_k,0), (i_1,\ldots,i_k,1), \ldots, (i_1,\ldots,i_k,i_j)\}.$$

We know $\int_{N(A(\mathcal{F})+\delta E)} x_j\, dV$ can be written as $|\mathcal{H}_j(A(\mathcal{F})) + \delta\mathcal{H}_j(E)|$ from the proof of Lemma 11 (See our full version [20]). Now, we denote $\overline{\mathcal{H}}_j(A)$ as

$$\overline{\mathcal{H}}_j(A) = \bigcup_{(i_1,\ldots,i_k)\in A} \{(i_1,\ldots,i_k,0),\ (i_1,\ldots,i_k,i_j)\}.$$

It can be verified that the convex hull of $\mathcal{H}_j(A)$ is equivalent to the convex hull of $\overline{\mathcal{H}}_j(A)$. Then we have

$$\int_{N(A(\mathcal{F})+\delta E)} x_j\, dV = |\overline{\mathcal{H}}_j(A(\mathcal{F})) + \delta\overline{\mathcal{H}}_j(E)|,$$

and the number of points in this subset is bounded by $(\delta+1)|\overline{\mathcal{H}}_j(A(\mathcal{F}))|$, which is no more than $2(\delta+1)|A(\mathcal{F})|$.

Computation of $p_{\mathcal{F}}$: We need to compute the integral $\int_{N(\widetilde{A}(\mathcal{F})+\delta\widetilde{E})} 1\, dV$, which is the volume of the convex hull of $\widetilde{A}(\mathcal{F}) + \delta\widetilde{E}$. As the number of points in $\widetilde{A}(\mathcal{F})$ is no more than $2|\widetilde{A}(\mathcal{F})|$, the number of points in $\widetilde{A}(\mathcal{F}) + \delta\widetilde{E}$ is bounded by $2(\delta+1)|A(\mathcal{F})|$.

**Computing the Volume of a Polyhedron.** Volume computation is #P-hard for a polytope $P \subseteq \mathbb{R}^d$ represented as the convex hull of vertices [18]. However, there exists an $O^*(n^4)$ polynomial-time approximation algorithm [31] (where the asterisk indicates that the dependence on error parameters and logarithmic factors in $n$ is not shown). For example, in cryptanalysis—and even for more complex polynomial equations—the exact volume can be computed quickly, typically within one second.

**Experiments.** We implemented our algorithms using SageMath 10.3 on a MacBook Pro equipped with an M1 chip with a maximum CPU clock rate of 3.2 GHz. The source code for the experiments is open-sourced and available at

https://github.com/fffmath/AsymptoticBounds.

We further compared our method with the heuristic approach [35,39]. Since the heuristic method does not always yield a polynomial of degree $k+1$ when $m$ is small, for computing $p_{\mathcal{F}}$, a natural idea is to interpolate the results of $p_{\mathcal{F}}(m)$ for $m = 0, \ldots, k+1$, then for $m = 1, \ldots, k+2$, and to terminate the heuristic method when the interpolated polynomials stabilize. We conducted experiments under different values of $k$ as the following Table 2. Our method shows significant time advantages, as these polynomials require large values of $m$ before becoming polynomial-like. For instance, in Exp. 5 - Exp. 8, the minimum required values of $m$ were 12, 12, 14, and 18, respectively. Moreover, the bounds computed by our approach are both *provable* and *efficient*.

**Table 2.** Running time for computing asymptotic upper bounds." - " means longer than 24 h. The details about the polynomials used in our experiments can be found in our full version [20].

| **Experiment** | $k$ | **Interpolation** [35] | **Ours** |
|---|---|---|---|
| Exp. 1 | 3 | 10.9 s | 0.2 s |
| Exp. 2 | 3 | 46.2 s | 0.04 s |
| Exp. 3 | 3 | 2238.2 s | 0.1 s |
| Exp. 4 | 3 | 828.3 s | 0.1 s |
| Exp. 5 | 4 | 33112.4 s | 0.2 s |
| Exp. 6 | 4 | 32451.7 s | 0.1 s |
| Exp. 7 | 4 | - | 0.1 s |
| Exp. 8 | 4 | - | 0.2 s |

## 5.2 Cryptanalytic Advances for CI-HNP

The Commutative Isogeny Hidden Number Problem (CI-HNP), introduced by Meers and Nowakowski [35], investigates the bit-security of isogeny-based key exchange protocols. The problem formulation concerns whether an adversary can recover a shared secret elliptic curve when given the most significant bits (MSBs) of the Diffie–Hellman style exchanged key. They focus on both CSIDH and CSURF key exchanges. Recently, the CSURF case has been continuously improved [38,39]. These results are all based on Coppersmith's method. Notably, they all used a new heuristic when computing the bounds in Coppersmith's method.

To minimize prerequisites on isogeny background, we present a self-contained and simplified definition for CI-HNP over CSURF; the original version appears in [35].

**Definition 10 (CI-HNP (CSURF)).** *Given a modulus $M \in \mathbb{N}$ and polynomials*

$$\begin{cases} f_1(x_1, x_2, x_3) := x_1^2 + a_1 x_1 x_2^2 + a_2 x_1 x_2 + a_3 x_1 + a_4 x_2^2 + a_5 x_2 + a_6, \\ f_2(x_1, x_2, x_3) := x_3^2 + b_1 x_1^2 x_3 + b_2 x_1 x_3 + b_3 x_3 + b_4 x_1^2 + b_5 x_1 + b_6, \end{cases}$$

*for some constants $a_i, b_i \in \mathbb{Z}$, the CI-HNP over CSURF is to solve roots $\mathbf{u}$ of $f_1$ and $f_2$ modular $M$. We say that $\alpha$ MSBs are required if the system of polynomial equations can be solved for $\|\mathbf{u}\|_\infty < M^{1-\alpha}$.*

In [35], their strategy can solve all small roots $u$ for $\|\mathbf{u}\|_\infty < M^{10/41}$, so their result implies that $31/41 \approx 75.61\%$ MSBs are required.

Next, we will show how to use our formulas to obtain improved results without introducing additional heuristics.

**Theorem 2.** *Given a modulus $M \in \mathbb{N}$ and polynomials*

$$\begin{cases} f_1(x_1, x_2, x_3) := x_1^2 + a_1 x_1 x_2^2 + a_2 x_1 x_2 + a_3 x_1 + a_4 x_2^2 + a_5 x_2 + a_6, \\ f_2(x_1, x_2, x_3) := x_3^2 + b_1 x_1^2 x_3 + b_2 x_1 x_3 + b_3 x_3 + b_4 x_1^2 + b_5 x_1 + b_6, \end{cases}$$

*for some constants $a_i, b_i \in \mathbb{Z}$, a bound $X \in \mathbb{N}$, then all small roots $\mathbf{u} = (u_1, u_2, u_3)$ of $f_1$ and $f_2$ modulo $M$ with $|u_i| < X$ can be found in polynomial time in $\log(M)$ under Assumption 1 if*

$$X < M^{0.2599}.$$

*Proof.* Using our Variant II in Sect. 4.3, we choose shift as $x_2$ in , i.e., $E = A(1 + x_2)$ and the order as $x_2 \prec_{\text{lex}} x_1 \prec_{\text{lex}} x_3$ to construct lattice $\mathcal{L}$.

Using our formulas for $\det(\mathcal{L}) < M^{m \dim(\mathcal{L})}$, we have:

$$\dim(\mathcal{L}) = 12t_1^3 + 7t_1^2t_2 + 28t_1^2 m + 10t_1t_2m + 16t_1m^2 + 3t_2m^2 + \frac{8}{3}m^3 + o(m^3),$$

$$p_1 = \frac{32}{3}t_1^4 + \frac{19}{3}t_1^3t_2 + \frac{104}{3}t_1^3 m + 15t_1^2t_2m + 33t_1^2 m^2 + 11t_1t_2m^2 + 12t_1m^3 + \frac{7}{3}t_2m^3 + \frac{3}{2}m^4 + o(m^4),$$

$$p_2 = 19t_1^4 + \frac{38}{3}t_1^3t_2 + 52t_1^3 m + 24t_1^2t_2m + 45t_1^2 m^2 + 14t_1t_2m^2 + 16t_1m^3 + \frac{8}{3}t_2m^3 + 2m^4 + o(m^4),$$

$$p_3 = \frac{34}{3}t_1^4 + 12t_1^3t_2 + \frac{7}{2}t_1^2t_2^2 + \frac{112}{3}t_1^3 m + 28t_1^2t_2m + 5t_1t_2^2 m + 36t_1^2 m^2 + 16t_1t_2m^2 + \frac{3}{2}t_2^2 m^2 + \frac{40}{3}t_1m^3 + \frac{8}{3}t_2m^3 + \frac{5}{3}m^4 + o(m^4),$$

$$p_{\mathcal{F}} = -10t_1^4 - 8t_1^3t_2 - 20t_1^3 m - 11t_1^2t_2m - 2t_1^2 m^2 - t_1t_2m^2 + \frac{16}{3}t_1m^3 + t_2m^3 + \frac{4}{3}m^4 + o(m^4).$$

Substituting $t_1 = 0.401\,m$ and $t_2 = 0.111\,m$, we obtain $X < M^{0.2599}$. □

We compare our results with previous work in Table 1. Our framework enables precise security parameter selection for isogeny-based protocols by eliminating heuristic assumptions in bound computation and providing the first non-heuristic improvement over previous work.

## 6 Conclusion

In this paper, we introduced novel techniques from additive combinatorics—namely, sumset theory and integer point counting in integral polytopes—into the analysis of Coppersmith's method. Our approach establishes the first provable and efficient algorithm for computing the asymptotic bounds of Coppersmith's method. As an application, we improve the cryptanalytic result for the Commutative Isogeny Hidden Number Problem.

**Open Problems.** Lastly, we state some open problems. The heuristic used for computing bounds in [38] remains unresolved; perhaps the introduced tools from sumset theory may inspire further research. In Sect. 4.3, we propose several variants. Of course, some variants have not been mentioned. Given a system of polynomial equations, determining which variant yields better bounds before computing the bounds is also an interesting problem.

**Acknowledgments.** We thank Shaoshi Chen, Long Guo, Xingjian Li, and Jesús de Loera for the discussion on Additive Combinatorics. This work is partially supported by the National Natural Science Foundation of China (No. 62372445, 62032009) and the Innovation Program for Quantum Science and Technology (2021ZD0302902).

## References

1. Ajtai, M.: The shortest vector problem in $L_2$ is NP-hard for randomized reductions. In: Proceedings of the Thirtieth Annual ACM Symposium on Theory of Computing, pp. 10–19 (1998)
2. Bajo, E., et al.: Weighted Ehrhardt theory: extending Stanley's nonnegativity theorem. Adv. Math. **444**, 109627 (2024)
3. Baldoni, V., Berline, N., De Loera, J., Köppe, M., Vergne, M.: How to integrate a polynomial over a simplex. Math. Comput. **80**(273), 297–325 (2011)
4. Barvinok, A.I.: Computation of exponential integrals. J. Math. Sci. **70**, 1934–1943 (1994)
5. Barvinok, A.I.: Partition functions in optimization and computational problems. Algebra i Analiz **4**, 3–53 (1992)
6. Blömer, J., May, A.: A tool kit for finding small roots of bivariate polynomials over the integers. In: Cramer, R. (ed.) EUROCRYPT 2005. LNCS, vol. 3494, pp. 251–267. Springer, Heidelberg (2005). https://doi.org/10.1007/11426639_15
7. Boneh, D., Durfee, G.: Cryptanalysis of RSA with private key d less than n/sup 0.292. IEEE Trans. Inf. Theory **46**(4), 1339–1349 (2000)
8. Boneh, D., Halevi, S., Howgrave-Graham, N.: The modular inversion hidden number problem. In: Boyd, C. (ed.) ASIACRYPT 2001. LNCS, vol. 2248, pp. 36–51. Springer, Heidelberg (2001). https://doi.org/10.1007/3-540-45682-1_3
9. Boneh, D., Venkatesan, R.: Hardness of computing the most significant bits of secret keys in Diffie-Hellman and related schemes. In: Koblitz, N. (ed.) CRYPTO 1996. LNCS, vol. 1109, pp. 129–142. Springer, Heidelberg (1996). https://doi.org/10.1007/3-540-68697-5_11
10. Brion, M., Vergne, M.: Lattice points in simple polytopes. J. Am. Math. Soc. **10**, 371–392 (1997)
11. Castryck, W., Decru, T.: CSIDH on the surface. In: Ding, J., Tillich, J.-P. (eds.) PQCrypto 2020. LNCS, vol. 12100, pp. 111–129. Springer, Cham (2020). https://doi.org/10.1007/978-3-030-44223-1_7
12. Coppersmith, D.: Finding a small root of a univariate modular equation. In: Maurer, U. (ed.) EUROCRYPT 1996. LNCS, vol. 1070, pp. 155–165. Springer, Heidelberg (1996). https://doi.org/10.1007/3-540-68339-9_14
13. Coppersmith, D.: Small solutions to polynomial equations, and low exponent RSA vulnerabilities. J. Cryptol. **10**(4), 233–260 (1997)
14. Coron, J.-S.: Finding small roots of bivariate integer polynomial equations revisited. In: Cachin, C., Camenisch, J.L. (eds.) EUROCRYPT 2004. LNCS, vol. 3027, pp. 492–505. Springer, Heidelberg (2004). https://doi.org/10.1007/978-3-540-24676-3_29
15. Coron, J.-S.: Finding small roots of bivariate integer polynomial equations: a direct approach. In: Menezes, A. (ed.) CRYPTO 2007. LNCS, vol. 4622, pp. 379–394. Springer, Heidelberg (2007). https://doi.org/10.1007/978-3-540-74143-5_21
16. De Loera, J.A.: The many aspects of counting lattice points in polytopes. Math. Semesterber. **52**(2), 175–195 (2005)
17. De Micheli, G., Heninger, N.: Recovering cryptographic keys from partial information, by example. Cryptology ePrint Archive (2020)
18. Dyer, M.E., Frieze, A.M.: On the complexity of computing the volume of a polyhedron. SIAM J. Comput. **17**(5), 967–974 (1988)
19. Ehrhart, E.: Sur les polyèdres rationnels homothétiques à n dimensions. CR Acad. Sci. Paris **254**, 616 (1962)

20. Feng, Y., Luo, H., Chen, Q., Nitaj, A., Pan, Y.: Computing asymptotic bounds for small roots in coppersmith's method via sumset theory. Cryptology ePrint Archive, Paper 2024/1330 (2024). https://eprint.iacr.org/2024/1330
21. Feng, Y., Nitaj, A., Pan, Y.: Partial prime factor exposure attacks on some RSA variants. Theoret. Comput. Sci. **999**, 114549 (2024)
22. Granville, A., Shakan, G., Walker, A.: Effective results on the size and structure of Sumsets. Combinatorica **43**(6), 1139–1178 (2023)
23. Han, S.P., Kirfel, C., Nathanson, M.B.: Linear forms in finite sets of integers. Ramanujan J. **2**, 271–281 (1998)
24. Heninger, N., Ryan, K.: The hidden number problem with small unknown multipliers: Cryptanalyzing mega in six queries and other applications. In: Boldyreva, A., Kolesnikov, V. (eds.) Public-Key Cryptography – PKC 2023. PKC 2023. LNCS, vol. 13940, pp. 147–176. Springer, Cham (2023). https://doi.org/10.1007/978-3-031-31368-4_6
25. Herrmann, M., May, A.: Maximizing small root bounds by linearization and applications to small secret exponent RSA. In: Nguyen, P.Q., Pointcheval, D. (eds.) PKC 2010. LNCS, vol. 6056, pp. 53–69. Springer, Heidelberg (2010). https://doi.org/10.1007/978-3-642-13013-7_4
26. Howgrave-Graham, N.: Finding small roots of univariate modular equations revisited. In: Darnell, M. (ed.) Cryptography and Coding 1997. LNCS, vol. 1355, pp. 131–142. Springer, Heidelberg (1997). https://doi.org/10.1007/BFb0024458
27. Howgrave-Graham, N.: Approximate integer common divisors. In: Silverman, J.H. (ed.) CaLC 2001. LNCS, vol. 2146, pp. 51–66. Springer, Heidelberg (2001). https://doi.org/10.1007/3-540-44670-2_6
28. Jochemsz, E., May, A.: A strategy for finding roots of multivariate polynomials with new applications in attacking RSA variants. In: Lai, X., Chen, K. (eds.) ASIACRYPT 2006. LNCS, vol. 4284, pp. 267–282. Springer, Heidelberg (2006). https://doi.org/10.1007/11935230_18
29. Khovanskii, A.G.: Newton polyhedron, Hilbert polynomial, and sums of finite sets. Funct. Anal. Appl. **26**(4), 276–281 (1992)
30. Lenstra, A.K., Lenstra, H.W., Lovász, L.: Factoring polynomials with rational coefficients. Math. Ann. **261**, 515–534 (1982)
31. Lovász, L., Vempala, S.: Simulated annealing in convex bodies and an o*(n4) volume algorithm. J. Comput. Syst. Sci. **72**(2), 392–417 (2006)
32. May, A.: Cryptanalysis of unbalanced RSA with small CRT-exponent. In: Yung, M. (ed.) CRYPTO 2002. LNCS, vol. 2442, pp. 242–256. Springer, Heidelberg (2002). https://doi.org/10.1007/3-540-45708-9_16
33. May, A.: New RSA vulnerabilities using lattice reduction methods. Ph.D. thesis, Citeseer (2003)
34. May, A., Nowakowski, J., Sarkar, S.: Approximate divisor multiples–factoring with only a third of the secret CRT-exponents. In: Dunkelman, O., Dziembowski, S. (eds.) Advances in Cryptology – EUROCRYPT 2022. LNCS, vol. 13277, pp. 147–167. Springer, Cham (2022). https://doi.org/10.1007/978-3-031-07082-2_6
35. Meers, J., Nowakowski, J.: Solving the Hidden Number Problem for CSIDH and CSURF via Automated Coppersmith. In: Guo, J., Steinfeld, R. (eds.) Advances in Cryptology – ASIACRYPT 2023. ASIACRYPT 2023. LNCS, vol. 14441, pp. 39–71. Springer, Singapore (2023). https://doi.org/10.1007/978-981-99-8730-6_2
36. Nathanson, M.B.: Growth of sumsets in abelian semigroups. arXiv preprint math/0002091 (2000)
37. Nathanson, M.B., Ruzsa, I.Z.: Polynomial growth of sumsets in abelian semigroups. J. de théorie des nombres de Bordeaux **14**(2), 553–560 (2002)

38. Ryan, K.: Solving multivariate coppersmith problems with known moduli. Cryptology ePrint Archive (2024)
39. Sarkar, S.: Enhanced bound for the commutative isogeny hidden number problem in CSURF. In: Mukhopadhyay, S., Stănică, P. (eds.) Progress in Cryptology – INDOCRYPT 2024. LNCS, vol. 15496, pp. 201–211. Springer, Cham (2024). https://doi.org/10.1007/978-3-031-80311-6_10
40. Takayasu, A., Lu, Y., Peng, L.: Small CRT-exponent RSA revisited. In: Coron, J.-S., Nielsen, J.B. (eds.) EUROCRYPT 2017. LNCS, vol. 10211, pp. 130–159. Springer, Cham (2017). https://doi.org/10.1007/978-3-319-56614-6_5

# New Results on the $\phi$-Hiding Assumption and Factoring Related RSA Moduli

Jun Xu[1,2(✉)], Jun Song[1,2], and Lei Hu[1,2]

[1] State Key Laboratory of Cyberspace Security Defense, Institute of Information Engineering, Chinese Academy of Sciences, Beijing 100085, China
{xujun,songjun,hulei}@iie.ac.cn

[2] School of Cyber Security, University of Chinese Academy of Sciences, Beijing 100049, China

**Abstract.** In this paper, we first propose a rigorous polynomial time algorithm based on the univariate Coppersmith theorem that factorizes an integer $N = PQ^r$ with unknown primes $P, Q$ and $r \geq 1$, for an arbitrary given prime $e > N^{\frac{1}{4r}}$ satisfying $e \mid \phi(N)$. Furthermore, the bound $e > N^{\frac{1}{4r}}$ is improved to $e > N^{\beta - r\beta^2}$ if the value of $\beta$ such that $Q \geq N^{\beta}$ is known. Moreover, these two bounds can also be obtained respectively when $e$ is no longer a prime number. Specifically, we address the scenario where $e$ is a square-free composite number with known factorization, as well as the case where $e$ is a composite number with known factorization, and the corresponding prime factors $P$ and $Q$ of $N$ satisfy $\gcd(P-1, Q-1) = 2$. In both cases, in order to make the corresponding algorithms polynomial time, we limit the number of prime factors of $e$ to $O(\log \log N)$ and $r$ to be any integer constant. When applied to the $\phi$-hiding assumption, our bounds are significantly better than previous results. When applied to standard RSA moduli, we extend the case where $e$, which was involved in the previous best bound $e > N^{\frac{1}{4}}$, is no longer a prime number. This can highlight the security vulnerability introduced by the function $\mathrm{RSA}_{N,e}$, as discussed by Kakvi et al. in [23], being at least $e_i$-to-1 lossy for some prime factors $e_i$ of $e$. When applied to decompose the semi-smooth RSA subgroup moduli, we provide a rigorous proof for the second bound presented by Naccache and Stern for the first time. We validate the effectiveness of algorithms through experiments.

**Keywords:** $\phi$-hiding assumption · RSA moduli · Coppersmith's method · the Adleman–Manders–Miller algorithm · Hensel lifting

## 1 Introduction

### 1.1 Motivation

At Eurocrypt 1999, the $\phi$-hiding assumption was proposed by Cachin, Micali, and Stadler for constructing an efficient private information retrieval scheme [9]. The $\phi$-hiding assumption refers to the difficulty in determining whether a given


Y. Tauman Kalai and S. F. Kamara (Eds.): CRYPTO 2025, LNCS 16000, pp. 33–66, 2025.
https://doi.org/10.1007/978-3-032-01855-7_2

prime $e$ divides $\phi(N)$ for a given integer $N$ with unknown factorization, where $\phi$ is the Euler function. For a given standard RSA modulus $N = PQ$ (i.e. primes $P, Q$ are balanced) and any given prime $e > N^{\frac{1}{4}}$, if $e$ divides $\phi(N)$, then one can factorize $N$ in polynomial time based on the univariate Coppersmith theorem (see [8, Corollary 14] and [15, Section 7]). Therefore, the $\phi$-hiding assumption shows a connection between known factors of $\phi(N)$ and decomposing the modulus $N$. The $\phi$-hiding assumption is related to many cryptographic schemes, including private information retrieval schemes [9,15], lossy trapdoor permutation [26], certified trapdoor permutations [23], laconic private set intersection [5], non-committing encryption [19] and factoring-based signature scheme [1]. Although plenty of cryptographic schemes have been designed based on the $\phi$-hiding assumption, there is a significant lack of research on the assumption itself and its variants.

At Asiacrypt 2008, Schridde and Freisleben analyzed a very special case of the $\phi$-hiding assumption for multi-power RSA moduli [34]. At Crypto 2010, Kiltz et al. first proposed another variant of $\phi$-hiding assumption, termed as the multi-prime $\phi$-hiding assumption, specifically tailored for multi-prime RSA moduli [25]. Later, this variant was analyzed in [20,36,38]. In the Journal of Cryptology published in 2019 [1, Section 5.3], Abdalla et al. pointed out that: *More precisely, we need e in the $\phi$-hiding assumption to be chosen as a power of a small prime number ... But to our knowledge, this new variant of the $\phi$-hiding assumption has not been analyzed and might actually not hold.* This means that researchers have proposed the requirement that the $e$ involved in $\phi$-hiding assumption can be non prime numbers.

On the other hand, some cryptographic schemes that rely on RSA modulus $N$ also embed information about known factors of $\phi(N)$. At ACM-CCS 1998, Naccache and Stern put forward a homomorphic encryption scheme based on the hardness of computing higher residues modulo a composite RSA integer [30]. In this scheme, the involved modulus $N = PQ$ has prime factors $P$ and $Q$ of equal bit-size. The corresponding trapdoor is obtained by injecting small prime factors in $P-1$ and $Q-1$. It is clear that the product of such small primes is a divisor of $\phi(N)$. At TCC 2005, this type of modulus mentioned by [30] was referred to by Groth [16] as semi-smooth RSA subgroup moduli, abbreviated as SS moduli, which is a special kind of RSA modulus. At Crypto 2016, Yamakawa et al. gave a reduction from the adversary-dependent decisional RSA subgroup (ad-DRSA) assumption to hardness of factorizing SS moduli [39]. If there exists a probabilistic polynomial time algorithm that breaks the ad-DRSA assumption, then one can find many small primes that divide $\phi(N)$, where $N = PQ$ is an SS modulus. Once there are enough such primes, the modulus $N$ will be decomposed based on the bivariate Coppersmith theorem. At ACISP 2020, Zhao et al. designed a homomorphic encryption scheme and lossy trapdoor functions based on the so-called SS moduli [41].

Takagi proposed a variant of RSA such that the modulus $N = PQ^r$ for $r > 1$ [35], referred to as multi-power RSA. He noticed that the decryption process can be significantly faster in this variant. In order to balance efficiency and security, an excessively large $r$ may compromise security, so it is usually set to $r$ equals 2. Many public key cryptographic schemes are based on the difficulty of decomposing large integers with the special form $N = PQ^2$, such as Okamoto's Esign [31], the Okamoto–Uchiyama Encryption [32], and a series of cryptography systems based on quadratic field, including NICE cryptosystems [18,22]. The modulus with the form $N = PQ^2$ is highly interesting due to its potential to enhance efficiency compared to RSA. No essential weaknesses have been identified in comparison to the standard RSA moduli. At Asiacrypt 2009, Castagnos et al. gave an algorithm in [11] based on binary quadratic forms to factor integers of the form $N = PQ^2$, which yields a key-recovery polynomial-time attack on NICE cryptosystems. This attack involves a provable variant of the Coppersmith method.

It is noteworthy that the task of *computing the squarefree part of an integer* (namely, given a positive integer $N$, finding positive integers $r$ and $s$ such that $N = rs^2$, where $r$ is squarefree) constitutes a classic problem in algorithmic number theory [4], due to its polynomial-time equivalence to the problem of determining the ring of integers of a number field [3].

### 1.2 Previous Cryptanalysis

**Analysis of the $\phi$-hiding Assumption.** At Asiacrypt 2008, Schridde and Freisleben analyzed the validity of the $\phi$-hiding assumption [34]. The involved modulus $N = PQ^r$ is a multi-power RSA modulus, where $r$ is even. The authors showed that, for any given prime $e$, there is a polynomial time algorithm to decide whether $e$ divides $P - 1$ with a high probability. The involved method is the Jacobi symbol rather than lattice method. The even number $r$ here is beneficial to the application of the Jacobi symbol. If $r$ is odd, their method will no longer work. Note that dividing $P-1$ by $e$ is a special case of dividing $\phi(N)$ by $e$. It implies that the assumption solved in the paper [34] is only a special case of the $\phi$-hiding assumption. It is worth noting that the algorithm proposed in [34] cannot be used to decompose moduli either.

At Asiacrypt 2012, Kakvi, Kiltz and May [23] presented a polynomial time algorithm based on the univariate Coppersmith theorem, given an arbitrary $N$ with unknown factorization and prime $e > N^{\frac{1}{4}}$, to certify whether the RSA function $\mathrm{RSA}_{N,e} : \mathbb{Z}_N^* \to \mathbb{Z}_N^*, x \to x^e \mod N$ defines a permutation over $\mathbb{Z}_N^*$. As is well known, the function $\mathrm{RSA}_{N,e}$ is a permutation over $\mathbb{Z}_N^*$ if and only if the prime $e$ and $\phi(N)$ are coprime (i.e. $e$ does not divide $\phi(N)$). It implies that the certification algorithm could also be utilized to solve the $\phi$-hiding assumption. Kakvi et al. extended the case where $e$ is a prime number to the case of composite numbers with known factorization. In this case, the composite number $e$ can be written as $e = \prod e_i^{z_i}$, where $e_i$'s are different primes and integers $z_i > 0$. Kakvi et al. wrote in [23, Section 1.1]: *We can give an efficient certification procedure if $e_i > N^{\frac{1}{4}}$, for all $i$. If, for one $i$, we have $e_i < N^{\frac{1}{4}}$, then* $\mathrm{RSA}_{N,e}$ *is (at least) $e_i$-to-1 (lossy) under the $\phi$-hiding assumption.*

In [27], Lu et al. improved the result for the generalized modulus $N = \prod_{i=1}^n P_i^{k_i}$, where $k_1, \cdots, k_n \geq 1$. If $\min\{k_1, \cdots, k_n\} = 1$, then the result of

Lu et al. is the same as that in [23]. If $\min\{k_1, \cdots, k_n\} \geq 2$, The results of Lu et al. have more advantages.

In [40], Zhang et al. gave the corresponding result for the moduli with the form $N = PQ^r$. If $r = 1$, the result of Zhang et al. matches that in [23]. If $r > 1$, Zhang et al.'s result is better.

**Factorization of SS Moduli.** In [30], Naccache and Stern gave a heuristic analysis that $N$ can be factorized if $e > N^{\frac{1}{2}}$, for a given composite $e$ without a known factorization, satisfying $e$ divides $\phi(N)$. Furthermore, if the exact splitting of $e$ is given, that is, $e = E_1E_2$ such that $E_1$ divides $P-1$ and $E_2$ divides $Q-1$, then $N$ can be heuristically decomposed if $e > N^{\frac{1}{4}}$.

In [39], Yamakawa et al. presented a rigorous proof of the first result of Naccache and Stern in [30], that is, $e > N^{\frac{1}{2}}$, using the bivariate Coppersmith method. However, how to provide a strict proof for the Naccache–Stern second result, i.e. $e > N^{\frac{1}{4}}$, is still an unresolved issue.

### 1.3 Our Contributions

In this paper, we first present new results for factorizing large integers with the form $N = PQ^r$ with $r \geq 1$, where $P, Q$ are unknown and distinct primes. Denote $Q \geq N^{\beta}$. We have $0 < \beta < \frac{1}{r}$. Our results depend on whether the specific value of $\beta$ is known.

For any given prime $e > N^{\frac{1}{4r}}$ satisfying $e \mid \phi(N)$, the integer $N$ can be factorized in polynomial time. If the specific value of $\beta$ is given, then the bound $e > N^{\frac{1}{4r}}$ will be improved to $e > N^{\beta - r\beta^2}$. For a standard RSA modulus $N = PQ$ ($P, Q$ are balanced, i.e. $r = 1$, $\beta = \frac{1}{2}$), these two bounds are the same, which matches the previous best bound $e > N^{\frac{1}{4}}$. When $\beta \neq \frac{1}{2r}$ for $r \geq 1$, the second bound $e > N^{\beta - r\beta^2}$ is better.

In addition, the above two bounds can be obtained separately, when the prime number $e$ is modified to a given square-free composite number with $O(\log \log N)$ prime factors. In this case, our factorization algorithms are polynomial time when the factorization of $e$ is known, for any integer constant $r$. The hypothesis on the number of prime factors of $e$ is reasonable because the average number of prime factors of a random integer is the one mentioned here: $O(\log \log N)$ [17].

Moreover, we also generalize the involved integer $e$ to a given composite with $O(\log \log N)$ prime factors (that is, some prime factors may be the same). The above two bounds are still achieved in polynomial time for any integer constant $r$. Here we assume primes $P$ and $Q$ satisfy $\gcd(P-1, Q-1) = 2$. For random primes $P$ and $Q$, the condition holds with a probability of $\frac{6}{\pi^2} \approx 61\%$. Hence the hypothesis is reasonable.

There are corresponding applications regarding the $\phi$-hiding assumption. For a given integer $N = PQ^r$ with unknown factorization, one can decide whether any given prime $e > N^{\frac{1}{4r}}$ divides $\phi(N)$ or not in polynomial time for any integer constant $r$. Further, if primes $P$ and $Q$ are balanced, then the bound $e > N^{\frac{1}{4r}}$

can be improved to $e > N^{\frac{1}{(r+1)^2}}$. To be specific, the bound $e > N^{\frac{1}{(r+1)^2}}$ is better than $e > N^{\frac{1}{4r}}$ for $r > 1$. These two bounds are the same for $r = 1$. In this case, the bound is $e > N^{\frac{1}{4}}$, which matches the previous best bound. In many cases, our results are significantly better than previous ones. For specific comparison, refer to Sect. 5. In addition, the above two bounds can be obtained separately when the given $e$ in the $\phi$-hiding assumption is no longer a prime number.

There are also relevant applications regarding the decomposition of certain types of RSA moduli. For a standard RSA modulus $N = PQ$ with the same bit-length for $P$ and $Q$, if a composite $e > N^{\frac{1}{4}}$ satisfies $e \mid \phi(N)$, then $N$ can be factorized in polynomial time, where $e$ with a known factorization contains $O(\log\log N)$ prime factors. This means that even if the prime factors of $e$ are all less than $N^{\frac{1}{4}}$, as long as $e$ is greater than $N^{\frac{1}{4}}$, the modulus $N$ can still be decomposed. Therefore, this actually points out the security threat posed by the function $\mathrm{RSA}_{N,e}$ mentioned by Kakvi et al. in [23] being at least one $e_i$-to-1 lossy, where $e_i$'s are prime factors of $e$.

Regarding SS moduli, we provide a rigorous proof for the second bound, which was originally proposed by Naccache and Stern in [30]. To the best of our knowledge, this is the first rigorous polynomial-time algorithm for such a bound. Based on this, we discuss the reduction from Crypto 2016 [39], decomposition of SS moduli instances [30], and the security of the the Naccache–Stern homomorphic scheme [12]. Details are in Sect. 6.

### 1.4 Technical Overview

The core of this work is to transform the relation $e \mid \phi(N)$ into the relation $e \mid Q - u$. Here $0 < u < e$ is a known integer or an element in a known set, where $e$ is a given integer, and $N = PQ^r$ is a given modulus, satisfying $r \geq 1$ and $P, Q$ are unknown primes. Once the relation $e \mid Q - u$ is obtained, we respectively utilize two univariate Coppersmith algorithms to factorize $N$, based on whether $\beta$ satisfying $Q \geq N^{\beta}$ is unknown or not. Due to the lack of heuristics in the univariate Coppersmith algorithms, the results we obtained are rigorous.

Here, we can assume $\gcd(e, N) = 1$. Otherwise, $N$ is factorized easily. It implies that the relation $e \mid \phi(N)$ is equivalent to the relation $e \mid (P-1)(Q-1)$. We consider the specific case of integer $e$ with a known factorization.

**Case 1: $e$ is a Prime Number.** In this case, $e \mid (Q-1)$ or $e \mid (P-1)$ based on $e \mid (P-1)(Q-1)$. If $e \mid (Q-1)$, then we write $Q = ey_0 + u$, where $u = 1$. Hence, the above transformation is finished. On the other hand, if $e \mid (P-1)$, then we can write $Q = ey_0 + u$, where $u^r \equiv N \mod e$. Hence, such a $u$ can be computed based on the Adleman–Manders–Miller (AMM) algorithm [2,10]. Therefore, the transformation is obtained. Case 1 corresponds to the proof of Theorem 1.

**Case 2: $e$ is a Square-free Composite Number.** In this case, from $e \mid (P-1)(Q-1)$, there must be two factors of $e$, $E_1$ and $E_2$, satisfying $e = E_1E_2$ such that $E_1 \mid (P-1)$ and $E_2 \mid (Q-1)$. In order for such tuple $(E_1, E_2)$ to be enumerated in polynomial time, we limit the number of prime factors of $e$ to

$O(\log\log N)$. When such tuple $(E_1, E_2)$ is found, we obtain

$$P = E_1k_1 + 1 \text{ and } Q = E_2k_2 + 1,$$

where $k_1, k_2$ are unknown integers, and $\gcd(E_1, E_2) = 1$ because $e$ is square-free. Through a series of modular operations (see Lemma 6), we ultimately obtain

$$P = ex_0 + s,$$

where integer $x_0$ is unknown, and integer $s$ is known satisfying $0 < s < e$. Since $P$ is a prime, it is easy to see $\gcd(e, s) = 1$. This is a very interesting observation. It transforms the partial information disclosure of $P$ and $Q$ into a relationship where $P$ has more information disclosure. Perhaps it also has independent applications.

On the other hand, according to division with remainder, we can write

$$Q = ey_0 + u.$$

Here integers $y_0, u$ are both unknown, where $0 < u < e$. The current task is how to calculate $u$ here. If $r = 1$, we get $u = s^{-1}N \mod e$. It means that the $u$ can be easily calculated. If $r > 1$, we have $u^r \equiv s^{-1}N \mod e$. For sake of discussion, we denote $b := Ns^{-1} \mod e$. Therefore, $b$ can be calculated publicly. We write $e = e_1e_2\cdots e_n$, where $e_i$'s are prime factors and $n$ is the number of prime factors. Then we have $u^r \equiv b \mod e_i$ for all $1 \le i \le n$. At this point, we use the AMM algorithm to compute the corresponding roots over prime field $\mathbb{F}_{e_i}$ for $i = 1, \cdots, n$. Then utilize the Chinese Remainder Theorem (CRT) to obtain all candidate values containing $u$ in the sense of modulo $e$. The number of candidates is bounded by $r^n$, where $n = O(\log\log N)$. It implies that the number is polynomial of $\log N$ for any integer constant $r$. Case 2 corresponds to the proof of Theorem 2.

**Case 3: $e$ is a General Composite Number.** In the case, we can also enumerate in polynomial time for the tuple $(E_1, E_2)$ to obtain $E_1 \mid (P-1)$ and $E_2 \mid (Q-1)$, where $e = E_1E_2$ and the number of prime factors of $e$ is $O(\log\log N)$. Here we assume $\gcd(P-1, Q-1) = 2$. Hence $\gcd(E_1, E_1)$ equals 1 or 2. The situation of $\gcd(E_1, E_2) = 2$ can be translated into that of $\gcd(E_1, E_2) = 1$. When $\gcd(E_1, E_2) = 1$, based on the analysis in Case 2, we can also get

$$P = ex_0 + s \text{ and } Q = ey_0 + u,$$

where $0 < s < e$ is known. If $r = 1$, the $u$ can be computed, the same as Case 2. If $r > 1$, in addition to using the AMM algorithm and CRT, we also need to use Hensel lifting. This is because there may be identical prime factors in $e$. The number of candidates for $u$ is also polynomial of $\log N$ for any integer constant $r$. Case 3 corresponds to the proof of Theorem 3.

To sum up, for Case 1, the overall time complexity is polynomial time, while for Cases 2 and 3, the time complexity is polynomial time for any given integer constant $r$.

### 1.5 Organization

We organize the paper as follows. In Sect. 2, we recall some preliminaries. Section 3 presents key lemmas for our main results. In Sect. 4, we provide main results for integer factorization. In Sect. 5, we employ main results to address the $\phi$-hiding assumption. In Sect. 6, we discuss how to apply main results to factorize RSA moduli and other special moduli cases. Section 7 presents experiments to support the main results.

## 2 Preliminaries

Here we first review results of finding small roots based on Coppersmith's method, the AMM algorithm, Hensel lifting, and then introduce $\phi$-hiding assumption and certified RSA permutation. Additionally, we recall semi-smooth RSA subgroup modulus and the Naccache–Stern homomorphic encryption algorithm, finally present a reduction from Crypto 2016.

### 2.1 Finding Small Roots

Coppersmith [14] gave a rigorous LLL-based method for extracting small roots of a modular univariate polynomial with a known modulus. May adopted the method of Howgrave-Graham's reformulation [21] and proposed the following result with general case.

**Lemma 1** ([14,29]). *Let $N$ be an integer of unknown factorization, which has a divisor $Q \geq N^{\beta}$, $0 < \beta \leq 1$. Let $0 < \mu < \frac{\beta}{7}$. Let $f(x)$ be a univariate monic polynomial of degree $\delta$. Then we can find all solution $x_0$ for the equation*

$$f(x) = 0 \bmod Q \text{ with } |x_0| \leq N^{\frac{\beta^2}{\delta} - \mu}$$

*in time $O(\mu^{-7}\delta^5 \log^2 N)$.*

At Asiacrypt 2015, Lu, Zhang, Peng and Lin generalized the modular equation $f(x) = 0 \mod Q$, and gave the following result [28].

**Lemma 2** ([28]). *For every $\mu > 0$, let $N$ be a sufficiently large composite integer (of unknown factorization) with a divisor $Q^r$, where $Q \geq N^{\beta}$ and $r \geq 1$. Let $f(x)$ be a univariate monic polynomial of degree $\delta$. Then one can find all solutions $x_0$ of the equation*

$$f(x) = 0 \bmod Q^v \text{ with } |x_0| \leq N^{\frac{rv\beta^2}{\delta} - \mu}$$

*in time $O(\mu^{-7}\delta^5 v^2 \log^2 N)$.*

In this paper, the corresponding $\delta = 1$ and $v = 1$. Hence, the runtime in Lemma 2 becomes $O(\mu^{-7} \log^2 N)$.

### 2.2 The Adleman–Manders–Miller Algorithm

Adleman, Manders and Miller proposed a square root extraction method over finite fields and described how to extend the square root method to the general $r$-th root extraction [2], where $r \geq 2$. In 2012, Cao, Sha and Fan revisited the AMM algorithm for the case of general $r$-th root extraction [10]. The Adleman–Manders–Miller $r$-th root extraction is presented in Algorithm 1. In the algorithm, an $r$-th non-residue is required as an additional input. The time complexity of this algorithm is $O(\log^4 p + r \log^3 p)$. It is worth noting that there is a significant difference between square root extraction and general $r$-th root extraction. For the case of $r > 2$, it is necessary to compute the discrete logarithm problem to find the desired intermediate value. Please refer to [2,10] for further details.

**Algorithm 1.** Adleman–Manders–Miller $r$-th root extraction algorithm in the prime field $\mathbb{F}_p$.

Input: $\mathbb{F}_p$ and a $r$-th residue $\delta$, $r \mid p-1$.
Output: A $r$-th root of $\delta$ .
1: Choose $\rho$ uniformly at random from $\mathbb{F}_p^*$.
2: if $\rho^{\frac{p-1}{r}} = 1$, go to 1.
3: Compute $t, s$ such that $p - 1 = r^t s$, where $(r, s) = 1$.
   Compute the least nonnegative integer $\alpha$ such that $s \mid r\alpha - 1$
   Compute $a \leftarrow \rho^{r^{t-1}s}$, $b \leftarrow \delta^{r\alpha-1}$, $c \leftarrow \rho^s$, $h \leftarrow 1$.
4: for i=1 to $t-1$
   compute $d = b^{r^{t-1-i}}$
   if $d = 1, j \leftarrow 0$,
   else $j \leftarrow -\log_a d$ (compute the discrete logarithm)
   $b \leftarrow b(c^r)^j$, $h \leftarrow hc^j$
   $c \leftarrow c^r$
   end for
5: return $\delta^\alpha \cdot h$

The goal of Algorithm 1 is to find a root of the modular univariate polynomial $x^r \equiv \delta \mod p$, where $p$ is a known prime and $r$ divides $p-1$. In fact, if $r$ does not divide $p-1$, then the corresponding root $x \in \mathbb{F}_p^*$ can be also found out. Let $g = \gcd(r, p-1)$. Clearly, $g$ divides $p-1$. According to the extended Euclidean algorithm, we have $g = s \cdot r + t \cdot (p-1)$, where the integers $s$ and $t$ can be publicly computed. Based on Fermat's little theorem, we get $x^{p-1} \equiv 1 \mod p$. Hence, we obtain that $x^g = x^{(s \cdot r + t \cdot (p-1))} \equiv \delta^s \mod p$, where $\delta' := \delta^s \mod p$ is a known integer. Note that $g \mid p-1$. If $g = 1$, then $x = \delta'$. For the case of $g > 1$, we utilize Algorithm 1 to find the root $x$ of the equation $x^g \equiv \delta' \mod p$.

### 2.3 Hensel Lifting

Hensel's lemma states that in some cases, we can lift the root to a root modulo any larger prime power.

**Lemma 3 (Hensel's Lemma [37]).** *Let $f(x)$ be a polynomial with integer coefficients. Let $p$ be a prime. Suppose that $f(c_1) = 0 \mod p$ for some $c_1$. If the derivative $f'(c_1) \not\equiv 0 \mod p$, then there exists a sequence $\{c_i\}_{i\in\mathbb{N}}$ of integers satisfying $c_{i+1} \equiv c_i \mod p^i$, and $f(c_{i+1}) \equiv 0 \mod p^{i+1}$ for all $i \geq 1$, where*

$$c_{i+1} \equiv c_i - \frac{f(c_i)}{f'(c_i)} \mod p^{i+1}. \tag{1}$$

*Moreover, $c_i$ is unique modulo $p^i$ for $i \geq 2$.*

The condition $f'(c) \not\equiv 0 \mod p$ means that $c$ is not a repeated root of the polynomial $f(x)$. Let $f(x) = x^r - \delta$, where $r, \delta$ are constant integers. Let $c$ be a root of $f(x)$ modulo $p$ satisfying $c \in \mathbb{F}_p^*$. Then $f'(c) \not\equiv 0 \mod p$ if and only if $r \not\equiv 0 \mod p$. Therefore, when $0 < r < p$, we have $f'(c) \not\equiv 0 \mod p$. The corresponding $f$ in this article meets the requirement $f'(c) \not\equiv 0 \mod p$.

### 2.4 The $\phi$-Hiding Assumption

We briefly introduce the $\phi$-hiding assumption and the corresponding problem. Please refer to papers [9,34] for more details.

**Definition 1 ($\phi$-Hiding Problem [9]).** *For a given integer $N$ with unknown factorization, and a given prime $e$, the problem is to decide whether $e$ divides $\phi(N)$ or not, where $\phi$ is the Euler function.*

For a standard RSA modulus $N = PQ$, that is, primes $P, Q$ have the same bit length, if a given prime $e > N^{\frac{1}{4}}$, the $\phi$-hiding problem can be solved in the polynomial time based on the Coppersmith method. The $\phi$-hiding problem is conjectured to be difficult when a given prime $e$ is much smaller than $N^{\frac{1}{4}}$.

**Definition 2 ($\phi$-Hiding Assumption [34]).** *Given an integer $N$ with unknown factorization, it is computationally hard to decide whether a prime $e$ with $2 < e \ll N^{\frac{1}{4}}$ divides $\phi(N)$ or not.*

At Asiacrypt 2008, Schridde and Freisleben analyzed the validity of the Phi-Hiding Assumption with multi-power RSA moduli [34]. To be specific, for a given modulus $N = PQ^r$, where $r$ is even, there is polynomial time algorithm to decide whether $e$ divides $P - 1$ with a high probability, for any given prime $e$.

### 2.5 Certified RSA Permutation

We introduce the definitions of trapdoor permutations and certified trapdoor permutations, and then present a connection between the certified RSA permutation and the $\phi$-hiding problem.

**Definition 3 (Trapdoor Permutation [24]).** *A family of trapdoor permutations is a triple of algorithms $(G, E, D)$ satisfying the following relation:*

1. *$G(\cdot)$ is a randomized algorithm that takes no input and generates a pair $(pk, sk)$, where pk is a public key and sk is a secret key;*
2. *$E(\cdot)$ is a deterministic algorithm such that, for any fixed public key pk, the mapping $x \to E(pk, x)$ is a bijection;*
3. *$D(\cdot)$ is a deterministic algorithm such that for every possible pair of keys $(pk, sk)$ generated by $G(\cdot)$ and for every $x$ we have $D(sk, E(pk, x)) = x$.*

A family of trapdoor permutations is said to be certified if the permutation can be verified in polynomial time given *pk*. The definition was given by Bellare and Yung.

**Definition 4 (Certified Trapdoor Permutation** [6,7]**).** *$(G, E, D, C)$ is called a family of certified trapdoor permutations if $(G, E, D)$ is a family of trapdoor permutations and $C(\cdot)$ is a deterministic polynomial-time algorithm such that, for an arbitrary pk (potentially not generated by $G(\cdot)$), returns 1 if and only if $(E(pk, \cdot))$ defines a permutation over domain $Dom_{pk}$.*

Let $(N, e)$ be a RSA public key, where $e$ is a given prime, and $N$ is a sufficiently large integer with unknown factorization. The goal is to certify whether the RSA function $\mathrm{RSA}_{N,e} : \mathbb{Z}_N^* \to \mathbb{Z}_N^*, x \to x^e \mod N$ defines a permutation over $\mathbb{Z}_N^*$. As is well known, the function $\mathrm{RSA}_{N,e}$ is a permutation over $\mathbb{Z}_N^*$ if and only if $\gcd(e, \phi(N)) = 1$. Note that $e$ is a prime. Hence, the function $\mathrm{RSA}_{N,e}$ is not a permutation if and only if $e$ divides $\phi(N)$. It means that the problem of certifying RSA permutation can be transformed into the corresponding $\phi$-hiding problem.

### 2.6 The Naccache–Stern Homomorphic Encryption

At ACM-CCS 1998, Naccache and Stern proposed an encryption algorithm (called the NS algorithm), which have two versions: one is deterministic and the other is probabilistic. Both versions are homomorphic encryption schemes. The expansion rate of probabilistic version is much better than those of the Goldwasser–Micali algorithm and Benaloh's algorithm. The NS algorithm mentioned later is a probabilistic version [12].

**Key Generation.** The process of key generation is as follows:

1. Choose $k$ small distinct odd primes $p_1, \cdots, p_k$, where $k$ should be even. These prime numbers have a bit length of at most 10.
2. Set $u = \prod_{i=1}^{\frac{k}{2}} p_i$ and $v = \prod_{i=\frac{k}{2}+1}^{k} p_i$, and $\sigma = uv = \prod_{i=1}^{k} p_i > 2^{160}$.
3. Choose two large primes $a$ and $b$ such that $P = 2au + 1$ and $Q = 2bv + 1$ are primes as well.
4. Set $N = PQ$ and select a semi-random integer $g \in \mathbb{Z}_n^*$ and the order of $g$ is $\phi(N)/4$, where $\phi(x)$ is the Euler function. Obviously, the integer $g$ is not a $p_i$th residue modulo $N$.

The public key is $(N, g, \sigma)$ and the private key is $(p_i, P, Q)$.

**Encryption.** The message $m$ is chosen from $\mathbb{Z}_\sigma$ and the sender selects a random integer $x \in \mathbb{Z}_n$ to randomize the ciphertext. Then computes the ciphertext $c \equiv g^m \cdot x^\sigma \mod N$.

**Decryption.** In order to get the message $m$, first calculate $w_i \equiv c^{\frac{\phi(N)}{p_i}} \mod N \equiv g^{\frac{m \cdot \phi(N)}{p_i}} \cdot x^{\frac{\sigma \cdot \phi(N)}{p_i}} \mod N$, where $i = 1, \cdots, k$. Clearly, the expression $x^{\sigma \cdot \phi(N)/p_i} \equiv 1 \mod N$ because $p_i | \sigma$. Note that the integer $m$ can be rewritten as $m_i + l_i p_i$, where $0 \leq m_i < p_i$. We can exhaustively search for the correct $m \equiv m_i \mod p_i$ by calculating whether $g^{m_i \cdot \phi(N)/p_i} \mod N$ equals $w_i$. Finally, recover the message $m$ by using CRT.

### 2.7 Semi-Smooth RSA Subgroup Moduli

At TCC 2015, the definition of semi-smooth RSA subgroup (SS) moduli was first introduced by Groth [16]. Here we briefly recall SS moduli as follows. Please refer to [16] for more details.

**Definition 5 (Groth [16]).** *For given integers $\ell_B$, $t_p$ and $t_q$, we say that a composite number $N = PQ = (2au+1)(2bv+1)$ is an $(\ell_B, t_p, t_q)$-semi-smooth RSA subgroup ($(\ell_B, t_p, t_q)$-SS) modulus when the following conditions are satisfied:*

1. *$P$ and $Q$ are different primes with the same bit-length such that* $\gcd(P-1, Q-1) = 2$.
2. *$a$ and $b$ are different primes large than $2^{\ell_B}$.*
3. *$u$ and $v$ are respectively products of $t_p$ and $t_q$ different $\ell_B$-bit primes. Here, an $\ell_B$-bit prime means a prime number between $2^{\ell_B - 1}$ and $2^{\ell_B}$. Note that* $\gcd(u, v) = 1$ *due to* $\gcd(P-1, Q-1) = 2$.

*Remark 1.* The type of modulus used in [30] is the SS modulus. To be specific, the involved moduli are $(10, 15, 15)$-SS moduli $N$, where the bit length of $N$ is 768. Furthermore, a challenge for decomposing a specific $(10, 15, 15)$-SS modulus with 768-bit was provided in [30, Section 5]. The difference is that the product $\sigma$ of $u$ and $v$ in the modulus involved in the NS algorithm is publicly available.

### 2.8 Reduction at Crypto 2016

At Crypto 2016, a reduction was given from the adversary-dependent decisional RSA subgroup (ad-DRSA) assumption to the factoring assumption. The idea of reduction is presented as follows. Please refer to [39, Section 3] for the specific definition of the ad-DRSA assumption and further details.

If there is a probabilistic polynomial time algorithm that breaks the ad-DRSA assumption, then one can find prime factors $e_i$ that divide $\phi(N)$, where the $N$ is the so-called semi-smooth RSA subgroup modulus. If there are enough prime factors $e_i$, then $N$ will be decomposed. It implies that there exists a probabilistic polynomial time algorithm to break the factoring assumption.

*Remark 2.* The type of modulus utilized in [39] is also the SS modulus. Specifically, the corresponding are $(15, 32, 32)$-SS moduli $N$ (where the bit length of $N$ is 1280) and $(15, 70, 70)$-SS moduli $N$ (where the bit length of $N$ is 2420), respectively.

## 3 Key Lemmas for Main Results

In this section, we first extend Lemma 1 and Lemma 2 to a generalized case. It is worth noting that here we do not need any information about the size of $Q$. In other words, if we denote $Q \geq N^{\beta}$, then the value of $\beta$ can remain unknown in Lemma 5.

To prove Lemma 5, we first establish the following result. It serves as an extension to [23, Lemma 5]. This result is derived from Lemma 2, with a more precise formulation provided by [28, Theorem 2].

**Lemma 4.** *For every $\mu > 0$, let $N$ be an integer of unknown factorization with divisor $Q^r : Q \geq N^{\beta}$ ($\beta \in (0, \frac{1}{r}]$ and $r \geq 1$). Further, let $e = N^{\gamma}$ with $e \mid (Q - \overline{u})$, where $\overline{u}$ is an integer satisfying $0 < \overline{u} < e$. Then there is an algorithm that, given $(N, e, \beta, \mu, \overline{u})$, outputs $Q$ in time $O(\mu^{-7} \log^2 N)$ provided that*

$$Q \leq N^{r\beta^2 + \gamma - \mu}.$$

*If this algorithm can not find a non-trivial factor of $N$, it outputs $\perp$.*

*Proof.* From $e \mid (Q - \overline{u})$, it follows that the polynomial $f(x) = ex + \overline{u}$ has a root $x_0$ modulo $Q$. By multiplying by $e^{-1}$ modulo $N$, we obtain a univariate monic polynomial of degree $\delta = 1$. Since $Q \leq N^{r\beta^2+\gamma-\mu}$, we have $x_0 = \frac{Q-\overline{u}}{e} < \frac{N^{r\beta^2+\gamma-\mu}}{N^{\gamma}} = N^{r\beta^2-\mu}$. Therefore, we can recover $x_0$ by Lemma 2 in time $O(\mu^{-7} \log^2 N)$. For every candidate of $x_0$, we check whether $\gcd(ex_0 + \overline{u}, N)$ gives us the divisor $Q$. Note that all candidate solutions originate from the roots of the polynomial generated by the Coppersmith lattice. Therefore, the upper bound on the number of candidate solutions is the degree of this polynomial, which corresponds to the lattice dimension. According to the proof process of [28, Theorem 2] (see Page 196), the lattice dimension is $O(\mu^{-1})$. Hence, the time of computing gcd is $O(\mu^{-1} \log^2 N)$, which is negligible compared to the running time of Coppersmith s algorithm. □

**Lemma 5.** *Let $N$ be an integer of unknown factorization with a divisor $Q^r$, where $r \geq 1$. For any fixed $\varepsilon > 0$, let $e < N$ be an integer such that $\gamma = \log_N e = \frac{1}{4r} + \varepsilon$ and $\gcd(e, N) = 1$. Let $\overline{u}$ be any given integer satisfying $0 < \overline{u} < e$. Given $N$, $e$ and $\overline{u}$, one can use Lemma 4 to decide whether $e$ divides $(Q - \overline{u})$ in time $O(\varepsilon^{-8} \log^2 N)$ .*

*Remark 3.* The result in Lemma 5 can be seen as an adaptation of [23, Theorem 3] and [27, Theorem 3], where [23,27] respectively discussed the cases of $r = 1$ and $r > 1$. There are two differences here. Firstly, the given integer $e$ does not necessarily need to be a prime number. Secondly, the given $\overline{u}$ may not be equal to 1.

The proof process of Lemma 5 is similar to those in [23,27]. For completeness, we provide the following analysis.

*Proof.* Initially, we observe that $e \mid (Q-\overline{u})$, which implies there exists an $x_0 \in \mathbb{Z}$ such that $Q = ex_0 + \overline{u}$. We now focus on finding $x_0$, a small root of the polynomial equation $f(x) = ex + \overline{u} \mod Q$, under the condition that $Q^r \mid N$.

In order to execute Coppersmith's algorithm, we need to know the value of $\beta$, which is the bit-size of the unknown divisor. However, the specific value of $\beta$ is unknown. By Lemma 4, we can check whether $e \mid (Q-\overline{u})$ for $Q$ within the specified range $[N^\beta, N^{r\beta^2+\gamma-\mu}]$. However, in this lemma, the target range of $Q$ is $[e, N^{\frac{1}{r}}]$ with $e = N^\gamma$, which is significantly broader than the former. To address this gap, we adopt the framework from Asiacrypt 2012 [23].

First we set the equality $r\beta^2 + \gamma - \mu = \frac{1}{r}$, which yields $\beta = \frac{\sqrt{1-r(\gamma-\mu)}}{r}$. Subsequently, we verify whether $Q$ lies in the interval $[N^{\frac{\sqrt{1-r(\gamma-\mu)}}{r}}, N^{\frac{1}{r}}]$ by executing the algorithm in Lemma 4. If the algorithm outputs $\perp$, we set $r\beta^2 + \gamma - \mu = \frac{\sqrt{1-r(\gamma-\mu)}}{r}$ to produce a new $\beta$, then we recheck whether $Q$ lies in the new interval.

In summary, we repeatedly execute the algorithm to cover the target range with a sequence of intervals $[N^{\beta_1}, N^{\beta_0}], \cdots, [N^{\beta_n}, N^{\beta_{n-1}}]$ where the $\beta_i$ are defined by the recurrence relation

$$\beta_{i+1} = \max\{\sqrt{\frac{\beta_i - (\gamma-\mu)}{r}}, \gamma\}$$

with $\beta_0 = \frac{1}{r}$.

To determine the number of invocations required by the algorithm in Lemma 4, we first prove that the sequence $\{\beta_i\}$ is monotonically decreasing.

Since $\gamma < \frac{1}{r} = \beta_0$ and $\sqrt{\frac{\beta_0-(\gamma-\mu)}{r}} < \sqrt{\frac{\beta_0}{r}} = \beta_0$, we have $\beta_1 < \beta_0$. Next, we demonstrate that if $\beta_i \le \beta_{i-1}$ holds, then $\beta_{i+1} \le \beta_i$. Given that $\beta_i \le \beta_{i-1}$, it follows that $\frac{\beta_i-(\gamma-\mu)}{r} \le \frac{\beta_{i-1}-(\gamma-\mu)}{r}$. By the monotonicity of the square root function, we obtain $\sqrt{\frac{\beta_i-(\gamma-\mu)}{r}} \le \sqrt{\frac{\beta_{i-1}-(\gamma-\mu)}{r}}$. Therefore, $\beta_{i+1} \le \beta_i$ since $\max\{\sqrt{\frac{\beta_i-(\gamma-\mu)}{r}}, \gamma\} \le \max\{\sqrt{\frac{\beta_{i-1}-(\gamma-\mu)}{r}}, \gamma\}$.

Considering that the sequence $\{\beta_i\}$ is monotonically decreasing and bounded below by $\gamma$, it must converge. We now analyze the length of interval $[\beta_i, \beta_{i-1}]$. At first, we define a "length function" $\Delta(\beta_{i-1}) = \beta_{i-1} - \beta_i \ge 0$, representing the length of the $i^{th}$ interval. It is obvious that

$$\Delta(\beta_{i-1}) = \beta_{i-1} - \beta_i = \beta_{i-1} - \sqrt{\frac{\beta_{i-1}-(\gamma-\mu)}{r}},$$

and the first two derivatives of $\Delta(\beta)$ are given by $\Delta'(\beta) = 1 - \frac{1}{2\sqrt{r}}(\beta-(\gamma-\mu))^{-\frac{1}{2}}$ and $\Delta''(\beta) = \frac{1}{4\sqrt{r}}(\beta-(\gamma-\mu))^{-\frac{3}{2}} > 0$. Through straightforward computation, we find that $\Delta(\beta)$ attains its minimum at the point $\beta^{(0)} = \frac{1}{4r} + \gamma - \mu$. Consequently, the length of interval $\Delta(\beta)$ is of size at least $\Delta(\beta^{(0)}) = \gamma - \mu - \frac{1}{4r}$. To ensure $\Delta(\beta^{(0)}) > 0$, the condition $\frac{1}{4r} < \gamma - \mu$ must hold.

Given that $\Delta(\beta^{(0)}) = \gamma - \mu - \frac{1}{4r}$ and the target range is $[e, N^{\frac{1}{r}}]$ with $e = N^{\gamma}$, we conclude that after the number of $\lceil \frac{\frac{1}{r}-\gamma}{\gamma-\mu-\frac{1}{4r}} \rceil + 1$ steps, the sequence $\{\beta_i\}$ stabilizes at $\beta = \gamma$. This implies that the entire range $[e, N^{\frac{1}{r}}]$ has been exhaustively verified.

To analyze the running time of the algorithm in Lemma 5, the choice of the parameter $\mu$ in Lemma 4 needs to be discussed. Given $\gamma = \frac{1}{4r} + \epsilon$ and the constraint $\frac{1}{4r} < \gamma - \mu$, we derive $\mu < \gamma - \frac{1}{4r} = \epsilon$. By selecting $\mu = \frac{1}{c}\epsilon$ with $c$ as a positive integer, the number of invocations of Lemma 4 can be bounded by

$$\lceil \frac{\frac{1}{r} - \gamma}{\gamma - \mu - \frac{1}{4r}} \rceil + 1 \leq \frac{\frac{1}{r}}{(c-1)\mu} + 1 = O(\mu^{-1}) = O(\epsilon^{-1}).$$

Since each iteration takes $O(\mu^{-7} \log^2 N)$ time, the total running time of the algorithm is $O(\mu^{-8} \log^2 N) = O(\epsilon^{-8} \log^2 N)$. □

Next, we present a new lemma, which will play an important role in proving Theorems 2 and 3 in our main results.

**Lemma 6.** *Let $N = PQ^r$ be a given integer with unknown factorization, where $P, Q$ are different primes, and $r \geq 1$ is an integer. Let $E_1, E_2$ be given positive integers satisfying $E_1E_2 > 1$, $\gcd(E_1E_2, N) = 1$ and $\gcd(E_1, E_2) = 1$, such that $E_1 \mid (P-1)$ and $E_2 \mid (Q-1)$. Then we have*

$$E_1E_2 \mid (P - s). \tag{2}$$

*Here, the integer $s := E_1(E_1^{-1}(N-1) \mod E_2) + 1$ satisfies $0 < s < E_1E_2$ and $\gcd(s, E_1E_2) = 1$, which can be publicly computed.*

*Proof.* From $E_1 \mid (P-1)$ and $E_2 \mid (Q-1)$, we have

$$P = E_1k_1 + 1,\ Q = E_2k_2 + 1, \tag{3}$$

where $k_1$ and $k_2$ are unknown integers. Plugging the relation (3) into $N = PQ^r$, we get $N = (E_1k_1 + 1)(E_2k_2 + 1)^r$. Then taking modulo $E_2$ on both sides, we get

$$N - 1 \equiv E_1k_1 \mod E_2. \tag{4}$$

Since $\gcd(E_1, E_2) = 1$, there exists $E_1^{-1}$ modulo $E_2$. Multiplying by $E_1^{-1}$ and taking modulo $E_2$ on both sides of (4), we have $k_1 \equiv E_1^{-1}(N-1) \bmod E_2$. Then we rewrite this relation as $k_1 = E_2x_0 + s_1$, where the integer $x_0$ is unknown, and the integer $s_1 := E_1^{-1}(N-1) \mod E_2$. Plugging the relation $k_1 = E_2x_0 + s_1$ into $P = E_1k_1 + 1$, we obtain $P = (E_1E_2)x_0 + s$. Note that $s = E_1s_1 + 1$, where $0 < s \leq E_1E_2$. In fact, if $s = E_1E_2$, then we can deduce $E_1E_2 = 1$ or $P$ based on the relation (2). Thus, $0 < s < E_1E_2$. Moreover, $s$ can be publicly computed. Finally, since $P$ is prime, the equation $P = (E_1E_2)x_0 + s$ implies $\gcd(s, E_1E_2) = 1$. □

# 4 Main Results

In this section, we present the factorization scenarios of the RSA modulus $N$, based on different cases where $e$, with known factorization, satisfies $e \mid \phi(N)$.

## 4.1 The Case that $e$ Is a Prime Number

We give the following result according to Coppersmith's method and the AMM algorithm.

**Theorem 1.** *Let $N = PQ^r$ be a given integer with unknown factorization, where $P, Q$ are different primes, $r \geq 1$ is a given integer, and $Q \geq N^\beta$ for $0 < \beta < \frac{1}{r}$. Let $e$ be a given prime satisfying $e \mid \phi(N)$. For any fixed $\varepsilon > 0$, we can factorize $N$ in time polynomial of $\varepsilon^{-1}$ and $\log N$, when one of the following two conditions is met:*

$$\begin{cases} e \geq N^{\frac{1}{4r}+\varepsilon} & (\beta \text{ is unknown}) \quad (5) \\ e \geq N^{\beta - r\beta^2+\varepsilon} & (\beta \text{ is known}) \quad (6) \end{cases}.$$

*Proof.* The Euler function of $N$ is $\phi(N) = Q^{r-1}(P-1)(Q-1)$, where $N = PQ^r$, and $P, Q$ are different primes. Assume $\gcd(e, N) = 1$. Otherwise, $N$ can be factorized by computing $\gcd(e, N)$. Note that the prime $e$ divides $\phi(N)$. Hence we get that $e$ divides $P - 1$ or $Q - 1$.

Now, we consider the situation where the specific value of $\beta$ is unknown. We first apply Lemma 5 to determine whether $e$ divides $Q-1$. If $e \mid (Q-1)$, then $N$ can be factorized when $e \geq N^{\frac{1}{4r}+\varepsilon}$. If $e \nmid (Q-1)$, then $e \mid (P-1)$. Furthermore, we may write $P = ex_0+1$, where $x_0$ is an unknown integer. We can also consider the case of $Q$ using division with remainder. That is, we write

$$Q = ey_0 + u. \quad (7)$$

Here, $x_0$ and $0 < u < e$ are unknown integers. Next we will show that the integer $u$ can be publicly computed.

According to the expressions $P = ex_0 + 1$, $Q = ey_0 + u$ and $N = PQ^r$, we deduce that

$$u^r \equiv N \mod e. \quad (8)$$

When $r = 1$, we directly conclude that $u$ is equal to $N \bmod e$. When $r > 1$, we employ the AMM algorithm in a finite field in $O(\log^4 e + r\log^3 e)$ time [10, Section 6], which is polynomially bounded[1] in $\log N$, to compute all roots of the univariate polynomial equation $y^r = N$ over the prime field $\mathbb{F}_e$. As is well known, the equation $y^r = N$ over $\mathbb{F}_e$ can have up to $r$ different roots. It implies that the number of all candidate values for $u$ is bounded by a polynomial of $\log N$.

[1] Note that $Q$ is a prime number, and the smallest prime number is 2. This implies that $2^r \leq Q^r < N$. Therefore, $r < \log N$.

If $e \geq Q$, then $u = Q$ based on the expression (7). For any given candidate value $\overline{u}$ of $u$, we compute $\gcd(\overline{u}, N)$. Then we can get the non-trivial factor of $N$ when $\overline{u} = u$. Since the maximum number of candidate values is exactly $r$, the computational complexity during this phase is $O(r \log^2 N)$.

If $e < Q$, we return to the expression (7). For any given candidate value $\overline{u}$ of $u$, we apply Lemma 5 to decide whether $e$ divides $Q - \overline{u}$ or not. Therefore, we can factorize $N$, when $\overline{u} = u$ and $e \geq N^{\frac{1}{4r}+\varepsilon}$. Since the number of candidate values is bounded by $r$, Lemma 5 must be invoked at most $r$ times. Thus, the running time in this process is $O(r\varepsilon^{-8} \log^2 N)$. This implies that the aforementioned gcd computation time becomes negligible in comparison.

The above analysis is aimed at situations where the specific value of $\beta$ satisfying $Q \geq N^\beta$ is unknown. Furthermore, if the specific value of $\beta$ is given, a better bound will be obtained.

Similar to the above analysis, we first apply Lemma 2 to verify whether $e$ divides $Q - 1$. If not, $e$ must divide $P - 1$. Subsequently, we express $Q$ in the form $Q = ey_0 + u$, where $0 < u < e$, $Q^r \mid N$ and $Q \geq N^\beta$. Then we have $0 < y_0 = \frac{Q-u}{e} = \frac{Q}{e} - \delta$, where $\delta := \frac{u}{e}$ satisfying $0 < \delta < 1$. Thus, we get $e = \frac{Q}{y_0+\delta}$. Notice that $ey_0 + u \equiv 0 \mod Q$. Taking modulo $e^{-1} \mod N$ on both sides, we get $y_0 + a \equiv 0 \mod Q$, where $a := ue^{-1} \mod N$ is known. It implies that there is a desired root $y_0$ in the univariate modular equation $y + a \equiv 0 \mod Q$. For any given candidate value $\overline{u}$ of $u$, we set $\overline{a} = \overline{u}e^{-1} \mod N$, and let

$$f(y) := y + \overline{a} \mod Q, \text{ where } Q^r \mid N. \tag{9}$$

Applying Lemma 2 to the expression (9), we can recover the desired root $y_0$ in polynomial time, when $\overline{a} = a$, and $|y_0| \leq N^{r\beta^2-\varepsilon}$. According to the Triangle inequality, we have $|y_0 + \delta| < |y_0| + 1 \leq N^{r\beta^2-\varepsilon} + 1$. For a large $N$, the term 1 here is negligible. Hence, for simplicity, we write $|y_0 + \delta| < N^{r\beta^2-\varepsilon}$. Based on $e = \frac{Q}{y_0+\delta}$ and $Q \geq N^\beta$, we have $e \geq N^{\beta - r\beta^2+\varepsilon}$.

Finally, we analyze the overall runtime of the above algorithm. For clarity, define $T_{\text{Cop}}$ as the runtime of Coppersmith's algorithm. To be specific,

$$T_{\text{Cop}} = \begin{cases} O(\varepsilon^{-8} \log^2 N) & (\beta \text{ is unknown}) \\ O(\varepsilon^{-7} \log^2 N) & (\beta \text{ is known}) \end{cases}, \tag{10}$$

based on Lemma 5 and Lemma 2, respectively. Let $T_{\text{AMM},r,e}$ denote the runtime of the AMM algorithm, defined as

$$T_{\text{AMM},r,e} = O(\log^4 e + r \log^3 e), \tag{11}$$

where $r$ is the polynomial degree and $e$ is the modulus.

For the case $r = 1$, we invoke Lemma 5 or Lemma 2 at most twice. Thus, the worst-case runtime is $2 \cdot T_{\text{Cop}}$, yielding:

$$\begin{cases} O(\varepsilon^{-8} \log^2 N) & (\beta \text{ is unknown}) \\ O(\varepsilon^{-7} \log^2 N) & (\beta \text{ is known}) \end{cases}.$$

This runtime is polynomial in $\varepsilon^{-1}$ and $N$.

For the case $r > 1$, the AMM algorithm is invoked once, and Lemma 5 or Lemma 2 is applied up to $r+1$ times. The worst-case runtime becomes $T_{\text{AMM},r,e} + (r+1) \cdot T_{\text{Cop}}$, resulting in:

$$\begin{cases} O\left(r\varepsilon^{-8}\log^2 N + \log^4 e + r\log^3 e\right) & (\beta \text{ is unknown}) \\ O\left(r\varepsilon^{-7}\log^2 N + \log^4 e + r\log^3 e\right) & (\beta \text{ is known}) \end{cases}.$$

Given $e \leq \phi(N) < N$ and $r < \log N$, the overall runtime remains polynomial in $\varepsilon^{-1}$ and $N$. □

*Remark 4.* Let us compare the bounds (5) and (6) in Theorem 1. We consider the exponent $\beta - r\beta^2$ in (6) as follows:

$$\beta - r\beta^2 = -r(\beta - \frac{1}{2r})^2 + \frac{1}{4r}.$$

When $\beta = \frac{1}{2r}$, $\beta - r\beta^2$ takes the maximum value $\frac{1}{4r}$. It implies that the bound (5) is the same as the bound (6). When $\beta \neq \frac{1}{2r}$, we have $\beta - r\beta^2 < \frac{1}{4r}$. Hence, the bound (6) is better than the bound (5). The reason for this is that the specific value of $\beta$ satisfies $Q \geq N^\beta$ is unknown. Therefore, it has to consider the worst-case scenario.

### 4.2 The Case that $e$ Is a Square-Free Composite Number

Interestingly, if the involved $e$ in Theorem 1 is a square-free composite number, the corresponding bound can also be obtained. However, the corresponding proof may be slightly more complex. It is necessary to involve the Chinese Remainder Theorem.

**Theorem 2.** *Define $N$ as in Theorem 1. Let $e$ be a given square-free composite number with known factorization satisfying $e \mid \phi(N)$, where the number of prime factors of $e$ is $O(\log\log N)$. For any fixed $\varepsilon > 0$, we can factorize $N$ in time polynomial of $\varepsilon^{-1}$ and $\log N$ for any integer constant $r$, when one of conditions (5) and (6) in Theorem 1 is satisfied.*

*Proof.* Since $e < N$, we may assume that $\gcd(e, N) = 1$; otherwise, $N$ can be factored by computing $\gcd(e, N)$. Since $e \mid \phi(N)$ and $\phi(N) = Q^{r-1}(P-1)(Q-1)$, it follows that $e \mid (P-1)(Q-1)$. Without loss of generality, we let $e = e_1 \cdot e_2 \cdots e_n = E_1E_2$ such that $E_1 \mid (P-1)$ and $E_2 \mid (Q-1)$, where $n = O(\log\log N)$ is the number of prime factors of $e$ and the $e_i$ are distinct. Consequently, $\gcd(E_1, E_2) = 1$. Under this coprimality condition ($\gcd(E_1, E_2) = 1$), there exist $2^n$ possible pairs of such $(E_1, E_2)$. Since $n = O(\log\log N)$, the total number of candidate pairs $2^n$ remains polynomial in $\log N$. For each candidate pair, we perform subsequent operations. If a candidate pair coincides with the correct pair $(E_1, E_2)$, the modulus $N$ can be factored via the following method.

For the correct pair $(E_1, E_2)$, since $E_1 \mid (P-1)$ and $E_2 \mid (Q-1)$, we derive the relation (2) in Lemma 6, i.e., $e \mid (P-s)$, where $e = E_1E_2$, and $s$ is a known integer satisfying $0 < s < e$ and $\gcd(e, s) = 1$. Rewriting this relation, we obtain

$$P = ex_0 + s, \tag{12}$$

where $x_0$ is an unknown integer.

If $e > P$, then $s = P$. Consequently, $N$ can be factored by computing $\gcd(s, N)$. This implies that only cases with $e \leq P$ require further analysis.

Similarly, we express

$$Q = ey_0 + u, \text{ where } Q^r \mid N. \tag{13}$$

Here, $y_0$ and $u$ (with $0 < u < e$) are unknown integers, termed the quotient and remainder, respectively. The subsequent analysis demonstrates that $u$ can be computed publicly.

Consistent with the previous analysis, it suffices to consider the case $e \leq Q$. Specifically, if $e > Q$, determining $u$ reveals $u = Q$. Subsequently, a non-trivial factor of $N$ can be efficiently computed via the Euclidean algorithm. Therefore, our analysis focuses exclusively on scenarios where $e \leq \min\{P, Q\}$, while cases with $e > \min\{P, Q\}$ are trivially resolvable.

Substituting expressions (12) and (13) into $N = PQ^r$, we derive $N = (ex_0 + s)(ey_0 + u)^r$. Reducing both sides modulo $e$, we obtain the congruence:

$$N \equiv su^r \mod e. \tag{14}$$

Now, we compute $u$ using equation (14). Given that $\gcd(s, e) = 1$, the modular inverse $s^{-1} \mod e$ exists. By multiplying both sides of equation (14) by $s^{-1} \mod e$ and reducing modulo $e$, we derive

$$u^r \equiv Ns^{-1} \mod e. \tag{15}$$

When $r = 1$, this simplifies to $u = Ns^{-1} \mod e$, meaning $u$ can be computed directly. For $r > 1$, $u$ remains computable, but the procedure becomes more involved. We address this scenario as follows.

Given $e = e_1 \cdot e_2 \cdots e_n$, where the $e_i$ are distinct known primes, define

$$b := Ns^{-1} \mod e,$$

a computable integer. From congruence (15), namely $u^r \equiv b \mod e$, we derive the system:

$$u^r \equiv b \mod e_i, 1 \leq i \leq n. \tag{16}$$

First, we utilize the AMM algorithm [2,10] in a finite field in $O(\log^4 e_i + r \log^3 e_i)$ time, which is bounded by a polynomial of $\log N$ since $1 \leq r < \log N$, to calculate all roots of the univariate polynomial equation $y^r = b$ over the prime field $\mathbb{F}_{e_i}$ $(1 \leq i \leq n)$. As is well known, the equation $y^r = b$ over $\mathbb{F}_{e_i}$ can have up to $r$ different roots. For any given root $U_{i,j}$ such that $U_{i,j}^r = b$ over $\mathbb{F}_{e_i}$

$(1 \leq j \leq r)$, that is, $U_{i,j}^r \equiv b \mod e_i$. In other words, we get the involved tuple $(U_{1,j_1}, \cdots, U_{n,j_n})$ satisfying

$$\begin{cases} U_{1,j_1}^r \equiv b \mod e_1, \\ U_{2,j_2}^r \equiv b \mod e_2, \\ \vdots \\ U_{n,j_n}^r \equiv b \mod e_n, \end{cases}$$

where $1 \leq j_1, j_2, \cdots, j_n \leq r$. Finally, we calculate all candidate values for $u$ using the CRT algorithm. To be specific, for any given tuple $(U_{1,j_1}, \cdots, U_{n,j_n})$, we calculate the corresponding candidate value $\overline{u}$ for $u$ in $O(\log^2 e)$ time as follows:

$$\overline{u} = \sum_{i=1}^{n} C_i U_{i,j_i} \mod e, \text{where } C_i := (e/e_i) \cdot ((e/e_i)^{-1} \mod e_i).$$

The number of all candidate values for $u$ is at most $r^n$. For $r > 1$, due to $n = O(\log\log N)$, we have $r^n = r^{O(\log\log N)}$. It implies that the number of all candidate values for $u$ is bounded by a polynomial of $\log N$ when $r$ is any integer constant.

We first analyze the case $r = 1$. From the prior analysis, $u$ can be directly computed in this scenario. Subsequently, we derive $e \mid (Q - u)$ from (13). For the case where the specific value of $\beta$ is unknown, when $e \geq N^{\frac{1}{4r}+\varepsilon}$, Lemma 5 allows us to recover the prime $Q$, thereby factorizing $N$. When the specific value of $\beta$ is known, we solve the univariate modular equation derived from (13) using Lemma 2. If $e \geq N^{\beta - r\beta^2 + \varepsilon}$, the desired root $y_0$ is obtained, from which $Q$ can be determined.

In the case $r = 1$, for any candidate pair $(E_1, E_2)$, we require exactly one application of Lemma 5 or Lemma 2. Given that there are $2^n$ candidate pairs, the total runtime becomes $2^n \cdot T_{\text{Cop}}$. Substituting equation (10), this yields

$$\begin{cases} O\left(2^n \varepsilon^{-8} \log^2 N\right) & (\beta \text{ is unknown}) \\ O\left(2^n \varepsilon^{-7} \log^2 N\right) & (\beta \text{ known}) \end{cases},$$

where $n = O(\log\log N)$. The runtime is polynomial in $\varepsilon^{-1}$ and $\log N$.

We now address the case $r > 1$. Following the analysis above, we can enumerate all candidate values containing $u$. Once these candidate values for $u$ are computed, we substitute them into equation (13):

$$Q = ey_0 + u \quad \text{where} \quad Q^r \mid N.$$

For the scenario where the specific value of $\beta$ is unknown, we apply Lemma 5 to verify whether $e$ divides $Q - \overline{u}$, where $\overline{u}$ denotes an arbitrary candidate value of $u$. Consequently, if $\overline{u} = u$ and $e \geq N^{\frac{1}{4r}+\varepsilon}$, we can factorize $N$.

When the specific value of $\beta$ is known, a tighter bound can be derived. Aligning with the proof methodology of Theorem 1, equation (13) allows us to factorize $N$ via Lemma 2 under the condition $e \geq N^{\beta - r\beta^2 + \varepsilon}$.

We now analyze the overall runtime for $r > 1$. For any candidate pair $(E_1, E_2)$, our procedure involves: 1. Applying the AMM algorithm to solve $y^r \equiv b \mod e_i$ for all $1 \le i \le n$. This step requires executing the AMM algorithm $n$ times, generating up to $r^n$ candidate roots. 2. Utilizing CRT at most $r^n$ times to construct candidates for the root of $y^r \equiv b \mod e$, resulting in a maximum of $r^n$ candidates. 3. Invoking Lemma 5 or Lemma 2 for each candidate, implying $r^n$ total applications.

Let $T_{\mathrm{CRT},e}$ denote the runtime of CRT under modulus $e$, defined as:

$$T_{\mathrm{CRT},e} = O(\log^2 e). \tag{17}$$

The total time complexity is bounded by

$$2^n \cdot \left( \sum_{i=1}^{n} T_{\mathrm{AMM},r,e_i} + r^n T_{\mathrm{CRT},e} + r^n T_{\mathrm{Cop}} \right). \tag{18}$$

From (11), the AMM runtime per modulus $e_i$ is $T_{\mathrm{AMM},r,e_i} = O(\log^4 e_i + r \log^3 e_i)$. Aggregating across all moduli:

$$\sum_{i=1}^{n} (\log^4 e_i + r \log^3 e_i) \le \log^4 e + r \log^3 e,$$

where $e = \prod_{i=1}^{n} e_i$.

According to (17), the runtime of CRT is given by $T_{\mathrm{CRT},e} = O(\log^2 e)$. Since $e < N$, it follows that $\log^2 e < \log^2 N$. Consequently, the term $r^n T_{\mathrm{CRT},e}$ in (18) is negligible compared to the term $r^n T_{\mathrm{Cop}}$, where

$$T_{\mathrm{Cop}} = \begin{cases} O(\varepsilon^{-8} \log^2 N) & (\beta \text{ is unknown}) \\ O(\varepsilon^{-7} \log^2 N) & (\beta \text{ is known}) \end{cases}$$

based on (10). Substituting these relations into (18), we obtain the following runtime complexities:

$$\begin{cases} O\left(2^n \left(r^n \varepsilon^{-8} \log^2 N + \log^4 e + r \log^3 e\right)\right) & (\beta \text{ is unknown}) \\ O\left(2^n \left(r^n \varepsilon^{-7} \log^2 N + \log^4 e + r \log^3 e\right)\right) & (\beta \text{ is known}) \end{cases},$$

with $n = O(\log \log N)$. For any fixed integer constant $r$, the overall runtime remains polynomial in $\varepsilon^{-1}$ and $\log N$.

□

### 4.3 The Case that $e$ Is a General Composite Number

We can also extend the result to general composite numbers $e$ with $O(\log \log N)$ prime factors. In other words, there may be several prime factors of $e$ that are the same. Therefore, Hensel lifting needs to be utilized. It is worth noting that we assume that the prime numbers $P$ and $Q$ satisfy $\gcd(P-1, Q-1) = 2$ in this case. For random primes $P$ and $Q$, the probability of such an assumption occurring is $\frac{6}{\pi^2}$, approximately equal to 61%.

**Theorem 3.** *Define $N$ as in Theorem 1, where unknown prime factors $P, Q$ satisfy* $\gcd(P-1, Q-1) = 2$. *Let $e$ be a given integer with known factorization such that $e \mid \phi(N)$, where the number of prime factors of $e$ is $O(\log\log N)$. For any fixed $\varepsilon > 0$, we can factorize $N$ in time polynomial of $\varepsilon^{-1}$ and $\log N$ for any integer constant $r$, when one of conditions (5) and (6) in Theorem 1 holds.*

*Proof.* We may assume that $\gcd(e, N) = 1$; otherwise, $N$ can be factorized. Observe that $e \mid \phi(N)$, where $\phi(N) = Q^{r-1}(P-1)(Q-1)$. This implies $e \mid (P-1)(Q-1)$. Without loss of generality, we partition $e = e_1 e_2 \cdots e_n = E_1 E_2$ such that $E_1 \mid (P-1)$ and $E_2 \mid (Q-1)$, where $n$ is the number of prime factors $e_i$. Given $\gcd(P-1, Q-1) = 2$, it follows that $\gcd(E_1, E_2) = 1$ or 2. In the case of $\gcd(E_1, E_2) = 1$, there are $2^n$ possibilities for such $(E_1, E_2)$. If $\gcd(E_1, E_2) = 2$, then the prime factors $e_1, \cdots, e_n$ contain two 2. Thus, there are $2^{n-2}$ possibilities for such $(E_1, E_2)$. Since $n = O(\log\log N)$, the total number of candidate pairs $(E_1, E_2)$ remains polynomial in $\log N$. For each candidate pair, we proceed as follows: If the candidate pair corresponds to the correct pair $(E_1, E_2)$, we demonstrate that $N$ can be factorized.

For the correct pair $(E_1, E_2)$, given the divisibility conditions $E_1 \mid (P-1)$ and $E_2 \mid (Q-1)$, we derive $P = E_1 k_1 + 1$ and $Q = E_2 k_2 + 1$, where $k_1$ and $k_2$ are unknown integers. Substituting these two relations into $N = PQ^r$, we obtain $N = (E_1 k_1 + 1)(E_2 k_2 + 1)^r$. By taking modulo $E_2$ on both sides, we derive the congruence

$$N - 1 \equiv E_1 k_1 \mod E_2.$$

Note that $\gcd(E_1, E_2) = 1$ or 2. Without loss of generality, we consider the case of $\gcd(E_1, E_2) = 1$. Otherwise, we let $E_1' = \frac{E_1}{2}$ and $E_2' = \frac{E_2}{2}$, where $\gcd(E_1', E_2') = 1$. Then we have $\frac{N-1}{2} \equiv E_1' k_1 \mod E_2'$. It means that the analysis in the case $\gcd(E_1, E_2) = 2$ is similar to that in the case of $\gcd(E_1, E_2) = 1$.

For the case of $\gcd(E_1, E_2) = 1$, based on the proof of Theorem 2, we can also obtain the relation (15), that is,

$$u^r \equiv N s^{-1} \mod e.$$

When $r = 1$, we get $u = N s^{-1} \mod e$. Hence, $u$ can be directly calculated. When $r > 1$, $u$ can also be computed as follows.

Note that $e = e_1 \cdot e_2 \cdots e_n$, where $e_i$'s are known primes. For the convenience of subsequent discussions, we rewrite $e = \widetilde{e}_1^{z_1} \cdot \widetilde{e}_2^{z_2} \cdots \widetilde{e}_t^{z_t}$, where $z_1 > 0, \cdots, z_t > 0$, and $\widetilde{e}_1, \cdots, \widetilde{e}_t$ are different primes satisfying $\{\widetilde{e}_1, \cdots, \widetilde{e}_t\} \subseteq \{e_1, \cdots, e_n\}$. Thus, $0 < t \le n$. We denote $b := N s^{-1} \mod e$. Clearly, the integer $b$ can be known. According to the expression (15), i.e. $u^r \equiv b \mod e$, we have $u^r \equiv b \mod \widetilde{e}_i, 1 \le i \le t$. We first use the AMM algorithm in a finite field in time $O(\log^4 \widetilde{e}_i + r\log^3 \widetilde{e}_i)$, which is bounded by a polynomial of $\log N$, to calculate all roots of the univariate polynomial equation $y^r = b$ over the prime field $\mathbb{F}_{\widetilde{e}_i}$ $(1 \le i \le t)$. As is well known, the equation $y^r = b$ over $\mathbb{F}_{\widetilde{e}_i}$ can have up to $r$ different roots. For any given root $U_{i,j}$ such that $U_{i,j}^r = b$ over $\mathbb{F}_{\widetilde{e}_i}$ $(1 \le j \le r)$, that is, $U_{i,j}^r \equiv b \mod \widetilde{e}_i$. Then, we can apply Hensel lifting to find the corresponding root $W_{i,j}$ such that $W_{i,j}^r \equiv b \mod \widetilde{e}_i^{z_i}$ $(1 \le i \le t, 1 \le j \le r)$ in time $O(\log r \cdot z_i^3 \log^2 \widetilde{e}_i)$, which is bounded by a polynomial[2] of $\log N$, where the integers $\widetilde{e}_1^{z_1}, \widetilde{e}_2^{z_2}, \cdots, \widetilde{e}_t^{z_t}$ are pairwise coprime[3]. In other words, we get the involved tuple $(W_{1,j_1}, \cdots, W_{t,j_t})$ satisfying

$$\begin{cases} W_{1,j_1}^r \equiv b \mod \widetilde{e}_1^{z_1}, \\ W_{2,j_2}^r \equiv b \mod \widetilde{e}_2^{z_2}, \\ \vdots \\ W_{t,j_t}^r \equiv b \mod \widetilde{e}_t^{z_t}, \end{cases}$$

where $1 \leq j_1, j_2, \cdots, j_t \leq r$. Finally, we calculate all candidate values for $u$ using CRT. To be specific, for any given tuple $(W_{1,j_1}, \cdots, W_{t,j_t})$, we calculate the corresponding candidate value $\overline{u}$ for $u$ in $O(\log^2 e)$ time:

$$\overline{u} = \sum_{i=1}^{t} C_i W_{i,j_i} \mod e, \text{where } C_i := (e/\widetilde{e}_i^{z_i}) \cdot ((e/\widetilde{e}_i^{z_i})^{-1} \mod \widetilde{e}_i^{z_i}).$$

In summary, for $r = 1$, we compute $u$ directly. For $r > 1$, we generate all candidate values for $u$, where the total number of candidates is bounded by $r^t$. Given $0 < t \leq n$ and $n = O(\log\log N)$, we have $r^t \leq r^n = r^{O(\log\log N)}$. This implies that the maximum number of candidates is polynomial in $\log N$ for any constant integer $r$. For each candidate $\overline{u}$, we apply Lemma 5 to verify whether $e \mid (Q - \overline{u})$. If successful, this allows us to factorize $N$ under the condition $e \geq N^{\frac{1}{4r}+\varepsilon}$.

When the specific value of $\beta$ (satisfying $Q \geq N^\beta$) is known, Lemma 2 yields the improved bound $e \geq N^{\beta - r\beta^2 + \varepsilon}$.

Finally, we analyze the time complexity. Analogous to Theorem 2, we must iterate through all candidate pairs $(E_1, E_2)$. Consequently, the total running time is $2^n$ multiplied by the time required per candidate.

In the situation $r = 1$, for each candidate pair $(E_1, E_2)$, we invoke either Lemma 5 or Lemma 2 once. The total runtime becomes $2^n \cdot T_{\text{Cop}}$, where $T_{\text{Cop}}$ is defined in (10). Specifically, the runtime complexity is derived as follows:

$$\begin{cases} O\left(2^n \varepsilon^{-8} \log^2 N\right) & (\beta \text{ is unknown}) \\ O\left(2^n \varepsilon^{-7} \log^2 N\right) & (\beta \text{ is known}) \end{cases},$$

where $n = O(\log\log N)$. The aforementioned expression coincides with the case of $r = 1$ in Theorem 2.

In the situation $r > 1$, the analysis is a bit more complex. For each given candidate of $(E_1, E_2)$, we perform the AMM algorithm for the case of each modulo $\widetilde{e}_i$, and then utilize Hensel lifting for the case of modulo $\widetilde{e}_i^{z_i}$, for all $1 \leq i \leq t$, where $\widetilde{e}_1, \cdots, \widetilde{e}_t$ are distinct primes, and $z_i \geq 1$. At this stage, the AMM algorithm is utilized $t$ times, and Hensel lifting is likewise implemented

[2] Since $e = \widetilde{e}_1^{z_1} \cdot \widetilde{e}_2^{z_2} \cdots \widetilde{e}_t^{z_t}$, we have $\widetilde{e}_i \leq e$ and $z_i \leq \log e$ for all $i$. Due to $e < N$ and $r < \log N$, the expression $\log r \cdot z_i^3 \log^2 \widetilde{e}_i$ is polynomially bounded in terms of $\log N$.

[3] If $z_i = 1$ for some $i \in \{1, \cdots, t\}$, then we do not need to use Hensel lifting. In the case, $W_{i,j} = U_{i,j}$.

$t$ times. This stage generates up to $r^t$ tuples. For any fixed tuple, we need to execute the CRT algorithm once. Therefore, CRT is executed at most $r^t$ times. This process obtains all candidate values including $u$, with a maximum of $r^t$. For each candidate value, Lemma 5 or Lemma 2 is utilized once. Therefore, a maximum of $r^t$ times are required.

Let $T_{\mathrm{Hen},r,\widetilde{e}_i,z_i}$ denote the execution time of Hensel lifting, where

$$T_{\mathrm{Hen},r,\widetilde{e}_i,z_i} = O(\log r \cdot z_i^3 \log^2 \widetilde{e}_i). \tag{19}$$

Here, $r$ is the polynomial degree and $\widetilde{e}_i$ is the lifted modulus. The total runtime is bounded by:

$$2^n \cdot \left( \sum_{i=1}^{t} T_{\mathrm{AMM},r,\widetilde{e}_i} + \sum_{i=1}^{t} T_{\mathrm{Hen},r,\widetilde{e}_i,z_i} + r^t \cdot T_{\mathrm{CRT},e} + r^t \cdot T_{\mathrm{Cop}} \right), \tag{20}$$

with $0 < t \leq n$.

First, we consider the AMM runtime. According to (11), we have $T_{\mathrm{AMM},r,\widetilde{e}_i} = O(\log^4 \widetilde{e}_i + r \log^3 \widetilde{e}_i)$. Note that

$$\sum_{i=1}^{t} (\log^4 \widetilde{e}_i + r \log^3 \widetilde{e}_i) \leq (\sum_{i=1}^{t} \log \widetilde{e}_i)^4 + r(\sum_{i=1}^{t} \log \widetilde{e}_i)^3 \leq \log^4 e + r \log^3 e,$$

where $e = \widetilde{e}_1^{z_1} \cdot \widetilde{e}_2^{z_2} \cdots \widetilde{e}_t^{z_t} \geq e_1 \cdot e_2 \cdots e_t$. Hence, we have

$$\sum_{i=1}^{t} T_{\mathrm{AMM},r,\widetilde{e}_i} = O(\log^4 e + r \log^3 e). \tag{21}$$

Next, we deal with the case of Hensel lifting. From (19), we get $T_{\mathrm{Hen},r,\widetilde{e}_i,z_i} = O(\log r \cdot z_i^3 \log^2 \widetilde{e}_i)$. Since

$$\sum_{i=1}^{t} z_i^3 \log^2 \widetilde{e}_i \leq \sum_{i=1}^{t} z_i^3 \log^3 \widetilde{e}_i = \sum_{i=1}^{t} (\log \widetilde{e}_i^{z_i})^3 \leq (\sum_{i=1}^{t} \log \widetilde{e}_i^{z_i})^3 = \log^3 e,$$

we deduce

$$\sum_{i=1}^{t} T_{\mathrm{Hen},r,\widetilde{e}_i,z_i} = O(\log r \log^3 e). \tag{22}$$

It implies that the term $\sum_{i=1}^{t} T_{\mathrm{Hen},r,\widetilde{e}_i,z_i}$ in (20) is negligible compared to the term $\sum_{i=1}^{t} T_{\mathrm{AMM},r,\widetilde{e}_i}$.

Finally, we address the situation of CRT. Based on (17), we have $T_{\mathrm{CRT},e} = O(\log^2 e)$. Given $e < N$, it follows that $\log^2 e < \log^2 N$. Therefore, the term $r^t T_{\mathrm{CRT},e}$ in (20) is negligible compared to the term $r^t T_{\mathrm{Cop}}$, where

$$T_{\mathrm{Cop}} = \begin{cases} O(\varepsilon^{-8} \log^2 N) & (\beta \text{ is unknown}) \\ O(\varepsilon^{-7} \log^2 N) & (\beta \text{ is known}) \end{cases}.$$

By substituting these relations and the upper bound of $t$ ($t = n$) into (20), we derive the following runtime complexities:

$$\begin{cases} O\left(2^n\left(r^n\varepsilon^{-8}\log^2 N + \log^4 e + r\log^3 e\right)\right) & (\beta \text{ is unknown}) \\ O\left(2^n\left(r^n\varepsilon^{-7}\log^2 N + \log^4 e + r\log^3 e\right)\right) & (\beta \text{ is known}) \end{cases},$$

where $n = O(\log\log N)$. The aforementioned expression coincides with the case of $r > 1$ in Theorem 2.

□

## 5 Application to the $\phi$-Hiding Assumption

In this section, we give new results to solve the corresponding $\phi$-hiding problem.

**Corollary 1.** *Let $N = PQ^r$ be a given integer with unknown factorization, where $P, Q$ are primes, and $r \geq 1$. For any fixed $\varepsilon > 0$, let*

$$e \geq N^{\frac{1}{4r}+\varepsilon}$$

*be a given prime. Then we can decide whether $e$ divides $\phi(N)$ or not in polynomial time.*

*Proof.* When $\gcd(e, N) \neq 1$, then $N$ can be efficiently factorized. In this case, we can easily decide whether $e \mid \phi(N)$. When $\gcd(e, N) = 1$, if the prime $e$ divides $\phi(N)$ and $e \geq N^{\frac{1}{4r}+\varepsilon}$, then $N$ can be decomposed in the polynomial time according to Theorem 1. It implies that the $\phi$-hiding problem is solved in polynomial time. □

**Corollary 2.** *Let $N = PQ^r$ be a given integer with unknown factorization, where primes $P, Q$ have the same bit-length, and $r \geq 1$. For any fixed $\varepsilon > 0$, let*

$$e \geq N^{\frac{1}{(r+1)^2}+\varepsilon}$$

*be a given prime. Then we can decide whether $e$ divides $\phi(N)$ or not in polynomial time.*

*Remark 5.* In Corollary 1, we do not need any information about the size of $Q$. It is worth noting that in this result, such information is known. This leads to a better result being obtained. Specifically, $\frac{1}{(r+1)^2} < \frac{1}{4r}$ for $r > 1$. For the case of $r = 1$, these two bounds are the same, that is, $e > N^{\frac{1}{4}}$. It matches the previous best result.

*Proof.* Similar to the above proof, we only deal with the case that $\gcd(e, N) = 1$. In this case, if the prime $e$ divides $\phi(N)$ and $e \geq N^{\beta - r\beta^2+\varepsilon}$, where the value of $\beta$ satisfying $Q \geq N^\beta$ is known, then $N$ can be decomposed in the polynomial time according to Theorem 1.

Notice that $P$ and $Q$ have the same bit-size. If $Q > P$, then $Q^{r+1} > PQ^r = N$. It means that $Q \geq N^{\frac{1}{r+1}}$. Thus, we can take $\beta = \frac{1}{r+1}$. In this case, the condition $e \geq N^{\beta - r\beta^2 + \varepsilon}$ becomes $e \geq N^{\frac{1}{(r+1)^2} + \varepsilon}$. If $Q < P$, then $Q < N^{\frac{1}{r+1}} < P < 2Q$. It implies that $Q > N^{\frac{1}{r+1} - \log_N 2}$. Hence, we can take $\beta = \frac{1}{r+1} - \log_N 2$. For a large $N$, $\log_N 2$ is negligible. In this situation, the condition $e \geq N^{\beta - r\beta^2 + \varepsilon}$ still becomes $e \geq N^{\frac{1}{(r+1)^2} + \varepsilon}$. To sum up, when the bit-size of $P$ and $Q$ is equal, the condition $e \geq N^{\beta - r\beta^2 + \varepsilon}$ reduces to $e \geq N^{\frac{1}{(r+1)^2} + \varepsilon}$. □

*Remark 6.* According to Theorem 2 and Theorem 3, the $\phi$-hiding problem can be solved when the involved $e$ is no longer a prime number. The corresponding bounds in Corollary 1 and Corollary 2 can be obtained, respectively. We omit the specific process.

Next, we will provide relevant comparisons with previous work.

**Comparison with** [34]**.** For $N = PQ^r$, where $r$ is an even number (e.g., $r = 2$), [34] can only handle the case where the prime $e$ divides $P - 1$, meaning $P$ hides $e$. Because it uses the Jacobi symbol, where the power of $Q$ happens to be even. If $e$ divides $Q - 1$, this method fails to work because the power of $P$ is no longer even (see [34, Theorem 2]). Our method can deal with both of these situations. Moreover, ours is related to decomposing $N$, but [34] cannot achieve it. Certainly, if $e$ exactly divides $P - 1$, the result of [34] yields significantly better than ours. However, this condition represents only a special case of the broader scenario where $e$ divides $\phi(N)$.

**Comparison with** [23]**.** The modulus $N$ considered in this article is a special case of modulus in [23], i.e. $N = PQ^r$ for $r \geq 1$ and $P, Q$ are unknown primes. For any given prime $e \geq N^{\frac{1}{4r} + \varepsilon}$, we can decide whether $\gcd(e, \phi(N)) = 1$ or not in polynomial time. When $r = 1$, the bound $N^{\frac{1}{4}}$ is the same as that in [23]. But when $r > 1$, our bound $N^{\frac{1}{4r}}$ is significantly better than the bound $N^{\frac{1}{4}}$ in [23, Theorem 3].

**Comparison with** [27]**.** The modulus $N = PQ^r$ involved in this paper is also a special case of Lu et al. [27]. Note that $\min\{1, r\} = 1$ for any positive integer $r$. In this case, we can determine whether $e \mid \phi(N)$ in polynomial time for $e > N^{\frac{1}{4r}}$. However, the condition of Lu et al. is $e > N^{\frac{1}{4}}$ only for a prime $e$. Hence, when $r > 1$, our bound $N^{\frac{1}{4r}}$ is significantly better than Lu et al.'s bound.

**Comparison with** [40]**.** For a multi-power RSA modulus $N = PQ^r$ (i.e., $P, Q$ are unknown different primes with the same bit-length), the success condition[4] in [40] is a given prime $e > N^{\frac{\gcd(r, e-1)}{(r+1)^2}}$. In this article, our working condition

[4] In fact, the bound given in [40] is $e \geq 2N^{\frac{\gcd(r, e-1)}{(r+1)^2} + \epsilon}$, where $\epsilon > 0$ is a enough small constant. Note that $2N^{\frac{\gcd(r, e-1)}{(r+1)^2} + \epsilon} = N^{\frac{\gcd(r, e-1)}{(r+1)^2} + \log_N 2 + \epsilon}$, where $\log_N 2$ is negligible for a sufficiently large $N$. For the sake of comparison, we only write $e > N^{\frac{\gcd(r, e-1)}{(r+1)^2}}$.

is a given integer $e > N^{\frac{1}{(r+1)^2}}$. Due to the exponent $\frac{1}{(r+1)^2} < \frac{\gcd(r,e-1)}{(r+1)^2}$ for $\gcd(r, e-1) > 1$, our bound is significantly better than that in [40] for this case.

## 6 Application to Factoring RSA Moduli

In this section, we present rigorous results for factoring the relevant RSA moduli.

**Corollary 3.** *Let $N = PQ$ be a given semi-smooth RSA subgroup modulus. For any fixed $\varepsilon > 0$, let*

$$e \geq N^{\frac{1}{4}+\varepsilon}$$

*be a given integer with a known factorization such that $e \mid \phi(N)$, where the number of prime factors of $e$ is $O(\log \log N)$. We can factorize $N$ in time polynomial of $\log N$.*

*Proof.* The semi-smooth RSA subgroup modulus $N = PQ$, where primes $P, Q$ have the same bit-length. Therefore, we can take $r = 1$ for the form $N = PQ^r$, and $\beta = \frac{1}{2}$ for $Q \geq N^{\beta}$ without loss of generality. The integer $e$, with $e \mid \phi(N)$, is square-free. Further, we have the condition $e \geq N^{\frac{1}{4}+\varepsilon}$ according to Theorem 2. □

**Corollary 4.** *Let $N = PQ$ be a given standard RSA modulus. For any fixed $\varepsilon > 0$, let*

$$e \geq N^{\frac{1}{4}+\varepsilon}$$

*be a given integer with a known factorization satisfying $e \mid \phi(N)$, where $e$ is the product of $O(\log \log N)$ different primes. We can factorize $N$ in polynomial time.*

*Proof.* The modulus $N = PQ$ satisfies that prime numbers $P, Q$ have the same bit length. It means that we can take $r = 1$ for the form $N = PQ^r$, and $\beta = \frac{1}{2}$ for $Q \geq N^{\beta}$ without loss of generality. Further, we obtain the condition $e \geq N^{\frac{1}{4}+\varepsilon}$ based on Theorem 2. □

**Corollary 5.** *Let $N = PQ$ be a given RSA modulus, where prime $P, Q$ have the same bit-length and satisfy $(P-1, Q-1) = 2$. For any fixed $\varepsilon > 0$, let*

$$e \geq N^{\frac{1}{4}+\varepsilon}$$

*be a given integer with a known factorization satisfying $e \mid \phi(N)$, where the number of prime factors of $e$ is $O(\log \log N)$. We can factorize $N$ in polynomial time.*

*Proof.* Note that prime numbers $P, Q$ have the same bit-length. Hence, we take $r = 1$, and $\beta = \frac{1}{2}$ for $Q \geq N^{\beta}$. Then we get the condition $e \geq N^{\frac{1}{4}+\varepsilon}$ based on Theorem 3. □

Next, we will provide relevant comparisons and discussions.

**Discussion on the Extension in** [23]**.** Kakvi et al. wrote in [23, section 1.1]: *Our certification algorithm works only for prime e but it can be extended to the case where the factorization of* $e = \prod e_i^{z_i}$ *is known. In that case we can give an efficient certification procedure if* $e_i \geq N^{\frac{1}{4}+\varepsilon}$*, for all i. If, for one i, we have* $e_i < N^{\frac{1}{4}}$*, then* $\text{RSA}_{N,e}$ *is (at least)* $e_i$*-to-1 (lossy) under the* $\phi$*-hiding assumption.* However, Corollary 4 or Corollary 5 shows that even if all prime factors $e_i$'s satisfy $e_i < N^{\frac{1}{4}}$, if a square-free composite $e$ divides $\phi(N)$ satisfying $e > N^{\frac{1}{4}}$, the standard RSA modulus $N$ can be effectively decomposed. Therefore, when designing cryptographic algorithms, it is important to avoid using such situation.

**Comparison with the Method in** [30]**.** Naccache and Stern provided a heuristic analysis to factorize an SS modulus $N$ in [30, Section 2.4], if a known integer $E_1$ divides $P-1$ and a known integer $E_2$ divides $Q-1$. The required condition is $e > N^{1/4}$, where $e = E_1E_2$. In Corollary 3, we propose a rigorous approach to address this issue. To our knowledge, this is the first time a rigorous method has been given. Even if the factors $E_1$ and $E_2$ are not given in advance, as long as the number of prime factors of $e$ (with known factorization) is $O(\log\log N)$, our algorithm can still decompose $N$ in polynomial time under the above condition.

**Discussion on the Reduction in** [39]**.** At Crypto 2016, Yamakawa, Yamada, Hanaoka and Kunihiro gave the following reduction. If there is a PPT algorithm that breaks the ad-DRSA assumption, then one can find primes that divides $\phi(N)$, where $N$ is the involved SS modulus. Based on the following Proposition 1, the SS modulus $N$ is factorized in polynomial time. In other words, there exists a PPT algorithm to break the factoring assumption.

**Proposition 1** ([39])**.** *Let P and Q be primes with the same bit-length and* $N = PQ$*. Let integer e be a divisor of* $\phi(N) = (P-1)(Q-1)$*. If there exists a positive constant c such that* $e > N^{\frac{1}{2}+c}$ *holds, then there exists a polynomial time algorithm that is given N and e, and factorize N.*

The proof of Proposition 1 heavily depends on the Coppersmith theorem for bivariate integer equations in [13, Theorem 3], which does not require knowledge of the specific decomposition of integer $e$. Although a heuristic proof has already appeared in [30, Section 2.4], Proposition 1 provides a rigorous proof for this result.

Here we present a rigorous proof for heuristic analysis in [30, Section 2.4]. The proof is very simple and does not require the Coppersmith method.

**Theorem 4.** *Let P and Q be primes with the same bit-length and* $N = PQ$*. Let integer e be a divisor of* $\phi(N) = (P-1)(Q-1)$*. If there exists a positive constant* $\epsilon = O(\frac{\log\log N}{\log N})$ *such that* $e > N^{\frac{1}{2}-\epsilon}$ *holds, then there exists a polynomial time algorithm that is given N and e, and factorize N.*

*Proof.* Let $\phi(N) = N+1-(P+Q) = ek$, where $k$ is an positive integer. Dividing both sides by $e$, we get $\frac{N+1}{e} - \frac{P+Q}{e} = k$. Then we rewriting the equation above, there is $\lfloor \frac{N+1}{e} \rfloor - \lfloor \frac{P+Q}{e} \rfloor + d = k$, where $d$ is an integer, obviously $|d| \leq 1$. Since primes $P$ and $Q$ have the same bit-length, we obtain $P + Q < 3\sqrt{N}$, which implies $\lfloor \frac{P+Q}{e} \rfloor < 3N^{\epsilon}$.

Considering that $N^{\epsilon}$ is relatively small and $\lfloor \frac{P+Q}{e} \rfloor$ is an integer, we can exhaustively enumerate $\lfloor \frac{P+Q}{e} \rfloor - d$ to obtain $k$. After $k$ is obtained, we compute $P + Q = N + 1 - ek$ and factorize $N$.

The time complexity of factoring $N$ using the quadratic formula to find the roots of a quadratic equation is $O(1)$. Then the overall time complexity would be determined by the value of $O(3N^{\epsilon})$ which is bounded by a polynomial of $\log N$. Therefore, this algorithm will run in polynomial time with $\epsilon = O(\frac{\log \log N}{\log N})$. □

It is worth mentioning that our method can efficiently factorize $N$ when $e > N^{\frac{1}{2}-\epsilon}$, where $\epsilon = O(\frac{\log \log N}{\log N})$. It implies that the result of Proposition 1 is slightly improved. Notice that Proposition 1 is used for the specific parameter setting in [39]. Therefore, replacing Proposition 1 with Theorem 4 will slightly affect the case of specific parameters.

Yamakawa et al. gave an asymptotic parameter setting in [39, Section 2]. For a security parameter $\lambda$, the bit length of modulus $N$ is $O(\lambda^3)$, and the bit length of primes $e_i$ is $\lceil 4 \log \lambda \rceil$, where the primes $e_i$ divide $\phi(N)$. We let $e$ be the product of different prime numbers $e_i$. Without loss of generality, we write $e = e_1 \cdot e_2 \cdots e_n$, where $n$ is the number of prime factors. It is obvious that the product $e$ divides $\phi(N)$. According to Corollary 3, when $e > N^{\frac{1}{4}}$ and $n = O(\log \log N)$, the modulus $N$ can be factorized in polynomial time. On the one hand, if the condition $e > N^{\frac{1}{4}}$ holds, we roughly need $n > \frac{1/4 \log N}{4 \log \lambda} = O(\frac{\lambda^3}{\log \lambda})$. On the other hand, if $n = O(\log \log N)$ is satisfied, then $n = O(\log \lambda)$. However, these two aspects are contradictory. This means that the result in Corollary 3 does not affect asymptotic parameter setting.

**Discussion on Factoring SS Moduli.** The type of modulus in [30,39] is SS modulus. For example, the moduli involved in [30] are (10, 15, 15)-SS 768-bit moduli, for 80-bit security. In [30, Section 5], Naccache and Stern provided a challenge for decomposing a specific (10, 15, 15)-SS 768-bit modulus $N = pq$. Note that there are a total of 75 prime numbers with 10-bit, of which 30 are used in the construction of modulus in the challenge. In other words, these primes divide $\phi(N) = (p-1)(q-1)$. Based on Corollary 3, we need to select at least 20 (due to $\frac{768}{4*10} \approx 19.2$) such prime numbers to implement the attack, where $\binom{75}{20} \approx 2^{59.5}$. Moreover, the worst-case possibility of accurately determining whether these prime numbers divide $p - 1$ or $q - 1$ is $2^{20}$. Note that $2^{59.5} \cdot 2^{20} \approx 2^{80}$. Afterwards, for each of the $2^{80}$ situations, we also need to use the Coppersmith-type algorithm, which takes up the majority of the time. Therefore, such a direct strategy does not seem to break the 80-bit security. In order to reduce the computational complexity of the solution, we need to accelerate the process of exhaustive search. We denote Pr as the probability of including $s$ desired prime numbers in $m$ prime numbers, where $m \leq 75$ and $s \geq 20$. In an average sense, there are $\frac{1}{\Pr}\binom{m}{s}2^s$ possibilities. Let $T_s$ be the running time of Coppersmith's method. Hence, the running time of the attack algorithm is approximately $\frac{1}{\Pr}\binom{m}{s}2^s T_s$. The minimum scenario for considering the running time is future work.

**Discussion on the Security of the Naccache–Stern Scheme.** The most notable characteristic of the NS probabilistic encryption lies in the fact that the factorization $\sigma$ of $\phi(N)$ is public. In the discussion on factoring SS moduli, we have explored that when $\sigma$ is unknown, exhaustive search becomes necessary. One must exhaustively search and combine correct prime numbers from 75 10-bit primes to find $E_1E_2 = \sigma$, ultimately enabling the factorization of the modulus $N$. However, when $\sigma$ is known, exhaustive search is unnecessary. Only the greatest common divisor between 75 primes and $\sigma$ needs to be found to decompose $\sigma$. Subsequently, one needs to find $E_1$ and $E_2$ such that $E_1 \cdot E_2 = \sigma'$, where $E_1|(P-1)$, $E_2|(Q-1)$, and $N^{1/4} < \sigma' < \sigma$. This process simply involves combining the factors of $\sigma$. To apply Theorem 3, one needs to combine at least $\lceil \frac{\log N}{4 \cdot 10} \rceil$ prime factors, and the worst-case probability of obtaining the correct combination is no more than $2^{\lceil \frac{\log N}{4 \cdot 10} \rceil}$ possibilities. Therefore, the time complexity of attacking probabilistic NS encryption systems, similar to SS moduli, can be derived. Denote $T_s$ as the running time of Coppersmith's method, the time complexity of attacking probabilistic NS encryption systems is approximately $75 \log 10 \cdot 2^{\lceil \frac{\log N}{4 \cdot 10} \rceil} T_s$, where $75 \log 10$ represents the time taken by the Euclidean algorithm to compute common factors. When the bit length of $N$ is 768, the time complexity is approximately $75 \log 10 \cdot 2^{20} T_s$. Since the actual implementation of the attack can utilize parallel computing to accelerate the exhaustive search process, this complexity is acceptable in real-world attacks.

## 7 Experiments

We implemented experiments in Sage 9.3 on Linux Ubuntu, utilizing an Intel(R) Core(TM) i5-9300H CPU @ 2.40GHz. Our implementations are publicly available at https://github.com/TearsJin/659A70AF5035D498. We performed multiple experiments under different parameters for Theorem 1, Theorem 2, and Theorem 3. The difference in these experiments lies in the variation of $e$. Each experiment consists of two phases: parameter generation and the attack. Since the experiments for these three theorems are similar, we have chosen the experiment of Theorem 2 for a detailed description. The lattice basis reduction algorithm used here is Ryan–Heninger's Flatter algorithm [33].

**Parameter Generation.** In order to generate the modulus $N = PQ^r$. Initially, we set the values of $k, \ell_b, B_Q, B_P$. Then we randomly select $k/2 - 1$ $\ell_b$-bit primes to form the set $S_Q = \{q_1, q_2, \dots, q_{k/2-1}\}$ and calculate the product $u = \prod_{q \in S_Q} q$. Subsequently, we choose a slightly larger prime $a$ of bit length $B_Q$ and another prime $q'$ of bit length $\ell_b$. Next, we compute $Q = 2auq' + 1$. If $Q$ is not a prime number, we repeat the process of selecting $q'$ until $Q$ becomes prime. The generation of $P$ follows the same process ($P = 2bvp' + 1$). Finally, we select an appropriate number of prime from the set $S_P \cup S_Q$ and calculate their product to obtain $e$.

For the experiment of Theorem 1, the parameter generation phase is largely similar to that of Theorem 2, with the difference being the need to replace prime $a$ with $ea'$ (or $b$ with $eb'$) to obtain a large prime $e$, such that $e \mid (Q-1)$ or $e \mid (P-1)$. For Theorem 3, the difference from Theorem 2 is that when selecting $S_p$, primes can be repeated (the same applies to $S_q$), but we must ensure that the primes selected for $P$ are not used for $Q$ (since $\gcd(P-1, Q-1) = 2$).

**Attack Phase.** In the attack, following the proof of Theorem 2, we factorize $e$ as $e = e_1 e_2 \cdots e_n$ after computing $b \equiv u^r \mod e$ using $E_1$ and $E_2$ (see Remark 7). Then, we employ the AMM algorithm to find the roots of the equation $u^r \equiv b \mod e_i$, where $1 \le i \le n$.

**Table 1.** Experimental results. "Thm." is the abbreviation of Theorem, "Bound" represents the asymptotic lower bound of $\gamma = \log_N e$, "Dim." signifies the maximum dimension of the lattice, "$T$" represents the number of runs for Flatter, and "$T_1, T_2, T_3$" represent the number of runs for the AMM algorithm, Hensel lifting and CRT, respectively.

| | $k, l_b, B_Q, B_P$ | $r$ | Bound | $\gamma$ | $\beta$ | Dim. | $T$ | $T_1$ | $T_2$ | $T_3$ | Total Time |
|---|---|---|---|---|---|---|---|---|---|---|---|
| | | | | | $\beta$ is unknown | | | | | | |
| Thm. 1 | 20,15,300,400 | 1 | 0.250 | 0.278 | 0.450 | 112 | 26 | - | - | - | 645s |
| Thm. 1 | 20,15,300,450 | 2 | 0.125 | 0.144 | 0.300 | 243 | 17 | $< 1$s | - | - | 6149 s |
| Thm. 1 | 20,15,300,752 | 3 | 0.083 | 0.102 | 0.199 | 222 | 13 | $< 1$s | - | - | 4778 s |
| Thm. 2 | 30,15,100,172 | 1 | 0.250 | 0.279 | 0.446 | 108 | 26 | - | - | - | 802s |
| Thm. 2 | 25,15,100,192 | 2 | 0.125 | 0.159 | 0.297 | 110 | 17408 | $< 5$s | - | $< 5$s | 7078 s |
| Thm. 3 | 30,18,50,50 | 1 | 0.250 | 0.278 | 0.500 | 115 | 26 | - | $< 1$s | - | 1321 s |
| Thm. 3 | 30,18,50,50 | 2 | 0.125 | 0.148 | 0.333 | 160 | 2176 | $< 2$s | $< 1$s | $< 1$s | 6214 s |
| | | | | | $\beta$ is known | | | | | | |
| Thm. 1 | 20,15,300,902 | 1 | 0.208 | 0.224 | 0.296 | 147 | 1 | - | - | - | 169s |
| Thm. 1 | 20,15,300,1010 | 1 | 0.200 | 0.213 | 0.277 | 275 | 1 | - | - | - | 1456 s |
| Thm. 1 | 20,15,300,2710 | 2 | 0.090 | 0.104 | 0.120 | 140 | 2 | $< 1$s | - | - | 224s |
| Thm. 1 | 20,10,300,301 | 2 | 0.111 | 0.133 | 0.333 | 119 | 2 | $< 1$s | - | - | 87s |
| Thm. 1 | 20,10,300,300 | 3 | 0.062 | 0.084 | 0.250 | 133 | 3 | $< 1$s | - | - | 162s |
| Thm. 1 | 20,20,300,300 | 4 | 0.040 | 0.061 | 0.200 | 144 | 4 | $< 1$s | - | - | 513s |
| Thm. 2 | 20,30,300,1504 | 1 | 0.186 | 0.217 | 0.248 | 34 | 1 | - | - | - | 3s |
| Thm. 2 | 20,20,300,300 | 1 | 0.250 | 0.267 | 0.500 | 193 | 1 | - | - | - | 417s |
| Thm. 2 | 20,20,300,301 | 2 | 0.111 | 0.152 | 0.333 | 47 | 4096 | $< 20$s | - | $< 1$s | 8123 s |
| Thm. 3 | 30,12,50,248 | 1 | 0.225 | 0.241 | 0.350 | 139 | 1 | - | $< 1$s | - | 75s |
| Thm. 3 | 30,18,50,50 | 2 | 0.111 | 0.146 | 0.333 | 57 | 128 | $< 1$s | $< 1$s | $< 1$s | 3123 s |

Since each equation has at most $r$ roots, we enumerate at most $r^n$ combinations in total. For each potential combination, we utilize CRT to compute $\overline{u}$, followed by employing Lemma 5 (referred to as the Iteration Algorithm) to solve the equation $f(y) = ey + \overline{u} \mod Q$. If $\beta$ is known, we use Coppersmith's method in Lemma 2 instead of the Iteration Algorithm.

For the experiment of Theorem 3, the attack phase require Hensel lifting for each potential combination. For the experiment of Theorem 1, we do not need to perform an exhaustive search for $E_1 E_2 = e$ and the CRT algorithm. The remaining steps align closely with the experiment of Theorem 2.

From Table 1, our results are comparable to prior works when $r = 1$, and the experimental data for $r > 1$ validate the theorems in our theoretical analysis. Furthermore, in terms of runtime, since our experiments use relatively small values of $r$, the AMM algorithm, Hensel lifting, and the CRT algorithm complete within seconds - significantly faster than Flatter. Thus, Flatter dominates the overall runtime.

According to Table 1, we observe that the first row corresponds to $\gamma = 0.278$ with an asymptotic lower bound of 0.250, yielding a gap of 0.028, while the lattice dimension is 112. In contrast, the second row shows $\gamma = 0.144$ with a smaller gap of 0.019 from the asymptotic lower bound, but a significantly larger lattice dimension of 243. These results demonstrate that as $\gamma$ approaches the asymptotic lower bound, the required lattice dimension increases.

*Remark 7.* It should be noted that at the beginning of the Theorem 2 and Theorem 3, we need to enumerate all possible factors $E_1$ and $E_2$ of $e$, and run the algorithm for all possible factors. However, considering that doing so would make the experimental time too long, we recorded the values of $E_1$ and $E_2$ when generating $e$, thus skipping this enumeration process.

We conduct comparative experiments against prior works [23,27,40] to demonstrate that the bound of our attack is significantly tighter than those of existing approaches when $r > 1$. The results are summarized in Table 2.

**Table 2.** Experimental results comparing with prior works. For integer $N = PQ^r$, primes $P$ and $Q$ have the same bit-length, and $e = N^\gamma$ is prime. The bounds in [40] are derived under the condition that $e$ is expressed as $e = rk + 1$ with $r \geq 1$, which implies $\gcd(r, e-1) = r$. Define "Bound" and "Dim." as in Table 1.

| | $k, l_b, B_Q, B_P$ | Bound ( [23,27,40], Ours) | $r$ | $\gamma$ | Dim. |
|---|---|---|---|---|---|
| Theorem 1 | 20,20,300,300 | (0.250, 0.250, 0.250, 0.250) | 1 | 0.267 | 174 |
| Theorem 1 | 20,20,300,300 | (0.250, 0.250, 0.222, 0.111) | 2 | 0.133 | 121 |
| Theorem 1 | 20,20,300,300 | (0.250, 0.250, 0.188, 0.062) | 3 | 0.082 | 171 |
| Theorem 1 | 20,20,300,300 | (0.250, 0.250, 0.160, 0.040) | 4 | 0.061 | 149 |

**Acknowledgments.** The authors gratefully acknowledge the anonymous reviewers for their insightful comments and are particularly indebted to Sabrina Kunzweiler for her invaluable suggestions. This work was supported by the National Natural Science Foundation of China (Grant No. 62272454, 12441106).

## References

1. Abdalla, M., Benhamouda, F., Pointcheval, D.: On the tightness of forward-secure signature reductions. J. Cryptol. **32**(1), 84–150 (2019)
2. Adleman, L.M., Manders, K.L., Miller, G.L.: On taking roots in finite fields. In: FOCS, IEEE Computer Society (1977) 175–178
3. Adleman, L.M., McCurley, K.S.: Open problems in number theoretic complexity. In: Discrete Algorithms and Complexity, pp. 237–262. Elsevier (1987)
4. Adleman, L.M., McCurley, K.S.: Open problems in number theoretic complexity, II. In: Adleman, L.M., Huang, M.-D. (eds.) ANTS 1994. LNCS, vol. 877, pp. 291–322. Springer, Heidelberg (1994). https://doi.org/10.1007/3-540-58691-1_70
5. Alamati, N., Branco, P., Döttling, N., Garg, S., Hajiabadi, M., Pu, S.: Laconic private set intersection and applications. In: Nissim, K., Waters, B. (eds.) TCC 2021. LNCS, vol. 13044, pp. 94–125. Springer, Cham (2021). https://doi.org/10.1007/978-3-030-90456-2_4
6. Bellare, M., Yung, M.: Certifying cryptographic tools: the case of trapdoor permutations. In: Brickell, E.F. (ed.) CRYPTO 1992. LNCS, vol. 740, pp. 442–460. Springer, Heidelberg (1993). https://doi.org/10.1007/3-540-48071-4_31
7. Bellare, M., Yung, M.: Certifying permutations: Noninteractive zero-knowledge based on any trapdoor permutation. J. Cryptol. **9**(3), 149–166 (1996)
8. Blömer, J., May, A.: A tool kit for finding small roots of bivariate polynomials over the integers. In: Cramer, R. (ed.) EUROCRYPT 2005. LNCS, vol. 3494, pp. 251–267. Springer, Heidelberg (2005). https://doi.org/10.1007/11426639_15
9. Cachin, C., Micali, S., Stadler, M.: Computationally private information retrieval with polylogarithmic communication. In: Stern, J. (ed.) Computationally private information retrieval with polylogarithmic communication. LNCS, vol. 1592, pp. 402–414. Springer, Heidelberg (1999). https://doi.org/10.1007/3-540-48910-X_28
10. Cao, Z., Sha, Q., Fan, X.: Adleman-Manders-Miller root extraction method revisited. In: Wu, C.-K., Yung, M., Lin, D. (eds.) Inscrypt 2011. LNCS, vol. 7537, pp. 77–85. Springer, Heidelberg (2012). https://doi.org/10.1007/978-3-642-34704-7_6
11. Castagnos, G., Joux, A., Laguillaumie, F., Nguyen, P.Q.: Factoring $pq^2$ with quadratic forms: nice cryptanalyses. In: Matsui, M. (ed.) Advances in Cryptology – ASIACRYPT 2009. LNCS, vol. 5912, pp. 469–486. Springer, Heidelberg (2009). https://doi.org/10.1007/978-3-642-10366-7_28
12. Koç, Ç.K., Özdemir, F., Ödemiş Özger, Z.: Naccache-Stern Algorithm. In: Partially Homomorphic Encryption, pp. 71–82. Springer, Cham (2021). https://doi.org/10.1007/978-3-030-87629-6_7
13. Coppersmith, D.: Finding a small root of a bivariate integer equation; factoring with high bits known. In: Maurer, U. (ed.) EUROCRYPT 1996. LNCS, vol. 1070, pp. 178–189. Springer, Heidelberg (1996). https://doi.org/10.1007/3-540-68339-9_16
14. Coppersmith, D.: Small solutions to polynomial equations, and low exponent RSA vulnerabilities. J. Cryptol. **10**(4), 233–260 (1997)

15. Gentry, C., Ramzan, Z.: Single-database private information retrieval with constant communication rate. In: Caires, L., Italiano, G.F., Monteiro, L., Palamidessi, C., Yung, M. (eds.) ICALP 2005. LNCS, vol. 3580, pp. 803–815. Springer, Heidelberg (2005). https://doi.org/10.1007/11523468_65
16. Groth, J.: Cryptography in subgroups of $\mathbb{Z}_n^*$. In: Kilian, J. (ed.) TCC 2005. LNCS, vol. 3378, pp. 50–65. Springer, Heidelberg (2005). https://doi.org/10.1007/978-3-540-30576-7_4
17. Hardy, G.H., Ramanujan, S.: The normal number of prime factors of a number $n$. Q. J. Math. **48**, 76–92 (1917)
18. Hartmann, M., Paulus, S., Takagi, T.: NICE - new ideal Coset encryption -. In: Koç, Ç.K., Paar, C. (eds.) NICE - new ideal coset encryption. LNCS, vol. 1717, pp. 328–339. Springer, Heidelberg (1999). https://doi.org/10.1007/3-540-48059-5_28
19. Hemenway, B., Ostrovsky, R., Rosen, A.: Non-committing encryption from $\phi$-hiding. In: Dodis, Y., Nielsen, J.B. (eds.) TCC 2015. LNCS, vol. 9014, pp. 591–608. Springer, Heidelberg (2015). https://doi.org/10.1007/978-3-662-46494-6_24
20. Herrmann, M.: Improved cryptanalysis of the multi-prime $\phi$ - hiding assumption. In: Nitaj, A., Pointcheval, D. (eds.) AFRICACRYPT 2011. LNCS, vol. 6737, pp. 92–99. Springer, Heidelberg (2011). https://doi.org/10.1007/978-3-642-21969-6_6
21. Howgrave-Graham, N.: Finding small roots of univariate modular equations revisited. In: Darnell, M. (ed.) Cryptography and Coding 1997. LNCS, vol. 1355, pp. 131–142. Springer, Heidelberg (1997). https://doi.org/10.1007/BFb0024458
22. Jacobson, M.J., Scheidler, R., Weimer, D.: An adaptation of the NICE cryptosystem to real quadratic orders. In: Vaudenay, S. (ed.) AFRICACRYPT 2008. LNCS, vol. 5023, pp. 191–208. Springer, Heidelberg (2008). https://doi.org/10.1007/978-3-540-68164-9_13
23. Kakvi, S.A., Kiltz, E., May, A.: Certifying RSA. In: Wang, X., Sako, K. (eds.) ASIACRYPT 2012. LNCS, vol. 7658, pp. 404–414. Springer, Heidelberg (2012). https://doi.org/10.1007/978-3-642-34961-4_25
24. Katz, J., Lindell, Y.: Introduction to Modern Cryptography, Second Edition. CRC Press (2014)
25. Kiltz, E., O'Neill, A., Smith, A.: Instantiability of RSA-OAEP under chosen-plaintext attack. In: Rabin, T. (ed.) CRYPTO 2010. LNCS, vol. 6223, pp. 295–313. Springer, Heidelberg (2010). https://doi.org/10.1007/978-3-642-14623-7_16
26. Kiltz, E., O'Neill, A., Smith, A.D.: Instantiability of RSA-OAEP under chosen-plaintext attack. J. Cryptol. **30**(3), 889–919 (2017)
27. Lu, Y., Kunihiro, N., Zhang, R., Peng, L., Ma, H.: Certifying variant of RSA with generalized moduli. In: Naccache, D., et al. (eds.) ICICS 2018. LNCS, vol. 11149, pp. 598–608. Springer, Cham (2018). https://doi.org/10.1007/978-3-030-01950-1_35
28. Lu, Y., Zhang, R., Peng, L., Lin, D.: Solving linear equations modulo unknown divisors: revisited. In: Iwata, T., Cheon, J.H. (eds.) ASIACRYPT 2015. LNCS, vol. 9452, pp. 189–213. Springer, Heidelberg (2015). https://doi.org/10.1007/978-3-662-48797-6_9
29. May, A.: Using LLL-reduction for solving RSA and factorization problems. In: Nguyen, P., Vallée, B. (eds.) The LLL Algorithm. Information Security and Cryptography, pp. 315–348. Springer, Berlin, Heidelberg (2010). https://doi.org/10.1007/978-3-642-02295-1_10
30. Naccache, D., Stern, J.: A new public key cryptosystem based on higher residues. In: CCS, pp. 59–66. ACM (1998)
31. Okamoto, T.: A fast signature scheme based on congruential polynomial operations. IEEE Trans. Inf. Theory **36**(1), 47–53 (1990)

32. Okamoto, T., Uchiyama, S.: A new public-key cryptosystem as secure as factoring. In: Nyberg, K. (ed.) EUROCRYPT 1998. LNCS, vol. 1403, pp. 308–318. Springer, Heidelberg (1998). https://doi.org/10.1007/BFb0054135
33. Ryan, K., Heninger, N.: Fast practical lattice reduction through iterated compression. In: Handschuh, H., Lysyanskaya, A. (eds.) Advances in Cryptology – CRYPTO 2023. CRYPTO 2023. LNCS, vol. 14083, pp. 3–36. Springer, Cham (2023). https://doi.org/10.1007/978-3-031-38548-3_1
34. Schridde, C., Freisleben, B.: On the validity of the $\phi$-hiding assumption in cryptographic protocols. In: ASIACRYPT, vol. 5350, pp. 344–354. LNCS, Springer, Cham (2008)
35. Takagi, T.: Fast RSA-type cryptosystem modulo $p^k q$. In: Krawczyk, H. (eds.) Advances in Cryptology — CRYPTO 1998. CRYPTO 1998. LNCS, vol. 1462, pp. 318–326. Springer, Berlin, Heidelberg (1998). https://doi.org/10.1007/BFb0055738CRYPTO
36. Tosu, K., Kunihiro, N.: Optimal bounds for multi-prime $\phi$-hiding assumption. In: Susilo, W., Mu, Y., Seberry, J. (eds.) ACISP 2012. LNCS, vol. 7372, pp. 1–14. Springer, Heidelberg (2012). https://doi.org/10.1007/978-3-642-31448-3_1
37. von zur Gathen, J., Gerhard, J.: Modern Computer Algebra (3. edn.). Cambridge University Press, Cambridge (2013)
38. Xu, J., Hu, L., Sarkar, S., Zhang, X., Huang, Z., Peng, L.: Cryptanalysis of multi-prime $\phi$-hiding assumption. In: ISC, vol. 9866, LNCS, pp. 440–453. Springer, Cham (2016)
39. Yamakawa, T., Yamada, S., Hanaoka, G., Kunihiro, N.: Adversary-dependent lossy trapdoor function from hardness of factoring semi-smooth RSA subgroup moduli. In: Robshaw, M., Katz, J. (eds.) CRYPTO 2016. LNCS, vol. 9815, pp. 3–32. Springer, Heidelberg (2016). https://doi.org/10.1007/978-3-662-53008-5_1
40. Zhang, X., Wang, L., Xu, J.: Certifying multi-power RSA. IET Inf. Secur. **13**(4), 330–335 (2019)
41. Zhao, X., Cao, Z., Dong, X., Shao, J., Wang, L., Liu, Z.: New assumptions and efficient cryptosystems from the $e$-th power residue symbol. In: Liu, J.K., Cui, H. (eds.) ACISP 2020. LNCS, vol. 12248, pp. 408–424. Springer, Cham (2020). https://doi.org/10.1007/978-3-030-55304-3_21

# PEGASIS: Practical Effective Class Group Action using 4-Dimensional Isogenies

Pierrick Dartois[1,2(✉)], Jonathan Komada Eriksen[5], Tako Boris Fouotsa[3], Arthur Herlédan Le Merdy[4], Riccardo Invernizzi[5], Damien Robert[1,2], Ryan Rueger[6,7], Frederik Vercauteren[5], and Benjamin Wesolowski[4]

[1] University of Bordeaux, CNRS, Bordeaux INP, IMB, UMR 5251, 33400 Talence, France
pierrick.dartois@u-bordeaux.fr
[2] INRIA, IMB, UMR 5251, 33400 Talence, France
damien.robert@inria.fr
[3] EPFL, LASEC, Lausanne, Switzerland
tako.fouotsa@epfl.ch
[4] ENS de Lyon, CNRS, UMPA, UMR 5669, Lyon, France
{arthur.herledan_le_merdy,benjamin.wesolowski}@ens-lyon.fr
[5] KU Leuven, COSIC, Heverlee, Belgium
{frederik.vercauteren,riccardo.invernizzi}@esat.kuleuven.be
[6] IBM Research Europe, Zurich, Switzerland
ryan@rueg.re
[7] Technische Universität München, Munich, Germany

**Abstract.** In this paper, we present the first practical algorithm to compute an effective group action of the class group of any imaginary quadratic order $\mathcal{O}$ on a set of supersingular elliptic curves primitively oriented by $\mathcal{O}$. Effective means that we can act with any element of the class group directly, and are not restricted to acting by products of ideals of small norm, as for instance in CSIDH. Such restricted effective group actions often hamper cryptographic constructions, e.g. in signature or MPC protocols.

Our algorithm is a refinement of the Clapoti approach by Page and Robert, and uses 4-dimensional isogenies. As such, it runs in polynomial time, does not require the computation of the structure of the class group, nor expensive lattice reductions, and our techniques allow it to be instantiated with the orientation given by the Frobenius endomorphism. This makes the algorithm practical even at security levels as high as CSIDH-4096. Our implementation in SageMath takes 1.5 s to compute a group action at the CSIDH-512 security level, 21 s at CSIDH-2048 level and around 2 min at the CSIDH-4096 level. This marks the first instantiation of an effective cryptographic group action at such high security levels. For comparison, the recent KLaPoTi approach requires around 200 s at the CSIDH-512 level in SageMath and 2 s in Rust.


Y. Tauman Kalai and S. F. Kamara (Eds.): CRYPTO 2025, LNCS 16000, pp. 67–99, 2025.
https://doi.org/10.1007/978-3-032-01855-7_3

## 1 Introduction

The simplicity and flexibility of the Diffie-Hellman key-agreement protocol [25] has made it ideally suited to create more advanced protocols, such as public-key encryption [28], digital signatures [53], password-authenticated key exchange [35], threshold encryption [24], threshold signatures [33,34], updatable encryption [9] and many more. These protocols are all based on the computational efficiency and commutativity of group exponentiation, combined with the computational hardness of the discrete logarithm problem.

Due to Shor's algorithm [54], the discrete logarithm problem is not quantum hard. To construct a post-quantum analogue of the Diffie-Hellman protocol, we need to remove the underlying group structure. One way to achieve this is to use a commutative group action instead. The vectorisation and parallelisation problems, which are analogues of the discrete-logarithm and computational Diffie-Hellman problems respectively, are assumed to be (superpolynomially, but sub-exponentially [38]) hard, even for quantum computers. Furthermore, both problems are equivalently hard for quantum computers [31,32,41]. Using group actions, it is possible to construct post-quantum analogues of the advanced protocols given above: public-key encryption [42], digital signatures [7], password-authenticated key-exchange [1], threshold encryption and signatures [23] and updatable encryption [39].

A group action is said to be *effective* (EGA) if, amongst other conditions, the action can be computed in polynomial time [2]. That is, if $G$ acts on $X$, we have a polynomial-time algorithm that computes $gx$ for any $g$ in $G$ and $x$ in $X$. If we only have a polynomial-time algorithm that can compute $g_i x$ for $\{g_1, \ldots, g_n\}$, a set of (polynomially many) generators of $G$, the action is said to be a *restricted effective* group action (REGA).

The most prominent instantiation of a REGA is given by the action of the class group of an imaginary quadratic order on a certain set of oriented elliptic curves, with the CSIDH protocol [12] (or its variant CSURF [11]) being the most efficient. In CSIDH, the orientation is given by the Frobenius endomorphism, and the set of oriented curves simply consists of the supersingular curves defined over $\mathbb{F}_p$, up to $\mathbb{F}_p$-isomorphism. Since we can only efficiently evaluate the action of ideals of smooth norm, CSIDH is indeed a REGA and not an EGA. This often results in difficulties in constructing post-quantum variants of protocols based on Diffie-Hellman: many of the previously mentioned examples really require an EGA, while other examples, such as the signature scheme SeaSign [21], resort to some form of rejection sampling to not leak information about the secret (as a workaround for being a REGA).

A three step approach to turn a REGA into an EGA was given by the signature scheme CSI-FiSh [7]: the first step computes the structure of the class group (which can be done in quantum polynomial time, but classically takes subexponential time), the second step computes a (very) short basis of the relation lattice (which takes exponential time, even quantumly) and the third step expresses any element as a product of the generators with small exponents, using the short basis. Step 1 has been done in practice for CSIDH-512, but further research [6,8,48] concludes that using a 512 bit prime for CSIDH does not achieve NIST level 1 security, with the latter two sources claiming that primes of more than 2000 bits are required. Since the computation of the class group is infeasible for such large primes, the primitive SCALLOP [20] and improvements [3,13] avoided such computation by using a (large prime conductor) suborder of an order with small discriminant, so that the class group structure comes for free. This approach however does not fundamentally solve steps 2 and 3 (see https://yx7.cc/blah/2023-04-14.html for an informal, but detailed discussion of this issue), and the highest level achieved in [3] is equivalent to CSIDH-1536, for which a single group action takes almost 12 min using a C++ implementation. This approach is therefore completely hopeless to instantiate practical effective group actions at higher security levels (even using a quantum computer).

**Our Contributions.** We describe a practical algorithm to compute the group action of any element in the class group of an imaginary quadratic order $\mathcal{O}$ on a set of supersingular elliptic curves over $\overline{\mathbb{F}}_p$ primitively oriented by $\mathcal{O}$. Our algorithm works for all orders of discriminant $\Delta_{\mathcal{O}}$ all the way up to $|\Delta_{\mathcal{O}}| \approx p$ and in particular, applies in the CSIDH/CSURF setting, where the orientation is given by Frobenius, and we have $\Delta_{\mathcal{O}} = -p$ or $\Delta_{\mathcal{O}} = -4p$. As such, we obtain the first EGA at security levels equivalent to CSIDH-2048 and CSIDH-4096. We implement the algorithm in SageMath, and show that it achieves a highly practical runtime, which scales well to higher security levels. Not only does our algorithm allow us to easily instantiate security levels far beyond what previous EGA instantiations were able to; the timings of our proof-of-concept SageMath implementation also outperform all other EGA instantiations (even compared to their highly optimized C++/Rust implementations) at corresponding security levels. Our implementation is publicly available at https://github.com/pegasis4d.

**Technical Overview.** Our work is based on the Clapoti framework [46], and proceeds by embedding the isogeny we wish to evaluate in an isogeny in dimension 4. In order to evaluate the action given by the ideal $\mathfrak{a} \subseteq \mathcal{O}$ on an elliptic curve $E$ using only one 4-dimensional $2^e$-isogeny, the Clapoti framework requires finding two other integral ideals $\mathfrak{b}, \mathfrak{c}$ equivalent to $\mathfrak{a}$ such that

$$uN(\mathfrak{b}) + vN(\mathfrak{c}) = 2^e, \tag{1}$$

with the restriction that $u, v$ are integers that can be written as the sum of two squares (in particular, they must be easy to factorise), and where $2^e < p$ (or more accurately, the full torsion group $E[2^e]$ should be defined over $\mathbb{F}_{p^{2k}}$ for a small $k$).

Several issues arise when trying to solve the above equation for $|\Delta_{\mathcal{O}}| \approx p$: even without the restriction on $u$ and $v$ being sums of squares, sometimes the equation simply has no solution. Indeed, since the smallest ideals equivalent to $\mathfrak{a}$ are already expected to have norm around $\sqrt{p}$, and a solution is guaranteed to exist only when $N(\mathfrak{b})N(\mathfrak{c}) < 2^e$, this contradicts the requirement $2^e < p$.

As such, imposing the extra condition for both $u$ and $v$ to be sums of squares further lowers the probability of finding a solution.

The main insight is that we can derive a related equation which is much easier to solve by exploiting the fact we can always efficiently compute small degree isogenies. We use this insight in two ways: first, we write $\mathfrak{b} = \mathfrak{b}_k\mathfrak{b}_e$ and $\mathfrak{c} = \mathfrak{c}_k\mathfrak{c}_e$ where $\mathfrak{b}_e$ and $\mathfrak{c}_e$ are ideals of smooth norm and compute the isogenies $\varphi_{\mathfrak{b}_e} : E \to E_1$ and $\varphi_{\mathfrak{c}_e} : E \to E_2$, simply using Elkies' algorithm [29] or Vélu's algorithm [55]. We can then apply the Clapoti framework to $E_1 \times E_2$ instead of $E \times E$, resulting in the equation

$$uN(\mathfrak{b}_k) + vN(\mathfrak{c}_k) = 2^e,$$

where now the product $N(\mathfrak{b}_k)N(\mathfrak{c}_k)$ is typically much smaller than $2^e$ since we have removed the norms of the ideals $\mathfrak{b}_e$ and $\mathfrak{c}_e$.

Second, we use the same insight to relax the conditions on $u$ and $v$: instead of requiring that each can be written as a sum of squares, we again allow to take out smooth factors $g_u$ and $g_v$ such that $u = g_u(x_u^2+y_u^2)$ and $v = g_v(x_v^2+y_v^2)$. Note that integers containing prime factors (to an odd power) which are 3 mod 4 can never be written as a sum of squares, so allowing factors like $3, 7, 11, 19, \ldots$ to be taken out of $u$ and $v$ drastically increases the probability that both $u/g_u$ and $v/g_v$ are sums of squares. Applying the above, allows us to solve the (relaxed) norm equation efficiently, even at the highest security levels.

With $u$ and $v$ of this form, we are able to efficiently construct a 2-dimensional $u$-isogeny $\Phi_u : E_1^2 \to E_u^2$ and a 2-dimensional $v$-isogeny $\Phi_v : E_2^2 \to E_v^2$. We then compute a 4-dimensional $2^e$-isogeny $F : E_u^2 \times E_v^2 \to E_{\mathfrak{a}}^2 \times E'^2$ that "embeds" $\Phi_u$, $\Phi_v$, $\varphi_{\mathfrak{b}_k} : E_1 \to E_{\mathfrak{a}}$ and $\varphi_{\mathfrak{c}_k} : E_2 \to E_{\mathfrak{a}}$, where $E_{\mathfrak{a}} := \mathfrak{a} \cdot E$. Using level-2 theta coordinates as in [17], the computation of $F$ is relatively fast. We finally extract the resulting curve $E_{\mathfrak{a}}$ from the codomain of $F$. For very high security levels, we remark that it is helpful to relax the conditions on $u, v$ and allow them to be arbitrary positive integers, at the cost of using more dimension-4 isogenies (see Sects. 4.2 and 6.4).

**Comparison with Related Work.** We briefly compare our algorithm with 2 related works: the original Clapoti framework [46] and the recent KLaPoTi algorithm [47] that relies on KLPT.

**Clapoti**: As described above our work is based on the Clapoti framework [46], which presents the first polynomial time algorithm to act with a random ideal $\mathfrak{a} \subseteq \mathcal{O}$ by finding two integral ideals $\mathfrak{b}, \mathfrak{c}$ equivalent to $\mathfrak{a}$ such that

$$uN(\mathfrak{b}) + vN(\mathfrak{c}) = M\,. \tag{2}$$

For a provably polynomial time algorithm, $M$ has to be chosen powersmooth, but in order to achieve a practical algorithm, one really is limited to $M = 2^e$ where the $2^e$-torsion is easily accessible, in particular, $2^e < p$. However, the expected number of solutions is $2^e/N(\mathfrak{b})N(\mathfrak{c})$ where $N(\mathfrak{b}), N(\mathfrak{c})$ are roughly $\sqrt{p}$ and thus if $p + 1 = f2^e$ even for small $f$, this equation simply will not have a solution. To illustrate this: for the 4000-bit parameter set, directly applying Clapoti will fail in 97% of the cases when $M = 2^e < p$, and this is without the restriction on $u$ and $v$ being sums of squares. If one adds this restriction on $u$ and $v$, the probability to find a solution is close to 0 since the probability that a pair $(u, v)$ each of size $\sqrt{p}$ is a sum of squares is proportional to $1/\log(p)$. Furthermore, note that it is impossible to test all pairs $(u, v)$ since this would involve factorisation, even further lowering the probability by another 2 to 3 orders of magnitude depending on the size of $p$. In conclusion: running Clapoti with $M = 2^e < p$ will almost always fail, and thus is not a practically efficient algorithm.

**KLaPoti**: A recent paper by Panny, Petit and Stopar [47] has also instantiated a primitive KLaPoTi based on Clapoti. KLaPoTi differs from PEGASIS in several aspects. The main ones are the way Eq. (1) is solved, the dimension of the isogeny used in the evaluation of the group action and the size of the base prime $p$. KLaPoTi relies on the KLPT algorithm [37] to solve Eq. (1), which now requires $u, v$ to be perfect squares. The fact that $u$ and $v$ are perfect squares allows to perform the group action computation using dimension-2 isogenies only. Nevertheless, the relatively large size of the solution obtained by this KLPT approach requires $|\Delta|^3 < 2^e$ where $\Delta$ is the discriminant of the order $\mathcal{O}$. This implies that KLaPoTi uses a base prime $p$ whose bitsize is 3 times larger than the one used in CSIDH and PEGASIS, and uses an order $\mathcal{O}$ of discriminant $\Delta$ with $|\Delta|^3 < 2^e < p$. This highly affects the performance and the key sizes in KLaPoTi. Even though PEGASIS performs the group action using 4-dimensional isogenies, the fact that $|\Delta| \approx 2^e \approx p$ in PEGASIS enables a group action computation which is more efficient. For example, to achieve similar security to CSIDH-512, KLaPoTi uses a prime $p$ of 1536 bits and a single group action computation takes approximately 3 min [47, Section 7.1] in SageMath, while PEGASIS uses a prime of about 512 bits and a single group action computation takes approximately 1.5 s.

**Organisation of Paper.** The rest of the paper is organized as follows. In Sect. 2 we recall the necessary background material. In Sect. 3 we describe our whole algorithm for general orientations. In Sect. 4, we detail an important subroutine, namely how to compute an isogeny of prescribed degree in dimension 2, before we in Sect. 5 specialise our algorithm for the CSIDH orientation. Finally, in Sect. 6 we detail some implementation choices before we present our timings.

**Full Version of the Paper.** Due to space limitations, this is an abbreviated version of the full version of the paper [18], which contains the missing proofs and an extended appendix with more details on theta coordinates and 4D isogenies; an extra variant of the algorithm; working exclusively over $\mathbb{F}_p$ and an in depth explanation on how parameters were chosen.

## 2 Preliminaries

For a general introduction to isogenies, especially in the context of cryptography, we refer the reader to [30].

### 2.1 Isogeny Class-Group Action on Oriented Curves

Classic results [56, Th. 4.5] tell us that the class-group $\mathrm{Cl}(\mathcal{O})$ of an imaginary quadratic order $\mathcal{O}$ acts freely and transitively on the set $\mathrm{Ord}_q(\mathcal{O})$ of *ordinary* elliptic curves $E/\mathbb{F}_q$ with endomorphism ring $\mathrm{End}(E) \cong \mathcal{O}$. In [14], generalising the work of [11,12], Colò and Kohel introduced the framework for a similar action, in which $\mathrm{Cl}(\mathcal{O})$ acts on a set of *supersingular* elliptic curves $E$ which contain $\mathcal{O}$ as a subring of $\mathrm{End}(E)$. We briefly recount this general construction, together with results from [45].

Let $\mathcal{O} = \mathbb{Z}[\alpha]$ be an imaginary quadratic order and $E/\mathbb{F}_{p^n}$ an elliptic curve. We call an injective morphism of rings $\iota \colon \mathcal{O} \xhookrightarrow{\mathrm{End}} (E)$ an $\mathcal{O}$*-orientation* and say it is *primitive* if $\iota(\alpha) = \omega$ is a primitive element of $\mathrm{End}(E)$ viewed as a lattice, *i.e.* $\omega$ does not factor through a (non-trivial) scalar multiplication. We call the pair $(E, \iota)$ a (primitively) $\mathcal{O}$-oriented elliptic curve.

Let $(E, \iota)$ be primitively $\mathcal{O}$-oriented and $\mathfrak{a}$ an integral invertible ideal of $\mathcal{O}$ with norm coprime to $p$. Let $\varphi_{\mathfrak{a}} \colon E \to E_{\mathfrak{a}}$ be the isogeny with kernel

$$E[\mathfrak{a}] = \bigcap_{\sigma \in \mathfrak{a}} \ker(\iota(\sigma))$$

and degree $\mathrm{N}(\mathfrak{a})$. Now consider the map $\mathcal{O} \to \mathrm{End}(E_{\mathfrak{a}}) : \gamma \mapsto \varphi_{\mathfrak{a}}\iota(\gamma)\widehat{\varphi_{\mathfrak{a}}}$. It is an injective morphism of additive groups, but sends $1 \mapsto [\deg(\varphi_{\mathfrak{a}})]$ and so is not a morphism of rings. We fix this by first noting that $\varphi_{\mathfrak{a}}\iota(\gamma)\widehat{\varphi_{\mathfrak{a}}}$ always factors through $[\deg(\varphi_{\mathfrak{a}})]$ and then defining $(\varphi_{\mathfrak{a}})_*(\iota)$ as the map given by $(\varphi_{\mathfrak{a}})_*(\iota)(\gamma) = \varphi_{\mathfrak{a}}\iota(\gamma)\widehat{\varphi_{\mathfrak{a}}}/[\deg(\varphi_{\mathfrak{a}})]$ to obtain a morphism of rings and thus a well-defined $\mathcal{O}$-orientation. Indeed, by diagram-chasing one verifies that $\ker(\varphi_{\mathfrak{a}})$ is invariant under $\omega = \iota(\alpha)$, demonstrating that $\varphi_{\mathfrak{a}}\iota(\gamma)\widehat{\varphi_{\mathfrak{a}}}(E[\deg(\varphi_{\mathfrak{a}})]) = \{0\}$ for all $\gamma$ in $\mathbb{Z}[\alpha]$, and that $\varphi_{\mathfrak{a}}\iota(\gamma)\widehat{\varphi_{\mathfrak{a}}}$ factors through $[\deg(\varphi_{\mathfrak{a}})]$. In fact, $(\varphi_{\mathfrak{a}})_*(\iota)$ is a *primitive* orientation [45, Prop. 3.5].

We say that the isogenies $\varphi_{\mathfrak{a}} \colon (E, \iota) \to (E_{\mathfrak{a}}, (\varphi_{\mathfrak{a}})_*(\iota))$ are $\mathcal{O}$*-oriented.* Likewise, an isomorphism $\varphi \colon E \xrightarrow{\sim} E'$ is called an $\mathcal{O}$*-isomorphism* $(E, \iota) \to (E', \iota')$ if $\iota' = \varphi_*(\iota) := (\gamma \mapsto \varphi\iota(\gamma)\hat{\varphi})$. Using this terminology, we define $\mathrm{SS}^{\mathrm{pr}}_{p^n}(\mathcal{O})$ to be the $\mathcal{O}$-isomorphism classes of primitively $\mathcal{O}$-oriented supersingular elliptic curves defined over $\mathbb{F}_{p^n}$. This set is non-empty if and only if $p$ is not split in $K = \mathcal{O} \otimes_{\mathbb{Z}} \mathbb{Q}$ and does not divide the conductor of $\mathcal{O}$ in $\mathcal{O}_K$ [45, Prop. 3.2].

We note that every class $[\mathfrak{a}]$ in the class-group $\mathrm{Cl}(\mathcal{O})$ is represented by an invertible integral ideal $\mathfrak{b}$ with norm $\mathrm{N}(\mathfrak{b})$ coprime to $p$ [16, Cor. 7.17]. Moreover, it is clear that principal ideals $\gamma\mathcal{O}$ correspond to endomorphisms $\varphi_{\gamma\mathcal{O}} = \iota(\gamma)$. Now the map

$$\mathrm{Cl}(\mathcal{O}) \times \mathrm{SS}^{\mathrm{pr}}_p(\mathcal{O}) \to \mathrm{SS}^{\mathrm{pr}}_p(\mathcal{O}) \qquad [\mathfrak{a}], (E, \iota) \mapsto \mathfrak{a} \cdot (E, \iota) := (E_{\mathfrak{a}}, (\varphi_{\mathfrak{a}})_*(\iota))$$

is well-defined; and when $SS_p^{pr}(\mathcal{O})$ is non-empty, the action is free with at most two orbits [45, Prop. 3.3, Th. 3.4]. Restricting to one of these orbits, we obtain a free and transitive group action.

The vectorisation problem of this action - given $(E, \iota), (E', \iota')$ compute $[\mathfrak{a}]$ such that $\mathfrak{a} \cdot (E, \iota) = (E', \iota')$ - is thought to be quantum resistant. This property led to several cryptographic constructions based on ideal class group actions [12–14,20] which define (restricted) effective group actions, as mentioned in Sect. 1. The first one to be introduced was CSIDH (Commutative Supersingular Isogeny Diffie-Hellman)[1] [12] where $\mathcal{O} = \mathbb{Z}[\sqrt{-p}]$ and the orientation induces an isomorphism $\mathcal{O} \xrightarrow{\sim} \mathrm{End}_{\mathbb{F}_p}(\mathcal{O})$, mapping $\sqrt{-p}$ to the Frobenius endomorphism of $(x, y) \mapsto (x^p, y^p)$ for all $E \in SS_p^{pr}(\mathcal{O})$. Even though these schemes are thought to be quantum resistant, the best known quantum attack against the underlying vectorisation problem is a subexponential algorithm due to Kuperberg [38]. For that reason, there is an uncertainty on the parameters required to ensure a sufficient security level for CSIDH (and other class group action schemes). As mentioned in Sect. 1, conservative sources [6,8,48] estimate that a 2000 bit prime $p$ is required to ensure a NIST-1 security level for CSIDH.

### 2.2 Polarised Isogenies Between Abelian Varieties

Every abelian variety $A$ has a *dual* $\widehat{A}$ of the same dimension and every isogeny $\varphi\colon A \to B$ has a *dual* $\widehat{\varphi}\colon \widehat{B} \to \widehat{A}$ of the same degree. If there exists a special kind of isogeny $\lambda_A\colon A \to \widehat{A}$ called a *polarisation*, we say $(A, \lambda_A)$ is a *polarised* abelian variety (PAV). When $\lambda_A$ is an isomorphism, we say it is a *principal* polarisation and call $A$ a *principally* polarised abelian variety (PPAV). Elliptic curves are exactly the 1-dimensional PPAVs; they are canonically principally polarised.

**Definition 2.1 (Polarised Isogenies).** *Let $\varphi\colon (A, \lambda_A) \to (B, \lambda_B)$ be an isogeny between PAVs. If there exists an integer $d$ such that $\widehat{\varphi}\lambda_B\varphi = [d]\lambda_A$, we say that $\varphi$ is $(\lambda_A, \lambda_B)$-*polarised *with* polarised degree $\deg_p(\varphi) = d$. *When $A, B$ are PPAVs we define the* polarised dual *of $\varphi$ to be $\widetilde{\varphi} = \lambda_A^{-1}\widehat{\varphi}\lambda_B\colon (B, \lambda_B) \to (A, \lambda_A)$. Then $\varphi$ is $(\lambda_A, \lambda_B)$-polarised with degree $d$ if $\widetilde{\varphi}\varphi = [d]$ in* $\mathrm{End}(A)$.

$(\lambda_A, \lambda_B)$-polarised isogenies of polarised degree $d$ are characterised by an isotropy condition of their kernel.

**Lemma 2.1** *Let $\varphi\colon (A, \lambda_A) \to (B, \lambda_B)$ be a $(\lambda_A, \lambda_B)$-polarised isogeny with polarised degree $d$ such that $p \nmid d$ and let $g := \dim(A)$. Then $\ker(\varphi)$ is a subgroup of cardinality $d^g$ of $A[d]$, isotropic with respect to the Weil pairing $e^{[d]\lambda_A}$ associated to the polarisation $[d]\lambda_A : A \to \widehat{A}$ (as defined in [40, p. 135]).*

*Conversely, if $A$ is a PPAV of dimension $g$ and $\varphi\colon A \to B$ has kernel $\ker(\varphi) \subseteq A[d]$ of cardinality $d^g$ and isotropic for $e^{[d]\lambda_A}$, then there exists a unique principal polarisation $\lambda_B$ on $B$ such that $\varphi : A \to B$ is a $(\lambda_A, \lambda_B)$-polarised isogeny with polarised degree $d$.*

[1] Note that CSIDH is based on the CRS protocol [15,52], which uses the full endomorphism ring of an ordinary curve instead of an orientation of a supersingular curve.

*Proof* The proof is given in the full version of the paper [18]. □

For brevity, we will drop mention of the polarisations when they are clear from context, and say *d-isogeny* to mean an isogeny with polarised degree $d$. In particular, it is implicit that the corresponding polarisation to a PAV denoted $A$ is $\lambda_A$. Between elliptic curves, the principal polarisation being canonical, the dual $\widehat{\varphi}$ and polarised dual $\widetilde{\varphi}$ of an isogeny can be identified and will both be denoted by $\widehat{\varphi}$; and the notions of degree and polarised degree are also the same.

We recall a standard result about factoring isogenies between PPAVs, which we will need to recall the Clapoti construction in the more general context of [46, Remark 2.10].

**Lemma 2.2 (Factoring Isogenies between PPAVs).** *Let $A, B$ be PPAVs defined over a field $k$ and $\varphi\colon A \to B$ be a $d$-isogeny between them. For every pair of positive coprime integers $d_1, d_2$ each being coprime to* $\mathrm{char}(k)$ *satisfying $d_1 d_2 = d$, there exists a PPAV $C$, a $d_1$-isogeny $\varphi_1\colon A \to C$ and a $d_2$-isogeny $\varphi_2\colon C \to B$, each uniquely defined up to isomorphism, such that $\varphi = \varphi_2 \circ \varphi_1$.*

*Proof* The proof is given in the full version of the paper [18]. □

### 2.3 Kani's Lemma and Embedding Isogenies Into Higher Degree

If $(\varphi_{ji})_{ij}$ is a matrix of polarised isogenies $\varphi_{ij}\colon A_i \to B_j$ between PPAVs, then its polarised dual is given by $(\widetilde{\varphi_{ij}})_{ij}$. Whether or not a $2 \times 2$ matrix of polarised isogenies is a polarised isogeny is the content of Kani's lemma.

**Lemma 2.3 (Kani, [49, Lemma 2.1]).** *Let $A_1, A_2, B_1, B_2$ be PPAVs defined over $k$ and let $\varphi_{ij}\colon A_i \to B_j$ be polarised $d_{ij}$-isogenies. The map*

$$\Phi = \begin{pmatrix} \varphi_{11} & \varphi_{21} \\ \varphi_{12} & \varphi_{22} \end{pmatrix} : A_1 \times A_2 \to B_1 \times B_2$$

*is a polarised isogeny if and only if $d_{11} = d_{22}, d_{12} = d_{21}$ and the corresponding square $S_\Phi$*

$$\begin{array}{ccc} A_1 & \xrightarrow{\varphi_{11}} & B_1 \\ {\scriptstyle -\varphi_{12}}\downarrow & & \downarrow{\scriptstyle \widetilde{\varphi_{21}}} \\ B_2 & \xrightarrow[\widetilde{\varphi_{22}}]{} & A_2 \end{array}$$

*commutes. In such cases, $\deg_p(\Phi) = d_{11} + d_{12}$ and we call $\Phi$ the* Kani-map *corresponding to the* Kani-square *$S_\Phi$. Further, if $d_{11} = d_{22}$ is coprime to $d_{12} = d_{21}$, we call the Kani-square a $(d_{11}, d_{12})$-*isogeny diamond. *Finally, when $d_{11}$ is coprime to $d_{12}$ and $d = d_{11} + d_{12}$ is coprime to the characteristic of $k$, then*

$$\ker(\Phi) = \{([d_{11}]x, \widetilde{\varphi_{21}}\varphi_{11}(x)) \mid x \in A_1[d]\}.$$

If $\Phi$ can be efficiently evaluated, then so can $\varphi_{ij}$, and $\Phi$ is said to *embed* $\varphi_{ij}$. In other words, $\Phi$ is an *efficient representation* of the $\varphi_{ij}$ in the sense of the following definition.

**Definition 2.2.** *Let $\mathscr{A}$ be an algorithm. Given a d-isogeny $\varphi : A \to B$ between PPAVs of dimension g defined over $\mathbb{F}_q$, an* efficient representation *of $\varphi$ with respect to $\mathscr{A}$ is some data $D_\varphi \in \{0,1\}^*$ of polynomial size in g, $\log(d)$ and $\log(q)$ such that for all $P \in A(\mathbb{F}_{q^k})$, $\mathscr{A}$ with input $(D_\varphi, P)$ returns $\varphi(P)$ in polynomial time in g, $\log(d)$, k and $\log(q)$.*

## 3 Our Algorithmic Approach

We now describe our algorithm for computing the class group action by a general orientation.

### 3.1 Applying Kani's Lemma in Dimension 4

The factorisation lemma (Lemma 2.2) gives us a strategy to embed arbitrary isogenies into higher dimension [46, Remark 2.10]. If $\varphi\colon A \to B$, $\psi\colon A \to C$ are isogenies between PPAVs with coprime polarised degrees, we can form a Kani-diamond by factoring the composition $\psi\widetilde{\varphi}$ as $\widetilde{\varphi'\psi'}$ whereby $\psi'\colon B \to D$ and $\varphi'\colon C \to D$ have polarised degrees $\deg_{\mathrm{p}}(\varphi') = \deg_{\mathrm{p}}(\varphi), \deg_{\mathrm{p}}(\psi) = \deg_{\mathrm{p}}(\psi')$. The kernel of the resulting Kani-map can be computed so long as $\psi\widetilde{\varphi}$ is known on $B[\deg_{\mathrm{p}}(\varphi) + \deg_{\mathrm{p}}(\psi)]$.

When computing the class-group action of $[\mathfrak{a}]$ on a primitively oriented elliptic curve $(E, \iota)$, the isogenies $\varphi, \psi$ are taken to be $\widehat{\varphi}_{\mathfrak{b}}, \widehat{\varphi}_{\mathfrak{c}}\colon E_{\mathfrak{a}} \to E$ where $\mathfrak{b}, \mathfrak{c}$ are representatives of $[\mathfrak{a}]$. The composition $\widehat{\varphi}_{\mathfrak{c}}\varphi_{\mathfrak{b}} = \varphi_{\bar{\mathfrak{c}}\mathfrak{b}}$ is an endomorphism on $E$ dictated by $\iota$ and so the kernel of the resulting 2-dimensional Kani-map can be computed so long as the $\mathrm{N}(\mathfrak{b})+\mathrm{N}(\mathfrak{c})$ torsion is accessible. For practically efficient computation (using [19] for instance), we must find ideals $\mathfrak{b}, \mathfrak{c}$ representing $[\mathfrak{a}]$ such that $\mathrm{N}(\mathfrak{b}) + \mathrm{N}(\mathfrak{c}) = 2^e$, where $2^{e+2} \mid p + 1$ in order to work over $\mathbb{F}_{p^2}$ (the reason we need $2^{e+2}$ to divide $p + 1$ is due to technicalities when using level-2 theta coordinates to compute higher-dimensional isogenies). However, finding ideals $\mathfrak{b}, \mathfrak{c}$ satisfying this norm equation is not easy in practice and can only be done with standard techniques when $p$ is much bigger than $|\mathrm{disc}(\mathcal{O})|$ (which is not suitable for CSIDH/CSURF, where $|\mathrm{disc}(\mathcal{O})| = p$ or $4p$).

***Goal:*** *solve the norm equation:*

$$u\mathrm{N}(\mathfrak{b}) + v\mathrm{N}(\mathfrak{c}) = 2^e \tag{3}$$

*with* $2^{e+2} \mid p+1$, $[\mathfrak{a}] = [\mathfrak{b}] = [\mathfrak{c}]$, $u, v > 0$, $\gcd(u\mathrm{N}(\mathfrak{b}), v\mathrm{N}(\mathfrak{c})) = 1$, *and such that we can build efficiently computable dimension-d isogenies $\Phi_u\colon E^d \to A_u, \Phi_v\colon E^d \to A_v$ of polarised degrees $u, v$.*

Indeed, the factoring lemma (Lemma 2.2) ensures that we have a $(u\mathrm{N}(\mathfrak{b}), v\mathrm{N}(\mathfrak{c}))$-isogeny diamond

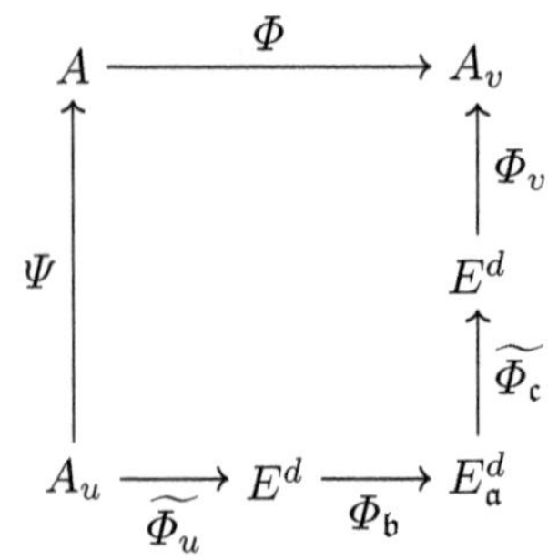

where $\Phi_{\mathfrak{b}} := \mathrm{diag}(\varphi_{\mathfrak{b}}), \Phi_{\mathfrak{c}} := \mathrm{diag}(\varphi_{\mathfrak{c}})\colon E^d \to E^d_{\mathfrak{a}}$, $\Phi$ is an $u\mathrm{N}(\mathfrak{b})$-isogeny and $\Psi$ is a $v\mathrm{N}(\mathfrak{c})$-isogeny. Hence, by Kani's Lemma 2.3, we can embed the compositions $\Phi_{\mathfrak{b}} \circ \widetilde{\Phi_u}$ and $\Phi_{\mathfrak{c}} \circ \widetilde{\Phi_v}$ into a $2d$-dimensional $2^e$-isogeny $F : A_u \times A_v \to E^d_{\mathfrak{a}} \times A$.

Except when $u$ and $v$ are perfect squares as in [47] (which does not make the norm equation much easier to solve), we cannot expect $\Phi_u$ and $\Phi_v$ to be one-dimensional. Using higher dimensions $d \geq 2$ appears necessary because it is difficult to construct (efficient representations of) outgoing 1-dimensional isogenies $\Phi_u, \Phi_v$ of large given degree $u, v$ on $E$ without knowing the endomorphism ring $\mathrm{End}(E)$: the only tools we have at our disposal to produce arbitrary-degree isogenies all require higher dimensions. In fact, a variant of this problem (construct a large *prime* degree isogeny on $E$) is conjectured to be cryptographically hard [4, Problem 2].

In any case, *Zarhin's trick* [27, Th. 11.29, Eq. (4)] would allow us to efficiently construct endomorphisms $\Phi_u, \Phi_v$ of $E^4$ with the prescribed polarised degrees $u, v$. However, we consider computing the corresponding 8-dimensional isogeny $F$ to be too expensive. Instead, we will see in Sect. 4 how to find solutions when $d = 2$. Consequently, we have to compute a 4-dimensional isogeny $F$, which can be done efficiently with level-2 theta coordinates [17]. As mentioned earlier, the algorithms to compute the $2^e$-isogeny $F$ require $2^{e+2}$-torsion points, so we need $2^{e+2}|p+1$ instead of $2^e|p+1$ to be able to work over $\mathbb{F}_{p^2}$.

Unfortunately, there do not always exist positive integer solutions $u, v$ to $u\mathrm{N}(\mathfrak{b}) + v\mathrm{N}(\mathfrak{c}) = 2^e$. Indeed, the *Frobenius coin problem* tells us that we are only guaranteed solutions when $2^e \geq \mathrm{N}(\mathfrak{b})\mathrm{N}(\mathfrak{c}) - \mathrm{N}(\mathfrak{b}) - \mathrm{N}(\mathfrak{c})$; on the other hand, when $\mathcal{O} = \mathbb{Z}[\sqrt{-p}]$ (as in CSIDH), the smallest representative of any class $[\mathfrak{a}]$ in $\mathrm{Cl}(\mathcal{O})$ is expected to be of size roughly $\sqrt{p}$. So, recalling that $2^{e+2} \mid p+1$, we see that we rarely have guaranteed solutions $u, v$. The solution we propose to overcome this difficulty is to give some additional freedom on the choice of ideals $\mathfrak{b}, \mathfrak{c}$ by factoring out their smooth part.

### 3.2 Factoring Out Easy Steps First

We will now describe how to compute the action of $[\mathfrak{a}]$ on $(E, \iota)$ in four dimensions. Throughout this section, $\mathfrak{b}, \mathfrak{c}$ are primitive[2] representatives of $[\mathfrak{a}]$.

[2] i.e. neither $\mathfrak{b}$ nor $\mathfrak{c}$ is contained in $N\mathcal{O}$ for any $N > 1$.

**The Idea.** Suppose we can factor $\mathfrak{b} = \mathfrak{b}_e\mathfrak{b}_k, \mathfrak{c} = \mathfrak{c}_e\mathfrak{c}_k$, so that the isogenies $\varphi_{\mathfrak{b}_e}: E \to E_1, \varphi_{\mathfrak{c}_e}: E \to E_2$ are efficiently computable (*e.g.* smooth degree) and so that we can find efficiently computable isogenies $\Phi_u: E_1^2 \to A_u, \Phi_v: E_2^2 \to A_v$ (*e.g.* integer-matrix endomorphisms) with polarised degrees $u, v$ satisfying

$$u\mathrm{N}(\mathfrak{b}_k) + v\mathrm{N}(\mathfrak{c}_k) = 2^e. \tag{4}$$

Then we can consider the following $(u\mathrm{N}(\mathfrak{b}), v\mathrm{N}(\mathfrak{c}))$-isogeny diamond

$$\begin{array}{ccccc}
A & & \xrightarrow{\quad\Phi\quad} & & A_v \\
\uparrow & & & & \uparrow \Phi_v \\
\Psi & & & & E_2^2 \\
 & & & & \uparrow \widetilde{\Phi_{\mathfrak{c}_k}} \\
A_u & \xrightarrow{\widetilde{\Phi_u}} & E_1^2 & \xrightarrow{\Phi_{\mathfrak{b}_k}} & E_{\mathfrak{a}}^2
\end{array}$$

where $\Phi_I$ is the 2-dimensional isogeny $\mathrm{diag}(\varphi_I, \varphi_I)$ given by the action of $I \subseteq \mathcal{O}$. Then, Kani's lemma yields a 4-dimensional isogeny

$$F := \begin{pmatrix} \Phi_{\mathfrak{b}_k} \circ \widetilde{\Phi_u} & \Phi_{\mathfrak{c}_k} \circ \widetilde{\Phi_v} \\ -\Psi & \widetilde{\Phi} \end{pmatrix} : A_u \times A_v \to E_{\mathfrak{a}}^2 \times A, \tag{5}$$

with kernel

$$\begin{aligned}
\ker(F) &= \left\{([u\mathrm{N}(\mathfrak{b}_k)]x, \Phi_v\widetilde{\Phi_{\mathfrak{c}_k}}\Phi_{\mathfrak{b}_k}\widetilde{\Phi_u}(x)) \mid x \in A_u[2^e]\right\} \\
&= \left\{([u\mathrm{N}(\mathfrak{b}_k)]x, \Phi_v\Phi_{\overline{\mathfrak{c}_k}\mathfrak{b}_k}\widetilde{\Phi_u}(x)) \mid x \in A_u[2^e]\right\} \\
&= \left\{([\mathrm{N}(\mathfrak{b}_k)]\Phi_u(y), \Phi_v\Phi_{\overline{\mathfrak{c}_k}\mathfrak{b}_k}(y)) \mid y \in E_1^2[2^e]\right\}.
\end{aligned} \tag{6}$$

Since $\mathfrak{b}, \mathfrak{c}$ both represent $[\mathfrak{a}]$, $\overline{\mathfrak{c}}\mathfrak{b} = \sigma\mathcal{O}$ is principal and we can evaluate $\varphi_{\overline{\mathfrak{c}}\mathfrak{b}} = \iota(\sigma)$. Having computed $\varphi_{\mathfrak{c}_e}$ and $\varphi_{\mathfrak{b}_e}$, we can evaluate

$$\mathrm{N}(\mathfrak{b}_e)\mathrm{N}(\mathfrak{c}_e)\varphi_{\overline{\mathfrak{c}_k}\mathfrak{b}_k} = \varphi_{\mathfrak{c}_e}\iota(\sigma)\widehat{\varphi_{\mathfrak{b}_e}}. \tag{7}$$

and compute $\ker(F)$ (more exactly points of $2^{e+2}$-torsion generating $\ker(F)$ as required in [17]). We refer to Sect. 5.2 for more details on the kernel computation in the case of CSIDH.

**The Algorithm.** By construction, $u\mathrm{N}(\mathfrak{b}_k) + v\mathrm{N}(\mathfrak{c}_k) = 2^e$ has at least as many positive integer solutions $u, v$ as $u\mathrm{N}(\mathfrak{b}) + v\mathrm{N}(\mathfrak{c}) = 2^e$. Indeed, every ideal appearing as $\mathfrak{b}_k$ can also be chosen as $\mathfrak{b}$ (with $\mathfrak{b}_e = 1$). More relevant, though, is that the norms of the ideals $\mathfrak{b}_k$ are smaller, and so we hope for more $u, v$ solutions.

The ideals $\mathfrak{b}_e, \mathfrak{c}_e$ should be chosen so that the corresponding isogenies $\varphi_{\mathfrak{b}_e}, \varphi_{\mathfrak{c}_e}$ are easy to compute, *e.g.* of smooth degrees. More precisely, letting $\mathfrak{B}$ be a set of small primes, we permit $\mathfrak{b}_e, \mathfrak{c}_e$ to be a product of ideals lying above the primes in $\mathfrak{B}$. Note that since $\mathfrak{b}_e, \mathfrak{c}_e$ are primitive, these primes will all be split in $\mathcal{O}$.

With this requirement we now proceed as follows (we refer to Sect. 5.1 for details).

1. Obtain a set $S$ of short representatives of $[\mathfrak{a}]$ (*e.g.* by Lagrange-reduction).
2. Factor each $\mathfrak{b}$ in $S$ as $\mathfrak{b} = \mathfrak{b}_e \mathfrak{b}_k$ maximising the norm of $\mathfrak{b}_e$.
3. Select a pair of ideals $\mathfrak{b} = \mathfrak{b}_e \mathfrak{b}_k$ and $\mathfrak{c} = \mathfrak{c}_e \mathfrak{c}_k$ from $S$ with $\mathrm{N}(\mathfrak{b}_k), \mathrm{N}(\mathfrak{c}_k)$ coprime, prioritizing those with the smallest $\mathrm{N}(\mathfrak{b}_k), \mathrm{N}(\mathfrak{c}_k)$.
4. Enumerate the positive integer solutions $u, v$ of $u\mathrm{N}(\mathfrak{b}_k) + v\mathrm{N}(\mathfrak{c}_k) = 2^e$.
5. Return a solution $u, v$ if it allows for the construction of $\Phi_u, \Phi_v$; else choose a different $\mathfrak{b}, \mathfrak{c}$ pair.

We briefly remark that this technique of splitting the isogeny computation into an easy 1-dimensional, followed by potentially expensive $(d \geq 2)$-dimensional computation also allows us to compute more isogenies $\Phi_u$ of prescribed polarised degree $u$. Indeed, the naïve approach of constructing $\Phi_u$ as a $2 \times 2$ integer-matrix

$$\begin{pmatrix} x_u & -y_u \\ y_u & x_u \end{pmatrix} \tag{8}$$

only permits $u = x_u^2 + y_u^2$ to be a sum of two squares. Composing $\Phi_u$ as the diagonal of some one-dimensional isogeny of sufficiently smooth degree $g_u$ (*e.g.* $\mathfrak{B}$-smooth), and then a matrix as above allows for polarised degrees $u = g_u(x_u^2 + y_u^2)$ (see Sect. 4.1).

### 3.3 Finding the Codomain Orientation

Once we have computed the 4-dimensional isogeny $F : A_u \times A_v \to E_\mathfrak{a}^2 \times A$ and extracted $E_\mathfrak{a}$ from its codomain (following the approach presented in the full version of the paper [18, Appendix B] in the case of CSIDH), we still have to compute the orientation $\iota_\mathfrak{a} := (\varphi_\mathfrak{a})_*(\iota)$ on $E_\mathfrak{a}$. In the case of CSIDH, this orientation is naturally given by the Frobenius endomorphism and does not need to be computed. However, this orientation is not that easy to determine in general.

Given a generator $\alpha \in \mathcal{O}$ of $\mathcal{O}$ (i.e. $\mathcal{O} = \mathbb{Z}[\alpha]$), we only have to compute an efficient representation of $\iota_\mathfrak{a}(\alpha)$, as defined in Definition 2.2. Assuming $|\mathrm{disc}(\mathcal{O})| \leq 2^{2f}$ with $2^f \mid p+1$, we can always find $\alpha$ of norm bounded by $2^{2f}$ and it suffices to evaluate $\iota_\mathfrak{a}(\alpha)$ on a basis of $E_\mathfrak{a}[2^f]$ to efficiently represent this endomorphism, *e.g.* using the higher dimensional interpolation algorithms from [50, Theorem 3.7 & Sect. 6.4]. Furthermore, if $e + 2 \leq f$, then knowing $\iota(\alpha)$ on the $2^f$-torsion is sufficient to compute the $2^{e+2}$-torsion lying above $\ker(F)$ given by Eq. (6) so to compute the action of any ideal on $E$. The same holds for $E_\mathfrak{a}$: the knowledge of $\iota_\mathfrak{a}(\alpha)$ on $E_\mathfrak{a}[2^f]$ is sufficient to propagate the ideal class group action further.

Now we explain how we compute $\iota_{\mathfrak{a}}(\alpha)$ on a basis of $E_{\mathfrak{a}}[2^f]$. Using the fact that $\bar{\mathfrak{c}}\mathfrak{b} = \sigma\mathcal{O}$, we obtain that

$$\iota_{\mathfrak{a}}(\alpha) = (\varphi_{\mathfrak{a}})_*(\iota) = \frac{1}{\mathrm{N}(\mathfrak{a})}\varphi_{\mathfrak{a}} \circ \iota(\alpha) \circ \widehat{\varphi}_{\mathfrak{a}} = \frac{1}{\mathrm{N}(\mathfrak{b})}\varphi_{\mathfrak{b}} \circ \iota(\alpha) \circ \widehat{\varphi}_{\mathfrak{b}}.$$

Let $(P_1, Q_1)$ and $(P_{\mathfrak{a}}, Q_{\mathfrak{a}})$ be two bases of $E_1[2^f]$ and $E_{\mathfrak{a}}[2^f]$ respectively. Then by Eq. (5), we have $F(\Phi_u(P_1, 0), 0) = ([u]\varphi_{\mathfrak{b}_k}(P_1), 0, *)$ so we can evaluate $[u]\varphi_{\mathfrak{b}_k}(P_1)$, hence $\varphi_{\mathfrak{b}_k}(P_1)$ by multiplying by an inverse of $u \mod 2^f$. We compute $\varphi_{\mathfrak{b}_k}(Q_1)$ similarly. Now, with (easy) discrete logarithm computations in $E_{\mathfrak{a}}[2^f]$, we may find $a, b, c, d \in \mathbb{Z}$ such that $\varphi_{\mathfrak{b}_k}(P_1) = [a]P_{\mathfrak{a}} + [b]Q_{\mathfrak{a}}$ and $\varphi_{\mathfrak{b}_k}(Q_1) = [c]P_{\mathfrak{a}} + [d]Q_{\mathfrak{a}}$. Then, a simple matrix inversion yields

$$\widehat{\varphi}_{\mathfrak{b}_k}(P_{\mathfrak{a}}) = [\delta \mathrm{N}(\mathfrak{b}_k)]([d]P_1 - [b]Q_1) \text{ and } \widehat{\varphi}_{\mathfrak{b}_k}(Q_{\mathfrak{a}}) = [\delta \mathrm{N}(\mathfrak{b}_k)](-[c]P_1 + [a]Q_1),$$

with $\delta$ an inverse of $ad - bc \mod 2^f$ (which does exist because $\mathrm{N}(\mathfrak{b}_k) = \deg(\varphi_{\mathfrak{b}_k})$ is odd, so $\varphi_{\mathfrak{b}_k}$ maps a $2^f$-torsion basis to a $2^f$-torsion basis). So we have computed $(\widehat{\varphi}_{\mathfrak{b}_k}(P_{\mathfrak{a}}), \widehat{\varphi}_{\mathfrak{b}_k}(Q_{\mathfrak{a}}))$. Similarly, knowing $\varphi_{\mathfrak{b}_e}$, we can compute the action of its dual $\widehat{\varphi}_{\mathfrak{b}_e}$ on the $2^f$-torsion provided that $\mathrm{N}(\mathfrak{b}_e)$ is odd. We can impose this condition by removing 2 from the set of allowed primes $\mathfrak{B}$. Hence, we can evaluate $\widehat{\varphi}_{\mathfrak{b}_e} \circ \widehat{\varphi}_{\mathfrak{b}_k} = \widehat{\varphi}_{\mathfrak{b}}$ on the basis $(P_{\mathfrak{a}}, Q_{\mathfrak{a}})$. We can then evaluate $[\mathrm{N}(\mathfrak{b})]\iota_{\mathfrak{a}}(\alpha) = \varphi_{\mathfrak{b}} \circ \iota(\alpha) \circ \widehat{\varphi}_{\mathfrak{b}} = \varphi_{\mathfrak{b}_k} \circ \varphi_{\mathfrak{b}_e} \circ \iota(\alpha) \circ \widehat{\varphi}_{\mathfrak{b}_e} \circ \widehat{\varphi}_{\mathfrak{b}_k}$ on $(P_{\mathfrak{a}}, Q_{\mathfrak{a}})$, using our knowledge of the action of $\iota(\alpha)$ on the $2^f$-torsion, of $\varphi_{\mathfrak{b}_e}$ and of $\varphi_{\mathfrak{b}_k}$ via $F$. Since $\mathrm{N}(\mathfrak{b}) = \mathrm{N}(\mathfrak{b}_e)\mathrm{N}(\mathfrak{b}_k)$ is odd, we can invert it modulo $2^f$ and finally obtain $(\iota_{\mathfrak{a}}(\alpha)(P_{\mathfrak{a}}), \iota_{\mathfrak{a}}(\alpha)(Q_{\mathfrak{a}}))$, as desired.

## 4 Computing 2-Dimensional Isogenies of Prescribed Polarised Degree

In this section, we explain how to construct dimension 2 isogenies $\Phi_u, \Phi_v$ of prescribed polarised degree $u, v$, in order to solve Eq. (3) (or more precisely the version in Eq. (4)).

We first treat an easy special case in Sect. 4.1. Then we explain in Sect. 4.2 how to treat the case of $u$ (or $v$) an arbitrary positive integer. The drawback of the latter approach is that it involves computing a 4-dimensional $2^e$-isogeny to build $\Phi_u$ in dimension 2.

### 4.1 The Simplest Case: When the Polarised Degree Is $\mathfrak{B}$-Good

Let us first assume that $u$ and $v$ are a sum of two squares. Then, given a curve $E$ and an integer $u = x_u^2 + y_u^2$, the endomorphism

$$M_u = \begin{pmatrix} x_u & -y_u \\ y_u & x_u \end{pmatrix} \tag{9}$$

on $E^2$ is such that $M_u \widetilde{M_u} = [u]$ is the multiplication by $u$ on each component. Hence $M_u$ induces an isogeny $\Phi_u$ of polarised degree $u$ as desired.

The probability that a random number $u$ can be written as sum of two squares is roughly $1/\sqrt{\log(u)} \approx 1/\sqrt{\log(p)/2}$. Unfortunately, writing $u$ as above requires the factorisation of $u$. If we instead restrict $u$ to be a prime, the probability goes down to the order of $1/\log(u)$. Since we need both $u$ and $v$ to be of this form, we expect to find a valid pair after $\approx \log(p)^2$ attempts. Looking at the size of the primes we are working with, this approach becomes soon too expensive.

Instead, we can adopt the same strategy as in Sect. 3.2 to relax our condition and aim for $\mathfrak{B}$-good values $u, v$, for a given set of small primes.

**Definition 4.1.** *Let $\mathfrak{B}$ be a set of small primes. We say that $u \in \mathbb{N}^*$ is* $\mathfrak{B}$-good *when $u$ is of the form $u = g_u(x_u^2 + y_u^2)$ where $x_u, y_u \in \mathbb{N}$ and $g_u \in \mathbb{N}^*$ is a product of primes in $\mathfrak{B}$.*

We may then write $u = g_u(x_u^2 + y_u^2)$ and $v = g_v(x_v^2 + y_v^2)$, as above, where $g_u$ and $g_v$ contain all the prime factors of $u, v$ that are in $\mathfrak{B}$. Recall that an integer can be written as a sum of two squares if and only if, in its prime power decomposition, there is no prime power $\ell^k$ such that $k$ is odd and $\ell \equiv 3 \mod 4$ [36, Ch. 2.15, Ex. 10]. We can then restrict $g_u$ and $g_v$ to primes that are 3 mod 4. Notice that small prime numbers are more likely to appear in the factorization of a number, and hence to cause failure of the sum of squares condition. Heuristically, by taking out factors 3, 7 and 11 we already increase the probability of finding a sum of squares by a factor 3. If we choose $\mathcal{O}$ such that these small primes are split in $\mathcal{O}$, we can easily compute isogenies of degrees $g_u$ and $g_v$ via the action of $\mathrm{Cl}(\mathcal{O})$. In particular, in the case of CSIDH, these isogenies are defined over $\mathbb{F}_p$ so they are even more efficient to compute (see Sect. 5.2).

Given a pair $u, v$ with no factors in $\mathfrak{B}$, we are now left with the task of determining if both numbers can be expressed as sums of two squares. As mentioned above, checking this condition requires factoring, which we cannot afford. We instead perform trial division up to a fixed bound ($10^4$ for the 500 and 1000 parameters, and $10^5$ for all the others), and then test what is left for primality. We observe that this procedure reduces the chances of finding a good pair by 2 to 3 orders of magnitude, as expected.

If the primality test succeeds, and all nonsquare factors are 1 mod 4, we can apply Cornacchia's algorithm to obtain $x_u$ and $y_u$ (respectively $x_v, y_v$). This strategy is further discussed in Sect. 5.2 in the case of CSIDH.

*Remark 4.1.* It is possible to relax the $\mathfrak{B}$-good condition on $(u, v)$ by allowing $u$ (resp. $v$) to take the form $g_u(ax_u^2 + by_u^2)$ (resp. $g_v(ax_v^2 + by_v^2)$), where $g_u, g_v, a, b \in \mathfrak{B}$, while ensuring that Kani's lemma remains applicable as in Sect. 3.1. Then, at the cost of computing 4 additional isogenies of degree $a$ and $b$ with Elkies' algorithm, we improve the likelihood that $u$ and $v$ are suitable for computing isogenies of degree $u$ and $v$ in dimension 2. Experiments have shown that allowing $a$ and $b$ to take values in $\{2, 3, 5, 7\}$ increases the probability of success by approximately a factor of 3. Further details on this construction can be found in the full version of the paper [18, Appendix C].

### 4.2 The General Case

We now treat the case of a general $u, v$. Although it is easy to construct $\Phi_u, \Phi_v$ in dimension 4, we saw in Sect. 3.1 that this would involve a dimension 8 isogeny for $F$. In this section we explain how to construct them in dimension 2, on $E^2$. For that, we extend the approach of QFESTA [43] from dimension 1 to dimension 2. A drawback is that our approach will be heuristic, although our implementation shows that the heuristic works well in practice.

Let $(E, \iota)$ be an $\mathcal{O}$-oriented supersingular elliptic curve. Let $\Delta = \mathrm{disc}(\mathcal{O})$ be the discriminant of $\mathcal{O}$. First, we show that we can heuristically build (efficient) endomorphisms on $E^2$ of polarised degree $N$, as long as $N \gg |\Delta|$. By construction, we can evaluate any endomorphism $\gamma \in \mathcal{O}$, which gives us a 1-dimensional isogeny $\iota(\gamma)$ of degree $N(\gamma)$. Since $\sqrt{\Delta} \in \mathcal{O}$, the quadratic form $\gamma \mapsto N(\gamma)$ restricts on the suborder $\mathbb{Z} + \sqrt{\Delta}\mathbb{Z}$ of $\mathcal{O}$ to the quadratic form $q(x, y) = x^2 + |\Delta|y^2$.

Now let $\gamma_1, \gamma_2 \in \mathcal{O}$ of norms $n_1, n_2$ respectively, and consider the endomorphism

$$\gamma = \begin{pmatrix} \iota(\gamma_1) & \iota(\overline{\gamma_2}) \\ -\iota(\gamma_2) & \iota(\overline{\gamma_1}) \end{pmatrix} \in \mathrm{End}(E^2).$$

Then, by [50, Lemma 3.2], its polarised dual is

$$\widetilde{\gamma} = \begin{pmatrix} \iota(\overline{\gamma_1}) & -\iota(\overline{\gamma_2}) \\ \iota(\gamma_2) & \iota(\gamma_1) \end{pmatrix},$$

so that $\widetilde{\gamma} \circ \gamma = [n_1 + n_2]$ in $\mathrm{End}(E^2)$ and $\gamma$ is an $(n_1+n_2)$-isogeny. In particular, we can build endomorphisms on $E^2$ of polarised degree $N$ as long as $N$ is represented by the quadratic form $q(x, y, z, t) = (x^2 + y^2) + |\Delta|(z^2 + t^2)$.

**Heuristic 1.** *Let $N \gg |\Delta|$. Then we can heuristically build an efficient endomorphism $\gamma \in \mathrm{End}(E^2)$ of polarised degree $N$.*

*Justification* Since $N \gg |\Delta|$, we can sample many small $z, t$ such that $(z^2 + t^2)|\Delta| < N$. Then if $m = N - |\Delta|(z^2 + t^2)$ is a sum of two squares, we can find $\gamma$ by the discussion above. This situation can be efficiently detected whenever $m$ is a prime congruent to 1 mod 4, which heuristically happens with probability $\approx 1/\log(N)$. Since $N \gg |\Delta|$, we can try with many different couples $(z, t)$ until one succeeds. □

In practice, we can use a direct adaptation of the algorithm `RepresentInteger` from [22] to find a solution of $(x^2 + y^2) + |\Delta|(z^2 + t^2) = N$.

Now by Lemma 2.2, if $\gamma$ is an efficiently represented endomorphism of $E^2$ of polarised degree $N = N_1 N_2$, with $N_1, N_2$ coprime, then it decomposes uniquely as $\gamma = \mu_2 \circ \gamma_1 = \mu_1 \circ \gamma_2$ where the $\gamma_i, \mu_i$ are isogenies of polarised degree $N_i$. Furthermore, by Kani's lemma (Lemma 2.3) the 4-dimensional isogeny

$$\Gamma = \begin{pmatrix} \gamma_1 & \widetilde{\mu_2} \\ -\gamma_2 & \widetilde{\mu_1} \end{pmatrix} \tag{10}$$

is of polarised degree $N_1 + N_2$. The kernel of $\Gamma$ is given by $\mathrm{Ker}\Gamma = \{(N_1 P, \gamma P) \mid P \in E^g[N_1 + N_2]\}$, so we can efficiently evaluate $\Gamma$ to obtain the 2-dimensional isogeny $\gamma_1$ of polarised degree $N_1$ as long as the $(N_1 + N_2)$-torsion on $E$ is smooth and accessible (*i.e.* defined over a small extension of $\mathbb{F}_p$). Hence, an efficient representation of $\gamma$ yields an efficient representation of $\gamma_1$ in the sense of Definition 2.2.

For simplicity, and because this matches our implementation choice, we will now restrict to the case where we look for $N_1 + N_2 = 2^e$ a power of two.

**Theorem 4.1.** *Assume that $E[2^e] \subseteq E(\mathbb{F}_{p^2})$ (with $e \geq 3$), that $2^{3e/2-1} \gg |\Delta|$, and that $u < 2^{e-1}$ is odd. Then, under Heuristic 1, we can efficiently represent an isogeny $\Phi_u$ of polarised degree $u$ on $E^2$.*

*Proof.* First consider $N = N_1 N_2$ with $N_1 = u, N_2 = 2^e - u$. Since $u$ is assumed to be odd, $N_1$ is coprime to $N_2$. If $N \gg |\Delta|$, we can use Heuristic 1 to build an endomorphism in dimension 2 of polarised degree $N$, which we split via a 4-dimensional isogeny of polarised degree $2^e$ to get $\Phi_u$.

If this is not the case, then since $2^{3e/2} \gg |\Delta|$ by assumption, this means that $u$ is smaller than $2^f$, with $f = \lceil e/2 \rceil$. We use a two step solution like in [26,44]. First we let $u_2 = u(2^f - u)$, then $2^f - 1 \leq u_2 < 2^{2f-2} \leq 2^{e-1}$. Then we let $N = u_2(2^e - u_2)$. By our choice of $f$, $N \geq 2^{3e/2-1}$, so $N \gg |\Delta|$ and we can use Heuristic 1 to build an endomorphism in dimension 2 of polarised degree $N$, which we split a first time (via a 4-dimensional isogeny of polarised degree $2^e$) to get a 2-dimensional isogeny $\Phi_{u_2}$ of polarised degree $u_2$, which we split again (via a 4-dimensional isogeny of polarised degree $2^f$) to get $\Phi_u$. □

*Remark 4.2.*

- To compute $\Gamma$ as defined in Eq. (10), we only need the $m$-torsion to be smooth and accessible on $E$, where $N_1 + N_2 \mid m^2$, see [51, § 6.3 and Appendix B]. This allows to relax the conditions on Theorem 4.1 to $u < 2^{2e}$ and $2^{3e-1} \gg \Delta$.
- In practice, for our application from Sect. 3, we have $u, v \approx \sqrt{|\Delta|}$. Furthermore, in the case of CSIDH, we have $\Delta = -p$, and we select $p$ such that $p = c2^f - 1$ for a small cofactor $c$. In particular, we can take $e = f$ in Theorem 4.1, so that $2^e \approx p$. In that case we already have $u(2^e - u) \gg p$, and we do not need the two step solution, nor the more relaxed torsion condition from the item above.

Combining Sect. 3 with Theorem 4.1, the resulting algorithm to compute the action of a quadratic ideal $\mathfrak{a} \subset \mathcal{O}$ on an $\mathcal{O}$-oriented elliptic curve is very similar to the algorithm used in [5] to convert a quaternionic ideal to an isogeny when the full endomorphism ring of $E$ is known. We make up for the lack of known endomorphisms on $E$ to build isogenies of suitable fixed degree by going up to dimension 2 and working on $E^2$. This doubling of dimension propagates to the rest of the algorithm, and we end up computing $\Phi_u, \Phi_v$ and $E_{\mathfrak{a}}$ via an isogeny of dimension 4, compared to dimension 2 in [5].

This change of dimension has important consequences for the fine-tuning of the algorithm. Indeed, as we have seen in Sect. 4.1, $\Phi_u$ (resp. $\Phi_v$) are much easier to compute whenever $u$ (resp. $v$) is a sum of two squares, or at least $\mathfrak{B}$-good in the sense of Definition 4.1. In particular, in that case we do not need to use a 4-dimensional isogeny to compute $\Phi_u$.

A similar situation happened in [5]: if $u$ was a sum of two squares we could compute $\Phi_u$ directly without going through a 2-dimensional isogeny. However, experiments showed that spending more time on the norm equation to find $u$ a sum of two squares did not compensate having to do one less 2-dimensional isogeny. The situation is different in our case, because a 4-dimensional $2^e$-isogeny is much slower than a 2-dimensional $2^e$-isogeny (by a factor roughly $\times 8$). Depending on the size of our parameters, experiments show that the optimal choices depend on the size of $\Delta$.

- If $\Delta$ is of moderate size, we look for $\mathfrak{B}$-good $u, v$, and only compute one 4-dimensional isogeny for $E_{\mathfrak{a}}$.
- If $\Delta$ is of large size, we look for only one of $u, v$ to be $\mathfrak{B}$-good, while we let the other one be arbitrary. This time computing $\varphi_{\mathfrak{a}}$ requires two 4-dimensional isogenies. For CSIDH, our experiments in Sect. 6.4 suggest this strategy becomes faster than the previous one for $p$ of 4000 bits. We remark that for very large $\Delta$, we expect that letting $u, v$ be arbitrary and computing three 4-dimensional isogenies would be the optimal choice.

In the case of CSIDH (detailed in Sects. 5 and 6), only the first choice is implemented and the computation stays reasonably efficient even for our biggest parameters ($p$ of 4000 bits) as long as the allowed set of small split primes $\mathfrak{B}$ is well chosen. We refer to Sect. 6.4 for further discussion on the above trade-off.

## 5 Our Algorithm Specialized to CSIDH

In this section, we apply our algorithm to the CSIDH setting, or more accurately, the CSURF setting [11]; we fix a prime of the form $p = c2^f - 1$ where $c$ is a small odd integer and $f \gg 1$ so that $p \equiv 7 \pmod 8$, and work with curves oriented by $\mathbb{Z}\left[\frac{1+\sqrt{-p}}{2}\right]$, where the orientation is given by sending $\sqrt{-p}$ to the Frobenius endomorphism. Not only does using the orientation given by Frobenius make evaluating the orientation very fast, but by using the maximal order instead of the typical CSIDH suborder $\mathbb{Z}[\sqrt{-p}]$, we are able to execute our whole algorithm over $\mathbb{F}_p$, by choosing a particularly suitable basis of $E[2^e]$, and working with $x$-only arithmetic. This is further detailed in Sect. 5.2 and in the full version of the paper [18, Appendix D]

At a high level, the three-step process is summarized as in Algorithm 1. We now describe the involved steps in more detail.

### 5.1 Step 1: the Norm Equation

In this section, we explain how to solve the norm equation (4) sketched in Sect. 3.2. This subsection is summarized in Algorithm 2. As in Sect. 4.1, we

**Algorithm 1.** EVALUATEACTION($E, \mathfrak{a}$)

**Input:** $E$ a supersingular elliptic curve over $\mathbb{F}_p$ defined on the surface.
**Input:** $\mathfrak{a} \subseteq \mathbb{Z}\left[\frac{1+\sqrt{-p}}{2}\right]$ an ideal.
**Output:** $\mathfrak{a} \star E$

1: Compute $\mathfrak{l} \subseteq \mathbb{Z}\left[\frac{1+\sqrt{-p}}{2}\right]$ an ideal of small norm. ▷ Precomputation
2: Set $E' := E$ and $\mathfrak{a}' = \mathfrak{a}$.
3: $\mathtt{fail}, \mathfrak{b}_e, \mathfrak{b}_k, \mathfrak{c}_e, \mathfrak{c}_k, u, v, e :=$ FINDUV($\mathfrak{a}'$) ▷ Step 1
4: **if** `fail` **then** ▷ Rerandomize the ideal
5:     Compute $\mathfrak{a}' = \mathfrak{a}'\mathfrak{l}$
6:     Compute $E' = \bar{\mathfrak{l}} \star E'$ using Elkies algorithm.
7:     **run** Line 3 on $E', \mathfrak{a}'$.
8: **end if**
9: `KernelData` := COMPUTEKERNELDATA($E', \mathfrak{b}_e, \mathfrak{b}_k, \mathfrak{c}_e, \mathfrak{c}_k, u, v, e$) ▷ Step 2
10: Compute the 4-dimensional isogeny $F$, defined by `KernelData`. ▷ Step 3
11: Extract $E_{\mathfrak{a}}$ from the codomain of $F$. ▷ See [18, Appendix B.4].
12: **return** $E_{\mathfrak{a}}$.

fix a set of small Elkies primes $\mathfrak{B}$, *i.e.* of primes that split in $\mathbb{Q}(\sqrt{-p})$. Notice that we can always impose $2 \in \mathfrak{B}$. We begin by creating a list of primitive ideals equivalent to $\mathfrak{a}$. More precisely, we obtain a list of equivalent ideals $\mathfrak{a}^{(i)}$ such that $\mathfrak{a}^{(i)} = \mathfrak{a}_e^{(i)}\mathfrak{a}_k^{(i)}$ and $N(\mathfrak{a}_k^{(i)})$ is a product of primes in $\mathfrak{B}$. We then want to find a pair $(i, j)$ such that for $N_1 = N(\mathfrak{a}_k^{(i)})$ and $N_2 = N(\mathfrak{a}_k^{(j)})$ (note that the smooth part has been removed from the norm), we can find positive integers $u, v$ solving the equation

$$uN_1 + vN_2 = 2^e. \tag{11}$$

Since generically $N_1N_2$ determines the minimal value for $e$ such that the above equation has a solution, we test pairs in order of increasing $N_1N_2$.

Given such a pair of norms $N_1, N_2$, we first check that they are coprime. Indeed, if $\gcd(N_1, N_2)$ is not a power of 2, Eq. (11) has no solutions. Since $2 \in \mathfrak{B}$ and we assume $N_1, N_2$ has no prime factors in $\mathfrak{B}$, this requirement simply becomes $\gcd(N_1, N_2) = 1$.

If $\gcd(N_1, N_2) = 1$, we can find $u_0$ and $v_0$ such that $u_0N_1 + v_0N_2 = 1$ via the extended Euclidean algorithm, and consequently $2^eu_0N_1 + 2^ev_0N_2 = 2^e$. Note that one of $u_0$ and $v_0$ will be negative and that we parametrize all possible solutions to the equation by writing

$$(2^eu_0 + kN_2)N_1 + (2^ev_0 - kN_1)N_2 = 2^e,$$

for some $k \in \mathbb{Z}$. This also allows to determine the minimal $e$ for which Eq. (11) has a solution by enumerating the set of $k$ for which both $u = 2^eu_0 + kN_2$ and $v = 2^ev_0 - kN_1$ are positive.

*Remark 5.1.* The exponent $e$ in Eq. (11) determines the number of four-dimensional 2-isogeny steps to be computed, so taking a lower exponent $e$ will be more efficient.

As remarked before and also observed in [5], solving Eq. (11) directly for $\mathfrak{a}^{(i)}$ and $\mathfrak{a}^{(j)}$, often fails since $N_1, N_2$ are in $O(\sqrt{p})$ and $2^e < p$, which makes the original Clapoti approach unpractical in our case. Removing factors in $\mathfrak{B}$, makes $N_1$ and $N_2$ much smaller and hence greatly increases the probability of finding solutions to Eq. (11): the number of expected solutions grows roughly as the product of all factors removed. This leads to the following tradeoff: the bigger the set of primes $\mathfrak{B}$, the higher the probability of finding a solution, but the more time is spent in the second step computing small degree isogenies. Furthermore, even if the probability of finding a solution for a given choice of $\mathfrak{B}$ is low, and in particular, we fail to find a solution, we can simply rerandomize the starting ideal (by some small ideal) and start over. More details about this approach are given below.

Assuming that we can find enough solution pairs $(u, v)$, for each one we have to determine whether $u$ and $v$ are $\mathfrak{B}$-good, *i.e.* if we can write $u = g_u(x_u^2 + y_u^2)$ and $v = g_v(x_v^2 + y_v^2)$ with the prime factors of $g_u$ and $g_v$ in $\mathfrak{B}$. Recall that a number can be expressed as a sum of two squares if and only if all its prime factors that are 3 mod 4 appear with an even exponent. The obvious choice is then to set $g_u$ (resp. $g_v$) to be the product of all prime factors that are 3 mod 4 and contained in $\mathfrak{B}$ and dividing $u$ (resp. $v$). To determine whether what is left contains more prime factors 3 mod 4 we would need to factor $u$, which is too expensive in general. As such we simply proceed by trial division up to a small bound, hoping that what is left at the end is a prime that is 1 mod 4 (note that we simply reject when it is 3 mod 4). If everything succeeds, we have found the factorization of $u$, and hence its decomposition as a sum of two squares. The same procedure applies to $v$. How to choose an optimal set $\mathfrak{B}$ is analyzed in greater detail in Sect. 6.1.

Once we have found a full solution, we proceed to the next step: we will denote the ideals $\mathfrak{a}^{(i)}, \mathfrak{a}^{(j)}$ as $\mathfrak{b}$ and $\mathfrak{c}$, so in particular, $N_1 = N(\mathfrak{b}_k)$ and $N_2 = N(\mathfrak{c}_k)$.

**Rerandomization** For some ideals, Eq. (11) may not have a solution with $u, v$ of the required shape. As already observed, increasing the bound $\mathfrak{B}$ is always a possible solution, though this quickly becomes expensive.

Another solution to this is to simply rerandomize the starting ideal $\mathfrak{a}$. Namely, if none of the sampled, equivalent ideals gives us a solution for Eq. (11), we can multiply $\mathfrak{a}$ by a non-principal ideal $\mathfrak{l}$ for which the action is easy to evaluate (*e.g.* an ideal above $\ell$, where $\ell$ is the smallest split prime). We obtain a new ideal $\mathfrak{a}' = \mathfrak{a}\mathfrak{l}$ and try to solve Eq. (11) for this ideal instead. If we manage to do so, we can simply run our algorithm on $\mathfrak{a}'$, using this solution, starting from the starting curve $E_{\bar{\mathfrak{l}}} = \bar{\mathfrak{l}} \star E$ instead, which is easy to compute by the choice of $\mathfrak{l}$. Otherwise, we can rerandomize again by computing $\mathfrak{a}'' = \mathfrak{l}\mathfrak{a}'$, and so on. As soon as Eq. (11) has a reasonable chance of being solved, this method takes care of failures quite efficiently, making Step 1 faster at the cost of a few Elkies steps. The average number of rerandomizations for different levels are reported in Table 2.

**Algorithm 2.** FINDUV($\mathfrak{a}$)

**Input:** $\mathfrak{a} \subseteq \mathbb{Z}\left[\frac{1+\sqrt{-p}}{2}\right]$ an ideal.
**Output:** Fail, flag indicating failure to find solution.
**Output:** $\mathfrak{b}_e, \mathfrak{b}_k, \mathfrak{c}_e, \mathfrak{c}_k \subseteq \mathbb{Z}\left[\frac{1+\sqrt{-p}}{2}\right]$ ideals, such that $\mathfrak{b}_e\mathfrak{b}_k \sim \mathfrak{c}_e\mathfrak{c}_k \sim \mathfrak{a}$.
**Output:** $u, v, e$ positive integers, such that $u \cdot N(\mathfrak{b}_k) + v \cdot N(\mathfrak{c}_k) = 2^e$, for $e < f - 3$.

Compute a list of short ideals $\mathfrak{a}^{(i)}$ equivalent to $\mathfrak{a}$
Write $\mathfrak{a}^{(i)} = \mathfrak{a}_e^{(i)}\mathfrak{a}_k^{(i)}$, such that $N(\mathfrak{a}_e^{(i)})$ is a product of primes in $\mathfrak{B}$
Sort the list by $N(\mathfrak{a}_k^{(i)})$
**for** all pairs $(i, j)$ with $1 \leq i < j \leq 10$ **do**
  Set $N_1 = N(\mathfrak{a}_k^{(i)})$, $N_2 = N(\mathfrak{a}_k^{(j)})$
  Find all pairs $(u, v)$ such that $uN_1 + vN_2 = 2^e$, with $e \leq f - 3$
  **for** each pair $(u, v)$ **do**
    Remove factors of $\mathcal{B}$ from $u, v$
    Perform trial division on $u, v$ ▷ Bound depends on security level
    **if** factors 3 mod 4 are found with odd exponent **then**
      Continue to next pair
    **end if**
    **if** remaining part of $u, v$ are both prime **then**
      **return** False, $\mathfrak{a}_e^{(i)}, \mathfrak{a}_k^{(i)}, \mathfrak{a}_e^{(j)}, \mathfrak{a}_k^{(j)}, u, v, e$
    **end if**
  **end for**
**end for**
**return** True, _, _, _, _, _, _, _.

### 5.2 Step 2: Computing Kernel Points

After determining a suitable pair of ideals $\mathfrak{b}, \mathfrak{c}$, our goal is to construct the 4-dimensional $2^e$-isogeny described in Sect. 3.2. We now detail how to derive the kernel of this isogeny. This subsection is summarized in Algorithm 3.

Let $E$ denote the starting curve on which we want to act with $\mathfrak{a}$, then we obtain the following diagram derived from the isogeny diamond in Sect. 3.2:

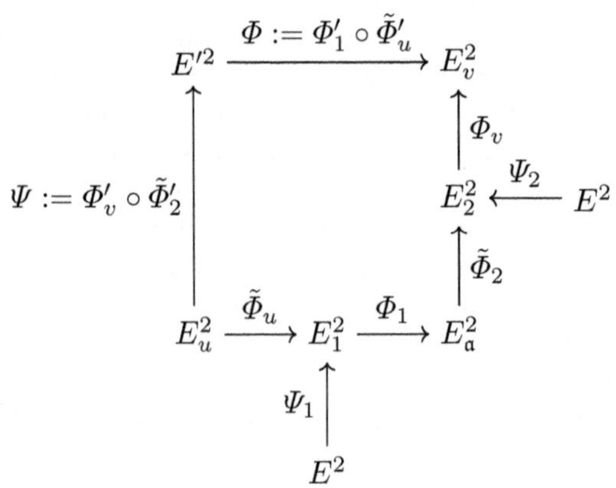

In the diagram above, we have:

- $\Psi_1 = \mathrm{diag}(\varphi_{\mathfrak{b}_e}, \varphi_{\mathfrak{b}_e})$, where $\varphi_{\mathfrak{b}_e}$ is the isogeny corresponding to the action of $\mathfrak{b}_e$; analogously, $\Psi_2 = \mathrm{diag}(\varphi_{\mathfrak{c}_e}, \varphi_{\mathfrak{c}_e})$;
- $\Phi_1 = \mathrm{diag}(\varphi_{\mathfrak{b}_k}, \varphi_{\mathfrak{b}_k})$ and $\Phi_2 = \mathrm{diag}(\varphi_{\mathfrak{c}_k}, \varphi_{\mathfrak{c}_k})$;
- $\Phi_u$ and $\Phi_v$ are isogenies of polarised degree $u$ and $v$ respectively; as explained in Sect. 4.1, we can write $\Phi_u = M_u \mathrm{diag}(\varphi_u, \varphi_u)$, with $\deg(\varphi_u) = g_u$, $\Phi_v = M_v \mathrm{diag}(\varphi_v, \varphi_v)$ with $\deg(\varphi_v) = g_v$, $M_u$ and $M_v$ being given by Eq. (9).

Further, the isogenies $\Phi$ and $\Psi$ are the isogenies of polarised degree $uN_1$ and $vN_2$ completing the square, whose existence is guaranteed by Lemma 2.2. In this setting we can also describe them explicitly, as the following lemma shows.

**Lemma 5.1.** *$\Phi$ is of the form $\Phi_1' \circ \widetilde{\Phi}_u'$, where:*

- *$\Phi_1' := \mathrm{diag}(\varphi_{\mathfrak{b}_k}', \varphi_{\mathfrak{b}_k}') : E_1'^2 \to E_v^2$ with $E_1' := [\overline{\mathfrak{b}}_k] \cdot E_v$ and $\varphi_{\mathfrak{b}_k}'$, the isogeny associated to the action of $\mathfrak{b}_k$ on $E_1'$;*
- *$\Phi_u' := M_u \mathrm{diag}(\varphi_u', \varphi_u') : E_1'^2 \to E'^2$, $M_u$ being given by Eq. (9) and $\varphi_u'$ being the isogeny of degree $g_u$ given by the action of the same ideal $I_u$ as $\varphi_u$ (as a product of Elkies primes).*

*$\Psi$ is of the form $\Phi_v' \circ \widetilde{\Phi}_2'$, where:*

- *$\Phi_2' := \mathrm{diag}(\varphi_{\mathfrak{c}_k}', \varphi_{\mathfrak{c}_k}') : E_2'^2 \to E_u^2$ with $E_2' := [\overline{\mathfrak{c}}_k] \cdot E_u$ and $\varphi_{\mathfrak{c}_k}'$, the isogeny associated to the action of $\mathfrak{c}_k$ on $E_2'$;*
- *$\Phi_v' := M_v \mathrm{diag}(\varphi_v', \varphi_v') : E_2'^2 \to E'^2$, $M_v$ being given by Eq. (9) and $\varphi_v'$ being the isogeny of degree $g_v$ given by the action of the same ideal $I_v$ as $\varphi_v$ (as a product of Elkies primes).*

*In particular, the common codomain of $\widetilde{\Phi}$ and $\Psi$ is a product of elliptic curves $E'^2$.*

*Proof.* The proof is given in the full version of the paper [18, Section 5.2]. □

Let $(P, Q)$ be a basis of $E_1[2^{e+2}]$ (recall from Sect. 3.1 that the theta isogeny algorithm requires the $2^{e+2}$-torsion to compute a $2^e$-isogeny, see [18, Appendix A] for more details). To compute the kernel of the isogeny in dimension 4, we need to compute the points

$$P_u = \varphi_u(P), \quad Q_u = \varphi_u(Q)$$

on $E_u$ and

$$P_v = \varphi_v \circ \widehat{\varphi}_{\mathfrak{c}_k} \circ \varphi_{\mathfrak{b}_k}(P), \quad Q_v = \varphi_v \circ \widehat{\varphi}_{\mathfrak{c}_k} \circ \varphi_{\mathfrak{b}_k}(Q),$$

on $E_v$.

**Isogenies of degree $g_u$ and $g_v$.** The isogenies $\varphi_u$ and $\varphi_v$ with $\deg(\varphi_u) = g_u$ and $\deg(\varphi_v) = g_v$ have no specific requirement other than their degree. Although it is possible to deal with all small primes via Vélu's algorithm [55], it is more efficient to restrict $\mathfrak{B}$ to Elkies primes (*i.e.* splitting primes in $\mathbb{Q}(\sqrt{-p})$) and we can use the correponding algorithm [29] to compute the small degree isogenies.

Note that $\varphi_u$ of degree $g_u$ and $\varphi_v$ of degree $g_v$ can be used to construct 2-dimensional isogenies of polarised degree $u = g_u(x_u^2 + y_u^2)$ and $v = g_v(x_v^2 + y_v^2)$ respectively by composition with matrices $M_u, M_v$ described in Sect. 4.1. However, we do not need to perform that step now, as it can be included in the 4-dimensional computation.

**Working over $\mathbb{F}_p$.** Note that, by definition, the isogenies $\varphi_{\mathfrak{b}}$ and $\varphi_{\mathfrak{c}}$ are $\mathbb{F}_p$-rational, and as noted above, our choice of primes in $\mathfrak{B}$ imply that $\varphi_u$ and $\varphi_v$ can also be chosen to be defined over $\mathbb{F}_p$. The main difficulty comes from evaluating these isogenies on a basis of $E[2^{e+2}]$, which is not defined over $\mathbb{F}_p$.

We will show that all operations can in fact be carried out over the Kummer line, where we have a rational basis. Let $f$ the largest integer so that $2^f \mid (p+1)$. By our choice of prime, the two eigenvalues of Frobenius on $E[2^{f-1}]$ are $\pm 1$. Thus, we can pick a basis $\langle P, Q \rangle = E[2^{f-1}]$ corresponding to the two eigenvectors of Frobenius; we let $P, Q$ be points of order $2^{f-1}$ satisfying

$$\pi(P) = P, \quad \pi(Q) = -Q. \tag{12}$$

Clearly, these points $P, Q$ are $\mathbb{F}_p$-rational on the Kummer line $E/\pm 1$, and together (adjusting by translation by a point of 2-torsion if needed) they form a basis of $E[2^{f-1}]$. This is where we use that we are on the surface. If we were on the floor, picking similar points would not give a basis, since in that case, $[2^{f-2}]P = [2^{f-2}]Q$, the unique rational point of 2-torsion.

In the full version of the paper [18, Appendix D.1] we show how to efficiently generate such a basis, based on a technique which is similar to how one usually computes bases of $E[2^f]$ over $\mathbb{F}_{p^2}$.

**Evaluating the Ideals.** The rest of this section will be devoted to the computation of $P_v, Q_v$. In particular, we need to evaluate $\widehat{\varphi}_{\mathfrak{c}_k} \circ \varphi_{\mathfrak{b}_k}$ on a basis of $E_1[2^{e+2}]$. From Eq. (7) we know that

$$\widehat{\varphi}_{\mathfrak{c}_k} \circ \varphi_{\mathfrak{b}_k} = \frac{1}{N(\mathfrak{b}_e)N(\mathfrak{c}_e)} \varphi_{\mathfrak{c}_e} \circ \iota(\sigma) \circ \widehat{\varphi}_{\mathfrak{b}_e} \tag{13}$$

with $\bar{\mathfrak{c}}\mathfrak{b} = \sigma\mathcal{O}$. By construction, $N(\mathfrak{b}_e)$ and $N(\mathfrak{c}_e)$ are both smooth, with all their factors in $\mathfrak{B}$. Let us assume for simplicity that they are also odd; the even case needs a bit more care and is detailed afterwards.

We detail how to evaluate the endomorphism $\iota(\sigma)$. First, assume that $\sigma$ is of the form $a+b\sqrt{-p}$, with $a, b \in \mathbb{Z}$. Explicitly, this is mapped to the endomorphism $[a] + [b]\pi$, where $\pi$ denotes the Frobenius endomorphism. Evaluating such an endomorphism on our choice of basis is particularly easy: with the same notation as in the previous section, the evaluation is simply given by

$$[a]P + [b]\pi(P) = [a]P + [b]P = [a+b]P,$$
$$[a]Q + [b]\pi(Q) = [a]Q + [b](-Q) = [a-b]Q.$$

Note in particular that we can evaluate this on the Kummer line. Although $\sigma$ is an element of the order $\mathbb{Z}[\frac{1+\sqrt{-p}}{2}]$, and hence is more generally of the form $a + b\sqrt{-p}$, where $a, b$ are in $\mathbb{Z}[\frac{1}{2}]$, *i.e.* are rational numbers with denominator at most 2, we show in [18, Appendix D.2] how to evaluate this on our basis (on the Kummer line) without having to use division points, which may not be $\mathbb{F}_p$-rational.

Further, note that since we are after the action on the $2^{e+2}$-torsion, we can compute $(N(\mathfrak{b}_e)N(\mathfrak{c}_e))^{-1} \pmod{2^{e+2}}$, to account for the division in Eq. (13). Hence, all that remains to evaluate $\widehat{\varphi}_{\mathfrak{c}_k} \circ \varphi_{\mathfrak{b}_k}$ is to describe how we efficiently recover the isogenies $\varphi_{\mathfrak{b}_e}$ and $\varphi_{\mathfrak{c}_e}$.

These isogenies are (by definition) the product of prime degree Elkies isogenies. More specifically, say that for a given prime $\ell$, we have $v_\ell(N(\mathfrak{b}_e)) = k$, *i.e.* $\ell$ divides $N(\mathfrak{b}_e)$ exactly $k$ times. Then $\mathfrak{b}_e$ will act with exactly $k$ degree-$\ell$ Elkies isogenies. We can also assume that all these isogenies will be in the same direction, since otherwise $\mathfrak{b}_e$ and consequently $\mathfrak{b}$ would factor through multiplication by $\ell$, and we assumed that $\mathfrak{b}$ was primitive (if it was not, the ideal $\mathfrak{b}/\ell$ would also be equivalent to $\mathfrak{a}$, but with smaller norm).

With Elkies' algorithm, we can return both kernel polynomials of degree $\ell$ determining the two Elkies isogenies of degree $\ell$. To check which polynomial corresponds to the correct isogeny, we check the eigenvalue of Frobenius, as described in the original CSIDH paper [12, Section 3]. In more detail, assume that $(\ell, \sqrt{-p} - \lambda) = \mathfrak{l} \subseteq \mathfrak{b}_e$, *i.e.* we wish to evaluate the action of $\mathfrak{l}$. Since the roots of the correct kernel polynomial $h(x)$ are precisely the $x$-coordinates of the points of order $\ell$, satisfying $\pi(P) = [\lambda]P$, we simply test this equality symbolically: we have the equality

$$(x^p, y^p) \equiv [\lambda](x, y) \pmod{h(x), y^2 - f(x)},$$

where $f(x)$ is the polynomial coming from the curve equation. If these values are not equal, we know that this kernel polynomial corresponds to the other eigenvalue. Note that when we are doing multiple $\ell$-isogenies, we need only check the eigenvalue of Frobenius for the first $\ell$-isogeny; after that, we can recognise the right kernel polynomial to be the one not corresponding to the previous $j$-invariant.

*Remark 5.2.* If $\mathfrak{b}_e$ and $\mathfrak{c}_e$ share some steps, we can perform those steps (corresponding to the action of the ideal $\mathfrak{b}_e + \mathfrak{c}_e$) in advance, and start evaluating the ideal action from the resulting curve. The advantage is twofold: first, we avoid evaluating the same ideal twice. Second, we do not need to evaluate the common part on points. We can instead start computing $P_u$ and $P_v$ directly from the codomain curve.

**Even Norm Part** We now explain how to deal with even normed ideals. For this, we write the ideal $\mathfrak{b}_e$ as

$$\mathfrak{b}_e = \mathfrak{b}_{e'}\mathfrak{b}_2$$

where $\mathfrak{b}_2$ is an ideal of norm $2^{f_\mathfrak{b}}$, and correspondingly for $\mathfrak{c}_e$. As explained in Remark 5.2, the shared steps of $\mathfrak{b}_e, \mathfrak{c}_e$ can be computed at the beginning, hence we can assume that $\mathfrak{b}_2$ and $\mathfrak{c}_2$ are coprime (*i.e.* the corresponding 2-isogenies go in "opposite" directions). Writing $f_{12} = f_\mathfrak{b} + f_\mathfrak{c}$, we get that

$$\widehat{\varphi}_{\mathfrak{c}_k} \circ \varphi_{\mathfrak{b}_k} = \frac{1}{N(\mathfrak{b}_{e'})N(\mathfrak{c}_{e'})2^{f_{12}}} \varphi_{\mathfrak{c}_e} \circ \iota(\sigma) \circ \widehat{\varphi}_{\mathfrak{b}_e}.$$

The only added difficulty that needs to be accounted for is that we cannot find an inverse to $2^{f_{12}}$ modulo $2^{e+2}$.

We fix this by taking a basis of a larger torsion group. Using the same technique as for the odd normed case, we can thus evaluate

$$[2^{f_{12}+1}] \circ \widehat{\varphi}_{\mathfrak{c}_k} \circ \varphi_{\mathfrak{b}_k} = \frac{1}{N(\mathfrak{b}_{e'})N(\mathfrak{c}_{e'})} \varphi_{\mathfrak{c}_e} \circ \iota(\sigma) \circ \widehat{\varphi}_{\mathfrak{b}_e},$$

and hence we can find the evaluation of $\widehat{\varphi}_{\mathfrak{c}_k} \circ \varphi_{\mathfrak{b}_k}$ on $E_1[2^{e+2}]$ by instead starting with a basis of $E[2^{e+2+f_{12}}]$. (We remark that by construction, we have $e + 2 + f_{12} \leq f$.)

**Algorithm 3.** $\textsc{ComputeKernelData}(E, \mathfrak{b}_e, \mathfrak{c}_e, \mathfrak{b}_k, \mathfrak{c}_k, u, v, e)$

**Input:** $E$ a supersingular elliptic curve over $\mathbb{F}_p$ defined on the surface.
**Input:** $\mathfrak{b}_e, \mathfrak{b}_k, \mathfrak{c}_e, \mathfrak{c}_k \subseteq \mathbb{Z}\left[\frac{1+\sqrt{-p}}{2}\right]$ ideals, such that $\mathfrak{b}_e\mathfrak{b}_k \sim \mathfrak{c}_e\mathfrak{c}_k$.
**Input:** $u, v, e$ positive integers, such that $u \cdot N(\mathfrak{b}_k) + v \cdot N(\mathfrak{c}_k) = 2^e$, for $e < f - 3$.
**Output:** `KernelData` necessary for computing the 4-dimensional isogeny.

Compute a basis $P, Q$ of $E[2^{f-1}]$. ▷ See [18, Appendix D] to sample special basis.
Compute the isogeny $\phi_{\mathfrak{b}_e} : E \to E_1$ using Elkies algorithm.
$P_1, Q_1 := \phi_{\mathfrak{b}_e}(P), \phi_{\mathfrak{b}_e}(Q)$.
Double $P_1, Q_1$ until they are of order $2^{e+2}$. ▷ Nr. of doublings depends on $\phi_{\mathfrak{b}_e}$.
Write $u = g_u(x_u^2 + y_u^2)$ and $v = g_v(x_v^2 + y_v^2)$.
Compute a random isogeny $\phi_u : E_1 \to E_u$ of degree $g_u$ using Elkies algorithm.
$P_u, Q_u := \phi_u(P_1), \phi_u(Q_1)$
Find a generator $\sigma$ of the principal ideal $\overline{\mathfrak{c}_e\mathfrak{c}_k}\mathfrak{b}_e\mathfrak{b}_k$.
Compute the isogeny $\phi_{\mathfrak{c}_e} : E \to E_2$, using Elkies algorithm.
Compute $d \equiv N(\mathfrak{c}_{e'})^{-1} \pmod{2^{e+2}}$, where $\mathfrak{c}_{e'}$ is the odd normed part of $\mathfrak{c}_e$.
$P_2, Q_2 := [d] \circ \phi_{\mathfrak{c}_e} \circ \sigma(P), [d] \circ \phi_{\mathfrak{c}_e} \circ \sigma(Q)$. ▷ See [18, Algorithm 4] for evaluating $\sigma$.
Double $P_2, Q_2$ until they are of order $2^{e+2}$. ▷ Nr. of doublings depends on $\phi_{\mathfrak{b}_e}$.
Compute a random isogeny $\phi_v : E_2 \to E_v$ of degree $g_v$ using Elkies algorithm.
Compute $P_v, Q_v = \phi_v(P_2), \phi_v(Q_2)$.
`KernelData` $:= [N(\mathfrak{b}_k), N(\mathfrak{c}_k), g_u, x_u, y_u, g_y, x_v, y_v, P_u, Q_u, P_v, Q_v]$.
**return** `KernelData`.

### 5.3 Step 3: Computing the 4-Dimensional Isogeny

In this step, we compute the 4-dimensional $2^e$-isogeny isogeny $F : A_u \times A_v \to E_\mathfrak{a}^2 \times A$ from Sect. 3.2 (defined in Eq. (5)). We can actually be much more explicit than in Sect. 3.2. From Sect. 5.2, we obtain that $A_u = E_u^2$, $A_v = E_v^2$ and $A = E'^2$. In particular

$$F = \begin{pmatrix} \Phi_1 \circ \tilde{\Phi}_u & \Phi_2 \circ \tilde{\Phi}_v \\ -\Phi'_v \circ \tilde{\Phi}'_2 & \Phi'_u \circ \tilde{\Phi}'_1 \end{pmatrix} : E_u^2 \times E_v^2 \to E_{\mathfrak{a}}^2 \times E'^2.$$

Equation (6) also becomes:

$$\begin{aligned} &\ker(F) \\ &= \Big\{([uN_1]\varphi_u(P), [uN_1]\varphi_u(Q), \\ &\quad [g_u]M_v \cdot M_u^T(\varphi_v \circ \widehat{\varphi}_{\mathfrak{c}_k} \circ \varphi_{\mathfrak{b}_k}(P), \varphi_v \circ \widehat{\varphi}_{\mathfrak{c}_k} \circ \varphi_{\mathfrak{b}_k}(Q))) \mid P, Q \in E_u[2^e]\Big\} \\ &= \Big\{([N_1]M_u(\varphi_u(P), \varphi_u(Q)), \\ &\quad M_v(\varphi_v \circ \widehat{\varphi}_{\mathfrak{c}_k} \circ \varphi_{\mathfrak{b}_k}(P), \varphi_v \circ \widehat{\varphi}_{\mathfrak{c}_k} \circ \varphi_{\mathfrak{b}_k}(Q))) \mid P, Q \in E_1[2^e]\Big\}. \end{aligned} \tag{14}$$

To compute $F$, we proceed with theta coordinates of level 2 and the algorithms from [17] (see also the full version of the paper [18, Appendix B]). These algorithms require a basis of an isotropic subgroup (for the Weil pairing) $K' \subset (E_u^2 \times E_v^2)[2^{e+2}]$ such that $[4]K' = \ker(F)$.

Let $(P, Q)$ be a basis of $E_1[2^{e+2}]$, $\zeta := e_{2^{e+2}}(P, Q)$, $\eta_1, \alpha$ be inverses of $N_1, uN_1$ modulo $2^{e+2}$ respectively, $(P_u, Q_u) := \varphi_u(P, Q)$ and $(P_v, Q_v) := \varphi_v \circ \widehat{\varphi}_{\mathfrak{c}_k} \circ \varphi_{\mathfrak{b}_k}(P, Q)$ the points computed in Step 2. Then, applying [18, Lemma A.1] to $F$ and the $\zeta$-symplectic basis $(x_1, x_2, y_1, y_2) := ((\varphi_{\mathfrak{b}_k}(P), 0), (0, \varphi_{\mathfrak{b}_k}(P)), ([\eta_1]\varphi_{\mathfrak{b}_k}(Q), 0), (0, [\eta_1]\varphi_{\mathfrak{b}_k}(Q)))$, we obtain a basis

$$\begin{aligned} T_1 &:= ([N_1 x_u]P_u, [N_1 y_u]P_u, [x_v]P_v, [y_v]P_v) \\ T_2 &:= ([-N_1 y_u]P_u, [N_1 x_u]P_u, [-y_v]P_v, [x_v]P_v) \\ T_3 &:= ([(1-2^e\alpha)x_u]Q_u, [(1-2^e\alpha)y_u]Q_u, [\eta_1 x_v]Q_v, [\eta_1 y_v]Q_v) \\ T_4 &:= ([-(1-2^e\alpha)y_u]Q_u, [(1-2^e\alpha)x_u]Q_u, [-\eta_1 y_v]Q_v, [\eta_1 x_v]Q_v), \end{aligned}$$

of an isotropic subgroup $K' \subset (E_u^2 \times E_v^2)[2^{e+2}]$ such that $[4]K' = \ker(F)$.

To compute $F$ and extract $E_{\mathfrak{a}}$ from its codomain, we take as input:

- The points $P_u, Q_u, P_v, Q_v$ computed in Step 2.
- The integers $N_1, N_2, g_u, x_u, y_u, g_v, x_v, y_v, e$ obtained from a solution of Eq. (11) obtained in Step 1.

This data is not only useful to compute $T_1, \ldots, T_4$ but also gluing and diagonal isogenies located in the beginning of the 2-isogeny chain $F$ that must be handled with care. For this technical reason, one must provide the data above and not $T_1, \cdots, T_4$ or kernel points of $F$ directly. We refer to the full version of the paper [18, Appendix B] for a detailed presentation of the computation of $F$ with level-2 theta coordinates (following the approach of [17]) and to [18, Appendix A] for a cryptographer friendly introduction to higher-dimensional isogeny computations with theta coordinates.

*Remark 5.3 (Working over $\mathbb{F}_p$).* Using the basis from Eq. (12) for our elliptic curves, we can work with rational theta null points all along our dimension 4 isogeny chain. This is one of the reasons to work on the surface: on the floor, the elliptic curve level 2 theta null points are not rational. Our kernel generators have Frobenius-eigenvalue $\pm 1$, so define $\mathbb{F}_p$-rational points on the Kummer variety and thus their theta-coordinates are $\mathbb{F}_p$-rational (recall that level-2 theta coordinates only give an embedding of the Kummer into projective space, not of the whole variety). This allows us to do the full dimension-4 isogeny computation over $\mathbb{F}_p$, with the exception of the gluing isogenies. Indeed, as currently implemented the gluing formulas mix points with eigenvalue 1 and points with eigenvalue $-1$, so we need to temporally work over $\mathbb{F}_{p^2}$. We expect that using more symmetric gluing formulas would allow us to stay over $\mathbb{F}_p$ even for gluing, but we leave that for future work.

## 6 Implementation Results

In this section we describe different implementation choices and their relative efficiency tradeoffs. We give concrete timings, and compare them with the current state of the art of group action primitives. Our implementation is publicly available at https://github.com/pegasis4d.

### 6.1 Parameter Choices

Since our algorithm relies on higher dimensional representations of isogenies, we start with choosing primes of the form $p = c2^f - 1$, ensuring that the full $2^f$-torsion is defined over $\mathbb{F}_{p^2}$. Furthermore, since the probability that Eq. (11) admits a solution, depends heavily on how close $2^f$ is to $p$, we restrict to the case where $c$ is small.

Among the possible choices for $c$ we retain those that maximize the number of small primes that split in $\mathcal{O}$, and in particular, primes that are 3 mod 4, since these will greatly increase the probability of finding $\mathfrak{B}$-good pairs $(u, v)$. Note that prime factors of $c$ will automatically be split.

To choose the set $\mathfrak{B}$, we proceed as follows: we only include split primes in $\mathfrak{B}$, which has 3 advantages: first, we can execute the whole algorithm over $\mathbb{F}_p$, instead of over $\mathbb{F}_{p^2}$, resulting in a major speed-up. Second, it allows us to use Elkies' algorithm to compute small degree isogenies without explicitly constructing kernel points over extensions of $\mathbb{F}_p$. Third: such split primes are the only ones that appear as factors of norms of primitive ideals in $\mathcal{O}$.

The number of primes to include in $\mathfrak{B}$ is mostly a tradeoff between steps 1 and 2: including more primes in $\mathfrak{B}$ makes Eq. (11) easier to solve (step 1 becomes faster), but step 2 will have more (and larger) Elkies isogenies to compute. For each parameter set, we started by setting $\mathfrak{B} = \{2, 3\}$ and progressively added primes until computing $\ell$-isogenies would become too expensive. We then selected the set with the best overall timing. The final choices are reported in Table 1. A more detailed discussion of the selection process can be found in the full version of the paper [18, Appendix E].

**Table 1.** Parameter sets used in our implementation for different bitsizes. The prime $p$ is of the form $p = c2^f - 1$ and $\mathfrak{B}$ is the set of small split primes used.

| Parameter set | $f$ | $c$ | $\mathfrak{B}$ |
|---|---|---|---|
| 500 | 503 | 33 | 2, 3, 7, 11, 13 |
| 1000 | 1004 | 15 | 2, 3, 5, 7, 11 |
| 1500 | 1551 | 9 | 2, 3, 5, 11 |
| 2000 | 2026 | 51 | 2, 3, 7, 11, 17 |
| 4000 | 4084 | 63 | 2, 3, 7, 11, 17, 19 |

### 6.2 Solving the Norm Equation

The first step (Sect. 5.1) begins with creating a reduced basis of the starting ideal $\mathfrak{a}$, followed by a search for small vectors. We are looking for short vectors of (reduced) norm roughly $\sqrt{p}$, but we allow them to be slightly larger at this point (up to $\log(p)\sqrt{p}$). We then attempt to solve Eq. (11) by taking pairs of the shortest vectors. In general, the more pairs, the higher the probability to find a solution. However, the first combinations will be the smallest ones, hence the ones with the highest probability of success. In practice, we observed that taking combinations only involving the 10 shortest vectors, and rerandomizing upon failure, was the most efficient choice for all parameter sets.

Finally, for each pair of $(u, v)$ that we obtain, we have to attempt to write $u/g_u$ and $v/g_v$ as sums of squares. For this, we do trial division on both with all prime factors up to $10^4$ for the 500 and 1000 bits parameters, and up to $10^5$ for all larger parameters. If we find factors 3 mod 4 (with odd exponent) not included in $\mathfrak{B}$, we immediately discard the pair. Otherwise, we test what is left for primality. If they are prime, we have the factorization of $(u, v)$ and hence their decomposition as sum of two squares. Otherwise, we move on to the next pair.

### 6.3 Implementation Results

The results of our SageMath 10.5 implementation can be found in Table 2; timings for each step are in seconds, and are obtained by averaging 100 runs on an Intel Core i5-1235U clocked at 4.0 GHz.

We conclude this section with a more detailed comparison with the other available isogeny-based EGAs in the literature. The comparison is summarised in Table 3. The timings for SCALLOP [20] were measured on an Intel i5-6440HQ processor clocked at 3.5 GHz, while the timings for SCALLOP-HD [13] were measured on an Intel Alder Lake CPU core clocked at 2.1 GHz, and the timings for PEARL-SCALLOP [3] were measured on an Intel i5-1038NG7 processor clocked at 2.0 GHz. The timings for the two versions of KLaPoTi [47] were all re-measured on the same hardware setup as the timings presented in Table 2.

PEGASIS is the first instantiation of an EGA at the 2000-bit and 4000-bit security level. In fact, it is even the first time that the full CSIDH group action

**Table 2.** Timings in seconds for SageMath 10.5 PEGASIS implementation to evaluate one group action at different prime sizes, measured on an Intel Core i5-1235U CPU with maximal clock speed of 4.0 GHz. The last column indicates the number of ideal-class rerandomizations required to find a solution in Step 1. These results are averaged over 100 runs. Step 1 is the time used to solve the norm equation, Step 2 is the time used to derive the kernel of the dimension 4 isogeny, and Step 3 is the time used to compute the dimension 4 isogeny.

| Prime size (bits) | Prime | Time (s) | | | | Rerand. |
|---|---|---|---|---|---|---|
| | | Step 1 | Step 2 | Step 3 | Total | |
| 508 | $3 \cdot 11 \cdot 2^{503} - 1$ | 0.097 | 0.48 | 0.96 | 1.53 | 0.17 |
| 1008 | $3 \cdot 5 \cdot 2^{1004} - 1$ | 0.21 | 1.16 | 2.84 | 4.21 | 0.07 |
| 1554 | $3^2 \cdot 2^{1551} - 1$ | 1.19 | 2.85 | 6.49 | 10.5 | 1.53 |
| 2031 | $3 \cdot 17 \cdot 2^{2026} - 1$ | 1.68 | 8.34 | 11.3 | 21.3 | 0.70 |
| 4089 | $3^2 \cdot 7 \cdot 2^{4084} - 1$ | 15.6 | 52.8 | 53.5 | 122 | 0.41 |

**Table 3.** Comparison of PEGASIS and other effective group actions in the literature. Timings in seconds of different implementations to evaluate one group action at different (rounded) prime sizes. The SCALLOP variants are starred because they were measured on different hardware setups. The results of both KLaPoTi and PEGASIS are averaged over 100 runs and measured on the same hardware.

| Paper | Language | Time (s) | | | | |
|---|---|---|---|---|---|---|
| | | Approx. prime size (bits) | | | | |
| | | 500 | 1000 | 1500 | 2000 | 4000 |
| SCALLOP [20]* | `C++` | 35 | 750 | | | |
| SCALLOP-HD [13]* | Sage | 88 | 1140 | | | |
| PEARL-SCALLOP [3]* | `C++` | 30 | 58 | 710 | | |
| KLaPoTi [47] | Sage | 207 | | | | |
| | Rust | 1.95 | | | | |
| **PEGASIS (This work)** | Sage | 1.53 | 4.21 | 10.5 | 21.3 | 121 |

can be computed at the 1000-bit level. However, as Table 3 shows, PEGASIS also significantly outperforms all earlier works at their security levels. The closest comparison comes with the Rust implementation of KLaPoTi. However, the fact that KLaPoTi was able to achieve a speedup by two orders of magnitude simply by switching from a high-level SageMath implementation to a low-level Rust implementation is also very promising for PEGASIS. Under the assumption that a comparable speedup would be possible for PEGASIS, we see that PEGASIS gives a highly-practical EGA, even at the highest security levels.

One of the main reasons of this efficiency gain is that unlike all the other EGA instantiations, we are able to use the orientation given by Frobenius. This has three key benefits:

- Evaluating the orientation is very efficient,
- We do not need to represent, nor push forward the orientation,
- We can work over $\mathbb{F}_p$.

The price to pay is the need to go up to dimension 4 to compute the action, but as Table 2 shows, it is still reasonably efficient. We stress that our implementation is only a proof of concept, to explore whether level 4000 was feasible in practice. In particular, we are missing many standard implementation tricks; as a simple example, we work with affine coordinates instead of projective coordinates. Despite this, our timings are very encouraging, and we hope a low level optimised implementation could even be made comparable in efficiency to a state-of-the-art implementation of CSIDH ran as a REGA, like in [10].

### 6.4 Further Improvements

As described in Sect. 4.2, it is possible to force only one among $u/g_u$ and $v/g_v$ to be a sum of squares, and perform the other isogeny in dimension 4. Note that such 4-dimensional isogeny will have only half of the length of the isogeny that we perform at the end, thus being twice as fast (at least, since the isogeny computation is quasi-linear in its length). On the other hand, steps 1 and 2 would both become much faster. This approach hence becomes promising as soon as the 4-dimensional isogeny computation has a cost comparable to step 2, which is the case for the 2000 and 4000 parameter (see Table 2). For such parameters, we computed the first two steps of the algorithm, with $\mathfrak{B} = \{2, 3, 7\}$ in both cases; the results are reported in Table 4. We note that the number of rerandomizations stays comparable whilst the total time for step 1 and step 2 notably decreases.

**Table 4.** Time taken to compute Step 1 and Step 2 when solving the norm equation with single sum of squares, measured in wall-clock seconds. The last column gives the number of rerandomizations needed. These results are averaged over 100 runs.

| Prime (bits) | Prime | Time (s) | | | Rerand. |
|---|---|---|---|---|---|
| | | Step 1 | Step 2 | Total | |
| 2031 | $3 \cdot 17 \cdot 2^{2026} - 1$ | 0.49 | 3.83 | 4.32 | 0.70 |
| 4089 | $3^2 \cdot 7 \cdot 2^{4084} - 1$ | 3.25 | 22.8 | 26.0 | 1.25 |

Estimating the cost of one $u$-isogeny in dimension 4 as half of the cost of step 3 in Table 2, we expect to reach 21.3 s for the 2000 parameter and 106.2 s for the 4000. This approach is hence comparable to ours in the former case, and even faster in the latter. We leave its implementation as future work. On the other hand, doing both $u$ and $v$ using 4-dimensional isogenies is less efficient at all security levels we considered.

**Acknowledgements.** This work was supported in part by the European Research Council (ERC) under the European Union's Horizon 2020 research and innovation programme (under grant agreement ISOCRYPT - No. 101020788, and grant agreement AGATHA CRYPTY - No. 101116169); by the Research Council KU Leuven grant C14/24/099 and by CyberSecurity Research Flanders with reference number VR20192203; by the Agence Nationale de la Recherche under grant ANR-22-PNCQ-0002 (HQI); by SNSF Consolidator Grant CryptonIs 213766. R. Invernizzi is funded by Research Foundation - Flanders (FWO) under a PhD Fellowship fundamental research (project number 1138925N).

## References

1. Abdalla, M., Eisenhofer, T., Kiltz, D., Kunzweiler, S., Riepel, D.: Password-authenticated key exchange from group actions. In: Dodis, Y., Shrimpton, T. (eds.) CRYPTO 2022, Part II, vol. 13508, LNCS, pp. 699–728. Springer, Cham (2022). https://doi.org/10.1007/978-3-031-15979-4_24
2. Alamati, N., De Feo, L., Montgomery, H., Patranabis, S.: Cryptographic group actions and applications. In: Moriai, S., Wang, H. (eds.) ASIACRYPT 2020, Part II, vol. 12492, LNCS, pp. 411–439. Springer, Cham, (2020). https://doi.org/10.1007/978-3-030-64834-3_14
3. Allombert, B., et al.: PEARL-SCALLOP: Parameter Extension Applicable in Real Life for SCALLOP (2024)
4. Basso, A., et al.: PRISM: Simple And Compact Identification and Signatures From Large Prime Degree Isogenies. Cryptology ePrint Archive, Report 2025/135 (2025). https://eprint.iacr.org/2025/135
5. Basso, A., et al.: SQIsign2D-West: The Fast, the Small, and the Safer. Cryptology ePrint Archive, Report 2024/760 (2024). https://eprint.iacr.org/2024/760
6. Boyle, E., Kohl, L., Scholl, P.: Homomorphic secret sharing from lattices without FHE. In: Ishai, Y., Rijmen, V. (eds.) EUROCRYPT 2019. LNCS, vol. 11477, pp. 3–33. Springer, Cham (2019). https://doi.org/10.1007/978-3-030-17656-3_1
7. Beullens, W., Kleinjung, T., Vercauteren, F.: CSI-FiSh: Efficient isogeny based signatures through class group computations. In: Galbraith, S.D., Moriai, S. (eds.) ASIACRYPT 2019. LNCS, vol. 11921, pp. 227–247. Springer, Cham (2019). https://doi.org/10.1007/978-3-030-34578-5_9
8. X. Bonnetain and A. Schrottenloher. "Quantum Security Analysis of CSIDH". In: *EUROCRYPT 2020, Part II*. Ed. by A. Canteaut and Y. Ishai. Vol. 12106. LNCS. Springer, Cham, May 2020, pp. 493–522. https://doi.org/10.1007/978-3-030-45724-2_17
9. Boyd, C., Davies, G.T., Gjøsteen, K., Jiang, Y.: Fast and secure updatable encryption. In: Micciancio, D., Ristenpart, T. (eds.) CRYPTO 2020. LNCS, vol. 12170, pp. 464–493. Springer, Cham (2020). https://doi.org/10.1007/978-3-030-56784-2_16
10. Campos, F., Hellenbrand, A., Meyer, M., Reijnders, K.: dCTIDH: Fast & Deterministic CTIDH. Cryptology ePrint Archive, Paper 2025/107 (2025). https://eprint.iacr.org/2025/107
11. Castryck, W., Decru, T.: CSIDH on the surface. In: Ding, J., Tillich, J.-P. (eds.) PQCrypto 2020. LNCS, vol. 12100, pp. 111–129. Springer, Cham (2020). https://doi.org/10.1007/978-3-030-44223-1_7

12. Castryck, W., Lange, T., Martindale, C., Panny, L., Renes, J.: CSIDH: an efficient post-quantum commutative group action. In: Peyrin, T., Galbraith, S. (eds.) ASIACRYPT 2018. LNCS, vol. 11274, pp. 395–427. Springer, Cham (2018). https://doi.org/10.1007/978-3-030-03332-3_15
13. Chen, M., Leroux, A., Panny, L.: SCALLOP-HD: group action from 2-dimensional isogenies. In: Tang, Q., Teague, V. (eds.) PKC 2024, Part II. LNCS, vol. 14603, pp. 190–216. Springer, Cham (2024). https://doi.org/10.1007/978-3-031-57725-3_7
14. Colò, L., Kohel, D.: Orienting supersingular isogeny graphs. Cryptology ePrint Archive, Report 2020/985 (2020). https://eprint.iacr.org/2020/985
15. Couveignes, J.-M.: Hard Homogeneous Spaces. Cryptology ePrint Archive, Report 2006/291 (2006). https://eprint.iacr.org/2006/291
16. Cox, D.A.: Primes of the Form x2+ny2: Fermat, Class Field Theory, and Complex Multiplication, 2nd edn., p. 349. Wiley, Hoboken (2013)
17. Dartois, P.: Fast computation of 2-isogenies in dimension 4 and cryptographic applications. Cryptology ePrint Archive, Paper 2024/1180 (2024). https://eprint.iacr.org/2024/1180
18. Dartois, P., et al.: PEGASIS: Practical Effective Class Group Action using 4-Dimensional Isogenies. Cryptology ePrint Archive, Paper 2025/401 (2025). https://eprint.iacr.org/2025/401
19. Dartois, P., Maino, L., Pope, G., Robert, D.: An Algorithmic Approach to (2, 2)-isogenies in the Theta Model and Applications to Isogeny-based Cryptography. Cryptology ePrint Archive, Paper 2023/1747 (2023). https://eprint.iacr.org/2023/1747
20. De Feo, L., et al.: SCALLOP: scaling the CSI-FiSh. In: Boldyreva, A., Kolesnikov, V., (eds.) PKC 2023, Part I. LNCS, vol. 13940, pp. 345–375. Springer, Cham (2023). https://doi.org/10.1007/978-3-031-31368-4_13
21. De Feo, L., Galbraith, S.D.: SeaSign: compact isogeny signatures from class group actions. In: Ishai, Y., Rijmen, V. (eds.) EUROCRYPT 2019. LNCS, vol. 11478, pp. 759–789. Springer, Cham (2019). https://doi.org/10.1007/978-3-030-17659-4_26
22. De Feo, L., Kohel, D., Leroux, A., Petit, C., Wesolowski, B.: SQISign: compact post-quantum signatures from quaternions and isogenies. In: Moriai, S., Wang, H. (eds.) ASIACRYPT 2020. LNCS, vol. 12491, pp. 64–93. Springer, Cham (2020). https://doi.org/10.1007/978-3-030-64837-4_3
23. De Feo, L., Kohel, D., Leroux, A., Petit, C., Wesolowski, B.: SQISign: compact post-quantum signatures from quaternions and isogenies. In: Moriai, S., Wang, H. (eds.) ASIACRYPT 2020. LNCS, vol. 12491, pp. 64–93. Springer, Cham (2020). https://doi.org/10.1007/978-3-030-64837-4_3
24. Desmedt, Y., Frankel, Y.: Threshold cryptosystems. In: Brassard, G. (ed.) CRYPTO 1989. LNCS, vol. 435, pp. 307–315. Springer, New York (1990). https://doi.org/10.1007/0-387-34805-0_28
25. Diffie, W., Hellman, M.E.: New directions in cryptography. IEEE Trans. Inf. Theory **22**(6), 644–654 (1976). https://doi.org/10.1109/TIT.1976.1055638
26. Duparc, M., Fouotsa, T.B.: SQIPrime: A dimension 2 variant of SQISignHD with non-smooth challenge isogenies. Cryptology ePrint Archive, Report 2024/773 (2024). https://eprint.iacr.org/2024/773
27. Edixhoven, B., van der Geer, G., Moonen, B.: Abelian Varieties (2012). http://van-der-geer.nl/~gerard/AV.pdf
28. ElGamal, T.: A public key cryptosystem and a signature scheme based on discrete logarithms. In: Blakley, G.R., Chaum, D. (eds.) CRYPTO 1984. LNCS, vol. 196, pp. 10–18. Springer, Heidelberg (1985). https://doi.org/10.1007/3-540-39568-7_2

29. Elkies, N.D.: Elliptic and modular curves over finite fields and related computational issues. In: Buell, D.A., Teitelbaum, J.T. (eds.) Computational Perspectives on Number Theory: Proceedings of a Conference in Honor of A. O. L. Atkin, vol. 7, pp. 21–76. AMS/IP Studies in Advanced Mathematics. American Mathematical Society, International Press (1998)
30. Feo, L.D.: Mathematics of Isogeny Based Cryptography (2017). arXiv: 1711.04062 [cs.CR]. https://arxiv.org/abs/1711.04062
31. Galbraith, S., Panny, L., Smith, B., Vercauteren, F.: Quantum Equivalence of the DLP and CDHP for Group Actions. Cryptology ePrint Archive, Report 2018/1199 (2018). https://eprint.iacr.org/2018/1199
32. Galbraith, S.D., Lai, Y.-F., Montgomery, H.: A simpler and more efficient reduction of DLog to CDH for Abelian group actions. In: Tang, Q., Teague, V. (eds.) PKC 2024, Part II. LNCS, vol. 14603, pp. 36–60. Springer, Cham (2024). https://doi.org/10.1007/978-3-031-57725-3_2
33. Gennaro, R., Jarecki, S., Krawczyk, H., Rabin, T.: Robust threshold DSS signatures. In: Maurer, U. (ed.) EUROCRYPT 1996. LNCS, vol. 1070, pp. 354–371. Springer, Heidelberg (1996). https://doi.org/10.1007/3-540-68339-9_31
34. Harn, L.: Group-oriented (t, n) threshold digital signature scheme and digital multisignature. IEE Proc. Comput. Digital Techn. **141**(5), 307–313 (1994)
35. Jablon, D.P.: Strong password-only authenticated key exchange. ACM SIGCOMM Comput. Commun. Rev. **26**(5), 5–26 (1996)
36. Jacobson, N.: Basic Algebra I, 2nd edn. Courier Corporation, Chelmsford (1984)
37. Kohel, D., Lauter, K., Petit, C., Tignol, J.-P.: On the quaternionisogeny path problem. LMS J. Comput. Math. **17**(A), 418–432 (2014). https://doi.org/10.1112/S1461157014000151
38. Kuperberg, G.: A subexponential-time quantum algorithm for the dihedral hidden subgroup problem. SIAM J. Comput. **35**(1), 170–188 (2005)
39. Leroux, A., Roméas, M.: Updatable encryption from group actions. In: Saarinen, M.-J., Smith-Tone, D. (eds.) Post-Quantum Cryptography - 15th International Workshop, PQCrypto 2024, Part II. LNCS, vol. 14772, pp. 20–53. Springer, Cham (2024). https://doi.org/10.1007/978-3-031-62746-0_2
40. Milne, J.S.: Abelian varieties. In: Cornell, G., Silverman, J.H. (eds.) Arithmetic Geometry, pp. 103–150. Springer. New York, NY (1986). https://doi.org/10.1007/978-1-4613-8655-1_5. ISBN: 978-1-4613-8655-1
41. Montgomery, H., Zhandry, M.: Full quantum equivalence of group action DLog and CDH, and more. In: Agrawal, S., Lin, D. (eds.) ASIACRYPT 2022, Part I. LNCS, vol. 13791, pp. 3–32. Springer, Cham (2022). https://doi.org/10.1007/978-3-031-22963-3_1
42. Moriya, T., Onuki, H., Takagi, T.: SiGamal: a supersingular isogeny-based PKE and its application to a PRF. In: Moriai, S., Wang, H. (eds.) ASIACRYPT 2020. LNCS, vol. 12492, pp. 551–580. Springer, Cham (2020). https://doi.org/10.1007/978-3-030-64834-3_19
43. Nakagawa, K., Onuki, H.: QFESTA: efficient algorithms and parameters for FESTA using quaternion algebras. In: Reyzin, L., Stebila, D. CRYPTO 2024, Part V. LNCS, vol. 14924, pp. 75–106. Springer, Cham (2024). https://doi.org/10.1007/978-3-031-68388-6_4
44. Nakagawa, K., Onuki, H.: SQIsign2D-East: A New Signature Scheme Using 2-dimensional Isogenies. Cryptology ePrint Archive, Report 2024/771 (2024). https://eprint.iacr.org/2024/771

45. Onuki, H.: On oriented supersingular elliptic curves. Finite Fields App. 69, 101777 (2021). https://doi.org/10.1016/j.ffa.2020.101777, https://www.sciencedirect.com/science/article/pii/S1071579720301465. ISSN: 1071-5797
46. Page, A., Robert, D.: Introducing Clapoti(s): Evaluating the isogeny class group action in polynomial time. Cryptology ePrint Archive, Report 2023/1766 (2023). https://eprint.iacr.org/2023/1766
47. Panny, L., Petit, C., Stopar, M.: KLaPoTi: An asymptotically efficient isogeny group action from 2-dimensional isogenies. IACR Cryptol. ePrint Arch. p. 1844 (2024). https://eprint.iacr.org/2024/1844
48. Peikert, C.: He gives C-sieves on the CSIDH. In: Canteaut, A., Ishai, Y. (eds.) EUROCRYPT 2020. LNCS, vol. 12106, pp. 463–492. Springer, Cham (2020). https://doi.org/10.1007/978-3-030-45724-2_16
49. Robert, D.: Some applications of higher dimensional isogenies to elliptic curves (overview of results). Cryptology ePrint Archive, Report 2022/1704 (2022). https://eprint.iacr.org/2022/1704
50. Robert, D.: Breaking SIDH in polynomial time. In: Hazay, C., Stam, M. EUROCRYPT 2023, Part V. LNCS, vol. 14008, pp. 472–503. Springer, Cham (2023). https://doi.org/10.1007/978-3-031-30589-4_17
51. Robert, D.: On the efficient representation of isogenies (a survey). Cryptology ePrint Archive, Report 2024/1071 (2024). https://eprint.iacr.org/2024/1071
52. Rostovtsev, A., Stolbunov, A.: Public-Key Cryptosystem Based on Isogenies. Cryptology ePrint Archive, Report 2006/145 (2006). https://eprint.iacr.org/2006/145
53. Schnorr, C.P.: Efficient identification and signatures for smart cards. In: Brassard, G. (ed.) CRYPTO 1989. LNCS, vol. 435, pp. 239–252. Springer, New York (1990). https://doi.org/10.1007/0-387-34805-0_22
54. Shor, P.W.: Algorithms for quantum computation: discrete logarithms and factoring. In: 35th FOCS, pp. 124–134. IEEE Computer Society Press, November 1994. https://doi.org/10.1109/SFCS.1994.365700
55. Vélu, J.: Isogénies entre courbes elliptiques. Comptes-rendus de l'Académie des Sciences **273**, 238–241 (1971). https://gallica.bnf.fr
56. Waterhouse, W.C.: Abelian varieties over finite fields. eng. In: Annales scientifiques de l'École Normale Supérieure **2**(4), 521–560 (1969). http://eudml.org/doc/81852

# Deterministic Algorithms for Class Group Actions

Marc Houben(✉)

Inria Bordeaux, Institut de Mathématiques de Bordeaux, Bordeaux, France
marc.houben@math.u-bordeaux.fr

**Abstract.** We present an algorithm for the CSIDH protocol that is fully deterministic and strictly constant time. It does not require dummy operations and can be implemented without conditional branches. Our proof-of-concept C implementation shows that a key exchange can be performed in a constant (i.e., fixed) number of finite field operations, independent of the secret keys. The algorithm relies on a technique reminiscent of the standard Montgomery ladder and applies to the computation of isogenies that divide an endomorphism of smooth degree represented by its kernel. We describe our method in the general context of class group actions on oriented elliptic curves, giving rise to a large family of non-interactive key exchanges different from CSIDH.

**Keywords:** Isogeny-based cryptography · orientations · class group actions

## 1 Introduction

CSIDH [20] is a key exchange protocol based on isogenies between elliptic curves. Its main advantages compared to other post-quantum candidates are its relatively small keys and that it is *non-interactive*. Its main disadvantages are that it is relatively slow, and that it admits subexponential quantum attacks [42,43,58]. Though the exact post-quantum security of CSIDH is still debated [9,10,23,56], this has led most recent work to focus on more conservative (i.e. larger) parameter choices [11,12], severely impacting estimates of its practical performance. Despite this, CSIDH public keys are still more compact than their lattice-based counterparts, even in the high-parameter range [11, Sec. 6]. Perhaps more importantly, the best lattice-based candidates do not provide non-interactive protocols; the first lattice-based non-interactive key exchange that is deemed practical is Swoosh [38], but involves keys several orders of magnitude greater than CSIDH's.

Because of its compact keys and non-interactive nature, CSIDH has enjoyed a considerable amount of attention in the years following its inception, with most research targeting practical performance improvements and resistance against side-channel attacks. The majority of research in the latter category focuses on constant-time implementations, with the first techniques [50] already appearing soon after the initial CSIDH paper (in fact, the original paper [20, Remark. 15]


Y. Tauman Kalai and S. F. Kamara (Eds.): CRYPTO 2025, LNCS 16000, pp. 100–130, 2025.
https://doi.org/10.1007/978-3-032-01855-7_4

already alludes to an approach based on dummy operations). The current literature on constant-time CSIDH is vast [4,9,11,12,22,23,28,29,39,40,49,51,53]. Approaches may be roughly divided into two categories: those based on *dummy operations*, i.e. useless operations whose results may be discarded, but whose effect is to mask algorithms with a variable running time, and those which are *dummy free*, i.e. without employing dummy operations. Those in the first category, e.g. CTIDH [4] and dCTIDH [12], are typically more efficient, but may be susceptible to *fault injections*: by actively corrupting the algorithm and checking if the output remains unchanged, we can detect which operations are dummy, thus revealing information about the secret key. We note that fault injections typically require a relatively strong attacker model and form its own subject of ongoing research [6,13,44–46]. Attempts at constant-time CSIDH in the dummy-free category are typically computationally more expensive; examples are dummy-free OAYT [53] and dCSIDH [11].

The main reason that achieving constant-time CSIDH is a non-trivial problem, is that existing algorithms for evaluating the protocol are inherently *probabilistic*: they require to sample points on elliptic curves of prescribed order;[1] a process that fails with non-zero probability. In fact, sampling points of prescribed order is not only expensive (as it requires multiplying curve points by large integers), but it also makes the protocol fundamentally *non-deterministic*. As a consequence, all existing constant-time implementations have a strictly *variable* running time, but employ various tricks to ensure that the running time does not depend on secret data. The current state-of-the-art constant-time implementations, dCSIDH [11] and dCTIDH [12], attempt to avoid the issue of sampling points entirely, by restricting to a small key space for which the required points of prescribed order may be precomputed. Although the running time of both algorithms does not depend on secret information, they do not fully manage to avoid the issue, since they still require to sample points on the public key curve.

## Our Contributions

- We present an algorithm for evaluating the CSIDH group action that avoids point sampling entirely. It is fully deterministic, strictly constant time, dummy free, and can be implemented without conditional branches. Moreover, it applies to the full CSIDH key space. Our approach does not require advanced techniques and can be seen as a minor modification of the original CSIDH algorithm [20, Alg. 2];
- We present our results in the general setting of class group actions on oriented elliptic curves, giving rise to a larger family of non-interactive key exchange protocols of which CSIDH can be seen as a special case;

[1] There are other approaches, such as using radical isogenies [16,17,28,37], but these suffer other drawbacks, such as scaling poorly with larger parameters, being expensive to make constant time (let alone dummy free) [28], and, for larger degrees, not being provably correct [37].

- We provide an unoptimized C implementation which executes a full CSIDH-512 key exchange in a constant number of finite field operations, independent of the secret key;
- We provide a proof-of-concept SageMath implementation of a non-interactive key exchange using supersingular elliptic curves with general orientations.

**Main Idea.** We will now describe the main idea behind our approach, which is most easily explained by considering the CSIDH variant CSURF [14]. Let

$$p = 8 \cdot \prod_{i=1}^{n} \ell_i - 1$$

be a prime number, where the $\ell_i$ denote small odd primes. Consider the supersingular elliptic curve $E/\mathbf{F}_p : y^2 = x^3 - x$. The ring of $\mathbf{F}_p$-rational endomorphisms of $E$ is $\mathcal{O} := \mathrm{End}_{\mathbf{F}_p}(E) = \mathbf{Z}\left[\frac{\pi-1}{2}\right]$, where $\pi : E \to E$ denotes the ($p$-)Frobenius endomorphism. CSURF works by acting on $E$ with elements of the ideal class group $\mathrm{Cl}(\mathcal{O})$ of the order $\mathcal{O}$. This is done by computing successive $\ell_i$-isogenies for various $\ell_i$, corresponding to the $\mathcal{O}$-ideals above $\ell_i$ given by

$$\mathfrak{l}_i = \left(\ell_i, \frac{\pi - 1}{2}\right) \quad \text{and} \quad \overline{\mathfrak{l}_i} = \left(\ell_i, \frac{\pi + 1}{2}\right).$$

Each $\ell_i$ always gives rise to two $\ell_i$-isogenies: the isogeny with kernel $E[\mathfrak{l}_i] := E[\ell_i] \cap E[(\pi - 1)/2]$, which is generated by an $\ell_i$-torsion point that is $\mathbf{F}_p$-rational, and the one with kernel $E[\overline{\mathfrak{l}_i}] := E[\ell_i] \cap E[(\pi + 1)/2]$, which is generated by an $\ell_i$-torsion point with $\mathbf{F}_p$-rational $x$-coordinate but (for odd $\ell_i$) $y$-coordinate in $\mathbf{F}_{p^2} \setminus \mathbf{F}_p$. The codomain of these isogenies are $[\mathfrak{l}_i] * E$ and $[\overline{\mathfrak{l}_i}] * E = [\mathfrak{l}_i]^{-1} * E$ respectively. Special about CSURF (compared to CSIDH) is that we can also act with 2-isogenies via the ideals above $\ell_0 := 2$. In the resulting key exchange protocol, the secret key is a vector of exponents $(a_0, \ldots, a_n) \in \mathbf{Z}^n$, and the public key is the curve $E_A := \prod_{i=0}^{n} [\mathfrak{l}_i]^{a_i} E$. It is computed as a chain of $\ell_i$-isogenies, by computing a point that generates the kernel of the correct isogeny at each step, and then applying, e.g., Vélu's formulae. To obtain (sufficiently many) such kernel generators is where random point sampling is required. We can slightly cheat by precomputing points $P \in E[(\pi - 1)/2]$ and $Q \in E[(\pi + 1)/2]$ of full order (i.e. order $\prod_{i=0}^{n} \ell_i$) on the base curve, and adding these to the public parameters of the scheme. This allows to perform the action by any ideal class with exponents in $\{-1, 0, 1\}$, as long as we push both points through each of the $\ell_i$-isogenies. Since every $\ell_i$-isogeny annihilates part of the available $\ell_i$-torsion, it seems that eventually (if $|a_i| \geq 2$ for at least one $i$), we are forced to sample a new point. This is where our trick comes in.

A remarkable property of the CSURF group action, first noticed in [54] and [21, Lem. 8], is that the ideal class corresponding to the exponent vector $(1, \ldots, 1)$ is trivial; in particular, we have $([\mathfrak{l}_0] \cdot \ldots \cdot [\mathfrak{l}_n]) * E = E$. This is because

$$\prod_{i=0}^{n} \mathfrak{l}_i = \left(\frac{\pi - 1}{2}\right) \mathcal{O}$$

as $\mathcal{O}$-ideals.[2] This implies that we may evaluate the action by an ideal class $(a_0, \ldots, a_n)$ with exponents $a_i \in \{0, 1\}$ in two different ways: either as $E' = \prod_{i=0}^{n}[\mathfrak{l}_i]^{a_i} * E$ or as $E' = \prod_{i=0}^{n}[\overline{\mathfrak{l}_i}]^{1-a_i} * E$, where the first isogeny, say $\varphi^+ : E \to E'$, has degree $\prod_{i=0}^{n} \ell_i^{a_i}$, and the second isogeny, say $\varphi^- : E \to E'$, has degree $\prod_{i=0}^{n} \ell_i^{1-a_i}$. Given the points $P \in E[(\pi - 1)/2]$ and $Q \in E[(\pi + 1)/2]$, we can compute $\varphi^+$, whose kernel is contained in $E[(\pi - 1)/2]$, from $P$. Similarly, we can compute $\varphi^-$, whose kernel is contained in $E[(\pi + 1)/2]$, from $Q$. More importantly, though, we have

$$E\left[\frac{\pi - 1}{2}\right] \cap E\left[\frac{\pi + 1}{2}\right] = \{0\},$$

which implies that the image $Q' := \varphi^+(Q) \in E'[(\pi+1)/2]$ still has order $\prod_{i=0}^{n} \ell_i$, and similarly for $P' := \varphi^-(P) \in E'[(\pi - 1)/2]$. Thus, by computing both $\varphi^+$ and $\varphi^-$ and pushing through the corresponding points, we refrain from losing torsion information. Iterating the procedure allows to compute the class group action for any $(a_0, \ldots, a_n) \in \mathbf{Z}^n$. See Fig. 1 for an example by picture.

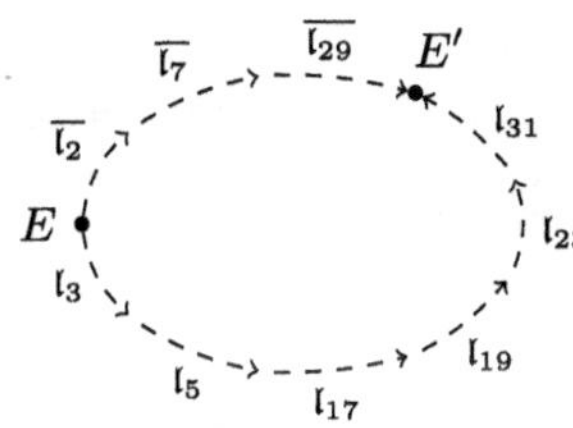


**Fig. 1.** Acting by the ideal class $(0, 1, 1, 0, 1, 1, 1, 0, 1)$ in "CSURF-32". Here we took $p = 8 \cdot 3 \cdot 5 \cdot 7 \cdot 17 \cdot 19 \cdot 23 \cdot 29 \cdot 31 - 1 \approx 2^{32}$, and $\mathfrak{l}_\ell$ and $\overline{\mathfrak{l}_\ell}$ denote the ideals $(\ell, \frac{\pi-1}{2})$ and $(\ell, \frac{\pi+1}{2})$ respectively. The bottom isogeny chain $\varphi^+$ corresponds to the original ideal class (going in the "positive" direction), whereas the top isogeny chain $\varphi^-$ corresponds to $(-1, 0, 0, -1, 0, 0, 0, -1, 0)$ (going in the "negative" direction).

Note that, since the degrees of $\varphi^+$ and $\varphi^-$ are complementary, this algorithm always computes the action by an ideal class with binary exponents (i.e. in $\{0, 1\}$) at the cost of *one* $\ell_i$-isogeny for every $\ell_i$. On a high level, and as we will more precisely see in Algorithm 1, this leads naturally to a Montgomery-ladder-style approach for computing the class group action; where the Montgomery ladder is based on the square-and-multiply (or double-and-add) algorithm, we obtain a method which could be described as isogeny-and-multiply.

[2] This can be explained by the fact that the algebraic norm of $(\pi - 1)/2$ is $(p+1)/4 = \prod_{i=0}^{n} \ell_i$.

In Sect. 3, we will present our algorithms in the general setting of class group actions on elliptic curves primitively oriented by an imaginary quadratic order $\mathcal{O} = \mathbf{Z}[\sigma]$. We will require that the generator $\sigma$, viewed as an endomorphism, has smooth degree and is represented either (i) by its kernel, or (ii) as the composition of two isogenies, both given by their kernels. We also need to assume that the kernel of $\sigma$ and its dual intersect trivially. This applies to CSURF by taking $\sigma = \frac{\pi-1}{2}$, and (with a minor adjustment) to CSIDH by taking $\sigma = \pi - 1$.

**Outline.** In Sect. 2 we introduce the necessary background on orientations and their associated class group actions. Section 3 contains the main results and described the algorithms in a general setting. Section 4 specializes to the case of CSIDH, and in Sect. 5 we consider parameters for other orientations. We point out directions for future research in Sect. 6.

## 2 Preliminaries

Throughout, we denote by $k$ a perfect field. Our main references are [31,52].

### 2.1 Isogenies

An isogeny is a non-constant morphism of elliptic curves. Given an elliptic curve $E/k$, isogenies with domain $E$ are uniquely determined up to post-composition by an isomorphism by their scheme-theoretic kernel, denoted $E[\varphi]$. For separable isogenies, this is the usual (group-theoretic) kernel, consisting of all points of $E(\overline{k})$ that map to the identity element on the codomain. We will often identify separable isogenies with their kernel, even though this only well-defines the underlying map up to post-composition with an isomorphism. Given separable isogenies $\varphi : E \to E_1$ and $\psi : E \to E_2$, the *pushforward* of $\psi$ by $\varphi$ is the isogeny $\varphi_*(\psi) : E_1 \to E_3$ with kernel $E_1[\varphi_*(\psi)] := \varphi(E[\psi])$. We have $\deg \varphi_*(\psi) = \deg \psi$ if and only if $E[\varphi] \cap E[\psi] = \{0\}$.

### 2.2 Orientations

Let $E/k$ be an elliptic curve and let $K$ be an imaginary quadratic number field. A $K$-*orientation* is a (necessarily injective) ring homomorphism

$$\iota : K \to \mathrm{End}^0(E) := \mathrm{End}(E) \otimes_{\mathbf{Z}} \mathbf{Q},$$

where $\mathrm{End}(E) = \mathrm{End}_{\overline{k}}(E)$ denotes the full endomorphism ring of $E$. The pair $(E, \iota)$ is called a $K$-*oriented elliptic curve*. Given an order $\mathcal{O} \subseteq K$, we call $\iota$ an $\mathcal{O}$-*orientation* if $\iota(\mathcal{O}) \subseteq \mathrm{End}(E)$. For any element $\sigma \in \mathcal{O}$, we have that $\deg \iota(\sigma) = N(\sigma)$, where $N : K \to \mathbf{Q}$ denotes the algebraic norm.

An $\mathcal{O}$-orientation is called *primitive* if it does not extend to a strictly larger order. That is, for any strict superorder $\mathcal{O}' \supsetneq \mathcal{O}$ in $K$, we have that $\iota(\mathcal{O}') \not\subseteq \mathrm{End}(E)$. A $K$-orientation is a primitive $\mathcal{O}$-orientation for a unique order, called the *primitive order*, given by $\mathcal{O}_{\mathrm{pr}} := \iota^{-1}(\mathrm{End}(E))$.

If $(E, \iota)$ is a $K$-oriented elliptic curve, and $\varphi : E \to E'$ is an isogeny, then we obtain an induced $K$-orientation $\varphi_*(\iota)$ on $E'$ given by

$$\varphi_*(\iota)(\alpha) := \varphi \circ \iota(\alpha) \circ \hat{\varphi} \otimes \frac{1}{\deg(\varphi)}. \tag{1}$$

Given two $K$-oriented elliptic curves $(E, \iota)$ and $(E', \iota')$, a *$K$-oriented isogeny* is an isogeny $\varphi : E \to E'$ for which $\varphi_*(\iota) = \iota'$. If $\varphi : (E, \iota) \to (E', \iota')$ is a $K$-oriented isogeny of prime degree $\ell$, then exactly one of the following is true:

(i) $\mathcal{O}_{\mathrm{pr}} = \mathcal{O}'_{\mathrm{pr}}$, in which case $\varphi$ is called *horizontal*;
(ii) $\mathcal{O}_{\mathrm{pr}} \subsetneq \mathcal{O}'_{\mathrm{pr}}$ and $[\mathcal{O}'_{\mathrm{pr}} : \mathcal{O}_{\mathrm{pr}}] = \ell$, in which case $\varphi$ is called *ascending*;
(iii) $\mathcal{O}'_{\mathrm{pr}} \subsetneq \mathcal{O}_{\mathrm{pr}}$ and $[\mathcal{O}_{\mathrm{pr}} : \mathcal{O}'_{\mathrm{pr}}] = \ell$, in which case $\varphi$ is called *descending.*

In general, a $K$-oriented isogeny of composite degree can be any composition of these three types of isogenies. In case the primitive orders of the domain and codomain are *comparable*, i.e. one is contained in the other, we will use the same terminologies (horizontal, ascending, descending) to describe the corresponding isogeny.

## 2.3 Class Group Actions

Let $\mathcal{O} \subseteq K$ be an imaginary quadratic order, and let $(E, \iota)$ be an $\mathcal{O}$-oriented elliptic curve. If $\mathfrak{a} \subseteq \mathcal{O}$ is an ideal, we define its kernel by

$$E[\mathfrak{a}] := \bigcap_{\alpha \in \mathfrak{a}} E[\iota(\alpha)],$$

and denote by $\varphi_{\mathfrak{a}} : E \to E'$ an isogeny with kernel $E[\mathfrak{a}]$. The curve $E'/\overline{k}$, unique up to isomorphism, is also denoted $\mathfrak{a} * E$. The induced $K$-oriented isogeny

$$(E, \iota) \to (\mathfrak{a} * E, (\varphi_{\mathfrak{a}})_*(\iota))$$

is horizontal if and only if $\mathfrak{a}$ is invertible (if $\mathfrak{a}$ is not invertible, then it is ascending). Moreover, if $\mathfrak{b}$ is an equivalent $\mathcal{O}$-ideal, then

$$(\mathfrak{a} * E, (\varphi_{\mathfrak{a}})_*(\iota)) \cong (\mathfrak{b} * E, (\varphi_{\mathfrak{b}})_*(\iota))$$

as $K$-oriented elliptic curves. This induces an action

$$\mathrm{Cl}(\mathcal{O}) \circlearrowleft \{(E, \iota) \mid E/\overline{k} \text{ ell. curve}, \iota \text{ an } \mathcal{O}\text{-orientation}\}/\cong$$

by the ideal class group $\mathrm{Cl}(\mathcal{O})$ of $\mathcal{O}$ on the set of $\mathcal{O}$-oriented elliptic curves over $\overline{k}$ up to $K$-oriented isomorphism, as soon as the latter set is nonempty. If we further restrict to primitive $\mathcal{O}$-orientations, then this action is free.

By a slight abuse of notation, given an $\mathcal{O}$-oriented curve $(E, \iota)$ and an element $\sigma \in \mathcal{O}$, we will denote by $E[\sigma] := E[\iota(\sigma)] = E[(\sigma)]$ the kernel of $\iota(\sigma)$. Similarly, if $(N, \sigma)$ is an $\mathcal{O}$-ideal, where $N \in \mathbf{Z}_{>0}$, we denote its kernel by $E[N, \sigma] := E[(N, \sigma)]$.

**Lemma 2.1.** *Let $E/k$ be an elliptic curve, primitively oriented by an imaginary quadratic order $\mathcal{O} = \mathbf{Z}[\sigma]$. Let $\ell$ be a prime number, different from the characteristic of $k$, such that $\ell \mid N(\sigma)$. Then*

*(i)* $E[\ell, \sigma] \cong \mathbf{Z}/\ell\mathbf{Z}$;
*(ii)* $E[\ell, \sigma] = E[\ell, \hat{\sigma}] \iff \ell \mid \mathrm{tr}(\sigma)$.

*Proof.* Since $\ell \mid N(\sigma)$, we have that $E[\ell, \sigma] \neq \{0\}$. If $E[\ell, \sigma] = E[\ell]$, then $\sigma$ factors through $[\ell]$, contradicting the assumption that the orientation is primitive, hence $E[\ell, \sigma]$ is cyclic of order $\ell$, proving (i). For (ii), note that $\sigma + \hat{\sigma} = [\mathrm{tr}(\sigma)]$, so $E[\sigma] \cap E[\hat{\sigma}] \subseteq E[\mathrm{tr}(\sigma)]$. It follows that $E[\ell, \sigma] \cap E[\ell, \hat{\sigma}] \neq \{0\}$ if and only if $\ell \mid \mathrm{tr}(\sigma)$. □

**Corollary 2.2.** *Let $E/k$ be primitively oriented by $\mathbf{Z}[\sigma]$, and suppose that $N(\sigma)$ is coprime to the characteristic of $k$. Then $E[\sigma]$ is cyclic, and $E[\sigma] \cap E[\hat{\sigma}] = \{0\} \iff \gcd(N(\sigma), \mathrm{tr}(\sigma)) = 1$.*

**Proposition 2.3.** *Let $\mathcal{O} = \mathbf{Z}[\sigma]$ be an imaginary quadratic order of conductor $f$. Let $I = (N, \sigma)$ be an $\mathcal{O}$-ideal, where $N \in \mathbf{Z}_{>0}$ and $N \mid N(\sigma)$. Then $I$ is invertible if and only if $\gcd(N, N(\sigma)/N, f) = 1$.*

*Proof.* Let $K$ be the fraction field of $\mathcal{O}$. Then $I$ is invertible if and only if $\mathcal{O}_L(I) := \{\alpha \in K \mid \alpha I \subseteq I\} = \mathcal{O}$ [32, Cor. 4.4]. Let $\alpha = x + y\sigma \in K$, where $x, y \in \mathbf{Q}$. Then

$$(x + y\sigma)\sigma = y\sigma^2 + x\sigma = -yN(\sigma) + (x + y\mathrm{tr}(\sigma))\sigma.$$

This is an element of $I$ if and only if $x + y\mathrm{tr}(\sigma) \in \mathbf{Z}$ and $N \mid yN(\sigma)$. The latter condition is equivalent to $y \in \frac{1}{N(\sigma)/N}\mathbf{Z}$. Similarly,

$$(x + y\sigma)N = xN + yN\sigma,$$

which is in $I$ if and only if $x \in \mathbf{Z}$ and $y \in \frac{1}{N}\mathbf{Z}$. Combining the conditions, we find that

$$x + y\sigma \in \mathcal{O}_L(I) \iff x \in \mathbf{Z} \text{ and } y \in \frac{1}{N}\mathbf{Z} \cap \frac{1}{N(\sigma)/N}\mathbf{Z} \cap \frac{1}{\mathrm{tr}\sigma}\mathbf{Z}.$$

Therefore $I$ is invertible if and only if $\gcd(N, N(\sigma)/N, \mathrm{tr}(\sigma)) = 1$. Now, let $\ell$ be a prime number such that $\ell \mid \gcd(N, N(\sigma)/N)$. The desired result will follow if we can show that $\ell \mid \mathrm{tr}(\sigma) \iff \ell \mid f$. Note that, since $\ell \mid \gcd(N, N(\sigma)/N)$, we must have $\ell^2 \mid N(\sigma)$. Thus, if $\ell \mid \mathrm{tr}(\sigma)$, then $\sigma/\ell$ is an algebraic integer (indeed, its norm and trace are both integral), hence $\ell \mid f$. Now suppose that $\ell \mid f$. Then $\ell^2 \mid \mathrm{Disc}(\sigma) = \mathrm{tr}(\sigma)^2 - 4N(\sigma)$. Since $\ell^2 \mid N(\sigma)$, it follows that $\ell \mid \mathrm{tr}(\sigma)$, completing the proof. □

**Corollary 2.4.** *Let $E/k$ be primitively oriented by an imaginary quadratic order $\mathcal{O} = \mathbf{Z}[\sigma]$ of conductor $f$. Let $K \subseteq E[\sigma]$ be a subgroup of order $d$. Then the $d$-isogeny $E \to E/K$ is horizontal if and only if* $\gcd(d, N(\sigma)/d, f) = 1$.

*Proof.* By Corollary 2.2, we have that $E[\sigma]$ is cyclic, so $K = E[d,\sigma] \subseteq E[\sigma]$ is the unique subgroup of order $d$. The result follows by applying the proposition to the ideal $I = (d, \sigma)$. □

*Example 2.5 (CSIDH).* Let $p \equiv 3 \pmod 8$. Let $E/\mathbf{F}_p$ be the supersingular elliptic curve $E : y^2 = x^3 + x$, and denote by $\pi \in \mathrm{End}(E)$ the Frobenius endomorphism. Then $E$ is primitively oriented by $\mathcal{O} = \mathbf{Z}[\pi]$. The minimal polynomial of $\pi$ is $X^2 + p = 0$, and the maximal order of $\mathbf{Q}(\pi)$ is $\mathbf{Z}\left[\frac{\pi-1}{2}\right]$. The conductor of $\mathcal{O}$ is $f = 2$. Let $\sigma := \pi - 1$. Then $E[\sigma] = E(\mathbf{F}_p)$. The ideal $I = (4, \pi - 1)$ corresponds to the unique subgroup of $E(\mathbf{F}_p)$ of order 4, which is generated by the point $P = (-1, \sqrt{-2})$. We have $N(\sigma) = p + 1 \equiv 4 \pmod 8$, so $\gcd(4, N(\sigma)/4, f) = \gcd(4, (p+1)/4, 2) = 1$, hence $I$ is invertible and the isogeny $E \to E/\langle P\rangle$ is horizontal. Since $\gcd(2, (p+1)/2, 2) = 2$, the isogeny $E \to E/\langle 2P\rangle = E/\langle(0,0)\rangle$ corresponding to the ideal $(2, \pi - 1)$ is not horizontal. Indeed, it is ascending; its codomain $E' : y^2 = x^3 - x$ is oriented by the maximal order. Figure 2 depicts the situation using the (in this case disconnected) 2-*isogeny volcano* [62].

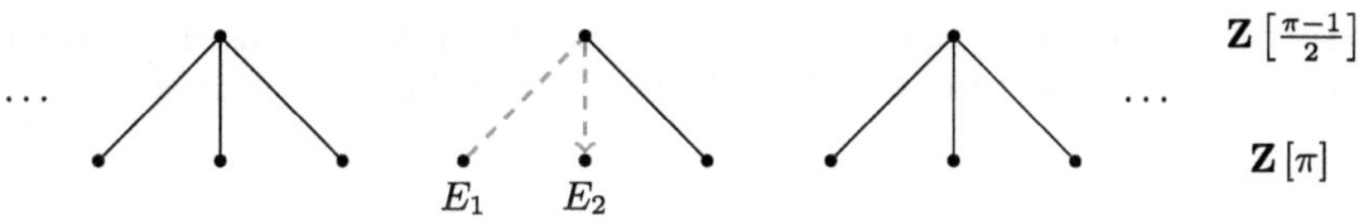


**Fig. 2.** The supersingular $\mathbf{F}_p$-rational 2-isogeny graph, also known as the 2-isogeny volcano, if $p \equiv 3 \pmod 8$. The curves at the *surface* (i.e. at the top) are primitively oriented by the maximal order, whereas the curves at the *floor* (i.e. at the bottom) are primitively oriented by the order of conductor 2. The dashed 4-isogeny $E_1 \to E_2$ is given by the invertible $\mathbf{Z}[\pi]$-ideal $(4, \pi - 1)$.

*Example 2.6 (CSURF).* Let $p \equiv 7 \pmod 8$. The supersingular elliptic curves over $\mathbf{F}_p$ (i.e. the supersingular curves over $\overline{\mathbf{F}_p}$ orientable by $\mathbf{Z}[\pi]$) again partition into two subsets, depending on whether the primitive order is $\mathbf{Z}[\pi]$ or $\mathcal{O}_K = \mathbf{Z}\left[\frac{\pi-1}{2}\right]$. In this situation, however, the prime 2 is split (instead of inert) in $\mathcal{O}_K$, which implies that the curves oriented by $\mathcal{O}_K$ admit horizontal 2-isogenies. This leads to an isogeny volcano of the shape depicted in Fig. 3.

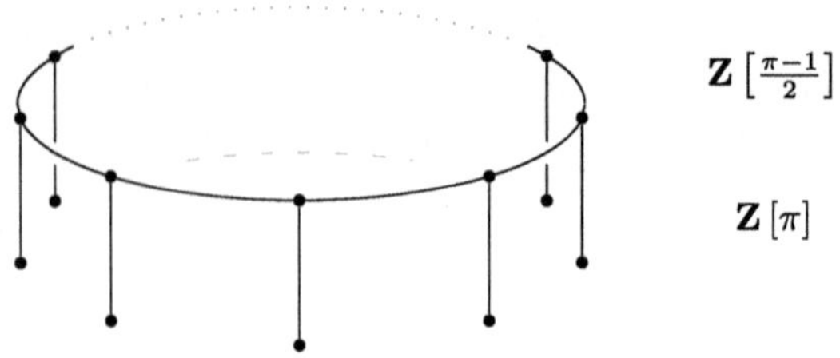


**Fig. 3.** The supersingular $\mathbf{F}_p$-rational 2-isogeny graph if $p \equiv 7 \pmod 8$.

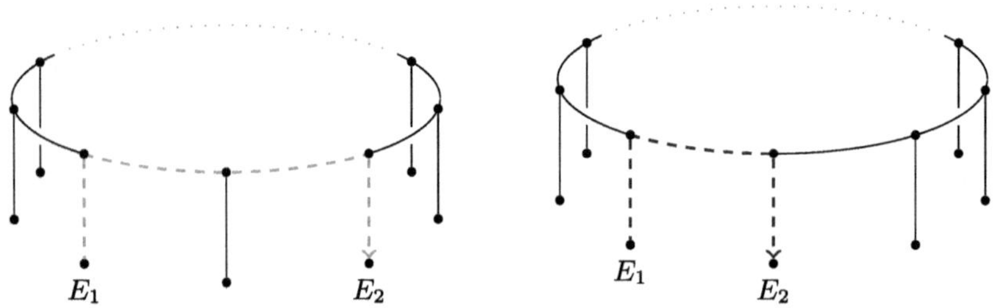


**Fig. 4.** Let $p \equiv 15 \pmod{32}$ (i.e. $p + 1$ is divisible by 16 but not by 32). The dashed isogeny on the left corresponds to the ideal $(16, \pi - 1)$, whereas the one on the right corresponds to the ideal $(8, \pi - 5)$. Note that both ideals are indeed invertible by Proposition 2.3; we have $16 \mid\mid (p + 1) = N(\pi - 1)$ and $8 \mid\mid (p + 25) = N(\pi - 5)$.

### 2.4 Representing Orientations

Let $E/\mathbf{F}_q$ be an elliptic curve and let $\mathcal{O}$ be an imaginary quadratic order. We say an *effective representation* of an orientation $\iota : \mathcal{O} \hookrightarrow \mathrm{End}(E)$ consists of the following data:

(i) The minimal polynomial $f \in \mathbf{Z}[X]$ of a generator $\sigma$ of $\mathcal{O}$ (or, equivalently, the norm and trace of $\sigma$);
(ii) An algorithm to evaluate $\iota(\sigma)$ on any point $P \in E(\mathbf{F}_{q^r})$ for any $r \in \mathbf{Z}_{>0}$.

There are several ways in which an orientation may be effectively represented. In particular, when it comes to condition (ii), a number of methods exist in the literature. In the case of CSIDH and CRS, we have that $\mathcal{O} = \mathbf{Z}[\pi]$ is generated by the Frobenius endomorphism, which may be represented as an explicit map $E \to E, (x, y) \mapsto (x^p, y^p)$. A generalization to this are $(d, \epsilon)$-structures [26], where an additional $d$-isogeny from the curve to its Frobenius conjugate is provided. In SCALLOP [36] and PEARL-SCALLOP [2], the orientation is given by the kernels of two (smooth degree) isogenies $\varphi_1 : E \to E_1, \varphi_2 : E \to E_2$

such that $\iota(\sigma) = \hat{\varphi}_2\varphi_1$. SCALLOP-HD [24] uses a two-dimensional representation. More precisely, we are given the images of $\iota(\sigma)$ on $E[2^e]$, together with an element $\tau = a + b\sigma \in \mathcal{O}$ such that $N(\sigma) + N(\tau) = 2^e$. This allows to represent $\iota(\sigma)$ by the $(2^e, 2^e)$-isogeny $E^2 \to E^2$ given by $\begin{pmatrix} \hat{\iota(\sigma)} & \hat{\iota(\tau)} \\ -\iota(\tau) & \iota(\sigma) \end{pmatrix}$ with kernel $\{(\iota(\sigma)(R), \iota(\tau)(R)) \mid R \in E[2^e]\}$. In OSIDH [31], on the other hand, public keys do not contain an effective representation of the orientation. In fact, it was shown that knowledge of such a representation renders the protocol insecure [52], and that this leads to a practically feasible (though exponential time) attack [35].

In this work, we consider two (closely related) types of effective representations. In both cases, we assume that the generator $\sigma$ of $\mathcal{O}$ has smooth norm. Firstly, we study the situation in which we are given the kernel of $\iota(\sigma)$ as a subgroup of $E$. This applies to CSIDH by taking $\sigma = \pi - 1$. Secondly, we study the case in which $\iota(\sigma)$ is written as the composition of two isogenies of smooth degree, again given by their kernel (or the kernel of the dual). This is the situation of (PEARL-)SCALLOP.

## 3 Deterministic Class Group Actions

Let $k$ be a perfect field. All elliptic curves in this section are assumed to be defined over $k$. For practical purposes, the field $k$ will always be a finite field $\mathbf{F}_q$, and for the described algorithms to be practical, all points and isogenies should be defined over $\mathbf{F}_q$ or over a small field extension of this field. What is relevant, however, is that we can efficiently perform field arithmetic, elliptic curve arithmetic (in particular, that we can multiply curve points by scalars), and that we can *compute* cyclic isogenies given a point that generates the kernel, in the sense that we can compute the codomain and evaluate the isogeny at points. In practice this could be realized by Vélu [63] or $\sqrt{\text{élu}}$ [7] formulae.

Let $E/k$ be an elliptic curve, primitively oriented by an imaginary quadratic order $\mathcal{O} = \mathbf{Z}[\sigma]$ of conductor $f$. Assume that $\gcd(N(\sigma), \operatorname{char} k) = 1$; in particular, the endomorphism $\iota(\sigma)$ is separable. Let $c := \gcd(N(\sigma), f)$ and write $N(\sigma) = c \cdot \prod_{i=1}^{n} \ell_i^{e_i}$ for primes $\ell_i \nmid f$ and $e_i \in \mathbf{Z}_{>0}$. This implies a factorization of the principal $\mathcal{O}$-ideal generated by $\sigma$ as

$$(\sigma) = (c, \sigma) \cdot \prod_{i=1}^{n} (\ell_i, \sigma)^{e_i} =: \mathfrak{c} \cdot \prod_{i=1}^{n} \mathfrak{l}_i^{e_i}. \tag{2}$$

Note that Proposition 2.3 implies that the ideal $\mathfrak{c} = (c, \sigma)$ is invertible; this ideal will become relevant once we consider the CSIDH protocol in Sect. 4. For the remainder of this section, however, we will assume that $c = \gcd(N(\sigma), f) = 1$, so that (2) simplifies as

$$(\sigma) = \prod_{i=1}^{n} (\ell_i, \sigma)^{e_i} = \prod_{i=1}^{n} \mathfrak{l}_i^{e_i}. \tag{3}$$

The ideal classes $[\mathfrak{l}_i]$ span a subgroup of the ideal class group $\mathrm{Cl}(\mathcal{O})$ of $\mathcal{O}$. Denote by $\varpi : \mathbf{Z}^n \to \mathrm{Cl}(\mathcal{O})$ the group homomorphism $(s_i)_{i=1}^n \mapsto \prod_{i=1}^n [\mathfrak{l}_i]^{s_i}$. Note that $(e_i)_{i=1}^n \in \ker \varpi$; in fact, under a mild condition on the trace of $\sigma$, it is "minimal" as an element of $\ker \varpi$ in the following sense.

**Proposition 3.1.** *Suppose that* $\mathrm{tr}(\sigma)^2 < 4(N(\sigma) - \sqrt{N(\sigma)})$. *Let* $0 \leq s_i \leq e_i$ *be integers. If* $(s_1, \ldots, s_n) \in \ker \varpi$, *then either* $s_i = 0$ *for all* $i$, *or* $s_i = e_i$ *for all* $i$.

*Proof.* Suppose to the contrary that $(s_1, \ldots, s_n) \in \ker \varpi$ where $s_i \neq 0$ and $s_j \neq e_j$ for some (not necessarily distinct) $1 \leq i, j \leq n$. Then $\prod_{i=1}^n \mathfrak{l}_i^{s_i} = (\tau)$ for some $\tau \in \mathbf{Z}[\sigma]$. Since $\sigma$ generates $\mathcal{O}$, we have that $\tau \notin \mathbf{Z}$. Possibly replacing $(s_1, \ldots, s_n)$ by $(e_1 - s_1, \ldots, e_n - s_n)$, we may assume that $N(\tau) \leq \sqrt{N(\sigma)}$. Now

$$4\sqrt{N(\sigma)} < 4N(\sigma) - \mathrm{tr}(\sigma^2) = |\mathrm{Disc}(\sigma)| \leq |\mathrm{Disc}(\tau)| \leq 4N(\tau) \leq 4\sqrt{N(\sigma)},$$

a contradiction. $\square$

Suppose henceforth that $\gcd(N(\sigma), \mathrm{tr}(\sigma)) = 1$, or, equivalently (since $\mathrm{Disc}(\mathcal{O}) = \mathrm{Disc}(\sigma) = \mathrm{tr}(\sigma)^2 - 4N(\sigma)$), that

$$\gcd(N(\sigma), \mathrm{Disc}(\mathcal{O})) = 1. \tag{4}$$

Since $\mathrm{Disc}(\mathcal{O}) = f^2 \mathrm{Disc}(\mathcal{O}_K)$, this is a stronger assumption than $\gcd(N(\sigma), f) = 1$. In particular, it implies that all primes in the factorization (3) are split. By Corollary 2.2, it follows that $E[\sigma]$ and $E[\hat{\sigma}]$ are cyclic and that

$$E[\sigma] \cap E[\hat{\sigma}] = \{0\}. \tag{5}$$

Our main focus will be on the following computational problem.

**Problem 3.2.** *Given an effective representation of the orientation by* $\mathbf{Z}[\sigma]$ *on* $E$, *together with a vector of integers* $(s_1, \ldots, s_n) \in \mathbf{Z}^n$, *compute the elliptic curve* $E' := \prod_{i=1}^n \mathfrak{l}_i^{s_i} * E$, *together with an effective representation of the (induced) orientation by* $\mathbf{Z}[\sigma]$ *on* $E'$.

Of course, the nature of this problem depends heavily on *how* the orientation is effectively represented. We consider two main cases. In the first case, we are given generators $P \in E[\sigma]$ and $Q \in E[\hat{\sigma}]$, say, over (a small field extension of) the base field $k$. In the second, the endomorphism $\iota(\sigma)$ has square degree $M^2$, and is given as the composition of two isogenies of degree $M$. Here, we assume that we are given kernels of both isogenies as well as of their duals.

### 3.1 Given Two Kernel Points

Suppose we are given generators $P \in E[\sigma]$ and $Q \in E[\hat{\sigma}]$. By (5), we have that $P$ and $Q$ form a basis for $E[N]$, where $N := N(\sigma) = \prod_{i=1}^n \ell_i^{e_i}$.

*Remark 3.3.* One may note that the data of $P$ and $Q$ *overdetermines* the information of a $\mathbf{Z}[\sigma]$-orientation. Indeed, we can compute $Q$ from $P$ using a probabilistic algorithm: if $R \in E[N]$ is a random point, then $\sigma(R) \in E[\hat{\sigma}]$. We can compute the order of $\sigma(R)$ (for example using the Weil pairing with $P$), and keep sampling points until the lcm of their orders is $N$. We then obtain $Q$ as a sum of suitable multiples of the $\sigma(R)$. However, our goal is to give a *deterministic* algorithm for Problem 3.2, and our eventual method will rely on the knowledge of both $P$ and $Q$.

Let $s_1, \ldots, s_n \in \mathbf{Z}$, and suppose that we want to compute the elliptic curve

$$E_A := \left[\prod_{i=1}^{n} \mathfrak{l}_i^{s_i}\right] * E = [\mathfrak{a}] * E,$$

together with a basis for $E_A[N]$ corresponding to a $\mathbf{Z}[\sigma]$-orientation on $E_A$. Recall that $\varpi : \mathbf{Z}^n \to \mathrm{Cl}(\mathcal{O})$ denotes the map $(s_1, \ldots, s_n) \mapsto [\prod \mathfrak{l}_i^{s_i}]$. By adding a suitable multiple of $(e_1, \ldots, e_n) \in \ker(\varpi)$, we may assume that $s_i \in \mathbf{Z}_{\geq 0}$ for all $i$. If $0 \leq s_i \leq e_i$ for all $i$, then computing $E_A$ is straightforward; since $P \in E[\sigma]$ has order $\prod \ell_i^{e_i}$, a suitable multiple $K$ of $P$ has order $\prod \ell_i^{s_i}$. The desired elliptic curve $E_A$ can then be computed as the codomain of an isogeny $\varphi_{\mathfrak{a}} : E \to E/\langle K \rangle \cong E_A$ with kernel $\langle K \rangle$ (for example using Vélu's formulas) as a chain of $\ell_i$-isogenies. What is less straightforward, is how to find generators for $E_A[\sigma]$ and $E_A[\hat{\sigma}]$, or how to compute the group action if $s_i > e_i$ for some $i$. Note that if we can solve the first problem, then we can solve the second, by applying the group action iteratively, so we will focus on the first. The crucial ingredient is the following.

**Proposition 3.4.** *Let $\mathcal{O} = \mathbf{Z}[\sigma]$ be an imaginary quadratic order, let $(E, \iota)$ be an $\mathcal{O}$-oriented elliptic curve, and let $\varphi : E \to E'$ be an isogeny. Assume that both $\varphi$ and $\iota(\sigma)$ are separable, and that $E[\sigma] \cap E[\varphi] = \{0\}$. Assume also that $\varphi_*(\iota)(\sigma) \in \mathrm{End}(E')$, where $\varphi_*(\iota)$ denotes the induced orientation on $E'$ as defined by* (1)*. Then, up to post-composition by an automorphism of $E'$, we have $\varphi_*(\iota)(\sigma) = \varphi_*(\iota(\sigma))$.*

*Proof.* We show that both isogenies have the same kernel. By definition of the pushforward, $E'[\varphi_*(\iota(\sigma))] = \varphi(E[\iota(\sigma)])$. Now note that

$$\#\varphi(E[\iota(\sigma)]) = \#E[\iota(\sigma)] = N(\sigma) = \#E'[\varphi_*(\iota)(\sigma)].$$

It thus suffices to prove that $\varphi(E[\iota(\sigma)]) \subseteq E'[\varphi_*(\iota)(\sigma)]$. So let $P \in \varphi(E[\iota(\sigma)])$. Then $P = \varphi(Q)$ for some $Q \in E[\iota(\sigma)]$. We find that

$$\varphi_*(\iota)(\sigma)(P) = \frac{1}{\deg(\varphi)} \varphi \circ \iota(\sigma) \circ \hat{\varphi} \circ \varphi(Q) = \varphi\left(\iota(\sigma)(Q)\right) = \varphi(0) = 0,$$

completing the proof. □

Now, let $\mathfrak{a} = \prod_{i=1}^{n} \mathfrak{l}_i^{s_i}$ be an $\mathcal{O}$-ideal, where $0 \leq s_i \leq e_i$ for all $i$. The kernel $K$ of the (necessarily horizontal) isogeny $\varphi_{\mathfrak{a}} : E \to E_A$ is contained in $E[\sigma]$, hence intersects $E[\hat{\sigma}]$ trivially. Applying the lemma, it follows that $\varphi_{\mathfrak{a}}(Q)$ generates $E_A[\hat{\sigma}]$. Similarly, the equivalent $\mathcal{O}$-ideal $\mathfrak{b} := \prod_i (\ell_i, \hat{\sigma})^{e_i - s_i}$ corresponds to an isogeny $\varphi_{\mathfrak{b}} : E \to E_A$ whose kernel is contained in $E[\hat{\sigma}]$, hence $\varphi_{\mathfrak{b}}(P)$ generates $E_A[\sigma]$. This gives rise to the following high-level description of an algorithm for evaluating the class group action.

(i) From $P \in E[\sigma]$, compute $K^+ := \left[\prod_{i=1}^{n} \ell_i^{e_i - s_i}\right] P$ of order $\prod_i \ell_i^{s_i}$.
(ii) From $Q \in E[\hat{\sigma}]$, compute $K^- := \left[\prod_{i=1}^{n} \ell_i^{s_i}\right] Q$ of order $\prod_i \ell_i^{e_i - s_i}$.
(iii) Compute $\varphi^+ : E \to E'$ with kernel $K^+$, and set $Q' := \varphi^+(Q)$.
(iv) Compute $\varphi^- : E \to E'$ with kernel $K^-$, and set $P' := \varphi^-(P)$.
(v) Return $E', P', Q'$.

In essence, we have factored the endomorphism $\iota(\sigma)$ as a product of two isogenies $\iota(\sigma) = \widehat{\varphi^-} \circ \varphi^+$. The pushforward of $\iota(\sigma)$ by $\varphi^-$ defines an orientation by $\mathbf{Z}[\sigma]$ on the codomain, and likewise for the pushforward of $\iota(\hat{\sigma})$ by $\varphi^+$ (cf. Fig. 5).

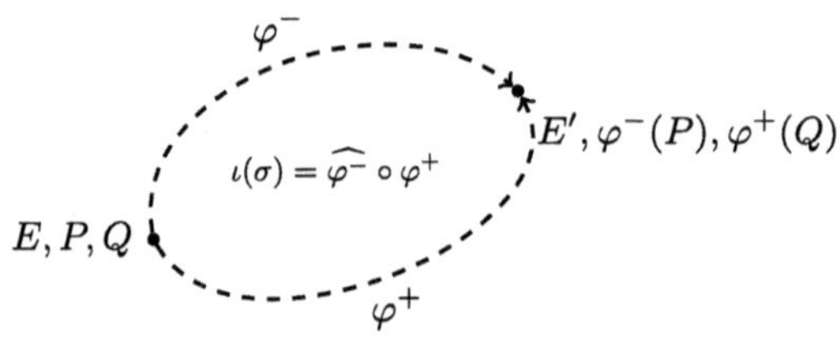


**Fig. 5.** Evaluating a class group action by factoring an endomorphism.

In practice, the isogenies in steps (iii) and (iv) of the algorithm would each be computed as a chain of $\ell_i$-isogenies. Since the total number of $\ell_i$-isogenies is always $e_i$, this can naturally be done in constant time (assuming that the cost of an $\ell_i$-isogeny only depends on $\ell_i$). The same holds for the point multiplications in steps (i) and (ii), given that they are executed as successive $\ell_i$-multiplications (and assuming that the cost of an $\ell_i$-multiplication only depends on $\ell_i$). In fact, this leads quite naturally to a "Montgomery-ladder"-style algorithm, where the classical square-and-multiply (or double-and-add) is replaced by isogeny-and-multiply. See Algorithm 1 for a complete description of the procedure. Here, the subroutine Eval-$\ell_i$-Isogeny denotes an algorithm that takes as input an elliptic curve $E$, a point $K \in E$ (of order $\ell_i$), and two points $P, Q \in E$, and returns the codomain $E'$ of a cyclic $\ell_i$-isogeny $\varphi : E \to E' \cong E/\langle K \rangle$ with kernel $\langle K \rangle$, as well as the evaluations $\varphi(P), \varphi(Q)$ of $\varphi$ at $P$ and $Q$.

*Remark 3.5.* As in the traditional Montgomery ladder, the conditional branch in the inner loop of Algorithm 1 can be replaced by a constant-time conditional swap (cswap) of two memory registers $R_0$ and $R_1$, in this case storing $(E^+, P^+, Q')$ and $(E^-, P^-, P')$ respectively, where the cswap-bit is $b \leftarrow j \leq s_i$.

**Algorithm 1.** Evaluating a class group action using two kernel points

**Input:** An elliptic curve $E/k$ primitively oriented by the order $\mathcal{O} = \mathbf{Z}[\sigma]$, where $N(\sigma) = \prod_{i=1}^{n} \ell_i^{e_i}$ is coprime to $\mathrm{Disc}(\mathcal{O})$ and char$k$; generators $P \in E[\sigma], Q \in E[\hat{\sigma}]$; a vector of integers $(s_1, \ldots, s_n) \in [0, e_i]^n$.
**Output:** The curve $E' := \left[\prod_i \mathfrak{l}_i^{s_i}\right] * E$; generators $P' \in E'[\sigma], Q' \in E'[\hat{\sigma}]$.

```
(E⁺, P⁺, Q') ← (E, P, Q);                       ▷ P⁺ ∈ E⁺[σ] and Q' ∈ E⁺[σ̂].
(E⁻, P⁻, P') ← (E, Q, P);                       ▷ P⁻ ∈ E⁻[σ̂] and P' ∈ E⁻[σ].
m ← ∏_i ℓ_i^{e_i};
for i = 1, ..., n do
    for j = 1, ..., e_i do
        if j ≤ s_i then
            m ← m/ℓ_i; K ← [m]P⁺;                          ▷ K has order ℓ_i.
            (E⁺, P⁺, Q') ← Eval-ℓ_i-Isogeny(E⁺, K, P⁺, Q');   ▷ "Isogeny"
            P⁻ ← [ℓ_i]P⁻;                                   ▷ "Multiply"
        else                          ▷ Same, but with E⁺ and E⁻ swapped.
            m ← m/ℓ_i; K ← [m]P⁻;
            (E⁻, P⁻, P') ← Eval-ℓ_i-Isogeny(E⁻, K, P⁻, P');
            P⁺ ← [ℓ_i]P⁺;
        end if
    end for
end for
assert E⁺ = E⁻;
return (E⁺, P', Q');
```

*Remark 3.6.* The main idea of factoring an endomorphism as in Fig. 5 essentially already appears in SCALLOP [36, Prop. 9], but it was not remarked that this leads to a constant-time evaluation of the ideal action.

### 3.2 Given Four Kernel Points

An endomorphism of an elliptic curve can sometimes be more efficiently represented as a composition of two isogenies. This is an idea that is also used in SCALLOP [36] and PEARL-SCALLOP [2], where it is called an "effective representation". We will consider the case where we are given points $P \in E[\sigma]$ and $Q \in E[\hat{\sigma}]$ such that $\iota(\sigma) = \widehat{\varphi_Q} \circ \varphi_P$, where $\varphi_P, \varphi_Q$ denote isogenies with kernels $\langle P \rangle, \langle Q \rangle$ respectively.

*Example 3.7.* To illustrate the advantage of such a representation over simply giving a generator of $E[\sigma]$, suppose that $E/\mathbf{F}_q$, where $q = p^2$, is a supersingular elliptic curve with $(p+1)^2$ points, so that $E/\mathbf{F}_q \cong \mathbf{Z}/(p+1)\mathbf{Z} \times \mathbf{Z}/(p+1)\mathbf{Z}$. Let $m \in \mathbf{Z}_{>0}$ such that $m \mid (p+1)$, and suppose that $\omega \in \mathrm{End}(E)$ is a cyclic endomorphism of degree $m^2$. Let $P, Q$ be generators of $E[\omega, m], E[\hat{\omega}, m]$ respectively, so that $\omega = \widehat{\varphi_Q} \circ \varphi_P$. Since $E[m] \subseteq E(\mathbf{F}_q)$, the points $P, Q$ are necessarily defined over $\mathbf{F}_q$, whereas a generator of $E[\omega]$, being of order $m^2$, may only be defined over a field extension (possibly of large degree).

As we will describe now, Algorithm 1 adapts naturally to this setting. Suppose again that $E/k$ is primitively oriented an imaginary quadratic order

$\mathcal{O} = \mathbf{Z}[\sigma]$ and that $\gcd(\mathrm{Disc}(\mathcal{O})\mathrm{char}k, N(\sigma)) = 1$, but now, suppose that $N(\sigma) = M^2$ is a perfect square, and let $N(\sigma) = \prod_{i=1}^n \ell_i^{2e_i}$ be its prime factorization. As before, we obtain a factorization of the principal $\mathcal{O}$-ideal generated by $\sigma$ into prime ideals as

$$(\sigma) = \prod_{i=1}^{n} (\ell_i, \sigma)^{2e_i} = \prod_{i=1}^{n} \mathfrak{l}_i^{2e_i}.$$

Let $P \in E[\sigma, M]$ and $Q \in E[\hat{\sigma}, M]$ be generators. Then $E/\langle P\rangle \cong E/\langle Q\rangle$. We will call this common elliptic curve the *companion curve* (of $E$), and we will denote it by $E_c$. Denote by $\varphi^+, \varphi^- : E \to E_c$ the isogenies with kernels $\langle P\rangle, \langle Q\rangle$ respectively. Under the map $\varpi : \mathbf{Z}^n \to \mathrm{Cl}(\mathcal{O})$ as before, they correspond to the ideal class $\varpi(e_1, \ldots, e_n) = \varpi(-e_1, \ldots, -e_n)$. The endomorphism $\iota(\sigma)$ is given by $\widehat{\varphi^-} \circ \varphi^+$, and the images of $P, Q$ under $\varphi^-, \varphi^+$ are generators for $E_c[\sigma, M]$ and $E_c[\hat{\sigma}, M]$ respectively, which we will denote by $P_c := \varphi^-(P)$ and $Q_c := \varphi^+(Q)$. A straightforward adaptation of Algorithm 1 to this setting results in Algorithm 2.

**Algorithm 2.** Evaluating a class group action using four kernel points

**Input:** An elliptic curve $E/k$ primitively oriented by the order $\mathcal{O} = \mathbf{Z}[\sigma]$, where $N(\sigma) = \prod_{i=1}^n \ell_i^{2e_i}$ is coprime to $\mathrm{Disc}(\mathcal{O})$ and $\mathrm{char}k$; generators $P \in E[\sigma, M], Q \in E[\hat{\sigma}, M], P_c \in E_c[\sigma, M], Q_c \in E_c[\hat{\sigma}, M]$; a vector of integers $(s_1, \ldots, s_n) \in [0, e_i]^n$.
**Output:** The curve $E' := \left[\prod_i \mathfrak{l}_i^{s_i}\right] * E$; generators $P' \in E'[\sigma, M], Q' \in E'[\hat{\sigma}, M]$.

```
(E⁺, P⁺, Q') ← (E, P, Q);            ▷ E⁺[σ] = ⟨P⁺⟩ and E⁺[σ̂] = ⟨Q'⟩.
(E⁻, P⁻, P') ← (E_c, Q_c, P_c);      ▷ E⁻[σ̂] = ⟨P⁻⟩ and E⁻[σ] = ⟨P'⟩.
m ← ∏_i ℓ_i^{e_i};
for i = 1, ..., n do
    for j = 1, ..., e_i do
        if j ≤ s_i then
            m ← m/ℓ_i; K ← [m]P⁺;
            (E⁺, P⁺, Q') ← Eval-ℓ_i-Isogeny(E⁺, K, P⁺, Q');
            P⁻ ← [ℓ_i]P⁻;
        else
            m ← m/ℓ_i; K ← [m]P⁻;
            (E⁻, P⁻, P') ← Eval-ℓ_i-Isogeny(E⁻, K, P⁻, P');
            P⁺ ← [ℓ_i]P⁺;
        end if
    end for
end for
assert E⁺ = E⁻;
return (E⁺, P', Q');
```

**Comparison to Algorithm 1.** In contrast with Algorithm 1, the output of Algorithm 2 is *not* of the same form as its input: what is missing is the companion curve $E'_c$ of $E'$, together with generators $P'_c \in E'_c[\sigma, M]$ and $Q'_c \in E'_c[\hat{\sigma}, M]$. However, this data can be computed by running the algorithm again, with the roles of $E_c$ and $E$ swapped. This can be easily seen on the level of ideal classes. Indeed, we have $E' = \varpi(s_1, \ldots, s_n) * E$, so

$$\varpi(s_1, \ldots, s_n)E_c = \varpi(s_1 + e_1, \ldots, s_n + e_n)E = \varpi(e_1, \ldots, e_n)E' = E'_c. \quad (6)$$

See Fig. 6 for a graphical representation of the situation.

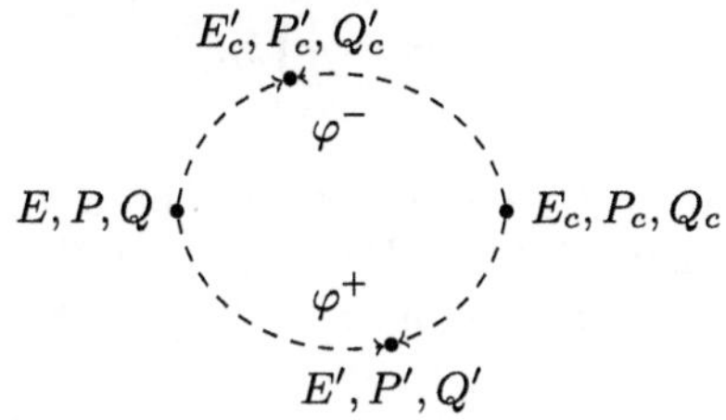


**Fig. 6.** Factoring the endomorphism $\sigma = \widehat{\varphi^-} \circ \varphi^+$ through its companion curve.

Recovering the full four-point representation $P' \in E'[\sigma, M], Q' \in E'[\hat{\sigma}, M], P'_c \in E'_c[\sigma, M], Q'_c \in E'_c[\hat{\sigma}, M]$ (which is required to apply the group action iteratively) thus costs two evaluations of Algorithm 2. From a high-level point of view, the cost of *one* execution of Algorithm 2 is equivalent to that of computing one isogeny of degree $M$ as a chain of $\ell_i$-isogenies (together with some evaluations of these isogenies at points and some elliptic curve arithmetic). More precisely, it consists of a factorization of the $M$-isogeny $\varphi^+$. In this sense, the two executions of Algorithm 2 have a combined cost equivalent to that of *one* evaluation of the (degree $M^2$) endomorphism $\iota(\sigma)$, which would be the same as the cost of one application of Algorithm 1 if we were granted access to full order generators (i.e. of order $M^2$) of $E[\sigma]$ and $E[\hat{\sigma}]$ over the base field.

Although the computational cost of evaluating an ideal class corresponding to an endomorphism of a fixed degree is equivalent between the two algorithms, the exponent range in Algorithm 2 is of half the size. This may seem to put Algorithm 2 at a strict computational disadvantage. However, it could be argued that from the point of view of post-quantum security, not the key space, but the size of $\mathrm{Cl}(\mathbf{Z}[\sigma])$ is the most relevant parameter. Algorithm 2 allows to double the value of $N(\sigma)$ (which, in case $\mathrm{tr}(\sigma)$ is chosen small, dictates the size of $|\mathrm{Disc}(\sigma)|$, and hence $\#\mathrm{Cl}(\mathbf{Z}[\sigma])$), without increasing the size of the base field or the degrees of the isogeny computations required. In contrast, increasing $N(\sigma)$ in Algorithm 1 forces the available torsion, and with it the size of the base field, to grow.

## 4 Application: Fully Deterministic CSIDH

Let $p$ be a prime number of the form $p = 4 \cdot \prod_{i=1}^{n} \ell_i - 1$, where $\ell_i$ are (small) primes. For example, CSIDH-512 as described in [20] uses the prime number

$$p := 4 \cdot \underbrace{(3 \cdot 5 \cdot \ldots \cdot 373)}_{\text{73 consecutive primes}} \cdot 587 - 1 \approx 2^{511}.$$

Let $E$ be the supersingular elliptic curve given by $E : y^2 = x^3 + x$. Denote by $\pi \in \mathrm{End}(E_0)$ the $p$-Frobenius endomorphism. As an algebraic integer, it satisfies the equation $\pi^2 + p = 0$. The curve $E$ is primitively oriented by the order $\mathcal{O} := \mathbf{Z}[\pi]$ of conductor $f = 2$. Consider the generator $\sigma := \pi - 1$ of $\mathcal{O}$. Then $N(\sigma) = p + 1 = 4 \cdot \prod_{i=1}^{n} \ell_i$, corresponding to a factorization (cf. Equation (2))

$$(\sigma) = \mathfrak{c} \cdot \prod_{i=1}^{n} \mathfrak{l}_i, \tag{7}$$

where $\mathfrak{c} := (4, \sigma)$ and $\mathfrak{l}_i := (\ell_i, \sigma)$. The subgroup $E[\sigma]$ is the group $E(\mathbf{F}_p)$ of $\mathbf{F}_p$-rational points. We have $E[\mathfrak{l}_i] = E[\ell_i](\mathbf{F}_p)$ and $E[\mathfrak{c}] = E[4](\mathbf{F}_p)$. Likewise, we denote $\overline{\mathfrak{l}_i} := (\ell_i, \hat{\sigma}) = (\ell_i, \pi + 1)$ and $\overline{\mathfrak{c}} = (4, \hat{\sigma}) = (4, \pi + 1)$ for the conjugate ideals, so that

$$(\hat{\sigma}) = \overline{\mathfrak{c}} \cdot \prod_{i=1}^{n} \overline{\mathfrak{l}_i}.$$

Note that, in this situation, we have $E[\sigma] \cap E[\hat{\sigma}] \neq \{0\}$, so that Algorithm 1 does not immediately apply. This slight inconvenience is a consequence of the fact that CSIDH works with curves at the *bottom* of their 2-isogeny volcano, cf. Example 2.5. Of course, this is not really an issue, since we could instead use a base curve on the surface of the volcano, e.g. the curve given by $y^2 = x^3 - x$, and instead do CSURF [14]. Curves on the surface are oriented by the maximal order $\mathcal{O}_K = \mathbf{Z}[\frac{\pi-1}{2}]$ and the factorization $(\frac{\pi-1}{2}) = \prod_i (\ell_i, \frac{\pi-1}{2})$ contains only prime ideals of odd norm. In any case, acting on curves on the surface or at the floor of the volcano produces group actions with equivalent security, cf. [14, Rem. 2]. We choose, however, to stick to the original description of the CSIDH protocol, and use an alternative approach; computing the isogeny given by $\mathfrak{c}$ using an explicit formula, rather than from its kernel.

### 4.1 Adjusting Algorithm 1

Let $0 \leq s_i \leq 1$ be integers, and consider the ideals

$$\mathfrak{a} = \prod_{i=1}^{n} \mathfrak{l}_i^{s_i} \quad \text{and} \quad \mathfrak{b} = \prod_{i=1}^{n} \overline{\mathfrak{l}_i}^{1-s_i}.$$

The elliptic curves $E' = [\mathfrak{a}] * E$ and $E'' = [\mathfrak{b}] * E$ are not isomorphic, but they are connected by the ideal $\mathfrak{c}$. Indeed, by Equation (7), we have that $[\mathfrak{c}][\mathfrak{a}][\mathfrak{b}]^{-1} = [(\sigma)] = 1$. In fact, given both $E'$ and $E''$ in Montgomery form, there is an explicit equation for the 4-isogeny $\varphi_4 : E' \to E''$ given by $\mathfrak{c}$, see e.g. [41, Eq. (21)]. We denote by Eval-4-Isogeny an algorithm that executes this isogeny. More precisely, it takes as input a (Montgomery) curve $E$ and a point $P \in E$, and outputs $\mathfrak{c} * E$ and $\varphi_{\mathfrak{c}}(P)$. This gives rise to Algorithm 3 for evaluating the CSIDH group action. Here, slightly abusing notation, we denote by $E^t(\mathbf{F}_p)$ the group $E[\pi+1] = E[\hat{\sigma}]$; the $x$-coordinates of the latter coincide with those of the rational points on a quadratic twist $E^t$ of $E$.

**Algorithm 3.** Deterministic CSIDH

**Input:** An elliptic curve $E/\mathbf{F}_p$; points $P \in E(\mathbf{F}_p), Q \in E^t(\mathbf{F}_p)$ of maximal odd order; an integer $B \in \mathbf{Z}_{>0}$; a vector of integers $(s_1, \ldots, s_n) \in [0, B]^n$.
**Output:** The curve $E' := \left[\prod_i \mathfrak{l}_i^{s_i}\right] * E$; points $P' \in E'(\mathbf{F}_p), Q' \in E'^t(\mathbf{F}_p)$ of maximal odd order.

```
(P', Q') ← (P, Q);
for j = 1, ..., B do
    (P⁺, P⁻) ← (P', Q');
    m ← ∏_i ℓ_i;
    for i = 1, ..., n do
        if j ≤ s_i then
            m ← m/ℓ_i; K ← [m]P⁺;
            (E⁺, P⁺, Q') ← Eval-ℓ_i-Isogeny(E⁺, K, P⁺, Q');
            P⁻ ← [ℓ_i]P⁻;
        else
            m ← m/ℓ_i; K ← [m]P⁻;
            (E⁻, P⁻, P') ← Eval-ℓ_i-Isogeny(E⁻, K, P⁻, P');
            P⁺ ← [ℓ_i]P⁺;
        end if
    end for
    (E⁻, P') ← Eval-4-Isogeny(E⁻, P');
    assert E⁺ = E⁻;
end for
return (E⁺, P', Q');
```

Replacing the conditional branch in the inner loop of Algorithm 3 by a cswap, cf. Remark 3.5, we obtain a branch-free, deterministic, dummy-free, constant-time algorithm for evaluating the CSIDH group action. At the expense of adding the points $P', Q'$ to the public key, this gives a *fully* deterministic variant (i.e. without sampling points) of the associated key exchange protocol.

*Remark 4.1.* Note that even though $P', Q'$ are images of a secret isogeny, the degree of this isogeny is not known (in fact, the degree *is* the secret), hence higher-dimensional isogeny interpolation methods [15,48,60] do not apply to recover the secret isogeny. At the expense of making the protocol slightly non-deterministic, a more cautious approach would be to scale $P', Q'$ by random scalars. An even more cautious approach would be to discard the points $P'$ and $Q'$ entirely, as they can be resampled anyway. In fact, we can combine this with an Elligator-style [8] sampling as in [11, Sec. 4.2] to compress public keys (i.e., find the smallest Elligator seed $u \in \mathbf{F}_p$ for which the corresponding $\mathbf{F}_p$-rational point has full order, and publish $u$ as part of the public key). In fact, given the points $P'$ and $Q'$, sampling new points of full order is faster, since we can check their order using the Weil pairing [59].

*Remark 4.2.* Similar to the first proposals for constant-time CSIDH [49], Algorithm 3 restricts to ideal classes with *non-negative* exponents. Assuming the size of the targeted key space is the same, this introduces a computational overhead by a factor of two compared to its variable-time counterpart. For large parameter CSIDH this may not be an issue in practice, since relatively small classical key spaces suffice [11]. Rather, the opposite issue arises: we are forced to compute an $\ell_i$-isogeny for every odd prime $\ell_i \mid (p+1)$, which may be expensive for large $p$.

A proof-of-concept unoptimized implementation in C of the CSIDH protocol as described in Algorithm 3 can be found in the GitHub repository [1]. Its main feature is that it executes a key exchange in a constant (i.e. fixed) number of finite field operations, independent of the secret key. Our code follows the prescription of Algorithm 3 almost exactly, without additional optimizations (such as strategies). Since our implementation is unoptimized, its running time is about twice that of the worst case of the variable-time CSIDH algorithm it is based on [55]. We leave optimizing the computational performance of the algorithm to future work. Nevertheless, in Sect. 4.2 we give a qualitative comparison to the state of the art on constant-time CSIDH.

### 4.2 Comparison to Existing Methods for CSIDH

We will give a comparison of Algorithm 3 to existing constant-time implementations of CSIDH. The literature on this topic is vast, with a significant amount of research dedicated to making the protocol more computationally efficient. Tricks include, but are not limited to, using different curve models [50], radical isogenies [16,17,28,37], (batching) strategies [25,29,39,49,53], Matryoshka isogenies [4,9,12], optimizing addition chains [22], and choosing primes with faster finite field arithmetic [11,12].

From the point of efficiency, the current state of the art are CTIDH [4], dCSIDH [11], and the most recent dCTIDH [12]. Out of these protocols, dCSIDH seems strongest in terms of security: it is constant-time, dummy free, and *almost* deterministic (it still requires random point sampling, but only on the public key curve). dCTIDH is *deterministic* in the same sense as dCSIDH, but uses dummy operations. CTIDH is constant-time, but probabilistic and also uses dummy operations. Although dCTIDH seems superior to CTIDH in any metric (it is even slightly faster), one disadvantage of dCTIDH compared to CTIDH, is that its keys have small $\ell^\infty$-norm, which gives rise to more memory-efficient attacks [27]. However, since dCTIDH is the current state of the art regarding efficiency, and dCSIDH seems strongest in terms of security, these will be the two main methods that we compare against.

**Disadvantages Compared to the State of the Art.** The main disadvantages of Algorithm 3 compared to dCTIDH and dCSIDH are as follows.

(i) Algorithm 3 seems incompatible with the approach of dCTIDH of exploiting the Matryoshka structure [9, Sec. 5.3] of Vélu's formulae; this is a powerful combinatorial trick that creates a larger key space at the cost of fewer isogenies (it is also the crucial ingredient for CTIDH's [4] efficiency).

(ii) To evaluate the group action using Algorithm 3 requires to evaluate an $\ell_i$-isogeny of every degree $\ell_i$ at least once. On the other hand, dCSIDH [11, Sec. 3.2] is free to employ any subset of the $\ell_i$ in the group action computation. The latter approach gives a possible advantage when the characteristic of the base field is large (i.e. when targeting high levels of quantum security).

**Advantages Compared to the State of the Art.** The main advantages of Algorithm 3 compared to dCTIDH and dCSIDH are as follows.

(i) It requires no random point sampling. Both dCSIDH and dCTIDH require to sample torsion points on the codomain curve after application of the group action. This is not only expensive, but also makes the algorithm, strictly speaking, non-deterministic and non-constant time.[3] Moreover, since random point sampling fails with higher probability for small order torsion points, the dCSIDH protocol avoids using isogenies of the smallest degrees, even though these are the cheapest.
(ii) It is fully dummy-free. The dCTIDH algorithm uses Matryoshka isogenies [12, Sec. 2.4], which is a method that relies inherently on dummy operations. Such operations may be susceptible to attacks based on fault injections.
(iii) It allows to evaluate the full (restricted effective) class group action. Both dCSIDH and dCTIDH restrict to a key space which is a subset of $\{-1, 0, 1\}^n$, which admits time-memory trade-offs for classical attacks [27]. Moreover, such a small key space means that sufficient classical security can only be guaranteed for larger parameters, thus targeting mainly a pessimistic post-quantum scenario for CSIDH.
(iv) It does not depend on the specific structure of Vélu's formulae. CTIDH and dCTIDH's Matryoshka isogenies rely strongly on the structure of Vélu isogeny formulas. Although Vélu and $\sqrt{\text{élu}}$ are the currently most widely employed methods for computing an isogeny from a kernel point, the subroutine Eval-$\ell_i$-Isogeny in Algorithm 3 may be replaced by any other such algorithm.
(v) It does not require constant-time elliptic curve arithmetic. CTIDH and dCTIDH mask the degree of an isogeny computation among a "batch" of different possible degrees (called WOMBats in [12]). Since the degree of the isogeny being computed influences the elliptic curve multiplication that needs to be performed (e.g. the cofactor multiplication to obtain a kernel point of the correct degree), this requires a form of constant-time elliptic curve arithmetic, where multiplications are performed in constant-time independent of the degree in a batch. This is a non-trivial problem that requires precomputing differential addition chains and padding those that perform too well with dummy operations. In Algorithm 3, the point multiplications are independent of the secret key. This allows to precompute and employ optimal differential additions chains for all of the multiplications.

[3] Of course, since point sampling only happens on a publicly known elliptic curve (the public key curve), its running time does not depend on secret information, and hence does not affect the security of the protocol.

**Fault Injections.** The main difference between dCSIDH and dCTIDH is that dCTIDH uses dummy operations. As noted in advantage (ii), such operations may be susceptible to fault injection attacks. In the CSIDH literature, several papers study fault injections targeting dummy operations [13,44–46]. However, this is not the only situation in which fault attacks may apply; another example is disorientation faults [6], which specifically target the random point sampling process. None of these these attacks directly apply to Algorithm 3, since it does not use dummy operations nor random point sampling. We argue, however, that more research is required to measure against different fault attacker models; a good starting point may be to study which fault attacks and countermeasures for the classical Montgomery ladder translate to the setting of Algorithm 3.

### 4.3 Public Key Validation

To prevent active attacks against the CSIDH protocol, we are required to *validate* public keys. In case the public key consists only of an elliptic curve, this involves a supersingularity test; see e.g. [5] for a survey of methods specific to CSIDH. If we are additionally given (the $x$-coordinates of) points $P$ and $Q$ as in Algorithm 3, then we also need to verify that:

(a) we have $P \in E(\mathbf{F}_p)$ and $Q \in E^t(\mathbf{F}_p)$;
(b) both $P$ and $Q$ have order $M = \prod_{i=1}^{n} \ell_i$.

Note that the combination of both claims already implies that $E$ is supersingular. In fact, the curves $E$ and $E^t$ have the same trace of Frobenius up to sign, so if $S \in E(\mathbf{F}_p) \cup E^t(\mathbf{F}_p)$ is a point of order $M \mid (p+1)$, then $M \mid \mathrm{tr}(\pi)$. Since $M = (p+1)/4 > 2\sqrt{p}$ (we can certainly assume $p \geq 67$ for all cryptographic purposes), it follows that $\mathrm{tr}(\pi) = 0$ by the Hasse–Weil bound.

In order to verify conditions (a) and (b), we can use the same approach as dCTIDH [12, Sec. 3.4]. We shortly summarize the idea here. Suppose that we are given two elements of $\mathbf{F}_p$, corresponding to the $x$-coordinates of two points $P, Q \in E(\mathbf{F}_{p^2})$, both uniquely defined up to multiplication by $-1$. After multiplying $P$ and $Q$ by $(p+1)/M = 4$, we can assume that the order of $P$ and $Q$ (is odd and) divides $M$. Now consider the reduced Tate pairing $t_M(P,Q) \in \mu_M \subseteq \mathbf{F}_{p^2}^\times$. Its order (as a root of unity) is $M$ if and only if $\langle P \rangle \neq \langle Q \rangle$ and $\mathrm{ord}(P) = \mathrm{ord}(Q) = M$, i.e. if and only if both (a) and (b) hold. We can compute the pairing using cubical arithmetic [64], and its order can be verified using product trees; see [59] for more details.

*Remark 4.3.* An attentive reader may notice that this does not determine which of $P$ and $Q$ is in $E(\mathbf{F}_p)$ and which is in $E^t(\mathbf{F}_p)$. Although this could be decided by one Legendre symbol computation, it is not strictly necessary from the standpoint of active security. Indeed, if we were to apply an ideal class $[\mathfrak{a}]$ with exponent vector $(s_1, \ldots, s_n)$ to a curve with the points $P$ and $Q$ swapped, then this amounts to replacing $s_i$ by $-s_i$, i.e. replacing $[\mathfrak{a}]$ by $[\mathfrak{a}]^{-1}$. If $E_B \cong [\mathfrak{b}]E_0$ — where $E_0/\mathbf{F}_p : y^2 = x^3 + x$ — is another supersingular elliptic curve over $\mathbf{F}_p$, then $([\mathfrak{a}]^{-1}E_B)^t \cong [\mathfrak{a}]E_B^t \cong [\mathfrak{a}]\left([\mathfrak{b}]^{-1}E_0\right)$. That is, an active attacker does not learn information from the action by $[\mathfrak{a}]$ on the invalid public key curve that could not already be obtained from the action on a valid public key curve.

## 5 General Orientations

### 5.1 Finding Practical Parameters for a Non-interactive Key Exchange

To set up a class group action by a general imaginary quadratic order for which Algorithms 1 or 2 apply, we first need to find an elliptic curve, assume over a finite field, together with an effective orientation. Ordinary elliptic curves only admit orientations by $\mathbf{Q}(\pi)$, where $\pi$ is the Frobenius endomorphism, which gives rise to the CRS scheme [34,61]. The problem of finding ordinary elliptic curves for which this orientation is "good" is a different problem outside of the scope of this paper, so we will restrict to the supersingular case. In general, the problem of finding an orientation by a given imaginary quadratic order on a supersingular elliptic curve, even if we know that an orientation exists, is difficult if the endomorphism ring of the curve is unknown; c.f. [3]. If the endomorphism ring is known, then embedding a given imaginary quadratic order essentially comes down to solving a quaternion norm equation, which can be done with Cornacchia's algorithm (modulo local obstructions); we will thus restrict to this case. Let $p \equiv 3 \pmod 4$ be a prime number such that $M := p + 1$ is smooth, say $M = 4 \cdot \prod_{i=1}^{n} \ell_i$. Let $E/\mathbf{F}_p$ be the supersingular elliptic curve given by $E : y^2 = x^3 + x$. Write $\mathbf{F}_q = \mathbf{F}_p(\sqrt{-1})$ for the finite field of $q = p^2$ elements. Denote by $\pi : E \to E, (x, y) \mapsto (x^p, y^p)$ the Frobenius endomorphism, and by $i : E \to E$ the automorphism $(x, y) \mapsto (-x, \sqrt{-1}y)$. Then $\mathrm{End}(E) \cong \mathbf{Z}[1, i, \frac{i+\pi}{2}, \frac{1+i\pi}{2}]$.

**Orienting the Curve.** Say we want to orient $E$ by an imaginary quadratic order $\mathcal{O} = \mathbf{Z}[\sigma]$ of discriminant $\mathrm{Disc}(\mathcal{O})$, or equivalently, we want to find an element of $\mathrm{End}(E)$ with prescribed norm $N$ and trace $t$ (where $t^2 - 4N = \mathrm{Disc}(\mathcal{O})$). For simplicity of the exposition, let us restrict to the case of embedding $\mathcal{O}$ into the suborder $\mathbf{Z}[1, i, \pi, i\pi]$ of $\mathrm{End}(E)$, i.e. we want to find an element $\sigma := a + bi + c\pi + di\pi$ such that $\mathrm{tr}(\sigma) = t$ and $N(\sigma) = N$, where tr and $N$ denote the (reduced) quaternion trace and norm respectively. The trace $t$ of $\sigma$ dictates the value of $a$ (hence must be necessarily be even). The norm equation now reads

$$N(\sigma) = a^2 + b^2 + p(c^2 + d^2) = N.$$

Regarding this equation modulo $p$, we find either zero, one, or two solutions for $b \pmod p$. Suppose we are in the latter case, and let $b \in \mathbf{Z}_{>0}$ be a lift of such a solution. The final step is to solve $m := \frac{N(\sigma)-(a^2+b^2)}{p} = c^2 + d^2$ for $c$ and $d$, for which Cornacchia's algorithm may be employed; a solution exists if and only if $m$ is positive and if every odd prime $p \equiv 3 \pmod 4$ divides $m$ an even number of times (i.e. the exponent of $p$ in the prime factorization of $m$ is even). In practice, we will only consider the situation where $m$ which is prime and $\equiv 1 \pmod 4$, since this can be verified efficiently. Moreover, as we explain below, we will search for $\sigma$ of *odd* trace, so that we actually must consider the full quaternion order $\mathbf{Z}[1, i, \frac{i+\pi}{2}, \frac{1+i\pi}{2}]$.

**Conditions on the Orientation.** Assume that the order $\mathcal{O} = \mathbf{Z}[\sigma]$ we orient by is maximal (i.e. of conductor $f = 1$); choosing an order of small conductor $> 1$ makes the class group larger, but does not benefit the security of the scheme, since we can always reduce to case of the maximal order by computing an ascending isogeny (see e.g. [36, Sec. 7] or [31, Sec. 5.1]). Moreover, if $\mathcal{O}$ is maximal then every $\mathcal{O}$-orientation is automatically primitive.

The size of the class group $\#\text{Cl}(\mathcal{O})$, which is asymptotically roughly proportional to $|\text{Disc}(\mathcal{O})|^{1/2}$ (the asymptotic average of $\#\text{Cl}(\mathcal{O})/|\text{Disc}(\mathcal{O})|^{1/2}$ is $\approx 0.46$ [30, p. 290]), dictates the (quantum) security of the group action; we thus want it to be large. Note that $\text{Disc}(\mathcal{O}) = \text{tr}(\sigma)^2 - 4N(\sigma)$, so we want to choose $N(\sigma)$ as large as possible and $\text{tr}(\sigma)$ as small as possible. For the first condition, the best we can do is $N(\sigma) = M^2$, assuming that we want to represent $\sigma$ using elements of $E(\mathbf{F}_q) = E[M]$ (as a composition of two isogenies given by their kernels). Once we have chosen $N(\sigma) = M^2$, we may try successive small traces $t$ and attempt to solve the norm equation using the procedure described above. Note that

$$|\text{Disc}(\mathcal{O})| = |\text{tr}(\sigma)^2 - 4N(\sigma)| = (2M - t)(2M + t). \tag{8}$$

In order for $\mathcal{O}$ to be maximal, we need the discriminant to be square-free, at least away from 2. Moreover, in certain cases, small prime divisors of the discriminant may introduce weaknesses through attacks using self-pairings [18,19], so we prefer to avoid those entirely. Most optimal would thus be the situation where $2M - t$ and $2M + t$ are both prime; if the trace $t$ is small, then both factors are of approximate size $2M$. Summarizing, we obtain the following procedure to find $\sigma = a + bi + c\frac{i+\pi}{2} + d\frac{1+i\pi}{2} \in \text{End}(E)$ with the desired properties.

(i) Let $t$ be the smallest odd prime number different from all $\ell_i$;
(ii) Check if $2M - t$ and $2M + t$ are both prime; if not, try the next smallest value of $t$.
(iii) Solve the norm equation with fixed trace $t = 2a + d$ modulo $p$, and lift the solution to $\mathbf{Z}$; if there is no solution, start over with the next value of $t$.
(iv) Rewrite the remaining equation as $c^2 + d^2 = m$ for some integer $m$. If $m$ is not a prime $\equiv 1 \pmod 4$, start over with the next value of $t$.
(v) Solve for $c$ and $d$ using Cornacchia's algorithm, and return the values of $a, b, c, d \in \mathbf{Z}$.

*Example 5.1.* Let

$$p = 4 \cdot \underbrace{(3 \cdot 5 \cdot \ldots \cdot 373)}_{\text{73 consecutive primes}} \cdot 587 - 1 \approx 2^{511}$$

be the CSIDH-512 prime. Write $M = p + 1$. Then $E/\mathbf{F}_p : y^2 = x^3 + x$ admits a (necessarily) primitive orientation by the (maximal) imaginary quadratic order

$\mathcal{O}$ of discriminant $\mathrm{Disc}(\mathcal{O}) = (2M+t)(2M-t)$, where $t = 2748817$ and $2M+t$ and $2M-t$ are both prime. Concretely, the orientation sends a generator of $\mathcal{O}$ of trace $t$ (and norm $M^2$) to the endomorphism $a + bi + c\frac{i+\pi}{2} + d\frac{1+i\pi}{2}$ of $E$, where[4]

$$
\begin{aligned}
a &= -477590666081226663362492096448380963510439585895055347230318425775059276959 55; \\
b &= 13330115377726222420483962441734730714600237606311941633063749684971410307471 0 \\
&\quad 86777423661614616351159775178954748483073397493132549795640957231967517242 95; \\
c &= 1041580612037323145011898281915055899570718561128782211612848453542759015507 40; \\
d &= 955181332162453326724984192896761927020879171790110694460636851550118581407 27.
\end{aligned}
$$

**Computing a Kernel Representation.** Once $\sigma \in \mathrm{End}(E)$ has been found, finding a representation as a composition of two isogenies given by their kernel is quite straightforward. Concretely, we want to find generators $P \in E[M, \sigma] \subseteq E(\mathbf{F}_q)$ and $Q \in E[M, \hat{\sigma}] \subseteq \mathbf{F}_q$. To do so, sample random points $R \in E(\mathbf{F}_q) = E[M]$. If $\sigma(R) \neq 0$, then it is a non-trivial element of $E[M, \hat{\sigma}]$. By sampling sufficiently many points and applying the endomorphisms $\sigma$ and $\hat{\sigma}$ by their explicit description as a map (in terms of the endomorphisms $i$ and $\pi$), we obtain generators $P$ and $Q$ as a sum of multiples of the sampled (image) points.

### 5.2 Non-interactive Key Exchange

With the effective orientation in place, we are ready to initiate a non-interactive key exchange protocol as follows.

**Setup.** Firstly, we compute the companion curve $E_c, P_c, Q_c$ from $E, P, Q$. Recall that, denoting $\varphi^+ : E \to E_c$ the isogeny with kernel $\langle P \rangle$ and by $\varphi^- : E \to E_c$ the isogeny with kernel $\langle Q \rangle$, we have that $P_c = \varphi^-(P)$ and $Q_c = \varphi^+(Q)$. We add $E_c, P_c, Q_c$ to the public parameters of the protocol. Given $E, P, Q, E_c, P_c, Q_c$, we can evaluate the action on $E$ by any ideal class of the form $\prod_{i=1}^n (\ell, \sigma)^{s_i}$, where $0 \leq s_i \leq 1$ for all $i$, using Algorithm 2 (note that, by assumption on the factorization of $M$, we are in the case where $e_i = 1$ for all $i$). This returns $E' = \prod_{i=1}^n (\ell, \sigma)^{s_i} E$ together with a representation of the orientation on $E'$ given by $P' \in E[\sigma]$ and $Q' \in E[\hat{\sigma}]$. Recall from Equation (6) that by acting by the same ideal class on $E_c, P_c, Q_c$, we obtain the companion curve $E'_c$ to $E'$. We can thus compute $E', P', Q', E'_c.P'_c, Q'_c$ using two applications of Algorithm 2, at a cost roughly equivalent to one evaluation of $\sigma$.

**The Protocol.** Let $B \in \mathbf{Z}_{>0}$ denote a bound on the exponent range of the ideals used; the private key space will be of size $(B+1)^n$.

[4] It may seem remarkable that the size of $b$ is about twice the size of the other constants. This is explained by the fact that it comes from the solution to a quadratic equation modulo $p$, specifically step (iii) of the algorithm, hence we expect its order of magnitude to be about $p$. The other constants are dominated by the solution to the Cornacchia equation $c^2 + d^2 = m$, where $m$ has size about $p$, so they have size about $\sqrt{p}$.

1. Alice's private key is a sequence of integers $(a_1, \dots, a_n) \in \{0, \dots, B\}^n$. She computes $E^A = \prod_{i=1}^n [(\ell_i, \sigma)]^{a_i} E$ together with $P^A \in E^A[\sigma]$ and $Q^A \in E^A[\hat{\sigma}]$ as well as $E_c^A = \prod_{i=1}^n [(\ell_i, \sigma)]^{a_i} E_c$ together with $P_c^A \in E_c^A[\sigma]$ and $Q_c^A \in E_c^A[\hat{\sigma}]$ using $2B$ applications of Algorithm 2. She sends $E^A, P^A, Q^A$ as well as $E_c^A, P_c^A, Q_c^A$ to Bob.
2. Bob's private key is a sequence of integers $(b_1, \dots, b_n) \in \{0, \dots, B\}^n$. He computes $E^B = \prod_{i=1}^n [(\ell_i, \sigma)]^{b_i} E$ together with $P^B \in E^B[\sigma]$ and $Q^B \in E^B[\hat{\sigma}]$ as well as $E_c^B = \prod_{i=1}^n [(\ell_i, \sigma)]^{b_i} E_c$ together with $P_c^B \in E_c^B[\sigma]$ and $Q_c^B \in E_c^B[\hat{\sigma}]$ using $2B$ applications of Algorithm 2. He sends $E^B, P^B, Q^B$ as well as $E_c^B, P_c^B, Q_c^B$ to Alice.
3. Alice computes $E^{AB} = \prod_{i=1}^n [(\ell_i, \sigma)]^{a_i} E^B$, using $2B$ applications of Algorithm 2. Her shared secret is the $j$-invariant $j(E^{AB})$ of $E^{AB}$,
4. Bob computes $E^{BA} = \prod_{i=1}^n [(\ell_i, \sigma)]^{b_i} E^A$ using $2B$ applications of Algorithm 2. His shared secret is $j(E^{BA}) = j(E^{AB})$.

A few remarks about the described protocol are in place.

(i) Although Bob requires $E_c^A, P_c^A, Q_c^A$ to execute Algorithm 2, they may be recomputed from $E^A, P^A, Q^A$ (at the cost of exactly two applications of Algorithm 2). At the expense of slightly increasing the cost of the shared key derivation step, this data may thus be removed from the public key.

(ii) The data $E^A, P^A, Q^A$ is essentially an SIDH public key, which may be further compressed using well-known techniques such as pairings [33].

(iii) Compared to CSIDH, the protocol works over $\mathbf{F}_{p^2}$ instead of $\mathbf{F}_p$, but only requires a prime $p$ of *half* the size for an equally sized class group. This makes the size of the base field equivalent to CSIDH's in terms of post-quantum security.

(iv) Compared to CSIDH, the classical key space is smaller in comparison to the size of the base field; it only depends on the characteristic $p$ (i.e. the number of $\ell_i$ in the factorization of $M = p + 1$). If post-quantum security (i.e. resistance to Kuperberg's algorithm) is the bottleneck, this may not be a practical issue; cf. [11, Sec. 3.1].

(v) Since the shared secret only depends on $E^{AB}$ and not on $E_c^{AB}$, one of the applications of Algorithm 2 in the shared key derivation step may be skipped (the very last one), making the actual cost equal to $2B - 1$ applications of Algorithm 2.

(vi) If Alice and Bob both use Vélu's formulae, they can ensure that their secret isogenies commute as maps (not just up to isomorphism), by [47, Thm. 3.1][5]. This guarantees that the points $P^{AB}, P^{BA} \in E^{AB}[\sigma]$ are equal, and similarly for $Q^{AB}, Q^{BA} \in E^{AB}[\hat{\sigma}]$. These points, which represent a $\mathbf{Z}[\sigma]$-orientation on $E^{AB}$, may thus be considered part the shared secret.

We have implemented the parameter search described in Sect. 5.1 and an unoptimized proof-of-concept of the key exchange protocol in SageMath, using the library [57] for Kummer line arithmetic. The associated code can be found in the GitHub repository [1].

[5] The reference only concerns the case where the degrees of the isogenies are coprime, but the proof does not seem to require this assumption.

## 6 Future Work

We highlight the following possible directions for future work.

(a) Re-analyze the quantum oracle cost for CSIDH. The cost of evaluating the CSIDH group action on a quantum computer is difficult to estimate and has been subject of debate since CSIDH's origin. The main difficulty is that evaluating the class group action in quantum superposition requires a constant-time, fully deterministic algorithm without conditional branches. In fact, the main bottleneck in the comprehensive analysis given by [9] is that random point sampling fails with non-zero probability, and with different probabilities for every degree $\ell_i$. This induces a large overhead on the quantum circuit in order to guarantee a quantum algorithm with sufficiently low overall failure rate, see [9, Sec. 6 & 7]. Algorithm 3 simplifies the situation considerably, since it naturally satisfies all properties required for evaluation on a quantum computer.[6] In fact, it gives a quantum algorithm with a failure rate of zero. It would be interesting to study the precise gain, together with an updated analysis of more recent tricks such as strategies and $\sqrt{\text{élu}}$, in the quantum oracle cost.[7]

(b) Study the practical performance of Algorithm 3. In view of Remark 4.2, we expect that Algorithm 3 performs best for primes $p$ for which the number of $\ell_i$ matches the (bit)size of the classical key space.

(c) Study the practicality of *higher-order factorizations* of endomorphisms. We have considered (Sect. 3.1 and 3.2) the cases where $\iota(\sigma)$ is the composition of either one or two isogenies explicitly given by their kernel. A generalization would be to consider an endomorphism of degree $M^r$ for some $r \in \mathbf{Z}_{>0}$, given as a composition of $r$ isogenies of degree $M$. The advantage of such an approach could be similar to the one described in Example 3.7; to increase the size of the orientation without increasing the size of the base field. The size of the public key (which now requires at least $r$ curves together with a kernel point), as well as the computational cost of the protocol, is linear in $r$. The size of the key space remains constant, but the size of the class group (and hence the quantum security of the group action) also grows linearly with $r$. At larger parameters, this may be more efficient than the current approach of increasing the size of the base field.

**Acknowledgements.** We thank Damien Robert for several helpful discussions. We also thank Steven Galbraith, Krijn Reijnders, and the anonymous CRYPTO'25 reviewers for their feedback on an earlier version of the paper. This work was financially supported by the France 2030 program, managed by the French National Research Agency under grant agreement No. ANR-22-PETQ-0008 PQ-TLS.

---

[6] Note that dCSIDH and dCTIDH cannot be readily implemented as a quantum oracle, since they still require random point sampling to evaluate exponent vectors outside of the range $\{-1, 0, 1\}^n$.

[7] A rough estimate building on [9] that includes $\sqrt{\text{élu}}$ is given in [23, Sec. 3.6].

## References

1. GitHub repository associated to this paper. https://github.com/houbenmr/DeterministicClassGroupActions
2. Allombert, B., et al.: PEARL-SCALLOP: Parameter Extension Applicable in Real-Life SCALLOP. Cryptology ePrint Archive, Report 2024/1744 (2024). https://eprint.iacr.org/2024/1744
3. Arpin, S., Clements, J., Dartois, P., Eriksen, J.K., Kutas, P., Wesolowski, B.: Finding orientations of supersingular elliptic curves and quaternion orders. DCC **92**(11), 3447–3493 (2024). https://doi.org/10.1007/s10623-024-01435-5
4. Banegas, G., et al.: CTIDH: faster constant-time CSIDH. IACR TCHES **2021**(4), 351–387 (2021). https://doi.org/10.46586/tches.v2021.i4.351-387, https://tches.iacr.org/index.php/TCHES/article/view/9069
5. Banegas, G., Gilchrist, V., Smith, B.: Efficient supersingularity testing over $\mathbb{F}_p$ and CSIDH key validation. Cryptology ePrint Archive, Report 2022/880 (2022). https://eprint.iacr.org/2022/880
6. Banegas, G., et al.: Disorientation faults in CSIDH. In: Hazay, C., Stam, M. (eds.) EUROCRYPT 2023, Part V. LNCS, vol. 14008, pp. 310–342. Springer, Cham (2023). https://doi.org/10.1007/978-3-031-30589-4_11
7. Bernstein, D.J., De Feo, L., Leroux, A., Smith, B.: Faster computation of isogenies of large prime degree. Cryptology ePrint Archive, Report 2020/341 (2020). https://eprint.iacr.org/2020/341
8. Bernstein, D.J., Hamburg, M., Krasnova, A., Lange, T.: Elligator: elliptic-curve points indistinguishable from uniform random strings. In: Sadeghi, A.R., Gligor, V.D., Yung, M. (eds.) ACM CCS 2013, pp. 967–980. ACM Press, November 2013. https://doi.org/10.1145/2508859.2516734
9. Bernstein, D.J., Lange, T., Martindale, C., Panny, L.: Quantum circuits for the CSIDH: Optimizing quantum evaluation of isogenies. In: Ishai, Y., Rijmen, V. (eds.) EUROCRYPT 2019, Part II. LNCS, vol. 11477, pp. 409–441. Springer, Cham (2019). https://doi.org/10.1007/978-3-030-17656-3_15
10. Bonnetain, X., Schrottenloher, A.: Quantum security analysis of CSIDH. In: Canteaut, A., Ishai, Y. (eds.) EUROCRYPT 2020, Part II. LNCS, vol. 12106, pp. 493–522. Springer, Cham (2020). https://doi.org/10.1007/978-3-030-45724-2_17
11. Campos, F., et al.: Optimizations and practicality of high-security CSIDH. CiC **1**(1), 5 (2024). https://doi.org/10.62056/anjbksdja
12. Campos, F., Hellenbrand, A., Meyer, M., Reijnders, K.: dCTIDH: Fast & Deterministic CTIDH. Cryptology ePrint Archive, Report 2025/107 (2025). https://eprint.iacr.org/2025/107
13. Campos, F., Kannwischer, M.J., Meyer, M., Onuki, H., Stöttinger, M.: Trouble at the CSIDH: Protecting CSIDH with dummy-operations against fault injection attacks. Cryptology ePrint Archive, Report 2020/1005 (2020). https://eprint.iacr.org/2020/1005
14. Castryck, W., Decru, T.: CSIDH on the surface. In: Ding, J., Tillich, J.-P. (eds.) PQCrypto 2020. LNCS, vol. 12100, pp. 111–129. Springer, Cham (2020). https://doi.org/10.1007/978-3-030-44223-1_7
15. Castryck, W., Decru, T.: An efficient key recovery attack on SIDH. In: Hazay, C., Stam, M. (eds.) EUROCRYPT 2023, Part V. LNCS, vol. 14008, pp. 423–447. Springer, Cham (2023). https://doi.org/10.1007/978-3-031-30589-4_15
16. Castryck, W., Decru, T., Houben, M., Vercauteren, F.: Horizontal racewalking using radical isogenies. In: Agrawal, S., Lin, D. (eds.) ASIACRYPT 2022, Part II.

LNCS, vol. 13792, pp. 67–96. Springer, Cham (2022). https://doi.org/10.1007/978-3-031-22966-4_3
17. Castryck, W., Decru, T., Vercauteren, F.: Radical isogenies. In: Moriai, S., Wang, H. (eds.) ASIACRYPT 2020, Part II. LNCS, vol. 12492, pp. 493–519. Springer, Cham (2020). https://doi.org/10.1007/978-3-030-64834-3_17
18. Castryck, W., Houben, M., Merz, S.P., Mula, M., van Buuren, S., Vercauteren, F.: Weak instances of class group action based cryptography via self-pairings. In: Handschuh, H., Lysyanskaya, A. (eds.) CRYPTO 2023, Part III. LNCS, vol. 14083, pp. 762–792. Springer, Cham (2023). https://doi.org/10.1007/978-3-031-38548-3_25
19. Castryck, W., Houben, M., Vercauteren, F., Wesolowski, B.: On the decisional Diffie-Hellman problem for class group actions on oriented elliptic curves. Res. Number Theory **8**(4), 99 (2022). https://doi.org/10.1007/s40993-022-00399-6
20. Castryck, W., Lange, T., Martindale, C., Panny, L., Renes, J.: CSIDH: an efficient post-quantum commutative group action. In: Peyrin, T., Galbraith, S. (eds.) ASIACRYPT 2018, Part III. LNCS, vol. 11274, pp. 395–427. Springer, Cham (2018). https://doi.org/10.1007/978-3-030-03332-3_15
21. Castryck, W., Panny, L., Vercauteren, F.: Rational isogenies from irrational endomorphisms. In: Canteaut, A., Ishai, Y. (eds.) EUROCRYPT 2020, Part II. LNCS, vol. 12106, pp. 523–548. Springer, Cham (2020). https://doi.org/10.1007/978-3-030-45724-2_18
22. Cervantes-Vázquez, D., Chenu, M., Chi-Domínguez, J.J., De Feo, L., Rodríguez-Henríquez, F., Smith, B.: Stronger and faster side-channel protections for CSIDH. In: Schwabe, P., Thériault, N. (eds.) LATINCRYPT 2019. LNCS, vol. 11774, pp. 173–193. Springer, Cham (2019). https://doi.org/10.1007/978-3-030-30530-7_9
23. Chávez-Saab, J., Chi-Domínguez, J.J., Jaques, S., Rodríguez-Henríquez, F.: The SQALE of CSIDH: sublinear Vélu quantum-resistant isogeny action with low exponents. J. Cryptogr. Eng. **12**(3), 349–368 (2022). https://doi.org/10.1007/s13389-021-00271-w
24. Chen, M., Leroux, A., Panny, L.: SCALLOP-HD: group action from 2-dimensional isogenies. In: Tang, Q., Teague, V. (eds.) PKC 2024, Part II. LNCS, vol. 14603, pp. 190–216. Springer, Cham (2024). https://doi.org/10.1007/978-3-031-57725-3_7
25. Cheng, H., Fotiadis, G., Großschädl, J., Ryan, P.Y.A., Rønne, P.B.: Batching CSIDH group actions using AVX-512. IACR TCHES **2021**(4), 618–649 (2021). https://doi.org/10.46586/tches.v2021.i4.618-649, https://tches.iacr.org/index.php/TCHES/article/view/9077
26. Chenu, M., Smith, B.: Higher-degree supersingular group actions. Cryptology ePrint Archive, Report 2021/955 (2021). https://eprint.iacr.org/2021/955
27. Chi-Domínguez, J.J., Esser, A., Kunzweiler, S., May, A.: Low memory attacks on small key CSIDH. In: Tibouchi, M., Wang, X. (eds.) ACNS 23International Conference on Applied Cryptography and Network Security, Part II. LNCS, vol. 13906, pp. 276–304. Springer, Cham (2023). https://doi.org/10.1007/978-3-031-33491-7_11
28. Chi-Domínguez, J.J., Reijnders, K.: Fully projective radical isogenies in constant-time. In: Galbraith, S.D. (ed.) CT-RSA 2022. LNCS, vol. 13161, pp. 73–95. Springer, Cham (2021). https://doi.org/10.1007/978-3-030-95312-6_4
29. Chi-Domínguez, J.J., Rodríguez-Henríquez, F.: Optimal strategies for CSIDH. Cryptology ePrint Archive, Report 2020/417 (2020). https://eprint.iacr.org/2020/417

30. Cohen, H.: A Course in Computational Algebraic Number Theory. Springer Publishing Company, Incorporated, Heidelberg (2010). https://doi.org/10.1007/978-3-662-02945-9
31. Colò, L., Kohel, D.: Orienting supersingular isogeny graphs. J. Math. Cryptol. **14**, 414–437 (2020). https://doi.org/10.1515/jmc-2019-0034
32. Conrad, K.: The conductor ideal of an order. Expos. Paper. **1**, 2 (2024). https://kconrad.math.uconn.edu/blurbs/gradnumthy/conductor.pdf
33. Costello, C., Jao, D., Longa, P., Naehrig, M., Renes, J., Urbanik, D.: Efficient compression of SIDH public keys. In: Coron, J.S., Nielsen, J.B. (eds.) EUROCRYPT 2017, Part I. LNCS, vol. 10210, pp. 679–706. Springer, Cham (2017). https://doi.org/10.1007/978-3-319-56620-7_24
34. Couveignes, J.M.: Hard homogeneous spaces. Cryptology ePrint Archive, Report 2006/291 (2006). https://eprint.iacr.org/2006/291
35. Dartois, P., De Feo, L.: On the security of OSIDH. In: Hanaoka, G., Shikata, J., Watanabe, Y. (eds.) PKC 2022, Part I. LNCS, vol. 13177, pp. 52–81. Springer, Cham (2022). https://doi.org/10.1007/978-3-030-97121-2_3
36. De Feo, L., et al.: SCALLOP: Scaling the CSI-FiSh. In: Boldyreva, A., Kolesnikov, V. (eds.) PKC 2023, Part I. LNCS, vol. 13940, pp. 345–375. Springer, Cham (2023). https://doi.org/10.1007/978-3-031-31368-4_13
37. Decru, T.: Radical isogeny *inline image* formulae. In: Reyzin, L., Stebila, D. (eds.) CRYPTO 2024, Part V. LNCS, vol. 14924, pp. 107–128. Springer, Cham (2024). https://doi.org/10.1007/978-3-031-68388-6_5
38. Gajland, P., de Kock, B., Quaresma, M., Malavolta, G., Schwabe, P.: SWOOSH: efficient lattice-based non-interactive key exchange. In: Balzarotti, D., Xu, W. (eds.) USENIX Security 2024. USENIX Association (2024)
39. Hutchinson, A., LeGrow, J.T., Koziel, B., Azarderakhsh, R.: Further optimizations of CSIDH: A systematic approach to efficient strategies, permutations, and bound vectors. In: Conti, M., Zhou, J., Casalicchio, E., Spognardi, A. (eds.) ACNS 20International Conference on Applied Cryptography and Network Security, Part I. LNCS, vol. 12146, pp. 481–501. Springer, Cham (2020). https://doi.org/10.1007/978-3-030-57808-4_24
40. Jalali, A., Azarderakhsh, R., Kermani, M.M., Jao, D.: Towards optimized and constant-time CSIDH on embedded devices. In: Polian, I., Stöttinger, M. (eds.) COSADE 2019. LNCS, vol. 11421, pp. 215–231. Springer, Cham (2019). https://doi.org/10.1007/978-3-030-16350-1_12
41. Jao, D., De Feo, L.: Towards quantum-resistant cryptosystems from supersingular elliptic curve isogenies. In: Yang, B.-Y. (ed.) PQCrypto 2011. LNCS, vol. 7071, pp. 19–34. Springer, Heidelberg (2011). https://doi.org/10.1007/978-3-642-25405-5_2
42. Kuperberg, G.: A subexponential-time quantum algorithm for the dihedral hidden subgroup problem. SIAM J. Comput. **35**(1), 170–188 (2005). https://doi.org/10.1137/S0097539703436345
43. Kuperberg, G.: Another subexponential-time quantum algorithm for the dihedral hidden subgroup problem. In: 8th Conference on the Theory of Quantum Computation, Communication and Cryptography (TQC 2013). Leibniz International Proceedings in Informatics (LIPIcs), vol. 22, pp. 20–34 (2013). https://doi.org/10.4230/LIPIcs.TQC.2013.20
44. LeGrow, J., Hutchinson, A.: An analysis of fault attacks on CSIDH. Cryptology ePrint Archive, Report 2020/1006 (2020). https://eprint.iacr.org/2020/1006

45. LeGrow, J.T.: A faster method for fault attack resistance in static/ephemeral CSIDH. J. Cryptogr. Eng. **13**(3), 283–294 (2023). https://doi.org/10.1007/s13389-023-00318-0
46. LeGrow, J.T., Hutchinson, A.: (Short Paper) analysis of a strong fault attack on static/ephemeral CSIDH. In: Nakanishi, T., Nojima, R. (eds.) IWSEC 2021. LNCS, vol. 12835, pp. 216–226. Springer, Cham (2021). https://doi.org/10.1007/978-3-030-85987-9_12
47. Leonardi, C.: A note on the ending elliptic curve in SIDH. Cryptology ePrint Archive, Report 2020/262 (2020). https://eprint.iacr.org/2020/262
48. Maino, L., Martindale, C., Panny, L., Pope, G., Wesolowski, B.: A direct key recovery attack on SIDH. In: Hazay, C., Stam, M. (eds.) EUROCRYPT 2023, Part V. LNCS, vol. 14008, pp. 448–471. Springer, Cham (2023). https://doi.org/10.1007/978-3-031-30589-4_16
49. Meyer, M., Campos, F., Reith, S.: On lions and elligators: an efficient constant-time implementation of CSIDH. In: Ding, J., Steinwandt, R. (eds.) Post-Quantum Cryptography - 10th International Conference, PQCrypto 2019. pp. 307–325. Springer, Cham (2019). https://doi.org/10.1007/978-3-030-25510-7_17
50. Meyer, M., Reith, S.: A faster way to the CSIDH. In: Chakraborty, D., Iwata, T. (eds.) INDOCRYPT 2018. LNCS, vol. 11356, pp. 137–152. Springer, Cham (2018). https://doi.org/10.1007/978-3-030-05378-9_8
51. Moriya, T., Onuki, H., Takagi, T.: How to construct CSIDH on Edwards curves. In: Jarecki, S. (ed.) CT-RSA 2020. LNCS, vol. 12006, pp. 512–537. Springer, Cham (2020). https://doi.org/10.1007/978-3-030-40186-3_22
52. Onuki, H.: On oriented supersingular elliptic curves. Finite Fields App. **69**, 101777 (2021). https://doi.org/10.1016/j.ffa.2020.101777
53. Onuki, H., Aikawa, Y., Yamazaki, T., Takagi, T.: (Short paper) A faster constant-time algorithm of CSIDH keeping two points. In: Attrapadung, N., Yagi, T. (eds.) IWSEC 19. LNCS, vol. 11689, pp. 23–33. Springer, Cham (2019). https://doi.org/10.1007/978-3-030-26834-3_2
54. Onuki, H., Takagi, T.: On collisions related to an ideal class of order 3 in CSIDH. In: Aoki, K., Kanaoka, A. (eds.) IWSEC 20. LNCS, vol. 12231, pp. 131–148. Springer, Cham (2020). https://doi.org/10.1007/978-3-030-58208-1_8
55. Panny, L.: An open-source implementation of the CSIDH protocol. https://yx7.cc/code/csidh/csidh-20180826.tar.xz
56. Peikert, C.: He gives C-sieves on the CSIDH. In: Canteaut, A., Ishai, Y. (eds.) EUROCRYPT 2020, Part II. LNCS, vol. 12106, pp. 463–492. Springer, Cham (2020). https://doi.org/10.1007/978-3-030-45724-2_16
57. Pope, G.: An implementation of isogenies between Kummer Lines of Montgomery curves using $x$-only arithmetic. https://github.com/GiacomoPope/KummerIsogeny
58. Regev, O.: A subexponential time algorithm for the dihedral hidden subgroup problem with polynomial space (2004). https://arxiv.org/pdf/quant-ph/0406151
59. Reijnders, K.: Effective pairings in isogeny-based cryptography. In: Aly, A., Tibouchi, M. (eds.) LATINCRYPT 2023. LNCS, vol. 14168, pp. 109–128. Springer, Cham (2023). https://doi.org/10.1007/978-3-031-44469-2_6
60. Robert, D.: Breaking SIDH in polynomial time. In: Hazay, C., Stam, M. (eds.) EUROCRYPT 2023, Part V. LNCS, vol. 14008, pp. 472–503. Springer, Cham (2023). https://doi.org/10.1007/978-3-031-30589-4_17
61. Rostovtsev, A., Stolbunov, A.: Public-Key Cryptosystem Based On Isogenies. Cryptology ePrint Archive, Report 2006/145 (2006). https://eprint.iacr.org/2006/145

62. Sutherland, A.: Isogeny volcanoes. Open Book Ser. **1**(1), 507–530 (2013). https://doi.org/10.2140/obs.2013.1.507
63. Vélu, J.: Isogénies entre courbes elliptiques. Comptes-Rendus de l'Académie des Sciences **273**, 238–241 (1971)
64. Robert, D.: Fast pairings via biextensions and cubical arithmetic (2024). https://eprint.iacr.org/2024/517

# More Efficient Isogeny Proofs of Knowledge via Canonical Modular Polynomials

Thomas den Hollander, Sören Kleine, Marzio Mula, Daniel Slamanig, and Sebastian A. Spindler(✉)

Research Institute CODE, Universität der Bundeswehr München, München, Germany
{thomasdh,soeren.kleine,marzio.mula, daniel.slamanig,s.spindler}@unibw.de

**Abstract.** Proving knowledge of a secret isogeny has recently been proposed as a means to generate supersingular elliptic curves of unknown endomorphism ring, but is equally important for cryptographic protocol design as well as for real world deployments. Recently, Cong, Lai and Levin (ACNS'23) have investigated the use of general-purpose (non-interactive) zero-knowledge proof systems for proving the knowledge of an isogeny of degree $2^k$ between supersingular elliptic curves. In particular, their approach is to model this relation via a sequence of $k$ successive steps of a walk in the supersingular isogeny graph and to show that the respective $j$-invariants are roots of the second modular polynomial. They then arithmetize this relation and show that this approach, when compared to state-of-the-art tailor-made proofs of knowledge by Basso et al. (EUROCRYPT'23), gives a 3-10× improvement in proof and verification times, with comparable proof sizes.

In this paper we ask whether we can further improve the modular polynomial-based approach and generalize its application to primes $\ell > 2$, as used in some recent isogeny-based constructions. We will answer these questions affirmatively, by designing efficient arithmetizations for each $\ell \in \{2, 3, 5, 7, 13\}$ that achieve an improvement over Cong, Lai and Levin of up to 48%.

Our main technical tool and source of efficiency gains is to switch from classical modular polynomials to canonical modular polynomials. Adapting the well-known results on the former to the latter polynomials, however, is not straight-forward and requires some technical effort. We prove various interesting connections via novel use of resultant theory, and advance the understanding of canonical modular polynomials, which might be of independent interest.

## 1 Introduction

More than twenty years have passed since the seminal works by Couveignes [24], Rostovstev, and Stolbunov [59] have introduced the idea of using maps between elliptic curves, called *isogenies*, for cryptographic purposes. Although their original attempts seemed too inefficient to compare with concurrent cryptosystems,


Y. Tauman Kalai and S. F. Kamara (Eds.): CRYPTO 2025, LNCS 16000, pp. 131–166, 2025.
https://doi.org/10.1007/978-3-032-01855-7_5

later efforts in this direction [16,43] gave birth to a rich, and still lively, branch of cryptography.

A strong reason for researchers to push into this field is that the main problem on which it is based – namely, recovering a secret isogeny between two given elliptic curves – is considered hard even for quantum computers. Moreover, compared with other proposals for post-quantum cryptography, isogenies enjoy shorter parameters which though come at the price of slower performance. Since its proposal, isogeny-based cryptography has evolved into a very active and dynamic field, and many different cryptographic applications have been proposed so far.

In this work we are focusing on non-interactive zero-knowledge proofs of knowledge of secret isogenies, which are an important tool for cryptographic protocol design. An immediate application of such proofs is the design of signature schemes obtained via the Fiat-Shamir heuristic, e.g. GPS signatures [37], CSI-FiSh [12] or SQISign [29]. Moreover, they can be used to construct related primitives such as verifiable random functions (VRFs), as recently demonstrated using isogenies by Levin and Pedersen [48].

They also enable cryptographic tools that otherwise require a trusted setup. More precisely, such proofs have been studied for settings where one wants to avoid a trusted setup to generate supersingular curves of unknown endomorphism ring [9,21]. Such curves are needed for several isogeny-based protocols ranging from hash functions [17] to verifiable delay functions (VDFs) [14,30], delay encryption schemes [15], and public-key encryption [35,54]. In all these applications it is central to the security that the trapdoor is discarded after the trusted setup – a requirement that is hard to enforce in practice. Basso et al. [9] propose to implement a sequential multi-party ceremony to replace the trusted setup. Loosely speaking, they consider a walk in the isogeny graph

$$E_0 \to E_1 \to \cdots \to E_k$$

that starts from some (known) curve $E_0$ and then each party $i$ takes the previous curve $E_{i-1}$, generates a random isogeny to a new curve $E_i$ and provides a proof that they know the isogeny from $E_{i-1}$ to $E_i$. Such a protocol can be used to replace a trusted setup as long as one of the parties in the chain can be assumed to be honest (i.e. discards its secret isogeny).[1]

Finally, such proofs are a central tool to enforce honest behavior in multi-party protocols, where parties are forced to demonstrate that certain values such as (partial) public keys are well formed, e.g. in distributed key generation schemes [4,5]. These proofs-of-possession (PoPs) are, moreover, an important measure to prevent rogue key attacks in multi-party signature protocols [58]. In practice, this is required in public-key infrastructures (PKIs) when requesting the issuance of a certificate. In current PKIs based on X.509 certificates [22], these so-called certificate signing requests realize these PoPs via signatures.

[1] This is a technique often used to avoid a trusted setup for generating the structured reference string (SRS) for succinct non-interactive argument of knowledge systems (zk-SNARKs) [41], and can be seen as a variant where one uses explicit zero-knowledge proofs for the updates [1] instead of knowledge assumptions [41].

While this only works for certifying signing keys, it becomes more relevant in a post-quantum setting – for example, when certifying KEM keys for KEMTLS [60], one explicitly requires zero-knowledge proofs [42].

### 1.1 Previous Work

In general one can distinguish between *tailor-made* approaches and *generic* (or *general-purpose*) approaches to prove knowledge of isogenies in zero-knowledge. Subsequently, we are only focusing on work directly relevant to our approach, and we refer the reader to a recent comprehensive survey of proofs of knowledge of isogenies by Beullens et al. [11] for a complete overview.

For tailor-made approaches, the most recent work is the one of Basso et al. [9], which builds on the SIDH proof of knowledge from [27,28] and achieves statistical zero-knowledge. One main limitation of this (and most previous approaches, with the exception of [29]) is that the small challenge space requires numerous parallel executions of the protocol in order to reduce the soundness error. Moreover, the knowledge soundness achieved in [9] is not exact but only relaxed, i.e. while the relation is intended to prove knowledge of a $d$-isogeny, one can only extract an $\ell^{2i}d$-isogeny for some small prime $\ell$ and $0 \leq i \leq n$.

The second approach is to take a general-purpose (non-interactive) zero-knowledge proof system that is capable of proving any language in $\mathsf{NP}$, such as a zk-SNARK, and prove the respective isogeny relation using this proof system. While tailor-made approaches might intuitively seem to be more efficient than such a generic approach, there has been enormous progress in the field of zk-SNARKs over the last decade (cf. [63] for a good overview). This has led Cong, Lai and Levin [21] (CLL henceforth) to look into how well such an approach can perform when concretely instantiated with various recent general-purpose zero-knowledge proof systems. As a starting point CLL take the work by Chavez-Saab, Rodríguez-Henríquez and Tibouchi [18], which constructs isogeny-based verifiable delay functions (VDFs) [14] using a succinct non-interactive argument (SNARG) system. For the evaluation of their VDF they require to prove isogeny walks between supersingular elliptic curves. In brief, for a small prime $\ell$ they consider the supersingular isogeny graph of $\ell$-isogenous supersingular elliptic curves (represented by their $j$-invariants) and want to prove a walk in this graph. Their idea now is to consider the $\ell^{th}$ modular polynomial $\Phi_\ell(X,Y) \in \mathbb{Z}[X,Y]$, for which it holds that two curves $E$ and $E'$ are $\ell$-isogenous (over an algebraic closure) if and only if their $j$-invariants satisfy $\Phi_\ell(j(E), j(E')) = 0$. Consequently, when aiming to prove a walk in the $\ell$-isogeny graph from some starting curve $E$ to some curve $E'$, we can efficiently represent it as a sequence of successive steps, i.e. a sequence of $j$-invariants $j_0, j_1, \ldots, j_k$ such that $\Phi_\ell(j_i, j_{i+1}) = 0$ for all $i \in \{0, \ldots, k-1\}$, and $j_0 = j(E)$ and $j_k = j(E')$. This means that the relation[2]

$$\mathcal{R}_{\ell^k\text{-IsoPath}} = \{((E, E'), \phi) \mid \phi \colon E \to E' \text{ is an isogeny of degree } \ell^k\}$$

[2] In $\mathcal{R}_{\ell^k\text{-IsoPath}}$ we consider all $\ell^k$-isogenies defined over a fixed algebraic closure.

can equivalently be represented by means of the relation

$$\mathcal{R}_{\ell^k\text{-ModPoly}} = \left\{ \left((E, E'), (j_i)_{i\in[k-1]}\right) \;\middle|\; \begin{array}{c} \Phi_\ell(j(E), j_1) = 0 \;\wedge \\ \Phi_\ell(j_{k-1}, j(E')) = 0 \\ \bigwedge_{i\in[k-2]} \; \Phi_\ell(j_i, j_{i+1}) = 0 \end{array} \right\}. \tag{1}$$

We note that in [18] the authors do not require the zero-knowledge and knowledge soundness properties for the VDF application, and thus a SNARG suffices. CLL then use the above relation for the specific case of an isogeny of degree $2^k$ to construct a rank-1 constraint system (R1CS), which is a very popular arithmetization method in state-of-the-art zk-SNARKs. They then take a number of existing plausibly post-quantum zero-knowledge argument systems and in particular Aurora [10], Ligero [3] and Limbo [31], which do not need to make additional structured cryptographic assumptions (e.g. such as lattice-based proof systems for R1CS [13,56]).

Although CLL focus on $\ell = 2$, it is not uncommon for isogeny-based protocols to involve, or at least allow for, other small primes. For instance, the KEM presented in [54] makes use of a 3-smooth isogeny as a public key, and a 5- or 7-smooth isogeny for encapsulation. Similarly, a 3-smooth isogeny is used for the encryption in the PKE schemes from [33] and [8, Algorithm 4]. More generally, while the choice $\ell = 2$ is usually done for simplicity, considering different small primes can provide greater flexibility and also allows for trade-offs in the efficiency between the building blocks and the isogeny proofs of knowledge.

The results in [21] show that the efficiency of this general-purpose approach when compared with the recent tailor-made approach in [9] achieves an order of magnitude improvement over proof and verification times, with slightly worse but still comparable proof sizes. Moreover, compared to existing tailor-made solutions, this approach provides a stronger notion of soundness, i.e. an exact instead of a relaxed one.

> *In this work we ask whether this is the best we can do when targeting R1CS and whether the approach can be generalized to prove the knowledge of isogenies of degree $\ell^k$ for primes $\ell$ greater than* 2.

### 1.2 Our Contributions

The goal of this paper is to improve on the state-of-the-art results of [21] for proving the knowledge of an isogeny, and we make the following contributions.

**Use of Canonical Modular Polynomials.** We consider canonical modular polynomials in place of the classical modular polynomials used in [18,21], and we show that constructing a proof of knowledge of the corresponding relation $\mathcal{R}_{\ell^k\text{-ModRoot}}$ is computationally equivalent to proving the relations $\mathcal{R}_{\ell^k\text{-IsoPath}}$ and $\mathcal{R}_{\ell^k\text{-ModPoly}}$ mentioned above. While the approach via classical modular polynomials stems directly from well-known theoretical results, the same results are not as readily available for the case of canonical polynomials.

Therefore we incorporate them and prove connections to the classical modular polynomials via novel use of resultant theory. We also spot a few gaps in the relevant literature and provide new proofs of some basic properties of the modular polynomials over finite fields. For example, we analyze the existence of edges of multiplicity at least three in the supersingular $\ell$-isogeny graph for small $\ell$ – which seems to be known to experts of the field, at least in a weaker form – and we study the relationship between multiple edges in the $\ell$-isogeny graph on the one hand and multiple roots of the $\ell^{th}$ canonical modular polynomial on the other hand. Hence this part might also be of interest beyond the concrete application in this paper.

**Improved and Generalized Isogeny Proofs of Knowledge.** By moving to canonical modular polynomials we obtain a more efficient arithmetization for the equivalent relation $\mathcal{R}_{\ell^k\text{-ModPoly}}$. Moreover, while [21] only consider isogenies of 2-power degrees, we generalize the approach to cover isogenies of degree $\ell^k$, where $\ell \in \{2, 3, 5, 7, 13\}$. This is of interest not only because such primes are used in some recent isogeny-based constructions [8,33,54], but also because here we reduce the number of constraints further, potentially yielding even more efficient proof systems.

We first encode our new relation into an R1CS over the field $\mathbb{F}_{p^2}$, and subsequently lift these arithmetizations to $\mathbb{F}_p \times \mathbb{F}_p$ in order to obtain a formulation that works over $\mathbb{F}_p$. We are able to exploit the structured nature of the canonical modular polynomials to optimize the resulting arithmetizations. We describe several techniques to minimize the non-zero entries in the constraint matrices when lifting, such as a basis change for product relations and a change of variables for linear relations, which may be applicable more broadly. To give some intuition, this translates to a concrete reduction in prover times from roughly 1.2 s to 700 ms and in verifier time from roughly 100 ms to 60 ms for the identification scheme over $\mathbb{F}_p$ described in [21]. Additionally, we provide a circuit for backtracking prevention that is three times more efficient compared to [21]. All these improvements are presented in Sect. 5.

As multiple of our proofs contain involved calculations, we verify the necessary computational claims with SageMath scripts that can be found in the accompanying GitHub repository[3].

### 1.3 High-Level Overview

To improve upon the previous approach of [21], we introduce the canonical modular polynomials $\Phi_\ell^c(X, j)$ and study how, for $\ell \in \{2, 3, 5, 7, 13\}$ and a fixed $j$-invariant, their roots relate to $\ell$-isogenies: First, we use resultant theory to arrive at the Multiplicity Theorem, which states that the number of $\ell$-isogenies $j_0 \to j_1$ agrees with the number of solutions of the equation system

$$\Phi_\ell^c(X, j_0) = 0 = \Phi_\ell^c(\ell^s/X, j_1), \tag{2}$$

[3] https://github.com/QuSAC/IsogenyPoKviaCanonicalModPolys.

with the integer exponent $s = 12/(\ell - 1)$.

Next, we argue why, in most cases, there are at most two such solutions/isogenies, which allows for efficient computation of these roots via the Euclidean algorithm. Then, except at the $j$-invariants 0 and 1728, the connection between the solutions and $\ell$-isogenies is made more explicit in the Reconstruction Theorem by systematically associating to a solution of the above system (2) a kernel polynomial describing an $\ell$-isogeny $j_0 \to j_1$. As we can recover the solution from the coefficients of said kernel polynomial, we use this result as our main tool to show that the solutions lie in $\mathbb{F}_{p^2}$ when considering supersingular $j$-invariants. Finally, we demonstrate how the developed theory can be leveraged to yield an efficient arithmetization by encoding (a slightly modified variant of) the equation system (2) as an R1CS over both $\mathbb{F}_{p^2}$ and $\mathbb{F}_p$, where we optimize the number of variables, constraints and non-zero entries.

## 2 Preliminaries

### 2.1 Isogeny Graphs and Classical Modular Polynomials

Let $K$ be a perfect field, and let $E_0, E_1$ be elliptic curves over $K$. An *isogeny* is a morphism of curves $\phi\colon E_0 \longrightarrow E_1$ which induces also a surjective group homomorphism on the sets of $\overline{K}$-rational points. An isogeny of degree $n$ is also called an *$n$-isogeny*, and two elliptic curves $E_0$ and $E_1$ over $K$ are called *$n$-isogenous* if there exists an $n$-isogeny $\phi\colon E_0 \longrightarrow E_1$. An isogeny of degree 1 is called an *isomorphism*, an isogeny $\phi\colon E \longrightarrow E$ is called an *endomorphism*, and an endomorphism of degree 1 is called an *automorphism*. We refer the interested reader to the full version of this article [32, Appendix A.1] for other standard definitions, properties and references on elliptic curves and isogenies.

We will say that two $n$-isogenies $\phi_1 : E \longrightarrow E_1$ and $\phi_2 : E \longrightarrow E_2$ are *equivalent* if they are the same up to post-composition with an isomorphism, i.e. if there exists an isomorphism $\sigma\colon E_1 \longrightarrow E_2$ such that $\phi_2 = \sigma \circ \phi_1$. The kernel of an isogeny $\phi$ can be represented by its *kernel polynomial* [45, §2.4], which is the square-free monic polynomial whose roots are precisely the $x$-coordinates of non-trivial points in the kernel of $\phi$. Closely related to kernel polynomials is the $n^{th}$ *division polynomial* $\psi_n$ of an elliptic curve $E$ (which we scale by $2y$ for even $n$ compared to the usual definition [65, p. 81], so that it is always a polynomial in $x$ only): It is the kernel polynomial of the multiplication-by-$n$ endomorphism scaled by the factor $n$ (resp. $2n$) for odd $n$ (resp. even $n$) as long as $\mathrm{char}(K)$ does not divide $n$.

To each elliptic curve $E$ defined over a field $K$ one can attach a *$j$-invariant* $j(E) \in K$ which can be computed efficiently from the coefficients of $E$. Two elliptic curves $E_0$ and $E_1$ are isomorphic if and only if $j(E_0) = j(E_1)$, and any $j_0 \in \overline{K}$ is the $j$-invariant of an elliptic curve defined over $K(j_0)$ [61, Proposition III.1.4]. By a slight abuse of terminology, we will often refer to the *number of non-equivalent $n$-isogenies $j_0 \to j_1$* to indicate the number of equivalence classes of $n$-isogenies starting from a fixed elliptic curve $E_0$ of $j$-invariant $j_0$ and landing on some elliptic curve of $j$-invariant $j_1$; note that the number of such equivalence classes does not depend on the choice of representative $E_0$ of $j_0$.

Now fix a prime $p$ and let $q = p^k$ for some positive integer $k$. An elliptic curve $E$ over $\mathbb{F}_q$ is called *supersingular* if the cardinality of $E(\mathbb{F}_q)$ is congruent to 1 modulo $p$ [65, Proposition 4.31]. Given a prime $\ell \neq p$, the *supersingular $\ell$-isogeny graph* $\mathcal{G}_\ell(p)$ is the directed multigraph defined as follows: The vertices of $\mathcal{G}_\ell(p)$ shall be the isomorphism classes of supersingular elliptic curves, which we parametrize by their $j$-invariants in $\mathbb{F}_{p^2}$ [61, Theorem V.3.1], and the number of edges $j_0 \to j_1$ is precisely the number of non-equivalent $\ell$-isogenies $j_0 \to j_1$.

The graph $\mathcal{G}_\ell(p)$ is connected, $(\ell+1)$-regular, and it is Ramanujan [19,57]. Furthermore, since every isogeny admits a dual isogeny [61, Theorem III.6.1-2], it can almost be considered as an undirected graph; however, curves of $j$-invariants 0 or 1728 have special automorphisms [61, Theorem III.10.1], which can cause asymmetries in the graph for $p \geq 5$: If we write $\mu(0) := 3$, $\mu(1728) := 2$ and $\mu(j) := 1$ for $j \notin \{0, 1728\}$, then there are $\mu(j_0)/\mu(j_1)$ times as many non-equivalent $\ell$-isogenies $j_0 \to j_1$ as there are non-equivalent $\ell$-isogenies $j_1 \to j_0$ (cf. [2, Formula (11)]).

In this paper we will consider random walks on $\mathcal{G}_\ell(p)$, i.e. sequences

$$j(E_0) \longrightarrow j(E_1) \longrightarrow \ldots \longrightarrow j(E_k)$$

of adjacent $j$-invariants in $\mathcal{G}_\ell(p)$. It is easy to check whether two given $j$-invariants belong to a pair of $\ell$-isogenous elliptic curves. To this end, one can use the so-called *classical modular polynomials* (see [55, §4.3], [2, §2.4] and [62, §2.3]): The $\ell^{th}$ classical modular polynomial $\Phi_\ell(X,Y)$ is a bivariate polynomial with integer coefficients whose roots are given by the pairs of $j$-invariants of $\ell$-isogenous elliptic curves – more precisely, given the prime $\ell$ and any two elliptic curves $E$, $E'$ over a field $K$ with $\mathrm{char}(K) \neq \ell$, the number of non-equivalent $\ell$-isogenies $E \to E'$ is equal to the multiplicity of $j(E')$ as a root of $\Phi_\ell(j(E), Y)$.

### 2.2 Resultants

Let $R$ be an integral domain and let $g, h \in R[X]$ be non-zero polynomials. The *Sylvester matrix* of $g$ and $h$ and especially its determinant, the *resultant* $\mathrm{res}(g,h)$ of $g$ and $h$, are important algebraic tools to detect common divisors between two polynomials. We only state the necessary properties here and give the theoretical background together with proofs for the below results in the full version of this article [32, Appendix B].

**Proposition 1.** *Let $R$ be an integral domain, let $g, h \in R[X]$ be non-zero polynomials and let $\varphi\colon R \to S$ be a ring homomorphism of integral domains, extended to a ring homomorphism $\varphi\colon R[X] \to S[X]$ via coefficient-wise application. Then the following holds:*

(a) *If $\varphi$ preserves the degrees of $g$ and $h$, then*

$$\mathrm{res}(\varphi(g), \varphi(h)) = \varphi(\mathrm{res}(g,h)).$$

(b) $\mathrm{res}(g,h) = 0$ *if and only if $g$ and $h$ share a common divisor of positive degree.*

*Remark 1.* We note that, as the *discriminant* of $g$ is defined as the resultant of $g$ and $\frac{\partial}{\partial X} g$ up to scaling, the above results also translate to the discriminant.

**Proposition 2.** *Let $R = K[Y]$ be a polynomial ring over a field $K$ and fix an element $y_0 \in K$. Additionally let $g, h \in R[X]$ be non-zero polynomials and extend the $K$-linear evaluation homomorphism $\varphi \colon R \to K$ given by $Y \mapsto y_0$ to a ring homomorphism $\varphi \colon R[X] \to K[X]$ via coefficient-wise application. Further suppose that $\varphi$ preserves the $X$-degrees of $g$ and $h$, and write*

$$m := \deg \gcd(\varphi(g), \varphi(h)).$$

*Then*

$$\left.\frac{\partial^k}{\partial Y^k}\right|_{Y=y_0} \mathrm{res}_X(g, h) = 0 \text{ for } k \in \{0, \ldots, m-1\}.$$

### 2.3 Zero-Knowledge Argument Systems and R1CS

As stated before, in this work we will use generic techniques to prove the knowledge of isogenies, improving and expanding on the previous results of [21]. Since our arithmetization is broadly applicable across different argument systems and we do not need any formal properties of an argument system throughout this work, we will omit a full formal treatment of zk-SNARKS. For a comprehensive formal treatment, readers are referred to the respective proof systems [3,10,66].

A *zk-SNARK* is a non-interactive argument system that is complete, knowledge-sound, zero-knowledge and succinct. The proving algorithm takes a statement and witness pair $(s, w)$ for some NP-relation and generates a proof $\pi$. There is a verification algorithm to check the validity of a proof. Completeness indicates that a valid proof can be generated from any pair $(s, w)$ in the relation. Knowledge soundness means that any prover that can generate a valid proof for a statement $s$ needs to know a corresponding witness $w$. Zero-knowledge means that the proof does not reveal any information about the witness. An argument system is succinct if the proof size is small and the proof can be verified efficiently. Usually, both proof size and verifier time are required to be polynomial in $|x|$ and polylogarithmic in $|w|$.

In this paper we design an efficient arithmetization in the form of a rank-1 constraint system (R1CS). This represents a popular choice of arithmetization and it allows us to cover many different proof systems. An R1CS is defined as follows:

**Definition 1** ([10]). *The relation $\mathcal{R}_{R1CS}$ is the set of pairs $((\mathbb{F}, k, n, m, A, B, C, v), w)$ where $\mathbb{F}$ is a finite field, $k, n, m \in \mathbb{N}$ denote the numbers of inputs, variables and constraints respectively ($k \leq n$), $A$, $B$, $C$ are $m \times (1+n)$-matrices over $\mathbb{F}$, $v \in \mathbb{F}^k$, and $w \in \mathbb{F}^{n-k}$, such that for all $i \in [m]$*

$$\left(\sum_{j=0}^{n} A_{ij} z_j\right) \cdot \left(\sum_{j=0}^{n} B_{ij} z_j\right) = \left(\sum_{j=0}^{n} C_{ij} z_j\right),$$

*where $(1, v, w) =: z = (z_j)_j \in \mathbb{F}^{1+n}$.*

It is worth noting that the efficiency of proving and verifying knowledge of a witness may depend on different aspects of the R1CS, depending on the proof system that is used. For example, the prover time of pairing-based SNARKs is usually $O(n)$, the proof size is constant, and the verifier time is $O(k)$ [40,50]. On the other hand, [3,10,67] have prover time proportional to the circuit size, which corresponds to the number of non-zero entries in the constraint matrices $A$, $B$ and $C$, which we will denote by nnz. Lastly, for [31] the proof size and prover and verifier times seem to be determined by the number of multiplications, corresponding to the number of R1CS constraints $m$. The efficiency of the arithmetization in [21] is only quantified through the number of constraints $m$ and optimized using this metric.

In this work, we will provide all of $n$, $m$ and nnz. When optimizing, we will focus on the latter two, since the number of variables is mostly relevant for the non-post-quantum secure pairing-based SNARKs. Often, optimizing for one metric also improves another, such as when a linear constraint can be removed to eliminate a variable, but this is not always the case. As we will see in Sect. 5, we achieve very efficient constraint systems in terms of all three metrics.

## 3 Canonical Modular Polynomials

The classical modular polynomials tend to have many non-vanishing coefficients, which makes these polynomials quite expensive to handle in an R1CS. To be more precise, the polynomial $\Phi_\ell(X, Y)$ is symmetric in $X$ and $Y$, of degree $\ell + 1$ in both variables [46, Theorem 5.2.3], and typically most of the possible mixed monomials $X^iY^j$ with $i, j \leq \ell$ occur. For example, the third classical modular polynomial is given by (see [20, Example 17.18])

$$\begin{aligned}\Phi_3(X, Y) = &-X^3Y^3 + X^4 + Y^4 + 2232(X^3Y^2 + X^2Y^3)\\ &- 1069956(X^3Y + XY^3) + 36864000(X^3 + Y^3)\\ &+ 2587918086X^2Y^2 + 8900222976000(X^2Y + XY^2)\\ &+ 452984832000000(X^2 + Y^2) - 770845966336000000XY\\ &+ 1855425871872000000000(X + Y).\end{aligned}$$

Luckily, there is a related class of polynomials called *canonical modular polynomials* $\Phi_\ell^c$ [47, §3.3.2][53, §2.2][55, §5.1-2], which are asymmetric and have a smaller degree in the second variable. To contrast our previous example, the third canonical modular polynomial is given by

$$\Phi_3^c(X, j) = X^4 + 36X^3 + 270X^2 + 756X + 729 - X \cdot j.$$

**The general (modular) construction.** In general, the $\ell^{th}$ canonical modular polynomial is constructed as follows: Letting $s = 12/\gcd(12, \ell - 1)$ denote the smallest non-zero natural number such that

$$\kappa := \frac{s \cdot (\ell - 1)}{12}$$

is an integer, and letting $\eta$ denote the Dedekind $\eta$ function, the function

$$f(\tau) := \ell^s \left( \frac{\eta(\ell \tau)}{\eta(\tau)} \right)^{2s}$$

is a modular function of weight 0 that is invariant under Möbius transformations of $\tau$ given by elements of

$$\Gamma_0(\ell) = \left\{ \begin{pmatrix} a & b \\ c & d \end{pmatrix} \in \mathrm{SL}_2(\mathbb{Z}) \colon c \equiv 0 \bmod \ell \right\}.$$

The finitely many cosets of $\mathrm{SL}_2(\mathbb{Z})/\Gamma_0(\ell)$ are represented by the matrices

$$S_n = \begin{pmatrix} 0 & -1 \\ 1 & n \end{pmatrix}, \ 0 \leq n < \ell, \quad \text{and} \quad S_\ell = \begin{pmatrix} 1 & 0 \\ 0 & 1 \end{pmatrix},$$

and one defines the canonical modular polynomial as

$$\Phi_\ell^c(X) := \prod_{n=0}^{\ell} (X - f(S_n(\tau))) = (X - f(\tau)) \prod_{n=0}^{\ell-1} \left( X - f\left( \frac{-1}{\tau + n} \right) \right).$$

This polynomial can now be expressed as a polynomial $\Phi_\ell^c(X, j)$ with integer coefficients in $X$ and the $j$-invariant $j = j(\tau)$, which itself is a modular function of weight 0 invariant under transformations given by matrices in $\mathrm{SL}_2(\mathbb{Z})$. Moreover, the degree of $\Phi_\ell^c(X, j)$ in the second variable $j$ is given by $\kappa$ (see [55, Eq. (5.1-2) and Lemma 5.7]).

**Restricting to $\ell \in \{2, 3, 5, 7, 13\}$.** The $\ell^{th}$ canonical modular polynomial thus has, for suitable coefficients $c_{i,m} \in \mathbb{Z}$, the form

$$\Phi_\ell^c(X, j) = \sum_{i=0}^{\ell+1} \sum_{m=0}^{\kappa} c_{i,m} X^i j^m.$$

In the case $\kappa = 1$, i.e. $\ell \in \{2, 3, 5, 7, 13\}$, these polynomials are hence quite small – we list them in the full version of this article [32, Appendix A.2], and hereafter we will work with these explicitly given polynomials directly.

**Lemma 1.** *Let $\ell \in \{2, 3, 5, 7, 13\}$. Setting $c_i := c_{i,0} \in \mathbb{Z}$, the $\ell^{th}$ canonical modular polynomial $\Phi_\ell^c(X, j)$ then is of the form*

$$\Phi_\ell^c(X, j) = X^{\ell+1} + \sum_{i=1}^{\ell} c_i X^i + \ell^s - X \cdot j = \Phi_\ell^c(X, 0) - X \cdot j.$$

*In particular, the rational function*

$$\Theta_\ell^c(X,j) := \Phi_\ell^c(\ell^s/X,j)\cdot X^{\ell+1}/\ell^s = X^{\ell+1} + \sum_{i=1}^{\ell} c_i \ell^{s\cdot(i-1)} X^{\ell+1-i} + \ell^{s\cdot\ell} - X^\ell \cdot j$$

*is a polynomial with integer coefficients. With* $\mathcal{J}_\ell(X) := \Phi_\ell^c(X,0)/X$ *we furthermore have that for any* $f \in K^\times$ *and* $j_0 \in K$*:*

$$j_0 = \mathcal{J}_\ell(f) \quad \textit{if and only if} \quad \Phi_\ell^c(f,j_0) = 0.$$

*Proof.* The claim on the form of $\Phi_\ell^c(X,j)$ follows from direct inspection, and the claim on the form of $\Theta_\ell^c(X,j)$ is an immediate consequence. Furthermore we have $\Phi_\ell^c(X,j) = X\cdot\mathcal{J}_\ell(X) - X\cdot j$, which implies the claim on $\mathcal{J}_\ell(X)$. □

Since the constant coefficients of $\Phi_\ell^c(X,j)$ and $\Theta_\ell^c(X,j)$ are powers of $\ell$, we obtain:

**Corollary 1.** *Let* $\ell \in \{2,3,5,7,13\}$, *assume* $\mathrm{char}(K) \neq \ell$ *and let* $j_0, j_1 \in K$ *be* $j$*-invariants with* $j_0 \neq j_1$*. Then*

$$\gcd(\Phi_\ell^c(X,j_0),\Phi_\ell^c(X,j_1)) = 1 = \gcd(\Theta_\ell^c(X,j_0),\Theta_\ell^c(X,j_1)).$$

**Roadmap for this Section.** In Subsect. 3.1 we investigate how, for a given $j_0 \in K$, the roots of $\Phi_\ell^c(X,j_0)$ relate to the number of $\ell$-isogenies $j_0 \to j_1$ to some $j_1 \in K$, culminating in the Multiplicity Theorem. Then we discuss in Subsect. 3.2 how many of the related $\ell$-isogenies can lead to the same target $j_1$ (Proposition 4, Theorem 1, Corollary 2) to argue how these roots can be computed efficiently. Finally, we analyze in Subsect. 3.3 in which field extension a root $f$ lies by giving a connection to kernel polynomials via the Reconstruction Theorem, which we then exploit together with previous results to determine the splitting behavior of $\Phi_\ell^c(X,j_0)$ for a supersingular $j$-invariant $j_0$ in Theorem 2.

In relation to $\ell$-isogenies, the above mentioned restriction to the five primes $\ell \in \{2,3,5,7,13\}$ satisfying $\kappa = 1$ also has a conceptual reason. In fact, these primes are precisely those for which the modular curve $X_0(\ell)$ has genus 0 by [64, Proposition 2.3.5]. In relation to the modular construction, this gives a high-level intuition of why we obtain a compact representation of $\ell$-isogenies: The elements of $X_0(\ell)$, which are the edges in $\mathcal{G}_\ell(p)$, can then be parametrized (up to issues at the 'ramified' points $j \in \{0,1728\}$) by $f \in \overline{\mathbb{F}_p}^\times$. This parametrization, which we will later analyze in the Reconstruction Theorem, has already been studied in the works of Fricke [36, Section 2, Chaps. 4-5], Mestre [52, §5], and Elkies [34, §4].

### 3.1 The Multiplicity Theorem

Unfortunately, it is no longer true that $\Phi_\ell^c(j_0,j_1) = 0$ if $j_0$ and $j_1$ are $\ell$-isogenous $j$-invariants in $\overline{\mathbb{F}_p}$. Instead, taking inspiration from the modular interpretation given e.g. by [47, p. 41], we will show that we need to find a common root $f$ of the two functions $\Phi_\ell^c(X, j_0)$ and $\Phi_\ell^c(\ell^s/X, j_1)$, where $s = 12/(\ell-1)$ is defined as above. To prove a more precise version of this claim, we first relate the classical modular polynomial to the canonical modular polynomial via resultant theory.

**Proposition 3.** *For any $\ell \in \{2, 3, 5, 7, 13\}$ we have, computing over the coefficient ring $R = \mathbb{Z}[J_0, J_1]$, the resultant equation*

$$\mathrm{res}_X(\Theta_\ell^c(X, J_1), \Phi_\ell^c(X, J_0)) = \ell^{s\cdot\ell} \cdot \Phi_\ell(J_0, J_1).$$

*In particular, suppose that we have a field $K$ of characteristic $\mathrm{char}(K) \notin [\ell]$ as well as $j_0, j_1 \in K$ with $m := \deg\gcd(\Phi_\ell^c(X, j_0), \Theta_\ell^c(X, j_1))$. Then*

$$\left.\frac{\partial^k}{\partial J_1^k}\right|_{J_1=j_1} \Phi_\ell(j_0, J_1) = 0 \text{ for } k \in \{0, \ldots, m-1\},$$

*i.e. there are at least $m$ non-equivalent $\ell$-isogenies from $j_0$ to $j_1$.*

*Proof.* The first claim is checked in the script `additional_computations.sage`. For the second claim we first apply the ring homomorphism $\mathbb{Z}[J_0] \to K$ defined by $J_0 \mapsto j_0$ in view of Proposition 1(a) to obtain in $K[J_1]$ the equality

$$\mathrm{res}_X(\Theta_\ell^c(X, J_1), \Phi_\ell^c(X, j_0)) = \ell^{s\cdot\ell} \cdot \Phi_\ell(j_0, J_1).$$

Now we consider the $K$-linear evaluation homomorphism $\varphi\colon K[J_1] \to K$ given by $J_1 \mapsto j_1$, extended via coefficient-wise application to $\varphi\colon K[J_1][X] \to K[X]$. As $\varphi$ preserves the $X$-degrees of $g := \Theta_\ell^c(X, J_1)$ and $h := \Phi_\ell^c(X, j_0)$, we are exactly in the situation of Proposition 2. With $\mathrm{char}(K) \notin [\ell]$ we thus deduce that $\mathrm{res}_X(g, h) = \ell^{s\cdot\ell} \cdot \Phi_\ell(j_0, J_1)$ has a root of multiplicity at least $m$ at $j_1$, and $\mathrm{char}(K) \neq \ell$ yields the claim. □

The previous relation will be the main tool in establishing the desired connection between the classical and the canonical modular polynomial. For the proof we need to analyze root multiplicities of the canonical modular polynomial in the next two results, which can also be found in [64, §4.3] in the language of modular curves.

**Lemma 2.** *Let $\ell \in \{2, 3, 5, 7, 13\}$, assume $\mathrm{char}(K) \neq \ell$ and let $j_0 \in K$. Then $\Phi_\ell^c(X, j_0)$ has a double root in $\overline{K}$ if and only if $j_0 = 0$ or $j_0 = 1728$.*

*Proof.* To simplify notation we may assume that $K$ is algebraically closed. In view of Lemma 1 we obtain the univariate polynomial

$$\mathcal{D}_\ell(X) := j + \tfrac{\partial}{\partial X}\Phi_\ell^c(X, j).$$

Now an element $f \in K$ is a double root of $\Phi_\ell^c(X, j_0)$ if and only if it is non-zero (due to $\mathrm{char}(K) \neq \ell$) and satisfies $\mathcal{J}_\ell(f) = j_0 = \mathcal{D}_\ell(f)$. From this we see that the double roots are precisely the common roots of $\Phi_\ell^c(X, j_0)$ and the polynomial

$$\mathcal{D}_\ell(X) \cdot X - \mathcal{J}_\ell(X) \cdot X = -\Phi_\ell^c(X, \mathcal{D}_\ell(X)),$$

which has leading coefficient $\ell$. In the script `additional_computations.sage` we check that there are $e, m, n \in \mathbb{N}$ such that

$$\text{res}_X(\Phi_\ell^c(X, J), -\Phi_\ell^c(X, \mathcal{D}_\ell(X))) = (-1)^\ell \cdot \ell^e \cdot (J - 0)^m \cdot (J - 1728)^n,$$

computed over the coefficient ring $R = \mathbb{Z}[J]$. Therefore $\text{char}(K) \neq \ell$ allows us to apply Proposition 1 (with the homomorphism $\mathbb{Z}[J] \to K$ given by the evaluation $J \mapsto j_0$) to deduce the claimed equivalence. □

The second result discusses the special $j$-invariants 0 and 1728; for an explicit list of the factors given below we refer the reader to the full version of the article [32, Appendix A.3].

**Lemma 3.** *For each $\ell \in \{2, 3, 5, 7, 13\}$ there are ($\ell$-dependent) monic polynomials $g_0$ and $g_{1728}$ in $\mathbb{Z}[X]$ of degree at most 2 and ($\ell$-dependent) monic non-constant polynomials $h_{0,\pm}$ and $h_{1728,\pm}$ in $\mathbb{Z}[X]$ such that*

$$\Phi_\ell^c(X, 0) = g_0 \cdot h_{0,+}^3, \quad \Theta_\ell^c(X, 0) = g_0 \cdot h_{0,-}^3$$

*and*

$$\Phi_\ell^c(X, 1728) = g_{1728} \cdot h_{1728,+}^2, \quad \Theta_\ell^c(X, 1728) = g_{1728} \cdot h_{1728,-}^2.$$

*Moreover, if $K$ is a field with $\text{char}(K) \notin \{2, 3, \ell\}$ and $j^* \in \{0, 1728\}$, then each $h_{j^*,\pm}$ has only simple roots, and does not share any roots with $g_{j^*}$ in $\overline{K}$.*

*Proof.* In the SageMath script `additional_computations.sage` we confirm the above factorizations as well as that, for $j^* \in \{0, 1728\}$, the prime factors of $\deg(h_{j^*,\pm})$ lie in $\{2, 3\}$, and that the prime factors of $\text{disc}(h_{j^*,\pm})$ and $\text{res}(g_{j^*}, h_{j^*,\pm})$ lie in $\{2, 3, \ell\}$. To prove the additional claim, we now make use of resultant theory once more by considering the unique homomorphism $\varphi\colon \mathbb{Z} \to K$. This homomorphism preserves the degree of $h_{j^*,\pm}$ and, as the prime factors of $\deg(h_{j^*,\pm})$ are contained in $\{2, 3\}$, the degree of $\frac{\partial}{\partial X} h_{j^*,\pm}$ due to our assumption on $\text{char}(K)$. Therefore this assumption and Proposition 1(a) (cf. Remark 1) yield

$$\text{disc}(\varphi(h_{j^*,\pm})) = \varphi(\text{disc}(h_{j^*,\pm})) \neq 0,$$

so $h_{j^*,\pm}$ cannot have a double root in $\overline{K}$ by Proposition 1(b). Similarly we obtain

$$\text{res}(\varphi(g_{j^*}), \varphi(h_{j^*,\pm})) = \varphi(\text{res}(g_{j^*}, h_{j^*,\pm})) \neq 0,$$

i.e. $g_{j^*}$ and $h_{j^*,\pm}$ cannot have a common root in $\overline{K}$ by Proposition 1(b). □

With the above preparations we are finally ready to state and prove the following crucial relation between the classical and canonical modular polynomial:

**Multiplicity Theorem.** *Let $\ell \in \{2, 3, 5, 7, 13\}$, let $K$ be a field of characteristic $\text{char}(K) \notin \{2, \ldots, \ell\}$ and let $j_0, j_1 \in K$. Then there are exactly as many non-equivalent $\ell$-isogenies $j_0 \to j_1$ as there are roots $f \in \overline{K}^\times$ of $\Phi_\ell^c(X, j_0)$ (counted with multiplicity) such that $\Phi_\ell^c(\ell^s/f, j_1) = 0$. In particular, $j_0$ and $j_1$ are $\ell$-isogenous if and only if there exists an $f \in \overline{K}^\times$ such that*

$$\Phi_\ell^c(f, j_0) = 0 = \Phi_\ell^c(\ell^s/f, j_1). \tag{MT}$$

*Proof.* To simplify notation we assume that $K$ is algebraically closed. As before we consider the polynomial $\Theta_\ell^c(X, j_1) = \Phi_\ell^c(\ell^s/X, j_1) \cdot X^{\ell+1}/\ell^s$ instead of the rational function $\Phi_\ell^c(\ell^s/X, j_1)$, noting that it has the same roots due to $\mathrm{char}(K) \neq \ell$. For any $j_0, j_1 \in K$ we write $\beta_\ell(j_0, j_1)$ for the number of roots of $\Phi_\ell^c(X, j_0)$ (counted with multiplicity) that are roots of $\Theta_\ell^c(X, j_1)$, and we write $\nu_\ell(j_0, j_1)$ for the number of non-equivalent $\ell$-isogenies from $j_0$ to $j_1$.

Hence our goal is to show that $\beta_\ell(j_0, j_1) = \nu_\ell(j_0, j_1)$; however, it suffices to prove the inequality $\beta_\ell(j_0, j_1) \leq \nu_\ell(j_0, j_1)$ for all $j_0, j_1 \in K$. Indeed, summing both quantities over all possible $j_1$ for a fixed $j_0 \in K$ then yields

$$\ell + 1 = \deg_X(\Phi_\ell^c(X, j_0)) = \sum_{j_1 \in K} \beta_\ell(j_0, j_1) \leq \sum_{j_1 \in K} \nu_\ell(j_0, j_1) = \ell + 1$$

in view of Lemma 1, and thus all inequalities have to be equalities.

To prove the inequalities, we first note that Proposition 3 immediately yields

$$\deg \gcd(\Phi_\ell^c(X, j_0), \Theta_\ell^c(X, j_1)) \leq \nu_\ell(j_0, j_1). \tag{3}$$

We will use this inequality in the following, but we need to work through a slightly tedious case distinction: First, if $j_0 \notin \{0, 1728\}$, then any root of $\Phi_\ell^c(X, j_0)$ is a simple root by Lemma 2, so

$$\beta_\ell(j_0, j_1) = \deg \gcd(\Phi_\ell^c(X, j_0), \Theta_\ell^c(X, j_1)) \leq \nu_\ell(j_0, j_1).$$

Next we consider an edge case: Let $\mathrm{char}(K) = 3$ and let $j_0 = j^* = 0 = 1728$ be the unique supersingular $j$-invariant in $K$ (cf. [61, §V.4]). Then all $\ell + 1$ non-equivalent $\ell$-isogenies starting from $j^*$ are loops, and one can directly verify that we have $\Theta_\ell^c(X, 0) = \Phi_\ell^c(X, 0)$ over $K$. Therefore, for $j_1 \neq j^*$, Corollary 1 yields

$$\beta_\ell(j^*, j^*) = \ell + 1 = \nu_\ell(j^*, j^*) \quad \text{and} \quad \beta_\ell(j^*, j_1) = 0 = \nu_\ell(j^*, j_1);$$

thus we may now assume $\mathrm{char}(K) \notin \{2, 3, \ell\}$. To proceed we recall the multiplicity factors

$$\mu(0) = 3, \quad \mu(1728) = 2 \quad \text{and} \quad \mu(j) = 1$$

for $j \in K \setminus \{0, 1728\}$, and consider a special $j$-invariant $j_0 = j^* \in \{0, 1728\}$. For $j^* \neq j_1$ any (distinct) root $f$ of $\Phi_\ell^c(X, j^*)$ such that $\Theta_\ell^c(f, j_1) = 0$ then has multiplicity $\mu(j^*)$ (resp. $\mu(j_1)$) as a root of $\Phi_\ell^c(X, j^*)$ (resp. of $\Theta_\ell^c(X, j_1)$). Indeed, if $j_1 \notin \{0, 1728\}$ the second claim follows from Lemma 2, and otherwise all multiplicities are derived from Lemma 3 since Corollary 1 and the assumption $j^* \neq j_1$ force $f$ to be a root of $h_{j^*,+}$ and $h_{j_1,-}$ (if $j_1 \in \{0, 1728\}$), which only have simple roots by our restriction on the characteristic.

With the inequality (3) and $\mu(1728) < \mu(0)$ we hence see that the roots of the greatest common divisor of $\Phi_\ell^c(X, 1728)$ and $\Theta_\ell^c(X, 0)$ all have multiplicity $\mu(1728)$, so we obtain

$$\beta_\ell(1728, 0) = \deg \gcd(\Phi_\ell^c(X, 1728), \Theta_\ell^c(X, 0)) \leq \nu_\ell(1728, 0).$$

Using the multiplicity-preserving correspondence $f \mapsto \ell^s/f$ between roots of $\Phi_\ell^c(X, j)$ and roots of $\Theta_\ell^c(X, j)$, we further deduce from the above analysis that

$$\beta_\ell(j^*, j_1) = \tfrac{\mu(j^*)}{\mu(j_1)} \cdot \beta_\ell(j_1, j^*) \leq \tfrac{\mu(j^*)}{\mu(j_1)} \cdot \nu_\ell(j_1, j^*) = \nu_\ell(j^*, j_1)$$

in all other cases with $j^* \neq j_1$, where the middle inequality has been derived in previous cases and the last equality is due to the larger automorphism groups at the special $j$-invariants 0 and 1728, as explained in Subsect. 2.1.

The final case to consider is $j^* = j_1$, where Lemma 3 also does the heavy lifting: Here any root $f$ of $\Phi_\ell^c(X, j^*)$ is either a root of $g_{j^*}$ – then with the same multiplicity for both $\Phi_\ell^c(X, j^*)$ and $\Theta_\ell^c(X, j^*)$ – or it is a root of both $h_{j^*,\pm}$, in which case its multiplicity for both $\Phi_\ell^c(X, j^*)$ and $\Theta_\ell^c(X, j^*)$ is $\mu(j^*)$ since each $h_{j^*,\pm}$ only has simple roots. Therefore we also deduce

$$\beta_\ell(j^*, j^*) = \deg \gcd(\Phi_\ell^c(X, j^*), \Theta_\ell^c(X, j^*)) \leq \nu_\ell(j^*, j^*)$$

from the inequality (3), and this finishes the proof. □

*Remark 2.* In fact, it is true for all primes $\ell \in \mathbb{N}$ and $\ell$-isogenous $j$-invariants $j_0, j_1 \in \overline{\mathbb{F}_p}$ that we can always find a common root of the system (MT). Indeed, we can first view $j_0$ and $j_1$ as reductions modulo $p$ of CM $j$-invariants $J_0, J_1 \in \mathbb{C}$ ([46, Theorem 13.5.14]) that are integral by [25, Theorem 11.1]. Now Eqs. (5.2–4) in [55, §5] show that there is a common solution $\tilde{f} \in \mathbb{C}$ that has to be integral as it satisfies the polynomial $\Phi_\ell^c(X, J_0)$; therefore it can be reduced to a solution $f \in \overline{\mathbb{F}_p}$ of the system (MT).

However, the restriction to $\kappa = 1$ is crucial for the other direction: For example, for $\ell = 11$, $p = 61$ the $j$-invariants $j_0 = 41$ and $j_1 = 37$ are not $\ell$-isogenous over $\overline{\mathbb{F}_p}$; in fact, they are not even isogenous since $j_0$ is supersingular, whereas $j_1$ is ordinary. Nonetheless, either root of the polynomial $X^2 + 3X - 27 \in \mathbb{F}_{p^2}[X]$ gives a solution to the system (MT).

In spite of that, experiments seem to suggest that there are still *at most* as many $\ell$-isogenies $j_0 \to j_1$ as there are roots from $j_0$ to $j_1$ (counted as in the Multiplicity Theorem). Note that this does not contradict our previous findings since Corollary 1 fails for $\kappa > 1$: For instance, in our example we have

$$\gcd(\Phi_{11}^c(X, 41), \Phi_{11}^c(X, 50)) = X^2 - 30X - 1 \in \mathbb{F}_p[X].$$

### 3.2 Isogeny Relations and Root Computation

Recall that our goal is to build an efficient proof of knowledge for isogenies of degree $\ell^k$ (where $\ell \in \{2, 3, 5, 7, 13\}$), or, equivalently, for the relation $\mathcal{R}_{\ell^k\text{-ModPoly}}$ (Eq. (1)). However, to apply the canonical modular polynomials we instead need to consider the relation

$$\mathcal{R}_{\ell^k\text{-ModRoot}} := \left\{ \begin{array}{c} ((E, E'), \\ ((j_i)_{i\in[k-1]}, (f_i)_{i\in[k]})) \end{array} \middle| \begin{array}{c} \Phi_\ell^c(f_1, j(E)) = 0 \;\wedge \\ \Theta_\ell^c(f_k, j(E')) = 0 \\ \bigwedge_{i\in[k-1]} \Theta_\ell^c(f_i, j_i) = 0 = \Phi_\ell^c(f_{i+1}, j_i) \end{array} \right\}.$$

With the Multiplicity Theorem we see that simply omitting the roots $(f_i)_{i\in[k]}$ from the witness brings us back to $\mathcal{R}_{\ell^k\text{-ModPoly}}$, so this new relation requires additional information from the prover. To gauge the related additional work for the prover, we will investigate two questions: *How many roots can the system* (MT) *have? And in which field do these roots lie?*

**How Many Roots?** To answer the first question in view of the Multiplicity Theorem, we investigate the number of $\ell$-isogenies between $j$-invariants more closely. The following result is a consequence of the well-known structure of *ordinary isogeny volcanoes*:

**Proposition 4.** *Let $\ell$ be a prime and suppose that we have two $j$-invariants $j_0, j_1 \in \overline{\mathbb{F}_p}$ for some prime $p \neq \ell$. If $j_0$ is ordinary, then the following holds:*

(a) *If $j_0 \notin \{0, 1728\}$ or $j_0 = j_1$, then there are at most two non-equivalent $\ell$-isogenies $j_0 \to j_1$.*
(b) *If $j_0 = 0 \neq j_1$, then there are at most three non-equivalent $\ell$-isogenies $j_0 \to j_1$ and at most one $\ell$-isogeny $j_1 \to j_0$ up to equivalence.*
(c) *If $j_0 = 1728 \neq j_1$, then there are at most two non-equivalent $\ell$-isogenies $j_0 \to j_1$ and at most one $\ell$-isogeny $j_1 \to j_0$ up to equivalence.*

*Proof.* This follows immediately from [62, Theorem 7 & Remark 8] (note, however, that for $\ell = 2$ there is exactly 1 vertex at the first level of the ordinary isogeny graph component containing 1728 – the second formula given in Remark 8 only holds for odd $\ell$). □

*Remark 3.* Müller claims in [55, Lemma 4.14] that the $\ell + 1$ non-equivalent $\ell$-isogenies defined on an ordinary curve over $\mathbb{F}_p$ with $j$-invariant not in $\{0, 1728\}$ map to $\ell + 1$ distinct $j$-invariants, i.e. to $\ell + 1$ non-isomorphic elliptic curves. However, if we consider $p = 29$, $\ell = 7$ and the two $j$-invariants $j_0 = 23$ and $j_1 = 12$ (noting that $1728 \equiv 17 \bmod 29$), then the curve

$$E_0 \colon y^2 = x^3 + 21x + 26$$

satisfies $j(E_0) = 23 = j_0$ and admits two 7-isogenies $\alpha_1$ and $\alpha_2$ to the elliptic curve

$$E_1 \colon y^2 = x^3 + 6x + 9$$

of $j$-invariant $j(E_1) = 12 = j_1$.

Importantly, the kernels of these two 7-isogenies are distinct (and hence the isogenies are not equivalent) since their kernel polynomials

$$x^3 + 2x^2 + 21x + 16 \quad \text{and} \quad x^3 + 14x^2 + 13x + 23$$

are distinct. The issue is that the endomorphism $\widehat{\alpha}_2 \circ \alpha_1$ of degree $7^2$ is not equivalent to the multiplication-by-7 isogeny [7] on $E_0$, which again can be checked by comparing the kernel polynomials of these two endomorphisms.

In general, Proposition 4 does not extend to supersingular $j$-invariants – the following example can, using the Multiplicity Theorem, easily be checked with both the classical and the canonical modular polynomial:

*Example 1.* For $\ell = 7$ and $p = 71$ there are 6 non-equivalent $\ell$-isogenies $0 \to 48$, 2 non-equivalent $\ell$-isogenies $48 \to 0$ and 4 non-equivalent $\ell$-isogenies $40 \to 40$.

Luckily, we can strictly limit when the claims of Proposition 4 do not transfer to supersingular $j$-invariants in our setting:

**Theorem 1.** *Let $\ell \leq 13$ be a prime. Then there is a prime $p_\ell < 4\ell^3$ (given in Table 1) such that for any prime $p > p_\ell$ and any two supersingular $j$-invariants $j_0, j_1 \in \mathbb{F}_{p^2}$ the following holds:*

(a) *If $j_0 \notin \{0, 1728\}$ or $j_0 = j_1$, then there are at most two non-equivalent $\ell$-isogenies $j_0 \to j_1$.*
(b) *If $j_0 = 0 \neq j_1$, then there are at most three non-equivalent $\ell$-isogenies $j_0 \to j_1$ and at most one $\ell$-isogeny $j_1 \to j_0$ up to equivalence.*
(c) *If $j_0 = 1728 \neq j_1$, then there are at most two non-equivalent $\ell$-isogenies $j_0 \to j_1$ and at most one $\ell$-isogeny $j_1 \to j_0$ up to equivalence.*

*Proof.* We first argue that for $j_0 \neq 0$ there are at most two non-equivalent $\ell$-isogenies $j_0 \to j_1$. If this were not the case, then $\Phi_\ell(j_0, Y)$ would have a triple root at $Y = j_1$, and in the full version of this article [32, Proposition 21] we use resultant theory to computationally check that this can only happen up to the prime $p_\ell < 4\ell^3$ given in Table 1 below.

In the script `additional_computations.sage` we check that $\Phi_\ell(0, 1728)$ does not have a prime factor larger than $p_\ell$, i.e. 0 and 1728 cannot be $\ell$-isogenous for $p > p_\ell$. Now consider $j_0 = 0$, which forces $p \equiv 2 \bmod 3$ (cf. [61, Example V.4.4]). For $\ell \in \{2, 3\}$ we check in the same script that, due to $p > p_\ell$, $\Phi_\ell(0, Y)$ has a triple root $j_1 \in \mathbb{F}_p \setminus \{0, 1728\}$, and for $\ell = 3$ a single root at 0. Since the number of non-equivalent $\ell$-isogenies $0 \to j_1$ is three times the number of non-equivalent $\ell$-isogenies $j_1 \to 0$, both claims hence hold for $j_0 = 0$ here.

For $\ell > 3$ we can use $p > p_\ell > 3\ell^2$ to apply [49, Theorem 2(2)], which directly yields claim (b) and further shows that – with $\left(\frac{\ell}{3}\right)$ denoting the Legendre symbol – there are exactly

$$(\ell + 1) - 3 \cdot \tfrac{1}{3}\left(\ell - \left(\tfrac{\ell}{3}\right)\right) = 1 + \left(\tfrac{\ell}{3}\right) \leq 2$$

non-equivalent $\ell$-isogenies $0 \to 0$, thus also finishing the proof of claim (a).

Finally, for $j_0 = 1728 \neq j_1$ we have already shown that there are at most two non-equivalent $\ell$-isogenies $1728 \to j_1$ and that 1728 is not $\ell$-isogenous to 0. Thus the number of non-equivalent $\ell$-isogenies $1728 \to j_1$ is exactly twice the number of non-equivalent $\ell$-isogenies $j_1 \to 1728$, and claim (c) follows. □

**Table 1.** Maximal primes $p_\ell$ for which a pair $(j_0, j_1)$ of non-zero $j$-invariants with at least three $\ell$-isogenies between them exists ($a$ is a square root of 349 modulo $p_\ell$).

| $\ell$ | 2 | 3 | 5 | 7 | 11 | 13 |
|---|---|---|---|---|---|---|
| $p_\ell$ | 13 | 53 | 379 | 1217 | 5101 | 8387 |
| $j_0$ | 5 | $6a + 28$ | $117a + 322$ | $379a + 173$ | $977a + 4220$ | $326a + 4482$ |
| $j_1$ | 5 | $47a + 28$ | $262a + 322$ | $838a + 173$ | $4124a + 4220$ | $8061a + 4482$ |

*Remark 4.* For any prime $\ell \in \mathbb{N}$ one can find a prime $p_\ell$ as in Theorem 1, and one has the bound $p_\ell < 4\ell^4$. Indeed, due to [49, Theorem 2] it suffices to consider the situation where we have at least three non-equivalent $\ell$-isogenies $j_0 \to j_1$ for $j_0 \notin \{0, 1728\}$ or $(j_0, j_1) = (0, 1728)$. In view of [7, Theorem 4.10] we can then construct two non-commuting endomorphisms of degree $\ell^2$ on a curve $E$ with $j(E) = j_0$ by composing two non-equivalent $\ell$-isogenies $j_0 \to j_1$ with a suitable $\ell$-isogeny $j_1 \to j_0$. Hence we obtain two embeddings of quadratic orders into the endomorphism ring of $E$ with distinct images, and these embeddings can be extended to optimal embeddings of (possibly larger) quadratic orders that still have distinct images as the endomorphisms do not commute. Thus Kaneko's bound [44, Theorem 2'] yields $4p_\ell \leq (-4\ell^2)^2$, i.e. $p_\ell < 4\ell^4$. In particular, by the discussion in Subsect. 2.1 this proves that 0 and 1728 cannot be $\ell$-isogenous for $p > 4\ell^4$.

Returning to our relation, let us suppose that we have two $j$-invariants $j_0, j_1 \in \overline{\mathbb{F}_p}$. As before we consider the polynomials

$$\Phi_\ell^c(X, j_0) \quad \text{and} \quad \Theta_\ell^c(X, j_1) = \Phi_\ell^c(\ell^s/X, j_1) \cdot X^{\ell+1}/\ell^s,$$

which have the same set of common solutions as the system (MT) due to $p \neq \ell$; these common solutions are, moreover, precisely the roots of the polynomial

$$\Gamma_\ell(j_0, j_1) := \gcd\left(\Phi_\ell^c(X, j_0), \Theta_\ell^c(X, j_1)\right) \in \mathbb{F}_p(j_0, j_1)[X].$$

The previous results now show that the degree of $\Gamma_\ell(j_0, j_1)$ is low in most cases:

**Corollary 2.** *Let $\ell \in \{2, 3, 5, 7, 13\}$, let $j_0, j_1 \in \overline{\mathbb{F}_p}$ for a prime $p > \ell$, and consider as above the gcd-polynomial $\Gamma_\ell(j_0, j_1) \in \overline{\mathbb{F}_p}[X]$. Then*

$$\deg \Gamma_\ell(j_0, j_1) = \min\{\nu_\ell(j_0, j_1), \nu_\ell(j_1, j_0)\}$$

*where $\nu_\ell(j, j')$ denotes the number of non-equivalent $\ell$-isogenies $j \to j'$. In particular:*

(a) $\deg \Gamma_\ell(j_0, j_1) \geq 1$ *if and only if $j_0$ and $j_1$ are $\ell$-isogenous.*
(b) *If $j_0$ is ordinary or $p > p_\ell$ (e.g. if $p \geq 4\ell^3$), then* $\deg \Gamma_\ell(j_0, j_1) \leq 2$.

*Proof.* The main claim is a direct consequence of the Multiplicity Theorem and the multiplicity analysis that was performed in its proof, noting that the minimum is necessary to account for higher root multiplicities at $j$-invariants 0 and 1728 (see also Lemma 3); hence claim (a) follows immediately. Moreover, Proposition 4 and Theorem 1 imply claim (b). □

*Remark 5.* Since we can always factor an $\ell^2$-isogeny into two $\ell$-isogenies (cf. [61, Corollary III.4.11]), the $j$-invariants $j_0$ for which there is some $j$-invariant $j_1$ with $\deg \Gamma_\ell(j_0, j_1) \geq 2$ correspond precisely to the $j$-invariants of $\ell^2$*-small* curves as defined in [51], where the authors also prove that these $j$-invariants form a vanishingly small, but generally non-empty subset of $\overline{\mathbb{F}_p}$ for large $p$.

For $\ell \in \{2, 3, 5, 7, 13\}$ we can bound the size of this set more precisely: By factoring the $J_1$-resultant

$$\mathrm{res}_{J_1}(\Phi_\ell(J_0, J_1), \tfrac{\partial}{\partial J_1}\Phi_\ell(J_0, J_1)) \in \mathbb{Z}[J_0],$$

we see that the $J_0$-degree sum of all its distinct irreducible factors is at most $\ell^2 + 1$ (cf. the script `additional_computations.sage`). Hence Proposition 1(a) shows that there are at most $\ell^2 + 1$ invariants $j_0 \in \overline{\mathbb{F}_p}$ that can belong to an $\ell^2$-small curve for $p > \ell$.

**Computing Roots.** Corollary 2 suggests the following efficient strategy to find a root $f$ of the system (MT) for two $\ell$-isogenous $j$-invariants $j_0, j_1 \in \overline{\mathbb{F}_p}$: If the $j$-invariants do not lie in $\mathbb{F}_{p^2}$, and are hence necessarily ordinary, or if we have $p \geq 4\ell^3$ (which is guaranteed for cryptographically large primes), we can simply compute the gcd-polynomial $\Gamma_\ell(j_0, j_1)$ and obtain a root either by directly reading it off (in the degree 1 case) or by using the quadratic formula (in the degree 2 case, which only occurs rarely by Remark 5). Otherwise we will see in the next section (Theorem 2) that $\Gamma_\ell(j_0, j_1) \in \mathbb{F}_{p^2}[X]$ splits into linear factors over $\mathbb{F}_{p^2}$ – this allows us to factor the polynomial over $\mathbb{F}_{p^2}$, e.g. using Berlekamp factorization. Note, however, that we are only interested in finding one root; thus we may, starting with $\Gamma_\ell(j_0, j_1)$, iteratively compute a partial factorization and only keep the factor of smallest degree at each step.

In view of the above results, we conclude that our new relation is practically equivalent to the relation $\mathcal{R}_{\ell^k\text{-ModPoly}}$, i.e. a user with knowledge of an $\ell$-isogeny $j$-invariant chain of length $k$ can efficiently compute the additional roots $(f_i)_{i\in[k]}$ needed to prove their knowledge with respect to the relation $\mathcal{R}_{\ell^k\text{-ModRoot}}$.

### 3.3 Isogeny Reconstruction and Splitting Behavior

**Where do the roots lie?** After we have now given an essentially optimal bound on the number of roots of the system (MT) in large characteristic, we next investigate where these roots lie. Due to Remark 5 and the Multiplicity Theorem, this question is easily answered in the overwhelming majority of cases: For a $j$-invariant $j_0$ and a root $f$ of $\Phi_\ell^c(X, j_0)$ such that there is only one non-equivalent $\ell$-isogeny to $j_1 = \mathcal{J}_\ell(\ell^s/f)$, $f$ is the unique root of the system given by the two polynomial equations $\Phi_\ell^c(X, j_0) = 0$ and $\Theta_\ell^c(\ell^s/X, j_1) = 0$, and hence lies in the field extension $\mathbb{F}_p(j_0, j_1)$. In fact, as $\mathcal{J}_\ell(f) = j_0$ and $\mathcal{J}_\ell(\ell^s/f) = j_1$ by Lemma 1, we have $\mathbb{F}_p(f) = \mathbb{F}_p(j_0, j_1)$.

To analyze the splitting behavior in general, however, additional work is required: As the following example shows, the field extension generated by the two $j$-invariants is not guaranteed to contain a root of the system (MT).

*Example 2.* Let $\ell = 3$, $p = 61$ and $j_0 = 9 \in \mathbb{F}_{61}$. Then we have the factorizations

$$\Phi_3(9, j_1) = (j_1 - 9)^2 \cdot (j_1 - 41)^2 \quad \text{and} \quad \Phi_3^c(X, 9) = (X^2 - 15X - 3) \cdot (X^2 - 10X + 1)$$

over $\mathbb{F}_{61}$. Further we have $\Gamma_3(9, 9) = X^2 - 15X - 3$ and $\Gamma_3(9, 41) = X^2 - 10X + 1$; these polynomials are irreducible over $\mathbb{F}_{61}$, i.e. their roots lie in $\mathbb{F}_{61^2} \setminus \mathbb{F}_{61}$.

As a remedy to this issue, the following result describes how we can reconstruct an $\ell$-isogeny from a common root $f$ of the system (MT) in most situations:

**Reconstruction Theorem.** *Let $\ell \in \{2, 3, 5, 7, 13\}$, let $K$ be a field of characteristic* $\mathrm{char}(K) \notin \{2, 3, \ell\}$*, let $j_0 \in K \setminus \{0, 1728\}$ be a $j$-invariant and let $f \in \overline{K}^\times$ be a root of $\Phi_\ell^c(X, j_0)$. Define the parameters*

$$A = -3j_0(j_0 - 1728) \quad \text{and} \quad B = -2j_0(j_0 - 1728)^2$$

*and the elliptic curve*

$$E\colon y^2 = x^3 + Ax + B.$$

*Then $j(E) = j_0$, and we can associate to $f$ a kernel polynomial $\phi_\ell(f)$ of degree $\lceil \frac{\ell-1}{2} \rceil$ that defines over $K(f)$ an $\ell$-isogeny from $E$ to a curve with $j$-invariant $\mathcal{J}_\ell(\ell^s/f)$. Moreover, $f$ can be expressed as a $K$-rational function in the coefficients $1 = s_0, s_1, \ldots, s_n$ of $\phi_\ell(f)$, i.e.*

$$K(f) = K(s_1, \ldots, s_n).$$

*Proof.* To limit confusion of variable names in this proof, we will write the canonical modular polynomial in the variables $T$ and $j$ (instead of the usual variables $X$ and $j$). This proof will be highly computational – the observational claims used along the way can be verified via the SageMath script `kernel_polynomials.sage`.

The discriminant of the curve $E$ is $2^{11} \cdot 3^5 \cdot j_0 \cdot (j_0 - 1728)$, which is non-zero by our assumptions. Hence $E$ is an elliptic curve and one easily verifies that $j(E) = j_0$.

To work computationally, we will consider the coefficient ring $\mathbb{Z}[T, T^{-1}]$ of Laurent polynomials over $\mathbb{Z}$; since the root $f$ is non-zero due to $\mathrm{char}(K) \neq \ell$, we can then apply the ring homomorphism $\mathbb{Z}[T, T^{-1}] \to K(f)$ given by evaluating $T$ at $f$. By Lemma 1 we can represent $j_0$ via the rational function

$$j_0(T) = \mathcal{J}_\ell(T) = \Phi_\ell^c(T, 0)/T;$$

now considering the coefficients of $E$ as elements of $\mathbb{Z}[T, T^{-1}]$, and hence $E = E(T)$ as a curve over $\mathbb{Q}(T)$, we can apply the following deciding trick, which is based on the ideas in [26] and [64, §3-4]: The $\ell^{th}$ division polynomial $\psi_\ell \in \mathbb{Q}(T)[x]$ of $E(T)$ has coefficients in $\mathbb{Z}[T, T^{-1}]$ and admits in $\mathbb{Z}[T, T^{-1}][x]$ a monic factor $\phi_\ell \in \mathbb{Z}[T, T^{-1}][x]$ of degree $\lceil \frac{\ell-1}{2} \rceil =: n$. Evaluating at $f$ hence yields the polynomial $\phi_\ell(f) \in K(f)[x]$ of degree $n$, and we want to show that this is a kernel polynomial.

For $\ell = 2$ we do this directly: Writing $\phi_2 = x - \xi$ and plugging the root $\xi$ into the $x$-coordinate of $E(T)$ yields $y^2 = 0$, so $(\xi(f), 0)$ is a 2-torsion point of $E(f)$ as desired.

To prove that $\phi_\ell(f)$ is a kernel polynomial for $\ell \geq 3$, we want to apply the *Kernel polynomial criterion* given in [64, §3.3], noting that $a = 2$ is a *semi-primitive root modulo* $\ell$ as stated on [64, p. 34].

Hence we first have to compute the action $[2]^*(x)$ of the [2]-endomorphism of $E$ on the $x$-coordinate. By the multiplication-by-2 formula given in [65, Theorem 3.6] we have

$$[2]^*(x) = \frac{x^4 - 2A(T)x^2 - 8B(T)x + A(T)^2}{4x^3 + 4A(T)x + 4B(T)} =: \frac{t_1(T)}{t_2(T)}$$

where $\mathrm{res}_x(t_1(T), t_2(T)) = 2^{22} \cdot 3^{10} \cdot j_0(T)^2 \cdot (j_0(T) - 1728)^2$ is the square of the discriminant of $E(T)$. In view of [65, Lemma 3.5], Proposition 1 thus shows that the polynomials $t_1(f)$ and $t_2(f)$ are coprime in $K(f)[x]$ due to our assumptions that $\mathrm{char}(K) \notin \{2, 3\}$ and $j_0 \notin \{0, 1728\}$.

Next we have to evaluate $\phi_\ell$ (in $x$) at $[2]^*(x)$, which gives

$$\phi_\ell\left(\frac{t_1(T)}{t_2(T)}\right) = \frac{1}{t_2(T)^n} \cdot \left[\phi_\ell\left(\frac{t_1(T)}{t_2(T)}\right) \cdot t_2(T)^n\right] =: \frac{1}{t_2(T)^n} \cdot h_\ell(T)$$

where $h_\ell(f)$ is coprime to $t_2(f)^n$ in $K(f)[x]$ since $t_1(f)$ and $t_2(f)$ are coprime. Now we define the monic polynomial

$$\tau_2(\phi_\ell(f)) := \gcd(\psi_\ell(f), h_\ell(f));$$

as $\psi_\ell(f)$ is the $\ell^{th}$ division polynomial of $E(f)$, we see with [64, Corollary 3.3.2] that $\phi_\ell(f)$ is a kernel polynomial of an $\ell$-isogeny if and only if $\tau_2(\phi_\ell(f)) = \phi_\ell(f)$.

However, by [64, Proposition 3.3.1] we also see that $\tau_2(\phi_\ell(f))$ is a monic polynomial of degree $n = \frac{\ell-1}{2}$, so it suffices to show that $\phi_\ell(f)$ divides $\tau_2(\phi_\ell(f))$. To this end, first note that $\phi_\ell(T)$ divides $\psi_\ell(T)$ over $\mathbb{Z}[T, T^{-1}]$ by construction, which allows us to deduce that $\phi_\ell(f)$ divides $\psi_\ell(f)$.

Furthermore we can check computationally that $\phi_\ell(T)$ divides $h_\ell(T)$ over $\mathbb{Z}[T, T^{-1}]$, and hence $\phi_\ell(f)$ also divides $h_\ell(f)$. Therefore the definition of $\tau_2(\phi_\ell(f))$ forces it to be divisible by $\phi_\ell(f)$, and we conclude that $\phi_\ell(f)$ is a kernel polynomial of an $\ell$-isogeny defined on $E(f)$.

Penultimately, we want to show that the isogeny defined by $\phi_\ell(f)$ maps to a curve of $j$-invariant $\mathcal{J}_\ell(\ell^s/f)$. This can be deduced directly from *Vélu's formulas* – more precisely, in [45, §2.4] Kohel describes the target curve in terms of $A$,

$B$ and the coefficients of $\phi_\ell(f)$. Applying these formulas, we see that the target curve is in short Weierstrass form with discriminant $\Delta = 2^{11} \cdot 3^5 \cdot f^{\ell-1} \cdot A \cdot B \neq 0$ and $j$-invariant $\mathcal{J}_\ell(\ell^s/f)$.

Finally, we refer to the full version of this article [32, Appendix A.4] for the ($\ell$-dependent) expressions of $f$ as a $K$-rational function in the coefficients of $\phi_\ell(f)$; here we only note that, as a kernel polynomial, $\phi_\ell(f)$ will never have any double roots, so $\mathrm{disc}(\phi_\ell(f)) \neq 0$ by Proposition 1(b) (in view of Remark 1). □

*Remark 6.* Note that we can also reconstruct $\ell$-isogenies from a root $f \in \overline{K}^\times$ of $\Phi_\ell^c(X, j_0)$ if we have $j_1 = \mathcal{J}_\ell(\ell^s/f) \notin \{0, 1728\}$. Indeed, in this case we first compute the dual isogeny (up to equivalence) by applying the above techniques to $\ell^s/f$, and then take its dual and precompose with the different automorphisms at $j_0$ to obtain the non-equivalent $\ell$-isogenies $j_0 \to j_1$ corresponding to $f$.

We now use the Reconstruction Theorem to analyze the splitting behavior of $\Phi_\ell^c(X, j_0)$, i.e. where its roots lie, for a supersingular $j$-invariant $j_0$.

**Theorem 2.** *Let $\ell \in \{2, 3, 5, 7, 13\}$, let $p \neq \ell$ be a prime and let $j_0 \in \mathbb{F}_{p^2}$ be a supersingular $j$-invariant. Then $\Phi_\ell^c(X, j_0)$ splits over $\mathbb{F}_{p^2}$.*

*Proof.* We first handle the case $j_0 \in \{0, 1728\}$: For $p \leq p_\ell$ we confirm the claim in the SageMath script `splitting_special.sage`, so we may assume $p > p_\ell$. By Theorem 1(b-c) and Corollary 2 we then see that $\Gamma_\ell(j_0, j_1) \in \mathbb{F}_{p^2}[X]$ has degree at most 1 for any supersingular $j_1 \neq j_0$, so the only roots of $\Phi_\ell^c(X, j_0)$ that may not lie in $\mathbb{F}_{p^2}$ are the roots of $\Gamma_\ell(j_0, j_0)$. However, by Corollary 2(b) this is a polynomial of degree at most 2 over $\mathbb{F}_p$.

Thus we may assume $j_0 \notin \{0, 1728\}$ and, in particular, $p \geq 5$. Now let $f \in \overline{\mathbb{F}_p}$ be a root of $\Phi_\ell^c(X, j_0)$. With the Reconstruction Theorem we can then associate to $f$ the kernel polynomial $\phi_\ell(f)$ of an $\ell$-isogeny defined on a curve $E$ over $\mathbb{F}_{p^2}$.

Moreover, the kernel of this isogeny is invariant under the action of the $p^2$-Frobenius isomorphism of $\overline{\mathbb{F}_p}$ on $E$. Indeed, this action is given by evaluation of the $p^2$-Frobenius endomorphism $\pi$ of $E$; due to [2, §4] we further see that $\pi$ has trace $\pm 2p$ since $j_0 \notin \{0, 1728\}$, so it acts on $E$ via scalar multiplication by $\pm p$ (cf. [2, §5]) and we conclude that any subgroup of $E(\overline{\mathbb{F}_p})$ is invariant under the action of $\pi$.

Therefore the coefficients of the kernel polynomial $\phi_\ell(f)$ lie in $\mathbb{F}_{p^2}$ as well, and with the second part of the Reconstruction Theorem we deduce $f \in \mathbb{F}_{p^2}$ as desired. □

We give an application, which can alternatively be proven by showing that any Legendre parameter of a supersingular $j$-invariant lies in $\mathbb{F}_{p^2}$ [6, Proposition 2.2].

**Corollary 3.** *Let $p$ be a prime and let $j_0 \in \mathbb{F}_{p^2}$ be a supersingular $j$-invariant. Then $j_0 - 1728$ is a square in $\mathbb{F}_{p^2}$.*

*Proof.* As all elements of $\mathbb{F}_p$ are squares in $\mathbb{F}_{p^2}$, we may assume $j_0 \notin \{0, 1728\}$ and, in particular, $p \geq 5$. Due to Proposition 1(a) we can thus compute the discriminant of $\Phi_2^c(X, j_0)$ by first computing the discriminant of $\Phi_2^c(X, J_0)$ over $\mathbb{Z}[J_0]$ and then reducing modulo $p$ and evaluating $J_0$ at $j_0$, which yields

$$\operatorname{disc}(\Phi_2^c(X, j_0)) = 2^2 \cdot j_0^2 \cdot (j_0 - 1728).$$

Now $\Phi_2^c(X, j_0)$ does not have multiple roots by Lemma 2 and splits into three linear factors over $\mathbb{F}_{p^2}$ by Theorem 2, so [39, Theorem 1.8] shows that $\operatorname{disc}(\Phi_2^c(X, j_0))$ must be a square in $\mathbb{F}_{p^2}$, and the claim follows. □

## 4 Proving Isogeny Knowledge via R1CS

In the previous section we have laid all the theoretical foundations for describing the R1CS that will enable us to build an efficient proof of knowledge for an $\ell$-isogeny walk with $k$ steps. Before we describe our approach based on canonical modular polynomials, we briefly revisit the strategy pursued in [21] for the prime $\ell = 2$.

### 4.1 Revisiting the Approach in [21]

The authors of [21] use the classical modular polynomial $\Phi_2(X, Y)$ to construct an R1CS to prove knowledge of a $2^k$-isogeny with respect to the relation $\mathcal{R}_{\ell^k\text{-ModPoly}}$ (cf. Eq. (1)). They do this by finding an efficient arithmetization to prove that $\Phi_2(j_i, j_{i+1}) = 0$ for a chain of $k + 1$ successive $j$-invariants. Here $j_0 = j(E_0)$ and $j_k = j(E_k)$ are part of the statement, and $j_i$ for $0 < i < k$ are part of the R1CS witness. We can recover the original isogeny by searching at each step for 2-isogenous elliptic curves $E_i$, $E_{i+1}$ where $j(E_i) = j_i$ and $j(E_{i+1}) = j_{i+1}$. On the other hand, such a chain of $j$-invariants can be found for any $2^k$-isogeny by iteratively computing 2-isogenies using kernel points. This means that the problem of finding such a chain of $j$-invariants is equivalent to finding an explicit isogeny $E_0 \to E_k$ of degree $2^k$.

In order to arithmetize, the authors express each step of the isogeny walk as an R1CS gadget, which is then employed for each link in the chain. Two tricks are used to optimize:

- The values $j_i$, $j_i^2$ and $j_i^3$ are computed for all $i \in \{0, \ldots, k\}$, as well as $j_i j_{i+1}$ for each $i < k$. The condition that $\Phi_2(j_i, j_{i+1}) = 0$ can then be expressed as a single R1CS constraint.
- To express the gadget over $\mathbb{F}_p$ as well as over $\mathbb{F}_{p^2}$, the authors use arithmetizations for products and squares that are more efficient than the naive approach of computing each cross term individually. In particular, the product $(x_1 + x_2\alpha)(y_1 + y_1\alpha)$, with $x_1, x_2, y_1, y_2 \in \mathbb{F}_p$ and $\alpha^2 = d$ some quadratic non-residue in $\mathbb{F}_p$, can be expressed in three products over $\mathbb{F}_p$. Squarings can be expressed in two products.

Our goal is now twofold: First, to further optimize the arithmetization for $\ell = 2$. Second, to construct efficient R1CS for more primes $\ell > 2$, more specifically for the primes $\ell \in \{2, 3, 5, 7, 13\}$, for which we have developed a good understanding of canonical modular polynomials in the previous section.

By Lemma 1, for $\ell \in \{2, 3, 5, 7, 13\}$ the $\ell^{th}$ canonical modular polynomial has the form

$$\Phi_\ell^c(X, j) = X^{\ell+1} + \textstyle\sum_{i=1}^{\ell} c_i X^i + \ell^s - X \cdot j.$$

In what follows we will write $c_0 = \ell^s$ and $c_{\ell+1} = 1$. In view of the Multiplicity Theorem the proof of knowledge with respect to relation $\mathcal{R}_{\ell^k\text{-ModRoot}}$ can be encoded step-wise via the system of Eqs. (MT).

Multiplying the equation $\Phi_\ell^c(\ell^s/X, j_1) = 0$ by $X^{\ell+1}/\ell^s$ to obtain $\Theta_\ell^c(X, j_1)$ as before, we obtain the equivalent system (where $c_i' = c_{\ell+1-i} \cdot \ell^{s(\ell-i)}$):

$$\textstyle\sum_{i=0}^{\ell+1} c_i X^i - j_0 \cdot X = 0 \wedge \sum_{i=0}^{\ell+1} c_i' X^i - j_1 \cdot X^\ell = 0. \tag{4}$$

We will reformulate these equations as an R1CS in the upcoming subsection. In our applications we consider supersingular $j$-invariants, which are known to be contained in $\mathbb{F}_{p^2}$. It is crucial for the effectivity of our method that in this situation the roots of the above equations still lie in the quadratic extension $\mathbb{F}_{p^2}$ of $\mathbb{F}_p$, rather than in a larger extension, as proven in Theorem 2.

### 4.2 Reformulation as an R1CS

**Advantages of Canonical Modular Polynomials.** Compared to the classical modular polynomials, the canonical modular polynomials have a structure that lends itself better to arithmetization. Concretely, as we will see, we can exploit their structure for the R1CS in three main ways:

- First, the total degree of the polynomials is lower, going from a single polynomial of total degree $2\ell$ to two polynomials of degree $\ell + 1$. This lowers the multiplicative complexity, which enables us to use fewer constraints.
- Second, whereas $\Phi_\ell$ is very dense, $\Phi_\ell^c$ and $\Theta_\ell^c$ are both polynomials in just $X$ in addition to a single term containing $j$. Hence there are fewer monomials to produce in the R1CS and the computed terms can more often be reused.
- Lastly, the structure described in Lemma 3 allows us to factor part of this polynomial as a square, improving arithmetization over $\mathbb{F}_p$.

**More efficient R1CS over $\mathbb{F}_{p^2}$.** We can compute the powers $1, X, X^2, \ldots, X^\ell$ together with the $j$-invariants $j$ and $j'$, and rewrite the equations as

$$X \cdot \left( \sum_{i=0}^{\ell} c_{i+1} X^i - j \right) + c_0 = 0, \tag{5}$$

$$X^\ell \cdot \left( \sum_{i=0}^{1} c_{\ell+i}' X^i - j' \right) + \sum_{i=0}^{\ell-1} c_i' X^i = 0. \tag{6}$$

To reduce the number of non-zero entries, we employ a change of variables and have the prover supply $y = j - c_1$ instead of $j$ and $y' = j' - c_1$ instead of $j'$. This eliminates the term $X$ from the first equation and the term $X^\ell$ from the second equation, since $c_1 = c'_\ell$. Clearly knowledge of a chain of $j$-invariants is equivalent to knowledge of a chain of $y$'s.

These equations are expressed as an R1CS as follows. The assignment vector $z$ has the form $z = (1\ X\ X^2\ \ldots\ X^\ell\ y\ y')^T$, and the corresponding constraint matrices are given by

$$A = \begin{pmatrix} 0\,1\,0 \cdots 0\,0\,0 \\ 0\,1\,0 \cdots 0\,0\,0 \\ \vdots \quad\ \vdots \quad\ \vdots \\ 0\,1\,0 \cdots 0\,0\,0 \\ 0\,0\,0 \cdots 1\,0\,0 \end{pmatrix}, \quad B = \begin{pmatrix} 0 & 1 & 0 & \cdots & 0 & 0 & 0 \\ 0 & 0 & 1 & \cdots & 0 & 0 & 0 \\ \vdots & & & \vdots & & & \vdots \\ 0 & c_2 & c_3 & \cdots & c_{\ell+1} & -1 & 0 \\ 0 & c'_{\ell+1} & 0 & \cdots & 0 & 0 & -1 \end{pmatrix},$$

and

$$C = \begin{pmatrix} 0 & 0 & 1 & 0 & \cdots & 0 & 0\,0 \\ 0 & 0 & 0 & 1 & \cdots & 0 & 0\,0 \\ \vdots & & & & \vdots & & \vdots \\ 0 & 0 & 0 & 0 & \cdots & 1 & 0\,0 \\ -c_0 & 0 & 0 & 0 & \cdots & 0 & 0\,0\,0 \\ -c'_0 & -c'_1 & -c'_2 & -c'_3 & \cdots & -c'_{\ell-1} & 0\,0\,0 \end{pmatrix}.$$

For an isogeny path of length $k$, each new step introduces a new value $y_{i+1}$ together with the $\ell$ powers of the current solution $X_i$. Moreover, we need $\ell - 1$ more constraints for checking the powers of the new variable $X_i$, together with two more constraints which encode the two Eqs. (4). There are $\ell + 1$, $2\ell + 2$ and $2\ell$ non-zero entries in $A$, $B$ and $C$, respectively. This means that we can arithmetize an $\ell^k$-isogeny for $\ell \in \{2, 3, 5, 7, 13\}$ in $(\ell+1)k+1$ variables, $(\ell+1)k$ constraints and $(5\ell+3)k$ non-zero entries in the R1CS.

In fact, we can do better for $\ell \in \{7, 13\}$, in the following way. We let $t = \frac{\ell+1}{2}$ and rewrite the two equations as

$$X^t \cdot \left( \sum_{i=0}^{t} c_{i+t} X^i \right) + \sum_{i=0, i \neq 1}^{t-1} c_i X^i - yX = 0, \tag{7}$$

$$X^t \cdot \left( \sum_{i=0, i \neq t-1}^{t} c'_{i+t} X^i - y' X^{t-1} \right) + \sum_{i=0}^{t-1} c'_i X^i = 0. \tag{8}$$

This way we need to compute the variables $X^2, \ldots, X^t, yX, y'X^{t-1}$, and we have $t + 1 + 2$ constraints ($t + 1$ consistency checks, and the two above equations). We have $t$ variables for the powers of $X$ and two for $yX$ and $y'X^{t-1}$, as well as one per $j$-invariant, through $y$. This gives a total of $(t + 3)k + 1$ variables. The $t + 1$ consistency checks can be computed in $3t + 3$, while the two other equations require $4t + 4$ non-zero entries in the constraint matrices. In total, this means $(t + 3)k + 1$ variables, $(t + 3)k$ constraints and $(7t + 7)k$ non-zero entries in the R1CS to arithmetize a walk of length $k$ for $\ell \in \{3, 5, 7, 13\}$.

### 4.3 Lifting to $\mathbb{F}_p \times \mathbb{F}_p$

So far, we have described efficient arithmetizations for proving isogenies that work over $\mathbb{F}_{p^2}$. While it is perfectly valid to use an R1CS over this field, this is not supported by all proof systems. Fortunately, we can lift any arithmetization over $\mathbb{F}_{p^2}$ to $\mathbb{F}_p \times \mathbb{F}_p$.

We represent elements in $\mathbb{F}_{p^2}$ as $x + y\alpha$ with $x, y \in \mathbb{F}_p$ and $\alpha^2 = d$ for some quadratic non-residue $d \in \mathbb{F}_p$. Linear operations over $\mathbb{F}_{p^2}$ translate directly to linear operations over $\mathbb{F}_p$, whereas a multiplication $(x_1+x_2\alpha)(y_1+y_2\alpha) = z_1+z_2\alpha$ would naively induce four multiplications for all cross terms $x_1y_1$, $x_1y_2\alpha$, $x_2y_1\alpha$ and $x_2y_2d$. As noted in [21], there exist well-known techniques to do this more efficiently. Multiplication can be performed using one auxiliary variable and three constraints by applying Karatsuba's algorithm:

$$\begin{aligned} u &= x_2y_2, \\ z_1 - du &= x_1y_1, \\ z_1 + z_2 + (1-d)u &= (x_1 + x_2)(y_1 + y_2). \end{aligned}$$

This immediately implies an upper bound for the cost of lifting: We can substitute this relation for every row of the original R1CS to obtain a new system with $m' = 3m$.

The number of variables becomes $n' = 2n + m$, since variables now have two components and we add one intermediate variable for every constraint. The number of non-zero entries for this new system is $\text{nnz}' \leq 4\,\text{nnz}$ due to the doubling of the number of variables, and because all variables are used at most twice in the above system of equations.

Squaring a variable can be performed more efficiently. For

$$z_1 + z_2\alpha = (x_1 + x_2\alpha)^2,$$

the following system of equations suffices:

$$\begin{aligned} z_2 &= 2x_1x_2, \\ z_1 + (d+1)/2z_2 &= (x_1 + x_2)(x_1 + dx_2). \end{aligned}$$

This uses just two constraints and nine non-zero entries, requiring no auxiliary variables.

**Optimized embedding into $\mathbb{F}_p$.** The above gadgets for multiplication and squaring can be used to reduce the number of constraints needed in the R1CS. However, we can achieve a further improvement by changing how we represent elements from $\mathbb{F}_{p^2}$ in $\mathbb{F}_p \times \mathbb{F}_p$. The basis change $(x_1, x_2) \to (x_1, x_1+x_2) = (x_1, x_s)$ saves one non-zero entry in the last constraint for the general product. This might seem minor, but since both coefficients of $x$ can themselves be a linear combination of many variables, this may lead to significant savings.

For a square, instead of avoiding a non-zero entry, we need to add an entry to express the output $z_2 = z_s - z_1$. Fortunately, although clearly this gives a tradeoff between the two bases, the embedding can be chosen separately per variable. In our case, this sum basis turns out to be at least as efficient as the regular basis almost everywhere.

**Exploiting $\Phi_\ell^c$'s structure.** The above gadgets and the sum basis help us to express the canonical modular polynomials efficiently in an R1CS over $\mathbb{F}_p \times \mathbb{F}_p$. Furthermore, for some $\ell$, the canonical modular polynomial can be rewritten using the structure described in Lemma 3 such that it utilizes more squares. This in turn minimizes the number of necessary constraints. For $\ell = 2$ over $\mathbb{F}_p \times \mathbb{F}_p$, we can write the entire system using two squares and one product. First, define $y = c_1 - c_2^2 \cdot (4c_3)^{-1} - j$ (and $y'$ accordingly). Then

$$c_3 \left(c_2 \cdot (2c_3)^{-1} + X\right)^2 + y + c_0 X^{-1} = 0,$$
$$c_3 \ell^{3s} \left(c_2 \ell^s \cdot (2c_3)^{-1} + X^{-1}\right)^2 + \ell^s y' + c_0 X = 0,$$

captures both polynomials in two squaring relations. We only need to compute the inverse $X^{-1}$ with a single additional multiplication. Over $\mathbb{F}_p \times \mathbb{F}_p$, the resulting system has $7k$ constraints and $7k + 2$ variables. In a similar fashion, for $\ell = 7$, we can use the fact that Eq. (7) can be written as a square plus the term $\tilde{y} = 1728 - j$. For $\ell = 13$, we can express 9 coefficients correctly using the square of a degree 7 polynomial, after which we only need to correct for the lowest degree terms.

**Computing powers of $X$.** To compute even powers, we can square directly. It is, however, also possible to use a squaring for odd powers, through the relation

$$b \left(a \cdot (2b)^{-1} X^i + X^{i+1}\right)^2 = a^2 \cdot (4b)^{-1} X^{2i} + a X^{2i+1} + b X^{2i+2}. \tag{9}$$

We hence obtain a linear combination of three powers, where we can freely choose $a \in \mathbb{F}_p$ and $b \in \mathbb{F}_p^\times$. By subtracting away $a^2 \cdot (4b)^{-1} X^{2i}$ and $b X^{2i+2}$, we obtain a constraint for the odd power $X^{2i+1}$. Of course, this method cannot be used for the products with $y$ or the highest power of $X$, i.e. $X^\ell$ or $X^t$, since here we cannot compensate for the even powers appearing on the right-hand side.

**Change of variables.** One disadvantage of the above method is that it increases the number of non-zero entries in the constraint matrices. To remedy this, we note that some powers of $X$ are only used in linear combinations with other powers, i.e. in a polynomial where all three powers are already present. As such, we make a change of variables and store the right-hand side of Eq. (9) directly instead of $X^{2i+1}$. We can then choose $a$ and $b$ appropriately such that they agree with the coefficients of one of the polynomials. For example, for $\ell = 5$ we define $Z = c_5(c_4 \cdot (2c_5)^{-1} X + X^2)^2$ and rewrite Eq. (5) as

$$X \cdot \left[c_2 X + \left(c_3 - c_4^2 \cdot (4c_5)^{-1}\right) X^2 + Z + X^5 - y\right] + c_0 = 0. \tag{10}$$

The advantage is twofold: We do not need to subtract powers from Eq. (9) when computing $X^3$, and we do not have to add an $X^4$ term to Eq. (10). We should only use this substitution for powers that are not necessary to compute higher powers: The above would be inefficient if we also required the value of $X^3$ directly to express $(X^3)^2 = X^6$. Concretely, we use this trick to replace $X^3$ for $\ell \in \{5, 7\}$ and $X^5$ for $\ell = 13$.

More generally, the number of non-zero entries can often be minimized through a change of variables. For example, since $jX$ and $j'X^{t-1}$ are both only used once, we can instead already add the terms of the linear combinations in which they will be used later. This is advantageous, since a linear combination uses fewer nnz in the outcome of a square than in its input, and is still cheaper in the outcome of a multiplication. This way, the intermediate variables that are unavoidable can be used as efficiently as possible.

### 4.4 Optimized Backtracking Prevention

In [21, Appendix A], the authors briefly discuss a method of enforcing that an isogeny is cyclic, which in our setting is equivalent to the condition that a walk is non-backtracking (cf. [23, Corollary 4.5]).

To do this, it is checked that for all $i \in \{1, \ldots, k-1\}$, it holds that $j_{i-1} \neq j_{i+1}$. The authors arithmetize this by testing that $j_{i-1} - j_{i+1} \neq 0$. To this end, the prover is required to supply a $b$ such that

$$b \cdot \prod_{i=1}^{k-1} (j_{i-1} - j_{i+1}) = b(j_0 - j_2)(j_1 - j_3)(j_2 - j_4) \cdots = 1.$$

If for any $i$, $j_{i-1} = j_{i+1}$, then the polynomial will be 0 for any $b$, and otherwise the prover can solve for $b$ by taking an inverse. This method uses $k-1$ constraints, $k-1$ variables and $4k-4$ non-zero entries over $\mathbb{F}_{p^2}$. When this method is lifted to $\mathbb{F}_p \times \mathbb{F}_p$, however, it uses $3(k-1)$ constraints and variables, and $18k-19$ non-zero entries. If we were to apply it to our system for $\ell = 2$, this would incur a 43% overhead on $m$ and $n$, and a 44% overhead on nnz.

To remedy this, note that it is not actually necessary to compute a product over $\mathbb{F}_{p^2}$ to test that every factor is non-zero. Instead, we can use the constraint

$$p(a, b) = b \prod_{i=1}^{k-1} \left(\Re(j_{i-1}) - \Re(j_{i+1}) + a\left(\Im(j_{i-1}) - \Im(j_{i+1})\right)\right) = 1.$$

If $j_{i-1} = j_{i+1}$ for any $i$, $p(a, b) = 0$. On the other hand, if for all $i$, $j_{i-1} \neq j_{i+1}$, then $p(a, b)$ is a non-zero polynomial. Fixing $b \neq 0$ and applying the Schwartz–Zippel lemma, there are at least $p - k + 1$ values of $a$ for which $p(a, b) \neq 0$, and for each such $a$ there then is a suitable $b$ to satisfy the constraint. We can either let the prover choose $a, b \in \mathbb{F}_p$ for perfect soundness and completeness, or let $a$ be a uniformly random constant. Now the prover just has to supply $b$, saving one constraint and variable per step. This incurs no soundness loss, since no value of $a$ helps a cheating prover. On the other hand, there is at most a $\frac{k-1}{p} \leq \text{negl}(\lambda)$ completeness loss. Finally, we can set $a = 0$ and save two nnz per step, but now the completeness loss depends on the distribution of the path's $j$-invariants.

## 5 Evaluation

We provide `constraints.sage`, which expresses and verifies all arithmetizations and automatically counts the number of constraints, variables and nnz. These results can be found in Table 2. We achieve significant improvements everywhere, ranging between 25% – 45% for the number of constraints and 27% – 48% for nnz, making our arithmetizations suitable for $\ell$-power isogenies for each prime $\ell \in \{2, 3, 5, 7, 13\}$, as well as mixed power isogenies. To additionally compare results for distinct $\ell$, we normalize by considering a security level $\lambda$, such that $\ell^k > 2^\lambda$. By increasing $\ell$ we can decrease $k$, reducing the number of constraints necessary for the relation $\mathcal{R}_{\text{R1CS}}$. These results can be found in Table 3. We see that moving to higher $\ell$ further improves efficiency for walks of similar degree.

In Table 4 we provide concrete prover and verifier times as well as proof sizes for Aurora [10] and Ligero [3]. We use the parameter sets `p434` and `p441+` from [21].[4] These results are projected based on the number of constraints $m$, which appears to be a common and reliable basis for comparison.[5]

**Table 2.** Our results compared to [21]. We consider the number of constraints $m$, the number of variables $n$ and the number of non-zero entries in the constraint matrices nnz.

| $\ell$ | Field | $m$ | | $n$ | | nnz | |
|---|---|---|---|---|---|---|---|
| | | [21] | Ours | [21] | Ours | [21] | Ours |
| 2 | $\mathbb{F}_{p^2}$ | $4k+2$ | $3k$ | $4k+3$ | $3k+1$ | $21k+6$ | $13k$ |
| 3 | | | $4k$ | | $4k+1$ | | $18k$ |
| 5 | | | $6k$ | | $6k+1$ | | $28k$ |
| 7 | | | $7k$ | | $7k+1$ | | $35k$ |
| 13 | | | $10k$ | | $10k+1$ | | $56k$ |
| 2 | $\mathbb{F}_p$ | $11k+5$ | $7k$ | $11k+7$ | $7k+2$ | $79k+23$ | $41k$ |
| 3 | | | $11k$ | | $11k+2$ | | $65k$ |
| 5 | | | $15k$ | | $15k+2$ | | $97k$ |
| 7 | | | $17k$ | | $17k+2$ | | $123k$ |
| 13 | | | $24k$ | | $24k+2$ | | $194k$ |

Finally, our additional circuit to prevent backtracking with variable $a$, reduces $m$ by one-third. The approach with constant $a$ and negligible completeness loss reduces $m$ by two-thirds. The full overview is found in Table 5.

[4] Measurements were done on a desktop PC on a single thread and based on academic implementation `libiop`. Because of this, we expect optimizations and multithreading to yield significant improvements.

[5] See e.g. [10,38] and https://github.com/scipr-lab/libiop for independent benchmarks.

**Table 3.** Our results compared to those of [21], normalized for security parameter $\lambda$.

| $\ell$ | Field | $m$ | | $n$ | | nnz | |
|---|---|---|---|---|---|---|---|
| | | [21] | Ours | [21] | Ours | [21] | Ours |
| 2 | $\mathbb{F}_{p^2}$ | $4\lambda + 2$ | $3\lambda$ | $4\lambda + 3$ | $3\lambda + 1$ | $21\lambda + 6$ | $13\lambda$ |
| 3 | | | $2.524\lambda$ | | $2.524\lambda + 1$ | | $11.357\lambda$ |
| 5 | | | $2.584\lambda$ | | $2.584\lambda + 1$ | | $12.059\lambda$ |
| 7 | | | $2.493\lambda$ | | $2.493\lambda + 1$ | | $12.467\lambda$ |
| 13 | | | $2.702\lambda$ | | $2.702\lambda + 1$ | | $15.133\lambda$ |
| 2 | $\mathbb{F}_p$ | $11\lambda + 5$ | $7\lambda$ | $11\lambda + 7$ | $7\lambda + 2$ | $79\lambda + 23$ | $41\lambda$ |
| 3 | | | $6.940\lambda$ | | $6.940\lambda + 2$ | | $41.010\lambda$ |
| 5 | | | $6.460\lambda$ | | $6.460\lambda + 2$ | | $41.776\lambda$ |
| 7 | | | $6.056\lambda$ | | $6.056\lambda + 2$ | | $43.813\lambda$ |
| 13 | | | $6.486\lambda$ | | $6.486\lambda + 2$ | | $52.426\lambda$ |

**Table 4.** An evaluation of our results compared to [21] for walks with $\ell = 2$. The results from $\mathbb{F}_{p^2}$ correspond to the identification protocol with parameter set `p434`, with path length $k = 216$ and security level $\lambda = 128$, while $\mathbb{F}_p$ corresponds to `p441+`. The timings and proof sizes are from [21] and subsequently projected from $m$.

| Field | | Aurora | | Ligero | |
|---|---|---|---|---|---|
| | | [21] | Ours | [21] | Ours |
| $\mathbb{F}_{p^2}$ | Prover time (ms) | 934 | 669 | 587 | 420 |
| | Verifier time (ms) | 99 | 74 | 847 | 634 |
| | Proof size (kB) | 194 | 178 | 1849 | 1599 |
| $\mathbb{F}_p$ | Prover time (ms) | 1216 | 727 | 427 | 255 |
| | Verifier time (ms) | 98 | 62 | 493 | 313 |
| | Proof size (kB) | 166 | 147 | 1733 | 1381 |

**Table 5.** The number of constraints $m$, variables $n$ and number of non-zero entries nnz used to prevent backtracking using the existing method from [21] and our methods. For variables, we do not include 1 and the $j$-invariants in the count.

| Field | Approach | $m$ | $n$ | nnz |
|---|---|---|---|---|
| $\mathbb{F}_{p^2}$ | [21] | $k - 1$ | $k - 1$ | $4k - 4$ |
| $\mathbb{F}_p$ | [21] | $3k - 3$ | $3k - 3$ | $18k - 19$ |
| | Ours, variable $a$ | $2k - 2$ | $2k - 1$ | $9k - 9$ |
| | Ours, constant $a$ | $k - 1$ | $k - 1$ | $6k - 6$ |
| | Ours, $a = 0$ | $k - 1$ | $k - 1$ | $4k - 4$ |

## 6 Conclusion and Open Problems

In this paper we improved on the state-of-the-art of using general-purpose zero-knowledge proof systems for proving knowledge of an isogeny via R1CS. We were able to generalize the approach of Cong, Lai and Levin [21] beyond $\ell = 2$ to prime numbers $\ell \in \{3, 5, 7, 13\}$ via the use of canonical modular polynomials. Moreover, we optimized the arithmetizations for the corresponding relation both over $\mathbb{F}_{p^2}$ and over $\mathbb{F}_p \times \mathbb{F}_p$.

In the course of our work we encountered interesting mathematical questions, some of which might hold in greater generality. For example, while Remark 4 argues that one can generalize Theorem 1 to any prime $\ell$ with the looser bound $p_\ell < 4\ell^4$, the growth trend displayed in Table 1 suggests that tighter bounds on the prime $p_\ell$ could be achievable – in fact, experimental data up to $\ell = 31$ suggests that the bound $p_\ell < 4\ell^3$ might hold in general.

It might be even more interesting to study the canonical modular polynomials (or different, equivalent polynomials) for primes $\ell$ such that $\kappa > 1$. In that case we do not know to what extent the Multiplicity Theorem still holds true. More precisely, we expect one inequality to still hold, but the other to fail generally, as discussed in Remark 2.

**Acknowledgements.** The last author would like to thank Jonathan Love, Travis Morrison and Eli Orvis for interesting discussions on the supersingular isogeny graph, which led to Remark 4, at the Leuven Isogeny Days 5. The authors further want to thank all anonymous reviewers for their feedback.

## References

1. Abdolmaleki, B., Glaeser, N., Ramacher, S., Slamanig, D.: Circuit-succinct universally composable NIZKs with updatable CRS. In: 2024 IEEE 37th Computer Security Foundations Symposium (CSF), pp. 527–542. IEEE Computer Society, Los Alamitos, CA, USA, July 2024. https://doi.org/10.1109/CSF61375.2024.00006
2. Adj, G., Ahmadi, O., Menezes, A.: On isogeny graphs of supersingular elliptic curves over finite fields. Finite Fields App. **55**, 268–283 (2019). https://doi.org/10.1016/J.FFA.2018.10.002
3. Ames, S., Hazay, C., Ishai, Y., Venkitasubramaniam, M.: Ligero: lightweight sublinear arguments without a trusted setup. In: Thuraisingham, B.M., Evans, D., Malkin, T., Xu, D. (eds.) ACM CCS 2017: 24th Conference on Computer and Communications Security, pp. 2087–2104. ACM Press, Dallas, TX, USA, October 31–November 2, 2017. https://doi.org/10.1145/3133956.3134104
4. Atapoor, S., Baghery, K., Cozzo, D., Pedersen, R.: Practical robust DKG protocols for CSIDH. In: Tibouchi, M., Wang, X. (eds.) ACNS 23: 21st International Conference on Applied Cryptography and Network Security, Part II. LNCS, vol. 13906, pp. 219–247. Springer, Cham, Switzerland, Kyoto, Japan (2023). https://doi.org/10.1007/978-3-031-33491-7_9
5. Atapoor, S., Baghery, K., Cozzo, D., Pedersen, R.: VSS from distributed ZK proofs and applications. In: Guo, J., Steinfeld, R. (eds.) Advances in Cryptology – ASIACRYPT 2023, Part I. LNCS, vol. 14438, pp. 405–440. Springer, Singapore (2023). https://doi.org/10.1007/978-981-99-8721-4_13

6. Auer, R., Top, J.: Legendre elliptic curves over finite fields. J. Number Theory **95**(2), 303–312 (2002). https://doi.org/10.1006/jnth.2001.2760
7. Bank, E., Camacho-Navarro, C., Eisenträger, K., Morrison, T., Park, J.: Cycles in the supersingular $l$-isogeny graph and corresponding endomorphisms. In: Balakrishnan, J.S., Folsom, A., Lalín, M., Manes, M. (eds.) Research Directions in Number Theory. AWMS, vol. 19, pp. 41–66. Springer, Cham (2019). https://doi.org/10.1007/978-3-030-19478-9_2
8. Basso, A., Maino, L.: POKÉ: A compact and efficient PKE from higher-dimensional isogenies. In: Fehr, S., Fouque, P.-A. (eds.) Advances in Cryptology – EUROCRYPT 2025, Part II. Lecture Notes in Computer Science, vol. 15602, pp. 94–123. Springer, Cham (2025). https://doi.org/10.1007/978-3-031-91124-8_4
9. Basso, A., et al.: Supersingular curves you can trust. In: Hazay, C., Stam, M. (eds.) Advances in Cryptology – EUROCRYPT 2023, Part II. Lecture Notes in Computer Science, vol. 14005, pp. 405–437. Springer, Cham, Switzerland, Lyon, France (2023). https://doi.org/10.1007/978-3-031-30617-4_14
10. Ben-Sasson, E., Chiesa, A., Riabzev, M., Spooner, N., Virza, M., Ward, N.P.: Aurora: Transparent succinct arguments for R1CS. In: Ishai, Y., Rijmen, V. (eds.) Advances in Cryptology – EUROCRYPT 2019, Part I. LNCS, vol. 11476, pp. 103–128. Springer, Cham, Switzerland, Darmstadt, Germany (2019). https://doi.org/10.1007/978-3-030-17653-2_4
11. Beullens, W., De Feo, L., Galbraith, S.D., Petit, C.: Proving knowledge of isogenies: a survey. Des. Codes Cryptogr. **91**(11), 3425–3456 (2023). https://doi.org/10.1007/S10623-023-01243-3
12. Beullens, W., Kleinjung, T., Vercauteren, F.: CSI-FiSh: efficient isogeny based signatures through class group computations. In: Galbraith, S.D., Moriai, S. (eds.) Advances in Cryptology – ASIACRYPT 2019, Part I. LNCS, vol. 11921, pp. 227–247. Springer, Cham (2019). https://doi.org/10.1007/978-3-030-34578-5_9
13. Beullens, W., Seiler, G.: LaBRADOR: Compact proofs for R1CS from module-SIS. In: Handschuh, H., Lysyanskaya, A. (eds.) Advances in Cryptology – CRYPTO 2023, Part V. LNCS, vol. 14085, pp. 518–548. Springer, Cham (2023). https://doi.org/10.1007/978-3-031-38554-4_17
14. Boneh, D., Bonneau, J., Bünz, B., Fisch, B.: Verifiable delay functions. In: Shacham, H., Boldyreva, A. (eds.) Advances in Cryptology – CRYPTO 2018, Part I. LNCS, vol. 10991, pp. 757–788. Springer, Cham (2018). https://doi.org/10.1007/978-3-319-96884-1_25
15. Burdges, J., De Feo, L.: Delay encryption. In: Canteaut, A., Standaert, F.X. (eds.) Advances in Cryptology – EUROCRYPT 2021, Part I. LNCS, vol. 12696, pp. 302–326. Springer, Cham (2021). https://doi.org/10.1007/978-3-030-77870-5_11
16. Castryck, W., Lange, T., Martindale, C., Panny, L., Renes, J.: CSIDH: an efficient post-quantum commutative group action. In: Peyrin, T., Galbraith, S. (eds.) Advances in Cryptology – ASIACRYPT 2018, Part III. LNCS, vol. 11274, pp. 395–427. Springer, Cham, Switzerland, Brisbane, Queensland, Australia (2018). https://doi.org/10.1007/978-3-030-03332-3_15
17. Charles, D.X., Lauter, K.E., Goren, E.Z.: Cryptographic hash functions from expander graphs. J. Cryptol. **22**, 93–113 (2009)
18. Chávez-Saab, J., Rodríguez-Henríquez, F., Tibouchi, M.: Verifiable isogeny walks: towards an isogeny-based postquantum VDF. In: AlTawy, R., Hülsing, A. (eds.) SAC 2021: 28th Annual International Workshop on Selected Areas in Cryptography. LNCS, vol. 13203, pp. 441–460. Springer, Cham (2022). https://doi.org/10.1007/978-3-030-99277-4_21

19. Codogni, G., Lido, G.: Spectral theory of isogeny graphs. arXiV:2308.13913v3 [math.NT], July 2024
20. Cohen, H., Frey, G., Avanzi, R.M., Doche, C., Lange, T., Nguyen, K., Vercauteren, F.: Handbook of elliptic and hyperelliptic curve cryptography. Discrete Math. Appl. (Boca Raton), Chapman & Hall/CRC, Boca Raton, FL (2006). https://doi.org/10.1201/9781420034981
21. Cong, K., Lai, Y.F., Levin, S.: Efficient isogeny proofs using generic techniques. In: Tibouchi, M., Wang, X. (eds.) ACNS 23: 21st International Conference on Applied Cryptography and Network Security, Part II. LNCS, vol. 13906, pp. 248–275. Springer, Cham (2023). https://doi.org/10.1007/978-3-031-33491-7_10
22. Cooper, D., Santesson, S., Farrell, S., Boeyen, S., Housley, R., Polk, W.: Internet x.509 public key infrastructure certificate and certificate revocation list (CRL) profile. RFC 5280, RFC Editor, May 2008. http://www.rfc-editor.org/rfc/rfc5280.txt
23. Costache, A., Feigon, B., Lauter, K., Massierer, M., Puskás, A.: Ramanujan graphs in cryptography. In: Balakrishnan, J.S., Folsom, A., Lalín, M., Manes, M. (eds.)
24. Couveignes, J.M.: Hard homogeneous spaces. Cryptology ePrint Archive, Paper 2006/291 (2006), https://eprint.iacr.org/2006/291
25. Cox, D.A.: Primes of the Form $x^2 + ny^2$. Fermat, Class Field Theory, and Complex Multiplication. Pure and Applied Mathematics: A Wiley Series of Texts, Monographs and Tracts, John Wiley & Sons, 2nd edn. (2013)
26. Cremona, J., Watkins, M.: Computing isogenies of elliptic curves (2005). http://magma.maths.usyd.edu.au/users/watkins/papers/isogs.ps
27. De Feo, L., Dobson, S., Galbraith, S.D., Zobernig, L.: SIDH proof of knowledge. In: Agrawal, S., Lin, D. (eds.) Advances in Cryptology – ASIACRYPT 2022, Part II. LNCS, vol. 13792, pp. 310–339. Springer, Cham (2022). https://doi.org/10.1007/978-3-031-22966-4_11
28. De Feo, L., Jao, D., Plût, J.: Towards quantum-resistant cryptosystems from supersingular elliptic curve isogenies. J. Math. Cryptol. **8**(3), 209–247 (2014). https://doi.org/10.1515/JMC-2012-0015
29. De Feo, L., Kohel, D., Leroux, A., Petit, C., Wesolowski, B.: SQISign: compact post-quantum signatures from quaternions and isogenies. In: Moriai, S., Wang, H. (eds.) Advances in Cryptology – ASIACRYPT 2020, Part I. LNCS, vol. 12491, pp. 64–93. Springer, Cham (2020). https://doi.org/10.1007/978-3-030-64837-4_3
30. De Feo, L., Masson, S., Petit, C., Sanso, A.: Verifiable delay functions from supersingular isogenies and pairings. In: Galbraith, S.D., Moriai, S. (eds.) Advances in Cryptology – ASIACRYPT 2019, Part I. LNCS, vol. 11921, pp. 248–277. Springer, Cham (2019). https://doi.org/10.1007/978-3-030-34578-5_10
31. Delpech de Saint Guilhem, C., Orsini, E., Tanguy, T.: Limbo: efficient zero-knowledge MPCitH-based arguments. In: Vigna, G., Shi, E. (eds.) ACM CCS 2021: 28th Conference on Computer and Communications Security, pp. 3022–3036. ACM Press, Virtual Event, Republic of Korea (2021). https://doi.org/10.1145/3460120.3484595
32. den Hollander, T., Kleine, S., Mula, M., Slamanig, D., Spindler, S.A.: More efficient isogeny proofs of knowledge via canonical modular polynomials. Cryptology ePrint Archive, Paper 2024/1738 (2024). https://eprint.iacr.org/2024/1738
33. Duparc, M., Fouotsa, T.B., Vaudenay, S.: SILBE: An updatable public key encryption scheme from lollipop attacks. In: Eichlseder, M., Gambs, S. (eds.) SAC 2024: 31st Annual International Workshop on Selected Areas in Cryptography, Part I. Lecture Notes in Computer Science, vol. 15516, pp. 151–177. Springer, Cham (2024). https://doi.org/10.1007/978-3-031-82852-2_7

34. Elkies, N.D.: Elliptic and modular curves over finite fields and related computational issues. In: Buell, D.A., Teitelbaum, J.T. (eds.) Computational Perspectives on Number Theory, Studies in Advanced Mathematics, vol. 7, pp. 21–76. American Mathematical Society (AMS) (1998)
35. Fouotsa, T.B., Moriya, T., Petit, C.: M-SIDH and MD-SIDH: countering SIDH attacks by masking information. In: Hazay, C., Stam, M. (eds.) Advances in Cryptology – EUROCRYPT 2023, Part V. LNCS, vol. 14008, pp. 282–309. Springer, Cham (2023). https://doi.org/10.1007/978-3-031-30589-4_10
36. Fricke, R.: Die elliptischen Funktionen und ihre Anwendungen: Zweiter Teil: Die algebraischen Ausführungen. Life Science and Basic Disciplines (German Language), Springer Berlin, Heidelberg, 1st edn. (2011). https://doi.org/10.1007/978-3-642-19561-7. (originally published by B.G. Teubner-Verlag (1922))
37. Galbraith, S.D., Petit, C., Silva, J.: Identification protocols and signature schemes based on supersingular isogeny problems. In: Takagi, T., Peyrin, T. (eds.) Advances in Cryptology – ASIACRYPT 2017, Part I. LNCS, vol. 10624, pp. 3–33. Springer, Cham (2017). https://doi.org/10.1007/978-3-319-70694-8_1
38. Golovnev, A., Lee, J., Setty, S.T.V., Thaler, J., Wahby, R.S.: Brakedown: linear-time and field-agnostic SNARKs for R1CS. In: Handschuh, H., Lysyanskaya, A. (eds.) Advances in Cryptology – CRYPTO 2023, Part II. LNCS, vol. 14082, pp. 193–226. Springer, Cham (2023). https://doi.org/10.1007/978-3-031-38545-2_7
39. Gow, R.: Some properties and uses of the discriminant of a polynomial. In: Ryan, R., Hurley, T., Rippon, P. (eds.) Irish Mathematical Society Bulletin. vol. 24, pp. 12–19. Irish Mathematical Society (1990)
40. Groth, J.: On the size of pairing-based non-interactive arguments. In: Fischlin, M., Coron, J.S. (eds.) Advances in Cryptology – EUROCRYPT 2016, Part II. LNCS, vol. 9666, pp. 305–326. Springer, Berlin (2016). https://doi.org/10.1007/978-3-662-49896-5_11
41. Groth, J., Kohlweiss, M., Maller, M., Meiklejohn, S., Miers, I.: Updatable and universal common reference strings with applications to zk-SNARKs. In: Shacham, H., Boldyreva, A. (eds.) Advances in Cryptology – CRYPTO 2018, Part III. LNCS, vol. 10993, pp. 698–728. Springer, Cham (2018). https://doi.org/10.1007/978-3-319-96878-0_24
42. Güneysu, T., Hodges, P.W., Land, G., Ounsworth, M., Stebila, D., Zaverucha, G.: Proof-of-possession for KEM certificates using verifiable generation. In: Yin, H., Stavrou, A., Cremers, C., Shi, E. (eds.) ACM CCS 2022: 29th Conference on Computer and Communications Security, pp. 1337–1351. ACM Press (2022). https://doi.org/10.1145/3548606.3560560
43. Jao, D., De Feo, L.: Towards quantum-resistant cryptosystems from supersingular elliptic curve isogenies. In: Yang, B.Y. (ed.) Post-Quantum Cryptography - 4th International Workshop, PQCrypto 2011, pp. 19–34. Springer, Berlin, Heidelberg (2011). https://doi.org/10.1007/978-3-642-25405-5_2
44. Kaneko, M.: Supersingular $j$-invariants as singular moduli mod $p$. Osaka J. Math. **26**(4), 849–855 (1989)
45. Kohel, D.: Endomorphism rings of elliptic curves over finite fields. Ph.D. thesis, University of California, Berkeley (1996). https://www.i2m.univ-amu.fr/perso/david.kohel/pub/thesis.pdf
46. Lang, S.: Elliptic Functions, Graduate Texts in Mathematics, vol. 112. Springer, New York, NY (1987). https://doi.org/10.1007/978-1-4612-4752-4
47. Lercier, R.: Algorithmique des courbes elliptiques dans les corps finis. Ph.D. thesis, Ecole Polytechnique, June 1997. https://univ-rennes.hal.science/tel-01101949

48. Levin, S., Pedersen, R.: Faster proofs and VRFs from isogenies. Cryptology ePrint Archive, Paper 2024/1626 (2024). https://eprint.iacr.org/2024/1626
49. Li, S., Ouyang, Y., Xu, Z.: Neighborhood of the supersingular elliptic curve isogeny graph at $j = 0$ and 1728. Finite Fields Appl. **61**, 101600 (2020). https://doi.org/10.1016/j.ffa.2019.101600
50. Lipmaa, H.: A unified framework for non-universal SNARKs. In: Hanaoka, G., Shikata, J., Watanabe, Y. (eds.) PKC 2022: 25th International Conference on Theory and Practice of Public Key Cryptography, Part I. LNCS, vol. 13177, pp. 553–583. Springer, Cham (2022). https://doi.org/10.1007/978-3-030-97121-2_20
51. Love, J., Boneh, D.: Supersingular curves with small noninteger endomorphisms. In: ANTS XIV: Proceedings of the Fourteenth Algorithmic Number Theory Symposium. Open Book Series, vol. 4, pp. 7–22. Mathematical Sciences Publishers (2020). https://msp.org/obs/2020/4-1/obs-v4-n1-p.pdf
52. Mestre, J.F.: La méthode des graphes. exemples et applications. In: Proceedings of the international conference on class numbers and fundamental units of algebraic number fields (Katata), pp. 217–242 (1986). https://wstein.org/papers/rank4/mestre-en.pdf. (english version (tr. Andrei Jorza))
53. Morain, F.: Calcul du nombre de points sur une courbe elliptique dans un corps fini: aspects algorithmiques. Journal de Théorie des Nombres de Bordeaux **7**(1), 255–282 (1995). http://www.jstor.org/stable/43972443
54. Moriya, T.: IS-CUBE: An isogeny-based compact KEM using a boxed SIDH diagram. Cryptology ePrint Archive, Paper 2023/1506 (2023). https://eprint.iacr.org/2023/1506
55. Müller, V.: Ein Algorithmus zur Bestimmung der Punktanzahl elliptischer Kurven über endlichen Körpern der Charakteristik größer drei. Ph.D. thesis, Universität des Saarlandes (1995). https://publikationen.sulb.uni-saarland.de/handle/20.500.11880/25777
56. Nguyen, N.K., Seiler, G.: Practical sublinear proofs for R1CS from lattices. In: Dodis, Y., Shrimpton, T. (eds.) Advances in Cryptology – CRYPTO 2022, Part II. LNCS, vol. 13508, pp. 133–162. Springer, Cham (2022). https://doi.org/10.1007/978-3-031-15979-4_5
57. Pizer, A.K.: Ramanujan graphs and Hecke operators. Bull. Am. Math. Soc. New Ser. **23**(1), 127–137 (1990). https://doi.org/10.1090/S0273-0979-1990-15918-X
58. Ristenpart, T., Yilek, S.: The power of proofs-of-possession: securing multiparty signatures against rogue-key attacks. In: Naor, M. (ed.) Advances in Cryptology – EUROCRYPT 2007. LNCS, vol. 4515, pp. 228–245. Springer, Berlin, Heidelberg (2007). https://doi.org/10.1007/978-3-540-72540-4_13
59. Rostovtsev, A., Stolbunov, A.: Public-key cryptosystem based on isogenies. Cryptology ePrint Archive, Paper 2006/145 (2006). https://eprint.iacr.org/2006/145
60. Schwabe, P., Stebila, D., Wiggers, T.: Post-quantum TLS without handshake signatures. In: Ligatti, J., Ou, X., Katz, J., Vigna, G. (eds.) ACM CCS 2020: 27th Conference on Computer and Communications Security, pp. 1461–1480. ACM Press, Virtual Event, USA (2020). https://doi.org/10.1145/3372297.3423350
61. Silverman, J.H.: The arithmetic of elliptic curves, Grad. Texts in Mathematics, vol. 106. Springer New York, NY, 2nd edn. (2009). https://doi.org/10.1007/978-0-387-09494-6
62. Sutherland, A.V.: Isogeny volcanoes. In: Howe, E.W., Kedlaya, K.S. (eds.) ANTS X. Proceedings of the Tenth Algorithmic Number Theory Symposium. The Open Book Series, vol. 1, pp. 507–530. Mathematical Sciences Publishers, November 2013. https://doi.org/10.2140/obs.2013.1.507

63. Thaler, J.: Proofs, arguments, and zero-knowledge. Found. Trends Priv. Secur. **4**(2–4), 117–660 (2022). https://doi.org/10.1561/3300000030
64. Tsukazaki, K.: Explicit isogenies of elliptic curves. Ph.D. thesis, University of Warwick, July 2013. http://webcat.warwick.ac.uk/record=b2688905~S1
65. Washington, L.C.: Elliptic Curves. Number Theory and Cryptography, 2nd edn. Chapman and Hall/CRC, Boca Raton (2008)
66. Xie, T., Zhang, J., Zhang, Y., Papamanthou, C., Song, D.: Libra: succinct zero-knowledge proofs with optimal prover computation. In: Boldyreva, A., Micciancio, D. (eds.) Advances in Cryptology – CRYPTO 2019, Part III. LNCS, vol. 11694, pp. 733–764. Springer, Cham (2019). https://doi.org/10.1007/978-3-030-26954-8_24
67. Xie, T., Zhang, Y., Song, D.: Orion: zero knowledge proof with linear prover time. In: Dodis, Y., Shrimpton, T. (eds.) Advances in Cryptology – CRYPTO 2022, Part IV. LNCS, vol. 13510, pp. 299–328. Springer, Cham (2022). https://doi.org/10.1007/978-3-031-15985-5_11

# KLPT$^2$: Algebraic Pathfinding in Dimension Two and Applications

Wouter Castryck[1(✉)], Thomas Decru[1], Péter Kutas[2,4], Abel Laval[3], Christophe Petit[3,4], and Yan Bo Ti[5,6]

[1] COSIC, KU Leuven, Leuven, Belgium
wouter.castryck@esat.kuleuven.be, decruthomas@gmail.com
[2] Faculty of Informatics, Eötvös Loránd University, Budapest, Hungary
kutasp@gmail.com
[3] Computer Science Department, Université Libre de Bruxelles, Brussels, Belgium
{abel.laval,christophe.petit}@ulb.be
[4] School of Computer Science, University of Birmingham, Birmingham, UK
[5] DSO National Laboratories, Singapore, Singapore
yanbo.ti@gmail.com
[6] Temasek Laboratories, National University of Singapore, Singapore, Singapore

**Abstract.** Following Ibukiyama, Katsura and Oort, all principally polarized superspecial abelian surfaces over $\overline{\mathbb{F}}_p$ can be represented by a certain type of $2 \times 2$ matrix $g$, having entries in the quaternion algebra $B_{p,\infty}$. We present a heuristic polynomial-time algorithm which, upon input of two such matrices $g_1, g_2$, finds a "connecting matrix" representing a polarized isogeny of smooth degree between the corresponding surfaces. Our algorithm should be thought of as a two-dimensional analog of the KLPT algorithm from 2014 due to Kohel, Lauter, Petit and Tignol for finding a connecting ideal of smooth norm between two given maximal orders in $B_{p,\infty}$.

The KLPT algorithm has proven to be a versatile tool in isogeny-based cryptography, and our analog has similar applications; we discuss two of them in detail. First, we show that it yields a polynomial-time solution to a two-dimensional analog of the so-called constructive Deuring correspondence: given a matrix $g$ representing a superspecial principally polarized abelian surface, realize the latter as the Jacobian of a genus-2 curve (or, exceptionally, as the product of two elliptic curves if it concerns a product polarization). Second, we show that, modulo a plausible assumption, Charles–Goren–Lauter style hash functions from superspecial principally polarized abelian surfaces require a trusted set-up. Concretely, if the matrix $g$ associated with the starting surface is known then collisions can be produced in polynomial time. We deem it plausible that all currently known methods for generating a starting surface indeed reveal the corresponding matrix. As an auxiliary tool, we present an efficient method for converting isogenies of powersmooth degree into the corresponding connecting matrix, a step for which a previous approach by Chu required super-polynomial (but sub-exponential) time.


Y. Tauman Kalai and S. F. Kamara (Eds.): CRYPTO 2025, LNCS 16000, pp. 167–200, 2025.
https://doi.org/10.1007/978-3-032-01855-7_6

# 1 Introduction

In isogeny-based cryptography, the core problem is that of finding an explicit isogeny between two isogenous elliptic curves over a finite field. Here, "explicit" often implicates that the degree of the isogeny is powersmooth, or a power of some small prescribed prime number $\ell$. For reasons of both security and efficiency, almost all cryptographic constructions restrict their focus to supersingular elliptic curves. Famously, Deuring [19] proved that such curves are (essentially) in one-to-one correspondence with maximal orders in the quaternion algebra $B_{p,\infty}$ ramified at $p$ and $\infty$; here $p$ denotes the field characteristic. Under this correspondence, isogenies correspond to ideals, and the isogeny-finding problem translates into finding a connecting ideal between two given maximal orders $\mathcal{O}_0, \mathcal{O}_1 \subset B_{p,\infty}$, where one then aims for integral ideals $I$ whose norm $\mathsf{n}(I)$ is powersmooth or a power of $\ell$. Interestingly, this quaternion version of the isogeny-finding problem can be dealt with efficiently: in 2014, Kohel, Lauter, Petit, and Tignol [33] proposed a polynomial-time algorithm, now commonly known as the KLPT algorithm, for solving exactly this problem.

This result has had an amplitude of consequences, both constructive and destructive. For example, it breaks the second pre-image resistance of the Charles–Goren–Lauter (CGL) hash function [21,22] when using an untrusted set-up. A more recent cryptanalytic example is the break of pSIDH [10].[1] More fundamentally, it has led to a key insight in isogeny-based cryptography. Namely, on one hand, given a maximal order in $B_{p,\infty}$, one can use the KLPT algorithm to compute a corresponding supersingular elliptic curve $E/\overline{\mathbb{F}}_p$ in polynomial time: this is called the constructive Deuring correspondence and it is practical for cryptographically sized values of $p$ [23]. On the other hand, the converse problem, namely computing the endomorphism ring of a given supersingular elliptic curve, is believed to be very hard. By now, we understand, in a heuristic-free way,[2] that this is in fact the central hard problem in (supersingular) isogeny-based cryptography [45]. That is, the Deuring correspondence is a one-way function, and it allows for trapdoors, e.g., in the form of secret isogenies to an easy base curve. This has sparked many important constructions, where we highlight the Galbraith–Petit–Silva (GPS) signature scheme [25] and SQIsign [18].

Recently, the field of isogeny-based cryptography was shaken up by the use of higher-dimensional principally polarized abelian varieties. Earlier works such as [7,11,24,43] studied these objects in their own right, but the real catalysts were the attacks on SIDH [5,35,39] which revealed a very powerful interplay between higher dimension and dimension one, i.e., the world of elliptic curves. Constructive applications followed soon, especially because the machinery allows for efficient representations of isogenies of arbitrary degree [40]. This has culminated in various new schemes, including SQIsign variants [1,17,20,37] improving over their ancestor in terms of speed, compactness, and security foundations.

---

[1] The attack from [10] does not invoke the KLPT algorithm directly; rather, it uses and adapts several of its subroutines.

[2] Modulo a reliance on the generalized Riemann hypothesis.

In view of these current trends, a higher-dimensional analog of the KLPT algorithm is an important lacking tool. The direct provocation for this research is the PhD thesis by Chu [11], who mentions this as a missing ingredient in a GPS-style signature scheme from superspecial principally polarized abelian surfaces. Here, the Deuring correspondence is to be replaced with a correspondence due to Ibukiyama, Katsura and Oort [29] describing principal polarizations and polarized isogenies in terms of $2 \times 2$ matrices with entries in $B_{p,\infty}$. Such a missing analog of KLPT is exactly the central result of our paper.

**Main Contributions:**

- *KLPT*$^2$. We provide a two-dimensional analog of the KLPT algorithm: upon input of two matrices $g_1, g_2$ representing two principally polarized superspecial abelian surfaces, the KLPT$^2$ algorithm heuristically finds, in polynomial time, a "connecting matrix" representing a polarized isogeny of reduced degree $N$. We provide versions both for $N = \ell^e$ (where $\ell$ is a small prescribed prime number) and for $N$ powersmooth. In both cases, the value of $N$ achieved is in $O(p^{25+o(1)})$. The main techniques are the following. First we observe that if the matrices $g_1, g_2$ are in a very special form, then finding a connecting matrix is easy (Lemma 3.3). This turns the problem into a transformation problem: instead of connecting two matrices, try to transform one matrix into a standard form. An important challenge is to bound the output degree in a way that only depends on $p$ and not on the sizes of the matrices $g_i$. This is handled using certain size reductions and solving certain Diophantine equations. One noteworthy ingredient is an algorithm that given $a, c \in \mathcal{O}$ (where $\mathcal{O}$ is a maximal order in $B_{p,\infty}$) that have coprime norm, finds $b, d \in \mathcal{O}$ such that the reduced norm of the matrix $\left(\begin{smallmatrix} a & b \\ c & d \end{smallmatrix}\right)$ is a power of $\ell$ (or powersmooth) in $O(p^{3+o(1)})$. Quite surprisingly, this problem is essentially equivalent to 1-dimensional KLPT (Sect. 3.2). We deem it very likely that the exponent $25 + o(1)$ can be improved, but leave such sharpenings for future work (and we note that future improvements on one-dimensional KLPT also improve our results).
- *Constructive Ibukiyama–Katsura–Oort (IKO) correspondence.* In Sect. 4.1, we describe an efficient algorithm for matrix-to-isogeny conversion for powersmooth degrees (thereby ticking off an unsurprising but missing ingredient in Chu's aforementioned signature scheme). Combined with our KLPT$^2$ algorithm, this yields a heuristic polynomial-time method for an analog of the constructive Deuring correspondence, described in Sect. 5.1: given a matrix $g$ representing a principally polarized superspecial abelian surface, we explicitly realize this surface as either the Jacobian of a genus-2 curve, or as a product of elliptic curves equipped with the product polarization.
- *Polynomial-time isogeny-to-matrix conversion for isogenies of smooth degree.* In order to transfer more advanced applications of KLPT to dimension two, one also needs an efficient solution to the converse problem: given a principally polarized superspecial abelian surface $A_1$ with known matrix $g_1$, along with a polarized isogeny $\varphi : A_1 \to A_2$, find a matrix $g_2$ corresponding to $A_2$ along with a connecting matrix corresponding to $\varphi$. In the special case

of $(\ell, \ell)$-isogenies, where $\ell$ denotes any small prime, we provide a simple and efficient method for computing such a connecting matrix, and then $g_2$ follows right away. This then naturally extends to a polynomial-time algorithm for isogeny-to-matrix conversion for polarized isogenies of powersmooth degree. In this way, we by-pass the need for invoking Chu's super-polynomial (but sub-exponential) time algorithm for the principal ideal problem (PIP) in quaternionic matrix rings [11, Chapter 2]. Finally, by mimicking a method due to Eisenträger, Hallgren, Lauter, Morrison and Petit [21, Algorithm 9], in Sect. 14 we lift this to a polynomial-time algorithm for isogeny-to-matrix conversion for polarized isogenies of arbitrary smooth degree, through a repeated application of $\text{KLPT}^2$.
- *Attacks on CGL style hash functions.* Section 5.4 describes our main application: an attack on CGL-type hash functions in dimension two, which were explicitly proposed in [7,13,24,34,43], in the case of an untrusted set-up. This is similar to the KLPT-based attacks [21,22] on the original CGL hash function. Concretely, if the starting surface comes with a known matrix $g$ (which seems a fair assumption to make in all untrusted instantiations) then we can use the $\text{KLPT}^2$ algorithm to find collisions. Unfortunately, it does not allow us to find second pre-images, due to the fact that $\text{KLPT}^2$ does not produce "good" chains of $(\ell, \ell)$-isogenies in the sense of [7] (see Corollary 5.4).

We conclude this introduction by noting that our $\text{KLPT}^2$ algorithm can be seen as a constructive proof (modulo heuristic assumptions) of the dimension-two case of Jordan and Zaytman's recent result that the graph of $(\ell, \dots, \ell)$-isogenies between superspecial principally polarized abelian varieties is connected [30].

**Outline**

We provide some background on the KLPT algorithm, principal polarizations, the Ibukiyama–Katsura–Oort correspondence, and quaternionic matrices in Sect. 2. We describe our generalization of KLPT to dimension two in Sect. 3 and discuss routines for matrix-to-isogeny and isogeny-to-matrix conversion in Sect. 4. We describe our applications of $\text{KLPT}^2$ in Sect. 5. This is the shortened proceedings version of a longer paper that can be found online [6], to which we refer for all the missing proofs, several accompanying remarks, and some natural directions for future research. The numbering of our theorems, lemmas, remarks etc. is consistent with that of the full version.

**Acknowledgments and Support**

We thank Jonathan Komada Eriksen, Riccardo Invernizzi, Gábor Ivanyos, Harun Kir, Gioella Lorenzon, Aurel Page, Krijn Reijnders, Damien Robert, Frederik Vercauteren and the anonymous reviewers for helpful insights and comments. Castryck and Decru are supported in part by the European Research Council (ERC) under the European Union's Horizon 2020 research and innovation programme (grant agreement ISOCRYPT – No. 101020788), by the Research Council KU Leuven grant C14/ 24/099, as well as by CyberSecurity Research Flanders with reference number VR20192203. Together with Kutas, they are also supported by the CELSA alliance through the MaCro project. Decru is partly supported by Fonds de la Recherche Scientifique (FRS-FNRS) and by Fonds voor Wetenschappelijk Onderzoek (FWO) with reference number 1245025N. Petit is partly supported by EPSRC through grant number EP/V011324/1 and FRS-FNRS through grant number T.0238.25. Kutas is partly supported by EPSRC through grant number EP/V011324/1, the Hungarian Ministry of Innovation and Technology Office within the framework of the Quantum Information National Laboratory Program and by the grant "EXCELLENCE-151343", and by János Bolyai Research Scholarship of the Hungarian Academy of Sciences.

## 2 Preliminaries

### 2.1 Deuring Correspondence and the KLPT Algorithm

For general background on quaternion algebras, we refer to [44]. For now, recall that a (rational) quaternion algebra $B$ is a central simple algebra of dimension 4 over $\mathbb{Q}$. An order in $B$ is a subring $\mathcal{O} \subset B$ containing 1 which has rank 4 as a $\mathbb{Z}$-module. An order is called maximal if it is maximal with respect to inclusion. The isomorphism class of a quaternion algebra is determined by its local behaviour: for which completions $\mathbb{Q}_v$ do we have that $B \otimes_{\mathbb{Q}} \mathbb{Q}_v$ is a division algebra? Such places $v$ are called ramified.[3] In this paper we will be concerned with $B_{p,\infty}$, the unique quaternion algebra up to isomorphism which is ramified at $\infty$ and at a fixed prime number $p$ (typically of cryptographic size). The endomorphism ring of every supersingular elliptic curve over $\overline{\mathbb{F}}_p$ is isomorphic to a maximal order $\mathcal{O} \subset B_{p,\infty}$. Under this isomorphism, the degree of an endomorphism corresponds to the norm[4] $\mathsf{n}(u)$ of the corresponding quaternion $u$.

*Example 2.1.* If $p \equiv 3 \bmod 4$ then one can realize the quaternion algebra $B_{p,\infty}$ as $\mathbb{Q}\langle 1, i, j, k\rangle$ with $i^2 = -1$, $j^2 = -p$ and $k = ij = -ji$. The elliptic curve $E_0 : y^2 = x^3 + x$ with $j(E_0) = 1728$ is supersingular. Here $\mathrm{End}(E_0) \cong \mathcal{O}_0$ with

$$\mathcal{O}_0 = \left\langle 1, i, \frac{i+j}{2}, \frac{1+k}{2} \right\rangle.$$

One isomorphism $\tau : \mathcal{O}_0 \xrightarrow{\cong} \mathrm{End}(E_0)$ arises by letting $\tau(i) : (x, y) \mapsto (-x, \sqrt{-1}y)$ and $\tau(j) : (x, y) \mapsto (x^p, y^p)$. As mentioned: $\mathsf{n}(u) = \deg(\tau(u))$ for all $u \in \mathcal{O}_0$.

The Deuring correspondence [19] asserts that this turns into a categorical equivalence between supersingular elliptic curves defined over $\overline{\mathbb{F}}_p$ (up to Galois conjugation) and maximal orders in $B_{p,\infty}$ (up to isomorphism or, equivalently, up to conjugation). On the elliptic curve side, the non-zero morphisms are isogenies $\varphi : E_0 \to E_1$. On the quaternion side, such an isogeny $\varphi$ corresponds to a rank-4 sub-$\mathbb{Z}$-module $I \subset B_{p,\infty}$ which is a left, resp. right, ideal of a maximal order $\mathcal{O}_0 \cong \mathrm{End}(E_0)$, resp. $\mathcal{O}_1 \cong \mathrm{End}(E_1)$. This ideal is then referred to as a connecting ideal of $\mathcal{O}_0$ and $\mathcal{O}_1$. Note that endomorphism rings can be embedded

[3] In the non-ramified cases we have $B \otimes_{\mathbb{Q}} \mathbb{Q}_v \cong \mathrm{M}_2(\mathbb{Q}_v)$.

[4] Or rather to its *reduced* norm in the sense of [44, Section 3.3]; throughout this paper, for simplicity, we will drop the adjective "reduced".

into $B_{p,\infty}$ in many ways: any embedding can be post-composed with conjugation. This warrants the notion of equivalent ideals: a left ideal $J \subset \mathcal{O}_0$ will be a right ideal of an order $\mathcal{O}_1' \cong \mathcal{O}_1$ if and only if there exists $\beta \in B_{p,\infty} \setminus \{0\}$ such that $J = I\beta$. On the geometric side, this corresponds to different isogenies connecting the same curves. The left ideals $I, J \subset \mathcal{O}_0$ are then said to be equivalent.

There is an explicit geometric view on Deuring's construction of the ideal $I$: it can be seen as the subset of $\mathrm{End}(E_0)$ that is obtained by post-composing $\varphi$ with all elements of $\mathrm{Hom}(E_1, E_0)$. Thus $I$ encodes the set of all isogenies $E_1 \to E_0$, and the norm of every element of $I$ is divisible by the degree of $\varphi$. More precisely, it can be shown that $\deg(\varphi)$ equals $\mathsf{n}(I) = \gcd\{\mathsf{n}(u) \mid u \in I\}$, the norm of $I$.

The Deuring correspondence implies that there is a natural quaternion analog of the $\ell$-isogeny pathfinding problem. Indeed, upon input of two maximal orders $\mathcal{O}_0, \mathcal{O}_1 \subset B_{p,\infty}$ connected by an ideal $I$, it amounts to finding an equivalent left ideal $J \subset \mathcal{O}_0$ of norm $\ell^e$ for some $e \geq 1$. An alternative viewpoint taking the geometric interpretation into account is as follows: when given one connecting ideal $I$, it is enough to find $\sigma \in I$ such that $\mathsf{n}(\sigma) = \mathsf{n}(I)\ell^e$. This is exactly the problem that is addressed by the KLPT algorithm [33].[5] It is then easy to check that $J = I\beta$ with $\beta = \bar{\sigma}/\,\mathsf{n}(I)$ is an equivalent ideal with norm $\ell^e$. Geometrically, under the above identification of $I$ with $\mathrm{Hom}(E_1, E_0)\varphi$, we can write $\sigma = \tau\varphi$ for a degree-$\ell^e$ isogeny $\tau : E_1 \to E_0$, and then $J$ corresponds to $\mathrm{Hom}(E_1, E_0)\varphi\hat{\sigma}/\deg(\varphi) = \mathrm{Hom}(E_1, E_0)\varphi\hat{\varphi}\hat{\tau}/\deg(\varphi) = \mathrm{Hom}(E_1, E_0)\hat{\tau}$.

*Remark 2.2.* This is an important view on KLPT as we will need it in exactly the version where it finds an element of prescribed norm in a certain ideal.

The way KLPT proceeds is as follows. Using a simple trick one can assume knowledge of a left ideal $I \subset \mathcal{O}_0$ of prime norm $N$, so we would like to find an element $\sigma \in I$ of norm $N\ell^e$. First one finds $\gamma \in \mathcal{O}_0$ whose norm is $N\ell^{e_0}$. Now the ideal $J = \mathcal{O}_0 N + \mathcal{O}_0\gamma$ has norm $N$. Locally, i.e., modulo $N$, $I$ and $J$ reduce to proper left ideals of the matrix ring $\mathrm{M}_2(\mathbb{Z}/N\mathbb{Z})$ and such ideals only differ by right-multiplication by an invertible element $\delta$. Such a $\delta$ can be computed locally and lifted to $\mathcal{O}_0$ (using an explicit isomorphism between $\mathcal{O}_0/N\mathcal{O}_0$ and $\mathrm{M}_2(\mathbb{Z}/N\mathbb{Z})$) which implies that $\gamma\delta \in I$. Now the key is that $\delta$ is determined modulo $N$ only, so what is left to do is choose an appropriate lifting such that $\mathsf{n}(\delta) = \ell^{e_1}$. This step is called *strong approximation* and in [33] it is carried out for special extremal orders $\mathcal{O}_0$, i.e., maximal orders containing an imaginary quadratic order with small discriminant (it can be modified to work for arbitrary orders, see [18, Section 5] and [10, Section 5]). Now it is clear that $\gamma\delta$ will fit our criteria with $e = e_0 + e_1$. The KLPT algorithm can ensure that $\ell^e \in O(p^{3+o(1)})$.[6]

### 2.2 Principally Polarized Abelian Varieties

For detailed background, we refer to [4,11,29,36]. An abelian variety over an algebraically closed field is a projective algebraic variety which is also an alge-

[5] In other applications of KLPT one searches for connecting ideals having powersmooth norm, but the approach is entirely the same.

[6] The original bound from KLPT is in the order of $p^{3.5}$, but an improvement due to Petit and Smith [38], reported in [9, Algorithm 13], reduces this to $p^{3+o(1)}$ as stated.

braic group. The notion generalizes that of an elliptic curve, which is an abelian variety of dimension one. However, for most uses (including in cryptography), the more relevant generalization is that of an abelian variety equipped with a *principal polarization*. Unfortunately, this notion does not admit a down-to-earth definition. Luckily, the exact construction is not really important for this paper, which is mostly algebraic in nature. Therefore, the reader who is unfamiliar with the notation and terminology below can just think of a polarization as a certain kind of isogeny (i.e., a finite surjective homomorphism) between $A$ and a companion abelian variety $\hat{A}$ called its dual.[7] We include a formal definition, e.g., to allow the reader to verify the proof of Theorem 2.8 further down:

**Definition 2.3.** *A* polarization *on a $g$-dimensional abelian variety $A$ is an isogeny of the form*

$$\begin{aligned} \lambda : A &\to \hat{A} = \mathrm{Pic}^0(A) \\ P &\mapsto [t_{-P}(D) - D] \end{aligned}$$

*with $D$ an ample divisor on $A$, where $t_{-P}$ denotes point-wise translation by $-P$. It can be shown that* $\deg(\lambda) = (D^g/g!)^2$ *with $D^g$ the self-intersection number of $D$. If this degree is equal to* 1 *then the polarization is called* principal. *Write* $\mathrm{PPol}(A)$ *for the set of principal polarizations on $A$.*

The reason why the notion of a principally polarized abelian variety still generalizes that of an elliptic curve is that, in the latter case, there is a unique principal polarization, called the canonical polarization. It is given by the negated Abel–Jacobi map: $P \mapsto [(\infty) - (P)]$. The uniqueness typically no longer holds in higher dimension. This is notoriously true for *superspecial* abelian varieties, which are our main objects of interest. A $g$-dimensional superspecial abelian variety is a variety which—as an unpolarized variety—is isomorphic to a product of $g$ supersingular elliptic curves. It can be shown that, for a fixed characteristic $p$, all such products are pairwise isomorphic as soon as $g \geq 2$ [41, Theorem 3.5]. However, this unique isomorphism class carries $\Theta(p^{g(g+1)/2})$ inequivalent principal polarizations (in the sense of Definition 2.7 below).

**Definition 2.4.** *A (polarized) isogeny between two principally polarized abelian varieties $(A, \lambda_A)$ and $(B, \lambda_B)$ is an isogeny $\varphi : A \to B$ that respects the polarizations, i.e., there exists a positive integer $N$ for which the following diagram commutes*

$$\begin{array}{ccc} A & \xrightarrow{\ \varphi\ } & B \\ {\scriptstyle [N]\lambda_A}\big\downarrow & & \big\downarrow{\scriptstyle \lambda_B} \\ \hat{A} & \xleftarrow[\ \hat{\varphi}\ ]{} & \hat{B} \end{array}$$

*Here, $\hat{\varphi}$ is the dual isogeny, defined by taking inverse image divisors under $\varphi$. One has* $\deg(\varphi) = N^g$, *and we call* $N = \mathrm{degrd}(\varphi)$ *the* reduced degree *of $\varphi$. If $N = 1$ then $\varphi$ is called a (polarized) isomorphism; we write $(A, \lambda_A) \cong (B, \lambda_B)$.*

[7] Not all isogenies $A \to \hat{A}$ are polarizations: a certain positivity condition should be satisfied. E.g., if $\lambda$ is a polarization, then $-\lambda$ is not. See [12, pp. 6–7] for a discussion.

*Remark 2.5.* Given a principally polarized abelian variety $(A, \lambda_A)$, an abelian variety $B$ and an isogeny $\varphi : A \to B$, in general there does not exist a principal polarization $\lambda_B : B \to \hat{B}$ such that $\varphi$ is polarized. If it does exist, then $\lambda_B$ is unique and called the induced principal polarization. Assuming that $\deg(\varphi) = N^g$ for some integer $N$ coprime with the field characteristic, a necessary and sufficient condition for existence [31, Proposition 1.1] is that $\ker(\varphi)$ is a maximal isotropic subgroup of $A[N]$, where isotropic means that $e_{N,\lambda_A}(P, Q) = 1$ for all $P, Q \in A[N]$, with $e_{N,\lambda_A} : A[N] \times A[N] \to \mu_N$ the $N$-Weil pairing with respect to the principal polarization $\lambda_A$. In this case $\mathrm{degrd}(\varphi) = N$.

*Remark 2.6.* An isogeny $\varphi$ is said to be an $(N_1, \ldots, N_r)$-isogeny, for certain integers $N_i$, if it is separable, polarized and $\ker(\varphi) \cong \bigoplus_{i=1}^{r} \mathbb{Z}/N_i\mathbb{Z}$. If $\mathrm{degrd}(\varphi)$ is a prime number $\ell$, then it concerns an $(\ell, \ldots, \ell)$-isogeny, where $r = g$.

For any isogeny $\varphi : A \to B$ and any choice of principal polarizations $\lambda_A$, $\lambda_B$, it is natural to consider the *adjoint* isogeny

$$\tilde{\varphi} = \lambda_A^{-1} \hat{\varphi} \lambda_B : B \to A$$

with respect to $\lambda_A$, $\lambda_B$. If $\varphi$ is polarized, then so is $\tilde{\varphi}$ and we have $\tilde{\varphi}\varphi = [\mathrm{degrd}(\varphi)]$ and $\varphi\tilde{\varphi} = [\mathrm{degrd}(\varphi)]$. In the context of elliptic curves, the adjoint isogeny can be identified with the dual isogeny $\hat{\varphi} : \hat{B} \to \hat{A}$ via the canonical polarization, with which any isogeny is compatible. This is not the case in higher dimensions. This forces us to make a clear distinction between the dual isogeny, which is independent from any polarization, and the adjoint isogeny, which depends on a choice of principal polarizations and which exhibits the common properties we are familiar with from the elliptic curve case.

If $\lambda$ is a principal polarization on an abelian variety $A$, then the adjoint operator $\mathrm{Ros}_\lambda : \alpha \mapsto \tilde{\alpha} = \lambda^{-1}\hat{\alpha}\lambda$, defines an involution of $\mathrm{End}(A)$ called the Rosati involution (with respect to $\lambda$).

**Definition 2.7.** *Two principal polarizations $\lambda_1$ and $\lambda_2$ on an abelian variety $A$ are said to be* equivalent *if $(A, \lambda_1) \cong (A, \lambda_2)$, i.e., there exists an automorphism $\alpha$ of $A$ such that $\hat{\alpha}\lambda_1\alpha = \lambda_2$. We write $\mathrm{PPol}^0(A)$ for the set of principal polarizations on $A$ up to equivalence.*

Turning our focus to dimension $g = 2$, we recall that principally polarized abelian surfaces can be classified as follows: they are isomorphic to either

- a product $E_1 \times E_2$ of two elliptic curves, equipped with the *product polarization*, coming from $D = (E_1 \times \{\infty\}) + (\{\infty\} \times E_2)$, or
- the Jacobian $\mathrm{Jac}(C)$ of a genus-2 curve, equipped with the canonical polarization, coming from $D = (u(C))$ with $u : C \hookrightarrow \mathrm{Pic}^0(C) \cong \mathrm{Jac}(C) : P \mapsto [(P) - (\infty)]$ the Abel–Jacobi map (where $\infty \in C$ denotes any base point).

With respect to product polarizations, the adjoint admits a very explicit description which follows from the proof of [3, Proposition 4.10]. Consider four elliptic curves $E_1, E_2, E_3, E_4$ and assume we have an isogeny $\varphi : E_1 \times E_2 \to E_3 \times E_4$, not necessarily polarized. We can write this isogeny in matrix form:

$$\varphi : \begin{pmatrix} P \\ Q \end{pmatrix} \mapsto \begin{pmatrix} \alpha_{13} & \alpha_{23} \\ \alpha_{14} & \alpha_{24} \end{pmatrix} \begin{pmatrix} P \\ Q \end{pmatrix}$$

where each $\alpha_{ij} : E_i \to E_j$ is a homomorphism (an isogeny or the zero map) of elliptic curves. With respect to the product polarizations on $E_1 \times E_2$ and $E_3 \times E_4$, we have

$$\tilde{\varphi} : \begin{pmatrix} P \\ Q \end{pmatrix} \mapsto \begin{pmatrix} \hat{\alpha}_{13} & \hat{\alpha}_{14} \\ \hat{\alpha}_{23} & \hat{\alpha}_{24} \end{pmatrix} \begin{pmatrix} P \\ Q \end{pmatrix},$$

so in this case the map $\varphi \mapsto \tilde{\varphi}$ can be thought of as a conjugate-transpose. The isogeny $\varphi$ is polarized if and only if

$$\begin{pmatrix} \hat{\alpha}_{13} & \hat{\alpha}_{14} \\ \hat{\alpha}_{23} & \hat{\alpha}_{24} \end{pmatrix} \begin{pmatrix} \alpha_{13} & \alpha_{23} \\ \alpha_{14} & \alpha_{24} \end{pmatrix} = \begin{pmatrix} [N] & 0 \\ 0 & [N] \end{pmatrix}$$

for some positive integer $N$. This integer necessarily equals $\operatorname{degrd}(\varphi)$, so that $\deg(\varphi) = N^2$. In general, by [32, Corollary 64] and [26, Proposition 3.9], we have

$$\deg(\varphi) = (\deg \alpha_{13} + \deg \alpha_{14})(\deg \alpha_{23} + \deg \alpha_{24}) - \deg(\hat{\alpha}_{23}\alpha_{13} + \hat{\alpha}_{24}\alpha_{14}). \quad (1)$$

### 2.3 Ibukiyama–Katsura–Oort Correspondence

In the remainder of the paper, we fix a prime $p \notin \{2, 3\}$ and a supersingular elliptic curve $E_0/\overline{\mathbb{F}}_p$. Let $B_{p,\infty}$ be the unique quaternion algebra (up to isomorphism) ramified exactly at $p$ and infinity. Then, as mentioned, $\operatorname{End}(E_0)$ is isomorphic through the Deuring correspondence to a maximal order $\mathcal{O}_0$ of $B_{p,\infty}$. Define $A_0 = E_0 \times E_0$ and consider the product polarization $\lambda_0$. By our previous discussion, the endomorphism ring of $A_0$ is isomorphic to $\mathrm{M}_2(\mathcal{O}_0)$ and under this isomorphism the Rosati involution (i.e., the adjoint operator) with respect to $\lambda_0$ corresponds to the conjugate-transpose.

Recall that, considered without their polarizations, all superspecial abelian surfaces in characteristic $p$ are isomorphic. Consequently, every principally polarized superspecial abelian surface $(A, \lambda_A)$ is isomorphic to $(A_0, \lambda)$ for some principal polarization $\lambda$ on $A_0$. Explicitly, if $\varphi : A_0 \to A$ is an (unpolarized) isomorphism, then we can take $\lambda = \hat{\varphi}\lambda_A\varphi$. The following method due to Ibukiyama, Katsura and Oort can be used to represent a principal polarization $\lambda$ on $A_0$ as a matrix with coefficients in $\mathcal{O}_0$. One considers the map

$$\begin{aligned} \mu : \operatorname{PPol}(A_0) &\to \operatorname{End}(A_0) \\ \lambda &\mapsto \lambda_0^{-1}\lambda, \end{aligned}$$

noting that the image $\lambda_0^{-1}\lambda$ can be identified with an element of $\mathrm{M}_2(\mathcal{O}_0)$.

**Theorem 2.8.** *The map $\mu$ is injective and its image, once transferred to the quaternion world through the Deuring correspondence, corresponds to*

$$\mathrm{Mat}(A_0) := \left\{ \begin{pmatrix} s & r \\ \bar{r} & t \end{pmatrix}, \quad s,t \in \mathbb{Z}_{>0}, r \in \mathcal{O}_0, st - r\bar{r} = 1 \right\} \quad \subset \mathrm{GL}_2(\mathcal{O}_0),$$

*i.e., $\mu$ determines a bijection between* $\mathrm{PPol}(A_0)$ *and* $\mathrm{Mat}(A_0)$.

*Proof.* This is [29, Corollary 2.9] specialized to principal polarizations (i.e., to ample divisors with self-intersection 2). □

*Remark 2.9.* An alternative way of specifying a principal polarization $\lambda$ on $A_0$ is through the Rosati involution it induces on $\mathrm{M}_2(\mathcal{O}_0)$. This datum is very explicitly encoded in the matrix $g = \mu(\lambda)$:

$$\mathrm{Ros}_\lambda(\alpha) = \lambda^{-1}\hat{\alpha}\lambda = (\lambda_0^{-1}\lambda)^{-1}(\lambda_0^{-1}\hat{\alpha}\lambda_0)(\lambda_0^{-1}\lambda) = g^{-1}\,\mathrm{Ros}_{\lambda_0}(\alpha)g = g^{-1}\alpha^* g,$$

where we recall that the Rosati involution with respect to the product polarization $\lambda_0$ indeed amounts to the conjugate-transpose $-^*$.[8] Conversely, given black-box access to $\mathrm{Ros}_\lambda$, one can reconstruct the matrix $g$ via linear system solving, by considering $g\,\mathrm{Ros}_\lambda(b_i) = b_i^* g$ for a $\mathbb{Z}$-basis $b_1, \ldots, b_{16}$ of $\mathrm{M}_2(\mathcal{O}_0)$.

In a natural way, the matrix representation extends to polarized isogenies. Let $\lambda_1, \lambda_2 \in \mathrm{PPol}(A_0)$ be represented by matrices $g_1, g_2 \in \mathrm{Mat}(A_0)$ and let $\varphi : (A_0, \lambda_1) \to (A_0, \lambda_2)$ be a polarized isogeny of reduced degree $N$. Being an endomorphism of $A_0$, we can identify $\varphi$ with a matrix $\gamma \in \mathrm{M}_2(\mathcal{O}_0)$, and the property $\hat{\varphi}\lambda_2\varphi = N\lambda_1$ readily translates into

$$(\lambda_0^{-1}\hat{\varphi}\lambda_0)\lambda_0^{-1}\lambda_2\varphi = N\lambda_0^{-1}\lambda_1.$$

Using $\lambda_0^{-1}\lambda_i = g_i$ and identifying $\varphi$ with $\gamma$, this can be rewritten as

$$\gamma^* g_2 \gamma = N g_1, \tag{2}$$

which is the chief equation of this entire paper. Conversely, whenever a matrix $\gamma \in \mathrm{M}_2(\mathcal{O}_0)$ satisfies (2), it determines a polarized isogeny $\varphi : (A_0, \lambda_1) \to (A_0, \lambda_2)$ of reduced degree $N$. In Sect. 4 we will discuss methods for converting polarized isogenies into matrices and vice versa.

We conclude with two remarks:

1. The equivalence relation for principal polarizations from Definition 2.7 naturally translates to the language of matrices as well: given $g_1, g_2 \in \mathrm{Mat}(A_0)$ encoding principal polarizations $\lambda_1, \lambda_2$ on $A_0$, we have

$$\lambda_1 \sim \lambda_2 \quad \Longleftrightarrow \quad \exists u \in \mathrm{GL}_2(\mathcal{O}_0), \quad u^* g_1 u = g_2.$$

   In this case, we say that the matrices are *congruent*; this terminology is taken from [27]. We then define $\mathrm{Mat}^0(A_0)$ as the set $\mathrm{Mat}(A_0)$ considered modulo congruence. Figure 1 summarizes the bijections that allow us to manipulate (isomorphism classes of) principally polarized superspecial abelian surfaces using only matrices with entries in $\mathcal{O}_0$.

[8] More generally, the adjoint of $\alpha$ with respect to $g_1 = \mu(\lambda_1)$, $g_2 = \mu(\lambda_2)$ is $g_1^{-1}\alpha^* g_2$.

2. Every supersingular elliptic curve in characteristic $p$ admits a model over $\mathbb{F}_{p^2}$, therefore the same is true for $A_0$ and the product polarization $\lambda_0$. When working with a model such that $\#A_0(\mathbb{F}_{p^2}) = (p \pm 1)^4$, as will be the case in practice, we know that all endomorphisms of $A_0$ are defined over $\mathbb{F}_{p^2}$ as well. Consequently, *every* principal polarization $\lambda = \lambda_0(\lambda_0^{-1}\lambda)$ is defined over $\mathbb{F}_{p^2}$. If $(A, \lambda_A)$ is a superspecial principally polarized abelian surface defined over $\mathbb{F}_{p^2}$ such that $\#A(\mathbb{F}_{p^2}) = (p \pm 1)^4$, then it is $\mathbb{F}_{p^2}$-isomorphic to $(A_0, \lambda)$ for some principal polarization $\lambda$ on $A_0$. See [4] for an extended discussion.

$$\left\{\begin{array}{c}\text{Superspecial}\\ \text{principally polarized}\\ \text{abelian surfaces}\\ (A,\lambda_A)\\ \text{up to polarized}\\ \text{isomorphism}\end{array}\right\} \longleftrightarrow \left\{\begin{array}{c}\text{Principal}\\ \text{polarizations}\\ \lambda \in \mathrm{PPol}(A_0)\\ \text{up to equivalence}\end{array}\right\} \overset{\mu}{\longleftrightarrow} \left\{\begin{array}{c}\text{Matrices}\\ g \in \mathrm{Mat}(A_0)\\ \text{up to congruence}\end{array}\right\}$$

**Fig. 1.** Classification of principally polarized superspecial abelian surfaces

### 2.4 Quaternionic Matrices and Determinants

When trying to define the determinant of a matrix

$$u = \begin{pmatrix} a & b \\ c & d \end{pmatrix} \in \mathrm{M}_2(B_{p,\infty}),$$

care is needed in view of the non-commutativity. Note that there is no ambiguity in the Hermitian case (i.e., for matrices that are invariant under taking the conjugate-transpose), which are always defined over a quadratic, hence commutative, subfield of $B_{p,\infty}$. In particular, it makes sense to consider $\det(uu^*)$ instead. Alternatively, one can consider the (reduced) norm $\mathcal{N}(u)$, defined as $\det(\iota(u \otimes 1))$, where

$$\iota : \mathrm{M}_2(B_{p,\infty}) \otimes_{\mathbb{Q}} \mathbb{C} \to \mathrm{M}_4(\mathbb{C})$$

is any isomorphism of $\mathbb{C}$-algebras. As the following lemma shows, this leads to the same result.

**Lemma 2.10.** $\det(uu^*) = \det(u^*u) = \mathsf{n}(a)\,\mathsf{n}(d) + \mathsf{n}(b)\,\mathsf{n}(c) - \mathsf{tr}(\bar{a}b\bar{d}c) = \mathcal{N}(u)$.

One notable consequence of the above lemma is that the map $u \mapsto \det(uu^*)$ is multiplicative; indeed this property is immediate for $\mathcal{N}(-)$. Another interesting corollary, for which we could not find an explicit reference, is the following:

**Corollary 2.11.** *Let $E/\overline{\mathbb{F}}_p$ be a supersingular elliptic curve and let* $\mathrm{End}(E) \cong \mathcal{O} \subset B_{p,\infty}$. *Let $u \in \mathrm{End}(E^2)$, which via this isomorphism can be identified with an element of* $\mathrm{M}_2(\mathcal{O})$. *Then* $\deg u = \mathcal{N}(u)$.

*Proof.* This follows from (1) and an explicit calculation, see [6] for details. □

The multiplicativity also applies to the usual determinant when applied to Hermitian matrices. Up to sign, this is easy to see using that $\mathcal{N}(g) = \det(g)^2$ for any Hermitian matrix $g$. But the signs match as well:

**Lemma 2.12.** *Let $u, g, h \in \mathrm{M}_2(B_{p,\infty})$ where $g, h$ are assumed Hermitian. Then*

- $\det(gh) = \det(g)\det(h)$,
- $\det(u^*gu) = \mathcal{N}(u)\det(g)$.

We end this section by showing that the "adjugate"[9] with respect to $\mathcal{N}(-)$ of an invertible matrix with entries in a subring $\mathcal{O} \subset B_{p,\infty}$ again has entries in $\mathcal{O}$.

**Lemma 2.13.** *If $u \in \mathrm{M}_2(\mathcal{O})$ is invertible in $\mathrm{M}_2(B_{p,\infty})$ then $u^{-1}\mathcal{N}(u) \in \mathrm{M}_2(\mathcal{O})$.*

## 3 Pathfinding in Dimension 2

The goal of this section (and the main goal of the paper) is the description of an algorithm which solves the *algebraic pathfinding problem* in dimension 2. That is, upon input of $g_1, g_2 \in \mathrm{Mat}(A_0)$, the goal is to find a matrix $\gamma \in \mathrm{M}_2(\mathcal{O}_0)$ and a smooth integer $N$ such that (2) holds. More precisely, we fix any small prime number $\ell$ and present the following solution, where $N$ is a power of $\ell$. Just as in the original KLPT algorithm, we assume that $\mathcal{O}_0$ is special extremal, i.e., it contains a quadratic order whose discriminant has a very small absolute value [33, §2.3]. In fact, for simplicity, we restrict to $p \equiv 3 \bmod 4$ and use the base curve $E_0 : y^2 = x^3 + x$ and maximal order $\mathcal{O}_0$ from Example 2.1. Note that the Gaussian integers $\mathbb{Z}[i]$ are contained in $\mathcal{O}_0$, so this order is of the desired kind.

**Theorem 3.1. (KLPT$^2$).** *There exists a polynomial-time algorithm which upon input $g_1, g_2 \in \mathrm{Mat}(A_0)$ and a prime number $\ell \neq p$, under plausible heuristic assumptions, returns $\gamma \in \mathrm{M}_2(\mathcal{O}_0)$ such that*

$$\gamma^* g_2 \gamma = \ell^e g_1$$

*where $\ell^e \in O(p^{25+o(1)})$.*

[9] We intentionally avoid the word "adjoint", because the matrix $u^{-1}\mathcal{N}(u)$ should not be confused with the adjoint $\tilde{u}$ of $u$ in the sense of Sect. 2.2. Firstly, the latter notion only makes sense when $u$ describes a polarized isogeny with respect to certain principal polarizations. Secondly, in case it does make sense, we have $\tilde{u}u = u\tilde{u} = \mathrm{degrd}(u)\mathbb{I}_2$, whereas $u^{-1}\mathcal{N}(u)u = uu^{-1}\mathcal{N}(u) = \deg(u)\mathbb{I}_2 = \mathrm{degrd}(u)^2\mathbb{I}_2$ in view of Corollary 2.11. Recall that $\tilde{u} = g_1^{-1}u^*g_2$ when working with respect to principal polarizations associated with $g_1, g_2 \in \mathrm{Mat}(A_0)$.

A proof-of-concept implementation of the algorithm can be found in:

https://github.com/KLPT2/KLPT2

Further down, in Theorem 3.15, we will present a variant for powersmooth $N$, which is often better-suited for (theoretically flavoured) applications.

Our implementation also supports the "plausible heuristic assumptions", which are hard to state out of context and will be highlighted during the description of the algorithm.

*Remark 3.2.* Our algorithm is randomized and expected to return a different matrix $\gamma$ on each iteration. Unfortunately, the output never corresponds to a "good" chain of $(\ell, \ell)$-isogenies in the sense of [7], i.e., we never have $\ker(\gamma) \cong (\mathbb{Z}/\ell^e\mathbb{Z})^2$, see Corollary 5.4. In fact, as far as we are aware, even the mere connectedness of the superspecial $(\ell, \ell)$-isogeny graph by good isogeny chains is an open problem [7, Conjecture 3].

### 3.1 Finding Connecting Matrices

Our proof strategy for Theorem 3.1 is based on the following lemma.

**Lemma 3.3.** *Let $h_1, h_2 \in \mathrm{M}_2(\mathcal{O}_0)$ be Hermitian matrices with equal upper-left entries and equal determinants, i.e., we have*

$$h_1 = \begin{pmatrix} D & r_1 \\ \bar{r}_1 & t_1 \end{pmatrix}, \quad h_2 = \begin{pmatrix} D & r_2 \\ \bar{r}_2 & t_2 \end{pmatrix}$$

*for $D, t_1, t_2 \in \mathbb{Z}, r_1, r_2 \in \mathcal{O}_0$ such that $Dt_1 - \mathsf{n}(r_1) = Dt_2 - \mathsf{n}(r_2)$. Then for*

$$\tau = \begin{pmatrix} D & r_1 - r_2 \\ 0 & D \end{pmatrix}$$

*we have $\tau^* h_2 \tau = D^2 h_1$.*

*Proof.* Explicit calculation; see the full version of our paper [6] for details. □

Note that in the above lemma we do not impose $\det(h_1) = \det(h_2) = 1$, so this is not always a special case of (2). We only want the two determinants to be equal, for reasons that will become apparent soon.

When given $g_1, g_2$, our goal is to transform them in a fashion such that Lemma 3.3 becomes applicable. This is aided by the following lemma:

**Lemma 3.4.** *Assume that $\delta^* g_2 \delta = N u^* g_1 u$ with $N \in \mathbb{Z}$, $u, \delta \in \mathrm{M}_2(\mathcal{O}_0)$. Then there exists $\gamma \in \mathrm{M}_2(\mathcal{O}_0)$ such that $\gamma^* g_2 \gamma = N \mathcal{N}(u)^2 g_1$.*

*Proof.* One can choose $\gamma = \delta u^{-1} \mathcal{N}(u)$. The equality $\gamma^* g_2 \gamma = N \mathcal{N}(u)^2 g_1$ is clearly satisfied and Lemma 2.13 implies that $\gamma \in \mathrm{M}_2(\mathcal{O}_0)$. □

This naturally leads to the following plan for solving the problem $\gamma^* g_2 \gamma = \ell^e g_1$. Namely, given $g \in \mathrm{Mat}(A_0)$ we want to find $u \in \mathrm{M}_2(\mathcal{O}_0)$ with the following properties:

- $\mathcal{N}(u) = \ell^{e_1}$ where $e_1$ does not depend on $g$ (but $u$ does).
- The top left entry of $u^* g u$ is $\ell^{e_2}$, where $e_2$ does not depend on $g$.

How does this solve our initial problem? First we transform $g_1$ and $g_2$ with an appropriate $u_1$ and $u_2$ in the above fashion. Then we invoke Lemma 3.3 as by design the two sides have the same top left entry and the same determinant, by Lemma 2.12. This yields a matrix $\tau \in \mathrm{M}_2(\mathcal{O}_0)$ such that

$$\tau^* u_2^* g_2 u_2 \tau = \ell^{2e_2} u_1^* g_1 u_1. \tag{3}$$

We can then apply Lemma 3.4 with $\delta = u_2\tau$ to return

$$\gamma = u_2 \tau u_1^{-1} \mathcal{N}(u_1), \tag{4}$$

which has reduced degree $\ell^{2(e_1+e_2)}$.

So now our focus is on a single

$$g = \begin{pmatrix} s & r \\ \bar{r} & t \end{pmatrix} \in \mathrm{Mat}(A_0),$$

where along the way we will explicitly bound $\ell^{e_1}, \ell^{e_2}$ by appropriate constants. First let us calculate what the top left entry of $u^* g u$ is.

**Lemma 3.6.** *Let* $u = \left(\begin{smallmatrix} a & b \\ c & d \end{smallmatrix}\right)$. *Then the top left corner of* $u^* g u$ *is given by*

$$s' := s \cdot \mathsf{n}(a) + t \cdot \mathsf{n}(c) + \mathsf{tr}(\bar{c}\bar{r}a).$$

*Proof.* This follows from a simple calculation. □

Note in particular that the top left corner $s'$ only depends on $a$ and $c$ (likewise, the bottom right corner $t'$ only depends on $b$ and $d$). This motivates the following rough strategy:

1. Find $a, c \in \mathcal{O}_0$ such that $s'$ is a fixed power of $\ell$.
2. Given $a, c$, find values for $b, d \in \mathcal{O}_0$ such that the reduced norm $\mathcal{N}(u)$ is another fixed power of $\ell$.

We first concentrate on Step 2, then come back to Step 1 in Sect. 3.4.

### 3.2 Controlling the Reduced Norm

Let us be given non-zero $a, c \in \mathcal{O}_0$, where we assume that $\mathsf{n}(a)$ and $\mathsf{n}(c)$ are coprime; this will indeed be ensured. In this section we explain how to find $x, y \in \mathcal{O}_0$ such that

$$\mathcal{N}\begin{pmatrix} a & x \\ c & y \end{pmatrix} = \mathsf{n}(a)\,\mathsf{n}(y) + \mathsf{n}(c)\,\mathsf{n}(x) - \mathsf{tr}(\bar{a}x\bar{y}c) = \ell^{e_0}$$

for some fixed power $\ell^{e_0}$ (we will eventually have $e_1 = 2e_0$). We do not solve this Diophantine equation directly. Instead, one can see that the problem amounts to a pathfinding problem in dimension 1, so that we can invoke the standard KLPT algorithm. Indeed, an easy calculation shows

$$\mathsf{n}(c)\mathcal{N}\begin{pmatrix} a & x \\ c & y \end{pmatrix} = \mathsf{n}(a\bar{c}y) + \mathsf{n}(\mathsf{n}(c)x) - \mathsf{tr}(\mathsf{n}(c)x\overline{a\bar{c}y}) = \mathsf{n}(\mathsf{n}(c)x - a\bar{c}y) \tag{5}$$

so it suffices to find an $\omega$ of norm $\mathsf{n}(c)\ell^{e_0}$ in the right $\mathcal{O}_0$-ideal $I$ generated by $\mathsf{n}(c)$ and $a\bar{c}$. Note that $I$ has norm $\mathsf{n}(c)$ because $\gcd(\mathsf{n}(a), \mathsf{n}(c)) = 1$. We can therefore find such an $\omega$ with $\ell^{e_0} \in O(p^{3+o(1)})$ using the KLPT algorithm (heuristically). Writing $\omega = \mathsf{n}(c)o_1 + a\bar{c}o_2$, we can then simply put $x = o_1, y = -o_2$.

Equation (5) seemingly comes out of the blue, but there is a conceptual explanation for it, which is discussed in the full version of the paper [6] and which may be key to future improvements of the KLPT$^2$ algorithm.

### 3.3 Reduction of the Matrix $g$

Thanks to the previous subsection, our task has been (essentially) reduced to finding $a, c \in \mathcal{O}_0$ in such a way that the top-left entry

$$s' = K((a,c)) := s \cdot \mathsf{n}(a) + t \cdot \mathsf{n}(c) + \mathsf{tr}(\bar{c}\bar{r}a) \tag{6}$$

of $u^*gu$ is some fixed power of $\ell$, only depending on $p$. Moreover, we want to make sure that $\mathsf{n}(a)$ and $\mathsf{n}(c)$ are non-zero and coprime. We see that $K$ is a quadratic form on $\mathcal{O}_0^2$, which is a free $\mathbb{Z}$-module of rank 8.

**Proposition 3.10.** *The quadratic form $K$ is positive definite and has determinant $(p/4)^4$.*

The goal of this subsection is to describe an intermediate step, where we wish to find a transformation matrix $u$ making $s'$ as small as possible. This can be achieved through lattice reduction: using Proposition 3.10, we see that (6) expresses $s'$ as the squared-Euclidean length of a vector in a lattice $\Lambda \subset \mathbb{R}^8$ having volume $(p/4)^2$.[10] By the Minkowski bound we can find a non-zero vector with $K$-value $s' < \frac{3}{2}\sqrt{p}$. Once $a, c$ realizing a small value of $s'$ are found, we can complement them with $b, d$ using the KLPT algorithm, as described in the previous subsection. However, remember that we want $\mathsf{n}(a)$ and $\mathsf{n}(c)$ to be coprime for this. Furthermore, to simplify the analysis in Theorem 3.13 below, we will want $s'$ to be a prime different from 2 and $\ell$. Therefore we need some extra margin; in the full version of our paper [6] we give a heuristic argumentation showing that $s' < \sqrt{p}(\ln p)^{1/4}$ should always be feasible.

Despite the smallness of $s'$, the other entries of $u^*gu$ may become quite large. Thus, we use an extra transformation to keep these values contained. For this we can use a matrix of the form $\left(\begin{smallmatrix} 1 & \alpha \\ 0 & 1 \end{smallmatrix}\right)$. To lighten notation, let us explain this step directly on $g$, rather than on $u^*gu$:

[10] E.g., this follows via the Cholesky decomposition of the matrix in the proof of Proposition 3.10.

$$\left(\begin{smallmatrix}1 & \alpha\\ 0 & 1\end{smallmatrix}\right)^* g \left(\begin{smallmatrix}1 & \alpha\\ 0 & 1\end{smallmatrix}\right) = \begin{pmatrix} s & \alpha s + r \\ \bar{\alpha} s + \bar{r} & \mathsf{n}(\alpha)s + \mathsf{tr}(\bar{\alpha} r) + t \end{pmatrix}$$

The main observation here is twofold. First $s$ does not change. Second $r$ changes to $\alpha s + r$, thus we can attain anything in $\mathcal{O}_0$ that is congruent to $r$ modulo $s$. In particular we can ensure that the coordinates $r_i, i = 1, \ldots, 4$ of $r$ with respect to the basis from Example 2.1 satisfy $|r_i| \leq s/2$. This implies that $\mathsf{n}(r) \leq s^2(p+5)/8$. Note that $\left(\begin{smallmatrix}1 & \alpha\\ 0 & 1\end{smallmatrix}\right) \in \mathrm{GL}_2(\mathcal{O}_0)$, hence we do not have to worry about the reduced norm in this step.

Applying this to

$$u^* g u = \begin{pmatrix} s' & r' \\ \bar{r}' & t' \end{pmatrix},$$

first note that

$$s't' - \mathsf{n}(r') = \mathcal{N}(u) = \ell^{e_0} \in O(p^{3+o(1)})$$

by the KLPT step, where we have used Lemma 2.12. Thus from $\mathsf{n}(r') \leq s'^2(p+5)/8$ and $s' \leq \sqrt{p}(\ln p)^{1/4}$, one finds that $t' \leq \ell^{e_0}/s' + s'(p+5)/8 \in O(p^{3+o(1)}/s')$.

Finally, we will also want that $\ell \nmid t'$, or equivalently $\ell \nmid \mathsf{n}(r')$. This is easy to achieve by slightly tweaking $\alpha$ if needed. Indeed, one easily checks that, by relaxing the bounds $|r_i| \leq s/2$ to $|r_i| \leq s$, it can be ensured that $\mathsf{tr}(r') \not\equiv -1 \bmod \ell$. Then, if it so happens that $\ell \mid \mathsf{n}(r')$, an extra transformation using $\left(\begin{smallmatrix}1 & 1\\ 0 & 1\end{smallmatrix}\right)$ will fix this issue.

In summary, by applying a suitable transformation $g \leftarrow u^* g u$, we can reduce to the case where $g$ has bounded entries satisfying some non-divisibility conditions, at the cost of increasing the determinant from 1 to a power of $\ell$. For clarity we give a definition for this case, while adding in another heuristic assumption, which should be satisfied with overwhelming probability:

**Definition 3.12.** *A matrix*

$$g = \begin{pmatrix} s & r \\ \bar{r} & t \end{pmatrix}, \quad s, t \in \mathbb{Z}_{>0}, r \in \mathcal{O}_0, st - r\bar{r} > 0$$

*is called* $\ell$-reduced

- $\det(g) = st - \mathsf{n}(r) = \ell^{e_0}$ *for some* $e_0 \geq 0$,
- $s \leq \sqrt{p}(\ln p)^{1/4}$ *is a prime number not dividing* $2\ell t$,
- $\mathsf{n}(r) \leq s^2 p$ *is not a multiple of* $\ell$.

The extra assumption is $s \nmid t$. Note that the conditions imply $s \nmid \mathsf{n}(r)$ and $\ell \nmid t$.

### 3.4 Controlling the Top-Left Entry and Finalizing the Algorithm

Starting from a reduced matrix $g$ as in Definition 3.12, with determinant $\ell^{e_0} \in O(p^{3+o(1)})$, we now show how to find a matrix $u$, of $\ell$-power reduced norm, such that $u^*gu$ has a top left corner equal to $\ell^{e_2}$ for some $e_2 \geq 0$. As discussed before, this amounts to solving the Diophantine equation

$$\ell^{e_2} = s\,\mathsf{n}(a) + t\,\mathsf{n}(c) + \mathsf{tr}(\bar{c}\bar{r}a) \tag{7}$$

in such a way that $\gcd(\mathsf{n}(a), \mathsf{n}(c)) = 1$, and complementing with appropriate $b, d$ via the KLPT algorithm.

**Theorem 3.13.** *Let $g \in \mathrm{M}_2(\mathcal{O}_0)$ be an $\ell$-reduced matrix as in Definition 3.12. There exists a (heuristic) polynomial-time algorithm that finds a solution to (7) with $\mathsf{n}(a)$ and $\mathsf{n}(c)$ coprime, provided that $\ell^{e_2} \in \Theta(p^{6.5+o(1)})$.*

*Proof.* We make the following restrictions: we take $a$ of the form $a_1 + a_2 i \in \mathbb{Z}[i]$ and we take $c$ of the form $c_1\bar{r}j + c_2\bar{r}k \in \bar{r}j\mathbb{Z}[i]$. Since $\mathsf{tr}(\bar{c}\bar{r}a)$ is zero for every such choice of $a, c$, equation (7) simplifies to $\ell^{e_2} = s\,\mathsf{n}(a) + t\,\mathsf{n}(c)$. We then solve the quadratic equation

$$t\,\mathsf{n}(c) = tp\,\mathsf{n}(r)(c_1^2 + c_2^2) \equiv \ell^{e_2} \bmod s.$$

Since $s$ is an odd prime and $s \nmid t, p, \mathsf{n}(r), \ell$, this provides us with an irreducible conic equation over $\mathbb{F}_s$ which always has a solution: this gives us $c$, with $c_1, c_2 \in \{0, \ldots, s-1\}$. Now we have that $\ell^{e_2} - t\,\mathsf{n}(c)$ is divisible by $s$, reducing to

$$\frac{\ell^{e_2} - t\,\mathsf{n}(c)}{s} = \mathsf{n}(a). \tag{8}$$

Since $a \in \mathbb{Z}[i]$ this can be solved using Cornacchia's algorithm, provided we know the factorization of $\ell^{e_2} - t\,\mathsf{n}(c)$. Thus we iterate until (8) has a solution and we can factor $\ell^{e_2} - t\,\mathsf{n}(c)$ efficiently. Here one expects a polylogarithmic number of iterations. The reason for the size constraints on $\ell^{e_2}$ is that one needs $\ell^{e_2} - t\,\mathsf{n}(c)$ to be positive, as otherwise it cannot be the sum of two squares. From

$$t\,\mathsf{n}(c) = t \cdot p \cdot \mathsf{n}(r) \cdot (c_1^2 + c_2^2) \in O\left(\frac{p^{3+o(1)}}{s} \cdot p \cdot s^2 p \cdot 2\,s^2\right) \subset O(p^{6.5+o(1)})$$

the bound follows. Note that (8) does not guarantee that $\gcd(\mathsf{n}(a), \mathsf{n}(c)) = 1$, so a number of retries, each time choosing different representants of $c_1, c_2 \bmod s$ (or choosing a genuinely different solution to the above quadratic equation over $\mathbb{F}_s$), may be needed. This does not affect the above asymptotic estimate. □

*Remark 3.14.* In particular, from (8) it is clear that $c$ should be chosen such that $\ell \nmid \mathsf{n}(c)$, for otherwise $\ell \mid \gcd(\mathsf{n}(a), \mathsf{n}(c))$. This is the reason for the condition $\ell \nmid \mathsf{n}(r)$ in Definition 3.12. It is interesting to specialize this to our main case of interest $\ell = 2$: both $\mathsf{n}(r)$ and $c_1^2 + c_2^2$ should be odd. Then, assuming $e_0, e_2 \geq 2$, equation (8) implies that

$$-t\,\mathsf{n}(c) = -tp\,\mathsf{n}(r)(c_1^2 + c_2^2) \equiv s\,\mathsf{n}(a) \bmod 4 \quad \Rightarrow \quad -t^2 p(c_1^2 + c_2^2) \equiv \mathsf{n}(a) \bmod 4,$$

showing that $\mathsf{n}(a) \equiv -1 \cdot 3 \cdot 1 \equiv 1 \bmod 4$. This is a necessary condition for the Cornacchia-step to succeed.

We are now ready to prove our main result:

*Proof of Theorem* 3.1: The algorithm to find $\gamma \in \mathrm{M}_2(\mathcal{O}_0)$ when given

$$g_1 = \begin{pmatrix} s_1 & r_1 \\ \bar{r}_1 & t_1 \end{pmatrix}, \quad g_2 = \begin{pmatrix} s_2 & r_2 \\ \bar{r}_2 & t_2 \end{pmatrix} \quad \in \mathrm{Mat}(A_0)$$

is summarized in Algorithm 1. From the preceding discussions, it should be clear that all steps are heuristically polynomial-time. As for the output length, note that the matrices $u_1, u_2$ produced in Step 7 have reduced norm $\ell^{e_1}$ with $e_1 = 2e_0$, and for $i = 1, 2$ the upper-left entry of $u_i^* g_i u_i$ equals $\ell^{e_2}$. Thus, from (4) we find that $\gamma$ has reduced degree

$$\ell^e = \ell^{2(e_1+e_2)} = (\ell^{e_0})^4 \cdot (\ell^{e_2})^2 \in O(p^{12+o(1)} \cdot p^{13+o(1)})$$

in view of the KLPT bound and Theorem 3.13. □

---

**Algorithm 1:** KLPT$^2$: An algorithm to solve the quaternion $\ell$-isogeny path problem in dimension 2

---

**Input** : $g_1, g_2 \in \mathrm{Mat}(A_0)$
**Output:** $\gamma \in \mathrm{M}_2(\mathcal{O})$ such that $\gamma^* g_2 \gamma = \ell^e g_1$ with $\ell^e \in O(p^{25+\varepsilon})$

1 **For** *i=1,2* **do**
2 Find $a, c$ using lattice reduction such that $\gcd(\mathsf{n}(a), \mathsf{n}(c)) = 1$, and $s_i\,\mathsf{n}(a) + t_i\,\mathsf{n}(c) + \mathsf{tr}(\bar{c}\bar{r}_i a) < \sqrt{p}(\ln p)^{1/4}$ is prime (not $2, \ell$).
3 Find $b, d$ using KLPT as described in Section 3.2 such that the reduced norm of $u := \left(\begin{smallmatrix} a & b \\ c & d \end{smallmatrix}\right)$ is $\ell^{e_0}$.
4 Find $\alpha$ such that $g' = \left(\begin{smallmatrix} s' & r' \\ \bar{r}' & t' \end{smallmatrix}\right) := \left(\begin{smallmatrix} 1 & 0 \\ \bar{\alpha} & 1 \end{smallmatrix}\right) u^* g_i u \left(\begin{smallmatrix} 1 & \alpha \\ 0 & 1 \end{smallmatrix}\right)$ is reduced.
5 Find $a', c'$ using lattice reduction such that $\gcd(\mathsf{n}(a'), n(c')) = 1$ and $s'\,\mathsf{n}(a') + t'\,\mathsf{n}(c') + \mathsf{tr}(\bar{c}'\bar{r}'a') = \ell^{e_2}$ using Theorem 3.13.
6 Find $b', d'$ using KLPT as described in Section 3.2 such that the reduced norm of $u' = \left(\begin{smallmatrix} a' & b' \\ c' & d' \end{smallmatrix}\right)$ is $\ell^{e_0}$.
7 Let $u_i = u\left(\begin{smallmatrix} 1 & \alpha \\ 0 & 1 \end{smallmatrix}\right)u'$.
8 Compute $\tau$ connecting $u_1^* g_1 u_1$ and $u_2^* g_2 u_2$ as in Lemma 3.3.
9 **Return** $\gamma := u_2 \tau u_1^{-1} \mathcal{N}(u_1)$ as in (4).

---

The algebraic pathfinding problem was studied here for $N = \ell^e$ similarly to the original KLPT algorithm. However, it is clear that both KLPT and Theorem 3.13 can be adjusted to any number that is big enough; see also [25].

Now by invoking powersmooth versions of KLPT and Theorem 3.13 we get a powersmooth degree isogeny, since the product of powersmooth numbers is still powersmooth. This implies the following version of Theorem 3.1:

**Theorem 3.15.** *There exists a (heuristic) polynomial-time algorithm which upon input* $g_1, g_2 \in \mathrm{Mat}(A_0)$ *and a smoothness bound* $B$ *returns* $\gamma \in \mathrm{M}_2(\mathcal{O}_0)$ *such that*

$$\gamma^* g_2 \gamma = N g_1$$

*where* $N \in O(p^{25+o(1)})$ *is* $B$*-powersmooth.*

## 4 Translating Between Matrices and Isogenies

The main applications of the standard KLPT algorithm go hand in hand with efficient methods for converting left (non-zero) ideals of $\mathcal{O}_0$ into isogenies emanating from $E_0$ and vice versa. Likewise, in order to put KLPT$^2$ to practical use, we need methods for translating appropriately chosen $2 \times 2$ matrices with entries in $\mathcal{O}_0$ to polarized isogenies emerging from $A_0$ and conversely.

The analogy with the elliptic curve case becomes more apparent when noting that $\mathrm{M}_2(\mathcal{O}_0)$ is a principal ideal ring. Consequently, we have a natural identification of left ideals $I \subset \mathrm{M}_2(\mathcal{O}_0)$ with their generating matrices $\gamma \in \mathrm{M}_2(\mathcal{O}_0)$, up to left-multiplication with elements of $\mathrm{GL}_2(\mathcal{O}_0)$. On a high level, the known approaches for translating between ideals and isogenies in dimension one carry over to dimension two. But in the case of isogeny-to-ideal conversion there is an important caveat: the ideal returned by the standard isogeny-to-ideal approaches is described in terms of multiple generators, and extracting a single generating matrix from this description is not a trivial task. Indeed, a large part of Chu's thesis [11, Chapter 2] is devoted to the design of a sub-exponential time algorithm for solving this instance of the principal ideal problem (PIP).

In this section, we describe some first routines for converting matrices to isogenies and vice versa; our main result is presented in Sect. 4.2, where we show how to by-pass the PIP for powersmooth-degree isogenies. Then, in Sect. 5, we will enhance these basic routines through the use of KLPT$^2$.

*Remark 4.1.* At several points in the remainder of this article, we use an unspecified algorithm which upon input of

- a principally polarized abelian surface $A$ over a finite field $\mathbb{F}_q$, described either as the Jacobian of an explicit genus-2 curve $C/\mathbb{F}_q$ (with the canonical polarization) or as the product of two explicit elliptic curves $E_1, E_2$ over $\mathbb{F}_q$ (with the product polarization),
- a subgroup $K \subset A(\mathbb{F}_q)$ which is also a maximal isotropic subgroup of $A[\ell^e]$ with respect to the $\ell^e$-Weil pairing, for some given prime power $\ell^e$,
- a point $P \in A(\mathbb{F}_q)$,

computes, in time polynomial in $\log q$ and $\ell$, the codomain of a polarized isogeny $\varphi$ with kernel $K$, again described as either an explicit Jacobian or an explicit product of two elliptic curves,[11] along with the image point $\varphi(P)$. E.g., if $\ell = 2$ then this can be done through an $e$-fold application of the classical formulae due to Richelot [42]; the occasional gluing and splitting steps can be handled using [28]. In general, it is hard to pinpoint one concrete reference for the complete statement, but the existence of such an algorithm is considered folklore, with all ingredients to be found in [14–16] and the aforementioned references.

### 4.1 Matrices to Polarized Isogenies from $A_0$

This is stated in [11, Section A.2] as a "required routine", but no details are given, even though the method is not too surprising. The input is a matrix $\gamma \in \mathrm{M}_2(\mathcal{O}_0)$ of reduced norm $N^2$, where $N = N_1 N_2 \cdots N_r$ is assumed powersmooth, i.e., the factors $N_i$ are pairwise coprime and bounded by $B$ for some constant $B = \mathrm{poly}(\log p)$. In view of Remark 2.5, we also assume that the kernel of $\gamma$, when identified with an endomorphism of $A_0$, is a maximal isotropic subgroup of $A_0[N]$ with respect to the $N$-Weil pairing for the product polarization $\lambda_0$. (If $\gamma$ fails to meet this condition, then our method will detect this along the way.) The desired output is a chain of polarized isogenies

$$A_0 \xrightarrow{\varphi_1} A_1 \xrightarrow{\varphi_2} A_2 \xrightarrow{\varphi_3} \dots \xrightarrow{\varphi_r} A_r \tag{9}$$

of respective reduced degrees $N_i$, such that $\ker(\gamma) = \ker(\varphi_r \circ \cdots \circ \varphi_2 \circ \varphi_1)$, where each $A_i$ is either a product $E_1 \times E_2$ of two elliptic curves equipped with the product polarization, or the Jacobian $\mathrm{Jac}(C)$ of a curve of genus 2 equipped with the canonical polarization. The method is summarized in Algorithm 2. We refer to the full version of our paper [6] for a more detailed discussion.

**Algorithm 2:** MatrixToIsogeny: powersmooth degree

**Input** : $\gamma \in \mathrm{M}_2(\mathcal{O}_0)$ with $\mathrm{degrd}(\gamma) = N_1 \cdots N_r$ powersmooth
**Output:** polarized isogenies $\varphi_r \circ \cdots \circ \varphi_1 : A_0 \to A_r$ with $\mathrm{degrd}\,\varphi_i = N_i$

$\tilde{\gamma} \leftarrow N\gamma^{-1}$, $\varphi_0 = \mathrm{id}$.
**For** $i = 1, \dots, r$ **do**
  $P_i, Q_i \leftarrow$ basis of $E_0[N_i]$.
  $S_i \leftarrow \tilde{\gamma}(\{(P_i, 0), (0, P_i), (Q_i, 0), (0, Q_i)\})$.
    // Generators of $(\ker\gamma)[N_i]$.
**For** $i = 1, \dots, r$ **do**
  $S_i \leftarrow (\varphi_{i-1} \circ \cdots \circ \varphi_0)(S_i)$.
  $\varphi_i \leftarrow$ isogeny $A_{i-1} \to A_i$ with kernel $\langle S_i \rangle$.
**Return** $\varphi_r \circ \cdots \circ \varphi_1 : A_0 \to A_r$.

[11] In general, it is possible that this concerns a pair of conjugate elliptic curves over $\mathbb{F}_{q^2}$, i.e., the codomain concerns a Weil restriction. But in our case, where we work with superspecial abelian surfaces over an extension of $\mathbb{F}_{p^2}$, this does not occur: the two elliptic curves are necessarily supersingular, hence can be defined over $\mathbb{F}_{p^2}$.

### 4.2 Polarized Isogenies from $A_0$ to Matrices

Conversely, given a chain of polarized isogenies emanating from $A_0$ as in (9), where the degrees $N_i = \deg \varphi_i$ are pairwise coprime and bounded by $B$, here the goal is to produce a matrix $\gamma \in \mathrm{M}_2(\mathcal{O}_0)$ such that $\ker(\gamma) = \ker(\varphi_r \cdots \varphi_2 \circ \varphi_1)$. Such a matrix is uniquely determined up to left-multiplication with an element of $\mathrm{GL}_2(\mathcal{O}_0)$ and will automatically satisfy

$$\gamma^* g_r \gamma = N \cdot \mathbb{I}_2$$

with $N = N_1 N_2 \cdots N_r$, for some representant $g_r \in \mathrm{Mat}(A_0)$ of the class in $\mathrm{Mat}^0(A_0)$ corresponding to the principally polarized abelian surface $A_r$. Note that $g_r$ can then be computed as $N\gamma^{*-1}\gamma^{-1} = N(\gamma\gamma^*)^{-1}$.

This conversion can be done as in Algorithm 3, which at a high level coincides with Chu's method from [11, Algorithm A.2.2]. Concerning Step 3, recall that $N_i \leq B$ implies that the elements of $G_i$ are defined over an extension field of degree $O(B^2)$. The main difference with Chu's method lies in how we handle Step 6, which we have labeled as the "key step". This is where Chu invokes a sub-exponential time algorithm for the PIP in $\mathrm{M}_2(\mathcal{O}_0)$, described in [11, Chapter 2]. We by-pass the need for invoking a PIP solver, by instead running the following polynomial-time method. It is clear that we can assume that $N_i = \ell^e$ equals a power of a prime number $\ell$.

---

**Algorithm 3:** IsogenyToMatrix: powersmooth degree

---

**Input** : chain $\varphi_r \circ \cdots \circ \varphi_1 : A_0 \to A_r$ of polarized isogenies
with $N_i := \mathrm{degrd}(\varphi_i) \leq B$ pairwise coprime

**Output:** $\gamma \in \mathrm{M}_2(\mathcal{O}_0)$ such that $\ker(\gamma) = \ker(\varphi_r \circ \cdots \circ \varphi_1)$,
$g_r \in \mathrm{Mat}(A_0)$ corresponding to $A_r$

1 $\gamma \leftarrow \mathbb{I}_2$.
2 **For** $i = 1, \ldots, r$ **do**
3 $\quad G_i \leftarrow (\tilde{\varphi}_{i-1} \circ \cdots \circ \tilde{\varphi}_2 \circ \tilde{\varphi}_1)(\ker \varphi_i) \subset A_0[N_i]$.
4 $\quad\quad$ `// Pulling back the kernel of` $\varphi_i$ `to` $A_0$.
5 $\quad K_i \leftarrow \gamma(G_i)$. `// Pushing the kernel forward under` $\gamma$.
6 $\quad \gamma_i \leftarrow$ matrix with kernel $K_i$. `// *** key step ***`
7 $\quad \gamma \leftarrow \gamma_i \gamma$.
8 **Return** $\gamma$, $N_1 \cdots N_r(\gamma\gamma^*)^{-1}$.

---

We first describe the method in case $e = 1$, i.e., $N_i = \ell$. Then $K_i \cong (\mathbb{Z}/\ell\mathbb{Z})^2$. Consider $A_0 = E_0^2$ together with the natural projection maps

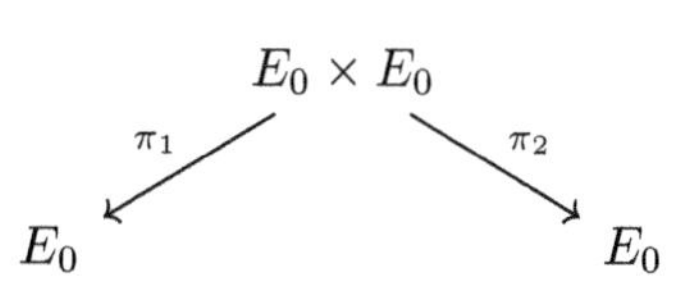

For each $j = 1, 2$ the projected subgroup $\pi_j(K_i) \subset E_0[\ell]$ is either trivial, a cyclic subgroup of order $\ell$, or all of $E_0[\ell]$. Moreover, if $\pi_1(K_i), \pi_2(K_i) \subsetneq E_0[\ell]$ then necessarily both groups are cyclic, i.e., $K_i = \langle (P, \infty), (\infty, Q) \rangle$ for order-$\ell$ points $P, Q \in E_0$. Based on this observation, we make a case distinction:

(i) Assume $\pi_1(K_i) = E_0[\ell]$. Let $P_1, P_2$ be a basis of $E_0[\ell]$. Then

$$(P_1, \lambda_{11}P_1 + \lambda_{12}P_2),\ (P_2, \lambda_{21}P_1 + \lambda_{22}P_2)\ \in K_i$$

for certain integers $\lambda_{jk}$, and these points necessarily generate $K_i$. We claim that we can find an endomorphism $a \in \mathcal{O}_0$ such that

$$a(P_j) = \lambda_{j1}P_1 + \lambda_{j2}P_2$$

for $j = 1, 2$, so that $K_i = \langle (P_1, a(P_1)), (P_2, a(P_2)) \rangle$ and then we can take

$$\gamma_i = \begin{pmatrix} \ell & 0 \\ -a & 1 \end{pmatrix}$$

whose kernel contains $K_i$ (but then for norm reasons equality must hold). The existence of $a$ follows because the $\ell^4$ elements of $\mathcal{O}_0/\ell\mathcal{O}_0$ all act differently on $E_0[\ell]$ (indeed, if two endomorphisms $a_1, a_2$ are such that $E_0[\ell] \subset \ker(a_1 - a_2)$, then necessarily $\ell \mid a_1 - a_2$). In practice, finding $a$ is just an easy linear algebra problem mod $\ell$ (express $a$ as an unknown linear combination of the basis from Example 2.1, evaluate at $P_1, P_2$, and solve for the coefficients).

(ii) Assume $\pi_2(K_i) = E_0[\ell]$: this is of course entirely analogous, leading to a matrix of the form

$$\gamma_i = \begin{pmatrix} 1 & -a \\ 0 & \ell \end{pmatrix}.$$

(iii) If $K_i = \langle (P, \infty), (\infty, Q) \rangle$ for order-$\ell$ points $P, Q \in E_0$, then we can easily find an endomorphism $b \in \mathcal{O}_0$ such that $b(Q) \notin \langle P \rangle$.[12] The matrix

$$\gamma_0 = \begin{pmatrix} 1 & b \\ 0 & 1 \end{pmatrix} \in \mathrm{GL}_2(\mathcal{O}_0)$$

transforms $K_i$ into the group $\gamma_0(K_i) = \langle (P, \infty), (b(Q), Q) \rangle$. This group satisfies $\pi_1(\gamma_0(K_i)) = E_0[\ell]$, so using (i) we can find a matrix $\gamma_0'$ such that $\gamma_0'(\gamma_0(K_i)) = 0$. Letting $\gamma_i = \gamma_0'\gamma_0$, for norm reasons we can conclude that $\ker(\gamma_i) = K_i$.

The case where $N_i = \ell^e$ for arbitrary $e \geq 1$ can be handled by iterating this procedure. For ease of exposition, let us first assume that

$$K_i \cong \frac{\mathbb{Z}}{\ell^e\mathbb{Z}} \times \frac{\mathbb{Z}}{\ell^e\mathbb{Z}}.$$

[12] We thank the ISOCRYPT brainstorm team for their help with this step.

Then the method is totally straightforward and can be found in Algorithm 4. Note that this algorithm does not assume that $\ell^e$ is polynomially bounded, i.e., we can drop the powersmoothness assumption, as long as the elements of $K_i$ are defined over $\mathbb{F}_{p^2}$ or a small-degree extension thereof.[13]

---

**Algorithm 4:** IsogenyToMatrix: $\ell$-power degree

---

**Input** : subgroup $K \cong (\mathbb{Z}/\ell^e\mathbb{Z})^2$ of $A_0$ generated by points defined over a small extension of $\mathbb{F}_{p^2}$

**Output:** $\gamma \in \mathrm{M}_2(\mathcal{O}_0)$ such that $\ker(\gamma) = K$

1 $\gamma \leftarrow \mathbb{I}_2, \; K_1 \leftarrow K$.

2 **For** $i = 1, \ldots, e$ **do**

3     $G_i \leftarrow \ell^{e-i} K_i$.

4     $\gamma_i \leftarrow$ matrix with kernel $G_i$. `// Method for` $(\ell, \ell)$`-subgroups.`

5     $\gamma \leftarrow \gamma_i \gamma, \; K_{i+1} \leftarrow \gamma_i(K_i)$.

6 **Return** $\gamma$.

---

This method can be easily adapted to work for arbitrary kernel types, i.e., of the form

$$K_i \cong \frac{\mathbb{Z}}{\ell^e\mathbb{Z}} \times \frac{\mathbb{Z}}{\ell^{e-f}\mathbb{Z}} \times \frac{\mathbb{Z}}{\ell^f\mathbb{Z}}$$

for some $f \in \{0 \ldots, \lfloor e/2 \rfloor\}$ [24, Proposition 2], again as long as this kernel is generated by points defined over a small extension of $\mathbb{F}_{p^2}$. (We can always reduce to the case of 3 or fewer generators: if there are 4 generators then the corresponding matrix $\gamma_i$ factors through $\ell\mathbb{I}_2$ and one can reduce to the case of reduced degree $\ell^{e-2}$.) The main caveat lies in Step 3 of Algorithm 4, where one should be more careful: indeed, in this case $\ell^{e-1}K_i \not\cong \mathbb{Z}/\ell\mathbb{Z} \times \mathbb{Z}/\ell\mathbb{Z}$. A clean workaround, which serves as a warm-up for Sect. 5.4, is to define the subgroup

$$K_i' = \langle \ell^{e-f}P, R \rangle \cong \frac{\mathbb{Z}}{\ell^f\mathbb{Z}} \times \frac{\mathbb{Z}}{\ell^f\mathbb{Z}}$$

with $P \in K_i$ any point of order $\ell^e$ and $R \in K_i$ any point of order $\ell^f$ that is not halvable in $K_i$. Since $e_{\ell^f,\lambda_0}(\ell^{e-f}P, R) = e_{\ell^e,\lambda_0}(P, R) = 1$, this concerns a maximal isotropic subgroup of $A_0[\ell^f]$. We can now run Algorithm 4 on input $K_i'$, returning a matrix $\gamma_i'$, and then rerun the algorithm on input

$$\gamma_i'(K_i') \cong K_i/K_i' \cong \frac{\mathbb{Z}}{\ell^{e-f}\mathbb{Z}} \times \frac{\mathbb{Z}}{\ell^{e-f}\mathbb{Z}},$$

after initializing $\gamma \leftarrow \gamma_i'$ rather than $\gamma \leftarrow \mathbb{I}_2$ in Step 1.

---

[13] Of course, this rationality assumption still comes with an implicit bound, i.e., of the kind $\ell^e \mid p^r - (-1)^r$ with $r$ the extension degree. In Sect. 5.2 we will use the KLPT[2] algorithm to get rid of this bound.

# 5 Applications of $\mathrm{KLPT}^2$

We are ready to discuss a number of applications of the $\mathrm{KLPT}^2$ algorithm.

## 5.1 Constructive IKO Correspondence

For elliptic curves, the *constructive Deuring correspondence* asks to solve the following problem: upon input of a maximal order $\mathcal{O} \subset B_{p,\infty}$, return a supersingular elliptic curve $E/\mathbb{F}_{p^2}$ such that $\mathrm{End}(E) \cong \mathcal{O}$. The KLPT algorithm can be turned into a heuristic polynomial-time algorithm for solving this problem. At a high level, the method works as follows. One starts from an elliptic curve $E_0/\mathbb{F}_{p^2}$ having a known, special extremal endomorphism ring $\mathrm{End}(E_0) \cong \mathcal{O}_0$. Using the KLPT algorithm, one computes a left ideal $I \subset \mathcal{O}_0$ of powersmooth norm $N$ connecting $\mathcal{O}_0$ and $\mathcal{O}$. This ideal can then be converted into an isogeny emerging from $E_0$ using the elliptic-curve counterpart of Algorithm 2. The codomain of this isogeny is a valid output for the constructive Deuring correspondence.

For *unpolarized* superspecial abelian surfaces, the direct analog of the constructive Deuring correspondence is void: all such surfaces are pairwise isomorphic and therefore share the same endomorphism ring, namely $\mathrm{M}_2(\mathcal{O}_0)$. However, in the principally polarized case, the endomorphism ring comes equipped with an extra datum: the Rosati involution, which as explained in Remark 2.9 is completely encoded in the matrix $g \in \mathrm{Mat}(A_0)$ corresponding to $\lambda$. Therefore, a more meaningful counterpart of the constructive Deuring correspondence reads:

**Theorem 5.1. (constructive IKO correspondence).** *There exists a (heuristic) polynomial-time algorithm which upon input $g \in \mathrm{Mat}(A_0)$, either finds two elliptic curves $E_1, E_2$ or finds a genus-2 curve $C$ such that for*

$$\begin{aligned}(A, \lambda) &= (E_1 \times E_2, \textit{product polarization}), \quad \textit{resp.}\\ (A, \lambda) &= (\mathrm{Jac}(C), \textit{canonical polarization}),\end{aligned}$$

*we have $(A, \lambda) \cong (A_0, \mu^{-1}(g))$, with $\mu$ the map from Theorem 2.8.*

*Proof.* Using our pathfinding algorithm from Theorem 3.15 we can find $\gamma \in \mathrm{M}_2(\mathcal{O}_0)$ such that

$$\gamma^* g \gamma = N\mathbb{I}_2,$$

with $N$ powersmooth. To produce the desired output, one then simply converts $\gamma$ into a polarized isogeny emanating from $A_0$ using Algorithm 2. If the codomain of this polarized isogeny is a product $E_1 \times E_2$, we output $E_1, E_2$; when landing on a Jacobian $\mathrm{Jac}(C)$, output $C$. □

## 5.2 Relaxing Powersmoothness Assumptions When Translating Between Matrices and Isogenies

**(i) Matrices to Isogenies from $A_0$ in Arbitrary Degree.** Let us be given a matrix $\gamma \in \mathrm{M}_2(\mathcal{O}_0)$ as in Sect. 4.1, but we drop the assumption that $N$ is powersmooth. We claim that, using KLPT$^2$, we can nevertheless convert $\gamma$ into a polarized isogeny $\varphi$ emanating from $A_0$. This mimicks well-known techniques from the elliptic curve case [21,45]. First, recall that a matrix $g \in \mathrm{Mat}(A_0)$ representing the codomain can be computed as $g = N(\gamma\gamma^*)^{-1}$. Then, using Theorem 3.15, we can find a matrix $\gamma'$ and a powersmooth integer $N'$ such that $\gamma'^* g \gamma' = N' \cdot \mathbb{I}_2$, and we know that $\gamma, \gamma'$ correspond to polarized isogenies $\varphi, \varphi'$ with the same codomain, i.e. $\varphi, \varphi' : A_0 \to A$, where $\mathrm{degrd}(\varphi) = N$ and $\mathrm{degrd}(\varphi') = N'$. We can compute $\varphi'$ as a composition of small-degree isogenies using Algorithm 2, which also reveals $A$. We have $N'\varphi = \varphi' \tilde{\varphi}' \varphi$ where we note that

$$\tilde{\varphi}'\varphi = \lambda_0^{-1}\hat{\varphi}'\lambda\varphi = \lambda_0^{-1}\hat{\varphi}'\lambda_0\,\lambda_0^{-1}\lambda\,\varphi \;\in \mathrm{End}(A_0)$$

can be identified with $\gamma'^* g\gamma \in \mathrm{M}_2(\mathcal{O}_0)$. Thus we can evaluate

$$\varphi(P) = \frac{1}{N'}\varphi'(\gamma'^* g\gamma P)$$

on any input point $P$ whose order is coprime with $N'$. This is enough for considering $\varphi$ as being known, e.g., in view of [39,40].

*Remark 5.2. (matrices to isogenies from $A_0$ in smooth degree).* If $N$ is smooth (but not powersmooth, so that Algorithm 2 may not be applicable) then the above "evaluation representation" of $\varphi$ may not be the preferred format. Rather, one may want an explicit decomposition $\varphi = \varphi_r \circ \cdots \circ \varphi_1$ into isogenies of small degree. A polynomial-time conversion between these formats is possible through a repeated use of a higher-dimensional analogue of [40, Corollary 6.8], but this seems impractical. Alternatively, this can be handled using multiple applications of KLPT$^2$ as outlined in Algorithm 5.

**(ii) Isogenies from $A_0$ to Matrices in Smooth Degree.** The KLPT$^2$ algorithm can also be used to convert polarized isogenies from $A_0$ into matrices when the degree is smooth, rather than powersmooth. For this we recycle a trick due to Eisenträger, Hallgren, Lauter, Morrison and Petit [21, Algorithm 9]; see also Wesolowski [45, Algorithm 3]. The method is detailed in Algorithm 6, where we note that Steps 3–9 are trivial at iteration $i = 1$.

### 5.3 Translating Between Matrices and Isogenies from Other Starting Surfaces

**(i) Matrices to Polarized Isogenies.** Next, let us be given a matrix $g_1 \in \mathrm{Mat}(A_0)$ and a matrix $\gamma \in \mathrm{M}_2(\mathcal{O}_0)$ of reduced norm $N^2$ (for arbitrary $N$), with the promise that $\gamma$ defines a polarized isogeny emanating from $(A_0, \lambda_1)$, where $\lambda_1 = \mu^{-1}(g_1)$ is the principal polarization corresponding to $g_1$. Our goal is to tackle the following enhanced version of the constructive IKO correspondence: return the top row in a commutative diagram of the form

**Algorithm 5:** MatrixToIsogeny: smooth degree

**Input** : $\gamma \in \mathrm{M}_2(\mathcal{O}_0)$ with $\mathrm{degrd}(\gamma) = N_1 N_2 \cdots N_e$ where $N_i \leq B$
**Output:** polarized isogenies $\varphi_e \circ \cdots \circ \varphi_1 : A_0 \to A_e$ with $\mathrm{degrd}\,\varphi_i = N_i$

**For** $i = 1, \ldots, e-1$ **do**
  $G_i \leftarrow (\ker \gamma)[N_i]$.
  $\gamma_i \leftarrow$ matrix with kernel $G_i$. `// Step 6 in Algorithm 3.`
  $\gamma \leftarrow \gamma\gamma_i^{-1}$.
$\gamma_e \leftarrow \gamma$, $\gamma \leftarrow \mathbb{I}_2$.
  `// Input` $\gamma$ `decomposed as` $\gamma_e \cdots \gamma_1$`; then reinitialize` $\gamma$.
**For** $i = 1, \ldots, e$ **do**
  $\gamma \leftarrow \gamma_i\gamma$.
  $g_i \leftarrow N_1 N_2 \cdots N_i (\gamma\gamma^*)^{-1}$. `// Codomain matrix of` $\varphi_i$.
  Find $\gamma' \in \mathrm{M}_2(\mathcal{O}_0)$ and powersmooth $N'$ coprime with $N_1 N_2 \cdots N_i$ s.t. $\gamma'^* g_i \gamma' = N' \cdot \mathbb{I}_2$. `// Mild strengthening of Thm 3.15.`
  Using Algorithm 2, convert $\gamma'$ to polarized isogeny $\varphi' : A_0 \to A_i$.
  $G_i \leftarrow \ker(\tilde{\gamma}\gamma')[N_i]$. `// Note` $\tilde{\gamma} = N_1 N_2 \cdots N_i \gamma^{-1}$.
  $\varphi_i \leftarrow$ adjoint of isogeny $A_i \to A_{i-1}$ with kernel $\varphi'(G_i)$.
**Return** $\varphi_e \circ \cdots \circ \varphi_1 : A_0 \to A_e$.

$$\begin{array}{ccc} \begin{array}{c}\mathrm{Jac}(C_1) \text{ or} \\ E_{11} \times E_{12}\end{array} & \xrightarrow{\varphi} & \begin{array}{c}\mathrm{Jac}(C_2) \text{ or} \\ E_{21} \times E_{22}\end{array} \\ \cong\downarrow & & \downarrow\cong \\ (A_0, \lambda_1) & \xrightarrow{\gamma} & (A_0, \lambda_2). \end{array}$$

That is, for $i = 1, 2$ one should return the underlying genus-2 curve $C_i$ or elliptic curves $E_{i1}, E_{i2}$, along with an efficient representation of $\varphi$. This can be done as follows. If $N$ is powersmooth, then using a mild strengthening of Theorem 3.15 we can compute a matrix $\kappa \in \mathrm{M}_2(\mathcal{O}_0)$ and a powersmooth integer $K$ such that $\gcd(K, N) = 1$ and $\kappa^* g_1 \kappa = K \cdot \mathbb{I}_2$. This implies that

$$(\gamma\kappa)^* g_2 (\gamma\kappa) = NK \cdot \mathbb{I}_2$$

with $g_2 = \mu(\lambda_2) = N\gamma^{*-1} g_1 \gamma^{-1}$. We can then run Algorithm 2 on input $\gamma\kappa$, first processing the factors of $K$, to end up with an isogeny that naturally factors as

$$(A_0, \lambda_0) \longrightarrow \begin{array}{c}\mathrm{Jac}(C_1) \text{ or} \\ E_{11} \times E_{12}\end{array} \xrightarrow{\varphi} \begin{array}{c}\mathrm{Jac}(C_2) \text{ or} \\ E_{21} \times E_{22}\end{array}:$$

hence the desired output. If $N$ is not powersmooth then we first apply Theorem 3.15 to replace $\gamma$ with a matrix $\gamma'$ of powersmooth reduced norm $N'^2$ (i.e., satisfying $\gamma'^* g_2 \gamma' = N' \cdot g_1$) and proceed as in Sect. 5.2.

**Algorithm 6:** IsogenyToMatrix: smooth degree

**Input** : chain $\varphi_r \circ \cdots \circ \varphi_1 : A_0 \to A_r$ of polarized isogenies with $N_i := \mathrm{degrd}(\varphi_i) \leq B$

**Output:** $\gamma \in \mathrm{M}_2(\mathcal{O}_0)$ such that $\ker(\gamma) = \ker(\varphi_r \circ \cdots \circ \varphi_1)$, $g_r \in \mathrm{Mat}(A_0)$ corresponding to $A_r$

$\gamma \leftarrow \mathbb{I}_2$.<br>
**For** $i = 1, \ldots, r$ **do**<br>
    $g_i \leftarrow N_1 \cdots N_{i-1}(\gamma\gamma^*)^{-1}$. `// Codomain matrix of` $\varphi_{i-1}$.<br>
    Find $\gamma' \in \mathrm{M}_2(\mathcal{O}_0)$ and powersmooth $N'$ with $\gcd(N', N_i) = 1$ and $\gamma'^* g_i \gamma' = N' \cdot \mathbb{I}_2$. `// Mild strengthening of Theorem 3.15.`<br>
    Using Algorithm 2, convert $\gamma'$ to polarized isogeny $\varphi' : A_0 \to A_{i-1}$.<br>
        `// Domain of` $\varphi_i$.<br>
    $G_i \leftarrow \tilde{\varphi}'(\ker \varphi_i) \subset A_0[N_i]$.<br>
        `// Pulling back the kernel of` $\varphi_i$ `to` $A_0$.<br>
    $K_i \leftarrow \gamma'(G_i)$. `// Pushing the kernel forward under` $\gamma'$.<br>
    $\gamma_i \leftarrow$ matrix with kernel $K_i$. `// Step 6 in Algorithm 3.`<br>
    $\gamma \leftarrow \gamma_i \gamma$<br>
**Return** $\gamma$, $N_1 \cdots N_r(\gamma\gamma^*)^{-1}$.

**(ii) Polarized Isogenies to Matrices.** We can easily extend the foregoing methods for isogeny-to-matrix conversion from $(A_0, \lambda_0)$ to any principally polarized starting surface $(A, \lambda)$, say given as a Jacobian $\mathrm{Jac}(C)$ or a product of elliptic curves $E_1 \times E_2$, as soon as a corresponding matrix $g \in \mathrm{Mat}(A_0)$ is known. As for the output matrix,

- let us recall from Sect. 4.2 that it is determined up to left-multiplication with an element of $\mathrm{GL}_2(\mathcal{O}_0)$ only,
- in addition, if in the method below one replaces $g$ with a different representant of its class in $\mathrm{Mat}^0(A_0)$, then this amounts to *right*-multiplication with an element of $\mathrm{GL}_2(\mathcal{O}_0)$.

The problem of isogeny-to-matrix conversion easily reduces to the case $(A, \lambda) = (A_0, \lambda_0)$. Indeed, by means of Theorem 3.1 we can find a matrix $\gamma'$ with reduced degree $2^e$ connecting $\mathbb{I}_2$ and $g$. Using Algorithm 5 this matrix can be converted into a polarized isogeny $\varphi' : (A_0, \lambda_0) \to (A, \lambda)$, represented as a chain of $(2,2)$-isogenies. Now if $\varphi$ is a polarized isogeny emanating from $(A, \lambda)$, then $\varphi \circ \varphi'$ is a polarized isogeny emanating from $(A, \lambda_0)$, and if $\gamma$ is a matrix corresponding to $\varphi \circ \varphi'$, then $\gamma\gamma'^{-1}$ is a matrix corresponding to $\varphi$.

### 5.4 Attacks on CGL Hash Functions

We now arrive at our main cryptographic application: finding collisions for two-dimensional variants of the Charles–Goren–Lauter (CGL) hash function [8], in the case of an untrusted set-up.

**CGL Hash Functions in Dimension Two.** In 2018, Takashima [43] proposed the first such variant, using random non-backtracking walks in the $(2,2)$-isogeny graph of superspecial principally polarized abelian surfaces. It was observed by Flynn and Ti [24] that such hash functions admit trivial collisions, coming from the fact that every $(4,2,2)$-isogeny admits three different decompositions into two $(2,2)$-isogenies. Therefore, starting with [7], all subsequent proposals restrict to "good" chains of $(2,2)$-isogenies, i.e., composing to a $(2^e,2^e)$-isogeny for some $e \geq 1$. This means that the kernel of every outgoing $(2,2)$-isogeny trivially intersects the kernel of the dual of the previous, incoming $(2,2)$-isogeny.[14]

Let us briefly detail how CGL hash functions in dimension two are currently constructed, generalizing from $(2,2)$-isogenies to $(\ell,\ell)$-isogenies for any small prime $\ell$. During set-up, an initial node in the graph is chosen, corresponding to some superspecial principally polarized abelian surface $A_1$, as well as $\ell^3$ "allowed" outgoing edges, corresponding to a subset of the set of $(\ell^2+1)(\ell+1)$ outgoing polarized $(\ell,\ell)$-isogenies from this initial node. At each node, the outgoing edges are sorted in some deterministic way; e.g. by comparing the invariants of all the neighbor nodes. The input message $\mathsf{mess}$ is mapped deterministically to $(m_1, m_2, \ldots, m_k) \in \{0,1,\ldots,\ell^3-1\}^*$, with some padding if necessary. To hash, one of the $\ell^3$ allowed edges is chosen according to the value of $m_1$, and we compute the corresponding neighbor node, yielding a new principally polarized abelian surface $A_2$. Using the value $m_2$, we choose one of the $\ell^3$ outgoing edges corresponding to an $(\ell,\ell)$-isogeny whose kernel trivially intersects the kernel of the dual of the previous $(\ell,\ell)$-isogeny. This results in a node corresponding to a surface $A_3$ and we repeat this process until we have landed on a node corresponding to a surface $A_{k+1}$. We deterministically map suitable invariants of $A_{k+1}$ to $\{0,1\}^n$, where $n \approx 3\log p$, and use this as the output of our hash function.

**KLPT² Produces "bad" Chains.** In dimension one, the KLPT algorithm can be used to compute second pre-images for the CGL hash function as soon as the endomorphism ring of the starting curve is known [21]. In dimension two, a very similar reasoning applies as soon as a matrix $g_1 \in \mathrm{Mat}(A_0)$ corresponding to the initial node is known: given a message $\mathsf{mess}_1$,

- using the method from Sect. 5.3(ii), one can compute a matrix $g_{k+1}$ corresponding to its hash value $A_{k+1}$,
- using KLPT² on input $g_1, g_{k+1}$, one then computes a connecting matrix $\gamma$ corresponding to a polarized isogeny of reduced degree $\ell^e$; with overwhelming probability this will be different from the isogeny hashing $\mathsf{mess}_1$,

[14] Rather than merely not coinciding with it: this is how "non-backtracking" was understood in Takashima's proposal [43].

– as outlined in Sect. 5.3(i), one can then effectively convert $\gamma$ into a chain of $(\ell,\ell)$-isogenies from $A_1$ to $A_{k+1}$.

But, alas, this chain will fail to hash a second pre-image $\mathsf{mess}_2$, because with overwhelming probability it will not be a "good" chain. Indeed, in general, KLPT$^2$ fails to return $(\ell^e,\ell^e)$-isogenies in view of Corollary 5.4 below:

**Lemma 5.3.** *Let $a, c \in \mathcal{O}_0$ be non-zero elements such that* $\gcd(\mathsf{n}(a),\mathsf{n}(c)) = 1$ *and assume that $\ell \nmid \mathsf{n}(a),\mathsf{n}(c)$. Let $b, d \in \mathcal{O}_0$ be such that*

$$\mathcal{N}(u) = \ell^{e_0}, \qquad u = \begin{pmatrix} a & b \\ c & d \end{pmatrix},$$

*computed by finding an element of norm $\mathsf{n}(c)\ell^{e_0}$ in $\mathsf{n}(c)\mathcal{O}_0 + a\bar{c}\mathcal{O}_0$ via the KLPT algorithm, as explained in Sect. 3.2. Assume that the degree-$\ell^{e_0}$ component of this element is cyclic (this is generically expected). Then* $\ker(u) \cong \mathbb{Z}/\ell^{e_0}\mathbb{Z}$.

**Corollary 5.4.** *Under the assumption from Lemma 5.3 that the KLPT algorithm produces cyclic isogenies, to describe the kernel of the matrix $\gamma \in \mathrm{M}_2(\mathcal{O}_0)$ returned by Algorithm 1, one needs at least* 3 *generators.*

Under plausible heuristic assumptions, one can be more precise about the structure of $\ker(\gamma)$. In the full version of our paper [6], we argue that

$$\ker(\gamma) \cong \frac{\mathbb{Z}}{\ell^{2e_1+2e_2}\mathbb{Z}} \times \frac{\mathbb{Z}}{\ell^{e_1+2e_2}\mathbb{Z}} \times \frac{\mathbb{Z}}{\ell^{e_1}\mathbb{Z}} \tag{10}$$

holds with a probability that is bounded (from below) by a constant only depending on $\ell$ and converging to 1 as $\ell \to \infty$. Consequently, this is expected to be true after a constant number of reruns of KLPT$^2$ if needed. Here the exponents $e_1, e_2$ are as in Sect. 3.1; recall from (4) that the final exponent $e$ arises as $2e_1+2e_2$ with $e_1 = 2e_0$. We stress that, while it is convenient to restrict to the shape (10) for expository purposes, our collision finding method outlined below can be adapted to any other isomorphism type.

**Collision Finding.** While second pre-images seem out of reach, the KLPT$^2$ algorithm still lends itself to finding collisions, as we now discuss. The first step is to run KLPT$^2$ on input $g_1, g_1$, resulting in a matrix $\gamma \in \mathrm{M}_2(\mathcal{O}_0)$ defining a polarized endomorphism

$$(A_0, \lambda_1) \longrightarrow (A_0, \lambda_1), \quad A_1 \cong (A_0, \lambda_1),\ g_1 = \mu(\lambda_1)$$

of reduced degree $\ell^e$. In view of the previous discussion, we can assume that $\ker(\gamma)$ is of isomorphism type (10).

Then the idea for converting $\gamma$ into a collision is inspired by the reasoning at the end of Sect. 4.2, where it was argued that there exists a subgroup of $\ker(\gamma)$ determining a polarized $(\ell^{e_1},\ell^{e_1})$-isogeny $\gamma_1 : (A_0,\lambda_1) \to (A_0,\lambda)$, through which $\gamma$ factors, in such a way that the remaining factor $\gamma_2 : (A_0,\lambda) \to (A_0,\lambda_1)$ is a polarized $(\ell^{e_1+2e_2}, \ell^{e_1+2e_2})$-isogeny. Thus we have two "good" paths $\gamma_1$, $\tilde{\gamma}_2$ emanating from $(A_0, \lambda_1)$ with the same codomain: this is the algebraic version of the desired collision. If we effectively succeed in finding $\gamma_1, \gamma_2$ then these matrices can be converted into two colliding isogenies emanating from $A_1$, by following the procedure described in Sect. 5.3.

In Sect. 4.2 we also had an explicit description of the subgroup $\ker(\gamma_1)$, namely

$$\langle \ell^{e_1+2e_2} P, R \rangle \tag{11}$$

where $P \in \ker(\gamma)$ is any point of order $\ell^e = \ell^{2e_0+2e_2}$ and $R$ is any point of order $\ell^{e_1}$ that cannot be divided by $\ell$ inside $\ker(\gamma)$. This explicit description is of lesser use to us, because the generators in (11) are in general defined over a huge-degree extension of $\mathbb{F}_{p^2}$ only. Before explaining our workaround, let us note that many other subgroups of $\ker(\gamma)$ are equally valid choices: the only crucial features are that

- the subgroup is isomorphic to $(\mathbb{Z}/\ell^{e_1}\mathbb{Z})^2$, i.e. $\gamma_1$ is a "good" chain of isogenies,
- it contains a point $R$ that is not divisible by $\ell$ in $\ker(\gamma)$, so that

$$\frac{\ker(\gamma)}{\ker(\gamma_1)} \cong (\mathbb{Z}/\ell^{e_1+2e_2}\mathbb{Z})^2,$$

  i.e., also the cofactor $\gamma_2$ is a "good" chain of isogenies, and
- it concerns a maximal isotropic subgroup with respect to the $\ell^{e_1}$-Weil pairing for $\lambda_1$, so that $\gamma_1$ is a polarized isogeny.

The following lemma shows that $\gamma_1$ can be built following a "greedy" approach.

**Lemma 5.6.** *Consider any subgroup $G \cong (\mathbb{Z}/\ell^{e_1}\mathbb{Z})^3$ of $A_0[\ell^{e_1}]$ and let $K_1 \subset G[\ell]$ be maximal isotropic with respect to the $\ell$-Weil pairing $e_{\ell,\lambda_1}$. Consider the following iterative procedure for $i \geq 2$: let $K_i$ be any subgroup of $G$ for which*

$$K_i \supset K_{i-1}, \qquad K_i \cong \frac{\mathbb{Z}}{\ell^i\mathbb{Z}} \times \frac{\mathbb{Z}}{\ell^i\mathbb{Z}}, \qquad e_{\ell^i,\lambda_1}|_{K_i \times K_i} = 1. \tag{12}$$

*Then, regardless of the choices made, this procedure can be repeated up to $i = e_1$, and for every $i$ we have that $K_i$ is maximal isotropic with respect $e_{\ell^i,\lambda_1}$.*

We start with any subgroup $K_1 \subset (\ker \gamma)[\ell]$ that

- is maximal isotropic with respect to $e_{\ell,\lambda_1}$,
- contains $\ell^{e_1-1}R \in K_1$, with $R$ a point that is not divisible by $\ell$ in $\ker(\gamma)$.

Then the subgroup $K_{e_1}$ produced by Lemma 5.6 will indeed be a suitable instance of $\ker(\gamma_1)$. A point of the form $\ell^{e_1-1}R$ can be found by taking any order-$\ell$ point independent of $\ker(\tau)$ and $\ker(u_1)$, and taking its image under $u_1$. Once $K_1$ is fixed, we look for a matrix $\kappa_1 \in \mathrm{M}_2(\mathcal{O}_0)$ with kernel $H_1 = K_1$. We then know that

$\gamma$ factors through $\kappa_1$, and continue with the remaining factor $\gamma\kappa_1^{-1}$: we look for any maximal isotropic subgroup $H_2 \cong (\mathbb{Z}/\ell\mathbb{Z})^2$, with corresponding matrix $\kappa_2$, which forms a "good" extension of $\kappa_1$. We then continue with $\gamma\kappa_1^{-1}\kappa_2^{-1}$, and so on. In this way we implicitly build a tower of subgroups $K_i = (\ker \kappa_i \circ \cdots \circ \kappa_1)$ as in Lemma 5.6. Eventually, this leads to (see the full version [6] for more details):

**Proposition 5.1.** *Assuming knowledge of a matrix $g_1 \in \mathrm{Mat}(A_0)$ corresponding to the initial node, under plausible heuristic assumptions, collisions for the two-dimensional variant of the CGL hash function can be produced in polynomial time.*

We deem it likely that all currently known ways for constructing a superspecial principally polarized abelian surface $A_1$ implicitly reveal an isogeny to $E_0^2$. This would be analogous to the current situation for supersingular elliptic curves [2]. See the full version of this paper [6] for an extended discussion.

## References


1. Basso, A., et al.: SQIsign2D-west: the fast, the small, and the safer. In: Chung, KM., Sasaki, Y. (eds.) ASIACRYPT 2024, Part III. LNCS, vol. 15486, pp. 339–370. Springer, Cham (2024). https://doi.org/10.1007/978-981-96-0891-1_11
2. Booher, J., et al.: Failing to hash into supersingular isogeny graphs. Comput. J. **67**(8), 2702–2719 (2024). https://doi.org/10.1093/comjnl/bxae038
3. Bouw, I., et al.: Bad reduction of genus three curves with complex multiplication. In: Bertin, M.J., Bucur, A., Feigon, B., Schneps, L. (eds.) Women in Numbers Europe. AWMS, vol. 2, pp. 109–151. Springer, Cham (2015). https://doi.org/10.1007/978-3-319-17987-2_5
4. Brock, B.: Superspecial curves of genera two and three. Ph.D. thesis, Princeton University (1994)
5. Castryck, W., Decru, T.: An efficient key recovery attack on SIDH. In: Hazay, C., Stam, M. (eds.) EUROCRYPT 2023, Part V. LNCS, vol. 14008, pp. 423–447. Springer, Cham (2023). https://doi.org/10.1007/978-3-031-30589-4_15
6. Castryck, W., Decru, T., Kutas, P., Laval, A., Petit, C., Ti, Y.B.: KLPT$^2$: algebraic pathfinding in dimension two and applications. Cryptology ePrint Archive, Paper 2025/372, 2025. Full version of this paper. https://eprint.iacr.org/2025/372
7. Castryck, W., Decru, T., Smith, B.: Hash functions from superspecial genus-2 curves using Richelot isogenies. J. Math. Cryptol. **14**(1), 268–292 (2020). https://doi.org/10.1515/jmc-2019-0021
8. Charles, D.X., Lauter, K.E., Goren, E.Z.: Cryptographic hash functions from expander graphs. J. Cryptol. **22**(1), 93–113 (2009). https://doi.org/10.1007/s00145-007-9002-x
9. Chavez-Saab, J., et al.: SQIsign: algorithm specifications and supporting documentation, v1.0. https://sqisign.org/
10. Chen, M., Imran, M., Ivanyos, G., Kutas, P., Leroux, A., Petit, C.: Hidden stabilizers, the isogeny to endomorphism ring problem and the cryptanalysis of pSIDH. In: Guo, J., Steinfeld, R. (eds.) ASIACRYPT 2023, Part III. LNCS, vol. 14440, pp. 99–130. Springer, Singapore (2023). https://doi.org/10.1007/978-981-99-8727-6_4

11. Chu, H.-W.: Algorithms for abelian surfaces over finite fields and their applications to cryptography. Ph.D. thesis, Pennsylvania State University (2021). https://etda.libraries.psu.edu/files/final_submissions/24383
12. Conrad, B.: Polarizations. Notes of the VIGRE Number Theory Working Group (2004). https://math.stanford.edu/~conrad/vigregroup/vigre04/polarization.pdf
13. Santos, M.C.-R., Costello, C., Smith, B.: Efficient $(3,3)$-isogenies on fast Kummer surfaces. Res. Num. Theor. **11** (2025). Article no. 25. https://doi.org/10.1007/s40993-024-00600-y
14. Cosset, R.: Applications des fonctions thêta à la cryptographie sur courbes hyperelliptiques. Ph.D. thesis, Université Henri Poincaré Nancy (2011). https://theses.hal.science/tel-00642951v1
15. Cosset, R., Robert, D.: Computing $(\ell, \ell)$-isogenies in polynomial time on Jacobians of genus 2 curves. Math. Comput. **84**(294), 1953–1975 (2015). http://www.jstor.org/stable/24489183
16. Couveignes, J.-M., Ezome, T.: Computing functions on Jacobians and their quotients. LMS J. Comput. Math. **18**(1), 555–577 (2015). https://doi.org/10.1112/S1461157015000169
17. Dartois, P., Leroux, A., Robert, D., Wesolowski, B.: SQIsignHD: new dimensions in cryptography. In: Joye, M., Leander, G. (eds.) EUROCRYPT 2024, Part I. LNCS, vol. 14651, pp. 3–32. Springer, Cham (2024). https://doi.org/10.1007/978-3-031-58716-0_1
18. De Feo, L., Kohel, D., Leroux, A., Petit, C., Wesolowski, B.: SQISign: compact post-quantum signatures from quaternions and isogenies. In: Moriai, S., Wang, H. (eds.) ASIACRYPT 2020, Part I. LNCS, vol. 12491, pp. 64–93. Springer, Cham (2020). https://doi.org/10.1007/978-3-030-64837-4_3
19. Deuring, M.: Die Typen der Multiplikatorenringe Elliptischer Funktionenkörper. Abhandlungen aus dem mathematischen Seminar der Universität Hamburg **14**, 197–272 (1941)
20. Duparc, M., Fouotsa, T.B.: SQIPrime: a dimension 2 variant of SQISignHD with non-smooth challenge isogenies. In: Chung, KM., Sasaki, Y. (eds.) ASIACRYPT 2024, Part III. LNCS, vol. 15486, pp. 396–429. Springer, Singapore (2024). https://doi.org/10.1007/978-981-96-0891-1_13
21. Eisenträger, K., Hallgren, S., Lauter, K., Morrison, T., Petit, C.: Supersingular isogeny graphs and endomorphism rings: reductions and solutions. In: Nielsen, J.B., Rijmen, V. (eds.) EUROCRYPT 2018. LNCS, vol. 10822, pp. 329–368. Springer, Cham (2018). https://doi.org/10.1007/978-3-319-78372-7_11
22. Eisenträger, K., Hallgren, S., Leonardi, C., Morrison, T., Park, J.: Computing endomorphism rings of supersingular elliptic curves and connections to path-finding in isogeny graphs. Open Book Ser. **4**, 215–232 (2020). https://doi.org/10.2140/obs.2020.4.215
23. Eriksen, J.K., Panny, L., Sotáková, J., Veroni, M.: Deuring for the people: supersingular elliptic curves with prescribed endomorphism ring in general characteristic. In: LuCaNT: LMFDB, Computation, and Number Theory, Contemporary Mathematics, pp. 339–365 (2023). https://doi.org/10.1090/conm/796/16008
24. Flynn, E.V., Ti, Y.B.: Genus two isogeny cryptography. In: Ding, J., Steinwandt, R. (eds.) PQCrypto 2019. LNCS, vol. 11505, pp. 286–306. Springer, Cham (2019). https://doi.org/10.1007/978-3-030-25510-7_16
25. Galbraith, S.D., Petit, C., Silva, J.: Identification protocols and signature schemes based on supersingular isogeny problems. In: Takagi, T., Peyrin, T. (eds.) ASIACRYPT 2017, Part I. LNCS, vol. 10624, pp. 3–33. Springer, Cham (2017). https://doi.org/10.1007/978-3-319-70694-8_1

26. Gaudry, P., Soumier, J., Spaenlehauer, P.-J.: Isogeny-based cryptography using isomorphisms of superspecial abelian surfaces. Cryptology ePrint Archive, Paper 2025/136 (2025). https://eprint.iacr.org/2025/136
27. Gélin, A., Howe, E., Ritzenthaler, C.: Principally polarized squares of elliptic curves with field of moduli equal to $\mathbb{Q}$. Open Book Ser. **2**(1), 257–274 (2019). https://doi.org/10.2140/obs.2019.2.257
28. Howe, E.W., Leprévost, F., Poonen, B.: Large torsion subgroups of split Jacobians of curves of genus two or three. Forum Mathematicum **12**(3), 315–364 (2000). https://doi.org/10.1515/form.2000.008
29. Ibukiyama, T., Katsura, T., Oort, F.: Supersingular curves of genus two and class numbers. Compositio Mathematica **57**(2), 127–152 (1986). http://eudml.org/doc/89752
30. Jordan, B.W., Zaytman, Y.: Isogeny graphs of superspecial abelian varieties and Brandt matrices. Mathematische Zeitschrift (2024, to appear). https://arxiv.org/pdf/2005.09031.pdf
31. Kani, E.: The number of curves of genus two with elliptic differentials. J. für die reine und angewandte Mathematik **485**, 93–121 (1997). https://doi.org/10.1515/crll.1997.485.93
32. Kani, E.: The moduli spaces of Jacobians isomorphic to a product of two elliptic curves. Collectanea Mathematica **67**, 21–54 (2015). https://doi.org/10.1007/s13348-015-0148-9
33. Kohel, D., Lauter, K., Petit, C., Tignol, J.-P.: On the quaternion isogeny path problem. LMS J. Comput. Math. **17**(A), 418–432 (2014). https://doi.org/10.1112/S1461157014000151
34. Kunzweiler, S., et al.: Radical 2-isogenies and cryptographic hash functions in dimensions 1, 2 and 3. In: Jager, T., Pan, J. (eds.) PKC 2025, Part III. LNCS, vol. 15676, pp. 265–299. Springer, Cham (2025). https://doi.org/10.1007/978-3-031-91826-1_9
35. Maino, L., Martindale, C., Panny, L., Pope, G., Wesolowski, B.: A direct key recovery attack on SIDH. In: Hazay, C., Stam, M. (eds.) EUROCRYPT 2023, Part V. LNCS, vol. 14008, pp. 448–471. Springer, Cham (2023). https://doi.org/10.1007/978-3-031-30589-4_16
36. Milne, J.: Abelian varieties, version 2.0 (2008). Course notes available at https://www.jmilne.org/math/CourseNotes/av.html
37. Nakagawa, K., et al.: SQIsign2D-east: a new signature scheme using 2-dimensional isogenies. In: Chung, KM., Sasaki, Y. (eds.) ASIACRYPT 2024, Part III. LNCS, vol. 15486, pp. 272–303. Springer, Cham (2024). https://doi.org/10.1007/978-981-96-0891-1_9
38. Petit, C., Smith, S.: An improvement to the quaternion analogue of the $\ell$-isogeny problem. Presentation at MathCrypt (2018)
39. Robert, D.: Breaking SIDH in polynomial time. In: Hazay, C., Stam, M. (eds.) EUROCRYPT 2023, Part V. LNCS, vol. 14008, pp. 472–503. Springer, Cham (2023). https://doi.org/10.1007/978-3-031-30589-4_17
40. Robert, D.: On the efficient representation of isogenies: a survey for NuTMiC 2024. In: Dębrowski, A., Pieprzyk, J., Pomykała, J. (eds.) NuTMiC 2024. LNCS, vol. 14966, pp. 3–84 (2025). https://doi.org/10.1007/978-3-031-82380-0_1
41. Shioda, T.: Supersingular K3 surfaces. In: Lønsted, K. (ed.) Algebraic Geometry. LNM, vol. 732, pp. 564–591. Springer, Heidelberg (1979). https://doi.org/10.1007/BFb0066664

42. Smith, B.: Explicit endomorphisms and correspondences. Ph.D. thesis, University of Sydney (2005). https://www.academia.edu/77805612/Explicit_endomorphisms_and_Correspondences
43. Takashima, K.: Efficient algorithms for isogeny sequences and their cryptographic applications. In: Takagi, T., Wakayama, M., Tanaka, K., Kunihiro, N., Kimoto, K., Duong, D.H. (eds.) Mathematical Modelling for Next-Generation Cryptography. MI, vol. 29, pp. 97–114. Springer, Singapore (2018). https://doi.org/10.1007/978-981-10-5065-7_6
44. Voight, J.: Quaternion Algebras. GTM, vol. 288. Springer, Cham (2021). https://doi.org/10.1007/978-3-030-56694-4
45. Wesolowski, B.: The supersingular isogeny path and endomorphism ring problems are equivalent. In: 2021 IEEE 62nd Annual Symposium on Foundations of Computer Science (FOCS), pp. 1100–1111. IEEE (2022). https://doi.org/10.1109/FOCS52979.2021.00109

# Code-Based Cryptography

# Sample Efficient Search to Decision for $k$LIN

Andrej Bogdanov[1](✉), Alon Rosen[2], and Kel Zin Tan[3]

[1] University of Ottawa, Ottawa, Canada
abogdano@uottawa.ca
[2] BIDSA, Bocconi University, Milan, Italy
alon.rosen@unibocconi.it
[3] National University of Singapore, Singapore, Singapore
kelzin@u.nus.edu

**Abstract.** The $k$LIN problem concerns solving noisy systems of random sparse linear equations mod 2. It gives rise to natural candidate hard CSP distributions and is a cornerstone of local cryptography. Recently, it was used in cryptographic constructions, under the name "sparse LPN".

For constant sparsity $k$ and inverse polynomial noise rate, both search and decision versions of $k$LIN are statistically possible and conjectured to be computationally hard for $n \ll m \ll n^{k/2}$, where $m$ is the number of $k$-sparse linear equations, and $n$ is the number of variables.

We show an algorithm that given access to a distinguisher for $(k-1)$LIN with $m$ samples, solves search $k$LIN with roughly $O(nm)$ samples. Previously, it was only known how to reduce from search $k$LIN with $O(m^3)$ samples, yielding guarantees for decision $k$LIN only when $m \ll n^{k/6}$.

The reduction succeeds even if the distinguisher has sub-constant advantage at a small additive cost in sample complexity. Our technique applies with some restrictions to Goldreich's function and $k$LIN with random coefficients over other finite fields.

**Keywords:** learning parity with noise · sparse LPN · local functions · random CSPs · search to decision · one-way functions · pseudorandom generators

A. Bogdanov—Supported by an NSERC Discovery Grant. Part of this work done while visiting Bocconi University, supported by the European Research Council (ERC) under the EU's Horizon 2020 research and innovation programme (Grant agreement No. 101019547).

A. Rosen—Work supported by European Research Council (ERC) under the EU's Horizon 2020 research and innovation programme (Grant agreement No. 101019547) and Cariplo CRYPTONOMEX grant.

K. Z. Tan—Work supported by the National Research Foundation, Singapore, under its NRF Fellowship programme, award no. NRF-NRFF14-2022-0010.


Y. Tauman Kalai and S. F. Kamara (Eds.): CRYPTO 2025, LNCS 16000, pp. 203–220, 2025.
https://doi.org/10.1007/978-3-032-01855-7_7

# 1 Introduction

The *learning parity with noise* problem asks to solve noisy random linear equations mod 2 [BFKL93]. The best known algorithms for it run in time $2^{O(n/\log n)}$, where $n$ is the number of variables [BKW03]. The running time does not improve even if the task is relaxed to distinguishing the output of the noisy equations from random. Equivalence of search and decision is established by means of an efficient sample-preserving algorithm for finding a solution given access to an efficient distinguisher [AIK09].

A well-known variant requires equations to involve only a small number $k$ of variables [Ale03]. Known as noisy $k$LIN, this "sparse learning parity with noise" problem lends itself to increased efficiency with no apparent loss in security, as long as the number $m$ of equations satisfies $m \ll n^{k/2}$.

The advantages of sparse equations were first advocated by Goldreich, who put forward the study of one-way functions in which each output bit is a predicate of $k$ input bits [Gol00]. Hardness of inversion depends on choice of the predicate and setting of parameters [MST06,BQ12,ABR16,AL18]. As in the dense case, one may ask whether the search task of inverting the candidate one-way function reduces to the decision task of distinguishing its output from random.

Applebaum reduced search of Goldreich's function with $m_s = O(m^3/\alpha^2)$ output bits to decision with $m$ output bits and advantage $\alpha$ [App13]. The reduction applies to noisy predicates including $k$LIN. In the constant advantage regime, $k$LIN decision and search become easy as soon as $m$ reaches $n^{k/2}$, so the guarantees are only meaningful when $m \ll n^{k/6}$. This has bearing on the sparsity, dimension, and number of output bits with which the function could be securely instantiated.

For the special case of $k$LIN, Bogdanov, Sabin, and Vasudevan [BSV19] obtained an efficient reduction with $m_s = O(m(m/\alpha)^{2/k})$, albeit one that only succeeds with $\exp(-\tilde{O}(m/\alpha)^{6/k})$ probability.

Beyond its natural appeal, interest in the noisy $k$LIN problem has recently piqued following proposals for basing advanced cryptographic primitives on it [DIJL23,DJ24,CHKV24].

## 1.1 Our Results

We show a search to decision reduction for noisy $k$LIN: an algorithm that given access to a distinguisher for $(k-1)$LIN with $m$ (sample, label) pairs, solves search $k$LIN with $m_s$ (sample, label) pairs and success probability $\alpha_s$, where $m_s$ and $\alpha_s$ depend on the rate $\eta \in [0, 1)$ of the noise added to the labels and on the advantage $\alpha \in [0, 1]$ of the distinguisher. Specifically,

- the number of (sample, label) pairs for search is $m_s = O(nm + n/\eta^2\alpha^{2(k-2)})$,
- the success probability of search is $\alpha_s = 1 - \exp(-\Omega(\alpha^2 n)) + n\exp(-\Omega(m))$.

For constant $k, \alpha$, and inverse polynomial noise rate $\eta$, this yields $m_s = O(mn)$. For $k = O(\log n)$, and constant $\alpha$ the number of samples grows polynomially, but even then gives meaningful search to decision tradeoffs. The reduction gives meaningful tradeoffs also for inverse polynomial $\alpha$, depending on the magnitude of $k$. We highlight the following:

- Our reduction applies more generally to local functions with deterministic predicates of a certain natural form, covering well-studied instantiations of Goldreich's function.
- It is of interest even in the noiseless setting. Even though the search variant of noiseless $k$LIN can be solved by Gaussian elimination beyond the statistical threshold of $O(n)$ examples, the distinguishing algorithm when $m$ exceeds $n^{k/2}$ is substantially simpler. It is an $\mathrm{AC}^0$ algorithm, while Gaussian Elimination is believed to require more power than $\mathrm{NC}^1$.
- It is a $\sqrt{n}$ factor away from being optimal in terms of the conjectured sample complexity for polynomial-time algorithms. In Sect. 6.1 we explain the difficulty in overcoming this barrier using our approach.

One could also consider what happens when the search algorithm has access to a *refuter* rather than to a distinguisher. A refuter is required to reject all "planted" $k$LIN instances and must accept a noticeable fraction of random ones. We show that in such a case, the sample complexity of the $k$LIN solver can be improved by an additional square factor in the advantage.

### 1.2 The $k$LIN Problem

Let $P\colon \{\pm 1\}^k \to \{\pm 1\}$ be a possibly randomized predicate. We are mainly interested in the noisy $k$LIN (also known as sparse LPN) predicate

$$P(z_1, \ldots, z_k) = z_1 \cdots z_k \cdot e$$

with noise rate $\eta = \mathbb{E}[e] > 0$. Our results will also apply to random instances of Goldreich's function, in which case the predicate is deterministic.

An *instance* with secret $\mathbf{s} = (s_1, \ldots, s_n) \in \{\pm 1\}^n$ is a collection of $m$ independent examples consisting of a sample $\mathbf{i}$ and a label $\ell$, each of the form

$$(\mathbf{i}; \ell) = (\mathbf{i}; P(\mathbf{s}_\mathbf{i})) = (i_1, \ldots, i_k; P(s_{i_1}, \ldots, s_{i_k})), \tag{1}$$

where $\mathbf{i} = (i_1, \ldots, i_k) \in [n]^k$ are independent indices sampled uniformly with replacement from $[n]$.

Our model deviates from the literature standard in that the indices $i_1, \ldots, i_k$ are sampled with repetition. Some $k$LIN examples will therefore effectively contain fewer than $k$ variables owing to cancellations. In Sect. 5 we explain why our main Theorem also extends in the more common model where each example depends on exactly $k$ variables.

The *search* problem asks to find $\mathbf{s}$ from $(\mathbf{i}_1, \ell_1), \ldots, (\mathbf{i}_m, \ell_m)$, and the *distinguishing* problem asks to tell apart the planted distribution (1) from the null distribution consisting of samples $\mathbf{i}_j$ with labels $\ell_j$ that are independent random bits.

There is no known efficient distinguisher of constant advantage when $m \ll n^{k/2}$, even though the distributions are statistically distinguishable provided $m > n/(1+H(\eta))$. Search $k$LIN is also efficiently solvable with high probability when $m_s \geq Kn^{k/2}$ for some constant $K$. One search algorithm with this sample complexity is described in Sect. 5.

The best known efficient distinguisher in the regime $m \ll n^{k/2}$ is somewhat model-dependent. In our model, the "collision finding" distinguisher that searches for repeated samples $(\mathbf{i}, \ell), (\mathbf{i}, \ell')$ and outputs $\ell \cdot \ell'$ has advantage $\Theta(\eta m^2 n^{-k})$ when $m < n^{k/2}$. This advantage is likely to be asymptotically optimal among all distinguishers of degree $\tilde{O}(n(n/m)^{2/(k-2)})$ for odd $k$ [FKO06, GKM22].[1]

It is plausible that the sample complexity required to solve the search and decision variants is asymptotically the same. Our main result provides a partial explanation. If decision $(k-1)$LIN can be solved efficiently with advantage $\Omega(\max\{m^{-1/2(k-2)}, n^{-1/2}\})$ then search $k$LIN can be solved given $O(n)$ times more samples.

### 1.3 Theorem Statements

Our main result is the following search to distinguishing reduction for noisy $k$LIN.

**Theorem 1.1.** *There is an efficient algorithm that, given access to a distinguisher for $(k-1)$LIN for $m$ examples with advantage $\alpha$, solves search $k$LIN given $O(nm + n/\eta^2\alpha^{2(k-2)})$ examples except with probability* $\exp(-\Omega(\alpha^2 n)) + n\exp(-\Omega(\eta^2 m))$, *assuming the secret is uniform over $\{\pm 1\}^n$.*

The main new idea is described in Sect. 3, which shows a sample-efficient reduction from approximate search to distinguishing. Section 4 shows how to extract the actual secret from an approximate one. This transformation was proposed by Bogdanov and Qiao [BQ12] and used by Applebaum [App13] in the context of amplification. Here we optimize the sample complexity in the regime of subconstant advantage. The proof of Theorem 1.1 is in Sect. 5. Theorem 5.1 in Sect. 5 provides an extension to other finite fields in the high advantage regime.

Our result generalizes to any (possibly randomized) predicates of the form

$$P(z_1, \ldots, z_k) = z_1 \cdot Q(z_2, \ldots, z_k). \tag{2}$$

These include $k$LIN as a special case but also other studied examples [CEMT14, AL18].

Predicate $Q$ admits a unique Fourier expansion [O'D14]

$$Q(z_2, \ldots, z_k) = \sum_S \hat{Q}(S) \prod_{i \in S} z_i, \tag{3}$$

[1] A quirk of our model is that there is a better distinguisher when $k$ is even: Look for the equation "0 = 1", i.e. an equation in which all the variables on the left cancel out. Such an equation is present with probability $\Theta(\eta m n^{-k/2})$. This distinguisher is ruled out in the distinct indices model.

with the Fourier coefficients given by $\hat{Q}(S) = \mathbb{E}\, Q(z_2, \ldots, z_k) \prod_{i \in S} z_i$. The expectation is taken over both the (uniform) choice of $z_2, \ldots, z_k$ and the potential randomness of $Q$.

Two parameters of interest are pure high degree $d(Q) = \min\{|S|: \hat{Q}(S) \neq 0\}$ and pure max-weight $\eta(Q) = \max_{S\colon |S|=d(Q)} |\hat{Q}(S)|$. Noisy $(k-1)$LIN has pure high degree $k-1$ and pure max-weight $\eta$.

**Theorem 1.2.** *There is an efficient algorithm that, given access to a distinguisher for predicate $Q$ for $m$ examples with advantage $\alpha$, solves search for predicate $P$ given $O(nm + n/\eta(Q)^2\alpha^{2(d(Q)-1)})$ examples except with probability $\exp(-\Omega(\alpha^2 n)) + n\exp(-\Omega(\eta(Q)^2 m))$, assuming the secret is uniform over all balanced strings of length $n$.*

The statement can be extended to almost balanced secrets, specifically secrets whose relative imbalance $|(s_1 + \cdots + s_n)/n|$ does not exceed $c_k \alpha^{d(Q)-1}$ for a sufficiently small constant $c_k$. Using arguments of Applebaum [App13] this is sufficient to obtain a variant of Theorem 1.2 for truly uniform secrets but with a messy dependence on $\alpha$.

Theorem 1.1 can in fact be derived from Theorem 1.2. Our proofs of the two diverge in Sect. 4 because the proof of Theorem 1.1 is somewhat simpler and more direct so we present it first.

*The Distinguisher's Advantage.* Theorems 1.1 and 1.2 are vacuous when the advantage of the distinguisher is $O(1/\sqrt{n})$. This is a natural limitation of our reduction, which makes only $O(n)$ black-box queries to the distinguisher.

In general, a $q$-query reduction to a $\alpha = o(1/\sqrt{q})$ advantage distinguisher cannot be expected to tell apart the planted from the null distribution (and therefore produce any distinguishing feature like a solution). The reason is that on any given query the distinguisher might reveal the correct answer with probability $\alpha$ and produce a random bit otherwise. The advantage of the reduction can then be no larger than the advantage in distinguishing an $\alpha$-biased coin from a $-\alpha$-biased one from $q$ flips, which is at most $O(q\alpha^2) = o(1)$.

The distinguisher's advantage can be amplified from $\alpha$ to $\alpha'$ at a multiplicative cost of $\Theta((\alpha'/\alpha)^2)$ in sample complexity [App13].

## 2 The Poisson Sample Model

It is more natural to state the search to distingushing reduction (Sect. 3) in the *Poisson sample model.* In this model the number of examples $m$ is not a priori fixed. It is a Poisson random variable Poisson$(\lambda n^k)$ of rate $\lambda n^k$.

Equivalently, conditioned on the secret $\mathbf{s}$, the number of occurrences of each of the $2n^k$ possible sample-label pairs $(\mathbf{i}; \ell)$ is an independent Poisson random variable of rate $\lambda \cdot p_{\ell|\mathbf{s}_\mathbf{i}}$. Here, $p_{\ell|\mathbf{z}}$ is the conditional probability that $P(\mathbf{z}) = \ell$ in the planted distribution and $p_{\ell|\mathbf{z}} = 1/2$ in the null distribution. We call $\lambda$ the *rate per sample.*

In our parameter setting of interest, the rate per sample $\lambda$ is on the order of $m/n^k$, which is much less than one. Most samples won't appear at all. Out of those that do most will appear once. The probability of a collision, i.e. of some sample appearing at least twice, is about $n^k\lambda^2/2 = \Theta(m^2/n^k)$.

The equivalence of the two descriptions is a consequence of the additivity of Poisson random variables: The sum of independent Poisson random variables of rates $\lambda_\tau$ is a Poisson random variable of rate $\sum \lambda_\tau$. Conversely, suppose each sample in a given collection is independently of type $\tau$ with probability $p_\tau$. If the size of the collection is Poisson($\sum \lambda_\tau$) then conditioned on the size, the samples are independently of type $\tau$, each with probability proportional to $\lambda_\tau$. In our application there are $2n^k$ types $\tau$, one corresponding to each possible sample-label pair $(i_1, \dots, i_k; \ell)$.

The Poisson and fixed sample models are equivalent up to constant factors in (average) sample complexity and statistical error that is inverse exponential in the number of samples. Here are the conversion algorithms between the two models.

*Fixed-to-Poisson.* The Poisson model with rate per sample $\lambda = m/2n^k$ is simulated by procedure *FtoP*: Choose the first $M$ examples for a Poisson$(m/2)$ random variable $M$ provided that $M \le m$, and fail if $M > m$.

**Claim 2.1.** *On input a fixed size m sample instance, FtoP produces an instance that is $e^{-m/8}$-statistically close to a Poisson instance of rate per sample $m/2n^k$.*

*Poisson-to-Fixed.* Conversely, the fixed number of samples model can be simulated by procedure *PtoF*: Choose a random subset of $m = \lambda n^k/2$ many (distinct) examples if at least this many are available and fail otherwise.

**Claim 2.2.** *On input a Poisson sample instance of rate per sample $\lambda$, PtoF produces an instance that is $e^{-\lambda n^k/12}$-close to a fixed sample instance of size $\lambda n^k/2$.*

Both claims follow from Poisson large deviation bounds [Can22, Theorem A.8]:

$$\Pr(\text{Poisson}(\lambda) \ge \lambda + x), \Pr(\text{Poisson}(\lambda) \le \lambda - x) \le \exp\bigl(-x^2/2(\lambda + x)\bigr). \quad (4)$$

*Proof (of Claim 2.1).* If an infinite number of fixed samples was available and the "provided that $M \le m$ condition was dropped the output would be perfectly Poisson of rate per sample $\lambda$. The statistical error is therefore bounded by the probability that the $M \le m$ condition fails, namely that a Poisson$(m/2)$ random variable is greater than $m$. By (4) this probability is at most $\exp(-m/8)$.

*Proof (of Claim 2.2).* The number $M$ of available examples is a Poisson$(\lambda n^k)$ random variable $M$. Conditioned on $M \ge m$ the output distribution perfectly follows that fixed number of samples model. The statistical error is therefore the probability that a Poisson$(\lambda n^k)$ random variable is less than $\lambda n^k/2$. By (4) this probability is at most $\exp(-\lambda n^k/12)$.

## 3 Approximate Search to Distinguishing Reduction

Our reduction uses the distinguisher to extract information about the equality of the secret entries $s_1$ and $s_j$ for all $j \neq 1$. The reduction maps $k$LIN instances in which $s_1$ and $s_j$ are equal and different into planted and random instances of $(k-1)$LIN, respectively. For this purpose the distinguisher is executed on the subset of examples that have $s_1$ or $s_j$ as their first variables, suitably preprocessed. This basic reduction is implemented by algorithm $S$ below. The advantage of working in the Poisson model is that the instances given from the distinguisher match one of the promised distributions (planted or random) perfectly.

The output of the reduction is an approximation $\hat{\mathbf{s}}$ of the secret $\mathbf{s}$. Our measure for the quality of approximation is the *overlap*

$$\langle \mathbf{s}, \hat{\mathbf{s}} \rangle = \frac{s_1\hat{s}_1 + \cdots + s_n\hat{s}_n}{n}.$$

**Proposition 3.1.** *If $D$ is a distinguisher for Goldreich's function with predicate $Q$, rate per sample $2\lambda$, and advantage $\alpha$ then the output of algorithm $S$ below has average overlap at least $\alpha$ with the secret $\mathbf{s}$ given samples for predicate $P$ with rate per sample $\lambda$, assuming the secret is uniformly random.*

**Algorithm** $S$**:** On input a multiset $C$ of samples $(i_1, \ldots, i_k; \ell)$,

Guess the value $\hat{s}_1 \in \{\pm 1\}$ of $s_1$.
Set $A = \{(i_2, \ldots, i_k; \ell \cdot \hat{s}_1) \colon (1, i_2, \ldots, i_k; \ell) \in C\}$.
For $j = 2$ up to $n$,
    Set $B_j = \{(i_2, \ldots, i_k; \ell \cdot \hat{s}_1) \colon (j, i_2, \ldots, i_k; \ell) \in C\}$.
    Set $\hat{s}_j$ to equal the output of $D$ on the collection of examples $A \cup B_j$.
Output $\hat{\mathbf{s}} = \hat{s}_1 \cdots \hat{s}_n$.

$A \cup B$ denotes union of multisets: If $x$ occurs with multiplicities $a$ and $b$ in $A$ and $B$, respectively, it occurs with multiplicity $a + b$ in $A \cup B$.

Given input $A \cup B_j$, the distinguisher has no information which examples came from $A$ and which examples came from $B_j$. If (the guess is correct and) $s_1$ equals $s_j$, $A \cup B_j$ is identically distributed to a planted instance. If $s_1$ does not equal $s_j$ the labels of the $A$-instances and $B_j$-instances take opposite values so $A \cup B_j$ is distributed identically to a random instance.

We view the distinguisher $D$ as a function into the interval $[-1, 1]$. Its advantage is given by $(\mathbb{E}[D(\text{planted})] - \mathbb{E}[D(\text{null})])/2$.

*Proof.* We show that, assuming $\hat{s}_1 = s_1$, for every $j \geq 2$, $A \cup B_j$ is identical to a planted distribution sample when $s_j = s_1$ and to a null distribution sample when $s_j \neq s_1$. By our assumption on $D$ and the uniformity of $s_j$ (given $s_1$),

$$\mathbb{E}[\hat{s}_j s_j] = \frac{1}{2}\,\mathbb{E}[\hat{s}_j s_1 | s_j = s_1] - \frac{1}{2}\,\mathbb{E}[\hat{s}_j s_1 | s_j \neq s_1] = \frac{1}{2}\,\mathbb{E}[\text{planted}] - \frac{1}{2}\,\mathbb{E}[\text{null}] = \alpha.$$

Therefore $\hat{\mathbf{s}}$ and $\mathbf{s}$ have average overlap $(1 + (n-1)\alpha)/n \geq \alpha$.

Assuming $\hat{s}_1 = s_1$, collection $A$ is a Poisson sample for Goldreich's function with predicate $Q$ with planted assignment $s$ rate per sample $\lambda$. If $s_j$ and $s_1$ are equal so is $B_j$. By additivity, $A \cup B_j$ is a Poisson sample for the planted distribution with rate per sample $2\lambda$.

If $s_2$ and $s_1$ are not equal then each sample-label pair $(i_2, \ldots, i_k; \ell) \in [n]^{k-1} \times \{\pm 1\}$ has Poisson$(\lambda p)$ occurrences in collection $A$ and Poisson$(\lambda(1-p))$ occurrences in collection $B_j$, where $p = p_{\ell|s_{i_2},\ldots,s_{i_k}}$. By additivity, $(i_2, \ldots, i_k; \ell)$ occurs Poisson$(\lambda p + \lambda(1-p)) =$ Poisson$(\lambda)$ times, independently among all such pairs. This is identical to the null distribution with rate per sample $2\lambda$.

Proposition 3.1 guarantees *average* overlap $\alpha$ between the output of $S$ and the secret. If $\alpha$ was as large as $1-\delta/n$ this would be sufficient to recover the secret except with probability $\delta$. Such large advantage can be attained by amplification at a *multiplicative* cost in sample complexity. We pursue an alternative route that entails only an additive cost, provided $\alpha$ is at least $1/\sqrt{n}$.

When $\alpha$ is small, it could be that this advantage is lopsided in the sense that in a $(1-\alpha)$ fraction of instances $S$ has no advantage at all and it completely recovers the secret in the rest.

The following variant of the reduction ensures that $S$ has good advantage on a large fraction of instances provided $\alpha$ is not too small. A secondary difference is that it also applies to secrets that are balanced, which is the setting of our Theorem 1.2.

**Theorem 3.2.** *If $D$ is a secret-independent distinguisher for Goldreich's function with predicate $Q$, rate per sample $2\lambda$, and advantage $\alpha$ then for at least one $i^\star \in [n]$ the output of algorithm $S^\star$ below has overlap at least $\Omega(\alpha)$ with the secret for all but a $3\exp(-\Omega(\alpha^2 n))$ fraction of instances, given samples for predicate $P$ with rate per sample $\lambda$, assuming the secret is uniformly random or a uniformly random balanced string.*

A distinguisher is *secret-independent* if its advantage does not depend on the secret conditioned on the samples. Namely, for every pair of secrets $\mathbf{s}$ and $\mathbf{s}'$,

$$\mathbb{E}[D(\mathbf{i}_1, Q(\mathbf{s}_{\mathbf{i}_1}), \ldots, \mathbf{i}_m, Q(\mathbf{s}_{\mathbf{i}_m}))] = \mathbb{E}[D(\mathbf{i}_1, Q(\mathbf{s}'_{\mathbf{i}_1}), \ldots, \mathbf{i}_m, Q(\mathbf{s}'_{\mathbf{i}_m}))].$$

In the proofs of the main theorems secret-independence is enforced by rerandomization.

The algorithm $S^\star$ is the same as $S$ with variable $s_{i^\star}$ playing the role of $s_1$.

**Algorithm** $S^\star$**:** On input a multiset $C$ of samples $(\mathbf{i}, \ell)$,

Guess the value $\hat{s}_{i^\star} \in \{\pm 1\}$ of $s_{i^\star}$.

Set $A_i = \{(i_2, \ldots, i_k; \ell \cdot \hat{s}_{i^\star}) \colon (i, i_2, \ldots, i_k; \ell) \in C\}$.

For $j \neq i^\star$, set $\hat{s}_j = D(A_{i^\star} \cup A_j)$.

Output $\hat{\mathbf{s}} = \hat{s}_1 \cdots \hat{s}_n$.

*Proof.* For an (unlabeled) sample collection $C = \{\mathbf{i}_1, \ldots, \mathbf{i}_m\}$ let $adv(C)$ be the advantage of the distinguisher on $C$:

$$adv(C) = \mathbb{E}[D(\mathbf{i}_1, Q(\mathbf{s}_{\mathbf{i}_1}), \ldots, \mathbf{i}_m, Q(\mathbf{s}_{\mathbf{i}_m}))] - \mathbb{E}[D(\text{null})].$$

By the secret-independence assumption, $adv(C)$ does not depend on $\mathbf{s}$.

If $A$ and $B$ are independent collections of examples (sample-label pairs) with sample rate $\lambda$ respectively, by assumption $adv(A \cup B)$ equals $\alpha$. By Markov's inequality, for at least a $\alpha/2$ fraction of multisets $A$, the advantage must be at least $\alpha/2$ over the choice of $B$ (conditioned on $A$). Call such a multiset $A$ good.

Assume for now that $\mathbf{s}$ is uniformly random. Let $I$ and $J$ be an arbitrary partition of the variables with $|I| = \alpha n/10$. As each $A_i$ is good with probability at least $\alpha/2$ and these events are independent across $i \in I$, there exists some $i^\star \in I$ for which $A_{i^\star}$ is good except with probability at most $(1-\alpha/2)^{|I|} \leq \exp(-\alpha|I|/2) = \exp(-\alpha^2 n/20)$.

Assuming $A_{i^\star}$ is good, by the argument in the proof of Proposition 3.1, for every $j \in J$, $\hat{s}_j = s_j$ with conditional probability at least $\alpha/2$. These events are now mutually independent conditioned on $A_{i^\star}$. By Hoeffding's bound, $\sum_{j\in J} s_j \hat{s}_j$ is at least $\alpha|J|/4$ except with probability $\exp(-\Omega(\alpha^2|J|)) = \exp(-\Omega(\alpha^2 n))$. If this happens the total overlap $\langle \hat{\mathbf{s}}, \mathbf{s}\rangle$ is at least

$$\frac{1}{n}\left(\frac{\alpha|J|}{4} - |I|\right) = \frac{1}{n}\left(\frac{\alpha n}{4} - (1+\alpha/4)|I|\right) \geq \frac{1}{n}\left(\frac{\alpha n}{4} - \frac{5}{4}|I|\right) = \frac{1}{n}\left(\frac{\alpha n}{4} - \frac{\alpha n}{8}\right) = \frac{\alpha}{8}$$

If $\mathbf{s}$ is uniform over balanced strings the partition of variables into $I$ and $J$ is no longer arbitrary. Let $P$ be a Binomial$((1-\alpha/10)n, 1/2)$ random variable. If both $P$ and $1-P$ are at most $n/2$ then $J$ is set to contain some $P$ variables of value $+1$ and some $(1-\alpha/10)n - P$ variables of value $-1$. The remaining variables are put in $I$. (If not the variables are partitioned arbitrarily.) The assignment to $x_j : j \in J$ is a uniformly random string except with the probability that $\max\{P, (1-P)\} > n/2$. By a Chernoff bound this is at most $2\exp(-\Omega(\alpha^2 n))$ and is subsumed into the failure probability.

# 4 Amplification of Overlap

We show how to recover the secret $\mathbf{s}$ in a planted instance given an $\alpha$-overlapping approximation $\hat{\mathbf{s}}$. Specializing to $k$LIN, the idea is to predict secret entry $s_{i_1}$ by the parity $s_{i_2} \cdots s_{i_k} \ell$ and amplify the prediction advantage to almost 1 using sufficiently many independent examples. By Proposition 4.4 below $\Omega(\alpha^{2(k-1)} \log n)$ examples suffice for this.

In Theorem 4.5 we improve the dependence of sample size on $\alpha$. To accomplish this the advantage is doubled in stages until it becomes constant at which point Proposition 4.4 is applied with constant $\alpha$. In Theorem 4.7 we extend the argument to other predicates of type (2), provided the secret is balanced.

### 4.1 Noisy Parities

We specialize $Q$ to the noisy parity predicate $z_2 \cdots z_{k-1}e$ with $\mathbb{E}\, e = \eta$. We use $\mathbf{s}$ to denote the secret of $k$-LIN instance $C$ throughout this section.

**Algorithm** *Amp*: On input a multiset $C$ of samples $(\mathbf{i}, \ell)$, and $\hat{\mathbf{s}} \in \{\pm 1\}^n$

For every $i \in [n]$,
    Let $s'_i$ be the majority of $\hat{s}_{i_2} \cdots \hat{s}_{i_k} \cdot \ell$ over $(i, i_2, \ldots, i_k; \ell) \in C$.
Output $\mathbf{s}' = s'_1 \cdots s'_n$.

**Proposition 4.1.** *There exists a constant $c > 0$ so that assuming $0 \le \langle \mathbf{s}, \hat{\mathbf{s}} \rangle = \alpha < c/3$, the output $\mathbf{s}'$ of Amp satisfies $\langle \mathbf{s}, \mathbf{s}' \rangle \ge 2\alpha$ except with probability $\exp(-\Omega(\alpha^2 n))$, provided $C$ contains $9/c^2\eta^2\alpha^{2(k-2)}$ samples whose first entry is $i$ for every $i \in [n]$.*

**Claim 4.2.** *Given a $k$-noisy parity example $(\mathbf{i}, \ell)$ with secret $\mathbf{s}$, and an $\hat{\mathbf{s}}$ such that $\langle \mathbf{s}, \hat{\mathbf{s}} \rangle = \alpha \ge 0$, $\mathbb{E}[s_{i_1} \cdot \ell \hat{s}_{i_2} \cdots \hat{s}_{i_k} \mid \mathbf{s}, \mathbf{s}'] = \eta \cdot \alpha^{k-1}$.*

*Proof.* The label $\ell$ equals $s_{i_1} s_{i_2} \cdots s_{i_k} e$. As the pairs $(s_i, \hat{s}_i)$ are mutually independent across $i$, $s_{i_1}$ cancels out and the expectation equals

$$\mathbb{E}[s_{i_2}\hat{s}_{i_2} | \mathbf{s}, \mathbf{s}'] \cdots \mathbb{E}[s_{i_k}\hat{s}_{i_k} | \mathbf{s}, \mathbf{s}']\, \mathbb{E}[e] = \eta\alpha^{k-1}$$

**Claim 4.3.** *There exists a constant $c > 0$ such that for every $\alpha > 0$ and odd $n$, $\mathbb{E}\,\mathrm{sign}(X_1 + \cdots + X_n) \ge \min\{c\alpha\sqrt{n}, c\}$, where $X_1, \ldots, X_n \in \{\pm 1\}^n$ are independent and $\alpha$-biased.*

*Proof.* As the expectation increases monotonically in $\alpha$, it is sufficient to prove the claim under the assumption $\alpha\sqrt{n} \le 1$. Theorem 5.19 in [O'D14] is the identity

$$\mathbb{E}\,\mathrm{sign}(X_1 + \cdots + X_n) = \frac{2n}{2^n} \binom{n-1}{(n-1)/2} \sum_{k \text{ odd}} (-1)^{(k-1)/2} \cdot \frac{1}{k} \cdot \binom{(n-1)/2}{(k-1)/2} \cdot \alpha^k.$$

The leading term $k = 1$ dominates the sum. The total contribution of the other terms can be generously upper bounded by

$$\sum_{k \ge 3 \text{ odd}} \binom{(n-1)/2}{(k-1)/2} \cdot \alpha^k = \alpha\big((1+\alpha^2)^{(n-1)/2} - 1\big) \le \alpha\bigg(\Big(1 + \frac{1}{n}\Big)^{n/2} - 1\bigg) \le 0.64\alpha.$$

By Stirling's approximation formula,

$$\mathbb{E}\,\mathrm{sign}(X_1 + \cdots + X_n) \ge 0.36\alpha \cdot \frac{2n}{2^n} \binom{n-1}{(n-1)/2} = \Omega(\alpha\sqrt{n}).$$

*Proof (of Proposition 4.1).* Let $c$ be the constant from Claims 4.2 and 4.3. By these two claims, for every $i$, either $\mathbb{E}[s_i s_i'] \geq c \geq 3\alpha$, or

$$\mathbb{E}[s_i s_i'] \geq c \cdot \eta \alpha^{k-1} \cdot \sqrt{\frac{9}{c^2 \eta^2 \alpha^{2(k-2)}}} = 3\alpha.$$

The statistics $\mathbb{E}[s_i s_i']$ are independent and at least $3\alpha$-biased across $i$. By Hoeffding's bound, $\langle \mathbf{s}, \mathbf{s}' \rangle \geq 2\alpha$ except with probability $\exp(-\Omega(\alpha^2 n))$.

**Proposition 4.4.** *If $\langle \mathbf{s}, \hat{\mathbf{s}} \rangle \geq c$, the output of Amp equals $\mathbf{s}$ except with probability $n \exp(-\Omega(\eta^2 c^{2(k-1)} r))$, provided $C$ contains at least $r$ samples whose first entry is $i$ for every $i \in [n]$.*

*Proof.* By Claim 4.2 and the Hoeffding bound, $\Pr[s_i \neq \hat{s}_i]$ is at most $\exp(-\Omega(c^2 r))$ for every $i$. The proposition follows by a union bound over $i$.

**Theorem 4.5.** *Assuming $\langle \mathbf{s}, \hat{\mathbf{s}} \rangle \geq \alpha$, algorithm Recover outputs $\mathbf{s}$ except with probability $\exp(-\Omega(\alpha^2 n)) + n \exp(-\Omega(\eta^2 r))$, provided $C$ contains at least $K/\eta^2 \alpha^{2(k-2)} + r$ samples whose first entry is $i$ for every $i \in [n]$ for some constant $K$.*

We say a set of samples is $\alpha$-sufficient if it contains $9/c^2\eta^2\alpha^{2(k-2)}$ samples whose first entry is $i$ for every $i$ if $\alpha < c/3$, and $r$ samples otherwise.

**Algorithm** *Recover*: On input a multiset $C$ of samples $(\mathbf{i}, \ell)$, and $\hat{\mathbf{s}} \in \{\pm 1\}^n$, and $\alpha > 0$

> While $\alpha < c/3$,
>
>     Replace $\hat{\mathbf{s}}$ by the output of *Amp* on a fresh $\alpha$-sufficient subsample of $C$.
>
>     Double $\alpha$.
>
> Output *Amp* on a fresh 1-sufficient subsample of $C$.

*Proof.* By Proposition 4.1, the invariant $\langle \mathbf{s}, \hat{\mathbf{s}} \rangle \geq \alpha$ is maintained throughout the while loop except with probability $\exp(-\Omega(\alpha^2 n)) + \exp(-\Omega((2\alpha)^2 n)) + \cdots = \exp(-\Omega(\alpha^2 n))$. By the end of the loop the overlap is then at least $2c/3$. By Proposition 4.4 the output then equals $\mathbf{s}$ except with additional probability $\Omega(-r)$.

The required number of samples that start with $i$ is

$$\frac{9}{c^2\eta^2} \cdot \left( \frac{1}{\alpha^{2(k-2)}} + \frac{1}{(2\alpha)^{2(k-2)}} + \cdots \right) + r \leq \frac{18}{c^2 \eta^2 \alpha^{2(k-2)}} + r.$$

### 4.2 Goldreich's Function

We generalize Theorem 4.5 to arbitrary $Q$ of type (2). The analogue of Proposition 4.1 is

**Proposition 4.6.** *There exists a constant $c > 0$ so that assuming $\mathbf{s}$ is balanced and $0 \leq \langle \mathbf{s}, \hat{\mathbf{s}} \rangle = \alpha < c/3$, the output $\mathbf{s}'$ of Amp satisfies $\langle \mathbf{s}, \mathbf{s}' \rangle \geq 2\alpha$ except with probability $\exp(-\Omega(\alpha^2 n))$, provided $C$ contains $9/c^2\eta(Q)^2\alpha^{2d(Q)}$ samples whose first entry is $i$ for every $i \in [n]$.*

Let $S^\star$ be the set of size $d(Q)$ (the pure high degree of $Q$) that maximizes $|\hat{Q}(S)|$ and $\sigma = \operatorname{sign} \hat{Q}(J)$.

**Algorithm** *Amp*: On input a multiset $C$ of samples $(\mathbf{i}, \ell)$, and $\hat{\mathbf{s}} \in \{\pm 1\}^n$
1 For every $i_1 \in [n]$,
2 Let $s'_{i_1}$ be the majority of $\ell \cdot \sigma \cdot \prod_{j \in S^\star} \hat{s}_{i_j}$ over $(i_1, i_2, \ldots, i_k; \ell) \in C$.
3 Output $\mathbf{s}' = s'_1 \cdots s'_n$.

*Proof.* We show the analogue of Claim 4.2: $\mathbb{E}\, s_{i_1} \ell \sigma \prod_{j \in S^\star} \hat{s}_{i_j} \geq \eta \alpha^d$. The conclusion then follows from Claim 4.3 as in the proof of Proposition 4.1.

Applying the Fourier expansion (3) of $Q$,

$$\begin{aligned}\mathbb{E}\, s_{i_1} \cdot \ell \cdot \sigma \cdot \prod_{j \in S^\star} \hat{s}_{i_j} &= \sum_S \sigma \hat{Q}(S)\, \mathbb{E} \prod_{j \in S} s_{i_j} \prod_{j \in S^\star} \hat{s}_{i_j} \\ &= \sigma Q(S^\star) \prod_{j \in S^\star} \mathbb{E}\, s_{i_j} \hat{s}_{i_j} - \sum_{S \neq S^\star} \hat{Q}(S) \cdot \mathbb{E} \prod_{j \in S} s_{i_j} \prod_{j \in S^\star} \hat{s}_{i_j}.\end{aligned}$$

As $\sigma$ is the sign of $Q(S^\star)$ the leading term equals $\eta \alpha^{|S^\star|} = \eta(Q) \alpha^{d(Q)}$. All other terms vanish: By independence,

$$\mathbb{E} \prod_{j \in S} s_{i_j} \prod_{j \in S^\star} \hat{s}_{i_j} = \prod_{j \in S \setminus S^\star} \mathbb{E}\, s_{i_j} \cdot \prod_{j \in S \triangle S^\star} \mathbb{E}\, s_{i_j} \hat{s}_{i_j} \cdot \prod_{j \in S^\star \setminus S} \mathbb{E}\, \hat{s}_{i_j}.$$

As $S \neq S^\star$ and $|S| \geq |S^\star|$ by the minimality of $S^\star$, the first product term is nonempty. Since $\mathbf{s}$ is balanced it evaluates to zero.

The analogue of Theorem 4.5 is

**Theorem 4.7.** *Assuming* $\mathbf{s}$ *is balanced and* $\langle \mathbf{s}, \hat{\mathbf{s}} \rangle \geq \alpha$, *algorithm Recover outputs* $\mathbf{s}$ *except with probability* $\exp(-\Omega(\alpha^2 n)) + n \exp(-\Omega(\eta(Q)^2 r))$, *provided* $C$ *contains at least* $K/\eta(Q)^2 \alpha^{2(d(Q)-1)} + r$ *samples whose first entry is* $i$ *for every* $i \in [n]$ *for some constant* $K$.

## 5 Proofs of Main Theorems

We compose the approximate search to distinguishing reduction and the amplification to prove Theorems 1.1 and 1.2. We also explain why Theorem 1.1 extends to the more common random $k$LIN model in which the sample indices $i_1, \ldots, i_k$ are distinct.

*Proof (of Theorem 1.1).* Partition the instance into two parts, $C_1$ of size Poisson$(mn)$ and $C_2$ in which for every $i \in [n]$ there are at least $K/\eta^2 \alpha^{2(k-2)} + m$ samples that start with $i$. By Claim 2.1 and the Hoeffding bound the samples in $C$ suffice for $C_1$ and $C_2$ except with probability $\exp(-\Omega(m))$.

To recover the secret, $S^\star$ is executed on $C_1$ to produce $\hat{\mathbf{s}}$. Then *Recover* is executed on $C_2$ and $\hat{\mathbf{s}}$ to recover the secret.

By Theorem 3.2, $\hat{\mathbf{s}}$ has $\Omega(\alpha)$ overlap with the secret except with probability $\exp(-\Omega(\alpha^2 n))$, provided it is given access to a secret-independent $(k-1)$LIN distinguisher for Poisson$(2m)$ many samples. Secret-independence is enforced by rerandomizing the secret, namely by shifting every label by $r_{i_1} \cdots r_{i_k}$ for a random secret $r$. This transformation preserves distinguishing advantage (under a uniform choice of secret). By Claim 2.2 a distinguisher for Poisson$(2m)$ samples can be realized from a distinguisher for $m$ samples except with probability $\exp(-\Omega(m))$. As the distinguisher is invoked by $S^\star$ less than $n$ times the overlap is as promised except with probability $n\exp(-\Omega(m))$.

Applying *Recover* on inputs $C_2$ and $\hat{\mathbf{s}}$ (which is independent of $C_2$) with $r = m$, by Theorem 4.5 the secret is recovered except with probability $\exp(-\Omega(\alpha^2 n)) + n\exp(-\Omega(\eta^2 m))$.

The main difference in the proof of Theorem 1.2 is in the enforcement of secret-independence. The transformation now consists of a random permutation of the sample entries, namely example $(i_2, \dots, i_k; \ell)$ is replaced by $(\pi(i_2), \dots, \pi(i_k); \ell)$ for a random permutation $\pi$ on $[n]$. As

$$(\pi(i_2), \dots, \pi(i_k); Q(s_{i_2}, \dots, s_{i_k}))$$

is identically distributed to

$$(i_2, \dots, i_k; Q(s_{\pi^{-1}(i_2)}, \dots, s_{\pi^{-1}(i_k)})),$$

the Hamming weight of $\mathbf{s}$ is a sufficient statistic of the permuted sample, so the distinguisher's advantage does not depend on $\mathbf{s}$ among balanced strings. The other difference is that Theorem 4.7 is used in lieu of Theorem 4.5 to analyze the amplification.

## 5.1 Extension to Exact Weight Instances

In the exact weight $k$LIN model the sample elements $(i_1, \dots, i_k)$ are chosen without repetition. One complication in the search to distinguishing reduction, for instance algorithm $S$, is that the samples of $A \cup B_j$ are no longer identically distributed as those of a random $(k-1)$LIN instance. Owing to the lack of repetitions, the average number of occurrences of indices 1 and $j$ ("variables" $s_i$ and $s_j$) is about half that of the other variables. The distinguisher is not guaranteed to provide any useful information on such an atypical instance. To mitigate this effect the reduction discards those examples in $A$ that include index $j$ and those examples in $B_j$ that include index 1.

For simplicity we describe the modification of algorithm $S$ to the exact weight setting. The modification to $S^\star$ is analogous.

**Algorithm** $S$**:** On input a multiset $C$ of samples $(i_1, \dots, i_k; \ell)$,

1 Guess the value $\hat{s}_1 \in \{\pm 1\}$ of $s_1$.

2 For $j = 2$ up to $n$,

3 Set $A_j = \{(i_2, \dots, i_k; \ell \cdot \hat{s}_1) \colon (1, i_2, \dots, i_k; \ell) \in C, j \notin \{i_2, \dots, i_k\}\}$.

4 Set $B_j = \{(i_2, \ldots, i_k; \ell \cdot \hat{s}_1) \colon (j, i_2, \ldots, i_k; \ell) \in C, 1 \notin \{i_2, \ldots, i_k\}\}$.
5 Set $\hat{s}_j$ to equal the output of $D$ on the collection of examples $A_j \cup B_j$.
6 Output $\hat{\mathbf{s}} = \hat{s}_1 \cdots \hat{s}_n$.

In step 5 the instance $A_j \cup B_j$ is implicitly interpreted as a $(k-1)$LIN instance over the $n-2$ variables $[n] \setminus \{i, j\}$. Assuming $C$ has rate per sample $\lambda$ (which in this setting means Poisson$(\lambda n(n-1)\cdots(n-k+1))$ many examples), $A_j \cup B_j$ is now identically distributed to a planted (resp., random) $(k-1)$LIN instance with $n-2$ variables of rate per sample

$$2\lambda \cdot \left(1 - \frac{1}{n-2}\right) \cdots \left(1 - \frac{1}{n-k+1}\right)$$

when $s_1$ equals (resp., does not equal) $s_j$. The slight loss in rate compared to rate $2\lambda$ in the proof of Proposition 3.1 does not affect the asymptotics of the result.

A minor complication also arises in amplification. In Claim 4.2 the indices are now not independent as they are conditioned on being distinct leading to a slightly worse lower bound of $\eta(\alpha - (k-1)/n)^{k-1}$. Again this only affects asymptotically insignificant quantities in Theorem 4.5.

We do not know how to extend the proof of Theorem 1.2 to the model in which indices are chosen without repetition. The reason is that the search-to-distinguishing reduction does not preserve the balance of the secret. It remains balanced in the case $s_1 \neq s_j$ but loses its balance when $s_1$ equals $s_j$.

### 5.2 Extension to Other Finite Fields

The $k$LIN problem naturally extends to other groups. When the group is a field $\mathbb{F}$, there is an alternative model in which the coefficients are not integers (representing the number of occurrences) but random nonzero field elements. In this $(k, \mathbb{F})$-LIN model the sample representing the left-hand side $a_1 x_{i_1} + \cdots + a_k x_{i_k}$ is specified by the sequence of coefficient-index pairs

$$\mathbf{i} = ((a_1, i_1), \ldots, (a_k, i_k))$$

where $a_1, \ldots, a_k$ are nonzero field elements and $i_1, \ldots, i_k$ are coordinates in $[n]$, all sampled uniformly and independently (with replacement).

The *search* problem asks to find $\mathbf{s} \in \mathbb{F}^n$ from $(\mathbf{i}_1, \ell_1), \ldots, (\mathbf{i}_m, \ell_m)$, whereas the *decision* problem asks to tell apart the planted distribution $(\mathbf{i}_1, \ell_1), \ldots, (\mathbf{i}_m, \ell_m)$ from the null distribution $(\mathbf{i}_1, b_1), \ldots, (\mathbf{i}_m, b_m)$ where $b_i$ is a random element from $\mathbb{F}$.

**Theorem 5.1.** *There is an algorithm of complexity $O((m+n)|\mathbb{F}|^2)$ that, given access to a distinguisher for $m$ $(k-1, \mathbb{F})$-LIN with advantage $1 - \delta/|\mathbb{F}|(n-1)$, solves $(k, \mathbb{F})$-LIN except with probability $\delta + \exp(-\Omega(m))$ from $4mn$ examples under any noise distribution.*

*Proof.* By Claims 2.1 and Claim 2.2, it is sufficient to prove the theorem in the Poisson sample model with rate per sample $\lambda = mn/(n(|\mathbb{F}|-1))^k$ for search and $(|\mathbb{F}|/(|\mathbb{F}|-1)) \cdot (\lambda/n)$ for distinguishing and that is what we will do. The reduction is then implemented by

**Algorithm** $S$**:** On input a multiset $C$ of examples and the value of $s_1 \in \mathbb{F}$,

1 Set $A = \{((a_2, i_2), \ldots, (a_k, i_k); \ell - a_1 \cdot s_1)\colon$
$\qquad ((a_1, 1), (a_2, i_2), \ldots, (a_k, i_k); \ell) \in C\}$
2 Keep each example in $A$ with probability $1/(|\mathbb{F}|-1)$ and discard otherwise.
3 For $j = 2$ up to $n$,
4 $\quad$ For $v$ ranging over $\mathbb{F}$,
5 $\qquad$ Set $B_j = \{((a_2, i_2), \ldots, (a_k, i_k); \ell - a_1 \cdot v)\colon$
$\qquad\qquad ((a_1, j), (a_2, i_2), \ldots, (a_k, i_k); \ell) \in C\}$
6 $\qquad$ If $D(A \cup B_j)$ accepts, set $\hat{s}_j = v$.
7 If all $\hat{s}_j$ have been uniquely set, output $\hat{\mathbf{s}}$.

The rate per sample of the reduction is as desired because the rates per sample of $A$ and $B_j$ are $\lambda/n(|\mathbb{F}|-1)$ and $\lambda/n$, respectively.

If $v = s_j$ then the examples in $A \cup B_j$ are identically distributed to planted $(k-1)$LIN because the label of every sample has been shifted by the discarded entry ($a_1 s_1$ for examples in $A$ and $a_j v = a_j s_j$ for samples in $B_j$).

If $v \neq s_j$ then the examples in $A \cup B_j$ follow the null distribution. For examples in $A$ the right-hand side follows the planted distribution $(a_2 s_{i_2} + \cdots + a_k s_{i_k}) + e$. For examples in $B_j$ this value is shifted by $a_1 \cdot (s_j - v)$ which is a uniform nonzero field element. Each example originates from $A$ with probability

$$\frac{1/(|\mathbb{F}|-1)}{1 + 1/(|\mathbb{F}|-1)} = \frac{1}{|\mathbb{F}|}.$$

The shift is therefore zero with probability $1/|\mathbb{F}|$ and a nonzero random field element otherwise. Its distribution is uniform over $\mathbb{F}$ and therefore so is the label itself.

As the advantage is assumed to equal $1 - \delta/|\mathbb{F}|(n-1)$, $D$ rejects at most a $\delta/|\mathbb{F}|(n-1)$ fraction of planted instances and accepts at most a $\delta/|\mathbb{F}|(n-1)$ fraction of null instances. By a union bound, except with probability $\delta$, line 6 triggers exactly when $v = s_j$ for all $j$. In that case $\hat{\mathbf{s}} = \mathbf{s}$.

Our algorithm works under the assumption that the value of the first secret $s_1$ is known. This assumption, however, can be removed by rerunning the algorithm with different values of $s_1$ over the field $\mathbb{F}$ (using the same set of samples) and taking the best answer. Therefore the algorithm time complexity is $O((m + n)|\mathbb{F}|^2)$ with $O(n|\mathbb{F}|^2)$ calls to the distinguisher.

To decrease the probability of failure for the search algorithm, we can construct a distinguishing algorithm with a success rate close to 1. A distinguisher of success rate $\alpha$ can be amplified into one of the desired rate $1-\delta$ at a multiplicative cost of $O((\log(n|\mathbb{F}|/\delta))/\alpha^2)$ in sample complexity. This is achieved through repetition and taking the majority of the predictions, followed by analysis with the Hoeffding bound.

# 6 Concluding Remarks

## 6.1 On the Sample Complexity Gap

In the constant advantage regime, our reduction solves $k$LIN from $O(mn)$ samples given a distinguisher for $m$ samples for $(k-1)$LIN. The best known efficient search algorithm for $k$LIN requires $\Omega(n^{k/2})$ samples, while the best known distinguisher for $(k-1)$LIN requires $\Omega(n^{(k-1)/2})$ samples. If our reduction's sample complexity were improved by a $\sqrt{n}$ factor our reduction would match the optimal sample complexity for search to decision. Towards understanding this gap it is instructive to revisit one efficient search algorithm for $k$LIN.

**Algorithm** *Search*: On input a multiset $C$ of samples $(i_1, \dots, i_k; \ell)$,
1 Set $A_i = \{(i_2, \dots, i_k; \ell) \colon (i, i_2, \dots, i_k; \ell) \in C\}$ for every $i$.
2 For every pair $i \neq j$,
3 Set $M_{ij} = \ell_i \cdot \ell_j$ if the same sample $(i_2, \dots, i_k)$ appears in $A_i$ and $A_j$ with labels $\ell_i$ and $\ell_j$.
4 Set $M_{ij} = 0$ if the samples in $A_i$ and $A_j$ are disjoint.
5 Derive $\hat{\mathbf{s}}$ from $M$ by spectral analysis.

The implementation of step 5 is not important for our purposes. $\hat{\mathbf{s}}$ can be taken to equal the sign of the top eigenvector of $M$ after rows with unusually many nonzero entries are removed (see e.g. [FO05, CRV15]).

Given $Kn^{k/2}$ samples for sufficiently large $K$, the output of this algorithm has $\Omega(1)$ overlap with the planted solution $\mathbf{s}$. The reason is that $M$ can be modeled as a sparse "stochastic block model" matrix with respect to the partition induced by the $+1$ and $-1$ of $\mathbf{s}$.

Like our reduction $S$, algorithm *Search* leverages noisy information $M_{ij}$ about $s_i s_j$ (equality of $s_i$ and $s_j$) to recover an approximation of the secret $\mathbf{s}$. There is however an important difference.

The *Search* algorithm ensures robustness against noise by using all pairwise predictions $M_{ij} \approx s_i s_j$. In contrast, reduction $S$ only uses information about the correlation of $s_j$ with $s_1$. The reason the additional information is ignored by the reduction is that an adversarial distinguisher with success rate $\alpha$ can refuse to reveal any useful information for a $(1-\alpha)$ fraction of $M$'s rows and columns. In contrast, the success of *Search* relies on the (almost) independence of the predictions $M_{ij}$. When $\alpha$ is on the order of $1/n$ as in the setting of algorithm *Search* an adversarial distinguisher yields essentially no information about $\mathbf{s}$.

## 6.2 The Unique Sample Model

Our instance model allows repeated samples. We assumed that the $k$LIN noise (more generally, the internal randomness of $P$) is chosen independently among repeated samples. An alternative model is one in which samples cannot repeat. The two models are $O(mn^{-2})$ statistically close. Our results carry over assuming the advantage $\alpha$ is at least as large. The best low-degree $k$LIN distinguisher in the unique sample model, however, has advantage $\Theta(m^4 n^{-2k})$. Our reduction is sensitive to the choice of model in the low-advantage regime $m^4n^{-2k} \ll \alpha \ll m^2n^{-k}$.

### 6.3 Exact $k$LIN and Refutation

We believe that our reduction is of interest even in the noiseless setting. Even though the search variant of noiseless $k$LIN can be solved by Gaussian elimination beyond the statistical threshold of $O(n)$ examples, the distinguishing algorithm is substantially simpler. It is an $\mathrm{AC}^0$ algorithm, while Gaussian Elimination is believed to require more power than $\mathrm{NC}^1$.

In the exact $k$LIN setting the distinguisher that seeks collisions is in fact a refuter. It rejects all planted $k$LIN instances but accepts an $\Omega(m^2n^{-k})$ fraction of random ones. If the distinguisher in Theorem 1.1 is a refuter of advantage $\alpha$, the sample complexity of the $k$LIN solver can be improved to $O(nm+n/\alpha^{(k-2)})$, economizing on an additional square factor in the advantage. Moreover the reduction can be implemented in $\mathrm{TC}^0$ at a slight loss in parameters.

**Acknowledgements.** We are grateful to Shuichi Hirahara, Nobutaka Shimizu, Nikhil Srivastava, Prashant Vasudevan, and Luca Trevisan for enlightening discussions. We thank the CRYPTO 2025 reviewers for their helpful suggestions.

## References

[ABR16] Applebaum, B., Bogdanov, A., Rosen, A.: A dichotomy for local small-bias generators. J. Cryptol. **29**(3), 577–596 (2016)

[AIK09] Applebaum, B., Ishai, Y., Kushilevitz, E.: Cryptography with constant input locality. J. Cryptol. **22**(4), 429–469 (2009)

[AL18] Applebaum, B., Lovett, S.: Algebraic attacks against random local functions and their countermeasures. SIAM J. Comput. **47**(1), 52–79 (2018)

[Ale03] Alekhnovich, M.: More on average case vs approximation complexity. In: 44th Symposium on Foundations of Computer Science (FOCS 2003), pp. 298–307 (2003)

[App13] Applebaum, B.: Pseudorandom generators with long stretch and low locality from random local one-way functions. SIAM J. Comput. **42**(5), 2008–2037 (2013)

[BFKL93] Blum, A., Furst, M., Kearns, M., Lipton, R.J.: Cryptographic primitives based on hard learning problems. In: Stinson, D.R. (ed.) CRYPTO 1993. LNCS, vol. 773, pp. 278–291. Springer, Heidelberg (1994). https://doi.org/10.1007/3-540-48329-2_24

[BKW03] Blum, A., Kalai, A., Wasserman, H.: Noise-tolerant learning, the parity problem, and the statistical query model. J. ACM **50**(4), 506–519 (2003)

[BQ12] Bogdanov, A., Qiao, Y.: On the security of Goldreich's one-way function. Comput. Complex. **21**(1), 83–127 (2012)

[BSV19] Bogdanov, A., Sabin, M., Vasudevan, P.N.: XOR codes and sparse learning parity with noise. In: Proceedings of 2019 ACM-SIAM Symposium on Discrete Algorithms (SODA), pp. 986–1004 (2019)

[Can22] Canonne, C.L.: Topics and techniques in distribution testing: a biased but representative sample. Found. Trends Commun. Inf. Theory **19**(6), 1032–1198 (2022)

[CEMT14] Cook, J., Etesami, O., Miller, R., Trevisan, L.: On the one-way function candidate proposed by goldreich. ACM Trans. Comput. Theory **6**(3), 14:1–14:35 (2014)

[CHKV24] Corrigan-Gibbs, H., Henzinger, A., Kalai, Y., Vaikuntanathan, V.: Somewhat homomorphic encryption from linear homomorphism and sparse LPN. IACR Cryptology ePrint Archive, p. 1760 (2024)

[CRV15] Chin, P., Rao, A., Vu, V.: Stochastic block model and community detection in sparse graphs: a spectral algorithm with optimal rate of recovery. In: Proceedings of The 28th Conference on Learning Theory, vol. 40, pp. 391–423 (2015)

[DIJL23] Dao, Q., Ishai, Y., Jain, A., Lin, H.: Multi-party homomorphic secret sharing and sublinear MPC from sparse LPN. In: Handschuh, H., Lysyanskaya, A. (eds.) 43rd Annual International Cryptology Conference, CRYPTO 2023, pp. 315–348 (2023). https://doi.org/10.1007/978-3-031-38545-2_11

[DJ24] Dao, Q., Jain, A.: Lossy cryptography from code-based assumptions. In: Reyzin, L., Stebila, D. (eds.) CRYPTO 2024, pp. 34–75 (2024). https://doi.org/10.1007/978-3-031-68382-4_2

[FKO06] Feige, U., Kim, J.H., Ofek, E.: Witnesses for non-satisfiability of dense random 3CNF formulas. In: Proceedings of the 47th IEEE Symposium on Foundations of Computer Science, FOCS 2006, pp. 497–508 (2006)

[FO05] Feige, U., Ofek, E.: Spectral techniques applied to sparse random graphs. Random Struct. Algorithms **27**(2), 251–275 (2005)

[GKM22] Guruswami, V., Kothari, P.K., Manohar, P.: Algorithms and certificates for Boolean CSP refutation: smoothed is no harder than random. In: STOC 2022: 54th Annual ACM SIGACT Symposium on Theory of Computing, pp. 678–689 (2022)

[Gol00] Goldreich, O.: Candidate one-way functions based on expander graphs. Electron. Colloquium Comput. Complex., TR00-090 (2000)

[MST06] Mossel, E., Shpilka, A., Trevisan, L.: On epsilon-biased generators in $NC^0$. Random Struct. Algorithms **29**(1), 56–81 (2006)

[O'D14] O'Donnell, R.: Analysis of Boolean Functions. Cambridge University Press (2014)

# Error Floor Prediction with Markov Models for QC-MDPC Codes

Sarah Arpin[1(✉)], Jun Bo Lau[2], Antoine Mesnard[3], Ray Perlner[4], Angela Robinson[4], Jean-Pierre Tillich[3], and Valentin Vasseur[5]

[1] Department of Mathematics, Virginia Polytechnic Institute and State University, Virginia, USA
sarpin@vt.edu
[2] COSIC, KU Leuven, Leuven, Belgium
[3] INRIA, Paris, France
[4] Computer Security Division, National Institute of Standards and Technology, Gaithersburg, USA
[5] Thales, Gennevilliers, France

**Abstract.** Quasi-cyclic moderate-density parity check (QC-MDPC) code-based encryption schemes under iterative decoders offer highly-competitive performance in quantum-resistant cryptography, but their IND-CCA2 security is an open question because the decoding failure rate (DFR) of these algorithms is not well-understood. The DFR decreases extremely rapidly as the blocklength increases, then decreases much more slowly in regimes known as the waterfall and error floor, respectively. The waterfall behavior is rather well predicted by a Markov model introduced by Sendrier and Vasseur [SV19b] but it does not capture the error floor behavior. Assessing precisely for which blocklength this error floor begins is crucial for the low DFRs sought in the context of cryptography.

By enriching the Markov model [SV19b] with information about near codewords we are able to capture this error-floor behavior for a step-by-step decoder. This decoder displays worse decoding performance than the parallel decoders used in practice but is more amenable to a Markov chain analysis. We already capture the error floor with a simplified model. A refined model taking into account certain structural features of the secret key is even able to give accurate key dependent predictions both in the waterfall and error floor regimes. We show that error floor behavior is governed by convergence to a near codeword when decoding fails.

We ran this model for the BIKE cryptosystem with this simpler step-by-step decoder to better ascertain whether the DFR is low enough to achieve IND-CCA2 security. Our model gives a DFR below $2^{-131.2}$, using a block length $r = 13477$ instead of the BIKE parameter $r = 12323$. This paper gives some strong evidence that the IND-CCA2 requirement can be met at the cost of a modest increase of less than 10% in the key size.


Y. Tauman Kalai and S. F. Kamara (Eds.): CRYPTO 2025, LNCS 16000, pp. 221–252, 2025.
https://doi.org/10.1007/978-3-032-01855-7_8

# 1 Introduction

## 1.1 Motivation

**The NIST PQC Standardization Process.** The U.S. National Institute of Standards and Technology (NIST) Post-Quantum Cryptography (PQC) standardization process, which began with 82 submissions, has selected two key encapsulation algorithms for standardization: CRYSTALS-Kyber and HQC. The BIKE cryptosystem was a candidate considered in round 4, a cryptosystem based on quasi-cyclic moderate-density parity check (QC-MDPC) codes which are decoded by an iterative Black-Grey-Flip (BGF) decoder [ABB+21,DGK20]. The BIKE cryptosystem offers competitive performance but lacks a formal security claim in the static-key setting.

**Estimating the DFR of BIKE.** Cryptosystems with a non-zero probability of decryption failures require careful analysis when proving IND-CCA2 security. In particular, the standard security proof [HHK17] requires the average failure probability to be below $2^{-\lambda}$ where $\lambda$ is the security parameter. BIKE is one such cryptosystem. A low DFR for BIKE is not just a theoretical concern, since a DFR sufficiently higher than $2^{-\lambda}$ enables the GJS key-recovery attack [GJS16], which exploits decoding failures in an IND-CCA security model.

The target DFR of $2^{-\lambda}$ is too small to measure directly, so another approach is needed to prove that the DFR of BIKE is below $2^{-\lambda}$. Previous work [SV19b,SV19a,DGK20] approximates the DFR by (i) directly measuring the average DFR for smaller code sizes by running the decoder (which is doable since the DFR is high enough to observe decoding failures) then (ii) extrapolating the behavior to estimate the DFR for larger parameters that are out of reach of experiments. However, the DFR falls into two regimes, making such extrapolations unreliable. The first regime is the *waterfall region*, where the DFR decays more than exponentially in the block size $n$ of the scheme (with other parameters fixed). The second regime is the *error floor* which kicks in when the block size is sufficiently large and where the decay is much slower (Fig. 1). The issue is that the experiments are done in the waterfall region and extrapolation is made under the hypothesis that for the BIKE parameters we are still in this region. This could lead to underestimation of the DFR and consequently, an underestimation of the block size needed to achieve a particular security parameter $\lambda$.

It remains an open problem to predict for which value of $n$ the error floor begins for BIKE. It is really a problem of predicting the iterative decoding performance of a QC-MDPC code. For LDPC codes (which have rows and columns of weight $O(1)$ compared to $O(\sqrt{n})$ for MDPC codes), with the same kind of decoder, the error floor phenomenon is better understood. For LDPC codes, the error floor is either due to the existence of low-weight codewords which would fool any decoder, or of small *near codewords*. They are also called trapping sets and are errors of small weight with a syndrome also of small weight [Ric03,HB18,VCN14]. Error vectors which have a large enough intersection with those codewords or near codewords are known to cause the error floor behavior in LDPC codes.

On the other hand, MDPC codes typically have no low-weight codewords or near codewords. However, BIKE is based on QC-MDPC codes, and this gives BIKE more structure than a random MDPC code. BIKE admits a parity-check matrix $\boldsymbol{H}$ formed by two circulant blocks. Such codes have codewords of weight equal to the row weight $w$ of $\boldsymbol{H}$ (which is of order $O(\sqrt{n})$) [SV19a,BBC+21]. There are near codewords of half the row weight which, due to the block-circulant structure, is also equal to the column weight $d$ of $\boldsymbol{H}$. In particular, the set of *near codewords* consists of error vectors where either the first or second half of bits is precisely a row of $\boldsymbol{H}$ and the rest of the bits are 0 [Vas21]. The lower bound[1] on the DFR based on those moderate-weight codewords is too low to be of concern for the BIKE parameters [BBC+21].

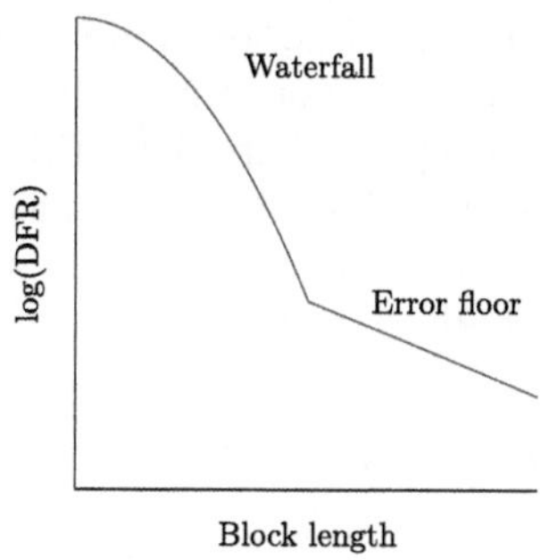


**Fig. 1.** Waterfall and error floor regions for decoding failure rate.

However, a clear explanation of the error floor for QC-MDPC has not been found to date even if the near codewords of [Vas21] could be a factor: the DFR conditioned on an error vector with large intersection with one of the near codewords was shown in [Vas21] to be non-negligible. Even if the contribution to the DFR of such events is bigger than the contribution to the DFR coming from the moderate-weight codewords, it is not enough to be of concern for BIKE parameters. Moreover [ABH+22] shows that for scaled-down BIKE parameters where the error floor can be observed experimentally, the errors that contribute to the DFR do not have large intersection with the near codewords of [Vas21].

Remarkably, the waterfall region is much better understood [SV19b,Vas21] by analyzing with a Markov chain approach a step-by-step decoder flipping bits one at a time. At each step a random position is considered and flipped according to whether the number of unsatisfied parity-checks involving this position (called the *counter* of the position) is greater than some threshold. To understand the rationale of this rule, denote by $\pi_0$ the probability that a parity-check involving an error free bit is not satisfied and denote by $\pi_1$ the probability that a parity-check involving a bit in error is not satisfied. The crucial observation is that

$$\pi_0 < \pi_1. \tag{1}$$

Due to the regular structure of $\boldsymbol{H}$ all bits are involved in the same number $d$ of parity checks. We therefore expect that the counter of an error free position behaves as a binomial random variable $\text{Bin}(d, \pi_0)$[2], whereas the counter of a

[1] It is the probability that the error covers at least half one of those codewords.

[2] $\text{Bin}(n, p)$ is the sum of $n$ i.i.d. Bernoulli variables $X_i$ of parameter $p$, that is $\mathbf{P}(X_i = 1) = p$ for all $i$ in $\{1, \cdots, n\}$.

position in error behaves as $\text{Bin}(d, \pi_1)$. Therefore a bit in error tends to be involved in more unsatisfied parity checks than a correct bit. In standard iterative decoding, all positions are considered at once and flipped or not according to the same rule. The fact that the decoder is step-by-step makes it much more amenable to a Markov-chain modeling whose states are the pairs $(s, t)$, $t$ being the number of errors and $s$ the syndrome weight of the error. This Markov-chain model closely predicts the DFR in the waterfall region but does not capture the error floor region. Roughly speaking, the DFR is predicted here by computing the resulting probability distributions of the pairs $(s, t)$. The predicted DFR is the probability to attain a state where $t$ is not zero at the end.

### 1.2 Our Approach

**Intuition: Convergence to Near Codewords in the Error Floor Regime.** Our work started with a fundamental observation, namely that in the toy examples for which we could observe the error floor phenomenon experimentally, the remaining error at the end of the iterative decoding process when decoding failed covered in many cases one of the near codewords put forward in [Vas21]. Interestingly enough, [ABH+22, Fig 3,4 and 5] shows that in the error floor regime, errors which result in a decoding failure tend to have a bigger intersection with at least one of those near codewords than a random error of the same size. There is a good justification for this behavior in Sect. 2.4.

[BBC+21] noted that there exist *bad counters* which can lead to decoding failures. We provide a full classification of such bad counters. The point is that we actually do not have two kinds of behaviors for the counters as explained before, but rather four different behaviors of the counters. At each decoding iteration, consider the near codeword $\boldsymbol{\nu}$ that is the closest to the actual error and denote by $u$ the size of its intersection with the actual error $\boldsymbol{e}$. As explained in Sect. 2.4, we expect the following four kinds of behavior:

1. The counters of the $u$ bits belonging to the support of $\boldsymbol{\nu}$ and $\boldsymbol{e}$ behave like the sum of two independent binomial variables $\text{Bin}(u-1, \pi_0) + \text{Bin}(d-u+1, \pi_1)$
2. The counters of the $d-u$ bits not in error but in the support of $\boldsymbol{\nu}$ behave as the sum of two binomial variables $\text{Bin}(u, \pi_1) + \text{Bin}(d-u, \pi_0)$.
3. The counters of the rest of the $t-u$ bits in error behave "as usual" as a binomial variable $\text{Bin}(d, \pi_1)$.
4. The counters of the rest of the $n-d-t+u$ bits that are not in error also behave as expected, namely as a binomial variable $\text{Bin}(d, \pi_0)$.

In other words, since $\pi_0 < \pi_1$, we expect an abnormal behavior from the $d$ bits which belong to the closest near codeword. Indeed, those that are in error are less likely to be corrected by the iterative decoding process than the others which are in error: their counter is somewhat in between a counter of a bit which is in error and a counter of a bit which is not in error. Similarly, the $d-u$ bits of the near codeword that are not in error have a greater chance to be wrongly flipped by the iterative decoding process than the other bits in error. This is even worse, because the more bits are in error in the near codeword, the more the bits involved in this near codeword behave as their opposite: those that are still not in error tend to look even more like bits which are in error. This leads to a snowball effect. As soon as enough bits are in error in the near codeword, there is a non negligible chance to end up at the end of the iterative decoding process with the whole near codeword being in error. Due to the peculiar structure of near codewords, the iterative decoding process gets stuck there.

This discussion suggests that errors which give rise to a decoding failure in the error floor region should be somewhat closer to one of those near codewords at the beginning, and the intersection size only increases during the decoding process. This is why we adapted the Markov model of [SV19b, Vas21] to also keep track of this parameter $u$ which is the biggest intersection of a near codeword with the residual error vector in the decoding process.

**Two New Markov Models.** We have followed two different but related approaches for keeping track of the size of the intersection of the error vector with the near codewords in a Markov model.

- The first approach uses the simple model for the counters described before together with a simplified model of the parity-check matrix. This simple model keeps track of the size $u$ of the intersection of the error with a single, randomly selected near codeword $\boldsymbol{\nu}$. We estimate the contribution to the DFR coming from $\boldsymbol{\nu}$. This is then used to account for the contributions coming from all near codewords. See Sect. 5.
- The second approach is much more involved. It computes the transition probabilities much more accurately. It takes into account the secret key structure by using the specific structure of the near codewords corresponding to a given key. The only simplifying assumption which is made is that in the error floor regime the decoding failure is dominated by errors which are close to a single near codeword, and that this does not change during the decoding process. In this case, the Markov model keeps track of the size $u$ of the intersection of the error with the closest near codeword. We capture the DFR in the error floor regime with high accuracy within this model. See Sect. 6.

**The Simple Markov Model.** The first approach has been tested with scaled-down BIKE parameters and by taking a random key $\boldsymbol{H}$. To simplify the computation of $\pi_0$ and $\pi_1$ we made the assumption that the columns of $\boldsymbol{H}$ are drawn uniformly at random up to fixed column weight $d$. This new Markov model captures the error floor region and provides a much more conservative estimate than the DFR estimate based on the Markov model of [SV19b, Vas21] which is too optimistic in the error floor regime. It turns out that the new DFR estimate is larger than the true estimate in both the waterfall and error floor regions (and not only in the waterfall regime as was the case for the Markov model of [SV19b, Vas21]). This is quite encouraging since even with this simple model there is a tool for choosing the parameters of BIKE in a conservative manner.

**A Key Dependent Markov Model.** One drawback of this simple Markov model is that it does not take into account the structure of the key. There are indeed weak keys [DGK20, Vas21, NSP+23, WWW23] where decoding behaves really badly. Moreover, there is a difference between the DFR of the best and worst key of the DFR in the few thousand of instances of the toy example we considered. This led us to refine the Markov model which allowed us to compute the transition probabilities more accurately.

One of the difficulties of having a Markov model working for all sorts of keys is that the near codewords split into two classes, those that have their support either in the first half of the code positions or in the second half. These two classes might affect the DFR in a very different way. To circumvent this problem, we added a bit to the Markov state, getting a state $(s, t, u, b)$ where $b = 0$ indicates that the closest near codeword has all its support in the first half of positions and 1 otherwise. At the expense of increasing the state space size and adding more involved transition probability formulas, we get a Markov model which captures now all possible keys. Remarkably, in the toy examples this model is still accurate for predicting the error floor for the step-by-step decoder and other variants: the majority decoder (the threshold for flipping being half the total number of equations involving a bit), the BGF decoder, or a decoder with a new custom threshold rule which improves the DFR by a significant amount.

Moreover, we can also use our model to examine what causes the DFR. We split the contribution of the DFR into two parts. The first one is the contribution $\text{DFR}_\text{e}$ to the DFR where decoding failed because it ended up covering a near codeword: The final state where we got blocked in the Markov chain was a state $(s, t, u, b)$ for which $u = d$. It can be viewed in some sense as the error-floor term in the DFR. The second one is the total DFR minus $\text{DFR}_\text{e}$: $\text{DFR}_\text{w} = \text{DFR} - \text{DFR}_\text{e}$, which can be viewed as the waterfall part of the DFR. Not only did our Markov model accurately predict the DFR, but did also predict well each term separately. Indeed, even in the error floor region where $\text{DFR}_\text{e}$ is really bigger than $\text{DFR}_\text{w}$, the $\text{DFR}_\text{w}$ term predicted by our model matches the $\text{DFR}_\text{w}$ term computed in the experiments. This is a further indication that the model predicts accurately the error floor and the waterfall behaviors. All in all, in this work, we conclude that the dominant contribution to the error floor for QC-MDPC codes under iterative decoders is due to convergence to a near codeword.

### 1.3 Summary of the Main Results

The simple Markov model we present here already captures the error floor regime and gives a conservative estimate of the DFR. On the other hand, the refined model which is key dependent is used to

- give an extremely close approximation of experimental data in the waterfall and error floor regimes, further improving upon the first model and [SV19b],
- estimate for the BIKE 1 parameters and with the previous BIKE 1 decoder using a single threshold function a DFR of about $2^{-91}$,
- show that for this decoding rule, there is an error floor behavior which appears already for slightly larger values of the block length than the one which was chosen and depending on the gap parameter $\delta$ of the decoder gives a contribution to the DFR which is between $2^{-100}$ and $2^{-120}$,

- improve this decoding rule by raising the minimum allowed threshold from 36 to 39 to show that for a slightly larger block length ($r = 13477$ instead of $r = 12323$), we obtain a DFR which is below $2^{-131.2}$ for a typical key.

These models predict and experiments confirm that the dominating cause of failures in the error floor regime in a wide range of parameters is due to convergence to near codewords. All models use the step-by-step decoder which is experimentally shown to produce more decoding failures than parallel decoders. The most impactful model is the refined model which matches the experimental data, also using a step-by-step decoder, remarkably well throughout both the error floor and waterfall regimes. This model is applied to the BIKE cryptosystem parameter sets to give a DFR approximation; it is expected that the DFR for the same parameter sets using a parallel bit-flipping decoder as specified in [ABB+21] and decoding rule based on iteration dependent threshold functions would result in a lower DFR than what is approximated by the model.

All in all, this paper solves a major issue for the fourth round candidate BIKE of the NIST PQC competition, namely to give a convincing prediction for the DFR of this cryptosystem. Being able to show that this quantity is below $2^{-\lambda}$ is a major concern for BIKE to prove its IND-CCA2 security. This paper gives some strong evidence that this requirement can be met at the cost of a modest increase of less than 10% in the key size, by raising a little bit the minimum threshold, and filtering out atypical keys during key generation.

## 2 Background

### 2.1 Notation

**Basic Notation.** Vectors and matrices are respectively denoted in bold letters and bold capital letters such as $\boldsymbol{a}$ and $\boldsymbol{A}$. Vectors are assumed to be row vectors and $\boldsymbol{x}^\intercal$ denotes the column vector which is the transpose of the row vector $\boldsymbol{x}$. For a matrix $\boldsymbol{A}$, the vector that is the transpose of the $j$-th column of $\boldsymbol{A}$ is denoted by $\boldsymbol{A}_j$. The entry at index $i$ of the vector $\boldsymbol{x}$ is denoted by $x_i$ or $x(i)$. The Schur (component-wise) product $(x_i y_i)_{1 \leqslant i \leqslant n}$ of two vectors $\boldsymbol{x} = (x_i)_{1 \leqslant i \leqslant n}$ and $\boldsymbol{y} = (y_i)_{1 \leqslant i \leqslant n}$ of the same length is denoted by $\boldsymbol{x} \star \boldsymbol{y}$. The Hamming weight $|\boldsymbol{x}|$ of a vector $\boldsymbol{x}$ is its number of nonzero entries.

**Probabilistic Notation.** $\text{Bin}(n, p)$ denotes a random variable following a binomial distribution with parameters $n$ and $p$, that is the sum $\sum_{i=1}^{n} X_i$ of $n$ i.i.d. Bernoulli variables with parameter $p$. Expressions like $\text{Bin}(n_1, p_1) + \text{Bin}(n_2, p_2)$ stand for the sum of the two independent binomial random variables $\text{Bin}(n_1, p_1)$ and $\text{Bin}(n_2, p_2)$. By abuse of notation, we write $X \sim Y$ when two random variables $X$ and $Y$ follow the same distribution. For a finite set $\mathscr{S}$, $x \xleftarrow{\$} \mathscr{S}$ means that $x$ is an element of $\mathscr{S}$ sampled uniformly at random in $\mathscr{S}$.

**Binary Linear Codes.** All codes considered here are binary and linear, which means that they are vector spaces over $\mathbb{F}_2$. A code $\mathscr{C}$ of length $n$ and dimension $k$ is a $k$-dimensional subspace of $\mathbb{F}_2^n$. We say that such a code is an $[n, k]$ code.

It is specified by a parity-check matrix which is a matrix whose kernel is $\mathscr{C}$, *i.e.* $\mathscr{C} = \{\boldsymbol{c} \in \mathbb{F}_2^n : \boldsymbol{H}\boldsymbol{c}^\intercal = 0\}$.

**Quasi-Cyclic Codes and Polynomial Notation.** On top of being binary and linear, all codes considered here are quasi-cyclic, *i.e.* their parity-check matrix is formed by blocks of circulant matrices. More precisely, they are double circulant codes, meaning that the parity-check matrix has the form $\boldsymbol{H} = \begin{pmatrix}\boldsymbol{C}_0 \, \boldsymbol{C}_1\end{pmatrix}$ where both $\boldsymbol{C}_0$ and $\boldsymbol{C}_1$ are circulant matrices. From now on, $r$ will denote the size of $\boldsymbol{C}_0$ and $\boldsymbol{C}_1$ and the length $n$ of the code will be $n = 2r$. $\boldsymbol{C}_0$ and $\boldsymbol{C}_1$ are also supposed to have the same column weight. This weight is denoted by $d$. The row weight $w$ of $\boldsymbol{H}$ is also constant and satisfies $w = 2d$. Such codes are conveniently represented by polynomials since $r \times r$ binary circulant matrices form a ring $\mathscr{R}$ isomorphic to $\mathbb{F}_2[x]/(x^r - 1)$, the isomorphism $\Psi$ being given by

$$\begin{pmatrix} c_0 & c_{r-1} & \cdots & c_2 & c_1 \\ c_1 & c_0 & c_{r-1} & & c_2 \\ \vdots & c_1 & c_0 & \ddots & \vdots \\ c_{r-2} & \vdots & \ddots & \ddots & c_{r-1} \\ c_{r-1} & c_{r-2} & \cdots & c_1 & c_0 \end{pmatrix} \mapsto c_0 + c_1 x + \cdots + c_{r-1}x^{r-1}.$$

We use this isomorphism to view $\boldsymbol{H} = \begin{pmatrix}\boldsymbol{C}_0 \, \boldsymbol{C}_1\end{pmatrix}$ as the pair $(h_0(x), h_1(x))$ where $h_0(x) = \Psi(\boldsymbol{C}_0)$ and $h_1(x) = \Psi(\boldsymbol{C}_1)$. We overload the notation from now on:

**Notation 1.** *We denote the parity-check matrix* $\boldsymbol{H} \stackrel{def}{=} (h_0, h_1)$. *We also write* $h_0(x) = \sum_{j=1}^{d} x^{l_j}$ *and* $h_1(x) = \sum_{j=1}^{d} x^{r_j}$, *where* $l_j$ *and* $r_j$ *run over the nonzero coefficients of* $h_0$ *and* $h_1$, *respectively.*

We likewise represent error vectors $\boldsymbol{e} = (e_0, \cdots, e_{n-1}) \in \mathbb{F}_2^n$ with polynomials

$$\boldsymbol{e} \rightsquigarrow e(x) = e_0(x) \oplus e_1(x) = \sum_{j=0}^{r-1} e_j x^j \oplus \sum_{j=0}^{r-1} e_{r+j} x^j \in (\mathbb{F}_2[x]/(x^r - 1))^2$$

We use here "$\oplus$" to denote a formal sum, and "$+$" to denote addition in the ring $\mathbb{F}_2[x]/(x^r - 1)$. The syndrome $\boldsymbol{s} = (s_0, \cdots, s_{r-1})$ of an error $\boldsymbol{e} = (e_0, ..., e_{n-1})$, *i.e.* $\boldsymbol{s}^\intercal = \boldsymbol{H}\boldsymbol{e}^\intercal$ is also represented as a polynomial $s(x) = \sum_{j=0}^{r-1} s_j x^j$ and

$$s(x) = e_0(x)h_0(x) + e_1(x)h_1(x). \tag{2}$$

Note that all polynomial operations are performed in the ring $\mathbb{F}_2[x]/(x^r - 1)$.

### 2.2 Iterative Decoders

The problem we will be interested to solve efficiently during the deciphering process is the syndrome decoding problem.

*Problem 2.1 (syndrome decoding problem (SDP)).* Given an $r \times n$ parity-check matrix $\boldsymbol{H} \in \mathbb{F}_2^{r \times n}$ and an error vector $\boldsymbol{e}$ sampled uniformly at random of weight $t$ with syndrome $\boldsymbol{s}^\intercal = \boldsymbol{H}\boldsymbol{e}^\intercal$, find a vector $\boldsymbol{e}'$ such that $\boldsymbol{H}\boldsymbol{e}'^\intercal = \boldsymbol{s}^\intercal$ and $|\boldsymbol{e}'| = t$.

Iterative, bit-flipping syndrome decoders generally solve the SDP by guessing that columns of $\boldsymbol{H}$ with *many* bits in common with $\boldsymbol{s}$ are likely affected by errors. Recall that $\boldsymbol{H}_i$ denotes the transpose of the $i$-th column of matrix $\boldsymbol{H}$, and define $\sigma_i(\boldsymbol{H}, \boldsymbol{s}) = |\boldsymbol{H}_i \star \boldsymbol{s}|$, the number of unsatisfied parity-check equations involving $i$. We will denote this quantity simply by $\sigma_i$ in what follows and say that it is the *counter* corresponding to bit $i$. The bit-flipping decoders initialize $\boldsymbol{e}' = \boldsymbol{0}$, compute $\sigma_j$ for all or some $j \in \{0, \ldots, n-1\}$, then flip the $j$-th bit $e'_j$ whenever $\sigma_j \geq T$, where $T$ is a given threshold function. We say a decoding failure has occurred whenever the output $\boldsymbol{e}'$ satisfies: $\boldsymbol{H}\boldsymbol{e}'^{\intercal} \neq \boldsymbol{s}^{\intercal}$ or $\boldsymbol{e}' \neq \boldsymbol{e}$.

The accuracy of bit-flipping decoders greatly depends on $T$. If the threshold is too high, the decoder ceases to flip bits before arriving at the correct vector $\boldsymbol{e}'$. If the threshold is too low, more bits are flipped than should be, again resulting in an incorrect vector $\boldsymbol{e}'$. $T$ is always chosen such that $T \geqslant \frac{d+1}{2}$. This ensures that the weight of $\Delta\boldsymbol{s}^{\intercal} \overset{\text{def}}{=} \boldsymbol{s}^{\intercal} + \boldsymbol{H}\boldsymbol{e}'^{\intercal}$ is strictly decreasing, so that we may expect it to reach 0 so that $\boldsymbol{H}\boldsymbol{e}'^{\intercal} = \boldsymbol{s}^{\intercal}$ at the end.

It is most common for iterative decoders to consider each column of $\boldsymbol{H}$ in comparison with $\boldsymbol{s}$ during each round of decoding. This can result in multiple bits of the guess $\boldsymbol{e}'$ being flipped in one round of decoding. The BIKE cryptosystem round 4 specification uses the Black-Grey-Flip (BGF) iterative decoder [DGK20]. A closed form analysis of the DFR of the BGF decoder remains an open problem.

In this work we analyze the step-by-step decoder - an iterative decoder which randomly selects one column of $\boldsymbol{H}$ for comparison with $\boldsymbol{s}$ during each decoding round: At most one bit is flipped per round. This simplifies the computation of the Markov chain transition probabilities by restricting the number of possible states in the next step. It is detailed in Algorithm 1.

**Algorithm 1** step-by-step decoder.

**Input:** $\boldsymbol{H} \in \mathbb{F}_2^{r\times n}$, $\boldsymbol{s} \in \mathbb{F}_2^r$, $t \in \{1, \ldots, n\}$
**Output:** $\boldsymbol{e} \in \mathbb{F}_2^n$ such that $\boldsymbol{H}\boldsymbol{e}^{\intercal} = \boldsymbol{s}^{\intercal}$ and $|\boldsymbol{e}| = t$ or $\perp$ (decoding failure)
**Require:** a threshold function $T$ such that $T \geqslant \frac{d+1}{2}$
**Ensure:** the weight of $\Delta\boldsymbol{s}^{\intercal} = \boldsymbol{s}^{\intercal} + \boldsymbol{H}\boldsymbol{e}'^{\intercal}$ decreases strictly in the algorithm below

```
e' ← 0, Δs ← s
while Δs ≠ 0 do
    ℰ ← {{0, ··· , n − 1} : |H_j ⋆ Δs| ⩾ T}          ▷ |H_j ⋆ Δs| is the counter σ_j
    if ℰ ≠ ∅ then
        j ←$ ℰ
        e'_j ← 1 − e'_j, Δs ← Δs + H_j              ▷ |Δs| has decreased by d − 2σ_j
    else return (⊥)                                  ▷ The decoder is then in a blocked state
if |e'| = t then return (e')
else return (⊥)
```

The step-by-step decoder has been studied in detail and experimental evidence [Vas21, Chap 7, Fig. 7.1] shows that for the classical bit flipping strategy, the step-by-step decoder performs significantly worse than the parallel version.

### 2.3 Near Codewords

Near codewords were introduced in the literature of iterative decoding as a way to formalize a collection of error vectors with lower-weight, nonzero syndrome than expected, which are therefore difficult to decode.

**Definition 2.2 (near codeword of type $(s,t)$).** *An error vector* $\mathbf{e} \in \mathbb{F}_2^n$ *is a near codeword of type* $(s,t)$ *if* $|\mathbf{e}| = t$ *and* $|\boldsymbol{H}\mathbf{e}^T| = s$.

MDPC codes are known to have minimum distance which is typically linear in the code-length $n$ and are unlikely to have small near codewords. This is not the case for QC-MDPC codes: the minimum distance is of order $O(\sqrt{n})$. This is because $h_1(x) \oplus h_0(x)$ belongs to the code of parity-check matrix $\boldsymbol{H} = (h_0, h_1)$. This leads one to suspect that such codes also have small-weight near codewords. This is indeed the case and that this is most likely the main issue for decoding as identified in [Vas21]. To define them, fix a parity-check matrix $\boldsymbol{H} = (h_0, h_1)$.

**Definition 2.3 (The set $\mathcal{N}$ of near codewords).** *The set* $\mathcal{N}$ *of near codewords is the union of all* $n$*-bit vectors with polynomial representations of the form* $x^i h_0(x) \oplus \mathbf{0}$ *and* $\mathbf{0} \oplus x^i h_1(x)$, *for all* $i \in \{0, ..., r-1\}$.

In this work, when we refer to a near codeword, we mean an element of $\mathcal{N}$.

**Unusually Low Syndrome Weight.** Elements of $\mathcal{N}$ are $(d,d)$-near codewords as per Definition 2.2: they are of weight $d$ and have syndrome weight $d$. Moreover, even errors $\boldsymbol{e}$ which have an overlap of size $u$ with a near codeword $\boldsymbol{\nu}$ of this kind (meaning that $|\boldsymbol{e} \star \boldsymbol{\nu}| = u$) have an unusually low weight syndrome. If $|\boldsymbol{e}| = t$, the syndrome weight can be as large as $d \cdot t$ and is always $\leqslant d \cdot t - u(u-1)$.

This can be read off directly from the polynomial representation of the syndrome. To verify the first claim, the near codeword $e(x) = x^i h_0(x) \oplus 0 \in \mathcal{N}$, for example, has syndrome $s(x) = (x^i h_0(x)) h_0(x) = x^i h_0^2(x)$, which is of weight $d$ as $h_0(x)$ has precisely $d$ nonzero coefficients, and in $\mathbb{F}_2[x]/(x^r - 1)$ squaring and multiplication by $x$ preserve the number of nonzero coefficients. To verify the second claim suppose that the near codeword $\boldsymbol{\nu}$ is say of the form $x^i h_0(x) \oplus 0$, the error $\boldsymbol{e}$ can be written as a polynomial as $e(x) = e_0(x) \oplus e_1(x)$, $x^i h_0(x) = a(x) + b(x)$ and $e_0(x) = a(x) + c(x)$ where $a(x)$ is the polynomial for the common part $\boldsymbol{e} \star \boldsymbol{\nu}$. The syndrome of $\boldsymbol{e}$ is

$$\begin{aligned} s(x) &= e_0(x)h_0(x) + e_1(x)h_1(x) \\ &= x^{r-i}(a(x) + b(x))(a(x) + c(x)) + e_1(x)h_1(x) \\ &= x^{r-i}\left(a(x)^2 + a(x)b(x) + a(x)c(x) + b(x)c(x)\right) + e_1(x)h_1(x). \end{aligned}$$

Recall here that we perform the polynomial computation over $\mathbb{F}_2[x]/(x^r - 1)$ and that $x^{r-i}x^i = 1$ in this ring. Let us denote by $|P|$ the weight of a polynomial $P$, namely the number of its non zero coefficients. The weight satisfies $|P \cdot Q| \leqslant |P| \cdot |Q|$ and $|P + Q| \leqslant |P| + |Q|$ for all polynomials $P$ and $Q$. Notice that $d \cdot t$ is exactly $|e_0| \cdot |h_0| + |e_1| \cdot |h_1| = |a|^2 + |a| \cdot |b| + |a| \cdot |c| + |b| \cdot |c| + |e_1| \cdot |h_1|$. The point is that $|a^2| = |a|$ because of the *forced cancellations* in the product $a(x)^2$. Indeed, as in the previous point, squaring preserves the number of nonzero coefficients. This implies that we have at least a drop of $|a|^2 - |a| = u(u-1)$ in the syndrome weight as claimed above.

### 2.4 Tanner Graphs

We use the language of *Tanner graphs* to fully explain the role of *bad counters*, first considered in [BBC+21, §4.1].

**Definition.** A Tanner graph is a very handy tool for analyzing iterative decoding of LDPC or MDPC codes. For LDPC codes, this notion dates back to Gallager who explained and studied his iterative decoding algorithms [Gal63] by using them. In a more general form, they have been defined in [Tan81]. It is a bipartite graph which represents the parity-check matrix $\boldsymbol{H} = (H_{i,j})_{\substack{0 \leqslant i < r \\ 0 \leqslant j < n}}$ of a code. It has two types of vertices, the *variable nodes* which are in bijection with the code positions $\{0, \cdots, n-1\}$, and the *check nodes* which are in bijection with the parity checks, *i.e.* the rows of $\boldsymbol{H}$. There is an edge between a variable node $j$ and the check node $i$ if and only if $H_{i,j} = 1$.

In our case, where $n = 2r$ and the parity-check matrix is formed by two circulant blocks, we can relate this to the polynomial notation established in Sect. 2.1 and index the variable nodes and check nodes a little bit differently. More specifically, the variable node associated to the $i$-th position is indexed by $x^i \oplus 0$ if $i < r$ and by $0 \oplus x^{i-r}$ if $i \geqslant r$. Polynomial notation is also used to index the check nodes. The check node associated to the $i$-th row of $\boldsymbol{H}$ is indexed by $x^i$. When $\boldsymbol{H} = (h_0, h_1)$, the set of check nodes adjacent to the variable node $x^i \oplus 0$ is the set of monomials in $x^i h_0(x)$ and the set of check nodes adjacent to the variable node $0 \oplus x^i$ is the set of monomials appearing in $x^i h_1(x)$. Note that the syndrome weight $|\boldsymbol{H}\boldsymbol{e}^\intercal|$ of an error $\boldsymbol{e}$ can be read off from the Tanner graph:

**Fact 1.** *Consider the subgraph of the Tanner graph induced by an error* $\mathbf{e}$*: It is formed by the variable nodes belonging to* $\mathbf{e}$ *and all the check nodes adjacent to it. The number of check nodes of odd degree in this graph is* $|\boldsymbol{H}\boldsymbol{e}^\intercal|$*. The counter of a bit is the number of check nodes in this subgraph that are of odd degree and that are adjacent to it in the complete Tanner graph.*

**Subgraph Induced by a Near Codeword.** The subgraph $\mathscr{G}$ of the Tanner graph induced by a near codeword $\boldsymbol{\nu}$ in $\mathcal{N}$ has a special structure. It has a unusually small number of check nodes for subgraphs induced by $d$ variable nodes. We detail below the structure when $\boldsymbol{\nu}$ is $h_0(x) \oplus 0$ and recall that $h_0(x) = \sum_{i=1}^{d} x^{l_i}$, but the general case can be deduced from this one, by a shift of the positions and/or replacing $l_i$ by $r_i$ in the case of a near codeword $0 \oplus x^m h_1(x)$.

**Fact 2.** *Consider the subgraph* $\mathscr{G}$ *of the Tanner graph induced by* $\boldsymbol{\nu} = h_0(x) \oplus 0$*. The variables nodes are the d variable nodes labeled* $x^{l_i} \oplus 0$ *for* $i \in \{1, \cdots, d\}$*. The check nodes are all the* $x^{l_i + l_j}$*. There are at most* $\binom{d+1}{2}$ *of them. Each pair* *of variable nodes* $(x^{l_i} \oplus 0, x^{l_j} \oplus 0)$ *in* $\mathscr{G}$ *has at least one check node in common, namely* $x^{l_i+l_j}$.

This simple fact has a number of consequences concerning the influence that near codewords have on the counters. It will be helpful here to distinguish four kind of bits.

**Definition 2.4.** *Given a near codeword* $\boldsymbol{\nu}$ *and a error vector* $\mathbf{e}$ *intersecting* $\boldsymbol{\nu}$ *in* $u$ *positions, we classify the* $n$ *error vector bits into the four categories:*

- $u$ bad bits: *the* $u$ *bits belonging to the supports of both* $\mathbf{e}$ *and* $\boldsymbol{\nu}$*;*
- $d - u$ suspicious bits: *the other* $d - u$ *bits of* $\boldsymbol{\nu}$ *(not in the support of* $\mathbf{e}$*);*
- $t - u$ normal bits in error: *the other* $t - u$ *bits of* $\mathbf{e}$ *(not in the support of* $\boldsymbol{\nu}$*);*
- $n - d - t + u$ good bits: *neither in* $\boldsymbol{\nu}$ *nor* $\mathbf{e}$.

Bad bits and suspicious bits really display an abnormal behavior concerning the counters due to Fact 2 which explains why they are a nuisance for iterative decoding. Indeed we expect that the counters $\sigma_j$ behave like (to simplify the discussion we assume that $\boldsymbol{\nu} = h_0(x) \oplus 0$).

bad bit: $\sigma_j \sim \text{Bin}(u-1, \pi_0) + \text{Bin}(d-u+1, \pi_1)$. The bad bit which is some $x^{l_i} \oplus 0$ is adjacent to $u - 1$ check nodes of the form $x^{l_i+l_j}$ where $x^{l_j} \oplus 0$ is another bad bit. The contributions of these two bits for this parity-check cancel out, and this parity-check behaves in first approximation as a parity adjacent to a bit which is not in error. Its probability for not being satisfied is therefore $\pi_0$. Similarly the bad bit is adjacent to the check node $x^{2l_i}$ and $d - u$ check nodes of the form $x^{l_i+l_j}$ where $x^{l_j} \oplus 0$ is now a suspicious bit. In both cases, the contribution of those bits to the parity-check is 1 and these $d - u + 1$ parity-checks should behave as parity-checks adjacent to a bit which is in error, in which case the probability of not being satisfied is $\pi_1$.

sus. bit: $\sigma_j \sim \text{Bin}(u, \pi_1) + \text{Bin}(d - u, \pi_0)$. This comes from the fact that the suspicious bit which is some $x^{l_i} \oplus 0$ is adjacent to $u$ check nodes of the form $x^{l_i+l_j}$ where $x^{l_j} \oplus 0$ is a bad bit (they contribute together to 1 in the parity-check) and to $d - u$ check nodes of the form $x^{l_i+l_j}$ where $x^{l_j} \oplus 0$ is another suspicious bit (they contribute together to 0 in the parity-check).

An illustration of this principle is given in the full version of the paper [ALM+25, App. D]. Notice that the greater $u$ is, the greater the chances are to flip a suspicious bit which further increases $u$. This is what we call the snowball effect leading to a potential convergence to a near codeword. This error is readily seen to uncorrectable by further steps of iterative decoding.

## 3 Convergence to a Near Codeword in $\mathcal{N}$ in the Error Floor

To verify the convergence to a near codeword in the error floor region we have tested parameters for which we can experimentally observe the error floor behavior. We have chosen a random QC-MDPC code with $r = 1723$, $d = 17$ and tested two decoding algorithms:

1. The majority step-by-step decoder: $T = \frac{d+1}{2} = 9$. It flips a bit every time it decreases the syndrome weight. For this decoder, we expect to hit the error floor faster than for other decoders because it has the most chance to flip suspicious bits, thus getting the snowball effect described in Sect. 2.4.
2. An improved step-by-step decoder which uses a better (more conservative) decoding threshold. It starts with a high threshold value $T_0$ which favors to flip bits which are more likely to be in error. It is only when no bit can be flipped that a threshold $T_1 \leqslant T_0$ is used. For a syndrome weight $s$, $T_0$ and $T_1$ are given by: $T_0 = \min\{\max(\lfloor \alpha \cdot s + \beta \rfloor, \frac{d+1}{2})\}$, where $\alpha \stackrel{\text{def}}{=} 0.006016213884791455$, $\beta \stackrel{\text{def}}{=} 8.797325112097532$, $T_1 = \frac{d+1}{2}$.

Figure 2 shows the experimental results obtained for both decoders. It is a striking illustration of the phenomenon of convergence to a near codeword in the error floor regime for both decoders. The curves corresponding to the "better threshold" decoder correspond to a threshold pair $(T_0, T_1)$ given above. Together with the experimental curve we have drawn two other curves: "Contrib. of ncw" is the contribution to the DFR coming solely from the convergence to a near codeword. This contribution dominates in the error floor regime since the DFR is almost identical to this curve in this region. This can also be seen by removing from the DFR the contribution from the near codewords. These are the curves referred to as "Contr. of other". These curves show both a waterfall phenomenon and that, as we move further in the error floor region, the DFR contribution coming from convergence to a near codeword dominates the DFR.

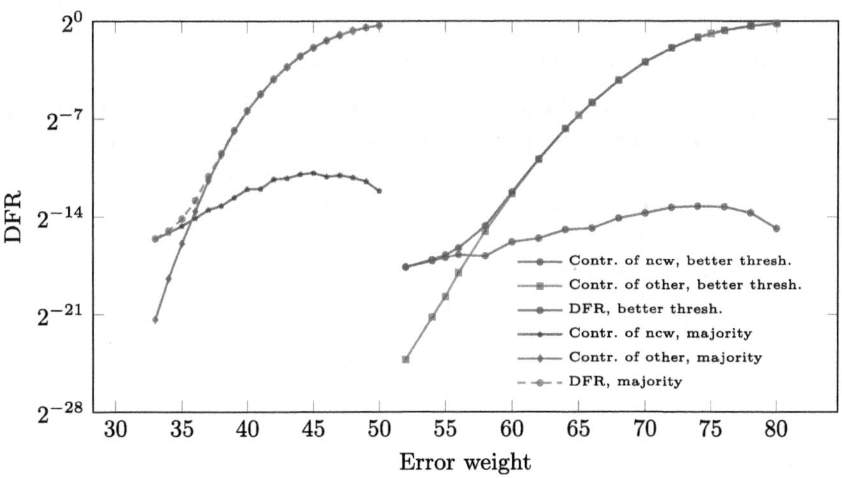


**Fig. 2.** DFR vs. error weight ($r = 1723$, $d = 17$), experimental curves.

# 4 Modeling Step-by-Step Decoding with a Markov Chain

## 4.1 The Markov Model

The Markov model introduced in [SV19b] kept track of the pair $(s, t)$ where $s$ and $t$ are respectively the syndrome weight and the error weight during the step-by-step decoding process. Here by error we mean the difference $\boldsymbol{e} - \boldsymbol{e}'$ between the true error $\boldsymbol{e}$ and the estimated error $\boldsymbol{e}'$ in Algorithm 1 and by syndrome we mean the syndrome of this difference, namely $\boldsymbol{H}(\boldsymbol{e} - \boldsymbol{e}')^{\intercal} = \boldsymbol{s}^{\intercal} - \boldsymbol{H}\boldsymbol{e}'^{\intercal}$ which is nothing but the vector $\Delta\boldsymbol{s}$ in Algorithm 1. This syndrome weight is therefore always decreasing during the decoding process and we hope to get an error weight of 0 at the end. The decoding process picks at random a certain error bit $j$ and checks if $\sigma_j \geqslant T(s)$. If it is the case, it flips it and the resulting syndrome has weight equal to $s + d - 2\sigma$. $t$ is either decreased or increased by 1 if the bit that is flipped was in error or not. It may also happen that all counters of the $n$ error bits are less than $T(s)$. In this case, we go to the blocked state and decoding has failed. If we get to the $(0, 0)$ state, decoding has succeeded.

This model does not take into account the crucial role of near codewords in the decoding process. Indeed, when the error has a large intersection with one of such near codewords, then it has also an influence on the syndrome weight which is smaller. For the two Markov models that we are considering, we are going to take near codewords into account in two ways: a first method consists in choosing a particular near codeword $\boldsymbol{\nu}$ and defines a quantity $u$ which is the size of the intersection of this near codeword with the residual error during iterative decoding. A second method defines $u$ as the size of the intersection of the error with the *closest* near codeword. In all cases, the Markov chain is defined in a similar way by letting the state be the triple $(s, t, u)$ (actually there is an additional bit $b$ in the definition of the state in the second method, but this is unessential for now). There are five transition cases:

- all bits have a counter which is too low to flip them. This we call the blocked state, denoted $\perp$. This corresponds to a decoding failure. This is an absorbing state of the Markov chain: once we are in this state, we stay in it. We denote by $p_{\perp}$ the probability that we are in this state.
- If there exists a bit which can be flipped, we choose one of such bits at random. We flip it and go to the state $(s + d - 2\sigma, t', u')$, where if it was a bad bit $t' = t - 1$ and $u' = u - 1$, a suspicious bit $t' = t + 1$ and $u' = u + 1$, a normal bit in error $t' = t - 1$ and $u' = u$, and a good bit $t' = t + 1$ and $u' = u$. Depending on whether the bit was respectively a bad bit, a normal bit in error, a suspicious bit or a good bit, we denote by $q_{\text{bad}}(\sigma)$, $q_{\text{err}}(\sigma)$, $q_{\text{sus}}(\sigma)$, $q_{\text{good}}(\sigma)$ the respective probabilities to flip the corresponding bit conditioned on the fact that there is at least one bit that we can flip. The corresponding transition probabilities are then $(1 - p_{\perp})q_{\cdot}(\sigma)$ where $\bullet \in \{\text{bad, err, sus, good}\}$.

The transitions are depicted in Fig. 3. All these probabilities can be computed easily once we have the counter probabilities $p_{\text{bad}}(\sigma)$, $p_{\text{err}}(\sigma)$, $p_{\text{sus}}(\sigma)$ and $p_{\text{good}}(\sigma)$ that a bit chosen uniformly at random among respectively the bad bits, the normal bits in error, the suspicious bits and the good bits, has a counter

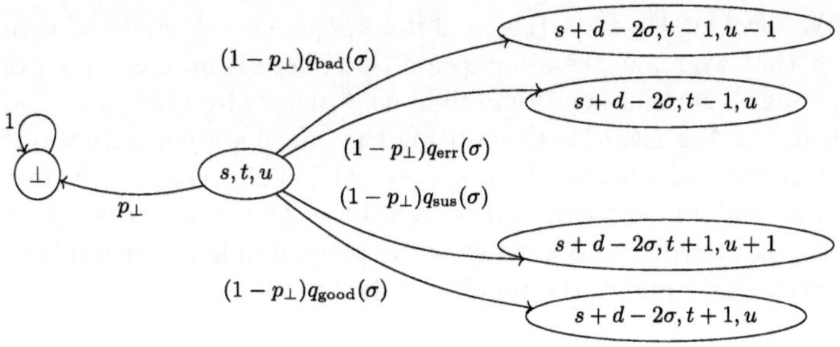


**Fig. 3.** Transition diagram starting with syndrome weight $s$, error weight $t$, and intersection $u$ with a $(d,d)$-near codeword $\boldsymbol{\nu}$.

equal to $\sigma$. If we let $p'_{\text{bad}}(\sigma)$, $p'_{\text{err}}(\sigma)$, $p'_{\text{sus}}(\sigma)$ and $p'_{\text{good}}(\sigma)$ the probabilities that a bit chosen uniformly at random has a counter equal to $\sigma$ and belongs respectively to the group **bad**, **norm**, **sus** and **good**, then clearly $p'_{\text{bad}}(\sigma) = \frac{u}{n}p_{\text{bad}}(\sigma)$, $p'_{\text{err}}(\sigma) = \frac{t-u}{n}p_{\text{err}}(\sigma)$, $p'_{\text{sus}}(\sigma) = \frac{d-u}{n(1-p)}p_{\text{sus}}(\sigma)$, $p'_{\text{good}}(\sigma) = \frac{(n-t)-(d-u)}{n(1-p)}p_{\text{good}}(\sigma)$. If we let $p \stackrel{\text{def}}{=} \sum_{\sigma<T}\left(p'_{\text{bad}}(\sigma)+p'_{\text{err}}(\sigma)+p'_{\text{sus}}(\sigma)+p'_{\text{good}}(\sigma)\right)$, then the transition probabilities of Fig. 3 are given by

$$p_\perp = \Big(\sum_{\sigma<T} p_{\text{bad}}(\sigma)\Big)^u \Big(\sum_{\sigma<T} p_{\text{err}}(\sigma)\Big)^{t-u} \Big(\sum_{\sigma<T} p'_{\text{sus}}(\sigma)\Big)^{d-u} \Big(\sum_{\sigma<T} p_{\text{good}}(\sigma)\Big)^{n-t-d+u},$$

$$q_{\text{bad}}(\sigma) = \frac{p'_{\text{bad}}(\sigma)}{1-p},\quad q_{\text{err}}(\sigma) = \frac{p'_{\text{err}}(\sigma)}{1-p},\quad q_{\text{sus}}(\sigma) = \frac{p'_{\text{sus}}(\sigma)}{1-p},\quad q_{\text{good}}(\sigma) = \frac{p'_{\text{good}}(\sigma)}{1-p}.$$

The probabilities of the counters $p_{\text{bad}}(\sigma)$, $p_{\text{err}}(\sigma)$, $p_{\text{sus}}(\sigma)$ and $p_{\text{good}}(\sigma)$ depend on the model and will be dealt with later in the paper.

### 4.2 Computing the DFR with the Help of the Markov Chain

Let us show now how to efficiently compute the stationary probability distribution $\mathbf{P}_\infty(\perp|s,t,u)$ which is the probability that, after an infinite number of iterations, we end up in the blocked state (where decoding fails). We let $\mathbf{P}(s',t',u'|s,t,u)$ be the probability of transitioning to state $(s',t',u')$ given that we were previously in state $(s,t,u)$. We make use of the following equality

$$\mathbf{P}_\infty(\perp|s,t,u) = \mathbf{P}(\perp|s,t,u) + \sum_{s',t',u'} \mathbf{P}_\infty(\perp|s',t',u') \cdot \mathbf{P}(s',t',u'|s,t,u) \quad (3)$$

along with the simple but crucial remark that the only transition probabilities $\mathbf{P}(s',t',u'|s,t,u)$ which are non zero have $s' < s$. This suggests to compute the probabilities $\mathbf{P}_\infty(\perp|s,t,u)$ by starting from $s = 0$ and increasing $s$ by 1 each time and the recursion formula (3) to compute the remaining ones. For $s = 0$ we set $\mathbf{P}_\infty(\perp|0,t,u) = 0$ if $t < 2d$ and $\mathbf{P}_\infty(\perp|0,t,u) = 1$ otherwise. The first rule accounts for the fact that there should be no codeword of weight less than

$w = 2d$. We also set $\mathbf{P}_\infty(\perp|s,t,u) = 0$ if $s < t(d-t+1)$ and $t \leqslant d$ to account for the fact that we make the assumption that there is no near-codeword of size $t < d$ which has a smaller syndrome than a subset of size $t$ of a near codeword of $\mathcal{N}$. This leads to Algorithm 2. Computing the initial state distribution $\mathbf{P}(s,t,u)$ is detailed in the full version of the paper [ALM+25, App. A]. Note that once this initial probability distribution is computed, the complexity for computing the DFR is just of order $O(E+S)$ where $E$ is the number of possible transitions in the Markov chain and $S$ the number of states.

**Algorithm 2.** Algorithm for computing the DFR

```
for all t, u do                                                  ▷ initialization
    if t < 2d then
        P∞(⊥|0, t, u) ← 0
    else
        P∞(⊥|0, t, u) ← 1
for all s, t, u s.t. s < t(d − t + 1) and t ⩽ d do
    P∞(⊥|0, t, u) ← 0
for s = 1 to s_max do                                            ▷ main loop
    for all t, u do
        P∞(⊥|s, t, u) ← Σ_{s'<s,t',u'} P∞(⊥|s', t', u') · P(s', t', u'|s, t, u) + P(⊥|s, t, u)
DFR ← Σ_{s,t,u} P∞(⊥|s, t, u) P(s, t, u).
```

## 5 A Simple Markovian Model

Since convergence to a near codeword dominates the error floor, it must be accounted for in a Markov state modeling the decoding process. Such states are triples $(s,t,u)$, where $s$ is the syndrome weight, $t$ is the error weight, and $u$ is the size of the intersection of the support of the error with a *fixed, random near codeword* $\boldsymbol{\nu}$. To amplify this effect by the size of the set of near codewords, we post-process the DFR obtained by this model together with a DFR obtained from a variant model which does not take into account the effect of near codewords. The equation used to combine these DFRs is given in Sect. 5.2. This is in contrast to the models used in Sect. 6), where only the effect of the closest near codeword is taken into account, and this remains the only near codeword which is assumed to have an effect on the decoding process.

**Model 1 (M).** *Let* $\mathbf{e}$ *be an error of weight* $t$ *with syndrome of weight* $s$*, and let* $\boldsymbol{\nu}$ *be a fixed random near codeword. Let* $u \stackrel{def}{=} |\mathbf{e} \star \boldsymbol{\nu}|$*. This model follows the values* $(s,t,u)$ *through the decoding process using a step-by-step decoder.*

**Model 2 (M0).** *Let* $\mathbf{e}$ *be an error of weight* $t$ *with syndrome of weight* $s$*. This model follows the same values as Model 1, but the value* $u$ *is set to 0 in the initial vector, so this model does not take into account the effect of a near codeword.*

Our model combining Models 1 and 2 according to the formula given in Sect. 5.2, is bound to see an error floor behavior: when the number of overlaps between an error vector and the near codeword becomes as large as possible (i.e., as $u$ approaches $d$), decoding fails, and the probability that $u = d$ at the beginning of decoding is lower bounded by $\frac{t^d}{n^d}$ where $t$ is the initial error weight. In the waterfall region, the DFR decays more than exponentially in $n$ with other parameters fixed and therefore this $\frac{t^d}{n^d}$ term is going to dominate and provoke an error floor phenomenon.

In summary: we distinguish bad, suspicious, normal, and good bits (Definition 2.4). We estimate the probabilities $\pi_0$ and $\pi_1$ to take into account $s$, $t$ and $u$. Recall $\pi_0$ is the probability that a parity-check adjacent to a given bit which is a good bit is not satisfied, and $\pi_1$ is the probability that a parity-check adjacent to a given bit which is a normal bit in error is not satisfied. The transition probabilities are obtained under the assumptions described in the following section.

### 5.1 Assumptions

The forced cancellations are a result of the quasi-cyclic structure of $\boldsymbol{H}$. For the remainder of Sect. 5, we make the heuristic assumption that the columns of $\boldsymbol{H}$ are drawn uniformly at random up to fixed column weight $d$.

For convenience of counting arguments, the error vector $\mathbf{e}$ may be permuted so that the bad, suspicious, normal, and good bits are collected. Let $\mathbf{Q}$ denote this permutation matrix. Likewise, the bits of the syndrome $\boldsymbol{s}$ may be permuted to collect the 1's and 0's. Let $\mathbf{P}$ denote this permutation matrix. Applying these permutations to the parity check matrix $\boldsymbol{H}$ and flipping the canceling pairs yields a matrix $\mathbf{H}'_{\text{eff}} := \mathbf{P}\boldsymbol{H}\mathbf{Q}$. Details may be found in the full version of the paper [ALM+25, App. C]. We use random variables to describe the columns of $\mathbf{H}'_{\text{eff}}$. Let $X_{\text{eff}} := \sum_{j \in \text{supp}(\boldsymbol{e})} \sigma_j - |\boldsymbol{s}|$. $X_{\text{eff}}$ measures the deviation from the ideal case where exactly one error is involved in each unsatisfied parity-check equation.

**Proposition 5.1.** *Assuming that the random variables that indicate the number of errors $|\boldsymbol{H}_i \star \mathbf{e}|$ for a given equation $i$ are independent and if $|\mathbf{e}| = t$, the expectation of $X_{\mathit{eff}}$ knowing $s$, $t$, and $u = |\mathbf{e} \star \boldsymbol{\nu}|$ is*

$$E[X_{\mathit{eff}}|s,t,u] = s \cdot \frac{\sum_l 2l\rho_{2l+1}}{\sum_l \rho_{2l+1}}, \text{ where} \tag{4}$$

$$\rho_l = \sum_{j=0}^{l} \binom{t-u}{j}\binom{u}{l-j}\left(\frac{d}{r}\right)^j\left(\frac{r-d}{r}\right)^{t-u-j}\left(\frac{d+1-u}{r}\right)^{l-j}\left(\frac{r-d-1+u}{r}\right)^{u-l+j} \tag{5}$$

*is the probability that any row in $\mathbf{H}'_{\mathit{eff}}$ restricted to the support of $\mathbf{e}$ has weight $l$.*

*Proof.* For any row $i \in \{0, \dots, r-1\}$ in $\mathbf{H}'_{\text{eff}}$, consider the $t$ columns corresponding to the support of $\boldsymbol{e}$. There are $t-u$ columns corresponding to bits in $\text{supp}(\boldsymbol{e})\backslash\text{supp}(\boldsymbol{\nu})$ and $u$ columns corresponding to bits in $\text{supp}(\boldsymbol{e}) \cap \text{supp}(\boldsymbol{\nu})$. All columns in $\text{supp}(\boldsymbol{e})\backslash\text{supp}(\boldsymbol{\nu})$ have weight $d$ and all columns in $\text{supp}(\boldsymbol{e}) \cap \text{supp}(\boldsymbol{\nu})$

have weight $d + 1 - u$ due to forced cancellations. Any entry in row $i$ on $\text{supp}(e) \setminus \text{supp}(\boldsymbol{\nu})$ has probability $\frac{d}{r}$ of being nonzero and probability $\frac{r-d}{r}$ of being zero. Any entry in row $i$ on $\text{supp}(\boldsymbol{e}) \cap \text{supp}(\boldsymbol{\nu})$ has probability $\frac{d+1-u}{r}$ of being nonzero and probability $\frac{r-d-1+u}{r}$ of being zero.

**Assumption 1.** *The counters $\sigma_j$ follow binomial distributions:*

$$\sigma_j \sim \begin{cases} \text{Bin}(d, \pi_0) & \textit{if } j \textit{ is a good bit} \\ \text{Bin}(d, \pi_1) & \textit{if } j \textit{ is a normal bit} \\ \text{Bin}(d-u, \pi_0) + \text{Bin}(u, \pi_1) & \textit{if } j \textit{ is a suspicious bit} \\ \text{Bin}(d-u+1, \pi_1) + \text{Bin}(u-1, \pi_0) & \textit{if } j \textit{ is a bad bit} \end{cases} \tag{6}$$

*where*

$$\pi_0 = \frac{s}{r}, \quad \pi_1 = \frac{s + \xi E[X_{\mathit{eff}}|s,t,u]}{s_{max}}, \quad s_{max} = d \cdot t - 2\binom{u}{2}$$

*for some constant $\xi$.*

*Remark 5.2.* The probability estimate $\pi_0$ in Assumption 1 is particularly pessimistic. Indeed, it is the probability that a *random* parity check is not satisfied, which is certainly an upper bound for the probability that a parity check corresponding to a bit which is not in error is unsatisfied. The model in Sect. 6 uses a more refined estimate of the probability $\pi_0$.

*Remark 5.3.* The constant $\xi$ in Assumption 1 is inherited from a refinement given in [Vas21] of the previous Markov model [SV19b]. Reducing the value of $\xi$ from 1 was intended to compensate for Non-Markovian effects relative to the state information $(s, t)$ used in that model, which would otherwise produce an overly optimistic DFR. The experimental data in Fig. 4 assumes the same value $\xi = 0.955$ used by [Vas21], which further contributes to the pessimism of Assumption 1 as reflected in our experimental data. There is no analogous factor to $\xi$ used in Sect. 6.

**Assumption 2.** *The step-by-step bit flipping decoder is a time homogeneous Markov chain, meaning that the transition probabilities are time invariant.*

**Markov end States.** There are two possible Markov end states that dominate the experiment findings: $(0, 0, 0)$ when we have successful decoding or $(d, d, d)$ when the state converges to a $(d, d)$-near codeword.

### 5.2 Markov Model Estimation of the DFR

Our simple Markov model experiments yield the decoding failure rate under the assumptions of models 2 and 1. Model 2 assumes no effect of the near codewords $\mathcal{N}$ on the decoding failure rate and Model 1 records the effect of a single near codeword on the decoding failure rate. Model 2 uses the same code but initializes the value of $u$ to 0 in the initial vector.

Let DFR(M) and DFR(M0) denote the respective decoding failure rates of Model 1 and 2. The true decoding failure rate denoted by DFR, is estimated by taking into account the existence of $|\mathcal{N}| = r$ near codewords. The difference $\text{DFR}(M) - \text{DFR}(M0)$ accounts for the number of decoding failures due to the existence of one near codeword, so $|\mathcal{N}|(\text{DFR}(M) - \text{DFR}(M0))$ gives the increase in DFR due to the existence of $|\mathcal{N}|$ near codewords. This gives the formula:

$$\text{DFR} = \text{DFR}(M0) + |\mathcal{N}|(\text{DFR}(M) - \text{DFR}(M0)). \tag{7}$$

This assumes an additive effect of the elements of $\mathcal{N}$ on DFR, and we refer to Eq. (7) as the *linear model* (see Fig. 4). We compare our data with experimental data obtained using [Vas24], as well as a previous Markov model [SV19b] which does not take into account the effect of the error having a large number of overlaps with a near codeword. The Simple Markov model gives a more conservative estimate for the DFR, in instances where models not taking into account the effect of near codewords underestimate the DFR.

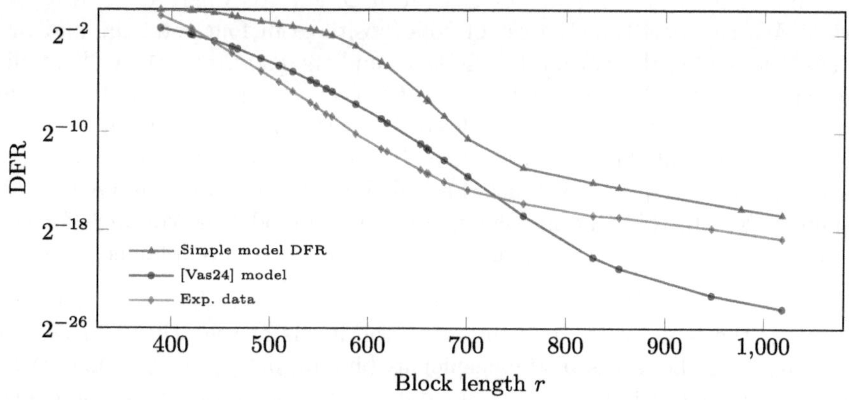


**Fig. 4.** Plot of experimental DFR data, Simple Markov model DFR, and the DFR of the Markov model described in [SV19b].

## 6 A Key Dependent Markov Model

The simplified model does not depend on the secret key. However, experimental evidence shows that the DFR is definitely key dependent: Even if it does not vary much for typical keys, there are rare keys for which this DFR behaves better and weak keys which behave significantly worse. In this section, we give a way to predict the iterative decoding performance which is key dependent. It makes use of the degree distribution of the subgraph $\mathscr{G}$ of the Tanner graph associated to the near codeword closest to $e' + e$ denoted in the whole section by $\boldsymbol{\nu}$.

### 6.1 Derivation of the Markov Chain Model

**The State Space.** The state space is the set of $(s, t, u, b)$ where $s = |\Delta\mathbf{s}|$ and $t = |\mathbf{e} + \mathbf{e}'|$ as before, $u = |(\mathbf{e} + \mathbf{e}') \star \boldsymbol{\nu}|$ and $b \in \{0, 1\}$ encodes whether or not $\boldsymbol{\nu}$ is $x^a h_0(x) \oplus 0$ (a *left near codeword*) or $0 \oplus x^b h_1(x)$ (a *right near codeword*). The structure of $\mathscr{G}$ depends on $b$. Its degree structure is given by the following proposition which follows immediately from Fact 2

**Proposition 6.1.** *The parity checks of even degree* $2m$ *in the subgraph* $\mathscr{G}$ *corresponding to a left near codeword are associated to sets of* $m$ *different pairs* $\{l_{a_1}, l_{b_1}\}, \cdots, \{l_{a_m}, l_{b_m}\}$ *such that* $l_{a_1} + l_{b_1} = \cdots = l_{a_m} + l_{b_m}$*, where the* $a_i$*'s and the* $b_i$*'s all belong to* $\{0, \cdots, d-1\}$ *and* $a_i \neq b_i$ *for all* $i \in \{1, \cdots, m\}$.

*The parity checks of odd degree* $2m+1$ *in* $\mathscr{G}$ *are associated to an* $a \in \{0, \cdots, d-1\}$ *and sets of* $m$ *different pairs* $\{l_{a_1}, l_{b_1}\}, \cdots, \{l_{a_m}, l_{b_m}\}$ *such that* $2l_a = l_{a_1} + l_{b_1} = \cdots = l_{a_m} + l_{b_m}$*, where* $a_i, b_i \in \{0, \cdots, d-1\}$ *and* $a_i \neq b_i$ *for all* $i \in \{1, \cdots, m\}$.

A similar proposition holds for right near codewords where the $r_i$'s replace the $l_i$'s. We can partition the set of code positions in four sets, the bad bits, the suspicious bits, the normal bits in error and the good bits. We will simplify notation in what follows and label a parity check $x^a$ simply by $a$. We assume from now on that the closest near-codeword $\boldsymbol{\nu}$ to the error intersects it in exactly $u$ positions and that the error has weight $t$. We also assume that $\boldsymbol{\nu} = h_0(x) \oplus 0$. The case $\boldsymbol{\nu} = 0 \oplus h_1(x)$ is similar. The label $x^a \oplus 0$ of a variable node is also simplified to $a$. In this section, we explain how we model the counters for each kind of bits. This will lead to Model 3 which is then used as explained in Sect. 4.

**The Case of Bad Bits.** We have three kinds of parity checks adjacent to a bad bit. If the label of the bad bit is $a_1$, the labels of the other bad bits are $a_2, \cdots, a_u$, and the labels of the suspicious bits are $a_{u+1}, \cdots, a_d$, then we can group the parity check nodes adjacent to $a_1$. The first group consists of a single parity check node of odd degree in $\mathscr{G}$ labeled $2a_1$. The second group consists of $(u-1)$ parity check nodes labeled $a_1 + a_2, \cdots, a_1 + a_u$. The third group consists of $(d-u)$ parity check nodes labeled $a_1 + a_{u+1}, \cdots, a_1 + a_d$.

We do not know the label $a_1, \cdots, a_u$, and we model the probability that the corresponding parity checks are unsatisfied by using the following lemma.

**Lemma 6.2.** *Let* $a$ *be a bad bit and let*

- $\rho^{b,1}_{\Delta,\ell}$ *be the probability that the parity check labeled* $2a$ *is adjacent to* $\ell$ *bits in error given that it is of degree* $\Delta$ *in* $\mathscr{G}$;
- $\rho^{b,2}_{\Delta,\ell}$ *be the probability that a parity check labeled* $a + b$ *of degree* $\Delta$ *in* $\mathscr{G}$ *is adjacent to* $\ell$ *bits in error given that it* $b$ *is another bad bit;*
- $\rho^{b,3}_{\Delta,\ell}$ *be the probability that a parity check labeled* $a + b$ *is adjacent to* $\ell$ *bits in error given that it is of degree* $\Delta$ *in* $\mathscr{G}$*, that* $b$ *is a suspicious bit;*

*Then*

$$\rho^{b,1}_{\Delta,\ell} = \frac{\sum_{j=1}^{\min(\Delta,\ell)} \binom{\Delta-1}{j-1}\binom{d-\Delta}{u-j}\binom{w-\Delta}{\ell-j}\binom{n-d-w+\Delta}{t-u-\ell+j}}{\binom{d-1}{u-1}\binom{n-d}{t-u}}$$

$$\rho^{b,2}_{\Delta,\ell} = \frac{\sum_{j=2}^{\min(\Delta,\ell)} \binom{\Delta-2}{j-2}\binom{d-\Delta}{u-j}\binom{w-\Delta}{\ell-j}\binom{n-d-w+\Delta}{t-u-\ell+j}}{\binom{d-2}{u-2}\binom{n-d}{t-u}}$$

$$\rho^{b,3}_{\Delta,\ell} = \frac{\sum_{j=1}^{\min(\Delta,\ell)} \binom{\Delta-2}{j-1}\binom{d-\Delta}{u-j}\binom{w-\Delta}{\ell-j}\binom{n-d-w+\Delta}{t-u-\ell+j}}{\binom{d-2}{u-1}\binom{n-d}{t-u}}.$$

*Proof.* The reasoning is similar in all three cases.

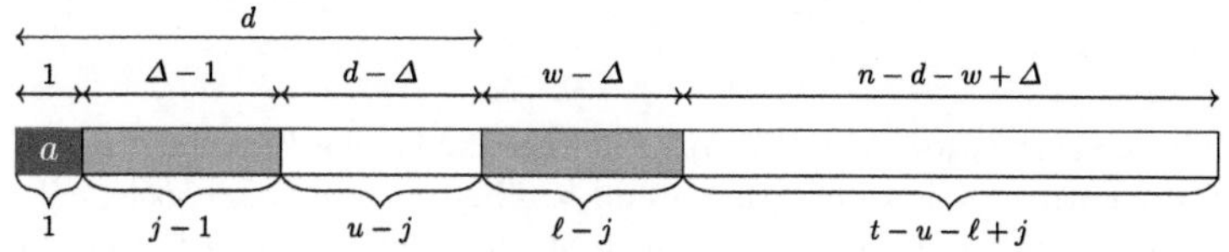


**Fig. 5.** The configuration of the error and the parity check. The black and pink are the positions of the parity check. The numbers on top are the block sizes. The numbers below are the number of errors in each block. The first block of size 1 is the bad bit $a$. The second block consists of the other positions involved in the parity check and the support of $\boldsymbol{\nu}$. The third block consists of the positions in the support of $\boldsymbol{\nu}$ not involved in the parity check equation. The fourth block consists of the positions of the parity check which are not in the support of $\boldsymbol{\nu}$. The last block contains the remaining positions.

*The Formula for* $\rho^{b,1}_{\Delta,\ell}$. We compute the probability that an error of weight $t$ which has weight $u$ on the $d$ bits of the near-codeword $\boldsymbol{\nu}$ and $t-u$ on the complement of the support of $\boldsymbol{\nu}$ intersects a given parity check of weight $w$ in exactly $\ell$ positions. The parity check $2a$ involves the bad bit $a$ we are interested in, plus $\Delta - 1$ other bits of $\boldsymbol{\nu}$. If we denote by $\rho^{b,1}_{\Delta,\ell,j}$ the probability that this error is also of weight $j$ on the $\Delta$ bits which belong at the same time to the support of the parity check labeled $2a$ and the support of $\boldsymbol{\nu}$, then we have

$$\rho^{b,1}_{\Delta,\ell,j} = \frac{\binom{\Delta-1}{j-1}\binom{d-\Delta}{u-j}\binom{w-\Delta}{\ell-j}\binom{n-d-w+\Delta}{t-u-\ell+j}}{\binom{d-1}{u-1}\binom{n-d}{t-u}}$$

This can be verified by counting the number of ways the $\binom{d-1}{u-1}\binom{n-d}{t-u}$ configurations of $t-1$ errors where there are $u-1$ errors among the $d-1$ bits of $\boldsymbol{\nu}$ other than the bad bit $a$ we are interested in satisfy all the needed constraints. Figure 5 gives a picture of the configuration we are interested in. This yields the formula for $\rho^{b,1}_{\Delta,\ell}$ by summing over all possible values of $j$.

*The Formula for* $\rho^{b,2}_{\Delta,\ell}$. We introduce $\rho^{b,2}_{\Delta,\ell,j}$, the probability that the error is also of weight $j$ on the $\Delta$ bits which belong to the support of the parity check labeled

$a+b$ and the support of $\boldsymbol{\nu}$. Then,

$$\rho^{b,2}_{\Delta,\ell,j} = \frac{\binom{\Delta-2}{j-2}\binom{d-\Delta}{u-j}\binom{w-\Delta}{\ell-j}\binom{n-d-w+\Delta}{t-u-\ell+j}}{\binom{d-2}{u-2}\binom{n-d}{t-u}}$$

Figure 6 displays the corresponding configuration. The difference is that now the parity check labeled $a+b$ contains two bits which are in error, namely $a$ and $b$.

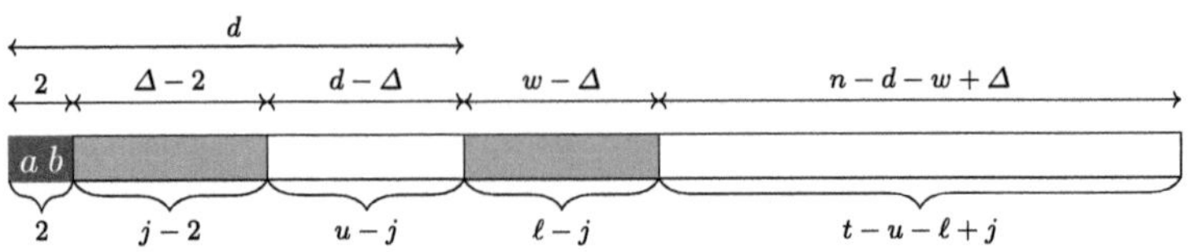


**Fig. 6.** The configuration of the error and the parity check, as in Fig. 5. The first block of size 2 corresponds to bad bits $a$ and $b$. The second block consists of the other positions involved in the parity check which are in the support of the near codeword $\boldsymbol{\nu}$. The last three blocks are as in Fig. 5.

*The Formula for* $\rho^{b,3}_{\Delta,\ell}$. This uses a similar reasoning, with the only difference that the parity check labeled $a+b$ contains by definition a bit which is in error, namely $a$ and a bit which is not in error, namely $b$. □

**Proposition 6.3.** *For* $g \in \{1,2,3\}$, *let* $\overline{\pi^{b,g}}$ *be the average probability that a parity check of group* $g$ *associated to a bad bit is unsatisfied. Then*

$$\overline{\pi^{b,1}} = \frac{1}{d}\sum_{a\in\boldsymbol{\nu}}\sum_{\ell}\rho^{b,1}_{\deg(2a),2\ell+1},$$

$$\overline{\pi^{b,g}} = \frac{1}{d(d-1)}\sum_{\substack{a\in\boldsymbol{\nu}\\ b\in\boldsymbol{\nu},\ b\neq a}}\sum_{\ell}\rho^{b,g}_{\deg(a+b),2\ell+1}, \quad \textit{for } g \geqslant 2,$$

*where* $\deg(c)$ *is the degree of the parity check node* $c$ *in* $\mathscr{G}$.

*Proof.* The probability that the parity check labeled $2a$ associated to a bad bit $a$ is unsatisfied is $\sum_{\ell}\rho^{b,1}_{\deg(2a),2\ell+1}$. The average is taken over all possible bits of the near codeword $\boldsymbol{\nu}$. The reasoning is the same for $\overline{\pi^{b,g}}$, the only difference is that we take the average over all possible edges leaving a variable node labeled $a$ to a check node labeled $a+b$ for all possible $b$'s different from $a$. □

**The Case of Suspicious Bits.** The case of a suspicious bit is similar to the case of a bad bit. We partition the parity checks associated to it in three groups, as we did for a bad bit. There is a single parity check in the first group associated to a suspicious bit $a$, namely the parity check labeled $2a$. The second group contains $d-u-1$ other parity checks labeled $a+b$ where $b$ is another suspicious bit. The last group contains $u$ parity check bits labeled $a+b$ where $b$ is a bad bit.

**Lemma 6.4.** *Let a be a suspicious bit and let*

- $\rho^{s,1}_{\Delta,\ell}$ *be the probability that the parity check labeled* $2a$ *in* $\mathcal{G}$ *is adjacent to* $\ell$ *bits in error given that it is of degree* $\Delta$ *in* $\mathcal{G}$*;*
- $\rho^{s,2}_{\Delta,\ell}$ *be the probability that a parity check labeled* $a+b$ *is adjacent to* $\ell$ *bits in error given that it is of degree* $\Delta$ *in* $\mathcal{G}$ *and* $b$ *is another suspicious bit;*
- $\rho^{s,3}_{\Delta,\ell}$ *be the probability that a parity check labeled* $a+b$ *is adjacent to* $\ell$ *bits in error given that it is of degree* $\Delta$ *in* $\mathcal{G}$*, that* $b$ *is a bad bit.*

*Then*

$$\rho^{s,1}_{\Delta,\ell} = \frac{\sum_{j=0}^{\min(\Delta,\ell)} \binom{\Delta-1}{j}\binom{d-\Delta}{u-j}\binom{w-\Delta}{\ell-j}\binom{n-d-w+\Delta}{t-u-\ell+j}}{\binom{d-1}{u}\binom{n-d}{t-u}}$$

$$\rho^{s,2}_{\Delta,\ell} = \frac{\sum_{j=0}^{\min(\Delta,\ell)} \binom{\Delta-2}{j}\binom{d-\Delta}{u-j}\binom{w-\Delta}{\ell-j}\binom{n-d-w+\Delta}{t-u-\ell+j}}{\binom{d-2}{u}\binom{n-d}{t-u}}$$

$$\rho^{s,3}_{\Delta,\ell} = \frac{\sum_{j=1}^{\min(\Delta,\ell)} \binom{\Delta-2}{j-1}\binom{d-\Delta}{u-j}\binom{w-\Delta}{\ell-j}\binom{n-d-w+\Delta}{t-u-\ell+j}}{\binom{d-2}{u-1}\binom{n-d}{t-u}}.$$

**Proposition 6.5.** *For* $g \in \{1,2,3\}$*, let* $\overline{\pi^{s,g}}$ *be the average probability that a parity check of group* $g$ *associated to a suspicious bit is unsatisfied. Then*

$$\overline{\pi^{s,1}} = \frac{1}{d}\sum_{a\in\boldsymbol{\nu}}\sum_{\ell}\rho^{s,1}_{\deg(2a),2\ell+1}$$

$$\overline{\pi^{s,g}} = \frac{1}{d(d-1)}\sum_{\substack{a\in\boldsymbol{\nu}\\ b\in\boldsymbol{\nu},\, b\neq a}}\sum_{\ell}\rho^{s,g}_{\deg(a+b),2\ell+1}, \text{ for } g \geqslant 2.$$

*Here* $\deg(c)$ *refers to the degree of the parity check node* $c$ *in* $\mathcal{G}$*.*

**The Case of Normal Bits in Error.** We do not need to distinguish several groups of parity checks in this case.

**Proposition 6.6.** *Let* $\rho^{e}_{\Delta,\ell}$ *be the probability that a parity check node of degree* $\Delta$ *in the subgraph* $\mathcal{G}$ *of the Tanner graph induced by* $\boldsymbol{\nu}$ *and adjacent to a normal bit in error contains exactly* $\ell$ *erroneous bits. A parity check not in* $\mathcal{G}$ *is said to be degree of* 0*. We also let* $\overline{\pi^{e}}$ *be the average of these probabilities over all edges of the Tanner graph leaving the bits which are not in* $\boldsymbol{\nu}$*.*

$$\rho^{e}_{\Delta,\ell} = \frac{\sum_{j=0}^{\min(\Delta,\ell-1)} \binom{\Delta}{j}\binom{d-\Delta}{u-j}\binom{w-\Delta-1}{\ell-j-1}\binom{n-d-w+\Delta}{t-u-\ell+j}}{\binom{d}{u}\binom{n-d-1}{t-u-1}} \quad (8)$$

$$\overline{\pi^{e}} = \frac{1}{d(n-d)}\sum_{\Delta}(w-\Delta)n_{\Delta}\sum_{\ell}\rho^{e}_{\Delta,2\ell+1}, \quad (9)$$

*where* $n_{\Delta}$ *is the number of check nodes in the subgraph* $\mathcal{G}$ *of the Tanner graph induced by* $\boldsymbol{\nu}$ *which are of degree* $\Delta$*.*

*Proof.* The reasoning for (8) is similar to what is done for Lemma 6.2 and is omitted. For computing the average of (8), observe that there are $d(n-d)$ edges in the Tanner graph leaving the $n-d$ positions which are not in $\boldsymbol{\nu}$. $\overline{\rho^e_{\Delta,\ell}}$ is nothing but the average probability over all edges that such an edge is adjacent to a check node which is not satisfied. If such a check node is of degree $\Delta$ in $\mathscr{G}$, then the probability that it is in error is exactly $\sum_\ell \rho^e_{\Delta,2\ell+1}$. There are exactly $(w-\Delta)n_\Delta$ edges of this kind that are adjacent to a check node of degree $\Delta$ in $\mathscr{G}$. This explains (9).

**The Case of Good Bits.** This case is similar to the case of normal bits in error.

**Proposition 6.7.** *Let $\rho^g_{\Delta,\ell}$ be the probability that a parity check node of $\mathscr{G}$ of degree $\Delta$ adjacent to a good bit contains exactly $\ell$ erroneous bits. We also let $\overline{\pi^g}$ be the average of these probabilities over all edges of the Tanner graph leaving the bits which are not in $\boldsymbol{\nu}$. We have*

$$\rho^g_{\Delta,\ell} = \frac{\sum_{j=0}^{\min(\Delta,\ell)} \binom{\Delta}{j}\binom{d-\Delta}{u-j}\binom{w-\Delta-1}{\ell-j}\binom{n-d-w+\Delta}{t-u-\ell+j}}{\binom{d}{u}\binom{n-d-1}{t-u}} \tag{10}$$

$$\overline{\pi^g} = \frac{1}{d(n-d)} \sum_\Delta (w-\Delta)n_\Delta \sum_\ell \rho^g_{\Delta,2\ell+1}, \tag{11}$$

This analysis of bad, suspicious, normal, and good bits yields the following model:

**Model 3.** *We model the counters $\sigma_i$ according to the type of bit:*

- *bad bit:* $\sigma_i \sim \mathrm{Bin}(1, \frac{s\overline{\pi^{b,1}}}{\mathbb{E}(s|t,u)}) + \mathrm{Bin}(u-1, \frac{s\overline{\pi^{b,2}}}{\mathbb{E}(s|t,u)}) + \mathrm{Bin}(d-u, \frac{s\overline{\pi^{b,3}}}{\mathbb{E}(s|t,u)})$
- *suspicious bit:* $\sigma_i \sim \mathrm{Bin}(1, \frac{s\overline{\pi^{s,1}}}{\mathbb{E}(s|t,u)}) + \mathrm{Bin}(d-u-1, \frac{s\overline{\pi^{s,2}}}{\mathbb{E}(s|t,u)}) + \mathrm{Bin}(u, \frac{s\overline{\pi^{s,3}}}{\mathbb{E}(s|t,u)})$
- *normal bit in error:* $\sigma_i \sim \mathrm{Bin}(d, \frac{s\overline{\pi^e}}{\mathbb{E}(s|t,u)})$
- *good bit:* $\sigma_i \sim \mathrm{Bin}(d, \frac{s\overline{\pi^g}}{\mathbb{E}(s|t,u)})$

*where $\mathbb{E}(s|t,u)$ is given by:*

$$\begin{aligned}\mathbb{E}(s|t,u) = \frac{1}{w}\Big(&u\overline{\pi^{b,1}} + u(u-1)\overline{\pi^{b,2}} + u(d-u)\overline{\pi^{b,3}} + (d-u)\overline{\pi^{s,1}}\\ &+ (d-u)(d-u-1)\overline{\pi^{s,2}} + (d-u)u\overline{\pi^{s,3}} + (t-u)d\overline{\pi^e} + (n+u-t-d)d\overline{\pi^g}\Big)\end{aligned}$$

### 6.2 Results

First, we checked this new model on the same toy example of Sect. 5 with a random key (see Fig. 7). It gives a much better behavior in the waterfall region than the previous model. We partition decoding failures both in the experiments and in the model in two parts: the decodings that failed because they converged to a near codeword ("Contr. of ncw") and the rest of the decoding failures (called "Contr. of other"). The models and the experiments agree remarkably well.

We also tested two different step-by-step decoders on the same code: one which uses the majority rule for the threshold, and another one which uses the decoder with two thresholds $T_0$ and $T_1$, see Fig. 2. There is a first conservative threshold to flip the bits initially, and a second threshold (actually the majority rule) to flip the bits when there are no more bit flips to perform with the first rule. This decoder is much better than the majority decoder.

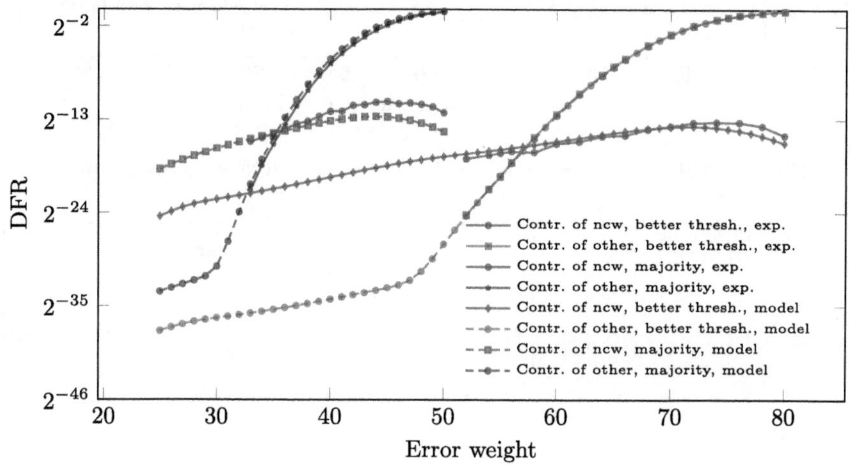


**Fig. 7.** DFR vs. error weight ($r = 1723$, $d = 17$), experiments vs. model.

In [Vas21] which compared parallel decoders to similar step-by-step decoders, the performance of the parallel decoders was much better than those of the step-by-step decoders. However, the step-by-step decoder with two thresholds used to draw Fig. 7 is rather competitive with the parallel BGF decoder of BIKE, see Fig. 8. This seems to confirm that there is a significant gain in choosing conservative thresholds in the early iterations, as observed in [Sen24]. The BGF decoder is slightly superior to the step-by-step decoder, with a somewhat steeper waterfall and a better error floor.

After all this experimental evidence, we ran the model of this section on a key chosen at random for the step-by-step decoder by choosing several different thresholds for various block sizes for $d = 71$ and $t = 134$. See Fig. 9.

We checked the influence of the gap parameter $\delta$ used for decoding. Here the threshold $T$ depends only on the syndrome weight $s$, the block length $r$, the error weight $t$ and the gap parameter $\delta$ as follows

$$T = \min\left(d, \max\left(\lfloor A_{r,t}(s) + \delta \rfloor, \frac{d+1}{2}\right)\right), \tag{12}$$

where $A_{r,t}(s)$ is an affine function $\alpha \cdot s + \beta$ of $s$ depending on $r$ and $t$ which is computed with the same method as for BIKE. For $t = 134$ and various values of $r$, the coefficients are given in the full version of the paper [ALM+25, App. B].

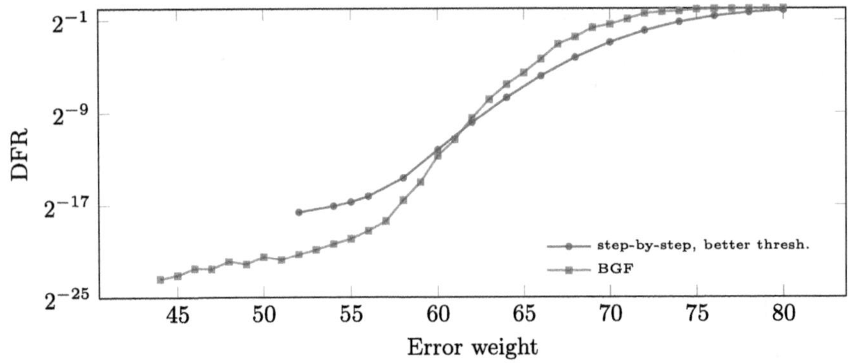


**Fig. 8.** DFR vs. error weight ($r = 1723$, $d = 17$), BGF vs. step-by-step.

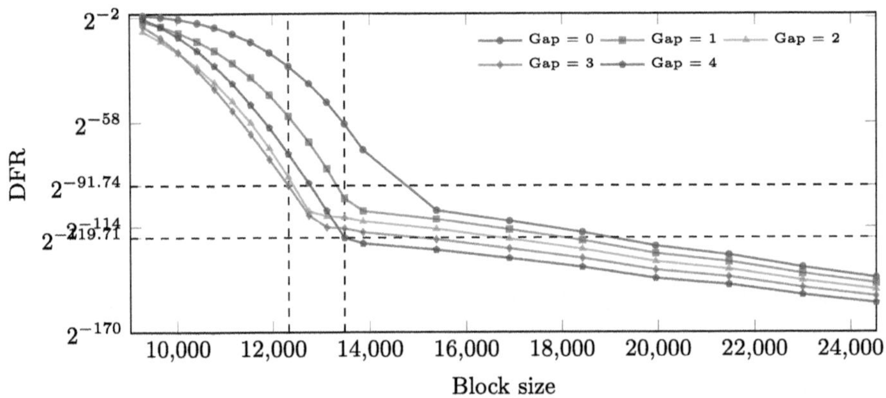


**Fig. 9.** DFR vs. block size ($d = 71$, $t = 134$).

Using the same gap parameter $\delta = 3$ as the one used in the latest BIKE decoder seems in the model to be optimal for the actual BIKE 1 parameter: $r = 12323$. It results in a DFR of about $2^{-91.7}$, unfortunately above $2^{-\lambda}$. Moreover, even if we increase the block length $r$ we do not improve the DFR by much, because the error floor kicks in right after this value of $r$. We attain a DFR of $2^{-114.1}$ with this gap for $r = 13109$, but need to go to $r = 18427$ to go below $2^{-\lambda}$. Using a gap $\delta$ equal to 4 allows to an error floor which appears a little bit later and allows to obtain a DFR which is about $2^{-119.6}$ for $r = 13477$. This $r$-value is less than 10 percent more than the actual BIKE parameter.

**Experimental Evidence for Cryptographic Parameters in the Waterfall Region.** However there is a caveat here. It appears that taking a larger threshold function affects the accuracy of the waterfall prediction. Indeed, we have performed two kinds of experiments for values of $r$ close to the BIKE 1 parameters and the same $d$ and $t$ as BIKE 1 so as to be able to observe experimentally the DFR. We are here at the beginning of the waterfall. Figure 10 shows that the model predicts accurately the waterfall behavior when $\delta = 1$, but the predictions become clearly optimistic when $\delta$ increases (here we show the value $\delta = 3$. More experimental evidence can be found in the full version of the paper [ALM+25].

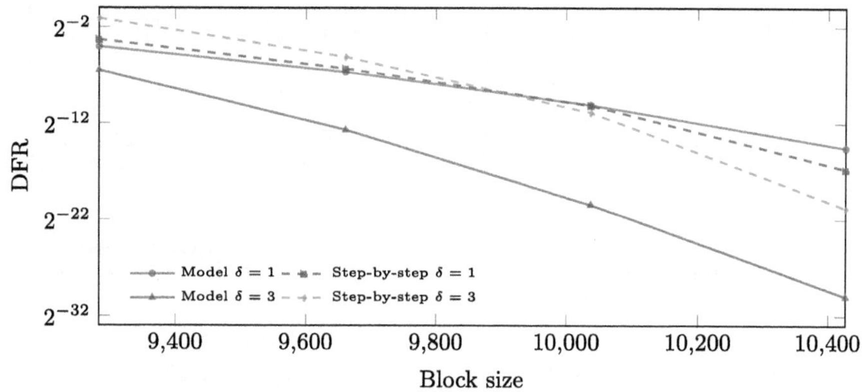


**Fig. 10.** Waterfall behavior ($d = 71$, $t = 134$), gap $\delta \in \{1, 3\}$.

**Evidence that the Error Floor Behavior is Always Captured Accurately.** To have a better understanding of the influence of $\delta$, we have performed a systematic study on the toy parameters $(r, d) = (1723, 17)$. First we have chosen $t = 65$ to be in the waterfall region. The results are displayed in Fig. 11a. There are several interesting features. The DFR is split in two parts as $\text{DFR} = \text{DFR}_\text{e} + \text{DFR}_\text{w}$, where $\text{DFR}_\text{e}$ corresponds to the convergence to a near codeword. It can be computed experimentally when $\text{DFR}_\text{e}$ is large enough. The Markov model can also give the corresponding contribution. The term $\text{DFR}_\text{w}$ (as "waterfall" contribution and "other" in legend of the figure) can be viewed as the waterfall contribution and is defined simply as $\text{DFR} - \text{DFR}_\text{e}$. In Fig. 11a we are in the waterfall region since $\text{DFR} \approx \text{DFR}_\text{w}$ or what amounts to the same $\text{DFR}_\text{e} \ll \text{DFR}_\text{w}$. The Markov chain predictions are slightly pessimistic when $\delta$ is in the interval $[0, 1]$ but become optimistic in the case $\delta \in [1, 3]$. However, what is remarkable is that the predictions for the error floor term $\text{DFR}_\text{e}$ are in general really accurate for a gap bigger than 0.5. This strongly suggests that the Markov model predicts accurately the error floor behavior irrespective of the gap parameter.

This has been further tested in Fig. 11b with $(r, d, t) = (1723, 17, 35)$. This time we are in the error floor since $\text{DFR}_\text{w} \ll \text{DFR}_\text{e}$. The predictions for the DFR are here rather accurate (even if a little bit pessimistic). The experimental DFR and predicted DFR agree this time for all values of the gap parameter between 0 and 3. This shows the accuracy of the error floor prediction for our model.

We can extend experiments much beyond the toy parameters by noticing that we can decompose the DFR as $\text{DFR} = \sum_{u=1}^{d} \text{DFR}(u)p(u)$, where $\text{DFR}(u)$

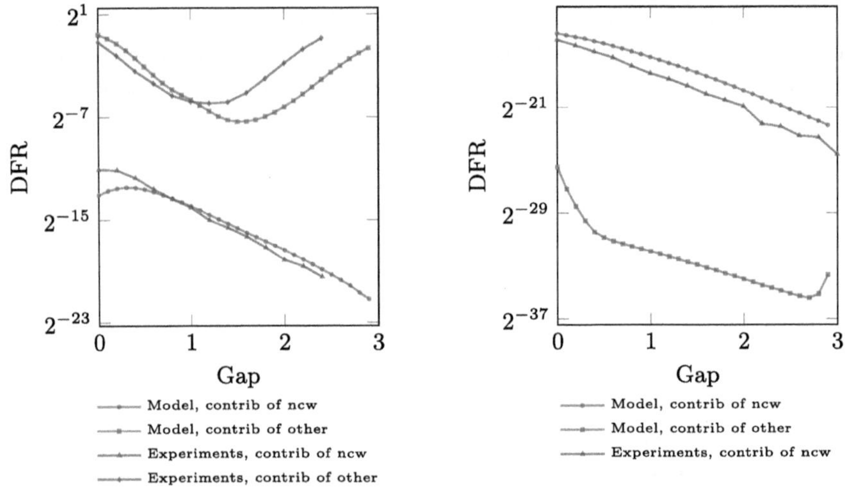


(a) Waterfall region
$(r, d, t) = (1723, 17, 65)$

(b) Error floor region
$(r, d, t) = (1723, 17, 35)$

**Fig. 11.** Experimental and model DFR for waterfall and error floor regions.

is the DFR conditioned on the event that the closest near-codeword intersects the error in exactly $u$ positions and $p(u)$ is the probability that this event occurs. We can tweak the initial distribution of the Markov chain so as to compute exactly $\text{DFR}(u)$. In the case where the dominating terms in this sum correspond to $u$'s for which $p(u)$ is small and the corresponding $\text{DFR}(u)$ are large enough, we can run experiments conditioned that the error intersects the closest near-codeword in exactly $u$ positions and check if $\text{DFR}(u)$ is indeed predicted correctly. This allows to make such verification way beyond DFR's that we can measure experimentally. This approach has permitted to expand significantly the regime of parameters that we can verify experimentally. We were able to increase the value of $d$ from 17 to 27, $t$ from 35 to 46 and $r$ from 1723 to 17053. All our parameters that have been found are such that we can verify the contribution of the $f(u) \stackrel{\text{def}}{=} \text{DFR}(u)p(u)$ around the value of $u$ for which this contribution attains its maximum. In all cases we get a remarkable prediction of $f(u) = \text{DFR}(u)p(u)$ for large values of $u$ and a good prediction around the maximum of $f(u)$ which is just a little bit pessimistic in this case. All in all, these experiments permit to verify values of DFR that are as low as $2^{-80}$ (Fig. 12).

We have also performed experiments for the cryptographic parameters. The Markov model predictions agree well for the $\text{DFR}(u)$ that we were able to check as Fig. 13 shows.

**Changing the Threshold Function.** A closer inspection of the affine function $A_{r,t}$ used in BIKE specification shows that for a large set of values of $s$ (roughly between 0 and more than 70 per cent of the typical initial syndrome value)

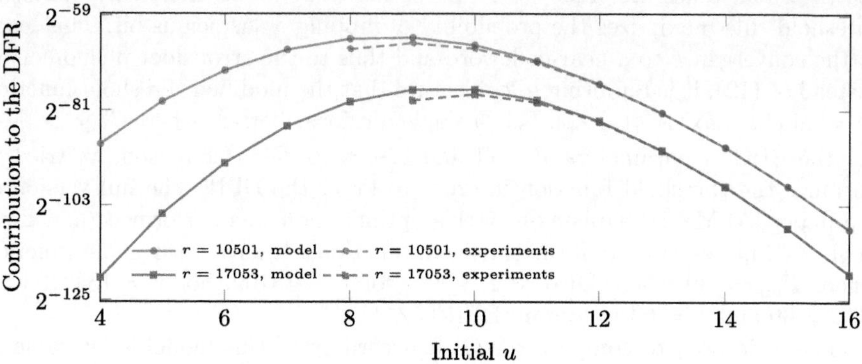


(a) $(d, t, \delta) = (27, 46, 0)$

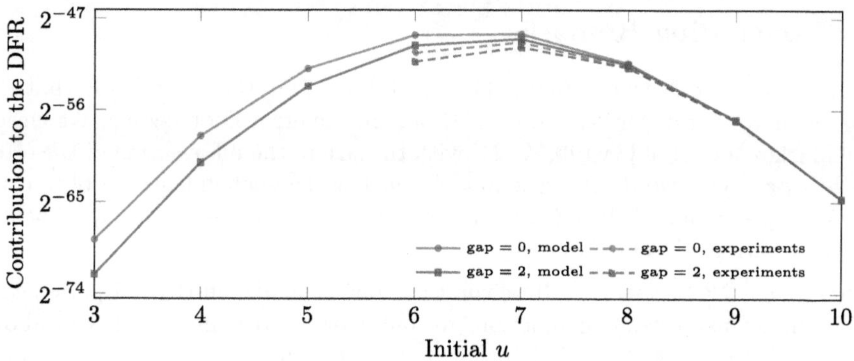


(b) $(r, d, t) = (9661, 19, 33)$

**Fig. 12.** Experimental and model DFR.

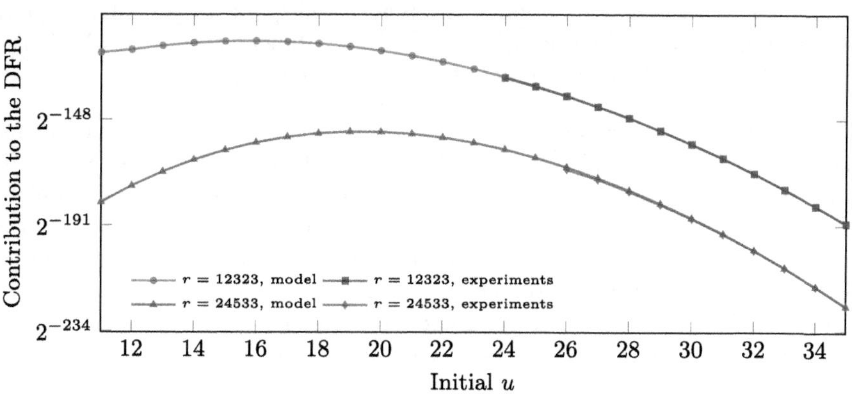


**Fig. 13.** $(d, t, \delta) = (71, 134, 3)$

the threshold takes the value $\frac{d+1}{2}$. This seems to be a bad choice: the majority threshold rule maximizes the probability of flipping a suspicious bit. This leads to the convergence to a near-codeword and thus to the error floor phenomenon. Instead of (12), it is tempting to conjecture that the modified threshold function $T = \min(d, \max(A_{r,t}(s) + \delta, T_{\min}))$ might perform better, where $T_{\min} > \frac{d+1}{2}$. For the BIKE 1 parameters, $d = 71$ and $\frac{d+1}{2} = 36$. For this reason, we tried to optimize the threshold function in order to lower the DFR. The full version of the paper [ALM+25] explains how this optimization was performed (and gives in §B.2 a full description of the threshold function). It gave a threshold function where $T_{\min} = 39$ where DFR $\approx 2^{-126.736}$ for $r = 13109$. For $r = 13477$, with $T_{\min} = 39$ and $\delta = 3.4$ we obtain DFR $\approx 2^{-131.259}$.

The code used to compute the DFR according to this model is available at https://github.com/vvasseur/qcmdpc_markov_ncw.

# 7 Concluding Remarks

*A New Accurate Markov Model.* This work highlights the central role that the near codewords put forward in [Vas21] play in the error floor regime. We enrich the Markov model of [SV19b, Vas21] with the size of the intersection of the error with a near codeword. Using a model which is key-dependent, we obtain an accurate prediction of the DFR in the error-floor regime, matching experimental data for various decoders and keys.

*Attaining a DFR below* $2^{-\lambda}$. If we run this Markov model on BIKE 1 parameters with the former threshold function, we fall short of reaching a DFR of about $2^{-91}$, which is below $2^{-\lambda}$. This problem cannot simply be addressed by taking slightly larger parameters, because the error floor kicks in just after the block size $r = 12323$ chosen for BIKE 1. However, this error floor seems to be due a threshold function taking its minimum possible value $\frac{d+1}{2}$ for a very large range of values of the syndrome weight $s$. This can be addressed adequately by increasing this minimum threshold value from 36 to 39 in the case of BIKE 1. In this case, a threshold function with an adjusted gap leads to a DFR for the step-by-step decoder which is below $2^{-131.2}$ for a block size $r = 13477$. This is slightly less than a 10% increase of the current BIKE 1 parameter.

*Analyzing a Parallel Decoder.* There are reasons to believe [Vas21] that the parallel decoders used in the actual BIKE implementation produce an even lower DFR. Whereas up to now, only the beginning of the waterfall region could be explored for cryptographic parameters, this work opens a new road for exploring the ability of various decoders to attain even more efficiently the needed $2^{-\lambda}$ DFR and for understanding the effect of various weak keys on the DFR. Concerning the first point, it could be interesting to consider the approach followed in [ABP24a] (for the full version see [ABP24b]) to analyze parallel decoders.

**Acknowledgements.** A. Mesnard and J.P. Tillich acknowledge the financial support of the French *Agence Nationale de la Recherche* through project ANR-22-PETQ-0008PQ-TLS. J. B. Lau acknowledges the financial support in part by the European

Research Council under the European Union's Horizon 2020 research and innovation programme (ISOCRYPT - No. 101020788), by the Research Council KU Leuven grant (C14/24/099) and by CyberSecurity Research Flanders (VR20192203). The authors would like to thank the anonymous reviewers and Paolo Santini for fruitful comments and discussion. S. Arpin acknowledges the support of the Commonwealth Cyber Initiative.

## References

ABB+21. Aragon, N., et al.: BIKE: bit flipping key encapsulation - SPEC V4.2 (2021). https://bikesuite.org/files/v4.2/BIKE_Spec.2021.07.26.1.pdf

ABH+22. Arpin, S., Billingsley, T.R., Hast, D.R., Lau, J.B., Perlner, R.A., Robinson, A.: A study of error floor behavior in QC-MDPC codes. In: Cheon, J.H., Johansson, T. (eds.) PQCrypto 2022, LNCS, vol. 13512, pp. 89–103. Springer, Cham (2022). https://doi.org/10.1007/978-3-031-17234-2_5

ABP24a. Annechini, A., Barenghi, A., Pelosi, G.: Bit-flipping decoder failure rate estimation for $(v, w)$−regular codes. In: Proceedings of IEEE International Symposium on Information Theory - ISIT, pp. 3374–3379. IEEE (2024)

ABP24b. Annechini, A., Barenghi, A., Pelosi, G.: Bit-flipping decoder failure rate estimation for $(v, w)$−regular codes. CoRR, abs/2401.16919 (2024)

ALM+25. Arpin, S., et al.: Error floor prediction with Markov models for QC-MDPC codes. Cryptology ePrint Archive, Paper 2025/153 (2025)

BBC+21. Baldi, M., Barenghi, A., Chiaraluce, F., Pelosi, G., Santini, P.: Performance bounds for QC-MDPC codes decoders. In: Wachter-Zeh, A., Bartz, H., Liva, G. (eds.) CBCrypto 2021. LNCS, vol. 13150, pp. 95–122. Springer, Cham (2021). https://doi.org/10.1007/978-3-030-98365-9_6

DGK20. Drucker, N., Gueron, S., Kostic, D.: QC-MDPC decoders with several shades of gray. In: Ding, J., Tillich, J.-P. (eds.) PQCrypto 2020. LNCS, vol. 12100, pp. 35–50. Springer, Cham (2020). https://doi.org/10.1007/978-3-030-44223-1_3

Gal63. Gallager, R.G.: Low Density Parity Check Codes. M.I.T. Press, Cambridge, Massachusetts (1963)

GJS16. Guo, Q., Johansson, T., Stankovski, P.: A key recovery attack on MDPC with CCA security using decoding errors. In: Cheon, J.H., Takagi, T. (eds.) ASIACRYPT 2016. LNCS, vol. 10031, pp. 789–815. Springer, Heidelberg (2016). https://doi.org/10.1007/978-3-662-53887-6_29

HB18. Hashemi, Y., Banihashemi, A.H.: Characterization of elementary trapping sets in irregular LDPC codes and the corresponding efficient exhaustive search algorithms. IEEE Trans. Inf. Theory **64**(5), 3411–3430 (2018)

HHK17. Hofheinz, D., Hövelmanns, K., Kiltz, E.: A modular analysis of the Fujisaki-Okamoto transformation. In: Kalai, Y., Reyzin, L. (eds.) TCC 2017. LNCS, vol. 10677, pp. 341–371. Springer, Cham (2017). https://doi.org/10.1007/978-3-319-70500-2_12

NSP+23. Nosouhi, M.R., et al.: Weak-key analysis for BIKE post-quantum key encapsulation mechanism. IEEE Trans. Inf. Forensics Secur. **18**, 2160–2174 (2023)

Ric03. Richardson, T.: Error floors of LDPC codes. In: Proceedings of the 41th Annual Allerton Conference on Communication, Control, and Computing, vol. 41, pp. 1426–1435 (2003)

Sen24. Sendrier, N.: BIKE decoding failure – weak keys & error floors. In: Slides of the Panel Discussion of the Fifth PQC Standardization Conference, April 2024

SV19a. Sendrier, N., Vasseur, V.: About low DFR for QC-MDPC decoding. Cryptology ePrint Archive, Paper 2019/1434 (2019). https://eprint.iacr.org/2019/1434

SV19b. Sendrier, N., Vasseur, V.: On the decoding failure rate of QC-MDPC bit-flipping decoders. In: Ding, J., Steinwandt, R. (eds.) PQCrypto 2019. LNCS, vol. 11505, pp. 404–416. Springer, Cham (2019). https://doi.org/10.1007/978-3-030-25510-7_22

Tan81. Tanner, R.M.: A recursive approach to low complexity codes. IEEE Trans. Inform. Theory **27**(5), 533–547 (1981)

Vas21. Vasseur, V.: Post-quantum cryptography: a study of the decoding of QC-MDPC codes. Ph.D. thesis, Université de Paris, March 2021

Vas24. Vasseur, V.: qcmdpc_markov Github codebase (2024). Accessed 26 Aug 2024

VCN14. Vasić, B., Chilappagari, S.K., Nguyen, D.V.: Chapter 6 - failures and error floors of iterative decoders. In: Declerq, D., Fossorier, M., Biglieri, E. (eds.) Academic Press Library in Mobile and Wireless Communications, pp. 299–341. Academic Press, Oxford (2014)

WWW23. Wang, T., Wang, A., Wang, X.: Exploring decryption failures of BIKE: new class of weak keys and key recovery attacks. In: Handschuh, H., Lysyanskaya, A. (eds.) CRYPTO 2023. LNCS, vol. 14083, pp. 70–100. Springer, Cham (2023). https://doi.org/10.1007/978-3-031-38548-3_3

# Highway to Hull: An Algorithm for Solving the General Matrix Code Equivalence Problem

Alain Couvreur[1,2(✉)] and Christophe Levrat[1,2]

[1] Inria, Saclay, France
{alain.couvreur,christophe.levrat}@inria.fr
[2] Laboratoire LIX, École Polytechnique, Institut Polytechnique de Paris, Palaiseau, France

**Abstract.** The matrix code equivalence problem consists, given two matrix spaces $\mathcal{C}, \mathcal{D} \subset \mathbb{F}_q^{m\times n}$ of dimension $k$, in finding invertible matrices $P \in \mathrm{GL}_m(\mathbb{F}_q)$ and $Q \in \mathrm{GL}_n(\mathbb{F}_q)$ such that $\mathcal{D} = P\mathcal{C}Q^{-1}$. Recent signature schemes such as MEDS and ALTEQ relate their security to the hardness of this problem. Recent works by Narayanan, Qiao and Tang on the one hand and by Ran and Samardjiska on the other hand tackle this problem. The former is restricted to the "cubic" case $k = m = n$ and succeeds in $\widetilde{\mathcal{O}}(q^{\frac{k}{2}})$ operations. The latter is an algebraic attack on the general problem whose complexity is not fully understood and which succeeds only on $\mathcal{O}(1/q)$ instances. We present a novel algorithm which solves the problem in the general case. Our approach consists in reducing the problem to the matrix code conjugacy problem, *i.e.* the case $P = Q$. For the latter problem, similarly to the permutation code equivalence problem in Hamming metric, a natural invariant based on the *Hull* of the code can be used. Next, the equivalence of codes can be deduced using a usual list collision argument. For $k = m = n$, our algorithm achieves the same time complexity as Narayanan *et al.* but with a lower space complexity. Moreover, ours extends to a much broader range of parameters.

## Introduction

In the last decades, so-called *equivalence problems* have frequently been used for cryptographic applications. The first examples probably come from multivariate cryptography with the Matsumoto-Imai [19] or HFE [22] schemes, whose security relies on the hardness of the polynomial isomorphism problem: deciding whether two spaces of polynomials are equivalent with respect to a linear or affine change of variables.

In recent years, we observed an intensification of this trend but also a diversification of the equivalence problems used for cryptography. In particular, in NIST's recent on-ramp call for signature[1], many signature schemes involve equivalence problems which are not the polynomial isomorphism one. For instance,

[1] https://csrc.nist.gov/Projects/pqc-dig-sig/round-1-additional-signatures.


Y. Tauman Kalai and S. F. Kamara (Eds.): CRYPTO 2025, LNCS 16000, pp. 253–283, 2025.
https://doi.org/10.1007/978-3-032-01855-7_9

*Hawk*'s [5] security rests among others on the hardness of the Lattice Isomorphism Problem (LIP), LESS [1] rests on the monomial equivalence of Hamming metric codes, MEDS [9] on the matrix code equivalence and ALTEQ [4] on the equivalence of alternate trilinear forms. The latter problem (equivalence of alternate trilinear forms) is in fact a sub-case of the former: the matrix code equivalence problem, which is the purpose of the present article. The two problems are actually proven to be polynomially equivalent [14, Prop. 8.3].

Given two matrix spaces $\mathcal{C}, \mathcal{D} \subset \mathbb{F}_q^{m\times n}$, the *matrix code equivalence problem* consists in deciding whether there exists $P \in \mathrm{GL}_m(\mathbb{F}_q)$ and $Q \in \mathrm{GL}_n(\mathbb{F}_q)$ such that $\mathcal{D} = P\mathcal{C}Q^{-1}$. The search version of the problem asks to return, if exists, a pair $(P, Q)$ providing the equivalence. Even though its use for cryptography is rather new, this problem has been known for a long time in algebraic complexity theory where it is usually formulated in an equivalent way as the 3–*tensor isomorphism* problem. This problem is assumed to be hard and is in particular known to be at least as hard as the monomial code equivalence problem (see [14] or [11]).

### Our Contribution

In this article, we present a new algorithm for solving the matrix code equivalence problem, or equivalently the 3–tensor isomorphism problem. Given equivalent $k$–dimensional $m \times n$ matrix spaces with entries in $\mathbb{F}_q$, we are able to solve the search equivalence problem in

$$\widetilde{\mathcal{O}}(q^{\max(\frac{k}{2},k-m+2)})$$

operations in $\mathbb{F}_q$. Note in particular that in the specific case $k = m = n$ which is the one that is used in the parameters of MEDS and ALTEQ, we achieve the time complexity $\widetilde{\mathcal{O}}(q^{\frac{k}{2}})$ which is the one achieved by Narayanan, Qiao and Tang [20]. However,

1. our algorithm rests on completely different invariants;
2. in the specific case $k = m = n$, the space complexity of our algorithm is $\mathcal{O}(nq^{\frac{n}{2}-1})$, which is is smaller than that of [20] by a factor $n^2$;
3. our result does not require the parameters $k, m, n$ to be equal, while this is necessary for Narayanan *et al.*'s algorithm to run.
   Note that, if the equivalence of alternate trilinear forms problem on which ALTEQ is built requires by design to have $k = m = n$, there is no need to instantiate MEDS with such a constraint on $k, m, n$. It turns out that MEDS' proposed parameters [9] satisfy this condition making them vulnerable to Narayanan *et al.*'s attack, but MEDS' designers could have easily circumvented the aforementioned attack just by breaking the symmetry on the parameters $k, m, n$. Still, the algorithm introduced in the present article attacks a much broader range of triples $k, m, n$.

A specificity of our algorithm is that, taking its inspiration from the Hamming metric counterpart of the code equivalence problem problem and Sendrier's famous *support splitting algorithm* [27], we use the *Hull* of the code, *i.e.* its intersection with its orthogonal space w.r.t some given bilinear form.

**Related works**

The schemes MEDS and ALTEQ [4,9] were both submitted to NIST's on-ramp call for digital signatures. Before, ALTEQ's and MEDS' specifications were respectively presented in the articles [30] and [10]. In [3], Beullens describes a new algorithm solving the trilinear form equivalence problem, harming the proposed parameters for ALTEQ. More recently, Narayanan, Qiao and Tang [20] presented an algorithm solving the same problem but also the matrix code equivalence problem in the case of $k$–dimensional spaces of $k \times k$ matrices. Their approach combines a collision list argument with a nice algebraic invariant and achieves a complexity in $\widetilde{\mathcal{O}}(q^{\frac{k}{2}})$. Finally, Ran and Samardjiska [24] designed an algorithm for the 3-tensor isomorphism problem which looks for triangles in tensor graphs. Such triangles exist in roughly $1/q$ of all instances of the problem. In these instances and for current parameters of MEDS and ALTEQ, their algorithm provides a speedup compared to all previous works.

# 1 The Matrix Code Equivalence Problem

**Definition 1.** *Let $m, n, k$ be positive integers. An $m \times n$ matrix code of dimension $k$ is a $k$-dimensional $\mathbb{F}_q$-linear subspace of $\mathbb{F}_q^{m\times n}$.*

**Definition 2 (Matrix code equivalence problem).** *Let $m, n, k$ be positive integers. Consider two $k$-dimensional linear subspaces $\mathcal{C}, \mathcal{D}$ of $\mathbb{F}_q^{m\times n}$. The matrix code equivalence problem $\mathsf{MCE}_{m,n,k}(\mathcal{C}, \mathcal{D})$ consists in finding (if exist) matrices $P \in \mathrm{GL}_m(\mathbb{F}_q), Q \in \mathrm{GL}_n(\mathbb{F}_q)$ such that*

$$\mathcal{D} = P\mathcal{C}Q^{-1}.$$

*When $m = n = k$, we call it the* cubic matrix code equivalence problem*:* $\mathsf{CMCE}_n(\mathcal{C}, \mathcal{D})$.

*Remark 1.* We may suppose that $m \leqslant n$. Indeed, if $\mathcal{D} = P\mathcal{C}Q^{-1}$ then

$$\mathcal{D}^\top = (Q^{-1})^\top \mathcal{C}^\top P^\top$$

so any algorithm solving the case $m \leqslant n$ can also be used, after transposing the whole problem, to solve the case $n \leqslant m$. In the remainder of this article, we will always suppose that $m \leqslant n$. Moreover, we may switch $\mathcal{C}$ and its dual $\mathcal{C}^\perp$ in order to have $\dim(\mathcal{C}^\perp) \leqslant \dim(\mathcal{C})$. Indeed, if $\mathcal{D} = P\mathcal{C}Q^{-1}$ then

$$\mathcal{D}^\perp = (P^{-1})^\top \mathcal{C}^\perp Q^\top.$$

Hence, the case where $mn - k = m = n$ may be reduced to an instance of $\mathsf{CMCE}$.

The $\mathsf{CMCE}$ problem is notably the basis of the former NIST signature scheme candidate MEDS. A polynomial-time equivalent problem [25], the *alternating trilinear form equivalence problem*, underpins the former NIST signature candidate ALTEQ. An attack against these problems was recently described by Naranayan, Qiao and Tang in [20].

### 1.1 Related Problems

**The Trilinear Forms Equivalence Problem**

**Definition 3 (Trilinear Form Equivalence Problem** (TFE)**).** *The* trilinear forms equivalence *problem* $\mathsf{TFE}_{m,n,k}$ *is the following. Given two trilinear forms* $f, g\colon \mathbb{F}_q^m \times \mathbb{F}_q^m \times \mathbb{F}_q^k \to \mathbb{F}_q$*, find three matrices* $(P, Q, R) \in \mathrm{GL}_m(\mathbb{F}_q) \times \mathrm{GL}_n(\mathbb{F}_q) \times \mathrm{GL}_k(\mathbb{F}_q)$ *such that for any* $x, y, z \in \mathbb{F}_q^m \times \mathbb{F}_q^n \times \mathbb{F}_q^k$*,*

$$f(Px, Qy, Rz) = g(x, y, z).$$

The following well-known result shows the the matrix code equivalence problem reduces to the trilinear forms equivalence problem with the same parameters.

**Lemma 1.** *The problem* $\mathsf{MCE}_{m,n,k}$ *admits a (deterministic) polynomial-time reduction to* $\mathsf{TFE}_{m,n,k}$*.*

**Alternate Trilinear Form Equivalence Problem** A sub-case of the trilinear form equivalence problem that has been considered for the design of ALTEQ is the *alternate trilinear forms equivalence problem* ATFE. An *alternate* trilinear form is a trilinear form $f : \mathbb{F}_q^n \times \mathbb{F}_q^n \times \mathbb{F}_q^n$ such that for any $x \in \mathbb{F}_q^n$,

$$f(x, x, \cdot) \equiv f(x, \cdot, x) \equiv f(\cdot, x, x) \equiv 0.$$

This is equivalent to the fact that, given any permutation $\sigma \in \mathfrak{S}_3$ (the group of permutation on 3 letters), and any triple $(x_1, x_2, x_3) \in (\mathbb{F}_q^n)^3$,

$$f(x_{\sigma(1)}, x_{\sigma(2)}, x_{\sigma(3)}) = \varepsilon(\sigma) f(x_1, x_2, x_3),$$

where $\varepsilon(\sigma)$ denotes the signature of the permutation $\sigma$. This definition leads to the following problem.

**Definition 4 (Alternate Trilinear Form Equivalence Problem** (ATFE)**).** *The alternate trilinear forms equivalence problem* $\mathsf{ATFE}_{m,n,k}$ *is the following. Given two alternate trilinear forms* $f, g\colon \mathbb{F}_q^m \times \mathbb{F}_q^m \times \mathbb{F}_q^k \to \mathbb{F}_q$*, find a matrix* $P \in \mathrm{GL}_n(\mathbb{F}_q)$ *such that for any* $x, y, z \in \mathbb{F}_q^m \times \mathbb{F}_q^n \times \mathbb{F}_q^k$*,*

$$f(Px, Py, Pz) = g(x, y, z).$$

**3–Tensor Isomorphism.** On the tensor product $\mathbb{F}_q^m \otimes \mathbb{F}_q^n \otimes \mathbb{F}_q^k$, there is a natural action of $\mathrm{GL}_m(\mathbb{F}_q) \times \mathrm{GL}_n(\mathbb{F}_q) \times \mathrm{GL}_k(\mathbb{F}_q)$, and the 3–tensor isomorphism problem consists in deciding whether two tensors $T_1, T_2 \in \mathbb{F}_q^m \otimes \mathbb{F}_q^n \otimes \mathbb{F}_q^k$ are in the same orbit with respect to the aforementioned group action. The 3–tensor isomorphism problem is well-known to be equivalent to the matrix code equivalence one. See [14, Fig. 2] for further details on the connections between various equivalence problems.

*Remark 2.* Note that the terminology of *cubic matrix code equivalence problem* introduced in Definition 2 refers to the corresponding tensors, which will be $n \times n \times n$, *i.e. cubic tensors.*

*Remark 3.* Rewriting an instance of MCE as an instance of TFE or of 3–tensor isomorphism shows that the problem is symmetric in the three parameters $m, n, k$. In particular, we may choose to permute $m, n, k$ as we like in our algorithm in order to minimize its complexity. Moreover, as we will explain in Lemma 2, we may also switch $k$ for $mn - k$.

### 1.2 Related Works on Attacks on MCE and ATFE

**About ALTEQ.** In article [30] in which the design of ALTEQ is established, various cryptanalysis techniques are considered to solve ATFE problem. They include algebraic attacks: computing the matrix $P$ as the solution of a quadratic system; or MinRank based attacks (re discussed further as "Leon–like techniques"). The authors then consider a collision search attack with a cost $\widetilde{\mathcal{O}}(q^{\frac{2n}{3}})$, which they claim to be the best possible. Finally, NIST proposal ALTEQ [4] selects parameters with respect to a finer analysis of algebraic and MinRank based attacks.

**About MEDS.** For the design of MEDS [10], the authors consider a graph-search based approach inspired from the works of Bouillaguet, Fouque and Véber [6] on the polynomial isomorphism problem for spaces of quadratic forms. This approach leads to an attack of complexity $\widetilde{\mathcal{O}}(q^{\frac{2}{3}(m+n)})$. Also, they consider the possibility of algebraic modelling which turns out to be harder than for ATFE since the unknown correspond to a pair of matrices $(P, Q)$ instead of a single one. They also study a "Leon–like" approach, a reference to Leon's algorithm [17] for determining code equivalence that consists in harvesting minimum weight codewords to determine the code equivalence. When transposed to the matrix code setting, the Hamming weight is replaced by the rank and such an approach is nothing but the aforementioned MinRank based technique, which, following a recent result from Beullens [2] on Hamming metric code equivalence, can be combined with a collision search technique. MEDS' parameter selection rests on the complexity of both algebraic attacks and Leon–like ones.

**Subsequent Attacks.** Recently, two attacks taking their inspiration from the Graph–based techniques of Bouillaguet, Fouque and Véber [6] appeared in the literature.

*Beullens' attack.* First, Beullens proposed a graph–search–based technique to solve ATFE. His attack turns out to be particularly efficient for small values of $n$. For instance, for $n$ odd, he could achieve a complexity in $\mathcal{O}(q^{(n-5)/2}n^{11} + q^{n-7}n^{6})$. This permitted to identify weak keys in [30].

*Narayanan, Qiao and Tang's attack.* In [20], the authors introduced a new algorithm solving both ATFE and MCE in the cubic case $k = m = n$. We conclude this section by sketching the principle of this algorithm in order to point out the need for being in the cubic case.

As already explained in § 1.1, the problem can be reformulated into that of the equivalence of two trilinear forms

$$f\colon \mathbb{F}_q^n \times \mathbb{F}_q^n \times \mathbb{F}_q^n \longrightarrow \mathbb{F}_q \quad \text{and} \quad g\colon \mathbb{F}_q^n \times \mathbb{F}_q^n \times \mathbb{F}_q^n \longrightarrow \mathbb{F}_q,$$

where we look for a triple $P, Q, R \in \mathrm{GL}_n(\mathbb{F}_q)$ such that for any $x, y, z \in \mathbb{F}_q^n$, $g(x, y, z) = f(Px, Qy, Rz)$.

The idea of the algorithm consists first in guessing a pair $(x_1, x_1') \in (\mathbb{F}_q^n)^2$ such that $x_1' = Px_1$ and $f(x_1, \cdot, \cdot)$ is a bilinear form of rank $n-1$. Next, due to the rank constraint, from $x_1$ can be deduced a unique $y_1$ (up to scalar multiplication) such that $f(x_1, y_1, \cdot) \equiv 0$. Similarly, they deduce a $z_1$ such that $f(\cdot, y_1, z_1) \equiv 0$, and an $x_2$ such that $f(x_2, \cdot, z_1) \equiv 0$ and so on. By this manner, they construct 3 sequences $x_1, \ldots, x_n$, $y_1, \ldots, y_n$ and $z_1, \ldots, z_n$ for $f$ and similarly construct $x_1', \cdots, x_n'$, $y_1', \ldots, y_n'$ and $z_1', \ldots, z_n'$ for $g$. Stacking these vectors as columns of $n \times n$ matrices, we get 6 matrices $X, Y, Z, X', Y'$ and $Z'$ that will be invertible with a high probability.

The key observation is that

$$X' = PX \quad Y' = QY \quad \text{and} \quad Z' = RZ.$$

Therefore, for any $x, y, z$

$$f(X'x, Y'y, Z'z) = f(PXx, QYy, QZz) = g(Xx, Yy, Zz).$$

Thus, (up to some action of diagonal matrices that we do not discuss here) the trilinear forms $f_{x_1} \stackrel{\text{def}}{=} f(X' \cdot, Y' \cdot, Z' \cdot)$ and $g_{x_1'} \stackrel{\text{def}}{=} g(X \cdot, Y \cdot, Z \cdot)$ coincide.

In view of this observation, the algorithm solving MCE consists in a collision search between two dictionaries. The first one collects pairs $(f_{x_1}, x_1)$, the left–hand term being the search key and the right–hand one being the corresponding value, and the second one collects pairs $(g_{x_1'}, x_1')$. Once such a collision is found, determining the equivalence becomes easy (see [20] for further details). The space complexity of their algorithm is essentially the expected size of the computed dictionaries. Each dictionary has length $q^{(n-2)/2}$, and its entries are pairs consisting of a point of $\mathbb{P}^n(\mathbb{F}_q)$ and a cubic 3-tensor of dimension $n \times n \times n$. Hence the total space complexity is $\mathcal{O}(n^3 q^{(n-2)/2})$.

*Conclusion about Narayanan, Qiao and Tang.* It should be emphasized that the crux of their algorithm rests on the unique possibility (up to scalar multiplication) of passing from $x_i$ to $y_i$, from $y_i$ to $z_i$ and from $z_i$ to $x_{i+1}$. Such a technique is possible only because at each step, the corresponding bilinear form is represented by a rank $n-1$ matrix of size $n \times n$. Hence, their approach strongly rests on the fact that they lie in the cubic case $k = m = n$.

*Ran and Samardjiska's attack.* In [24], the authors describe a graph-based algorithm which solves the 3-tensor isomorphism problem in a specific case, namely when the graphs of the two isomorphic tensors contain cycles of length 3. This only happens in $\sim 1/q$ of all instances. However, contrary to [20], they are not limited to the cubic case. Their article contains a generic algorithm for the tensor isomorphism problem, and two versions adapted specifically to the MCE and ATFE problems. They all rely on the same *modus operandi*:

- first, model by algebraic equations the existence of triangles in the graphs associated with the two tensors, and solve these using Gröbner basis techniques in order to construct lists of triangles found in each tensor's graph;
- then, for each pair of triangles in the two lists, try to construct the isometry by solving a system of linear and quadratic equations.

The authors provide timings showing that their attack is more efficient with real-world parameters than the previous ones, even going as far as breaking the designed Level I parameters of ALTEQ in under half an hour. However, this only applies to those $1/q$ of all instances in which the considered tensors do have triangles in their associated graphs.

*Comparison with the present work.* We do not expect our work to beat the time complexity of [20] or [24] in the cases where they apply. However, our algorithm solves the MCE problem in a very broad range of parameters, and is not restricted to the cubic case like [20] or to those (very rare) tensors whose graphs contain triangles like [24]. Moreover, it improves upon the space complexity of [20] by a factor $\Theta(n^2)$.

## 2 Technical Overview

In this article, we propose an algorithm to solve $\mathsf{MCE}_{m,n,k}(\mathcal{C},\mathcal{D})$ for the range of parameters $m, n, k$ such that $n \geqslant m$ and

$$k < m^2 - 1 \text{ or } mn - k < m^2 - 1$$

(see Remark 5). This includes the cubic case, *i.e.*, $k = m = n$, in which the complexity of our algorithm turns out to be similar to that of [20].

### 2.1 Preliminaries

Our algorithm will use in a crucial way the notion of *dual matrix code* and that of *Hull*. We give both definitions below. Recall that the *trace* $\mathrm{Tr}(M)$ of a square matrix $M$ is the sum of its diagonal coefficients.

**Definition 5.** *Let $\mathcal{C} \subset \mathbb{F}_q^{m\times n}$ be a linear code. The* dual *of $\mathcal{C}$ is the code*

$$\mathcal{C}^{\perp} \stackrel{def}{=} \{M \in \mathbb{F}_q^{m\times n} \mid \forall C \in \mathcal{C}, \mathrm{Tr}(M^{\top}C) = 0\}.$$

**Definition 6.** *Let $\mathcal{C} \subset \mathbb{F}_q^{m\times m}$ be a matrix code. We will call* hull *of $\mathcal{C}$ the code*

$$h(C) = \{M \in \mathcal{C} \mid \forall C \in \mathcal{C}, \operatorname{Tr}(MC) = 0\}.$$

*Remark 4.* Beware that the hull is **not** the intersection of $\mathcal{C}$ with its dual as defined in Definition 5. It is the intersection with another orthogonal subspace, this time with respect to the bilinear form $(X, Y) \mapsto \operatorname{Tr}(XY)$.

The definition of the hull (Definition 6) is the only place of the article where this nonstandard bilinear form is used. Besides, every dual or orthogonal complement which appears in the article is taken with respect to the usual inner product $(X, Y) \mapsto \operatorname{Tr}(X^\top Y)$.

The subsequent lemmas yield two key observations for our algorithms:

1. if two codes are equivalent, so are their duals;
2. if two codes are conjugate, so are their hulls.

**Lemma 2.** *Let $\mathcal{C}, \mathcal{D} \subset \mathbb{F}_q^{m\times n}$ be two $\mathbb{F}_q$-vector spaces, and $P \in \mathrm{GL}_m(\mathbb{F}_q)$, $Q \in \mathrm{GL}_n(\mathbb{F}_q)$ be matrices such that $\mathcal{D} = P\mathcal{C}Q^{-1}$. Then*

$$\mathcal{D}^\perp = (P^{-1})^\top \mathcal{C}^\perp Q^\top.$$

*Proof.* Since $\mathcal{C}$ and $\mathcal{D}$ have the same dimension, so do $\mathcal{D}^\perp$ and $(P^{-1})^\top \mathcal{C}^\perp Q^\top$. Hence, it is enough to prove that one of these spaces is included in the other. Consider any $B \in \mathcal{D}$ and $A \in \mathcal{C}^\perp$. There is a matrix $C \in \mathcal{C}$ such that $B = PCQ^{-1}$. We have:

$$\begin{aligned}
\operatorname{Tr}(B^\top (P^{-1})^\top A Q^\top) &= \operatorname{Tr}((Q^{-1})^\top C^\top P^\top (P^{-1})^\top A Q^\top) \\
&= \operatorname{Tr}((Q^{-1})^\top C^\top A Q^\top) \\
&= \operatorname{Tr}(C^\top A) = 0. && \text{(since } A \in \mathcal{C}^\perp)
\end{aligned}$$

Hence, $\mathcal{D} \subseteq (P^{-1})^\top \mathcal{C}^\perp Q^\top$. □

**Lemma 3.** *Let $\mathcal{C}, \mathcal{D} \subset \mathbb{F}_q^{m\times m}$ be two $\mathbb{F}_q$-vector spaces. Let $P \in \mathrm{GL}_m(\mathbb{F}_q)$ be a matrix such that $\mathcal{D} = P\mathcal{C}P^{-1}$. Then*

$$h(\mathcal{D}) = P h(\mathcal{C}) P^{-1}.$$

*Proof.* Let $C \in h(\mathcal{C})$, and set $D = PCP^{-1} \in \mathcal{D}$. Let us show that $D \in h(\mathcal{D})$. Let $B \in \mathcal{D}$. There exists $A \in \mathcal{C}$ such that $B = PAP^{-1}$. We have

$$\begin{aligned}
\operatorname{Tr}(BD) &= \operatorname{Tr}(PAP^{-1}PCP^{-1}) \\
&= \operatorname{Tr}(AC) = 0. && \text{(since } C \in h(\mathcal{C}))
\end{aligned}$$

The other inclusion is proved in the same way. □

The following proposition, which says that roughly $1/q$ of all codes have a one-dimensional hull, is a consequence of results presented in [26]. It is explained in Appendix B, and will be crucial in the complexity analysis.

In the sequel, we denote by $\ker(\mathrm{Tr})$ the subspace of $\mathbb{F}_q^{m\times m}$ of matrices whose trace is zero.

**Proposition 1.** *The proportion of* $m \times m$ *matrix codes contained in* $\ker(\mathrm{Tr})$ *and whose hull has dimension 1 is asymptotically equal to*

$$\frac{1}{q}\left(1+\mathcal{O}\left(\frac{m^2}{q^{(m^2-1)/2}}\right)\right).$$

## 2.2 Summary of the Algorithm

We are given two $k$-dimensional subspaces $\mathcal{C}, \mathcal{D}$ of $\mathbb{F}_q^{m\times n}$. Our aim is to find two matrices $P \in \mathrm{GL}_m(\mathbb{F}_q)$ and $Q \in \mathrm{GL}_n(\mathbb{F}_q)$ verifying $\mathcal{D} = P\mathcal{C}Q^{-1}$. If we have found a suitable matrix $P$, computing $Q$ can be done using linear algebra (see Sect. 5). The strategy for finding $P$ consists first in guessing a pair $(A, B) \in \mathcal{C}^{\perp} \times \mathcal{D}^{\perp}$ such that $B = (P^{-1})^{\top} A Q^{\top}$, that is, a pair $A, B$ which match with respect to the equivalence $\mathcal{D}^{\perp} = (P^{-1})^{\top}\mathcal{C}^{\perp}Q^{\top}$ given by Lemma 2. With such a pair at hand, one can reduce the equivalence problem to the conjugacy problem of the codes

$$\mathcal{C}_A \stackrel{\text{def}}{=} \mathcal{C}A^{\top} \qquad \text{and} \qquad \mathcal{D}_B \stackrel{\text{def}}{=} \mathcal{D}B^{\top}. \tag{1}$$

Indeed, if $B = PAQ^{-1}$ we prove in Lemma 4 further that $\mathcal{D}_B = P\mathcal{C}_A P^{-1}$. Solving a matrix code conjugacy problem in this context is generally as hard as solving $\mathsf{MCE}$ [14], but it is easy in a particular case: when the hull of both codes has dimension 1, we may easily find conjugate generators of these two hulls. The two main steps in order to find $P$ are the following.

1. From $\mathcal{C}, \mathcal{D}$, construct two conjugate codes $\mathcal{C}_A, \mathcal{D}_B$ with one-dimensional hull.
2. Compute a matrix $R$ that conjugates these hulls and deduce a matrix $P$ such that that $\mathcal{D}_B = P\mathcal{C}_A P^{-1}$.

*First step.* We begin by finding two matrices $A \in \mathcal{C}^{\perp}$ and $B \in \mathcal{D}^{\perp}$ such that the codes $\mathcal{C}_A$ and $\mathcal{D}_B$ of (1) have conjugate hulls. For any $A$, one may find at least one such $B$, which is $(P^{-1})^{\top} A Q^{\top}$.

In order to determine these matrices $A$ and $B$, we construct a dictionary whose keys are (normalized and suitably chosen) polynomials $\chi \in \mathbb{F}_q[t]$ of degree $m$. The values corresponding to a key $\chi$ are the pairs $(A, U) \in \mathbb{F}_q^{m\times n} \times \mathbb{F}_q^{m\times m}$ such that the hull $h(\mathcal{C}_A)$ is one-dimensional and generated by the matrix $U$ with characteristic polynomial $\chi$. Then, we apply the same process to $\mathcal{D}$ and look for collisions. This step is explained in detail in Sect. 3.

*Second step.* Once we have a pair of matrices $(A, B) \in \mathcal{C}^\perp \times \mathcal{D}^\perp$ such that $h(\mathcal{C}_A)$ and $h(\mathcal{C}_B)$ are one-dimensional and generated by conjugate matrices $U$ and $V$, we may easily compute a matrix $R \in \mathrm{GL}_m(\mathbb{F}_q)$ such that $V = RUR^{-1}$. We also impose in the collision search that the characteristic polynomial $\chi$ of $U, V$ is squarefree so that $U, V$ are both diagonalizable in an extension of $\mathbb{F}_q$. In this context, we will observe that the matrix $P$ we are looking for, *i.e.* the one such that $\mathcal{D}_B = P\mathcal{C}_A P^{-1}$, is the product of $R$ by some invertible matrix which can be expressed as $f(U)$ for some polynomial $f \in \mathbb{F}_q[t]$ of degree less than $m$. The calculation of this polynomial is explained in Sect. 4.

### 2.3 A Comment on Matrix Code Equivalence *v.s.* Matrix Code Conjugacy

A remark that arises from our work, is that the equivalence problem seems to become much easier when reducing from general matrix code equivalence (*i.e.* arbitrary $P, Q$) to matrix code conjugacy (*i.e.* $m = n$ and $P = Q$). It is interesting to observe that from a complexity theory point of view the two problems are polynomially equivalent [14, Thm. A]. Still, the use of the hull gives a heuristic polynomial-time algorithm that solves a proportion $\mathcal{O}(1/q)$ of instances of the conjugacy problem (the $1/q$ coming from the fact that a random matrix code has a one-dimensional hull with probability $\mathcal{O}(1/q)$).

This phenomenon could be compared with what happens in classical coding theory, where two problems arise : the *permutation equivalence problem* (finding a permutation matrix sending a code to another) and the *monomial equivalence problem* (finding a monomial matrix, *i.e.* the product of a permutation matrix and a nonsingular diagonal matrix sending one code to another). When the ground field cardinality $q$ is polynomial in the code length, the two problems are known to be polynomially equivalent [28] but Sendrier's *Support Splitting algorithm* [27] is on average efficient on the former while being completely inefficient on the latter.

### 2.4 Complexity and Impact

The complexity of the algorithm is dominated by the collision search in the first step. Given a uniformly random code $\mathcal{C}$ and a uniformly random full-rank matrix $A \in \mathcal{C}^\perp$, the codes $\mathcal{C}_A$ are uniformly distributed among the matrix codes in $\ker(\mathrm{Tr}) \subset \mathbb{F}_q^{m \times m}$. Among these, a proportion of approximately $1/q$ have a one-dimensional hull. By an argument similar to the birthday paradox, computing two lists of length roughly $q^{(k^\perp - 2)/2}$ is enough to find some collisions. This requires picking matrices $A$, and for each of these, computing the hull of $\mathcal{C}_A$. The total time complexity, given in Theorem 1, is

$$\widetilde{\mathcal{O}}\left(q^{\max(\frac{k^\perp}{2}, k^\perp - m + 2)}\right)$$

operations in $\mathbb{F}_q$, where $k^\perp \stackrel{\text{def}}{=} mn - k$ is the dimension of the dual code $\mathcal{C}^\perp$. In the cubic case $m = n = k$, by switching $\mathcal{C}$ and $\mathcal{C}^\perp$, this complexity can be reduced to $\widetilde{\mathcal{O}}\left(q^{n/2}\right)$. The space complexity is

$$\mathcal{O}\left((k^{\perp}+m+1)q^{\min(\frac{k^{\perp}}{2}-1,m-3)}\right)$$

elements of $\mathbb{F}_q$, which is essentially the size of the computed dictionaries. In the cubic case, this amounts to $\mathcal{O}\left(nq^{\frac{n}{2}-1}\right)$ elements of $\mathbb{F}_q$. This reduces the space complexity of [20] by a factor $n^2$, which, with the initial cubic parameters of MEDS-128, is about 200.

## 3 Reducing to Probably Conjugate Spaces

We look at $k$-dimensional matrix codes inside $\mathbb{F}_q^{m\times n}$. Given a code of dimension $k$, we will denote by $k^{\perp}=mn-k$ the dimension of its dual.

### 3.1 Structure of the Reduction

Lemma 2 shows that the instances $(\mathcal{C},\mathcal{D})$ and $(\mathcal{C}^{\perp},\mathcal{D}^{\perp})$ of MCE are equivalent. In particular, for complexity reasons, we may switch $(\mathcal{C},\mathcal{D})$ for $(\mathcal{C}^{\perp},\mathcal{D}^{\perp})$: we will systematically choose the instance with the highest dimension. Indeed, since collision search is performed on the dual codes, we fit in the situation where the codes have the smallest possible duals. Thus from now on, we suppose

$$k^{\perp}\leqslant k.$$

Lemma 2 also shows that given $A\in\mathcal{C}^{\perp}$, the matrix $B=(P^{-1})^{\top}AQ^{\top}$ belongs to $\mathcal{D}^{\perp}$. The key of the algorithm lies in the following lemma.

**Lemma 4.** *Let* $(A,B)\in\mathcal{C}^{\perp}\times\mathcal{D}^{\perp}$ *such that* $B=(P^{-1})^{\top}AQ^{\top}$. *Then, the codes*

$$\mathcal{C}_A\overset{def}{=}\mathcal{C}A^{\top}\quad\textit{and}\quad\mathcal{D}_B\overset{def}{=}\mathcal{D}B^{\top}\quad\textit{satisfy}\quad\mathcal{D}_B=P\mathcal{C}_AP^{-1}.$$

*Proof.* This is a straightforward computation. □

The aim of the first step of our algorithm is to find pairs $(A,B)$ such that $\mathcal{C}_A$ and $\mathcal{D}_B$ are two conjugate $k$-dimensional codes, in order to find $P$. Given any $\mathcal{C}_A$, $\mathcal{D}_B$, finding a matrix $P$ such that $\mathcal{D}_B=P\mathcal{C}_AP^{-1}$ is complicated: this is the code conjugacy problem (see for instance [14]). However, it is much easier if one knows a distinguished pair of conjugate elements $U\in\mathcal{C}_A$, $V\in\mathcal{D}_B$. In order to find such a pair $(U,V)$, we need to find conjugate one-dimensional subspaces in both $\mathcal{C}_A$ and $\mathcal{D}_B$. We can do this when the hulls of both $\mathcal{C}_A$ and $\mathcal{D}_B$ are one-dimensional, since, as shown in Lemma 3, the hulls of two conjugate matrix codes are conjugate.

*Remark 5.* By construction, there is an inclusion $\mathcal{C}_A\subset\ker(\mathrm{Tr})$. Moreover, in order to have a one-dimensional hull, we need this inclusion to be a strict. Since we require $\mathcal{C}_A$ to have the same dimension as $\mathcal{C}$, this means that our algorithm in this form only works for

$$k<m^2-1.$$

Given an instance $(\mathcal{C}, \mathcal{D})$ of $\mathsf{MCE}_{m,n,k}$, our goal is to find matrices $P \in \mathrm{GL}_m(\mathbb{F}_q)$ and $Q \in \mathrm{GL}_n(\mathbb{F}_q)$ such that $\mathcal{D} = P\mathcal{C}Q^{-1}$. The method below allows us to reduce the problem to the case where $m = n$, $P = Q$, and $\mathcal{C}$ and $\mathcal{D}$ have non trivial conjugate hulls. The reduction consists in the following steps.

1. Construct a dictionary $\{\chi : (A, U)\}$, where $\mathcal{C}_A = \mathcal{C}A^\top$ has a one–dimensional hull, $U \in \mathbb{F}_q^{m\times m} \setminus \{0\}$ generates this hull and $\chi \in \mathbb{F}_q[t]_{\leqslant m}$ is the characteristic polynomial of $U$, which we require to be squarefree. This is done in a very straightforward way: pick $A$ at random, compute $h(\mathcal{C}_A)$ and if it is one-dimensional and generated by a matrix $U$, compute its characteristic polynomial $\chi_U$ and add the entry $(\chi\colon (A, U))$ to the dictionary. To make the second step easier, we only keep $A$ when $\chi$ is separable. The precise procedure is explained in Algorithm 2. In order to find collisions more easily, we normalize the characteristic polynomials as explained in Appendix A: this reduces the number of possible characteristic polynomials to approximately $q^{m-3}$ (see Lemma 15).
2. Pick random matrices $B \in \mathcal{D}^\perp$, and if the hull of $\mathcal{D}B^\top$ is one-dimensional, check if the characteristic polynomial of one of its generators is a key in the dictionary. The aforementioned conditions on the characteristic polynomials directly imply that the generators $U, V$ of $h(\mathcal{C}_A), h(\mathcal{D}_B)$ having the same characteristic polynomial $\chi$ are conjugate: for each collision, we immediately compute $R \in \mathrm{GL}_m(\mathbb{F}_q)$ such that $V = RUR^{-1}$. The collision-finding procedure is described in Algorithm 3.

This yields a list of tuples $(A, B, U, V, R)$ such that the codes $\mathcal{C}_A$ and $\mathcal{D}_B$ have one-dimensional hulls respectively generated by matrices $U, V$ such that $V = RUR^{-1}$. To these tuples, we then apply an algorithm of Sect. 4 which allows to find a suitable matrix $P$ such that $\mathcal{D}_B = P\mathcal{C}_AP^{-1}$. In order to compute $Q$, we now need to solve $\mathcal{D} = (P\mathcal{C}) \cdot Q$, where $P\mathcal{C}$ is known. This is an easy problem, which is solved by linear algebra as explained in Sect. 5.

---

**Algorithm 1:** ComputeNormalizedCharpoly

---

**Data:** $k$-dimensional code $\mathcal{C} \subset \ker(\mathrm{Tr}) \subset \mathbb{F}_q^{m\times m}$ such that $\dim h(\mathcal{C}) = 1$
**Result:** Pair $(\chi, U)$ where $U \in \mathbb{F}_q^{m\times m}$ generates $h(\mathcal{C})$, and $\chi \in \mathbb{F}_q^{m-2} - \{0\}$ represents $U$'s characteristic polynomial

---

Compute a generator $U$ of $h(\mathcal{C})$
Compute char. polynomial $a_0 + a_1t + \cdots + a_{m-3}t^{m-3} + t^m$ of $U$
Set $\chi = (a_{m-3}, a_{m-4}, \ldots, a_0) \in \mathbb{F}_q^{m-2} - \{0\}$
$\lambda =$ Normalize$(U, \chi)$ using Algorithm 7
**return** $(\lambda \diamond \chi, \lambda U)$ (where $\diamond$ is defined further below Eq. $(\star\star\star)$)

---

**Algorithm 1.** Computes the normalized generator of the hull of a code with one-dimensional hull.

**Algorithm 2:** ConstructDict

**Data:** $k$-dimensional code $\mathcal{C} \subset \mathbb{F}_q^{m \times n}$, integer $L$
**Result:** Dictionary $\{\chi : (A, U)\}$ with $L$ keys
where $U \in \mathbb{F}_q^{m \times m}$ generates $h(\mathcal{C}_A)$ and has characteristic polynomial $\chi$

```
Dict = {}
Compute a basis of C^⊥
while length(Dict) < L do
    Pick a random A ∈ C^⊥
    if rk(A) = m and dim(C_A) = k then
        if dim h(C_A) = 1 then
            (χ, U) = ComputeNormalizedCharpoly(C_A)
            if gcd(χ(t), χ'(t)) = 1 and χ ∉ Dict then
                Add entry (χ : (A, U)) to Dict
return Dict
```

**Algorithm 2.** Constructs a dictionary whose keys are separable polynomials, and whose values are pairs of matrices $(A, U)$ such that $h(\mathcal{C}_A) = \mathbb{F}_q U$.

**Algorithm 3:** Finding $P$

**Data:** $k$-dimensional code $\mathcal{D} \subset \mathbb{F}_q^{m \times n}$, integer $N$, dictionary Dict
**Result:** Triple $(A, B, P) \in (\mathbb{F}_q^{m \times n})^2 \times (\mathbb{F}_q^{m \times m})^2 \times \mathrm{GL}_m(\mathbb{F}_q)$ s.t. $\mathcal{D}_B = P\mathcal{C}_A P^{-1}$

```
i = 0
while i < N do
    Pick a random B ∈ D^⊥
    if rk(B) = m and dim(D_B) = k then
        if dim h(D_B) = 1 then
            i = i + 1
            (χ, V) = ComputeNormalizedCharpoly(D_B)
            if χ is a key of Dict with value A then
                Use one of the Algorithms of Section 4 to deduce P
                if success then
                    return (A, B, P)
return ⊥
```

**Algorithm 3.** Returns a triple $(A, B, P)$ where $\mathcal{D}_B = P\mathcal{C}_A P^{-1}$.

### 3.2 Distribution of the Computed Matrix Spaces and Polynomials

In this section, we discuss the distribution of the matrix spaces and characteristic polynomials obtained using the algorithms above. Given a vector space $V$ and an integer $d$, we denote by $\mathrm{Gr}_d(V)$ (resp. $\mathrm{Gr}_{\leqslant d}(V)$) the set of all $d$-dimensional (resp. at most $d$-dimensional) linear subspaces of $V$. We prove that given a uniformly random $\mathcal{C} \in \mathrm{Gr}_k(\mathbb{F}_q^{m \times n})$ and $A \in \mathcal{C}^\perp$ such that $\mathcal{C}_A$ has one-dimensional hull (and some mild additional conditions), the distribution of the characteristic polynomials of a generator of these hulls is asymptotically uniform with respect to $q$.

Given a matrix $A \in \mathbb{F}_q^{m\times n}$, we define the map

$$\begin{aligned}\phi_A\colon \mathbb{F}_q^{m\times n} &\longrightarrow \mathbb{F}_q^{m\times m}\\ M &\longmapsto MA^\top.\end{aligned}$$

For a $k$-dimensional code $\mathcal{C} \subset \mathbb{F}_q^{m\times n}$ and a matrix $A \in \mathbb{F}_q^{m\times n}$, we consider in our reduction the code $\phi_A(\mathcal{C}) = \mathcal{C}_A \subset \mathbb{F}_q^{m\times m}$. This amounts to considering the map

$$\begin{aligned}\Phi\colon \mathrm{Gr}_k(\mathbb{F}_q^{m\times n}) \times \mathbb{F}_q^{m\times n} &\longrightarrow \mathrm{Gr}_{\leqslant k}(\mathbb{F}_q^{m\times m})\\ (\mathcal{C}, A) &\longmapsto \phi_A(\mathcal{C}) = \mathcal{C}_A.\end{aligned}$$

We will choose $A$ to have full rank $m$ (recall that $m \leqslant n$). This entails that $\phi_A$ is surjective. The preimages of a $k$-dimensional code $\mathcal{D} \subset \mathbb{F}_q^{m\times m}$ under $\Phi$ are exactly the pairs $(\mathcal{C}, A)$ such that $\mathcal{C} \subset \phi_A^{-1}(\mathcal{D})$ and $\mathcal{C} \cap \ker(\phi_A) = 0$. We now set

$$X \stackrel{\text{def}}{=} \{(\mathcal{C}, A) \in \mathrm{Gr}_k(\mathbb{F}_q^{m\times n}) \times \mathbb{F}_q^{m\times n} \mid A \in \mathcal{C}^\perp,\ \mathrm{rk}(A) = m,\ \mathcal{C} \cap \ker(\phi_A) = 0\}.$$

**Lemma 5.** *The restricted map*

$$f_1 = \Phi_{|X}\colon X \to \mathrm{Gr}_k(\ker(\mathrm{Tr})), \tag{$\star$}$$

*where* $\mathrm{Gr}_k(\ker(\mathrm{Tr}))$ *denotes the set of $k$–dimensional spaces of $m \times m$ matrices whose trace is zero, is surjective and equidistributed (i.e. each element of its image has the same number of preimages).*

*Proof.* Given $\mathcal{D} \in \mathrm{Gr}_k(\mathbb{F}_q^{m\times m})$ whose elements have trace zero, any element $(\mathcal{C}, A) \in \Phi_{|X}^{-1}(\mathcal{D})$ satisfies $A \in \mathcal{C}^\perp$. Given a rank $m$ matrix $A \in \mathbb{F}_q^{m\times n}$, the codes $\mathcal{C}$ such that $\mathcal{C}A^\top = \mathcal{D}$ and $(\mathcal{C}, A) \in X$ are exactly the complementary subspaces of $\ker(\phi_A)$ in $\phi_A^{-1}(\mathcal{D})$. The number of elements in $\Phi_{|X}^{-1}(\mathcal{D})$ is the number of rank $m$ matrices in $\mathbb{F}_q^{m\times n}$ multiplied by the number of complementary subspaces of an $m(n-m)$-dimensional subspace in a $(k + m(n-m))$-dimensional $\mathbb{F}_q$-vector space. The latter number is nonzero and does not depend on a particular choice of $\mathcal{D}$. Hence, the map $f_1$ is surjective and equidistributed. □

**Lemma 6.** *In a code $\mathcal{C}_A \subset \ker(\mathrm{Tr})$, any element in the hull of $\mathcal{C}_A$ satisfies* $\mathrm{Tr}(U^2) = 0$.

*Proof.* This is a direct consequence of the definition of the hull (Definition 6).

**Lemma 7.** *If $q$ is not a power of 2, the map*

$$f_2\colon \{\mathcal{C} \in \mathrm{Gr}_k(\ker(\mathrm{Tr})) \mid \dim h(\mathcal{C}) = 1\} \to \{U \in \mathbb{F}_q^{m\times m} \mid \mathrm{Tr}(U) = \mathrm{Tr}(U^2) = 0\}/\mathbb{F}_q^\times \tag{$\star\star$}$$

*which sends $\mathcal{C}$ to a generator of $h(\mathcal{C})$ (modulo the action of $\mathbb{F}_q^\times$) is equidistributed. In particular, as soon as the set on the left is nonempty, $f_2$ is surjective.*

*Proof.* We work in $\ker(\mathrm{Tr})$ with the non-degenerate bilinear form $(X, Y) \mapsto \mathrm{Tr}(XY)$. Consider any two matrices $U_1, U_2$ such that $\mathrm{Tr}(U_i) = \mathrm{Tr}(U_i^2) = 0$. To prove equidistribution, it is enough to construct a bijection between their preimages under this map. The map $\mathbb{F}_q U_1 \to \mathbb{F}_q U_2$ which sends $U_1$ to $U_2$ is an isometry with respect to the aforementioned bilinear form. Since $\mathrm{char}(\mathbb{F}_q) \neq 2$, Witt's extension theorem [15, Thm. 5.2] ensures that this map extends to an isometry $g$ of $\ker(\mathrm{Tr})$. Then, the map

$$\{\mathcal{C} \subset \ker(\mathrm{Tr}) \mid h(\mathcal{C}) = \mathbb{F}_q U_1\} \to \{\mathcal{C} \subset \ker(\mathrm{Tr}) \mid h(\mathcal{C}) = \mathbb{F}_q U_2\}$$

which sends $\mathcal{C}$ to $g(\mathcal{C})$ is a bijection. □

*Remark 6.* Recall that Proposition 1 states that asymptotically, $1/q$ of all matrix codes in $\mathrm{Gr}_k(\ker \mathrm{Tr})$ have a one-dimensional hull. Hence, the number of these codes is equivalent to $q^{k(m^2-1-k)-1}$ when $q \to \infty$. Therefore, for big enough $q$, such codes exist, and the map $f_2$ is always surjective.

**Lemma 8.** *Let $\chi \in \mathbb{F}_q[t]$ be a separable polynomial of degree $m$ such that $\chi(0) \neq 0$. The number of matrices $U$ with characteristic polynomial $\chi$ is asymptotically (when $q \to \infty$) equivalent to $q^{m^2-m}$.*

*Proof.* Let $U$ be a matrix with characteristic polynomial $\chi$. Since $\chi$ is separable, it is also the minimal polynomial of $U$, and the matrices with characteristic polynomial $\chi$ are conjugates of $U$. There are as many conjugates of $U$ as elements in the quotient

$$\mathrm{GL}_m(\mathbb{F}_q)/\{P \in \mathrm{GL}_m(\mathbb{F}_q) \mid PUP^{-1} = U\}.$$

Since $U$ has a separable characteristic polynomial, any matrix which commutes with $U$ is a polynomial in $U$ [16, Cor. IV.E.8]. We are looking for the cardinality of $\mathbb{F}_q[U] \cap \mathrm{GL}_m(\mathbb{F}_q)$. A classical consequence of Cayley Hamilton theorem entails that $\mathbb{F}_q[U] \cap \mathrm{GL}_m(\mathbb{F}_q)$ is nothing but the group $\mathbb{F}_q[U]^\times$ of invertible elements of the ring $\mathbb{F}_q[U]$. Hence, the polynomials $f \in \mathbb{F}_q[t]/(\chi)$ such that $f(U)$ is not invertible are those that are divisible by an irreducible factor of $\chi$. Their number is maximal when $U$ is diagonalizable over $\mathbb{F}_q$, in which case there are less than $mq^{m-1}$ such polynomials. Hence, $\mathbb{F}_q[U] \cap \mathrm{GL}_m(\mathbb{F}_q)$ has at least $q^m - mq^{m-1} = q^m(1 - m/q)$ elements; since it always has less than $q^m$ elements, its cardinality is equivalent to $q^m$, and that of $\mathrm{GL}_m(\mathbb{F}_q)/(\mathbb{F}_q[U] \cap \mathrm{GL}_m(\mathbb{F}_q))$ is equivalent to $q^{m^2-m}$. □

Consider the set of matrices $U \in \mathrm{GL}_m(\mathbb{F}_q)$ such that $\mathrm{Tr}(U) = \mathrm{Tr}(U^2) = 0$, up to scalar multiplication. The characteristic polynomial $\chi_U \in \mathbb{F}_q[t]$ of such a matrix $U$ is of the form $t^m + a_{m-3}t^{m-3} + \cdots + a_1 t + a_0$, with $a_0 \neq 0$ since $U$ is invertible. For any $\lambda \in \mathbb{F}_q^\times$, the characteristic polynomial of $\lambda U$ is

$$\chi_{\lambda U} = t^m + \lambda^3 a_{m-3} t^{m-3} + \cdots + \lambda^{m-1} a_1 t + \lambda^m a_0.$$

Hence, there is a map

$$f_3\colon \{U \in \mathrm{GL}_m(\mathbb{F}_q) \mid \mathrm{Tr}(U) = \mathrm{Tr}(U^2) = 0\}/\mathbb{F}_q^\times \longrightarrow \mathbb{F}_q^{m-2}/\mathbb{F}_q^\times$$
$$U \longmapsto (a_{m-3}, \dots, a_0) \qquad (\star\star\star)$$

where $\mathbb{F}_q^\times$ acts on $\mathbb{F}_q^{m-2}$ via $\lambda \diamond (a_{m-3}, \dots, a_0) = (\lambda^3 a_{m-3}, \dots, \lambda^m a_0)$. Its image is $(\mathbb{F}_q^{m-2} - (\mathbb{F}_q^{m-3} \times \{0\}))/\mathbb{F}_q^\times$. Lemma 8 asserts that any element of the form $(a_{m-3}, \dots, u_0)$ corresponding to a separable polynomial has $\sim q^{m^2-m}$ preimages under $f_3$.

Denote by

$$\mathrm{Sep}_{q,m} \subset (\mathbb{F}_q^{m-2} - (\mathbb{F}_q^{m-3} \times \{0\}))/\mathbb{F}_q^\times$$

the set of classes of separable characteristic polynomials with nonzero constant coefficient.

*Remark 7.* We give more details about this construction in Appendix A. In particular, we show in Lemma 15 that the set $\mathrm{Sep}_{q,m}$ has $\sim q^{m-3}$ elements. In Algorithm 1, we use a unique representative of each class of characteristic polynomials. The way of computing such a normalized representative is also explained in Appendix A and presented in Algorithm 7.

**Proposition 2.** *Suppose $q$ is not a power of 2. Denote by*

$$f_q = f_3 \circ f_2 \circ f_1 \colon X \to \mathbb{F}_q^{m-2}/\mathbb{F}_q^\times$$

*the map which sends $(\mathcal{C}, A)$ to the equivalence class of the tuple of coefficients of the characteristic polynomial of a generator of the hull of $\mathcal{C}_A$. The maps $f_1, f_2, f_3$ are defined in $(\star), (\star\star), (\star\star\star)$. The map*

$$f_{q|f_q^{-1}(\mathrm{Sep}_{q,m})} \colon f_q^{-1}(\mathrm{Sep}_{q,m}) \to \mathrm{Sep}_{q,m}$$

*is asymptotically equidistributed, i.e.*

$$\min_{\chi \in \mathrm{Sep}_{q,m}} |f_q^{-1}(\chi)| \underset{q\to\infty}{\sim} \max_{\chi \in \mathrm{Sep}_{q,m}} |f_q^{-1}(\chi)|.$$

*Proof.* It is a direct consequence of Lemmas 5, 7 and 8. □

*Remark 8.* The elements produced by Algorithm 2 are characteristic polynomials obtained by picking uniformly random elements of $f_q^{-1}(\mathrm{Sep}_{q,m})$ and computing a normalized representative of their image under the map $f$. Hence, Proposition 2 shows that given uniformly random inputs $\mathcal{C} \in \mathrm{Gr}_k(\mathbb{F}_q^{m\times n})$, the distribution of normalized characteristic polynomials $\chi \in \mathrm{Sep}_{q,m}$ produced by Algorithm 2 is asymptotically uniform.

*Remark 9.* The result above shows that the distribution of the computed characteristic polynomials is asymptotically uniform for random $\mathcal{C}$ and $A$. But in practice, a fixed code $\mathcal{C}$ is given to us. In that case, we have not said anything about the distribution of the codes $\mathcal{C}A^\top$ yet. In the special case $m = n$, the map

$$\psi_\mathcal{C} : \mathcal{C}^\perp \cap \mathrm{GL}_m(\mathbb{F}_q) \to \mathrm{Gr}_k(\mathbb{F}_q^{m\times m})$$

sending $A$ to $\mathcal{C}A^\top$ is equidistributed. Indeed, given two codes $\mathcal{D}_1 = \mathcal{C}A_1^\top \in \mathrm{Gr}_k(\mathbb{F}_q^{m\times m})$ and $\mathcal{D}_2 = \mathcal{C}A_2^\top$, the map

$$\begin{aligned} \psi_\mathcal{C}^{-1}(\mathcal{D}_1) &\longrightarrow \psi_\mathcal{C}^{-1}(\mathcal{D}_2) \\ B_1 &\longmapsto A_2 A_1^{-1} B_1 \end{aligned}$$

is a bijection.

### 3.3 Complexity Analysis

In this section, the symbol $\sim$ always denotes asymptotic equivalence, and the notation $o(\cdot)$ denotes asymptotic domination, with respect to the parameter $q$. We make the following assumption, justified by Remarks 8 and 9.

**Assumption 1.** *Given a code $\mathcal{C}$, distinct full-rank matrices $A$ yield distinct codes $\mathcal{C}_A = \mathcal{C}A^\top$ and the characteristic polynomials $\chi$ are uniformly distributed among the codes $\mathcal{C}_A$ with one-dimensional hull. For this, we require $k \leqslant m^2 - 2$: otherwise, the codes $\mathcal{C}A^\top$ would be the full* $\ker(\mathrm{Tr})$ *as soon as $A$ has full rank, and could not have a one-dimensional hull.*

We are going to answer the following questions:

1. How many matrices $A$ do we need to sample to find enough characteristic polynomials?
2. How many operations are needed to compute the dictionary?
3. What is the total complexity of running Algorithms 2 and 3 with the parameters answering the previous questions?

**How many matrices $A$ do we need to sample in order to find enough characteristic polynomials?** For any $A \in \mathcal{C}^\perp$ and any $\lambda \in \mathbb{F}_q^\times$, $\mathcal{C}_A = \mathcal{C}_{\lambda A}$. Hence, the total number of codes $\mathcal{C}_A$, $A \in \mathcal{C}^\perp$ is less than

$$\frac{1}{q-1}(\#\mathcal{C}^\perp - 1) = \frac{q^{k^\perp} - 1}{q-1} \sim q^{k^\perp - 1}$$

where $k^\perp = \dim(\mathcal{C}^\perp) = mn - k$. The number of $\mathcal{C}_A$ with one-dimensional hull is therefore equivalent to $q^{k^\perp - 2}$ by Proposition 1. The total number of possible classes of separable characteristic polynomials is $\sim q^{m-3}$ (see Lemma 15).

Thus, the dictionary constructed in Algorithm 2 will have size $L \leqslant q^{m-3}$. Then, according to the usual list collision arguments, the number $L'$ of one-dimensional hulls to check in Algorithm 3 should satisfy

$$LL' \sim q^{k^{\perp}-2}.$$

We have to treat two cases separately:

(*i*) $k^{\perp} - 2 \leqslant 2(m-3)$, where the dictionary constructed by Algorithm 2 will not need to cover all the possible characteristic polynomials and we take

$$L \sim q^{\frac{k^{\perp}}{2}-1} \quad \text{and} \quad L' \sim q^{\frac{k^{\perp}}{2}-1};$$

(*ii*) $k^{\perp} - 2 > 2(m-3)$, where there are not enough different characteristic polynomials to have $L \sim L'$, and we take

$$L \sim q^{m-3} \quad \text{and} \quad L' \sim q^{k^{\perp}-m+1}.$$

**Lemma 9.** *Let $r$ be an integer. The average number of matrices to sample in Algorithm 2 in order to get $r$ distinct characteristic polynomials is $\sim qr$ if $r = o(q^{m-3})$ and $\sim qr\log(r)$ if $r \sim q^{m-3}$.*

*Proof.* The latter case is a classical result usually called *coupon collector's problem*, while for the former we prove a variant. Denote by

$$N_{\chi} \sim q^{m-3}$$

the total number of possible characteristic polynomials with the shape $X^m + a_{m-3}X^{m-3} + \cdots + a_0$, by $M \leqslant (q^{k^{\perp}} - 1)/(q-1)$ the number of elements in $(\mathcal{C}^{\perp} - \{0\})/\mathbb{F}_q^{\times}$ with full rank and by $S_r$ the number of matrices $A$ we have to sample in order to get $r$ different characteristic polynomials of matrices spanning one-dimensional hulls of codes $\mathcal{C}_A$. Denote by $s_j$ the number of matrices to sample after having a list of $j-1$ distinct polynomials in order to get the $j$-th one. We seek to compute the expected value

$$\mathbb{E}(S_r) = \mathbb{E}(s_1) + \cdots + \mathbb{E}(s_r).$$

The random variable $s_j$ follows a geometric distribution: it is the first success of a Bernoulli variable. The parameter $p_j$ of this variable is computed as follows: it is the proportion, among all the elements of $(\mathcal{C}^{\perp} - \{0\})/\mathbb{F}_q^{\times}$, of those (equivalence classes of) matrices $A$ yielding a code $\mathcal{C}_A$ with one-dimensional hull and characteristic polynomial that is not among the $j$ polynomials already in the list. From Proposition 1, the number of full–rank matrices $A$ that yield a code $\mathcal{C}_A$ with one-dimensional hull is

$$M\left(\frac{1}{q} + \mathcal{O}\left(\frac{m^2}{q^{(m^2+1)/2}}\right)\right).$$

Under Assumption 1, the number of matrices that yield a code $\mathcal{C}_A$ with a one-dimensional hull and one of the $j$ characteristic polynomials already in the list is

$$j \cdot \frac{M\left(\frac{1}{q} + \mathcal{O}\left(\frac{m^2}{q^{(m^2+1)/2}}\right)\right)}{N_\chi}.$$

Hence

$$\begin{aligned}
p_j &= \frac{1}{M}\left[\frac{M}{q} + \mathcal{O}\left(\frac{m^2 M}{q^{(m^2+1)/2}}\right) - j\frac{M}{qN_\chi} + \frac{j}{N_\chi}\mathcal{O}\left(\frac{m^2 M}{q^{(m^2+1)/2}}\right)\right] \\
&= \frac{1}{q}\left(1 - \frac{j}{N_\chi}\right) + \mathcal{O}\left(\frac{m^2}{q^{(m^2+1)/2}}\right) \\
&\sim \frac{1}{q}\left(1 - \frac{j}{N_\chi}\right) \qquad \left(\text{since } \tfrac{1}{qN_\chi} \sim \tfrac{1}{q^{m-2}}\right) \\
&\sim \frac{N_\chi - j}{qN_\chi}.
\end{aligned}$$

The expected value of the geometric random variable $s_j$ with parameter $p_j$ is $1/p_j$. Hence, using the fact that $r = o(N_\chi)$,

$$\begin{aligned}
\mathbb{E}(S_r) &\sim qN_\chi\left(\frac{1}{N_\chi} + \cdots + \frac{1}{N_\chi - r + 1}\right) \\
&\sim qN_\chi \log\left(\frac{N_\chi}{N_\chi - r}\right) \\
&\sim -qN_\chi \log\left(1 - r/N_\chi\right) \sim qr.
\end{aligned}$$

□

## Complexity of Computing the Dictionary

**Lemma 10.** *The average complexity of Algorithm 2 with input a $k$-dimensional code $\mathcal{C} \subset \mathbb{F}_q^{m\times n}$ and a desired list length $L$ is*

$$\begin{aligned}
&\mathcal{O}(qLk(nm^{\omega-1} + km^2)) \quad \text{if } L = o(q^{m-3}) \\
&\mathcal{O}(q^{m-2}km(nm^{\omega-1} + km^2)) \quad \text{if } L \sim q^{m-3}.
\end{aligned}$$

*Proof.* In order to get $L$ distinct characteristic polynomials, Lemma 9 tells us that we need to sample $\sim qL$ matrices $A$ if $L = o(q^{m-3})$ and $\sim qL\log L$ if $L \sim q^{m-3}$. In this last case, this requires to sample $\sim mq^{m-2}$ matrices. For each of these, we first need to compute a basis $(C_1, \ldots, C_k)$ of $\mathcal{C}A^\top$, which is given by $k$ products of a matrix of size $m \times n$ by a matrix of size $n \times m$; this requires $\mathcal{O}(knm^{\omega-1})$ operations in $\mathbb{F}_q$. Then, we need to compute $\mathcal{C}_A \cap \mathcal{C}_A^\perp$, which is given by the kernel of the (symmetric) Gram matrix $(\mathrm{Tr}(C_iC_j))_{1\leqslant i,j\leqslant k}$. Computing the diagonal entries of a given product $C_iC_j$ requires $\mathcal{O}(m^2)$ operations in $\mathbb{F}_q$. Hence, the Gram matrix is computed in $\mathcal{O}(k^2m^2)$ operations in $\mathbb{F}_q$. Computing its kernel takes $\mathcal{O}(k^\omega)$ operations in $\mathbb{F}_q$. When the hull has dimension 1, we then only need to compute the characteristic polynomial of the generator we have found, which is done in $\mathcal{O}(m^\omega)$ operations [21, Thm. 1.1], and to normalize it. This normalization can be precomputed for a proportion $(1-2/q)$ of all cases (see Remark 12). So sampling one matrix takes $\mathcal{O}(knm^{\omega-1}+k^2m^2+k^\omega+m^\omega)$ operations, which, since $k \leqslant m^2$ and $m \leqslant n$ gives $\mathcal{O}(k(nm^{\omega-1}+km^2))$. Multiplying this by the number of sampled matrices (mentioned in the beginning of the present proof) yields the result. □

**Total Complexity of This Reduction Step** Recall that we allowed ourselves to replace $\mathcal{C}$ with $\mathcal{C}^\perp$ if needed, in order to ensure that $k^\perp \leqslant k$ and that we need $k < m^2-1$ for the algorithm to work (see Remark 5).

**Theorem 1.** *Suppose that $m \leqslant n$ and $k^\perp \leqslant k < m^2-1$ and that Assumption 1 holds. Under Assumption 2, Algorithm 3 takes an expected complexity of*

$$\mathcal{O}\left(km(nm^{\omega-1}+km^2)q^{\max(\frac{k^\perp}{2},k^\perp-m+2)}+m^{2\omega}q^{k^\perp-m+1}\right)$$

*operations in $\mathbb{F}_q$, and a space complexity of*

$$\mathcal{O}\left((k^\perp+m+1)q^{\min(\frac{k^\perp}{2}-1,m-3)}\right)$$

*elements of $\mathbb{F}_q$.*

*Remark 10.* One can get rid of Assumption 2 by replacing the techniques of Subsect. 4.1 by those of Subsect. 4.2 at the cost of another sub-exponential term in the time complexity (Lemma 13). Namely, this would give an overall complexity of

$$\mathcal{O}\left(km(nm^{\omega-1}+km^2)q^{\max(\frac{k^\perp}{2},k^\perp-m+2)}+q^{k^\perp-m+1}k^{\omega-1}m^2q^{3\sqrt{m}/\sqrt{\log m}\log q}\right)$$

operations in $\mathbb{F}_q$.

*Proof.* We consider separately Cases (i) and (ii) introduced in Page 18. The time complexity of Algorithm 2, given by Lemma 10, is

$$\mathcal{O}\left(k(nm^{\omega-1}+km^2)q^{\max(\frac{k^\perp}{2},k^\perp-m+2)}\right).$$

The cost of Algorithm 3 depends on the number of "false positives" encountered, *i.e.* situations where we find for $h(\mathcal{D}_B)$ a characteristic polynomial which is an entry of the dictionary but running an Algorithm of Sect. 4 shows that $\mathcal{D}_B$ is not a conjugate of the code $\mathcal{C}_A$ corresponding to that entry. For each key of the dictionary, there are $\sim q^{k^\perp-2}/q^{m-3} = q^{k^\perp-m+1}$ one-dimensional hulls corresponding to this key, roughly all of which are false positives.

In Case (i), Algorithm 3 costs

$$\mathcal{O}\left(km(nm^{\omega-1}+km^2)q^{\frac{k^\perp}{2}}+m^{2\omega}q^{k^\perp-m+1}\right).$$

In Case (ii), recall that the algorithms of Sect. 4, whose complexities are given in Lemma 11, have to be called on average $q^{k^\perp - m+1}$ times. Here, the complexity of calling the algorithms of Sect. 4 outweighs that of computing the dictionary, and the time complexity of Algorithm 3 is

$$\mathcal{O}(m^{2\omega} q^{k^\perp - m+1}).$$

The space complexity is simple to compute: it is dominated by the number $L$ of entries in the dictionary. There are $\mathcal{O}(q^{\min(\frac{k^\perp}{2}-1, m-3)})$ such entries, which consist of a matrix $A \in \mathcal{C}^\perp$ and a characteristic polynomial. To reduce space complexity, one may store in each of these entries only the coordinates of the matrix $A$ in a basis of $\mathcal{C}^\perp$ as well as the characteristic polynomial of the generator of $h(\mathcal{C}_A)$, which amounts to $k^\perp + m + 1$ field elements per entry. □

## 4 Finding the Right Matrix

In order to shorten the notations, we now denote by $\mathcal{C}, \mathcal{D}$ the codes $\mathcal{C}_A, \mathcal{D}_B$. We are in the following situation: we are given two codes $\mathcal{C}, \mathcal{D} \subset \mathbb{F}_q^{m \times m}$ with one-dimensional hulls generated respectively by matrices $U, V$ and a matrix $R \in \mathrm{GL}_m(\mathbb{F}_q)$ such that $V = RUR^{-1}$. Our aim is to decide whether $\mathcal{C}_A$ and $\mathcal{D}_B$ are conjugate by some matrix $P \in \mathrm{GL}_m(\mathbb{F}_q)$, and if they are, find such a matrix.

In this section, we propose two approaches. The first one is based on multivariate polynomial system solving and has a polynomial time complexity conditioned by some assumption. The second one is based on diagonalization arguments, has a sub-exponential time complexity but does not rest on any assumption.

### 4.1 First Approach: Using Polynomial System Solving

The one-dimensional hulls of the codes $\mathcal{C}$ and $\mathcal{D}$ are respectively generated by conjugate matrices $U, V \in \mathrm{GL}_m(\mathbb{F}_q)$ having a squarefree characteristic polynomial. We can compute a matrix $R \in \mathrm{GL}_m(\mathbb{F}_q)$ such that $V = RUR^{-1}$, hence $h(\mathcal{D}) = Rh(\mathcal{C})R^{-1}$. We are looking for a matrix $P \in \mathrm{GL}_m(\mathbb{F}_q)$ such that $\mathcal{D} = P\mathcal{C}P^{-1}$. We know that the matrix $P \in \mathbb{F}_q^{m \times m}$ we are looking for satisfies $V = PUP^{-1}$. Therefore, there exists a matrix $T \in \mathbb{F}_q^{m \times m}$ which commutes with $U$ such that $P = RT$. Since the characteristic polynomial of $U$ is separable, we can write $T = f(U)$, where $f = \alpha_0 + \alpha_1 t + \cdots + \alpha_{m-1} t^{m-1} \in \mathbb{F}_q[t]$ (see [16, Cor. IV.E.8]). We know $R$ and search for a polynomial $f$ such that

$$\mathcal{D} = Rf(U)\mathcal{C}f(U)^{-1}R^{-1}. \qquad (\circ)$$

A usual argument (for instance by Cayley-Hamilton Theorem) shows that there exists a polynomial $g$ of degree $< m$ such that $f(U)^{-1} = g(U)$. Then, we can solve the following system whose unknowns are the coefficients of $f, g$:

$$Rf(U)\mathcal{C}g(U)R^{-1} \subset \mathcal{D}. \qquad (2)$$

The above system is bilinear in the $m$ coefficients of $f$ and the $m$ coefficients of $g$. Thus, when linearizing, this yields $m^2$ unknowns while $\mathcal{C}, \mathcal{D} \in \mathbb{F}_q^{m\times m}$ both have dimension $k$ (recall that for short we denote $\mathcal{C}_A, \mathcal{D}_B$ by $\mathcal{C}, \mathcal{D}$), hence the system has $k(m^2-k)$ equations which exceeds $m^2$ as soon as $1 < k < m^2 - 1$. Thus, the linearized system is over-constrained, which encourages to make the following assumption.

**Assumption 2.** *The linearized version of System* (2) *has a space of solutions of dimension* 1 *when* $\mathcal{C}, \mathcal{D}$ *are conjugate and no nonzero solution otherwise.*

**Lemma 11.** *Under Assumption 2, the calculation of the polynomial* $f$ *and hence of the matrix* $P$ *requires* $\mathcal{O}(m^{2\omega})$ *operations in* $\mathbb{F}_q$*".*

### 4.2 Second Approach: Using Diagonalization

Our strategy may be broken down into the following two steps:

1. Since their characteristic polynomial is separable, $U$ and $V$ are diagonalizable over an extension of $\mathbb{F}_q$: we may reduce to the case where they are diagonal.
2. We find the matrix $P$, which is $R$ multiplied by some element of $\mathbb{F}_q[U]$, by considering its action on some subspaces of $\mathcal{C}$.

**Reducing to Diagonal Matrices.** Under the assumption that $U, V$ have a squarefree characteristic polynomial, there is a diagonal matrix $\Delta$ and a matrix $S \in \mathrm{GL}_m(\mathbb{F}_{q'})$ both defined over an extension $\mathbb{F}_{q'}$ of $\mathbb{F}_q$ such that $V = S\Delta S^{-1}$. Such matrices $S, \Delta$ are easily computable. Therefore,

$$U = R^{-1}VR = R^{-1}S\Delta S^{-1}R$$

and ($\circ$) is equivalent to

$$\mathcal{D} = Sf(\Delta)S^{-1}R\mathcal{C}R^{-1}Sf(\Delta)^{-1}S^{-1}$$

*i.e.*,

$$S^{-1}\mathcal{D}S = f(\Delta)\cdot S^{-1}R\mathcal{C}R^{-1}S\cdot f(\Delta)^{-1}.$$

We may compute bases of $\mathcal{D}' = S^{-1}\mathcal{D}S$ and $\mathcal{C}' = S^{-1}R\mathcal{C}R^{-1}S$. The problem at hand is now to compute $f \in \mathbb{F}_q[t]$ of degree at most $m-1$ such that, given codes $\mathcal{C}', \mathcal{D}' \subset \mathbb{F}_q^{m\times m}$ of dimension $k$ and a diagonal matrix $\Delta$,

$$\mathcal{D}' = f(\Delta)\mathcal{C}'f(\Delta)^{-1}.$$

The reduction is summed up in the algorithm below.

**Algorithm 4:** REDUCING TO DIAGONAL MATRICES

**Data:** Codes $\mathcal{C}, \mathcal{D} \subset \mathbb{F}_q^{m \times m}$
Matrices $U, V \in \mathbb{F}_q^{m \times m}$ with separable characteristic polynomial s.t. $h(\mathcal{C}) = \mathbb{F}_q \cdot U$ and $h(\mathcal{D}) = \mathbb{F}_q \cdot V$
Matrix $R \in \mathrm{GL}_m(\mathbb{F}_q)$ such that $V = RUR^{-1}$
**Result:** Tuple $(\mathcal{C}', \mathcal{D}', \Delta, S)$ where:
$S \in \mathrm{GL}_m(\mathbb{F}_{q'})$ for some extension $\mathbb{F}_{q'}/\mathbb{F}_q$,
$\Delta \in \mathrm{GL}_m(\mathbb{F}_{q'})$ diagonal, $V = S\Delta S^{-1}$, $\mathcal{C}' = S^{-1}R\mathcal{C}R^{-1}S$ and $\mathcal{D}' = S^{-1}\mathcal{D}S$.

Compute field extension $\mathbb{F}_{q'}$ of $\mathbb{F}_q$ over which $U$ is diagonalizable
Compute $S \in \mathrm{GL}_m(\mathbb{F}_{q'})$ and diagonal $\Delta \in \mathbb{F}_{q'}^{m \times m}$ s.t. $V = S\Delta S^{-1}$
Compute bases of $\mathcal{C}' = S^{-1}R\mathcal{C}R^{-1}S$ and $\mathcal{D}' = S^{-1}\mathcal{D}S$
**return** $(\mathcal{C}', \mathcal{D}', \Delta, S)$

**Conjugating by the Right Matrix.** Replacing $q, \mathcal{C}, \mathcal{D}$ with $q', \mathcal{C}', \mathcal{D}'$, we are now left with the following problem. We are given codes $\mathcal{C}, \mathcal{D} \subset \mathbb{F}_q^{m \times m}$ of dimension $k$ and a diagonal matrix $\Delta$, and need to find a polynomial $f \in \mathbb{F}_q[t]$ such that $\deg(f) < m$ and $\mathcal{D} = f(\Delta)\mathcal{C}f(\Delta)^{-1}$. Note that if a polynomial $f$ verifies this, any scalar multiple of $f$ does, so we may assume that $f$ is monic. We may write

$$\Delta = \begin{pmatrix} \delta_1 & & & \\ & \delta_2 & & \\ & & \ddots & \\ & & & \delta_m \end{pmatrix}$$

and since $\Delta$ is diagonal,

$$f(\Delta) = \begin{pmatrix} f(\delta_1) & & & \\ & f(\delta_2) & & \\ & & \ddots & \\ & & & f(\delta_m) \end{pmatrix}.$$

Our strategy is the following:

- Find the entries of $f(\Delta)$.
- Knowing $\Delta$, retrieve $f$ using Lagrange interpolation.

We may easily find a set $\Lambda$ of $k-1$ non-diagonal indexes $(i,j) \in \{1 \ldots m\}^2$ such that the respective intersections $\mathcal{C}(\Lambda), \mathcal{D}(\Lambda)$ of $\mathcal{C}, \mathcal{D}$ with the subspace $E_\Lambda$ of $\mathbb{F}_q^{m \times m}$ defined by the equations $\{x_{i,j} = 0\}_{(i,j) \in \Lambda}$ are one-dimensional.

**Lemma 12.** *The subspaces $\mathcal{C}(\Lambda), \mathcal{D}(\Lambda)$ satisfy*

$$f(\Delta)\mathcal{C}(\Lambda)f(\Delta)^{-1} = \mathcal{D}(\Lambda).$$

*Proof.* Since $\Delta$ is diagonal, so is $f(\Delta)$, and conjugating a matrix by $f(\Delta)$ does not change those of its entries which are equal to zero. Hence,

$$f(\Delta)E_\Lambda f(\Delta)^{-1} = E_\Lambda.$$

The result now follows from the equalities below.

$$\begin{aligned} f(\Delta)\mathcal{C}(\Lambda)f(\Delta)^{-1} &= f(\Delta)(\mathcal{C} \cap E_\Lambda)f(\Delta)^{-1} \\ &= (f(\Delta)\mathcal{C}f(\Delta)^{-1}) \cap (f(\Delta)E_\Lambda f(\Delta)^{-1}) \\ &= (f(\Delta)\mathcal{C}f(\Delta)^{-1}) \cap E_\Lambda \\ &= \mathcal{D}(\Lambda). \end{aligned}$$

□

We now pick a matrix $C = (c_{ij})_{i,j} \in \mathcal{C}(\Lambda)$, and a matrix $D = (d_{ij})_{i,j} \in \mathcal{D}(\Lambda)$. After multiplying by an element of $\mathbb{F}_q$, we may suppose that they have the same characteristic polynomial, and solve $Df(\Delta) = f(\Delta)C$. This means solving the system of $m(m-1)/2 - (k-1)$ equations

$$d_{ij}f(\lambda_j) = f(\lambda_i)c_{ij} \qquad (1 \leqslant i < j \leqslant m, (i,j) \notin S)$$

which yields the $m$ values $f(\delta_1), \ldots, f(\delta_m)$ up to a scalar multiple. We then find a polynomial $f$ corresponding to these values using Lagrange interpolation.

*Remark 11.* Note that in some rare cases, in particular if $k$ is very small, the matrix $C$ could have too many zeros for the system to determine $f$ uniquely. In that case, picking another set $S$ of coordinates does the trick.

**Algorithm 5:** FIND THE RIGHT POLYNOMIAL

**Data:** Codes $\mathcal{C}, \mathcal{D} \subset \mathbb{F}_q^{m\times m}$
Diagonal $\Delta = \mathrm{Diag}(\delta_1, \ldots, \delta_n) \in \mathbb{F}_q^{m\times m}$ s.t. $\delta \in \mathcal{C}$ and $\Delta \in \mathcal{D}$
**Result:** Polynomial $f \in \mathbb{F}_q[t]$ such that $\mathcal{D} = f(\Delta)\mathcal{C}f(\Delta)^{-1}$ (if exists)

```
while true do
    Pick set Λ of k − 1 random non diagonal indexes (i, j) ∈ {1, ..., m}^2
    Compute C(Λ) = C ∩ {x_ij = 0}_(i,j)∈Λ, D(Λ) = D ∩ {x_ij = 0}_(i,j)∈Λ
    if dim C(Λ) = dim D(Λ) = 1 then
        Pick C ∈ C(Λ), D ∈ D(Λ) with the same characteristic polynomial (if
          exist)
        Solve system d_ij u_j = u_i c_ij for (i, j) ∈ {1 ... m}^2
        if The system has no solution then
            return ⊥
        Compute polynomial f such that f(δ_i) = u_i
        return f
```

**Algorithm 6:** FIND THE RIGHT $P$

**Data:** Codes $\mathcal{C}, \mathcal{D} \subset \mathbb{F}_q^{m\times m}$
Matrices $U, V \in \mathbb{F}_q^{m\times m}$ with separable characteristic polynomial s.t. $h(\mathcal{C}) = \mathbb{F}_q \cdot U$ and $h(\mathcal{D}) = \mathbb{F}_q \cdot V$
Matrix $R \in \mathrm{GL}_m(\mathbb{F}_q)$ such that $V = RUR^{-1}$
**Result:** A matrix $P$ (if exists), such that $\mathcal{D} = P\mathcal{C}P^{-1}$

Compute $(\mathcal{C}', \mathcal{D}', \Delta, S)$ using Algorithm 4 with inputs $(\mathcal{C}, \mathcal{D}, U, V, R)$
Compute $f$ using Algorithm 5 with inputs $(\mathcal{C}', \mathcal{D}', \Delta)$
**if** $f = \perp$ **then**
  **return** $\perp$
**return** $Sf(\Delta)S^{-1}R$

**Complexity Analysis.**

**Lemma 13.** *Given conjugate codes $\mathcal{C}, \mathcal{D} \subset \mathbb{F}_q^{m\times m}$ with one-dimensional hulls and generators of these hulls with separable characteristic polynomials, the average complexity of finding $P \in \mathbb{F}_q^{m\times m}$ such that $\mathcal{D} = P\mathcal{C}P^{-1}$ using Algorithm 6 is*

$$\tilde{\mathcal{O}}(k^{\omega-1}m^2 q^{3\sqrt{m}/(\sqrt{\log m}\log q)}).$$

*Proof.* The smallest field extension $\mathbb{F}_{q'}$ over which the matrix $U$ is diagonalizable is the splitting field of its characteristic polynomial, which has degree $m$. The average degree $d$ of the splitting field of a monic polynomial of degree $m$ over $\mathbb{F}_q$ verifies [12, Thm. 2]

$$d = \exp\left(C\sqrt{m/\log(m)} + \mathcal{O}\left(\sqrt{m}\log(\log m)/\log(m)\right)\right)$$

where $C < 3$. This shows that $d = \mathcal{O}(q^{3\sqrt{m}/(\sqrt{\log m}\log q)})$. We can do all the computations over $\mathbb{F}_{q^d}$, which means the number of $\mathbb{F}_q$-operations will be that of $\mathbb{F}_{q^d}$-operations multiplied by $\tilde{\mathcal{O}}(d)$ (using FFT-based algorithm for polynomial arithmetic, see for instance [13, Thm. 8.23]). Diagonalizing $U$ and $V$ is done in time $\mathcal{O}(m^\omega)$. Computing the subspaces $\mathcal{C} \cap E_\Lambda$, $\mathcal{D} \cap E_\Lambda$ is just linear algebra and requires $\mathcal{O}(k^{\omega-1}m^2)$ operations in $\mathbb{F}_{q^d}$. Solving the system of equations takes $\mathcal{O}(m)$ multiplications in $\mathbb{F}_{q^d}$. In total, the complexity is $\tilde{\mathcal{O}}(dk^{\omega-1}m^2)$. □

## 5 Recovering $Q$ once We Know $P$

Note first that, given a code $\mathcal{C}_A$, the probability that a random code $\mathcal{D}$ is a conjugate of $\mathcal{C}_A$ is less than

$$|\,\mathrm{GL}_m(\mathbb{F}_q)|/|\,\mathrm{Gr}_k(\mathbb{F}_q^{m\times m})| \sim q^{m^2-k(m^2-k)}.$$

This is less than $q^{-m^2}$ for any $m \geqslant 3$ and $2 \leqslant k \leqslant m^2-2$. Thus, it is highly unlikely that we find matrices $A, B, P$ such that $\mathcal{D}_B = P\mathcal{C}_A P^{-1}$ without there existing a matrix $Q$ such that $\mathcal{D} = PCQ^{-1}$, and on average, the first $(A, B, P)$ found will be correct.

The problem we are now trying to solve is the following: given two $k$-dimensional codes $\mathcal{C}, \mathcal{D} \subset \mathbb{F}_q^{m\times n}$, find a matrix $Q \in \mathrm{GL}_m(\mathbb{F}_q)$ such that $\mathcal{D} = \mathcal{C}Q$. Let $(C_1, \ldots, C_k)$ be a basis of $\mathcal{C}$. Given any invertible matrix $Q \in \mathbb{F}_q^{n\times n}$ such that $C_1Q, \ldots, C_kQ \in \mathcal{D}$, we have $\mathcal{C}Q = \mathcal{D}$. Define the linear map

$$\begin{aligned} \psi_{\mathcal{C}} \colon \mathbb{F}_q^{n\times n} &\longrightarrow (\mathbb{F}_q^{m\times n})^k \\ Q &\longmapsto (C_1Q, \ldots, C_kQ). \end{aligned}$$

The suitable matrices $Q$ are exactly the elements of $\psi_{\mathcal{C}}^{-1}(\mathcal{D}^k) \cap \mathrm{GL}_n(\mathbb{F}_q)$. Concretely, computing the space $\psi_{\mathcal{C}}^{-1}(\mathcal{D}^k)$ requires $\mathcal{O}(n^2 \cdot (mnk)^{\omega-1})$ operations in $\mathbb{F}_q$. Then, an invertible matrix $Q$ is generally found quite easily by picking a random element in this space. Note that it may happen that invertible elements are rare in such a space. However, we claim that this situation is rather unlikely to happen. Moreover, even in the worst cases, the problem of finding such a $Q$ can be done in polynomial time as explained in [7, Thm. 3.7] and [11].

**Acknowledgements.** The authors express their deep gratitude to Matthieu Lequesne who suggested the title. They also thank the anonymous referees for their very helpful comments. The second author is funded by Inria and the French Cybersecurity Agency (ANSSI). This work benefited from the financial support of the French government and the *Agence Nationale de la Recherche (ANR)* through the *Plan France 2030* via the project ANR-22-PETQ-0008. The authors are part of a collaborative research project *Barracuda* with reference ANR-21-CE39-0009-BARRACUDA. The first author is partially funded by Horizon-Europe MSCA-DN project *Encode.*

## A Normalizing Matrices and Characteristic Polynomials

We consider the map introduced in Sect. 3.2

$$\begin{aligned} \{U \in \mathbb{F}_q^{m\times m} \mid \mathrm{Tr}(U) = \mathrm{Tr}(U^2) = 0\}/\mathbb{F}_q^\times &\longrightarrow (\mathbb{F}_q^{m-2} - (\mathbb{F}_q^{m-3} \times \{0\}))/\mathbb{F}_q^\times \\ U &\longmapsto (a_{m-3}, \ldots, a_0) \end{aligned}$$

where the characteristic polynomial of $U$ is $t^m + a_{m-3}t^{m-3} + \cdots + a_1t + a_0$ and $\mathbb{F}_q^\times$ acts on $\mathbb{F}_q^{m-2}$ via $\lambda \diamond (a_{m-3}, \ldots, a_0) = (\lambda^3 a_{m-3}, \ldots, \lambda^m a_0)$.

**Lemma 14.** *The set* $(\mathbb{F}_q^{m-2} - (\mathbb{F}_q^{m-3} \times \{0\}))/\mathbb{F}_q^\times$ *has*

$$q + q^2 + \cdots + q^{m-3} \sim q^{m-3}$$

*elements.*

*Proof.* The set $(\mathbb{F}_q^{m-2}/\mathbb{F}_q^\times) - \{(0, \ldots, 0)\}$ is a subset of the set of $\mathbb{F}_q$-rational points of the weighted projective space $\mathbb{P}_{3,\ldots,m}^{m-3}$ of dimension $m - 3$ and weights $3, \ldots, m$ over $\mathbb{F}_q$ [23, Lem. 6]. By [23, Lem. 7], this has $(q^{m-2} - q)/(q - 1)$ elements. □

**Lemma 15.** *The subset* $\mathrm{Sep}_{q,m} \subset (\mathbb{F}_q^{m-2} - (\mathbb{F}_q^{m-3} \times \{0\}))/\mathbb{F}_q^\times$ *of classes of separable polynomials has* $\sim q^{m-3}$ *elements.*

*Proof.* The monic inseparable polynomials of degree $m$ over $\mathbb{F}_q$ are the points of an open subset of a hypersurface of degree $2m-2$ in $\mathbb{P}^m$ [18, §1]. The set of inseparable polynomials whose coefficients of degree $m-1, m-2$ vanish is the intersection of this with two hyperplanes that do not contain it. Hence, it is an open subset of a hypersurface of degree $\leqslant 2m-2$ in $\mathbb{P}^{m-2}$, and has

$$\mathcal{O}\left((2m-2)q^{m-3}\right)$$

elements by the Serre bound [29, Théorème]. Since every element of $\mathbb{P}^{m-3}_{3,\ldots,m}(\mathbb{F}_q)$ has exactly $q-1$ preimages in $\mathbb{F}_q^{m-2}$ [23, Lem. 7], this means that there are $\mathcal{O}(mq^{m-4})$ classes of inseparable polynomials in $\mathbb{P}^{m-3}_{3,\ldots,m}(\mathbb{F}_q)$. Hence, by Lemma 14, $\mathrm{Sep}_{q,m}$ has $q^{m-3} - \mathcal{O}(mq^{m-4}) \sim q^{m-3}$ elements. □

Here is how to choose and compute a normalized representative of any element $\chi = (a_{m-3}, \ldots, a_0) \in \mathbb{F}_q^{m-2}$ modulo $\mathbb{F}_q^\times$. First, the normalized representative of 0 is itself. Now, consider $\chi \in \mathbb{F}_q^{m-2} - \{0\}$. Denote by $i_0 < i_1 < \cdots < i_\ell$ the indices such that $a_{m-i_j} \neq 0$. Choose a generator $g$ of $\mathbb{F}_q^\times$, and write $a_{m-i_j} = g^{s_j}$.

- If $i_0$ is prime to $q-1$, there is a unique $\lambda \in \mathbb{F}_q^\times$ such that $\lambda^{i_0} a_{m-i_0} = 1$; this $\lambda$ is $g^{-s_0 \cdot i_0^{-1} \bmod q}$. In that case, we choose $\chi' = \lambda \diamond \chi$ to be the normalized representative of $\chi$.
- If $d_0 \stackrel{\text{def}}{=} \gcd(i_0, q-1) > 1$, there are $d_0$ elements $\lambda$ satisfying this property. Let us describe how to find the right one.
  1. Here is how to compute one such $\lambda$. Write $i_0 = d_0 i_0'$, and denote by $j_0'$ the inverse of $i_0'$ modulo $q-1$. The set $\mathbb{F}_q^\times/(\mathbb{F}_q^\times)^{i_0}$ has $d_0$ elements: the equivalence classes of $1, g, \ldots, g^{d_0-1}$. Compute the Euclidean division $s_0 = s_0' \cdot d_0 + r_0$ of $s_0$ by $d_0$. Then the element $\lambda_0 \stackrel{\text{def}}{=} g^{-s_0' j_0'}$ satisfies $\lambda_0^{i_0} a_{m-i_0} = g^{r_0}$. Any product of $\lambda_0$ by a $d_0$-th root of unity in $\mathbb{F}_q$ still satisfies this relation.
  2. Now let $a_{m-i_1}$ be the next nonzero coefficient of $\chi$. We want to normalize $a_{m-i_1}\lambda_0^{i_1} = g^{s_1}$ by multiplying it by a $d_0$-th root of unity. Set $d_1 = \gcd(d_0, i_1)$. For any integer $\delta$, denote by $\mu_\delta(\mathbb{F}_q)$ the group of $\delta$-th roots of unity in $\mathbb{F}_q$. The set
$$\mathbb{F}_q^\times/\mu_{d_0}(\mathbb{F}_q)^{i_1} = \mathbb{F}_q^\times/\mu_{d_0/d_1}(\mathbb{F}_q)$$
has $(q-1)d_1/d_0$ elements. Write $i_1 = d_1 i_1'$ and denote by $j_1'$ the inverse of $i_1'$ modulo $d_0$. Compute the Euclidean division $s_1 = s_1' \cdot d_1(q-1)/d_0 + r_1$. The element $\alpha_1 = g^{-s_1' j_1' (q-1)/d_0}$ satisfies $\alpha_1^{i_1} g^{s_1} = g^{r_1}$. Set $\lambda_1 \stackrel{\text{def}}{=} \lambda_0 \alpha_1$. We have $\lambda_1^{i_0} a_{m-i_0} = g^{r_0}$ and $\lambda_1^{i_1} a_{m-i_1} = g^{r_1}$.
  3. If $d_1 \neq 1$, continue with $d_2 = \gcd(d_1, i_2)$. Stop after the $k$-th step if $k = \ell$ or $d_k = 1$. Return $\chi' = \lambda_k \diamond \chi$. The algorithm is summed up below.

The element $\chi' \in \mathbb{F}_q^{m-2}$ returned by this algorithm is equivalent to $\chi$. More generally, given equivalent inputs in $\mathbb{F}_q^{m-2}$, it returns the same output.

**Algorithm 7:** NORMALIZE

**Data:** Matrix $U \in \mathbb{F}_q^{m\times m}$, tuple $\chi = (a_{m-3}, \dots, a_0) \in \mathbb{F}_q^{m-2} - \{0\}$
Generator $g$ of $\mathbb{F}_q^\times$
**Result:** Matrix $U' \in \mathbb{F}_q^{m\times m}$, tuple $\chi' \in \mathbb{F}_q^{m-2} - \{0\}$

```
Set d = q − 1, i = 2 and λ = 1
while d ≠ 1 and (a_{m−i−1}, ..., a_1) ≠ (0, ..., 0) do
    Set i = min{j ∈ {i + 1 ... m} | a_{m−j} ≠ 0}
    Parse λ^i a_{m−i} = g^s
    Set d' = gcd(d, i) and i' = i/d'
    Compute inverse j' ∈ Z of i' modulo d
    Compute Euclidean division s = s' · (q − 1)d'/d + r
    Set λ ← λ g^{−s' j' (q−1)/d}
    Set d ← d', i ← i + 1
return λU, (λ^3 a_{m_3}, ..., λ^m a_0)
```

*Remark 12.* The complexity of Algorithm 7 is $\mathcal{O}(m \log(q)^2)$. To reduce its impact on the complexity of our attack, one can precompute the normalization of the most frequent characteristic polynomials. For instance, on may compute in advance the suitable $\lambda$ for vectors $(a_{m-3}, \dots, a_0)$ such that $a_{m-3}, a_{m-4} \neq 0$. Since 3 and 4 are coprime, a unique $\lambda$ is found knowing only $a_{m-3}, a_{m-4}$: constructing a dictionary $\{(a_{m-3}, a_{m-4}) : \lambda\}$ allows to precompute the normalization for $(q-1)^2 q^{m-4} \sim q^{m-2}$ elements of $\mathbb{F}_q^{m-2}$, that is, almost all of them.

## B Proportion of Codes with One-Dimensional Hull

This section explains how the following proposition can be deduced from a similar statement found in the literature.

**Proposition 1.** *The proportion of $m \times m$ matrix codes contained in* $\ker(\mathrm{Tr})$ *and whose hull has dimension 1 is asymptotically equal to*

$$\frac{1}{q}\left(1 + \mathcal{O}\left(\frac{m^2}{q^{(m^2-1)/2}}\right)\right).$$

Sendrier's work [26] gives detailed results about the number of codes with a hull of given dimension. His results are proven in the case of codes inside $\mathbb{F}_q^n$ with the usual inner product. In our case however, we consider $\mathbb{F}_q^{m\times m}$ endowed with the bilinear form $(X, Y) \mapsto \mathrm{Tr}(XY)$. Denoting by $\sigma_{n,i}$ the number of totally isotropic $[n, k]_q$-codes for a given bilinear form, the number $A_{n,k,1}$-codes whose intersection with their orthogonal complement has dimension 1 is equal to [26, Theorem 2]

$$A_{n,k,1} = \sum_{i=1}^{k} \begin{bmatrix} n-2i \\ k-i \end{bmatrix} \begin{bmatrix} i \\ 1 \end{bmatrix} (-1)^{i-1} q^{(i-1)(i-2)/2} \sigma_{n,i}$$

where $\begin{bmatrix} n \\ k \end{bmatrix}$ is the *Gaussian binomial coefficient* which denotes the number of $k$-dimensional linear subspaces of $\mathbb{F}_q^n$. The proof of this result does not involve the nature of the considered non-degenerate bilinear form. Sendrier goes on to show [26, Theorem 3], using asymptotic results based on explicit values of $\sigma_{n,i}$ specific to a bilinear form of discriminant 1, that for $1 \leqslant k \leqslant n/2$,

$$A_{n,k,1} q^{k(k+1)/2} = \left( \begin{bmatrix} n \\ k \end{bmatrix} \begin{bmatrix} k \\ 1 \end{bmatrix} \prod_{i=0}^{k-1} (q^i - (i \mod 2)) \right) \left( 1 + \mathcal{O}\left( \frac{k}{q^{n/2-1}} \right) \right).$$

There are different formulas of $\sigma_{n,i}$ given in [26, Theorem 1] depending on the remainders of $n, q$ modulo 2 and 4 and on the size of $k$. However, they are asymptotically equivalent, which yields this uniform result. For a bilinear form of different discriminant, these formulas are simply permuted; a general expression may be found in [8, IV, Proposition 3.5]. This does not change the asymptotic result above. Moreover, for $k \geqslant n/2$, the number of $[n, k]$-codes with one-dimensional hull is that of $[n, n-k]$-codes with one-dimensional hull, since the hull of a code $\mathcal{C}$ is exactly that of its dual. In particular, this means that for any $k$ such that $1 \leqslant k \leqslant n-1$,

$$\frac{A_{n,k,1}}{\begin{bmatrix} n \\ k \end{bmatrix}} = \frac{1}{q} \left( 1 + \mathcal{O}\left( \frac{\min(k, n-k)}{q^{n/2-1}} \right) \right)$$

or equivalently, that the proportion of codes whose hull has dimension 1 is asymptotically equivalent to $1/q$.

## References


1. Baldi, M., et al.: LESS (Linear Equivalence Signature Scheme). NIST, Post–Quantum Cryptography : Additional Digital Signature Schemes (2023). https://www.less-project.com/
2. Beullens, W.: Not enough LESS: An improved algorithm for solving code equivalence problems over FQ. In: Dunkelman, O., Jacobson, Jr., M.J., O'Flynn, C. (eds.) Selected Areas in Cryptography, pp. 387–403. Springer International Publishing, Cham (2021)
3. Beullens, W.: Graph-theoretic algorithms for the alternating trilinear form equivalence problem. In: Handschuh, H., Lysyanskaya, A. (eds.) Advances in Cryptology – CRYPTO 2023, pp. 101–126. Springer Nature Switzerland, Cham (2023)
4. Bläser, M., Duong, D.H., Narayanan, A.K., Plantard, T., Qiao, Y., Sipasseuth, A., Tang, G.: ALTEQ. NIST, Post–Quantum Cryptography : Additional Digital Signature Schemes (2023). https://csrc.nist.gov/csrc/media/Projects/pqc-dig-sig/documents/round-1/spec-files/ALTEQ-Spec-web.pdf
5. Bos, J.W., et al.: Hawk: a signature scheme inspired by the lattice isomorphism problem. NIST, Post–Quantum Cryptography : Additional Digital Signature Schemes (2023). https://hawk-sign.info/
6. Bouillaguet, C., Fouque, P.A., Véber, A.: Graph-theoretic algorithms for the "Isomorphism of Polynomials" problem. In: Johansson, T., Nguyen, P.Q. (eds.) Advances in Cryptology – EUROCRYPT 2013, pp. 211–227. Springer Berlin Heidelberg, Berlin, Heidelberg (2013)

7. Brooksbank, P.A., Wilson, J.B., O'Brien, E.A.: Testing isomorphism of graded algebras. Trans. Amer. Math. Soc. **372**(11), 8067–8090 (2019)
8. Caldero, P., Germoni, J.: Nouvelles histoires hédonistes de groupes et de géométries. Mathématiques en devenir, Calvage et Mounet (2018). https://hal.science/hal-02161089
9. Chou, T., et al.: MEDS (Matrix Equivalence Digital Signature Scheme). NIST, Post–Quantum Cryptography : Additional Digital Signature Schemes (2023). https://www.meds-pqc.org/
10. Chou, T., et al.: Take your MEDS: digital signatures from matrix code equivalence. In: El Mrabet, N., De Feo, L., Duquesne, S. (eds.) Progress in Cryptology - AFRICACRYPT 2023, pp. 28–52. Springer Nature Switzerland, Cham (2023)
11. Couvreur, A., Debris-Alazard, T., Gaborit, P.: On the hardness of code equivalence problems in rank metric (2020). https://hal.archives-ouvertes.fr/hal-02997801, preprint
12. Dixon, J.D., Panario, D.: The degree of the splitting field of a random polynomial over a finite field. Electron. J. Comb., R70–R70 (2004)
13. von zur Gathen, J., Gerhard, J.: Modern Computer Algebra. Cambridge University Press, 3rd edn. (2013)
14. Grochow, J., Qiao, Y.: On the complexity of isomorphism problems for tensors, groups, and polynomials I: tensor isomorphism-completeness. SIAM J. Comput. **52**(2), 568–617 (2023)
15. Grove, L.C.: Classical Groups and Geometric Algebra, vol. 39. American Mathematical Soc. (2002)
16. Kerr, M.: Algebra I Lecture Notes. https://www.math.wustl.edu/~matkerr/5031/index.html
17. Leon, J.: Computing automorphism groups of error-correcting codes. IEEE Trans. Inform. Theory **28**(3), 496–511 (1982)
18. López, A., Maisner, D., Nart, E., Xarles, X.: Orbits of Galois Invariant n-Sets of P1 under the action of PGL2. Finite Fields Appl. **8**(2), 193–206 (2002). https://doi.org/10.1006/ffta.2001.0335
19. Matsumoto, T., Imai, H.: Public quadratic polynomial-tuples for efficient signature-verification and message-encryption. In: Advances in Cryptology— EUROCRYPT'88: Workshop on the Theory and Application of Cryptographic Techniques Davos, Switzerland, May 25–27, 1988 Proceedings 7, pp. 419–453. Springer (1988)
20. Narayanan, A.K., Qiao, Y., Tang, G.: Algorithms for matrix code and alternating trilinear form equivalences via new isomorphism invariants. In: Joye, M., Leander, G. (eds.) Advances in Cryptology – EUROCRYPT 2024, pp. 160–187. Springer Nature Switzerland, Cham (2024)
21. Neiger, V., Pernet, C.: Deterministic computation of the characteristic polynomial in the time of matrix multiplication. J. Complexity **67**, 101572 (2021). https://doi.org/10.1016/j.jco.2021.101572
22. Patarin, J.: Hidden fields equations (HFE) and isomorphisms of polynomials (IP): two new families of asymmetric algorithms. In: Maurer, U. (ed.) EUROCRYPT 1996. LNCS, vol. 1070, pp. 33–48. Springer, Heidelberg (1996). https://doi.org/10.1007/3-540-68339-9_4
23. Perret, M.: On the number of points of some varieties over finite fields. Bull. Lond. Math. Soc. **35**(3), 309–320 (2003). https://doi.org/10.1112/S0024609302001820
24. Ran, L., Samardjiska, S.: Rare structures in tensor graphs. In: Chung, K.M., Sasaki, Y. (eds.) Advances in Cryptology – ASIACRYPT 2024, pp. 66–96. Springer Nature Singapore, Singapore (2025)

25. Ran, L., Samardjiska, S., Trimoska, M.: Algebraic algorithm for the alternating trilinear form equivalence problem. In: Esser, A., Santini, P. (eds.) Code-Based Cryptography, pp. 84–103. Springer Nature Switzerland, Cham (2023)
26. Sendrier, N.: On the dimension of the hull. SIAM J. Discrete Math. **10**(2), 282–293 (1997). https://doi.org/10.1137/S0895480195294027
27. Sendrier, N.: Finding the permutation between equivalent linear codes: the support splitting algorithm. IEEE Trans. Inform. Theory **46**(4), 1193–1203 (2000)
28. Sendrier, N., Simos, D.E.: The hardness of code equivalence over and its application to code-based cryptography. In: Post-Quantum Cryptography 2013. Lecture Notes Comput. Sci., vol. 7932, pp. 203–216. Springer (2013)
29. Serre, J.P.: Lettre à M. Tsfasman. Astérisque 198, 199–200 (1989)
30. Tang, G., Duong, D.H., Joux, A., Plantard, T., Qiao, Y., Susilo, W.: Practical post-quantum signature schemes from isomorphism problems of trilinear forms. In: Dunkelman, O., Dziembowski, S. (eds.) Advances in Cryptology – EUROCRYPT 2022, pp. 582–612. Springer International Publishing, Cham (2022)

# Stationary Syndrome Decoding for Improved PCGs

Vladimir Kolesnikov[1], Stanislav Peceny[1(✉)], Srinivasan Raghuraman[2], and Peter Rindal[3]

[1] Georgia Institute of Technology, Atlanta, GA, USA
kolesnikov@gatech.edu
[2] Visa Research and MIT, Cambridge, MA, USA
[3] Visa Research, Foster City, CA, USA

**Abstract.** Syndrome decoding (SD), and equivalently Learning Parity with Noise (LPN), is a fundamental problem in cryptography, which states that for a field $\mathbb{F}$, some compressing public matrix $\mathbf{G} \in \mathbb{F}^{k \times n}$, and a secret sparse vector $\boldsymbol{e} \in \mathbb{F}^n$ sampled from some *noise* distribution, $\mathbf{G}\boldsymbol{e}$ is indistinguishable from uniform. Recently, the SD has gained significant interest due to its use in pseudorandom correlation generators (PCGs).

In pursuit of better efficiency, we propose a new assumption called *Stationary Syndrome Decoding* (SSD). In SSD, we consider $q$ correlated noise vectors $\boldsymbol{e}_1, \ldots, \boldsymbol{e}_q \in \mathbb{F}^n$ and associated instances $\mathbf{G}_1\boldsymbol{e}_1, \ldots, \mathbf{G}_q\boldsymbol{e}_q$ where the noise vectors are restricted to having non-zeros in the same small subset of $t$ positions $L \subset [n]$. That is, for all $i \in L$, $\boldsymbol{e}_{j,i}$ is uniformly random, while for all other $i$, $\boldsymbol{e}_{j,i} = 0$.

Although naively reusing the noise vector renders SD and LPN insecure via simple Gaussian elimination, we observe known attacks do not extend to our correlated noise. We show SSD is unconditionally secure against so-called linear attacks, e.g., advanced information set decoding and representation techniques (Esser and Santini, Crypto 2024). We further adapt the state-of-the-art nonlinear attack (Briaud and Øygarden, Eurocrypt 2023) to SSD and demonstrate both theoretically and experimentally resistance to the attack.

We apply SSD to PCGs to amortize the cost of noise generation protocol. For OT and VOLE generation, each instance requires $O(t)$ communication instead of $O(t \log n)$. For suggested parameters, we observe a 1.5× improvement in the running time or between 6 and 18× reduction in communication. For Beaver triple generation using Ring LPN, our techniques have the potential for substantial amortization due to the high concrete overhead of the Ring LPN noise generation.

## 1 Introduction

Syndrome Decoding (SD), or equivalently Learning Parity with Noise (LPN), are standard assumptions in code-based cryptography. SD states that for some public matrix $\mathbf{G} \in \mathbb{F}^{k \times n}$, where $k < n$, and a secret sparse vector


Y. Tauman Kalai and S. F. Kamara (Eds.): CRYPTO 2025, LNCS 16000, pp. 284–317, 2025.
https://doi.org/10.1007/978-3-032-01855-7_10

$\boldsymbol{e} \in \mathbb{F}^n$ with a Hamming weight $|\boldsymbol{e}| \approx t$, $\mathbf{G}\boldsymbol{e}$ is pseudorandom. Recently, SD has seen increased interest due to its applications in secure multi-party computation (MPC) [RS21, DILO22, ANO+22, AS22, BDSW23], zero knowledge [YSWW21, WYKW21] [WYY+22, BDSW23], and post-quantum signatures [FJR22, CCJ23].

MPC enables parties that do not trust each other to compute on their private data without disclosing any information to the other parties. MPC has gained relevance in both academia and industry (e.g., for online auctions, electronic voting, privacy-preserving machine learning); its potential remains largely untapped due to the significantly higher costs compared to plaintext computation.

Most efficient MPC protocols work in the preprocessing model, where parties first preprocess cryptographic material that is independent of both the function and its inputs. This preprocessing phase typically involves generating random instances of oblivious transfers (OTs), oblivious linear evaluations (OLE), vector oblivious linear evaluations (VOLE), or Beaver triples. Once the function and inputs are known, the parties compute the function securely using the correlated randomness of the preprocessed material.

Preprocessing is often the computational bottleneck in MPC. A recent line of work on pseudorandom correlation generators (PCGs) shows great promise in significantly reducing preprocessing costs. PCGs offer sublinear communication and compelling computational overheads. While they have led to substantial improvements, PCGs are still far from matching the cost of honest majority or plaintext computation. *In this work, one of our goals is to reduce the cost of MPC by minimizing the costs associated with PCGs.*

State-of-the-art PCG constructions intimately rely on the Syndrome Decoding (SD) assumption. These PCGs make use of this assumption by having the parties interactively generate a secret sharing of the sparse vector $\boldsymbol{e}$ and then locally compute a sharing of $\mathbf{G}\boldsymbol{e}$. This final sharing forms, in part, the preprocessed materials. The computational overhead of this process has two main parts; generating the secret $\boldsymbol{e}$ with sublinear communication and performing the multiplication $\mathbf{G}\boldsymbol{e}$. Consequently, existing works optimize PCGs either by adding structure to $\mathbf{G}$ to accelerate the multiplication or by changing the distribution of $\boldsymbol{e}$ to improve the efficiency of generating a sharing of it. In our work, we take the latter approach. We amortize the cost of computing $\boldsymbol{e}$ across $q$ SD instances.

To achieve this, we propose and cryptanalyze a new assumption called the Stationary Syndrome Decoding (SSD). Intuitively, SSD allows for reusing the non-zero coordinates of a noise vector $\boldsymbol{e}$ across multiple SD instances, provided that the noise at each coordinate is uniformly drawn for each SD instance. For example, consider $\mathbb{F}_7$, $n = 12$, and $t = 4$. The noise vectors could be:

$$\boldsymbol{e}_1 = \left(0\,1\,0\,3\,0\,0\,0\,0\,6\,3\,0\,0\right),$$
$$\boldsymbol{e}_2 = \left(0\,0\,0\,1\,0\,0\,0\,0\,2\,4\,0\,0\right),$$
$$\ldots,$$
$$\boldsymbol{e}_q = \left(0\,4\,0\,6\,0\,0\,0\,0\,0\,3\,0\,0\right)$$

We refer to this assumption as stationary because the noise positions remain fixed across instances, e.g. at positions $L = \{2, 4, 9, 10\}$ in the example above. Note that the noisy values of $\boldsymbol{e}_i$ are sampled uniformly from $\mathbb{F}$, *including zero*. Without delving into details, the stationary nature of the noise positions enables us to reuse the bulk of the work required to generate a sharing of $\boldsymbol{e}$, such as the OTs and the GGM tree expansion. This can indirectly speed up the time to multiply $\mathbf{G}\boldsymbol{e}$ due to better parameter selection.

We believe the resilience of SSD to known LPN/SD attacks to be both unanticipated and significant. While we are not the first to consider the hardness of LPN and SD with structured noise, our assumption arguably has more implications due to the noise being highly correlated. This suggests the intriguing possibility of LPN and SD with other highly correlated noise distributions and the potential impact they can have on various constructions.

### 1.1 Contribution

Our core contribution is the introduction of the Stationary Syndrome Decoding assumption. First, we provide supporting evidence for its hardness. We show that SSD is resilient against all linear attacks [Pra62,Ste89,Jab01,BKW03,Lyu05] [FKI07,ABG+14,BR17,ES24] and adaptations of the state-of-the-art algebraic attacks of [BØ23].

Then, we show that SSD has significant efficiency implications for pseudorandom correlation generators (PCGs). In particular, we start with the communication and computation implications for degree-1 correlations, such as VOLE, OT, and binary OLE. Next, we discuss the same implications for degree-2 correlations, such as general OLE and Beaver triples. We also show that SSD can result in much better cache/memory utilization of PCGs.

*Degree 1 Correlations.* Let $n$ be the length and $t$ the Hamming weight of the noise vector $\boldsymbol{e}$. To generate $q$ noise vectors with the SSD assumption, our construction requires a single "base VOLE" of size $tq$ and $t\log_2(n/t)$ base OTs. To generate $q$ noise vectors using the standard SD construction also requires the same size base VOLE correlation, but $q$ times more base OTs. I.e., we can reuse all OTs across the $q$ instances. As a result, our construction requires an amortized $2\log_2(n/t)$ times less data to be sent when generating the sharing of $\boldsymbol{e}$. Our experiments show $6.4-7.5\times$ reduction in communication for OT and $10.7-17.6\times$ for VOLE, for a standard choice of parameters. We refer to [KPRR25] for more detail.

*Degree 2 Correlations.* The setup for degree 2 correlations from Ring-LPN [BCG+20,BBC+24,LXYY25], e.g. Beaver triples over $\mathbb{F}_p$, is significantly more complex and requires the generation of a weight $t' := t^2$ noise vector (product of two $t$-sparse vectors), in contrast to the simpler degree 1 setup, which only requires a weight $t$ noise vector. Moreover, the natural implementation requires $O(nt)$ local work instead of $O(n)$ in the degree 1 case. The recent implementation of [RR] demonstrates that the dominant cost is simply generating the noise vector using $O(nt)$ calls to a PRG. Some works starting with [SGRR19,BCG+20] suggested the use of so-called batch codes, such as cuckoo hashing, to reduce this overhead back to $O(n)$ at the expense of more work being performed in MPC, e.g. $O(\mathsf{poly}(t'))$. Alternatively, [BGH+25] gives a distributed multi-point function, which requires only $O(n)$ calls to a PRG and $O(nt)$ simple operations. However, the concrete costs of generating the distributed point function keys remain very high and likely require new protocol improvements.

To reduce the high concrete cost of these protocols, we propose using SSD, similarly to the degree-1 case, to amortize this expensive setup across the $q$ instances. In particular, the vast majority of the work performed within MPC can be performed once and then reused across the $q$ instances. This brings down the amortized overheads from at least $O(t' \log(n/t) + \mathsf{poly}(t'))$ to $O(t')$ communication and from $O(nt)$ to $O(n)$ computation. We believe this is an extremely promising direction for future exploration. We refer to [KPRR25] for more detail.

*Cache and Memory Utilization.* To achieve the desired sublinear communication overhead of PCGs, it has been necessary to generate the correlations in large batches, e.g. $n \approx 2^{20}$. However, SSD reduces this necessity as it is more communication efficient, and therefore allows for a smaller $n$ while achieving the same relative communication overhead. This in turn results in non-trivial performance improvements as the overall protocol can better fit into CPU cache. Our implementation shows that by executing $q = 2^5$ instances of size $n = 2^{15}$ binary OLEs rather than a large batch of $n = 2^{20}$, we can reduce wall-clock time for degree 1 correlations by 1.5 times while achieving the same relative communication overhead. Moreover, we expect speedup for degree 2 correlation to be even larger due to the larger amount of local computation along with the more complex setup protocol.

## 2 Related Work

In Sect. 3, we review existing works on syndrome decoding (SD) and related attacks. In this section, we focus on approaches aimed at improving pseudorandom correlation generators (PCGs), which serve as the motivating application of SD in our work. The majority of PCGs use essentially the same protocols [BCGI18, BCG+19b, BCG+19a, BCG+20, CRR21, BCG+22, RRT23]. They generate a secret sharing of a sparse vector $\boldsymbol{e}$ times either a scalar $\Delta$ or in [BCG+20] by another sparse vector. This sharing is then compressed by a linear function $\mathbf{G}$. Thus, to improve PCG performance, the focus has been to improve the generation of the shared sparse vector and the time required to multiply by $\mathbf{G}$. All prior works have focused on improving the generation of a *single* SD instance.

Thus far, the most impactful optimization for generating the secret sharing of $\boldsymbol{e}$ [AFS05, HOSS18, Ds17, BCGI18, SGRR19, BCG+19b, BCG+20, BCG+22] has been the idea of the regular noise distribution [AFS05] that replaces the Bernoulli/exact distributions (see Sect. 3.4). In the context of secure computation, this optimization was first used by TinyKeys [HOSS18] and later by [BCGI18] for PCGs. The regular noise distribution is so beneficial because it allows the generation of the sharing of $\Delta \boldsymbol{e}$ to consist of $O(n)$ AES calls across $t$ distributed point functions. This is in contrast with other noise distributions that require $O(t)$ distributed point functions and as much as $O(tn)$ AES calls, or the use of more complicated batch codes such as cuckoo hashing [SGRR19].

Another line of work tries to optimize the time it takes to multiply matrix $\mathbf{G}$ and $\boldsymbol{e}$ [BCGI18,BCG+19b,BCG+19a,BCG+20,CRR21,BCG+22,RRT23]. The original LPN assumption states that $\mathbf{G}$ is uniform, and therefore $\mathbf{G} \cdot \boldsymbol{e}$ requires $O(n^2)$ time. However, it is widely accepted that $\mathbf{G}$ can be replaced by the generator matrix of a code with high minimum distance, unless that code has strongly algebraic structure, such as the Reed-Solomon code, which can be efficiently decoded with the Berlekamp-Massey algorithm [Ber68]. By changing $\mathbf{G}$ to be a generator matrix, it is theoretically possible to compute $\mathbf{G} \cdot \boldsymbol{v}$ for any $\boldsymbol{v}$ in $O(n)$ time. However, practical considerations typically result in time $O(nc)$ where $c$ is somehow related to $\log n$ or the security parameter. [BCGI18,BCG+19b,BCG+19a] propose to rely on LDPC or quasi-cyclic codes as their security is well-studied and they offer reasonable performance. [BCG+22] propose using a type of turbo code that they call expand-accumulate, which not only significantly improves costs but also provably has high minimum distance. [RRT23] further improve on this code by replacing accumulation with a so-called convolution, which significantly increases minimum distance, and hence allows for more favorable parameters and performance. Our work differs from all these works in that we amortize PCG cost across *multiple* SD instances. I.e., we amortize out the cost of generating the noise vectors $\boldsymbol{e}$ across $q$ instances.

## 3 Preliminaries

### 3.1 Notation

Most of our notation follows standard conventions. Specifically, matrices are denoted using bold, non-italic, uppercase letters, while vectors are represented by bold, italic, lowercase letters. E.g., $\mathbf{G}$ is a matrix and $\boldsymbol{v}$ is a vector. We index matrices and vectors with subscript and use 1-based indexing, e.g., $\mathbf{M}_{i,j}$ or $\boldsymbol{v}_i$. $|\boldsymbol{v}|$ represents the Hamming weight of a vector. $||\boldsymbol{v}||$ represents the length of a vector or size of a set. $\boldsymbol{v}||\boldsymbol{u}$ denotes the concatenation of vectors $\boldsymbol{v}, \boldsymbol{u}$. $\boldsymbol{v} \odot \boldsymbol{u}$ and $\boldsymbol{v} \cdot \boldsymbol{u}$ denote the component-wise and dot product multiplications, respectively. $[a, b]$ denotes the sequence of natural numbers $a, \ldots, b$ and $[n]$ the sequence $[1, n]$. $[a, b]_{\mathbb{R}}$ denotes the inclusive range from $a$ to $b$ over the real numbers. $\kappa$ is the computational security parameter. $[\![x]\!]$ denotes a two-out-of-two secret sharing of $x \in \mathbb{F}$. A sender party holds a share $[\![x]\!]_{\mathsf{s}} \in \mathbb{F}$, while the receiver party holds $[\![x]\!]_{\mathsf{r}} \in \mathbb{F}$ such that $x = [\![x]\!]_{\mathsf{s}} + [\![x]\!]_{\mathsf{r}}$.

We denote variables of multivariate polynomials in bold, non-italic font, e.g., $\mathbf{x}, \mathbf{e}, \mathbf{z}$. A polynomial $f \in \mathbb{F}[\mathbf{x}]$ is in italics. When given concrete values, we denote $\mathbf{x}$ as $\boldsymbol{x}$. We use the graded lexicographic monomial ordering, where $\mathbf{x}^{\boldsymbol{\alpha}} > \mathbf{x}^{\boldsymbol{\beta}}$ if and only if $\sum_i \alpha_i > \sum_i \beta_i$, or $\sum_i \alpha_i = \sum_i \beta_i$ and the left-most non-zero entry of $\boldsymbol{\alpha} - \boldsymbol{\beta}$ is positive. $f_i$ will denote the $i$th smallest monomial in $f$. Let $\mathsf{LM}(f)$ denote the *largest monomial* in $f$ (without its coefficient) and $\mathsf{LT}(f)$ denote the *largest term* in $f$ (with its coefficient). A set $\mathcal{F} \subseteq \mathbb{F}[\mathbf{x}]$ of polynomials will be in calligraphy font (along with distributions). $\mathcal{M} := \{\mathbf{x}^{\boldsymbol{\alpha}} : \boldsymbol{\alpha} \in \mathbb{N}^n\} = \{\mathbf{x}_1^{\alpha_1} \cdot \ldots \cdot \mathbf{x}_n^{\alpha_n} : \boldsymbol{\alpha} \in \mathbb{N}^n\}$ denotes the set of monomials.

### 3.2 Distributions and Bias

A distribution $\mathcal{D}$ is associated with a set $X$ and each $x \in X$ is associated with a probability $p(x) \in [0,1]_{\mathbb{R}}$ s.t. $\sum_{x \in X} p(x) = 1$. Let $\mathsf{Dist}[X]$ denote the set of all probability distributions over set $X$. We can sample an element $x$ from $\mathcal{D}$, denoted as $x \leftarrow \mathcal{D}$, such that $\Pr[x \leftarrow \mathcal{D}] = p(x)$. In places, we will also treat $\mathcal{D}$ as a random variable in the natural way. When $X$ is a set, we use $x \leftarrow X$ to denote sampling from the uniform distribution $\mathcal{U}$ over $X$, i.e., $p(x) = 1/|X|$.

We will make use of the notion of $\mathsf{bias}$, which measures how much a distribution $\mathcal{D}$ is correlated with a linear function $\boldsymbol{v}$. Given a distribution $\mathcal{D}$ over $\mathbb{F}^n$ and a non-zero vector $\boldsymbol{v} \in \mathbb{F}^n$, the bias of $\mathcal{D}$ with respect to $\boldsymbol{v}$, denoted as $\mathsf{bias}_{\boldsymbol{v}}(\mathcal{D})$, is equal to: $\mathsf{bias}_{\boldsymbol{v}}(\mathcal{D}) := \left| \underset{\boldsymbol{d} \leftarrow \mathcal{D}}{\mathbb{E}}[\chi(\boldsymbol{v} \cdot \boldsymbol{d})] \right|$. where $\chi : \mathbb{F} \to \mathbb{C}$ is a non-trivial character of $\mathbb{F}^n$, e.g., $\chi(x) := \exp \frac{2\pi i \mathsf{Tr}(x)}{p}$ for a field with $p^k$ elements and field trace $\mathsf{Tr}(x) := x + x^p + \ldots + x^{p^{k-1}}$. In the binary case, this simplifies to $\mathsf{bias}_{\boldsymbol{v}}(\mathcal{D}) = |\Pr[\boldsymbol{v} \cdot \boldsymbol{x} = 0] - 1/2|$. By $\mathsf{bias}(\mathcal{D})$, we denote the largest bias of $\mathcal{D}$ with respect to any non-zero $\boldsymbol{v}$: $\mathsf{bias}(\mathcal{D}) = \max_{\boldsymbol{v} \neq \mathbf{0}} (\mathsf{bias}_{\boldsymbol{v}}(\mathcal{D}))$ We now present bias for a distribution $\sum_{i \leq t} \mathcal{D}_i$, obtained by taking $t$ independent distributions $\mathcal{D}_1, \ldots, D_t$ over $\mathbb{F}^n$, sampling $\boldsymbol{d}_i \leftarrow \mathcal{D}_i$ and outputting the sum $\boldsymbol{d} = \sum_{i \in [t]} \boldsymbol{d}_i$. One can generalize [Shp09]'s lemma for $\mathbb{F}_2^n$ to arbitrary $\mathbb{F}^n$.

**Lemma 1.** *For $t$ independent distributions $\mathcal{D}_1, \ldots, \mathcal{D}_t$ over $\mathbb{F}^n$, the bias of a distribution $\mathcal{D} := \sum_{i \in [t]} \mathcal{D}_i$ is bounded by $\mathsf{bias}(\mathcal{D}) \leq \prod_i \mathsf{bias}(\mathcal{D}_i)$ and that $\mathsf{bias}_{\boldsymbol{v}} \leq \prod_i \mathsf{bias}_{\boldsymbol{v}_i}(\mathcal{D}_i)$ for non-zero $\boldsymbol{v}_i \in \mathbb{F}^n$.*

*Proof.*

$$
\begin{aligned}
\mathsf{bias}(\mathcal{D}) &= \mathsf{bias}\left(\sum_i \mathcal{D}_i\right) \\
&= \max_{v \neq 0} \left| \underset{\boldsymbol{d}_i \leftarrow \mathcal{D}_i}{\mathbb{E}} [\chi(\boldsymbol{v} \cdot (\boldsymbol{d}_1 + \ldots + \boldsymbol{d}_t))] \right| \\
&= \max_{v \neq 0} \left| \underset{\boldsymbol{d}_i \leftarrow \mathcal{D}_i}{\mathbb{E}} [\chi(\boldsymbol{v} \cdot \boldsymbol{d}_1) \cdot \ldots \cdot \chi(\boldsymbol{v} \cdot \boldsymbol{d}_t)] \right| \qquad (1) \\
&\leq \max_{v_1 \neq 0} \left| \underset{\boldsymbol{d}_1 \leftarrow \mathcal{D}_1}{\mathbb{E}} [\chi(\boldsymbol{v}_1 \cdot \boldsymbol{d}_1)] \right| \cdot \ldots \cdot \max_{v_1 \neq 0} \left| \underset{\boldsymbol{d}_t \leftarrow \mathcal{D}_t}{\mathbb{E}} [\chi(\boldsymbol{v} \cdot \boldsymbol{d}_t)] \right| \qquad (2) \\
&= \prod_i \mathsf{bias}(\mathcal{D}_i)
\end{aligned}
$$

where (1) follows from $\chi(x+y) = \chi(x)\chi(y)$ and (2) follows from the independence of $\mathcal{D}_i$ and the triangle inequality. The proof of $\mathsf{bias}_{\boldsymbol{v}}(\mathcal{D})$ immediately follows. □

### 3.3 Coding Theory

Let $\mathcal{C}$ be a linear code that consists of a set of codewords $\boldsymbol{v}$ such that $\mathcal{C} := \{\boldsymbol{v} := \boldsymbol{x}\mathbf{G} \mid \boldsymbol{x} \in \mathbb{F}^k\}$, where $\boldsymbol{x}$ is any input of length $k$, $\mathbf{G} \in \mathbb{F}^{k \times n}$ is a *generator matrix* of $\mathcal{C}$, and $\mathbb{F}$ is some field. A matrix $\mathbf{H} \in \mathbb{F}^{m \times n}$, whose kernel is $\mathcal{C} := \{\boldsymbol{v} \mid \mathbf{H}\boldsymbol{v} := 0^m\}$, is called a *parity check matrix*. The code generated by $\mathbf{H}$ is called the dual code of $\mathcal{C}$. From $\mathbf{G}$, we can construct $\mathbf{H}$ and vice versa. It follows that $\mathbf{G}\mathbf{H}^T = 0$. The *minimum distance* $d$ of a linear code $\mathcal{C}$ represents the minimum number of positions of some codeword $\boldsymbol{v}$ that must be modified to get another codeword $\boldsymbol{v}'$. Equivalently, $d$ can be defined as the minimum weight non-zero codeword or as the minimum number of linearly dependent columns of $\mathbf{H}$. A *dual distance* of the matrix $\boldsymbol{A}$ is the largest integer $d$ such that every subset of $d$ rows of $\boldsymbol{A}$ is linearly independent. It is also the minimum distance of the dual of the code generated by $\boldsymbol{A}$.

### 3.4 Syndrome Decoding

*Syndrome Decoding (SD),* or equivalently the *dual* learning parity with noise (LPN) formulation, states that for some field $\mathbb{F}$, a public matrix $\mathbf{G} \in \mathbb{F}^{k \times n}$ that is a generator of a linear error-correcting code, and a private weight-$t$ sparse noise vector $\boldsymbol{e} \in \mathbb{F}^n$ sampled from some noise distribution, $(\mathbf{G}, \mathbf{G}\boldsymbol{e})$ is indistinguishable from $(\mathbf{G}, \boldsymbol{b})$, where $\boldsymbol{b} \leftarrow \mathbb{F}^k$ is uniformly random.

**Definition 1 (Syndrome Decoding Assumption ($\mathsf{SD}$)).** *Syndrome Decoding is parameterized by an implicit computational security parameter $\kappa$, a field $\mathbb{F}$, dimensions $n, k \in \mathbb{N}$ with $k < n$, and distributions $\mathcal{D} \in \mathsf{Dist}[\mathbb{F}^n]$, $\mathcal{G} \in \mathsf{Dist}[\mathbb{F}^{k \times n}]$. For samples $\mathbf{e} \leftarrow \mathcal{D} \in \mathbb{F}^n$ and $\mathbf{G} \leftarrow \mathcal{G} \in \mathbb{F}^{k \times n}$, the $(n, k, \mathbb{F}, \mathcal{D}, \mathcal{G})$-$\mathsf{SD}$ assumption states:*

$$\{(\mathbf{G}, \boldsymbol{b}) \mid \boldsymbol{b} := \mathbf{G} \cdot \boldsymbol{e}\} \approx \{(\mathbf{G}, \boldsymbol{b}) \mid \boldsymbol{b} \leftarrow \mathbb{F}^k\}$$

*where $\approx$ denotes computational indistinguishability.*

The $\mathsf{SD}$ assumption is known to be false for some choices of $\mathcal{G}$ and $\mathcal{D}$. For example, this is the case when $\mathbf{G}$ has small minimum distance, is a Reed-Solomon code, or $\boldsymbol{e}$ is too sparse.

*Learning Parity with Noise (LPN)* is a fundamental cryptographic assumption introduced by [BFKL94] and is equivalent to SD. LPN states that for some field $\mathbb{F}$, some public matrix $\boldsymbol{A} \in \mathbb{F}^{n \times m}$, a random secret vector $\boldsymbol{s} \leftarrow \mathbb{F}^m$, and a random secret weight-$t$ sparse noise vector $\boldsymbol{e} \in \mathbb{F}^n$, $(\boldsymbol{A}, \boldsymbol{A}\boldsymbol{s} + \boldsymbol{e})$ is indistinguishable from $(\boldsymbol{A}, \boldsymbol{b})$, where $\boldsymbol{b} \leftarrow \mathbb{F}^n$ is uniformly random. In the original formulations both $\boldsymbol{A}$ and $\boldsymbol{s}$ were uniformly random and each position of $\boldsymbol{e}$ was sampled from the Bernoulli with parameters $t/n$ so that in expectation $|\boldsymbol{e}| = t$. However, fruitful lines of research have shown that better performance can be achieved by adding structure to these distributions. Commonly, $\boldsymbol{A}$ is the transpose of a parity check matrix $\mathbf{H}$ of a linear error-correcting code with high minimum distance and fast encoding, e.g., [BCG+22, CRR21, RRT23]. Additionally, to improve performance of certain protocols $\boldsymbol{e}$ is often sampled from some noise distribution, e.g., regular [AFS05] as we will explain later.

**Definition 2 (Learning Parity with Noise Assumption (LPN)).** *Learning Parity with Noise is parameterized by an implicit computational security parameter $\kappa$, a field $\mathbb{F}$, dimensions $n, m \in \mathbb{N}$ with $n > m$, and distributions $\mathcal{D} \in \mathsf{Dist}[\mathbb{F}^n]$, $\mathcal{H} \in \mathsf{Dist}[\mathbb{F}^{n\times m}]$. For samples $\boldsymbol{e} \leftarrow \mathcal{D} \in \mathbb{F}^n$, $\boldsymbol{A} \leftarrow \mathcal{H} \in \mathbb{F}^{n\times m}$, and $\boldsymbol{s}_i \leftarrow \mathbb{F}^m$, the $(n, m, \mathbb{F}, \mathcal{D}, \mathcal{H})$-LPN assumption states:*

$$\{(\boldsymbol{A}, \boldsymbol{b}) \mid \boldsymbol{b} := \boldsymbol{A} \cdot \boldsymbol{s} + \boldsymbol{e}\} \approx \{(\boldsymbol{A}, \boldsymbol{b}) \mid \boldsymbol{b} \leftarrow \mathbb{F}^n\}$$

*where $\approx$ denotes computational indistinguishability.*

*LPN and SD Equivalence.* Recall that for a linear error-correcting code, the matrix $\boldsymbol{A}$ from the LPN formulation is the transpose of a parity check matrix $\mathbf{H} = \boldsymbol{A}^\mathsf{T}$, while $\mathbf{G}$ from the SD formulation is the generator. The key observation is that $\mathbf{G}\mathbf{H}^\mathsf{T} = 0$. Then, $\mathbf{G}(\mathbf{H}^\mathsf{T}\boldsymbol{s}+\boldsymbol{e}) = (\mathbf{G}\mathbf{H}^T)\boldsymbol{s}+\mathbf{G}\boldsymbol{e} = \mathbf{G}\boldsymbol{e} = \boldsymbol{b}$. Similarly, given a SD sample $(\mathbf{G}, \boldsymbol{b})$, one can define the equivalent LPN instance by sampling a uniform $\hat{\boldsymbol{s}} \in \mathbb{F}^m$ and outputting $(\boldsymbol{A}, \hat{\boldsymbol{b}})$ where $\hat{\boldsymbol{b}} := \boldsymbol{A}\hat{\boldsymbol{s}} + \hat{\mathbf{e}}$ and $\hat{\mathbf{e}}$ is an arbitrary solution to $\mathbf{G}\hat{\mathbf{e}} = \hat{\boldsymbol{b}}$. Correctness follows from the fact that there exists some $\boldsymbol{s} \in \mathbb{F}^m$ s.t. $\boldsymbol{A}\boldsymbol{s} + \boldsymbol{e} = \boldsymbol{A}\hat{\boldsymbol{s}} + \hat{\mathbf{e}}$.

*Noise Distributions.* Three choices for the noise distribution are dominant in the literature: Bernoulli, exact, and regular. In secure computation applications, their choice greatly impacts efficiency. Let $t$ be the desired sparsity of the error vector $\boldsymbol{e}$ of size $n$, consisting of elements from some field $\mathbb{F}$:

- *Bernoulli* is the classic noise distribution. Each $\boldsymbol{e}_i \in \mathbb{F}$ is sampled with $\mathsf{Ber}_{t/n}$, i.e., 0 with probability $1 - t/n$ and otherwise uniformly from $\mathbb{F} \setminus \{0\}$.
- *Exact* noise distribution evolved from the Bernoulli distribution and fixes the Hamming weight of the noise vector $|\boldsymbol{e}| = t$, I.e., $\boldsymbol{e} \leftarrow \{\boldsymbol{e} \in \mathbb{F}^n \mid |\boldsymbol{e}| = t\}$.
- *Regular* is the distribution of choice for pseudorandom correlation generators (PCG) as the noise vector is much cheaper to implement under secure computation than in the exact case (details to follow). $\boldsymbol{e}$ consists of $t$ same-size blocks $\boldsymbol{e}_1, ..., \boldsymbol{e}_t \in \mathbb{F}^{n/t}$, where each $\boldsymbol{e}_i$ is a uniformly random unit vector. I.e., $\boldsymbol{e}_i \leftarrow \{\boldsymbol{e}_i \in \mathbb{F}^{n/t} \mid |\boldsymbol{e}_i| = 1\}$.

Interestingly, there is not a clearly best noise distribution when it comes to security. [ES24] recently showed that regular noise can actually be harder for some parameter regimes, and vice versa.

### 3.5 Linear Attacks

Cryptanalyzing LPN is a thriving area of research. Many attacks have been proposed of which the most effective are those based on Gaussian elimination/BKW algorithm [BKW03, Lyu05] and information set decoding (ISD) [Pra62, Ste89].

When introducing a new LPN variant, it would be laborious to prove security against each possible attack. Fortunately, the majority of known attacks fit in the *linear test framework.* These include, among others, attacks based on Gaussian elimination and the BKW algorithm [BKW03, Lyu05], attacks based on covering codes and information set decoding [Pra62, Ste89], statistical decoding [Jab01, FKI07], and finding correlations with low degree polynomials [ABG+14, BR17]. In this framework, the adversary is given the matrix $\boldsymbol{A}$, arbitrarily preprocesses it, and then outputs a test vector $\boldsymbol{v}$. Now, the framework states that the distinguisher, who tries to distinguish the LPN sample from uniformly random, can be implemented by a simple linear test $\boldsymbol{v} \cdot (\boldsymbol{A}\boldsymbol{s} + \boldsymbol{e})$ and by checking if the output is biased, e.g., equals zero more than random chance.

One advantage of the linear test framework is that when LPN is initialized with a code that has high minimum distance $d$, then it cannot be distinguished from uniform except with negligible probability. Note that high minimum distance is not a necessary condition for security. It is well-known that small minimum distance can result in secure LPN as long as the *pseudominimum distance* is high. Pseudominimum distance represents the weight of the smallest codeword that is efficiently computable. In other words, small minimum distance codewords can exist as long as they cannot be efficiently found. We note that while the linear test framework covers the large majority of known attacks, there are some notable exceptions such as when the underlying code is strongly algebraic (e.g., Reed-Solomon) or the noise is structured (e.g., regular). Stationary syndrome decoding, which we introduce in this paper, has a highly structured noise, and thus requires analysis beyond the linear test framework.

To illustrate how the linear test framework captures various attacks, we next review how to cast state-of-the-art ISD algorithms as linear tests. First, the SD problem $(\mathbf{G}, \mathbf{G} \cdot \boldsymbol{e})$ is converted into its equivalent LPN formulation $(\boldsymbol{A}, \boldsymbol{b} := \boldsymbol{A}\boldsymbol{s} + \boldsymbol{e})$, see above. A subset of $m := n - k$ rows of $\boldsymbol{A}$ are selected, called an *information set* $I \subset [n]$, with the hope that this set does not intersect the non-zeros of the noise vector $\boldsymbol{e}$, i.e. $\boldsymbol{e}_i = 0$ for $i \in I$. One can then use Gaussian elimination to solve for the noisy positions of $\boldsymbol{e}$ by considering the corresponding $m \times m$ submatrix $\boldsymbol{A}'$, which consists of the rows in the information set i.e. $\boldsymbol{A}' := (\boldsymbol{A}_{I_1} /\!/ ... /\!/ \boldsymbol{A}_{I_m})$. One then solves the system $\boldsymbol{A}' \cdot \boldsymbol{s} = \boldsymbol{b}_I$ using Gaussian elimination and checks if $\boldsymbol{e}' := \boldsymbol{A}\boldsymbol{s} - \boldsymbol{b}$ is a $t$-sparse vector, which implies $\boldsymbol{e}' = \boldsymbol{e}$ w.h.p. This algorithm can be implemented in the linear test framework, for example, by simply checking if $\boldsymbol{e}'_1 = 0$, which is linear in the original SD problem since $\boldsymbol{e}'$ is linear in $\mathbf{G}\boldsymbol{e}$.

When ISD is naively implemented, each information set guess requires a costly Gaussian elimination step. Advanced ISD algorithms [Ste89, FS09a, BLP11] [MMT11, BJMM12, MO15, BM18, ES24] typically improve efficiency through a combination of techniques, such as reducing the overall search space, optimizing the process of finding the right information set, or amortizing the cost of Gaussian elimination by reusing partial computations across multiple *related* information sets. This avoids the need to restart the linear algebra from scratch for each attempt. While processing each individual set still takes at least

$O(1)$ time, the overall approach becomes significantly more efficient. As a result, in the linear test framework, these attacks can be structured so that each test effectively runs in $O(1)$ time as well.

Importantly, we note that the noise parameter $t$ suggested by the linear test framework tends to be highly conservative. For example, [LWYY22] shows that in SD, a choice of $t \approx 60$ should provide the same level of bit-security against linear tests as opposed to $t \approx 170$ required by the linear test framework. In this work, we adopt a more conservative approach and choose parameters according to the linear test framework to ensure provable security guarantees. However, we are also not aware of any concrete speedup for ISD-styled algorithms when applied to SSD, which suggests more aggressive parameters could be considered.

### 3.6 Algebraic Preliminaries

Recent work by Briaud and Øygarden [BØ23] represents one such attack that does not fit within the linear test framework. The attack is based on algebraic geometry and leverages the regular structure of noise in LPN and SD. At the highest level, the attack represents LPN/SD as a system of linear and non-linear polynomials and then solves for the noise vector $\boldsymbol{e}$. [BØ23]'s work is a crucial prerequisite to analyze the security of our assumption against algebraic attacks. For that reason, we first provide an overview of the concepts necessary to understand [BØ23]'s attack before reviewing their attack. For those less familiar with agebraic geometry we provide a self-contained introduction in [KPRR25].

*Macaulay Matrix.* The Macaulay matrix is an essential primitive for solving non-linear systems of equations. Let $\mathcal{M} := \{\mathbf{x}^\alpha : \alpha \in \mathbb{N}^n\}$ be the set of all monomials. Let $\mathsf{coeff}(f, m)$ represent the coefficient of a monomial $m \in \mathcal{M}$ in a polynomial $f \in \mathcal{A}$. For finite subsets $\mathcal{F} := \{f_1, \dots, f_p\} \subset \mathcal{A}$ and $\mathcal{S} := \{s_1, \dots, s_q\} \subset \mathcal{M}$, the Macaulay matrix $\mathsf{Macaulay}(\mathcal{F}, \mathcal{S})$, is defined as

$$\mathsf{Macaulay}(\mathcal{F}, \mathcal{S}) := \begin{pmatrix} \mathsf{coeff}(f_1, s_1) & \dots & \mathsf{coeff}(f_1, s_q) \\ \vdots & \ddots & \vdots \\ \mathsf{coeff}(f_p, s_1) & \dots & \mathsf{coeff}(f_p, s_q) \end{pmatrix}$$

Note that $\mathcal{S}$ need not have all the monomials in $\mathcal{F}$.

*XL Algorithm and Gröbner Bases.* Techniques based on Gröbner bases and the closely related XL algorithm [CKPS00] can be used to solve systems of polynomial equations. Both approaches usually depend on the Macaulay matrix (see [KPRR25]). For the systems we consider, the XL algorithm is more performant, and hence our discussion focuses on XL.

Let $\mathcal{F} := \{f_1, \dots, f_p\}$ such that $\mathcal{F} \subseteq \mathcal{A}$ be a system of polynomial equations, i.e., $f_1(\mathbf{x}) = \dots = f_p(\mathbf{x}) = 0$. The XL algorithm can be split into two phases. The first phase maps the non-linear system $\mathcal{F}$ to a linear system. We start by multiplying each $f_i$ by arbitrary monomials such that the resulting polynomials are of degree at most $d$. $d$ is carefully selected and input to the algorithm such that this step produces enough new equations. Note that finding the right $d$ is often challenging and constitutes a significant effort for the approach. We then linearize the system by treating its monomials as new variables and save their coefficients in the Macaulay matrix. The second phase is standard. We proceed by solving the linear system with Gaussian elimination and obtain a polynomial in one variable. We solve this polynomial using some factorization algorithm and obtain a root, substitute, and repeat this process to solve for the remaining variables. The full algorithm is presented in Fig. 1.

$\mathsf{XL}(\mathcal{F} = \{f_1, \ldots, f_p\} \subset \mathcal{A}, d_{\mathsf{wit}} \in \mathbb{N}):$

1. Expand the system to degree $d_{\mathsf{wit}}$ by computing, $\mathcal{I}_{\leq d_{\mathsf{wit}}} := \{mf_i : m \in \mathcal{M}, f_i \in \mathcal{F}, \mathsf{deg}(mf_i) \leq d_{\mathsf{wit}}\} = \{h \in \mathcal{I} : \mathsf{deg}(h) \leq d_{\mathsf{wit}}\}$.
2. Obtain the Macaulay matrix $\mathbf{M} := \mathsf{Macaulay}(\mathcal{I}_{\leq d_{\mathsf{wit}}}, \mathcal{M}_{\leq d_{\mathsf{wit}}}) \in \mathbb{F}^{p \times q}$ where $\mathcal{M}_{\leq d_{\mathsf{wit}}} := \{m \in \mathcal{M} : \mathsf{deg}(m) \leq d_{\mathsf{wit}}\}$ and $q := |\mathcal{M}_{\leq d_{\mathsf{wit}}}|$. We now have a linear system $\mathbf{M} \cdot \mathbf{z} = 0$ where $\mathbf{z}_1, \ldots, \mathbf{z}_q$ are relabelings of the $\mathcal{M}_{\leq d_{\mathsf{wit}}}$.
3. For $i \in [n]$ :
   (a) Reorder $\mathbf{M}, \mathbf{z}$ such that $(\mathbf{z}_1, \ldots, \mathbf{z}_{d_{\mathsf{wit}}+1}) = (1, \mathbf{x}_i^1, \ldots, \mathbf{x}_i^{d_{\mathsf{wit}}})$.
   (b) Perform Wiedemann Gaussian elimination [Wie86] on $\mathbf{M}$ where $(\mathbf{z}_1, \ldots, \mathbf{z}_{d_{\mathsf{wit}}+1}) = (1, \mathbf{x}_i^1, \ldots, \mathbf{x}_i^{d_{\mathsf{wit}}})$ are eliminated last. Output $\perp$ if the first row of $\mathbf{M}$ is not of the form $(\mathbf{M}_{1,1}, \ldots, \mathbf{M}_{1,d_{\mathsf{wit}}+1}, 0, \ldots 0)$.
   (c) Solve the univariate polynomial system $\sum_{j \in [d_{\mathsf{wit}}+1]} \mathbf{M}_{1,j} \mathbf{x}_i^{j-1} = 0$ using factoring algorithms. Let $x_i$ be one of the roots.
   (d) Substitute $x_i$ in for $\mathbf{x}_i$ and simplify $\mathbf{M}$.
4. Output $(x_1, \ldots, x_n)$.

**Fig. 1.** The XL algorithm [CKPS00] for solving quadratic system of equations.

As briefly discussed above, for XL to be successful we need to select $d$ carefully such that we produce in the first phase enough linearly independent equations in relation to the number of monomials. In other words, $p \geq q$ in the Macaulay matrix so that we can apply Gaussian elimination. The threshold for large enough $d$ is called the witness degree $d_{\mathsf{wit}}$ and we use [BØ23]'s definition below.

**Definition 3 (Witness Degree** [BØ23]**).** *Consider an affine system of polynomials $\mathcal{F} := \{f_1, \ldots, f_p\}$ with coefficients in $\mathbb{F}$, the ideal $\mathcal{I} := \langle \mathcal{F} \rangle$, and some $d \in \mathbb{N}$. Now consider:*

$$\mathcal{I}_{\leq d} := \{h \in \mathcal{I} : \mathsf{deg}(h) \leq d\}$$

$$\mathcal{J}_{\leq d} := \left\{ h \in \mathcal{I} : \exists g_i \ s.t. \ h = \sum_{i \in [p]} g_i f_i; \forall i \in [p], \mathsf{deg}(g_i) \leq d - \mathsf{deg}(f_i) \right\}$$

*The witness degree $d_{\mathsf{wit}}$ is the smallest $d \in \mathbb{N}$ for which it holds that $\mathcal{I}_{\leq d} = \mathcal{J}_{\leq d}$ and $\mathsf{LM}(\mathcal{I}_{\leq d}) = \mathsf{LM}(\mathcal{I})$, where $\mathsf{LM}(\cdot)$ (for some graded ordering) denotes the* *monomial ideal generated by the leading monomials of all polynomials in the input ideal.*

Intuitively, $d_{\mathsf{wit}}$ guarantees that everything we need to know about the structure of an ideal can be captured by polynomials of degree at most $d_{\mathsf{wit}}$. Note that the witness degree $d_{\mathsf{wit}}$ is related to the degree of regularity $d_{\mathsf{reg}}$ (see [KPRR25]). The key difference is that $d_{\mathsf{reg}}$ is usually used for homogeneous systems solved with Gröbner bases, while $d_{\mathsf{wit}}$ is suitable also for affine systems solved with XL.

The runtime of the XL algorithm is largely determined by the cost of Gaussian elimination. As the systems we consider have a single solution and are sparse, we can use the Wiedemann algorithm [Wie86] to perform the Gaussian elimination, and find a solution in $3 \cdot \mathsf{maxRowWeight}(\mathbf{M}) \cdot q^2$ , where 3 is a constant standard in the literature (see [BØ23]), $\mathsf{maxRowWeight}(\mathbf{M}) := \mathsf{max}(\{|\mathbf{M}_i| : i \in [p]\})$ is the maximum number of non-zero entries across the rows of the Macaulay matrix $\mathbf{M}$, and $q$ is the number of columns in the Macaulay matrix.

### 3.7 Algebraic Attacks

[BØ23] *'s Attack.* The attack solves for the noise vector $\boldsymbol{e} \in \mathbb{F}^n$ in a polynomial system representing a single instance of regular-noise SD. Recall that a regular $\boldsymbol{e} = \boldsymbol{e}_1 || \dots || \boldsymbol{e}_t$ can be viewed as $t$ vectors $\boldsymbol{e}_1, \dots, \boldsymbol{e}_t$ each of size $n/t$ and Hamming weight $|\boldsymbol{e}_i| = 1$. The system consists of $k$ linear parity check equations $\mathbf{G}\boldsymbol{e} - \boldsymbol{b} = 0$ and $\binom{n/t}{2}t$ quadratic equations encoding the regular structure of $\boldsymbol{e}$, i.e., $\boldsymbol{e}_{i,j_1}\boldsymbol{e}_{i,j_2} = 0$ for all $i \in [t]$ and $j_1 < j_2 \in [n/t]$.[1] These two sets of equations represent the complete system of polynomial equations to solve regular syndrome decoding over a large field $\mathbb{F}$. Over $\mathbb{F}_2$, we additionally encode that the sum of each block equals 1, i.e., $\sum_{j \in [n/t]} \boldsymbol{e}_{i,j} - 1 = 0$, for all $i \in [t]$. We cannot do this over larger fields as we do not know the values of the non-zero coordinates. We also include field equations $\boldsymbol{e}_{i,j}^2 - \boldsymbol{e}_{i,j} = 0$, for all $i \in [t]$ and $j \in [n/t]$. More generally, we can include $\boldsymbol{e}_{i,j}^{||\mathbb{F}||} - \boldsymbol{e}_{i,j} = 0$ for any $\mathbb{F}$. However, for large $\mathbb{F}$, the degree of the field equations is much higher than $d_{\mathsf{wit}}$, and hence they have no contribution.

We note that the main contribution to the polynomial system comes from the $k$ parity check equations. Hence, the attack is more effective for instances with a non-constant rate such as in primal LPN. The presented system is for the dual setting. To attack the primal setting, we simply convert the primal instance into an equivalent dual instance and then solve for the presented polynomial system. We now present the polynomial systems for large $\mathbb{F}$ and $\mathbb{F}_2$ formally.

**Modeling 1 (Polynomial System over a Large Field $\mathbb{F}$).** *Let $(\mathbf{G}, \boldsymbol{b})$ be a regular syndrome decoding instance over a large $\mathbb{F}$. Let $\mathcal{F} := \mathcal{R} \cup \mathcal{S}$ be a set of polynomials such that:*

- *$\mathcal{R}$ is the set of $k$ linear parity check equations $\mathbf{G}\boldsymbol{e} - \boldsymbol{b} = 0$.*

[1] $\boldsymbol{e}_{i,j}$ represents $j$th element of $i$th block $\boldsymbol{e}_i$ of $\boldsymbol{e}$.

- $\mathcal{S}$ *is the set of* $t\binom{n/t}{2}$ *quadratic equations that encode the regularity of the noise vector* $\mathbf{e}$, *i.e.,* $\mathbf{e}_{i,j_1}\mathbf{e}_{i,j_2} = 0$ *for all* $i \in [t]$ *and* $j_1 < j_2 \in [n/t]$.

**Modeling 2 (Polynomial System over $\mathbb{F}_2$).** *Let* $(\mathbf{G}, \boldsymbol{b})$ *be a regular syndrome decoding instance over* $\mathbb{F}_2$. *Let* $\mathcal{F} := \mathcal{R} \cup \mathcal{S} \cup \mathcal{V} \cup \mathcal{W}$ *be a set of polynomials such that:*

- $\mathcal{R}$ *and* $\mathcal{S}$ *are the same sets as in Modeling 1.*
- $\mathcal{V}$ *is the set of* $n$ *field equations* $\mathbf{e}_{i,j}^2 - \mathbf{e}_{i,j} = 0$ *for all* $i \in [t]$ *and* $j \in [n/t]$.
- $\mathcal{W}$ *is the set of* $t$ *linear equations* $\sum_{j\in[n/t]} \mathbf{e}_{i,j} - 1 = 0$, *for all* $i \in [t]$. *They express that each of the* $t$ *blocks has Hamming weight* 1.

[BØ23] solve these polynomial systems with XL Wiedemann. To apply XL Wiedemann, [BØ23] estimate the witness degree $d_{\mathsf{wit}}$ at which the polynomial system is solved. This is [BØ23]'s key contribution. It also determines the cost of XL Wiedemann as $d_{\mathsf{wit}}$ determines the size of the Macaulay matrix.

The $d_{\mathsf{wit}}$ estimate is the index of the first $\leq 0$ coefficient in the Hilbert series $\mathcal{HS}_{\mathcal{A}/\mathcal{I}}(z)$, where $\mathcal{I} := \langle \mathcal{F}^{(h)} \rangle$ in Modeling 1 and Modeling 2 respectively. Thus, $d_{\mathsf{wit}}$ can be simply retrieved if we know the Hilbert series. Recall that unfortunately Hilbert series are often difficult to compute. By using the assumption that the relevant Macaulay matrices have maximal rank and using the knowledge of regular and semi-regular sequences, [BØ23] arrive at the following Hilbert series.

**Theorem 1 (Hilbert Series for Modeling 1).** *Assuming the Macaulay matrix has maximum rank, the Hilbert series of the homogeneous ideal* $\mathcal{I} := \langle \mathcal{F}^{(h)} \rangle$, *where* $\mathcal{F}$ *is the Modeling 1 polynomial system, is*

$$\mathcal{HS}_{\mathcal{A}/\mathcal{I}}(\mathbf{z}) := (1-\mathbf{z})^k \cdot \left(1 + \frac{n}{t} \cdot \frac{\mathbf{z}}{1-\mathbf{z}}\right)^t,$$

*truncated after the first* $\leq 0$ *coefficient.*

**Theorem 2 (Hilbert Series for Modeling 2).** *Assuming the Macaulay matrix has maximum rank, the Hilbert series of the homogeneous ideal* $\mathcal{I} := \langle \mathcal{F}^{(h)} \rangle$, *where* $\mathcal{F}$ *is the Modeling 2 polynomial system, is*

$$\mathcal{HS}_{\mathcal{A}/\mathcal{I}}(\mathbf{z}) := \frac{(1 + (n/t - 1)\mathbf{z})^t}{(1+\mathbf{z})^k},$$

*truncated after the first* $\leq 0$ *coefficient.*

As presented, the complexity of the algorithm that solves Modeling 1 and Modeling 2 is too high to be competitive with more established attacks. In other words, the witness degree is too high and needs to be reduced to potentially decrease the complexity of the overall algorithm. With that in mind, [BØ23] present a hybrid approach, which consists of repeatedly guessing a few noise-free elements of $\boldsymbol{e}$ and invoking XL Wiedemann until successfully computing $\boldsymbol{e}$.

More specifically, parameterized by $f \in [t]$ and $\mu \in [n/t]$, the hybrid approach guesses $\mu$ noise-free positions in the first $f$ blocks of $\mathbf{e}$ (i.e., add new equations for each guessed noise-free $\mathbf{e}_{i,j} = 0$ to $\mathcal{F}$). Let $p$ be the probability that the guessed positions are all noise-free. We then expect to repeat the XL Wiedemann $O(p^{-1})$ times. The hope is that the loss from rerunning XL Wiedemann is superseded by the decreased degree at which the system is solved. As before, the degree $d_{\mathsf{wit}}$ is derived from the Hilbert series, which for Modeling 1 changes to

$$\mathcal{HS}_{\mathcal{A}/\mathcal{I}}(\mathbf{z}) := \left[ (1-\mathbf{z})^k \cdot \left(1 + \left(\frac{n}{t} - \mu\right) \cdot \frac{\mathbf{z}}{1-\mathbf{z}}\right)^f \cdot \left(1 + \frac{n}{t} \cdot \frac{\mathbf{z}}{1-\mathbf{z}}\right)^{t-f} \right],$$

truncated after the first $\leq 0$ coefficient. For Modeling 2, it changes to

$$\mathcal{HS}_{\mathcal{A}/\mathcal{I}}(\mathbf{z}) := \left[ \frac{(1 + (n/t - 1 - \mu)\mathbf{z})^f \cdot (1 + (n/t - 1)\mathbf{z})^{t-f}}{(1+\mathbf{z})^k} \right],$$

also truncated after the first $\leq 0$ coefficient.

## 4 Overview

In this work, we introduce a new assumption that we call the stationary syndrome decoding (SSD), analyze its security, and present its implications for different applications. The high-level idea of SSD is straightforward. We consider $q$ instances of syndrome decoding (SD). SSD states that it is secure to reuse the noisy *positions* of the noise vector $\mathbf{e}$ across all $q$ instances as long as their corresponding *values* are sampled uniformly for each instance. More formally:

**Definition 4 (Stationary Syndrome Decoding (SSD)).** *Stationary Syndrome Decoding is parameterized by an implicit computational security parameter $\kappa$, a field $\mathbb{F}$, dimensions $n, k, q \in \mathbb{N}$ with $k < n$, and distributions $\mathcal{L} \in \mathsf{Dist}[\{0,1\}^n]$, $\mathcal{G} \in \mathsf{Dist}[\mathbb{F}^{k\times n}]$. For sample $L \leftarrow \mathcal{L}$ and for $i \in [q]$, sample $\mathbf{e}_i \leftarrow L \odot \mathbb{F}^n$, $\mathbf{G}_i \leftarrow \mathcal{G} \in \mathbb{F}^{k\times n}$. The $(n, k, q, \mathbb{F}, \mathcal{L}, \mathcal{G})$-SSD assumption states:*

$$\{(\mathbf{G}_i, \boldsymbol{b}_i) \mid \boldsymbol{b}_i := \mathbf{G}_i \cdot \boldsymbol{e}_i\}_{i\in[q]} \approx \{(\mathbf{G}_i, \boldsymbol{b}_i) \mid \boldsymbol{b}_i \leftarrow \mathbb{F}^k\}_{i\in[q]}$$

*where $\approx$ denotes computational indistinguishability.*

The applications we consider will restrict $\mathcal{L}$ to being a subset containing sparse vectors, typically with $O(\kappa)$ ones. It is not hard to show that this definition is equivalent to the following LPN-styled definition.

Like SD (Sect. 3.4), the SSD assumption is false for some choices of $\mathcal{G}$ and $\mathcal{L}$. This definition serves as template that we make concrete in Sect. 5 and 6. We give concrete parameters in Sect. 7 for when we believe that SSD holds.

**Definition 5 (Stationary Learning Parity with Noise (SLPN)).** *Stationary Learning Parity with Noise is parameterized by an implicit computational* *security parameter $\kappa$, a field $\mathbb{F}$, dimensions $n, m, q \in \mathbb{N}$ with $n > m$, and distributions $\mathcal{L} \in \mathsf{Dist}[\{0,1\}^n]$, $\mathcal{H} \in \mathsf{Dist}[\mathbb{F}^{n \times m}]$. For sample $L \leftarrow \mathcal{L}$ and for $i \in [q]$, sample $\boldsymbol{e}_i \leftarrow L \odot \mathbb{F}^n$, $\boldsymbol{A}_i \leftarrow \mathcal{H} \in \mathbb{F}^{n \times m}$ and $\boldsymbol{s}_i \leftarrow \mathbb{F}^m$. The $(n, m, q, \mathbb{F}, \mathcal{L}, \mathcal{H})$-SLPN assumption states:*

$$\{(\boldsymbol{A}_i, \boldsymbol{b}_i) \mid \boldsymbol{b}_i := \boldsymbol{A}_i \cdot \boldsymbol{s}_i + \boldsymbol{e}_i\}_{i \in [q]} \approx \{(\boldsymbol{A}_i, \boldsymbol{b}_i) \mid \boldsymbol{b}_i \leftarrow \mathbb{F}^n\}_{i \in [q]}$$

*where $\approx$ denotes computational indistinguishability.*

In particular, the equivalence holds when $\mathbf{G}_i$ is the generator matrix for the parity check matrix $\boldsymbol{A}_i^{\top}$, see Sect. 3.4. Note that the more standard definitions of regular LPN and SD can be obtained simply by restricting $q$ to be one and requiring non-zero noise. Conversely, Definition 6 shows that one can similarly reframe SSD, SLPN in terms of the standard LPN formulation $(\mathbf{G}, \mathbf{G} \cdot \boldsymbol{e}) \approx (\mathbf{G}, \$)$ with specially structured noise $\boldsymbol{e}$ and matrices $\mathbf{G}$.

In the rest of this section, we justify at a high level SSD's security (Sect. 4.1) and discuss SSD's implications for the performance of pseudorandom correlation generators (Sect. 4.2).

### 4.1 The Security of SSD

The majority of known attacks on SD and LPN fall into two categories: linear and non-linear. For the parameter regime that PCGs commonly use, linear attacks are typically more efficient. Interestingly, SSD enjoys provable immunity to all of these attacks. As discussed in Sect. 3.5, these attacks can be shown to be equivalent to sampling the generator matrices $\mathbf{G}_1, \ldots, \mathbf{G}_q \in \mathbb{F}^{k \times n}$ and invoking an adversary $\mathcal{A}(\mathbf{G})$ which outputs a test vector $\boldsymbol{v} \in \mathbb{F}^{kq}$. The distinguisher is then implemented as $\boldsymbol{v} \cdot (\boldsymbol{b}_1 || \ldots || \boldsymbol{b}_q)$. I.e., if the output is correlated with the linear function $\boldsymbol{v} = (\boldsymbol{v}_1 || \ldots || \boldsymbol{v}_q)$, then the adversary $\mathcal{A}$ wins. We provably show no $\mathcal{A}$ exists that has noticeable advantage. The core idea is that any such attacker has to essentially come up with a codeword $\boldsymbol{v}_i$ of $\mathbf{G}_i$ that does not intersect the noise.[2] However, from the distribution of the noise, this is unlikely, even if the noise is correlated. SSD is particularly interesting because it targets a weakness of linear attacks such as information set decoding (ISD). At a high level, linear attacks come down to guessing a noise-free set of positions in $\boldsymbol{e}$, which are the non-zeros of $\boldsymbol{v}_i$, and then checking for linear correlations. However, this does not allow an attacker to take advantage of the new information that SSD provides. For a linear attacker, all $\boldsymbol{v}_i$ must be codewords, and therefore the new instances are no easier to attack than the first.

The situation with respect to non-linear attacks is more complicated. State-of-the-art techniques encode the problem statement into a system of non-linear equations and use algebraic techniques for solving the system, e.g., Gröbner bases. [BØ23] recently proved bounds on the running time of the XL [CKPS00] algorithm (see Sect. 3.6 and Fig. 1), when applied to the SD problem with regular

[2] Here we abuse notation and redefine $\boldsymbol{v}_i \in \mathbb{F}^n$ as a codeword of $\mathbf{G}_i$ that corresponds to a test vector $\mathbf{G}_i \boldsymbol{v}_i$ in the SD setting. See Sect. 5 for formal detail.

noise. They show that when $\mathbf{G} \in \mathbb{F}^{k \times n}$ has non-constant rate, e.g., $k = (1 - \epsilon)n$, then the XL algorithm can outperform linear attacks.

Given that our system can be seen as an even more structured version of regular noise SD, it is imperative that we understand how such attacks scale when adapted to use the additional structure. To achieve this, we define a system of equations that encodes the structure of the SSD problem and then prove bounds on the required running time to solve such systems using the XL algorithm. We show that XL is not noticeably better at solving SSD compared to SD.

### 4.2 Pseudorandom Correlation Generator (PCG) from SSD

We now explain at a high level how SSD improves the performance of PCGs and defer the full details to [KPRR25]. Typically, the end goal is to generate a secret sharing of a random vector $\boldsymbol{v}$ times a scalar $\Delta$, i.e., $[\![\boldsymbol{v}\Delta]\!]$. We will first compute a secret sharing of a $t$-sparse vector $\boldsymbol{e}$ times $\Delta$, i.e., $[\![\boldsymbol{e}\Delta]\!]$. The final result is obtained by computing $[\![\boldsymbol{v}\Delta]\!] = \mathbf{G}[\![\boldsymbol{e}\Delta]\!]$, i.e., $\boldsymbol{v} = \mathbf{G}\boldsymbol{e}$. $\boldsymbol{e}, \boldsymbol{v}$ will be known to the receiver while $\Delta$ is known to the sender. Many useful degree 1 PCGs, e.g., for OT, binary OLE, and VOLE, are directly obtained from $[\![\boldsymbol{v}\Delta]\!]$.

In more detail, let $n' := n/t$. The receiver samples $t$ subvectors $\boldsymbol{e}_1, \ldots, \boldsymbol{e}_t \in \mathbb{F}^{n'}$ of Hamming weight 1 and defines $\boldsymbol{e} := \boldsymbol{e}_1 || \ldots || \boldsymbol{e}_t \in \mathbb{F}^n$. The secret sharing $[\![\boldsymbol{e}\Delta]\!]$ is generated by evaluating $t$ so-called punctured PRFs [GGM84, BCG+19a] (PPRF) or a distributed point function (DPF), where the input to the $i$th PPRF is the index of the non-zero in $\boldsymbol{e}_i$ from the receiver and $\Delta$ from the sender. The output is $[\![\boldsymbol{e}_i\Delta]\!]$ and we obtain $[\![\boldsymbol{e}\Delta]\!] := [\![\boldsymbol{e}_1\Delta]\!] || \ldots || [\![\boldsymbol{e}_t\Delta]\!]$. A single instance of such PPRF protocol requires $\log_2 n'$ oblivious transfers (OTs).

Without going into detail, the PPRF protocol generates a GGM tree with $n'$ leaves. A version of the GGM tree will be held by both parties and is generated by applying a PRG to the value of each parent node and assigning the result to its children. In total, $2n'$ PRG calls are made to evaluate the full tree. Additionally, the parties perform an OT for each level of the GGM tree, which allows the receiver to know all but one of the seeds at each level. These missing seeds all lie on the path from the root to the leaf node that corresponds to the non-zero of $\boldsymbol{e}_i$. The expansion of the GGM tree is largely independent of the value assigned to the leaf, in this case a sharing of $\Delta$. SSD can be used to optimize this process by only expanding the tree once and then repeatedly derandomizing the leaf value for each instance, a $2\times$ reduction in the number of PRG calls and requiring no additional OTs. See [KPRR25] for a more detailed description.

Many applications require billions of correlations. However, due to memory constraints, it is often inefficient to have $n > 2^{24}$ and as such it is common to have $q$ PCG instances each of fixed size $n$, e.g., $n = 2^{20}$. This comes at the cost of requiring $qt \log_2 n/t$ OTs and communication. The SSD assumption allows us to reduce the overhead back down to $t \log_2 n/t$ OTs in total and an amortized $t$ communication per instance (i.e., $\log_2 n/t$ times less than SD). This is because the bulk of the work in the PPRF protocol is dependent on the locations of the non-zeros in $\boldsymbol{e}$ but *not their values*. As such, because SSD states that the location does not need to change, we obtain significant savings. We additionally obtain a much more cache-friendly construction that results in significant computational savings. This is because the ability to reuse the bulk of the setup makes it more attractive to use smaller values of $n$, which improves the cache efficiency.

We also obtain significant improvements for degree 2 PCGs such as non-binary OLEs and Beaver triples that rely on the Ring LPN assumption. This setting requires a very expensive setup to compute a sharing of two sparse polynomials $\boldsymbol{e} \cdot \boldsymbol{e}'$. If we apply the SSD assumption to this setting, the vast majority of the setup can be reused, dramatically decreasing the overhead.

## 5 Linear Attacks

We now demonstrate that our assumption is resilient to linear attacks. We focus on the restricted case of regular noise for efficiency. Our argument lies in showing that the linear test framework adversary gains no significant advantage from SLPN/SSD. It will be convenient to recast SSD in terms of standard SD with structured noise and structured $\mathbf{G}$.

**Definition 6 (Canonical Representation).** *We say $(n', m', \mathbb{F}, \mathcal{D}, \mathcal{H}')$-LPN is the Canonical Representation of $(n, m, q, \mathbb{F}, \mathcal{L}, \mathcal{H})$-SLPN if $n' = nq, m' = mq, \mathcal{D} = \{\boldsymbol{e}_1 || ... || \boldsymbol{e}_q : \boldsymbol{d} \leftarrow \mathcal{L}, \boldsymbol{e}_i \leftarrow \boldsymbol{d} \odot \mathbb{F}^n\}, \mathcal{H}' = \{\mathsf{diag}(\boldsymbol{A}_1, ..., \boldsymbol{A}_q) : \boldsymbol{A}_i \leftarrow \mathcal{H}\}$ where $\mathsf{diag}$ denotes the function that places $\boldsymbol{A}_1, ..., \boldsymbol{A}_q$ along the diagonal of a $n' \times m'$ matrix.*

*Similarly, we say $(n', k', \mathbb{F}, \mathcal{L}, \mathcal{G}')$-SD is the Canonical Representation of $(n, k, q, \mathbb{F}, \mathcal{D}, \mathcal{G})$-SSD if $n' = nq, k' = kq, \mathcal{D} = \{\boldsymbol{e}_1 || ... || \boldsymbol{e}_q : \boldsymbol{d} \leftarrow \mathcal{L}, \boldsymbol{e}_i \leftarrow \boldsymbol{d} \odot \mathbb{F}^n\}, \mathcal{G}' = \{\mathsf{diag}(\mathbf{G}_1, ..., \mathbf{G}_q) : \mathbf{G}_i \leftarrow \mathcal{G}\}$.*

It is not hard to show that the canonical representation is equivalent.

**Definition 7 (Security against Linear Tests).** *Security against Linear Tests is parameterized by an implicit security parameter $\kappa$, a finite field $\mathbb{F}$, dimensions $n, m \in \mathbb{N}$ with $n > m$, and subsets $\mathcal{D} \subset \mathbb{F}^n$, $\mathcal{H} \subseteq \mathbb{F}^{n \times m}$. We say that the $(n, m, \mathbb{F}, \mathcal{D}, \mathcal{H})$-LPN assumption is secure against linear attacks*

$$\Pr[\mathit{bias}(\mathcal{D}_{\boldsymbol{A}}) > \epsilon : \boldsymbol{A} \leftarrow \mathcal{H}] \leq \delta$$

*where $\epsilon, \delta$ are negligible and $\mathcal{D}_{\boldsymbol{A}}$ is the distribution induced by $\boldsymbol{s} \leftarrow \mathbb{F}^m, \boldsymbol{e} \leftarrow \mathcal{D}$ and outputting the LPN sample $\boldsymbol{A}\boldsymbol{s} + \boldsymbol{e}$.*

We note that one can also consider a computational version of linear test by restricting $\mathcal{D}$ to being efficient. This will then correspond to using the pseudo-minimum distance in the following.

**Theorem 3 (Security of SLPN against Linear Tests with Regular Noise).** *Let $\mathbb{F}$ be a finite field, $\mathcal{H} \subseteq \mathbb{F}^{n \times m}$ be a set of matrices with dual distance at least $d$ with probability at least $\delta$, $\mathcal{D} \in \{0, 1\}^n$ be the set of regular weight $t$ vectors, then $(n, m, q, \mathbb{F}, \mathcal{D}, \mathcal{H})$-SLPN is secure against attacks in the $(\epsilon, \delta)$-linear test framework of Definition 7 (in canonical representation) where*

$$\epsilon = (1 - d/n)^t$$

*Proof.* To prove SLPN secure against linear attacks, we split our proof into two cases and prove them separately. First, we consider the number of LPN instances $q = 1$ and only then $q > 1$.

*Non-stationary Noise,* $q = 1$. Let $d \in [n]$ be the minimum number of linearly dependent rows in $\boldsymbol{A}$. We show that there does not exist a $\boldsymbol{v}$ such that $\boldsymbol{v}\cdot(\mathbf{As} + \mathbf{e})$ is distinguishable from uniform. We consider two cases.

**Non-codeword** $\boldsymbol{v}$. Let us define the code $\mathcal{C} = \{\boldsymbol{c} \in \mathbb{F}^n : \boldsymbol{cA} = 0\} = \{\boldsymbol{m}\mathbf{G} : \boldsymbol{m} \in \mathbb{F}^k\}$. This implies that all $\boldsymbol{c} \in \mathcal{C}$ are mapped to zero when multiplied from the right by $\boldsymbol{A}$, that is $\boldsymbol{c}^\mathsf{T}\boldsymbol{A} = 0^m$. Conversely, for $\boldsymbol{v} \notin \mathcal{C}$ it holds that $\boldsymbol{v}^\mathsf{T}\boldsymbol{A} \neq 0^m$. Therefore, $\boldsymbol{v}^\mathsf{T}\boldsymbol{As} = \boldsymbol{u}^\mathsf{T}\boldsymbol{s} = r$ where $\boldsymbol{u} \in \mathbb{F}^m$ is some non-zero vector. Since $\boldsymbol{s}$ is uniform, it follows that so is $r$, and therefore $\max_{v \notin \mathcal{C}}(\mathsf{bias}_{\boldsymbol{v}}(\boldsymbol{As} + \boldsymbol{e})) = 0$.

**Codeword** $\boldsymbol{v}$. As just described, when $\boldsymbol{v}$ is a codeword the randomness contributed by $\boldsymbol{s}$ vanishes. That is, $\boldsymbol{v}^\mathsf{T}(\boldsymbol{As} + \boldsymbol{e}) = \boldsymbol{v}^\mathsf{T}\boldsymbol{e}$. To prove that the construction is secure against linear attacks we must show that $\boldsymbol{v} \cdot \boldsymbol{e}$ has negligible bias. Let $\boldsymbol{e}_i$ and $\boldsymbol{v}_i$ denote the $i$th regular block of $\boldsymbol{e}, \boldsymbol{v}$, respectively, and let $\mathcal{D}_i$ denote the distribution of $\boldsymbol{e}_i$. Lemma 1 states that the overall $\mathsf{bias}_{\boldsymbol{v}}(\mathcal{D})$ is bounded as $\mathsf{bias}_{\boldsymbol{v}}(\mathcal{D}) \leq \prod_{i\in[t]} \mathsf{bias}_{\boldsymbol{v}_i}(\mathcal{D}_i)$. We have $\mathsf{bias}_{\boldsymbol{v}_i}(\mathcal{D}_i) = \left|\mathop{\mathbb{E}}_{\boldsymbol{e}_i \leftarrow \mathcal{D}_i}[\chi(\boldsymbol{v}_i \cdot \boldsymbol{e}_i)]\right|$. Let $d_i$ denote the Hamming weight of $\boldsymbol{v}_i$. Recall that we have one noisy location in $\boldsymbol{e}_i$ (possibly with value zero), and therefore the probability the noisy location intersects $\boldsymbol{v}_i$ is $d_i/(n/t)$. Conditioned on intersecting, $\boldsymbol{v}_i \cdot \boldsymbol{e}_i$ is uniform over $\mathbb{F}$, and therefore the bias is 0. Otherwise, $\boldsymbol{v}_i \cdot \boldsymbol{e}_i = 0$ and $\chi(\boldsymbol{v}_i \cdot \boldsymbol{e}_i) = 1$. It follows that $\mathsf{bias}_{\boldsymbol{v}_i}(\mathcal{D}_i) = 1 - d_i/(n/t)$ and

$$\max_{v\in\mathcal{C}}(\mathsf{bias}_{\boldsymbol{v}}(\mathcal{D})) \leq \prod_i 1 - d_i/(n/t) \leq \left(1 - \frac{d}{n}\right)^t$$

Note that this differs from the traditional regular noise bias for $q = 1$ as we allow the noise value to be 0. For $\mathbb{F}_2$ and non-zero noise, $\Pr[\boldsymbol{v}_i\cdot\boldsymbol{e}_1 = 1] = d_i/(n/t)$ and $\chi(\boldsymbol{v}_i \cdot \boldsymbol{e}_1) = -1$. It follows that $\mathbb{E}[\chi(\boldsymbol{v}_i \cdot \boldsymbol{e}_i)] = -d_i/(n/t) + (1 - d_i/(n/t)) = 1 - 2d_i/(n/t)$ and overall $\mathsf{bias}_{\boldsymbol{v}}(\mathcal{D}) \leq (1 - 2d/n)^t$.

*Stationary Noise,* $q > 1$. As in the $q = 1$ case, it is clear that $\boldsymbol{v} \cdot (\boldsymbol{As} + \boldsymbol{e})$ is uniform when $\boldsymbol{v}$ is *not* a concatenation of $q$ codewords. This is because $\boldsymbol{v}$ does not map $\boldsymbol{s}$ to zero. Now let $\boldsymbol{v}_1, ..., \boldsymbol{v}_q$ denote the codewords of $\boldsymbol{v}$, i.e. $\boldsymbol{v}_i\boldsymbol{A}_i = 0^m$ and $\boldsymbol{v} = (\boldsymbol{v}_1||...||\boldsymbol{v}_q)$. As in the $q = 1$ case, if $\boldsymbol{v}$ intersects $\boldsymbol{e}$, then the result is uniformly random, and therefore has zero bias. Since (a) $\boldsymbol{v}$ is non-zero, and hence at least one $\boldsymbol{v}_i$ is non-zero, and (b) the bias of each block with non-zero $\boldsymbol{v}_i$ is at most $\left(1 - \frac{d}{n}\right)^t$, then the overall bias is at most this as well. Note that while the noisy locations between blocks do not change, their values in each block are uniformly random, and the overall bias is bounded as the maximum over the bias of each non-zero block. □

Note that given Theorem 3 and the equivalence of SLPN and SSD (see Sect. 4), the security of SSD against linear tests with regular noise is straightforward.

### 5.1 Other Linear Attacks

Given that our assumption introduces additional structure it is worth considering the existence of other attacks that could be considered linear while not fit into the linear test framework. Consider the SSD problem and the $q$ outputs $\boldsymbol{b}_1, ..., \boldsymbol{b}_q$, i.e. $\boldsymbol{b}_i = \mathbf{G}_i \boldsymbol{A}_i \boldsymbol{s}_i + \mathbf{G}_i \boldsymbol{e}_i$ for generator $\mathbf{G}_i$ of parity check $\boldsymbol{A}_i$. There exists a hidden subset $\mathbf{G}'_1, ..., \mathbf{G}'_q$ of $\mathbf{G}_1, ..., \mathbf{G}_q$ where $\mathbf{G}'_i := (\mathbf{G}_{i,*,L_1}, \dots \mathbf{G}_{i,*,L_t}) \in \mathbb{F}^{m \times t}$ and $\mathbf{G}_{i,*,L_j}$ is the $j$th "noisy column" of $\mathbf{G}_i$. We then have $\boldsymbol{b}_i = \mathbf{G}'_i \cdot \boldsymbol{c}_i$ where $\boldsymbol{c}_i \in \mathbb{F}^t$ are the $t$ noisy values in $\boldsymbol{e}_i$, i.e. $\boldsymbol{c}_{i,j} = \boldsymbol{e}_{i,L_j}$. Similarly, we can write this as one large linear equation $\boldsymbol{b} = \mathbf{G}' \cdot \boldsymbol{c}$. with $\mathbf{G}' = \mathsf{diag}(\mathbf{G}'_1, ..., \mathbf{G}'_t)$. Given that $|\boldsymbol{b}| > |\boldsymbol{c}|$, the pseudorandomness of $\boldsymbol{b}$ clearly depends on $\mathbf{G}'$ being hidden. We consider a special case where pseudorandomness breaks down.

Consider instantiating the SSD assumption where the space of generator matrices is the singleton set $\mathcal{G} = \{\mathbf{G}\}$. Therefore $\mathbf{G}_1, ..., \mathbf{G}_q$ above are all the same. This additionally means that $\mathbf{G}'$ can be expressed as an $m \times t$ matrix as opposed to a $qm \times qt$ matrix. In particular, consider $\mathbf{C} = (\boldsymbol{c}_1, ..., \boldsymbol{c}_q), \mathbf{B} = (\boldsymbol{b}_1, ..., \boldsymbol{b}_q)$ and observe that $\mathbf{B} = \mathbf{G}' \cdot \mathbf{C}$. Although the subset corresponding to $\mathbf{G}'$ is not known, $\mathbf{G}'$ is now fixed and does not grow with $q$. Therefore, when $q = t$, we can assume that $\mathsf{span}(\mathbf{B}) = \mathsf{span}(\mathbf{G}')$. This also means that $\boldsymbol{b}_{t+1} \in \mathsf{span}(\boldsymbol{b}_1, ..., \boldsymbol{b}_t)$, i.e. $\boldsymbol{b}_{t+1}$ can be distinguished. Because $m < t$, one would not expect this to happen for random $\boldsymbol{b}_i$.

Although this attack is clearly in some sense linear, it is not possible to perform it in the linear attack framework. Determining the coefficients $\boldsymbol{v} \in \mathbb{F}^t$ such that $\boldsymbol{b}_{t+1} = \langle(\boldsymbol{b}_1, ..., \boldsymbol{b}_t, \boldsymbol{v})\rangle$ is a function of the output, which the linear test adversary does not have. Linear test adversaries must first fix $\boldsymbol{v}$ before seeing $\boldsymbol{b}$. This exemplifies that although the linear test framework captures the majority of traditional attacks on LPN and SD, new attacks become possible when additional structure is added. To prevent this relatively trivial attack, it is critical that the family of codes be large and relatively uncorrelated.

Consider $\mathcal{G} = \mathbb{F}^{m \times n}$, i.e. the uniform distribution. Then clearly the linear attack $\mathcal{A}(\boldsymbol{b}_1, ..., \boldsymbol{b}_{t+1})$ described above is impossible. Each new $\boldsymbol{b}_i$ is the sum of an independent and uniformly random subset $\mathbf{G}'_i$. Any adversary breaking security must crucially rely on the fact that the $\mathbf{G}'_i$ matrices are correlated via the secret $L$ and public parameters $\mathbf{G}_1, ..., \mathbf{G}_q$.

More generally, existing codes used for PGCs [BCG+19a, BCG+22, RRT23] all sample their codes from an extremely large sample space. In particular, many more random bits are used to sample $\mathbf{G}_i$ than are present in $\boldsymbol{b}_i$. This suggests that it is extremely unlike that linear correlations would exist. Given that each is constructed using a randomly sampled seed, e.g. $\mathbf{G}_i = \mathsf{CodeGen}(\mathsf{H}(i))$ for a random oracle $\mathsf{H}$, then such linear attacks in the output should not be feasible.

## 6 Algebraic Attacks

In this section, we show that SSD is resilient against the recent algebraic attack of [BØ23]. We first modify [BØ23]'s attack so that it takes advantage of the stationary noise across instances. We then show that the structured stationary noise provides negligible advantage. More specifically, we start by presenting our modified system in Sect. 6.1. We continue by computing our system's Hilbert series in Sect. 6.2, use it to estimate the witness degree in Sect. 6.3, repeat the same procedure for the hybrid approach in Sect. 6.4, and then evaluate the attack's impact on SSD's security in Sect. 6.5.

### 6.1 Formulating Our Polynomial System

Recall that we restrict the noise to be at locations $L \in \mathcal{L}$ such that the locations are regular. Consider arbitrary matrices $\mathbf{G}_i \in \mathbb{F}^{k \times n}$ sampled from $\mathcal{G}$ and error vectors $\boldsymbol{e}_i \in \mathbb{F}^n$, where each $\boldsymbol{e}_i \leftarrow L \odot \mathbb{F}^n$ is a vector with *at most* $t$ non-zeros. That is, $\boldsymbol{e}_i = \boldsymbol{e}_{i,1}||\dots||\boldsymbol{e}_{i,t}$ where $||\boldsymbol{e}_{i,j}|| = n/t$ and $|\boldsymbol{e}_{i,j}| \leq 1$. We are given

$$(\mathbf{G}_1, \dots, \mathbf{G}_q, \boldsymbol{b}_1, \dots, \boldsymbol{b}_q),$$

where $\boldsymbol{b}_i = \mathbf{G}_i \cdot \boldsymbol{e}_i$.

We now formulate a system of polynomial equations to solve for $\boldsymbol{e}_i$ for $i \in [q]$, i.e., the system has $qn$ unknowns. We first consider in Modeling 3 the case where SSD is parameterized over a large field $\mathbb{F}$, and then in Modeling 4 the case where it is parameterized over $\mathbb{F}_2$.

**Modeling 3 (SSD over a Large Field $\mathbb{F}$).** *Let $(\mathbf{G}_1, \dots, \mathbf{G}_q, \boldsymbol{b}_1, \dots, \boldsymbol{b}_q)$ be an SSD instance with regular noise locations $L$ over a large $\mathbb{F}$. Let $\mathcal{F} := \mathcal{R} \cup \mathcal{S}$ be a set of polynomials such that:*

- *$\mathcal{R}$ is the linear equations $\langle \mathbf{G}_{i,j}, \mathbf{e}_i \rangle - \boldsymbol{b}_{i,j} = 0$, for all $i \in [q]$ and $j \in [k]$.*
- *$\mathcal{S}$ is the set of $q^2 t \binom{n/t}{2} = q^2 n^2/2t - q^2 n/2$ quadratic equations $\mathbf{e}_{i,v,j}\mathbf{e}_{i',v,j'} = 0$, for all $i, i' \in [q], v \in [t]$, and $j < j' \in [n/t]$, implied by the structured noise constraint $L$.*

Modeling 4 optimizes the system for $\mathbb{F}_2$ by including the field equations $\mathbf{e}_{i,v,j}^2 - \mathbf{e}_{i,v,j} = 0$, for all $i \in [q]$, $v \in [t]$, and $j \in [n/t]$. This ensures that the ideal $\langle \mathcal{F} \rangle$ generated by Modeling 4 is zero-dimensional. However, for large $\mathbb{F}$, as noted prior, these equations will have no contribution.

**Modeling 4 (SSD over $\mathbb{F}_2$).** *Let $(\mathbf{G}_1, \dots, \mathbf{G}_q, \boldsymbol{b}_1, \dots, \boldsymbol{b}_q)$ be a SSD instance with regular noise over $\mathbb{F}_2$. Let $\mathcal{F} := \mathcal{R} \cup \mathcal{S} \cup \mathcal{V}$ be a set of polynomials such that:*

- *$\mathcal{R}$ and $\mathcal{S}$ are the same sets as in Modeling 3.*
- *$\mathcal{V}$ is the field equations $\mathbf{e}_{i,v,j}^2 - \mathbf{e}_{i,v,j} = 0$ for all $i \in [q]$, $v \in [t]$, and $j \in [n/t]$.*

Compared to the prior work modeling for binary fields (Modeling 2), we observe that SSD appears slightly harder because we no longer restrict $\boldsymbol{e}$ to being regular with exact weight $t$ (i.e. the noisy positions are sampled uniformly, and thus can be zero). This eliminates $t$ linear equations that prior attacks [ES24, BØ23] were able to use.

### 6.2 Computing Hilbert Series

We now compute the Hilbert series (Sect. 3.6) of the homogeneous ideals associated with Modeling 3 and Modeling 4. Our computation uses a template similar to [BØ23] that estimates the Hilbert series of the ideals associated with Modeling 1 and Modeling 2. Note that $\mathcal{F}$, neither in the case of a large $\mathbb{F}$ nor $\mathbb{F}_2$, is a regular or semi-regular system (Sect. 3.6). To see why, consider $f_1 := \mathbf{e}_{1,1,1}\mathbf{e}_{1,1,2}$ and $f_2 := \mathbf{e}_{1,1,2}\mathbf{e}_{1,1,3}$ that come from the structured noise constraint $\mathcal{S}$. Recall that the regularity and semi-regularity of $\mathcal{F}$ is independent of the order in which we consider the polynomials in the system. Now, $\mathbf{e}_{1,1,1}f_2 = 0$ in $\mathcal{A}/\langle f_1 \rangle$, but $\mathbf{e}_{1,1,1} \neq 0$ in $\mathcal{A}/\langle f_1 \rangle$, and hence $\mathcal{F}$ is not a regular system. If $\mathcal{F}$ were to be a semi-regular system, then its degree of regularity can be no more than 3 using the aforementioned examples of $f_1, f_2$. However, $\mathbf{e}_{1,1,1}\mathbf{e}_{1,2,1}\mathbf{e}_{1,3,1} \notin \langle \mathcal{F} \rangle$ (with high probability). Thus, as long as $t \geq 3$ (or even $q \geq 3$, etc.), the system is not semi-regular either. As a result, we cannot use the Hilbert series from Sect. 3.6 and require a more sophisticated analysis.

**Hilbert Series for Modeling 3.** Recall Modeling 3's polynomial system $\mathcal{F} := \mathcal{R} \cup \mathcal{S}$. We first compute by monomial counting the Hilbert series $\mathcal{HS}_{\mathcal{A}/\langle \mathcal{S} \rangle}(\mathbf{z})$ of the quotient ring $\mathcal{A}/\langle \mathcal{S} \rangle$ resulting from the structured noise equations $\mathcal{S}$. After we compute the Hilbert series corresponding to $\mathcal{S}$, we need to incorporate the linear parity-check equations $\mathcal{R}$ to get the final Hilbert series. To do that, we follow [BØ23]'s approach. We formalize as Assumption 1 an assumption that the parity-check equations $\mathcal{R}$ behave well in the quotient ring $\mathcal{A}/\langle \mathcal{S} \rangle$ formed by the structured noise equations $\mathcal{S}$. Note its similarity with the definition of semi-regularity over large $\mathbb{F}$.

**Assumption 1.** *Let $\mathcal{F} := \mathcal{R} \cup \mathcal{S}$ be an instance of Modeling 3 and $d_{\mathsf{reg}}$ be the degree of regularity of the zero-dimensional ideal $\langle \mathcal{F} \rangle$. Let $\mathcal{R}^{(\mathsf{h})} := \{r_1, \ldots, r_{qk}\}$ be the set of homogenized parity check equations. Our assumption states that for $i \in [qk]$; if $gr_i = 0$ in $\mathcal{A}/\langle \mathcal{S}, r_1, \ldots, r_{i-1} \rangle$ with $\mathsf{deg}(gr_i) < d_{\mathsf{reg}}$, then $g = 0$ in $\mathcal{A}/\langle \mathcal{S}, r_1, \ldots, r_{i-1} \rangle$.*

We now state and derive the final Hilbert series.

**Theorem 4.** *For $\mathcal{F}$ associated with Modeling 3, the Hilbert series of the homogeneous ideal $\langle \mathcal{F}^{(\mathsf{h})} \rangle$ under Assumption 1 is*

$$\mathcal{HS}_{\mathcal{A}/\langle \mathcal{F}^{(\mathsf{h})} \rangle}(\mathbf{z}) = (1-\mathbf{z})^{qk} \cdot \left(1 + \frac{n}{t}\left(\frac{1}{(1-\mathbf{z})^q} - 1\right)\right)^t,$$

*truncated after the first $\leq 0$ coefficient. We call $(1-\mathbf{z})^{qk} \cdot \left(1 + \frac{n}{t}\left(\frac{1}{(1-\mathbf{z})^q} - 1\right)\right)^t$ the generating series of $\langle \mathcal{F}^{(\mathsf{h})} \rangle$.*

Theorem 4 immediately follows from the proofs of Lemma 2 and Lemma 3.

**Lemma 2.** *For the set $\mathcal{S}$ associated with the structural equations of Modeling 3, the Hilbert series of the homogeneous ideal $\langle \mathcal{S}^{(\mathsf{h})} \rangle$ is*

$$\mathcal{HS}_{\mathcal{A}/\langle \mathcal{S}^{(\mathsf{h})} \rangle}(\mathbf{z}) = \left(1 + \frac{n}{t}\left(\frac{1}{(1-\mathbf{z})^q} - 1\right)\right)^t.$$

*Proof.* Note that $\mathcal{S}$ is already homogenized, i.e., $\mathcal{S} = \mathcal{S}^{(\mathsf{h})}$. Recall that $\mathcal{HS}(\mathbf{z}) = \sum_d \mathcal{HF}(d) \cdot \mathbf{z}^d$ and the $\mathcal{HF}(d) = \mathsf{dim}(\mathcal{A}_d/\langle \mathcal{S}^{(\mathsf{h})} \rangle_d)$ is the size of the vector space basis $B_d \subset \{[\mathbf{x}^{\boldsymbol{\alpha}}] : \boldsymbol{\alpha} \in \mathbb{N}^n\}$ s.t. $\mathsf{span}(B_d) = \mathcal{A}_d/\langle \mathcal{S}^{(\mathsf{h})} \rangle_d$.

Let us first restrict our attention to a specific block $v \in [t]$ and let $\mathcal{S}_v$ be the subset of $\mathcal{S}$ that only considers block $v$. Because $\mathcal{S}_v = \{\mathbf{e}_{i,v,j}\mathbf{e}_{i',v,j'} : i, i' \in [q], j < j' \in [n/t]\}$, the quotient $\mathcal{A}/\langle \mathcal{S}_v^{(\mathsf{h})} \rangle$ cannot contain any monomials with $\mathbf{e}_{i,v,j}\mathbf{e}_{i',v,j'}$ as a factor. That is, for a fixed $v$ no monomial contains more than one $j$ index. If we then consider a specific degree $d$ and all of the $q$ instances, the admissible monomials are $B_{d,v} := \left\{\prod_{i\in[q]} \mathbf{e}_{i,v,j}^{\alpha_i} : j \in [n/t], \boldsymbol{\alpha} \in (\mathbb{N} \cup \{0\})^q, d = \sum_{i\in[q]} \alpha_i\right\}$. Let us count the number of such monomials for a specific $v \in [t], j \in [n/t], d > 0$. We will use a balls in bins argument to count $|\{\boldsymbol{\alpha} \in (\mathbb{N} \cup \{0\})^q : d = \sum_k \alpha_k\}|$. One can view this as counting the ways to assign $d$ balls into $q$ bins, i.e., bins $\alpha_1, \ldots, \alpha_q$. The number of ways to do this is $\binom{q+d-1}{d}$ and hence the number of monomials of the form $\prod_{i\in[q]} \mathbf{e}_{i,v,j}^{\alpha_i}$ for a fixed $v, j$ is $\binom{q+d-1}{d}$. Therefore, if we consider all $j \in [n/t]$ for the fixed block $v$, we have $|B_{d,v}| = \frac{n}{t} \cdot \binom{q+d-1}{d}$. Thus, the Hilbert series "for one block," say $v$, is

$$\mathcal{HS}_{\mathcal{A}/\langle \mathcal{S}_v^{(\mathsf{h})} \rangle}(\mathbf{z}) = 1 + \frac{n}{t} \cdot \sum_{d=1}^{\infty} \binom{q+d-1}{d} \mathbf{z}^d$$

where the one is from the constant monomial. We can find a closed form expression for the infinite sum inductively as follows. Consider $q = 1$. After substituting $q = 1$ into the infinite sum in $\mathcal{HS}_{\mathcal{A}/\langle \mathcal{S}^{(\mathsf{h})} \rangle, v}$, we get $\eta_1 = \sum_{d=1}^{\infty} \binom{1+d-1}{d} \mathbf{z}^d = \frac{\mathbf{z}}{1-\mathbf{z}}$. We claim that for arbitrary $q$, $\eta_q = \frac{1}{(1-\mathbf{z})^q} - 1$, which clearly holds for $q = 1$. Now, in pursuit of the inductive step, consider

$$\begin{aligned}
\mathbf{z} + \eta_q &= \mathbf{z} + \sum_{d=1}^{\infty} \binom{q+d-1}{d} \mathbf{z}^d \\
&= \mathbf{z} + q\mathbf{z} + \binom{q+1}{2} \mathbf{z}^2 + \ldots \\
&= \left((q+1)\mathbf{z} + \binom{q+2}{2} \mathbf{z}^2 + \ldots\right) - \left((q+1)\mathbf{z}^2 + \binom{q+2}{2} \mathbf{z}^3 + \ldots\right) \qquad (3) \\
&= \sum_{d=1}^{\infty} \binom{q+d}{d} \mathbf{z}^d - \sum_{d=1}^{\infty} \binom{q+d}{d} \mathbf{z}^{d+1} \\
&= (1-\mathbf{z}) \sum_{d=1}^{\infty} \binom{q+d}{d} \mathbf{z}^d \\
&= (1-\mathbf{z}) \eta_{q+1}
\end{aligned}$$

where (3) follows from $\binom{q+d}{d} - \binom{q+d-1}{d-1} = \binom{q+d-1}{d}$. Therefore, $\eta_{q+1} = \frac{\mathbf{z}+\eta_q}{1-\mathbf{z}} = \frac{1}{(1-\mathbf{z})^{q+1}} - 1$. Hence, $\mathcal{HS}_{\mathcal{A}/\langle \mathcal{S}_v^{(\mathsf{h})}\rangle}(\mathbf{z}) = 1 + \frac{n}{t}\left(\frac{1}{(1-\mathbf{z})^q} - 1\right)$. Finally, a general monomial of degree $d$ is a product of monomials for distinct blocks with the sum of their degrees equal to $d$. Relying on the same symbolic argument as in [FS09b], which gives the generating series of a Cartesian product, we have

$$\mathcal{HS}_{\mathcal{A}/\langle \mathcal{S}^{(\mathsf{h})}\rangle}(\mathbf{z}) = \left(1 + \frac{n}{t}\left(\frac{1}{(1-\mathbf{z})^q} - 1\right)\right)^t$$

□

**Lemma 3.** *For $\mathcal{F}$ associated with Modeling 3, the Hilbert series of the homogeneous ideal $\langle \mathcal{F}^{(\mathsf{h})}\rangle$ under Assumption 1 is*

$$\mathcal{HS}_{\mathcal{A}/\langle \mathcal{F}^{(\mathsf{h})}\rangle}(\mathbf{z}) = (1-\mathbf{z})^{qk} \cdot \mathcal{HS}_{\mathcal{A}/\langle \mathcal{S}^{(\mathsf{h})}\rangle}(\mathbf{z}),$$

*truncated after the first $\leq 0$ coefficient.*

*Proof.* Our proof is a straightforward modification and expansion of [BØ23]. Let $\mathcal{R}^{(\mathsf{h})} := \{r_1, \ldots, r_{qk}\}$ be the set of homogenized parity check equations. Let $\mathcal{I}(0)$ denote the ideal $\langle \mathcal{S}^{(\mathsf{h})}\rangle$ and $\mathcal{I}(j)$, $j \in [qk]$, denote the ideal $\langle \mathcal{S}^{(\mathsf{h})}, r_1, \ldots, r_j\rangle$. We will show Assumption 1 implies that for $j \in [qk]$, $d < d_{\mathsf{reg}}$, there exists a short exact sequence

$$0 \to \mathcal{A}_{d-1}/\mathcal{I}(j-1)_{d-1} \xrightarrow{\alpha} \mathcal{A}_d/\mathcal{I}(j-1)_d \xrightarrow{\beta} \mathcal{A}_d/\mathcal{I}(j)_d \to 0.$$

We prove this as follows. Let $\alpha : \mathcal{A}_{d-1}/\mathcal{I}(j-1)_{d-1} \to \mathcal{A}_d/\mathcal{I}(j-1)_d$ be the map

$$\alpha([f]) := [r_j f].$$

Firstly, $\alpha$ is well-defined as if $f_1 \in [f]$, then $f_1 = f + g$ for some $g \in \mathcal{I}(j-1)_{d-1}$. Then, $r_j f_1 = r_j f + r_j g$. By definition, $r_j g \in \mathcal{I}(j-1)_d$ since $r_j$ is homogenous and linear. Therefore, $[r_j f_1] = [r_j f]$. Secondly, $\alpha$ is injective. Suppose $\alpha([f]) = \alpha([f'])$, i.e., $[r_j f] = [r_j f']$. This implies that $r_j f - r_j f' \in \mathcal{I}(j-1)_d$, which in turn from Assumption 1 implies that $f - f' \in \mathcal{I}(j-1)_{d-1}$, i.e., $[f] = [f']$.

Let $\beta : \mathcal{A}_d/\mathcal{I}(j-1)_d \to \mathcal{A}_d/\mathcal{I}(j)_d$ be the map defined as

$$\beta([f]) := [f].$$

Again, $\beta$ is well-defined as if $f_1 \in [f]$, then $f_1 - f \in \mathcal{I}(j-1)_d$. Since $\mathcal{I}(j-1)_d \subseteq \mathcal{I}(j)_d$, $f_1 - f \in \mathcal{I}(j)_d$ and hence $[f_1] = [f]$. Also, $\beta$ is trivially surjective as $[f]$ is mapped to $[f]$.

Finally, we claim that $\mathsf{ker}(\beta) = \mathsf{im}(\alpha)$. To this end, we prove two statements. First, $\mathsf{im}(\alpha) \subseteq \mathsf{ker}(\beta)$. This is because if $[h] \in \mathsf{im}(\alpha)$, there exists an $f$ such that $[h] = [r_j f]$. Now, $\beta([h]) = \beta([r_j f]) = [0]$ as $r_j \in \mathcal{I}(j)$. Next, $\mathsf{ker}(\beta) \subseteq \mathsf{im}(\alpha)$. Suppose $[h] \in \mathsf{ker}(\beta)$. Then, $\beta([h]) = [h] = [0]$, i.e., $h \in \mathcal{I}(j)_d$. This implies that there exist $g \in \mathcal{S}^{(\mathsf{h})}$ and $f_1, \ldots, f_j$ such that $h = f_1 r_1 + \ldots + f_j r_j + g$. Let $g'$ denote the homogenous degree-$d$ part of $g$ and $f'_1, \ldots, f'_j$ denote the homogenous degree-$(d-1)$ parts of $f_1, \ldots, f_j$. Then, $h = f'_1 r_1 + \ldots + f'_j r_j + g$, i.e., $h - f'_j r_j \in \mathcal{I}(j-1)_d$. Therefore, $[h] = [r_j f'_j]$ and hence $\alpha([f'_j]) = [h]$, i.e., $[h] \in \mathsf{im}(\alpha)$.

Therefore, $0 \to \mathcal{A}_{d-1}/\mathcal{I}(j-1)_{d-1} \xrightarrow{\alpha} \mathcal{A}_d/\mathcal{I}(j-1)_d \xrightarrow{\beta} \mathcal{A}_d/\mathcal{I}(j)_d \to 0$ is indeed a short exact sequence. By the Hilbert function property for short exact sequences (Sect. 3.6), we have

$$\mathcal{HF}_{\mathcal{A}/\mathcal{I}(j-1)}(d-1) - \mathcal{HF}_{\mathcal{A}/\mathcal{I}(j-1)}(d) + \mathcal{HF}_{\mathcal{A}/\mathcal{I}(j)}(d) = 0.$$

Let $h_{d,j} := \mathcal{HF}_{\mathcal{A}/\mathcal{I}(j)}(d) = \mathsf{dim}(\mathcal{A}_d/\mathcal{I}(j)_d)$. Then, $h_{d,j} := h_{d,j-1} - h_{d-1,j-1}$. Let $\mathcal{G}_j$ be the generating series for $h_{d,j}$, i.e., let $\mathcal{G}_j(\mathbf{z}) = \sum_{d=0}^{\infty} h_{d,j}\mathbf{z}^d$. Note that $\mathcal{G}_j = \mathcal{HS}_{\mathcal{A}/\mathcal{I}(j)}$. We have

$$\begin{aligned}
\mathcal{G}_j(\mathbf{z}) &= \sum_{d=0}^{\infty} h_{d,j}\mathbf{z}^d \\
&= \sum_{d=0}^{\infty} (h_{d,j-1} - h_{d-1,j-1})\mathbf{z}^d \\
&= \sum_{d=0}^{\infty} h_{d,j-1}\mathbf{z}^d - \sum_{d=1}^{\infty} h_{d-1,j-1}\mathbf{z}^d \\
&= \sum_{d=0}^{\infty} h_{d,j-1}\mathbf{z}^d - \mathbf{z} \cdot \sum_{d=0}^{\infty} h_{d,j-1}\mathbf{z}^d \\
&= (1-\mathbf{z}) \cdot \mathcal{G}_{j-1}(\mathbf{z}).
\end{aligned}$$

Therefore, we get $\mathcal{HS}_{\mathcal{A}/\mathcal{I}(qk)}(\mathbf{z}) = (1-\mathbf{z})^{qk} \cdot \mathcal{HS}_{\mathcal{A}/\langle \mathcal{S}^{(\mathsf{h})}\rangle}(\mathbf{z})$. Note that by definition $\mathcal{I}(qk) = \langle \mathcal{S}^{(\mathsf{h})}, r_1, \ldots, r_{qk}\rangle = \langle \mathcal{F}^{(\mathsf{h})}\rangle$. Hence, the lemma follows. □

**Hilbert Series for Modeling** 4. We defer the presentation of Modeling 4 to [KPRR25] and note that it follows a similar methodology.

### 6.3 Estimating Witness Degree

As described earlier, following [BØ23], we will use the witness degree $d_{\mathsf{wit}}$ of the input polynomial system to estimate the cost of the XL Wiedemann approach. The systems $\mathcal{F}$ in Modeling 3 and Modeling 4 admit unique solutions for the range of parameters of interest. If $(a_1, \ldots, a_n)$ is a unique solution of the polynomial system, it has the reduced Gröbner basis $\{\mathbf{x}_1 - a_1, \ldots, \mathbf{x}_n - a_n\}$.[3] If $\mathcal{I} := \langle \mathcal{F}\rangle$, we have $\mathsf{LM}(\mathcal{I}_{\leq 1}) = \mathsf{LM}(\mathcal{I})$ and $\mathsf{dim}(\mathcal{I}_{\leq d}) = \mathsf{dim}(\mathcal{A}_{\leq d}) - 1$. In particular, we can say that $d_{\mathsf{wit}}$ is the smallest degree such that the rank of the Macaulay matrix is equal to the number of columns minus one.

[3] In the case of Modeling 4, the field equations ensure that the ideal is radical, and the claim from Hilbert's Nullstellensatz. In the case of Modeling 3, we assume that the system is sufficiently overdetermined to ensure this.

As in [BØ23], our Assumption 1 and [KPRR25]'s Assumption 2 associated with Modeling 4 imply that the relevant Macaulay matrix has maximal rank. Now, consider the Hilbert series from Theorem 4 and 5 (see [KPRR25]) prior to truncation. The coefficient in a term of degree $d < d_{\mathsf{reg}}$ is the number of columns that cannot be reduced in the Macaulay matrix of degree $d$. When $d \geq d_{\mathsf{reg}}$, the coefficient measures the number of "excess" rows after full reduction. We therefore estimate the witness degree $d_{\mathsf{wit}}$ as

$$d_{\mathsf{wit}} = \min \left\{ d \in \mathbb{N} : \sum_{j \in [d+1]} [\mathbf{z}^{j-1}](\mathcal{HS}(\mathbf{z})) \leq 0 \right\}$$

where $[\mathbf{z}^{j-1}](\mathcal{HS}(\mathbf{z}))$ denotes the coefficient of $\mathbf{z}^{j-1}$ in the Hilbert series from Theorem 4 and 5 (see [KPRR25]) prior to truncation. We have experimentally verified these estimates as we discuss in Sect. 6.5.

### 6.4 Hybrid Approach

Following [BØ23], we also present a hybrid approach, which consists of repeatedly guessing a few noise-free positions of $L$ (and therefore $\boldsymbol{e}$) and invoking XL Wiedemann until successfully computing $\boldsymbol{e}$. Parameterized by $f \in [t]$ and $\mu \in [\frac{n}{t}]$, the hybrid approach guesses $\mu$ noise-free positions in the first $f$ blocks of $\boldsymbol{e}$ and adds the equations $\boldsymbol{e}_{i,v,j} = 0$ for those $f$ blocks $v$ and $\mu$ positions $j$ in every instance $i$ to $\mathcal{F}$. Let us determine a bound $p_{f,\mu}$ on the probability that the guessed positions are all noise-free. There are at least $\frac{n}{t} - 1$ noise-free positions in each block. Therefore, the probability that the $\mu$ positions guessed in any given block are noise-free is at least $\frac{\binom{\frac{n}{t}-1}{\mu}}{\binom{\frac{n}{t}}{\mu}} = 1 - \frac{\mu t}{n}$. This means that the probability that all the positions guessed are noise-free is at least $p_{f,\mu} = \left(1 - \frac{\mu t}{n}\right)^f$. We then expect to repeat the XL Wiedemann $O(p_{f,\mu}^{-1})$ times.

We now need to derive the Hilbert series of this modified system. We discuss this hybrid approach for Modeling 3 and note that the case of Modeling 4 is similar. Consider the impact of our guessing on Lemma 2. For a fixed block $v$, the number of $j$ that are not fixed by our guess is now $\frac{n}{t} - \mu$ and not $\frac{n}{t}$ in the first $f$ blocks and still $\frac{n}{t}$ in the last $t - f$. To make Lemma 3 work, we augment Assumption 1 as in [BØ23] with Assumption 2. This ensures that fixing variables does not introduce unexpected cancelations at higher degrees among the parity-check equations in $\mathcal{R}$. For any invertible matrix $\mathbf{P}$, $f \in [t]$, and $\mu \in [\frac{n}{t}]$, let $\overline{\mathbf{P}_{f,\mu}^{-1}}$ denote the map that applies $\mathbf{P}^{-1}$ and then fixes the initial $\mu$ variables to 0 in the last $f$ blocks of $\mathbf{e}$.

**Assumption 2.** *Let $\mathcal{R}$ be the set of parity-check equations from Modeling 3. For every permutation matrix $\mathbf{P}$ which stabilizes each block of $\mathbf{e}$, $f \in [t]$, and $\mu \in [\frac{n}{t}]$, we assume $\mathcal{R}^{(\mathsf{h})} \circ \overline{\mathbf{P}_{f,\mu}^{-1}}$ satisfies Assumption 1 in the ring $\mathcal{A} \circ \overline{\mathbf{P}_{f,\mu}^{-1}}$.*

Under Assumption 2, the Hilbert series for Modeling 3 now becomes

$$\mathcal{HS}_{A/\langle \mathcal{F}^{(h)}\rangle,\text{hyb},f,\mu}(\mathbf{z}) = (1-\mathbf{z})^{qk} \cdot \left(1 + \left(\frac{n}{t} - \mu\right)\left(\frac{1}{(1-\mathbf{z})^q} - 1\right)\right)^f \cdot \left(1 + \frac{n}{t}\left(\frac{1}{(1-\mathbf{z})^q} - 1\right)\right)^{t-f},$$

truncated after the first $\leq 0$ coefficient. As before, the degree $d_{\mathsf{wit}}$ is derived from the Hilbert series. We refer to [BØ23] for further details.

### 6.5 Attack's Evaluation

We now evaluate our algebraic attack. We write scripts in the Magma Computational Algebra System V2.28-13 [BCP97] to (1) experimentally verify our Hilbert series and (2) compute the time complexity of the attack. We plan to open-source our Magma scripts along with our PCG code (see Sect. 8). In all our experiments, we use the free online Magma calculator, and hence our computation is restricted to $\leq 2$ minutes. Thus, we were able to run our scripts only on smaller parameters.

We first experimentally verify our Hilbert series from Sect. 6.4 is correct. We compare the output with the output of Magma's `HilbertSeries(·)`. We verify the hybrid version of our Hilbert series over $\mathbb{F}_{101}$ and for the same systems as [BØ23] in Table 7 (we can similarly verify over $\mathbb{F}_2$). The key difference is that we also add a parameter $q \geq 1$ ($q = 1$ for [BØ23]) to our system, which represents the number of SD instances. The largest $q$ we test for is 4 as for larger $q$ the `HilbertSeries(·)` function exceeds our computational resources. For $\mathbb{F}_{101}$, we confirm our Hilbert series is the same for all the tested systems $(q, n, k, t, f, \mu)$, and hence Assumption 1 holds:

$$(4,30,15,5,0,0), (4,30,20,5,0,0), (3,40,20,5,0,0),$$
$$(4,40,30,5,0,0), (3,49,30,7,0,0), (3,48,30,8,0,0),$$
$$(2,40,25,10,0,0), (1,84,50,12,3,2), (3,56,30,7,2,3),$$
$$(2,56,30,7,6,3), (3,70,40,10,5,2), (4,70,40,10,5,3)$$

We next focus on the efficiency of the algebraic attack. We run 2 experiments. For both, we consider $\mathbb{F}_{2^{128}}$ and $\mathbb{F}_2$ and the XL hybrid approach of Sect. 6.4. In each, we find the $(f, \mu)$ that results in the most efficient attack. We pick syndrome decoding parameters $n$, $k = n/2$ given our computational restrictions.

In the first experiment (Fig. 2), we show how the witness degree $d_{\mathsf{wit}}$ and the complexity of the XL Hybrid algorithm changes with increasing $q$. We fix $n = 2^{16}$, $k = 2^{15}$, fix $t = 69$ such that we get XL complexity of 128 with $q = 1$, and then vary $q = \{1, 2, 2^4, 2^7, 2^{10}\}$. Our results show that in fact the complexity of the XL algorithm increases with larger $q$. This implies that the attack is not able to take advantage of the additional information and becomes slower because the system of equations gets larger with increasing $q$, and hence more expensive for XL to solve. Another interesting aspect is that for all runs the best $f = t$. I.e., we should guess noise-free positions in all blocks. It is not surprising that this holds in the constant rate SD setting, where the amount of noise $t$ is smaller than in the non-constant rate LPN setting that [BØ23] emphasize. Overall, note that to get 128-bit security we require $t = 69$, which is substantially less than what is suggested by the linear test (Sect. 8). This implies that the algebraic attack may not be the ideal choice for our setting.

| | $\mathbb{F}_{2^{128}}$ $(t = 69)$ | | | $\mathbb{F}_2$ $(t = 69)$ | | |
|---|---|---|---|---|---|---|
| $q$ | $d_{\text{wit}}$ | $(f, \mu)$ | XL Hybrid | $d_{\text{wit}}$ | $(f, \mu)$ | XL Hybrid |
| 1 | 2 | (69,410) | 128 | 2 | (69,410) | 128 |
| 2 | 2 | (69,410) | 132 | 2 | (69,410) | 132 |
| $2^4$ | 2 | (69,410) | 144 | 2 | (69,410) | 144 |
| $2^7$ | 2 | (69,410) | 156 | 2 | (69,410) | 156 |
| $2^{10}$ | 2 | (69,410) | 168 | 2 | (69,410) | 168 |

**Fig. 2.** This experiment shows how the witness degree $d_{\text{wit}}$ and the complexity of the XL algorithm changes with increasing $q$. We set our parameters $n$, $k$ following standard choices in SD. I.e., we fix $n = 2^{16}$, $k = 2^{15}$, fix $t = 69$ such that we get XL complexity of 128 with $q = 1$, and then vary $q = \{1, 2, 2^4, 2^7, 2^{10}\}$. We consider $\mathbb{F}_{2^{128}}$ and $\mathbb{F}_2$, hybrid evaluation, and search all $(f, \mu)$ for the most efficient attack for each $q$. Note the results for $\mathbb{F}_{2^{128}}$ and $\mathbb{F}_2$ are identical.

The first experiment showed that we get the best attack by attacking a single SD instance. In the second experiment (see Fig. 3), we thus show the amount of noise $t$ necessary to get 128 bits of security for different $n$, $k$, and $q$ fixed to 1. We then repeat the same runs for $q = 2^{10}$ to show how $t$ changes.

| | | | $\mathbb{F}_{2^{128}}$ | | | | | | $\mathbb{F}_2$ | | | | | |
|---|---|---|---|---|---|---|---|---|---|---|---|---|---|---|
| | | | $q = 1$ | | | $q = 2^{10}$ | | | $q = 1$ | | | $q = 2^{10}$ | | |
| $n$ | $k$ | $d_{\text{wit}}$ | $(f, \mu)$ | XL | $t$ | $(f, \mu)$ | XL | $t$ | $(f, \mu)$ | XL | $t$ | $(f, \mu)$ | XL | $t$ |
| $2^{10}$ | $2^9$ | 2 | (101, 4) | 128 | 107 | (58,7) | 127 | 58 | (101, 4) | 128 | 107 | (58,7) | 127 | 58 |
| $2^{12}$ | $2^{11}$ | 2 | (89, 20) | 127 | 90 | (46,37) | 128 | 46 | (89, 20) | 127 | 90 | (46,37) | 128 | 46 |
| $2^{14}$ | $2^{13}$ | 2 | (74, 192) | 128 | 74 | (34,191) | 128 | 34 | (79, 91) | 128 | 79 | (34,191) | 128 | 34 |
| $2^{16}$ | $2^{15}$ | 2 | (69, 410) | 128 | 69 | (24,1364) | 128 | 24 | (69, 410) | 128 | 69 | (24,1364) | 128 | 24 |

**Fig. 3.** This experiment picks standard SD's $n$, $k$ parameters used for PCGs (i.e. $k = n/2$) and computes how much noise $t$ is necessary to get XL complexity of $\approx 128$ for $q = 1$ and $q = 2^{10}$. We consider $\mathbb{F}_{2^{128}}$ and $\mathbb{F}_2$, XL hybrid evaluation, and search all $(f, \mu)$ for the most efficient attack for each parameter setting.

## 7 Parameter Selection

We use our findings in Sect. 5 on SSD security against linear tests to choose the appropriate amount of noise $t$ for Fig. 4 and 5. To get 128 bits of security, we need $t = 176$ for OT generated with the SD assumption and $t = 400$ otherwise. Importantly, note from Theorem 3 that $q$ does not impact the choice of $t$. We also note that the parameters from the linear test framework tend to be conservative. E.g., [LWYY22]'s work suggests $t \approx 60$ gives 128 bits of security against known linear attacks, while our algebraic attacks in Sect. 6.5 suggest $t \approx 60$ depending on $n$. Moreover, the best attack strategy is to simply attack a single instance.

The main difference between SD and SSD parameters arises in small fields, e.g. $\mathbb{F}_2$. In this case, since our noise is sampled uniformly instead of set to 1, one must increase the noise to compensate. This difference vanishes over large fields, and fixed parameters for SD and SSD appear to give the same security level.

This suggests that one can instantiate SSD using the same parameters as SD for large fields, or increase the noise by the statistical security parameter for small fields so that each instance is expected to have at least as many non-zeros as in SD. However, for the time being, we opt for being conservative and choosing parameters based on the linear test framework.

## 8 Experimental Evaluation

*Implementation & Setting.* We present a detailed description of how to adapt existing PCG protocols in [KPRR25]. The crux for degree 1 PCG protocols is (1) generating a sharing of $\Delta\mathbf{e}$ and (2) compressing it by the generator matrix $\mathbf{G}$. SSD optimizes the generation of $[\![\Delta\mathbf{e}]\!]$ across $q$ PCG instances. Thus, we implement our SSD-based $[\![\Delta\mathbf{e}]\!]$ generation. Our implementation extends the libOTe framework [RR]. We use libOTe's implementation of OT from [Roy22]'s SoftSpokenOT and VOLE from [RRT23]'s work on expand-convolute codes for the base correlations (OT, subfield VOLE for $\mathbb{F}_2$, and VOLE for $\mathbb{F}_{2^{128}}$).

We conduct our experiments on an HP Victus machine running Windows 11, equipped with a 12th Gen Intel(R) Core(TM) i7-12650H CPU at 2.30GHz and 15.6GB of usable RAM. The parties execute sequentially on the same thread and on the same laptop. The wall-clock time reflects the combined runtime of both parties. We also report the total communication summed across both parties. Each data point is sampled over 10 runs, and we present their arithmetic mean.

*Communication.* We now express our communication costs analytically. Both protocols require the same constant number of rounds. The exact number depends on the instantiation but can be as small as 2.

We denote the depth of the GGM tree $d = \lceil \log_2(n/t) \rceil$. For OT with SSD, we generate $dt$ base OTs for the GGM tree, send $256dt$ additional bits for the GGM tree, and generate subfield VOLE of size $qt$. As we are working over $\mathbb{F}_2$, we implement the subfield VOLE via $qt$ base OTs. We also communicate $128tq$ bits during the expansion to get $[\![\Delta\mathbf{e}]\!]$. In total, we need $(d + q)t$ base OTs and $256dt + 128qt$ bits. In contrast, OT with SD requires $qdt$ base OTs and $256qt(d + 1)$ additional bits, but with a mildly smaller $t$. For VOLE with SSD, we also generate $dt$ base OTs for the GGM tree, send $256dt$ additional bits for the GGM tree, and communicate $128tq$ bits during the expansion. However, we

| Protocol | $q$ | Assumption | #OTs | #VOLE | Time (ns/o) Setup | Expand | Mult. | Comm. (b/o) Setup | Expand |
|---|---|---|---|---|---|---|---|---|---|
| OT $e \in \mathbb{F}_2^n$ $\Delta \in \mathbb{F}_{2^{128}}$ | $2^4$ | SSD, $t = 400$ | 4400 | 6400 | 0.09 | 11.36 | 52.63 | 0.18 | 0.46 |
| | | SD, $t = 176$ | 33792 | 0 | 0.20 | 17.24 | 52.63 | 0.52 | 2.24 |
| | $2^8$ | SSD, $t = 400$ | 4400 | 102400 | 0.04 | 11.88 | 52.75 | 0.10 | 0.21 |
| | | SD, $t = 176$ | 540672 | 0 | 0.19 | 16.91 | 52.75 | 0.52 | 2.24 |
| | $2^{12}$ | SSD, $t = 400$ | 4400 | 1638400 | 0.04 | 12.11 | 52.73 | 0.10 | 0.20 |
| | | SD, $t = 176$ | 8650752 | 0 | 0.19 | 16.74 | 52.73 | 0.52 | 2.24 |
| VOLE $e \in \mathbb{F}_{2^{128}}^n$ $\Delta \in \mathbb{F}_{2^{128}}$ | $2^4$ | SSD, $t = 400$ | 4400 | 6400 | 0.53 | 11.55 | 52.63 | 1.18 | 0.46 |
| | | SD, $t = 400$ | 70400 | 6400 | 0.89 | 17.63 | 54.58 | 2.19 | 4.70 |
| | $2^8$ | SSD, $t = 400$ | 4400 | 102400 | 0.19 | 11.91 | 52.75 | 0.08 | 0.21 |
| | | SD, $t = 400$ | 1126400 | 102400 | 0.59 | 17.29 | 54.61 | 1.15 | 4.70 |
| | $2^{12}$ | SSD, $t = 400$ | 4400 | 1638400 | 0.26 | 12.20 | 52.73 | 0.01 | 0.20 |
| | | SD, $t = 400$ | 18022400 | 1638400 | 0.66 | 17.15 | 54.65 | 1.08 | 4.70 |

**Fig. 4.** This experiment compares the runtime and communication costs of generating OT and VOLE with SSD vs. SD. It fixes $n = 2^{19}$, $k = 2^{18}$ and varies the number of batches $q \in \{2^4, 2^8, 2^{12}\}$. The cost is split into base correlations (OT, (subfield) VOLE), expanding the seeds to get a sharing of $\Delta e$, and multiplying the result by $\mathbf{G}$. The time (nanoseconds) and communication (bits) are expressed per output, i.e. divided by $qk$. $t$ is selected such that we get 128 bits of security.

| Protocol | $k$ | Assumption | #OTs | #VOLE | Time (ns/o) Setup | Expand | Mult. | Comm. (b/o) Setup | Expand |
|---|---|---|---|---|---|---|---|---|---|
| OT $e \in \mathbb{F}_2^n$ $\Delta \in \mathbb{F}_{2^{128}}$ | $2^{14}$ | SSD, $t = 400$ | 2800 | 409600 | 0.58 | 11.90 | 33.48 | 1.58 | 3.17 |
| | | SD, $t = 176$ | 1441792 | 0 | 2.04 | 32.17 | 33.48 | 5.50 | 24.84 |
| | $2^{16}$ | SSD, $t = 400$ | 3600 | 102400 | 0.15 | 11.95 | 49.61 | 0.41 | 0.84 |
| | | SD, $t = 176$ | 450560 | 0 | 0.64 | 20.59 | 49.61 | 1.72 | 7.58 |
| | $2^{18}$ | SSD, $t = 400$ | 4400 | 25600 | 0.05 | 11.80 | 52.80 | 0.12 | 0.26 |
| | | SD, $t = 176$ | 135168 | 0 | 0.19 | 17.81 | 52.80 | 0.52 | 2.24 |
| VOLE $e \in \mathbb{F}_{2^{128}}^n$ $\Delta \in \mathbb{F}_{2^{128}}$ | $2^{14}$ | SSD, $t = 400$ | 2800 | 409600 | 3.22 | 11.93 | 33.48 | 0.32 | 3.17 |
| | | SD, $t = 400$ | 2867200 | 409600 | 7.25 | 32.55 | 37.30 | 11.24 | 50.20 |
| | $2^{16}$ | SSD, $t = 400$ | 3600 | 102400 | 0.79 | 11.88 | 49.61 | 0.31 | 0.84 |
| | | SD, $t = 400$ | 921600 | 102400 | 2.07 | 21.30 | 52.05 | 3.81 | 15.67 |
| | $2^{18}$ | SSD, $t = 400$ | 4400 | 25600 | 0.26 | 11.62 | 52.80 | 0.31 | 0.26 |
| | | SD, $t = 400$ | 281600 | 25600 | 0.64 | 18.32 | 54.49 | 1.36 | 4.70 |

**Fig. 5.** This experiment compares the runtime and communication costs of generating OT and VOLE with SSD vs. SD. It fixes $qk = 2^{24}$, and varies $q$, $k$ such that $(q, k) \in \{(2^{10}, 2^{14}), (2^8, 2^{16}), (2^6, 2^{18})\}$. The cost is split into base correlations (OT, (subfield) VOLE), expanding the seeds to get a sharing of $\Delta e$, and multiplying the result by $\mathbf{G}$. The time (nanoseconds per output) and communication (bits per output), i.e. total divided by $qk$. $t$ is selected such that we get 128 bits of security.

also consume $qt$ base VOLE correlations, which cannot be implemented with base OTs as we are not working over $\mathbb{F}_2$. Thus, in total we need $dt$ base OTs, $qt$ VOLE correlations, and $256dt + 128qt$ bits. In contrast, VOLE with SD requires $qdt$ base OTs, $qt$ VOLE correlations, and $256qt(d + 1)$ bits of communication.

*Experiments.* We consider two experiments. The first (Fig. 4) fixes a batch size of $n = 2^{19}, k = 2^{18}$ and varies the number of batches $q \in \{2^4, 2^8, 2^{12}\}$. We compare our new SSD-based OT and VOLE protocols to the traditional SD protocols. We report the number of base correlations required, i.e. OTs and (subfield) VOLE. We break down the time required to compute base correlations, expand the seeds to compute $[\![\Delta e]\!]$, and compress the error vector using expand-convolute codes [RRT23]. We report time as the number of nanoseconds per output element. We also report the communication overhead as bits per output element. The second experiment (Fig. 5) reports the same quantities but for varied batch size $k \in \{2^{14}, 2^{16}, 2^{18}\}$ and a fixed $qk = 2^{24}$.

*Discussion.* First, we discuss observations that apply to both experiments. Note that for OT from SD we need no base VOLEs as the noisy elements of $\boldsymbol{e}$ are always 1 (recall this is not the case for OT from SSD). For all other settings, we need $qt$ base VOLEs. Furthermore, note that for SSD and a fixed $k, n$, the number of base OTs stays the same for different $q$ as all can be reused. Next, note that the setup for SSD is cheaper for OTs than for VOLEs as for OTs we generate the base VOLEs also with OTs. For VOLE, the multiplication by $\mathbf{G}$ is slightly more expensive for SD than for SSD as we cannot run the multiplication for SD over $\mathbb{F}_2$. Lastly, the parameter $t$ differs for SD and SSD when generating OTs. We select $t$ using our equations in Sect. 5 to get 128 bits of security assuming $\mathbf{G}$ has a relative pseudominimum distance of 0.2. We now discuss observations specific to each experiment.

- **Experiment 1.** We reduce the total communication $\approx 4.3 - 9.4\times$ for OT and $\approx 4.2 - 28.6\times$ for VOLE. To compute $[\![\Delta e]\!]$ (Setup+Expand in Fig. 4), we reduce runtime $\approx 1.4 - 1.5\times$. For the parameters in this experiment, multiplying $[\![\Delta e]\!]$ by $\mathbf{G}$ is the runtime bottleneck, and thus we reduce total runtime $\approx 1.1\times$ for both OT and VOLE. Our improvement can be significantly larger for different parameters (see Experiment 2).
- **Experiment 2.** We reduce communication $\approx 6.4 - 7.5\times$ for OT and $\approx 10.7 - 17.6\times$ for VOLE. To compute $[\![\Delta e]\!]$, we reduce runtime $\approx 1.5 - 2.7\times$. Notably, the runtime improvement increases for higher $q$ and smaller $k$. This implies that for fixed $qk$, it is preferable to create more smaller instances (i.e. large $q$ and small $k$) rather than fewer large ones. This is further exacerbated by the fact that for small instances, multiplying by $\mathbf{G}$ is also cheaper (33 nanoseconds per output (ns/o) for $k = 2^{14}$ vs. 52 ns/o for $k = 2^{18}$).
To generate $2^{24}$ OTs, the fastest $(q, k)$ configuration with respect to runtime results in about 5 b/o and a total of 45 ns/o for SSD and 68 ns/o for SD resulting in $1.5\times$ improvement in throughput. For VOLE, we similarly get $\approx 1.5\times$ throughput improvement.

**Acknowledgments.** This work is supported in part by a Visa research award and NSF awards CNS-2246354, and CCF-2217070.

## References


ABG+14. Akavia, A., Bogdanov, A., Guo, S., Kamath, A., Rosen, A.: Candidate weak pseudorandom functions in ac0 $\odot$ mod2. In: *Proceedings of the 5th Conference on Innovations in Theoretical Computer Science*, ITCS '14, pp. 251–260, New York, NY, USA (2014). Association for Computing Machinery

AFS05. Augot, D., Finiasz, M., Sendrier, N.: A family of fast syndrome based cryptographic hash functions. In: *Mycrypt* (2005)

ANO+22. Abram, D., Nof, A., Orlandi, C., Scholl, P., Shlomovits, O.: Low-bandwidth threshold ECDSA via pseudorandom correlation generators. In: *2022 IEEE Symposium on Security and Privacy*, pp. 2554–2572. IEEE Computer Society Press (2022)

AS22. Abram, D., Scholl, P.: Low-communication multiparty triple generation for SPDZ from ring-LPN. In: Hanaoka, G., Shikata, J., Watanabe, Y. (eds.) PKC 2022. Part I, volume 13177 of LNCS, pp. 221–251. Springer, Heidelberg (2022)

BBC+24. Bombar, M., Bui, D., Couteau, G., Couvreur, A., Ducros, C., Schreiber, S.S.: FOLEAGE: $\mathbb{F}_4$OLE-based multi-party computation for boolean circuits. In: LNCS, pp. 69–101 (2024)

BCG+19a. Boyle, E., et al.: Efficient two-round OT extension and silent non-interactive secure computation. In: Cavallaro, L., Kinder, J., Wang, X., Katz, J., (eds.) *ACM CCS 2019*, pp. 291–308. ACM Press (2019)

BCG+19b. Boyle, E., Couteau, G., Gilboa, N., Ishai, Y., Kohl, L., Scholl, P.: Efficient pseudorandom correlation generators: silent OT extension and more. In: Boldyreva, A., Micciancio, D. (eds.) CRYPTO 2019. Part III, volume 11694 of LNCS, pp. 489–518. Springer, Heidelberg (2019)

BCG+20. Boyle, E., Couteau, G., Gilboa, N., Ishai, Y., Kohl, L., Scholl, P.: Efficient pseudorandom correlation generators from ring-LPN. In: Micciancio, D., Ristenpart, T. (eds.) CRYPTO 2020. Part II, volume 12171 of LNCS, pp. 387–416. Springer, Heidelberg (2020)

BCG+22. Boyle, E., et al.: Correlated pseudorandomness from expand-accumulate codes. In: Dodis, Y., Shrimpton, T. (eds.) CRYPTO 2022. Part II, volume 13508 of LNCS, pp. 603–633. Springer, Heidelberg (2022)

BCGI18. Boyle, E., Couteau, G., Gilboa, N., Ishai, Y.: Compressing vector OLE. In: Lie, D., Mannan, M., Backes, M., Wang, X., (eds.), *ACM CCS 2018*, pp. 896–912. ACM Press (2018)

BCP97. Bosma, W., Cannon, J., Playoust, C.: The Magma algebra system. I. The user language. *J. Symbolic Comput.* **24**(3-4), 235–265 (1997). Computational algebra and number theory (London (1993)

BDSW23. Baum, C., Dittmer, S., Scholl, P., Wang, X.: Sok: vector ole-based zero-knowledge protocols. Des. Codes Crypt. **91**(8), 3527–3561 (2023)

Ber68. Berlekamp, E.R.: *Algebraic Coding Theory*. McGraw-Hill Series in Systems Science. McGraw-Hill (1968)

BFKL94. Blum, A., Furst, M.L., Kearns, M.J., Lipton, R.J.: Cryptographic primitives based on hard learning problems. In: Stinson, D.R. (ed.) CRYPTO'93. LNCS, vol. 773, pp. 278–291. Springer, Heidelberg (1994)

BGH+25. Boyle, E., Gilboa, N., Hamilis, M., Ishai, Y., Tu, Y.: Improved constructions for distributed multi-point functions . In: *2025 IEEE Symposium on Security and Privacy (SP)*, pp. 2414–2432, Los Alamitos, CA, USA (2025). IEEE Computer Society

BJMM12. Becker, A., Joux, A., May, A., Meurer, A.: Decoding random binary linear codes in $2^{n/20}$: How $1 + 1 = 0$ improves information set decoding. In: Pointcheval, D., Johansson, T. (eds.) EUROCRYPT 2012. LNCS, vol. 7237, pp. 520–536. Springer, Heidelberg (2012)

BKW03. Blum, A., Kalai, A., Wasserman, H.: Noise-tolerant learning, the parity problem, and the statistical query model. In: *Journal of the ACM* (2003)

BLP11. Daniel, J.: Bernstein, Tanja Lange, and Christiane Peters. smaller decoding exponents: ball-collision decoding. In: Rogaway, P. (ed.) CRYPTO 2011. LNCS, vol. 6841, pp. 743–760. Springer, Heidelberg (2011)

BM18. Both, L., May, A.: Decoding linear codes with high error rate and its impact for LPN security. In: Lange, T., Steinwandt, R. (eds.) PQCrypto 2018. LNCS, vol. 10786, pp. 25–46. Springer, Cham (2018). https://doi.org/10.1007/978-3-319-79063-3_2

BØ23. Briaud, P., Øygarden, M.: A new algebraic approach to the regular syndrome decoding problem and implications for PCG constructions. In: Hazay, C., Stam, M. (eds.) EUROCRYPT 2023. Part V, volume 14008 of LNCS, pp. 391–422. Springer, Heidelberg (2023)

BR17. Bogdanov, A., Rosen, A.: *Pseudorandom Functions: Three Decades Later*, pp. 79–158. Springer International Publishing, Cham (2017)

CCJ23. Carozza, E., Couteau, G., Joux, A.: Short signatures from regular syndrome decoding in the head. In Carmit Hazay and Martijn Stam, editors, Advances in Cryptology - EUROCRYPT **2023**, 532–563 (2023)

CKPS00. Courtois, N., Klimov, A., Patarin, J., Shamir, A.: Efficient algorithms for solving overdefined systems of multivariate polynomial equations. In: Preneel, B. (ed.) EUROCRYPT 2000. LNCS, vol. 1807, pp. 392–407. Springer, Heidelberg (2000)

CRR21. Couteau, G., Rindal, P., Raghuraman, S.: Silver: silent VOLE and oblivious transfer from hardness of decoding structured LDPC codes. In: Malkin, T., Peikert, C. (eds.) CRYPTO 2021. LNCS, vol. 12827, pp. 502–534. Springer, Cham (2021). https://doi.org/10.1007/978-3-030-84252-9_17

DILO22. Dittmer, S., Ishai, Y., Steve, L., Ostrovsky, R.: Authenticated garbling from simple correlations. In: Dodis, Y., Shrimpton, T. (eds.) CRYPTO 2022. Part IV, volume 13510 of LNCS, pp. 57–87. Springer, Heidelberg (2022)

Ds17. Doerner, J., shelat, A..: Scaling ORAM for secure computation. In: Thuraisingham, B.M., Evans, D., Malkin, T., Xu, D., (eds.). *ACM CCS 2017*, pp. 523–535. ACM Press (2017)

ES24. Esser, A., Santini, P.: Not just regular decoding: asymptotics and improvements of regular syndrome decoding attacks. In Leonid Reyzin and Douglas Stebila, editors, Advances in Cryptology - CRYPTO **2024**, 183–217 (2024)

FJR22. Feneuil, T., Joux, A., Rivain, M.: Syndrome decoding in the head: shorter signatures from zero-knowledge proofs. In: Dodis, Y., Shrimpton, T. (eds.) CRYPTO 2022. Part II, volume 13508 of LNCS, pp. 541–572. Springer, Heidelberg (2022)

FKI07. Fossorier, M.P.C., Kobara, K., Imai, H.: Modeling bit flipping decoding based on nonorthogonal check sums with application to iterative decoding attack of mceliece cryptosystem. *IEEE Trans. Info. Theory* **53**(1), 402–411 (2007)

FS09a. Finiasz, M., Sendrier, N.: Security bounds for the design of code-based cryptosystems. In: Matsui, M. (ed.) ASIACRYPT 2009. LNCS, vol. 5912, pp. 88–105. Springer, Heidelberg (2009)

FS09b. Flajolet, P., Sedgewick, R.: Analytic Combinatorics. Cambridge University Press (2009)

GGM84. Goldreich, O., Goldwasser, S., Micali, S..: How to construct random functions (extended abstract). In: *25th FOCS*, pp. 464–479. IEEE Computer Society Press (1984)

HOSS18. Hazay, C., Orsini, E., Scholl, P., Soria-Vazquez, E.: TinyKeys: a new approach to efficient multi-party computation. In: Shacham, H., Boldyreva, A. (eds.) CRYPTO 2018. Part III, volume 10993 of LNCS, pp. 3–33. Springer, Heidelberg (2018)

Jab01. Jabri, A.A.: A statistical decoding algorithm for general linear block codes. In: Honary, B., (ed.), *Cryptography and Coding*, pp. 1–8, Berlin, Heidelberg (2001). Springer Berlin Heidelberg

KPRR25. Kolesnikov, V., Peceny, S., Raghuraman, S., Rindal, P.: Stationary syndrome decoding for improved PCGs. Cryptology ePrint Archive, Paper 2025/295 (2025)

LWYY22. Liu, H., Wang, X., Yang, K., Yu, Y.: The hardness of LPN over any integer ring and field for PCG applications. Cryptology ePrint Archive, Report 2022/712 (2022). https://eprint.iacr.org/2022/712

LXYY25. Li, Z., Xing, C., Yao, Y., Yuan, C.: Efficient pseudorandom correlation generators for any finite field. In: *Annual International Conference on the Theory and Applications of Cryptographic Techniques*, pp. 145–175. Springer (2025)

Lyu05. Lyubashevsky, V.: The parity problem in the presence of noise, decoding random linear codes, and the subset sum problem. In: Chekuri, C., Jansen, K., Rolim, J.D.P., Trevisan, L., (eds.) *Approximation, Randomization and Combinatorial Optimization. Algorithms and Techniques*, pp. 378–389 (2005)

MMT11. May, A., Meurer, A., Thomae, E.: Decoding random linear codes in $\tilde{\mathcal{O}}(2^{0.054n})$. In: Lee, D.H., Wang, X., (eds.), *ASIACRYPT 2011*, vol. 7073 of *LNCS*, pp. 107–124. Springer, Heidelberg (2011)

MO15. May, A., Ozerov, I.: On computing nearest neighbors with applications to decoding of binary linear codes. In: Oswald, E., Fischlin, M. (eds.) EUROCRYPT 2015. Part I, volume 9056 of LNCS, pp. 203–228. Springer, Heidelberg (2015)

Pra62. Prange, E.: The use of information sets in decoding cyclic codes. In: *IRE Transactions on Information Theory* (1962)

Roy22. Roy, L.: SoftSpokenOT: quieter OT extension from small-field silent VOLE in the minicrypt model. In: Dodis, Y., Shrimpton, T. (eds.) CRYPTO 2022. Part I, volume 13507 of LNCS, pp. 657–687. Springer, Heidelberg (2022)

RR. Rindal, P., Roy, L.: libOTe: an efficient, portable, and easy to use Oblivious Transfer Library. https://github.com/osu-crypto/libOTe

RRT23. Raghuraman, S., Rindal, P., Tanguy, T.: Expand-convolute codes for pseudorandom correlation generators from LPN. In: Handschuh, H., Lysyanskaya, A. (eds.) CRYPTO 2023. Part IV, volume 14084 of LNCS, pp. 602–632. Springer, Heidelberg (2023)

RS21. Rindal, P., Schoppmann, P.: VOLE-PSI: fast OPRF and circuit-PSI from vector-OLE. In: Canteaut, A., Standaert, F.-X. (eds.) EUROCRYPT 2021. Part II, volume 12697 of LNCS, pp. 901–930. Springer, Heidelberg (2021)

SGRR19. Schoppmann, P., Gascón, A., Reichert, L., Raykova, M.: Distributed vector-OLE: Improved constructions and implementation. In: Cavallaro,

L., Kinder, J., Wang, X., Katz, J., (eds.) *ACM CCS 2019*, pp. 1055–1072. ACM Press (2019)

Shp09. Shpilka, A.: Constructions of low-degree and error-correcting $\epsilon$-biased generators. In: *computational complexity* (2009)

Ste89. Stern, J.: A method for finding codewords of small weight. In: Cohen, G., Wolfmann, J., (eds.) *Coding Theory and Applications*, pp. 106–113, Berlin, Heidelberg (1989). Springer Berlin Heidelberg

Wie86. Wiedemann, D.: Solving sparse linear equations over finite fields. In: *IEEE Transac- tions on Information Theory* (1986)

WYKW21. Weng, C., Yang, K., Katz, J., Wang, X.: Wolverine: fast, scalable, and communication-efficient zero-knowledge proofs for Boolean and arithmetic circuits. In: *42nd IEEE Symposium on Security and Privacy, SP 2021, San Francisco, CA, USA, 24-27 May 2021*, pp. 1074–1091. IEEE (2021)

WYY+22. Weng, C., Yang, K., Yang, Z., Xie, X., Wang, X.: AntMan: interactive zero-knowledge proofs with sublinear communication. In: Yin, H., Stavrou, A., Cremers, C., Shi, E.,(eds.) *ACM CCS 2022*, pp. 2901–2914. ACM Press (2022)

YSWW21. Yang, K., Sarkar, P., Weng, C., Wang, X.: QuickSilver: efficient and affordable zero-knowledge proofs for circuits and polynomials over any field. In: Vigna, G., Shi, E., (eds.) *ACM CCS 2021*, pp. 2986–3001. ACM Press (2021)

# Lattice-Based Cryptography

# On Gaussian Sampling for $q$-ary Lattices and Linear Codes with Lee Weight

Maiara F. Bollauf[1], Maja Lie[2(✉)], and Cong Ling[2]

[1] University of Tartu, Tartu, Estonia
maiara.bollauf@ut.ee

[2] Imperial College London, London, England
{m.lie22,c.ling}@imperial.ac.uk

**Abstract.** We show that discrete Gaussian sampling for a $q$-ary lattice is equivalent to codeword sampling for a linear code over $\mathbb{Z}_q$ with the Lee weight profile. This insight allows us to derive the theta series of a $q$-ary lattice from the Lee weight distribution of the associated code. We design a novel Gaussian sampler for $q$-ary lattices assuming an oracle that computes the symmetrized weight enumerator of the associated code. We apply this sampler to well-known lattices, such as the $E_8$, Barnes-Wall, and Leech lattice, highlighting both its advantages and limitations, which depend on the underlying code properties. For certain root lattices, we show that the sampler is indeed efficient, forgoing the need to assume an oracle. In many cases, our sampler achieves a significant speed-up compared to state-of-the-art sampling algorithms in cryptographic applications.

**Keywords:** Lattice Gaussian sampling · Lee weight · $q$-ary lattice · Schur product · Theta series

## 1 Introduction

Lattice Gaussian sampling refers to the process of sampling vectors from a discrete Gaussian distribution with a specified width $s$, defined over a lattice $\Lambda$. This technique plays a fundamental role in lattice-based cryptography. Namely, Gaussian sampling over lattices with the appropriate choice of width $s$ enables the solution of the *closest vector problem* (CVP) and the *shortest vector problem* (SVP) [2,3] and it is also one of the main tools used in worst-to-average case reductions for lattice problems [26]. Additionally, it is being used in the construction of several lattice-based cryptographic protocols, such as signature schemes, as it can be used to hide information about the lattice basis [15].

The width $s$ of a Gaussian sampler over a lattice determines how wide the distribution we sample from is. It is challenging for most lattices to sample over discrete Gaussian distributions when $s$ is not so large. In practical terms, the security of the SVP or approximate SVP relies on the fact that it should be


Y. Tauman Kalai and S. F. Kamara (Eds.): CRYPTO 2025, LNCS 16000, pp. 321–352, 2025.
https://doi.org/10.1007/978-3-032-01855-7_11

difficult for an adversary to obtain a lattice point within a radius $s\sqrt{n}$, where $n$ refers to the lattice dimension [30].

Micciancio and Regev [26] define the *smoothing parameter* of a lattice, which is the minimum amount of Gaussian noise that, when added to a lattice, produces a distribution close to uniform over $\mathbb{R}^n/\Lambda$. Klein's algorithm can be used to sample from an arbitrary lattice for $s$ sufficiently large, but $s$ may be well above the smoothing parameter [8]. Recently, Ducas and van Woerden [11] introduced a hash-then-sign signature scheme based on the *lattice isomorphism problem* (LIP), which can be implemented with any lattice that has an efficient Gaussian sampler with small sampling widths. Tight sampling for lattices would enhance the security of the LIP-based signature scheme, as it would be able to withstand attacks down to small approximation factors [11].

Lattice-based cryptographic protocols typically require sampling at or above the smoothing parameter. The smoothing parameter is defined in terms of the *theta series*, a lattice geometric invariant. Roughly, the theta series of a lattice $\Lambda$ characterizes the number of points in $\Lambda$ with a given (Euclidean) norm. Unfortunately, for a general lattice, we may not know its theta series and, therefore, do not have a tight estimation for the smoothing parameter. As a consequence, when sampling from a general lattice, the width $s$ may significantly exceed the smoothing parameter when, ideally, it should be as close to the smoothing parameter as possible to achieve improved security.

Gaussian sampling over $\mathbb{Z}$ for a fixed width $s$ is usually efficient since it can use precomputed data [28,30], while for general lattices, the complexity increases. Therefore, one can sample efficiently over the $\mathbb{Z}^n$ lattice utilizing one-dimensional samplers of $\mathbb{Z}$ [8, Sec. 5.1]. One-dimensional samplers of $\mathbb{Z}$ and its shifts are often used as subroutines in samplers for other lattices as well.

Lattice-based cryptography typically uses *q-ary lattices*, which only involves integer arithmetic modulo $q$. $\Lambda$ is called a $q$-ary lattice if $q\mathbb{Z}^n \subseteq \Lambda \subseteq \mathbb{Z}^n$. Such a lattice can be expressed equivalently in the form $q\mathbb{Z}^n + \mathcal{C}$, where $\mathcal{C}$ is a linear code in $\mathbb{Z}_q^n$. In lattice theory, techniques to obtain lattices via codes are denoted as Constructions A, B, C, D, and E, where each letter refers to the linear codes that are being employed (see [10, Ch. 5]). We will extensively work with Construction A obtained from a single linear $q$-ary code $\mathcal{C} \subseteq \mathbb{Z}_q^n$, Construction B from two nested binary codes, and Construction D from several nested binary codes.

Ling *et al.* proposed a lattice Gaussian sampler using coset decomposition for large enough $s$ [21,22]. In particular, [21] presented a sampler for Construction A in which codewords are sampled uniformly at random and proved that the resultant distribution is close to a lattice Gaussian if $s$ exceeds the smoothing parameter of $q\mathbb{Z}$[1]; it exemplified the method by considering the checkerboard lattice $\mathrm{D}_n$ and Gosset lattice $\mathrm{E}_8$ and remarked that the method can be extended to Construction D. Campello and Belfiore [9] proposed an efficient method for sampling from the 2-ary Construction A and 4-ary Construction B lattices for any width $s$. These constructions include the $\mathrm{D}_n$, and the Barnes-Wall lattices

[1] In fact, [21] addressed a general version of Construction A where the quotient $\mathbb{Z}/q\mathbb{Z}$ is replaced with $\Lambda_1/\Lambda_2$ for a pair of nested lattices $\Lambda_2 \subseteq \Lambda_1$.

$E_8$ and $BW_{16}$ (they also considered sampling from $A_2$ and the Leech lattice using coset decomposition). Their method relies on the relationship between the theta series of the lattice and the Hamming weight enumerator of the underlying binary linear code. In [13], Espitau *et al.* gave a general framework for efficient Gaussian sampling over lattices using extensions of lattices and new bounds on the smoothing parameter from lattice filtrations, assuming $s$ is large enough as in [21]. The authors used their framework to build efficient samplers for the $A_n, D_n$, and $E_n$ lattices as base cases. Their method can also be used to sample from the family of Barnes-Wall lattices $BW_{2^n}$.

### 1.1 Our Contribution

A smaller width $s$ leads to tighter security arguments, so ideally we want to sample as close as possible to the smoothing parameter of $\Lambda$. This paper proposes a new unrestricted sampler for $q$-ary lattices. By using the code formula of the $q$-ary lattice, we simplify the theta series calculation for some families of $q$-ary lattices and express the theta series in terms of the Lee weight enumerator of the underlying $q$-ary codes. We extend these former results to $q$-ary lattices obtained via Construction A for $q \geq 2$ and Construction D. Our method requires computing the Lee weight enumerator of some code, and this computation does not depend on the choice of sampling width $s$. As a consequence, we improve the efficiency of the current state-of-the-art sampling for root lattices. For Construction D, we build upon [9,13,21] by leveraging lattice filtrations in such a way that we can apply the samplers recursively. More specifically, our contributions are three-fold:

1. On the reduction front, we present polynomial-time reductions between Gaussian sampling on $q$-ary lattices and sampling codewords of a linear code with respect to the Lee weight profile, thereby establishing equivalence of the two problems. Recently, linear codes in the Lee metric have received attention in code-based cryptography. It is known that (the decision version of) the problem of finding codewords with a given Lee weight is NP-complete [36]. In practice, this Lee weight is chosen to be on the Lee-metric GV bound [32]. Since finding codewords with a specified Lee weight profile is at least as hard, this implies that Gaussian sampling for $q$-ary lattices is, in general, a computationally hard problem.
2. On the algorithmic front, we use the aforementioned reduction to design a new sampler in which one can sample with an arbitrary width $s$. For the $q$-ary ($q = 2$ and $q = 4$, respectively) lattices obtained via Construction A and B from binary codes, our sampler coincides with the method of coset decomposition explored in [9]. Then, we expand the sampling via cosets technique to another $q$-ary lattice family, Construction D, and show that it depends on the Lee weight distribution of the underlying codes in different levels of the filtration.
3. Our proposed sampler, when applied to root lattices and small dimensional $q$-ary lattices, represents an improvement compared to [13,21] which restricts $s$ according to the maximum smoothing parameter of the lattice filtration.

Comparison between our sampling procedure and the one presented in [13] is performed for known families of lattices (selected results are given in Table 1). The complexity, limitations, and advantages in the cryptographic context are also addressed.

**Table 1.** Comparison of complexity and sampling width. The upper bound on speed-up is obtained by counting the number of calls to a $\mathbb{Z}$ sampler, ignoring the overhead of codeword sampling. Note that upper bounds (UB) on speed-up for $\mathrm{BW}_{16}$ and $\Lambda_{24}$ are rather conservative since the sampling widths are different. See Sect. 7 for details. The Lee weight profile (LWP) table stores the information for the symmetric weight enumerator of the associated code. We estimate its size in bits. Note that the LWP table size is computed for a single coset $\mathbf{t} = \mathbf{0}$, so we include the number of cosets for each lattice.

| | **Complexity** | **Sampling Width** $s$ | | | |
|---|---|---|---|---|---|
| **Lattice** | Speed-up (UB) | [13] | This work | **LWP Table Size** | **#Cosets** |
| $\mathrm{A}_2$ | 18× | $\approx \eta_\epsilon(\mathrm{A}_2)$ | $= \eta_\epsilon(\mathrm{A}_2)$ | - | 2 |
| $\mathrm{E}_8$ | 22× | $\approx \eta_\epsilon(\mathrm{E}_8)$ | $= \eta_\epsilon(\mathrm{E}_8)$ | 14 bits | $2^4$ |
| $\mathrm{D}_n$ | 2× | $\approx \eta_\epsilon(\mathrm{D}_n)$ | $= \eta_\epsilon(\mathrm{D}_n)$ | - | 2 |
| $\Lambda_{24}$ | 2× | $\approx \eta_\epsilon(\mathrm{E}_8)$ | $= \eta_\epsilon(\Lambda_{24})$ | 34 bits | $2^{12}$ |
| $\mathrm{BW}_{16}$ | 11× | $> \eta_\epsilon(\mathrm{BW}_8)$ | $= \eta_\epsilon(\mathrm{BW}_{16})$ | 17 bits | $2^{11}$ |

In summary, our Gaussian sampler can output a lattice vector for arbitrary sampling width $s$ for any $q$-ary lattice $\Lambda$, since any such lattice can be expressed as $\Lambda = q\mathbb{Z}^n + \mathcal{C}$, where $\mathcal{C}$ is a linear code over $\mathbb{Z}_q^n$ [27]. We note that our sampling method is limited by the need to compute the Lee weight profiles of a potentially very large code (or its cosets). For random codes, this may not be known or efficient to compute. The *Schur* (or element-wise) product can be used to compute Lee weight profiles offline.

In this paper, we start with a theoretical and general $q$-ary sampler and apply our technique to known families of lattices to illustrate the improvements. Section 2 provides some preliminaries on codes and lattices; in Sect. 3, we prove the equivalence of lattice and code sampling, and in Sect. 4 we derive the theta series of a $q$-ary lattice from the symmetrized weight enumerator of the associated code(s). In Sect. 5, we present our samplers for Constructions A, B, and D lattices and employ the technique to remarkable lattices in Sect. 6. Comparisons and improvements with respect to the state-of-the-art are in Sect. 7.

### 1.2 Technical Overview

*Lee Weight.* Here we give an intuition why the somewhat mysterious Lee weight comes into play, using the trivial example of Gaussian sampling from the integers $\mathbb{Z}$. Sampling an integer $y \in \mathbb{Z}$ may be realized in two steps: firstly, we sample $j = y \mod q$ from $\mathbb{Z}_q = \{0, 1, \ldots, q-1\}$ for $q \in \mathbb{N}$; secondly, we sample an integer from the coset $q\mathbb{Z} + j$. Now we focus on the first step, assuming the second step is efficient. The probability of sampling a coset $q\mathbb{Z} + j$ is given by the theta function $\Theta_{q\mathbb{Z}+j}(z)$ for some $z$ defined properly.

The Lee weight of $j \in \mathbb{Z}_q$ is defined as $w_{\text{Lee}}(j) = \min\{j, q-j\}$. It resembles the Euclidean distance (which is relevant for lattices) more than the conventional Hamming distance [18]. The Gaussian function is even symmetric so that $\Theta_{q\mathbb{Z}+j}(z) = \Theta_{q\mathbb{Z}+q-j}(z)$. This coincides with the fact that $j$ and $-j = q - j$ in $\mathbb{Z}_q$ have the same Lee weight. Therefore, we only need the knowledge of the Lee weight, i.e., we sample from the coset $q\mathbb{Z} + j$ with probability $\Theta_{q\mathbb{Z}+w_{\text{Lee}}(j)}(z)$.

Our Gaussian sampling method for $q$-ary lattices generalizes the above idea, taking into account the underlying codes. For Construction D with multiple levels, we run recursion on the second step.

In more detail, our method relies on the structure of a $q$-ary lattice $q\mathbb{Z}^n + \phi(\mathcal{C})$, where $\phi$ is the natural embedding[2] from $\mathbb{Z}_q^n$ to $\mathbb{Z}^n$. Our key observation is that the theta series of a $q$-ary lattice can be obtained from the symmetrized weight enumerator of the associated code $\mathcal{C} \subseteq \mathbb{Z}_q^n$. We prove this by observing that the coset $q\mathbb{Z}^n + \phi(\mathbf{c})$, where $\mathbf{c} \in \mathcal{C}$, is isometric to a direct sum decomposition of many copies of $q\mathbb{Z} \pm j$ for $j \in \mathbb{Z}_q \hookrightarrow \mathbb{Z}$ (Lemma 1). Isometry preserves the lattice geometry and, thus, the theta series.

Our Gaussian sampling method for $q$-ary lattices uses many of these $q\mathbb{Z} + j$ samplers, with sampling probability depending only on (a product of) theta series of the form $\Theta_{q\mathbb{Z}+w_{\text{Lee}}(j)}(z)$ and the number $n_j(\mathbf{c})$ of coordinates in $\mathbf{c}$ with Lee weight equal to $j$. These $n_j(\mathbf{c})$ define the *Lee weight profile* and are exactly the exponents in the symmetrized weight enumerator of the code $\mathcal{C}$. Therefore, we can sample from $q\mathbb{Z}^n + \phi(\mathcal{C})$ by selecting some coset representative $\phi(\mathbf{c})$ with probability defined by its theta series, and this depends on the $n_j(\mathbf{c})$.

The use of the Lee norm in [33] is relevant to lattices but in a different context. It is interesting that the Lee norm is analogous to the $\ell_1$-norm while Gaussian sampling and lattice problems are usually concerned with the $\ell_2$-norm. These norms do not generally coincide, but we are able to overcome this discrepancy because we use Lee weight profiles rather than Lee weight directly. Other authors [17] have also made reductions between coding problems with respect to Lee distance and lattice problems in a different context[3].

*Theta Series.* Some families of lattices have well-documented theta series in the literature, such as the Constructions A and B lattices from binary codes. We extend it to a general Construction A lattice $q\mathbb{Z}^n + \mathcal{C}$ with $q \geq 2$ and connect

[2] Throughout this paper, even when we do not mention the mapping $\phi$, it is always implicit.

[3] These reductions use lattice problems in their $\ell_1$-norm formulation.

with the symmetrized weight enumerator of the respective code over $\mathbb{Z}_q$. Moving forward, we consider a $L$-level Construction D lattice with code formula [14,20][4]:

$$\Lambda_{\mathrm{D}} = 2^L\mathbb{Z}^n + 2^{L-1}\mathcal{C}_L + \ldots + 2\mathcal{C}_2 + \mathcal{C}_1, \tag{1}$$

where $\mathcal{C}_1, \mathcal{C}_2, \ldots, \mathcal{C}_L$ are binary linear codes that are *closed under Schur product* (more details follow below). In general, for $L \geq 3$, the theta series of $\Lambda_{\mathrm{D}}$ is unknown. Nonetheless, by performing case analysis, we can obtain a general form for the theta series of a 3-level Construction D lattice. Thus, the probability of a coset of such a lattice depends on the Lee weight of a linear code over $\mathbb{Z}_8$ defined by $4\mathcal{C}_3 + 2\mathcal{C}_2 + \mathcal{C}_1$. The same analysis shows that the probability of a coset of an $L$-level Construction D lattice depends on the Lee weight of a code over $\mathbb{Z}_{2^L}$. This is a generalization of the fact that the coset of Construction A and B lattices depend only on the Hamming weight of a code over $\mathbb{F}_2$ [9].

The Lee weight distribution of a code allows us to sample a coset representative of the lattice. In (1), we consider a filtration $\Lambda_1 \subseteq \Lambda_2 \subseteq \ldots \subseteq \Lambda_L$ where $\Lambda_1 = 2^L\mathbb{Z}^n + 2^{L-1}\mathcal{C}_L = 2^{L-1}(2\mathbb{Z}^n + \mathcal{C}_L)$ is a scaled Construction A lattice, $\Lambda_2 = 2^L\mathbb{Z}^n + 2^{L-1}\mathcal{C}_L + 2^{L-2}\mathcal{C}_{L-1}$, and we proceed recursively such that in each subsequent lattice we add the next (scaled) code until we get $\Lambda_L$ as the whole lattice $\Lambda_{\mathrm{D}}$. Let $\mathbf{c}$ be a coset representative. In the end, the sampler outputs a vector from $\mathcal{D}_{2^L\mathbb{Z}^n+\mathbf{c},s}$ using one-dimensional samplers of $\mathbb{Z}$ and its shifts. Recursive application of sampling via coset decomposition using Lee weight enables exact sampling of a Construction D lattice for any width $s > 0$.

### 1.3 Open Questions

Lattice and code-based cryptography are closely related. Lately, techniques from lattice-based cryptography were used to break FuLeeca [18], the first digital signature scheme based on the Lee metric. Meanwhile, the new connection discovered in this work shows that code sampling in the Lee metric and lattice Gaussian sampling are equally hard. To the best of our knowledge, no such relation has been shown before. It is an interesting open question whether code sampling in the Lee metric can be used to construct provably secure cryptosystems[5].

Our sampling algorithms rely on knowledge of the Lee weight profile or symmetrized weight enumerator of a code or its coset, but existing methods to compute these are computationally expensive. Enhancing their efficiency would result in faster lattice Gaussian samplers. While we have made some progress in this paper using the Schur product, further exploration is left for future work.

In [11], Ducas and van Woerden hypothesize that instantiating the LIP signature scheme with efficiently decodable lattices may lead to resistance against attacks down to smaller approximation factors. The Barnes-Wall lattices are remarkable, which makes it desirable to have a sampler for these lattices with a

[4] Note that this is a subclass of Construction D since not all Construction D lattices admit a code formula. See [10, p. 232] for the general definition.

[5] In fact, as noted in [18], an open question remains on how to adapt the GPV framework [15] to the Lee metric.

small sampling width $s$. With our sampler, we can set $s$ just above the smoothing parameter, but in practice, sampling requires us to sample codewords with respect to Lee weight (a hard problem in general). As a consequence, high-dimensional Barnes-Wall lattices remain a challenge for tight sampling with our method, and in this case, [13] provides wider and more efficient samplers. Optimizations of our samplers for Barnes-Wall lattices and security gain analysis of instantiating LIP with these remarkable lattices remain open questions.

## 2 Preliminaries

### 2.1 Notation

We denote by $\mathbb{N}$, $\mathbb{Z}$, and $\mathbb{R}$ the set of naturals, integers, and reals, respectively. Also, $[a : b] \triangleq \{a, a+1, \ldots, b\}$ for $a, b \in \mathbb{Z}$, $a \leq b$. The ring of integers modulo $q$ for $q \in \mathbb{N}$ is $\mathbb{Z}_q = \{0, 1, \ldots, q-1\}$. Vectors are boldfaced, e.g., $\mathbf{x}$ and matrices are represented by capital sans serif letters, e.g. $\mathsf{X}$. The symbol $+$ represents the element-wise addition over $\mathbb{R}$ and $\star$ denotes the Schur product between two elements in $\mathbb{F}_2^n$, i.e., $\mathbf{x} \star \mathbf{y} = (x_1 y_1, \ldots, x_n y_n)$, for $\mathbf{x}, \mathbf{y} \in \mathbb{F}_2^n$.

### 2.2 Linear Codes

The definitions and properties presented here are based on [10,23,35].

A ($q$-ary) *linear code* $\mathcal{C}$ of length $n$ over a finite field $\mathbb{F}_q$ ($q$ is a prime power) is a linear subspace $\mathcal{C} \subseteq \mathbb{F}_q^n$. When $q$ is not prime, we can also define linear codes over rings simply as additive subgroups of $\mathbb{Z}_q^n$. Throughout this paper, $q$ will be a prime or a power of prime. We call a $q$-ary linear code $\mathcal{C}$ an $(n, k)_q$ code, where $n$ is the length and $k$ is the dimension of the code.

We consider two different weights: Hamming and Lee. The *Hamming weight* of a codeword $\mathbf{c} \in \mathcal{C}$, denoted by $w_{\mathrm{H}}(\mathbf{c})$, is defined as the number of its nonzero coordinates. We will initially restrict our attention to binary codes. The Hamming weight enumerator of a code is a function that describes the weight profile of a binary code $\mathcal{C}$ in terms of the Hamming weight.

**Definition 1 (Hamming Weight Enumerator).** *Let $\mathcal{C}$ be a $(n, k)_2$ code. The Hamming weight enumerator of $\mathcal{C}$ is given by*

$$W_{\mathcal{C}}(x, y) = \sum_{\mathbf{c} \in \mathcal{C}} x^{n - w_{\mathrm{H}}(\mathbf{c})} y^{w_{\mathrm{H}}(\mathbf{c})} = \sum_{w=0}^{n} A_w x^{n-w} y^w$$

*where $A_w(\mathcal{C}) = \#\{\mathbf{c} \in \mathcal{C} : w_{\mathrm{H}}(\mathbf{c}) = w\}$, with $w \in [0 : \ell]$, is the number of codewords in $\mathcal{C}$ that have Hamming weight $w$.*

For codes over $\mathbb{Z}_q$, we define the Lee weight, which provides a more granular description of the nonzero coordinates of a codeword.

**Definition 2 (Lee Weight).** *The Lee weight of $c \in \mathbb{Z}_q$ is $w_{\mathrm{Lee}}(c) = \min\{c, q - c\}$. This can be naturally extended to a vector, i.e., given $\mathbf{c} = (c_1, c_2, \ldots, c_n) \in \mathbb{Z}_q^n$, its Lee weight is $w_{\mathrm{Lee}}(\mathbf{c}) = \sum_{j=1}^{n} w_{\mathrm{Lee}}(c_j)$.*

**Definition 3 (Lee Weight Profile).** *Let $\mathcal{C}$ be a linear code over $\mathbb{Z}_q$ of length $n$. The Lee weight profile of $\mathbf{c} \in \mathcal{C}$ is the tuple*

$$[n_0(\mathbf{c}), n_1(\mathbf{c}), \ldots, n_\ell(\mathbf{c})], \quad \ell = \lceil q/2 \rceil$$

*where $n_w(\mathbf{c}) = \#\{i \colon w_{\mathrm{Lee}}(c_i) = w\}$, with $w \in [0:\ell]$, i.e., it refers to the number of coordinates of $\mathbf{c}$ that are $\pm w$.*

When $q = 2, 3$, Lee weight coincides exactly with Hamming weight. The notion of Lee weight allows us to define additional weight enumerators.

**Definition 4 (Symmetrized Weight Enumerator).** *The symmetrized weight enumerator of a linear code $\mathcal{C}$ over $\mathbb{Z}_q$ of length $n$ is given by*

$$\mathrm{swe}_{\mathcal{C}}(x_0, x_1, \ldots, x_\ell) = \sum_{\mathbf{c} \in \mathcal{C}} x_0^{n_0(\mathbf{c})} x_1^{n_1(\mathbf{c})} \cdots x_{\ell-1}^{n_{\ell-1}(\mathbf{c})} x_\ell^{n_\ell(\mathbf{c})}$$

*where $n_w(\mathbf{c})$, with $w \in [0:\ell]$ as in Definition 3, and $\ell = \lceil q/2 \rceil$.*

Consider $\boldsymbol{\alpha} \in \mathbb{F}_2^n$. Then $\omega_{\boldsymbol{\alpha}}(\mathbf{c}_1, \ldots, \mathbf{c}_r)$ as the number of occurrences of $\boldsymbol{\alpha}$ as a row in the matrix of column vectors $\mathbf{c}_1, \ldots, \mathbf{c}_r$. For example, for the matrix with column vectors given by $\mathbf{c}_1 = (1,0,0), \mathbf{c}_2 = (1,1,0)$, and $\mathbf{c}_3 = (1,1,1)$, we have that $\omega_{1,1,1}(\mathbf{c}_1, \mathbf{c}_2, \mathbf{c}_3) = 1$ and $\omega_{1,0,0}(\mathbf{c}_1, \mathbf{c}_2, \mathbf{c}_3) = 0$.

Over multiple binary codes, we can define a generalized version of the *joint weight enumerator* or originally, *j-fold weight enumerator* [12] as follows.

**Definition 5 (Joint Weight Enumerator).** *Consider $j$ binary linear codes $\mathcal{C}_1, \ldots, \mathcal{C}_j \subseteq \mathbb{F}_2^n$. We define their joint weight enumerator to be*

$$\mathrm{jwe}_{\mathcal{C}_1,\ldots,\mathcal{C}_j}(\mathbf{x}) = \sum_{\mathbf{c}_1 \in \mathcal{C}_1} \cdots \sum_{\mathbf{c}_j \in \mathcal{C}_j} \prod_{\boldsymbol{\alpha} \in \mathbb{F}_2^j} x_{\boldsymbol{\alpha}}^{\omega_{\boldsymbol{\alpha}}(\mathbf{c}_1,\ldots,\mathbf{c}_j)} = \sum_{\substack{(\mathbf{c}_1,\ldots,\mathbf{c}_j) \\ \in \mathcal{C}_1 \times \ldots \times \mathcal{C}_j}} \prod_{\boldsymbol{\alpha} \in \mathbb{F}_2^j} x_{\boldsymbol{\alpha}}^{\omega_{\boldsymbol{\alpha}}(\mathbf{c}_1,\ldots,\mathbf{c}_j)},$$

*where $\mathbf{x} = (x_{\boldsymbol{\alpha}})$ is a $2^j$-tuple of variables with $\boldsymbol{\alpha} = (\alpha_1, \ldots, \alpha_j) \in \mathbb{F}_2^j$.*

Notice that $\mathrm{jwe}_{\mathcal{C}_1}(x_0, x_1)$ is the ordinary Hamming weight enumerator of a binary code $\mathcal{C}_1$ and $\mathrm{jwe}_{\mathcal{C}_1,\mathcal{C}_2}(\mathbf{x}) = \mathrm{jwe}_{\mathcal{C}_1,\mathcal{C}_2}(x_{00}, x_{01}, x_{10}, x_{11})$ is the biweight enumerator of two binary codes $\mathcal{C}_1$ and $\mathcal{C}_2$ [23, pp. 147-148].

For codes $\mathcal{C} \subseteq \mathbb{Z}_4^n$ constructed via $\mathcal{C} = 2\mathcal{C}_2 + \mathcal{C}_1$, where $\mathcal{C}_1, \mathcal{C}_2 \subseteq \mathbb{F}_2^n$ are linear codes, there is a natural relationship between the joint and the symmetrized weight enumerators, namely $\mathrm{jwe}_{\mathcal{C}_1,\mathcal{C}_2}(x_{00}, x_{01}, x_{10}, x_{11}) \triangleq \mathrm{jwe}_{\mathcal{C}_1,\mathcal{C}_2}(x_0, x_2, x_1, x_1) = \mathrm{swe}_{\mathcal{C}}(x_0, x_1, x_2)$. Indeed,

$$\omega_{0,0}(\mathbf{c}_1, \mathbf{c}_2) = n_0(\mathbf{c}), \quad \omega_{1,0}(\mathbf{c}_1, \mathbf{c}_2) + \omega_{1,1}(\mathbf{c}_1, \mathbf{c}_2) = n_1(\mathbf{c}), \quad \omega_{0,1}(\mathbf{c}_1, \mathbf{c}_2) = n_2(\mathbf{c}),$$

where we use the fact that the Lee weight of 1 and 3 in $\mathbb{Z}_4$ is the same (i.e., $3 \equiv -1 \bmod 4$), so we get

$$\begin{aligned}
\mathrm{swe}_{\mathcal{C}}(x_0, x_1, x_2) &= \sum_{\mathbf{c} \in \mathcal{C}} x_0^{n_0(\mathbf{c})} x_1^{n_1(\mathbf{c})} x_2^{n_2(\mathbf{c})} \\
&= \sum_{\mathbf{c}_1 \in \mathcal{C}_1} \sum_{\mathbf{c}_2 \in \mathcal{C}_2} x_0^{\omega_{0,0}(\mathbf{c}_1,\mathbf{c}_2)} x_1^{\omega_{1,0}(\mathbf{c}_1,\mathbf{c}_2)+\omega_{1,1}(\mathbf{c}_1,\mathbf{c}_2)} x_2^{\omega_{0,1}(\mathbf{c}_1,\mathbf{c}_2)} \\
&= \mathrm{jwe}_{\mathcal{C}_1,\mathcal{C}_2}(x_0, x_2, x_1, x_1) = \mathrm{jwe}_{\mathcal{C}_1,\mathcal{C}_2}(x_{00}, x_{01}, x_{10}, x_{11}). \qquad (2)
\end{aligned}$$

From now on we will denote $\omega_{\boldsymbol{\alpha}}(\mathbf{c}_1, \ldots, \mathbf{c}_j) = \omega_{\alpha_1,\ldots,\alpha_j}(\mathbf{c}_1, \ldots, \mathbf{c}_j)$ simply by $\omega_{\alpha_1,\ldots,\alpha_j}$, when the vectors $\mathbf{c}_1, \ldots, \mathbf{c}_j$ are clear from the context.

Next, we present the Reed-Muller codes, which are crucial to the construction of Barnes-Wall lattices.

**Definition 6 (Reed-Muller Code).** *A Reed-Muller code* RM$(r, m)$ *of order* $r$ *and length* $2^m$ *is a binary code defined as*

$$\mathrm{RM}(r,m) = \begin{cases} \mathbb{F}_2^{2^r}, & m = r \\ \{(\mathbf{u}, \mathbf{u}+\mathbf{v}) : \mathbf{u} \in \mathrm{RM}(r, m-1), \mathbf{v} \in \mathrm{RM}(r-1, m-1)\}, & m > r. \end{cases}$$

The $(\mathbf{u}, \mathbf{u}+\mathbf{v})$-construction is called *Plotkin construction.* A Reed-Muller code RM$(r, m)$ has dimension $k = \sum_{j \le r} \binom{m}{j}$ and cardinality $2^k$. Examples of Reed-Muller codes are: the universe codes RM$(m, m)$, the repetition codes RM$(0, m)$, and the parity-check codes RM$(1, m)$.

## 2.3 Lattices

A *real n-dimensional lattice* $\Lambda$ is a discrete additive subgroup of $\mathbb{R}^n$ [10]. The *dual lattice* is $\Lambda^* = \{\mathbf{x} \in \mathbb{R}^n : \forall \mathbf{y} \in \Lambda, \langle \mathbf{x}, \mathbf{y} \rangle \in \mathbb{Z}\}$. The *theta series* of a lattice is a series whose coefficients are the number of lattice points of a given Euclidean norm. It is the lattice analog of the weight enumerator of a linear code.

**Definition 7 (Theta Series).** *The theta series of an n-dimensional lattice* $\Lambda$ *is*

$$\Theta_\Lambda(z) = \sum_{\mathbf{x} \in \Lambda} e^{\pi i z \|\mathbf{x}\|^2},$$

*where* $\mathrm{Im}(z) > 0$.

In particular, when $z$ is purely imaginary, i.e., $z = i\tau$ and $\tau > 0$

$$\Theta_\Lambda(i\tau) = \sum_{\mathbf{x} \in \Lambda} e^{-\pi\tau \|\mathbf{x}\|^2}. \tag{3}$$

The theta series $\Theta_{\Lambda+\mathbf{t}}(z)$ for a coset $\Lambda+\mathbf{t}$ where $\mathbf{t} \in \mathbb{R}^n$ is defined analogously.

It is often relevant to express the theta series of a lattice in terms of the Jacobi theta functions [10, pp. 102-105]:

$$\vartheta_3(\xi|z) = \sum_{m \in \mathbb{Z}} e^{2mi\xi + \pi i z m^2}, \; \vartheta_2(z) = \sum_{m \in \mathbb{Z}} e^{\pi i z (m+1/2)^2},$$
$$\vartheta_3(z) = \vartheta_3(0|z) = \sum_{m \in \mathbb{Z}} e^{\pi i z m^2}, \; \vartheta_4(z) = \sum_{m \in \mathbb{Z}} (-1)^{m^2} e^{\pi i z m^2},$$

where $\mathrm{Im}(z) > 0$ and $\xi \in \mathbb{C}$. Observe that $\vartheta_3(z)$ coincides with the theta series of the one-dimensional lattice $\mathbb{Z}$ and $\vartheta_2(z)$ refers to the shift $\mathbb{Z} + 1/2$.

The function $\psi_k(z) = \Theta_{\mathbb{Z}+1/k}(z) = \sum_{m\in\mathbb{Z}} e^{\pi i z(m+1/k)^2}$ for $k \in \mathbb{Z}\setminus\{0\}$ is also useful in our context. Note that

$$\Theta_{\mathbb{Z}+1/k}(z) = \Theta_{\mathbb{Z}+(k-1)/k}(z) \tag{4}$$

because $\Theta_{\mathbb{Z}+(k-1)/k}(z) = \Theta_{\mathbb{Z}+1-1/k}(z) = \Theta_{\mathbb{Z}-1/k}(z)$ and we have the identity that $\psi_k(z) = \psi_{-k}(z)$ [10, p. 105]. For a general shift $t \in \mathbb{R}$ and considering $z = i\tau$ to be pure imaginary (3) with $\tau > 0$, we have the one dimensional theta series [7, Eq. (2.2.5)]

$$\Theta_{\mathbb{Z}+t}(i\tau) = \sum_{m\in\mathbb{Z}} e^{-\pi\tau(m+t)^2} = \tau^{-1/2}\sum_{k=-\infty}^{\infty} e^{2\pi ikt-\pi k^2/\tau} = \tau^{-1/2}\vartheta_3(\pi t|i\tau^{-1}).$$

In this paper, we focus on real lattices, but the lattice constructions can be extended to lattices over complex numbers. Lattices constructed from linear codes are of particular interest since the underlying code structure allows a simpler characterization of some of the lattice properties, like the theta series. These lattices are exactly the $q$-ary lattices [27].

Particularly, we consider lattices that can be expressed in terms of a code formula due to the connection with partition chains (or lattice filtrations [14,31]).

**Definition 8 (Partition Chain/Filtration).** *A partition chain*

$$\Lambda_L/\Lambda_{L-1}/\ldots/\Lambda_0$$

*is a sequence of lattices such that each is a sublattice of the previous one, that is,* $\Lambda_0 \subseteq \ldots \subseteq \Lambda_L$. *This is also called a filtration of the lattice* $\Lambda_L$.

A partition chain induces a coset decomposition such that every element of a lattice $\Lambda_L$ can be written as a sum of an element from $\Lambda_0$ and a coset representative from each partition $[\Lambda_j/\Lambda_{j-1}]$, where $j \in [1:L]$ [14, p. 1127]. The partition chain $\mathbb{Z}/2\mathbb{Z}/4\mathbb{Z}/\ldots$ induces the binary decomposition of an integer, so we can write any $x \in \mathbb{Z}$ as a sum $x_0 + 2x_1 + 4x_2 + \ldots$. A $2^L$*-ary lattice* is an integer lattice that has $2^\ell\mathbb{Z}^n$ as a sublattice for some $\ell$ (clearly, this is true for $\ell = L$), and the smallest such $\ell$ is called the *depth* or *level* of the lattice. To be mathematically precise, we define $\phi : \mathbb{Z}_q^n \to \mathbb{Z}^n$ as the natural embedding which simply maps a congruence class to its corresponding integer, for $q \geq 2$.

**Definition 9 (Construction A).** *Let* $q \geq 2$ *and* $\mathcal{C} \subseteq \mathbb{Z}_q^n$ *be a linear code, then*

$$\Lambda_{\mathrm{A}}(\mathcal{C}) = q\mathbb{Z}^n + \phi(\mathcal{C})$$

*defines a lattice, referred to as (q-ary) Construction A.*

**Definition 10 (Construction B).** *Let* $\mathcal{P}_n$ *be the* $(n, n-1)_2$ *parity-check code and* $\overline{\mathcal{C}} \subset \mathbb{F}_2^n$ *be doubly even code, i.e., the weight of every codeword in* $\overline{\mathcal{C}}$ *is divisible by 4. Notice that* $\overline{\mathcal{C}} \subset \mathcal{P}_n$. *Thus, the Construction B lattice is such that*

$$\Lambda_{\mathrm{B}}(\overline{\mathcal{C}}) = 4\mathbb{Z}^n + 2\phi(\mathcal{P}_n) + \phi(\overline{\mathcal{C}}).$$

Using partitions of binary lattices modulo 2 and 4, we can express Construction A and B lattices in terms of a code formula since the lattice cosets $[\Lambda_j/\Lambda_{j-1}]$ form binary linear codes for $j \in [1:L]$ where $L = 1, 2$ respectively [14, Lemma 3, pp. 1132-1133].

The code formula in Definition 10 can be extended to $L$ binary linear codes [14], which leads to the following definition of Construction D, provided that the underlying linear codes satisfy some multiplicative conditions [20, Th. 1].

**Definition 11 (Construction D).** *The code formula*

$$2^L\mathbb{Z}^n + 2^{L-1}\phi(\mathcal{C}_L) + \ldots + 2\phi(\mathcal{C}_2) + \phi(\mathcal{C}_1)$$

*defines a lattice $\Lambda_{\mathrm{D}}$ if and only if every binary linear code $\mathcal{C}_j \subseteq \mathbb{F}_2^n$ is pairwise closed under the Schur product, i.e. $\mathbf{c}_j \star \mathbf{c}'_j \triangleq (c_{j,1}c_{j',1}, \ldots, c_{j,n}c_{j',n}) \in \mathcal{C}_{j+1}$ for all $\mathbf{c}_j, \mathbf{c}'_j \in \mathcal{C}_j$, $j \in [1 : L-1]$. Particularly, this implies that $\mathcal{C}_1 \subseteq \mathcal{C}_2 \subseteq \ldots \subseteq \mathcal{C}_L$.*

From now on, we drop the notation of $\phi$ for simplicity, but the map is implied. Observe that both Constructions B and D can be seen as a particular case of the $q$-ary Construction A if we consider $\mathcal{C} = 2\mathcal{P}_n + \overline{\mathcal{C}}$ and $q = 4$ for Construction B, and $\mathcal{C} = 2^{L-1}\mathcal{C}_L + \cdots + 2\mathcal{C}_2 + \mathcal{C}_1$ and $q = 2^L$ for Construction D. In both cases, the set of codes satisfy the Schur product condition, which implies that the code $\mathcal{C}$ is linear over the respective $\mathbb{Z}_q$.

By the code formula, we can write any lattice vector $\mathbf{x} \in \Lambda_{\mathrm{D}}$ as $\mathbf{x} = 2^L\mathbf{z} + 2^{L-1}\mathbf{c}_L + \ldots + 2\mathbf{c}_2 + \mathbf{c}_1$ where $\mathbf{z} \in \mathbb{Z}^n$ and $\mathbf{c}_j$ is a codeword of $\mathcal{C}_j$, for all $j \in [1 : L]$. Therefore, we can express $\Lambda_{\mathrm{D}}$ as a disjoint union of its coset representatives as follows:

$$\Lambda_{\mathrm{D}} = \bigcup_{\mathbf{c}_L \in \mathcal{C}_L} \cdots \bigcup_{\mathbf{c}_1 \in \mathcal{C}_1} 2^L\mathbb{Z}^n + 2^{L-1}\mathbf{c}_L + \ldots + 2\mathbf{c}_2 + \mathbf{c}_1 = \bigcup_{\mathbf{c} \in \mathcal{C}} 2^L\mathbb{Z}^n + \mathbf{c} \tag{5}$$

where $\mathcal{C} = 2^{L-1}\mathcal{C}_L + \cdots + 2\mathcal{C}_2 + \mathcal{C}_1$ is a linear code over $\mathbb{Z}_{2^L}$.

The Barnes-Wall lattices are a remarkable example of Construction D lattices, known to have efficient bounded-distance decoding algorithms [25]. Since some families of Reed-Muller codes are nested and closed under the Schur product, the following code formulas define a lattice by Theorem 11. They correspond to the real Barnes-Wall lattices of dimension $n = 2^{m+1}$ [19]:

$$\mathrm{BW}_n = \Lambda(0, m) = \begin{cases} 2^{m/2}\mathbb{Z}^{2^{m+1}} + \sum\limits_{\substack{1 \leq r \leq m \\ m-r \text{ odd}}} \mathrm{RM}(r, m+1)2^{\frac{r-1}{2}}, & \text{if m even} \\ 2^{(m+1)/2}\mathbb{Z}^{2^{m+1}} + \sum\limits_{\substack{1 \leq r \leq m \\ m-r \text{ even}}} \mathrm{RM}(r, m+1)2^{\frac{r-1}{2}}, & \text{if m odd.} \end{cases}$$

## 2.4 Discrete Gaussian Distributions

The theta series is closely related to the discrete Gaussian distribution over a lattice. The Gaussian function is given by $\rho_s(\mathbf{x}) = e^{-\pi\|\mathbf{x}\|^2/s^2}$ for $\mathbf{x} \in \mathbb{R}^n$. Further, we can define the Gaussian function over a discrete set $S$ as $\rho_s(S) \triangleq \sum_{\mathbf{x}\in S} \rho_s(\mathbf{x})$. The *discrete Gaussian distribution* over a lattice coset $\Lambda + \mathbf{t}$ for $\mathbf{t} \in \mathbb{R}^n$ is the discrete distribution with support over the coset. The probability of choosing a vector $\mathbf{y} \in \Lambda + \mathbf{t}$ according to this distribution is[6]

$$\mathcal{D}_{\Lambda+\mathbf{t},s}(\mathbf{y}) \triangleq \frac{\rho_s(\mathbf{y})}{\rho_s(\Lambda+\mathbf{t})} = \frac{\rho_s(\mathbf{y})}{\Theta_{\Lambda+\mathbf{t}}\left({}^{i}/{}_{s^2}\right)}, \tag{6}$$

where $\rho_s(\Lambda + \mathbf{t})$ is a normalisation factor. We now recall some properties of the lattice Gaussian distribution.

**Proposition 1.** *[9, Prop. 1] For the lattice Gaussian distribution, it holds that*

1. $\mathcal{D}_{\alpha(\Lambda+\mathbf{t}),s}(\alpha\mathbf{y}) = \mathcal{D}_{\Lambda+\mathbf{t},s/\alpha}(\mathbf{y})$,
2. $\mathcal{D}_{(\Lambda_1+\mathbf{t}_1)\oplus(\Lambda_2+\mathbf{t}_2)}(\mathbf{y}_1,\mathbf{y}_2) = \mathcal{D}_{\Lambda_1+\mathbf{t}_1}(\mathbf{y}_1)\mathcal{D}_{\Lambda_2+\mathbf{t}_2}(\mathbf{y}_2)$.

The smoothing parameter is a lattice measure based on the Gaussian distribution [26].

**Definition 12 (Smoothing Parameter).** *For an $n$-dimensional lattice $\Lambda$, and a positive real $\varepsilon > 0$, the smoothing parameter $\eta_\varepsilon(\Lambda)$ is the smallest $s$ such that $\rho_{1/s}(\Lambda^* \setminus \{\mathbf{0}\}) \leq \varepsilon$.*

In the sampling context, if a noisy vector is sampled from a Gaussian distribution with a width at least as large as the smoothing parameter and then reduced modulo the fundamental parallelepiped of the lattice, the resulting distribution will be nearly uniform.

## 3 Reductions

We show that the problem of lattice sampling for $q$-ary lattices can be reduced to that of code sampling. Combined with a straightforward reduction in the other direction, this implies the two problems are equivalent.

For clarity, let us fix the lattice $\Lambda_{\mathrm{A}} = \Lambda_{\mathrm{A}}(\mathcal{C}) = q\mathbb{Z}^n + \mathcal{C}$ with $\mathcal{C} \subseteq \mathbb{Z}_q^n$ a linear code and $q \geq 2$, and give definitions of the two problems. We also let the shift $\mathbf{t} \in \mathbb{Z}_q^n$ without loss of generality.

**Definition 13 (Gaussian Sampling for $q$-ary Lattices).** *Given some lattice $\Lambda_{\mathrm{A}} = q\mathbb{Z}^n + \mathcal{C}$, a shift $\mathbf{t} \in \mathbb{Z}_q^n$ and sampling width $s > 0$, the Gaussian sampling problem asks to sample a vector $\mathbf{x} \in \Lambda_{\mathrm{A}} + \mathbf{t}$ from the distribution $\mathcal{D}_{\Lambda_{\mathrm{A}}+\mathbf{t},s}$.*

[6] In literature, there is a slightly different definition $\mathcal{D}_{\Lambda,s,\mathbf{t}}(\mathbf{x})$ with a center $\mathbf{t}$, where $\mathbf{x} \in \Lambda$. It is easy to see $\mathcal{D}_{\Lambda,s,\mathbf{t}}(\mathbf{x}) = \mathcal{D}_{\Lambda-\mathbf{t},s}(\mathbf{x}-\mathbf{t})$, namely, they are a shifted version of each other. In this paper, we follow the definition (6) since it is used in the GPV framework [15].

**Definition 14 (Sampling for $q$-ary Linear Codes).** *Given a linear code $\mathcal{C} \subseteq \mathbb{Z}_q^n$, a shift $\mathbf{t} \in \mathbb{Z}_q^n$ and a parameter $s$, the code sampling problem with respect to the Lee weight profile asks to sample a vector $\boldsymbol{\nu} \in \mathcal{C} + \mathbf{t}$ with probability given by*

$$\mathcal{L}_{\mathcal{C}+\mathbf{t},s}(\boldsymbol{\nu}) \triangleq \frac{\Theta_{q\mathbb{Z}}(z)^{n_0(\boldsymbol{\nu})}\Theta_{q\mathbb{Z}+1}(z)^{n_1(\boldsymbol{\nu})}\dots\Theta_{q\mathbb{Z}+\ell}(z)^{n_\ell(\boldsymbol{\nu})}}{\sum_{\boldsymbol{\nu}\in\mathcal{C}+\mathbf{t}}\Theta_{q\mathbb{Z}}(z)^{n_0(\boldsymbol{\nu})}\Theta_{q\mathbb{Z}+1}(z)^{n_1(\boldsymbol{\nu})}\dots\Theta_{q\mathbb{Z}+\ell}(z)^{n_\ell(\boldsymbol{\nu})}}$$

*where $z = {}^{i}/_{s^2}$, $n_j(\boldsymbol{\nu})$ are the entries of the Lee weight profile of $\boldsymbol{\nu}$ and $\ell = \lceil {}^{q}/_{2} \rceil$. We denote the induced distribution as $\mathcal{L}_{\mathcal{C}+\mathbf{t},s}$.*

Define $\mathcal{D}_{\Lambda_{\mathrm{A}}+\mathbf{t},s}(S) \triangleq \sum_{\mathbf{x}\in S}\mathcal{D}_{\Lambda_{\mathrm{A}}+\mathbf{t},s}(\mathbf{x})$ over a discrete set $S$.

**Lemma 1 (Key Lemma).** *Given a linear $q$-ary code $\mathcal{C} \subseteq \mathbb{Z}_q^n$, a vector $\mathbf{t} \in \mathbb{Z}_q^n$ and $\boldsymbol{\nu} \in \mathcal{C} + \mathbf{t}$, we have*[7]

$$\mathcal{D}_{\Lambda_{\mathrm{A}}+\mathbf{t},s}(q\mathbb{Z}^n + \boldsymbol{\nu}) = \mathcal{L}_{\mathcal{C}+\mathbf{t},s}(\boldsymbol{\nu}).$$

*Proof.* Consider $\boldsymbol{\nu} \in \mathcal{C}+\mathbf{t}$, then the $j$-th coordinate of $q\mathbf{z}+\boldsymbol{\nu}$, where $\mathbf{z} \in \mathbb{Z}^n$ and $j \in [1:n]$, is

$$qz_j + \nu_j = \begin{cases} qz_j, & \text{if } \nu_j = 0 \\ qz_j + 1, & \text{if } \nu_j = 1 \\ \vdots & \\ qz_j + (q-1), & \text{if } \nu_j = q-1. \end{cases}$$

For each $qz_j + \nu_j$, we derive a corresponding theta series for the one-dimensional lattice coset $q\mathbb{Z} + \nu_j$. We have that

$$\Theta_{q\mathbb{Z}}(z) = \vartheta_3(q^2 z),$$
$$\Theta_{q\mathbb{Z}+j}(z) = \Theta_{q\mathbb{Z}+q-j}(z), \quad j = 1, 2, \dots, q-1$$

and the second equality follows from an analogous argument to the proof of (4).

For a fixed $\boldsymbol{\nu}$, we can write

$$\Theta_{q\mathbb{Z}^n+\boldsymbol{\nu}}(z) = \sum_{\mathbf{z}\in\mathbb{Z}^n} e^{\pi i z\|q\mathbf{z}+\boldsymbol{\nu}\|^2}. \tag{7}$$

We have that $q\mathbb{Z}^n + \boldsymbol{\nu}$ is isometric to the decomposition given by[8]

$$q\mathbb{Z}^{n_0(\boldsymbol{\nu})} \oplus \left(q\mathbb{Z}^{n_1(\boldsymbol{\nu})} + \left(1^{n_1(\boldsymbol{\nu})}\right)\right) \oplus \dots \oplus \left(q\mathbb{Z}^{n_\ell(\boldsymbol{\nu})} + \left(\ell^{n_\ell(\boldsymbol{\nu})}\right)\right),$$

where $\ell = \lceil {}^{q}/_{2} \rceil$ and we interpret $j^{n_j(\boldsymbol{\nu})}$ to be a vector with $n_j(\boldsymbol{\nu})$ entries of $\pm j$. It follows that

[7] Formally, $\mathbf{t} \in \mathbb{Z}^n$, but we can assume $\mathbf{t} \in \mathbb{Z}_q^n$ without loss of generality [30].

[8] Direct sum decomposition does not preserve order, but this is not relevant for the computation of the theta series.

$$
\begin{aligned}
\Theta_{q\mathbb{Z}^n+\boldsymbol{\nu}}(z) &= \Theta_{q\mathbb{Z}^{n_0(\boldsymbol{\nu})}}(z)\Theta_{q\mathbb{Z}^{n_1(\boldsymbol{\nu})}+(1^{n_1(\boldsymbol{\nu})})}(z) \times \cdots \times \Theta_{q\mathbb{Z}^{n_\ell(\boldsymbol{\nu})}+(\ell^{n_\ell(\boldsymbol{\nu})})}(z) \\
&= \Theta_{q\mathbb{Z}}(z)^{n_0(\boldsymbol{\nu})}\Theta_{q\mathbb{Z}+1}(z)^{n_1(\boldsymbol{\nu})} \times \cdots \times \Theta_{q\mathbb{Z}+\ell}(z)^{n_\ell(\boldsymbol{\nu})}
\end{aligned} \tag{8}
$$

where the second equality follows by direct sum decomposition and using the fact that $\Theta_{\Lambda_1 \oplus \Lambda_2}(z) = \Theta_{\Lambda_1}(z)\Theta_{\Lambda_2}(z)$.

The proof is completed by observing that for $z = {}^{i}/{s^2}$,

$$
\mathcal{D}_{\Lambda_{\mathrm{A}}+\mathbf{t},s}(q\mathbb{Z}^n + \boldsymbol{\nu}) = \frac{\Theta_{q\mathbb{Z}^n+\boldsymbol{\nu}}(z)}{\sum_{\boldsymbol{\nu}\in\mathcal{C}+\mathbf{t}} \Theta_{q\mathbb{Z}^n+\boldsymbol{\nu}}(z)} = \mathcal{L}_{\mathcal{C}+\mathbf{t},s}(\boldsymbol{\nu}).
$$

□

**Theorem 1 (Equivalence of Lattice and Code Sampling).** *The Gaussian sampling problem for a Construction A lattice $\Lambda_{\mathrm{A}} + \mathbf{t}$ with $\mathcal{C} \subseteq \mathbb{Z}_q^n$ a linear code and $q \geq 2$ is equivalent to the problem of sampling codewords over $\mathcal{C} + \mathbf{t}$ with respect to their Lee weight profiles.*

*Proof.* We show the equivalence between lattice sampling (LS) and code sampling (CS) by establishing two reductions with polynomial running time. We use A → B to denote that problem A is reduced to problem B, i.e., an oracle for solving problem B can also be used as a subroutine to solve problem A efficiently.

(CS → LS): This reduction is simple, we just sample $\mathbf{x} \in \Lambda_{\mathrm{A}} + \mathbf{t}$ with probability $\mathcal{D}_{\Lambda_{\mathrm{A}}+\mathbf{t},s}(\mathbf{x})$, then return a vector $\boldsymbol{\nu} = \mathbf{x} \mod q$. The probability of obtaining $\boldsymbol{\nu}$ is $\mathcal{D}_{\Lambda_{\mathrm{A}}+\mathbf{t},s}(q\mathbb{Z}^n + \boldsymbol{\nu})$, since this is the probability that a point drawn from the discrete Gaussian in $\Lambda_{\mathrm{A}} + \mathbf{t}$ lies in the coset $q\mathbb{Z}^n + \boldsymbol{\nu}$. As proven in Lemma 1, $\mathcal{D}_{\Lambda_{\mathrm{A}}+\mathbf{t},s}(q\mathbb{Z}^n + \boldsymbol{\nu}) \propto \Theta_{q\mathbb{Z}}(z)^{n_0(\boldsymbol{\nu})}\Theta_{q\mathbb{Z}+1}(z)^{n_1(\boldsymbol{\nu})} \ldots \Theta_{q\mathbb{Z}+\ell}(z)^{n_\ell(\boldsymbol{\nu})}$ where the $n_j(\boldsymbol{\nu})$ are the entries of the Lee weight profile of $\boldsymbol{\nu}$. This probability depends on the Lee weight profile of $\boldsymbol{\nu}$ only.

(LS → CS): We can decompose a Construction A lattice as a disjoint union of cosets $\Lambda_{\mathrm{A}} = \Lambda_{\mathrm{A}}(\mathcal{C}) = \bigcup_{\mathbf{c}\in\mathcal{C}} q\mathbb{Z}^n + \mathbf{c}$. We sample from $\Lambda_{\mathrm{A}} + \mathbf{t}$ via coset decomposition:

1. Sample a coset representative $\boldsymbol{\nu} \in \mathcal{C} + \mathbf{t}$ with probability
$$
\mathcal{L}_{\mathcal{C}+\mathbf{t},s}(\boldsymbol{\nu}) = \mathcal{D}_{\Lambda_{\mathrm{A}}+\mathbf{t},s}(q\mathbb{Z}^n + \boldsymbol{\nu}).
$$
2. Sample a vector $\mathbf{x}$ from $\mathcal{D}_{q\mathbb{Z}^n+\boldsymbol{\nu},s}$ of the form $\mathbf{x} = q\mathbf{z} + \boldsymbol{\nu}$, where $\mathbf{z} \in \mathbb{Z}^n$.

This outputs a lattice vector $\mathbf{x} = q\mathbf{z} + \boldsymbol{\nu} \in q\mathbb{Z}^n + \boldsymbol{\nu}$ with probability $\mathcal{D}_{\Lambda_{\mathrm{A}}+\mathbf{t},s}(q\mathbb{Z}^n + \boldsymbol{\nu}) \cdot \mathcal{D}_{q\mathbb{Z}^n+\boldsymbol{\nu},s}(\mathbf{z} + \boldsymbol{\nu}) = \mathcal{D}_{\Lambda_{\mathrm{A}}+\mathbf{t},s}(\mathbf{z} + \boldsymbol{\nu}) = \mathcal{D}_{\Lambda_{\mathrm{A}}+\mathbf{t},s}(\mathbf{x})$ as desired. □

If we view any multilevel lattice construction (B or D) as a Construction A lattice with $q = 2^L$, then from Theorem 1 it follows that sampling a Construction D lattice is also equivalent to sampling codewords with respect to their Lee weight profiles. We omit the details.

## 4 Theta Series of $q$-ary Lattices

The theta series is the key lattice measure underlying our sampling method. In general, it is challenging to calculate the theta series of an arbitrary lattice $\Lambda$, but a closed formula is known for some well-studied lattices, which can lead to a better estimation of the smoothing parameter and improved samplers.

We now expand on the theta series of some families of $q$-ary lattices obtained from linear codes. We start with showing that the theta series of a Construction A lattice with $q \geq 2$ can be written in terms of the symmetrized weight enumerator of the associated linear code over $\mathbb{Z}_q$, based on [24].

**Theorem 2 (Theta Series of a Construction A Lattice for $q \geq 2$).** *The theta series of a Construction A lattice $\Lambda_{\mathrm{A}} \triangleq \Lambda_{\mathrm{A}}(\mathcal{C}) = q\mathbb{Z}^n + \mathcal{C}$ is given by*

$$\Theta_{\Lambda_{\mathrm{A}}}(z) = \mathrm{swe}_{\mathcal{C}}(\Theta_{\mathbb{Z}}(q^2 z), \Theta_{\mathbb{Z}+1/q}(q^2 z), \ldots, \Theta_{\mathbb{Z}+\ell/q}(q^2 z)),$$

*where $\ell = \lceil q/2 \rceil$.*

*Proof.* We can write

$$\Theta_{\Lambda_{\mathrm{A}}}(z) = \sum_{\mathbf{c}\in\mathcal{C}} \sum_{\mathbf{z}\in\mathbb{Z}^n} e^{\pi i z \|q\mathbf{z}+\mathbf{c}\|^2} = \sum_{\mathbf{c}\in\mathcal{C}} \Theta_{q\mathbb{Z}^n+\mathbf{c}}(z). \tag{9}$$

Using (8), we have

$$\Theta_{\Lambda_{\mathrm{A}}}(z) = \sum_{\mathbf{c}\in\mathcal{C}} \Theta_{q\mathbb{Z}}(z)^{n_0(\mathbf{c})} \Theta_{q\mathbb{Z}+1}(z)^{n_1(\mathbf{c})} \cdots \Theta_{q\mathbb{Z}+\ell}(z)^{n_\ell(\mathbf{c})}.$$

Notice that this is the symmetrized weight enumerator of the linear code $\mathcal{C} \subseteq \mathbb{Z}_q^n$ evaluated at the corresponding shifts of theta series. □

The two main challenges in calculating the theta series of any $q$-ary lattice obtained via Construction A are i) characterizing the symmetrized weight enumerator of a $q$-ary code $\mathcal{C}$ involves going through all the codewords of $\mathcal{C}$, and ii) the theta series of shifts of $q\mathbb{Z}$, i.e., $\Theta_{q\mathbb{Z}+c}(z)$ have some simplifications via the well-known Jacobi-theta functions [10, pp. 102-105], but not always. We present next some cases where this calculation is simplified due to these properties.

For the binary Construction A ($q = 2$), the symmetrized weight enumerator is simply the Hamming weight enumerator of the binary linear code $\mathcal{C}$. Moreover, $\Theta_{\mathbb{Z}}(q^2 z) = \vartheta_3(4z)$ and $\Theta_{\mathbb{Z}+1/q}(q^2 z) = \vartheta_2(4z)$, and from [10, Th. 3, Ch. 7] and without the scaling factor $1/\sqrt{2}$, we get the theta series of $\Lambda_{\mathrm{A}}(\mathcal{C})$.

**Theorem 3 (Theta Series of Binary Construction A Lattice).** *Consider an $(n, k)_2$ code $\mathcal{C}$, then the theta series of $\Lambda_{\mathrm{A}}(\mathcal{C})$ is given by*

$$\Theta_{\Lambda_{\mathrm{A}}(\mathcal{C})}(z) = W_{\mathcal{C}}(\vartheta_3(4z), \vartheta_2(4z)).$$

Given that the parity-check code $\mathcal{P}_n$ defines the Construction B lattice, its theta series can be written only in terms of the Hamming weight enumerator of the doubly-even code $\overline{\mathcal{C}} \subseteq \mathcal{P}_n$, according to [10, Th. 15, Ch. 7].

**Theorem 4 (Theta Series of a Construction B Lattice).** *Consider an $(n,k)_2$ doubly even code $\overline{\mathcal{C}}$. The theta series of $\Lambda_{\mathrm{B}}(\overline{\mathcal{C}})$ is*

$$\Theta_{\Lambda_{\mathrm{B}}(\overline{\mathcal{C}})}(z) = \tfrac{1}{2}W_{\overline{\mathcal{C}}}(\vartheta_3(4z), \vartheta_2(4z)) + \tfrac{1}{2}\vartheta_4(4z)^n.$$

Naturally, the same procedure can be applied to Construction D lattices. We show that its theta series can also be written as symmetrized weight enumerator of the linear code $\mathcal{C} \subseteq \mathbb{Z}_{2^L}^n$, provided that $\mathcal{C} = 2^{L-1}\mathcal{C}_L + \ldots + 2\mathcal{C}_2 + \mathcal{C}_1$ and $\mathcal{C}_j$ are binary linear codes closed under the Schur product, for $j \in [1:L]$. If we consider the $j$-th coordinate of a lattice vector $2^L\mathbf{z} + \mathbf{c}$ where $\mathbf{c} \in \mathcal{C}$, we get

$$2^L z_j + c_j = \begin{cases} 2^L z_j, & \text{if } (c_{1,j}, \ldots, c_{2^L,j}) = (0,0,\ldots,0) \\ 2^L z_j + 1, & \text{if } (c_{1,j}, \ldots, c_{2^L,j}) = (1,0,\ldots,0) \\ \vdots & \\ 2^L z_j + (2^L - 1), & \text{if } (c_{1,j}, \ldots, c_{2^L,j}) = (1,1,\ldots,1). \end{cases}$$

Let $\boldsymbol{\alpha} = (\alpha_1, \alpha_2, \ldots, \alpha_L) \in \mathbb{F}_2^L$ and recall that $\omega_{\boldsymbol{\alpha}}(\mathbf{c}_1, \ldots, \mathbf{c}_L)$ is the number of occurrences of $\boldsymbol{\alpha}$ as a row in the matrix of column vectors $\mathbf{c}_1, \ldots, \mathbf{c}_L$. Also, since $n_w(\mathbf{c})$ is the number of coordinates that have Lee weight $w$, it follows that

$$n_w(\mathbf{c}) = \omega_{\alpha_1,\ldots,\alpha_L}(\mathbf{c}_1, \ldots, \mathbf{c}_L) + \omega_{\tilde{\alpha}_1,\ldots,\tilde{\alpha}_L}(\mathbf{c}_1, \ldots, \mathbf{c}_L),$$

where $i = 2^{L-1}\alpha_L + \ldots + 2\alpha_2 + \alpha_1$ and $2^L - i = 2^{L-1}\tilde{\alpha}_L + \ldots + 2\tilde{\alpha}_2 + \tilde{\alpha}_1$. Therefore, we have that for the $\mathbb{Z}_{2^L}$-linear code $\mathcal{C} = 2^{L-1}\mathcal{C}_L + \ldots + 2\mathcal{C}_2 + \mathcal{C}_1$ with each $\mathcal{C}_j$ a binary linear code, we can write the Lee weight profile of $\mathbf{c} \in \mathcal{C}$ either as $[n_0(\mathbf{c}), n_1(\mathbf{c}), \ldots, n_\ell(\mathbf{c})]$ as in Definition 3 or equivalently, as

$$[\omega_{0,\ldots,0}(\mathbf{c}_1, \ldots, \mathbf{c}_L), \omega_{1,0,\ldots,0}(\mathbf{c}_1, \ldots, \mathbf{c}_L) + \omega_{0,1,\ldots,1}(\mathbf{c}_1, \ldots, \mathbf{c}_L), \ldots \\ \ldots, \omega_{1,\ldots,1}(\mathbf{c}_1, \ldots, \mathbf{c}_L)].$$

We can also rewrite (7) as a joint weight enumerator over $L$ binary codes.

**Theorem 5 (Theta Series of a Construction D Lattice).** *The theta series of a Construction D lattice $\Lambda_{\mathrm{D}} = 2^L\mathbb{Z}^n + 2^{L-1}\mathcal{C}_L + \ldots + 2\mathcal{C}_2 + \mathcal{C}_1$ is given by*

$$\Theta_{\Lambda_{\mathrm{D}}}(z) = \mathrm{jwe}_{\mathcal{C}_1,\ldots,\mathcal{C}_L}(\Theta_{\mathbb{Z}+t_{\boldsymbol{\alpha}}/2^L})$$

*where $\boldsymbol{\alpha} \in \mathbb{F}_2^L$ and $t_{\boldsymbol{\alpha}} = 2^{L-1}\alpha_L + \ldots + 2\alpha_2 + \alpha_1$.*

*Proof.* We have that

$$\begin{aligned} \Theta_{\Lambda_{\mathrm{D}}}(z) &= \sum_{\mathbf{c}\in\mathcal{C}} \Theta_{2^L\mathbb{Z}^n+\mathbf{c}}(z) \\ &= \sum_{\mathbf{c}\in\mathcal{C}} \Theta_{2^L\mathbb{Z}}(z)^{n_0(\mathbf{c})} \cdots \Theta_{2^L\mathbb{Z}+2^L-1}(z)^{n_{2^L-1}(\mathbf{c})} \\ &= \sum_{\mathbf{c}_1\in\mathcal{C}_1} \cdots \sum_{\mathbf{c}_L\in\mathcal{C}_L} \Theta_{2^L\mathbb{Z}}(z)^{\omega_{0,\ldots,0}(\mathbf{c}_1,\ldots,\mathbf{c}_L)} \cdots \Theta_{2^L\mathbb{Z}+2^L-1}(z)^{\omega_{1,\ldots,1}(\mathbf{c}_1,\ldots,\mathbf{c}_L)} \\ &= \sum_{\mathbf{c}_1\in\mathcal{C}_1} \cdots \sum_{\mathbf{c}_L\in\mathcal{C}_L} \prod_{\boldsymbol{\alpha}\in\mathbb{F}_2^L} \Theta_{\mathbb{Z}+t_{\boldsymbol{\alpha}}/2^L}(z)^{\omega_{\boldsymbol{\alpha}}(\mathbf{c}_1,\ldots,\mathbf{c}_L)} \\ &= \mathrm{jwe}_{\mathcal{C}_1,\ldots,\mathcal{C}_L}(\Theta_{\mathbb{Z}+t_{\boldsymbol{\alpha}}/2^L}). \end{aligned}$$

□

Theorem 5 can be also expressed in terms of the symmetrized weight enumerator over the code $\mathcal{C} = 2^{L-1}\mathcal{C}_L + \ldots + 2\mathcal{C}_2 + \mathcal{C}_1 \subseteq \mathbb{Z}_{2^L}^n$ as proposed in Theorem 2. The main difference between the code formula Construction D and Construction A for $q \geq 2$ is that we have an identity between the symmetrized weight enumerator of a single linear code over $\mathbb{Z}_{2^L}^n$ and the joint weight enumerator of multiple binary codes $\mathcal{C}_j$, for $j \in [1 : L]$. This does not hold in general for Construction A with $q \geq 2$ because we cannot always decompose a $q$-ary code $\mathcal{C} \subseteq \mathbb{Z}_q^n$ into a sum of binary codes. Such a particular property will further allow a simplification of the Gaussian sampling.

For the particular case of Theorem 5 for $L = 2$, we recover the theta series for a 2-level Construction D lattice [6, Th. 22]. For instance, the theta series of $\frac{1}{2}(4\mathbb{Z}^n + 2\mathcal{C}_2 + \mathcal{C}_1)$[9] is given by

$$
\begin{aligned}
\Theta_{\frac{1}{2}(4\mathbb{Z}^n+2\mathcal{C}_2+\mathcal{C}_1)}(z) &= \sum_{\mathbf{c}_1\in\mathcal{C}_1}\sum_{\mathbf{c}_2\in\mathcal{C}_2} \vartheta_3(4z)^{\omega_{0,0}}\left(\frac{\vartheta_2(z)}{2}\right)^{\omega_{1,0}+\omega_{1,1}}\vartheta_2(4z)^{\omega_{0,1}} \\
&= \mathrm{swe}_{\mathcal{C}}(\vartheta_3(4z), {}^{\vartheta_2(z)}/_2, \vartheta_2(4z)), \\
&\overset{(a)}{=} \mathrm{jwe}_{\mathcal{C}_1,\mathcal{C}_2}(\vartheta_3(4z), \vartheta_2(4z), {}^{\vartheta_2(z)}/_2, {}^{\vartheta_2(z)}/_2),
\end{aligned} \tag{10}
$$

for $\mathcal{C} = {}^1/_2(\mathcal{C}_1 + 2\mathcal{C}_2)$. In $(a)$ we have used the identity from (2). Notice that $\Theta_{2\mathbb{Z}+1/2}(z) = \Theta_{\mathbb{Z}+1/4}(4z) = \Theta_{\mathbb{Z}+3/4}(4z) = \psi_4(4z)$, and then we apply the identity $\psi_4(z) = \frac{\vartheta_2(z/4)}{2}$ [10, p. 105]. In particular, considering $\mathcal{C}_1 = \overline{\mathcal{C}}$ and $\mathcal{C}_2 = \mathcal{P}_n$, where $\overline{\mathcal{C}}$ is a doubly even code, we recover the theta series of Construction B presented in Theorem 4.

Next, we use Theorem 5 to express the theta series of the Barnes-Wall lattice $\mathrm{BW}_{128}$, which is a 3-level Construction D.

*Example 1.* Consider the Barnes-Wall lattice $\mathrm{BW}_{128} = 8\mathbb{Z}^{128} + 4\,\mathrm{RM}(5,7) + 2\,\mathrm{RM}(3,7) + \mathrm{RM}(1,7)$ where $\mathrm{RM}(r,7)$ is a Reed-Muller code of length $2^7$ of order $r$ for $r = 1, 3, 5$ [16]. Hence, via coset decomposition,

$$
\mathrm{BW}_{128} = \bigcup_{\mathbf{c}_3\in\mathcal{C}_3}\bigcup_{\mathbf{c}_2\in\mathcal{C}_2}\bigcup_{\mathbf{c}_1\in\mathcal{C}_1} 8\mathbb{Z}^{128} + 4\mathbf{c}_3 + 2\mathbf{c}_2 + \mathbf{c}_1
$$

and we define $\mathbf{c} \triangleq 4\mathbf{c}_3 + 2\mathbf{c}_2 + \mathbf{c}_1$. The theta series for each of the one-dimensional cosets is given by

$$
\begin{aligned}
&\Theta_{8\mathbb{Z}}(z) = \vartheta_3(64z), \quad \Theta_{8(\mathbb{Z}+1/8)}(z) = \Theta_{8(\mathbb{Z}+7/8)}(z) = \psi_8(64z), \\
&\Theta_{8(\mathbb{Z}+1/4)}(z) = \Theta_{8(\mathbb{Z}+3/4)}(z) = \psi_4(64z) = {}^{\vartheta_2(16z)}/_2, \\
&\Theta_{8(\mathbb{Z}+3/8)}(z) = \Theta_{8(\mathbb{Z}+5/8)}(z) = ({}^z/_i)^{-1/2}\,\vartheta_3\left({}^{3\pi}/_8 | z\right), \quad \Theta_{8(\mathbb{Z}+1/2)}(z) = \vartheta_2(64z).
\end{aligned}
$$

Hence, the theta series of a fixed coset of $\mathrm{BW}_{128}$ is

[9] The constant ${}^1/_2$ is used simply to obtain a volume-one lattice.

$$\begin{aligned}\Theta_{8\mathbb{Z}^{128}+\mathbf{c}}(z) &= \sum_{\mathbf{z}\in\mathbb{Z}^{128}} e^{\pi i z\|8\mathbf{z}+\mathbf{c}\|^2}\\ &=\vartheta_3(64z)^{\omega_{0,0,0}}\vartheta_2(64z)^{\omega_{0,0,1}}\left(\vartheta_2(16z)/2\right)^{\omega_{0,1,0}+\omega_{0,1,1}}\\ &\quad\times\psi_8(64z)^{\omega_{1,0,0}(\mathbf{c})+\omega_{1,1,1}}\Theta_{\mathbb{Z}+\frac{3}{8}}(64z)^{\omega_{1,1,0}+\omega_{1,0,1}}. \end{aligned} \tag{11}$$

The overall theta series is obtained by summing over all codewords $\mathbf{c} \in \mathcal{C}$.

$$\begin{aligned}\Theta_{\mathrm{BW}_{128}}(z) &= \sum_{\mathbf{c}\in\mathcal{C}}\sum_{\mathbf{z}\in\mathbb{Z}^{128}} e^{\pi i z||8\mathbf{z}+\mathbf{c}||^2}\\ &= \mathrm{swe}_{\mathcal{C}}\left(\vartheta_3(64z), \vartheta_2(64z), \vartheta_2(16z)/2, \psi_8(64z), \Theta_{\mathbb{Z}+3/8}(64z)\right),\end{aligned}$$

where $\mathcal{C} = 4\,\mathrm{RM}(5,7) + 2\,\mathrm{RM}(3,7) + \mathrm{RM}(1,7)$. ◊

For Gaussian sampling over a $q$-ary lattice $\Lambda$, the theta series we are interested in is $\Theta_{\Lambda+\mathbf{t}}(z)$, where $\mathbf{t} \in \mathbb{Z}_q^n$. The results of this section then correspond to $\mathbf{t} = \mathbf{0}$. For $\mathbf{t} \neq \mathbf{0}$ and a binary Construction A, one can calculate the weight enumerator of the coset $\mathcal{C} + \mathbf{t}$ of a code $\mathcal{C} \subseteq \mathbb{Z}_2^n$ with $\mathbf{t} \in \mathbb{Z}_2^n$ according to the extended version [5, Appendix A], and then obtain the theta series of $\Lambda_{\mathrm{A}}(\mathcal{C}) + \mathbf{t}$ via Theorem 3. For larger alphabets $q > 2$, expressing the symmetrized weight enumerator of a coset $\mathcal{C} + \mathbf{t}$ of a $q$-ary code $\mathcal{C}$ is more challenging and might not have a closed form. In this case, we assume an oracle for computing the symmetrized weight enumerator of a coset.

### 4.1 Smoothing Parameter

The smoothing parameter $\eta_\epsilon(\Lambda)$ is computed by finding $s$ such that $\Theta_{\Lambda^*}(is^2) - 1 = \epsilon$ where $\Theta_{\Lambda^*}(is^2) = \sum_{\mathbf{x}\in\Lambda^*} e^{-\pi\tau\|\mathbf{x}\|^2}$ with $\tau = s^2$ in (3). For a general Construction A lattice, its dual is also a Construction A lattice up to a scaling of $1/\sqrt{q}$ (more details in the extended version [5, Appendix B]). That is,

$$\Lambda_{\mathrm{A}}^* = \Lambda_{\mathrm{A}}(\mathcal{C})^* = (q\mathbb{Z}^n + \mathcal{C})^* = q\mathbb{Z}^n + \mathcal{C}^\perp = \Lambda_{\mathrm{A}}(\mathcal{C}^\perp),$$

where $\mathcal{C}^\perp = \{\mathbf{c}' \in \mathbb{Z}_q^n : \langle \mathbf{c}, \mathbf{c}'\rangle \equiv 0 \bmod q,\ \text{for all } \mathbf{c} \in \mathcal{C}\}$.

The theta series of the dual of $\Lambda_{\mathrm{A}}(\mathcal{C})$ is then given by

$$\Theta_{\Lambda_{\mathrm{A}}^*}(z) = \mathrm{swe}_{\mathcal{C}^\perp}(\Theta_{\mathbb{Z}}(q^2z), \Theta_{\mathbb{Z}+1/q}(q^2z), \ldots, \Theta_{\mathbb{Z}+\ell/q}(q^2z))$$

where $\ell = \lceil q/2 \rceil$. We can obtain the symmetrized weight enumerator of $\mathcal{C}^\perp$ from the symmetrized weight enumerator of $\mathcal{C}$ using MacWilliams identities [23, Th. 12] for $q < 5$. Now we set $z = is^2$ and solve for $s$ such that $\Theta_{\Lambda^*}(is^2) - 1 = \epsilon$. For $q \geq 5$, we cannot apply the MacWilliams identities [1], but we can solve for $s$ using a formulation involving the primal lattice instead [22]. Typically in cryptography, the modulus $q$ is chosen such that $q \geq 5$.

For the sake of comparison, Fig. 1 represents the smoothing parameters of two lattices, $\mathrm{E}_8$ and the Leech $\Lambda_{24}$. Sampling using a width $s$ smaller than the precise smoothing parameter may cause inconsistencies since most properties of the Gaussian distribution require sampling *above* the smoothing parameter. We observe that the approximations presented in [13] are usually fair for small values of $\epsilon$.

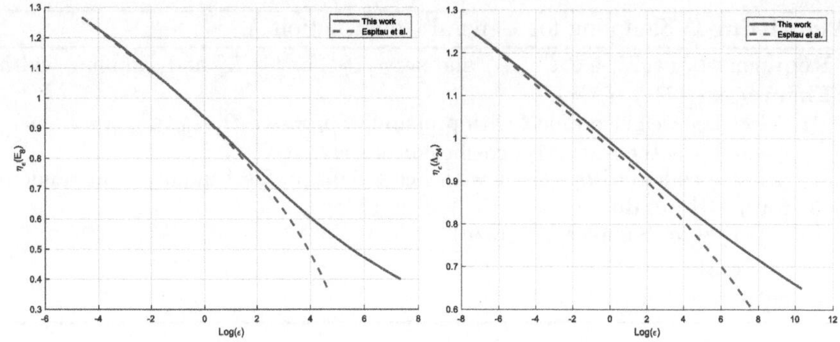


(a) $E_8$ lattice (b) $\Lambda_{24}$ lattice

**Fig. 1.** Smoothing parameters. The log scale refers to the natural logarithm.

# 5 Sampling Algorithms for $q$-ary Lattices

The reduction in Sect. 3 suggests an algorithm for lattice Gaussian sampling. Let $\Lambda = \bigcup_{\mathbf{c}\in\mathcal{C}} \Lambda' + \mathbf{c}$ be a disjoint union of cosets. To sample from $\Lambda + \mathbf{t}$, we now consider the decomposition with respect to the coset $\mathcal{C} + \mathbf{t}$. Sample first a vector $\boldsymbol{\nu} \in \mathcal{C} + \mathbf{t}$ with probability $\mathcal{D}_{\Lambda+\mathbf{t},s}(\Lambda' + \boldsymbol{\nu})$, then sample a lattice vector $\mathbf{x}' \in \Lambda'$ with probability $\mathcal{D}_{\Lambda'+\boldsymbol{\nu},s}(\mathbf{x}' + \boldsymbol{\nu})$ to output a vector $\mathbf{x} = \mathbf{x}' + \boldsymbol{\nu}$, with target probability $\mathcal{D}_{\Lambda+\mathbf{t},s}(\Lambda' + \boldsymbol{\nu}) \cdot \mathcal{D}_{\Lambda'+\boldsymbol{\nu},s}(\mathbf{x}' + \boldsymbol{\nu}) = \mathcal{D}_{\Lambda+\mathbf{t},s}(\mathbf{x})$.

## 5.1 Sampling General Construction A with $q \geq 2$

Algorithm 1 describes the coset decomposition sampling over a shift of a general Construction A lattice with code formula $q\mathbb{Z}^n + \mathcal{C}$. When $\mathbf{t} = \mathbf{0}$, the probability of sampling a coset corresponding to a codeword $\mathbf{c} \in \mathcal{C}$ depends on its Lee weight profile (see Sect. 3). We can compute the Lee weight profiles of the code offline using the Schur product, for example, according to the extended version [5, Appendix C], and store this information.

For $\mathbf{t} \neq \mathbf{0}$, we can use the symmetrized weight enumerator of the coset $\mathcal{C} + \mathbf{t}$. When $q = 2$, it is simply the Hamming weight enumerator of the coset of a code (see the extended version [5, Appendix A])[10]. When $q < 5$, we can use a similar approach as in the binary case to compute the symmetrized weight enumerator of $\mathcal{C} + \mathbf{t}$, but for $q \geq 5$ we assume access to an oracle that performs this calculation offline, since we cannot rely on the well-known relationship between a code and its dual [1].

In Algorithm 1, we let $\tilde{\boldsymbol{\nu}}$ be *any* codeword in $\mathcal{C} + \mathbf{t}$ that has Lee weight profile $\boldsymbol{\ell}$ and $\mathcal{D}_{q\mathbb{Z}^n+(\mathcal{C}+\mathbf{t}),s}(q\mathbb{Z}^n + \tilde{\boldsymbol{\nu}})$ be the probability that we sample a lattice vector in any coset whose representative has Lee weight profile $\boldsymbol{\ell}$. By Lemma 1, $\mathcal{D}_{q\mathbb{Z}^n+(\mathcal{C}+\mathbf{t}),s}(q\mathbb{Z}^n + \tilde{\boldsymbol{\nu}})$ is proportional to a term in the symmetrized weight enumerator of $\mathcal{C} + \mathbf{t}$ with exponents defined by the coordinates of $\boldsymbol{\ell}$. We select

[10] When $q = 2$ and $\mathbf{t} = \mathbf{0}$, we recover the Construction A sampler from [9].

**Algorithm 1:** Sampling for General Construction A

**Require:** $\Lambda_{\mathrm{A}} = q\mathbb{Z}^n + \mathcal{C}, \mathcal{C} \subseteq \mathbb{Z}_q^n$ and $\mathrm{swe}_{\mathcal{C}+\mathbf{t}}(\cdot)$ for $\mathbf{t} \in \mathbb{Z}_q^n$ and sampling width $s$
**Ensure:** $\mathbf{x} \leftarrow \mathcal{D}_{\Lambda_{\mathrm{A}}+\mathbf{t},s}(\mathbf{x})$
1: Select Lee weight profile $\boldsymbol{\ell}$ with probability $p_{\boldsymbol{\ell}} = A_{\boldsymbol{\ell}} \cdot \mathcal{D}_{q\mathbb{Z}^n+(\mathcal{C}+\mathbf{t}),s}(q\mathbb{Z}^n + \tilde{\boldsymbol{\nu}})$ where $A_{\boldsymbol{\ell}}$ is the respective coefficient of $\mathrm{swe}_{\mathcal{C}+\mathbf{t}}(\cdot)$
2: Select a codeword $\boldsymbol{\nu} \in \mathcal{C} + \mathbf{t}$ with Lee weight profile $\boldsymbol{\ell}$ uniformly at random
3: **for** $j \in [1:n]$ **do**
  $x_j \leftarrow q \cdot \mathrm{Sampler}_{\mathbb{Z}+\nu_j/q}(s/q)$
**end**
4: **return** $\mathbf{x} = (x_1, \ldots, x_n)$

$\boldsymbol{\ell}$ with probability $\mathcal{D}_{q\mathbb{Z}^n+(\mathcal{C}+\mathbf{t}),s}(q\mathbb{Z}^n + \tilde{\boldsymbol{\nu}})$ weighted by the number of codewords $A_{\boldsymbol{\ell}}$ with Lee weight profile $\boldsymbol{\ell}$. We then select a single codeword $\boldsymbol{\nu}$ associated to $\boldsymbol{\ell}$ uniformly over all such $A_{\boldsymbol{\ell}}$ codewords. We output a final lattice vector $\mathbf{x} = q\mathbf{z}+\boldsymbol{\nu}$ with $\mathbf{z} \in \mathbb{Z}^n$, by sampling $q\mathbb{Z}^n + (\mathcal{C} + \mathbf{t})$ using one dimensional $\mathbb{Z}$-samplers. The correctness of Algorithm 1 follows by applying the reduction in Theorem 1 with the general method of coset decomposition sampling.

*Example 2.* Consider the $\mathrm{D}_n$ lattice, obtained via binary Construction A as $\mathrm{D}_n = 2\mathbb{Z}^n + \mathcal{P}_n$, where $\mathcal{P}_n$ is the parity-check code and a shift $\mathbf{t} = \mathbf{0}$. There are $\binom{n}{2m}$ vectors of weight $2m$ in $\mathcal{P}_n$. The probability of selecting such coset is

$$p_{2m} = \binom{n}{2m} \frac{\Theta_{\mathbb{Z}+1/2}(4z)^{2m} \Theta_{\mathbb{Z}}(4z)^{n-2m}}{\Theta_{\mathrm{D}_n}(z)}$$

as given in [9, Eq. 3]. Hence, to sample in $\mathrm{D}_n$, we proceed as in Algorithm 2, according to [9]. ◊

Sampling in $\mathrm{D}_n + \mathbf{t}$, where $\mathbf{t} \neq \mathbf{0}$ will be discussed next.

**Algorithm 2:** Sampling over $\mathrm{D}_n$

**Require:** $\mathrm{D}_n = 2\mathbb{Z}^n + \mathcal{P}_n$ and sampling width $s$
**Ensure:** $\mathbf{x} \leftarrow \mathcal{D}_{\mathrm{D}_n,s}(\mathbf{x})$
1: Select $m \in \{1, \ldots, \lfloor n/2 \rfloor\}$ with probability $p_{2m}$
2: Select a subset $\mathcal{J} \subset \{1, \ldots, n\}$ with size $2m$
3: **for** $j \in \mathcal{J}$ **do**
  $x_j \leftarrow 2 \cdot \mathrm{Sampler}_{\mathbb{Z}+1/2}(s/2)$
**end**
4: **for** $j \in \{1, \ldots, n\} \setminus \mathcal{J}$ **do**
  $x_j \leftarrow 2 \cdot \mathrm{Sampler}_{\mathbb{Z}}(s/2)$
**end**
5: **return** $\mathbf{x} = (x_1, \ldots, x_n)$

### 5.2 Sampling Construction B Lattices

The Construction B lattice can be written as $\Lambda_{\mathrm{B}}(\overline{\mathcal{C}}) = 2\,\mathrm{D}_n + \overline{\mathcal{C}}$. Thus, sampling from $\Lambda_{\mathrm{B}}$ requires base samplers of the $\mathrm{D}_n$ lattice [9, Alg. 7]. Campello and Belfiore provide a sampler for $\Lambda_{\mathrm{B}}(\overline{\mathcal{C}})$ when $\mathbf{t} = \mathbf{0}$, which we summarize below.

Note that any permutation of coordinates is an automorphism of $\mathrm{D}_n$ [10, p. 118] and the addition by a lattice vector is an affine automorphism [10, p. 91], so it follows that $2\,\mathrm{D}_n + \mathbf{c} \simeq 2\,\mathrm{D}_n + (1^w, 0^{n-w})$ as lattices since $\overline{\mathcal{C}}$ is doubly even, so the sum of the coordinates of $\mathbf{c}$ is even and therefore $\mathbf{c} \in \mathrm{D}_n$. It follows that the theta series of a coset $2\,\mathrm{D}_n + \mathbf{c}$ depends only on the Hamming weight $w = w_{\mathrm{H}}(\mathbf{c})$. The theta series of $2(\mathrm{D}_n + \mathbf{c}/2)$ [9, Sec. VI] is

$$\begin{aligned}\Theta_{\mathrm{D}_n + \mathbf{c}/2}(z) &= \Theta_{\mathrm{D}_w + (\frac{1}{2}^w)}(4z)\Theta_{\mathrm{D}_{n-w}}(4z)\\ &\quad + \Theta_{\mathrm{D}_w + \left(\frac{3}{2}^1, \frac{1}{2}^{w-1}\right)}(4z)\Theta_{\mathrm{D}_{n-w} + (1^1, 0^{n-w-1})}(4z).\end{aligned}$$

Let $\mathcal{D}_{\Lambda_{\mathrm{B}},s}(2\,\mathrm{D}_n(\mathbf{c}) + (1^w, 0^{n-w})) = \Theta_{2\,\mathrm{D}_n + (1^w, 0^{n-w})}(z)/\Theta_{\Lambda_{\mathrm{B}}}(z)$ be the probability that a lattice vector sampled from the distribution on $\Lambda_{\mathrm{B}}$ lies in the coset $2\,\mathrm{D}_n + (1^w, 0^{n-w})$. The sampling procedure works by sampling a Hamming weight $w$ with probability $p_w = A_w \mathcal{D}_{\Lambda_{\mathrm{B}},s}(2\,\mathrm{D}_n + (1^w, 0^{n-w}))$, similar to the procedure for Construction A. The sampler selects a codeword $\mathbf{c} \in \overline{\mathcal{C}}$ uniformly from the set of all codewords of Hamming weight $w$. Next, we decompose $\mathrm{D}_n = (\mathrm{D}_w \oplus \mathrm{D}_{n-w}) \bigcup (\overline{\mathrm{D}}_w \oplus \overline{\mathrm{D}}_{n-w})$ where $\overline{\mathrm{D}}_n = \mathrm{D}_n + (1^1, 0^{n-1})$ by [9, Eq. (9)]. We then sample from $\mathrm{D}_w \oplus \mathrm{D}_{n-w}$ with probability $p_{\mathrm{even},w} \triangleq \mathcal{D}_{2\,\mathrm{D}_n + \mathbf{c},s}((2\,\mathrm{D}_w + (1^w)) \oplus 2\,\mathrm{D}_{n-w})$. Additionally, we sample from the complementary part with probability $1 - p_{\mathrm{even},w}$. This allows us to sample from a shift of a $\mathrm{D}_n$ lattice.

We now apply this idea to sampling a shift of $\mathrm{D}_n + \mathbf{t}$ where $\mathbf{t} \in \mathbb{Z}_2^n$. By replacing $\mathbf{c}/2$ with $\mathbf{t}$, we get that the theta series $\mathrm{D}_n + \mathbf{t}$ is

$$\Theta_{\mathrm{D}_n + \mathbf{t}}(z) = \Theta_{\mathrm{D}_w + \mathbf{1}}(4z)\Theta_{\mathrm{D}_{n-w}}(4z) + \Theta_{\mathrm{D}_w + (2^1, 1^{w-1})}(4z)\Theta_{\mathrm{D}_{n-w} + (1^1, 0^{n-w-1})}(4z)$$

where $w = w_{\mathrm{H}}(\mathbf{t})$. Note that since $\mathbf{t}$ is not necessarily a codeword in $\overline{\mathcal{C}}$, we may have that $w$ is odd. We decompose $\mathrm{D}_n$ as before. After that, we sample from $\mathrm{D}_w \oplus \mathrm{D}_{n-w}$ with probability $p_{\mathrm{even},w} \triangleq \mathcal{D}_{\mathrm{D}_n + \mathbf{t},s}((\mathrm{D}_w + (1^w)) \oplus \mathrm{D}_{n-w})$, and from the complementary part of the decomposition with probability $1 - p_{\mathrm{even},w}$. Notice that if $w$ is even, sampling $\mathrm{D}_n + \mathbf{t}$ is equivalent to sampling $\mathrm{D}_n$ when $\mathbf{t} = \mathbf{0}$.

### 5.3 Sampling Construction D Lattices for $L \geq 2$

Decomposing a linear $q$-ary code using a code formula offers significant advantages in the sampling process when $\mathbf{t} = \mathbf{0}$, as was the case for Construction B, and now we extend to a multilevel Construction D lattice. Consider a filtration of sublattices of a Construction D lattice of the form

$$\begin{aligned}2^L\mathbb{Z}^n + 2^{L-1}\mathcal{C}_L &\subseteq 2^L\mathbb{Z}^n + 2^{L-1}\mathcal{C}_L + 2^{L-2}\mathcal{C}_{L-2} \subseteq \ldots\\ &\subseteq 2^L\mathbb{Z}^n + 2^{L-1}\mathcal{C}_L + \ldots + 2\mathcal{C}_2 + \mathcal{C}_1 \triangleq \Lambda_{\mathrm{D}}\end{aligned}$$

where we notice that the first lattice in the filtration is a shifted Construction A lattice scaled by $2^{L-1}$ for $L \geq 1$.

Our sampler begins at the first level of the filtration and samples $\mathbf{c}_L \in \mathcal{C}_L$ with respect to a scaled Construction A lattice. The sampler proceeds to sample the next codeword by considering the next level of the filtration, and so on. After we have sampled $\mathbf{c}_j$ for $j \in [1 : L]$, we sample a lattice point from the overall lattice using base samplers of $\mathbb{Z}^n$ or $\mathrm{D}_n$.

To illustrate, we present a summary of the method for $L = 2$ in Algorithm 3. Note that in line 7, $\omega_{0,0}$ is simply $n - w_H(\mathbf{c}_1 + 2\mathbf{c}_2)$ and one can use the Hamming weight instead of calculating the Lee weight profile in this case.

**Algorithm 3:** Sampling for $L = 2$

**Require:** $\Lambda_{\mathrm{D}} = 4\mathbb{Z}^n + 2\mathcal{C}_2 + \mathcal{C}_1$, $\mathcal{C}_1 \subseteq \mathcal{C}_2$ closed under Schur product, $W_{\mathcal{C}_2}(\cdot)$, $\mathrm{swe}_{2\mathcal{C}_2+\mathcal{C}_1}(\cdot)$ and sampling width $s$
**Ensure:** $\mathbf{x} \leftarrow \mathcal{D}_{\Lambda_{\mathrm{D}},s}(\mathbf{x})$
1: $\Lambda_1 \leftarrow 4\mathbb{Z}^n + 2\mathcal{C}_2$
2: $A_w \leftarrow \#\{\mathbf{c}_2 \in \mathcal{C}_2 : w_{\mathrm{H}}(\mathbf{c}_2) = w\}$
3: $\mathcal{S}_w \leftarrow \{\mathbf{c}_2 \in \mathcal{C}_2 : w_{\mathrm{H}}(\mathbf{c}_2) = w\}$
4: Sample a weight $w$ with probability $p_w = A_w \cdot \mathcal{D}_{\Lambda_1,s}(4\mathbb{Z}^n + 2\tilde{\mathbf{c}}_2)$
5: Sample $\mathbf{c}_2 \leftarrow \mathcal{S}_w$ uniformly at random
6: $\Lambda_2 \leftarrow 4\mathbb{Z}^n + 2\mathcal{C}_2 + \mathcal{C}_1 = \Lambda_{\mathrm{D}}$
7: $A_{\boldsymbol{\ell}} \leftarrow \#\{\mathbf{c}_1 \in \mathcal{C}_1 : [\omega_{0,0}, w_{\mathrm{H}}(\mathbf{c}_1), \omega_{0,1}] = \boldsymbol{\ell}\}$
8: $\mathcal{S}_{\boldsymbol{\ell}} \leftarrow \{\mathbf{c}_1 \in \mathcal{C}_1 : [\omega_{0,0}, w_{\mathrm{H}}(\mathbf{c}_1), \omega_{0,1}] = \boldsymbol{\ell}\}$
9: Sample Lee weight profile $\boldsymbol{\ell}$ with probability $p_{\boldsymbol{\ell}} = A_{\boldsymbol{\ell}} \cdot \frac{\mathcal{D}_{\Lambda_{\mathrm{D}},s}(4\mathbb{Z}^n+2\mathbf{c}_2+\tilde{\mathbf{c}}_1)}{\mathcal{D}_{\Lambda_1,s}(4\mathbb{Z}^n+2\tilde{\mathbf{c}}_2)}$
10: Sample $\mathbf{c}_1 \leftarrow \mathcal{S}_{\boldsymbol{\ell}}$ uniformly at random
11: $\mathbf{c} \leftarrow 2\mathbf{c}_2 + \mathbf{c}_1$
12: **for** $j \in [1 : n]$ **do**
    $x_j \leftarrow 4 \cdot \mathrm{Sampler}_{\mathbb{Z}+c_j/4}(s/4)$
  **end**
13: **return** $\mathbf{x} = (x_1, \ldots, x_n)$

Alternatively, we can directly use $\mathcal{C} = 2\mathcal{C}_2 + \mathcal{C}_1$ as a code over $\mathbb{Z}_4$ and sample in a single step without defining conditional probabilities. In this case, we can sample the 2-level lattice $\Lambda_{\mathrm{D}} = 4\mathbb{Z}^n + 2\mathcal{C}_2 + \mathcal{C}_1$ by using Algorithm 1 with $q = 4$ and $\mathcal{C} = 2\mathcal{C}_2 + \mathcal{C}_1$. The correctness of Algorithm 3 is analogous to the correctness of Algorithm 4, by restricting it to two levels. We next provide the description and correctness proof for Algorithm 4.

For a 3-level Construction D lattice $\Lambda_{\mathrm{D}} = 8\mathbb{Z}^n + 4\mathcal{C}_3 + 2\mathcal{C}_2 + \mathcal{C}_1$, we repeat what was done for $L = 2$ to sample with respect to the first two levels of the filtration. Next, we sample with respect to the third and final filtration, which is the entire lattice $\Lambda_{\mathrm{D}}$, under the condition that $\mathbf{c}_3$ and $\mathbf{c}_2$ were previously sampled in the first two steps. The theta series of a coset in this lattice is, according to (11)

$$\Theta_{8\mathbb{Z}^n+4\mathbf{c}_3+2\mathbf{c}_2+\mathbf{c}_1}(z) = \vartheta_3(64z)^{\omega_{0,0,0}}\psi_8(64z)^{\omega_{1,0,0}+\omega_{1,1,1}}\left(\frac{\vartheta_2(16z)}{2}\right)^{\omega_{0,1,0}+\omega_{0,1,1}}$$
$$\Theta_{\mathbb{Z}+\frac{3}{8}}(64z)^{\omega_{1,1,0}+\omega_{1,0,1}}\vartheta_2(64z)^{\omega_{0,0,1}}$$

where $\mathbf{c}_1 \in \mathcal{C}_1$. The probability of a coset depends on the frequency values $\omega_{\boldsymbol{\alpha}}(\mathbf{c}_1, \mathbf{c}_2, \mathbf{c}_3)$, where $\boldsymbol{\alpha} \in \mathbb{F}_2^3$. Now, let $A_{\mathbf{k}}$ be the number of Lee weight profiles $\mathbf{k}$ defined by these frequency values and let $\tilde{\mathbf{c}}_1 \in \mathcal{C}_1$ be any codeword having weight profile $\mathbf{k}$ with respect to fixed $\mathbf{c}_3, \mathbf{c}_2$. Define the conditional probability that we select a vector from a discrete Gaussian on $8\mathbb{Z}^n + 4\mathcal{C}_3 + 2\mathcal{C}_2 + \mathcal{C}_1$ which lies in a coset of the form $8\mathbb{Z}^n + 4\mathbf{c}_3 + 2\mathbf{c}_2 + \tilde{\mathbf{c}}_1$ given that we have previously sampled $\mathbf{c}_3, \mathbf{c}_2$. The probability that we have already sampled $\mathbf{c}_3$ and $\mathbf{c}_2$ is the probability that step 1 outputs $\mathbf{c}_3$ and step 2 outputs $\mathbf{c}_2$. Overall, it follows that

$$p_{\text{cond}_2} \triangleq \frac{\mathcal{D}_{8\mathbb{Z}^n+4\mathcal{C}_3+2\mathcal{C}_2+\mathcal{C}_1,s}(8\mathbb{Z}^n + 4\mathbf{c}_3 + 2\mathbf{c}_2 + \tilde{\mathbf{c}}_1)}{\mathcal{D}_{8\mathbb{Z}^n+4\mathcal{C}_3+2\mathcal{C}_2,s}(8\mathbb{Z}^n + 4\mathbf{c}_3 + 2\tilde{\mathbf{c}}_2)}.$$

We sample $\mathbf{c}_1$ in two steps: first, we choose a Lee weight profile $\mathbf{k}$ with probability $p_{\mathbf{k}} = A_{\mathbf{k}} \cdot p_{\text{cond}_2}$, then we sample a codeword $\mathbf{c}_1$ uniformly from all codewords in $\mathcal{C}_1$ that have Lee weight profile $k$ with respect to $\mathbf{c}_3, \mathbf{c}_2$. This selects a codeword $\mathbf{c}_1 \in \mathcal{C}_1$ with probability $p_{\mathbf{k}}/A_{\mathbf{k}}$.

The final step is to sample a vector from $\mathcal{D}_{8\mathbb{Z}^n+4\mathbf{c}_3+2\mathbf{c}_2+\mathbf{c}_1,s}$ by recursively applying one-dimensional samplers of $\mathbb{Z}$ and its shifts. The sampler outputs a lattice vector of total probability

$$\mathcal{D}_{\Lambda_1,s}(8\mathbb{Z}^n + 4\mathbf{c}_3) \cdot \frac{\mathcal{D}_{\Lambda_2,s}(8\mathbb{Z}^n+4\mathbf{c}_3+2\mathbf{c}_2)}{\mathcal{D}_{\Lambda_1,s}(8\mathbb{Z}^n+4\mathbf{c}_3)} \cdot \frac{\mathcal{D}_{\Lambda_D,s}(8\mathbb{Z}^n+\mathbf{c})}{\mathcal{D}_{\Lambda_2,s}(8\mathbb{Z}^n+4\mathbf{c}_3+2\mathbf{c}_2)}\cdot$$
$$\mathcal{D}_{8\mathbb{Z}^n+4\mathbf{c}_3+2\mathbf{c}_2+\mathbf{c}_1,s}(8\mathbf{z} + \mathbf{c}) = \mathcal{D}_{\Lambda_D,s}(8\mathbb{Z}^n + \mathbf{c})\mathcal{D}_{8\mathbb{Z}^n+\mathbf{c},s}(8\mathbf{z} + \mathbf{c})$$
$$= \mathcal{D}_{\Lambda_D,s}(8\mathbf{z} + \mathbf{c}),$$

where $\Lambda_1 \subseteq \Lambda_2 \subseteq \Lambda_D = 8\mathbb{Z}^n + 4\mathcal{C}_3 + 2\mathcal{C}_2 + \mathcal{C}_1$ is the lattice filtration that we consider and $\mathbf{c} = 4\mathbf{c}_3 + 2\mathbf{c}_2 + \mathbf{c}_1$. This yields a sampling method that does not restrict the sampling width $s$ since it samples exactly from the true distribution of the lattice. We can extend this sampling technique to higher levels, as in Algorithm 4. The computation of Lee weight profiles can be performed offline, and the frequency of each Lee weight profile is contained in the symmetrized weight enumerator. This information is used in the online phase of sampling to define the relevant probabilities. We also sample codewords corresponding to a chosen Lee weight profile in the online phase.

### 5.4 Algorithm Complexity

For a general $L$-level Construction D lattice, we sample by recursively selecting codewords to obtain a coset representative $\mathbf{c} = 2^L\mathbf{c}_L + \ldots + 2\mathbf{c}_2 + \mathbf{c}_1$, then we sample a final lattice vector via one-dimensional samplers over the integers. Sampling these codewords depends on Lee weight profiles. In general, we may

**Algorithm 4:** Sampling for $L \geq 3$

**Require:** $\Lambda_{\text{D}} = 2^L\mathbb{Z}^n + 2^{L-1}\mathcal{C}_L + \ldots + 2\mathcal{C}_2 + \mathcal{C}_1$, $\mathcal{C}_j$ closed under Schur product for $j \in [1:L]$, $W_{\mathcal{C}_L}(\cdot)$, symmetrized weight enumerators of linear combinations of $\mathcal{C}_L, \ldots, \mathcal{C}_1$, sampling width $s$

**Ensure:** $\mathbf{x} \leftarrow \mathcal{D}_{\Lambda_{\text{D}},s}(\mathbf{x})$

1: Sample $\mathbf{c}_L$ and $\mathbf{c}_{L-1}$ as in Algorithm 3

2: $\Lambda_3 \leftarrow 2^L\mathbb{Z}^n + 2^{L-1}\mathcal{C}_L + 2^{L-2}\mathcal{C}_{L-1} + 2^{L-3}\mathcal{C}_{L-2}$

3: $A_{\mathbf{k}} \leftarrow \#\{\mathbf{c}_{L-2} \in \mathcal{C}_{L-2} : [\omega_{0,0,0}, \omega_{1,0,0} + \omega_{1,1,1}, \omega_{0,1,0} + \omega_{0,1,1}, \omega_{1,1,0} + \omega_{1,0,1}, \omega_{0,0,1}] = \mathbf{k}\}$

4: $\mathcal{S}_{\mathbf{k}} \leftarrow \{\mathbf{c}_{L-2} \in \mathcal{C}_{L-2} : [\omega_{0,0,0}, \omega_{1,0,0} + \omega_{1,1,1}, \omega_{0,1,0} + \omega_{0,1,1}, \omega_{1,1,0} + \omega_{1,0,1}, \omega_{0,0,1}] = \mathbf{k}\}$

5: Sample a Lee weight profile $k$ with probability
$p_{\mathbf{k}} = A_{\mathbf{k}} \cdot \frac{\mathcal{D}_{\Lambda_3,s}(2^L\mathbb{Z}^n + 2^{L-1}\mathbf{c}_L + 2^{L-2}\mathbf{c}_{L-1} + 2^{L-3}\tilde{\mathbf{c}}_{L-2})}{\mathcal{D}_{\Lambda_2,s}(2^L\mathbb{Z}^n + 2^{L-1}\mathbf{c}_L + 2^{L-2}\tilde{\mathbf{c}}_{L-1})}$

6: Sample $\mathbf{c}_{L-2} \leftarrow \mathcal{S}_{\mathbf{k}}$ uniformly at random

7: Repeat lines 4-8 for $\Lambda_4 \subseteq \ldots \subseteq \Lambda_{L-1} \subseteq \Lambda_L = \Lambda_{\text{D}}$

8: $\mathbf{c} \leftarrow 2^L\mathbf{c}_L + \ldots + 2\mathbf{c}_2 + \mathbf{c}_1$

9: **for** $j \in [1:n]$ **do**

  $x_j \leftarrow 2^L \cdot \text{Sampler}_{\mathbb{Z}+c_j/2^L}(s/2^L)$

**end**

10: **return** $\mathbf{x} = (x_1, \ldots, x_n)$

not have this information. Considering the Schur product of codewords might be an alternative; see the extended version [5, Appendix C].

In terms of complexity, Algorithm 4 first samples $\mathbf{c}_L$ with respect to its Hamming weight. We can compute the Hamming weight enumerator of $\mathcal{C}_L$ offline. To sample a codeword of a given weight, we can use a lookup table of the codewords sorted by weight. The online lookup time is $O(\log|\mathcal{C}_L|) = O(k_L)$ where $k_L$ is the dimension of $\mathcal{C}_L$, but the storage complexity of the table is at least the size of the code, which is exponential in $k_L$. Clearly, this is not polynomial, but we present cases where we can avoid using such lookup tables and still sample with respect to Hamming weight efficiently in Sect. 6.

Algorithm 4 proceeds to recursively sample from cosets of $\mathcal{C}_{L-1}, \ldots, \mathcal{C}_1$ with respect to Lee weight profiles. We can compute Lee weight profiles offline using, for example, the Schur product over $\mathcal{C}_{L-1}, \ldots, \mathcal{C}_1$. We need to compute the Lee weight profiles of $\mathcal{C}_L$ with $\mathcal{C}_{L-1}$ in the second step, then repeat with $\mathcal{C}_L, \mathcal{C}_{L-1}$ and $\mathcal{C}_{L-2}$ in the third step, and so on. However, notice that we can recover the Lee weight profiles in each step by simply performing the computation over all of the codes $\mathcal{C}_L, \ldots, \mathcal{C}_1$. That is, instead of first computing the Lee weight profiles for $\mathcal{C}_L, \mathcal{C}_{L-1}$ then $\mathcal{C}_L, \mathcal{C}_{L-1}, \mathcal{C}_{L-2}$ and so on, we can compute the Lee weight profiles for $\mathcal{C}_L, \ldots, \mathcal{C}_1$ once, then to get the LWP of $\mathcal{C}_L, \mathcal{C}_{L-1}$, for example, we can look at the subset of LWP when $\mathbf{c}_{L-2} = \ldots = \mathbf{c}_1 = \mathbf{0}$. This gives us the Lee weight profile of some codeword $2^{L-1}\mathbf{c}_L + 2^{L-2}\mathbf{c}_{L-1} + \mathbf{0} + \ldots + \mathbf{0}$. The complexity of this larger computation is $O(n \cdot |\mathcal{C}_L| \cdot \ldots \cdot |\mathcal{C}_1|) = O(n2^{k_L+\ldots+k_1})$ where $k_j$ is the dimension of $\mathcal{C}_j$, $j \in [1 : L]$. This is much larger than $O(k_L 2^{k_L})$, so the overall offline complexity is given by $O(n2^{k_L+\cdots+k_1})$.

The online complexity is harder to estimate since, in general, it is not efficient to sample codes of a given Hamming weight or of a given Lee weight profile. For a binary code, a very loose upper bound is $(n+1)(2+\lfloor \log_2 n \rfloor + k)$, where $k$ is the code dimension and $n$ is the code length. Observe that for the Leech lattice, for example, we need only 38 bits, while the upper bound gives 450 bits, considering $\mathbf{t} = 0$. For some small and root lattices, we can do much better (see Table 1).

We point out that computing Lee weight profiles do not depend on the sampling width $s$, so the choice of $s$ does not impact the offline complexity of the sampler. On the other hand, we can simplify the overall sampling procedure if we allow $s$ to be sufficiently above smoothing. For sufficiently large values of $s$, we can sample by choosing codewords uniformly at random, since the sampled lattice vectors now appear uniformly distributed over $\mathbb{R}^n/\Lambda$. This comes at a loss of increasing the sampling width.

*Limitations.* As a consequence, the sampling algorithm for Construction D with arbitrary $q$ and level $L$ is not usually efficient. This is expected since the major challenge of our sampling method relies on sampling codewords with respect to Lee weight profiles, which is a hard problem. Even for the simplest case when $L = 1$, we may not be able to sample a codeword of specific Hamming weight efficiently. However, given that the codewords can be sampled efficiently, the sampling method is consequently efficient and in particular, we can make the sampling width $s$ close to the smoothing parameter of the associated lattice. Therefore, speed-ups on our proposed sampling method depends on efficient sampling with respect to the Lee weight profiles of a code over $\mathbb{Z}_q$. Sampling codewords can be done efficiently for codes of reasonably small dimensions by enumeration or codes with some special structure [9, p. 167]. For example, the $(n, n-1)_2$ code consists of all $n$-tuples with an even number of non-zero coordinates. Due to its special structure, we can sample such a code by randomly sampling a subset of coordinates of even size. It is unclear how to optimize the computation of Lee weight profiles using the properties of the Schur product for certain structured codes. We provide some details for this in the extended version [5, Appendix C.2].

## 6 Sampling Remarkable Lattices

We apply our sampler to some remarkable lattices. Recall that our method only considers lattices that can be expressed via a code formula as in (1).

### 6.1 Sampling Root Lattices

The $\mathrm{D}_n$ lattice is constructed from the $(n, n-1)_2$ even weight code $\mathcal{C}_1$. We can sample $\mathrm{D}_n$ using Algorithm 2.

We can efficiently sample the exceptional root lattices $E_7$ and $E_8$. The Barnes-Wall lattice in dimension 8 will cover the case of $E_8$. We can build $E_7$ from Construction A using the $(7,4)_2$ Hamming code.

Alternatively, we can use the fact that $E_n \triangleq D_n^+$ from [10,13] when $n$ is even. All cosets of $D_n + (1/2, \dots, 1/2)$ have equal theta series by [9, Prop. 3]. Denote the probability that a lattice point in $D_n^+$ lies in the $D_n$ part of the decomposition as $\mathcal{D}_{D_n^+,s}(D_n) = \Theta_{D_n}(z)/\Theta_{D_n^+}(z)$. With probability $\mathcal{D}_{D_n^+,s}(D_n)$, sample from $D_n$. Otherwise, sample from $D_n + (1/2, \dots, 1/2)$. This is done by sampling $\mathbf{c} \in \mathcal{P}_n$ uniformly at random since all cosets of $D_n + (1/2, \dots, 1/2)$ have equal theta series.

To sample from $E_8 + \mathbf{t}$, we have that $E_8 + \mathbf{t} = D_8^+ + \mathbf{t}$. With probability $\mathcal{D}_{E_8 + \mathbf{t},s}(D_8 + \mathbf{t}) = \Theta_{D_8 + \mathbf{t}}(z)/\Theta_{E_8 + \mathbf{t}}(z)$, we use the sampler for $D_8 + \mathbf{t}$ as in Sect. 5.2. Otherwise we modify the sampler from Sect. 5.2 to sample from $D_8 + (1/2, \dots, 1/2) + \mathbf{t}$. Since the associated code is the even weight code and $q = 2$, the symmetrized weight enumerator corresponds to the Hamming weight enumerator, which is easy to obtain in this case. There is no need to store this information in a table; to sample a codeword of some even weight $w$, we randomly select $w$-out-of-$n$ coordinates to be nonzero.

### 6.2 Sampling Leech Lattice

We propose an alternative way to [9, Sec. VII] of sampling the Leech lattice $\Lambda_{24}$. We can write a scaled version of the Leech lattice as

$$\Lambda_{24} = (\mathbf{0} + 2\mathcal{G}_{24} + 4\mathcal{P}_{24} + 8\mathbb{Z}^{24}) \cup (\mathbf{1} + 2\mathcal{G}_{24} + 4\mathcal{O}_{24} + 8\mathbb{Z}^{24}), \tag{12}$$

where $\mathcal{G}_{24}$ is the $(24,12)_2$ Golay code, $\mathcal{P}_{24}$ is the $(24,23)_2$ parity-check code and $\mathcal{O}_{24}$ is a coset of $\mathcal{P}_{24}$ containing all codewords in $\mathbb{F}_2^{24}$ with odd weights, i.e., $\mathcal{O}_{24} = \{\mathbf{x} \in \mathbb{F}_2^{24} : \sum_{j=1}^{24} x_j \equiv 1 \bmod 2\} = (1, 0, \dots, 0) + \mathcal{P}_{24} \triangleq (1, 0^{23}) + \mathcal{P}_{24}$. We adopt the notation $(x_1^{n_1}, x_2^{n_2})$ to represent a vector where the first $n_1$ coordinates are $x_1$ followed by $n_2$ coordinates $x_2$.

We can rewrite $\Lambda_{24}$ as

$$\begin{aligned}
\Lambda_{24} &= (\mathbf{0} + 2\mathcal{G}_{24} + 4\mathcal{P}_{24} + 8\mathbb{Z}^{24}) \cup (\mathbf{1} + 2\mathcal{G}_{24} + 4\mathcal{O}_{24} + 8\mathbb{Z}^{24}) \\
&= (\mathbf{0} + 2\mathcal{G}_{24} + 4\mathcal{P}_{24} + 8\mathbb{Z}^{24}) \cup (\mathbf{1} + 2\mathcal{G}_{24} + 4\mathcal{P}_{24} + (4, 0^{23}) + 8\mathbb{Z}^{24}) \\
&= (\mathbf{0} + 2\mathcal{G}_{24} + 4\mathcal{P}_{24} + 8\mathbb{Z}^{24}) \cup (\mathbf{1} + 2\mathcal{G}_{24} + 4(2\mathbb{Z}^{24} + \mathcal{P}_{24} + (1, 0^{23}))) \\
&= 2\Lambda_B(\mathcal{G}_{24}) \cup (\mathbf{1} + 2\mathcal{G}_{24} + 4\overline{D}_{24}),
\end{aligned}$$

where $\overline{D}_n = D_n + (1, 0^{n-1})$. By the decomposition given by $D_n = (D_w \oplus D_{n-w}) \cup (\overline{D}_w \oplus \overline{D}_{n-w})$ in [9], we have that

$$\begin{aligned}
\overline{D}_n &= D_n + (1, 0^{n-1}) \\
&= (D_w + (1, 0^{w-1}) \oplus D_{n-w}) \cup (\overline{D}_w + (1, 0^{w-1}) \oplus \overline{D}_{n-w}) \\
&= (\overline{D}_w \oplus D_{n-w}) \cup (D_w + (2, 0^{w-1}) \oplus \overline{D}_{n-w}) \\
&\cong (\overline{D}_w \oplus D_{n-w}) \cup (D_w \oplus \overline{D}_{n-w}),
\end{aligned}$$

since $(2, 0^{w-1}) \in \mathrm{D}_w$. Consider a coset of the form $4\overline{D}_{24}+2\mathbf{c}+\mathbf{1}$. By [9, Eq. (10)], we have that

$$\begin{aligned}\Theta_{\overline{\mathrm{D}}_{24}+c/2+(1/4^{24})}(16z) &= \Theta_{\mathrm{D}_w+(3/2,1/2^{w-1})+(1/4^w)}(16z)\Theta_{\mathrm{D}_{n-w}+(1/4^{n-w})}(16z)\\ &\quad+\Theta_{\mathrm{D}_w+(1/2^w)+(1/4^w)}(16z)\Theta_{\mathrm{D}_{n-w}+(1,0^{n-w-1})+(1/4^{n-w})}(16z)\\ &= \Theta_{\mathrm{D}_w+(7/4,3/4^{w-1})}(16z)\Theta_{\mathrm{D}_{n-w}+(1/4^{n-w})}(16z)\\ &\quad+\Theta_{\mathrm{D}_w+(3/4^w)}(16z)\Theta_{\mathrm{D}_{n-w}+(5/4,1/4^{n-w-1})}(16z),\end{aligned}$$

so the theta series depends on the Hamming weight $w$ of $\mathbf{c} \in \mathcal{G}_{24}$. The Hamming weight distribution of the Golay code is well known, which can be read off of the Hamming weight enumerator $W_{\mathcal{G}_{24}}(x,y) = x^{24} + 759x^8y^{16} + 2576x^{12}y^{12} + 759x^{16}y^8 + y^{24}$ [34]. We can store this information in 38 bits (Table 1) by considering the symmetries of the Golay code.

### 6.3 Sampling Barnes-Wall Lattices

*Dimensions 4 and 8.* The Barnes-Wall lattices $\mathrm{BW}_4$ and $\mathrm{BW}_8$ are simply Construction A lattices from RM(1, 2) and RM(1, 3), respectively. Reed-Muller codes of order 1 have codewords with weight either $0, n/2$ or $n$. When $w = 0, n$ we have either $\mathbf{0}$ or $\mathbf{1}$. When $w = n/2$, there are $2^{m+1}-2$ codewords of weight $w$. These are all of the codewords in RM$(1, m)$ except the all-ones or all-zeros codeword. We can sample from this weight class using rejection sampling with $(2^{m+1}-2)/2^{m+1}$ iterations. As $m$ increases, this goes to 1. For $\mathrm{BW}_8 \triangleq \mathrm{E}_8$, storing the weight enumerator of the code takes 14 bits (Table 1). To briefly explain, given that the weight enumerator of the $(8, 4)_2$ Hamming code is $W_{\mathcal{H}_8}(x, y) = x^8 + 14x^4y^4 + y^8$, the table looks like {(0,1),(4,14),(8,1)}, where the first coordinate corresponds to the Hamming weight (since the code is binary) and the second is the number of codewords with that weight.

*Dimension 16.* The Barnes-Wall lattice $\mathrm{BW}_{16}$ is a Construction B lattice given by the code formula $4\mathbb{Z}^{16} + 2\,\mathrm{RM}(3, 4) + \mathrm{RM}(1, 4)$, since RM(1, 4) is a doubly even code. Therefore, we can apply the sampler proposed in Sect. 5.2 and need only to sample a codeword of fixed weight $w$ from RM(1, 4). To do this, we apply rejection sampling with = 1.067 iterations. Since this lattice is Construction B, we only need to store the Hamming weight information of the code RM(1, 4) by Theorem 4. This requires 17 bits of storage (Table 1).

*Dimension 32.* The Barnes-Wall lattice $\mathrm{BW}_{32}$ has the code formula $4\mathbb{Z}^{32} + 2\,\mathrm{RM}(3, 5) + \mathrm{RM}(1, 5)$ where RM(3, 5) is not the parity-check code. Therefore, we are in the case of Sect. 5.3, which requires us to sample a codeword $\mathbf{c}_2 \in \mathrm{RM}(3, 5)$ first by Hamming weight and $\mathbf{c}_1 \in \mathrm{RM}(1, 5)$ by computing Lee weight profiles. For sampling $\mathbf{c}_2$ by Hamming weight, we can enumerate the codewords of weight $w$ using design theory, which is detailed in the extended version [5, Appendix D]. We can compute Lee weight profiles for the second step offline or even move this step online since the size of RM(1, 5) is only twice the dimension of the lattice. The storage for the Lee weight profile requires around 418 bits.

*Dimensions* $\geq$ *64.* As the dimensions of the Barnes-Wall lattices grow, so do the dimensions of the Reed-Muller codes used to construct them. The online complexity will increase in response since we need to sample with respect to a chosen Lee weight profile over large codes.

Similarly to Barnes-Wall lattices, we briefly mention a family of Construction D lattices not addressed in the work of [13], denoted as $\mathrm{B}_n$ with $n = 2^m$, which are built from a tower of BCH codes. When the dimensions of the associated BCH codes are reasonably small, our sampler can be applied efficiently. These lattices are considered good packings in the sense that they are dense and have efficient decoding algorithms [4,29].

## 7 Improvements to State-of-the-Art Sampling

We discuss the improvements of our sampling method in some families of lattices, focusing on efficiency and restrictions on the sampling width. A summary is presented in Table 1 and supporting Sage [34] code can be found here https://github.com/mlie22/q-ary-sampling.

Given that the samplers in [13] mostly rely on $\mathbb{Z}$ samplers and do not require much additional computation whereas we require sampling codewords, we estimate a lower bound for the running time of our sampling algorithms by counting the number of calls to a $\mathbb{Z}$ sampler, which is used in a black-box manner. We assume the weight enumerators of all cosets of a linear code are known and ignore the costs of sampling codewords (which is cheap for small lattices), so this will give a reasonable estimate of the speed-up. Instead of explicitly stating these costs, we give some explanation on how one might sample codewords efficiently in several cases.

*Root Lattices.* In [13], the authors provide base samplers for the root lattices $\mathrm{D}_n$ ($n \geq 1$) and $\mathrm{E}_n$ ($n = 6, 7, 8$). We can sample these lattices with the method proposed in Sect. 5.2 using $n$ one-dimensional samplers of $\mathbb{Z}$ or $\mathbb{Z} + 1/2$. This is compared to the sampler in [13], which performs $n$ one-dimensional samplers of $\mathbb{Z}$ twice on average. The width of the sampler in [13] is approximately the smoothing parameter $s \approx \eta_\epsilon(\mathrm{D}_n)$, whereas the sampler proposed in Sect. 5.2 allows us to choose $s = \eta_\epsilon(\mathrm{D}_n)$ exactly. In terms of the number of calls to a $\mathbb{Z}$ sampler, our sampler is approximately twice as fast as [13]. This is supported by simulations performed in [34] for $n = 8, 16, 24$.

We can sample from $\mathrm{E}_7$ as a Construction A lattice with the $(7, 4)_2$ Hamming code. The codewords of weight 3 form a 1-(7,3,3) design, so every codeword of weight 3 uniquely decodes to a block in the design (see the extended version [5, Appendix D]). We can sample a codeword of weight 3 by sampling a block in the design via a choosing procedure as in [9, Sec. VII], then decoding. To sample a codeword of weight 4, we add the all-ones vector to a codeword of weight 3 due to the code's symmetry. Overall, we require 7 one-dimensional samplers of shifts of $\mathbb{Z}$ whereas [13] requires repeating the $\mathrm{E}_8$ base sampler four times on average, which results in 64 one-dimensional $\mathbb{Z}$ samplers, so our sampler is roughly 9 times faster. Our simulation compares by sampling 100,000 samples 8.64 times faster.

Regarding the $\mathrm{E}_8$ (or $\mathrm{BW}_8$) lattice, an improved gadget framework was proposed in [13, Sec. 10]. It was shown a gain of 9 bits in security and 113 bytes of the signature size for EAGLE-1024 while maintaining tight sampling. We can replace their $\mathrm{E}_8$ sampler with our sampler, which is more efficient and still samples at the smoothing parameter, preserving the security gains.

Recall that $\mathrm{E}_8$ is a Construction A lattice given by the code formula $2\mathbb{Z}^8 + \mathrm{RM}(1,3)$. Using the Construction A sampler, we first sample a weight $w \in \{0,4,8\}$, and then we sample a codeword with the corresponding weight. If $w = 0.8$, we obtain either an all-zero or an all-one codeword. Otherwise, all remaining codewords have weight 4. We apply rejection sampling to obtain a codeword of weight 4 with 1.143 iterations on average. The sampler then applies 8 one-dimensional samplers of $\mathbb{Z}$ and $\mathbb{Z} + 1/2$. Without the small cost of sampling codewords via rejection sampling, the complexity of our $\mathrm{E}_8$ sampler is dominated by sampling over the integers 8 times. In contrast, the sampling method from [13] requires sampling a shift of $\mathrm{D}_8$ with rejection sampling repeated 11 times to optimize the sampling width, which itself uses 8 samplers over $\mathbb{Z}$ twice on average. As a result, we expect our algorithm to be around 22 times faster. In fact, our simulations showed that our algorithm obtains 100,000 samples $\approx 25$ times faster than [13].

*Barnes-Wall Lattices Up to Dimension 64.* For the Barnes-Wall lattices of dimension 4,8, and 16, our sampler coincides with the Construction A and B samplers. In the state-of-the-art sampling of [13], the authors apply their idea of domain extension to sample a Barnes-Wall lattice $\mathrm{BW}_n$ using $\mathrm{BW}_{n/2}$ twice. They can sample a distribution of statistical distance at most $6\epsilon$ to $\mathcal{D}_{\mathrm{BW}_n,s}$ given that they have a discrete Gaussian sampler of $\mathrm{BW}_{n/2}$ with $s > \eta_\epsilon(\mathrm{BW}_{n/2})$ [13, Cor. 1].

Compared to the state-of-the-art sampling in [13], we can improve the sampling for $\mathrm{BW}_4$ and $\mathrm{BW}_8$ using Construction A sampling. To sample $\mathrm{BW}_{16}$ in [13], we sample $\mathrm{BW}_8$ which requires, on average, 16 one-dimensional $\mathbb{Z}$ samplers due to rejection sampling and gets repeated 11 times on average to optimize the sampling width $s \approx \eta_\epsilon(\mathrm{E}_8)$. Compared with our sampler for $\mathrm{BW}_{16}$, we sample a shift of $\mathrm{D}_{16}$ since this is a Construction B lattice, which translates to 16 one-dimensional samplers of shifts of $\mathbb{Z}$. In fact, we find that for general $\mathrm{BW}_n$, if we can sample with respect to Lee weight profiles efficiently, we estimate our sampler to be 11 times faster than in [13]. For our simulation with $\mathrm{BW}_{16}$, we obtain 100,000 samples 9.41 times faster than [13], which is reasonably close to our expectation.

*Leech Lattice.* The running time of sampling the Leech lattice for Espitau et al. [13] is dominated by the complexity of a $\mathrm{E}_8$ sampler by their choice of filtration $2\,\mathrm{E}_8 \subset T_\theta \subset T$ where $T_\theta \cong T \cong E_8$ [13, Sec. 8.2.3]. This requires 3 calls to an $E_8$ sampler and samples at a width that is approximately the smoothing parameter of $\mathrm{E}_8$ [13, Alg. 12], which is above $\eta_\epsilon(\Lambda_{24})$.

Recall $\Lambda_{24} = \Lambda_B(\mathcal{G}_{24}) \cup (\mathbf{1} + 2\mathcal{G}_{24} + 4\overline{\mathrm{D}}_{24})$. We sample from the Construction B part, as detailed in [9, p. 169], or from the $\mathbf{1} + 2\mathcal{G}_{24} + 4\overline{D}_{24}$ part using the Hamming weight of codewords in $\mathcal{G}_{24}$ following the procedure in [9, Sec. 6]. This samples twice as fast with $s = \eta_\epsilon(\Lambda_{24})$ since we require 24 samplers of a shift of $\mathrm{D}_n$, which in turn requires 24 one-dimensional samplers of shifts of $\mathbb{Z}$ [9, Alg. 7]. In comparison, the $\mathrm{E}_8$ sampler in [13] requires, on average, 16 one-dimensional $\mathbb{Z}$ samplers, which get called upon three times to sample the Leech lattice.

*Hexagonal Lattice.* Even if $\mathrm{A}_2$ is not a Construction A lattice, we include it for completeness since we use a technique based on coset decomposition [9, Sec. V].

Espitau et al. [13] propose an efficient sampler for the $\mathrm{A}_2$ root lattice, which the authors apply to sample in $\mathcal{R}_m = \mathbb{Z}[\zeta_m]$ where $m = 2^\ell 3^k$ for MITAKA. Using the fact that $\mathcal{R}_m \cong \bigoplus_{i=1}^{m/6} \mathcal{R}_3$, they sample in $\mathcal{R}_m$ by independently sampling $\mathrm{A}_2$ $m/6$ times [13, Sec. 9]. The width of the proposed $\mathrm{A}_2$ sampler is at the smoothing parameter $\eta_\epsilon(\mathrm{A}_2)$ for sufficiently small $\epsilon$ [13, p. 40] and, on average, requires 9 repetitions of the $\mathrm{E}_8$ sampler to acquire four samples in $\mathrm{A}_2$.

Following [9, Sec. V], we have the coset decomposition $\mathrm{A}_2 = \bigcup_{\mathbf{t}\in\mathcal{T}} \Lambda' + \mathbf{t}$ where $\Lambda' = \mathbb{Z} \oplus \sqrt{3}\mathbb{Z}$ and $\mathcal{T} = \{(0,0), (1/2, \sqrt{3}/2)\}$. Sample $\mathbf{t} = (0,0)$ with probability $\mathcal{D}_{\mathrm{A}_2,s}(\mathbb{Z} \oplus \sqrt{3}\mathbb{Z})$, then sample $\mathbf{x} \in \mathbb{Z} \oplus \sqrt{3}\mathbb{Z}$ from $\mathcal{D}_{\mathbb{Z}\oplus\sqrt{3}\mathbb{Z},s}(\mathbf{x})$ using two (scaled) one-dimensional samplers of $\mathbb{Z}$. Otherwise, sample $\mathbf{t} = (1/2, \sqrt{3}/2)$ with remaining probability $\mathcal{D}_{\mathrm{A}_2,s}(\mathbb{Z} \oplus \sqrt{3}\mathbb{Z} + \mathbf{t})$ and a lattice vector $\mathbf{x} + \mathbf{t}$ with probability $\mathcal{D}_{\mathbb{Z}\oplus\sqrt{3}\mathbb{Z}+\mathbf{t},s}(\mathbf{x} + \mathbf{t})$. We can sample $\mathbf{x} + \mathbf{t}$ with two (scaled) one-dimensional samplers of $\mathbb{Z} + 1/2$. This outputs four samples in $\mathrm{A}_2$ approximately 18 times faster. This comes from the fact that to obtain four samples of $\mathrm{A}_2$, the coset decomposition sampler requires 8 samplers over a shift of $\mathbb{Z}$ whereas the sampler in [13] repeats an $\mathrm{E}_8$ sampler 9 times on average which itself requires 2 repetitions of 8 samplers over $\mathbb{Z}$. In terms of the number of samplings over the integers, we expect our sampler to be 18 times faster. We compared our algorithm with the running time of the $\mathrm{E}_8$ sampler in [13], repeated the expected 9 times, which is the main work behind their $\mathrm{A}_2$ sampler. Our simulation showed that it performed better than estimated and was $\approx 32$ times faster over 100,000 samples. We do not use any table to store information about weight enumerators in this case, since no such table exists.

**Acknowledgments.** The authors are grateful to Antonio Campello and Franciele do Carmo Silva for helpful discussions. This work was supported in part by the Estonian Research Council through grant PRG2531 and in part by the Engineering and Physical Sciences Research Council (EPSRC) [grant numbers EP/X037010/1 and EP/Y004477/1]. Maja Lie acknowledges support from the Engineering and Physical Sciences Research Council (EPSRC) [grant number EP/W524323/1] and Imperial College London's I-X Centre for AI in Science. This work was done partially when Maiara Bollauf was a postdoctoral fellow at Simula UiB.

## References


1. Abdelghany, N., Wood, J.A.: Failure of the MacWilliams identities for the Lee weight enumerator over $\mathbb{Z}_m$, $m \geq 5$. Discret. Math. **343**(11), 112036 (2020)
2. Aggarwal, D., Dadush, D., Regev, O., Stephens-Davidowitz, N.: Solving the shortest vector problem in $2^n$ time using discrete Gaussian sampling: extended abstract. In: Proceedings of the Forty-Seventh Annual ACM Symposium on Theory of Computing – STOC 2015, pp. 733–742. Association for Computing Machinery, New York (2015)
3. Aggarwal, D., Dadush, D., Stephens-Davidowitz, N.: Solving the closest vector problem in $2^n$ time – the discrete Gaussian strikes again! In: 2015 IEEE 56th Annual Symposium on Foundations of Computer Science, pp. 563–582 (2015)
4. Barnes, E.S., Sloane, N.J.A.: New lattice packings of spheres. Can. J. Math. **35**(1), 117–130 (1983)
5. Bollauf, M.F., Lie, M., Ling, C.: On Gaussian sampling for q-ary lattices and linear codes with Lee weight. Cryptology ePrint Archive, Paper 2025/087 (2025). https://eprint.iacr.org/2025/087
6. Bollauf, M.F., Lin, H.Y., Ytrehus, Ø.: Secrecy gain of formally unimodular lattices from codes over the integers modulo 4. IEEE Trans. Inf. Theory **70**(5), 3309–3329 (2023)
7. Borwein, J., Borwein, P.: Pi and the AGM: A Study in Analytic Number Theory and Computational Complexity. Wiley-Interscience and Canadian Mathematics Series of Monographs and Texts. Wiley, New York (1987)
8. Brakerski, Z., Langlois, A., Peikert, C., Regev, O., Stehlé, D.: Classical hardness of learning with errors. In: Proceedings of the Forty-Fifth Annual ACM Symposium on Theory of Computing – STOC 2013, pp. 575–584. Association for Computing Machinery, New York (2013)
9. Campello, A., Belfiore, J.: Sampling algorithms for lattice Gaussian codes. In: 24th International Zurich Seminar on Communications, pp. 165–169 (2016)
10. Conway, J., Sloane, N.: Sphere Packings, Lattices and Groups, 3rd edn. Springer, New York (1999)
11. Ducas, L., van Woerden, W.: On the lattice isomorphism problem, quadratic forms, remarkable lattices, and cryptography. In: Dunkelman, O., Dziembowski, S. (eds.) EUROCRYPT 2022. LNCS, vol. 13277, pp. 643–673. Springer, Cham (2022). https://doi.org/10.1007/978-3-031-07082-2_23
12. Duke, W.: On codes and Siegel modular forms. Int. Math. Res. Not. **1993**(5), 125–136 (1993)
13. Espitau, T., Wallet, A., Yu, Y.: On Gaussian sampling, smoothing parameter and application to lattice signatures. In: Guo, J., Steinfeld, R. (eds.) Advances in Cryptology - ASIACRYPT 2023, pp. 65–97. Springer, Singapore (2023)
14. Forney, D.: Coset codes I: introduction and geometrical classification. IEEE Trans. Inf. Theory **34**(5), 1123–1151 (1989)
15. Gentry, C., Peikert, C., Vaikuntanathan, V.: Trapdoors for hard lattices and new cryptographic constructions. In: Proceedings of the Fortieth Annual ACM Symposium on Theory of Computing – STOC 2008, pp. 197–206. Association for Computing Machinery, New York (2008)
16. Harshan, J., Viterbo, E., Belfiore, J.: Construction of Barnes-Wall lattices from linear codes over rings. In: 2012 IEEE International Symposium on Information Theory, pp. 3110–3114. IEEE (2012)

17. Horlemann, A.L., Khathuria, K., Newman, M., Sakzad, A., Cabello, C.V.: Lattice-based vulnerabilities in Lee metric post-quantum cryptosystems. Cryptology ePrint Archive, Paper 2024/1495 (2024). https://eprint.iacr.org/2024/1495
18. Hörmann, F., van Woerden, W.: FuLeakage: breaking FuLeeca by learning attacks. In: Reyzin, L., Stebila, D. (eds.) CRYPTO 2024. LNCS, vol. 14925, pp. 253–286. Springer, Cham (2024). https://doi.org/10.1007/978-3-031-68391-6_8
19. Hu, S., Nebe, G.: Strongly perfect lattices sandwiched between Barnes-Wall lattices. J. Lond. Math. Soc. **101**, 1068–1089 (2018)
20. Kositwattanarerk, W., Oggier, F.E.: Connections between Construction D and related constructions of lattices. Des. Codes Crypt. **73**, 441–455 (2013)
21. Ling, C., Belfiore, J.C.: Achieving AWGN channel capacity with lattice Gaussian coding. IEEE Trans. Inf. Theory **60**(10), 5918–5929 (2014)
22. Ling, C., Luzzi, L., Belfiore, J.C., Stehlé, D.: Semantically secure lattice codes for the Gaussian wiretap channel. IEEE Trans. Inf. Theory **60**(10), 6399–6416 (2014)
23. MacWilliams, F.J., Sloane, N.J.A.: The Theory of Error-Correcting Codes. North-Holland, Amsterdam (1977)
24. Maher, D.P.: Lee polynomials of codes and theta functions of lattices. Can. J. Math. **30**(4), 738–747 (1978)
25. Micciancio, D., Nicolosi, A.: Efficient bounded distance decoders for Barnes-Wall lattices. In: 2008 IEEE International Symposium on Information Theory, pp. 2484–2488 (2008)
26. Micciancio, D., Regev, O.: Worst-case to average-case reductions based on Gaussian measures. SIAM J. Comput. **37**(1), 267–302 (2007)
27. Micciancio, D., Regev, O.: Lattice-Based Cryptography, pp. 147–191. Springer, Heidelberg (2009)
28. Micciancio, D., Walter, M.: Gaussian sampling over the integers: efficient, generic, constant-time. In: Katz, J., Shacham, H. (eds.) CRYPTO 2017. LNCS, vol. 10402, pp. 455–485. Springer, Cham (2017). https://doi.org/10.1007/978-3-319-63715-0_16
29. Mook, E., Peikert, C.: Lattice (list) decoding near Minkowski's inequality. IEEE Trans. Inf. Theory **68**, 863–870 (2020)
30. Peikert, C.: An efficient and parallel gaussian sampler for lattices. In: Rabin, T. (ed.) CRYPTO 2010. LNCS, vol. 6223, pp. 80–97. Springer, Heidelberg (2010). https://doi.org/10.1007/978-3-642-14623-7_5
31. Regev, O., Stephens-Davidowitz, N.: A reverse Minkowski theorem. In: Proceedings of the 49th Annual ACM SIGACT Symposium on Theory of Computing – STOC 2017, pp. 941–953. Association for Computing Machinery, New York (2017)
32. Ritterhoff, S., et al.: FuLeeca: a Lee-based signature scheme. In: Esser, A., Santini, P. (eds.) Code-Based Cryptography, pp. 56–83. Springer, Cham (2023). https://doi.org/10.1007/978-3-031-46495-9_4
33. Shparlinski, I.E., Steinfeld, R.: Noisy Chinese remaindering in the Lee norm. J. Complex. **20**(2), 423–437 (2004)
34. The Sage Developers: SageMath, the Sage Mathematics Software System (2022). https://www.sagemath.org
35. Wan, Z.X.: Quaternary Codes. World Scientific, Singapore (1997)
36. Weger, V., Khathuria, K., Horlemann, A.L., Battaglioni, M., Santini, P., Persichetti, E.: On the hardness of the Lee syndrome decoding problem. Adv. Math. Commun. **18**(1), 233–266 (2024)

# Wagner's Algorithm Provably Runs in Subexponential Time for SIS$^\infty$

Léo Ducas[1,2], Lynn Engelberts[1,3](✉), and Johanna Loyer[1]

[1] Centrum Wiskunde & Informatica, Amsterdam, The Netherlands
{l.ducas,lynn.engelberts}@cwi.nl, johanna.loyer@inria.fr
[2] Leiden University, Leiden, The Netherlands
[3] QuSoft, Amsterdam, The Netherlands

**Abstract.** At CRYPTO 2015, Kirchner and Fouque claimed that a carefully tuned variant of the Blum-Kalai-Wasserman (BKW) algorithm (JACM 2003) should solve the Learning with Errors problem (LWE) in slightly subexponential time for modulus $q = n^{\Theta(1)}$ and narrow error distribution, when given enough LWE samples. Taking a modular view, one may regard BKW as a combination of Wagner's algorithm (CRYPTO 2002), run over the corresponding dual problem, and the Aharonov-Regev distinguisher (JACM 2005). Hence the subexponential Wagner step alone should be of interest for solving this dual problem – namely, the Short Integer Solution problem (SIS) – but this appears to be undocumented so far.

We re-interpret this Wagner step as walking backward through a chain of projected lattices, zigzagging through some auxiliary superlattices. We further randomize the bucketing step using Gaussian randomized rounding to exploit the powerful discrete Gaussian machinery. This approach avoids sample amplification and turns Wagner's algorithm into an approximate discrete Gaussian sampler for $q$-ary lattices.

For an SIS lattice with $n$ equations modulo $q$, this algorithm runs in subexponential time $\exp(O(n/\log\log n))$ to reach a Gaussian width parameter of, say, $s = q/\mathrm{polylog}(n)$ only requiring $m = n+\omega(n/\log\log n)$ many SIS variables. For instance, this directly provides a provable algorithm for solving the Short Integer Solution problem in the infinity norm (SIS$^\infty$) for norm bounds $\beta = q/\mathrm{polylog}(n)$. This variant of SIS underlies the security of the NIST post-quantum cryptography standard ML-DSA, also known as Dilithium. Despite its subexponential complexity, Wagner's algorithm does not appear to threaten ML-DSA's concrete security.

**Keywords:** Wagner's algorithm · Discrete Gaussian sampling · Short Integer Solution problem (SIS) · Lattice-based cryptography · Cryptanalysis

## 1 Introduction

The Short Integer Solution problem (SIS) is a fundamental problem in lattice-based cryptography. It was introduced by Ajtai [Ajt96], along with an average-


Y. Tauman Kalai and S. F. Kamara (Eds.): CRYPTO 2025, LNCS 16000, pp. 353–384, 2025.
https://doi.org/10.1007/978-3-032-01855-7_12

case to worst-case reduction from SIS (in the average case) to the problem of finding a short basis in an arbitrary lattice (in the worst case). Since then, a plethora of cryptographic schemes have been based on the presumed average-case hardness of SIS. The SIS problem asks to find an integer vector of norm at most $\beta$ that satisfies a set of $n$ equations in $m$ variables modulo $q$. The average-case to worst-case reductions [Ajt96, MR07] consider SIS in the Euclidean norm, with norm bound $\beta$ significantly smaller than $q$. However, when it comes to practical cryptographic schemes, designers are often tempted to consider SIS instances outside of the asymptotic coverage of the reduction, or even to consider variants of the problem. This is the case for the new NIST standard ML-DSA (formerly known as Dilithium [DKL+18]), which considers SIS in the $\ell_\infty$-norm with norm bound $\beta$ rather close to the modulus $q$.

The dual of the latter SIS variant is commonly known as the Learning with Errors problem (LWE) [Reg05] with narrow error distribution, say ternary errors. This version of LWE was proven to be solvable in slightly subexponential time by Kirchner and Fouque [KF15] using a variant of the Blum-Kalai-Wasserman algorithm (BKW) [BKW03], at least when the number of samples $m$ is large enough. More precisely, it was claimed in [KF15] that $m$ linear in $n$ suffices, but a subsequent work of Herold, Kirshanova, and May [HKM18] found an issue in the proof. They resolved the issue only for $m \geq Cn \log n$ (for some constant $C > 0$), leaving open whether fewer samples would suffice. Whether this limitation on the number of samples is fundamental or an artifact of the proof remains unclear.

Our work was triggered by the folklore interpretation of BKW as a combination of Wagner's algorithm [Wag02], run over the dual lattice, and the Aharonov-Regev distinguisher [AR05]. This raises a natural question: using the tricks of Kirchner and Fouque but only in the Wagner part of the algorithm, can one (provably) solve interesting instances of SIS in subexponential time?

### 1.1 Contributions

We answer the above question positively, namely we prove that a variant of Wagner's algorithm solves SIS with $n$ equations modulo $q = n^{\Theta(1)}$ in subexponential time $\exp(O(n/\log\log n))$ for $\ell_\infty$-norm bound $\beta = q/\mathrm{polylog}(n)$ and only requiring $m = n + \omega(n/\log\log n)$ many SIS variables. We also achieve subexponential complexity for ISIS and $\mathrm{SIS}^\times$ for an $\ell_2$-norm bound $\beta = \sqrt{n} \cdot q/\mathrm{polylog}(n)$. In fact, in each of these applications, the $\mathrm{polylog}(n)$ factor in the norm bound can be replaced, for instance, by $2^{\log(n)^c}$ for an arbitrary constant $c < 1$. All prior algorithms (including heuristic ones) for these problems had exponential asymptotic complexity $\exp(\Omega(n))$.

Beyond these applications, we also provide a significant revision of the ideas and techniques at hand. First, we propose a more abstract interpretation of Wagner for lattices using a zigzag through a chain of projected lattices and superlattices, depicted in Fig. 1. This emphasizes that the key principle of the algorithm is not tied to SIS, and its subexponential complexity really stems from the ease of constructing the appropriate chain of lattices in the case of SIS lattices.

Furthermore, we circumvent the sample-amplification technique [Lyu05], and instead follow in the footsteps of [ADRS15, ADS15, AS18, ALS21, ACKS21] by relying on discrete-Gaussian techniques to obtain provable results. Specifically, we use discrete Gaussian sampling and rounding to maintain precise control of the distribution of vectors throughout the chain of lattices.

Finally, we consider whether this approach threatens the concrete security of the NIST standard ML-DSA. As detailed in the full version [DEL25], despite its subexponential complexity and despite removing all the overhead introduced for provability, this algorithm is far less efficient against the concrete parameters of ML-DSA than standard lattice-reduction attacks.

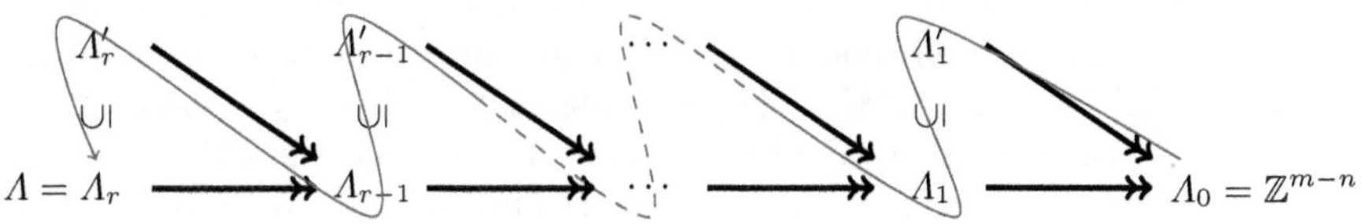


**Fig. 1.** Wagner's algorithm interpreted over a chain of projected lattices $\Lambda_i$ and auxiliary superlattices $\Lambda'_i$. Thick black double-arrows denote surjective orthogonal projections between lattices. The red curvy arrow denotes the path taken by the algorithm. It starts with (short) vectors in $\mathbb{Z}^{m-n}$, and follows the zigzag path until it generates (short) vectors in the lattice $\Lambda$, which, in our application, correspond to SIS solutions.

### 1.2 Technical Overview

The Short Integer Solution problem in the infinity norm is defined as follows.

*Problem 1.1* ($\mathrm{SIS}^\infty_{n,m,q,\beta}$). Let $n, m, q \in \mathbb{N}$ with $m \geq n$, and let $\beta > 0$. Given a uniformly random matrix $\mathbf{A} \in \mathbb{Z}_q^{n\times m}$, the problem $\mathrm{SIS}^\infty_{n,m,q,\beta}$ asks to find a nonzero vector $\mathbf{x} \in \mathbb{Z}^m$ satisfying $\mathbf{Ax} = \mathbf{0} \bmod q$ and $\|\mathbf{x}\|_\infty \leq \beta$.

This problem can be phrased as a short vector problem, as it is equivalent to finding a nonzero vector of norm at most $\beta$ in the $q$-ary lattice $\Lambda_q^\perp(\mathbf{A}) := \{\mathbf{x} \in \mathbb{Z}^m : \mathbf{Ax} = \mathbf{0} \bmod q\}$. It is trivial when $\beta > q$, as $(q, 0, \ldots, 0)$ is a solution, and becomes vacuously hard (i.e., typically no solution exists) when $\beta$ is too small.

Consider an instance of the $\mathrm{SIS}^\infty_{n,m,q,\beta}$ problem for some given $\mathbf{A} \in \mathbb{Z}_q^{n\times m}$. When $\mathbf{A}$ is of full rank[1] we can, without loss of generality, assume that $\mathbf{A}$ is written in systematic form, i.e., $\mathbf{A} = [\mathbf{A}' \mid \mathbf{I}_n]$ with $\mathbf{A}' \in \mathbb{Z}_q^{n\times(m-n)}$. With this writing of $\mathbf{A}$, we see that the problem of finding $\mathbf{x} \in \mathbb{Z}_q^m$ satisfying $\mathbf{Ax} = \mathbf{0} \bmod q$ and $\|\mathbf{x}\|_\infty \leq \beta$ is equivalent to finding $\mathbf{z} \in \mathbb{Z}_q^{m-n}$ satisfying $\|\mathbf{x}(\mathbf{z})\|_\infty \leq \beta$ where $\mathbf{x}(\mathbf{z}) := (\mathbf{z}; -\mathbf{A}'\mathbf{z})$.[2]

[1] This happens with overwhelming probability when $m-n = \omega(1)$: a uniformly random matrix in $\mathbb{Z}_q^{n\times m}$ (with $m \geq n$) is of full rank with probability at least $1 - 1/q^{m-n}$.

[2] We use the notation $(\mathbf{a}; \mathbf{b})$ for the vertical concatenation of vectors $\mathbf{a}$ and $\mathbf{b}$.

**Wagner-Style Algorithms for SIS.** Wagner's generalized birthday algorithm [Wag02] addresses the problem of finding elements in a list $L_0 \subseteq \mathbb{Z}_q^n$ that sum up to zero.[3] The same technique was independently used in [BKW03] to solve a dual problem.

Given an SIS instance $\mathbf{A} = [\mathbf{A}' \mid \mathbf{I}_n] \in \mathbb{Z}_q^{n \times m}$, divide the rows of the parity-check matrix $\mathbf{A}$ into $r$ blocks of equal size $n/r$, as illustrated in Fig. 2 (for $b_j := n/r$). The algorithm then iteratively solves smaller SIS instances corresponding to the parity-check matrices $\mathbf{A}_i = [\mathbf{A}'_i \mid \mathbf{I}_{in/r}]$, for $i = 1$ up to $r$, where $\mathbf{A}'_i$ is defined by the first $i$ blocks of rows of $\mathbf{A}'$. Specifically, the algorithm begins by filling an initial list $L_0$ with short vectors. Then, in iteration $i$, it computes, for each vector $\mathbf{x} \in L_{i-1} \subseteq \mathbb{Z}_q^{m-n+(i-1)n/r}$, the unique (modulo $q$) vector $\mathbf{y} \in \mathbb{Z}^{n/r}$ such that $\mathbf{A}_i(\mathbf{x}; \mathbf{y}) = \mathbf{0} \bmod q$. This vector $\mathbf{y}$ is likely to be of high norm since it is uniformly distributed modulo $q$. The algorithm then searches for pairs of such vectors $\mathbf{x}'_1 = (\mathbf{x}_1; \mathbf{y}_1)$, $\mathbf{x}'_2 = (\mathbf{x}_2; \mathbf{y}_2)$ that satisfy $\mathbf{y}_1 = \mathbf{y}_2 \bmod q$, to then add $\mathbf{x}'_1 - \mathbf{x}'_2 = (\mathbf{x}_1 - \mathbf{x}_2; \mathbf{0})$ to the list $L_i$. This ensures that the difference vector $\mathbf{x}'_1 - \mathbf{x}'_2$ remains short, as $\mathbf{x}_1$ and $\mathbf{x}_2$ are short and the rest has norm zero. The final list $L_r$ contains vectors $\mathbf{x} \in \mathbb{Z}_q^m$ that satisfy $\mathbf{A}\mathbf{x} = \mathbf{0} \bmod q$, providing potential nonzero and short solutions to the original SIS problem.

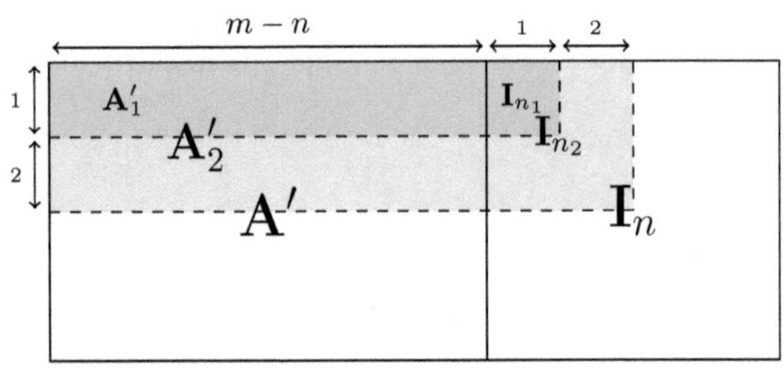


**Fig. 2.** Illustration of the parity-check matrices $\mathbf{A}_i := [\mathbf{A}'_i \mid \mathbf{I}_{n_i}]$, where $\mathbf{A}'_i$ is the matrix defined by the first $n_i := \sum_{j=1}^{i} {}_j$ rows of $\mathbf{A}'$. (Without the generalized lazy-modulus switching technique, the ${}_j$ are set equal to $n/r$.) Each iteration $i$ of the algorithm solves an SIS instance given by parity-check matrix $\mathbf{A}_i$, until ultimately the whole matrix $\mathbf{A} = \mathbf{A}_r$ is covered.

*Lazy-Modulus Switching.* The aforementioned approach constructs the lists $L_i$ by combining vectors that lie in the same *bucket*, where the bucket of $(\mathbf{x}; \mathbf{y})$ for $\mathbf{x} \in L_{i-1}$ is labeled by the value of $\mathbf{y}$ modulo $q$. The vectors in $L_i$ are then guaranteed to be of the form $(\mathbf{x}'; \mathbf{0})$, but this is not necessary for the algorithm to succeed: a form like $(\mathbf{x}'; \mathbf{y}')$ with both $\mathbf{x}'$ and $\mathbf{y}'$ being short suffices. Based on this observation, the authors of [AFFP14] consider using a smaller modulus

[3] Although Wagner originally considered the case $\mathbb{Z}_2^n$, the algorithm for $\mathbb{Z}_q^n$ follows the same principle.

$p < q$, and combine $(\mathbf{x}_1; \mathbf{y}_1)$ and $(\mathbf{x}_2; \mathbf{y}_2)$ if $\lfloor \frac{p}{q}\mathbf{y}_1 \rceil = \lfloor \frac{p}{q}\mathbf{y}_2 \rceil \bmod p$, where the operation $\lfloor \cdot \rceil$ denotes rounding each coordinate to its nearest integer modulo $p$. This modified condition for combining vectors may result in a nonzero 'rounding error' in the $\mathbf{y}'$-part, which is traded for a reduced number of buckets: $p^{n/r}$ instead of $q^{n/r}$.

Two concurrent works [KF15, GJMS17] generalize this *lazy-modulus switching* technique by considering different moduli $p_1, \ldots, p_r$ (not necessarily prime). In this approach, the matrix $\mathbf{A}$ is divided into $r$ blocks of respective size $b_1, \ldots, b_r$. The rounding errors induced by iteration $i$ are at most $q/p_i$, and may double in each subsequent iteration when the vectors are combined. Hence, it makes sense to use decreasing moduli $p_i$ to balance the accumulation of rounding error. Each step requires (more than) $p_i^{b_i}$ vectors to find collisions in $\mathbb{Z}_{p_i}^{b_i}$, leading to increasing block sizes $b_i$. This increasing choice of $b_i$'s is central to the subexponential complexity claim of [KF15].

**A Naive Analysis.** Algorithm 1 is a rephrased version of the algorithm of [KF15] without the LWE dual-distinguishing step. Let us attempt to analyze it in order to highlight the core of the issue.

**Algorithm 1:** Wagner-Style Algorithm for SIS

**Input** : Integers $n, m, q$;
Full-rank matrix $\mathbf{A} = [\mathbf{A}' \mid \mathbf{I}_n] \in \mathbb{Z}_q^{n \times m}$;
Integer parameters $N, r, (p_i)_{i=1}^r, (b_i)_{i=1}^r$ with $\sum_{i=1}^r b_i = n$
**Output:** List of vectors $\mathbf{x} \in \mathbb{Z}_q^m$ such that $\mathbf{Ax} = \mathbf{0} \bmod q$ and $\|\mathbf{x}\|_\infty \leq 2^r$

```
Initialize a list L_0 with 3^r N independent, uniform samples from {-1,0,1}^(m-n)
for i = 1,...,r do
    L_i := ∅
    Initialize empty buckets B(c) for each c ∈ Z_{p_i}^{b_i}
    for x ∈ L_{i-1} do                                          // Bucketing
        Compute the unique y ∈ Z_q^{b_i} satisfying A_i(x; y) = 0 mod q
        Compute c = ⌊(p_i/q) y⌉ mod p_i
        Append x' := (x; y) to B(c)
    for c ∈ Z_{p_i}^{b_i} do                                    // Combining
        for each two vectors x'_1, x'_2 in B(c) do
            Append x'_1 - x'_2 to the list L_i
            Remove x'_1 and x'_2 from B(c)
return L_r
```

*List Construction.* Since each vector in $L_i$ is either paired or left alone in a bucket, it follows that $|L_i| \leq 2|L_{i+1}| + p_i^{b_i}$. Thus, by initializing a list $L_0$ of size $3^r N$, we obtain at least $N$ vectors in $L_r$, assuming $N \geq \max_i p_i^{b_i}$.

*Bucketing and Combining.* At the beginning of each iteration $i \in \{1, \dots, r\}$, the algorithm initializes some empty lists $B(\mathbf{c})$, the *buckets*, each labeled by a vector (coset) $\mathbf{c} \in \mathbb{Z}_{p_i}^{b_i}$. Every iteration works in two phases. First, the 'for'-loop over the $\mathbf{x} \in L_{i-1}$ performs the *bucketing* phase: the vectors are added to a bucket according to their corresponding $\mathbf{y}$-value. In the *combining* phase, the 'for'-loop over each bucket representative $\mathbf{c} \in \mathbb{Z}_{p_i}^{b_i}$ takes differences of vectors $\mathbf{x}'_1, \mathbf{x}'_2$ belonging to the same bucket. Since $\mathbf{A}\mathbf{x}'_1 = \mathbf{0} \bmod q$ and $\mathbf{A}\mathbf{x}'_2 = \mathbf{0} \bmod q$, the difference vector $\mathbf{x}'_1 - \mathbf{x}'_2$ also satisfies $\mathbf{A}(\mathbf{x}'_1 - \mathbf{x}'_2) = \mathbf{0} \bmod q$ by linearity. Moreover, if two vectors $\mathbf{x}'_1 = (\mathbf{x}_1; \mathbf{y}_1)$, $\mathbf{x}'_2 = (\mathbf{x}_2; \mathbf{y}_2)$ belong to the same bucket $B(\mathbf{c})$, then they satisfy $\mathbf{c} = \lfloor \frac{p_i}{q} \mathbf{y}_1 \rceil = \lfloor \frac{p_i}{q} \mathbf{y}_2 \rceil \bmod p_i$. In particular, $\mathbf{y}_1$ and $\mathbf{y}_2$ are 'close' to each other, ensuring their difference is short: we have $\|\mathbf{y}_1 - \mathbf{y}_2\|_\infty \leq q/p_i$, and thus $\|\mathbf{x}'_1 - \mathbf{x}'_2\|_\infty \leq \max\{2\|\mathbf{x}_1\|_\infty, 2\|\mathbf{x}_2\|_\infty, q/p_i\}$. By induction over the $r$ iterations, it follows that the algorithm outputs vectors $\mathbf{x} \in L_r$ satisfying

$$\|\mathbf{x}\|_\infty \leq \max_{0 \leq i \leq r} 2^{r-i} \frac{q}{p_i}, \tag{1}$$

where we define $p_0 = q$.

**Time Complexity of Algorithm** 1. Equation (1) shows that the choice of the number of iterations $r$ and the moduli $p_i$ influences the maximal norm of the vectors. These parameters also affect the algorithm's time complexity, along with the other parameters that need to be chosen. Although the algorithm parameters $p_i, b_i, r$ and $N$ should be integers to make sense, we consider them as real numbers for simplicity in this introductory section.

*Parameter Selection.* Let the target norm for the SIS problem be $\beta = \frac{q}{f}$ for some factor $f > 1$. Note that the problem is easiest when $f = 1$ (norm $q$) and harder when $f$ increases (i.e., the norm $q/f$ becomes shorter). The bound on the output norms given in Eq. (1) is minimized when both terms are balanced: $2^r = 2^{r-i} q/p_i$. Therefore we set $p_i := q/2^i$. One can generate $p_i^{b_i}$ distinct vectors modulo $p_i$ with $b_i$ coordinates, so to keep the number of samples comparable at each step $i$, we set $N = p_i^{b_i}$. This implies $b_i = \frac{\log N}{\log p_i} = \frac{\log_2 N}{\log_2(q) - i}$. By the choice of the $p_i$, the final vectors have a norm of at most $2^r$. To ensure that it is at most $\beta = q/f$, we must choose $r$ such that $2^r \leq \frac{q}{f}$. We set $r := \log_2(q/f) - 1$. We must also ensure that $n = n_r = \sum_{i=1}^r b_i$. Since the $b_i$ increase with $i$, we can bound their sum by $n = \sum_{i=1}^r b_i \leq \int_1^{r+1} \frac{\log_2 N}{\log_2(q) - x} \mathrm{d}x = (\log_2 N) \cdot \ln\left(\frac{\log_2(q) - 1}{\log_2(q) - (r+1)}\right)$.[4] Thus,

$$n \leq \log_2(N) \cdot \ln\left(\frac{\log_2 q}{\log_2 f}\right).$$

Rewriting, we conclude that taking $\log_2(N) = \frac{n}{\ln\ln(q) - \ln\ln(f)}$ suffices. Up to rounding of the parameters (as they need to be integers), we would get the following statement.

[4] For $f$ an increasing function, $\int_0^r f(x)\,\mathrm{d}x \leq \sum_{i=1}^r f(i) \leq \int_1^{r+1} f(x)\,\mathrm{d}x$. Also, for $A, B, a, b > 0$, $\int_a^b \frac{A}{B-x} \mathrm{d}x = A \ln\left(\frac{B-a}{B-b}\right)$.

**Tentative Theorem.** *Let $n, m, q \in \mathbb{N}$ and $f > 1$. There exists an algorithm that, given $\mathbf{A} \in \mathbb{Z}_q^{n\times m}$, returns a (possibly zero) vector $\mathbf{x} \in \mathbb{Z}_q^m$ such that $\mathbf{Ax} = \mathbf{0} \bmod q$ and $\|\mathbf{x}\|_\infty \leq \frac{q}{f}$ in time*

$$T = 2^{\frac{n}{\ln\ln(q)-\ln\ln(f)}} \cdot \mathrm{poly}(n, \log q).$$

*Important Remark.* There is a catch! The output list of the algorithm contains a SIS solution only if at least one of the output vectors is *nonzero*. So it remains to be proven that the vectors do not all cancel out to zero. At the first iteration, the set $\{-1,0,1\}^{m-n}$ is significantly larger than the number of buckets, hence differences of vectors from a same bucket are unlikely to be zero vectors. However, from the second iteration onward, specifying the vector distributions is far from straightforward.

This issue does not arise in the original works of [Wag02, BKW03], where $m$ was assumed to be as large as the initial list size $|L_0|$, and the initial list is simply filled with standard unit vectors (i.e., vectors with one coordinate equal to 1 and zeros elsewhere). These vectors are linearly independent and hence cannot cancel each other out. In the case of solving ternary LWE with [BKW03] rather than SIS with [Wag02], this situation can be emulated using a sample-amplification technique from [Lyu05]. However, according to [HKM18], this requires at least $m = \Theta(n \log n)$ samples to start with; the argument of [KF15] that this should work for $m = \Theta(n)$ has been shown to be flawed in [HKM18].

Yet, at least heuristically, it is not clear why this approach should fail when $m = \Theta(n)$. There is enough entropy to avoid collision at the first step, and entropy should intuitively increase at a later stage: after all, the vectors are getting larger. But to adequately formalize this intuition, we shift our perspective on the algorithm.

**From Parity-Check Perspective to Lattices.** As mentioned before, the SIS problem is equivalent to a short vector problem which asks to find a nonzero vector of norm at most $\beta$ in the lattice $\Lambda := \{\mathbf{x} \in \mathbb{Z}^m \colon \mathbf{Ax} = \mathbf{0} \bmod q\}$. We consider the sequence of lattices $\Lambda_0 = \mathbb{Z}^{m-n}, \ldots, \Lambda_r = \Lambda$ with $\Lambda_i := \{\mathbf{x} \in \mathbb{Z}^{m-n+n_i} \colon \mathbf{A}_i\mathbf{x} = \mathbf{0} \bmod q\}$ for $i \geq 1$. Each parity-check matrix $\mathbf{A}_i$ adds a block of $b_i$ new coordinates, making $\Lambda_{i-1}$ a projection of $\Lambda_i$. It is easy to sample bounded vectors in $\Lambda_0 := \mathbb{Z}^{m-n}$; for example, one can sample in $\{-1,0,1\}^{m-n}$, as Algorithm 1 did. The goal is to use these initial samples to go back through the projections toward $\Lambda$ (recall Fig. 1), while keeping the norms bounded.

While one can lift a vector from $\Lambda_{i-1}$ to $\Lambda_i$, such a lifted vector would not be short because the lattice $\Lambda_i$ we are lifting over is too sparse. Instead, what happens in Algorithm 1 is that we implicitly lift to a denser lattice $\Lambda_i' \supseteq \Lambda_i$, and then take the difference of two vectors in the same coset of the quotient $\Lambda_i'/\Lambda_i$ to fall again in $\Lambda_i$. More explicitly, setting $\mathbf{c} = \lfloor \frac{p_i}{q}\mathbf{y} \rceil$ as in Algorithm 1, note that the vector $(\mathbf{x}, \mathbf{y} - \frac{q}{p_i}\mathbf{c})$ lives in the lattice $\Lambda_i' = \Lambda_i + (\{0\}^{m-n+n_{i-1}} \times \frac{q}{p_i}\mathbb{Z}^{b_i})$ which satisfies $|\Lambda_i'/\Lambda_i| = p_i^{b_i}$. Furthermore, the coset of that vector in the quotient $\Lambda_i'/\Lambda_i$ is exactly determined by $\mathbf{c} \bmod p_i$.

This provides a clean and pleasant interpretation of the algorithm as walking in a commutative diagram shown in Fig. 1. It further provides the framework to deploy the full machinery of discrete Gaussian distributions over lattices: the initial samples can easily be made Gaussian over $\mathbb{Z}^{m-n}$, the lifting step as well using the randomized Babai algorithm [GPV08,EWY23], and the combination step preserves Gaussians using convolution lemmas [Pei10, MP13], as already used in [ADRS15,ADS15,ACKS21,AS18,ALS21] to solve short vector problems. There are further technicalities to control the independence between the samples, which we handle using the (conditional) similarity notion introduced in [ALS21]. This permits to control all the distributions throughout the algorithm, leading to provable conclusions. In particular, a careful choice of the algorithm's parameters guarantees, with high probability, that the final distribution is not concentrated at zero [PR06, Lemma 2.11].

### 1.3 Organization of the Paper

Section 2 provides the necessary background. In Sect. 3, we present our Gaussian sampler and analyze its asymptotic time complexity. In Sect. 4, we then use the Gaussian sampler to asymptotically solve several variants of SIS, carefully avoiding the 'canceling out to zero' issue. In the appendix of the full version [DEL25], we discuss the impact of the attack on the concrete security of ML-DSA.

## 2 Preliminaries

*Notation.* We write $\|\cdot\|_2$ and $\|\cdot\|_\infty$ for the Euclidean and infinity norm of a vector, respectively. For a positive integer $N$, we define $[N] := \{1, \dots, N\}$. We use the notation $X = e^{\pm\delta}$ as shorthand for $X \in [e^{-\delta}, e^{\delta}]$. For $x = (x_1, \dots, x_N)$ and $i \in [N]$, we define $x_{-i} := (x_1, \dots, x_{i-1}, x_{i+1}, \dots, x_N)$, and we define $x_{-\{i,j\}}$ analogously. For events $E_0, E_1$, we use the convention that $\Pr[E_0 \mid E_1] = 0$ if $\Pr[E_1] = 0$.

*Asymptotic Notation.* Let $f$ and $g$ be functions that map positive integers to positive real numbers. We write $f(n) = O(g(n))$ if there exist constants $c, n_0 > 0$ such that $f(n) \le c \cdot g(n)$ for every integer $n \ge n_0$. Similarly, we write $f(n) = \Omega(g(n))$ if there exist constants $c, n_0 > 0$ such that $f(n) \ge c \cdot g(n)$ for every integer $n \ge n_0$. We say that $f(n) = \Theta(g(n))$ if both $f(n) = O(g(n))$ and $f(n) = \Omega(g(n))$. We define $\text{poly}(f(n)) := f(n)^{O(1)}$ and $\text{polylog}(f(n)) := \log(f(n))^{O(1)}$. We define $\tilde{O}(f(n)) := O(f(n) \cdot \text{polylog}(f(n)))$ and $\tilde{\Omega}(f(n)) := \Omega(f(n)/\text{polylog}(f(n)))$. We write $f(n) = o(g(n))$ if, for all constants $c > 0$, there exists $n_0 > 0$ such that $f(n) < c \cdot g(n)$ for every integer $n \ge n_0$. We write $f(n) = \omega(g(n))$ if, for all constants $c > 0$, there exists $n_0 > 0$ such that $f(n) > c \cdot g(n)$ for every integer $n \ge n_0$.

### 2.1 Similarity of Distributions

Inspired by [ALS21], we consider the notions of *similarity* and *conditional similarity*, which we define below, to measure the pointwise distance between two distributions. These concepts are slightly stronger than statistical distance (see Remark 2.1), and are particularly useful for handling small independencies arising from 'bucket-and-combine' type of algorithms (like each iteration of Wagner-style algorithms).

**Definition 2.1 (Similar).** *Let $D$ be a probability distribution over a set $\mathcal{X}$, and let $\delta \geq 0$ be a real. A random variable $X \in \mathcal{X}$ is $\delta$-similar to $D$ if, for all $x \in \mathcal{X}$, it holds that*

$$\Pr_X[X = x] = e^{\pm\delta} \cdot \Pr_{Y \sim D}[Y = x].$$

*Remark 2.1 (Similarity implies Closeness in Statistical Distance).* The notion of $\delta$-similarity is a stronger notion than being within statistical distance $\delta$, where we recall that the statistical distance between two discrete random variables $X, Y$ is defined as $\frac{1}{2}\sum_{x\in\mathcal{X}} |\Pr[X = x] - \Pr[Y = x]|$. Indeed, for all $\delta \in [0, 1]$, being $\delta$-similar implies being within statistical distance $\delta$, since for any such $\delta$ we have $[e^{-\delta}, e^{\delta}] \subseteq [1 - 2\delta, 1 + 2\delta]$.

The next definition is closely related to [ALS21, Definition 4.1], but we remark that we use different terminology and that we made the definition more general.

**Definition 2.2 (Conditionally Similar).** *Let $D$ be a probability distribution over a set $\mathcal{X}$, and let $\delta \geq 0$ be a real. Discrete random variables $X_1, \ldots, X_N \in \mathcal{X}$ are* conditionally $\delta$-similar to independent samples from $D$ *if, for all $i \in [N]$ and $x \in \mathcal{X}^N$, it holds that*

$$\Pr_{X_1,\ldots,X_N}[X_i = x_i \mid X_{-i} = x_{-i}] = e^{\pm\delta} \cdot \Pr_{Y\sim D}[Y = x_i].$$

In particular, being conditionally 0-similar (i.e., $\delta = 0$) is equivalent to being independently distributed according to $D$.

*Remark 2.2 (Conditional Similarity implies Marginal Similarity).* For $N = 1$, conditional similarity coincides with Definition 2.1. More generally, for all $N \geq 1$ and $\delta \geq 0$, conditional $\delta$-similarity implies marginal $\delta$-similarity. Indeed, if $X_1, \ldots, X_N \in \mathcal{X}$ are conditionally $\delta$-similar to independent samples from a distribution $D$ on $\mathcal{X}$, then, for all $i \in [N]$ and $x \in \mathcal{X}$, we have $\Pr[X_i = x] = \sum_{y\in\mathcal{X}^{N-1}} \Pr[X_i = x|X_{-i} = y] \Pr[X_{-i} = y] = e^{\pm\delta} \cdot \Pr_{Y\sim D}[Y = x]$.

A useful property of similarity and conditional similarity is that these notions are closed under convex combinations (as already observed in [ALS21]).

**Lemma 2.1.** *Let $D$ be a probability distribution over a set $\mathcal{X}$, and let $\delta \geq 0$ be a real. Let $\mathcal{E}$ be a finite or countably infinite set of mutually exclusive and collectively exhaustive events. If discrete random variables $X_1, \ldots, X_N \in \mathcal{X}$ satisfy*

$$\Pr_{X_1,\ldots,X_N}[X_i = x_i \mid X_{-i} = x_{-i} \text{ and } E] = e^{\pm\delta} \cdot \Pr_{Y\sim D}[Y = x_i]$$

*for all* $i \in [N]$, $x \in \mathcal{X}^N$, *and* $E \in \mathcal{E}$, *then* $X_1, \ldots, X_N$ *are conditionally* $\delta$*-similar to independent samples from* $D$.

*Proof.* Suppose that the premise is true for random variables $X_1, \ldots, X_N$. Then, for all $i \in [N]$ and $x \in \mathcal{X}^N$, we have

$$\Pr_{X_1,\ldots,X_N}[X_i = x_i \mid X_{-i} = x_{-i}] = \sum_{E \in \mathcal{E}} \Pr_{X_1,\ldots,X_N}[X_i = x_i \text{ and } E \mid X_{-i} = x_{-i}]$$

$$= \sum_{E \in \mathcal{E}} \Pr_{X_1,\ldots,X_N}[X_i = x_i \mid E \text{ and } X_{-i} = x_{-i}] \cdot \Pr_{X_1,\ldots,X_N}[E \mid X_{-i} = x_{-i}]$$

$$= e^{\pm\delta} \cdot \Pr_{Y \sim D}[Y = x_i]$$

since $\sum_{E \in \mathcal{E}} \Pr[E \mid X_{-i} = x_{-i}] = \frac{\sum_{E \in \mathcal{E}} \Pr[E \text{ and } X_{-i} = x_{-i}]}{\Pr[X_{-i} = x_{-i}]} = 1$. □

The following property can be viewed as the data-processing inequality for conditional similarity.

**Lemma 2.2.** *Let* $D$ *be a probability distribution over a set* $\mathcal{X}$, *and let* $\delta \geq 0$ *be a real. If discrete random variables* $X_1, \ldots, X_N \in \mathcal{X}$ *are conditionally* $\delta$*-similar to independent samples from* $D$, *then*

$$\Pr_{X_1,\ldots,X_N}[f(X_i) = 1] = e^{\pm\delta} \cdot \Pr_{Y \sim D}[f(Y) = 1]$$

*for all* $i \in [N]$ *and all functions* $f \colon \mathcal{X} \to \{0, 1\}$.

*Proof.* Suppose that $X_1, \ldots, X_N$ are conditionally $\delta$-similar to independent samples from $D$. Let $i \in [N]$ and let $f \colon \mathcal{X} \to \{0, 1\}$ be an arbitrary function. Define $f^{-1}(1) := \{x \in \mathcal{X} \colon f(x) = 1\}$. Then

$$\begin{aligned}
\Pr_{X_1,\ldots,X_N}[f(X_i) = 1] &= \sum_{x \in \mathcal{X}} \Pr_{X_1,\ldots,X_N}[f(X_i) = 1 \text{ and } X_i = x] \\
&= \sum_{x \in f^{-1}(1)} \Pr_{X_1,\ldots,X_N}[X_i = x] \\
&= e^{\pm\delta} \cdot \sum_{x \in f^{-1}(1)} \Pr_{Y \sim D}[Y = x] \\
&= e^{\pm\delta} \cdot \Pr_{Y \sim D}[f(Y) = 1].
\end{aligned}$$

□

## 2.2 Lattices

Given $k$ linearly independent vectors $\mathbf{b}_1, \ldots, \mathbf{b}_k \in \mathbb{R}^n$, let $\mathbf{B} \in \mathbb{R}^{n \times k}$ be the matrix whose columns are the $\mathbf{b}_i$. The *lattice* associated to $\mathbf{B}$ is the set $\mathcal{L}(\mathbf{B}) := \mathbf{B}\mathbb{Z}^k = \left\{\sum_{i=1}^k z_i \mathbf{b}_i \colon z_i \in \mathbb{Z}\right\} \subseteq \mathbb{R}^n$ of all integer linear combinations of these vectors. We say that $\mathbf{B}$ is a *basis* for a lattice $\mathcal{L}$ if $\mathcal{L} = \mathcal{L}(\mathbf{B})$. We say that $\mathcal{L}$ has *rank* $k$ and *dimension* $n$. If $n = k$, then $\mathcal{L}$ is said to be of *full rank*. We define $\mathrm{span}_{\mathbb{R}}(\mathcal{L}(\mathbf{B})) = \mathrm{span}_{\mathbb{R}}(\mathbf{B}) = \{\mathbf{B}\mathbf{x} \colon \mathbf{x} \in \mathbb{R}^n\}$. We define the *dual* of $\mathcal{L}$ by $\mathcal{L}^* := \{\mathbf{y} \in \mathrm{span}_{\mathbb{R}}(\mathcal{L}) \colon \forall \mathbf{x} \in \mathcal{L}, \langle \mathbf{x}, \mathbf{y} \rangle \in \mathbb{Z}\}$, which is a lattice.

*First Successive Minimum.* Given a lattice $\mathcal{L}$, we write $\lambda_1(\mathcal{L}) := \inf\{\|\mathbf{x}\|_2 : \mathbf{x} \in \mathcal{L} \setminus \{\mathbf{0}\}\}$ for the Euclidean norm of a shortest lattice vector. We define $\lambda_1^\infty(\mathcal{L})$ similarly for the infinity norm.

*Projections and Primitive Sublattices.* For $S \subseteq \mathbb{R}^n$, we write $\pi_S$ for the projection onto $\mathrm{span}_{\mathbb{R}}(S)$ and $\pi_S^\perp$ for the projection orthogonal to $\mathrm{span}_{\mathbb{R}}(S)$. We say that a sublattice $\mathcal{S}$ of a lattice $\mathcal{L} \subseteq \mathbb{R}^n$ is *primitive* if $\mathcal{S} = \mathrm{span}_{\mathbb{R}}(\mathcal{S}) \cap \mathcal{L}$. It implies that there exists a sublattice $\mathcal{C} \subseteq \mathcal{L}$ such that $\mathcal{S} \oplus \mathcal{C} = \mathcal{L}$ (i.e., $\mathcal{S} + \mathcal{C} = \mathcal{L}$ and $\mathcal{S} \cap \mathcal{C} = \{\mathbf{0}\}$). We then say that $\mathcal{C}$ is a *complement* to $\mathcal{S}$.

*Relevant q-ary Lattices.* We say that a lattice $\mathcal{L} \subseteq \mathbb{R}^n$ is *q-ary* if $q\mathbb{Z}^n \subseteq \mathcal{L} \subseteq \mathbb{Z}^n$. The two relevant types of $q$-ary lattices considered in this work are as follows: for $\mathbf{A} \in \mathbb{Z}_q^{n\times m}$, we define the full-rank $q$-ary lattices

$$\Lambda_q^\perp(\mathbf{A}) := \{\mathbf{x} \in \mathbb{Z}^m : \mathbf{A}\mathbf{x} = 0 \bmod q\} \subseteq \mathbb{Z}^m,$$
$$\Lambda_q(\mathbf{A}) := \{\mathbf{y} \in \mathbb{Z}^m : \exists \mathbf{s} \in \mathbb{Z}_q^n, \mathbf{y} = \mathbf{A}^\top \mathbf{s} \bmod q\} = \mathbf{A}^\top \mathbb{Z}^n + q\mathbb{Z}^m \subseteq \mathbb{Z}^m.$$

They are duals up to appropriate scaling: namely, $\Lambda_q(\mathbf{A}) = q \cdot (\Lambda_q^\perp(\mathbf{A}))^*$.

If $m \geq n$ and $\mathbf{A}$ is of full rank, we can assume without loss of generality that $\mathbf{A} = [\mathbf{A}' \mid \mathbf{I}_n]$ for some $\mathbf{A}' \in \mathbb{Z}_q^{n\times(m-n)}$. Then a basis of $\Lambda_q^\perp(\mathbf{A})$ is given by

$$\begin{pmatrix} 0 & \mathbf{I}_{m-n} \\ q\mathbf{I}_n & -\mathbf{A}' \end{pmatrix}.$$

### 2.3 Discrete Gaussian Distribution and Smoothness

In the following, when the subscripts $s$ and $\mathbf{c}$ are omitted, they are respectively taken to be 1 and $\mathbf{0}$.

For any real $s > 0$ and $\mathbf{c} \in \mathbb{R}^n$, we define the Gaussian function on $\mathbb{R}^n$ centered at $\mathbf{c}$ with parameter $s$ by

$$\forall \mathbf{x} \in \mathbb{R}^n,\ \rho_{s,\mathbf{c}}(\mathbf{x}) := \exp(-\pi\|(\mathbf{x}-\mathbf{c})/s\|_2^2).$$

For any countable set $A$, we define $\rho_{s,\mathbf{c}}(A) = \sum_{\mathbf{x}\in A} \rho_{s,\mathbf{c}}(\mathbf{x})$. Note that $\rho_{s,\mathbf{c}}(\mathbf{x}) = \rho_s(\mathbf{x}-\mathbf{c})$, and thus $\rho_{s,\mathbf{c}}(A) = \rho_s(A-\mathbf{c})$.

For any real $s > 0$, $\mathbf{c} \in \mathbb{R}^n$, and full-rank lattice $\mathcal{L} \subseteq \mathbb{R}^n$, we define the discrete Gaussian distribution over $\mathcal{L}$ centered at $\mathbf{c}$ with parameter $s$ by

$$\forall \mathbf{x} \in \mathcal{L},\ D_{\mathcal{L},s,\mathbf{c}}(\mathbf{x}) := \frac{\rho_{s,\mathbf{c}}(\mathbf{x})}{\rho_{s,\mathbf{c}}(\mathcal{L})} = \frac{\rho_s(\mathbf{x}-\mathbf{c})}{\rho_s(\mathcal{L}-\mathbf{c})}$$

and it is 0 for $\mathbf{x} \notin \mathcal{L}$.

Similarly, for any $\mathbf{t} \in \mathbb{R}^n$, we define $D_{\mathcal{L}-\mathbf{t},s,\mathbf{c}}(\mathbf{y}) := \frac{\rho_{s,\mathbf{c}}(\mathbf{y})}{\rho_{s,\mathbf{c}}(\mathcal{L}-\mathbf{t})}$ for $\mathbf{y} \in \mathcal{L}-\mathbf{t}$. (Note that $D_{\mathcal{L},s,\mathbf{c}} \equiv \mathbf{c} + D_{\mathcal{L}-\mathbf{c},s}$.)

*Infinity Norm of Discrete Gaussian Samples.* We can tail-bound the infinity norm of a discrete Gaussian sample using the following lemma, where we define $\mathcal{B}_n^\infty := \{\mathbf{x} \in \mathbb{R}^n : \|\mathbf{x}\|_\infty \leq 1\}$.

**Lemma 2.3** ([Ban95, **Lemma 2.10**]). *For any full-rank lattice $\mathcal{L} \subseteq \mathbb{R}^n$ and real $R > 0$,*

$$\frac{\rho(\mathcal{L} \setminus R \cdot \mathcal{B}_n^\infty)}{\rho(\mathcal{L})} < 2n \cdot e^{-\pi R^2}.$$

*Smoothness.* The work of [MR07] introduced a lattice quantity known as the smoothing parameter. More precisely, for any full-rank lattice $\mathcal{L} \subseteq \mathbb{R}^n$ and real $\varepsilon > 0$, we define the *smoothing parameter* $\eta_\varepsilon(\mathcal{L})$ as the smallest real $s > 0$ such that $\rho_{1/s}(\mathcal{L}^* \setminus \{\mathbf{0}\}) \leq \varepsilon$.

Intuitively, it gives a lower bound on $s$ such that $D_{\mathcal{L},s}$ 'behaves like' a continuous Gaussian distribution, in a specific mathematical sense. The following lemma justifies the name of the smoothing parameter.

**Lemma 2.4 (Implicit in** [MR07, **Lemma 4.4**]). *For any full-rank lattice $\mathcal{L} \subseteq \mathbb{R}^n$, real $\varepsilon \in (0,1)$, real $s \geq \eta_\varepsilon(\mathcal{L})$, and $\mathbf{c} \in \mathbb{R}^n$,*

$$\frac{\rho_{s,\mathbf{c}}(\mathcal{L})}{\rho_s(\mathcal{L})} \in \left[\frac{1-\varepsilon}{1+\varepsilon}, 1\right].$$

For $s$ slightly above smoothing, we can upper bound the probability of the most likely outcome of the discrete Gaussian distribution.

**Lemma 2.5 (Min-entropy** [PR06, **Lemma 2.11**]). *For any full-rank lattice $\mathcal{L} \subseteq \mathbb{R}^n$, reals $\varepsilon > 0$ and $s \geq 2\eta_\varepsilon(\mathcal{L})$, center $\mathbf{c} \in \mathbb{R}^n$, and vector $\mathbf{x} \in \mathbb{R}^n$,*

$$\Pr_{X \sim D_{\mathcal{L},s,\mathbf{c}}}[X = \mathbf{x}] \leq \frac{1+\varepsilon}{1-\varepsilon} \cdot 2^{-n}.$$

In particular, for $\mathbf{x} = \mathbf{0}$, Lemma 2.5 gives an upper bound on the probability that a discrete Gaussian sample is zero (if the standard deviation $s$ is large enough).

*Sampling and Combining.* In our algorithms, we sample from (scalings of) $\mathbb{Z}^n$ using the exact Gaussian sampler from [BLP+13].

**Lemma 2.6 (Implicit in** [BLP+13, **Lemma 2.3**]). *There is a randomized algorithm that, given a real $s \geq \sqrt{\ln(2n+4)/\pi}$ and $\mathbf{c} \in \mathbb{R}^n$, returns a sample from $D_{\mathbb{Z}^n,s,\mathbf{c}}$ in expected time* $\mathrm{poly}(n, \log s, \log \|\mathbf{c}\|_\infty)$.

Our analysis uses a variant of the convolution lemma [MP13, Theorem 3.3] (see also [Pei10, Theorem 3.1]) that bounds how similar the difference of two discrete Gaussians is to a discrete Gaussian. It is a slightly tighter result than [ALS21, Lemma 2.14].

**Lemma 2.7 (Explicit Variant of Convolution Lemma).** *Let $\mathcal{L} \subseteq \mathbb{R}^n$ be a full-rank lattice and let $s \geq \sqrt{2}\eta_\varepsilon(\mathcal{L})$ for some real $\varepsilon > 0$. For $i = 1, 2$, let $\mathcal{L} + \mathbf{c}_i$ be an arbitrary coset of $\mathcal{L}$ and $Y_i$ an independent sample from $D_{\mathcal{L}+\mathbf{c}_i,s}$. Then the distribution of $Y_1 - Y_2$ satisfies*

$$\forall \mathbf{y} \in \mathcal{L} + \mathbf{c}_1 - \mathbf{c}_2,\ \Pr[Y_1 - Y_2 = \mathbf{y}] \in \left[\frac{1-\varepsilon}{1+\varepsilon}, \frac{1+\varepsilon}{1-\varepsilon}\right] \cdot D_{\mathcal{L}+\mathbf{c}_1-\mathbf{c}_2,\sqrt{2}s}(\mathbf{y}).$$

It follows, for instance, that $Y_1 - Y_2$ is $3\varepsilon$-similar to $D_{\mathcal{L}+\mathbf{c}_1-\mathbf{c}_2,\sqrt{2}s}$ when $\varepsilon \leq \frac{1}{2}$.

*Proof.* Let $D_1 := D_{\mathcal{L}+\mathbf{c}_1,s}$ and $D_2 := D_{\mathcal{L}+\mathbf{c}_2,s}$. For $Y_1 \sim D_1$ and $Y_2 \sim D_2$, the distribution of $Y_1 - Y_2$ has support $\mathcal{L} + \mathbf{c}_1 - \mathbf{c}_2$. For all $\mathbf{x} \in \mathcal{L} + \mathbf{c}_1 - \mathbf{c}_2$, we have

$$\begin{aligned}
\Pr_{\substack{Y_1\sim D_1\\ Y_2\sim D_2}}[Y_1 - Y_2 = \mathbf{x}] &= \sum_{\mathbf{y}_1 \in \mathcal{L}+\mathbf{c}_1} \Pr_{\substack{Y_1\sim D_1\\ Y_2\sim D_2}}[Y_1 = \mathbf{y}_1 \text{ and } Y_1 - Y_2 = \mathbf{x}] \\
&= \sum_{\mathbf{y}_1 \in \mathcal{L}+\mathbf{c}_1} \Pr_{Y_1\sim D_1}[Y_1 = \mathbf{y}_1] \cdot \Pr_{\substack{Y_1\sim D_1\\ Y_2\sim D_2}}[Y_1 - Y_2 = \mathbf{x} \mid Y_1 = \mathbf{y}_1] \\
&= \sum_{\mathbf{y}_1 \in \mathcal{L}+\mathbf{c}_1} \frac{\rho_s(\mathbf{y}_1)}{\rho_s(\mathcal{L}+\mathbf{c}_1)} \cdot \frac{\rho_s(\mathbf{y}_1 - \mathbf{x})}{\rho_s(\mathcal{L}+\mathbf{c}_2)} \qquad \text{(def. of } D_1, D_2\text{)} \\
&= \rho_{\sqrt{2}s}(\mathbf{x}) \cdot \sum_{\mathbf{y}_1 \in \mathcal{L}+\mathbf{c}_1} \frac{\rho_{s/\sqrt{2}}(\mathbf{y}_1 - \mathbf{x}/2)}{\rho_s(\mathcal{L}+\mathbf{c}_1)\cdot\rho_s(\mathcal{L}+\mathbf{c}_2)} \qquad (2) \\
&= \rho_{\sqrt{2}s}(\mathbf{x}) \cdot \frac{\rho_{s/\sqrt{2}}(\mathcal{L}+\mathbf{c}_1 - \mathbf{x}/2)}{\rho_s(\mathcal{L}+\mathbf{c}_1)\cdot\rho_s(\mathcal{L}+\mathbf{c}_2)}
\end{aligned}$$

where Eq. (2) holds since $\rho_s(\mathbf{v}_1)\cdot\rho_s(\mathbf{v}_1 - \mathbf{v}_2) = \rho_s(\mathbf{v}_2/\sqrt{2})\cdot\rho_s(\sqrt{2}\mathbf{v}_1 - \mathbf{v}_2/\sqrt{2}) = \rho_{\sqrt{2}s}(\mathbf{v}_2)\cdot\rho_{s/\sqrt{2}}(\mathbf{v}_1 - \mathbf{v}_2/2)$ for all $\mathbf{v}_1, \mathbf{v}_2 \in \mathbb{R}^n$. Since $s \geq \sqrt{2}\eta_\varepsilon(\mathcal{L})$, $\rho_{s/\sqrt{2}}(\mathcal{L} + \mathbf{c}_1 - \mathbf{x}/2) \in \left[\frac{1-\varepsilon}{1+\varepsilon}, 1\right] \cdot \rho_{s/\sqrt{2}}(\mathcal{L})$ by Lemma 2.4. Hence,

$$\Pr_{\substack{Y_1\sim D_1\\ Y_2\sim D_2}}[Y_1 - Y_2 = \mathbf{x}] \in \left[\frac{1-\varepsilon}{1+\varepsilon}, 1\right] \cdot \rho_{\sqrt{2}s}(\mathbf{x}) \cdot \frac{\rho_{s/\sqrt{2}}(\mathcal{L})}{\rho_s(\mathcal{L}+\mathbf{c}_1)\cdot\rho_s(\mathcal{L}+\mathbf{c}_2)}.$$

Summing both sides implies $1 \in \left[\frac{1-\varepsilon}{1+\varepsilon}, 1\right] \cdot \rho_{\sqrt{2}s}(\mathcal{L}+\mathbf{c}_1-\mathbf{c}_2) \cdot \frac{\rho_{s/\sqrt{2}}(\mathcal{L})}{\rho_s(\mathcal{L}+\mathbf{c}_1)\cdot\rho_s(\mathcal{L}+\mathbf{c}_2)}$, i.e., $\frac{\rho_{s/\sqrt{2}}(\mathcal{L})}{\rho_s(\mathcal{L}+\mathbf{c}_1)\cdot\rho_s(\mathcal{L}+\mathbf{c}_2)} \in \left[1, \frac{1+\varepsilon}{1-\varepsilon}\right] \cdot \frac{1}{\rho_{\sqrt{2}s}(\mathcal{L}+\mathbf{c}_1-\mathbf{c}_2)}$. It follows that

$$\Pr_{\substack{Y_1\sim D_1\\ Y_2\sim D_2}}[Y_1 - Y_2 = \mathbf{x}] \in \left[\frac{1-\varepsilon}{1+\varepsilon}, \frac{1+\varepsilon}{1-\varepsilon}\right] \cdot \frac{\rho_{\sqrt{2}s}(\mathbf{x})}{\rho_{\sqrt{2}s}(\mathcal{L}+\mathbf{c}_1-\mathbf{c}_2)}$$

as we wanted to show. □

## 2.4 Bounds on Smoothing Parameters of Relevant Lattices

The following lemma gives a bound on the smoothing parameter of $\mathbb{Z}^n$. (Note that it can also be viewed as a special case of Lemma 2.9 below.)

**Lemma 2.8 (Special Case of [MR07, Lemma 3.3]).** *For any real* $\varepsilon > 0$,

$$\eta_\varepsilon(\mathbb{Z}^n) \leq \sqrt{\frac{\ln(2n(1+1/\varepsilon))}{\pi}}.$$

The next lemma gives an upper bound on $\eta_\varepsilon(\mathcal{L})$ in terms of $\lambda_1^\infty(\mathcal{L}^*)$. It will be used to obtain an upper bound on the smoothing parameter of the lattices $\Lambda_i$ that we consider.

**Lemma 2.9 (Part of [Pei08, Lemma 3.5]).** *For any full-rank lattice* $\mathcal{L} \subseteq \mathbb{R}^n$ *and real* $\varepsilon > 0$,

$$\lambda_1^\infty(\mathcal{L}^*) \cdot \eta_\varepsilon(\mathcal{L}) \leq \sqrt{\frac{\ln(2n(1+1/\varepsilon))}{\pi}}.$$

The lattices $\Lambda_i$ considered in this work are of the form $\Lambda_i = \Lambda_q^\perp(\mathbf{A}_i)$ for some matrices $\mathbf{A}_i$, and we recall that their dual lattice is of the form $\frac{1}{q}\Lambda_q(\mathbf{A}_i)$. We obtain the following lower bound on $\lambda_1^\infty(\Lambda_q(\mathbf{A}))$ for random matrices $\mathbf{A} \in \mathbb{Z}_q^{n\times m}$.

**Lemma 2.10 (Variant of [GPV08, Lemma 5.3]).** *Let* $n, m, q$ *be positive integers with* $q$ *prime and* $q^{1-n/m} \geq 6$. *For a uniformly random* $\mathbf{A} \in \mathbb{Z}_q^{n\times m}$,

$$\lambda_1^\infty(\Lambda_q(\mathbf{A})) > \frac{q^{1-n/m} \cdot 2^{-n/m}}{3}$$

*except with probability* $< 2^{-n}$.

*In particular, if* $m \geq n$, *then the right-hand side is lower bounded by* $\frac{q^{1-n/m}}{6}$.

*Proof.* For some positive real $B$ to be determined, let $S := \{\mathbf{y} \in \mathbb{Z}^m : \|\mathbf{y}\|_\infty \leq B\}$, and note that $|S| = (2B+1)^m$. For all $\mathbf{s} \in \mathbb{Z}_q^n \setminus \{\mathbf{0}\}$, $\Pr[\mathbf{A}^\top \mathbf{s} \bmod q \in S] = |S| \cdot q^{-m} = (2B+1)^m \cdot q^{-m}$. Taking the union bound over all $\mathbf{s} \in \mathbb{Z}_q^n \setminus \{\mathbf{0}\}$ gives

$$\begin{aligned}\Pr[\lambda_1^\infty(\Lambda_q(\mathbf{A})) \leq B] &= \Pr[\exists \mathbf{s} \in \mathbb{Z}_q^n \setminus \{\mathbf{0}\} \text{ such that } \mathbf{A}^\top \mathbf{s} \bmod q \in S] \\ &\leq |\mathbb{Z}_q^n \setminus \{\mathbf{0}\}| \cdot (2B+1)^m \cdot q^{-m} \\ &< (2B+1)^m \cdot q^{n-m}.\end{aligned}$$

Let $B := \frac{1}{3} q^{1-n/m} \cdot 2^{-n/m}$, and observe that $q^{1-n/m} \geq 6$ implies $q^{1-n/m} \cdot 2^{-n/m} \geq 3$ for all $m \geq n$. It follows that $B \geq 1$ and thus $\Pr[\lambda_1^\infty(\Lambda_q(\mathbf{A})) \leq B] < (3B)^m \cdot q^{n-m} = 2^{-n}$ as desired. The last part is immediate. □

**Lemma 2.11 (Smoothing Parameter of $\Lambda_q^\perp(\mathbf{A})$).** *Let* $n, m, q$ *be positive integers with* $q$ *prime,* $m \geq n$, *and* $q^{1-n/m} \geq 6$. *Let* $\varepsilon \leq \frac{1}{4m}$ *be a positive real. For a uniformly random* $\mathbf{A} \in \mathbb{Z}_q^{n\times m}$,

$$\eta_\varepsilon(\Lambda_q^\perp(\mathbf{A})) < \sqrt{\frac{72\ln(1/\varepsilon)}{\pi}} \cdot q^{n/m}$$

*except with probability* $< 2^{-n}$.

*Proof.* Since $m \geq n$, for a uniformly random $\mathbf{A} \in \mathbb{Z}_q^{n\times m}$, Lemma 2.10 implies $\lambda_1^\infty(\Lambda_q(\mathbf{A})) > \frac{1}{6}q^{1-n/m}$, except with probability $< 2^{-n}$. Since the dual of $\mathcal{L} := \Lambda_q^\perp(\mathbf{A})$ is $\mathcal{L}^* = \frac{1}{q}\Lambda_q(\mathbf{A})$, we obtain $\lambda_1^\infty(\mathcal{L}^*) > \frac{1}{6}q^{-n/m}$. Furthermore, by Lemma 2.9 (recall that $\mathcal{L}$ is full-rank and has dimension $m$), we have

$$\lambda_1^\infty(\mathcal{L}^*) \cdot \eta_\varepsilon(\mathcal{L}) \leq \sqrt{\frac{\ln(2m(1+1/\varepsilon))}{\pi}}$$

which is $\leq \sqrt{\frac{2\ln(1/\varepsilon)}{\pi}}$ for $\varepsilon \leq \frac{1}{4m}$. The statement follows. □

## 3 Wagner-Style Gaussian Sampler

In Sect. 1.2, we presented a warm-up version of the Wagner-style algorithm, which returns $N$ short vectors in $\Lambda_q^\perp(\mathbf{A})$. However, these vectors are possibly all equal to $\mathbf{0}$. We now show that a variant of that algorithm, using discrete Gaussians, allows us to avoid that issue. In particular, we present a Wagner-style algorithm for sampling $N$ vectors from a distribution that is essentially $D_{\Lambda_q^\perp(\mathbf{A}),s}$ when $s$ is sufficiently large. Such samples can be shown to be short and nonzero with high probability. Specifically, we present an algorithm for sampling from $D_{\Lambda_q^\perp(\mathbf{A}),s}$ in expected subexponential time for $m = n+\omega(n/\log\log n)$, $q = n^{\Theta(1)}$, and $s = q/f$ for some $f = \omega(1)$.

Recall that, for some $r \in \mathbb{N}$ and $b_1, \ldots, b_r$ such that $n = \sum_{i=1}^r b_i$, we define the $q$-ary lattices

$$\Lambda_0 = \mathbb{Z}^{m-n} \quad \text{and} \quad \Lambda_i = \Lambda_q^\perp(\mathbf{A}_i) = \{\mathbf{x} \in \mathbb{Z}^{m-n+n_i} : \mathbf{A}_i\mathbf{x} = \mathbf{0} \bmod q\} \tag{3}$$

for $i = 1, \ldots, r$, where $\mathbf{A}_i \in \mathbb{Z}_q^{n_i\times(m-n+n_i)}$ is the matrix corresponding to the first $n_i := \sum_{j=1}^i b_j$ SIS equations (recall Fig. 2).

Our approach to sample $N$ vectors from $D_{\Lambda_q^\perp(\mathbf{A}),s}$ for a given parameter $s$ is to start from many vectors sampled from $D_{\Lambda_0,s_0}$, where $s_0$ is such that $s = \sqrt{2^r}s_0$. Then, we iteratively (for $i \in \{1,\ldots,r\}$) transform a list of vectors that are conditionally similar to independent samples from $D_{\Lambda_{i-1},\sqrt{2^{i-1}}s_0}$ into a list of samples that are conditionally similar to independent samples from $D_{\Lambda_i,\sqrt{2^i}s_0}$. Then, after the last iteration, the list contains samples that are conditionally similar to independent samples from $D_{\Lambda_q^\perp(\mathbf{A}),s}$, as desired. (Using Lemma 2.5, we can then bound the probability that one such sample is nonzero.)

As explained in Sect. 1.2, mapping vectors in $\Lambda_{i-1}$ to vectors in $\Lambda_i$ will be done by first lifting the vectors in $\Lambda_{i-1}$ to vectors in a suitable superlattice $\Lambda_i' \supseteq \Lambda_i$, and then combining them into vectors in $\Lambda_i$. Specifically, for some $p_i \in \mathbb{N}$, the lattices $\Lambda_i'$ are defined by $\Lambda_i' = \mathcal{L}(\mathbf{B}_i')$ for

$$\mathbf{B}_i' := \begin{pmatrix} \mathbf{0} & \mathbf{I}_{m-n} \\ \mathbf{D}_i & -\mathbf{A}_i' \end{pmatrix} \text{ with } \mathbf{D}_i := \begin{pmatrix} \mathbf{0} & q\mathbf{I}_{n_{i-1}} \\ \frac{q}{p_i}\mathbf{I}_{b_i} & \mathbf{0} \end{pmatrix} \tag{4}$$

The first $b_i$ columns of $\mathbf{B}'_i$ generate (an embedding into $\mathbb{R}^{m-n+n_i}$ of) $\frac{q}{p_i}\mathbb{Z}^{b_i}$, which is a primitive sublattice of $\Lambda'_i$ that we denote by $\mathcal{S}$. Consider the projected lattice $\mathcal{P} = \pi_{\mathcal{S}}^{\perp}(\Lambda'_i)$, and note that it is (an embedding of) $\Lambda_{i-1}$. Thus, we can consider ways to lift from $\Lambda_{i-1}$ to $\Lambda'_i$; in Sect. 3.1, we consider a randomized way of lifting that preserves discrete Gaussian distributions.

From there, we would like to produce samples in $\Lambda_i$, rather than $\Lambda'_i$. A natural approach is to bucket our samples according to their cosets in the quotient $\Lambda'_i/\Lambda_i$, and then take differences within those buckets. Using standard analysis of convolutions of discrete Gaussians, we show in Sect. 3.2 that these differences are still essentially discrete Gaussian, yet with a width parameter increased by a factor of $\sqrt{2}$.

In Sect. 3.3, we then lay out the resulting Gaussian variant of Wagner's algorithm, and demonstrate its correctness and time complexity, under certain smoothing constraints on the parameters. Finally, in Sect. 3.4 we provide a choice of parameters that satisfy these constraints and allow for a subexponential-time algorithm for sampling from $D_{\Lambda_q^{\perp}(\mathbf{A}),s}$.

### 3.1 Discrete-Gaussian Lifting

Algorithm 2 below lifts vectors from $\Lambda_{i-1}$ to vectors in $\Lambda'_i$. It revisits the GPV sampling algorithm [GPV08] with a reinterpretation of the induction: rather than reducing the problem in dimension $n$ to two instances in dimensions 1 and $n-1$, we consider arbitrary splits in dimensions $n'$ and $n-n'$. Algorithm 2 can be viewed as a special case of [EWY23, Alg. 2], and our Lemma 3.1 is a variant of [EWY23, Theorem 1], where we analyze the conditional similarity of the output with respect to the discrete Gaussian (instead of merely looking at the statistical distance).

In particular, Lemma 3.1 (with $\delta = 0$ and $N = 1$) shows that Algorithm 2 turns a sample from $D_{\mathcal{P},s}$ into a sample that is $3\varepsilon$-similar to (and thus within statistical distance $3\varepsilon$ from) $D_{\mathcal{L},s}$, whenever $s \geq \eta_\varepsilon(\mathcal{S})$ for $0 < \varepsilon \leq \frac{1}{2}$.

**Lemma 3.1 (Complexity and Distribution of** DGLift**).** *Let $\mathcal{L} \subseteq \mathbb{R}^n$ be a lattice and let $\mathcal{P} = \pi_{\mathcal{S}}^{\perp}(\mathcal{L})$ for a primitive sublattice $\mathcal{S} \subseteq \mathcal{L}$. For a real $s > 0$, let $\mathcal{A}$ be a randomized algorithm that, given $\mathbf{c} \in \operatorname{span}(\mathcal{S})$, returns a sample from $D_{\mathcal{S},s,\mathbf{c}}$. Then* DGLift$(\mathcal{P}, \mathcal{L}, s, \cdot)$ *(Algorithm 2) is a randomized algorithm that, given a vector $\mathbf{x} \in \mathcal{P}$, outputs a vector $\mathbf{x}'$ in $\mathcal{L}$. It uses one query to $\mathcal{A}$, and all other operations run in polynomial time.*

*Moreover, for any reals $\delta \geq 0$ and $0 < \varepsilon \leq \frac{1}{2}$ satisfying $s \geq \eta_\varepsilon(\mathcal{S})$, if $X_1, \ldots, X_N \in \mathcal{P}$ are conditionally $\delta$-similar to independent samples from $D_{\mathcal{P},s}$, then the distribution of $X'_1, \ldots, X'_N$ for $X'_i :=$* DGLift$(\mathcal{P}, \mathcal{L}, s, X_i)$ *is conditionally $(\delta + 3\varepsilon)$-similar to independent samples from $D_{\mathcal{L},s}$.*

We will invoke the above lemma with $\mathcal{S} = \frac{q}{p_i}\mathbb{Z}^{b_i}$, hence an exact polynomial-time sampler is available whenever $s \geq \frac{q}{p_i}\sqrt{\ln(2b_i+4)/\pi}$ by Lemma 2.6.

**Algorithm 2:** DGLift$(\mathcal{P}, \mathcal{L}, s, \mathbf{x})$

**Input :** Lattices $\mathcal{P}, \mathcal{L}$, where $\mathcal{P} = \pi_{\mathcal{S}}^{\perp}(\mathcal{L})$ for a primitive sublattice $\mathcal{S} \subseteq \mathcal{L}$;
Real $s > 0$;
Vector $\mathbf{x} \in \mathcal{P}$

**Output:** Vector $\mathbf{x}' \in \mathcal{L}$ such that $\pi_{\mathcal{S}}^{\perp}(\mathbf{x}') = \mathbf{x}$

```
Let C be a complement to S
Compute the unique y ∈ C such that π_S^⊥(y) = x        // Lifting
Sample z ~ D_{S,s,x−y}                                  // Sampling
return x' := z + y
```

*Proof.* Consider Algorithm 2, where we use algorithm $\mathcal{A}$ for the sampling step, and let $\mathcal{C}$ be the complement of $\mathcal{S}$ that it considers. Note that $\pi_{\mathcal{S}}^{\perp}$ induces a bijection from $\mathcal{C}$ to $\mathcal{P}$, and that both directions can be computed in polynomial time. The claim on time and query complexity of Algorithm 2 is thus immediate.

For correctness, we remark that any output vector $\mathbf{x}' = \mathbf{z} + \mathbf{y}$ belongs to $\mathcal{L}$, since $\mathbf{z} \in \mathcal{S} \subseteq \mathcal{L}$ and $\mathbf{y} \in \mathcal{C} \subseteq \mathcal{L}$. Furthermore, $\mathbf{x}' = \pi_{\mathcal{S}}(\mathbf{x}') + \pi_{\mathcal{S}}^{\perp}(\mathbf{x}')$ with $\pi_{\mathcal{S}}(\mathbf{x}') = \mathbf{z} + \pi_{\mathcal{S}}(\mathbf{y})$ and $\pi_{\mathcal{S}}^{\perp}(\mathbf{x}') = \pi_{\mathcal{S}}^{\perp}(\mathbf{y}) = \mathbf{x}$, so the output is as desired.

For the remainder of the proof, let $f(\mathbf{x}) :=$ DGLift$(\mathcal{P}, \mathcal{L}, s, \mathbf{x})$. We remark that $\mathcal{S} \oplus \mathcal{C} = \mathcal{L}$ implies that any $\mathbf{v} \in \mathcal{L}$ can be uniquely written as $\mathbf{v} = \mathbf{v}_{\mathcal{S}} + \mathbf{v}_{\mathcal{C}}$ for $\mathbf{v}_{\mathcal{S}} \in \mathcal{S}$ and $\mathbf{v}_{\mathcal{C}} \in \mathcal{C}$ (and we define $\mathbf{v}_{\mathcal{S}}, \mathbf{v}_{\mathcal{C}}$ as such).

We first observe that for all $\mathbf{x} \in \mathcal{P}$ and $\mathbf{x}' \in \mathcal{L}$, the probability that DGLift on input $\mathbf{x}$ outputs $\mathbf{x}'$ is

$$\Pr[f(\mathbf{x}) = \mathbf{x}'] = \Pr_{Z \sim D_{\mathcal{S},s,\mathbf{x}-\mathbf{y}(\mathbf{x})}}[Z = \mathbf{x}' - \mathbf{y}(\mathbf{x})] = \begin{cases} \frac{\rho_s(\pi_{\mathcal{S}}(\mathbf{x}'))}{\rho_s(\mathcal{S} + \pi_{\mathcal{S}}(\mathbf{x}'_{\mathcal{C}}))} & \text{if } \mathbf{x} = \pi_{\mathcal{S}}^{\perp}(\mathbf{x}') \\ 0 & \text{otherwise} \end{cases} \tag{5}$$

where $\mathbf{y}(\mathbf{x})$ denotes the unique $\mathbf{y} \in \mathcal{C}$ such that $\pi_{\mathcal{S}}^{\perp}(\mathbf{y}) = \mathbf{x}$. Indeed, note that $\mathbf{x}' - \mathbf{y}(\mathbf{x}) \in \mathcal{S}$ if and only if $\mathbf{x}'_{\mathcal{C}} = \mathbf{y}(\mathbf{x})$ if and only if $\mathbf{x} = \pi_{\mathcal{S}}^{\perp}(\mathbf{x}'_{\mathcal{C}})$ if and only if $\mathbf{x} = \pi_{\mathcal{S}}^{\perp}(\mathbf{x}')$. Therefore, $\Pr_{Z \sim D_{\mathcal{S},s,\mathbf{x}-\mathbf{y}(\mathbf{x})}}[Z = \mathbf{x}' - \mathbf{y}(\mathbf{x})] = \frac{\rho_s(\mathbf{x}' - \mathbf{x})}{\rho_s(\mathcal{S} - \mathbf{x} + \mathbf{y}(\mathbf{x}))} = \frac{\rho_s(\pi_{\mathcal{S}}(\mathbf{x}'))}{\rho_s(\mathcal{S} - \mathbf{x} + \mathbf{y}(\mathbf{x}))}$ if $\mathbf{x} = \pi_{\mathcal{S}}^{\perp}(\mathbf{x}')$ and 0 otherwise. Since $\mathbf{x} = \pi_{\mathcal{S}}^{\perp}(\mathbf{x}')$ implies $\mathbf{y}(\mathbf{x}) = \mathbf{x}'_{\mathcal{C}}$, and thus $\mathbf{y}(\mathbf{x}) - \mathbf{x} = \pi_{\mathcal{S}}(\mathbf{y}(\mathbf{x})) = \pi_{\mathcal{S}}(\mathbf{x}'_{\mathcal{C}})$, Eq. (5) follows.

Next, we prove the following intermediate claim.

*Claim.* For $s \geq \eta_\varepsilon(\mathcal{S})$, we have $\rho_s(\mathcal{P}) \cdot \rho_s(\mathcal{S}) \in \left[1, \frac{1+\varepsilon}{1-\varepsilon}\right] \cdot \rho_s(\mathcal{L})$.

*Proof (of Claim).* By Eq. (5), if the input is a random variable $X \sim D$ for some distribution $D$ on $\mathcal{P}$, then for all $\mathbf{x}' \in \mathcal{L}$, we have

$$\Pr_{X,Z}[f(X) = \mathbf{x}'] = \Pr_{X,Z}[X = \pi_{\mathcal{S}}^{\perp}(\mathbf{x}')] \cdot \Pr_{X,Z}[f(X) = \mathbf{x}' \mid X = \pi_{\mathcal{S}}^{\perp}(\mathbf{x}')]$$

$$= \Pr_{X \sim D}[X = \pi_{\mathcal{S}}^{\perp}(\mathbf{x}')] \cdot \frac{\rho_s(\pi_{\mathcal{S}}(\mathbf{x}'))}{\rho_s(\mathcal{S} + \pi_{\mathcal{S}}(\mathbf{x}'_{\mathcal{C}}))}$$

$$\in \left[1, \frac{1+\varepsilon}{1-\varepsilon}\right] \cdot \Pr_{X \sim D}[X = \pi_{\mathcal{S}}^{\perp}(\mathbf{x}')] \cdot \frac{\rho_s(\pi_{\mathcal{S}}(\mathbf{x}'))}{\rho_s(\mathcal{S})}. \quad \text{(Lemma 2.4)}$$

In particular, if $D$ is $D_{\mathcal{P},s}$, then we have (for all $\mathbf{x}' \in \mathcal{L}$) that $\Pr[f(X) = \mathbf{x}'] \in \left[1, \frac{1+\varepsilon}{1-\varepsilon}\right] \cdot \frac{\rho_s(\mathbf{x}')}{\rho_s(\mathcal{P})\rho_s(\mathcal{S})}$ since $\pi_{\mathcal{S}}^{\perp}(\mathbf{x}') + \pi_{\mathcal{S}}(\mathbf{x}') = \mathbf{x}'$. Finally, summing both sides over all $\mathbf{x}' \in \mathcal{L}$ yields $1 \in \left[1, \frac{1+\varepsilon}{1-\varepsilon}\right] \cdot \frac{\rho_s(\mathcal{L})}{\rho_s(\mathcal{P})\rho_s(\mathcal{S})}$, which proves the claim. □

We now proceed with the main proof. Suppose that the input consists of $N$ random variables conditionally $\delta$-similar to independent samples from $D_{\mathcal{P},s}$. By Eq. (5), we know that for all $\mathbf{x}' \in \mathcal{L}^N$ and any $I \subseteq [N]$,

$$\begin{aligned}
&\Pr_{(X_1,Z_1),\ldots,(X_N,Z_N)}[\forall j \in I, f(X_j) = \mathbf{x}'_j] \\
&= \Pr_{X_1,\ldots,X_N}[\forall j \in I, X_j = \pi_{\mathcal{S}}^{\perp}(\mathbf{x}'_j)] \cdot \Pr_{Z_1,\ldots,Z_N}[\forall j \in I, f(\pi_{\mathcal{S}}^{\perp}(\mathbf{x}'_j)) = \mathbf{x}'_j] \\
&= \Pr_{X_1,\ldots,X_N}[\forall j \in I, X_j = \pi_{\mathcal{S}}^{\perp}(\mathbf{x}'_j)] \cdot \prod_{j \in I} \frac{\rho_s(\pi_{\mathcal{S}}(\mathbf{x}'_j))}{\rho_s(\mathcal{S} + \pi_{\mathcal{S}}(\mathbf{x}'_{j,\mathcal{C}}))} \qquad (6)
\end{aligned}$$

since the $Z_j$ are independent when the values of the $X_j$ are fixed. (Here, we write $\mathbf{x}'_{j,\mathcal{C}}$ for the unique $\mathbf{c} \in \mathcal{C}$ such that $\mathbf{x}'_j = \mathbf{s} + \mathbf{c}$ for $(\mathbf{s}, \mathbf{c}) \in \mathcal{S} \times \mathcal{C}$.) To conclude the proof, take any $i \in [N]$ and $\mathbf{x}' \in \mathcal{L}^N$. Then

$$\begin{aligned}
&\Pr_{X_1,\ldots,X_N}[f(X_i) = \mathbf{x}'_i \mid \forall j \in [N] \setminus \{i\}, f(X_j) = \mathbf{x}'_j] \\
&= \frac{\Pr_{X_1,\ldots,X_N}[\forall j \in [N], f(X_j) = \mathbf{x}'_j]}{\Pr_{X_1,\ldots,X_N}[\forall j \in [N] \setminus \{i\}, f(X_j) = \mathbf{x}'_j]} && \text{(def. conditional probability)} \\
&= \frac{\Pr_{X_1,\ldots,X_N}[\forall j \in [N], X_j = \pi_{\mathcal{S}}^{\perp}(\mathbf{x}'_j)]}{\Pr_{X_1,\ldots,X_N}[\forall j \in [N] \setminus \{i\}, X_j = \pi_{\mathcal{S}}^{\perp}(\mathbf{x}'_j)]} \cdot \frac{\rho_s(\pi_{\mathcal{S}}(\mathbf{x}'_i))}{\rho_s(\mathcal{S} + \pi_{\mathcal{S}}(\mathbf{x}'_{i,\mathcal{C}}))} && \text{(Equation (6))} \\
&= \Pr_{X_1,\ldots,X_N}[X_i = \pi_{\mathcal{S}}^{\perp}(\mathbf{x}'_i) \mid \forall j \in [N] \setminus \{i\}, X_j = \pi_{\mathcal{S}}^{\perp}(\mathbf{x}'_j)] \cdot \frac{\rho_s(\pi_{\mathcal{S}}(\mathbf{x}'_i))}{\rho_s(\mathcal{S} + \pi_{\mathcal{S}}(\mathbf{x}'_{i,\mathcal{C}}))} \\
&= e^{\pm\delta} \cdot \frac{\rho_s(\pi_{\mathcal{S}}^{\perp}(\mathbf{x}'_i))}{\rho_s(\mathcal{P})} \cdot \frac{\rho_s(\pi_{\mathcal{S}}(\mathbf{x}'_i))}{\rho_s(\mathcal{S} + \pi_{\mathcal{S}}(\mathbf{x}'_{i,\mathcal{C}}))} && \text{(by assumption)} \\
&= e^{\pm\delta} \cdot \frac{\rho_s(\mathbf{x}'_i)}{\rho_s(\mathcal{P})\rho_s(\mathcal{S} + \pi_{\mathcal{S}}(\mathbf{x}'_{i,\mathcal{C}}))} \\
&\in \left[e^{-\delta}, e^{\delta} \cdot \frac{1+\varepsilon}{1-\varepsilon}\right] \cdot \frac{\rho_s(\mathbf{x}'_i)}{\rho_s(\mathcal{P})\rho_s(\mathcal{S})} && \text{(by Lemma 2.4)} \\
&\subseteq \left[e^{-\delta} \cdot \frac{1-\varepsilon}{1+\varepsilon}, e^{\delta} \cdot \frac{1+\varepsilon}{1-\varepsilon}\right] \cdot \frac{\rho_s(\mathbf{x}'_i)}{\rho_s(\mathcal{L})}. && \text{(by the claim)}
\end{aligned}$$

Since $\left[\frac{1-\varepsilon}{1+\varepsilon}, \frac{1+\varepsilon}{1-\varepsilon}\right] \subseteq [e^{-3\varepsilon}, e^{3\varepsilon}]$ for all $0 < \varepsilon \leq \frac{1}{2}$, the lemma follows. □

### 3.2 Combining to a Sublattice

We now show that, given many independent discrete Gaussian samples from a lattice $\mathcal{L}'$, we can construct many vectors in a *full-rank* sublattice $\mathcal{L} \subseteq \mathcal{L}'$ whose distributions are (conditionally) similar to a discrete Gaussian over $\mathcal{L}$.

By the convolution lemma [Pei08, MP13] (more precisely, by Lemma 2.7), the difference of two independent samples from $D_{\mathcal{L}',s}$ follows a distribution similar to $D_{\mathcal{L}',\sqrt{2}s}$. If we condition on the result being in the sublattice $\mathcal{L}$, then this distribution can in fact be shown to be similar to $D_{\mathcal{L},\sqrt{2}s}$.

Motivated by this fact, we consider an algorithm (Algorithm 3) that first buckets its input vectors in $\mathcal{L}'$ with respect to their cosets modulo the sublattice $\mathcal{L}$, and then (carefully) combines pairs of vectors in the same cosets to obtain vectors in $\mathcal{L}$.[5] If we start with at least $3|\mathcal{L}'/\mathcal{L}|$ vectors from $\mathcal{L}'$, then the number of output vectors is only a constant factor smaller, as shown by Lemma 3.2. Furthermore, if the input vectors are conditionally similar to independent samples from $D_{\mathcal{L}',s}$, the output vectors are conditionally similar to independent samples from $D_{\mathcal{L},\sqrt{2}s}$, as shown by Lemma 3.3.

**Algorithm 3:** BucketAndCombine($\mathcal{L}', \mathcal{L}, L$)

**Input** : Full-rank lattices $\mathcal{L} \subseteq \mathcal{L}'$ in $\mathbb{R}^d$;
A list $L$ with $N$ vectors $\mathbf{x}_1, \ldots, \mathbf{x}_N \in \mathcal{L}'$ for some integer $N \geq 3|\mathcal{L}'/\mathcal{L}|$
**Output:** A list $L_{out}$ with $\lfloor N/3 \rfloor$ vectors in $\mathcal{L}$

```
Initialize empty lists B(c) for each coset c ∈ L'/L
for i = 1, ..., N do                                              // Bucketing
    Let c_i := x_i mod L
    Append x_i to B(c_i)
Initialize an empty list L_out
for i = 1, ..., N do                                              // Combining
    if B(c_i) contains at least two elements and |L_out| < ⌊N/3⌋ then
        Let x, x' be the first two elements in B(c_i)
        Append y := x − x' to L_out
        Remove x and x' from B(c_i)
return L_out
```

**Lemma 3.2 (Correctness of Algorithm 3).** *Algorithm 3 is correct. That is, given two full-rank lattices $\mathcal{L} \subseteq \mathcal{L}'$ in $\mathbb{R}^d$ and a list of $N$ vectors in $\mathcal{L}'$, it returns a list of $\lfloor N/3 \rfloor$ vectors in $\mathcal{L}$ if $N \geq 3|\mathcal{L}'/\mathcal{L}|$.*

*Proof.* By construction, each element of $L_{out}$ is of the form $\mathbf{y} = \mathbf{x} - \mathbf{x}'$ for $\mathbf{x} = \mathbf{x}' \bmod \mathcal{L}$, so $\mathbf{y} \in \mathcal{L}$. It thus remains to show that the output list $L_{out}$ always consists of $\lfloor N/3 \rfloor$ elements. Suppose, for contradiction, that the algorithm

[5] Algorithm 3 is just a reformulation of [ALS21, Algorithm 2] with a different number of output vectors (and output vectors of the form $\mathbf{x} - \mathbf{x}'$ instead of $\mathbf{x} + \mathbf{x}'$).

returns a list of size $\ell$ for some $\ell \in \{0, \dots, \lfloor N/3 \rfloor - 1\}$. Then the number of elements in $L$ that are used as part of the output is $2\ell$, so there must be $N-2\ell$ list elements that are not used. (Here, we talk about list elements instead of vectors, since two list elements may correspond to the same vector.) Their corresponding cosets must be distinct (since otherwise the algorithm would have been able to find more than $\ell$ output elements), so $N - 2\ell \le |\mathcal{L}'/\mathcal{L}| \le N/3$. It follows that $\lfloor N/3 \rfloor \le N/3 \le \ell$, which is a contradiction. Hence, the algorithm always succeeds to construct $\lfloor N/3 \rfloor$ output vectors. □

The following is a variant of [ALS21, Lemma 4.5], suitable for our purposes.

**Lemma 3.3 (Distribution of Output).** *Let $\mathcal{L} \subseteq \mathcal{L}'$ be full-rank lattices in $\mathbb{R}^d$. Let $N \ge 3|\mathcal{L}'/\mathcal{L}|$ be a positive integer, and let $\delta \ge 0$, $0 < \varepsilon \le \frac{1}{2}$, and $s \ge \sqrt{2}\eta_\varepsilon(\mathcal{L}')$ be reals.*

*If the input list consists of $N$ random variables on $\mathcal{L}'$ that are conditionally $\delta$-similar to independent samples from $D_{\mathcal{L}',s}$, then Algorithm 3 returns a list of $\lfloor N/3 \rfloor$ vectors from $\mathcal{L}$ that are conditionally $(4\delta + 3\varepsilon)$-similar to independent samples from $D_{\mathcal{L},\sqrt{2}s}$.*

Our proof makes use of the following fact: given a sample $X$ from a distribution similar to $D_{\mathcal{L}',s}$, if we condition on $X = \mathbf{c} \bmod \mathcal{L}$ for some $\mathcal{L} \subseteq \mathcal{L}'$ and $\mathbf{c} \in \mathcal{L}'$, then this distribution is similar to $D_{\mathcal{L}+\mathbf{c},s}$. More generally, conditioning on cosets preserves conditional similarity.

**Lemma 3.4 (Conditioning on Cosets).** *Let $\mathcal{L} \subseteq \mathcal{L}'$ be full-rank lattices in $\mathbb{R}^d$. Let $N$ be a positive integer, and let $\delta \ge 0$ and $s > 0$ be reals. Suppose that $X_1, \dots, X_N \in \mathcal{L}'$ are discrete random variables that are conditionally $\delta$-similar to independent samples from $D_{\mathcal{L}',s}$. Then, for all $i \in [N]$, all $\mathbf{c} \in (\mathcal{L}'/\mathcal{L})^N$, and all $\mathbf{x} \in (\mathcal{L}')^N$ satisfying $\mathbf{x}_j = \mathbf{c}_j \bmod \mathcal{L}$ for all $j \in [N]$,*

$$\Pr[X_i = \mathbf{x}_i \mid X_{-i} = \mathbf{x}_{-i} \text{ and } \forall j \in [N], X_j = \mathbf{c}_j \bmod \mathcal{L}] = e^{\pm 2\delta} \cdot \frac{\rho_s(\mathbf{x}_i)}{\rho_s(\mathcal{L} + \mathbf{c}_i)}.$$

*Proof.* Suppose that $X = (X_1, \dots, X_N)$ consists of $N$ random variables on $\mathcal{L}'$ that are conditionally $\delta$-similar to independent samples from $D_{\mathcal{L}',s}$. Then, by definition, we have for all $i \in [N]$ and all $\mathbf{x} \in (\mathcal{L}')^N$ that

$$\Pr[X_i = \mathbf{x}_i \mid X_{-i} = \mathbf{x}_{-i}] = e^{\pm\delta} \cdot \frac{\rho_s(\mathbf{x}_i)}{\rho_s(\mathcal{L}')}. \tag{7}$$

Consider arbitrary $i \in [N]$, $\mathbf{c} \in (\mathcal{L}'/\mathcal{L})^N$, and $\mathbf{x} \in (\mathcal{L}')^N$ satisfying $\mathbf{x}_j = \mathbf{c}_j \bmod \mathcal{L}$ for all $j \in [N]$. Then, by definition of conditional probability,

$$\begin{aligned}
&\Pr[X_i = \mathbf{x}_i \mid X_{-i} = \mathbf{x}_{-i} \text{ and } \forall j \in [N], X_j = \mathbf{c}_j \bmod \mathcal{L}] \\
&= \frac{\Pr[X_i = \mathbf{x}_i \text{ and } X_{-i} = \mathbf{x}_{-i} \text{ and } \forall j \in [N], X_j = \mathbf{c}_j \bmod \mathcal{L}]}{\Pr[X_{-i} = \mathbf{x}_{-i} \text{ and } \forall j \in [N], X_j = \mathbf{c}_j \bmod \mathcal{L}]} \\
&= \frac{\Pr[X_i = \mathbf{x}_i \text{ and } X_{-i} = \mathbf{x}_{-i}]}{\Pr[X_{-i} = \mathbf{x}_{-i} \text{ and } X_i = \mathbf{c}_i \bmod \mathcal{L}]} \qquad (\text{as } \mathbf{x}_j = \mathbf{c}_j \bmod \mathcal{L}\, \forall j \in [N])
\end{aligned}$$

$$= \frac{\Pr[X_i = \mathbf{x}_i \mid X_{-i} = \mathbf{x}_{-i}]}{\sum_{\mathbf{v} \in \mathcal{L}+\mathbf{c}_i} \Pr[X_i = \mathbf{v} \mid X_{-i} = \mathbf{x}_{-i}]}$$
$$= e^{\pm 2\delta} \frac{\rho_s(\mathbf{x}_i)/\rho_s(\mathcal{L}')}{\rho_s(\mathcal{L}+\mathbf{c}_i)/\rho_s(\mathcal{L}')}$$

where we apply Eq. (7) twice (to both the numerator and denominator) to obtain the last line. The conclusion then immediately follows. □

*Proof (of Lemma 3.3).* Correctness (on arbitrary input) follows from Lemma 3.2. Let $Y_1, \ldots, Y_M$ be the random variables corresponding to the vectors in the output list (in order), where $M := \lfloor N/3 \rfloor$. We want to show that, for all $j \in [M]$ and $\mathbf{y} \in \mathcal{L}^M$,

$$\Pr_{X_1,\ldots,X_N}[Y_j = \mathbf{y}_j \mid Y_{-j} = \mathbf{y}_{-j}] = e^{\pm(4\delta+3\varepsilon)} D_{\mathcal{L},\sqrt{2}s}(\mathbf{y}_j).$$

By Lemma 2.1, it suffices to show that for all $\mathbf{c}_1, \ldots, \mathbf{c}_N \in \mathcal{L}'/\mathcal{L}$ such that $\Pr_{X_1,\ldots,X_N}[\forall i \in [N], X_i = \mathbf{c}_i \bmod \mathcal{L}] > 0$, we have, for all $j \in [M]$, $\mathbf{y} \in \mathcal{L}^M$,

$$\Pr_{X_1,\ldots,X_N}[Y_j = \mathbf{y}_j \mid Y_{-j} = \mathbf{y}_{-j} \text{ and } \forall i \in [N], X_i = \mathbf{c}_i \bmod \mathcal{L}]$$
$$= e^{\pm(4\delta+3\varepsilon)} D_{\mathcal{L},\sqrt{2}s}(\mathbf{y}_j). \tag{8}$$

Consider any $\mathbf{c}_1, \ldots, \mathbf{c}_N \in \mathcal{L}'/\mathcal{L}$ such that $\Pr_{X_1,\ldots,X_N}[\forall i \in [N], X_i = \mathbf{c}_i \bmod \mathcal{L}] > 0$. Note that the output (in particular, the way the vectors are paired) is entirely determined by the cosets $(\mathbf{c}_1, \ldots, \mathbf{c}_N)$ for $\mathbf{c}_i := \mathbf{x}_i \bmod \mathcal{L}$. In particular, for any permutation $\pi \colon [N] \to [N]$ such that $(\mathbf{x}'_1, \ldots, \mathbf{x}'_N) := (\mathbf{x}_{\pi(1)}, \ldots, \mathbf{x}_{\pi(N)})$ satisfies $\mathbf{y}_j = \mathbf{x}'_{2j-1} - \mathbf{x}'_{2j}$ for all $j \in [M]$, we have that $\mathbf{x}'_1, \ldots, \mathbf{x}'_{2M}$ is entirely determined by the cosets $(\mathbf{c}_1, \ldots, \mathbf{c}_N)$. (The order of the vectors $\mathbf{x}'_{2M+1}, \ldots, \mathbf{x}'_N$ does not affect the algorithm's output.) Without loss of generality, we therefore redefine $(\mathbf{x}_1, \ldots, \mathbf{x}_N)$ as $(\mathbf{x}'_1, \ldots, \mathbf{x}'_N)$ for such a permutation (allowing us to write $\mathbf{y}_j = \mathbf{x}_{2j-1} - \mathbf{x}_{2j}$ for all $j \in [M]$).

Let $D$ be the distribution of the input variables $X = (X_1, \ldots, X_N)$ *conditional on* $X_i = \mathbf{c}_i \bmod \mathcal{L}$ for all $i \in [N]$. By the conditional similarity assumption and by Lemma 3.4, for all $i \in [N]$ and all $\mathbf{x} \in (\mathcal{L}')^N$ satisfying $\mathbf{x}_j = \mathbf{c}_j \bmod \mathcal{L}$ for all $j \in [N]$, we have

$$\Pr_{X \sim D}[X_i = \mathbf{x}_i \mid X_{-i} = \mathbf{x}_{-i}] = e^{\pm 2\delta} D_{\mathcal{L}+\mathbf{c}_i,s}(\mathbf{x}_i), \tag{9}$$

which we repeatedly use below.

To show that Eq. (8) holds for all $j \in [M]$, $\mathbf{y} \in \mathcal{L}^M$, and thus to finish the proof, it suffices (by another application of Lemma 2.1) to show that for all $j \in [M]$, $\mathbf{y} \in \mathcal{L}^M$, and all $\mathbf{v} \in (\mathcal{L}')^{N-2}$ satisfying $\Pr[X_{-\{2j-1,2j\}} = \mathbf{v} | Y_{-j} = \mathbf{y}_j] > 0$, we have

$$\Pr_{X \sim D}[Y_j = \mathbf{y}_j \mid Y_{-j} = \mathbf{y}_{-j} \text{ and } X_{-\{2j-1,2j\}} = \mathbf{v}] = e^{\pm(4\delta+3\varepsilon)} D_{\mathcal{L},\sqrt{2}s}(\mathbf{y}_j).$$

So take any $j \in [M]$ and $\mathbf{y} \in \mathcal{L}^M$, and any such $\mathbf{v} \in (\mathcal{L}')^{N-2}$. Since $X_{-\{2j-1,-2j\}}$ determines all the entries of $Y_{-j}$, we have that $\Pr[X_{-\{2j-1,2j\}} = \mathbf{v} | Y_{-j} = \mathbf{y}_j] > 0$ implies $\Pr[Y_{-j} = \mathbf{y}_{-j} \mid X_{-\{2j-1,2j\}} = \mathbf{v}] = 1$. Hence,

$$\begin{aligned} &\Pr_{X\sim D}[Y_j = \mathbf{y}_j \mid Y_{-j} = \mathbf{y}_{-j} \text{ and } X_{-\{2j-1,2j\}} = \mathbf{v}] \\ &= \Pr_{X\sim D}[Y_j = \mathbf{y}_j \mid X_{-\{2j-1,2j\}} = \mathbf{v}]. \end{aligned}$$

Writing $\mathbf{c} := X_{2j-1} \bmod \mathcal{L} = X_{2j} \bmod \mathcal{L}$, we have

$$\begin{aligned} &\Pr_{X\sim D}[Y_j = \mathbf{y}_j \mid X_{-\{2j-1,2j\}} = \mathbf{v}] \\ &= \Pr_{X\sim D}[X_{2j-1} - X_{2j} = \mathbf{y}_j \mid X_{-\{2j-1,2j\}} = \mathbf{v}] \\ &= \sum_{\mathbf{x}\in\mathcal{L}+\mathbf{c}} \Pr_{X\sim D}[X_{2j-1} = \mathbf{x} \text{ and } X_{2j} = \mathbf{x} - \mathbf{y}_j \mid X_{-\{2j-1,2j\}} = \mathbf{v}] \\ &= e^{\pm 2\delta} \cdot \sum_{\mathbf{x}\in\mathcal{L}+\mathbf{c}} D_{\mathcal{L}+\mathbf{c},s}(\mathbf{x}) \cdot \Pr_{X\sim D}[X_{2j} = \mathbf{x} - \mathbf{y}_j \mid X_{-\{2j-1,2j\}} = \mathbf{v}] \end{aligned}$$

by definition of conditional probability and Eq. (9) (for $i := 2j - 1$). Then,

$$\begin{aligned} &\Pr_{X\sim D}[X_{2j} = \mathbf{x} - \mathbf{y}_j \mid X_{-\{2j-1,2j\}} = \mathbf{v}] \\ &= \sum_{\mathbf{z}\in\mathcal{L}+\mathbf{c}} \Pr_{X\sim D}[X_{2j-1} = \mathbf{z} \text{ and } X_{2j} = \mathbf{x} - \mathbf{y}_j \mid X_{-\{2j-1,2j\}} = \mathbf{v}] \\ &= e^{\pm 2\delta} \cdot D_{\mathcal{L}+\mathbf{c},s}(\mathbf{x} - \mathbf{y}_j) \cdot \sum_{\mathbf{z}\in\mathcal{L}+\mathbf{c}} \Pr_{X\sim D}[X_{2j-1} = \mathbf{z} \mid X_{-\{2j-1,2j\}} = \mathbf{v}] \\ &= e^{\pm 2\delta} \cdot D_{\mathcal{L}+\mathbf{c},s}(\mathbf{x} - \mathbf{y}_j) \end{aligned}$$

using again the definition of conditional probability and Eq. (9). We complete the proof by noting that Lemma 2.7 and $\frac{1+\varepsilon}{1-\varepsilon} \le e^{3\varepsilon}$ for $\varepsilon \le \frac{1}{2}$ imply

$$\begin{aligned} \Pr_{X\sim D}[Y_j = \mathbf{y}_j \mid X_{-\{2j-1,2j\}} = \mathbf{v}] &= e^{\pm 4\delta} \cdot \sum_{\mathbf{x}\in\mathcal{L}+\mathbf{c}} D_{\mathcal{L}+\mathbf{c},s}(\mathbf{x}) \cdot D_{\mathcal{L}+\mathbf{c},s}(\mathbf{x} - \mathbf{y}_j) \\ &= e^{\pm 4\delta} \cdot \Pr_{(X_1,X_2)\sim(D_{\mathcal{L}+\mathbf{c},s})^2}[X_1 - X_2 = \mathbf{y}_j] \\ &= e^{\pm(4\delta+3\varepsilon)} \cdot D_{\mathcal{L},\sqrt{2}s}(\mathbf{y}_j). \end{aligned}$$

$\square$

### 3.3 The Algorithm: Wagner as a Gaussian Sampler

We are now ready to present our Gaussian sampler, laid out as Algorithm 4.

---

**Algorithm 4:** Wagner-Style Gaussian Sampler

---

**Input** : Integers $n, m, q$;
Full-rank matrix $\mathbf{A} = [\mathbf{A}' \mid \mathbf{I}_n] \in \mathbb{Z}_q^{n\times m}$;
Integer parameters $N, r, (p_i)_{i=1}^r, (b_i)_{i=1}^r$ with $\sum_{i=1}^r b_i = n$;
Real parameter $s_0 > 0$

**Output:** List of vectors in $\Lambda_q^\perp(\mathbf{A})$

Let $\Lambda_0 := \mathbb{Z}^{m-n}$
Initialize a list $L_0$ with $3^r N$ independent samples from $D_{\Lambda_0, s_0}$
**for** $i = 1, \ldots, r$ **do**
  Let $\Lambda_i$ be defined as in Equation (3)
  Let $\Lambda_i' = \mathcal{L}(\mathbf{B}_i')$ for $\mathbf{B}_i'$ defined as in Equation (4)
  $L_{i-1}' := \emptyset$
  **for** $\mathbf{x} \in L_{i-1}$ **do** // Lift
    Sample $\mathbf{x}' \sim \mathrm{DGLift}(\Lambda_{i-1}, \Lambda_i', s_{i-1}, \mathbf{x})$ ▷ Algorithm 2
    Append $\mathbf{x}'$ to $L_{i-1}'$
  $L_i = \mathrm{BucketAndCombine}(\Lambda_i', \Lambda_i, L_{i-1}')$ ▷ Algorithm 3 // Combine
  $s_i := \sqrt{2} s_{i-1}$
**return** $L_r$

---

*Remark 3.1.* In our applications of Algorithm 4, we consider input parameter $s_0$ satisfying $s_0 \geq \sqrt{\ln(2(m-n)+4)/\pi}$ and $\sqrt{2^{i-1}} s_0 \geq \frac{q}{p_i}\sqrt{\ln(2b_i+4)/\pi}$ for all $i \in [r]$. This allows us to use the exact sampler from Lemma 2.6 to sample from $D_{\Lambda_0, s_0}$ (in the initialization) and from $D_{\frac{q}{p_i}\mathbb{Z}^{b_i}, \sqrt{2^{i-1}}s_0}$ (in iterations $i = 1, \ldots, r$).

**Theorem 3.1 (Correctness of One Iteration).** *Let $\delta \geq 0$ and $0 < \varepsilon \leq \frac{1}{2}$ be reals. For $i \in [r]$, consider iteration $i$ of Algorithm 4 with well-defined parameters. If $s_{i-1} \geq \max(\eta_\varepsilon(\frac{q}{p_i}\mathbb{Z}^{b_i}), \sqrt{2}\eta_\varepsilon(\Lambda_i'), \frac{q}{p_i}\sqrt{\ln(2b_i+4)/\pi})$ and $L_{i-1}$ consists of $|L_{i-1}| \geq 3p_i^{b_i}$ vectors in $\Lambda_{i-1}$ that are conditionally $\delta$-similar to independent samples from $D_{\Lambda_{i-1}, s_{i-1}}$, then $L_i$ consists of $\lfloor |L_{i-1}|/3 \rfloor$ vectors in $\Lambda_i$ that are conditionally $(4\delta + 15\varepsilon)$-similar to independent samples from $D_{\Lambda_i, \sqrt{2}s_{i-1}}$.*

*Proof.* Let $\mathcal{S}$ be the embedding of $\frac{q}{p_i}\mathbb{Z}^{b_i}$ in $\mathbb{R}^{m-n+n_i}$ and $\mathcal{P}$ the embedding of $\Lambda_{i-1}$ in $\mathbb{R}^{m-n+n_i}$. Note that $\mathcal{S}$ is a primitive sublattice of $\Lambda_i'$ and that $\mathcal{P} = \pi_{\mathcal{S}}^\perp(\mathcal{C})$ for some complement $\mathcal{C}$ to $\mathcal{S}$. Since $s_{i-1} \geq \eta_\varepsilon(\frac{q}{p_i}\mathbb{Z}^{b_i}) = \eta_\varepsilon(\mathcal{S})$, the application of the algorithm from Lemma 3.1 turns the $|L_{i-1}|$ random variables on $\Lambda_{i-1}$ into $|L_{i-1}|$ random variables on $\Lambda_i'$ that are conditionally $(\delta + 3\varepsilon)$-similar to $D_{\Lambda_i', s_{i-1}}$. Here, as oracle to sample from $D_{\frac{q}{p_i}\mathbb{Z}^{b_i}, s_{i-1}, \mathbf{c}}$ (exactly), we use Lemma 2.6 to sample from $D_{\mathbb{Z}^{b_i}, \frac{p_i}{q}s_{i-1}, \frac{p_i}{q}\mathbf{c}}$, and multiply the resulting vector by $\frac{q}{p_i}$. This is justified since we assume $\frac{p_i}{q}s_{i-1} \geq \sqrt{\ln(2b_i+4)/\pi}$.

By Lemma 3.3 (where we use that $s_{i-1} \geq \sqrt{2}\eta_\varepsilon(\Lambda_i')$), the output list $L_i$ of BucketAndCombine consists of $\lfloor |L_{i-1}|/3 \rfloor$ vectors in $\Lambda_i$ that are conditionally

$\delta'$-similar to independent samples from $D_{\Lambda_i,\sqrt{2}s_{i-1}}$, where $\delta' = 4(\delta + 3\varepsilon) + 3\varepsilon = 4\delta + 15\varepsilon$. □

**Theorem 3.2 (Correctness of Algorithm** 4**).** *Let $0 < \varepsilon \le \frac{1}{2}$ be a real, and $r$ an integer. If the input parameters satisfy $N \ge p_i^{b_i}$, $s_0 \ge \sqrt{\ln(2(m-n)+4)/\pi}$, and $\sqrt{2^{i-1}}s_0 \ge \max(\eta_\varepsilon(\frac{q}{p_i}\mathbb{Z}^{b_i}), \sqrt{2}\eta_\varepsilon(\Lambda_i'), \frac{q}{p_i}\sqrt{\ln(2b_i+4)/\pi})$ for all $i \in [r]$, then Algorithm 4 returns a list of size $N$ consisting of vectors that are conditionally $4^r 5\varepsilon$-similar to independent samples from $D_{\Lambda_q^\perp(\mathbf{A}),\sqrt{2^r}s_0}$.*

*Proof.* To obtain the list $L_0$, we use the exact $D_{\mathbb{Z}^{m-n},s_0}$-sampler from Lemma 2.6, which takes time $\mathrm{poly}(m-n, \log s_0)$. This is justified since we assume $s_0 \ge \sqrt{\ln(2(m-n)+4)/\pi}$.

We show by induction that, for each iteration $i \in \{1,\dots,r\}$, the output list $L_i$ consists of $3^{r-i}N$ vectors in $\Lambda_i$ that are conditionally $\delta_i$-similar to independent samples from $D_{\Lambda_i,s_i}$ for $\delta_i := (4^i - 1)5\varepsilon$. The theorem then immediately follows, since $(4^r - 1)5\varepsilon \le 4^r 5\varepsilon$.

By assumption, $|L_0| = 3^r N \ge 3^r p_1^{b_1} \ge 3p_1^{b_1}$ and $s_0 \ge \max(\eta_\varepsilon(\frac{q}{p_1}\mathbb{Z}^{b_1}), \sqrt{2}\eta_\varepsilon(\Lambda_1'), \frac{q}{p_1}\sqrt{\ln(2b_1+4)/\pi})$. Therefore, Theorem 3.1 implies that the output list $L_1$ of iteration $i = 1$ consists of $3^{r-1}N$ vectors in $\Lambda_1$ that are conditionally $15\varepsilon$-similar to independent samples from $D_{\Lambda_1,s_1}$. Since $\delta_1 = 15\varepsilon$, this proves the base case.

Consider any $i \in \{2,\dots,r\}$, and suppose the claim holds for all $1 \le j \le i-1$. By the induction hypothesis and assumption, $|L_{i-1}| = 3^{r-(i-1)}N \ge 3^{r-(i-1)}p_i^{b_i} \ge 3p_i^{b_i}$ and $s_{i-1} = \sqrt{2^{i-1}}s_0 \ge \max(\eta_\varepsilon(\frac{q}{p_i}\mathbb{Z}^{b_i}), \sqrt{2}\eta_\varepsilon(\Lambda_i'), \frac{q}{p_i}\sqrt{\ln(2b_i+4)/\pi})$. Therefore, by Theorem 3.1, the output list $L_i$ of iteration $i$ consists of $3^{r-i}N$ vectors in $\Lambda_i$. By the induction hypothesis the vectors in $L_{i-1}$ are conditionally $\delta_{i-1}$-similar to independent samples from $D_{\Lambda_{i-1},s_{i-1}}$, so by Theorem 3.1 the vectors in $L_i$ are conditionally $(4\delta_{i-1} + 15\varepsilon)$-similar to independent samples from $D_{\Lambda_i,s_i}$. Since $4\delta_{i-1} + 15\varepsilon = 4(4^{i-1} - 1)5\varepsilon + 15\varepsilon = (4^i - 1)5\varepsilon = \delta_i$, the claim follows. □

*Remark 3.2 (Expected Runtime).* Using the exact sampler from Lemma 2.6 ensures that all vectors processed by Algorithm 4 have expected bitsize at most $\mathrm{poly}(m, r, \log s_0, \log q)$ when the parameters satisfy $p_i \le q$ for all $i \in [r]$. Hence, the expected runtime of Algorithm 4 is at most $(3^r N + \sum_{i=1}^r |L_{i-1}|) \cdot \mathrm{poly}(m, r, \log s_0, \log q) = 3^r N \cdot \mathrm{poly}(m, r, \log s_0, \log q)$.

### 3.4 Putting It All Together

We now have all the ingredients to prove the existence of a subexponential-time algorithm for sampling from a distribution conditionally similar to $D_{\Lambda_q^\perp(\mathbf{A}),s}$ for random (full-rank) matrices $\mathbf{A}$. We write the width $s$ of the desired discrete Gaussian distribution as $s = q/f$ for some $f > 1$, and remark that the difficulty of sampling with width $q/f$ increases with $f$. Below, we demonstrate that subexponential complexity is feasible when $q/f$ and $m$ are above a certain threshold.

We note that $q^{1-n/m} \ge 2^{\Theta(\log n/\log\log n)}$ for the parameters of interest, which tends to infinity as $n$ grows (so the assumption $q^{1-n/m} \ge 6$ is not too restrictive).

**Theorem 3.3.** *For $n \in \mathbb{N}$, let $m \geq n$ be an integer and $q = \mathrm{poly}(n)$ be a prime such that $q^{1-n/m} \geq 6$. Let $f > 1$ and $\varepsilon \leq \frac{1}{m}$ be positive reals such that $\frac{q}{f} \geq \sqrt{\ln(1/\varepsilon)}$. There exists a value of $N$ satisfying*

$$\log_2(N) = \frac{n/2}{\ln(\ln(q)) - \ln(\ln(f) + \frac{1}{2}\ln\ln(1/\varepsilon)) - O(1)} \tag{10}$$

*such that, if $m \geq n + 2\log_2 N$, there is a randomized algorithm that, given a uniformly random full-rank matrix $\mathbf{A} \in \mathbb{Z}_q^{n\times m}$, with probability at least $1-2^{-\tilde{\Omega}(n)}$ returns $N$ vectors in $\Lambda_q^\perp(\mathbf{A})$. The output vectors are conditionally $q^4\varepsilon$-similar to independent samples from $D_{\Lambda_q^\perp(\mathbf{A}),\frac{q}{f}}$. This algorithm has time and memory complexity $N \cdot \mathrm{poly}(m)$.*

*Proof.* We first provide a choice of parameters for Algorithm 4 (instantiated with the exact sampler from Lemma 2.6) and show that the conditions of Theorem 3.2 are satisfied.

*Choice of Parameters.* For $\varepsilon' := \varepsilon/5$, let $N$ be the smallest integer such that

$$\log_2(N/q) \geq \frac{n/2}{\ln(\ln(q)) - \ln(\ln(f) + \frac{1}{2}\ln(\frac{144}{\pi}\ln(3/\varepsilon')) + \frac{1}{2})}.$$

Then $N$ satisfies Eq. (10) for sufficiently large $n$. Let $s_0 := \frac{q/f}{\sqrt{2^r}}$, where[6]

$$r := \lfloor 2\log_2(q/f) - \log_2(\tfrac{144}{\pi}\ln(3/\varepsilon'))\rfloor.$$

For $i \in [r]$, define $p_i := \lfloor q/\sqrt{2^i}\rfloor$. For $i \in [r-1]$, define $b_i := \lceil \frac{\log_2(N)}{\log_2(q)-i/2} - 1\rceil$, and define $b_r := n - \sum_{i=1}^{r-1} b_i$ so that $\sum_{i=1}^{r} b_i = n$. Note that $p_i, b_i$ are integers.

To show that these parameters satisfy the conditions of Theorem 3.2, we consider sufficiently large $n$ so that $\varepsilon' \leq \frac{1}{6}$ (i.e., $\varepsilon \leq \frac{5}{6}$) and assume $2\log_2(N) \leq m - n$.

*Verifying that $N$ is Large Enough.* We claim that $N \geq p_i^{b_i}$ for all $i \in [r]$. For all $i \in [r-1]$, this claim follows immediately from the definition of $b_i$: $b_i \leq \frac{\log_2(N)}{\log_2(q)-i/2} \leq \frac{\log_2(N)}{\log_2(p_i)}$. So it remains to show that $b_r \leq \frac{\log_2(N)}{\log_2(p_r)}$. By definition,

$$\begin{aligned}\log_2(N/q) &\geq \frac{n/2}{\ln(\ln(q)) - \ln\left(\ln(f) + \frac{1}{2}\ln(\frac{144}{\pi}\ln(3/\varepsilon')) + \frac{1}{2}\right)} \\ &\geq \frac{n/2}{\ln(\log_2(q)) - \ln(\log_2(f) + \frac{1}{2}\log_2(\frac{144}{\pi}\ln(3/\varepsilon')) + \frac{1}{2})}\end{aligned}$$

[6] For all interesting parameters, we have $r \geq 1$. For the rare setting of parameters for which $r < 1$, we replace $r$ by $r+10$. (This suffices since, for any valid parameters, the assumption $q/f \geq \sqrt{\ln(1/\varepsilon)}$ ensures that $2\log_2(q/f) - \log_2(144\ln(3/\varepsilon')/\pi) + 10 \geq 1$ when $n \geq 2$.) Note that increasing $r$ by a constant additive factor does not affect the proof; in particular, Eq. (11) would still hold as it decreases with $r$.

$$\geq \frac{n/2}{\ln\left(\frac{2\log_2(q)}{2\log_2(q)-r}\right)} \tag{11}$$

since $r \geq 2\log_2(q/f) - \log_2(\frac{144}{\pi}\ln(3/\varepsilon')) - 1$. In particular, using known facts of integrals (recall Footnote 7 on page 6) we obtain

$$n \leq 2\log_2(N/q) \cdot \ln\left(\frac{2\log_2(q)}{2\log_2(q)-r}\right) = \int_0^r \frac{2\log_2(N/q)}{2\log_2(q)-x}dx \leq \sum_{i=1}^{r} \frac{2\log_2(N/q)}{2\log_2(q)-i}.$$

Since $\frac{2\log_2(N/q)}{2\log_2(q)-i} \leq \frac{2\log_2(N)}{2\log_2(q)-i} - 1 \leq b_i$, we obtain $n \leq \sum_{i=1}^{r-1} b_i + \frac{2\log_2(N/q)}{2\log_2(q)-r}$, and thus $b_r = n - \sum_{i=1}^{r-1} b_i \leq \frac{2\log_2(N/q)}{2\log_2(q)-r} \leq \frac{2\log_2(N)}{2\log_2(q)-r} \leq \frac{\log_2(N)}{\log_2(p_r)}$, as desired.

*Verifying the Smoothing Conditions of Theorem* 3.2. To show that the smoothing conditions in Theorem 3.2 are satisfied with probability $1 - 2^{-\tilde{\Omega}(n)}$, it suffices to show that the following holds (for large enough $n$):

(I) $s_0 \geq \sqrt{\ln(2(m-n)+4)/\pi}$ and $\sqrt{2^{i-1}}s_0 \geq \frac{q}{p_i}\sqrt{\ln(2b_i+4)/\pi}$ for all $i \in [r]$.
(II) With probability $1 - 2^{-\tilde{\Omega}(n)}$, $\sqrt{2^{i-1}}s_0 \geq \sqrt{2}\max(\eta_{\varepsilon'/3}(\frac{q}{p_i}\mathbb{Z}^{b_i}), \eta_{\varepsilon'/3}(\Lambda_{i-1}))$ for all $i \in [r]$.

Indeed, if $\sqrt{2^{i-1}}s_0 \geq \sqrt{2}\max(\eta_{\varepsilon'/3}(\frac{q}{p_i}\mathbb{Z}^{b_i}), \eta_{\varepsilon'/3}(\Lambda_{i-1}))$ (for any $i \in [r]$), then $\sqrt{2^{i-1}}s_0 \geq \max(\eta_{\varepsilon'}(\frac{q}{p_i}\mathbb{Z}^{b_i}), \sqrt{2}\eta_{\varepsilon'}(\Lambda_i'))$ by [EWY23, Proposition 2] (with the embedding of $\frac{q}{p_i}\mathbb{Z}^{b_i}$ in $\mathbb{R}^{m-n+n_i}$ as sublattice) and because $\eta_{\varepsilon'/3}(\frac{q}{p_i}\mathbb{Z}^{b_i}) \geq \eta_{\varepsilon'}(\frac{q}{p_i}\mathbb{Z}^{b_i})$.

To prove (I) and (II), we use that our choice of $r$ implies $s_0 \geq \sqrt{\frac{144\ln(3/\varepsilon')}{\pi}}$. Furthermore, we emphasize that $\varepsilon \leq \frac{1}{m}$ implies $\varepsilon' \leq \frac{3}{4m}$, so $\varepsilon' \leq \min(\frac{3}{4(m-n)}, \frac{3}{4b_1})$ and $\varepsilon' \leq \min(\frac{3}{4(m-n+n_{i-1})}, \frac{3}{4b_i})$ for all $i \in \{2, \ldots, r\}$. (Hence, we can apply the results from Sect. 2.4 to bound the parameters $\eta_{\varepsilon'}(\frac{q}{p_i}\mathbb{Z}^{b_i})$ and $\eta_{\varepsilon'}(\Lambda_i')$.)

Consider any $i \in [r]$. By Lemma 2.8 (with dimension $b_i$ and using that $\varepsilon' \leq \frac{3}{4b_i}$), we obtain $\sqrt{2}\eta_{\varepsilon'/3}(\frac{q}{p_i}\mathbb{Z}^{b_i}) \leq \frac{q}{p_i}\sqrt{\frac{4\ln(3/\varepsilon')}{\pi}} \leq \sqrt{2^{i-1}}\sqrt{\frac{32\ln(3/\varepsilon')}{\pi}} \leq \sqrt{2^{i-1}}s_0$ (since $p_i = \lfloor q/\sqrt{2^i}\rfloor \geq (q/\sqrt{2^i})/2$ whenever $p_i \geq 2$, and thus $\frac{q}{p_i} \leq 2\sqrt{2^i}$). Furthermore, for $i = 1$, we have by Lemma 2.8 that $\sqrt{2}\eta_{\varepsilon'/3}(\Lambda_0) = \sqrt{2}\eta_{\varepsilon'/3}(\mathbb{Z}^{m-n}) < \sqrt{\frac{4\ln(3/\varepsilon')}{\pi}} \leq s_0$. Since $\varepsilon' \leq \frac{3}{4m}$ we have $\frac{3}{\varepsilon'} \geq 2m \geq 2(m-n)+4$ and $\frac{3}{\varepsilon'} \geq 4m \geq 4n \geq 2n+4 \geq 2b_i+4$ for all $i \in [r]$. Hence, $s_0 \geq \sqrt{\frac{4\ln(3/\varepsilon')}{\pi}}$ implies $s_0 \geq \sqrt{\frac{\ln(3/\varepsilon')}{\pi}} \geq \sqrt{\frac{\ln(2(m-n)+4)}{\pi}}$, and $\sqrt{2^{i-1}}s_0 \geq \frac{q}{p_i}\sqrt{\frac{4\ln(3/\varepsilon')}{\pi}}$ implies $\sqrt{2^{i-1}}s_0 \geq \frac{q}{p_i}\sqrt{\frac{\ln(3/\varepsilon')}{\pi}} \geq \frac{q}{p_i}\sqrt{\frac{\ln(2b_i+4)}{\pi}}$ for all $i \in [r]$. Thus, (I) holds for $n \geq 2$.

Next, we observe that $q^{\frac{n_j}{m-n+n_j}} \leq \sqrt{2^j}$ for all $j \in [r]$. Indeed, for all $j \in [r]$, we have $n_j \leq jb_j$, so $\frac{n_j}{j}(2\log_2(q) - j) \leq b_j(2\log_2(q) - j) \leq 2\log_2(N) \leq m -$

$n$. Since $\frac{n_j}{j}(2\log_2(q) - j) \leq m - n$ if and only if $q^{\frac{n_j}{m-n+n_j}} \leq \sqrt{2^j}$, the claim follows. Thus, for each $i \in \{2, \dots, r\}$, Lemma 2.11 and the previous claim imply that $\sqrt{2}\eta_{\varepsilon'/3}(\Lambda_{i-1}) < \sqrt{\frac{144\ln(3/\varepsilon')}{\pi}} q^{\frac{n_{i-1}}{m-n+n_{i-1}}} \leq \sqrt{\frac{144\ln(3/\varepsilon')}{\pi}}\sqrt{2^{i-1}} \leq \sqrt{2^{i-1}}s_0$, except with probability $< 2^{-n_{i-1}}$.

Therefore, the union bound implies that, with probability at least $1 - \sum_{i=1}^{r-1} 2^{-n_i}$, $\sqrt{2^{i-1}}s_0 \geq \sqrt{2}\max(\eta_{\varepsilon'/3}(\frac{q}{p_i}\mathbb{Z}^{b_i}), \eta_{\varepsilon'/3}(\Lambda_{i-1}))$ for all $i \in [r]$. Note that $1 - \sum_{i=1}^{r-1} 2^{-n_i} \geq 1 - r2^{-b_1} = 1 - 2^{-\tilde{\Omega}(n)}$ since $\log_2(r) = \log_2\log_2(n) + O(1)$, $b_1 = \Omega(\frac{\log_2 N}{\log_2 n})$, and $\log_2(N) = \Omega(\frac{n}{\log_2\log_2(n)})$, so (II) holds as well.[7]

*Conclusion of the Proof.* Theorem 3.2 then implies that the output of this algorithm consists of at least $N$ vectors in $\Lambda_q^\perp(\mathbf{A})$ that are conditionally $4^r 5\varepsilon'$-similar to independent samples from $D_{\Lambda_q^\perp(\mathbf{A}),\sqrt{2^r}s_0}$. Since $4^r \leq q^4$, we obtain that they are conditionally $\delta$-similar for $\delta = q^4 5\varepsilon' = q^4\varepsilon$-similar.

Finally, the expected runtime of Algorithm 4 is at most $3^r N \cdot \mathrm{poly}(m, r, \log s_0, \log q)$ by Remark 3.2. Since $r = O(\log q)$, $s_0 \leq q$, and $q = \mathrm{poly}(m)$, it follows that the time and memory complexity are both upper bounded by $N \cdot \mathrm{poly}(m)$. □

## 4 Asymptotic Application to Cryptographic Problems

We now apply our previous result on Gaussian sampling for SIS lattices to solving various variants of SIS in subexponential time. We also discuss why our result does not directly lead to a provable subexponential-time algorithm for LWE with narrow error distribution.

### 4.1 Implications for SIS$^\infty$

The following theorem instantiated with $m = n + \omega(n/\log\log n)$ such that[8] $m = \mathrm{poly}(n)$, $q = n^{\Theta(1)}$, $\beta = q/\mathrm{polylog}(n)$, and a sufficiently small $\varepsilon = 1/\mathrm{poly}(n)$ provides a subexponential-time algorithm for $\mathrm{SIS}^\infty_{n,m,q,\beta}$. In fact, our subexponential complexity holds for even smaller norm bounds: for instance, we can achieve $\beta = q/2^{\log(n)^c}$ for any constant $c < 1$.

**Theorem 4.1.** *For $n \in \mathbb{N}$, let $m = n + \omega(n/\ln\ln n)$ be integer and $q = n^{\Theta(1)}$ be prime such that $q^{1-n/m} \geq 6$. Let $f > 1$ and $\varepsilon \leq \frac{1}{mq^4}$ be positive reals such*

[7] It also follows that $\eta_{\varepsilon/4}(\Lambda_q^\perp(\mathbf{A})) < \frac{q}{f}$. Indeed, another application of Lemma 2.11 yields $\eta_{\varepsilon/4}(\Lambda_q^\perp(\mathbf{A})) < \sqrt{72\ln(4/\varepsilon)/\pi}q^{n/m}$, except with probability $< 2^{-n}$, but this does not affect the lower bound on the success probability. By the aforementioned fact, we have $q^{n/m} \leq \sqrt{2^r}$, so by definition of $r$ we obtain $\eta_{\varepsilon/4}(\Lambda_q^\perp(\mathbf{A})) < \frac{q}{f}$.

[8] Note that one may always decrease $m$ by ignoring SIS variables, hence the condition $m = \mathrm{poly}(n)$ comes with no loss of generality.

*that* $\ln(f\sqrt{\ln(1/\varepsilon)}) = O(\ln(n)^c)$ *for some* $c < 1$*. There exists an algorithm that solves* $\mathrm{SIS}^{\infty}_{n,m,q,\beta}$ *for* $\beta := \frac{q}{f}\sqrt{\ln m}$ *in expected time*

$$T = 2^{\frac{n/2}{\ln(\ln(q)) - \ln\left(\ln(f) + \frac{1}{2}\ln\ln(1/\varepsilon)\right) - O(1)}} \cdot \mathrm{poly}(m)$$

*with success probability* $1 - \frac{1}{\Omega(n)}$*.*

*Proof.* Apply Theorem 3.3 with input $n, m, q, f, \varepsilon$ to the $\mathrm{SIS}^{\infty}_{n,m,q,\beta}$ instance $\mathbf{A}$. With probability at least $1 - 2^{-\tilde{\Omega}(n)}$, it returns a list of vectors $\mathbf{x}_1, \ldots, \mathbf{x}_N$ in $\Lambda_q^{\perp}(\mathbf{A})$ (so they are solutions to $\mathbf{A}\mathbf{x} = \mathbf{0} \bmod q$) that are conditionally $q^4\varepsilon$-similar to independent samples from $D_{\Lambda_q^{\perp}(\mathbf{A}),s}$ for $s := \frac{q}{f}$. In particular, it follows that the first vector $\mathbf{x}_1$ follows a distribution $D$ that is $q^4\varepsilon$-similar to $D_{\Lambda_q^{\perp}(\mathbf{A}),s}$ (recall Remark 2.2). By Footnote 10 we have $\frac{q}{f} > \eta_{\varepsilon/4}(\Lambda_q^{\perp}(\mathbf{A}))$. We note that we may, without loss of generality, assume $\frac{q}{f} > 2\eta_{\varepsilon/4}(\Lambda_q^{\perp}(\mathbf{A}))$ by replacing the role of the constant 144 in the proof of Theorem 3.3 by a larger constant.

Since $D$ is $q^4\varepsilon$-similar to $D_{\Lambda_q^{\perp}(\mathbf{A}),s}$, Lemma 2.2 (together with the fact that $e^{-x} \geq 1 - x$ for all $x \in \mathbb{R}$) implies

$$\begin{aligned}\Pr[\|\mathbf{x}_1\|_\infty \leq \beta \wedge \mathbf{x}_1 \neq \mathbf{0}] &\geq e^{-q^4\varepsilon} \Pr_{X \sim D_{\Lambda_q^{\perp}(\mathbf{A}),s}}[\|X\|_\infty \leq \beta \wedge X \neq \mathbf{0}] \\ &\geq \Pr_{X \sim D_{\Lambda_q^{\perp}(\mathbf{A}),s}}[\|X\|_\infty \leq \beta \wedge X \neq \mathbf{0}] - q^4\varepsilon \\ &\geq \Pr_{X \sim D_{\Lambda_q^{\perp}(\mathbf{A}),s}}[\|X\|_\infty \leq \beta \wedge X \neq \mathbf{0}] - \frac{1}{m}.\end{aligned}$$

We now show that $\Pr_{X \sim D_{\Lambda_q^{\perp}(\mathbf{A}),s}}[\|X\|_\infty \leq \beta \wedge X \neq \mathbf{0}] \geq 1 - \frac{2}{m^2} - \frac{1}{2^{m-1}}$, from which it follows that $\mathbf{x}_1$ is a solution to $\mathrm{SIS}^{\infty}$ with probability at least $1 - \frac{2}{m^2} - \frac{1}{2^{m-1}} - \frac{1}{m} \geq 1 - \frac{3}{m} \geq 1 - \frac{3}{n}$ when $n \geq 2$ (where we use that $m \geq n$), thereby proving the theorem.

It remains to prove our claim. We have

$$\Pr_{X \sim D_{\Lambda_q^{\perp}(\mathbf{A}),s}}[\|X\|_\infty \leq \beta \wedge X \neq \mathbf{0}] \geq \Pr_{X \sim D_{\Lambda_q^{\perp}(\mathbf{A}),s}}[\|X\|_\infty \leq \beta] - \Pr_{X \sim D_{\Lambda_q^{\perp}(\mathbf{A}),s}}[X = \mathbf{0}].$$

Since $s = \frac{q}{f} > 2\eta_{\varepsilon/4}(\Lambda_q^{\perp}(\mathbf{A}))$, Lemma 2.5 implies $\Pr_{X \sim D_{\Lambda_q^{\perp}(\mathbf{A}),s}}[X = \mathbf{0}] \leq \frac{1+\varepsilon/4}{1-\varepsilon/4} \cdot 2^{-m} \leq \frac{1}{2^{m-1}}$ (as $\frac{1+x/4}{1-x/4} \leq 2$ for all $x \in [0,1]$). Also, Lemma 2.3 yields $\Pr_{X \sim D_{\Lambda_q^{\perp}(\mathbf{A}),s}}[\|X\|_\infty \leq \beta] > 1 - 2me^{-\pi(\frac{\beta f}{q})^2} \geq 1 - \frac{2}{m^2}$, where we use that $\beta = \frac{q}{f}\sqrt{\ln m}$. Our claim follows. □

One may remark that our application of Lemma 2.3 makes us lose a $\sqrt{\ln m}$ factor on the norm bound to reach a constant success probability per sample. It would be tempting to only aim for a success probability barely greater than $1/N$ instead, however, the proof would then require $\varepsilon \approx 1/N$, which would make the algorithm exponential. This is admittedly a counterintuitive situation, and plausibly a proof artifact.

### 4.2 Implications for SIS$^\times$ and ISIS in $\ell_2$ Norm

Regarding the $\ell_2$-norm, for the same parameters as above, our Gaussian sampler outputs vectors of length less than $\beta = \sqrt{m} \cdot q/f$ for any $f = \text{polylog}(n)$ in subexponential time. However, SIS in $\ell_2$-norm is trivial for such a bound; for example, $(q, 0, \ldots, 0)$ is a valid solution.

Yet, some schemes [ETWY22] have used the inhomogeneous version of SIS (ISIS) for bounds $\beta > q$, which was shown [DEP23] to be equivalent to solving SIS$^\times$, a variant of SIS where the solution must be nonzero modulo $q$. The work of [DEP23] notes that the problem becomes trivial when $\beta \geq q\sqrt{n/12}$ and proposes a heuristic attack that is better than pure lattice reduction when $\beta > q$; however, it appears to run in exponential time in $n$ for $\beta = q\sqrt{n}/\text{polylog}(n)$. Our Gaussian sampler directly yields a provably subexponential-time algorithm in that regime.

**Theorem 4.2.** *For $n \in \mathbb{N}$, let $m = n + \omega(n/\ln \ln n)$ be integer and $q = n^{\Theta(1)}$ be prime such that $q^{1-n/m} \geq 6$. Let $f > 1$ and $\varepsilon \leq \frac{1}{mq^4}$ be positive reals such that $\ln(f\sqrt{\ln(1/\varepsilon)}) = O(\ln(n)^c)$ for some $c < 1$. There exists an algorithm that solves $\text{SIS}^\times_{n,m,q,\beta}$ and $\text{ISIS}_{n,m,q,\beta}$ for $\beta := \frac{q}{f}\sqrt{m}$ in expected time*

$$T = 2^{\frac{n/2}{\ln(\ln(q)) - \ln\left(\ln(f) + \frac{1}{2}\ln\ln(1/\varepsilon)\right) - O(1)}} \cdot \text{poly}(m)$$

*with success probability $1 - \frac{1}{\Omega(n)}$.*

The proof is essentially equivalent to that of Theorem 4.1, up to the invocation of Lemma 2.3 used to tail-bound the norm of a discrete Gaussian, which should be replaced by a similar tail-bound for the $\ell_2$-norm [Ban93, Lemma 1.5].

Note again here that one may always choose $m = n(1 + o(1))$ without loss of generality even when the given $m$ is much larger, simply by ignoring some SIS variables. Hence, reaching the norm bound $\beta = q\sqrt{m}/\text{polylog}(n)$ also permits to reach $\beta = q\sqrt{n}/\text{polylog}(n)$.

### 4.3 Potential Implications for LWE

Having obtained a discrete Gaussian sampler for SIS lattices, one may be tempted to apply the dual distinguisher of [AR05] and directly obtain a subexponential-time algorithm for LWE with narrow secrets. This is in fact problematic as such a distinguisher needs to consider subexponentially many samples simultaneously, so some naive reasoning using the data-processing inequality would force one to instantiate our Gaussian sampler with $\varepsilon = 2^{-\tilde{\Omega}(n)}$ rather than $\varepsilon = n^{-\Theta(1)}$. Unfortunately, for such small $\varepsilon$ our Gaussian sampler has exponential complexity.

This issue resonates with the one raised in [HKM18] regarding the proof of [KF15] when the parameter $m$ is linear in $n$; namely, their issue is about reaching exponentially small statistical distance. However, it is technically different:

in our case, it cannot be fixed by increasing $m$ to $\Theta(n \log n)$. Tracking down the limiting factor leads to blaming the poor smoothing parameters of $\frac{q}{p_i}\mathbb{Z}^{b_i}$. Thanks to the generality of our framework, it is plausible that this superlattice of $q\mathbb{Z}^{b_i}$ can be replaced by one of similar index with a much better smoothing parameter. We hope that future work will finally be able to provably fix the claim of [KF15] for $m$ linear in $n$.

**Acknowledgments.** The authors are grateful to Ronald de Wolf and the anonymous reviewers for their valuable comments on the manuscript. LD and JL were supported by the ERC Starting Grant 947821 (ARTICULATE). LE was supported by the Dutch National Growth Fund (NGF), as part of the Quantum Delta NL program.

## References

ACKS21. Aggarwal, D., Chen, Y., Kumar, R., Shen, Y.: Improved (provable) algorithms for the shortest vector problem via bounded distance decoding. In: 38th International Symposium on Theoretical Aspects of Computer Science (STACS 2021), volume 187 of *LIPIcs*, pp. 4:1–4:20. Schloss Dagstuhl - Leibniz-Zentrum für Informatik (2021)

ADRS15. Aggarwal, D., Dadush, D., Regev, O., Stephens-Davidowitz, N.: Solving the shortest vector problem in $2^n$ time using discrete Gaussian sampling: extended abstract. In: Proceedings of the Forty-Seventh Annual ACM Symposium on Theory of Computing, STOC 2015, pp. 733–742. ACM (2015)

ADS15. Aggarwal, D., Dadush, D., Stephens-Davidowitz, N.: Solving the closest vector problem in $2^n$ time - the discrete Gaussian strikes again! In: 2015 IEEE 56th Annual Symposium on Foundations of Computer Science, pp. 563–582. IEEE Computer Society (2015)

AFFP14. Albrecht, M.R., Faugère, J.-C., Fitzpatrick, R., Perret, L.: Lazy modulus switching for the BKW algorithm on LWE. In: Krawczyk, H. (ed.) PKC 2014. LNCS, vol. 8383, pp. 429–445. Springer, Heidelberg (2014). https://doi.org/10.1007/978-3-642-54631-0_25

Ajt96. Ajtai, M.: Generating hard instances of lattice problems (extended abstract). In: Proceedings of the Twenty-Eighth Annual ACM Symposium on Theory of Computing, STOC 1996, pp. 99–108. Association for Computing Machinery (1996)

ALS21. Aggarwal, D., Li, Z., Stephens-Davidowitz, N.: A $2^{n/2}$-time algorithm for $\sqrt{n}$-SVP and $\sqrt{n}$-hermite SVP, and an improved time-approximation tradeoff for (H)SVP. In: Canteaut, A., Standaert, F.-X. (eds.) EUROCRYPT 2021. LNCS, vol. 12696, pp. 467–497. Springer, Cham (2021). https://doi.org/10.1007/978-3-030-77870-5_17

AR05. Aharonov, D., Regev, O.: Lattice problems in NP $\cap$ coNP. J. ACM (JACM) **52**(5), 749–765 (2005)

AS18. Aggarwal, D., Stephens-Davidowitz, N.: Just take the average! An embarrassingly simple $2^n$-time algorithm for SVP (and CVP). In: 1st Symposium on Simplicity in Algorithms (SOSA 2018), volume 61 of *Open Access Series in Informatics*, pp. 12:1–12:19. Schloss Dagstuhl - Leibniz-Zentrum für Informatik (2018)

Ban93. Banaszczyk, W.: New bounds in some transference theorems in the geometry of numbers. Math. Ann. **296**, 625–635 (1993)

Ban95. Banaszczyk, W.: Inequalites for convex bodies and polar reciprocal lattices in $\mathbb{R}^n$. Discrete Comput. Geom. **13**, 217–231 (1995)

BKW03. Blum, A., Kalai, A., Wasserman, H.: Noise-tolerant learning, the parity problem, and the statistical query model. J. ACM (JACM) **50**(4), 506–519 (2003)

BLP+13. Brakerski, Z., Langlois, A., Peikert, C., Regev, O., Stehlé, D.: Classical hardness of learning with errors. In: Proceedings of the Forty-Fifth Annual ACM Symposium on Theory of Computing, STOC 2013, pp. 575–584. ACM (2013)

DEL25. Ducas, L., Engelberts, L., Loyer, J.: Wagner's algorithm provably runs in subexponential time for $SIS^\infty$. Cryptology ePrint Archive, Paper 2025/575 (2025). Full version

DEP23. Ducas, L., Espitau, T., Postlethwaite, E.W.: Finding short integer solutions when the modulus is small. In: Handschuh, H., Lysyanskaya, A. (eds.) CRYPTO 2023. LNCS, vol. 14083, pp. 150–176. Springer, Cham (2023). https://doi.org/10.1007/978-3-031-38548-3_6

DKL+18. Ducas, L., et al.: CRYSTALS-Dilithium: a lattice-based digital signature scheme. IACR Trans. Cryptogr. Hardw. Embed. Syst., 238–268 (2018)

ETWY22. Espitau, T., Tibouchi, M., Wallet, A., Yu, Y.: Shorter hash-and-sign lattice-based signatures. In: Dodis, Y., Shrimpton, T. (eds.) CRYPTO 2022. LNCS, vol. 13508, pp. 245–275. Springer, Cham (2022). https://doi.org/10.1007/978-3-031-15979-4_9

EWY23. Espitau, T., Wallet, A., Yang, Yu.: On Gaussian sampling, smoothing parameter and application to signatures. In: Guo, J., Steinfeld, R. (eds.) ASIACRYPT 2023. LNCS, vol. 14444, pp. 65–97. Springer, Singapore (2023). https://doi.org/10.1007/978-981-99-8739-9_3

GJMS17. Guo, Q., Johansson, T., Mårtensson, E., Stankovski, P.: Coded-BKW with sieving. In: Takagi, T., Peyrin, T. (eds.) ASIACRYPT 2017. LNCS, vol. 10624, pp. 323–346. Springer, Cham (2017). https://doi.org/10.1007/978-3-319-70694-8_12

GPV08. Gentry, C., Peikert, C., Vaikuntanathan, V.: Trapdoors for hard lattices and new cryptographic constructions. In: Proceedings of the Fortieth Annual ACM Symposium on Theory of Computing, STOC 2008, pp. 197–206. ACM (2008)

HKM18. Herold, G., Kirshanova, E., May, A.: On the asymptotic complexity of solving LWE. Des. Codes Crypt. **86**(1), 55–83 (2018)

KF15. Kirchner, P., Fouque, P.-A.: An improved BKW algorithm for LWE with applications to cryptography and lattices. In: Gennaro, R., Robshaw, M. (eds.) CRYPTO 2015. LNCS, vol. 9215, pp. 43–62. Springer, Heidelberg (2015). https://doi.org/10.1007/978-3-662-47989-6_3

Lyu05. Lyubashevsky, V.: The parity problem in the presence of noise, decoding random linear codes, and the subset sum problem. In: Chekuri, C., Jansen, K., Rolim, J.D.P., Trevisan, L. (eds.) APPROX/RANDOM 2005. LNCS, vol. 3624, pp. 378–389. Springer, Heidelberg (2005). https://doi.org/10.1007/11538462_32

MP13. Micciancio, D., Peikert, C.: Hardness of SIS and LWE with small parameters. In: Canetti, R., Garay, J.A. (eds.) CRYPTO 2013. LNCS, vol. 8042, pp. 21–39. Springer, Heidelberg (2013). https://doi.org/10.1007/978-3-642-40041-4_2

MR07. Micciancio, D., Regev, O.: Worst-case to average-case reductions based on Gaussian measures. SIAM J. Comput. **37**(1), 267–302 (2007)

Pei08. Peikert, C.: Limits on the hardness of lattice problems in $l_p$ norms. Comput. Complex. **17**(2), 300–351 (2008)

Pei10. Peikert, C.: An efficient and parallel gaussian sampler for lattices. In: Rabin, T. (ed.) CRYPTO 2010. LNCS, vol. 6223, pp. 80–97. Springer, Heidelberg (2010). https://doi.org/10.1007/978-3-642-14623-7_5

PR06. Peikert, C., Rosen, A.: Efficient collision-resistant hashing from worst-case assumptions on cyclic lattices. In: Halevi, S., Rabin, T. (eds.) TCC 2006. LNCS, vol. 3876, pp. 145–166. Springer, Heidelberg (2006). https://doi.org/10.1007/11681878_8

Reg05. Regev, O.: On lattices, learning with errors, random linear codes, and cryptography. In: Proceedings of the Thirty-Seventh Annual ACM Symposium on Theory of Computing, STOC 2005, pp. 84–93. ACM (2005)

Wag02. Wagner, D.: A generalized birthday problem. In: Yung, M. (ed.) CRYPTO 2002. LNCS, vol. 2442, pp. 288–304. Springer, Heidelberg (2002). https://doi.org/10.1007/3-540-45708-9_19

# Refined Attack on LWE with Hints: Constructing Lattice via Gaussian Elimination

Jinzheng Cao, Haodong Jiang, and Qingfeng Cheng(✉)

Information Engineering University, Zhengzhou 450001, China
qingfengc2008@sina.com

**Abstract.** This work presents an improved attack on LWE with hints. Our attack follows a generic and efficient framework that converts an arbitrary number of perfect hints, modular hints, and approximate hints into a problem on lattice. Based on the approach, we give a complexity estimator for solving LWE with hints, and exploit the "too many hints" regime with a new method of converting this phenomenon to lattice. The essential component of our work is an improved hint integration method, which decomposes LWE with hints into the SIS part and the LWE part. This new perspective on LWE with hints offers an insight on how hints help us solve the problem, and motivates us to efficiently reduce its dimension via Gaussian elimination instead of LLL reduction. We demonstrate the performance of our attack on LWE instances up to cryptographic dimensions. Experiments show that our method runs significantly faster than the method proposed by May and Nowakowski at Asiacrypt 2023. For example, given 200 perfect hints about CRYSTALS-KYBER 512, our method reduces the running time from 7 h to 1 h. When we use our method to solve NTRU, we achieve a 10 times acceleration given 200–350 perfect hints. Furthermore, our method requires fewer hints to carry out successful attacks in the too many hints regime. These results stresses the importance to protect post-quantum cryptography schemes against leakage.

**Keywords:** LWE · Lattice based attack · Post-quantum cryptography

## 1 Introduction

As a hard problem on lattice, the Learning with Errors (LWE) problem has been playing a central role in the development of post-quantum cryptography. The most important applications of LWE include fully homomorphic encryption, key encapsulation mechanism, and digital signature schemes [16,20]. NIST recently announced the standardization of schemes CRYSTALS-KYBER [3], CRYSTALS-DILITHIUM [21], and FALCON [21] as post-quantum cryptosystems. Among them, LWE provides security basis for CRYSTALS-KYBER and CRYSTALS-DILITHIUM [17]. Therefore, analyzing the complexities of LWE and its variants has become a vital area of research [5,10,12,14,22].


Y. Tauman Kalai and S. F. Kamara (Eds.): CRYPTO 2025, LNCS 16000, pp. 385–416, 2025.
https://doi.org/10.1007/978-3-032-01855-7_13

The small secret version of LWE problem asks to find the secret vector $\mathbf{s}$ given a list of samples $(\mathbf{A}, \mathbf{b}, q) \in \mathbb{Z}_q^{m \times n} \times \mathbb{Z}_q^m \times \mathbb{N}$ with $\mathbf{b} = \mathbf{A} \cdot \mathbf{s} + \mathbf{e} \mod q$, where $\mathbf{s} \in \mathbb{Z}_q^n$ and $\mathbf{e} \in \mathbb{Z}_q^m$ have small entries. In real-world cryptography, side-channel leakage is an important factor that reduces the hardness of LWE [9,11]. Analyzing LWE's resilience to side-channel attacks is therefore one of the key questions raised in the standardization and deployment of lattice-based post-quantum cryptography. Numerous works have been proposed to address this question. At the early stage, researchers used ad-hoc methods [1,4,8,18] to analyze specific cryptosystems, and they usually required a large amount of leakage. The first systematic framework to quantify LWE's information leakage was offered by Dachman-Soled, Ducas, Gong, and Rossi (DDGR) [6]. Their work formulates different kinds of side-channel leakage as "hints" parameterized with known values $\mathbf{v}, l, m_i$ and unknown value $\epsilon$. The DDGR paper mainly focuses on the following typical kinds of hints:

- perfect hints: $< \mathbf{s}, \mathbf{v} >= l$;
- modular hints: $< \mathbf{s}, \mathbf{v} >= l \bmod m_i$;
- mod-$q$ hints: $< \mathbf{s}, \mathbf{v} >= l \bmod q$;
- approximate hints: $< \mathbf{s}, \mathbf{v} >= l + \epsilon$.[1]

The basic idea of DDGR is successively integrating hints into the primal attack lattice. For each hint, the framework computes dual basis twice, which may be slow when many hints are involved. Dachman-Soled et al. [7] analyzed the framework from a geometric perspective, and applied it to more side-channel attacks on LWE. May and Nowakowski (MN) [13] improved the framework by designing a more efficient lattice construction method. In particular, they proposed a linear algebra approach for mod-$q$ hints. Given $k$ hints, it reduces the dimension of LWE from $n$ to $n - k$. However, this efficient method is not applicable to perfect hints and modular hins. In these cases, MN uses a LLL-based approach which is significantly slower. Another key contribution of MN is discovering the "too many hints" regime, where enough hints are provided to make solving LWE efficient in practice.

While DDGR and MN already provide impressive frameworks of integrating LWE with hints, they still leave us with interesting problems to explore. On the one hand, the pioneer work of DDGR gives a theoretical proof about hint integration, but it can only process one hint at a time. On the other hand, the MN method is faster when integrating numerous hints, but it fails to give a generic framework for mod-$q$ hints and other hints. Moreover, its correctness relies on assumptions about the quality of the LWE matrix. To make theses assumptions hold, the MN method scales the matrix by multiplying its blocks with a factor. Building on the existing works, we expect to efficiently process LWE with hints with a direct proof of correctness. To analyze the impact of hints on LWE's hardness with our framework, we also need a complexity estimator to predict the average time cost of solving LWE with hints.

[1] The DDGR paper defines approximate hints as $< \mathbf{s}, \mathbf{v} > +e = l$, which is equivalent with our definition when $\epsilon = -e$.

**Our Contributions.** The purpose of this article is to propose a generic approach that processes perfect hints, modular hints, and approximate hints in a provable and efficient way. Motivated by previous approaches of DDGR and MN, we provide a hint-processing method under minimum assumptions. Figure 1 gives an outline about our framework of solving LWE with hints. We now discuss each of our contributions in detail.

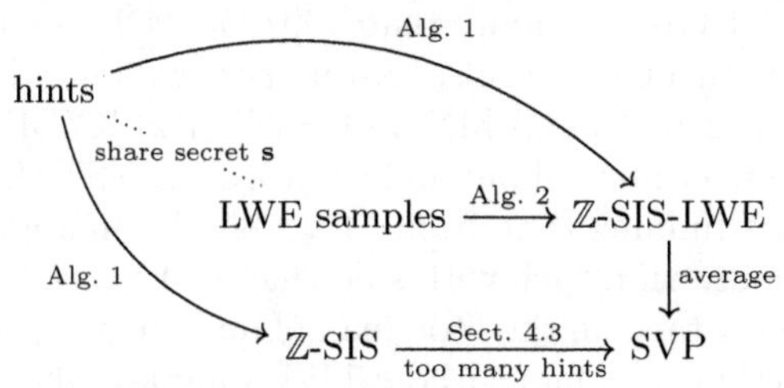


**Fig. 1.** Our framework of attacking LWE with hints

*Refined Lattice Construction from Hints.* We introduce a novel framework to extract information from the hints themselves before integrating hints with LWE. From a theoretical point of view, we transform the hints to a special variant of Small Integer Solution (SIS) problem called $\mathbb{Z}$-SIS, whose secret vector is identical to the corresponding LWE. Therefore, our framework decouples hints from the LWE problem by building $\mathbb{Z}$-SIS instances before including LWE samples, see Algorithm 1. This simplifies and clarifies how hints provide additional information that helps us solve LWE. Building on the $\mathbb{Z}$-SIS lattice, we propose Algorithm 2 to combine the LWE problem and the $\mathbb{Z}$-SIS problem generated by various kinds of hints. This transforms the LWE with hint instance to an SVP instance, leading to the final recovery of the secret vector. In particular, our method constructs the lattice by only computing the row echelon form of a smaller block by Gaussian elimination, whereas previous methods have to run LLL reductions on the whole basis. This approach brings several advantages: First, we have a more direct and succint approach to construct the lattice. Second, the method has a non-heuristic proof of correctness under minimum assumptions. Moreover, this generic method is able to unify perfect hints, modular hints, mod-$q$ hints, and approximate hints.

*Estimator of LWE with Hints.* To capture the impact of our framework on LWE's hardness, we establish a complexity estimator for recovering the secret vectors from LWE with hints. First, we evaluate the qualities of the $\mathbb{Z}$-SIS lattices to illustrate the shortness of new secret vectors. Then, the estimator is proposed to predict the required BKZ block sizes for recovering the secret vectors. Interestingly, we can apply this estimator to exploit a special case of the too many hints regime, where the perfect hints themselves are already enough to recover the secret vector without including any LWE samples. Given approximately $n/2$

hints for $n$ dimensional LWE, our method recovers the secret vector from the $\mathbb{Z}$-SIS lattice efficiently. Motivated by the analysis, we propose Algorithm 3 to solve the LWE problem if many hints are given.

*New Experimental Results.* We demonstrate concrete efficiency by comparing the implementation of our method with DDGR and MN. We run a series of experimental tests on a desktop computer with Intel Core i9-12900H and 16 GB of RAM. On CRYSTALS-KYBER 512, our lattice construction method uses less than 1 min, while DDGR uses more than 100 min, MN uses 1–100 min. Our full attacks on LWE with hints are also faster. For example, Fig. 2 compares the running time of our attacks and MN on CRYSTALS-KYBER 512 with perfect hints. Given 200 perfect hints about an instance of CRYSTALS-KYBER 512, our method reduces the running time from 7 h to 1 h. As an application, we use our framework to simulate an attack with side-channel leakage from power analysis. We further test our attack on the "too many hints" regime, where secret vectors are extracted directly from hints without LWE samples. The results demonstrate the advantages of our method.

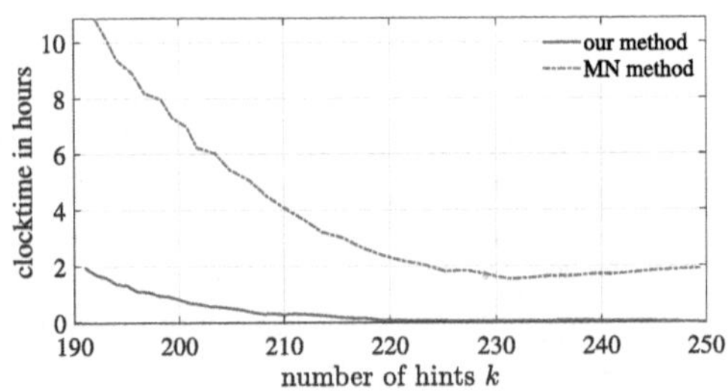


**Fig. 2.** Running time for attacking CRYSTALS-KYBER 512 with perfect hints

**Organization of the Paper.** The rest of this paper is organized as follows. Section 2 describes the preliminaries about lattices and LWE. Section 3 presents our framework of solving LWE with hints. Section 4 analyzes the complexity of our method for solving LWE, and discusses the special case of too many hints regime. Section 5 compares the experimental results of our method with previous works. We conclude the paper in Sect. 6.

## 2 Preliminaries

We use lower-case bold vectors to denote vectors, and upper-case bold vectors to denote matrices. We denote the Euclidean norm of vector $\mathbf{b}$ as $\|\mathbf{b}\|$.

### 2.1 Lattice

**Definition 1 (Lattice).** *Let $\mathbf{b}_1, \mathbf{b}_2, \ldots, \mathbf{b}_n \in \mathbb{R}^m$ be linearly independent vectors, we define the basis matrix as $\mathbf{B} = [\mathbf{b}_1, \mathbf{b}_2, \ldots, \mathbf{b}_n] \in \mathbb{R}^{n\times m}$. The lattice generated by $\mathbf{B}$ is $\mathcal{L}(\mathbf{B}) = \{\sum_{i=1}^{n} x_i \mathbf{b}_i : x_i \in \mathbb{Z}\}$.*

Two basis $\mathbf{B}_1, \mathbf{B}_2 \in \mathbb{R}^{n\times m}$ generate the same lattice if and only if there is a unimodular matrix $\mathbf{U} \in \mathbb{Z}^{n\times n}$ such that $\mathbf{B}_2 = \mathbf{U} \cdot \mathbf{B}_2$. The volume of $\mathcal{L}(\mathbf{B})$ is defined as $\mathrm{Vol}(\mathcal{L}(\mathbf{B})) = \sqrt{\det(\mathbf{B}\mathbf{B}^T)} = \prod_{i=1}^{n} \|\mathbf{b}_i^*\|$, where $\mathbf{b}_i^*$ denotes the Gram-Schmidt orthogonalized vectors of $\mathbf{b}_i$. When $m = n$, the volume of the lattice is the determinant of basis $\det(\mathbf{B})$. The volume of a lattice is independent from the choice of basis.

Most hard lattice problems can be reduced to finding short vectors in lattices. The $i$-th successive minimum of lattice $\mathcal{L}$ is defined as $\lambda_i(\mathcal{L}) = \min\{r > 0 : \mathcal{L}$ contains $i$ linearly independent vectors of length $\leq r\}$. The shortest vector of $\mathcal{L}$ is the vector $\mathbf{v} \in \mathcal{L}$ of length $\|\mathbf{v}\| = \lambda_1(\mathcal{L})$. In the Shortest Vector Problem (SVP), we are asked to find vector $\mathbf{v}$.

**Definition 2 (Shortest Vector Problem, SVP).** *Given a basis $\mathbf{B}$ of a lattice $\mathcal{L}$, find a non-zero lattice vector $\mathbf{v} \in \mathcal{L}$ of minimal length $\lambda_1(\mathcal{L})$.*

In practice, the shortest vector can usually be found by lattice basis reduction algorithms such as LLL and BKZ. We use the Gaussian heuristic to estimate the length of the shortest vector in a random lattice.

**Gaussian heuristic.** Given a $d$-dimensional lattice $\mathcal{L}$ and a measurable body $K \subset \mathbb{R}^d$, then it holds that $|K \cap \mathcal{L}| \approx \mathrm{Vol}(K)/\det(\mathcal{L})$. When taking $K$ as a $d$-dimensional ball of volume $\det(\mathcal{L})$, the Gaussian heuristic derives $\mathrm{vol}(K)/\det(\mathcal{L}) = 1$, so the length of the shortest vector $\lambda_1(\mathcal{L})$ can be estimated from the radius of the ball:

$$\lambda_1(\mathcal{L}) \approx \frac{\Gamma(\frac{d}{2}+1)^{\frac{1}{d}} \det(\mathcal{L})^{\frac{1}{d}}}{\sqrt{\pi}} \approx \sqrt{\frac{d}{2\pi e}} \det(\mathcal{L})^{1/d}.$$

We denote the estimated length of the shortest vector in lattice $\mathcal{L}$ as $\mathrm{GH}(\mathcal{L})$.

### 2.2 LWE

**Definition 3 (Learning with Errors, LWE).** *Let $n, m, q \in \mathbb{Z}$, and let $\chi$ be a distribution on $\mathbb{Z}$ with zero mean and standard deviation $\sigma$. Given $\mathbf{A} \in \mathbb{Z}^{n\times m}$ and $\mathbf{b} \equiv \mathbf{s}\mathbf{A} + \mathbf{e} \mod q$, where $\mathbf{e} \leftarrow \chi^m$, the LWE problem is to find secret vector $\mathbf{s}$ and noise $\mathbf{e}$. The tuple $(\mathbf{A}, \mathbf{b}, q)$ is called an LWE instance.*

In this work, we consider a special case called small secret LWE, where the secret vector $\mathbf{s}$ is also sampled from $\chi^n$ and has small entries. It is the setting of most practical LWE-based schemes.

The most common method to solve LWE is the primal attack, which reduces LWE to an SVP instance on a LWE lattice.

**Definition 4 (LWE Lattice).** *For an LWE instance* $(\mathbf{A}, \mathbf{b}, q)$ *where* $\mathbf{A} \in \mathbb{Z}^{n \times m}$*, the LWE lattice is a lattice generated by basis*

$$\mathbf{B}^{\mathrm{LWE}} = \begin{bmatrix} q\mathbf{I}_m & \mathbf{0} & \mathbf{0} \\ \mathbf{A} & \mathbf{I}_n & \mathbf{0} \\ \mathbf{b} & \mathbf{0} & 1 \end{bmatrix}. \quad (1)$$

We can verify that the LWE lattice contains vector $\mathbf{v} = [-\mathbf{e}, \mathbf{s}, -1]$. By definition, $\mathbf{e}$ and $\mathbf{s}$ have small entries, so the expected norm of $\mathbf{v}$ is significantly short in lattice $\mathcal{L}(\mathbf{B}^{\mathrm{LWE}})$. Therefore, we can recover the LWE secret by solving the SVP instance in $\mathcal{L}(\mathbf{B}^{\mathrm{LWE}})$.

### 2.3 LWE with Hints

We review existing works about LWE with hints. The notion of LWE's hints was first proposed by Dachman-Soled, Ducas, Gong, and Rossi (DDGR) in [6]. Sorting by different types of side-channel leakage, the information about LWE secret $\mathbf{s}$ can be formulated as hints. In our work, we specifically focus on the following types of hints:

1. Perfect hint: A tuple $\overline{\mathbf{v}} = (\mathbf{v}, l) \in \mathbb{Z}^n \times \mathbb{Z}$ with $<\mathbf{v}, \mathbf{s}>= l$.
2. Approximate hint: A tuple $\overline{\mathbf{v}} = (\mathbf{v}, l) \in \mathbb{Z}^n \times \mathbb{Z}$ with $<\mathbf{v}, \mathbf{s}>= l + \epsilon$.
3. Modular hint: A tuple $\overline{\mathbf{v}} = (\mathbf{v}, l, m) \in \mathbb{Z}^n \times \mathbb{Z} \times \mathbb{N}$ with $<\mathbf{v}, \mathbf{s}>\equiv l \mod m_i$.
4. Mod-$q$ hint: We call modular hint $\overline{\mathbf{v}} = (\mathbf{v}, l, m_i)$ a mod-$q$ hint if $m_i = q$.

Notably, we suppose that coordinates in every hint vector $\mathbf{v}$ are independently and uniformly distributed over $[-\frac{q-1}{2}, \frac{q-1}{2}]$, since special forms of hints may affect the hardness of LWE in more complicated ways [15]. We are particularly interested in using these hints to help us recover $\mathbf{s}$. DDGR provides the pioneering work which constructs a new lattice with each hint successively by computing dual basis. In this way, one can obtain a new LWE lattice with lower dimension or/and larger determinant. Therefore, the new instance will be easier than the initial one. However, these transformations are quite expensive, for the DDGR framework is only capable of processing one hint at a time. MN [13] provides a practical approach which processes all hints in one stroke.

## 3 Improved Framework for Processing Hints

Our goal is to extract information from the hints with a succint and efficient method. We will eventually propose a framework of converting LWE with hints to a problem on lattice. While previous works [6,13] provide algorithms with advanced features, they also leave us interesting questions: How LWE hints provide information about the LWE's secret vector, and whether it is possible to construct an algorithm that is both succint and fast for various hints. We try to discuss these topics from a hint-centric view: Instead of adding hints to the LWE lattice following DDGR and MN methods, we exploit the information provided by the hints even before involving any LWE samples. As a result, we provide a method that constructs a lattice from perfect, modular hints and approximate hints as fast as mod-$q$ hints without requiring additional assumptions like MN.

Subsection 3.1 discusses individual constructions of lattice basis for differnet types of hints. Subsection 3.2 summarizes these methods with a generic algorithm which processes perfect hints, modular hints, and approximate hints in one stroke. Subsection 3.3 provides our algorithm that integrates hints with LWE samples.

### 3.1 Direct Constructions of $\mathbb{Z}$-SIS from Hints

We begin by specifying techniques to extract information from perfect hints, approximate hints, modular hints, and mod-$q$ hints respectively. Recall that MN provides a straightforward method for mod-$q$ hints, which only uses matrix inversions and multiplications. The method is possible because the submatrix $\mathbf{V}_1$ is invertible in $\mathbb{Z}_q$. For other kinds of hints, however, MN is unable to continue with this methodology, for there is no guarantee that $\mathbf{V}_1$ is still invertible. In substitution, they propose a LLL-based method which involves more assumptions. Moreover, the method has to use a multiplication factor to scale the lattice, leading to larger entries and more computation. On the other hand, the DDGR framework is able to provably integrate various kinds hints, but is slow for multiple hints.

To deal with the shortcomings of previous works, we propose a novel method to exploit various types of hints, with a non-heuristic proof of its correctness. The motivation of our method is that instead of including hints into the LWE lattice in the first place, we start from a lattice constructed only from hints. This means that we interpret hints as equations which independently provide information about the secret vector. This perspective gives us a formal understanding about the contribution of hints to the recovery of LWE secret. To initiate our framework, we formally define a lattice problem called $\mathbb{Z}$-SIS problem, which is a variant of the SIS problem.

**Definition 5 ($\mathbb{Z}$-Small Integer Solution, $\mathbb{Z}$-SIS).** *Given $\nu \in \mathbb{R}$, matrix $\mathbf{V} \in \mathbb{Z}^{n\times k}$, vector $\ell \in \mathbb{Z}^k$, the $\mathbb{Z}$-SIS problem $(\mathbf{V}, \ell, \nu)$ is to find a vector $\mathbf{x}$ such that $\|x\| \le \nu$ and $\mathbf{x} \cdot \mathbf{V} = \ell$.*

Intuitively, Definition 5 asks to find a short vector $\mathbf{x} \in \mathbb{Z}^n$ that satisfies $\mathbf{x} \cdot \mathbf{V} = \ell$. Obviously the problem is derived from the common SIS problem which is defined over $\mathbb{Z}_q^k$. We observe that perfect hints $\overline{\mathbf{v}}_i = (\mathbf{v}_i, l_i) \in \mathbb{Z}^n \times \mathbb{Z}, i = 1, \ldots, k$ can be interpreted as a $\mathbb{Z}$-SIS instance, where $\mathbf{V} = \begin{bmatrix} | & & | \\ \mathbf{v}_1^T & \ldots & \mathbf{v}_k^T \\ | & & | \end{bmatrix}$, $\ell = [l_1, \ldots, l_k]$. Further, we can verify that the $\mathbb{Z}$-SIS instance shares the same secret vector $\mathbf{s}$ with the corresponding LWE instance.

**Proposition 1.** *Given n-dimensional LWE instance* $(\mathbf{A}, \mathbf{b}, q)$ *and perfect hints* $\overline{\mathbf{v}}_i = (\mathbf{v}_i, l_i) \in \mathbb{Z}^n \times \mathbb{Z}, i = 1, \ldots, k$, *let* $\mathbf{V} = \begin{bmatrix} | & & | \\ \mathbf{v}_1^T & \cdots & \mathbf{v}_k^T \\ | & & | \end{bmatrix}, \ell = [l_1, \ldots, l_k], \epsilon > 0$. *The secret vector* $\mathbf{s}$ *of LWE is also the target vector of* $\mathbb{Z}$*-SIS* $(\mathbf{V}, \ell, \nu)$ *when* $\nu = (1+\epsilon)\sigma\sqrt{n}$.

*Proof.* By definition of perfect hints, we have $\mathbf{s} \cdot \mathbf{V} = \ell$. We also know $\mathbf{s}$ is short: $\mathbb{E}[\|\mathbf{s}\|] \leq \sigma\sqrt{n}$ since $\mathbf{s}$ is sample with zero mean and standard deviation $\sigma$. Putting together, $\mathbf{s}$ is a target vector of $\mathbb{Z}$-SIS $(\mathbf{V}, \ell, \nu)$. □

*Remark 1.* Note that the $\mathbb{Z}$-SIS instance can be constructed only from hints even before we make use of the LWE instance $(\mathbf{A}, \mathbf{b}, q)$, while it still has the same secret vector $\mathbf{s}$ with LWE. This demonstrates that hints already provide information about the secret in themselves. Similar with LWE, the $\mathbb{Z}$-SIS problem can be solved by lattice algorithms. In fact, we construct the $\mathbb{Z}$-SIS lattice basis directly from the perfect hint matrix $\mathbf{H}$:

$$\mathbf{H} = \left[\begin{array}{ccc|c|c} | & & | & & 0 \\ \mathbf{v}_1^T & \cdots & \mathbf{v}_k^T & \begin{array}{c}\mathbf{0} \\ \hline \mathbf{I}_{n-k}\end{array} & \vdots \\ | & & | & & 0 \\ \hline l_1 & \cdots & l_k & 0 \ldots 0 & 1 \end{array}\right] = \left[\begin{array}{c|c|c} \mathbf{V}_1 & \mathbf{0} & \\ \hline \mathbf{V}_2 & \mathbf{I}_{n-k} & \mathbf{0} \\ \hline \ell & 0 \ldots 0 & 1 \end{array}\right]. \tag{2}$$

We can verify that lattice $\mathcal{L}(\mathbf{H})$ contains vector $[\mathbf{s}, -1] \cdot \mathbf{H} = [0^k, s_{k+1}, \ldots, s_n, -1]$. After extracting $s_{k+1}, \ldots, s_n$, we can recover $s_1, \ldots, s_k$ by linear algebra. In the following discussion, we describe our methods to extract $\mathbb{Z}$-SIS lattices from different types of hints.

**Perfect Hints.** Our starting point is a novel method to extract useful information from perfect hints. It is worth noting that Eq. (2) rewrites the $\mathbf{V}$ block as $\begin{bmatrix} \mathbf{V}_1 \\ \mathbf{V}_2 \end{bmatrix}$ similar with the case of mod-$q$ hints in MN method. However, unlike MN method for mod-$q$ hints, we are not able to reduce the $\mathbf{V}_1$ block to $\mathbf{I}$ since the invertibility of $\mathbf{V}_1$ is not certain. Fortunately, we are still able to reduce the $\mathbf{V}$ block to its Row Echelon Form. The application of this form of matrices is the major technical difference between our method and DDGR/MN.

**Definition 6 (Row Echelon Form, REF).** *An integer matrix* $\mathbf{B}$ *is in Row Echelon Form when any zero rows are below all non-zero rows, and the leading (first non-zero) entry of each row has only zeroes below it.*

The REF of a matrix can be obtained by performing Gaussian elimination. Based on the property of REF, we give a constructive proof about the existence of $\mathbb{Z}$-SIS lattice. Recall that MN's fast approach for mod-$q$ hints relies on computing $\mathbf{V}_1^{-1}$ in $\mathbb{Z}_q$, but $\mathbf{V}_1^{-1}$ is invalid when hints are defined over $\mathbb{Z}$. In contrast, the REFs of matrices still exist. We now use REF to construct a sublattice which contains the target vector.

**Theorem 1.** *Given* $\mathbf{H}$ *as defined in Eq.* (2), $\mathcal{L}(\mathbf{H})$ *contains a sublattice* $\mathcal{L}_{\mathbf{H},k} = \{[v_1, \ldots, v_{n+1}] \in \mathcal{L}(\mathbf{H}) : v_1 = \ldots = v_k = 0\}$.

*Proof.* We prove the existence of sublattice $\mathcal{L}_{\mathbf{H},k}$ with a construction of its basis. By reducing $\mathbf{V}$ to its REF, we obtain a unimodular matrix $\mathbf{U_V}$ such that

$$\mathbf{U_V} \cdot \mathbf{V} = \mathbf{U_V} \cdot \left[\begin{array}{c}\mathbf{V}_1 \\ \hline \mathbf{V}_2\end{array}\right] = \left[\begin{array}{c}\mathbf{V}'_k \\ \hline \mathbf{0}_{(n-k)\times k}\end{array}\right]$$

is the REF of $\mathbf{V}$. It is clear that the $k$ columns of $\mathbf{V}$ are independent, so $\mathbf{V}'_k$ is a $k$-dimensional diagonal matrix. Consequently, a *unique* vector $\mathbf{s}' = [s'_1, \ldots, s'_k]$ can be obtained by solving liear equation system $\mathbf{s}' \cdot \mathbf{V}'_k = \ell$. It can be verified that $\mathbf{s}'$ is composed of the first $k$ entries of $\mathbf{s} \cdot \mathbf{U}_\mathbf{V}^{-1}$. We next construct an $(n+1)$-dimensional unimodular matrix

$$\mathbf{U}_1 = \begin{bmatrix} 1 & & \\ & \ddots & \\ -\mathbf{s}' & \mathbf{0}_{n-k} & 1 \end{bmatrix} \cdot \begin{bmatrix} \mathbf{U_V} & \mathbf{0} \\ \mathbf{0} & 1 \end{bmatrix}, \tag{3}$$

such that

$$\mathbf{U}_1 \cdot \left[\begin{array}{c}\mathbf{V}_1 \\ \hline \mathbf{V}_2 \\ \hline \ell\end{array}\right] = \begin{bmatrix} 1 & & \\ & \ddots & \\ -\mathbf{s}' & \mathbf{0}_{n-k} & 1 \end{bmatrix} \cdot \left[\begin{array}{c}\mathbf{V}'_k \\ \hline \mathbf{0} \\ \hline \ell\end{array}\right] = \left[\begin{array}{c}\mathbf{V}'_k \\ \hline \mathbf{0} \\ \hline \mathbf{0}\end{array}\right].$$

When we multiply $\mathbf{H}$ with $\mathbf{U}_1$, we obtain

$$\mathbf{U}_1 \cdot \mathbf{H} = \left[\begin{array}{c|c|c}\mathbf{V}'_k & \mathbf{J}'_1 & \mathbf{0} \\ \hline \mathbf{0} & \mathbf{J}'_2 & \\ \hline \mathbf{0} & \mathbf{s}'' & 1\end{array}\right] = \left[\begin{array}{c|c}\mathbf{V}'_k & \mathbf{J}'_1 | \mathbf{0} \\ \hline \mathbf{0} & \mathbf{B}_{\text{SIS}}\end{array}\right]. \tag{4}$$

Note that $\mathbf{V}'_k$ is upper triangular, so the last $(n-k+1)$ rows actually form the basis of sublattice $\mathcal{L}_{\mathbf{H},k} = \{[v_1, \ldots, v_{n+1}] \in \mathcal{L}(\mathbf{H}) : v_1 = \ldots = v_k = 0\}$. □

It is straightforward that the target vector $\mathbf{v} = [\mathbf{s}, -1] \cdot \mathbf{H} = [0^k, s_{k+1}, \ldots, s_n, -1]$ is also in the sublattice $\mathcal{L}_{\mathbf{H},k}$. Therefore, the proof of Theorem 1 actually provides a lattice construction method, which works as follows:

1. Reduce $\mathbf{V}$ to REF, obtain the transformation matrix $\mathbf{U_V}$.
2. Construct $\mathbf{U}_1$ as described in Eq. (3).
3. Compute matrix $\mathbf{U}_1 \cdot \mathbf{H}$, remove its first $k$ rows and $k$ columns.

*Remark 2.* In the third step, we remove the first $k$ columns in order to get a square matrix. The remaining $(n-k+1)$-dimensional matrix

$$\mathbf{B}_{\text{SIS}} = \begin{bmatrix} \mathbf{J}'_2 & \mathbf{0} \\ \mathbf{s}'' & 1 \end{bmatrix}$$

is equivalent to the basis of $\mathcal{L}_{\mathbf{H},k}$ since the first $k$ entries of vectors in $\mathcal{L}_{\mathbf{H},k}$ are all zeroes. We claim that $\mathcal{L}(\mathbf{B}_{\text{SIS}})$ is the $\mathbb{Z}$-SIS lattice, and the target vector is

$$\mathbf{v}_{\text{SIS}} = [s_{k+1}, \ldots, s_n, -1].$$

Since our construction doesn't involve LLL reduction, it can be performed by direct linear algebra operations. In particular, we only need the equations $< \mathbf{v}_i, \mathbf{s} >= l_i$ to hold, and require no more assumptions. This provides a more direct and succint proof of correctness than the method of MN.

**Approximate Hints.** We extend our method to a more practical circumstance – hints with noise. In [6], this case is formulated as approximate hints: $< \mathbf{v}, \mathbf{s} >= l + \epsilon$. Based on this definition, we can define the approximate variant of $\mathbb{Z}$-SIS problem: Given $\nu \in \mathbb{R}$, matrix $\mathbf{V} \in \mathbb{Z}^{n \times k}$, vector $\ell \in \mathbb{Z}^k$, the approximate $\mathbb{Z}$-SIS problem $(\mathbf{V}', \ell', \nu)$ is to find a vector $\mathbf{x}$ such that $\|x\| \leq \nu$ and $\mathbf{x} \cdot \mathbf{V}' + \mathbf{e}' = \ell'$, $\mathbf{e}' = [\epsilon_1, \ldots, \epsilon_k]$.

Our framework can handle these hints by adapting the method for perfect hints. Given $n$-dimensional LWE instance $(\mathbf{A}, \mathbf{b}, q)$, perfect hints $\overline{\mathbf{v}}_i = (\mathbf{v}_i, l_i) \in \mathbb{Z}^n \times \mathbb{Z}, i = 1, \ldots, k_1$, and approximate hints $\overline{\mathbf{v}}'_i = (\mathbf{v}'_i, l'_i) \in \mathbb{Z}^n \times \mathbb{Z}, i = 1, \ldots, k_2$, we build a hint matrix

$$\mathbf{H} = \left[\begin{array}{ccc|ccc|c|c} | & & | & | & & | & \mathbf{0} & 0 \\ \mathbf{v}_1^T & \cdots & \mathbf{v}_{k_1}^T & (\mathbf{v}'_1)^T & \cdots & (\mathbf{v}'_{k_2})^T & \overline{\mathbf{I}_{n-k_1-k_2}} & \vdots \\ | & & | & | & & | & & 0 \\ \hline l_1 & \cdots & l_{k_1} & l'_1 & \cdots & l'_{k_2} & 0 \ldots 0 & 1 \end{array}\right] = \left[\begin{array}{c|c|c|c} \mathbf{V}_1 & \mathbf{V}'_1 & \mathbf{0} & \\ \mathbf{V}_2 & \mathbf{V}'_2 & \mathbf{I}_{n-k_1-k_2} & \mathbf{0} \\ \ell & \ell' & 0 \ldots 0 & 1 \end{array}\right]. \tag{5}$$

Following the same steps in the proof of Theorem 1, we get a unimodular matrix $\mathbf{U}_1$ such that

$$\mathbf{U}_1 \cdot \mathbf{H} = \left[\begin{array}{cc|c|c} \mathbf{V}''_{k_1+k_2} & & \mathbf{J}'_1 & \mathbf{0} \\ \mathbf{0} & & \mathbf{J}'_2 & \\ \hline \mathbf{0} & \ell'' & \mathbf{s}'' & 1 \end{array}\right], \tag{6}$$

where $\begin{bmatrix} \mathbf{V}'' \\ \mathbf{0} \end{bmatrix}$ is the REF of block $\begin{bmatrix} \mathbf{V}_1 \ \mathbf{V}'_1 \\ \mathbf{V}_2 \ \mathbf{V}'_2 \end{bmatrix}$. We predict the target short vector has form $[\mathbf{s}, -1] \cdot \mathbf{H} = [0^{k_1}, \epsilon_1, \ldots, \epsilon_{k_2}, s_{k_1+k_2+1}, \ldots, s_n, -1]$. Meanwhile, we know $\mathbf{V}''$ is a non-singular diagonal matrix. Following the methodology for perfect hints, we remove the first $k_1$ rows and first $k_1$ columns of $\mathbf{U}_1 \cdot \mathbf{H}$, and denote the new matrix as $\mathbf{B}_{\text{SIS}}$. It holds that sublattice $\mathcal{L}(\mathbf{B}_{\text{SIS}})$ contains the short vector $[\epsilon_1, \ldots, \epsilon_{k_2}, s_{k_1+k_2+1}, \ldots, s_n, -1]$. As a result, we convert the mixture of perfect hints and approximate hints to a $\mathbb{Z}$-SIS lattice.

*Remark 3.* The process of constructing $\mathbf{B}_{\text{SIS}}$ illustrates the difference between perfect hints and approximate hints. While both hints reduce the dimension of output coordinates of $\mathbf{s}$, the $k_2$ approximate hints add an additional noise entries $[\epsilon_1, \ldots, \epsilon_{k_2}]$. If the hints noises $\epsilon_i$ are smaller than LWE noises $e_i$, we can get a shorter output vector.

**Modular Hints.** So far we have constructed a $\mathbb{Z}$-SIS instance from perfect hints. Similarly, the method can be applied to modular hints. We first discuss how to construct $\mathbb{Z}$-SIS basis from modular hints $\overline{\mathbf{v}}_i = (\mathbf{v}_i, l_i, m_i) \in \mathbb{Z}^n \times \mathbb{Z} \times \mathbb{N}$, then discuss the difference between mod-$q$ hints and general modular hints under our framework. The basic idea for modular hints is consistent with [13]: to lift eqation $< \mathbf{v}_i, \mathbf{s} >\equiv l_i \mod m_i$ to $< \mathbf{v}_i, \mathbf{s} > +r_i m_i = l_i$ over the integers. These hints form a $\mathbb{Z}$-SIS instance$(\mathbf{V}_{\text{mod}}, \ell, \nu)$, where

$$\mathbf{V}_{\text{mod}} = \begin{bmatrix} m_1 & & \\ & \ddots & \\ & & m_k \\ | & & | \\ \mathbf{v}_1^T & \dots & \mathbf{v}_k^T \\ | & & | \end{bmatrix}.$$

We construct the modular hint matrix

$$\mathbf{H} = \left[\begin{array}{ccc|c|c} m_1 & & & & 0 \\ & \ddots & & \mathbf{0} & vdots \\ & & m_k & & \\ \hline | & & | & & \vdots \\ \mathbf{v}_1^T & \dots & \mathbf{v}_k^T & \mathbf{I}_n & \\ | & & | & & 0 \\ \hline l_1 & \dots & l_k & 0\dots0 & 1 \end{array}\right] = \left[\begin{array}{c|c|c} \mathbf{V}_{\text{mod}} & \frac{\mathbf{0}}{\mathbf{I}_n} & \begin{matrix}0\\ \vdots \\ 0\end{matrix} \\ \hline \ell & 0\dots0 & 1 \end{array}\right] = \left[\begin{array}{c|c} \mathbf{H}_0 & \mathbf{0} \\ \hline \ell \, \mathbf{0} & 1 \end{array}\right]. \tag{7}$$

Again, we are interested in recovering a sublattice $\mathcal{L}_{\mathbf{H},k} = \{[v_1, \dots, v_{n+k+1}] \in \mathcal{L}(\mathbf{H}) : v_1 = \dots = v_k = 0\}$, which contains the secret vector $[0, \dots, 0, s_1, \dots, s_n, -1]$ of the $\mathbb{Z}$-SIS instance. By reducing $\mathbf{V}_{\text{mod}}$ to its REF, we obtain a $(k+n)$-dimensional transformation matrix $\mathbf{U}_{\mathbf{V}}$ such that

$$\mathbf{U}_{\mathbf{V}} \cdot \mathbf{H}_0 = \mathbf{U}_{\mathbf{V}} \cdot \left[\begin{array}{ccc|c} m_1 & & & \\ & \ddots & & \mathbf{0} \\ & & m_k & \\ \hline | & & | & \\ \mathbf{v}_1^T & \dots & \mathbf{v}_k^T & \mathbf{I}_n \\ | & & | & \end{array}\right] = \begin{bmatrix} \mathbf{V}'_k & \mathbf{J}'_1 \\ \mathbf{0} & \mathbf{J}'_2 \end{bmatrix}.$$

Similar with the perfect hint case, we can compute a unique vector $\mathbf{s}' = [s'_1, \dots, s'_k]$ such that $\mathbf{s}' \cdot \mathbf{V}'_k = \ell$. Therefore, we construct an $(n+k+1)$-dimensional unimodular matrix $\mathbf{U}_1$ the same as Equation (3), such that

$$\mathbf{U}_1 \cdot \mathbf{H} = \left[\begin{array}{c|c|c} \mathbf{V}'_k & \mathbf{J}'_1 & \mathbf{0} \\ \mathbf{0} & \mathbf{J}'_2 & \\ \hline \mathbf{0} & \mathbf{s}'' & 1 \end{array}\right] = \left[\begin{array}{c|c|c} \mathbf{V}'_k & \mathbf{J}'_1 & \mathbf{0} \\ \hline \mathbf{0} & \multicolumn{2}{c}{\mathbf{B}_{\text{SIS}}} \end{array}\right]. \tag{8}$$

The block $\mathbf{B}_{\text{SIS}}$ is the basis of the sublattice that contains the secret vector $[s_1, \dots, s_n, -1]$

**Mod-$q$Hints.** Now we solve a challenge left by [13]: to unify general modular hints with mod-$q$ hints. In particular, we put mod-$q$ hints into our framework for hints, and explain how these hints affect the $\mathbb{Z}$-SIS basis. Then, we compare our method of processing mod-$q$ hints with the MN method.

Given mod-$q$ hints $\overline{\mathbf{v}}_i = (\mathbf{v}_i, l_i, q), i = 1, \ldots, k$, we construct the following modular hint matrix:

$$\mathbf{H} = \left[\begin{array}{c|c|c} q\mathbf{I}_k & \mathbf{0} & \mathbf{0} \\ \mathbf{V} & \mathbf{I}_n & \mathbf{0} \\ \hline \ell & 0\ldots0 & 1 \end{array}\right] = \left[\begin{array}{c|c} \mathbf{H}_0 & \mathbf{0} \\ \hline \ell\,|\,\mathbf{0} & 1 \end{array}\right]. \tag{9}$$

The matrix generates a vector $[r_1, \ldots, r_k, s_1, \ldots, s_n, -1] \cdot \mathbf{H} = [0^k, s_1, \ldots, s_n, -1]$. Note that submatrix $\mathbf{H}_0$ has form $\begin{bmatrix} q\mathbf{I}_k & \mathbf{0} \\ \mathbf{V} & \mathbf{I}_n \end{bmatrix}$, i.e. it is a $q$-ary lattice basis. After computing the REF, the matrix $\mathbf{U}_\mathbf{V} \cdot \mathbf{H}_0$ can be presented as

$$\mathbf{U}_\mathbf{V} \cdot \mathbf{H}_0 = \begin{bmatrix} \mathbf{I}_n & \mathbf{J}'_{n\times k} \\ \mathbf{0} & q\mathbf{I}_k \end{bmatrix} = \left[\begin{array}{c|c|c} \mathbf{I}_k & \mathbf{0} & \mathbf{J}'_1 \\ \hline & \mathbf{I}_{n-k} & \mathbf{J}'_2 \\ \hline & & q\mathbf{I}_k \end{array}\right]. \tag{10}$$

We construct an $(n+k+1)$-dimensional unimodular matrix

$$\mathbf{U}_1 = \begin{bmatrix} 1 & & \\ & \ddots & \\ -\ell & \mathbf{0}_n & 1 \end{bmatrix} \cdot \begin{bmatrix} \mathbf{U}_\mathbf{V} & \mathbf{0} \\ \mathbf{0} & 1 \end{bmatrix}, \tag{11}$$

which satisfies

$$\begin{aligned} \mathbf{U}_1 \cdot \mathbf{H} &= \begin{bmatrix} 1 & & \\ & \ddots & \\ -\ell & \mathbf{0}_n & 1 \end{bmatrix} \cdot \left[\begin{array}{c|c|c|c} \mathbf{I}_k & \mathbf{0} & \mathbf{J}'_1 & \mathbf{0} \\ \hline \mathbf{0} & \mathbf{I}_{n-k} & \mathbf{J}'_2 & \mathbf{0} \\ \hline & & q\mathbf{I}_k & \mathbf{0} \\ \hline \ell & & & 1 \end{array}\right] = \left[\begin{array}{c|c|c|c} \mathbf{I}_k & \mathbf{0} & \mathbf{J}'_1 & \mathbf{0} \\ \hline & \mathbf{I}_{n-k} & \mathbf{J}'_2 & \mathbf{0} \\ \hline & & q\mathbf{I}_k & \mathbf{0} \\ \hline & & -\ell\cdot\mathbf{J}'_1 & 1 \end{array}\right] \\ &= \left[\begin{array}{c|c|c|c} \mathbf{I}_k & \mathbf{0} & \mathbf{J}'_1 & \mathbf{0} \\ \hline \mathbf{0} & \multicolumn{3}{c}{\mathbf{B}} \end{array}\right]. \end{aligned} \tag{12}$$

Following the procedures discussed above, we should obtain a submatrix

$$\mathbf{B} = \begin{bmatrix} \mathbf{I}_{n-k} & \mathbf{J}'_2 & \\ & q\mathbf{I}_k & \\ & -\ell\cdot\mathbf{J}'_1 & 1 \end{bmatrix}$$

from the matrix in Eq. (12). Then, we provide a new observation based on the $q\mathbf{I}_k$ block in $\mathbf{B}$. Recall that $\mathcal{L}(\mathbf{B})$ contains the target vector $\mathbf{v} = [s_1, \ldots, s_n, -1]$. Therefore, there exist a list of coefficients $\{s'_1, \ldots, s'_{n-k}, t_1, \ldots, t_k\}$, such that

$$\begin{aligned}[s_1,\ldots,s_n,-1] =&[s'_1,\ldots,s'_{n-k},t_1,\ldots,t_k,-1]\cdot\begin{bmatrix}\mathbf{I}_{n-k} & \mathbf{J}'_2 & \\ & q\mathbf{I}_k & \\ & -\ell\cdot\mathbf{J}'_1 & 1\end{bmatrix}\\ =&[s'_1,\ldots,s'_{n-k}]\cdot\begin{bmatrix}\mathbf{I}_{n-k}\ \mathbf{J}'_2\ \mathbf{0}\end{bmatrix}+[t_1,\ldots,t_k]\cdot\begin{bmatrix}\mathbf{0}\ q\mathbf{J}'_k\ \mathbf{0}\end{bmatrix}\\ &+\begin{bmatrix}\mathbf{0}\ \ell\cdot\mathbf{J}'_1\ -1\end{bmatrix}\\ =&[s'_1,\ldots,s'_{n-k}]\cdot\begin{bmatrix}\mathbf{I}_{n-k}\ \mathbf{J}'_2\ \mathbf{0}\end{bmatrix}+\begin{bmatrix}\mathbf{0}\ \ell\cdot\mathbf{J}'_1\ -1\end{bmatrix}\bmod q.\end{aligned} \tag{13}$$

Let $\mathbf{A}_1, \mathbf{A}_2$ present the first $(n-k)$ rows and last $k$ rows of LWE matrix $\mathbf{A}$ respectively. Multiplying both hands of Eq. (13) by $\begin{bmatrix}\mathbf{A}\\ \mathbf{b}\end{bmatrix}=\begin{bmatrix}\mathbf{A}_1\\ \mathbf{A}_2\\ \mathbf{b}\end{bmatrix}$, we obtain

$$\begin{aligned}-\mathbf{e}\equiv[s'_1,\ldots,s'_n,-1]\cdot\begin{bmatrix}\mathbf{A}\\ \mathbf{b}\end{bmatrix}\equiv&[s'_1,\ldots,s'_{n-k}]\cdot(\mathbf{A}_1+\mathbf{J}'_2\mathbf{A}_2)\\ &-\left(\mathbf{b}-\ell\cdot\mathbf{J}'_1\mathbf{A}_2\right)\bmod q.\end{aligned} \tag{14}$$

This equation holds because LWE is defined over $\mathbb{Z}_q$, and $\begin{bmatrix}\mathbf{0}\ q\mathbf{J}'_k\ \mathbf{0}\end{bmatrix}\cdot\begin{bmatrix}\mathbf{A}\\ \mathbf{b}\end{bmatrix}= q\mathbf{J}'_k\mathbf{A}_2\equiv 0 \bmod q$. As a result, we can reorganize Eq. (13) to form an LWE instance:

$$\mathbf{b}'\equiv[s'_1,\ldots,s'_{n-k}]\cdot\mathbf{A}'+\mathbf{e}\bmod q, \tag{15}$$

where $\mathbf{A}'=\mathbf{A}_1+\mathbf{J}'_2\mathbf{A}_2$, $\mathbf{b}'=\mathbf{b}-\ell\cdot\mathbf{J}'_1\mathbf{A}_2$. The new LWE secret vector $[s'_1,\ldots,s'_{n-k}]$ is composed of $(n-k)$ entries of the original LWE instance. Therefore, we use the mod-$q$ hints to construct an $(n-k)$-dimensional LWE instance with the same noise.

*Remark 4.* Although our framework and MN framework both produce a $(n-k)$-dimensional LWE instance with $k$ mod-$q$ hints, we adopt different methodologies. MN gives a specialized method based on column operations over $\mathbb{Z}_q$, and this method is not applicable to other types of hints. In contrast, we interpret the mod-$q$ hints as a case in our general framework, and process them with row operations over $\mathbb{Z}$ consistent with perfect hints and modular hints. In theory, our method explains the reason why mod-$q$ hints are able to reduce LWE dimension—by producing $[\mathbf{0}, q, \mathbf{0}]$ rows in the $\mathbb{Z}$-SIS basis. In practice, our method is equivalent to lifting MN method from $\mathbb{Z}_q$ to $\mathbb{Z}$: In the process of computing REF of $\mathbf{H}_0$, we reduce the first $k$ columns to $\mathbf{I}_k$, see Eq. (10). It is consistent with the MN method. In practical LWE with hints instances, we usually use the mod-$q$ hints to decrease the dimension, then consider general modular hints.

### 3.2 Generic Construction of $\mathbb{Z}$-SIS from Hints.

Summarizing the individual methods in Subsects. 3.1, we provide a generic algorithm that extracts a $\mathbb{Z}$-SIS instance from a mixture of modular hints, perfect hints, and approximate hints. Given modular hints $\overline{\mathbf{v}}_i=(\mathbf{v}_i, l_i^{\mathbf{v}}, m_i)\in$

**Algorithm 1:** Generic $\mathbb{Z}$-SIS construction

**Input:** modular hints $\overline{\mathbf{v}}_i = (\mathbf{v}_i, l_i^{\mathbf{v}}) \in \mathbb{Z}^n \times \mathbb{Z} \times \mathbb{N}, i = 1, \ldots, k_1$; perfect hints $\overline{\mathbf{w}}_i = (\mathbf{w}_i, l_i^{\mathbf{w}}) \in \mathbb{Z}^n \times \mathbb{Z}, i = 1, \ldots, k_2$, approximate hints $\overline{\mathbf{y}}_i = (\mathbf{y}_i, l_i^{\mathbf{y}}) \in \mathbb{Z}^n \times \mathbb{Z}, i = 1, \ldots, k_3$, $k_2 + k_3 < n$

**Output:** basis of a sublattice $\mathcal{L}'$ which contains vector $[\epsilon_1, \ldots, \epsilon_{k_3}, s_{k_2+k_3+1}, \ldots, s_n, -1]$ and corresponding transformation matrix

1 construct mixed hint matrix $\mathbf{H}$ as in Equation (16)

2 reduce $\mathbf{H}_0$ to obtain a unimodular matrix $\mathbf{U} \in \mathbb{Z}^{(n+k_1)\times(n+k_1)}$, such that $\mathbf{U} \cdot \mathbf{H}_0 = \begin{bmatrix} \mathbf{H}_0' \\ \mathbf{0} \end{bmatrix}$ is the REF of $\mathbf{H}_0$, denote the first $(k_1 + k_2)$ rows and $(k_1 + k_2)$ columns of $\mathbf{H}_0'$ as $\mathbf{H}_0''$

3 solve equation $\mathbf{x} \cdot \mathbf{H}_0'' = [\ell_{\mathbf{v}} | \ell_{\mathbf{w}}]$, compute matrix

$$\mathbf{U}_{\text{reduce}} = \begin{bmatrix} 1 & & \\ & \ddots & \\ -\mathbf{x} & \mathbf{0}_{n-k_2} & 1 \end{bmatrix} \cdot \begin{bmatrix} \mathbf{U} & \mathbf{0} \\ \mathbf{0} & 1 \end{bmatrix}, \mathbf{H}_{\text{reduce}} = \mathbf{U}_{\text{reduce}} \cdot \mathbf{H}$$

4 remove the first $(k_1 + k_2)$ rows and $(k_1 + k_2)$ columns of $\mathbf{H}_{\text{reduce}}$, obtain matrix $\mathbf{B}_{\text{SIS}}$

5 remove the first $k_1$ rows and $k_1$ columns of $\mathbf{U}_{\text{reduce}}$, obtain matrix $\mathbf{U}_{\text{SIS}}$

6 return $(\mathbf{B}_{\text{SIS}}, \mathbf{U}_{\text{SIS}})$

---

$\mathbb{Z}^n \times \mathbb{Z} \times \mathbb{N}, i = 1, \ldots, k_1$, perfect hints $\overline{\mathbf{w}}_i = (\mathbf{w}_i, l_i^{\mathbf{w}}) \in \mathbb{Z}^n \times \mathbb{Z}, i = 1, \ldots, k_2$, and approximate hints $\overline{\mathbf{y}}_i = (\mathbf{y}_i, l_i^{\mathbf{y}}) \in \mathbb{Z}^n \times \mathbb{Z}, i = 1, \ldots, k_3$, we construct an $(n + k_1 + 1) \times (n + k_1 + 1)$ *mixed hint matrix*:

$$\mathbf{H} = \left[\begin{array}{c|c|c|c|c} \begin{matrix} m_1 & & \\ & \ddots & \\ & & m_{k_1} \end{matrix} & \mathbf{0} & \mathbf{0} & \mathbf{0} & \mathbf{0} \\ \hline \mathbf{V} & \mathbf{W} & \mathbf{Y} & \begin{matrix} \mathbf{0} \\ \hline \mathbf{I}_{n-k_2-k_3} \end{matrix} & \mathbf{0} \\ \hline \ell_{\mathbf{v}} & \ell_{\mathbf{w}} & \ell_{\mathbf{y}} & \mathbf{0} & 1 \end{array}\right] = \left[\begin{array}{c|c|c} \mathbf{H}_0 & \begin{matrix} \mathbf{0} \\ \hline \mathbf{I}_{n-k_2-k_3} \end{matrix} & \mathbf{0} \\ \hline \ell_{\mathbf{v}}\ \ell_{\mathbf{w}}\ \ell_{\mathbf{y}} & \mathbf{0} & 1 \end{array}\right], \tag{16}$$

with $\begin{bmatrix} \mathbf{V} \\ \hline \ell_{\mathbf{v}} \end{bmatrix} = \begin{bmatrix} | & & | \\ \mathbf{v}_1^T & \cdots & \mathbf{v}_{k_1}^T \\ | & & | \\ \hline l_1^{\mathbf{v}} & \cdots & l_{k_1}^{\mathbf{v}} \end{bmatrix}$, $\begin{bmatrix} \mathbf{W} \\ \hline \ell_{\mathbf{w}} \end{bmatrix} = \begin{bmatrix} | & & | \\ \mathbf{w}_1^T & \cdots & \mathbf{w}_{k_2}^T \\ | & & | \\ \hline l_1^{\mathbf{w}} & \cdots & l_{k_2}^{\mathbf{w}} \end{bmatrix}$, $\begin{bmatrix} \mathbf{Y} \\ \hline \ell_{\mathbf{y}} \end{bmatrix} = \begin{bmatrix} | & & | \\ \mathbf{y}_1^T & \cdots & \mathbf{y}_{k_3}^T \\ | & & | \\ \hline l_1^{\mathbf{y}} & \cdots & l_{k_3}^{\mathbf{y}} \end{bmatrix}$.

On a high level, our method extracts a sublattice in the following steps, see Algorithm 1.

1. transform block $\mathbf{H}_0$ to its REF;
2. use rows of the REF to ruduce the first $(k_1 + k_2)$ entries of the last row to zeros;
3. take the bottom-right block of size $(n - k_2 + 1) \times (n - k_2 + 1)$ as output.

Note that the algorithm outputs both $\mathbf{B}_{\text{SIS}}$ and $\mathbf{U}_{\text{SIS}}$, but only one is necessary since one can be recovered from the other. We output the two matrices together because we will use them later in Algorithm 3.

**Correctness of Algorithm.** Algorithm 1 constructs the $\mathbb{Z}$-SIS lattice basis starting from matrix $\mathbf{H}$ as in Eq. (16), where modular hints $\overline{\mathbf{v}}_i = (\mathbf{v}_i, l_i^{\mathbf{v}}, m_i)$ are lifted to perfect hints $< \mathbf{v}_i, \mathbf{s} > + r_i m_i = l_i$, and inserted at the first $k_1$ columns of $\mathbf{H}$. Similarly, perfect hints and approximate hints are arranged as described in Eq. (5). Therefore, the correctness of the algorithm can be proved following the same method as Theorem 1. Since the first $(k_1 + k_2)$ columns are linearly independent, the proof is still ensured by the REF of $\mathbf{H}_0$, and doesn't require additional assumptions. Summarizing the discussion, we obtain the following result.

**Theorem 2.** *Given* $\mathbf{H}$ *as defined in Eq.* (16), *Algorithm 1 produces a sublattice* $\mathcal{L}_{\mathbf{H}}^{(k_1,k_2,k_3)} = \{[v_1, \ldots, v_{n+k_1+1}] \in \mathcal{L}(\mathbf{H}) : v_1 = \ldots = v_{k_1+k_2} = 0\}$.

**Dimension of $\mathbf{B}_{\text{SIS}}$.** In Step 2 and Step 3, Algorithm 1 produces $(n-k_2+1)$ rows whose first $(k_1 + k_2)$ entries are zeros. These rows vectors form the basis of the $(n-k_2+1)$-dimensional sublattice $\mathcal{L}_{\mathbf{H}}^{(k_1,k_2,k_3)} = \{[v_1, \ldots, v_{n+k_1+1}] \in \mathcal{L}(\mathbf{H}) : v_1 = \ldots = v_{k_1+k_2} = 0\}$. Recall that our target vector $[r_1, \ldots, r_{k_1}, s_1, \ldots, s_n, -1] \cdot \mathbf{H} = [0^{k_1+k_2}, \epsilon_1, \ldots, \epsilon_{k_3}, s_{k_2+k_3+1}, \ldots, s_n, -1]$ is also in $\mathcal{L}_{\mathbf{H}}^{(k_1,k_2,k_3)}$. For simplicity, we remove the zero columns to obtain matrix $\mathbf{B}_{\text{SIS}}$. In conclusion, the dimension of $\mathbf{B}_{\text{SIS}}$ is reduced by each perfect hint, while modular hints and approximate hints don't affect its dimension.

**Complexity of Lattice Construction.** We are also interested in the running time of producing $\mathbf{B}_{\text{SIS}}$ compared with the MN method. As our algorithm shows, the cost of constructing the lattice is dominated by REF reduction. Given $k_1$ modular hints and $k_2$ perfect hints, the hint matrix has dimension $d = n + k_1$.

- Our method needs to perform Gaussian elimination on a $d \times (k_1 + k_2)$ block $\mathbf{H}_0$, which has time complexity $O(d^3)$.
- The MN method, on the other hand, needs to run LLL on the $(d+1) \times (d+1)$ matrix $\mathbf{H}$. By now the fastest LLL variant [19] has time complexity $O((d + 1)^\omega (p + d + 1)^{1+\epsilon})$, where $\omega \in (2, 3], p = O(\log \|\mathbf{H}\|_{\max})$.

Asymptotically, our method is faster than the LLL-based lattice construction by MN. Also note that MN asks to multiply the first $k_1 + k_2$ columns of $\mathbf{H}$ by $\left\lceil 2^{\frac{d+1}{2}} \text{gh}(\mathcal{L}(\mathbf{H})) \right\rceil$, which may further increase the cost of MN construction.

### 3.3 Integrating Hints and LWE

So far we have introduced our framework that uses hints to construct an instance of $\mathbb{Z}$-SIS problem. We now consider a fact that we can't ensure whether the $\mathbb{Z}$-SIS instance itself is easy to solve since the hints are randomly generated. In order to finally recover the secret vector, we combine the $\mathbb{Z}$-SIS problem with LWE samples.

**Technical Overview.** Based on the $\mathbb{Z}$-SIS construction, we give an algorithm to produce a lattice basis that integrates LWE samples and hints. The main technique is reusing the transformation matrix of Algorithm 1 to rearrange the LWE samples.

As we have verified in Proposition 1, one can combine $\mathbb{Z}$-SIS and LWE mainly because the two problems have the same secret vector $\mathbf{s}$. Take the perfect hints as an example, we have

$$[\mathbf{s}, -1] \cdot \left[\begin{array}{c} \mathbf{V} \\ \hline \ell \end{array}\right] = 0^k, \tag{17}$$

and

$$[\mathbf{s}, -1] \cdot \left[\begin{array}{c} \mathbf{A} \\ \hline \mathbf{b} \end{array}\right] \equiv -\mathbf{e} \bmod q. \tag{18}$$

---

**Algorithm 2:** $\mathbb{Z}$-SIS-LWE integration

**Input:** $n$-dimensional LWE instance $(\mathbf{A}, \mathbf{b}, q)$, number of LWE samples $m$; modular hints $\overline{\mathbf{v}}_i = (\mathbf{v}_i, l_i^{\mathbf{v}}, m_i) \in \mathbb{Z}^n \times \mathbb{Z} \times \mathbb{N}, i = 1, \ldots, k_1$; perfect hints $\overline{\mathbf{w}}_i = (\mathbf{w}_i, l_i^{\mathbf{w}}) \in \mathbb{Z}^n \times \mathbb{Z}, i = 1, \ldots, k_2$; approximate hints $\overline{\mathbf{y}}_i = (\mathbf{y}_i, l_i^{\mathbf{y}}) \in \mathbb{Z}^n \times \mathbb{Z}, i = 1, \ldots, k_3$

**Output:** basis of a lattice $\mathcal{L}$ which contains vector $[-e_1, \ldots, -e_m, \epsilon_1, \ldots, \epsilon_{k_3}, s_{k_2+k_3+1}, \ldots, s_n, -1]$

1. use Algorithm 1 to compute $(\mathbf{B}_{\mathrm{SIS}}, \mathbf{U}_{\mathrm{SIS}})$
2. compute $\mathbf{B}_0 = \mathbf{U}_{\mathrm{SIS}} \cdot \left[\begin{array}{c|c|c|c} \mathbf{A} & \mathbf{Y} & \begin{array}{c} \mathbf{0} \\ \hline \mathbf{I}_{n-k_2-k_3} \end{array} & \mathbf{0} \\ \hline \mathbf{b} & \ell_{\mathbf{y}} & \mathbf{0} & 1 \end{array}\right]$, remove its first $k_2$ rows to get matrix $\mathbf{B}_1$
3. construct matrix $\mathbf{B}_2 = \left[\begin{array}{c|c} q\mathbf{I}_m & \mathbf{0} \\ \hline \multicolumn{2}{c}{\mathbf{B}_1} \end{array}\right]$
4. return $\mathbf{B}_2$

---

Intuitively, we can combine the two problems by pairing the two equations in matrix $\left[\begin{array}{c|c} \mathbf{A} & \mathbf{V} \\ \hline \mathbf{b} & \ell \end{array}\right]$. It is also the technique used in the MN method [13]. Under our framework, however, we separate the processing of hints as Algorithm 1. It is worth noting that the algorithm performs a series of linear transformations on block $\mathbf{V}$ in order to extract a sublattice. Therefore, we need to transform the LWE samples accordingly to ensure we still have the identical secret vector. In particular, since Algorithm 1 produces a transformation matrix $\mathbf{U}_{\mathrm{SIS}}$ as a part of the output, we can reuse this transformation matrix to process the LWE matrix accordingly. We summarize our method in Algorithm 2. Note that the correctness of the algorithm is ensured by reusing the transformation matrix $\mathbf{U}_{\mathrm{SIS}}$, since it helps us produce vectors that are still bounded by the hints. More details about the proof of correctness can be found in the full version of this paper. Furthermore, our method in Algorithm 2 only requires an REF reduction over $(n+k_1)\times k_1$ matrix, while MN needs to run LLL reduction on a matrix with large entries (because MN multiplies the matrix by a large number to ensure the quality of LLL's output).

**Features and Impacts.** Compared with DDGR and MN, our method is improved in the following aspects:

- First, on a high level, our method puts perfect hints, approximate hints, modular hints, and mod-$q$ hints into a unified framework.
- Second, we adopt a hint-centric point of view that separates hints from the LWE background, and formulates the $\mathbb{Z}$-SIS problem to explain how hints help us recover the secret vector.
- Third, we provide a fast lattice construction method based on REF reduction. In contrast, DDGR needs expensive operations like dual lattice computation. MN relies on assumptions about the hint matrix, and needs to multiplying factors to balance its blocks.

**Table 1.** Methods of integrating LWE with hints

| | DDGR | MN | Our method |
|---|---|---|---|
| key approach | dual basis | LLL reduction | REF reduction |
| dimension reduce | √ | √ | √ |
| determinant increase | √ | √ | √ |
| non-heuristic correctness | √ | | √ |
| multiple hints | | √ | √ |

Table 1 compares technical details of DDGR [6], MN [13], and our method. It shows that our method combines theoretical correctness and efficiency by choosing propoer lattice construction approach. Summarizing our analysis, we can grasp the hints' contribution to attacking LWE from a new aspect: Since $\mathbb{Z}$-SIS and LWE share the same secret vector, the hints provide more constraints on the secret vector in the form of a $\mathbb{Z}$-SIS instance. It is notable that $\mathbb{Z}$-SIS is constructed only from hints, so we claim that hints provide information about the secret vector regardless of the LWE samples.

## 4 Complexity Analysis of LWE with Hints

This section discusses the impact of hints on the hardness of LWE, and tries to give an estimator which predicts the required BKZ block sizes for solving LWE with hints. Subsection 4.1 evaluates the qualities of the $\mathbb{Z}$-SIS lattice. Subsection 4.2 exploits the results to build the complexity estimator. Subsection 4.3 discusses the special case of too many hints regime.

### 4.1 Evaluation of $\mathbb{Z}$-SIS Lattice

In order to predict the required BKZ block sizes, we should first have a thorough understanding about the lattice basis we build. We start by discussing the quality of $\mathbb{Z}$-SIS lattices, then extend to $\mathbb{Z}$-SIS-LWE lattices. By evaluating the lattice's volume and dimension compared with the expected norm of the target vector, we will be able to predict the required block size for successful key recovery.

**Perfect Hints.** Theorem 1 implies that our construction of $\mathbb{Z}$-SIS basis $\mathbf{B}_{\text{SIS}}$ reduces the dimension by $k$. It remains to predict the volume of the lattice, which also affect the hardness of solving $\mathbb{Z}$-SIS. According to Eq. (2), the determinant of matrix $\mathbf{H}$ is up to its $\mathbf{V}_1$ submatrix:

$$\det(\mathbf{H}) = \det(\mathbf{V}_1) \cdot \det(\mathbf{I}_{n-k}) = \det(\mathbf{V}_1).$$

Through Eq. (4), we obtain $\det(\mathbf{B}_{\text{SIS}}) = \frac{\det(\mathbf{H})}{\det(\mathbf{V}'_k)} = \frac{\det(\mathbf{V}_1)}{\det(\mathbf{V}'_k)}$. In the following discussion, Lemma 1 and Theorem 3 will describe the quality of $\mathbf{V}'_k$, Lemma 2 will predict $\det(\mathbf{V}_1)$. Combining these results allows us to evaluate $\det(\mathbf{B}_{\text{SIS}})$.

**Lemma 1 (Lemma 2.5 in [13]).** *Let $k, n$ be integers with $1 \leq k < n$. Let $\mathbf{B} \in \mathbb{Z}^{n\times k}$ be a matrix, whose entries are independent and uniformly distributed over $\{-B, \ldots, B-1\}$ for some $B \in \mathbb{N}$. Then it holds that $\Pr[\mathcal{L}(\mathbf{B}) = \mathbb{Z}^k] > (1 - 2^{2+k-n}) + o(1)$ as $B \to \infty$.*

**Theorem 3.** *Let $\mathbf{H} = \text{Hint}(\overline{\mathbf{v}}_1, \ldots, \overline{\mathbf{v}}_k) \in \mathbb{Z}^{(n+1)\times(n+1)}$ be a perfect hint matrix, where coordinates of $\mathbf{v}_i$'s are independent and uniformly distributed over $\{-\frac{q-1}{2}, \ldots, \frac{q-1}{2}\}$. When $k < n$, the determinant of perfect $\mathbb{Z}$-SIS lattice basis $\mathbf{B}_{\text{SIS}}$ satisfies*

$$\Pr[\det(\mathbf{B}_{\text{SIS}}) = \det(\mathbf{V}_1)] > (1 - 2^{2+k-n}) + o(1).$$

*Proof.* Equation (4) implies $\det(\mathbf{B}_{\text{SIS}}) = \frac{\det(\mathbf{H})}{\det(\mathbf{V}'_k)} = \frac{\det(\mathbf{V}_1)}{\det(\mathbf{V}'_k)}$. It also holds that $\mathbf{V}'_k$ is the basis of the sublattice $\mathcal{L}'$ generated by $\mathbf{V} = \begin{bmatrix} | & & | \\ \mathbf{v}_1^T & \ldots & \mathbf{v}_k^T \\ | & & | \end{bmatrix}$. Since the coordinates of $\mathbf{v}_i$'s are independent and uniformly distributed over $\{-\frac{q-1}{2}, \ldots, \frac{q-1}{2}\}$, Lemma 1 implies $\Pr[\det(\mathbf{B}_{\text{SIS}}) = \det(\mathbf{V}_1)] = \Pr[\det(\mathbf{V}'_k) = 1] = \Pr[\mathcal{L}' = \mathbb{Z}^k] > (1 - 2^{2+k-n}) + o(1)$ as $q \to \infty$. This proves the theorem. □

Theorem 3 allows us to predict $\det(\mathbf{B}_{\text{SIS}})$ with $\det(\mathbf{V}_1)$. However, $\det(\mathbf{V}_1)$ itself is relatively hard to evaluate since its entries are random. Asymptotically, we give an estimation based on the assumption of random matrices.

**Lemma 2 (Sect.4 in [13]).** *Let $M_{k,q} = \{\mathbf{B} \in \mathbb{Z}^{k\times k} : \det \mathbf{B} \neq 0, \mathbf{B}$ has entries in $\{-(q-1)/2, (q-1)/2\}$ for odd positive integer $q$. If $\mathbf{B}$ is uniformly distributed over $M_{k,q}$. Then it holds that $\mathbb{E}[\ln(|\det \mathbf{B}|)] \sim \frac{k}{2} \ln\left(\frac{q^2-1}{12e} k\right)$, as $k \to \infty$.*

Since entries of $\mathbf{V}_1$ are uniformly distributed in $\{-(q-1)/2, (q-1)/2\}$, Lemma 2 implies that $\mathbb{E}[\ln(|\det(\mathbf{B}_{\text{SIS}})|)] = \mathbb{E}[\ln(|\det(\mathbf{V}_1)|)] \sim \frac{k}{2} \ln\left(\frac{q^2-1}{12e}k\right)$. This gives us an evaluation on the volume of the $\mathbb{Z}$-SIS lattice.

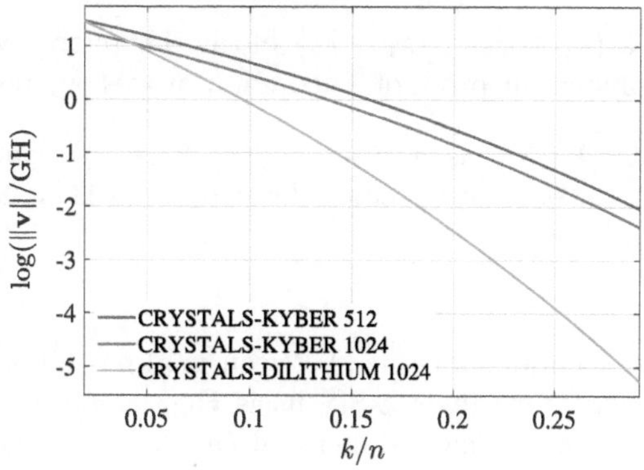


**Fig. 3.** Estimated shortness of $\mathbf{v}_{\text{SIS}}$

**Proposition 2.** *For $k \lesssim n/2$, we estimate* $\text{Vol}(\mathcal{L}(\mathbf{B}_{\text{SIS}})) \approx \left(\frac{q^2-1}{12e}k\right)^{\frac{k}{2}}$.

Based on the discussion, we know the volume of $\mathbb{Z}$-SIS lattice is mainly affected by the number of hints $k$. Meanwhile, the norm of target vector $\mathbf{v}_{\text{SIS}} = [s_{k+1}, \ldots, s_n, -1]$ can be estimated as $\mathbb{E}[\|\mathbf{v}_{\text{SIS}}\|] \approx \sigma\sqrt{n-k}$. Combining the results, we can evaluate the hardness of $\mathbb{Z}$-SIS by comparing the target vector with the Gaussian heuristic of $\mathcal{L}(\mathbf{B}_{\text{SIS}})$ denoted as GH. Figure 3 shows the comparison between the target vectors' norms and lattice volumes for various LWE parameters. When enough hints are provided (e.g. $k \approx 0.15n$ for KYBER, and $k \approx 0.1n$ for DILITHIUM), we expect to have $\mathbb{E}[\|\mathbf{v}_{\text{SIS}}\|] < \text{GH}$, which means recovering $\mathbf{v}_{\text{SIS}}$ can be reduced to SVP. We will discuss the conditions of recovering these problems with more detail in Sect. 4.

**Approximate Hints.** We can directly apply the analysis on perfect hints to approximate hints. Although we have verified that approximate hints don't decrease the dimension of target vector, they lead to a hint matrix similar with perfect hints. The following corollary presents our result.

**Corollary 1.** *Let* $\mathbf{H} = \text{Hint}(\overline{\mathbf{v}}_1, \ldots, \overline{\mathbf{v}}_{k_1}, \overline{\mathbf{v}}'_1, \ldots, \overline{\mathbf{v}}'_{k_2}) \in \mathbb{Z}^{(n+1)\times(n+1)}$ *be a hint matrix built by $k_1$ perfect hints and $k_2$ approximate hints, where coordinates of hints are independent and uniformly distributed over* $\{-\frac{q-1}{2}, \ldots, \frac{q-1}{2}\}$. *When $k < n$, the determinant of perfect $\mathbb{Z}$-SIS lattice basis $\mathbf{B}_{\text{SIS}}$ satisfies*

$$\Pr[\det(\mathbf{B}_{\text{SIS}}) = \det([\mathbf{V}_1|\mathbf{V}'_1])] > (1 - 2^{2+k_1+k_2-n}) + o(1).$$

*Proof.* Equation (5) gives the hint matrix

$$\mathbf{H} = \left[\begin{array}{c|c|c|c} \mathbf{V}_1 & \mathbf{V}_1' & \mathbf{0} & \\ \mathbf{V}_2 & \mathbf{V}_2' & \mathbf{I}_{n-k_1-k_2} & \mathbf{0} \\ \hline \ell & \ell' & 0\ldots0 & 1 \end{array}\right],$$

where $[\mathbf{V}_1|\mathbf{V}_1']$ is a $(k_1+k_2)\times(k_1+k_2)$ block. Therefore, we have $\det(\mathbf{H}) = \det([\mathbf{V}_1|\mathbf{V}_1'])$. Applying our proof of Theorem 3 proves our result. □

Since the block $[\mathbf{V}_1|\mathbf{V}_1']$ is a $(k_1+k_2)\times(k_1+k_2)$ random matrix with entries in $\{-\frac{q-1}{2},\ldots,\frac{q-1}{2}\}$, we predict the volume of $\mathbf{B}_{\text{SIS}}$ as $\text{Vol}(\mathcal{L}(\mathbf{B}_{\text{SIS}})) \approx \left(\frac{q^2-1}{12e}(k_1+k_2)\right)^{\frac{k_1+k_2}{2}}$.

**Modular Hints.** A major difference between modular hints and perfect hints is that the dimension of modular $\mathbb{Z}$-SIS basis $\mathbf{B}_{\text{SIS}}$ is still $(n+1)$. In contrast, the perfect $\mathbb{Z}$-SIS basis has lower dimension $(n-k+1)$. The cause for this is that the modular hint matrix includes $k$ additional rows

$$\left[\begin{array}{ccc|c} m_1 & & & \\ & \ddots & & \mathbf{0} \\ & & m_k & \end{array}\right]$$

through lifting. Then, the lattice construction procedure reduces $k$ dimensions. The final output is still an $(n+1)$-dimensional $\mathbf{B}_{\text{SIS}}$.

**Proposition 3.** *Let $\overline{\mathbf{v}}_i = (\mathbf{v}_i, l_i, m_i) \in \mathbb{Z}^n\times\mathbb{Z}\times\mathbb{N}$ be modular hints, $gcd(m_i,q) = 1, i = 1,\ldots,k$. Our method obtains a $\mathbb{Z}$-SIS basis $\mathbf{B}_{\text{SIS}}$ whose dimension is $(n+1)$.*

Another impact of the additional rows is that $\mathbf{B}_{\text{SIS}}$'s determinant is dominated by the moduli $\{m_1,\ldots,m_k\}$.

**Theorem 4.** *Let $\overline{\mathbf{v}}_i = (\mathbf{v}_i, l_i, m_i) \in \mathbb{Z}^n\times\mathbb{Z}\times\mathbb{N}$ be modular hints, $\gcd(m_i,q) = 1, i = 1,\ldots,k$. The determined of modular $\mathbb{Z}$-SIS basis satisfies $\Pr[\det(\mathbf{B}_{\text{SIS}}) = \prod_{i=1}^k m_i] > (1-2^{2+k-n}) + o(1)$.*

*Proof.* Equation (7) implies $\det(\mathbf{H}) = \prod_{i=1}^k m_i$. Similar with the perfect hint case, we have $\prod_{i=1}^k m_i = \det(\mathbf{H}) = \det(\mathbf{V}_k')\ \det(\mathbf{B}_{\text{SIS}})$ from Eq. (8). Since the entries of $\mathbf{V}$ are uniformly distributed over $\{-\frac{q-1}{2},\ldots,\frac{q-1}{2}\}$, it holds that $\Pr[\det(\mathbf{B}_{\text{SIS}}) = \prod_{i=1}^k m_i] = \Pr[\det(\mathbf{V}_k') = 1] \geq \Pr[\mathcal{L}(\mathbf{V}) = \mathbb{Z}^k] > (1-2^{2+k-n}) + o(1)$. This proves the theorem. □

**Mixed Hints** Given $k_1$ modular hints $\overline{\mathbf{v}}_i = (\mathbf{v}_i, l_i^{\mathbf{v}}, m_i)$, $k_2$ perfect hints $\overline{\mathbf{w}}_i = (\mathbf{w}_i, l_i^{\mathbf{w}})$, and $k_3$ approximate hints $\overline{\mathbf{y}}_i = (\mathbf{y}_i, l_i^{\mathbf{w}})$, Algorithm 2 produces a $(n - k_2 + 1)$-dimensional $\mathbb{Z}$-SIS lattice basis. The determinant of this basis can be analyzed following the same method as above. When we write the first $(k_2 + k_3)$ rows of block $[\mathbf{W}|\mathbf{Y}]$ as $[\mathbf{W}_1|\mathbf{Y}_1]$, the determinant of $\mathbf{B}_{\text{SIS}}$ can be estimated as $\prod_{i=1}^{k_1} m_i \cdot \det([\mathbf{W}_1|\mathbf{Y}_1])$ by Lemma 1. The analysis follows the proof of Theorem 3 and Theorem 4. Since the hints are randomly chosen, the determinant of $\mathbf{W}_1$ can be estimated as $\left(\frac{q^2-1}{12e}(k_2+k_3)\right)^{\frac{(k_2+k_3)}{2}}$. Summarizing the intermediate results, we evaluate the determinant of $\mathbf{B}_{\text{SIS}}$ as $\prod_{i=1}^{k_1} m_i \cdot \left(\frac{q^2-1}{12e}(k_2+k_3)\right)^{\frac{(k_2+k_3)}{2}}$.

### 4.2 Complexity Estimator for LWE with Hints

The lattice-based attack on LWE interprets its hardness as the shortness of the secret vector in the corresponding lattice. In particular, we evaluate the hardness quantitatively by predicting the BKZ block size $\beta$ required to recover the secret vector. Applying the analysis in [2], we estimate that secret vector $\mathbf{t}$ can be found if

$$\sqrt{\beta/d}\,\|\mathbf{t}\| \approx \sqrt{\beta}\sigma \leqslant \delta^{2\beta-d}\det(\mathbf{B}_2)^{1/d}, \tag{19}$$

where $d = m + n - k_2$, $\delta = (((\pi\beta)^{1/\beta}\beta)/(2\pi e))^{1/(2(\beta-1))}$. We can read from the equation that for given $\sigma$, the hints mainly affect size of lattice $d$ and volume of $\mathbb{Z}$-SIS-LWE lattice $\mathcal{L}(\mathbf{B}_2)$. While $d$ is relatively easy to predict based on amount of hints, the value of $\det(\mathbf{B}_2)$ is more involved. We now provide a theoretical evaluation of this lattice.

**Quality of the $\mathbb{Z}$-SIS-LWE lattice.** Intuitively, the new lattice has lower dimension than basic Primal attack. The hints also increase the volume of the lattice. On the other hand, the target vector will have smaller norm since its dimension is reduced. We first analyze the volume of the new lattice, which is illustrated in Theorem 5.

**Theorem 5 (Volume of $\mathbb{Z}$-SIS-LWE lattice).** *Let matrix $\mathbf{B}_2$ be the output of Algorithm 2, it holds that* $\det(\mathbf{B}_2) = q^m \cdot \det(\mathbf{B}_{\text{SIS}})$.

*Proof.* Line 2 of Algorithm 2 gives equation

$$\begin{bmatrix}\mathbf{B}'_1\\ \mathbf{B}_1\end{bmatrix} = \mathbf{U}_{\text{SIS}} \cdot \left[\begin{array}{cc|c|c}\mathbf{A} & \mathbf{Y} & \begin{array}{c}\mathbf{0}\\ \hline \mathbf{I}_{n-k_2-k_3}\end{array} & \mathbf{0}\\ \hline \mathbf{b} & \ell_{\mathbf{y}} & \mathbf{0} & 1\end{array}\right] = \begin{bmatrix}\mathbf{A}' & \mathbf{B}'_{\text{SIS}}\\ \mathbf{A}'' & \mathbf{B}_{\text{SIS}}\end{bmatrix}.$$

Then, step 3 in Algorithm 2 produces $\mathbf{B}_2$:

$$\mathbf{B}_2 = \left[\begin{array}{c|c} q\mathbf{I}_m & \mathbf{0}\\ \hline \multicolumn{2}{c}{\mathbf{B}_1}\end{array}\right] = \begin{bmatrix} q\mathbf{I}_m & \\ \mathbf{A}'' & \mathbf{B}_{\text{SIS}}\end{bmatrix}.$$

This implies that $\det(\mathbf{B}_2) = q^m \cdot \det(\mathbf{B}_{\text{SIS}})$. $\square$

From Theorem 5, we know that the volume of the integrated lattice is determined by

- determinant of $\mathbf{B}_{\mathrm{SIS}}$, i.e. number and type of hints as discussed in Subsect. 4.2;
- number of LWE samples.

We also need to estimate the norm of target vector $\mathbf{t} = [-e_1, \ldots, -e_m, \epsilon_1, \ldots, \epsilon_{k_3}, s_{k_2+k_3+1}, \ldots, s_n, -1]$. Since we are mainly interested in the "short secret LWE", we let $e_i$ and $s_j$ are sampled from the same distribution $\chi$ with standard deviation $\sigma$, and $\epsilon_i$ are sampled from a distribution with standard deviation $\sigma_1$. It follows that

$$\mathbb{E}[\|\mathbf{t}\|] \leq \sqrt{\sigma^2(m+n-k_2-k_3) + \sigma_1^2 k_3 + 1}.$$

In particular, if $\sigma_1 = \sigma$, we estimate $\mathbb{E}[\|\mathbf{t}\|] \approx \sigma\sqrt{m+n-k_2}$ for simplicity.

**The LWE with Hints Estimator.** Combining the results of Theorem 5 with Eq. (19), we rewrite the condition of recovering $\mathbf{t}$ as

$$\begin{aligned} \sqrt{\beta/d}\,\|\mathbf{t}\| \approx \sqrt{\beta}\sigma &\leqslant \delta^{2\beta-d}\det(\mathbf{B}_2)^{1/d} \\ &= \delta^{2\beta-d} q^{m/d} \det\left(\mathbf{B}_{\mathrm{SIS}}\right)^{1/d}, \end{aligned} \tag{20}$$

where $d = m+n-k_2$, $\delta = (((\pi\beta)^{1/\beta}\beta)/(2\pi e))^{1/(2(\beta-1))}$. Therefore, we are able to estimate the required block sizes for given LWE instances by choosing the minimum $\beta$ value that satisfies Eq. (20). For example, we run a simulation on the LWE instances generated in CRYSTALS-KYBER 512. It is also the KEM scheme accepted by NIST (ML-KEM).

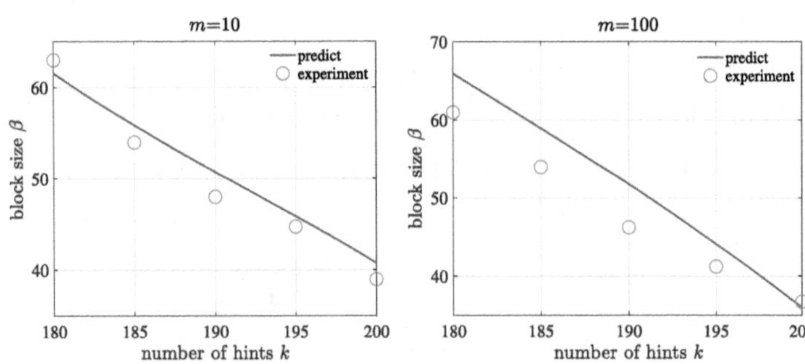


**Fig. 4.** Experimental verification of the estimator

We verify experimentally the prediction made by the estimator by comparing the predictions with experimental results. Figure 4 gives an example of our experiments on CRYSTALS-KYBER 512 with perfect hints.

### 4.3 Revision of the Too Many Hints Regime

Based on our general analysis on LWE with hints, we extend to an important scenario in literature: LWE with significantly many hints (for example $k \approx n/2$). MN [13] named this case as the "too many hints" regime, claiming that for many mod-$q$ hints and perfect hints, we can use LLL or BKZ with small blocks to solve the problem. Although MN notices the "too many hints" phenomenon, their framework simply describes it as reading the target vector from the output of LLL without further analysis. In this work, we take the example of perfect hints, and explain the gap between average LWE with hints and the too many hints regime under our framework:

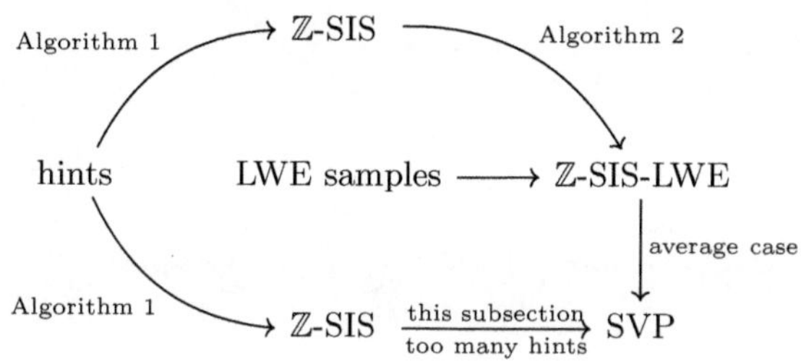


**Fig. 5.** Our method to integrate LWE with hints

Recall that Algorithm 1 is able to construct $\mathbb{Z}$-SIS lattices from any amount of hints. It naturally applies to too many hints. Then, the $\mathbb{Z}$-SIS lattice itself already forms a solvable SVP instance in the too many hints regime. Therefore, it is not necessary to combine $\mathbb{Z}$-SIS with LWE as the average case in Subsect. 3.3. In this case, we propose Algorithm 3 to recover the secret vector. Figure 5 illustrates our method of processing the hints.

**Evaluation of Too Many Hints.** We now give a theoretical analysis of the condition of the too many hints regime. Given $k$ perfect hints, we have proved in Sect. 3 that a lattice $\mathcal{L}(\mathbf{B}_{\text{SIS}})$ can be constructed. It contains the target vector

$$\mathbf{v}_{\text{SIS}} = [s_{k+1}, \ldots, s_n, -1].$$

In average cases, it's hard to identify $\mathbf{v}_{\text{SIS}}$ as the shortest vector since the amount of hints is small. The too many hints regime, on the other hand, allows us to discuss the shortness of vector $\mathbf{v}_{\text{SIS}}$. In particular, by "short" we mean $\mathbf{v}_{\text{SIS}}$ is the *unique shortest vector* in $\mathcal{L}(\mathbf{B}_{\text{SIS}})$. A vector is a $\gamma$-unique shortest vector in a lattice $\mathcal{L}$ when it is of norm $\lambda_1(\mathcal{L})$, and there are no other independent lattice vectors of norm between $\lambda_1(\mathcal{L})$ and $\gamma\lambda_1(\mathcal{L})$. The $\gamma$-unique Shortest Vector Problem ($\gamma$-uSVP) is a search problem in which we are asked to find a $\gamma$-unique shortest vector given the promise that it exists in a lattice. In our situation, we predict the value $\lambda_2(\mathcal{L}(\mathbf{B}_{\text{SIS}}))$ with Gaussian heuristic

$$\lambda_2(\mathcal{L}(\mathbf{B}_{\text{SIS}})) \approx \sqrt{\frac{n-k}{2\pi e}} \det(\mathbf{B}_{\text{SIS}})^{1/(n-k)}.$$

Similar with Subsect. 4.2, we predict $\lambda_1(\mathcal{L}(\mathbf{B}_{\text{SIS}}))$ with the norm of $\mathbf{v}_{\text{SIS}}$

$$\lambda_1(\mathcal{L}(\mathbf{B}_{\text{SIS}})) = \|\mathbf{v}_{\text{SIS}}\| \approx \sigma\sqrt{n-k}.$$

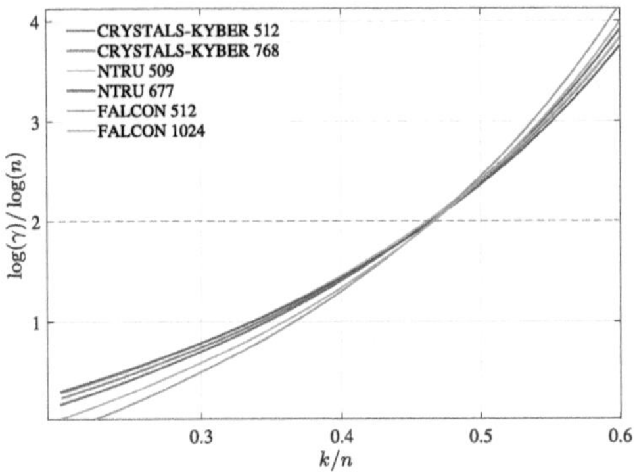


**Fig. 6.** Estimated $\gamma$ for $\mathcal{L}(\mathbf{B}_{\text{SIS}})$ with different numbers of hints

Subsequently, we can estimate the gap $\gamma = \lambda_2(\mathcal{L}(\mathbf{B}_{\text{SIS}}))/\lambda_1(\mathcal{L}(\mathbf{B}_{\text{SIS}}))$. Figure 6 illustrates the expected $\gamma$'s after converting $k$ hints to $\mathbf{B}_{\text{SIS}}$ basis. As shown in the figure, more hints lead to a larger $\frac{\log(\gamma)}{\log(n)}$ value, i.e. we expect to find an unusually short vector in the lattice $\mathcal{L}(\mathbf{B}_{\text{SIS}})$. Particularly, when we obtain $k \approx 0.4n$ perfect hints, $\mathcal{L}(\mathbf{B}_{\text{SIS}})$ forms a strong uSVP instance with $\gamma > n^2$. Therefore, we estimate the required number of hints $k$ should satisfy:

$$\begin{aligned} \gamma = \frac{\lambda_2(\mathcal{L}(\mathbf{B}_{\text{SIS}}))}{\lambda_1(\mathcal{L}(\mathbf{B}_{\text{SIS}}))} &\approx \frac{\sqrt{\frac{n-k}{2\pi e}} \det(\mathbf{B}_{\text{SIS}})^{1/(n-k)}}{\sigma\sqrt{n-k}} \\ &\approx \frac{\left(\frac{q^2-1}{12e}k\right)^{\frac{k}{2(n-k)}}}{\sigma\sqrt{2\pi e(n-k)}} > 2. \end{aligned} \tag{21}$$

Based on the analysis above, we summarize our explanation about what happens in the too many hints regime.

- In the *average case*, the secret vector $\mathbf{v}_{\text{SIS}}$ may not be significantly short in lattice $\mathcal{L}(\mathbf{B}_{\text{SIS}})$. We have to combine it with more LWE samples to construct an SVP instance.
- In the *too many hints case*, lattice $\mathcal{L}(\mathbf{B}_{\text{SIS}})$ already forms an uSVP instance with large $\gamma$. This allows us to extract $\mathbf{v}_{\text{SIS}}$ solely from $\mathcal{L}(\mathbf{B}_{\text{SIS}})$.
- In other words, "too many hints" is achieved when hints provide enough information about $\mathbf{s}$ independent from LWE.

**Algorithm 3:** Strategy for LWE with too many hints

**Input:** $n$-dimensional LWE instance $(\mathbf{A}, \mathbf{b}, q)$, number of LWE samples $m$; modular hints $\overline{\mathbf{v}}_i = (\mathbf{v}_i, l_i^{\mathbf{v}}, m_i) \in \mathbb{Z}^n \times \mathbb{Z} \times \mathbb{N}$, $i = 1, \ldots, k_1$; perfect hints $\overline{\mathbf{w}}_i = (\mathbf{w}_i, l_i^{\mathbf{w}}) \in \mathbb{Z}^n \times \mathbb{Z}, i = 1, \ldots, k_2$; approximate hints $\overline{\mathbf{y}}_i = (\mathbf{y}_i, l_i^{\mathbf{y}}) \in \mathbb{Z}^n \times \mathbb{Z}, i = 1, \ldots, k_3$, BKZ blocksize $\beta$

**Output:** the secret vector of LWE with hints instance

use Algorithm 1 to compute $(\mathbf{B}_{\text{SIS}}, \mathbf{U}_{\text{SIS}})$

run LLL reduction on $\mathbf{B}_{\text{SIS}}$, get output basis $\mathbf{B}_{\text{LLL}} = \mathbf{U}_{\text{LLL}} \cdot \mathbf{B}_{\text{SIS}}$

**if** *row vector* $\mathbf{b}$ *in* $\mathbf{B}_{\text{LLL}}$ *is the target vector* **then**

  return $\mathbf{b}$ `// strict too many hints regime`

**end**

run BKZ-$\beta$ reduction on $\mathbf{B}_{\text{SIS}}$, get output basis $\mathbf{B}_{\text{BKZ}} = (\mathbf{U}_{\text{BKZ}} \cdot \mathbf{U}_{\text{LLL}}) \cdot \mathbf{B}_{\text{SIS}}$

**if** *row vector* $\mathbf{b}$ *in* $\mathbf{B}_{\text{BKZ}}$ *is the target vector* **then**

  return $\mathbf{b}$ `// broader too many hints regime`

**end**

compute $\mathbf{B}_0 = \mathbf{U}_{\text{SIS}} \cdot \left[\begin{array}{c|c|c|c} \mathbf{A} & \mathbf{Y} & \begin{array}{c} \mathbf{0} \\ \hline \mathbf{I}_{n-k_2-k_3} \end{array} & \mathbf{0} \\ \hline \mathbf{b} & \ell_{\mathbf{y}} & \mathbf{0} & 1 \end{array}\right]$, remove its first $k_2$ rows to get matrix $\mathbf{B}_1$

construct matrix $\mathbf{B}_2 = \left[\begin{array}{c|c} q\mathbf{I}_m & \mathbf{0} \\ \hline \multicolumn{2}{c}{\mathbf{U} \cdot \mathbf{B}_1} \end{array}\right]$, where $\mathbf{U} = \mathbf{U}_{\text{BKZ}} \cdot \mathbf{U}_{\text{LLL}}$

run BKZ-$\beta$ reduction on $\mathbf{B}_2$, get output basis $\mathbf{B}_3$

**if** *row vector* $\mathbf{b}$ *in* $\mathbf{B}_3$ *is the target vector* **then**

  return $\mathbf{b}$ `// average case`

**end**

**Strategy to Exploit Too Many Hints.** Under the MN framework, the strict sense of too many hints regime is defined as recovering the secret vector directly in the lattice construction step, i.e. using LLL reduction. Otherwise, they have to run BKZ on a lattice with both hints and LWE samples following the average case. By reducing the hints to $\mathbb{Z}$-SIS, our work allows us to consider a broader sense of too many hints. Even if the secret is not recovered by LLL on the $\mathbb{Z}$-SIS lattice, we can still try slightly stronger reductions like BKZ on the lattice without adding LWE samples. Based on the discussion, we propose a new strategy to solve possible instances of too many hints. The strategy follows 3 main steps, see Algorithm 3.

1. If the instance is strictly in the too many hints regime, we can directly recover the secret vector by LLL on $\mathbf{B}_{\text{SIS}}$;
2. If not, we run BKZ on the basis to test if it is in the broader too many hints regime;
3. If the instance is not in the too many hints regime, pass the parameters to Algorithm 2 as an average LWE with hints instance.

Each step performs a stronger reduction and try to verify if it is in the too many hints regime. In this process, we reuse the transformation matrix of the last step by keeping $\mathbf{U}_{\text{LLL}}$ and $\mathbf{U}_{\text{BKZ}}$.

# 5 Experimental Results

We provide experimental data for our implementation of $\mathbb{Z}$-SIS construction from Sect. 3, and the implementation of combining $\mathbb{Z}$-SIS with LWE as described in Sect. 4. Our experiments are performed on a desktop computer with Intel Core i9-12900H and 16 GB of RAM. Generally, its single-core performance is close to the platform used in the work of MN. For each setting, we present the average data of 50 experiments on single threads. The source code is available at https://gitee.com/jinzhengcao/refined-attack-on-lwe-with-hints.git.

## 5.1 Results for Constructing $\mathbb{Z}$-SIS

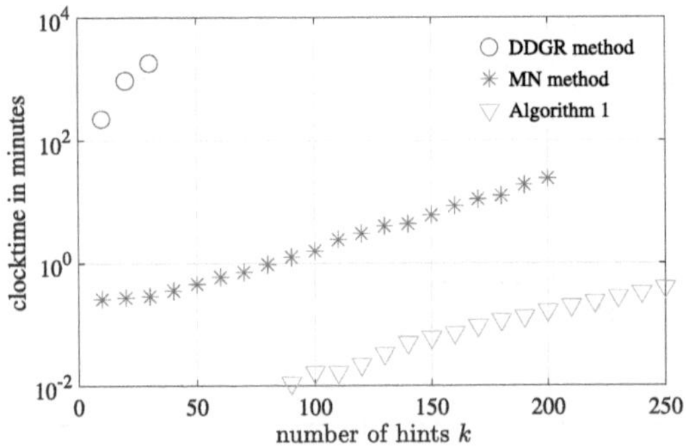


**Fig. 7.** Runtime of constructing $\mathbb{Z}$-SIS lattices for CRYSTALS-KYBER 512

We first test our method of constructing $\mathbb{Z}$-SIS lattices from hints presented in Sect. 3. Figure 7 depicts our running time for processing hints of CRYSTALS-KYBER 512 with Algorithm 1. Compared with the sequential method of DDGR and the LLL-based method of MN, our method is significantly faster. Particularly, our time cost is lower than 1 min for up to 250 hints. We explain that the speed-up is possible for two reasons:

- The MN method runs LLL on a $(n+1) \times (n+1)$ matrix to extract a sublattice, while we only need to compute REF by Gaussian elimination.
- The MN method needs to multiply the matrix with a large factor, which is not required in our method.

Based on the comparison of, we expect that the running time of construcing $\mathbb{Z}$-SIS in the whole attack should be marginal.

### 5.2 Results for Full Attacks

We now test the overall performance of attacking LWE with hints. We mainly focus on perfect hints to give comparable results. Our attack includes the following steps:

- Lattice construction, which is described in Algorithm 1 and Algorithm 2.
- LLL preprocessing, where we adopt the fast LLL variant implemented by [19].
- BKZ reduction, with the implementation of fpylll [23].

Note that we adopt the progressive BKZ strategy to achieve better efficiency, i.e. we run several BKZ tours with $\beta$ increasing. This reduction is stronger than the assumption of theoretical BKZ simulator which considers single BKZ tours, so the block sizes in the experiments are smaller than our estimator.

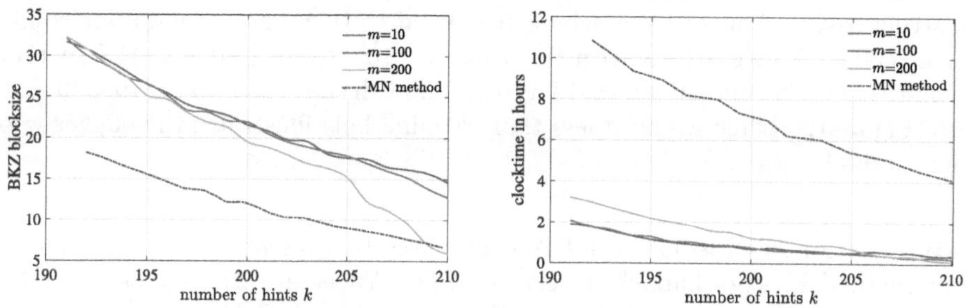


(a) BKZ blocksize (b) Time

**Fig. 8.** Experiments on CRYSTALS-KYBER 512 with perfect hints

**Experiments on PQC Standards.** Figure 8 presents the BKZ blocksizes and time for experiments on CRYSTALS-KYBER 512 with perfect hints. In our experiments, the number of hints $k$ increases from 191 to 210. For every setting, we try integrating different numbers of LWE samples ($m = 10, 100, 200$). Generally, more LWE samples require smaller block and slightly more time. We also compare our results with MN, and it shows that our method is significantly faster. Another observation is that the actual BKZ blocksizes are significantly smaller than our evaluation in Subsect. 4.2, especially when number of samples $m$ is large. We explain this phenomenon with the fact that BKZ algorithm can omit some unnecessary samples in itself, as described in [6].

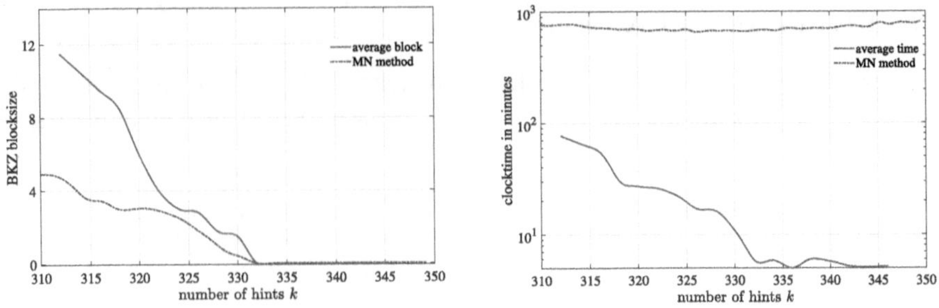


(a) BKZ blocksize (b) Time

**Fig. 9.** Average BKZ blocksize and time for NTRU 701

Our method is also applicable to NTRU with hints by considering NTRU as a structured variant of LWE where $\mathbf{b}$ is fixed to $\mathbf{0}$. Figure 9 shows our results of attacking NTRU-HRSS with $n = 701$, $m = 10$. Recall that the MN method requires $m = 701$ and about 11–13 h to accomplish the attack with 310–330 hints [13, Figure 12], while we need less than 80 min. This illustrates the efficiency of our method.

**Application to Side-Channel Attack.** We also present an example of using our method in side-channel attacks. In 2024, Yu et al. [24] proposed a CPU frequency leakage attacks against NTT in lattice-based KEMs. For secret vector $\mathbf{s}_0$, the attack produces a matrix $\mathbf{N}$ and vector $\hat{\mathbf{s}}_0$ such that

$$\hat{\mathbf{s}}_0 = \mathbf{N} \cdot \mathbf{s}_0 \bmod q.$$

While the approach of [24] was successful in extracting these linear equations, the authors were unable to actually solve large LWE instances with them. In particular, the literature evaluated the security loss under MN framework, and proposed that CYSTALS-KYBER 512 can be attacked with 406 equations. It is worth noting that they considered the equations as modular hints. We try to recover the LWE secret key by exploiting the following techniques. First, instead of regarding the equations as modular hints, we consider them as mod-$q$ hints. Second, our framework allows us to control the size of the lattice basis by adjusting the number of LWE samples $m$. Third, since the literature didn't provide data from real attacks, we sample random linear equations to conduct experiments. As we have analyzed, the hints reduces the dimension of the LWE lattice. Table 2 shows the experimental results of recovering secret vectors from CYSTALS-KYBER 512. In our experiments, we are able to efficiently find the secret with $\geq$380 hints, which is lower than the bound offered in [24]. Given fewer than 380 hints, the cost of solving the problem grows dramatically.

**Table 2.** Attacking CYSTALS-KYBER 512 with leakage in [24]

| #hints | #LWE samples | $\beta$ | time |
|---|---|---|---|
| 410 | 90 | 26 | 5 min |
| 400 | 90 | 31 | 22 min |
| 390 | 90 | 47 | 3 h |
| 380 | 130 | 46 | 4 h |
| 370 | 130 | 58 | 35 h |

### 5.3 Results for Too Many Hints

We also test our method on the "too many hints" regime. In Subsect. 4.3, we claim that this phenomenon is possible because a large amount of hints produce a $\mathbb{Z}$-SIS instance that is already solvable by lattice basis reduction. Furthermore, given about $n/2$ hints, we expect to recover the secret vector with LLL. We run experiments on CRYSTALS-KYBER 512 by the method in Subsect. 4.3 – first construct a $\mathbb{Z}$-SIS lattice using Algorithm 1, then run LLL/BKZ on the lattice. Figure 10 presents the required BKZ blocksizes and time to recover the secret vector from the $\mathbb{Z}$-SIS lattice. BKZ blocksize 0 denotes LLL reduction. In the grey area of too many hints regime, we can recover the secret key with LLL. In the white area where fewer hints are provided, we can still recover the secret from hints with BKZ reduction. We call this phenomenon the broad sense of too many hints regime.

Given a large number of hints (approximately $> 230$ in our experiments), we can recover the secret vectors directly by LLL reduction. In other words, they are in the too many hints regime as described in MN. Note that the MN method needs about 2 h for too many hints instances [13, Figure 6], while we use about 3 min. Our time consumption for other instances are also lower. For 210–230 hints, we enter the broader sense of too many hints regime, where we require about 5–30 min. The main reason of the speed-up is that the MN method runs LLL on a $(n+1)\times(n+1)$ matrix, while we run LLL on a $(n-k+1)\times(n-k+1)$ matrix after extracting the sublattice.

**Table 3.** Bounds of $k$ for too many hints regime

| scheme | predict | MN method | our method | time |
|---|---|---|---|---|
| KYBER 512 | 235 | 233 | 230 | 2.1 m |
| KYBER 768 | 354 | 390 | 376 | 9.8 m |
| NTRU 509 | 234 | 230 | 226 | 2.3 m |
| NTRU 677 | 310 | 334 | 325 | 3.8 m |
| FALCON 512 | 238 | 231 | 227 | 1.8 m |
| FALCON 1024 | 477 | 560 | 540 | 27.8 m |
| DILITHIUM 1024 | 348 | 463 | 450 | 44.9 m |

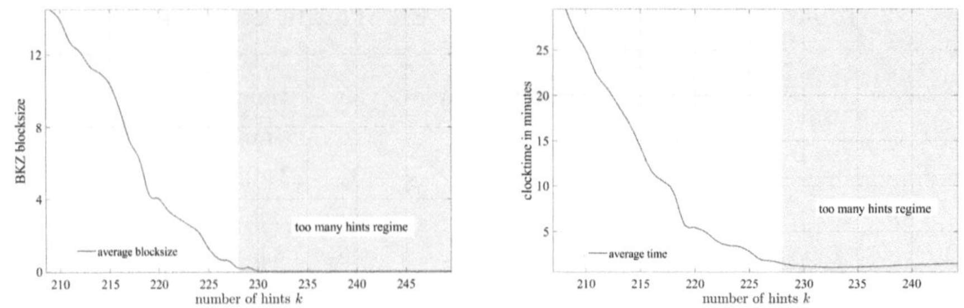


(a) BKZ blocksize (b) Time

**Fig. 10.** Average BKZ blocksize and time for CRYSTALS-KYBER 512 with only hints

We extend the experimental to more schemes. Table 3 lists our experiments for various lattice-based schemes, and compares the required number of hints $k$ for LLL to recover the key with the predicted bound. Generally, the experimental data matches with our predictions, and requires fewer hints than the MN method [13]. For higher dimensions (for example $n = 1024$), the experimental $k$ values slightly differ from the prediction. This is probably caused by the performance of LLL lattice basis reduction on larger lattices.

## 6 Conclusion

In this paper, we develop a novel framework for LWE with perfect hints, modular hints, mod-$q$ hints, and approximate hints. This framework is built on our theoretical analysis of LWE with hints, which guides us in understanding how these hints provide information about the LWE secret key. Through our work, we offer an algorithm that converts LWE with hints to an SVP instance with probable correctness. Furthermore, our algorithm constructs the lattice faster than previous works by choosing REF reduction as a main technique instead of LLL reduction. Compared with algorithms proposed by DDGR and MN, our method processes all hints in one stroke with REF reduction and ensures theoretical correctness at the same time. This combines the advantages of both of the existing algorithms. Experimental results demonstrate that our method is faster than DDGR and MN on cryptographic LWE instances. On CRYSTALS-KYBER 512 with about 200 hints, we reduce the running time from hours to minutes.

**Acknowledgements.** The work of Haodong Jiang was supported by the National Key R&D Program of China under Grant No. 2024YFB4504600. The work of Qingfeng Cheng (Corresponding Author) was supported by the National Natural Science Foundation of China under Grant No. 62472438, and the Natural Science Foundation of Henan under Grant No. 242300421414.

## References


1. Albrecht, M.R., Deo, A., Paterson, K.G.: Cold boot attacks on ring and module LWE keys under the NTT. IACR TCHES **2018**(3), 173–213 (2018). https://doi.org/10.13154/tches.v2018.i3.173-213
2. Albrecht, M.R., Göpfert, F., Virdia, F., Wunderer, T.: Revisiting the expected cost of solving uSVP and applications to LWE. In: Takagi, T., Peyrin, T. (eds.) ASIACRYPT 2017. LNCS, vol. 10624, pp. 297–322. Springer, Cham (2017). https://doi.org/10.1007/978-3-319-70694-8_11
3. Bos, J., et al.: Crystals - Kyber: a CCA-secure module-lattice-based KEM. In: 2018 IEEE European Symposium on Security and Privacy, pp. 353–367 (2018). https://doi.org/10.1109/EuroSP.2018.00032
4. Bos, J.W., Friedberger, S., Martinoli, M., Oswald, E., Stam, M.: Assessing the feasibility of single trace power analysis of Frodo. In: Cid, C., Jacobson Jr., M.J. (eds.) Selected Areas in Cryptography – SAC 2018. LNCS, vol. 11349, pp. 216–234. Springer, Cham (2019). https://doi.org/10.1007/978-3-030-10970-7_10
5. Cao, J., Cheng, Q., Weng, J.: Optimizing $c$-sum BKW and faster quantum variant for LWE. IACR Commun. Cryptol. **1**(3) (2024). https://doi.org/10.62056/a6qj5w7sf
6. Dachman-Soled, D., Ducas, L., Gong, H., Rossi, M.: LWE with side information: attacks and concrete security estimation. In: Micciancio, D., Ristenpart, T. (eds.) CRYPTO 2020. LNCS, vol. 12171, pp. 329–358. Springer, Cham (2020). https://doi.org/10.1007/978-3-030-56880-1_12
7. Dachman-Soled, D., Gong, H., Hanson, T., Kippen, H.: Revisiting security estimation for LWE with hints from a geometric perspective. In: Handschuh, H., Lysyanskaya, A. (eds.) Advances in Cryptology – CRYPTO 2023. LNCS, vol. 14085, pp. 748–781. Springer, Cham (2023). https://doi.org/10.1007/978-3-031-38554-4_24
8. Groot Bruinderink, L., Hülsing, A., Lange, T., Yarom, Y.: Flush, gauss, and reload – a cache attack on the BLISS lattice-based signature scheme. In: Gierlichs, B., Poschmann, A.Y. (eds.) CHES 2016. LNCS, vol. 9813, pp. 323–345. Springer, Heidelberg (2016). https://doi.org/10.1007/978-3-662-53140-2_16
9. Hermelink, J.: Side-channel and fault attacks in modern lattice-based cryptography. Ph.D. thesis, Bundeswehr University Munich, Neubiberg (Munich), Germany (2024). https://athene-forschung.unibw.de/148513
10. Jain, A., Lin, H., Saha, S.: A systematic study of sparse LWE. In: Reyzin, L., Stebila, D. (eds.) Advances in Cryptology – CRYPTO 2024. LNCS, vol. 14922, pp. 210–245. Springer, Cham (2024). https://doi.org/10.1007/978-3-031-68382-4_7
11. Kundu, S., Chowdhury, S., Saha, S., Karmakar, A., Mukhopadhyay, D., Verbauwhede, I.: Carry your fault: a fault propagation attack on side-channel protected LWE-based KEM. IACR TCHES **2024**(2), 844–869 (2024). https://doi.org/10.46586/TCHES.V2024.I2.844-869
12. Lu, M., Yang, J.: Memory-sample lower bounds for LWE. In: Reyzin, L., Stebila, D. (eds.) Advances in Cryptology – CRYPTO 2024. LNCS, vol. 14924, pp. 158–182. Springer, Cham (2024). https://doi.org/10.1007/978-3-031-68388-6_7
13. May, A., Nowakowski, J.: Too many hints – when LLL breaks LWE. In: Guo, J., Steinfeld, R. (eds.) Advances in Cryptology – ASIACRYPT 2023. LNCS, vol. 14441, pp. 106–137. Springer, Singapore (2023). https://doi.org/10.1007/978-981-99-8730-6_4
14. Murphy, S., Player, R.: A central limit approach for ring-LWE noise analysis. IACR Commun. Cryptol. **1**(2) (2024). https://doi.org/10.62056/ay76c0kr

15. Nguyen, T.T.Q.: Concrete security of some lattice-based cryptographic constructions. Ph.D. thesis (2024). http://www.theses.fr/2024NORMC248. These de doctorat dirigee par Roux-Langlois, Adeline et Giraud, Christophe Informatique Normandie 2024
16. Park, J., van Leeuwen, B., Zajonc, O.: FINALLY: a multi-key FHE scheme based on NTRU and LWE. IACR Commun. Cryptol. **1**(3) (2024). https://doi.org/10.62056/aebn-4c2h
17. Peikert, C., Pepin, Z.: Algebraically structured LWE, revisited. J. Cryptol. **37**(3), 28 (2024). https://doi.org/10.1007/S00145-024-09508-3
18. Ravi, P., Jhanwar, M.P., Howe, J., Chattopadhyay, A., Bhasin, S.: Exploiting determinism in lattice-based signatures: practical fault attacks on PQM4 implementations of NIST candidates. In: 2019 ACM Asia Conference on Computer and Communications Security, pp. 427–440. Association for Computing Machinery (2019). https://doi.org/10.1145/3321705.3329821
19. Ryan, K., Heninger, N.: Fast practical lattice reduction through iterated compression. In: Handschuh, H., Lysyanskaya, A. (eds.) Advances in Cryptology – CRYPTO 2023. LNCS, vol. 14083, pp. 3–36. Springer, Cham (2023). https://doi.org/10.1007/978-3-031-38548-3_1
20. Saeidi, Z., Mashhadi, S.: Two meaningful secret image sharing schemes based on integer wavelet transform and LWE. Comput. Appl. Math. **43**(3), 149 (2024). https://doi.org/10.1007/S40314-024-02664-Z
21. Soni, D., Basu, K., Nabeel, M., Aaraj, N., Manzano, M., Karri, R.: FALCON. In: Hardware Architectures for Post-Quantum Digital Signature Schemes, pp. 31–41. Springer, Cham (2021). https://doi.org/10.1007/978-3-030-57682-0_3
22. Steiner, M.J.: The complexity of algebraic algorithms for LWE. In: Joye, M., Leander, G. (eds.) Advances in Cryptology – EUROCRYPT 2024. LNCS, vol. 14653, pp. 375–403. Springer, Cham (2024). https://doi.org/10.1007/978-3-031-58734-4_13
23. The FPLLL development team: fpylll, a Python wraper for the fplll lattice reduction library, Version: 0.5.6 (2021). https://github.com/fplll/fpylll
24. Yu, T., Cheng, C., Yang, Z., Wang, Y., Pan, Y., Weng, J.: Hints from hertz: Dynamic frequency scaling side-channel analysis of number theoretic transform in lattice-based kems. IACR Cryptol. ePrint Archive **70** (2024). https://eprint.iacr.org/2024/070

# Uncompressing Dilithium's Public Key

Paco Azevedo-Oliveira[1,2(✉)], Andersson Calle Viera[1,3], Benoît Cogliati[1], and Louis Goubin[2]

[1] Thales DIS, Meudon, France
{andersson.calle-viera,benoit-michel.cogliati}@thalesgroup.com
[2] Laboratoire de Mathématiques de Versailles, UVSQ, CNRS, Université Paris-Saclay, 78035 Versailles, France
paco.azevedo-oliveira@thalesgroup.com, louis.goubin@uvsq.fr
[3] Sorbonne Université, CNRS, Inria, LIP6, 75005 Paris, France

**Abstract.** The Dilithium signature scheme – recently standardized by NIST under the name ML-DSA – owes part of its success to a specific mechanism that allows an optimization of its public key size. Namely, among the data of the MLWE instance $(\mathbf{A}, \mathbf{t})$, which is at the heart of the construction of Dilithium, the least significant part of $\mathbf{t}$ – denoted by $\mathbf{t}_0$ – is not included in the public key. The verification algorithm had been adapted accordingly, so that it should not require the knowledge of $\mathbf{t}_0$. However, since it is still required to compute valid signatures, it has been made part of the secret key. The knowledge of $\mathbf{t}_0$ has no impact on the black-box cryptographic security of Dilithium, as can be seen in the security proof. Nevertheless, it does allow the construction of much more efficient side-channel attacks. Whether it is possible to recover $\mathbf{t}_0$ thus appears to be a sensitive question. In this work, we show that each Dilithium signature leaks information on $\mathbf{t}_0$, then we construct an attack that retrieves it from Dilithium signatures. Experimentally, depending on the Dilithium security level, between 200 000 and 500 000 signatures are sufficient to recover $\mathbf{t}_0$ on a desktop computer.

## 1 Introduction

**Dilithium.** Following NIST's Post-Quantum Cryptography standardization process, the Dilithium signature scheme [BDK+21] has been selected as one of the winners under the name ML-DSA. It belongs to the family of lattice-based signature schemes, and is an application of the Fiat-Shamir with aborts [Lyu09] to the Module Learning-With-Errors (MLWE) problem. In general, the public key of such a scheme is an (M)LWE instance, which is to say a (matrix, vector) pair $(\mathbf{A}, \mathbf{t})$ such that two "small" *secret* vectors $\mathbf{s}_1$ and $\mathbf{s}_2$ exist such that $\mathbf{t} = \mathbf{A}\mathbf{s}_1 + \mathbf{s}_2$. One of the main selling points of Dilithium is its compressed public key. Indeed, the vector $\mathbf{t}$ is split coefficient-wise into a high and a low part, respectively denoted by $\mathbf{t}_1$ and $\mathbf{t}_0$. The Dilithium public key finally corresponds to the seed that was used to generate the matrix $\mathbf{A}$, along with $\mathbf{t}_1$, while $\mathbf{t}_0$ is considered to be part of the secret key. The generation of the signature and its


Y. Tauman Kalai and S. F. Kamara (Eds.): CRYPTO 2025, LNCS 16000, pp. 417–443, 2025.
https://doi.org/10.1007/978-3-032-01855-7_14

verification must be adapted so that the verifier is able to verify the signature without knowledge of $\mathbf{t}_0$.

**On the Status of $\mathbf{t}_0$.** As stated previously, $\mathbf{t}_0$ is considered as a part of the secret key. However, the security proof of Dilithium [BDK+21] assumes that the whole vector $\mathbf{t}$ is given in the public key, which means that this compression is not intended to increase the security of Dilithium. Moreover, Lyubashevsky mentions $\mathbf{t}_0$ in a conference given in 2022 [Lyu22]: "$\mathbf{t}_0$ are not given but they are not secret, some information is leaked with every signature. The security proof assumes that $\mathbf{t}_0$ is public.". This is further emphasized by the NIST draft standard for ML-DSA [NIS23], which states that $\mathbf{t}_0$ "can be reconstructed from a small number of signatures and, therefore, need not be regarded as secret". Unfortunately, it seems that this claim has never been formally studied. While this may seem benign due to the fact that the formal security of Dilithium does not rely on the secrecy of $\mathbf{t}_0$, it seems that its knowledge can be useful in the context of side-channel attacks.

Some papers assume that $\mathbf{t}_0$ is known to the attacker: in [RRB+19] we can read: "note that the security analysis of DILITHIUM is done with the assumption that the whole of $\mathbf{t}$ is declared as the public key. In addition to this, some information about $\mathbf{t}_0$ is leaked with every published signature and thus the whole of $\mathbf{t}$ can be reconstructed by just observing several signatures generated using the same secret key", but unfortunately again there is no argument or proof.

Others articles remain conservative and study their attacks in both cases: with or without the knowledge of $\mathbf{t}_0$. For example, in [EAB+23] the authors state that: "In Subsect. 5.3, we derive the impact of fully secret $\mathbf{t}_0$ on the complexity of the (reduced) RLWE instance. We hope that this approach gives a complete view to the reader about the applicability of the attack to Dilithium." There are even papers that explicitly ask for a clarification of the role of $\mathbf{t}_0$ in the side-channel literature on Dilithium. In particular in [WNGD23]: "Our results demonstrate the necessity of protecting the secret key of Dilithium from single-trace attacks. They also prompt a reassessment of the role of $\mathbf{t}_0$ in the security of Dilithium implementations."

Finally, at least one paper considers that it is unrealistic to assume that a "real" attacker can find $\mathbf{t}_0$ in a side-channel setting. In [RJH+18] we read: "Thus, it might indeed be possible that the whole of $\mathbf{t}$ leaks as part of the signature and observations of sufficiently many signatures might lead to the recovery of the complete LWE instance, $\mathbf{t}$. But again, we expect the number of signatures and the computational effort to be very high, which cannot be expected in a practical SCA setting".

In conclusion, there is no consensus on the role of $\mathbf{t}_0$ in the case of side-channel attacks.

**Our Contribution.** In this article, we study the possibility of recovering $\mathbf{t}_0$ from signatures corresponding to arbitrary messages. In more detail, from each signature, we extract inequalities on the coefficients of $\mathbf{t}_0$, until we get a system of linear non-equalities that admit $\mathbf{t}_0$ as its only solution. In order to solve the system, we rely on Linear Programming. The key takeaways of our work are the following:

1. Between 200 000 and 500 000 signatures are needed to reliably recover the value of $\mathbf{t}_0$, depending on the security level.
2. As a consequence, this results in a very large system of inequalities, which is computationally heavy to solve. We built a more efficient approach that builds a sequence of filtered systems of inequalities that have an increasingly smaller number of solutions until $\mathbf{t}_0$ becomes the unique solution.

Overall, our method is relatively simple yet non-trivial, and allows to find $\mathbf{t}_0$ in all our experiments, each time in less than 4 hours on a desktop computer. Our result shows two points: firstly it confirms the fact that not knowing $\mathbf{t}_0$ does not strengthen Dilithium's security (which is not really surprising) and, more importantly, it shows that $\mathbf{t}_0$ can be quickly recovered in practice. Therefore assuming that it can be recovered by a physical attacker is a sound assumption.

**On the Impact of $\mathbf{t}_0$.** This result has various impacts on the Dilithium side-channel state-of-the-art.

- First, in [MGTF19] the authors show that knowledge of the secret key portion $\mathbf{s}_1$ is sufficient to forge arbitrary signatures. Therefore most papers in the state-of-the-art, try to recover $\mathbf{s}_1$, other papers such as [BCVC+23] target $\mathbf{t}_0 - \mathbf{s}_2$, so that $\mathbf{s}_1$ can be found using the relation:

$$\mathbf{A}\mathbf{s}_1 = \mathbf{t}_1 2^d + (\mathbf{t}_0 - \mathbf{s}_2).$$

  Retrieving $\mathbf{t}_0$ shows that, given enough Dilithium signatures, $\mathbf{s}_2$ also allows to forge arbitrary signatures. This could give rise to new attacks, targeting $\mathbf{s}_2$ directly.
- Secondly, as some papers already used the knowledge of $\mathbf{t}_0$ to create attacks, it justifies that some already published attacks are applicable in practice and improved. For example: In [BAE+24] the authors describe a profiled attack targeting $\mathbf{s}_1$, on page 12 they write: "While this work focuses on describing the recovery of $\mathbf{s}_1$ from the relation$\mathbf{z} = \mathbf{y} + c\mathbf{s}_1$, a similar attack applies to recover $\mathbf{s}_2$, [...]. This approach requires knowledge of $\mathbf{t}_0$, a part of the public key which is not explicitly revealed by the signer but not necessarily sensitive or to remain secret...". Thus knowing $\mathbf{t}_0$ allows the attack to be carried out on $\mathbf{s}_1$ and $\mathbf{s}_2$. [EAB+23] describes a differential fault in the nonce generation. The attack is described theoretically with or without knowledge of $\mathbf{t}_0$, one can read on page 11: "In our attack, the knowledge of $\mathbf{t}_0$ is not required for the MLWE to RLWE reduction part of our attack as $\mathbf{t}_0$ can be embedded into the additive noise vector (moving $\mathbf{t}_0$ to the right part of Eq. 6). However, it has an impact on the resulting security of the RLWE problem making it harder to solve.". Furthermore, due to the limitations of their computing power, the attack without knowledge of $\mathbf{t}_0$ could only be carried out for Dilithium-V (see [EAB+23], page 6). Our results imply that the attack is feasible in practice for all security levels. [WNGD23] builds a deep learning profiled power

attack, as one can read page 3: "In our opinion, the main contribution of this paper is highlighting the possibility of recovering the complete secret vector $\mathbf{s}_1$ from a single trace with a non-negligible probability (9% in our experiments) in the case when $\mathbf{t}_0$ is known.". The attack works without $\mathbf{t}_0$'s knowledge, but requires more execution traces: it is no longer a "single trace attack". [RRB+19] describes a fault-based attack on the public key generation. This attack is impossible without knowing $\mathbf{t}_0$, as one can read on page 8: "There is a subtle but considerable difference with respect to publicly revealed LWE instances in the Dilithium scheme. The public key reveals only $\mathbf{t}_1$, the $d$ higher order bits of $\mathbf{t}$, while $\mathbf{t}_0$ (the lower order component) is part of the secret key. Even on ensuring nonce-reuse, we would not be able to trivially solve for the secret $\mathbf{s}$ from the faulty public key.". Finally in [AOVCG25], the authors use knowledge of $\mathbf{t}_0$ to find $\mathbf{s}_1$ with a fault attack. The attack would not have been possible without the knowledge of $\mathbf{t}_0$.

- In addition regarding countermeasures, the papers studying Dilithium masking [MGTF19, CGTZ23], and [ABC+23] do not protect $\mathbf{t}_0$ (because it does not reveal any information about the secret key). Our results provide additional justification for this phenomenon, as $\mathbf{t}_0$ could be recovered even when masked. Furthermore, when considering the protections needed for implementations, especially on constrained devices such as smart cards, attacks using knowledge of $\mathbf{t}_0$ must be considered as realistic as other attacks. Finally, [WGD24] builds upon a preliminary version of this paper. The authors used a profiled deep learning-assisted side-channel analysis on the unpacking procedure to successfully recover the least significant bit (LSB) of each coefficient of $\mathbf{t}_0$. When this LSB leakage is integrated into our attack, it effectively eliminates the need for the final filtering phase. As stated by the authors: "knowing the LSBs reduces the total number of signatures required to recover $\mathbf{t}_0$ by approximately half", demonstrating the substantial practical advantage conferred by leveraging even minimal side-channel leakage on $\mathbf{t}_0$.

Investigating if finding an approximate $\mathbf{t}_0$ with our method and efficiently combining it with part of others existing attacks using the knowledge of $\mathbf{t}_0$ could be an interesting new research direction. This hybrid approach could lead to building new efficient attacks and is left for future work.

*Outline.* This paper is organized as follows. In Sect. 2, we redefine the basic notions about Dilithium and recall some results from linear programming which will be useful in the rest of this article. In Sect. 3, we define and motivate the problem we will solve in the rest of the article. In Sect. 4, we propose an approach based on linear programming tools. Finally, Sect. 5 presents the experimental results obtained for this new attack and a brief discussion of our results.

## 2 Preliminary Requirements

In this section we begin by briefly introducing the notations and main functions used in Dilithium. For a detailed description of Dilithium, the reader is referred to [BDK+21]. We then review the main definitions and results of linear programming, which will be used in the next section.

### 2.1 Notations, Hints and Inequalities

**Definition 1.** *Let $\alpha$ be an even (resp. odd) integer. We define $r' := r \bmod^{\pm}(\alpha)$ the unique $-\frac{\alpha}{2} < r' \leq \frac{\alpha}{2}$ (resp. $-\frac{\alpha-1}{2} \leq r' \leq \frac{\alpha-1}{2}$) such that $r' = r \mod (\alpha)$. We will speak of centered reduction modulo $\alpha$. We define $r'' := r \bmod^{+}(\alpha)$ the unique $0 \leq r'' < \alpha$ such that $r'' = r \mod (\alpha)$.*

**Definition 2.** *We define $\phi_n = x^n + 1$ with $n$ a power of 2 and $q$ a prime, and introduce the following rings:*

$$\mathcal{R} := \mathbb{Z}[x]/(\phi_n) \text{ and } \mathcal{R}_q := \mathbb{Z}_q[x]/(\phi_n).$$

**Notation 1.** *For an integer $l \in \mathbb{N}^*$ and for an element $\mathbf{t}_0 \in \mathcal{R}^l$, we will note $\mathbf{t}_0 = (\mathbf{t}_0^{[0]}, ..., \mathbf{t}_0^{[l-1]}) \in \mathcal{R}^l$ and $\mathbf{t}_{0,i}^{[j]}$ will be the i-th coefficient of the polynomial $\mathbf{t}_0^{[j]}$.*

**Notation 2.** *We will note $[\![$ statement $]\!]$ the boolean operator which evaluates to 1 if statement is true, and to 0 otherwise.*

**Definition 3.** *For $w \in \mathbb{Z}_q$:*

$$||w||_\infty := |w \bmod^{\pm} (q)|.$$

*For $\boldsymbol{w} = \sum w_i x^i \in \mathcal{R}$:*

$$||\boldsymbol{w}||_\infty := \max ||w_i \bmod^{\pm}(q)||_\infty \text{ and } ||\boldsymbol{w}|| := \left(\sum ||w_i||_\infty^2\right)^{1/2}$$

*and for $\mathbf{w} = (\mathbf{w}^{[0]}, ..., \mathbf{w}^{[l-1]}) \in \mathcal{R}^l$,*

$$||\mathbf{w}||_\infty := \max ||\mathbf{w}^{[i]}||_\infty \text{ and } ||\mathbf{w}|| := \left(\sum ||\mathbf{w}^{[i]}||^2\right)^{1/2}.$$

*Finally, we define two sets $S_\eta, \tilde{S}_\eta \subset \mathcal{R}$ as follows:*

$$S_\eta := \{\boldsymbol{w} \in \mathcal{R} \mid ||\boldsymbol{w}||_\infty \leq \eta\} \text{ and } \tilde{S}_\eta := \{\boldsymbol{w} \bmod^{\pm} (2\eta) \mid \boldsymbol{w} \in \mathcal{R}\}.$$

Dilithium is a signature scheme based on structured lattices, we will therefore manipulate matrices and vectors of $\mathcal{R}$ or $\mathcal{R}_q$, with the values of $n$ and $q$ fixed at $n = 256$ and $q = 2^{23} - 2^{13} + 1 = 8\,380\,417$ regardless of the security level. In addition, to reduce the size of the public key and to generate the signature Dilithium uses algorithms that splits elements in $\mathbb{Z}_q$. The first and most natural way is to use bit decomposition: for $r \in \mathbb{Z}_q$ and $d \in \mathbb{N}^*$, $r = r_1 2^d + r_0$ where $r_0 = r \bmod^{\pm} 2^d$ and $r_1 = (r - r_0)/2^d$. This is done with the algorithm $\texttt{Power2Round}_q$ defined in Algorithm 1 and is used to reduce the size of the public key $\mathbf{t}$.

Since the public key is not "completely" known to the verifier, the signer must add "hints" to the signature to allow its verification. Given $r \in \mathbb{Z}_q$ and a small element $z \in \mathbb{Z}_q$, the verifier must calculate the high bits of $z+r$ without knowing $z$. To do this, the authors have decided to use a slightly different split: for an even $\alpha$ divisor of $q-1$ and $r \in \mathbb{Z}_q$ they define $r = r_1\alpha + r_0$ with $r_0 = r \bmod^{\pm}(\alpha)$ and $r_1 = (r - r_0)/\alpha$. We will call $r_1$ the high bits of $r$ and $r_0$ the low bits of $r$. As shown in Fig. 1, for $z \in \mathbb{Z}_q$ such that $|z| \leq \alpha/2$, adding $z$ to $r$ can only increase or decrease the high bits of $r$ by $\pm 1$. With this simple tweak one can calculate the high bits of $r + z$, only with the knowledge of $z$ and a hint bit $h \in \{0, 1\}$. Algorithm 1 give the description of the algorithms and Lemma 1 recall the main property used.

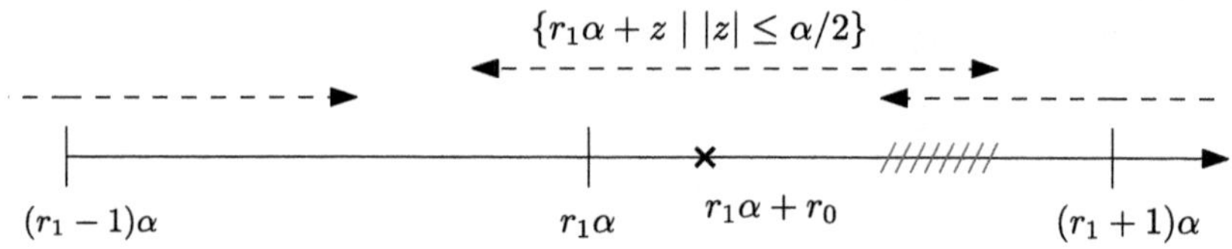


**Fig. 1.** carry caused by $z$

**Algorithm 1.** Supporting algorithms for Dilithium

$\texttt{Power2Round}_q(r, d)$:
- $r = r \bmod^+ q$
- $r_0 = r \bmod^{\pm} 2^d$
- **return** $((r - r_0)/2^d, r_0)$

$\texttt{Decompose}_q(r, \alpha)$:
- $r = r \bmod^+ q$
- $r_0 = r \bmod^{\pm} \alpha$
- **if** $r - r_0 = q - 1$ **then**
  - $r_1 = 0$
  - $r_0 = r_0 - 1$
- **else** $r_1 = (r - r_0)/\alpha$
- **return** $(r_1, r_0)$

$\texttt{HighBits}_q(r, \alpha)$:
- $(r_1, r_0) = \texttt{Decompose}_q(r, \alpha)$
- **return** $r_1$

$\texttt{LowBits}_q(r, \alpha)$:
- $(r_1, r_0) = \texttt{Decompose}_q(r, \alpha)$
- **return** $r_0$

$\texttt{MakeHint}_q(z, r, \alpha)$:
- $r_1 = \texttt{HighBits}_q(r, \alpha)$
- $v_1 = \texttt{HighBits}_q(r + z, \alpha)$
- **return** $[\![r_1 \neq v_1]\!]$

$\texttt{UseHint}_q(h, r, \alpha)$:
- $m = (q - 1)/\alpha$
- $(r_1, r_0) = \texttt{Decompose}_q(r, \alpha)$
- **if** $h = 1$ and $r_0 > 0$ **then**
  - **return** $(r_1 + 1) \bmod^+ m$
- **if** $h = 1$ and $r_0 \leq 0$ **then**
  - **return** $(r_1 - 1) \bmod^+ m$
- **return** $r_1$

**Lemma 1.** *[LDK+22] Let $q$ and $\alpha$ be two positive integers such that $q > 2\alpha$, $q \equiv 1 \bmod (\alpha)$ and $\alpha$ even. Let $\mathbf{r}$ and $\mathbf{z}$ be two vectors of $\mathcal{R}_q$ such that $||\mathbf{z}||_\infty \leq \alpha/2$*

*and let* $\mathbf{h}, \mathbf{h}'$ *be bit vectors. So the algorithms* $\texttt{HighBits}_q$ , $\texttt{MakeHint}_q$, $\texttt{UseHint}_q$ *satisfy the properties:*

$$\texttt{UseHint}_q(\texttt{MakeHint}_q(\mathbf{z}, \mathbf{r}, \alpha), \mathbf{r}, \alpha) = \texttt{HighBits}_q(\mathbf{r} + \mathbf{z}, \alpha).$$

### 2.2 Algorithm Description

**Key Generation:** The key generation algorithm is described in Algorithm 2. Dilithium is based on the Module-LWE problem, a variant of the LWE problem introduced by Regev in [Reg05], which we will not recall here. From some seeds, $\mathbf{A} \in \mathcal{R}_q^{k\times l}$ and $\mathbf{s}_1 \in S_\eta^l$ and $\mathbf{s}_2 \in S_\eta^k$ are generated and then $\mathbf{t} = \mathbf{A}\mathbf{s}_1 + \mathbf{s}_2$ is computed. Two optimisations are made to the public key, which is traditionally $(\mathbf{A}, \mathbf{t})$, to reduce its size. The first optimisation, the most natural, consists of transmitting only the seed used to generate the matrix $\mathbf{A}$. For the second optimisation, only $\mathbf{t}_1$ (the high part of $\mathbf{t}$ computed with $\texttt{Power2Round}_q$) is considered to be part of the public key. This reduces the size of the public key by half at the cost of adding a few bits at the time of signing, so that the verifier does not need the knowledge of $\mathbf{t}_0$.

**Algorithm 2.** KeyGen

**Ensure:** $(pk, sk)$
1: $\zeta \leftarrow \{0,1\}^{256}$
2: $(\rho, \rho', K) \in \{0,1\}^{256} \times \{0,1\}^{512} \times \{0,1\}^{256} := \mathrm{H}(\zeta)$
3: $\mathbf{A} \in \mathcal{R}_q^{k\times l} := \texttt{ExpandA}(\rho)$
4: $(\mathbf{s}_1,\, \mathbf{s}_2) \in S_\eta^l \times S_\eta^k := \texttt{ExpandS}(\rho')$
5: $\mathbf{t} := \mathbf{A}\,\mathbf{s}_1 + \mathbf{s}_2$
6: $(\mathbf{t}_1,\, \mathbf{t}_0) := \texttt{Power2Round}_q(\mathbf{t},\, d)$
7: $tr \in \{0,1\}^{256} := \mathrm{H}(\rho \,||\, \mathbf{t}_1)$
8: **return** $pk = (\rho,\, \mathbf{t}_1)$, $sk = (\rho, K, tr, \mathbf{s}_1, \mathbf{s}_2, \mathbf{t}_0)$

**Signature:** The signature algorithm is described in Algorithm 3. The signer derives a masking vector $\mathbf{y} \in \mathcal{R}_q^l$, from which it calculates $\mathbf{w}_1$, the high bits of $\mathbf{w} := \mathbf{A}\,\mathbf{y}$ and then a challenge $c \in \mathcal{R}$ which is a sparse polynomial whose coefficients are in $\{-1, 0, 1\}$. It then calculates $\mathbf{z} := \mathbf{y} + c\,\mathbf{s}_1$, the main part of the signature, which verifies the following equation, used for verification:

$$\texttt{HighBits}_q(\mathbf{Az} - c\mathbf{t},\, 2\,\gamma_2) = \texttt{HighBits}_q(\mathbf{Ay} - c\mathbf{s}_2,\, 2\,\gamma_2).$$

The signer then checks that $\mathbf{z}$ does not give information about the secret key; if it does, it starts again by drawing another masking vector. Once $\mathbf{z}$ has passed the tests, we have the following equation:

$$\mathbf{w}_1 = \texttt{HighBits}_q(\mathbf{Ay} - c\mathbf{s}_2,\ 2\gamma_2) = \texttt{HighBits}_q(\mathbf{Az} - c\mathbf{t},\ 2\gamma_2).$$

Since $\mathbf{t}_0$ is not known, anyone attempting to verify the signature cannot directly compute $\texttt{HighBits}_q(\mathbf{Az} - c\mathbf{t},\ 2\gamma_2)$. Using the method described in Subsect. 2.1, the signer adds $\mathbf{h} = \texttt{MakeHint}_q(-c\mathbf{t}_0, \mathbf{Ay} - c\mathbf{s}_2 + c\mathbf{t}_0, 2\gamma_2)$ to the signature, to allow the verifier to calculate $\texttt{HighBits}_q(\mathbf{Az} - c\mathbf{t},\ 2\gamma_2)$, without the knowledge of $\mathbf{t}_0$.

Finally, the signature is composed of the seed $\tilde{c}$, used to sample the challenge polynomial, the response vector $\mathbf{z}$, and the hint vector $\mathbf{h}$.

---

**Algorithm 3.** Sig

---

**Require:** $sk, M$
**Ensure:** $\sigma = (\tilde{c}, \mathbf{z}, \mathbf{h})$
$\mathbf{A} \in \mathcal{R}_q^{k \times l} := \texttt{ExpandA}(\rho)$
$\mu \in \{0,1\}^{512} := \mathrm{H}(tr \,||\, M)$
$\kappa := 0,\ (\mathbf{z}, \mathbf{h}) := \perp$
$\rho' \in \{0,1\}^{512} := \mathrm{H}(K \,||\, \mu)$
**while** $(\mathbf{z}, \mathbf{h}) = \perp$ **do**
  $\mathbf{y} \in \tilde{S}_{\gamma_1}^{l} := \texttt{ExpandMask}(\rho',\ \kappa)$
  $\mathbf{w} := \mathbf{A}\,\mathbf{y}$
  $\mathbf{w}_1 = \texttt{HighBits}_q(\mathbf{w},\ 2\gamma_2)$
  $\tilde{c} \in \{0,1\}^{256} := \mathrm{H}(\mu \,||\, \mathbf{w}_1)$
  $c \in B_\tau := \texttt{SampleInBall}(\tilde{c})$
  $\mathbf{z} := \mathbf{y} + c\,\mathbf{s}_1$
  $\mathbf{r}_0 := \texttt{LowBits}_q(\mathbf{w} - c\mathbf{s}_2,\ 2\gamma_2)$
  **if** $\|\mathbf{z}\|_\infty \geq \gamma_1 - \beta$ or $\|\mathbf{r}_0\|_\infty \geq \gamma_2 - \beta$ **then**
    $(\mathbf{z}, \mathbf{h}) := \perp$
  **else**
    $\mathbf{h} := \texttt{MakeHint}_q(-c\mathbf{t}_0, \mathbf{w} - c\mathbf{s}_2 + c\mathbf{t}_0, 2\gamma_2)$
    **if** $\|c\,\mathbf{t}_0\|_\infty \geq \gamma_2$ or $|\mathbf{h}|_{\mathbf{h}_j = 1} > \omega$ **then**
      $(\mathbf{z}, \mathbf{h}) := \perp$
  $\kappa := \kappa + l$
**return** $\sigma = (\tilde{c}, \mathbf{z}, \mathbf{h})$

---

**Verification:** The verification algorithm is described in Algorithm 4. To verify the signature, the verifier begins by reconstructing the matrix $\mathbf{A}$ and the polynomial $c$ on which the signer has committed. Using the vector $\mathbf{h}$ of the signature and $\texttt{UseHint}_q$, $\mathbf{w}_1 = \texttt{HighBits}_q(\mathbf{Az} - c\mathbf{t},\ 2\gamma_2)$ is recalculated. Finally, the signature will be accepted if it is possible to reconstruct the correct $c$ from $\mathbf{w}_1$ and if $\mathbf{z}$ meets the security conditions imposed during signature generation.

**Algorithm 4.** Ver

**Require:** $pk, \sigma$

$\mathbf{A} \in \mathcal{R}_q^{k \times l} :=$ ExpandA$(\rho)$

$\mu \in \{0,1\}^{512} := \mathrm{H}(\mathrm{H}(\rho \,||\, \mathbf{t}_1) \,||\, M)$

$c :=$ SampleInBall$(\tilde{c})$

$\mathbf{w}_1' :=$ UseHint$_q(\mathbf{h}, \mathbf{Az} - c\mathbf{t}_1 \cdot 2^d, 2\gamma_2)$

**return** $[\![ ||\mathbf{z}||_\infty < \gamma_1 - \beta ]\!]$ and $[\![ \tilde{c} = \mathrm{H}(\mu \,||\, \mathbf{w}_1') ]\!]$ and $[\![ |\mathbf{h}|_{\mathbf{h}_j=1} \leq \omega ]\!]$

**Remark 1.** *As shown above, in the formal definition of Dilithium,* $\mathbf{t}_0$ *is considered to be secret data even though it reveals nothing about the other polynomials of the secret key. Therefore, in a side channel attack, an attacker cannot use knowledge of* $\mathbf{t}_0$ *to attack a Dilithium implementation. Despite this, a large proportion of papers on side-channel or fault-based attacks against Dilithium [BVC+23] [RRB+19] [EAB+23] make the assumption that* $\mathbf{t}_0$ *is known. In the rest of the paper we will show that* $\mathbf{t}_0$ *can indeed be considered as part of the public key, since it can be reconstructed from Dilithium signatures.*

## 2.3 An Overview of Polyhedral Theory

A polyhedron is a set of points verifying a finite number of inequalities, in other words: an instersection of a finite number of half-spaces. We are interested in this geometrical object because in Sect. 3 we will show that by querying Dilithium signatures generated under the same secret key, we will collect inequalities on the coefficients of the polynomial vector $\mathbf{t}_0$. $\mathbf{t}_0$ will therefore be in a bounded polyhedron, traditionally called a polytope. Obtaining information about this polytope will allow us to find $\mathbf{t}_0$ in Sect. 4. We refer to [NW88] for general definitions and unproven propositions.

**Definition 4.** *A polyhedron* $P \subset \mathbb{R}^n$ *is the set of points that satisfy a finite number of linear inequalities,* $P = \{x \in \mathbb{R}^n : \ Ax \leq b\}$ *where* $(A, b)$ *is a* $m \times (n+1)$ *matrix.*

**Definition 5.** *A polyhedron* $P \subset \mathbb{R}^n$ *is bounded if there exists an* $w \in \mathbb{R}_+$ *such that* $P \subset \{x \in \mathbb{R}^n : \ -w \leq x_j \leq w \text{ for } j = 0, ..., n-1\}$*. A bounded polyhedron is called a polytope.*

**Definition 6.** *Let* $P \subset \mathbb{R}^n$ *be a polytope, we call the diameter of* $P$ *and we note* $diam(P)$ *the quantity:*

$$diam(P) = \max_{p_1, p_2 \in P} ||p_1 - p_2||_\infty$$

**Definition 7.** *A polyhedron* $P$ *is of dimension* $k$*, denoted by* $dim(P) = k$*, if the maximum number of affinely independent points in* $P$ *is* $k + 1$*.*

**Remark 2.** *The definition of diameter and dimension provide an estimation on the number of elements in a polytope. In our case, we are going to collect inequalities verified by* $\mathbf{t}_0$*, so we will obtain a polytope containing* $\mathbf{t}_0$*. Estimating the dimension and diameter of this polytope allows us to obtain an estimation on the coefficients of* $\mathbf{t}_0$*.*

### 2.4 The Basics of Linear Programming

The general linear programming problem is to find:

$$z_{LP} = \max\{cx : \ Ax \leq b, \ x \in \mathbb{R} \ \}$$

where $A$ is a $m \times n$ matrix and $c, b$ are $1 \times n$ and $m \times 1$ matrices. This problem is well defined is the sense that if it is feasible and does not have unbounded optimal values, then it has an optimal solution. In the rest of this paper, we will note $(LP)$ and write it in the following form:

$$\begin{aligned} &\text{maximize } cx \\ &\text{subject to } Ax \leq b \\ &\qquad\qquad\quad x \in \mathbb{R} \end{aligned}$$

**Remark 3.** *Let $P$ be a polytope described by a set of inequalities. Trivialy, finding an $x \in P$ (i.e. a point that satisfies all the inequalities that form the description of $P$) is an $(LP)$ problem, as it can be solved by maximizing any function on $P$. Minimising a function on $P$ is also an $(LP)$ problem as it is sufficient to maximise its opposite.*

**Proposition 1.** *Let $P = \{x \in \mathbb{R}^n \mid Ax \leq b\}$ be a polytope, upper-bounding the dimension of $P$ or calculating the diameter of $P$ are two $(LP)$ problems (Fig. 2).*

$$\begin{aligned} &\text{minimize } x_i \\ &\text{subject to } Ax \leq b \\ &\qquad\qquad\quad x \in \mathbb{R}^n \end{aligned} \qquad\qquad \begin{aligned} &\text{maximize } x_i \\ &\text{subject to } Ax \leq b \\ &\qquad\qquad\quad x \in \mathbb{R}^n \end{aligned}$$

**Fig. 2.** The $2 \times 256$ $(LP)$ problems related to $P$.

*Proof.* For $i \in \{0, \ldots, n-1\}$, by solving the following two $(LP)$ problems: Calculating $\text{card}(\{i \in \{0, \ldots, n-1\} : \ \exists w_i \in \mathbb{R}, \forall x \in P, \ x_i = w_i\})$ allows to upper-bound the dimension of $P$. Solving the same $(LP)$ problems allow also to calculate the diameter of $P$. □

**Notation 3.** *Let $P \subset \mathbb{R}^n$ be a polytope. The procedure for calculating a point by minimizing the null function on $P$ is denoted* `lp_guess`*, and we denote* `calculate_diam` *the procedure which consists in computing the diameter of $P$.*

## 3 Problem Definition and Existing Solutions

In the rest of the paper, we study the case of an attacker who tries to recover $\mathbf{t}_0$ based on knowledge of $pk = (\rho, \mathbf{t}_1)$ and a certain number of Dilithium signatures $\{\sigma_i\}_{i \in I}$ signed under the corresponding secret key $sk = (\rho, K, tr, \mathbf{s}_1, \mathbf{s}_2, \mathbf{t}_0)$. In this section we show that each Dilithium signature provides information on the coefficients of $\mathbf{t}_0$, in the form of inequalities on its coefficients. Naturally, we will try to exploit this leakage of information by using linear programming theory to propose a solution.

**Proposition 2.** *Let $j \in \{0,\ldots,k-1\}$ and $i \in \{0,\ldots,255\}$ and $\sigma = (\tilde{c},\mathbf{z},\mathbf{h})$ be a signature of* Sig.

- *If* $\mathbf{h}_i^{[j]} = 0$*:*
$$|(-c\mathbf{t}_0)_i^{[j]} + \texttt{LowBits}_q(\mathbf{Az} - c\mathbf{t}_1 \cdot 2^d, 2\,\gamma_2)_i^{[j]}| \leq \gamma_2 - \beta - 1.$$
- *If* $\mathbf{h}_i^{[j]} = 1$ *and* $\texttt{LowBits}_q(\mathbf{Az} - c\mathbf{t}_1 \cdot 2^d, 2\,\gamma_2)_i^{[j]} > 0$*:*
$$(-c\mathbf{t}_0)_i^{[j]} \geq \gamma_2 + \beta + 1 - \texttt{LowBits}_q(\mathbf{Az} - c\mathbf{t}_1 \cdot 2^d, 2\,\gamma_2)_i^{[j]} \geq 0.$$
- *If* $\mathbf{h}_i^{[j]} = 1$ *and* $\texttt{LowBits}_q(\mathbf{Az} - c\mathbf{t}_1 \cdot 2^d, 2\,\gamma_2)_i^{[j]} < 0$*:*
$$(-c\mathbf{t}_0)_i^{[j]} \leq -(\gamma_2 + \beta + 1) - \texttt{LowBits}_q(\mathbf{Az} - c\mathbf{t}_1 \cdot 2^d, 2\,\gamma_2)_i^{[j]} \leq 0.$$

**Remark 4.** $\mathbf{A}$ *and* $\mathbf{t}_1$ *are publicly known and* $c, \mathbf{z}, \mathbf{h}$ *belongs to the signature, so an attacker can calculate* $\texttt{LowBits}_q(\mathbf{Az} - c\mathbf{t}_1 \cdot 2^d, 2\,\gamma_2)$*. Since* $\gamma_2$ *and* $\beta$ *are known parameters, an attacker can calculate the bound of the inequality obtained on* $\mathbf{t}_0$*.*

*Proof.* Let $\sigma = (\tilde{c},\mathbf{z},\mathbf{h})$ be a signature of Sig, $j \in \{0,\ldots,k-1\}$ and $i \in \{0,\ldots,255\}$.

- If $\mathbf{h}_i^{[j]} = 0$, by definition of $\mathbf{h}_i^{[j]}$:
$$\texttt{HighBits}_q(\mathbf{Az} - c\mathbf{t}, 2\,\gamma_2)_i^{[j]} = \texttt{HighBits}_q(\mathbf{Az} - c\mathbf{t}_1 \cdot 2^d, 2\,\gamma_2)_i^{[j]}.$$
Using the relation $\mathbf{Az} - c\mathbf{t} = \mathbf{Az} - c\mathbf{t}_1 \cdot 2^d - c\mathbf{t}_0$ and decomposing $\mathbf{Az} - c\mathbf{t}$, $\mathbf{Az} - c\mathbf{t}_1 \cdot 2^d$ with their high and low bits, we obtain the following relation:
$$\texttt{LowBits}_q(\mathbf{Az} - c\mathbf{t}, 2\,\gamma_2)_i^{[j]} = \texttt{LowBits}_q(\mathbf{Az} - c\mathbf{t}_1 \cdot 2^d, 2\,\gamma_2)_i^{[j]} - (c\mathbf{t}_0)_i^{[j]},$$
and by definition of the signature:
$$|\texttt{LowBits}_q(\mathbf{Az} - c\mathbf{t}, 2\,\gamma_2)_i^{[j]}| < \gamma_2 - \beta.$$
So we finally obtain:
$$|-(c\mathbf{t}_0)_i^{[j]} + \texttt{LowBits}_q(\mathbf{Az} - c\mathbf{t}_1 \cdot 2^d, 2\,\gamma_2)_i^{[j]}| \leq \gamma_2 - \beta - 1.$$
- If $\mathbf{h}_i^{[j]} = 1$ and $\texttt{LowBits}_q(\mathbf{Az} - c\mathbf{t}_1 \cdot 2^d, 2\,\gamma_2)_i^{[j]} > 0$, by definition of $\mathbf{h}_i^{[j]}$:
$$\texttt{HighBits}_q(\mathbf{Az} - c\mathbf{t}, 2\,\gamma_2)_i^{[j]} = \texttt{HighBits}_q(\mathbf{Az} - c\mathbf{t}_1 \cdot 2^d, 2\,\gamma_2)_i^{[j]} + 1.$$

Using the relation $\mathbf{Az} - c\mathbf{t} = \mathbf{Az} - c\mathbf{t}_1 \cdot 2^d - c\mathbf{t}_0$ and decomposing $\mathbf{Az} - c\mathbf{t}, \mathbf{Az} - c\mathbf{t}_1 \cdot 2^d$ with their high and low bits, we obtain the following relation:

$$\texttt{LowBits}_q(\mathbf{Az} - c\mathbf{t}, 2\gamma_2)_i^{[j]} = \texttt{LowBits}_q(\mathbf{Az} - c\mathbf{t}_1 \cdot 2^d, 2\gamma_2)_i^{[j]} - (c\mathbf{t}_0)_i^{[j]} - 2\gamma_2$$

By definition of the signature:

$$|\texttt{LowBits}_q(\mathbf{Az} - c\mathbf{t}, 2\gamma_2)_i^{[j]}| < \gamma_2 - \beta.$$

By replacing $\texttt{LowBits}_q(\mathbf{Az} - c\mathbf{t}, 2\gamma_2)_i^{[j]}$ with the equation above and using the fact that $||\texttt{LowBits}_q(\mathbf{Az} - c\mathbf{t}, 2\gamma_2)||_\infty \leq \gamma_2$ and $||c\mathbf{t}_0||_\infty < \gamma_2$, we get:

$$(-c\mathbf{t}_0)_i^{[j]} \geq \gamma_2 + \beta + 1 - \texttt{LowBits}_q(\mathbf{Az} - c\mathbf{t}_1 \cdot 2^d, 2\gamma_2)_i^{[j]} \geq 0.$$

- If $\mathbf{h}_i^{[j]} = 1$ and $\texttt{LowBits}_q(\mathbf{Az} - c\mathbf{t}_1 \cdot 2^d, 2\gamma_2)_i^{[j]} < 0$:
  By definition of $\mathbf{h}_i^{[j]}$:

  $$\texttt{HighBits}_q(\mathbf{Az} - c\mathbf{t}, 2\gamma_2)_i^{[j]} = \texttt{HighBits}_q(\mathbf{Az} - c\mathbf{t}_1 \cdot 2^d, 2\gamma_2)_i^{[j]} - 1.$$

  Using the same reasoning, we obtain:

  $$\texttt{LowBits}_q(\mathbf{Az} - c\mathbf{t}, 2\gamma_2)_i^{[j]} = \texttt{LowBits}_q(\mathbf{Az} - c\mathbf{t}_1 \cdot 2^d, 2\gamma_2)_i^{[j]} - (c\mathbf{t}_0)_i^{[j]} + 2\gamma_2$$

  and therefore:

  $$|\texttt{LowBits}_q(\mathbf{Az} - c\mathbf{t}_1 \cdot 2^d, 2\gamma_2)_i^{[j]} - (c\mathbf{t}_0)_i^{[j]} + 2\gamma_2| < \gamma_2 - \beta.$$

  Finally, because $||\texttt{LowBits}_q(\mathbf{Az} - c\mathbf{t}, 2\gamma_2)||_\infty \leq \gamma_2$ and $||c\mathbf{t}_0||_\infty < \gamma_2$:

  $$(-c\mathbf{t}_0)_i^{[j]} \leq -(\gamma_2 + \beta + 1) - \texttt{LowBits}_q(\mathbf{Az} - c\mathbf{t}_1 \cdot 2^d, 2\gamma_2)_i^{[j]} \leq 0.$$

□

The reasoning above, for the second case is summarised in Fig. 3. In red the impossible values of $(-c\mathbf{t}_0)_i^{[j]}$ according to the value of $\mathbf{h}_i^{[j]}$. In purple, the impossible values of $(-c\mathbf{t}_0)_i^{[j]}$ according to the generation of the signature.

To measure the frequency with which we obtain an inequality on the coefficient of $\mathbf{t}_0$, we collected 10 000 signatures for an equal number of random messages for 10 random keys, for the three security level of Dilithium. The practical results are summarised in Table 1 below. For the sake of clarity, we have split the inequalities obtained for coefficients of $\mathbf{h}$ equal to 0 (on the left) from the inequalities obtained for coefficients of $\mathbf{h}$ equal to 1 (on the right).

**Remark 5.** *To visualise the information obtained, we can study the following problem: an attacker knows all the coefficients of* $\mathbf{t}_0^{[0]}$ *except the first two,* $\mathbf{t}_{0,0}^{[0]}$ *and* $\mathbf{t}_{0,1}^{[0]}$*. He queries signatures and obtains inequalities on the two missing coefficients, which can be represented as a point in the set of solutions to the inequalities it has collected.*

*In Fig. 4, the two coefficients the attacker is seeking are* $(-961, 1631)$ *and the white part represents the polytope of solutions for* 10, 50 *and* 100 *collected inequalities. As can be seen in the third image, we have an increasingly complex algebraic description (several dozen inequalities, most of which are not useful) of a simple geometric object (a polytope with* 5 *faces).*

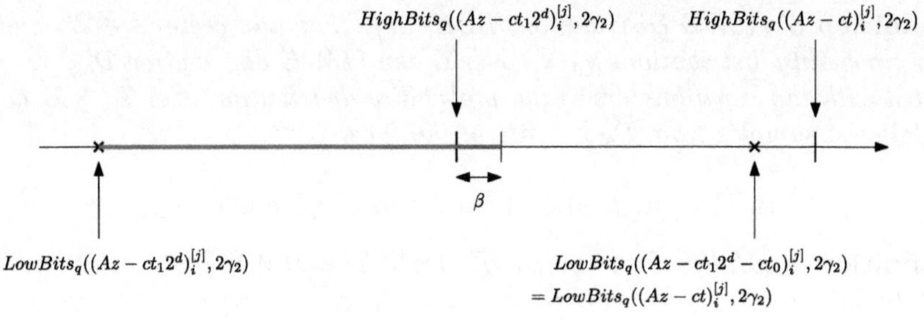


**Fig. 3.** Idea to obtain inequalities on $\mathbf{t}_0$.

**Table 1.** Average number of inequalities per signature, over 10 000 signatures, for different security levels.

| NIST Level | II | III | V |
|---|---|---|---|
| Average inequality obtained | $1\,922 + 63$ | $2\,996 + 38$ | $3\,984 + 56$ |

### 3.1 A State-of-the-Art Solution?

The paper [BDE+18] studies the following problem: A vector $\mathbf{s} \in \mathbb{Z}^n$ is fixed and secret, given $m$ samples $(\mathbf{a}_0, \langle \mathbf{a}_0, \mathbf{s}\rangle + e_0), \ldots, (\mathbf{a}_{m-1}, \langle \mathbf{a}_{m-1}, \mathbf{s}\rangle + e_{m-1})$, where for all $i$ in $\{0, \ldots, m-1\}$, $\mathbf{a}_i \in \mathbb{Z}^n$ and $e_i \in \mathbb{Z}$ follows a probability distribution $(\chi_a)^n$ and $\chi_e$ respectively, is it possible to find $\mathbf{s}$? The paper answers yes to the question (under assumptions detailed later) and gives the answer in two steps: from the point of view of information theory, it gives a minimum bound for $m$ (the number of samples required). Then they give a practical way of finding s where the number of samples required is only slightly higher than the theoretical bound. For the practical solution, they use the method of least squares. To avoid overloading the paper, only the main results of the article are given.

**Remark 6.** *It is natural to relate this problem to the problem of finding* $\mathbf{t}_0$. *Each signature gives inequalities on a linear combination of the coefficients of* $\mathbf{t}_0$. *Consequently, each signature provides an approximate value on a linear combination of the coefficients of the polynomials of* $\mathbf{t}_0$.

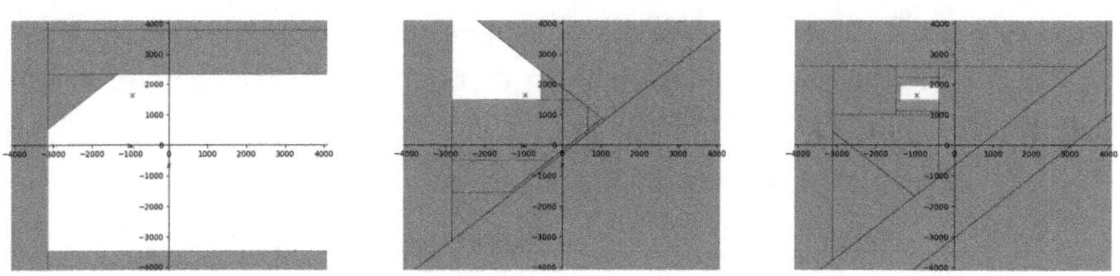

**Fig. 4.** Polytope containing $(\mathbf{t}_{0,0}^{[0]}, \mathbf{t}_{0,1}^{[0]})$ for 10, 50 and 100 inequalities.

**Definition 8** *(ILWE Distribution [BDE+18]). For any vector* $\mathbf{s} \in \mathbb{Z}^n$ *and any two probability distributions* $\chi_a, \chi_e$ *over* $\mathbb{Z}$*, the ILWE distribution* $\mathcal{D}_{\mathbf{s},\chi_a,\chi_e}$ *associated with those parameters is the probability distribution over* $\mathbb{Z}^n \times \mathbb{Z}$ *defined as follows: samples from* $\mathcal{D}_{\mathbf{s},\chi_a,\chi_e}$ *are of the form*

$$(\mathbf{a}, b) = (\mathbf{a}, \langle \mathbf{a}, \mathbf{s} \rangle + e) \quad \textit{with} \quad \mathbf{a} \leftarrow \chi_a^n \textit{ and } e \leftarrow \chi_e.$$

**Definition 9** *(ILWE Problem [BDE+18]). The ILWE problem is the computational problem parametrized by* $n, m, \chi_a, \chi_e$ *in which, given* $m$ *samples* $\{(\mathbf{a}_i, b_i)\}_{0 \le i \le m-1}$ *from a distribution of the form* $\mathcal{D}_{\mathbf{s},\chi_a,\chi_e}$ *for some* $\mathbf{s} \in \mathbb{Z}^n$*, one is asked to recover the vector* $\mathbf{s}$*.*

**Definition 10** *(Subgaussian random variable [BDE+18]).*
*A random variable* $X$ *over* $\mathbb{R}$ *is said to be* $\zeta$*−subgaussian for some* $\zeta > 0$ *if the following bound holds for all* $s \in \mathbb{R}$ *:*

$$\mathbb{E}[\exp(sX)] \le \exp(\frac{\zeta^2 s^2}{2}).$$

*A random vector* $\mathbf{x} \in \mathbb{R}^n$ *is called a* $\zeta$*−subgaussian random vector if for all vectors* $\mathbf{u} \in \mathbb{R}^n$ *with* $||\mathbf{u}||_2 = 1$*, the inner product* $\langle \mathbf{u}, \mathbf{x} \rangle$ *is a* $\zeta$*−subgaussian random variable.*

**Theorem 1** *([BDE+18]). Suppose that* $\chi_a$ *is a* $\zeta_a$*−subgaussian and* $\chi_e$ *is* $\zeta_e$*−subgaussian, and let* $(\mathbf{M}, \mathbf{b} = \mathbf{Ms}+\mathbf{e})$ *the data constructed from* $m$ *samples of the ILWE distribution* $\mathcal{D}_{\mathbf{s},\chi_a,\chi_e}$ *for some* $\mathbf{s} \in \mathbb{Z}^n$*. There exist constants* $C, C' > 0$ *such that if:*

$$m \ge Cn \quad \textit{and} \quad m \ge C' \times \frac{\sigma_e^2}{\sigma_a^2} \log(n)$$

*then the least square estimators* $\tilde{\mathbf{s}} = (\mathbf{M}^T\mathbf{M})^{-1}\mathbf{M}^T\mathbf{b}$ *satisfies* $||\mathbf{s} - \tilde{\mathbf{s}}||_\infty < 1/2$*, and hence* $\lceil \tilde{\mathbf{s}} \rfloor = \mathbf{s}$*, with probability at least* $1 - 1/n$*.*

**Building the ILWE System.** After collecting enough signatures, we will have multiple inequalities on the $k$ polynomials of $\mathbf{t}_0$ independently, so we can split the problem into $k$ smaller ones, one for each polynomial of the vector $\mathbf{t}_0$. For the sake of clarity, let us explain the methodology for a single polynomial of the vector $\mathbf{t}_0 = (\mathbf{t}_0^{[0]}, \dots, \mathbf{t}_0^{[k-1]})$. We select a signature that gives an inequality on $\mathbf{t}_0^{[0]}$. Let $\sigma = (\tilde{c}, \mathbf{z}, \mathbf{h})$ be a signature and $i \in \{0, \dots, 255\}$ such that $\mathbf{h}_i^{[0]} = 1$ and $\texttt{LowBits}_q(\mathbf{Az} - c\mathbf{t}_1 \cdot 2^d, 2\gamma_2)_i^{[0]} > 0$:

$$(-c\mathbf{t}_0)_i^{[0]} \ge \gamma_2 + \beta + 1 - \texttt{LowBits}_q(\mathbf{Az} - c\mathbf{t}_1 \cdot 2^d, 2\gamma_2)_i^{[0]}, \quad (1)$$

$$\sum_{j=0}^{n-1} \mathbf{t}_{0,j}^{[0]} (-cx^j)_i \ge \gamma_2 + \beta + 1 - \texttt{LowBits}_q(\mathbf{Az} - c\mathbf{t}_1 \cdot 2^d, 2\gamma_2)_i^{[0]}. \quad (2)$$

Since the polynomial $c$ is known, $\sigma$ gives us an inequality on the coefficients of $\mathbf{t}_0^{[0]}$. The case of $\mathbf{h}_i^{[0]} = 0$ and $\texttt{LowBits}_q(\mathbf{Az} - c\mathbf{t}_1 \cdot 2^d, 2\gamma_2) < 0$ are treated in the same way. Thus, with these signatures, we can construct two matrices $\mathbf{M}_+$ and $\mathbf{M}_-$ and four vectors $\mathbf{e}_+$, $\mathbf{b}_+$ and $\mathbf{e}_-$, $\mathbf{b}_-$ such that $\mathbf{b}_+ = \mathbf{M}_+\mathbf{t}_0^{[0]} + \mathbf{e}_+$ and $\mathbf{b}_- = \mathbf{M}_-\mathbf{t}_0^{[0]} + \mathbf{e}_-$. Each row of one of these matrices representing an inequality collected on $\mathbf{t}_0^{[0]}$. For the rest of this part, we assume that we have concatenated $\mathbf{M}_+, \mathbf{b}_+, \mathbf{e}_+$ and $\mathbf{M}_-, \mathbf{b}_-, \mathbf{e}_-$ to obtain $\mathbf{M}, \mathbf{b}, \mathbf{e}$ such that:

$$\mathbf{b} = \mathbf{M}\mathbf{t}_0^{[0]} + \mathbf{e}.$$

**Remark 7.** *To strictly apply Theorem 1, it must be proved that the coefficients of the matrix* $\mathbf{M}$*, as well as the error vector* $\mathbf{e}$*, follow subgaussian distributions, and then estimate the corresponding standard deviations* $\sigma_a$ *and* $\sigma_e$*. As always when moving from theory to practice, certain simplifications are necessary.*

**Estimating Probability Distributions.** We want now to calculate, if not estimate, the variance of the distribution followed by the coefficients of the matrix $\mathbf{M}$ and the error vector $\mathbf{e}$. Each row of the matrix $\mathbf{M}$ is built using the coefficients of a vector $c$ generated with a Dilithium signature. Therefore, each line of $\mathbf{M}$ has its coefficients in $\{-1, 0, 1\}$, of which $\tau$ coefficients will be $\pm 1$ (with equiprobability), the remainder being at zero. It is not true that the coefficients of the matrix $\mathbf{M}$ are independent. For example, the number of zeros in each row of $M$ will always be $256 - \tau$. Even worse, by retrieving an inequality from a zero coefficient of $\mathbf{h}$, consecutive rows of the matrix $\mathbf{M}$ will be identical. Nevertheless, we make the heuristic assumption that it is the case, so that we can explicitly calculate the law followed by the coefficients of the matrix $\mathbf{M}$.

**Lemma 2.** *Let* $m \in \mathbb{N}$ *be the number of collected inequalities on* $\mathbf{t}_0^{[0]}$*, and* $\tau$ *the numbers of non-zero coefficient in* $c$*. Under the heuristic assumptions described above, the coefficients of the matrix* $\mathbf{M} = (a_{i,j})_{0 \le i \le m-1, 0 \le j \le n-1}$ *follow the law below:*

$$\mathbb{P}(a_{i,j} = 0) = \frac{256 - \tau}{256} \quad \textit{and} \quad \mathbb{P}(a_{i,j} = 1) = \mathbb{P}(a_{i,j} = -1) = \frac{\tau}{2 \times 256}.$$

*Furthermore, this distribution is subgaussian and its variance can be calculated explicitly:*

$$\sigma_a^2 = \frac{\tau}{256}.$$

*Proof.* According to [BDE+18], any real variable whose probability distribution has a mean of zero and is carried by a segment is subgaussian, which is the case for $a_{i,j}$. In addition, the variance formula gives:

$$\sigma_a^2 = \mathbb{E}(a_{i,j}^2) = \frac{\tau}{256}.$$

□

To demonstrate that the vector $\mathbf{e}$ is subgaussian, according to [BDE+18] it is sufficient to show that it has null expectation and that it is carried by a segment. Since $\mathbf{e}$ is defined by parts (depending on the inequalities we recover), it is sufficient to show that each part is subgaussian. In order not to overload this section, we will only give details of the inequalities obtained for coefficients of $\mathbf{h}$ at 0. Let $\sigma = (\tilde{c}, \mathbf{z}, \mathbf{h})$ be a signature of $\texttt{Sig}$ and $i \in \{0, \ldots, 255\}$ such that $\mathbf{h}_i^{[0]} = 0$:

$$|(-c\mathbf{t}_0)_i^{[0]} + \texttt{LowBits}_q(\mathbf{Az} - c\mathbf{t}_1 \cdot 2^d, 2\,\gamma_2)_i^{[0]}| \leq \gamma_2 - \beta - 1.$$

The coefficients of $\mathbf{t}_0^{[0]}$ are fixed in $\{-2^{12}+1, \ldots, 2^{12}\}$ and from the generation of the signature $||c\mathbf{t}_0||_\infty < \gamma_2$, so we can assume that $(-c\mathbf{t}_0)_i^{[0]}$ follows a discrete Gaussian distribution centered and is carried by $\{-\gamma_2+1, \ldots, \gamma_2-1\}$. If we also assume that all the coefficients of $\texttt{LowBits}_q(\mathbf{Az} - c\mathbf{t}_1 \cdot 2^d, 2\,\gamma_2)$ follow a uniform distribution in $\{-\gamma_2+1, \ldots, \gamma_2\}$, then $\gamma_2 - \beta - 1 - \texttt{LowBits}_q(\mathbf{Az} - c\mathbf{t}_1 \cdot 2^d, 2\,\gamma_2)_i^{[0]}$ follows a uniform distribution in $\{-\beta-1, \ldots, (2\gamma_2-\beta-1)-1\}$ By the same reasoning, $-(\gamma_2 - \beta - 1) - \texttt{LowBits}_q(\mathbf{Az} - c\mathbf{t}_1 \cdot 2^d, 2\,\gamma_2)_i^{[0]}$ follows a uniform distribution in $\{-(2\gamma_2 - \beta - 1), \ldots, \beta\}$. Finally, even if it means adding 1/2 to the error obtained, the error vector obtained from the inequalities where the coefficient of $\mathbf{h}$ is zero has a null expectation and is carried by the following segment: $\{-(3\gamma_2 - \beta - 2), \ldots, 3\gamma_2 - \beta - 2\}$. With the same assumptions and the same reasoning, we can show that the error vector obtained for the inequalities given by the coefficients of $\mathbf{h}$ at 1 is also of zero expectation and is carried by the segment $\{-(3\gamma_2 + \beta), \ldots, 3\gamma_2 + \beta\}$. Finally, the error vector obtained by concatenating all the inequalities has zero expectation and is carried by the segment $\{-(3\gamma_2 + \beta), \ldots, 3\gamma_2 + \beta\}$. According to [BDE+18], $\mathbf{e}$ is $(3\gamma_2 + \beta)$-subgaussian and:

$$\sigma_e^2 \leq (3\gamma_2 + \beta)^2.$$

Table 2 summarises the different values of $\tau$, $\sigma_a$ and $\sigma_e$ (theoretical and experimental) according to the different security levels.[1]

**Table 2.** Value of the standard deviation according to the level of security.

| NIST Level | II | III | V |
|---|---|---|---|
| $\tau$ | 39 | 49 | 60 |
| $\sigma_a^2$ (theory) | 0.1523 | 0.19141 | 0.234375 |
| $\sigma_a^2$ (exp.) | 0.1523 | 0.19139 | 0.234372 |
| upper bound on $\sigma_e^2$ | 81 666 779 076 | 617 575 939 600 | 617 456 494 656 |
| $\sigma_e^2$ (exp.) | 11 411 519 137 | 30 832 793 508 | 30 752 629 506 |

[1] For each experimental measurement, the results are averages over 5 keys and the unbiased sample variance was calculated using 500 000 samples.

It will be possible to find $\mathbf{t}_0$ using Theorem 1 with $\Omega((\sigma_e/\sigma_a)^2\log(n))$ inequalities. However, as can be seen in Table 3 the variance of the error is significantly higher than the variance of the coefficients of the matrix $\mathbf{M}$. As it would be necessary to collect at least $m = (\sigma_e/\sigma_a)^2$ inequalities over $\mathbf{t}_0$, the size of the matrix $\mathbf{M} = (a_{i,j})_{0\leq i\leq m-1, 0\leq j\leq n-1}$ makes it impossible to calculate the least square estimator in practice (because it would be necessary to manipulate matrices of a size close to $m$). Furthermore according to [BDE+18], from an information-theoretic point of view, with fewer than $m = (\sigma_e/\sigma_a)^2$ inequalities it is not possible to distinguish the distribution of $\mathcal{D}_{\mathbf{t}_0,\chi_a,\chi_e}$ from $\mathcal{D}_{\mathbf{s},\chi_a,\chi_e}$ with $\mathbf{s} \neq \mathbf{t}_0$.

**Table 3.** Theoretical bound to distinguish $\mathbf{t}_0$.

| NIST Level | I | III | V |
|---|---|---|---|
| $\sigma_e^2/\sigma_a^2 \times \log(n)$ | $2^{39}$ | $2^{40}$ | $2^{39}$ |

**Remark 8.** *The ILWE system obtained is far too "noisy", but in our case we get more than an approximation of a linear combination of certain coefficients of* $\mathbf{t}_0$*, we also know whether this approximation is greater (in the case of a "upper inequality") or lower (in the case of a "lower inequality") than the value we are seeking. This detail changes the situation: taking this information into account by reformulating the problem of finding* $\mathbf{t}_0$ *into a linear programming problem will allow us to create an attack that will require far fewer inequalities than the ILWE method.*

Nevertheless, this section shows that the distribution of the inequalities obtained for $\mathbf{t}_0$ follows a subgaussian distribution centered around the expected value. This result will be important in Sect. 4 when it comes to demonstrating the termination of our attack.

## 4 An Attack Methodology

The natural approach is to recover enough inequalities on $\mathbf{t}_0$ to form a system $(LP)$ for which it is the unique solution. As we shall see later, this "naive" solution is not possible in our case.

**Building the (LP) System.** After collecting enough signatures, we will have multiple inequalities on the $k$ polynomials of $\mathbf{t}_0$ independently, so we can split the problem into $k$ smaller ones, one for each polynomial of the vector $\mathbf{t}_0$. We explain the methodology for a single polynomial of the vector $\mathbf{t}_0 = (\mathbf{t}_0^{[0]}, ..., \mathbf{t}_0^{[k-1]})$. We select a signature that gives an inequality on $\mathbf{t}_0^{[0]}$. Let $\sigma = (\tilde{c}, \mathbf{z}, \mathbf{h})$ be such a signature, with $i$ such that $\mathbf{h}_i^{[0]} = 1$. Assuming $\texttt{LowBits}_q(\mathbf{Az} - c\mathbf{t}_1 \cdot 2^d, 2\gamma_2)_i^{[0]} > 0$, one has

$$(-c\mathbf{t}_0)_i^{[0]} \geq \gamma_2 + \beta + 1 - \texttt{LowBits}_q(\mathbf{Az} - c\mathbf{t}_1 \cdot 2^d, 2\gamma_2)_i^{[0]}, \tag{3}$$

$$\sum_{j=0}^{n-1} \mathbf{t}_{0,j}^{[0]}(-cx^j)_i \geq \gamma_2 + \beta + 1 - \texttt{LowBits}_q(\mathbf{Az} - c\mathbf{t}_1 \cdot 2^d, 2\gamma_2)_i^{[0]}. \tag{4}$$

Since the polynomial $c$ is known, $\sigma$ gives an inequality on the coefficients of $\mathbf{t}_0^{[0]}$. The other two inequalities are treated in the same way. Thus, with these signatures, we can construct two matrices $\mathbf{M}_+$ and $\mathbf{M}_-$ and two vectors $\mathbf{b}_+$ and $\mathbf{b}_-$ such that $\mathbf{t}_0^{[0]} \in \{\mathbf{x} \in \{-2^{12}+1, \ldots, 2^{12}\}^n \mid \mathbf{M}_+\mathbf{x} \geq \mathbf{b}_+ \text{ and } \mathbf{M}_-\mathbf{x} \leq \mathbf{b}_-\}$. Each row of one of these matrices representing an inequality collected on $\mathbf{t}_0^{[0]}$. In particular, if we collect enough inequalities for $\mathbf{t}_0^{[0]}$ to be the only solution, we can find $\mathbf{t}_0^{[0]}$ by solving the following $(LP)$ problem of dimension $n = 256$ (Fig. 5):

$$\begin{aligned} &\text{maximize } 0 \\ &\text{subject to } \mathbf{M}_+\mathbf{x} \geq \mathbf{b}_+ \\ &\qquad\qquad\quad \mathbf{M}_-\mathbf{x} \leq \mathbf{b}_- \\ &\qquad\qquad\quad \mathbf{x} \in [-2^{12}+1, 2^{12}]^n \end{aligned}$$

**Fig. 5.** The $(LP)$ problem related to $\mathbf{t}_0^{[0]}$.

**Results Using the Naive Approach.** Unless a huge number of inequalities is collected, as can be seen in the Table 4, $\mathbf{t}_0$ will never be the only solution. Nevertheless, we can assume that we know $\mathbf{t}_0$, in order to estimate the size of the polytope containing it. In Table 4, the attack time takes into account the time required to generate the signatures and the time required to build and solve the $k$ $(LP)$ systems associated with $\mathbf{t}_0$, however the number of inequalities only includes inequalities associated with $\mathbf{t}_0^{[0]}$ and $\tilde{\mathbf{t}}_0^{[0]}$ is the polynomial obtained by minimizing the null function on the polytope defined by the inequalities collected on $\mathbf{t}_0^{[0]}$. For the sake of clarity, we have split the inequalities obtained for coefficients of $\mathbf{h}$ equal to 0 (on the left) from the inequalities obtained for coefficients of $\mathbf{h}$ equal to 1 (on the right).

The method provides us with a point close to $\mathbf{t}_0^{[0]}$ (because $\mathbf{t}_0^{[0]}$ is in the polytope constructed by the (LP) system by definition). Unfortunately, it is not possible to increase the number of inequalities endlessly, as the calculation time depends polynomially on the number of inequalities.

**Remark 9.** *If we denote $P$ the polytope obtained on $\mathbf{t}_0^{[0]}$ with a large number of inequalities, most of the inequalities we collect are not "useful" in the sense that*

**Table 4.** Attack times and size of the $(LP)$ system on $\mathbf{t}_0$.

| Number of signatures | Number of inequalities | $\|\|\mathbf{t}_0^{[0]} - \tilde{\mathbf{t}}_0^{[0]}\|\|_\infty$ | Attack time |
|---|---|---|---|
| 24 | $9\,953 + 389$ | $5\,649$ | 0h0m23s |
| 117 | $48\,456 + 1\,915$ | $1\,031$ | 0h3m52s |
| 583 | $241\,541 + 9\,378$ | 247 | 1h55m47s |

*$P$ remains unchanged whether the inequality is taken into account or not. This is illustrated in Fig. 4: with 100 inequalities collected, only 5 of them are actually useful in describing the polytope of solutions. By collecting lots of inequalities, we get an increasingly complex algebraic description (a growing set of inequalities) of a simple geometric object: a polytope with a few faces that approximates $\mathbf{t}_0^{[0]}$. We need a way of selecting "useful" and "useless" inequalities to reduce the complexity of solving the $(LP)$ problem associated with $\mathbf{t}_0^{[0]}$.*

### 4.1 Useful Inequalities

In this subsection we assume that we know $\tilde{\mathbf{t}}_0^{[0]} \in \mathcal{R}_q$ and $C$ such that $\|\tilde{\mathbf{t}}_0^{[0]} - \mathbf{t}_0^{[0]}\|_\infty \leq C$. In other words, $\mathbf{t}_0^{[0]} \in B_\infty(\tilde{\mathbf{t}}_0^{[0]}, C)$. Given an inequality on $\mathbf{t}_0$, we want to determine efficiently if the intersection between $B_\infty(\tilde{\mathbf{t}}_0^{[0]}, C)$ and the set of solutions of the inequality is non-trivial.

**Definition 11.** *Let $\tilde{\mathbf{t}}_0^{[0]} \in \mathcal{R}_q$ and $C \in \mathbb{R}_+$. We say that an inequality on $\mathbf{t}_0^{[0]}$ of the form $\{\mathbf{a}^\intercal\mathbf{x} - b \geq 0\}$ (resp. $\{\mathbf{a}^\intercal\mathbf{x} - b \leq 0\}$) is useful with respect to $\tilde{\mathbf{t}}_0^{[0]}$ and $C$ if and only if:*

$$B_\infty(\tilde{\mathbf{t}}_0^{[0]}, C) \not\subset \{\mathbf{x} \in \mathbb{R}^n \mid \mathbf{a}^\intercal\mathbf{x} - b \geq 0\ \} \text{ (resp. } \mathbf{a}^\intercal\mathbf{x} - b \leq 0)$$

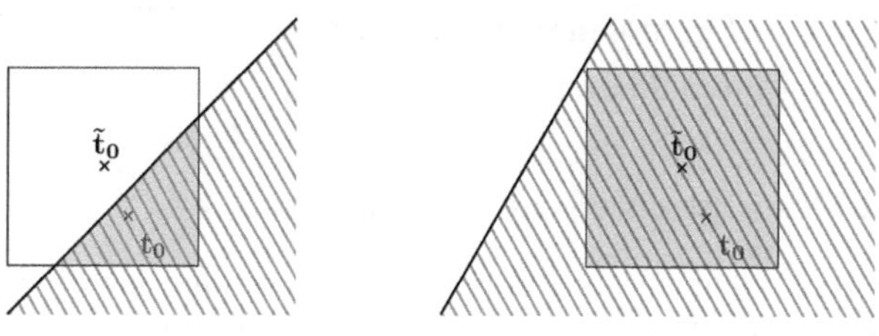


**Fig. 6.** On the left, a useful inequality. On the right a useless inequality.

**Remark 10.** *This definition is very natural and is illustrated with Fig. 6.*

**Proposition 3.** *An inequality on* $\mathbf{t}_0^{[0]}$ *of the form* $\{\mathbf{a}^\intercal\mathbf{x} - b \geq 0\}$ *is useful with respect to* $\tilde{\mathbf{t}}_0^{[0]}$ *and* $C$ *if and only if:*

$$\mathbf{a}^\intercal\tilde{\mathbf{t}}_0^{[0]} - C||\mathbf{a}^\intercal||_\infty^* < b.$$

*An inequality on* $\mathbf{t}_0^{[0]}$ *of the form* $\{\mathbf{a}^\intercal\mathbf{x} - b \leq 0\}$ *is useful with respect to* $\tilde{\mathbf{t}}_0^{[0]}$ *and* $C$ *if and only if:*

$$\mathbf{a}^\intercal\tilde{\mathbf{t}}_0^{[0]} + C||\mathbf{a}^\intercal||_\infty^* > b,$$

*where* $||.||_\infty^*$ *denote the operator norm.*

*Proof.* Let $f : \mathbf{x} \mapsto \mathbf{a}^\intercal\mathbf{x} - b$, then:

$$B_\infty(\tilde{\mathbf{t}}_0^{[0]}, C) \subset \{\mathbf{x} \in \mathbb{R}^n \mid f(\mathbf{x}) \geq 0\} \iff \inf_{||\mathbf{u}||_\infty \leq 1}(f(\tilde{\mathbf{t}}_0^{[0]} + C\mathbf{u})) \geq 0.$$

In addition,

$$\begin{aligned}\inf_{||\mathbf{u}||_\infty \leq 1}(\mathbf{a}^\intercal(\tilde{\mathbf{t}}_0^{[0]} + C\mathbf{u}) - b) &= \mathbf{a}^\intercal\tilde{\mathbf{t}}_0^{[0]} - C \sup_{||\mathbf{u}||_\infty \leq 1}(\mathbf{a}^\intercal(-\mathbf{u})) - b \\ &= \mathbf{a}^\intercal\tilde{\mathbf{t}}_0^{[0]} - C||\mathbf{a}^\intercal||_\infty^* - b.\end{aligned}$$

This concludes the first relation, and the same reasoning can be used to deduce the second result. □

**Remark 11.** *Proposition 3 allows us to calculate efficiently whether an inequality on* $\mathbf{t}_0$ *is useful or not with respect to* $\tilde{\mathbf{t}}_0$ *and* $C$*. Finally, it is important to note that the definitions and propositions stated here remain when the infinite norm is replaced by another norm, even if these formulations are not useful for us.*

**Notation 4.** *We will note* `generate_useful_ineq`$(\delta, \tilde{\mathbf{t}}_0^{[0]}, C)$ *the procedure for generating* $\delta$ *useful inequalities with respect to* $\tilde{\mathbf{t}}_0^{[0]}$ *and* $C$*.*

### 4.2 Formal Description of the Attack

With the different tools we need now defined, the main idea behind the attack strategy can be summed up in one sentence: 'Collect, guess, filter, repeat.' More precisely we will:

- Collect inequalities to obtain a polytope $P_0$. By definition, $\mathbf{t}_0^{[0]} \in P_0$.
- Calculate (or estimate heuristically) the diameter of $P_0$ to obtain $C$ and $\tilde{\mathbf{t}}_0^{[0]}$ such that $\mathbf{t}_0^{[0]} \in B_\infty(\tilde{\mathbf{t}}_0^{[0]}, C)$.

- Collect useful inequalities with respect to $\tilde{\mathbf{t}}_0^{[0]}$ and $C$ to obtain $P_1$ and by construction $\mathbf{t}_0^{[0]} \in P_1$.
- Repeat until the polytope $P$ verifies $diam(P) \leq 1/2$, in which case $\mathbf{t}_0^{[0]}$ as been recovered.

---

**Algorithm 5.** `Recovering` $\mathbf{t}_0^{[0]}$

---

**Ensure:** $\mathbf{t}_0^{[0]}$
**Require:** An inequality step $\delta$

$\tilde{\mathbf{t}}_0^{[0]} = 0$
$C, diam = 2^{12}$
$P = \{-2^{12} + 1 \leq x_i \leq 2^{12}\}_{i=0,\ldots,255}$
**while** $C \geq 1$ **do**
  $\Delta = \delta$
  **while** $diam > C/2$ **do**
    $P =$ `generate_useful_ineq`$(\Delta, \tilde{\mathbf{t}}_0^{[0]}, C)$
    $diam =$ `calculate_diam`$(P)$
    $\Delta = 2 \times \Delta$
  $C = C/2$
  $\tilde{\mathbf{t}}_0^{[0]} =$ `round(lp_guess(P))`
**return** $\tilde{\mathbf{t}}_0^{[0]}$

---

**Proposition 4.** *With probability* 1, *for any* $\delta \in \mathbb{N}^*$, *Algorithm 5 terminates in a finite number of steps with probability 1, giving* $\mathbf{t}_0^{[0]}$.

*Proof.* According to Sect. 3, the error between the sum of some of the coefficients of $\mathbf{t}_0^{[0]}$ and the bound of the inequality obtained follows a subgaussian distribution. In particular, there are inequalities which are equalities verified by certain coefficients of $\mathbf{t}_0^{[0]}$. Thus the procedure `generate_useful_ineq` finishes in a finite time for any value of $\delta$ and $C > 0$. This ensures that Algorithm 5 finishes after a finite number of steps. In addition, at step $i$ of Algorithm 5: $\mathbf{t}_0^{[0]} \in B_\infty(\tilde{\mathbf{t}}_0^{[0]}, 2^{12-i})$ so that at the last step $\mathbf{t}_0^{[0]} \in B_\infty(\tilde{\mathbf{t}}_0^{[0]}, 1/2)$ and therefore $\mathbf{t}_0^{[0]} = \tilde{\mathbf{t}}_0^{[0]}$. □

**Remark 12.** *Algorithm 5 is useful because it can be proved that it systematically finds* $\mathbf{t}_0^{[0]}$. *Unfortunately, in practice it is too complex to be used, as each call to the function* `calculate_diam` *requires the solution of* $2 \times 256$ *(LP) problems, each potentially containing several hundred thousand inequalities. Rather than calculating the size of the polytope containing* $\mathbf{t}_0^{[0]}$ *at each step, we estimate the number of inequalities needed to make the size of the corresponding polytope small enough, without having to calculate it explicitly. This is formally described in Algorithm 6.*

**Algorithm 6.** `Recovering` $\mathbf{t}_0^{[0]}$ `heuristically`

**Ensure:** A candidate for $\mathbf{t}_0^{[0]}$
**Require:** An inequality step sequence $(\delta_i)_{i\in\{1,\ldots,m\}}$, a radius sequence $C_m < C_{m-1} < \cdots < C_1 = 2^{12}$.

$\tilde{\mathbf{t}}_0^{[0]} = 0$
$i = 1$
$P = \{-2^{12}+1 \leq x_i \leq 2^{12}\}_{i=1,\ldots,256}$
**while** $i \leq m$ **do**
  $P =$ `generate_useful_ineq`$(\delta_i, \tilde{\mathbf{t}}_0^{[0]}, C_i)$
  $i = i + 1$
  $\tilde{\mathbf{t}}_0^{[0]} =$ `round(lp_guess(P))`
**return** $\tilde{\mathbf{t}}_0^{[0]}$

**Remark 13.** *If the sequence is not chosen carefully it may be that* $\mathbf{t}_0 \notin B_\infty(\tilde{\mathbf{t}}_0^{[0]}, C)$ *at some step of Algorithm 6. As Fig. 7 shows, if at any stage of the algorithm we have an* $\tilde{\mathbf{t}}_0^{[0]}$ *and* $C$ *such that* $\mathbf{t}_0^{[0]} \notin B_\infty(\tilde{\mathbf{t}}_0^{[0]}, C)$*, collecting useful inequalities with respect to* $\tilde{\mathbf{t}}_0^{[0]}$ *and* $C$ *can lead to a point which deviates from* $\mathbf{t}_0^{[0]}$*, or even worse: an (LP) system without solution.*

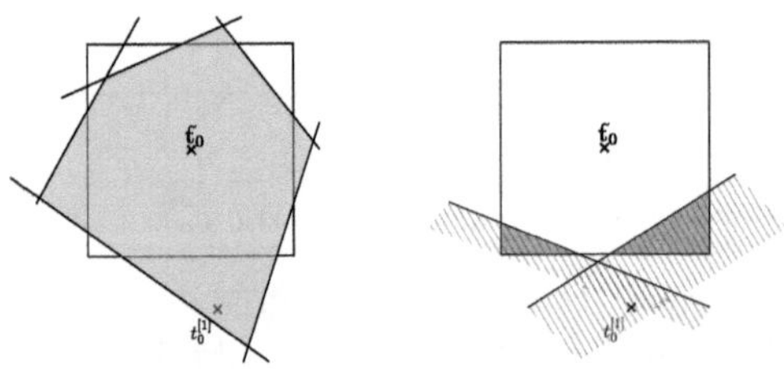

**Fig. 7.** $(LP)$ system for a poorly choosen $(\delta_i)$.

## 5 Experimental Results

We have used the reference implementation of Dilithium [DKL+22] to generate signatures and to solve the $(LP)$ problems linked to $\mathbf{t}_0$ we have decided to use lp_solve [MB04], a free linear programming solver in $C$. Our attack method applies independently of lp_solve and any other solver could have been chosen. All the tests and results presented in this section were carried out on a laptop computer equipped with an Intel(R) Core(TM) i7-10850H 2.70GHz CPU. The code to collect the signatures and perform the attack is available at https://github.com/anders1901/Attack_t0.

### 5.1 Attack on Dilithium-2

In this section we present the results obtained by applying Algorithm 6 with different choices of filtration ($C_i$) and inequality ($\delta_i$) sequence. This gives rise to time/signature/memory trade-offs. To reduce the number of signatures required we decided to store the signatures generated at each stage of the algorithm since the same inequality can be useful for different filtration, again an attacker could do without it at the cost of having to collect more signatures.

**Remark 14.** *The choices of the different sequences* $(C_i)$ *and* $(\delta_i)$ *are heuristic and are given as an example. Nothing prevents trying out other sequences and testing the results obtained.*

**Attack Methodology 1:** The most conservative method is to follow as directly as possible Algorithm 5.We therefore choose to divide the radius by two at each stage *i.e.* $(C_i) = (4096, 2048, \ldots, 2, 1)$. We also choose a constant inequality sequence, which we have set at 50 000. In other words, at each step we collect 50 000 inequalities on each of the polynome of $\mathbf{t}_0$ before solving the $k$ associated $(LP)$ problems. Table 5 shows the results obtained for the first 10 KAT keys.

**Table 5.** Average results of the attack on $\mathbf{t}_0$.

| Signatures | Inequalities selected | Recovery probability | Average time | Median time |
|---|---|---|---|---|
| 474 026 | 418 219 + 239 719 | 1 | 1h13m10s | 1h12m55s |

For greater clarity, we detail the results of Algorithm 6 for the first key of the KAT in Table 6. For this table only, the knowledge of $\mathbf{t}_0$ was used to illustrate the correctness of Algorithm 6. In Table 6, Time includes time to generate signatures as well as time to solve the $k = 4$ $(LP)$ problems at each step of Algorithm6 and in "Inequalities selected" we detail the number of inequalities from zero and non-zero hints, for the polynomial $\mathbf{t}_0^{[0]}$. With our choice of parameters, this attack time is largely dominated by signature collection time.

**Attack Methodology 2:** Another method of attack consists of choosing a more "relaxed" sequence, at the cost of querying more signature at each step of Algorithm 6. This method is useful in a context where the attacker have a large computing capacity and need to find $\mathbf{t}_0$ with as few signatures as possible. For our tests, to maintain a manageable attack time we have chosen the sequence $(C_i) = (2^{12} = 4096, 2048, \ldots, 16, 8)$ with the associated sequence inequalities: $(\delta_i) = (50\,000, \ldots, 50\,000, 150\,000)$. Table 7 shows the results obtained for the first 10 KAT keys. Again, we detail the results of the attack calculation for the first key of the KAT in Table 8, to compare it with the previous attack method.

For both methods, if we had sought to find $\mathbf{t}_0$ without filtration, each of the 4 (LP) problems associated would have contained at least 170 000 signatures.

**Table 6.** Detailed results of Algorithm 6 on the first KAT key.

| Round | $C_i$ | Signatures | Inequalities selected | $\|\|\mathbf{t}_0 - \tilde{\mathbf{t}}_0\|\|_\infty$ | Time |
|---|---|---|---|---|---|
| 1 | 4096 | 117 | 48 456 + 1 915 | 837 | 2m17s |
| 2 | 2048 | 234 | 46 612 + 3 731 | 431 | 1m56s |
| 3 | 1024 | 468 | 43 112 + 7 433 | 234 | 1m57s |
| 4 | 512 | 937 | 37 172 + 13 540 | 119 | 1m58s |
| 5 | 256 | 1 879 | 32 057 + 18 844 | 53 | 2m11s |
| 6 | 128 | 3 743 | 28 787 + 21 863 | 27 | 2m37s |
| 7 | 64 | 7 485 | 27 125 + 23 434 | 13 | 3m23s |
| 8 | 32 | 14 989 | 26 250 + 23 434 | 7 | 3m32s |
| 9 | 16 | 30 023 | 26 055 + 24 700 | 3 | 4m15s |
| 10 | 8 | 60 200 | 25 735 + 25 098 | 1 | 5m7s |
| 11 | 4 | 119 843 | 25 660 + 25 229 | 1 | 6m44s |
| 12 | 2 | 238 674 | 25 437 + 25 009 | 0 | 13m34s |
| 13 | 1 | 475 856 | 25 634 + 25 247 | 0 | 12m23s |
| Total | - | 475 856 | 457 373 + 253 581 | - | 0h51m17s |

**Table 7.** Average results of the attack on $\mathbf{t}_0$.

| Signatures | inequalities selected | Recovery probability | Average time | Median time |
|---|---|---|---|---|
| 179 354 | 392 696 + 213 943 | 1 | 1h26m53s | 1h24m8s |

According to Sect. 3 we obtain on average 496 inequalities per polynomial, resulting in four huge $(LP)$ systems of at least $170\,000 \times 496 = 84\,362\,500$ inequalities each, which is much more costly to solve than our sequence of small systems. Indeed, thanks to our natural definitions of "useful" inequalities, we were able to find an equivalent representation of each of the polytopes containing a polynomial of $\mathbf{t}_0$ with only 50 000 to 150 000 inequalities.

### 5.2 Attack on Dilithium-3 and Dilthium-5

The theory remains true regardless of the security level of Dilithium, therefore there should be no conceptual differences in treating different security levels. To provide complete results we tested the attack method presented in Subsect. 5.1 with the other two security levels of Dilithium. For the two security levels we tested the same sequence $(C_i) = (2^{12} = 4096, 2048, \ldots, 16, 2)$ associated with the following sequence of inequalities $(\delta_i) = (60\,000, \ldots, 60\,000)$. Table 9 and Table 10 show the results obtained.

**Remark 15.** *The attack is slightly less effective on Dilithum security levels* 3 *and* 5, *which is not surprising:* $\mathbf{t}_0$ *contains* 6 *and* 8 *polynomials respectively, instead of* 4 *for level* 2, *so there are just as many* $(LP)$ *problems to solve at*

**Table 8.** Detailed results of the attack on the first KAT key.

| Round | $C_i$ | Signatures | Inequalities selected | $\|\|\mathbf{t}_0 - \tilde{\mathbf{t}}_0\|\|_\infty$ | Time |
|---|---|---|---|---|---|
| 1 | 4096 | 117 | 48 456 + 1 915 | 1031 | 4m16s |
| 2 | 2048 | 234 | 46 612 + 3 731 | 495 | 4m2s |
| 3 | 1024 | 468 | 43 112 + 7 433 | 262 | 3m48s |
| 4 | 512 | 937 | 37 172 + 13 540 | 135 | 3m44s |
| 5 | 256 | 1 879 | 32 057 + 18 844 | 62 | 3m53s |
| 6 | 128 | 3 743 | 28 787 + 21 863 | 37 | 3m53s |
| 7 | 64 | 7 485 | 27 125 + 23 434 | 19 | 4m7s |
| 8 | 32 | 14 989 | 26 250 + 23 434 | 10 | 4m48s |
| 9 | 16 | 30 023 | 26 055 + 24 700 | 4 | 5m27s |
| 10 | 8 | 179 515 | 76 487 + 74 192 | 0 | 47m5s |
| Total | - | 179 515 | 392 113 + 213 853 | - | 1h25m3s |

**Table 9.** Average results of the attack on $\mathbf{t}_0$ for Dilithium-3.

| Signatures | inequalities selected | Recovery probability | Average time | Median time |
|---|---|---|---|---|
| 523 534 | 398 704 + 210 140 | 1 | 1h 30min 05sec | 1h 30min 33sec |

**Table 10.** Average results of the attack on $\mathbf{t}_0$ for Dilithium-5.

| Signatures | inequalities selected | Recovery probability | Average time | Median time |
|---|---|---|---|---|
| 513 106 | 481 181 + 249 566 | 1 | 3h 21min 23sec | 3h 22min 52sec |

*each step. It should also be noted that the other security levels are slower to sign messages.*

## 6 Conclusion

Even if the state of art of attacks against Dilithium continues to evolve, the corresponding ML-DSA standard has recently been published. Dilithium has thus become a leading standard, and as such, is implemented in a quickly growing number of products, some of which are vulnerable to side-channel attacks. In order to design and implement effective protections against such attacks, it is necessary to have a complete knowledge of the data that are available to potential attackers. In particular, as discussed in the introduction, the question of the exact vulnerability level of one of the secret key vectors $\mathbf{t}_0$ was up to now one of the grey areas that was greatly in need of clarification.

Our paper shows that $\mathbf{t}_0$ can be reconstructed from sufficiently many Dilithium signatures (between 200 000 and 500 000, depending on the security level) and in just a few hours of computation. In other words, in theory as in practice, it is reasonable to consider $\mathbf{t}_0$ as part of the public key. The results are not surprising but, in our opinion, it is striking that the attack is so effective. For instance, for Dilithium 2, $\mathbf{t}_0$ is a vector of 4 polynomials of degree 256, whose coefficients belong to the interval $\{-2^{12}+1,\ldots,2^{12}\}$, so that the set of potential solutions is enormous. Despite this, in all our experiments, we were able to find $\mathbf{t}_0$ in a few hours, with less than 200 000 signatures.

Finally, even if the various filtration techniques we used are efficient enough to recover $\mathbf{t}_0$ with a realistic complexity, there is still room for optimization in terms of both the number of signatures and the computation time.

**Acknowledgments.** This research was funded in part by the France 2030 program under grant agreement No. ANR-22-PETQ-0008 PQ-TLS and by the ANRT (Association nationale de la recherche et de la technologie).

## References

[ABC+23] Azouaoui, M., et al.: Protecting Dilithium against leakage: Revisited sensitivity analysis and improved implementations. IACR Trans. Cryptogr. Hardw. Embedd. Syst. **2023**(4), 58–79 (2023)

[AOVCG25] Azevedo-Oliveira, P., Viera, A.C., Cogliati, B., Goubin, L.: Finding a polytope: a practical fault attack against dilithium. Cryptology ePrint Archive, Paper 2025/195 (2025)

[BAE+24] Bronchain, O., Azouaoui, M., ElGhamrawy, M., Renes, J., Schneider, T.: Exploiting small-norm polynomial multiplication with physical attacks: application to crystals-dilithium. IACR Trans. Cryptogr. Hardw. Embedd. Syst. **2024**(2), 359–383 (2024)

[BCVC+23] Berzati, A., Viera, A.C., Chartouny, M., Madec, S., Vergnaud, D., Vigilant, D.: Exploiting intermediate value leakage in dilithium: a template-based approach. IACR Trans. Cryptogr. Hardw. Embed. Syst. **2023**(4), 188–210 (2023)

[BDE+18] Bootle, J., Delaplace, C., Espitau, T., Fouque, P.-A., Tibouchi, M.: LWE without modular reduction and improved side-channel attacks against BLISS. In: Peyrin, T., Galbraith, S. (eds.) ASIACRYPT 2018. LNCS, vol. 11272, pp. 494–524. Springer, Cham (2018). https://doi.org/10.1007/978-3-030-03326-2_17

[BDK+21] Bai, S., et al.: Algorithm specifications and supporting documentation (version 3.1) (2021). https://pq-crystals.org/dilithium/data/dilithium-specification-round3-20210208.pdf

[BVC+23] Berzati, A., Viera, A.C., Chartouny, M., Madec, S., Vergnaud, D., Vigilant, D.: Exploiting intermediate value leakage in dilithium: a template-based approach. IACR TCHES **2023**(4), 188–210 (2023)

[CGTZ23] Coron, J.-S., Gérard, F., Trannoy, M., Zeitoun, R.: Improved gadgets for the high-order masking of dilithium. IACR Trans. Cryptogr. Hardw. Embed. Syste. **2023**(4), 110–145 (2023)

[DKL+22] Ducas, L., et al.: PQ-CRYSTALS, Dilithium (2022). https://github.com/pq-crystals/dilithium. GitHub repository. Accessed 15 Dec 2022

[EAB+23] ElGhamrawy, M., et al.: From MLWE to RLWE: a differential fault attack on randomized & deterministic dilithium. IACR TCHES **2023**(4), 262–286 (2023)

[LDK+22] Lyubashevsky, V., et al.: CRYSTALS-DILITHIUM. Technical report, National Institute of Standards and Technology (2022). https://csrc.nist.gov/Projects/post-quantum-cryptography/selected-algorithms-2022

[Lyu09] Lyubashevsky, V.: Fiat-Shamir with aborts: applications to lattice and factoring-based signatures. In: Matsui, M. (ed.) ASIACRYPT 2009. LNCS, vol. 5912, pp. 598–616. Springer, Heidelberg (2009). https://doi.org/10.1007/978-3-642-10366-7_35

[Lyu22] Lyubashevsky, V.: NIST Conference. NIST Website (2022). https://www.nist.gov/video/fourth-pqc-standardization-conference-virtual-day-1-part-1

[MB04] Berkelaar, P.N.M., Eikland, K.: lp solve (2004). https://lpsolve.sourceforge.net/5.5. Open source (Mixed-Integer) Linear Programming system

[MGTF19] Migliore, V., Gérard, B., Tibouchi, M., Fouque, P.-A.: Masking dilithium. In: Deng, R.H., Gauthier-Umaña, V., Ochoa, M., Yung, M. (eds.) Applied Cryptography and Network Security, pp. 344–362. Springer, Cham (2019)

[NIS23] NIST. Fips 204 (draft): Module-lattice-based digital signature standard. Federal Inf. Process. Stds. (NIST FIPS), National Institute of Standards and Technology, Gaithersburg, MD (2023). https://nvlpubs.nist.gov/nistpubs/FIPS/NIST.FIPS.204.ipd.pdf

[NW88] Nemhauser, G.L., Wolsey, L.A.: Integer and combinatorial optimization. In: Wiley Interscience Series in Discrete Mathematics and Optimization (1988)

[Reg05] Regev, O.: On lattices, learning with errors, random linear codes, and cryptography. In: Proceedings of the Thirty-Seventh Annual ACM Symposium on Theory of Computing, STOC '05, pp. 84–93. Association for Computing Machinery, New York, NY, USA (2005)

[RJH+18] Ravi, P., Jhanwar, M.P., Howe, J., Chattopadhyay, A., Bhasin, S.: Side-channel assisted existential forgery attack on dilithium - a NIST PQC candidate. Cryptology ePrint Archive, Paper 2018/821 (2018). https://eprint.iacr.org/2018/821

[RRB+19] Ravi, P., Roy, D.B., Bhasin, S., Chattopadhyay, A., Mukhopadhyay, D.: Number "not used" once - practical fault attack on pqm4 implementations of NIST candidates. In: Polian, I., Stöttinger, M. (eds.) COSADE 2019. LNCS, vol. 11421, pp. 232–250. Springer, Heidelberg (2019)

[WGD24] Wang, R., Gärtner, J., Dubrova, E.: Decompressing dilithium's public key with fewer signatures using side channel analysis. Cryptology ePrint Archive, Paper 2024/2046 (2024)

[WNGD23] Wang, R., Ngo, K., Gärtner, J., Dubrova, E.: Single-trace side-channel attacks on CRYSTALS-dilithium: myth or reality? Cryptology ePrint Archive, Paper 2023/1931 (2023)

# Assessing the Impact of a Variant of MATZOV's Dual Attack on Kyber

Kevin Carrier[1(✉)], Charles Meyer-Hilfiger[2], Yixin Shen[3], and Jean-Pierre Tillich[2]

[1] ETIS UMR 8051, CY Cergy-Paris Université, ENSEA, CNRS, Cergy, France
kevin.carrier@cyu.fr
[2] Project COSMIQ, Inria de Paris, Paris, France
{charles.meyer-hilfiger,jean-pierre.tillich}@inria.fr
[3] Univ. Rennes, Inria, CNRS, IRISA, Rennes, France
yixin.shen@inria.fr

**Abstract.** The dual attacks on the Learning With Errors (LWE) problem are currently a subject of controversy. In particular, the results of [27], which claim to significantly lower the security level of Kyber [34], a lattice-based cryptosystem currently being standardized by NIST, are not widely accepted. The analysis behind their attack depends on a series of assumptions that, in certain scenarios, have been shown to contradict established theorems or well-tested heuristics [18].

In this paper, we introduce a new dual lattice attack on LWE, drawing from ideas in coding theory. Our approach revisits the dual attack proposed by [27], replacing modulus switching with an efficient decoding algorithm. This decoding is achieved by generalizing polar codes over $\mathbb{Z}_q$, and we confirm their strong distortion properties through benchmarks. This modification enables a reduction from small-LWE to plain-LWE, with a notable decrease in the secret dimension. Additionally, we replace the enumeration step in the attack by assuming the secret is zero for the portion being enumerated, iterating this assumption over various choices for the enumeration part.

We make an analysis of our attack without using the flawed independence assumptions used in [27] and we fully back up our analysis with experimental evidences.

Lastly, we assess the complexity of our attack on Kyber; showing that the security levels for Kyber-512/768/1024 are 3.5/11.9/12.3 bits below the NIST requirements (143/207/272 bits) in the same nearest-neighbor cost model as in [27,34]. All in all the cost of our attack matches and even slightly beat in some cases the complexities originally claimed by the attack of [27].

The work of KC and JPT was funded by the French Agence Nationale de la Recherche through ANR JCJC DECODE (ANR-22-CE39-0004-01) for KC and ANR-22-PETQ-0008 PQ-TLS for JPT. The work of CMH was funded by the French Agence de l'innovation de défense and by Inria. The work of YS was funded by EPSRC grant EP/W02778X/2 and the France 2030 program managed by the French National Research Agency under grant agreement ANR-22-PETQ-0008 PQ-TLS.


Y. Tauman Kalai and S. F. Kamara (Eds.): CRYPTO 2025, LNCS 16000, pp. 444–476, 2025.
https://doi.org/10.1007/978-3-032-01855-7_15

**Keywords:** Post-Quantum Cryptography · Learning With Errors · Dual Attack · Fast Fourier Transform · Polar Code

# 1 Introduction

## 1.1 Background

**The LWE Problem.** In this paper, we address the Learning With Errors (LWE) problem originally introduced by Regev in [32]. It revolves around the task of finding $\mathbf{s} \in \mathbb{Z}_q^n$ given $(\mathbf{A}, \mathbf{b}) \in \mathbb{Z}_q^{m\times n} \times \mathbb{Z}_q^m$ with $\mathbf{b} = \mathbf{A}\mathbf{s} + \mathbf{e}$ where $\mathbf{e}$ is of small Euclidean norm. This problem can be seen as the decoding problem for the code $\mathcal{C}(\mathbf{A})$ generated by the columns of $\mathbf{A}$ (*i.e.* $\mathcal{C}(\mathbf{A}) \triangleq \{\mathbf{A}\mathbf{x},\ \mathbf{x} \in \mathbb{Z}_q^n\}$) and the Euclidean distance, where we are asked to find the codeword (*i.e.* the element of $\mathcal{C}$) which is close in Euclidean distance to $\mathbf{b}$. We are particularly interested in the case where $\mathbf{s}$ is short too which is called the small LWE problem. This problem has emerged as a fundamental challenge in cryptography. Notably, it underpins the construction of various cryptographic primitives and is conjectured to withstand attacks from quantum computers [26]. Our motivation for exploring this problem stems particularly from the need to gauge the security level of KYBER, a lattice-based cryptosystem that is being standardized by the NIST[1].

**Dual Attacks.** The most efficient cryptanalysis techniques against LWE(-like) problems are "primal" and "dual" lattice attacks. The primal attack corresponds to lattice reduction being performed on the "primal" lattice $\Lambda_q(\mathbf{A})$ which is Construction $A$ of the $q$-ary lattice obtained from $\mathcal{C}(\mathbf{A})$, namely

$$\begin{aligned}\Lambda_q(\mathbf{A}) &= \{\mathbf{y} \in \mathbb{Z}^m \ :\ \exists \mathbf{c} \in \mathcal{C}(\mathbf{A}) \text{ such that } \mathbf{y} = \mathbf{c} \mod q\} \\ &= \{\mathbf{y} \in \mathbb{Z}^m \ :\ \exists \mathbf{s} \in \mathbb{Z}_q^n \text{ such that } \mathbf{y} = \mathbf{A}\mathbf{s} \mod q\}.\end{aligned}$$

Dual attacks mean that lattice reduction is performed over the dual lattice $\Lambda_q(\mathbf{A})^\vee$, which in this case, up to a $q$-multiplicative factor, is nothing but Construction $A$ applied to the dual code $\mathcal{C}(\mathbf{A})^\perp \triangleq \{\mathbf{x} \in \mathbb{Z}_q^m \ :\ \mathbf{A}^\top\mathbf{x} = \mathbf{0}\}$:

$$\begin{aligned}\Lambda_q(\mathbf{A})^\vee &\triangleq \{\mathbf{x} \in \mathbb{R}^m \ :\ \langle \mathbf{x}, \mathbf{y}\rangle \in \mathbb{Z},\ \forall \mathbf{y} \in \Lambda_q(\mathbf{A})\} \\ &= \tfrac{1}{q}\{\mathbf{x} \in \mathbb{Z}^m \ :\ \mathbf{A}^\top\mathbf{x} = \mathbf{0} \mod q\}.\end{aligned}$$

The lattice $\{\mathbf{x} \in \mathbb{Z}^m \ :\ \mathbf{A}^\top\mathbf{x} = \mathbf{0} \mod q\}$ is known under the name of the orthogonal lattice of $\mathbf{A}$, *i.e.* $\Lambda_q^\perp(\mathbf{A}) \triangleq \{\mathbf{x} \in \mathbb{Z}^m \ :\ \mathbf{A}^\top\mathbf{x} = \mathbf{0} \mod q\}$.

Dual attacks were introduced in [30]. In its simplest form, a dual attack is a distinguisher attack which is given either $(\mathbf{A}, \mathbf{A}\cdot\mathbf{s} + \mathbf{e})$ or $(\mathbf{A}, \mathbf{u})$ where $(\mathbf{A}, \mathbf{u})$ are uniform and $\mathbf{e}$ is short, and answers if we are in the first or the second case. It starts by computing many short $\mathbf{x}_j$'s in the dual lattice $\Lambda_q(\mathbf{A})^\vee$ and

[1] https://csrc.nist.gov/projects/post-quantum-cryptography.

the associated $\langle \mathbf{x}_j, \mathbf{b} \rangle$'s. Those short vectors are obtained by lattice reduction of $\Lambda_q(\mathbf{A})^\vee$ or what is basically equivalent $\Lambda_q^\perp(\mathbf{A})$. In the second case, we expect that these scalar products are uniformly distributed in $\mathbb{Z}_q$. On the other hand in the first case since $\langle \mathbf{x}_j, \mathbf{b} \rangle = \langle \mathbf{x}_j, \mathbf{A}\mathbf{s} + \mathbf{e} \rangle = \langle \mathbf{A}^\top \mathbf{x}_j, \mathbf{s} \rangle + \langle \mathbf{x}_j, \mathbf{e} \rangle = \langle \mathbf{x}_j, \mathbf{e} \rangle \mod q$, we get scalar products of small vectors which are tilted towards small entries.

There have been a sequence of developments in dual attacks, for instance by combining these attacks with a guessing stage [3] consisting in splitting the support of $\mathbf{s}$ in two parts $\begin{pmatrix} \mathbf{s}_{\mathsf{enu}} \\ \mathbf{s}_{\mathsf{lat}} \end{pmatrix}$ and guessing one part of this support. $\mathbf{A}$ is split accordingly $\mathbf{A} = [\mathbf{A}_{\mathsf{enu}} \ \ \mathbf{A}_{\mathsf{lat}}]$. This allows to only perform lattice reduction on Construction A of the code generated by $\begin{bmatrix} \mathbf{Id}_m \\ \mathbf{A}_{\mathsf{lat}}^\top \end{bmatrix}$. That means we only look for short vectors $\begin{pmatrix} \mathbf{x} \\ \mathbf{y}_{\mathsf{lat}} \end{pmatrix}$ such that $\mathbf{A}_{\mathsf{lat}}{}^\top \mathbf{x} = \mathbf{y}_{\mathsf{lat}} \mod q$. Define $\mathbf{y}_{\mathsf{enu}}$ by $\mathbf{y}_{\mathsf{enu}} = \mathbf{A}_{\mathsf{enu}}^\top \mathbf{x}$. The point is that looking for such vectors is faster because of the dimension reduction. We then guess $\mathbf{s}_{\mathsf{enu}}$ and check whether the $\langle \mathbf{x}, \mathbf{b} \rangle - \langle \mathbf{y}_{\mathsf{enu}}, \mathbf{s}_{\mathsf{enu}} \rangle$'s are tilted towards small values or not. This comes from the fact that

$$\begin{aligned} \langle \mathbf{x}, \mathbf{b} \rangle &= \langle \mathbf{x}, \mathbf{A}_{\mathsf{enu}} \mathbf{s}_{\mathsf{enu}} + \mathbf{A}_{\mathsf{lat}} \mathbf{s}_{\mathsf{lat}} + \mathbf{e} \rangle = \langle \mathbf{A}_{\mathsf{enu}}^\top \mathbf{x}, \mathbf{s}_{\mathsf{enu}} \rangle + \langle \mathbf{A}_{\mathsf{lat}}^\top \mathbf{x}, \mathbf{s}_{\mathsf{lat}} \rangle + \langle \mathbf{x}, \mathbf{e} \rangle \\ &= \langle \mathbf{y}_{\mathsf{enu}}, \mathbf{s}_{\mathsf{enu}} \rangle + \langle \mathbf{y}_{\mathsf{lat}}, \mathbf{s}_{\mathsf{lat}} \rangle + \langle \mathbf{x}, \mathbf{e} \rangle \mod q \end{aligned} \tag{1}$$

In [20] this was generalized to broader secret distributions paired with additional improvements on the exhaustive search. [21] applied a Fast Fourier Transform-style algorithm to the search over $\mathbf{s}_{\mathsf{enu}}$ and the search space is significantly reduced by roughly considering only the most significant bits of $\mathbf{s}_{\mathsf{enu}}$. [27] replaced this step with "modulus switching" [5,9], yielding significant performance gains. The algorithm can be described as follows.

*The MATZOV template.* Let $n_{\mathsf{enu}}, n_{\mathsf{fft}}, n_{\mathsf{lat}}$ be some positive integers such that $n_{\mathsf{enu}} + n_{\mathsf{fft}} + n_{\mathsf{lat}} = n$. The matrix $\mathbf{A}$ and the secret $\mathbf{s}$ are divided accordingly:

$$\mathbf{A} \stackrel{\triangle}{=} \left[\mathbf{A}_{\mathsf{enu}} \ \mathbf{A}_{\mathsf{fft}} \ \mathbf{A}_{\mathsf{lat}}\right] \in \mathbb{Z}_q^{m \times n_{\mathsf{enu}}} \times \mathbb{Z}_q^{m \times n_{\mathsf{fft}}} \times \mathbb{Z}_q^{m \times n_{\mathsf{lat}}}, \tag{2}$$

$$\mathbf{s} \stackrel{\triangle}{=} \begin{pmatrix} \mathbf{s}_{\mathsf{enu}} \\ \mathbf{s}_{\mathsf{fft}} \\ \mathbf{s}_{\mathsf{lat}} \end{pmatrix} \in \mathbb{Z}_q^{n_{\mathsf{enu}}} \times \mathbb{Z}_q^{n_{\mathsf{fft}}} \times \mathbb{Z}_q^{n_{\mathsf{lat}}}. \tag{3}$$

The objective is to guess the part $\mathbf{s}_{\mathsf{enu}}$ of the secret vector but to do that, we need to be able to distinguish between a right and a wrong guess. By performing lattice reduction on the lattice generated by $\begin{bmatrix} \mathbf{Id}_m & \mathbf{0} \\ \mathbf{A}_{\mathsf{lat}}^\top & q\mathbf{Id}_{n_{\mathsf{lat}}} \end{bmatrix}$, we obtain a set $\mathscr{S}$ of vectors $\begin{pmatrix} \mathbf{x} \\ \mathbf{y} \end{pmatrix}$ such that $\mathbf{x}$ and $\mathbf{y}$ are of small Euclidean norm in $\mathbb{Z}_q^m$ and $\mathbb{Z}_q^{n_{\mathsf{lat}}}$ respectively and are such that $\mathbf{y} = \mathbf{A}_{\mathsf{lat}}^\top \mathbf{x}$. Similarly to Eq. (1), we have

$$\langle \mathbf{x}, \mathbf{b} - \mathbf{A}_{\mathsf{enu}} \mathbf{s}_{\mathsf{enu}} \rangle - \left\langle \mathbf{A}_{\mathsf{fft}}^\top \mathbf{x}, \mathbf{s}_{\mathsf{fft}} \right\rangle = \langle \mathbf{x}, \mathbf{e} \rangle + \langle \mathbf{y}, \mathbf{s}_{\mathsf{lat}} \rangle . \tag{4}$$

Since $(\mathbf{x}, \mathbf{y})$ and $(\mathbf{e}, \mathbf{s}_{\mathsf{lat}})$ are short, Eq. (4) is biased towards zero, raising the issue of finding efficiently $\mathbf{s}_{\mathsf{enu}}$ and $\mathbf{s}_{\mathsf{fft}}$ such that the left-hand term in (4) is small.

One can notice that (4) actually gives us many small-LWE sample[2] $(\mathbf{a}', b') \in \mathbb{Z}_q^{n_{\mathsf{fft}}} \times \mathbb{Z}_q$ with secret $\mathbf{s}' \in \mathbb{Z}_q^{n_{\mathsf{fft}}}$ and error $e' \in \mathbb{Z}_q$ where

$$\mathbf{a}' \triangleq \mathbf{A}_{\mathsf{fft}}^{\top}\mathbf{x}, \tag{5}$$

$$b' \triangleq \langle \mathbf{x}, \mathbf{b} - \mathbf{A}_{\mathsf{enu}}\mathbf{s}_{\mathsf{enu}} \rangle, \tag{6}$$

$$\mathbf{s}' \triangleq \mathbf{s}_{\mathsf{fft}}, \tag{7}$$

$$e' \triangleq \langle \mathbf{x}, \mathbf{e} \rangle + \langle \mathbf{y}, \mathbf{s}_{\mathsf{lat}} \rangle . \tag{8}$$

Thus, we can distinguish a correct and an incorrect guess for $\mathbf{s}_{\mathsf{enu}}$ and recover $\mathbf{s}_{\mathsf{fft}}$ by solving this small-LWE instance. Since $n_{\mathsf{enu}}$ is small enough, $\mathbf{s}_{\mathsf{enu}}$ can be exhaustively searched. Once $\mathbf{s}_{\mathsf{enu}}$ is identified, $\mathbf{s}_{\mathsf{fft}}$ is recovered by solving the above small-LWE instance. Specifically, this involves exhaustively searching for a $\mathbf{z} \in \mathbb{Z}_q^{n_{\mathsf{fft}}}$ such that the vector $\left(\langle \mathbf{x}, \mathbf{b} - \mathbf{A}_{\mathsf{enu}}\mathbf{s}_{\mathsf{enu}} \rangle - \langle \mathbf{A}_{\mathsf{fft}}^{\top}\mathbf{x}, \mathbf{z} \rangle\right)_{(\mathbf{x},\mathbf{y}) \in \mathscr{S}}$ has a small Euclidean norm. One approach to speed up the search is to use a Fourier transform. The method introduces an evaluation function $E$, which assigns a real value to each guess $\widetilde{\mathbf{s}_{\mathsf{enu}}} \in \mathbb{Z}_q^{n_{\mathsf{enu}}}$:

$$E(\widetilde{\mathbf{s}_{\mathsf{enu}}}) \triangleq \max_{\mathbf{z} \in \mathbb{Z}_q^{n_{\mathsf{fft}}}} F_{\widetilde{\mathbf{s}_{\mathsf{enu}}}}(\mathbf{z}) \tag{9}$$

where

$$F_{\widetilde{\mathbf{s}_{\mathsf{enu}}}}(\mathbf{z}) \triangleq \sum_{(\mathbf{x},\mathbf{y}) \in \mathscr{S}} \cos\left(\frac{2\pi}{q}\left(\langle \mathbf{x}, \mathbf{b} - \mathbf{A}_{\mathsf{enu}}\widetilde{\mathbf{s}_{\mathsf{enu}}} \rangle - \langle \mathbf{A}_{\mathsf{fft}}^{\top}\mathbf{x}, \mathbf{z} \rangle\right)\right). \tag{10}$$

MATZOV's algorithm essentially consists in finding $\widetilde{\mathbf{s}_{\mathsf{enu}}} \in \mathbb{Z}_q^{n_{\mathsf{enu}}}$ such that $E(\widetilde{\mathbf{s}_{\mathsf{enu}}}) \geq T$, where $T \in \mathbb{N}$ is a threshold chosen around the expected value of $E$ when evaluated on the correct guess, namely $T \approx E(\mathbf{s}_{\mathsf{enu}})$. The key idea is that we expect $E(\mathbf{s}_{\mathsf{enu}})$ to be significantly larger than $E(\widetilde{\mathbf{s}_{\mathsf{enu}}})$ when $\widetilde{\mathbf{s}_{\mathsf{enu}}}$ is incorrect, *i.e.* when $\widetilde{\mathbf{s}_{\mathsf{enu}}} \neq \mathbf{s}_{\mathsf{enu}}$. Indeed, for the correct guess, Eq. (4) shows that $\langle \mathbf{x}, \mathbf{b} - \mathbf{A}_{\mathsf{enu}}\mathbf{s}_{\mathsf{enu}} \rangle - \langle \mathbf{A}_{\mathsf{fft}}^{\top}\mathbf{x}, \mathbf{s}_{\mathsf{fft}} \rangle \bmod q$ is biased toward zero. Consequently, each term in the sum in Eq. (10) will be biased toward 1, resulting in a large total value for $\mathbb{E}\left(F_{\mathbf{s}_{\mathsf{enu}}}(\mathbf{s}_{\mathsf{fft}})\right)$. On the other hand, if $\widetilde{\mathbf{s}_{\mathsf{enu}}} \neq \mathbf{s}_{\mathsf{enu}}$, then for all $\mathbf{z} \in \mathbb{Z}_q^{n_{\mathsf{fft}}}$, $\langle \mathbf{x}, \mathbf{b} - \mathbf{A}_{\mathsf{enu}}\widetilde{\mathbf{s}_{\mathsf{enu}}} \rangle - \langle \mathbf{A}_{\mathsf{fft}}^{\top}\mathbf{x}, \mathbf{z} \rangle \bmod q$ is uniformly distributed over $\mathbb{Z}_q$, meaning that $\mathbb{E}\left(F_{\widetilde{\mathbf{s}_{\mathsf{enu}}}}(\mathbf{z})\right) = 0$.

*Modulus Switching.* The point of using the evaluation function $E$ is that $F_{\widetilde{\mathbf{s}_{\mathsf{enu}}}}$ can be computed efficiently with a Fast Fourier Transform (FFT). However, the large input space $\mathbb{Z}_q^{n_{\mathsf{fft}}}$ makes the FFTcostly. This size can be reduced, though at the cost of slightly weakening the bias of $F_{\mathbf{s}_{\mathsf{enu}}}(\mathbf{s}_{\mathsf{fft}})$.

[2] By using $N$ samples $\{(\mathbf{a}_i', b_i')\}_{i \in [\![1,N]\!]}$, we can rewrite the LWE instance with a matrix $\mathbf{A}' \triangleq [\mathbf{a}_1' \cdots \mathbf{a}_N']$ and a vector $\mathbf{b}' \triangleq (b_1' \cdots b_N')^{\top}$.

To do that, MATZOV proposes to reduce the size of the field $\mathbb{Z}_q$ by using a *modulus switching* technique: instead of considering $F_{\widetilde{\mathbf{s}_{\mathsf{enu}}}}$, they consider

$$\begin{aligned} F^{(\mathsf{ms})}_{\widetilde{\mathbf{s}_{\mathsf{enu}}}} : \mathbb{Z}_p^{n_{\mathsf{fft}}} &\longrightarrow \mathbb{R} \\ \mathbf{z} &\longmapsto \sum_{(\mathbf{x},\mathbf{y})\in\mathscr{S}} \cos\left(\frac{2\pi}{p}\left(\frac{p}{q}\left\langle \mathbf{x}, \mathbf{b} - \mathbf{A}_{\mathsf{enu}}\widetilde{\mathbf{s}_{\mathsf{enu}}}\right\rangle - \left\langle \left\lfloor \frac{p}{q}\mathbf{A}_{\mathsf{fft}}^\top \mathbf{x} \right\rceil, \mathbf{z}\right\rangle\right)\right) \end{aligned}$$

where $p \leq q$ is a smaller modulus and $\lfloor\cdot\rceil$ stands for the integer rounding operation. Thus, for the wrong guess $\widetilde{\mathbf{s}_{\mathsf{enu}}} \neq \mathbf{s}_{\mathsf{enu}}$ and for all $\mathbf{z} \in \mathbb{Z}_p^{n_{\mathsf{fft}}}$, $F^{(\mathsf{ms})}_{\widetilde{\mathbf{s}_{\mathsf{enu}}}}(\mathbf{z})$ is still expected to be 0 whereas for the good guess $\mathbf{s}_{\mathsf{enu}}$ we have, from Eq. (4),

$$\begin{aligned} &F^{(\mathsf{ms})}_{\mathbf{s}_{\mathsf{enu}}}(\mathbf{s}_{\mathsf{fft}} \bmod p) \\ &= \sum_{(\mathbf{x},\mathbf{y})\in\mathscr{S}} \cos\left(\frac{2\pi}{p}\left(\frac{p}{q}\langle \mathbf{x}, \mathbf{e}\rangle + \frac{p}{q}\langle \mathbf{y}, \mathbf{s}_{\mathsf{lat}}\rangle + \left\langle \frac{p}{q}\mathbf{A}_{\mathsf{fft}}^\top\mathbf{x} - \left\lfloor \frac{p}{q}\mathbf{A}_{\mathsf{fft}}^\top \mathbf{x}\right\rceil, \mathbf{s}_{\mathsf{fft}}\right\rangle\right)\right) \\ &= \sum_{(\mathbf{x},\mathbf{y})\in\mathscr{S}} \cos\left(\frac{2\pi}{q}\left(\langle \mathbf{x}, \mathbf{e}\rangle + \langle \mathbf{y}, \mathbf{s}_{\mathsf{lat}}\rangle + \left\langle \mathbf{A}_{\mathsf{fft}}^\top\mathbf{x} - \frac{q}{p}\left\lfloor \frac{p}{q}\mathbf{A}_{\mathsf{fft}}^\top \mathbf{x}\right\rceil, \mathbf{s}_{\mathsf{fft}}\right\rangle\right)\right). \end{aligned}$$

Even if it means reducing the threshold a little, we can still expect $F^{(\mathsf{ms})}_{\mathbf{s}_{\mathsf{enu}}}(\mathbf{s}_{\mathsf{fft}} \bmod p) \geq T$ since the additional term $\left\langle \mathbf{A}_{\mathsf{fft}}^\top\mathbf{x} - \frac{q}{p}\left\lfloor \frac{p}{q}\mathbf{A}_{\mathsf{fft}}^\top \mathbf{x}\right\rceil, \mathbf{s}_{\mathsf{fft}}\right\rangle$ is also biased toward zero. Indeed, it is the scalar product of two short vectors; in particular:

$$d_{\mathsf{ms}} \triangleq \mathbb{E}\left(\left\|\mathbf{A}_{\mathsf{fft}}^\top\mathbf{x} - \frac{q}{p}\left\lfloor \frac{p}{q}\mathbf{A}_{\mathsf{fft}}^\top \mathbf{x}\right\rceil\right\|\right) \approx \frac{q}{p}\sqrt{\frac{n_{\mathsf{fft}}}{12}} \tag{11}$$

since we can make the approximation that each of the coordinates of $\frac{p}{q}\mathbf{A}_{\mathsf{fft}}^\top\mathbf{x} - \left\lfloor \frac{p}{q}\mathbf{A}_{\mathsf{fft}}^\top \mathbf{x}\right\rceil$ are drawn uniformly at random in $]-0.5, 0.5]$.

Finally, [27] claims that the security level of NIST candidates like Kyber could be significantly lowered. However, this result is not widely accepted, as the analysis relies on assumptions which turn out to be false according to [18].

**Dual Attacks in Code-Based Cryptography and Analysis.** Dual attacks in lattice based cryptography can be viewed as the lattice based analogue of statistical decoding in code-based cryptography which dates back to Al Jabri [23]. In this case, short codewords $\mathbf{h}$ in the dual code are computed, where short is with respect to the Hamming distance. The goal is to solve the decoding problem $\mathbf{b} = \mathbf{A}\mathbf{s} + \mathbf{e}$ where $\mathbf{b}$ and $\mathbf{A}$ are given whereas $\mathbf{s}$ and $\mathbf{e}$ are unknown and $\mathbf{e}$ is of small Hamming weight (rather than of small Euclidean norm for the LWE problem). The issue is to recover $\mathbf{s}$. Here too, the inner product $\langle \mathbf{h}, \mathbf{b}\rangle$ is biased towards zero. This is used to solve the decoding problem very much in the same way as it is used to solve the LWE problem. Similarly to what happened in lattice based cryptography, dual attacks became much more effective through a splitting strategy which allowed to look for short codewords in a smaller code [10]. In an analogous way to what was done in lattice based cryptography, these attacks were analyzed by making assumptions and in particular independence assumptions [10, Ass. 3.7] which are close to the independence assumptions made for analyzing MATZOV's attack [27, Ass. 4.4, Ass. 5.8]. In the lattice based case, these assumptions were shown to contradict some theorems in certain regimes or well-tested heuristics in some other regimes [18].

Note that it was already noticed in [10, §3.4] that the i.i.d. Bernoulli model used for analyzing dual attacks in code-based cryptography is not always accurate. However, it was conjectured there that the difference between this ideal model and experiments has no impact on the asymptotic analysis of the decoding based on this model. This was proved to be wrong in [29]. However, this paper gave at the same time an approach for analyzing rigorously dual attacks in coding theory by bringing in a duality equation [29, Prop. 1.3] shedding some light on the fundamental quantities manipulated by the decoder. This allowed to obtain a proof of the correctness of a slightly modified version of the dual attack proposed in [10]. Dual attacks for solving the decoding problem have been further improved in [11] and the approach of [29] has been carried over to this improved dual attack. [11] can be viewed as a somewhat improved version of the MATZOV attack in the context of codes, where the modulus switching part is replaced by an optimal lossy source encoder. It is worthwhile to note that [11, Section 8] shows that the fundamental duality equation [29, Prop. 1.3] used to analyze dual attacks for codes also carries over to the lattice setting and could serve as a tool to analyze dual attacks for lattices. Moreover, at the same time, a series of papers [17,31] provide some new ideas to properly analyze dual attacks in lattices. In particular, concurrently to [11, Section 8], [17] provided, in a more in-depth work and using comparable but not identical reasoning, similar heuristics to predict the behavior of these attacks.

### 1.2 Our Contribution

Our purpose here is to come up with a variation of the MATZOV algorithm, that improves it and which also helps analyzing it. This is obtained by a lattice based analogue of [11], replacing the modulus switching by lossy source encoding/using the relevant quantizer based on polar coding. We use the duality approach [11,17, 29] to analyze our new dual attack to avoid relying on independence assumptions. This duality approach allows us to derive a new simple heuristic that is backed up by experimental evidence and which is essentially a generalization of the heuristics made in [11,17]. All in all, it turns out that the complexities claimed in [27] can be achieved and even slightly surpassed with our algorithm, which dents the parameters of KYBER by a few bits, as predicted in [27].

**A Lossy Source Coding/Quantizer Approach.** Similarly to [11] we observe that the FFT approach factorizing the common computations for computing all the $F_{\widetilde{\mathbf{s}_{\mathsf{enu}}}}(\mathbf{z})$ for $\mathbf{z} \in \mathbb{Z}_q^{n_{\mathsf{fft}}}$ is probably suboptimal, since the $\mathbf{z}$ such that $F_{\widetilde{\mathbf{s}_{\mathsf{enu}}}}(\mathbf{z})$ is maximum is likely to be attained for $\mathbf{z} = \mathbf{s}_{\mathsf{fft}}$ which is of rather small norm. The problem is that the fast FFT algorithm doesn't leverage the fact that we only need to compute it for small $\mathbf{z}$'s which have the same Euclidean norm as $\mathbf{s}_{\mathsf{fft}}$. In a sense, the modulus switching approach of [27] is a way to alleviate this phenomenon since $\mathbf{s}_{\mathsf{fft}} \mod p$ is more uniformly distributed in $\mathbb{Z}_p^{n_{\mathsf{fft}}}$ than $\mathbf{s}$ is in $\mathbb{Z}_q^{n_{\mathsf{fft}}}$. A further refinement of this method, in the spirit of [22, Section 5.5], involves approximating the relevant $\mathbf{z} \in \mathbb{Z}_q^{n_{\mathsf{fft}}}$ vectors with sufficiently close codewords. This also allows to reduce the size $q^{n_{\mathsf{fft}}}$ of the space over which the fast Fourier transform is applied.

Basically the lossy source/quantizing approach can be explained as follows. We choose a linear code $\mathcal{C}_{\mathsf{lsc}}$ generated by the matrix $\mathbf{G} \in \mathbb{Z}_q^{n_{\mathsf{fft}} \times k_{\mathsf{fft}}}$, *i.e.* $\mathcal{C}_{\mathsf{lsc}} \triangleq \{\mathbf{G}\mathbf{u}_{\mathsf{lsc}} : \mathbf{u}_{\mathsf{lsc}} \in \mathbb{Z}_q^{k_{\mathsf{fft}}}\}$ so that we can find efficiently, for any $\mathbf{y}_{\mathsf{fft}} \in \mathbb{Z}_q^{n_{\mathsf{fft}}}$, a $\mathbf{u}_{\mathsf{lsc}} \in \mathbb{Z}_q^{k_{\mathsf{fft}}}$ such that $\mathbf{G}\mathbf{u}_{\mathsf{lsc}}$ is close to $\mathbf{y}_{\mathsf{fft}}$. $\mathbf{G}\mathbf{u}_{\mathsf{lsc}}$ can be viewed as a "quantization" of $\mathbf{y}_{\mathsf{fft}}$ and $\mathcal{C}_{\mathsf{lsc}}$ as a lossy source code or code used for quantization. We apply this quantization to all pairs of short dual vectors $(\mathbf{x}, \mathbf{y})$ in $\mathscr{S}$ and compute for all such $\mathbf{x}$'s a corresponding $\mathbf{u}_{\mathsf{lsc}} \in \mathbb{Z}_q^{k_{\mathsf{fft}}}$ such that

$$\left|\left|\mathbf{A}_{\mathsf{fft}}^\top \mathbf{x} - \mathbf{G}\mathbf{u}_{\mathsf{lsc}}\right|\right| \approx d_{\mathsf{lsc}} \tag{12}$$

where $d_{\mathsf{lsc}}$ is the decoding distance of the lossy source code. The point is that the left hand term in (4) can be rewritten as

$$\begin{aligned}
&\langle \mathbf{x}, \mathbf{b} - \mathbf{A}_{\mathsf{enu}}\mathbf{s}_{\mathsf{enu}} \rangle - \left\langle \mathbf{A}_{\mathsf{fft}}^\top \mathbf{x}, \mathbf{s}_{\mathsf{fft}} \right\rangle & (13)\\
&= \langle \mathbf{x}, \mathbf{b} - \mathbf{A}_{\mathsf{enu}}\mathbf{s}_{\mathsf{enu}} \rangle - \langle \mathbf{G}\mathbf{u}_{\mathsf{lsc}}, \mathbf{s}_{\mathsf{fft}} \rangle - \langle \mathbf{e}_{\mathsf{lsc}}, \mathbf{s}_{\mathsf{fft}} \rangle & (14)\\
&= \langle \mathbf{x}, \mathbf{b} - \mathbf{A}_{\mathsf{enu}}\mathbf{s}_{\mathsf{enu}} \rangle - \left\langle \mathbf{u}_{\mathsf{lsc}}, \mathbf{G}^\top \mathbf{s}_{\mathsf{fft}} \right\rangle - \langle \mathbf{e}_{\mathsf{lsc}}, \mathbf{s}_{\mathsf{fft}} \rangle & (15)
\end{aligned}$$

where $\mathbf{e}_{\mathsf{lsc}} \triangleq \mathbf{A}_{\mathsf{fft}}^\top \mathbf{x} - \mathbf{G}\mathbf{u}_{\mathsf{lsc}}$. If we use (4) we see that

$$\langle \mathbf{x}, \mathbf{b} - \mathbf{A}_{\mathsf{enu}}\mathbf{s}_{\mathsf{enu}} \rangle - \left\langle \mathbf{u}_{\mathsf{lsc}}, \mathbf{G}^\top \mathbf{s}_{\mathsf{fft}} \right\rangle = \langle \mathbf{x}, \mathbf{e} \rangle + \langle \mathbf{y}, \mathbf{s}_{\mathsf{lat}} \rangle + \langle \mathbf{e}_{\mathsf{lsc}}, \mathbf{s}_{\mathsf{fft}} \rangle. \tag{16}$$

So we expect that the left-hand term $\langle \mathbf{x}, \mathbf{b} - \mathbf{A}_{\mathsf{enu}}\mathbf{s}_{\mathsf{enu}} \rangle - \left\langle \mathbf{u}_{\mathsf{lsc}}, \mathbf{G}^\top \mathbf{s}_{\mathsf{fft}} \right\rangle$ is still small. In other words, we once again performed a reduction to an LWE problem. Indeed, Eq. (16) can be interpreted as an LWE sample $(\mathbf{a}', b') \in \mathbb{Z}_q^{k_{\mathsf{fft}}} \times \mathbb{Z}_q$, with secret $\mathbf{s}' \in \mathbb{Z}_q^{k_{\mathsf{fft}}}$ and error term $e' \in \mathbb{Z}_q$, where

$$\mathbf{a}' \triangleq \mathbf{u}_{\mathsf{lsc}}, \tag{17}$$

$$b' \triangleq \langle \mathbf{x}, \mathbf{b} - \mathbf{A}_{\mathsf{enu}}\mathbf{s}_{\mathsf{enu}} \rangle, \tag{18}$$

$$\mathbf{s}' \triangleq \mathbf{G}^\top \mathbf{s}_{\mathsf{fft}}, \tag{19}$$

$$e' \triangleq \langle \mathbf{x}, \mathbf{e} \rangle + \langle \mathbf{y}, \mathbf{s}_{\mathsf{lat}} \rangle + \langle \mathbf{e}_{\mathsf{lsc}}, \mathbf{s}_{\mathsf{fft}} \rangle. \tag{20}$$

The advantage of this reduction is that it drastically reduces the dimension of the problem. However, it is important to note that the secret $\mathbf{s}'$ is no longer small, but uniformly distributed over $\mathbb{Z}_q^{k_{\mathsf{fft}}}$; thus, this new problem becomes a plain-LWE problem. We can now solve it using a technique similar to the one previously described. This motivates to replace $F_{\widetilde{\mathbf{s}_{\mathsf{enu}}}}$ by

$$\begin{aligned}
F_{\widetilde{\mathbf{s}_{\mathsf{enu}}}}^{(\mathsf{lsc})} : \mathbb{Z}_q^{k_{\mathsf{fft}}} &\longrightarrow \mathbb{R}\\
\mathbf{z} &\longmapsto \sum_{(\mathbf{x},\mathbf{y}) \in \mathscr{S}} \cos\left(\frac{2\pi}{q}\left(\langle \mathbf{x}, \mathbf{b} - \mathbf{A}_{\mathsf{enu}}\widetilde{\mathbf{s}_{\mathsf{enu}}} \rangle - \langle \mathbf{u}_{\mathsf{lsc}}, \mathbf{z} \rangle\right)\right).
\end{aligned} \tag{21}$$

Again, for the wrong guess $\widetilde{\mathbf{s}_{\mathsf{enu}}} \neq \mathbf{s}_{\mathsf{enu}}$ and for all $\mathbf{z} \in \mathbb{Z}_p^{k_{\mathsf{fft}}}$, $F^{(\mathsf{lsc})}_{\widetilde{\mathbf{s}_{\mathsf{enu}}}}(\mathbf{z})$ is still expected to be 0 whereas for the good guess $\mathbf{s}_{\mathsf{enu}}$ we have, from Eq. (16), that

$$F^{(\mathsf{lsc})}_{\mathbf{s}_{\mathsf{enu}}}\left(\mathbf{G}^\top \mathbf{s}_{\mathsf{fft}}\right) = \sum_{(\mathbf{x},\mathbf{y})\in\mathscr{S}} \cos\left(\tfrac{2\pi}{q}\left(\langle \mathbf{x}, \mathbf{e}\rangle + \langle \mathbf{y}, \mathbf{s}_{\mathsf{lat}}\rangle + \langle \mathbf{e}_{\mathsf{lsc}}, \mathbf{s}_{\mathsf{fft}}\rangle\right)\right) \tag{22}$$

which is still expected to be large because the additional term $\langle \mathbf{e}_{\mathsf{lsc}}, \mathbf{s}_{\mathsf{fft}}\rangle$ is biased towards zero.

The pro and cons of this approach is that on the positive side:

- It allows us to choose large values for $n_{\mathsf{fft}}$, since we are now not limited by the $q^{n_{\mathsf{fft}}}$ term in the complexity coming from evaluating $F_{\widetilde{\mathbf{s}_{\mathsf{enu}}}}$ but by a smaller $q^{k_{\mathsf{fft}}}$ term. This in turn allows us to decrease the $n_{\mathsf{lat}}$ term and therefore the cost of lattice reduction.
- It allows us to solve radically the problem that $\mathbf{s}_{\mathsf{fft}}$ is not uniformly distributed in $\mathbb{Z}_q^{n_{\mathsf{fft}}}$. If $k_{\mathsf{fft}}$ is low enough, it can namely be verified that the likely argmax $\mathbf{G}^\top \mathbf{s}_{\mathsf{fft}}$ of $F^{(\mathsf{lsc})}_{\mathbf{s}_{\mathsf{enu}}}(\mathbf{z})$ is uniformly distributed in $\mathbb{Z}_q^{k_{\mathsf{fft}}}$. This solves one source of suboptimality of this approach.

  On the negative side, it increases the noise term in the right-hand side of (16) expressing the quantity $\langle \mathbf{x}, \mathbf{b} - \mathbf{A}_{\mathsf{enu}}\mathbf{s}_{\mathsf{enu}}\rangle - \left\langle \mathbf{u}_{\mathsf{lsc}}, \mathbf{G}^\top \mathbf{s}_{\mathsf{fft}}\right\rangle$. This is due to the additional term $\langle \mathbf{e}_{\mathsf{lsc}}, \mathbf{s}_{\mathsf{fft}}\rangle$ which appears there. We therefore expect $F^{(\mathsf{lsc})}_{\mathbf{s}_{\mathsf{enu}}}\left(\mathbf{G}^\top \mathbf{s}_{\mathsf{fft}}\right)$ to be smaller than $F_{\mathbf{s}_{\mathsf{enu}}}(\mathbf{s}_{\mathsf{fft}})$ and will need to make $\mathscr{S}$ bigger to distinguish it from other values of $F^{(\mathsf{lsc})}_{\widetilde{\mathbf{s}_{\mathsf{enu}}}}(\mathbf{z})$.

The last point above makes it clear that we want to make the additional noise term $\langle \mathbf{e}_{\mathsf{lsc}}, \mathbf{s}_{\mathsf{fft}}\rangle$ as small as possible. But of course for a given $k_{\mathsf{fft}}$, there is a lower bound of what we can achieve. It can namely be proven (see Eq. (39) in Sect. 2) that the best we can do is to choose, for a given $k_{\mathsf{fft}}$, the decoding distance $d_{\mathsf{lsc}}$ such that

$$d_{\mathsf{lsc}} \approx q^{1-\frac{k_{\mathsf{fft}}}{n_{\mathsf{fft}}}} \cdot \sqrt{\frac{n_{\mathsf{fft}}}{2\pi e}}. \tag{23}$$

This can be compared to the modulus switching approach. For a same FFT complexity, meaning roughly that $k_{\mathsf{fft}}$ is such that $p^{n_{\mathsf{fft}}} = q^{k_{\mathsf{fft}}}$, we have

$$d_{\mathsf{ms}} \approx \frac{q}{p}\sqrt{\frac{n_{\mathsf{fft}}}{12}} \approx 0.28867\frac{q\sqrt{n_{\mathsf{fft}}}}{p} \tag{24}$$

$$d_{\mathsf{lsc}} \approx \frac{q}{p}\sqrt{\frac{n_{\mathsf{fft}}}{2\pi e}} \approx 0.24197\frac{q\sqrt{n_{\mathsf{fft}}}}{p} \tag{25}$$

Equations (24) and (25) show that the lossy source coding approach yields a smaller value for $\|\langle \mathbf{e}_{\mathsf{lsc}}, \mathbf{s}_{\mathsf{fft}}\rangle\|$ than modulus switching, as $d_{\mathsf{lsc}} < d_{\mathsf{ms}}$. However, unlike modulus switching, we need to construct a code that can be decoded efficiently up to the optimal decoding distance $d_{\mathsf{lsc}}$. A classical approach involves using a Cartesian product of small random codes. This solution achieves asymptotically the optimal decoding distance $d_{\mathsf{lsc}}$ but with a sub-exponential complexity that is not so negligible (super-polynomial). In Sect. 3.3, we propose an alternative solution using polar codes, which can achieve a decoding distance very close to $d_{\mathsf{lsc}}$ in quasi-linear time.

It should be noted that the modulus switching strategy can really be viewed as a quantizing approach. In the modulus switching technique, we approximate $\mathbf{A}_{\mathsf{fft}}^\top \mathbf{x}$ by $\frac{q}{p}\left\lfloor \frac{p}{q}\mathbf{A}_{\mathsf{fft}}^\top \mathbf{x}\right\rceil$, *i.e.* we quantize/approximate a point in $\mathbb{R}^{n_{\mathsf{fft}}}$ by a point in the lattice $\frac{q}{p}\mathbb{Z}^{n_{\mathsf{fft}}}$. On the other hand, in the case of the lossy source code approach we approximate a point in $\mathbb{Z}_q^{n_{\mathsf{fft}}}$ by a codeword in $\mathcal{C}_{\mathsf{lsc}}$. If we express this as a quantizer, this means that we quantize/approximate a point in $\mathbb{R}^{n_{\mathsf{fft}}}$ by a lattice point in Construction A applied to $\mathcal{C}_{\mathsf{lsc}}$. The second quantizer just turns out to be much better than the first quantizer in terms of the distortion/quantizing distance which is achieved.

**Getting Rid of Independence Assumptions in the Analysis and Results.** In [27], it is argued that dual attacks can substantially lower the security level of certain NIST candidates, such as Kyber. However, this claim remains contested, as their analysis relies on assumptions that, according to [18], have been proven to be incorrect. Specifically, [18] highlights a flawed independence assumption, which can be stated as follows:

**Assumption 1.1 (Independence Assumption).** *Let $\Lambda$ be a full-rank lattice of dimension $n$, and let $\mathbf{r}$ be a random variable distributed according to* $\text{Unif}(\mathbb{R}^n/\Lambda)$ *or* $\mathcal{B}_\alpha{}^n$*, where the $\mathcal{B}_\alpha$ are i.i.d. centered binomial variables. Assume that* $\left(e^{2i\pi\langle \mathbf{w},\mathbf{r}\rangle}\right)_{\mathbf{w}\in\Lambda}$ *are mutually independent.*

In dual attacks, evaluation functions involve sums of terms like those described in the assumption. Assuming independence when the terms are not independent can lead to significant miscalculations in estimating false positives passing the evaluation function. This issue is highlighted in [18], which shows that predictions of such scoring functions are inaccurate in certain regimes.

Recent papers [11,17,29] present new approaches to analyze dual attacks accurately, without relying on the independence assumption. Specifically, let

$$F(\mathbf{x}) \triangleq \sum_{\mathbf{w}\in\Lambda\cap\mathscr{B}} e^{2i\pi\langle \mathbf{w},\mathbf{r}(\mathbf{x})\rangle} \tag{26}$$

define a scoring function, where $\Lambda$ is a full-rank lattice of dimension $n$, $\mathscr{B}\subseteq\mathbb{R}^n$ a set of small vectors, and $\mathbf{r}(\mathbf{x})\in\mathbb{R}^n$, all depending on the specific dual attack method under consideration. It can be observed that $F(\mathbf{x})$ remains invariant when any vector from the dual lattice of $\Lambda$ is added to $\mathbf{r}(\mathbf{x})$. Indeed, for any $\mathbf{w}^\vee\in\Lambda^\vee$, we have

$$\langle \mathbf{w},\mathbf{r}(\mathbf{x})+\mathbf{w}^\vee\rangle = \langle \mathbf{w},\mathbf{r}(\mathbf{x})\rangle + \langle \mathbf{w},\mathbf{w}^\vee\rangle = \langle \mathbf{w},\mathbf{r}(\mathbf{x})\rangle\,. \tag{27}$$

Thus, it is reasonable to conclude that $\langle \mathbf{w},\mathbf{r}(\mathbf{x})\rangle$ depends on the structure of the coset $\Lambda^\vee+\mathbf{r}(\mathbf{x})$, and in particular, on its shortest vector. One way to see this is by invoking the Poisson summation formula:

$$F(\mathbf{x}) = \frac{1}{\mathsf{Vol}(\Lambda)}\cdot\sum_{\mathbf{w}^\vee\in\Lambda^\vee+\mathbf{r}(\mathbf{x})} \widehat{\mathbb{1}_{\mathscr{B}}}\left(\mathbf{w}^\vee\right). \tag{28}$$

In [11,17], it was observed that the Fourier transform of the indicator function can be expressed in terms of Bessel functions, depending only on the input's length. Consequently, $F(\mathbf{x})$ is essentially related to the length enumerator of the vectors in $\Lambda^\vee + \mathbf{r}(\mathbf{x})$, particularly the shortest. We distinguish between correct and incorrect candidates by noting that $\mathbf{r}(\mathbf{x})$ is notably small when $\mathbf{x}$ is the desired vector, and random otherwise. Therefore, for the correct guess, the shortest vector in $\Lambda^\vee + \mathbf{r}(\mathbf{x})$ is $\mathbf{r}(\mathbf{x})$, while for incorrect guesses, it corresponds to the typical shortest vector in a random coset of a random lattice.

This approach allowed us to analyze our evaluation functions thoroughly (see Sect. 4). However, to simplify calculations, we make approximations that we validate through simulations. Finally, we control the number of false positives in our attack, ensuring they remain negligible. By doing so, we achieve results close to those of MATZOV (see Sect. 5). Furthermore, as they did previously, we apply our attack to the parameters of KYBER and confirm the claim in [27], which asserts that KYBER's security does not meet the NIST's requirements.

## 2 Notation and Preliminaries

**Basic Notation.** We denote vectors by bold lowercase letters and matrices by bold uppercase letters, *e.g.* $\mathbf{v}$ and $\mathbf{M}$. We consider the vectors as column vectors and therefore row vectors are denoted $\mathbf{v}^\top$. The concatenation of vectors $\mathbf{x}$ and $\mathbf{y}$ is denoted as $(\mathbf{x}, \mathbf{y})$. The components of the vector $\mathbf{x} \in \mathbb{R}^n$ are denoted by $x_i$ for $i \in [\![1, n]\!]$ where $[\![a, b]\!]$ are the integers between $a$ and $b$.

For any $x \in \mathbb{Z}_q$, denote by $\widehat{x} \in x + q\mathbb{Z}$ the unique integer such that $|\widehat{x}| \leq \frac{q-1}{2}$. We extend this notion to vectors $\mathbf{x} \in \mathbb{Z}_q^n$ componentwise. In other words, $\widehat{\mathbf{x}}$ is the lift from $\mathbb{Z}_q$ to $\mathbb{Z}$ centered on $\mathbf{0}$. We define $\|\mathbf{x}\|$ for $\mathbf{x} \in \mathbb{Z}_q^n$ as

$$\|\mathbf{x}\| \triangleq \|\widehat{\mathbf{x}}\| \triangleq \sqrt{\sum_{i=1}^{n} \widehat{x_i}^2} \triangleq \sqrt{\sum_{i=1}^{n} \operatorname*{argmin}_{j \in \mathbb{Z}} ((x_i + jq)^2)} \tag{29}$$

**The Learning With Error Problem.** Let us define more formally the LWE problem here. It starts by defining an LWE oracle that produces samples according to the following distribution:

**Definition 2.1 (LWE oracle).** *Let $q, n, m \in \mathbb{N}$, and let $\chi_s, \chi_e$ be distributions over $\mathbb{Z}_q$. We first draw $\mathbf{s} \in \mathbb{Z}_q^n$ with coordinates drawn independently from each other according to the distribution $\chi_s$ and then draw $m$ LWE samples $(\mathbf{a}_i, b_i) \in \mathbb{Z}_q^n \times \mathbb{Z}_q$ where the $\mathbf{a}_i$'s are drawn uniformly at random in $\mathbb{Z}_q^n$ and $b_i = \langle \mathbf{a}_i, \mathbf{s} \rangle + e_i$ where the $e_i$'s are drawn independently according to the distribution $\chi_e$. We let $\mathbf{A} \in \mathbb{Z}_q^{m \times n}$ be the matrix where the $i$-th row is $\mathbf{a}_i$. The pair $(\mathbf{A}, \mathbf{b})$ is the output of the oracle and satisfies $\mathbf{b} \triangleq \mathbf{A}\mathbf{s} + \mathbf{e}$.*

We then define the Search-LWE problem as follows:

**Problem 2.2 (Search-LWE).** *Given a sample $(\mathbf{A}, \mathbf{b})$ drawn from an oracle LWE$(q, n, m, \chi_s, \chi_e)$, the goal is to recover the secret vector $\mathbf{s}$.*

In the literature, the LWE oracle is sometimes defined by replacing the matrix $\mathbf{A} \in \mathbb{Z}_q^{m\times n}$ by a vector $\mathbf{a} \in \mathbb{Z}_q^n$. Then the LWE problems are stated for an arbitrary number of calls to the oracle. If the LWE oracle is called $m$ times, then the situation is actually the same as above.

**The Centered Binomial Distribution.** In the LWE oracle, the distributions $\chi_s$ and $\chi_e$ depend on the context. Historically, the secret vector $\mathbf{s}$ was distributed uniformly in $\mathbb{Z}_q^n$ and the noise vector $\mathbf{e}$ was short. It is quite common today to consider the case where $\mathbf{s}$ is also short; we are then talking about Small-LWE problem. In recent cryptosystems, particularly those involved in the NIST Post-Quantum Standardization Process, the distributions for $\chi_s$ and $\chi_e$ are centered binomial distributions. Note that in KYBER, the distribution for the secret vector and the error vector is the same.

**Definition 2.3 (Centered Binomial Distribution).** *The centered binomial distribution $\mathcal{B}_\alpha$ of parameter $\alpha \in [\![0, \frac{q-1}{2}]\!]$ is defined as $\mathcal{B}_\alpha \sim \sum_{i=1}^{\alpha}(X_i - Y_i)$ where the $X_i$'s and $Y_i$'s are i.i.d. as uniform over $\{0,1\}$. In particular, for all $i \in [\![-\alpha, \alpha]\!]$, we have $\mathbb{P}(\mathcal{B}_\alpha = i) = 2^{-2\alpha}\binom{2\alpha}{\alpha+i}$. Note that $\mathcal{B}_\alpha$ has mean 0 and standard deviation $\sigma \triangleq \sqrt{\frac{\alpha}{2}}$.*

**Coding Background.** To simplify the discussion, we assume that $q$ is a prime number implying that $\mathbb{Z}_q$ has the structure of a finite field. A linear code $\mathcal{C}$ of length $n$ and dimension $k$ is a subspace of $\mathbb{Z}_q^n$ of dimension $k$. We say that $\mathcal{C}$ is an $[n,k]_q$-code and its rate is $R \triangleq \frac{k}{n}$. A generator matrix $\mathbf{G}$ for $\mathcal{C}$ is a full rank matrix in $\mathbb{Z}_q^{n\times k}$ such that $\mathcal{C} = \{\mathbf{Gu} : \mathbf{u} \in \mathbb{Z}_q^k\}$, and a parity-check matrix $\mathbf{H}$ for $\mathcal{C}$ is a full rank matrix in $\mathbb{Z}_q^{(n-k)\times n}$ such that $\mathcal{C} = \{\mathbf{c} \in \mathbb{Z}_q^n : \mathbf{Hc} = \mathbf{0}\}$.

**Definition 2.4 (Dual Code).** *Let $\mathcal{C}$ be an $[n,k]_q$-code. The dual code $\mathcal{C}^\perp$ of $\mathcal{C}$ is defined as the following $[n, n-k]_q$-code:*

$$\mathcal{C}^\perp \triangleq \{\mathbf{h} \in \mathbb{Z}_q^n : \forall \mathbf{c} \in \mathcal{C}, \langle \mathbf{c}, \mathbf{h}\rangle = 0\} \tag{30}$$

**Lattice Background.** A lattice $\Lambda$ is a discrete subgroup of $\mathbb{R}^d$. In particular, for a matrix $\mathbf{B} \in \mathbb{R}^{d\times d}$, the lattice $\Lambda(\mathbf{B})$ is defined as:

$$\Lambda(\mathbf{B}) \triangleq \{\mathbf{Bx} : \mathbf{x} \in \mathbb{Z}^d\} \tag{31}$$

The matrix $\mathbf{B}$ is called a basis if it has full column rank.

The volume of a full-rank lattice $\Lambda \subset \mathbb{R}^d$ is the Euclidean volume of its fundamental Voronoï region $\mathsf{Vor}(\Lambda) \triangleq \{\mathbf{v} \in \mathbb{R}^d : \|\mathbf{v}\| \leq \|\mathbf{v}-\mathbf{x}\|, \forall \mathbf{x} \in \Lambda\}$. For a full-rank lattice $\Lambda(\mathbf{B})$, it is the volume of the fundamental $d$-dimensional parallelepiped defined by the column vectors of $\mathbf{B}$ (or any other basis of $\Lambda$). It is also the determinant of the matrix $\mathbf{B}$:

$$\mathsf{Vol}(\Lambda(\mathbf{B})) \triangleq \mathsf{Vol}(\mathsf{Vor}(\Lambda(\mathbf{B}))) = \det(\mathbf{B}) \tag{32}$$

The dual $\Lambda^\vee$ of a lattice $\Lambda$ is defined as

**Definition 2.5 (Dual Lattice).** *The dual $\Lambda^\vee$ of a lattice $\Lambda \subset \mathbb{R}^d$ is*

$$\Lambda^\vee \triangleq \{\mathbf{x} \in \mathrm{span}(\Lambda) \,:\, \forall \mathbf{y} \in \Lambda,\ \langle \mathbf{x}, \mathbf{y} \rangle \in \mathbb{Z}\}\,. \tag{33}$$

We can construct a lattice from a linear code through Construction A:

**Definition 2.6 (Construction A).** *Let $\mathcal{C}$ be an $[n,k]_q$-code. The lattice $\Lambda$ obtained by Construction A applied to $\mathcal{C}$ is given by*

$$\Lambda(\mathcal{C}) \triangleq \{\mathbf{x} \in \mathbb{R}^n \,:\, \mathbf{x} \equiv \mathbf{c} \bmod q,\ \mathbf{c} \in \mathcal{C}\}\,. \tag{34}$$

Note that if $\mathcal{C}$ is defined by a systematic generator matrix $\mathbf{G} \triangleq \begin{bmatrix} \mathbf{Id}_k \\ \mathbf{A} \end{bmatrix} \in \mathbb{Z}_q^{n\times k}$, then the lattice $\Lambda(\mathcal{C})$ that is obtained through Construction A is also the lattice $\Lambda(\mathbf{B})$ generated by

$$\mathbf{B} \triangleq \left[\begin{array}{c|c} \mathbf{Id}_k & \mathbf{0} \\ \hline \mathbf{A} & q\mathbf{Id}_{n-k} \end{array}\right]. \tag{35}$$

Clearly finding the closest point in Euclidean distance to some $\mathbf{y} \in \mathbb{Z}_q^n$ in $\mathcal{C}$ also amounts to find the closest lattice point in $\Lambda(\mathcal{C})$ of $\mathbf{y}$. The algorithm for performing this task when $\mathbf{y}$ belongs to $\mathbb{R}^n$ is known as a mean-squared-error (MSE) quantizer for $\Lambda(\mathcal{C})$. To analyze its performance, first notice that the fundamental Voronoï region $V$ of a lattice $\Lambda(\mathcal{C})$ associated to code $\mathcal{C}$ of dimension $k$ over $\mathbb{Z}_q^n$ has volume $\mathsf{Vol}\,(V) \triangleq \mathsf{Vol}\,(\Lambda(\mathcal{C})) = q^{n-k}$ [14]. The average decoding distance $\omega$ provided by the mean-square quantizer for $\Lambda$ can be assessed by the normalized second moment $G \triangleq G(\Lambda(\mathcal{C}))$, which is defined as

$$G \triangleq \frac{1}{n \cdot \mathsf{Vol}\,(V)^{\frac{2}{n}}} \int_V \frac{\|\mathbf{v}\|^2}{\mathsf{Vol}\,(V)} d\mathbf{v}. \tag{36}$$

It is known that

$$G \geq \frac{1}{2\pi e} \tag{37}$$

and is achieved asymptotically for lattices generated by Construction A from $q$-ary random codes when $q$ gets big [35]. The case where the equality is achieved in Eq. (37) really corresponds to the case when the equality

$$|\mathcal{C}| \cdot \mathsf{Vol}\,(\mathsf{Ball}_\omega^n) = q^n \tag{38}$$

is met, *i.e.* when the average decoding distance is

$$\omega \triangleq \sqrt{\int_V \frac{\|\mathbf{v}\|^2}{\mathsf{Vol}\,(V)} d\mathbf{v}} = \sqrt{\frac{n}{2\pi e}} \cdot q^{1-\frac{k}{n}} + o(1)\,. \tag{39}$$

It corresponds therefore to the lattice analogue of the Gilbert-Varshamov distance.

**Short Vector Sampler.** Dual attacks heavily depend on lattice reduction algorithms, such as BKZ, to find short vectors in a lattice or its dual. Our improvements in this paper do not address these algorithms. Instead, we will use Algorithm 1 to obtain short vectors and refer the reader to [21, 27] for implementation details.

---

**Algorithm 1.** Short Vectors Sampling Procedure [21]

**Input:** A basis $\mathbf{B} = \left[\mathbf{b}_0 \ldots \mathbf{b}_{d-1}\right]$ for a lattice and $2 \leq \beta_{\mathsf{bkz}}, \beta_{\mathsf{sieve}} \in \mathbb{Z} \leq d$.

**Output:** A list of $N_{\mathsf{sieve}}(\beta_{\mathsf{sieve}}) \triangleq \left(\sqrt{\frac{4}{3}}\right)^{\beta_{\mathsf{sieve}}}$ vectors from the lattice.

1: Randomize the basis $\mathbf{B}$.
2: Run BKZ-$\beta_{\mathsf{bkz}}$ to obtain a reduced basis $\mathbf{b}'_0, \ldots, \mathbf{b}'_{d-1}$.
3: Run a sieve in dimension $\beta_{\mathsf{sieve}}$ on the sublattice spanned by $\mathbf{b}'_0, \ldots, \mathbf{b}'_{\beta_{\mathsf{sieve}}-1}$ to obtain a list $L$ of $N_{\mathsf{sieve}}(\beta_{\mathsf{sieve}})$ vectors.
4: **return** $L$

---

The parameter $\beta_{\mathsf{bkz}}$ controls the block size in the BKZ algorithm, with the cost scaling exponentially with it. The sieving algorithm outputs $N_{\mathsf{sieve}}(\beta_{\mathsf{sieve}})$ short vectors in the lattice and its complexity also scales exponentially with $\beta_{\mathsf{sieve}}$. The magnitude $N_{\mathsf{sieve}}(\beta_{\mathsf{sieve}})$ also grows exponentially with $\beta_{\mathsf{sieve}}$ but slower than the cost of sieving. We will write $T_{\mathsf{BKZ}}(d, \beta_{\mathsf{bkz}})$ for the cost of running BKZ-$\beta_{\mathsf{bkz}}$ in dimension $d$ and $T_{\mathsf{sieve}}(\beta_{\mathsf{sieve}})$ for the cost of sieving in dimension $\beta_{\mathsf{sieve}}$. One possible instantiation of the lattice sieve algorithm is [8] which has a cost of $2^{0.292\,\beta_{\mathsf{sieve}}+o(\beta_{\mathsf{sieve}})}$. Thus, according to the best known algorithms we have $T_{\mathsf{BKZ}}(d, \beta_{\mathsf{bkz}}) \in \text{poly}(d) \cdot 2^{\Theta(\beta_{\mathsf{bkz}})}$ and $T_{\mathsf{sieve}}(\beta_{\mathsf{sieve}}) \in 2^{\Theta(\beta_{\mathsf{sieve}})}$. More specifically, we take these complexities from [27, Lemma 4.1, Assumption 7.3].

**Lemma 2.7 (Short Vectors Sampling Complexity).** *Let* $\mathbf{B}$ *be a basis of a d-dimensional lattice. Then, the running time* $T_{\mathsf{sample}}$ *of Algorithm 1 for outputting* $N_{\mathsf{sieve}}(\beta_{\mathsf{sieve}})$ *short vectors is*

$$T_{\mathsf{sample}}\left(d, \beta_{\mathsf{bkz}}, \beta_{\mathsf{sieve}}\right) = T_{\mathsf{BKZ}}(d, \beta_{\mathsf{bkz}}) + T_{\mathsf{sieve}}(\beta_{\mathsf{sieve}}) \tag{40}$$

*where*

- ▷ $T_{\mathsf{BKZ}}(d, \beta_{\mathsf{bkz}}) = C_{\mathsf{prog}}^2 \cdot (d - \beta_{\mathsf{bkz}} + 1) \cdot T_{\mathsf{NNS}}({\beta_{\mathsf{bkz}}}^{\mathsf{eff}})$,
- ▷ $T_{\mathsf{sieve}}(\beta_{\mathsf{sieve}}) = C_{\mathsf{prog}} \cdot T_{\mathsf{NNS}}\left(\beta_{\mathsf{sieve}}\right)$,
- ▷ $N_{\mathsf{sieve}}(\beta) = \left(\sqrt{\frac{4}{3}}\right)^{\beta}$ *is the expected number of sieve results,*
- ▷ $T_{\mathsf{NNS}}\left(\beta\right)$ *is the time complexity for finding all close pairs in dimension* $\beta$ *(see [2] with improvement of MATZOV [27, Section 6]),*
- ▷ $C_{\mathsf{prog}} = 1/\left(1 - 2^{-0.292}\right)$ *is the number of close pairs search to run,*
- ▷ *and* $\beta^{\mathsf{eff}}$ *is the optimal sieve dimension to use for solving the Shortest Vector Problem (SVP) for lattices in dimension* $\beta$.

Note that in [15], it is estimated that $\beta^{\text{eff}} = \beta - \frac{\beta \log(4/3)}{\log(\beta/(2\pi e))}$.

*The lengths of the short vectors produced by Algorithm* 1. Assuming that the Gaussian Heuristic (GH) and the Geometric Series Assumption[3] (GSA) [33] hold for a $d$-dimensional lattice, applying $\mathsf{BKZ}$-$\beta$ to it produces vectors $\mathbf{x}$ of average length [13]:

$$\|\mathbf{x}\| \approx \delta(\beta)^d \cdot \mathsf{Vol}\left(\Lambda\right)^{\frac{1}{d}}, \tag{41}$$

where $\delta(\beta) = \left(\frac{\beta}{2\pi e}\left(\pi\beta\right)^{\frac{1}{\beta}}\right)^{\frac{1}{2(\beta-1)}}$ is the root-Hermite factor[4]. With these assumptions, the expected length of the returned short vectors is given by:

**Lemma 2.8 (Length of the sampled short vectors [27, Lemma 4.2]).** *Let $\Lambda$ be a d-dimensional lattice. Then, Algorithm 1 outputs at least $N$ vectors of expected length $\ell$ given by*

$$\ell \triangleq \mathsf{Vol}\left(\Lambda\right)^{1/d} \cdot \sqrt{\frac{4}{3}} \cdot \delta(\beta_{\mathsf{sieve}})^{\beta_{\mathsf{sieve}}-1} \cdot \delta(\beta_{\mathsf{bkz}})^{d-\beta_{\mathsf{sieve}}}. \tag{42}$$

In our attack, we select $\beta_{\mathsf{bkz}}$ and $\beta_{\mathsf{sieve}}$ such that $T_{\mathsf{BKZ}}(d, \beta_{\mathsf{bkz}}) = T_{\mathsf{sieve}}(\beta_{\mathsf{sieve}})$. Under the same GH and GSA assumptions, we derive the following lemma:

**Lemma 2.9.** *The short vectors produced by Algorithm 1 are in a sublattice $\Lambda'$ of dimension $\beta_{\mathsf{sieve}}$ and expected volume*

$$\mathsf{Vol}\left(\Lambda'\right) = \left(\mathsf{Vol}\left(\Lambda\right)^{\frac{1}{d}} \cdot \delta(\beta_{\mathsf{bkz}})^{d-\beta_{\mathsf{sieve}}}\right)^{\beta_{\mathsf{sieve}}}. \tag{43}$$

**Fast Fourier Transform.** Dual lattice attacks widely use discrete Fourier transforms:

**Definition 2.10 (Discrete Fourier Transform).** *The discrete Fourier transform $\widehat{f}$ of a function $f \colon \mathbb{Z}_q^n \longrightarrow \mathbb{C}$ is defined as*

$$\widehat{f}\left(\mathbf{x}\right) = \sum_{\mathbf{a} \in \mathbb{Z}_q^n} f(\mathbf{a}) e^{-\frac{2i\pi}{q}\langle \mathbf{x}, \mathbf{a}\rangle}. \tag{44}$$

The effectiveness of our dual attacks is heavily dependent on the speed at which we can compute discrete Fourier transforms. In [27, Ass. 7.4], it is estimated that a Fast Fourier Transform ($\mathsf{FFT}$) over $\mathbb{Z}_q^n$ requires $n \cdot q^{n+1}$ multiplications. Note that this is clearly suboptimal for large prime $q$'s: while this is not a problem in [27] as $q$ is reduced thanks to modulus switching, here, we drop modulus switching resulting in $q$ being big and imposed by the original $\mathsf{LWE}$ instance (*i.e.* $q = 3329$ for KYBER). This motivates us to give the following finer estimation for the cost of an $\mathsf{FFT}$ over $\mathbb{Z}_{3329}^n$.

---

[3] The GSA may lead us to underestimate the final complexity of a few bits (see [18, Appendix A.3]).

[4] Experiments in [1] show that these assumptions hold for $d > \beta$ and $\beta \to \infty$ and in particular, it hold with good accuracy for $\beta > 50$.

**Proposition 2.11 (Complexity of the FFT).** *Let $q = 3329$. There exists an FFT over $\mathbb{Z}_q$ with complexity given by:*

$$N_{\mathsf{FFT}}^{(\mathsf{add})} = 240500 \quad and \quad N_{\mathsf{FFT}}^{(\mathsf{mul})} = 115928, \tag{45}$$

*the number of additions and multiplications, respectively.*

*By using the algorithm in [19, §2.3.2] that reduces the calculation of an FFT over $\mathbb{Z}_q^n$ to FFT's over $\mathbb{Z}_q$, we deduce that the total cost to perform a discrete Fourier transform over $\mathbb{Z}_q^n$ is*

$$n\, q^{n-1}\, N_{\mathsf{FFT}}^{(\mathsf{add})} \quad and \quad n\, q^{n-1}\, N_{\mathsf{FFT}}^{(\mathsf{mul})} \tag{46}$$

*additions and multiplications, respectively. Finally, by supposing as in [27, Ass. 7.4] that the cost of an addition and a multiplication are*

$$C_{\mathsf{add}} = 160 \quad and \quad C_{\mathsf{mul}} = 1024, \tag{47}$$

*respectively, the total cost of an FFT over $\mathbb{Z}_q^n$ is*

$$C_{\mathsf{FFT}} = C_{\mathsf{add}}\, n\, q^{n-1}\, N_{\mathsf{FFT}}^{(\mathsf{add})} + C_{\mathsf{mul}}\, n\, q^{n-1}\, N_{\mathsf{FFT}}^{(\mathsf{mul})}. \tag{48}$$

We obtained the number of additions and multiplications required for an FFT over $\mathbb{Z}_{3329}$, namely $N_{\mathsf{FFT}}^{(\mathsf{add})}$ and $N_{\mathsf{FFT}}^{(\mathsf{mul})}$, by slightly modifying the FFTW software. This software basically allows one to enumerate a large number of FFT's and we simply selected the one that minimized the cost $C_{\mathsf{FFT}}$[5].

# 3 Our Dual Attack Algorithm

In this section, we present our algorithm for solving the search LWE problem. Unlike MATZOV, we do not use modulus switching to reduce the modulus size. As noted in the introduction, we expect that a good lossy source code/quantizer results in a smaller additional noise term $\langle \mathbf{e}_{\mathsf{fft}}, \mathbf{s}_{\mathsf{fft}} \rangle$ compared to modulus switching. However, modulus switching may still offer benefits: it has certain advantages, such as improved FFT efficiency when the modulus is a power of two, which is not the case in the starting LWE problem for KYBER. Additionally, modulus switching provides more flexibility in choosing the parameter $k_{\mathsf{fft}}$. Although a hybrid approach combining both techniques is possible, we do not pursue it in this paper due to the complexity it would add to the analysis.

## 3.1 Overview of the Algorithm

Our algorithm begins by partitioning the set of coordinates $I \triangleq [\![1, n]\!]$ of the secret $\mathbf{s}$ into $I_{\mathsf{enu}}$, $I_{\mathsf{fft}}$ and $I_{\mathsf{lat}}$, with sizes $n_{\mathsf{enu}}$, $n_{\mathsf{fft}}$ and $n_{\mathsf{lat}}$, respectively. The

[5] We give more details on how this result was obtained in https://github.com/kevin-carrier/CodedDualAttack/tree/main/claimFFT.

three parts of the vector $\mathbf{s}$ are denoted as $\mathbf{s}_{\mathsf{enu}}$, $\mathbf{s}_{\mathsf{fft}}$ and $\mathbf{s}_{\mathsf{lat}}$ respectively. Similarly, we divide the columns of $\mathbf{A}$ to obtain $\mathbf{A}_{\mathsf{enu}}$, $\mathbf{A}_{\mathsf{fft}}$ and $\mathbf{A}_{\mathsf{lat}}$. As described in the introduction, our algorithm basically tries to guess a value $\widetilde{\mathbf{s}_{\mathsf{enu}}}$ for $\mathbf{s}_{\mathsf{enu}}$ by computing an associated score for $\widetilde{\mathbf{s}_{\mathsf{enu}}}$ namely the maximum value of the score function, $\max_{\mathbf{z}\in\mathbb{Z}_q^{k_{\mathsf{fft}}}} F_{\widetilde{\mathbf{s}_{\mathsf{enu}}}}(\mathbf{z})$ and making a decision on this value. Apart from the lossy source code approach described above, we depart from the MATZOV algorithm in the two following ways: firstly, we will make the bet that $\mathbf{s}_{\mathsf{enu}} = \mathbf{0}$, that is, we only consider $\widetilde{\mathbf{s}_{\mathsf{enu}}} = \mathbf{0}$ whereas MATZOV enumerates and tests several values $\widetilde{\mathbf{s}_{\mathsf{enu}}}$ taken by decreasing likelihood. Secondly, in our algorithm, we will select $I_{\mathsf{lat}}$ once and for all (instead of changing it at each iteration), and then iterate $R$ times with different choices for $I_{\mathsf{enu}}$ and $I_{\mathsf{fft}}$ on the remaining positions, this allows us to reuse the computed dual vectors for each iteration. The skeleton of the whole algorithm is given in Algorithm 2.

**Algorithm 2.** The code based dual attack to solve LWE

**Input:** a sample $(\mathbf{A}, \mathbf{b}) \in \mathbb{Z}_q^{m\times n} \times \mathbb{Z}_q^m$ produced by an LWE $(q, n, m, \mathcal{B}_\alpha, \mathcal{B}_\alpha)$ oracle.
**Parameters:** some positive integers $R$, $T$, $\beta_{\mathsf{bkz}}$, $\beta_{\mathsf{sieve}}$, $n_{\mathsf{enu}}$, $n_{\mathsf{fft}}$, $k_{\mathsf{fft}}$, $n_{\mathsf{lat}}$, $d_{\mathsf{lsc}}$ and an $[n_{\mathsf{fft}}, k_{\mathsf{fft}}]_q$ linear code with generator matrix $\mathbf{G}$.
**Output:** the secret vector $\mathbf{s}$.

choose $I_{\mathsf{lat}} \subseteq [\![1, n]\!]$ such that $|I_{\mathsf{lat}}| = n_{\mathsf{lat}}$;
$\mathscr{S} \leftarrow$ SET_OF_SHORT_LATTICE_VECTORS$(\mathbf{A}, I_{\mathsf{lat}})$;
**repeat** $R$ **times**
  choose a partition $I_{\mathsf{enu}} \cup I_{\mathsf{fft}}$ of $[\![1, n]\!] \setminus I_{\mathsf{lat}}$ with $|I_{\mathsf{enu}}| = n_{\mathsf{enu}}$, $|I_{\mathsf{fft}}| = n_{\mathsf{fft}}$;
  $\mathbf{A}_{\mathsf{enu}}, \mathbf{A}_{\mathsf{fft}} \leftarrow$ select the columns of $\mathbf{A}$ indexed by $I_{\mathsf{enu}}$ and $I_{\mathsf{fft}}$ respectively;
  $\mathscr{L} \leftarrow$ LWE_SAMPLES$(\mathscr{S}, \mathbf{A}_{\mathsf{fft}}, \mathbf{G})$;
  V $\leftarrow$ SOLVE_LWE_WITH_FFT$(\mathscr{L})$;
  **if** V $\geq T$ **then**
    $\mathbf{s}_{\mathsf{enu}} \leftarrow \mathbf{0}$
    $(\mathbf{s}_{\mathsf{fft}}, \mathbf{s}_{\mathsf{lat}}) \leftarrow$ SUB_LWE_SOLVER$(\left[\mathbf{A}_{\mathsf{fft}}\ \mathbf{A}_{\mathsf{lat}}\right], \mathbf{b})$
    **return** $(\mathbf{s}_{\mathsf{enu}}, \mathbf{s}_{\mathsf{fft}}, \mathbf{s}_{\mathsf{lat}}, I_{\mathsf{enu}}, I_{\mathsf{fft}}, I_{\mathsf{lat}})$
**end repeat**

We now give details on the procedures SET_OF_SHORT_LATTICE_VECTORS, LWE_SAMPLES, SOLVE_LWE_WITH_FFT and SUB_LWE_SOLVER.

**The Lattice Reduction Function SET_OF_SHORT_LATTICE_VECTORS.** This function outputs a set $\mathscr{S}$ of pairs of short vectors $(\mathbf{x}, \mathbf{y})$ obtained by performing the short vectors sampler Algorithm 1 with the appropriate choice of parameters on the lattice $\mathsf{lat}(\mathbf{B})$ where the lattice basis $\mathbf{B} \in \mathbb{R}^{(m+n_{\mathsf{lat}})\times(m+n_{\mathsf{lat}})}$ is given by Construction A:

$$\mathbf{B} \triangleq \left[\begin{array}{c|c} \mathbf{Id}_m & \mathbf{0} \\ \hline {\mathbf{A}_{\mathsf{lat}}}^\top & q\mathbf{Id}_{n_{\mathsf{lat}}} \end{array}\right]. \tag{49}$$

This gives pairs $(\mathbf{x}, \mathbf{y}) \in \mathbb{Z}^m \times \mathbb{Z}^{n_{\mathsf{lat}}}$ for which both $\mathbf{x}$ and $\mathbf{y}$ are short and satisfy $\mathbf{y} = \mathbf{A}_{\mathsf{lat}}^\top \mathbf{x} \mod q$. For the rest of this paper we denote by $N$ the expected size of $\mathscr{S}$. From Lemma 2.7, we have

**Notation 3.1.**

$$N \triangleq N_{\mathsf{sieve}}\left(\beta_{\mathsf{sieve}}\right) \triangleq \left(\sqrt{\frac{4}{3}}\right)^{\beta_{\mathsf{sieve}}}. \tag{50}$$

**Producing New LWE Samples with LWE_SAMPLES.** Each pair $(\mathbf{x}, \mathbf{y})$ of short vectors in $\mathscr{S}$ yields one LWE sample by decoding $\mathbf{A}_{\mathsf{fft}}^\top \mathbf{x}$ in the code $\mathcal{C}_{\mathsf{lsc}}$ generated by $\mathbf{G}$. This yields an output $\mathbf{u}_{\mathsf{lsc}} \in \mathbb{Z}_q^{k_{\mathsf{fft}}}$ such that $\mathbf{e}_{\mathsf{lsc}} \triangleq \mathbf{A}_{\mathsf{fft}}^\top \mathbf{x} - \mathbf{G}\mathbf{u}_{\mathsf{lsc}}$ is of small norm, say close to some $d_{\mathsf{lsc}}$. The new LWE sample is given by the pair $(\mathbf{u}_{\mathsf{lsc}}, \langle \mathbf{x}, \mathbf{b} \rangle)$. It is readily seen that, when $\mathbf{s}_{\mathsf{enu}} = \mathbf{0}$ we have

$$\langle \mathbf{x}, \mathbf{b} \rangle = \left\langle \mathbf{u}_{\mathsf{lsc}}, \mathbf{G}^\top \mathbf{s}_{\mathsf{fft}} \right\rangle + \langle \mathbf{x}, \mathbf{e} \rangle + \langle \mathbf{y}, \mathbf{s}_{\mathsf{lat}} \rangle + \langle \mathbf{e}_{\mathsf{lsc}}, \mathbf{s}_{\mathsf{fft}} \rangle \tag{51}$$

which corresponds to an LWE sample with secret $\mathbf{G}^\top \mathbf{s}_{\mathsf{fft}}$ and noise $e' = \langle \mathbf{x}, \mathbf{e} \rangle + \langle \mathbf{y}, \mathbf{s}_{\mathsf{lat}} \rangle + \langle \mathbf{e}_{\mathsf{lsc}}, \mathbf{s}_{\mathsf{fft}} \rangle$. All these samples $(\mathbf{u}_{\mathsf{lsc}}, \langle \mathbf{x}, \mathbf{b} \rangle)$ are then put in a list $\mathscr{L}$ which is the output of LWE_SAMPLES.

**Solving the Induced LWE Instance with SOLVE_LWE_WITH_FFT.** This procedure outputs a real number $V$ which indicates to us how noisy the aforementioned LWE samples are. This is done by searching exhaustively for the solution $\mathbf{G}^\top \mathbf{s}_{\mathsf{fft}}$ by computing the score function for all $\mathbf{z} \in \mathbb{Z}_q^{k_{\mathsf{fft}}}$:

$$F_{\mathbf{0}}^{(\mathsf{lsc})}(\mathbf{z}) \triangleq \sum_{(\mathbf{u}_{\mathsf{lsc}}, b) \in \mathscr{L}} \cos\left(\frac{2\pi}{q}\left(b - \langle \mathbf{u}_{\mathsf{lsc}}, \mathbf{z} \rangle\right)\right), \tag{52}$$

and returning its maximum value, $V = \max_{\mathbf{z} \in \mathbb{Z}_q^{k_{\mathsf{fft}}}} F_{\mathbf{0}}^{(\mathsf{lsc})}(\mathbf{z})$. If $\mathbf{s}_{\mathsf{enu}} = \mathbf{0}$ we expect that this maximum value is achieved for $\mathbf{z} = \mathbf{G}^\top \mathbf{s}_{\mathsf{fft}}$. The score function is efficiently computed with an FFT as follows. First we compute a function $f_{\mathbf{0}}^{(\mathsf{lsc})}$ defined for $\mathbf{a} \in \mathbb{Z}_q^{k_{\mathsf{fft}}}$ as

$$f_{\mathbf{0}}^{(\mathsf{lsc})}(\mathbf{a}) \triangleq \sum_{(\mathbf{a}, b)\,:\,(\mathbf{a}, b) \in \mathscr{L}} e^{\frac{2i\pi}{q} b}, \tag{53}$$

then we compute the FFT of $f_{\mathbf{0}}^{(\mathsf{lsc})}$ and take its real part. It is readily seen that

$$F_{\mathbf{0}}^{(\mathsf{lsc})} = \mathfrak{Re}\left(\widehat{f_{\mathbf{0}}^{(\mathsf{lsc})}}\right). \tag{54}$$

**Recovering the Rest of the Secret with SUB_LWE_SOLVER.** At this point, we expect that, under the condition that our parameters are well-chosen, if $V \geq T$ (here $T$ will be chosen around the expected value of $F_{\mathbf{0}}^{(\mathsf{lsc})}(\mathbf{G}^\top \mathbf{s}_{\mathsf{fft}})$ when $\mathbf{s}_{\mathsf{enu}} = \mathbf{0}$) then with overwhelming probability, $\mathbf{s}_{\mathsf{enu}} = \mathbf{0}$. In other words, we recovered $n_{\mathsf{enu}}$ positions of the secret from the original LWE problem $(\mathbf{A}, \mathbf{b})$ of dimension $m \times n$. Note that when $\mathbf{s}_{\mathsf{enu}} = \mathbf{0}$ we can write

$$\mathbf{b} = \mathbf{A}\mathbf{s} + \mathbf{e} = \begin{bmatrix}\mathbf{A}_{\mathsf{fft}} & \mathbf{A}_{\mathsf{lat}}\end{bmatrix} \begin{pmatrix}\mathbf{s}_{\mathsf{fft}} \\ \mathbf{s}_{\mathsf{lat}}\end{pmatrix} + \mathbf{e}. \tag{55}$$

As such, if indeed $\mathbf{s}_{\mathsf{enu}} = \mathbf{0}$, we can recover $\mathbf{s}_{\mathsf{fft}}$ and $\mathbf{s}_{\mathsf{lat}}$ by solving the new LWE problem given by $\left(\begin{bmatrix}\mathbf{A}_{\mathsf{fft}} & \mathbf{A}_{\mathsf{lat}}\end{bmatrix}, \mathbf{b}\right)$, which has strictly smaller dimension $m \times (n - n_{\mathsf{enu}})$. We don't specify a particular algorithm for the SUB_LWE_SOLVER routine, since it will be called at most once, and solving an LWE instance with smaller dimension and with error distribution $\mathcal{B}_\alpha$ has complexity negligible compared to the other computations in Algorithm 2.

### 3.2 Correctness of the Algorithm

The following lemma gives parameter conditions for Algorithm 2 to succeed.

**Lemma 3.2.** *Suppose* $(\mathbf{A}, \mathbf{b})$ *is sampled from an* LWE$(q, n, m, \mathcal{B}_\alpha, \mathcal{B}_\alpha)$*-oracle, and* SUB_LWE_SOLVER *returns* $\mathbf{s}_{\mathsf{fft}}$ *and* $\mathbf{s}_{\mathsf{lat}}$ *with probability* $1 - \mu$ *when the bet* $\mathbf{s}_{\mathsf{enu}} = \mathbf{0}$ *is valid and the secret meets the threshold, namely* $F_{\mathbf{0}}^{(\mathsf{lsc})}(\mathbf{G}^\top \mathbf{s}_{\mathsf{fft}}) \geq T$. *The probability that our algorithm succeeds in recovering the secret* $\mathbf{s}$*, is lower bounded by*

$$P_{\mathsf{success}} \triangleq \eta \cdot P_{\mathsf{good}} \cdot (1 - \mu) - \varepsilon \tag{56}$$

*where*

$$p_0 \triangleq \mathbb{P}\left(\mathcal{B}_\alpha = 0\right) = 2^{-2\alpha}\binom{2\alpha}{\alpha}, \qquad \varepsilon \triangleq R \cdot q^{k_{\mathsf{fft}}} \cdot P_{\mathsf{wrong}}, \tag{57}$$

$$\eta \triangleq \left(1 - \sum_{t=0}^{n_{\mathsf{enu}}+n_{\mathsf{fft}}} \left(1 - \frac{\binom{t}{n_{\mathsf{enu}}}}{\binom{n_{\mathsf{enu}}+n_{\mathsf{fft}}}{n_{\mathsf{enu}}}}\right)^R \binom{n_{\mathsf{enu}} + n_{\mathsf{fft}}}{t} p_0^t (1 - p_0)^{n_{\mathsf{enu}}+n_{\mathsf{fft}}-t}\right), \tag{58}$$

$$P_{\mathsf{good}} \triangleq \mathbb{P}\left(F_{\mathbf{0}}^{(\mathsf{lsc})}\left(\mathbf{G}^\top \mathbf{s}_{\mathsf{fft}}\right) \geq T \,|\mathbf{s}_{\mathsf{enu}} = \mathbf{0}\right), \tag{59}$$

$$P_{\mathsf{wrong}} \triangleq \mathbb{P}\left(F_{\mathbf{0}}^{(\mathsf{lsc})}\left(\mathbf{z}\right) \geq T \,|\mathbf{s}_{\mathsf{enu}} \neq \mathbf{0}\right) \tag{60}$$

*and where* $\mathbf{z}$ *is taken uniformly at random in* $\mathbb{Z}_q^{k_{\mathsf{fft}}}$*. We will use Approximations 4.8 and 4.9 to estimate* $P_{\mathsf{good}}$ *and* $P_{\mathsf{wrong}}$*, respectively.*

*Proof.* For $i \in [\![1, R]\!]$, let us denote the following events for each iteration $i$:

- $A_i$: "$s_{\mathsf{enu}} = \mathbf{0}$";
- $B_i$: "$F_{\mathbf{0}}^{(\mathsf{lsc})}(\mathbf{G}^\top \mathbf{s}_{\mathsf{fft}}) \geq T$";
- $C_i$: "sub-LWE finds the secret";
- $D_i$: "$\exists \mathbf{z} \in \mathbb{Z}_q^{k_{\mathsf{fft}}},\ F_{\mathbf{0}}^{(\mathsf{lsc})}(\mathbf{z}) \geq T$";

Using the union bound on the probability that the algorithm fails and taking the complement of this event yields that the probability that our algorithm succeeds is lower bounded by

$$\mathbb{P}\left(\left(\bigcup_i (A_i \cap B_i \cap C_i)\right) \cap \left(\bigcap_i (A_i \cup \overline{D_i})\right)\right)$$
$$\geq \mathbb{P}\left(\bigcup_i (A_i \cap B_i \cap C_i)\right) - \mathbb{P}\left(\bigcup_i (\overline{A_i} \cap D_i)\right)$$

Next, applying the union bound again and considering that we run $R$ iterations, we can upper bound $\mathbb{P}\left(\bigcup_i (\overline{A_i} \cap D_i)\right)$ by $Rq^{k_{\mathsf{fft}}} P_{\mathsf{wrong}}$, which gives the $-\varepsilon$ term in the inequality stated in the lemma. On the other hand, it is straightforward to lower bound the first term:

$$\begin{aligned}\mathbb{P}\left(\bigcup_i (A_i \cap B_i \cap C_i)\right) &= \mathbb{P}\left(\bigcup_i (A_i \cap B_i \cap C_i) \mid \bigcup_i A_i\right) \cdot \mathbb{P}\left(\bigcup_i A_i\right)\\ &\geq \mathbb{P}\left(B_{i_0} \cap C_{i_0} \mid A_{i_0}\right) \cdot \mathbb{P}\left(\bigcup_i A_i\right)\\ &= \mathbb{P}\left(C_{i_0} \mid A_{i_0}, B_{i_0}\right) \cdot \mathbb{P}\left(B_{i_0} \mid A_{i_0}\right) \cdot \mathbb{P}\left(\bigcup_i A_i\right)\\ &= (1-\mu) \cdot P_{\mathsf{good}} \cdot \mathbb{P}\left(\bigcup_i A_i\right)\end{aligned}$$

Let $n_0$ denote the number of zeros in $\mathbf{s}_{[\![1,n]\!]\setminus I_{\mathsf{lat}}}$. Then, we have

$$\begin{aligned}\mathbb{P}\left(\bigcup_i A_i\right) = 1 - \mathbb{P}\left(\bigcap_i \overline{A_i}\right) &= 1 - \sum_{t=0}^{n_{\mathsf{enu}}+n_{\mathsf{fft}}} \mathbb{P}\left(\bigcap_i \overline{A_i} \mid n_0 = t\right) \cdot \mathbb{P}(n_0 = t)\\ &= 1 - \sum_{t=0}^{n_{\mathsf{enu}}+n_{\mathsf{fft}}} \left(1 - \frac{\binom{t}{n_{\mathsf{enu}}}}{\binom{n_{\mathsf{enu}}+n_{\mathsf{fft}}}{n_{\mathsf{enu}}}}\right)^R \cdot \mathbb{P}(n_0 = t)\end{aligned}$$

Clearly, $n_0$ follows a binomial distribution with parameter $n_{\mathsf{enu}} + n_{\mathsf{fft}}$ and $p_0$. This concludes the proof. □

Note that Lemma 3.2 does not impose any constraints on $N$ and $T$. However, we must choose them carefully. First, if $R \cdot q^{k_{\mathsf{fft}}} \cdot P_{\mathsf{wrong}} \geq 1$ or if $P_{\mathsf{good}}$ is too small, then the lower bound we obtain for the probability of success of our dual attack is 0, which means we cannot actually guarantee a success. This is why, in Sect. 5, we select $N$ and $T$ that ensure a high probability of success. In particular, we set $\eta \geq 0.62$ and $\varepsilon$ close to 0, ensuring a success probability of at least $0.3(1-\mu)$. Furthermore, it is worth noting that the condition "$R \cdot q^{k_{\mathsf{fft}}} \cdot P_{\mathsf{wrong}}$ is much smaller than 1" resolves the indistinguishability issue raised in [18].

### 3.3 Which Codes Should We Use?

In Algorithm 2, one could ask: which code should we use for $\mathcal{C}_{\mathsf{lsc}}$ ? In terms of the decoding distance alone, the answer would be, just use a random code of dimension $k_{\mathsf{fft}}$ in $\mathbb{Z}_q^{n_{\mathsf{fft}}}$. In this case, we would obtain the decoding distance $d \approx q^{1-\frac{k_{\mathsf{fft}}}{n_{\mathsf{fft}}}}\sqrt{\frac{n_{\mathsf{fft}}}{2\pi e}}$ (see Eq. (39)) attaining the bound (37) or (38). However, the decoding algorithm we could use in this case would be too complex for our purpose. We could instead use a product code structure as in [8]. Contrarily to what happens in the latter case, where spherical codes can be used, we are in a situation where more structured codes could do the job better. A natural answer is given here by polar codes.

The generator matrix of such a code in length $n$ which is a power of 2 and an arbitrary code dimension $k$ is obtained as follows. We define a generator matrix $\mathbf{G}$ for our code as $\mathbf{G} \triangleq \mathbf{K}_1 \otimes \cdots \otimes \mathbf{K}_{\log_2(n)} \cdot \mathbf{F}$ where $\otimes$ stands for the Kronecker product, $\mathbf{K}_i \triangleq \begin{bmatrix} 1 & 1 \\ \alpha_i & 0 \end{bmatrix}$ and $\alpha_i$'s are some invertible elements chosen uniformly at random in $\mathbb{Z}_q^*$. The matrix $\mathbf{F} \in \mathbb{Z}_q^{n \times k}$ is an expansion matrix such that for all $\mathbf{m} \in \mathbb{Z}_q^k$, $\mathbf{Fm}$ is exactly $\mathbf{m}$ on $k$ positions and 0 on the others (that are the *frozen* positions). Since the code length we need is not necessarily a power of 2, we adjust it by puncturing the code (*i.e.* we remove as many rows of the generator matrix as needed).

Furthermore, the Successive Cancellation (SC) decoder which is classically used to decode polar codes in the error correction scenario can be turned with a simple modification into an algorithm for finding a close codeword (but not necessarily the closest one) [25]. This is precisely what is needed in our context. It needs a noise model to instantiate it, and this can be done for our Euclidean metric by using the Gaussian noise model. To get even closer to the optimal decoding distance, we have improved the decoding process: firstly we turn the SC algorithm into a probabilistic decoder, then we call it several times to get a list of codeword candidates and choose the closest one from this list. Additional details about our list decoder can be found in Appendix A of the extended version of this paper [12]. Our procedure induces a new small constant factor $L$ in the whole complexity which is the size of the decoding list; but in return this additional cost allows us to achieve a better decoding distance. The complexity for decoding is given by:

**Lemma 3.3 (Decoding polar codes).** *List decoding an $[n_{\mathsf{fft}}, k_{\mathsf{fft}}]_q$ polar code by using $L$ probabilistic SC decoders can be done with time complexity of order*

$$T_{\mathsf{dec}}(q, n_{\mathsf{fft}}, k_{\mathsf{fft}}) = 3 \cdot L \cdot \left(C_{\mathrm{mul}} \cdot N_{\mathit{FFT}}^{(\mathrm{mul})}(q) + C_{\mathrm{add}} \cdot N_{\mathit{FFT}}^{(\mathrm{add})}(q)\right) \cdot n'_{\mathsf{fft}} \log_2(n'_{\mathsf{fft}}) \quad (61)$$

*where $n'_{\mathsf{fft}}$ is the smallest power of 2 greater than $n_{\mathsf{fft}}$ and $N_{\mathit{FFT}}^{(\mathrm{mul})}(q)$ is the number of multiplications we need to achieve a discrete Fourier transform over $\mathbb{Z}_q$.*

The proof of this lemma directly follows from [12, Lemma A.4].

By using similar arguments as in [25], it can be proven that for $n_{\mathsf{fft}}$ tending to infinity and constant $\frac{k_{\mathsf{fft}}}{n_{\mathsf{fft}}}$, the average distance achieved by our decoder is

$$d_{\mathsf{lsc}} = \sqrt{\frac{n_{\mathsf{fft}}}{2\pi e}} \cdot q^{1-\frac{k_{\mathsf{fft}}}{n_{\mathsf{fft}}}} \cdot (1 + o(1)) \tag{62}$$

This result is essentially due to the polarization phenomenon (see [12, Appendix A] again). However, Eq. (62) is not precise enough to accurately estimate the full complexity of our dual attack due to the $o(1)$ term. For this reason, we provide a C implementation[6] and present experimental results demonstrating that polar codes are perfectly suited to our case. The experiments we conducted use the exact codes required for our dual attacks, and our optimization suggests choosing $L = 1$. To justify the use of polar codes in this context, we verified that the total complexity of our dual attack closely matches the ideal scenario, where decoding at the distance $d_{\mathsf{lsc}} \triangleq \sqrt{\frac{n_{\mathsf{fft}}}{2\pi e}} \cdot q^{1-\frac{k_{\mathsf{fft}}}{n_{\mathsf{fft}}}}$ would incur the same cost as using polar codes.

## 4 Analysis of Our Dual Attack

### 4.1 Complexity of Our Dual Attack

A general formula for the complexity of our algorithm using polar codes for $\mathcal{C}_{\mathsf{lsc}}$ is given by the following theorem:

**Theorem 4.1 (Complexity of Algorithm 2).** *Using the same notations as in the correctness Lemma 3.2 and by supposing that the cost of one call to* SUB_LWE_SOLVER *is negligible, the average time complexity of Algorithm 2 is upper bounded by*

$$T_{\mathsf{sample}} + R \cdot (N \cdot T_{\mathsf{dec}} + T_{\mathsf{FFT}}) \tag{63}$$

*where*

- ▷ $T_{\mathsf{sample}} \triangleq T_{\mathsf{sample}}(m+n_{\mathsf{lat}}, \beta_{\mathsf{bkz}}, \beta_{\mathsf{sieve}})$ *is the cost to produce* $N = N_{\mathsf{sieve}}(\beta_{\mathsf{sieve}})$ *short vectors in* $\Lambda(\mathbf{B})$*. This cost is given by Lemma 2.7;*
- ▷ $T_{\mathsf{dec}} \triangleq T_{\mathsf{dec}}(q, n_{\mathsf{fft}}, k_{\mathsf{fft}})$ *is the cost for decoding a random vector in* $\mathbb{Z}_q^{n_{\mathsf{fft}}}$ *in* $\mathcal{C}_{\mathsf{lsc}}$ *generated by* $\mathbf{G}$*. This cost is given by Lemma 3.3;*
- ▷ $T_{\mathsf{FFT}}$ *is the cost of an* FFT *over* $\mathbb{Z}_q^{k_{\mathsf{fft}}}$ *and is given by Proposition 2.11;*

### 4.2 Computing an Accurate Approximation of $P_{\mathsf{good}}$ and $P_{\mathsf{wrong}}$

In this subsection, we provide an accurate estimation of the probabilities $P_{\mathsf{good}}$ and $P_{\mathsf{wrong}}$ that appear in Theorem 4.1. First, let's recall the expression of the score function:

[6] https://github.com/kevin-carrier/CodedDualAttack/tree/main/PolarCodeOverZq.

$$F_{\widetilde{\mathbf{s}_{\mathsf{enu}}}}^{(\mathsf{lsc})}\left(\mathbf{G}^\top \widetilde{\mathbf{s}_{\mathsf{fft}}}\right) \triangleq \sum_{(\mathbf{x},\mathbf{y})\in\mathscr{S}} \cos\left(\frac{2\pi}{q}\left(\langle \mathbf{x}, \mathbf{b} - \mathbf{A}_{\mathsf{enu}}\widetilde{\mathbf{s}_{\mathsf{enu}}}\rangle - \left\langle \mathbf{u}_{\mathsf{lsc}}, \mathbf{G}^\top \widetilde{\mathbf{s}_{\mathsf{fft}}}\right\rangle\right)\right) \tag{64}$$

$$= \sum_{(\mathbf{x},\mathbf{y})\in\mathscr{S}} \cos\left(\frac{2\pi}{q}\left(\langle \mathbf{x}, \mathbf{b} - \mathbf{A}_{\mathsf{enu}}\widetilde{\mathbf{s}_{\mathsf{enu}}}\rangle - \langle \mathbf{c}_{\mathsf{lsc}}, \widetilde{\mathbf{s}_{\mathsf{fft}}}\rangle\right)\right) \tag{65}$$

where
$\mathscr{S}$ is a set of $N$ short vectors drawn from $\{(\mathbf{x},\mathbf{y}) \in \Lambda(\mathbf{B}) \,:\, \|(\mathbf{x},\mathbf{y})\| \leq d_{\mathsf{lat}}\}$. Here, $\mathbf{c}_{\mathsf{lsc}} \triangleq \mathbf{G}\mathbf{u}_{\mathsf{lsc}}$ is a codeword in $\mathcal{C}_{\mathsf{lsc}} \subseteq \mathbb{Z}_q^{n_{\mathsf{fft}}}$, obtained by decoding $\mathbf{A}_{\mathsf{fft}}^\top \mathbf{x}$ using our polar code decoder. It is important to note that, according to Lemma 2.9, the short lattice vectors in $\mathscr{S}$ generated by Algorithm 1 are not uniformly distributed within $\Lambda(\mathbf{B}) \cap \mathsf{Ball}_{d_{\mathsf{lat}}}^{m+n_{\mathsf{lat}}}$; instead, they belong to a $\beta_{\mathsf{sieve}}$-dimensional sublattice $\Lambda(\mathbf{B}') \subseteq \Lambda(\mathbf{B})$, where $\mathbf{B}' \in \mathbb{R}^{(m+n_{\mathsf{lat}})\times\beta_{\mathsf{sieve}}}$. More precisely, we make the following assumption regarding the distribution of vectors in $\mathscr{S}$:

**Assumption 4.2.** *We assume that the set $\mathscr{S}$ consists of $N$ vectors uniformly sampled from*

$$\{\mathbf{w} \in \Lambda(\mathbf{B}') \,:\, \|\mathbf{w}\| \leq d_{\mathsf{lat}}\},$$

*where $\mathbf{B}' \in \mathbb{R}^{(m+n_{\mathsf{lat}})\times\beta_{\mathsf{sieve}}}$ is a basis of a $\beta_{\mathsf{sieve}}$-dimensional sublattice of $\Lambda(\mathbf{B})$, and volume as stated in Lemma 2.9. The radius $d_{\mathsf{lat}} \triangleq \frac{\ell(\beta_{\mathsf{sieve}}+1)}{\beta_{\mathsf{sieve}}}$ corresponds to that of a $\beta_{\mathsf{sieve}}$-dimensional Euclidean ball, within which the average vector length $\ell$ is given in Lemma 2.8.*

Additionally, we assume that the probability distribution of the output of our polar code decoder has radial symmetry. This means that the probability depends only on the distance between the returned codeword and the word to be decoded, not on the specific direction. Through experimentation, we observed that this distance closely follows a normal distribution. Based on these observations, we make the following assumption:

**Assumption 4.3.** *Let $\mathbf{u}$ be any vector from $\mathbb{Z}_q^{n_{\mathsf{fft}}}$, and let $\mathrm{Dec}(\mathbf{u})$ represent the random variable corresponding to the output of our polar code decoding algorithm. The distribution of $\|\mathbf{u} - \mathrm{Dec}(\mathbf{u})\|$ does not depend on $\mathbf{u}$ and we assume that it can be smoothed and approximated by the normal distribution $\mathcal{N}(\mu_{\mathsf{lsc}}, \sigma_{\mathsf{lsc}}^2)$, where $\mu_{\mathsf{lsc}}$ is the mean and $\sigma_{\mathsf{lsc}}$ is the standard deviation, both determined through simulations. We also assume that the conditional distribution of $\mathbf{u} - \mathrm{Dec}(\mathbf{u})$ given that $\|\mathbf{u} - \mathrm{Dec}(\mathbf{u})\| = d_{\mathsf{lsc}}$ is uniform over $(\Lambda(\mathcal{C}_{\mathsf{lsc}}) + \mathbf{u}) \cap \mathsf{Sphere}_{d_{\mathsf{lsc}}}^{n_{\mathsf{fft}}}$.*

**First-Level Approximation of the Score Function.** The score function $F_{\widetilde{\mathbf{s}_{\mathsf{enu}}}}^{(\mathsf{lsc})}\left(\mathbf{G}^\top \widetilde{\mathbf{s}_{\mathsf{fft}}}\right)$, as recalled in Eq. (65), is a random variable influenced by multiple sources of randomness:

(i) the randomness in the short vector sampling Algorithm 1 that generates $\mathscr{S}$,
(ii) the inherent randomness in the polar code decoder Dec,

(iii) the randomness in the LWE instance, particularly in the choice of the matrix $\mathbf{A}$,
(iv) the randomness of the guess $\widetilde{\mathbf{s}_{\mathsf{enu}}}$, which primarily arises from the selection of $I_{\mathsf{enu}}$,
(v) the randomness of the guess $\widetilde{\mathbf{s}_{\mathsf{fft}}}$.

We denote by $\mathbb{E}_{\mathscr{S},\mathrm{Dec}}(\cdot)$ the conditional expectation over the randomness sources (i) and (ii). Thus, a first-level approximation of the score function is:

**Approximation 4.4 (First-Level Approximation).** *The score function $F^{(\mathsf{lsc})}_{\widetilde{\mathbf{s}_{\mathsf{enu}}}}\left(\mathbf{G}^\top\widetilde{\mathbf{s}_{\mathsf{fft}}}\right)$ can be approximated by its conditional expectation*

$$\mathbb{E}_{\mathscr{S},\mathrm{Dec}}\left(F^{(\mathsf{lsc})}_{\widetilde{\mathbf{s}_{\mathsf{enu}}}}\left(\mathbf{G}^\top\widetilde{\mathbf{s}_{\mathsf{fft}}}\right)\right) \tag{66}$$

*where the expectation is taken over the randomness of the polar code decoder and the short vector sampler.*

**Lemma 4.5.** *The conditional expectation in Approximation 4.4 can be expressed as*

$$\mathbb{E}_{\mathscr{S},\mathrm{Dec}}\left(F^{(\mathsf{lsc})}_{\widetilde{\mathbf{s}_{\mathsf{enu}}}}\left(\mathbf{G}^\top\widetilde{\mathbf{s}_{\mathsf{fft}}}\right)\right) = \sum_{\substack{\left(\mathbf{w}^\vee_{\mathsf{lat}},\mathbf{w}^\vee_{\mathsf{lsc}}\right)\in \\ \Lambda(\mathbf{B}^{\mathsf{tmp}}_{\mathsf{global}})^\vee + \frac{\left(\mathbf{B}'^\top\mathbf{r}_{\mathsf{lat}},\mathbf{B}^\top_{\mathsf{lsc}}\mathbf{r}_{\mathsf{lsc}}\right)}{q}}} \widehat{f_{\mathsf{lat}}}\left(\mathbf{w}^\vee_{\mathsf{lat}}\right)\cdot\widehat{f_{\mathsf{lsc}}}\left(\mathbf{w}^\vee_{\mathsf{lsc}}\right), \tag{67}$$

*where*

$$f_{\mathsf{lat}}\left(\mathbf{w}_{\mathsf{lat}}\right) \triangleq \mathbb{P}\left(\mathbf{B}'\mathbf{w}_{\mathsf{lat}}\in\mathscr{S}\right),\quad f_{\mathsf{lsc}}\left(\mathbf{w}_{\mathsf{lsc}}\right) \triangleq \mathbb{P}\left(\mathbf{u}-\mathrm{Dec}\left(\mathbf{u}\right)=\mathbf{B}_{\mathsf{lsc}}\mathbf{w}_{\mathsf{lsc}}\right), \tag{68}$$

$$\left(\mathbf{r}_{\mathsf{lat}},\mathbf{r}_{\mathsf{lsc}}\right) \triangleq \mathbf{r} \triangleq \left(\mathbf{e}+\mathbf{A}_{\mathsf{enu}}(\mathbf{s}_{\mathsf{enu}}-\widetilde{\mathbf{s}_{\mathsf{enu}}})+\mathbf{A}_{\mathsf{fft}}(\mathbf{s}_{\mathsf{fft}}-\widetilde{\mathbf{s}_{\mathsf{fft}}}),\mathbf{s}_{\mathsf{lat}},\widetilde{\mathbf{s}_{\mathsf{fft}}}\right), \tag{69}$$

*and*

$$\mathbf{B}^{\mathsf{tmp}}_{\mathsf{global}} \triangleq \begin{bmatrix} \mathbf{Id}_{\beta_{\mathsf{sieve}}} & \mathbf{0} \\ \mathbf{A}^\top_{\mathsf{fft}}\mathbf{B}'_{[m]} & \mathbf{Id}_{n_{\mathsf{fft}}} \end{bmatrix}. \tag{70}$$

*Here, $\mathbf{r}_{\mathsf{lat}}$ corresponds to the first $m+n_{\mathsf{lat}}$ coordinates of $\mathbf{r}$, while $\mathbf{r}_{\mathsf{lsc}}$ corresponds to its last $n_{\mathsf{fft}}$ coordinates. Additionally, under Assumption 4.3, we have that the random variable $\mathbf{u}-\mathrm{Dec}(\mathbf{u})$ is independent of $\mathbf{u}$ and follows the distribution induced by the polar code decoder.*

*Proof.* For any vector in $\Lambda(\mathbf{B}')$, let $\mathbf{x}$ and $\mathbf{y}$ denote its first $m$ coordinates and its next $n_{\mathsf{lat}}$ coordinates, respectively. Taking the conditional expectation over the randomness of both the polar code decoder and the short vector sampler, we obtain:

$$\begin{aligned}
&\mathbb{E}_{\mathscr{S},\mathrm{Dec}}\left(F^{(\mathsf{lsc})}_{\widetilde{\mathbf{s}_{\mathsf{enu}}}}\left(\mathbf{G}^\top \widetilde{\mathbf{s}_{\mathsf{fft}}}\right)\right)\\
&= \sum_{\substack{(\mathbf{x},\mathbf{y})\in\Lambda(\mathbf{B}')\\ \mathbf{c}_{\mathsf{lsc}}\in\Lambda(\mathcal{C}_{\mathsf{lsc}})}} \mathbb{P}\left((\mathbf{x},\mathbf{y})\in\mathscr{S} \text{ and } \mathrm{Dec}\left(\mathbf{A}_{\mathsf{fft}}^\top\mathbf{x}\right)=\mathbf{c}_{\mathsf{lsc}}\right) \cdot \cos\left(\tfrac{2\pi}{q}\left(\langle \mathbf{x}, \mathbf{b}-\mathbf{A}_{\mathsf{enu}}\widetilde{\mathbf{s}_{\mathsf{enu}}}\rangle - \langle \mathbf{c}_{\mathsf{lsc}}, \widetilde{\mathbf{s}_{\mathsf{fft}}}\rangle\right)\right)\\
&= \sum_{\substack{(\mathbf{x},\mathbf{y})\in\Lambda(\mathbf{B}')\\ \mathbf{w}_{\mathsf{lsc}}\in\Lambda(\mathcal{C}_{\mathsf{lsc}})+\mathbf{A}_{\mathsf{fft}}^\top\mathbf{x}}} \mathbb{P}\left((\mathbf{x},\mathbf{y})\in\mathscr{S} \text{ and } \mathbf{A}_{\mathsf{fft}}^\top\mathbf{x}-\mathrm{Dec}\left(\mathbf{A}_{\mathsf{fft}}^\top\mathbf{x}\right)=\mathbf{w}_{\mathsf{lsc}}\right) \cdot \cos\left(\tfrac{2\pi}{q}\left(\langle \mathbf{x}, \mathbf{b}-\mathbf{A}_{\mathsf{enu}}\widetilde{\mathbf{s}_{\mathsf{enu}}}\rangle - \left\langle \mathbf{A}_{\mathsf{fft}}^\top\mathbf{x}-\mathbf{w}_{\mathsf{lsc}}, \widetilde{\mathbf{s}_{\mathsf{fft}}}\right\rangle\right)\right)\\
&= \sum_{\substack{(\mathbf{x},\mathbf{y})\in\Lambda(\mathbf{B}')\\ \mathbf{w}_{\mathsf{lsc}}\in\Lambda(\mathcal{C}_{\mathsf{lsc}})+\mathbf{A}_{\mathsf{fft}}^\top\mathbf{x}}} \mathbb{P}\left((\mathbf{x},\mathbf{y})\in\mathscr{S}\right)\cdot\mathbb{P}\left(\mathbf{A}_{\mathsf{fft}}^\top\mathbf{x}-\mathrm{Dec}\left(\mathbf{A}_{\mathsf{fft}}^\top\mathbf{x}\right)=\mathbf{w}_{\mathsf{lsc}}\right) \cdot \cos\left(\tfrac{2\pi}{q}\left(\langle \mathbf{x}, \mathbf{b}-\mathbf{A}_{\mathsf{enu}}\widetilde{\mathbf{s}_{\mathsf{enu}}}\rangle - \left\langle \mathbf{A}_{\mathsf{fft}}^\top\mathbf{x}-\mathbf{w}_{\mathsf{lsc}}, \widetilde{\mathbf{s}_{\mathsf{fft}}}\right\rangle\right)\right)
\end{aligned}$$

where the last equality holds because of the independence of the decoding noise $\mathbf{u}-\mathrm{Dec}(\mathbf{u})$ from $\mathbf{u}$. Next, we simplify the inner expression inside the cosine:

$$\begin{aligned}
&\langle \mathbf{x}, \mathbf{b}-\mathbf{A}_{\mathsf{enu}}\widetilde{\mathbf{s}_{\mathsf{enu}}}\rangle - \left\langle \mathbf{A}_{\mathsf{fft}}^\top\mathbf{x}-\mathbf{w}_{\mathsf{lsc}}, \widetilde{\mathbf{s}_{\mathsf{fft}}}\right\rangle\\
&= \langle \mathbf{x}, \mathbf{e}+\mathbf{A}_{\mathsf{enu}}(\mathbf{s}_{\mathsf{enu}}-\widetilde{\mathbf{s}_{\mathsf{enu}}})+\mathbf{A}_{\mathsf{lat}}\mathbf{s}_{\mathsf{lat}}+\mathbf{A}_{\mathsf{fft}}\mathbf{s}_{\mathsf{fft}}\rangle - \left\langle \mathbf{A}_{\mathsf{fft}}^\top\mathbf{x}-\mathbf{w}_{\mathsf{lsc}}, \widetilde{\mathbf{s}_{\mathsf{fft}}}\right\rangle\\
&= \langle \mathbf{x}, \mathbf{e}+\mathbf{A}_{\mathsf{enu}}(\mathbf{s}_{\mathsf{enu}}-\widetilde{\mathbf{s}_{\mathsf{enu}}})+\mathbf{A}_{\mathsf{fft}}(\mathbf{s}_{\mathsf{fft}}-\widetilde{\mathbf{s}_{\mathsf{fft}}})\rangle + \left\langle \mathbf{A}_{\mathsf{lat}}^\top\mathbf{x}, \mathbf{s}_{\mathsf{lat}}\right\rangle + \langle \mathbf{w}_{\mathsf{lsc}}, \widetilde{\mathbf{s}_{\mathsf{fft}}}\rangle\\
&= \langle (\mathbf{x},\mathbf{y},\mathbf{w}_{\mathsf{lsc}}), \mathbf{r}\rangle \bmod q
\end{aligned}$$

where $\mathbf{r}$ is as defined in Eq. (69). So, we obtain

$$\mathbb{E}_{\mathscr{S},\mathrm{Dec}}\left(F^{(\mathsf{lsc})}_{\widetilde{\mathbf{s}_{\mathsf{enu}}}}\left(\mathbf{G}^\top \widetilde{\mathbf{s}_{\mathsf{fft}}}\right)\right) = \sum_{\substack{(\mathbf{x},\mathbf{y})\in\Lambda(\mathbf{B}')\\ \mathbf{w}_{\mathsf{lsc}}\in\Lambda(\mathcal{C}_{\mathsf{lsc}})+\mathbf{A}_{\mathsf{fft}}^\top\mathbf{x}}} \mathbb{P}\left((\mathbf{x},\mathbf{y})\in\mathscr{S}\right)\cdot\mathbb{P}\left(\mathbf{A}_{\mathsf{fft}}^\top\mathbf{x}-\mathrm{Dec}\left(\mathbf{A}_{\mathsf{fft}}^\top\mathbf{x}\right)=\mathbf{w}_{\mathsf{lsc}}\right) \cdot \cos\left(2\pi\left\langle(\mathbf{x},\mathbf{y},\mathbf{w}_{\mathsf{lsc}}), \tfrac{\mathbf{r}}{q}\right\rangle\right).$$

We observe that if $(\mathbf{x},\mathbf{y})\in\Lambda(\mathbf{B}')$ and $\mathbf{w}_{\mathsf{lsc}}\in\Lambda(\mathcal{C}_{\mathsf{lsc}})+\mathbf{A}_{\mathsf{fft}}^\top\mathbf{x}$, then it follows that $(-\mathbf{x},-\mathbf{y})\in\Lambda(\mathbf{B}')$ and $-\mathbf{w}_{\mathsf{lsc}}\in\Lambda(\mathcal{C}_{\mathsf{lsc}})-\mathbf{A}_{\mathsf{fft}}^\top\mathbf{x}$. Furthermore, the probabilities involved in the formula are invariant under negation. This allows us to express the cosine function in its exponential form, which yields

$$\mathbb{E}_{\mathscr{S},\mathrm{Dec}}\left(F^{(\mathsf{lsc})}_{\widetilde{\mathbf{s}_{\mathsf{enu}}}}\left(\mathbf{G}^\top \widetilde{\mathbf{s}_{\mathsf{fft}}}\right)\right) = \sum_{\substack{(\mathbf{x},\mathbf{y})\in\Lambda(\mathbf{B}')\\ \mathbf{w}_{\mathsf{lsc}}\in\Lambda(\mathcal{C}_{\mathsf{lsc}})+\mathbf{A}_{\mathsf{fft}}^\top\mathbf{x}}} \mathbb{P}\left((\mathbf{x},\mathbf{y})\in\mathscr{S}\right)\cdot\mathbb{P}\left(\mathbf{A}_{\mathsf{fft}}^\top\mathbf{x}-\mathrm{Dec}\left(\mathbf{A}_{\mathsf{fft}}^\top\mathbf{x}\right)=\mathbf{w}_{\mathsf{lsc}}\right)\cdot e^{2i\pi\left\langle(\mathbf{x},\mathbf{y},\mathbf{w}_{\mathsf{lsc}}),\frac{\mathbf{r}}{q}\right\rangle}$$

and so, replacing $(\mathbf{x},\mathbf{y})$ by $\mathbf{B}'\mathbf{w}_{\mathsf{lat}}$, we obtain

$$\mathbb{E}_{\mathscr{S},\mathrm{Dec}}\left(F^{(\mathsf{lsc})}_{\widetilde{\mathbf{s}_{\mathsf{enu}}}}\left(\mathbf{G}^\top \widetilde{\mathbf{s}_{\mathsf{fft}}}\right)\right) = \sum_{(\mathbf{w}_{\mathsf{lat}},\mathbf{w}_{\mathsf{lsc}})\in\Lambda(\mathbf{B}^{\mathsf{tmp}}_{\mathsf{global}})} f_{\mathsf{lat}}(\mathbf{w}_{\mathsf{lat}})\cdot f_{\mathsf{lsc}}(\mathbf{w}_{\mathsf{lsc}})\cdot e^{2i\pi\left\langle(\mathbf{B}'\mathbf{w}_{\mathsf{lat}},\mathbf{B}_{\mathsf{lsc}}\mathbf{w}_{\mathsf{lsc}}),\frac{\mathbf{r}}{q}\right\rangle}.$$

Note that the function $f_{\mathsf{lsc}}$ is defined in terms of a vector $\mathbf{u}$, which in this case depends on $\mathbf{w}_{\mathsf{lat}}$. However, the error vector produced by our polar code decoder is independent of the vector being decoded; that means the distribution $f_{\mathsf{lsc}}$ does not depend on $\mathbf{u}$. Finally, following [11,17], we can apply the Poisson summation formula to obtain Eq. (67). □

**Second-Level Approximation of the Score Function.** By estimating the Fourier transforms $\widehat{f_{\mathsf{lat}}}$ and $\widehat{f_{\mathsf{lsc}}}$ from Lemma 4.5, we derive a new approximation of the score function:

**Approximation 4.6 (Second-Level Approximation).** *Based on Approximation 4.4, Assumptions 4.2 and 4.3, and assuming the Gaussian Heuristic holds, we have*

$$F^{(\mathsf{lsc})}_{\widetilde{\mathbf{s}_{\mathsf{enu}}}}\left(\mathbf{G}^{\top}\widetilde{\mathbf{s}_{\mathsf{fft}}}\right) \approx N \cdot \sum_{\substack{i \geq 0 \\ j \geq 0}} N_{i,j} \cdot \int_0^{\infty} \psi_{\mathsf{lsc}}(d_{\mathsf{lsc}}) \cdot \Phi_{d_{\mathsf{lsc}}}(i,j) dd_{\mathsf{lsc}} \tag{71}$$

*where*

$$\Phi_{d_{\mathsf{lsc}}}(i,j) \stackrel{\triangle}{=} \Upsilon_{\frac{\beta_{\mathsf{sieve}}}{2}}\left(\tfrac{2\pi}{q} d_{\mathsf{lat}} i\right) \cdot \Upsilon_{\frac{n_{\mathsf{fft}}}{2}-1}\left(\tfrac{2\pi}{q} d_{\mathsf{lsc}} j\right), \tag{72}$$

$$\Upsilon_n(x) \stackrel{\triangle}{=} \frac{\Gamma(n+1)\, J_n(x)}{(x/2)^n} = \sum_{\ell=0}^{+\infty} \frac{(-1)^{\ell}(x/2)^{2\ell}}{\ell! \prod_{s=1}^{\ell}(n+s)}, \tag{73}$$

$$N_{i,j} \stackrel{\triangle}{=} \left| \left\{ (\mathbf{w}_{\mathsf{lat}}, \mathbf{w}_{\mathsf{lsc}}) \in q\Lambda\left(\mathbf{B}_{\mathsf{global}}\right)^{\vee} + \mathbf{r}_{\mathsf{proj}} \subseteq \operatorname{span}\left(\mathbf{B}'\right) \times \mathbb{R}^{n_{\mathsf{fft}}} : \|\mathbf{w}_{\mathsf{lat}}\| = i \text{ and } \|\mathbf{w}_{\mathsf{lsc}}\| = j \right\} \right|, \tag{74}$$

*with* $\mathbf{r}_{\mathsf{proj}}$, *the orthogonal projection on* $\operatorname{span}(\mathbf{B}_{\mathsf{global}}) = \operatorname{span}(\mathbf{B}') \times \mathbb{R}^{n_{\mathsf{fft}}}$ *of*

$$\mathbf{r} \stackrel{\triangle}{=} \left(\mathbf{e} + \mathbf{A}_{\mathsf{enu}}(\mathbf{s}_{\mathsf{enu}} - \widetilde{\mathbf{s}_{\mathsf{enu}}}) + \mathbf{A}_{\mathsf{fft}}(\mathbf{s}_{\mathsf{fft}} - \widetilde{\mathbf{s}_{\mathsf{fft}}}), \mathbf{s}_{\mathsf{lat}}, \widetilde{\mathbf{s}_{\mathsf{fft}}}\right), \tag{75}$$

*and*

$$\mathbf{B}_{\mathsf{global}} \stackrel{\triangle}{=} \begin{array}{c} \quad\ \ \beta_{\mathsf{sieve}} \qquad n_{\mathsf{fft}} \\ \left[\begin{array}{c|c} \mathbf{B}' & \mathbf{0} \\ \hline \mathbf{A}_{\mathsf{fft}}^{\top} \cdot \mathbf{B}'_{[m]} & \mathbf{B}_{\mathsf{lsc}} \end{array}\right] \begin{array}{l} m + n_{\mathsf{lat}} \\ n_{\mathsf{fft}} \end{array} \end{array}$$

*Here:*

- $\mathbf{B}' \in \mathbb{R}^{(m+n_{\mathsf{lat}}) \times \beta_{\mathsf{sieve}}}$ *is a lattice basis for the sampled short vectors,*
- $\mathbf{B}'_{[m]}$ *consists of the first* $m$ *rows of* $\mathbf{B}'$,
- *and* $\mathbf{B}_{\mathsf{lsc}}$ *is a basis of the lattice* $\Lambda(\mathcal{C}_{\mathsf{lsc}})$.

To justify the above approximation, we first show that under Assumptions 4.2 and 4.3, and assuming the Gaussian Heuristic holds, the following two approximations hold:

$$\widehat{f_{\mathsf{lat}}}\left(\mathbf{w}_{\mathsf{lat}}^{\vee}\right) \approx N \cdot \Upsilon_{\frac{\beta_{\mathsf{sieve}}}{2}}\left(2\pi d_{\mathsf{lat}}\left\|\mathbf{B}'\left(\mathbf{B}'^{\top}\mathbf{B}'\right)^{-1}\mathbf{w}_{\mathsf{lat}}^{\vee}\right\|\right), \tag{76}$$

$$\widehat{f_{\mathsf{lsc}}}\left(\mathbf{w}_{\mathsf{lsc}}^{\vee}\right) \approx \int_0^{\infty} \psi_{\mathsf{lsc}}(d_{\mathsf{lsc}}) \cdot \Upsilon_{\frac{n_{\mathsf{fft}}}{2}-1}\left(\tfrac{2\pi}{q} d_{\mathsf{lsc}}\left\|\mathbf{B}_{\mathsf{lsc}}^{-\top}\mathbf{w}_{\mathsf{lsc}}^{\vee}\right\|\right) dd_{\mathsf{lsc}}. \tag{77}$$

Details on these calculations are provided in the full version [12].

Therefore, by leveraging Approximation 4.4 and Lemma 4.5, together with Approximations (76) and (77), we obtain the justification for Approximation 4.6. First, we observe that for all $(\mathbf{w}_{\mathsf{lat}}^{\vee}, \mathbf{w}_{\mathsf{lsc}}^{\vee}) \in \Lambda(\mathbf{B}_{\mathsf{global}}^{\mathsf{tmp}})^{\vee} + \frac{(\mathbf{B}'^{\top}\mathbf{r}_{\mathsf{lat}}, \mathbf{B}_{\mathsf{lsc}}^{\top}\mathbf{r}_{\mathsf{lsc}})}{q}$, we have

$$q\left(\mathbf{B}'\left(\mathbf{B}'^{\top}\mathbf{B}'\right)^{-1}\mathbf{w}_{\mathsf{lat}}^{\vee}, \mathbf{B}_{\mathsf{lsc}}^{-\top}\mathbf{w}_{\mathsf{lsc}}^{\vee}\right) \in q\Lambda(\mathbf{B}_{\mathsf{global}})^{\vee} + \mathbf{r}_{\mathsf{proj}},$$

And so, combining all the terms and making the appropriate variable change, we obtain

$$F_{\widetilde{\mathbf{s}_{\mathsf{enu}}}}^{(\mathsf{lsc})}\left(\mathbf{G}^{\top}\widetilde{\mathbf{s}_{\mathsf{fft}}}\right) \approx$$

$$N \cdot \int_0^{\infty} \psi_{\mathsf{lsc}}(d_{\mathsf{lsc}}) \cdot \sum_{\substack{(\mathbf{w}_{\mathsf{lat}}^{\vee}, \mathbf{w}_{\mathsf{lsc}}^{\vee}) \in \\ q\Lambda(\mathbf{B}_{\mathsf{global}})^{\vee} + \mathbf{r}_{\mathsf{proj}}}} \Upsilon_{\frac{\beta_{\mathsf{sieve}}}{2}}\left(\tfrac{2\pi}{q} d_{\mathsf{lat}}\left\|\mathbf{w}_{\mathsf{lat}}^{\vee}\right\|\right) \cdot \Upsilon_{\frac{n_{\mathsf{fft}}}{2}-1}\left(\tfrac{2\pi}{q} d_{\mathsf{lsc}}\left\|\mathbf{w}_{\mathsf{lsc}}^{\vee}\right\|\right) dd_{\mathsf{lsc}}.$$

We conclude by noting that the inner sum depends only on the lengths of $\mathbf{w}_{\mathsf{lat}}^{\vee}$ and $\mathbf{w}_{\mathsf{lsc}}^{\vee}$, that we denote $i$ and $j$, respectively.

**Third-Level Approximation of the Score Function.** Recall that Approximation 4.6 gives

$$F_{\widetilde{\mathbf{s}_{\mathsf{enu}}}}^{(\mathsf{lsc})}\left(\mathbf{G}^{\top}\widetilde{\mathbf{s}_{\mathsf{fft}}}\right) \approx N \cdot \int_0^{\infty} \psi_{\mathsf{lsc}}(d_{\mathsf{lsc}}) \cdot \sum_{i,j} N_{i,j} \cdot \Phi_{d_{\mathsf{lsc}}}(i,j) dd_{\mathsf{lsc}} \tag{78}$$

where $N_{i,j}$ is a random variable representing the number of pairs $(\mathbf{w}_{\mathsf{lat}}^{\vee}, \mathbf{w}_{\mathsf{lsc}}^{\vee}) \in q\Lambda\left(\mathbf{B}_{\mathsf{global}}\right)^{\vee} + \mathbf{r}_{\mathsf{proj}} \subseteq \mathrm{span}\left(\mathbf{B}'\right) \times \mathbb{R}^{n_{\mathsf{fft}}}$ such that $\|\mathbf{w}_{\mathsf{lat}}^{\vee}\| = i$ and $\|\mathbf{w}_{\mathsf{lsc}}^{\vee}\| = j$.

Describing the distribution in Eq. (78) is quite complex. To simplify this, we propose the following model:

**Model 4.7.** *We assume that* $F_{\widetilde{\mathbf{s}_{\mathsf{enu}}}}^{(\mathsf{lsc})}\left(\mathbf{G}^{\top}\widetilde{\mathbf{s}_{\mathsf{fft}}}\right)$ *approximately follows the same distribution as* $\mathcal{D} + \mathcal{N}(0, N/2)$*, where* $\mathcal{N}(0, N/2)$ *denotes a normal distribution with mean* 0 *and standard deviation* $\sqrt{N/2}$*, and*

$$\mathcal{D} \triangleq N \cdot \int_0^{\infty} \psi_{\mathsf{lsc}}(d_{\mathsf{lsc}}) \cdot \left(\max_{i,j \,:\, N_{i,j}=1}\left(\Phi_{d_{\mathsf{lsc}}}(i,j)\right)\right) dd_{\mathsf{lsc}}. \tag{79}$$

*We recall that* $\psi_{\mathsf{lsc}}$ *refers to the probability density function of* $\mathcal{N}(\mu_{\mathsf{lsc}}, \sigma_{\mathsf{lsc}}^2)$.

Based on Approximation 4.6 and Model 4.7, we can make the following two approximations, with probabilities calculated over the randomness of the guesses $I_{\mathsf{enu}}$ and $\widetilde{\mathbf{s}_{\mathsf{fft}}}$, as well as over the randomness of the LWE instance:

**Approximation 4.8 (Good Guess).** *If we make the good guess* $(\widetilde{\mathbf{s}_{\mathsf{enu}}}, \widetilde{\mathbf{s}_{\mathsf{fft}}}) = (\mathbf{s}_{\mathsf{enu}}, \mathbf{s}_{\mathsf{fft}})$ *and if we choose* $T$ *around the expectation of* $F^{(\mathsf{lsc})}_{\mathbf{s}_{\mathsf{enu}}}(\mathbf{G}^\top \mathbf{s}_{\mathsf{fft}})$*, namely by defining*

$$\frac{T}{N} = \frac{\exp\left(\frac{-\alpha(\pi\mu_{\mathsf{lsc}}/q)^2}{1+2\alpha(\pi\sigma_{\mathsf{lsc}}/q)^2}\right)}{\sqrt{1+2\alpha(\pi\sigma_{\mathsf{lsc}}/q)^2}} \cdot \int_0^1 \beta_{\mathsf{sieve}} \cdot t^{\beta_{\mathsf{sieve}}-1} \cdot e^{-\alpha\left(\frac{\pi d_{\mathsf{lat}} t}{q}\right)^2} dt, \tag{80}$$

*then*

$$P_{\mathsf{good}} \triangleq \mathbb{P}\left(F^{(\mathsf{lsc})}_{\mathbf{s}_{\mathsf{enu}}}(\mathbf{G}^\top \mathbf{s}_{\mathsf{fft}}) \geq T\right) \approx 0.5 \tag{81}$$

**Approximation 4.9 (Wrong Guess).** *If we make the wrong guess* $(\widetilde{\mathbf{s}_{\mathsf{enu}}}, \widetilde{\mathbf{s}_{\mathsf{fft}}}) \neq (\mathbf{s}_{\mathsf{enu}}, \mathbf{s}_{\mathsf{fft}})$*, then*

$$P_{\mathsf{wrong}} \triangleq \mathbb{P}\left(F^{(\mathsf{lsc})}_{\widetilde{\mathbf{s}_{\mathsf{enu}}}}(\mathbf{G}^\top \widetilde{\mathbf{s}_{\mathsf{fft}}}) \geq T\right) \tag{82}$$

$$\approx \int_{-\infty}^{+\infty} \int_0^{+\infty} \min\left(1, \int_{\mathcal{E}(T-t)} \lambda(x)\mu(y) d(x,y)\right) \cdot \frac{e^{\frac{-t^2}{N} - \frac{(d_{\mathsf{lsc}}-\mu_{\mathsf{lsc}})^2}{2\sigma^2_{\mathsf{lsc}}}}}{\pi\sigma_{\mathsf{lsc}}\sqrt{2N}} dd_{\mathsf{lsc}}\, dt \tag{83}$$

*where*

$$\mathcal{E}(T-t) \triangleq \left\{(x,y) \in \mathbb{R}^2_+ \ : \ N \cdot \Phi_{d_{\mathsf{lsc}}}(x,y) \geq T - t\right\}, \tag{84}$$

$$\lambda(x) \triangleq \frac{2 \cdot \delta\left(\beta_{\mathsf{bkz}}\right)^{\beta_{\mathsf{sieve}}(m+n_{\mathsf{lat}}-\beta_{\mathsf{sieve}})} \cdot \pi^{\frac{\beta_{\mathsf{sieve}}}{2}} \cdot x^{\beta_{\mathsf{sieve}}-1}}{q^{\beta_{\mathsf{sieve}} \cdot \frac{m}{m+n_{\mathsf{lat}}}} \cdot \Gamma\left(\frac{\beta_{\mathsf{sieve}}}{2}\right)}, \tag{85}$$

*and*

$$\mu(y) \triangleq \frac{2 \cdot \pi^{\frac{n_{\mathsf{fft}}}{2}} \cdot y^{n_{\mathsf{fft}}-1}}{q^{k_{\mathsf{fft}}} \cdot \Gamma\left(\frac{n_{\mathsf{fft}}}{2}\right)}. \tag{86}$$

On the one hand, the rationale behind Approximation 4.8 is that if we make the good guess $(\widetilde{\mathbf{s}_{\mathsf{enu}}}, \widetilde{\mathbf{s}_{\mathsf{fft}}}) = (\mathbf{s}_{\mathsf{enu}}, \mathbf{s}_{\mathsf{fft}})$, then there exists an element $\mathbf{r}_{\mathsf{proj}} \in q\Lambda\left(\mathbf{B}_{\mathsf{global}}\right)^\vee + \mathbf{r}_{\mathsf{proj}}$ which has particulary small length. Thus, in Eq. (80), we chose $T$ as the expected score $\mathbb{E}\left(F^{(\mathsf{lsc})}_{\mathbf{s}_{\mathsf{enu}}}(\mathbf{G}^\top \mathbf{s}_{\mathsf{fft}})\right)$ of the good guess. Experiments confirm the score's expectation closely matches its median, justifying Approximation 4.8. On the other hand, to obtain Approximation 4.9, we first observe that, under Model 4.7, $P_{\mathsf{wrong}}$ arises as the convolution of the probability density function of the normal distribution $\mathcal{N}(0, N/2)$ with the survival function of $\mathcal{D}$. We then show that the distribution of $\mathcal{D}$ is governed by the lengths of short vectors in the coset $q\Lambda(\mathbf{B}_{\mathsf{global}})^\vee + \mathbf{r}_{\mathsf{proj}}$, where $\mathbf{r}_{\mathsf{proj}}$ is no longer the shortest vector in the lattice coset.

In the full version of this paper [12], we provide additional details on the calculations leading to Approximations 4.8 and 4.9.

**Validating Our Analysis Through Simulations.** We verify here the soundness of Approximation 4.9 for $P_{\text{wrong}}$, which is crucial for estimating the number of false candidates. To this end, we implemented and ran Algorithm 2, computing an experimental value for $P_{\text{wrong}}$, namely $\frac{\left|\{\mathbf{z}\in\mathbb{Z}_q^{k_{\text{fft}}} : F_{\mathbf{0}}^{(\text{lsc})}(\mathbf{z})\geq T\}\right|}{q^{k_{\text{fft}}}}$ for different values of $T$. We plotted it against its theoretical approximation in Fig. 1. Notably, we found that the experimental and theoretical estimates are in agreement, though the plot on the right suggests that our analysis may be slightly optimistic.

We used the g6k library [4] to generate short vectors in a lattice and used polar codes, along with the decoder described in Sect. 3.3, for the auxiliary code $\mathcal{C}_{\text{lsc}}$. We provide the program used to generate Fig. 1 in the GitHub repository[7].

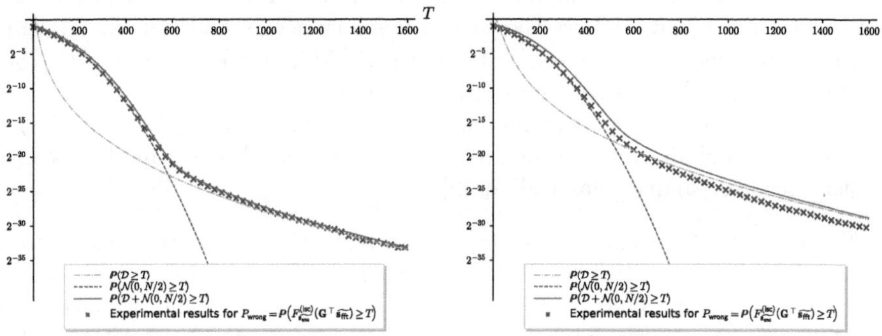


**Fig. 1.** Experimental validation of Approximation 4.9 for $P_{\text{wrong}}$. The solid lines represent our theoretical model, while the crosses indicate results obtained from simulations. The theoretical model is drawn using the observed values for $d_{\text{lat}}$ and $d_{\text{lsc}}$. In particular, $d_{\text{lsc}}$ follows a normal distribution with mean $\mu_{\text{lsc}}$ and standard deviation $\sigma_{\text{lsc}}$ that are derived from the observed decoding distances of the $[n_{\text{fft}}, k_{\text{fft}}]_q$ polar codes used in the experiments. The experimental data were obtained by running 4000 iterations of Algorithm 2, with each iteration using an input $(\mathbf{A}, \mathbf{b})$ taken uniformly at random in $\mathbb{Z}_q^{m\times n} \times \mathbb{Z}_q^m$. Parameters used are: – on the left: $q = 241$, $m = 40$, $n = 43$, $n_{\text{lat}} = 35$, $n_{\text{enu}} = 0$, $n_{\text{fft}} = 8$, $k_{\text{fft}} = 3$, $N = 25971$, $\beta_{\text{bkz}} = 32$, $\beta_{\text{sieve}} = 44$, $d_{\text{lat}} = 42.00$, $\mu_{\text{lsc}} = 23.94$ and $\sigma_{\text{lsc}} = 3.38$, – on the right: $q = 241$, $m = 40$, $n = 50$, $n_{\text{lat}} = 42$, $n_{\text{enu}} = 0$, $n_{\text{fft}} = 8$, $k_{\text{fft}} = 3$, $N = 25970$, $\beta_{\text{bkz}} = 35$, $\beta_{\text{sieve}} = 41$, $d_{\text{lat}} = 58.60$, $\mu_{\text{lsc}} = 23.87$ and $\sigma_{\text{lsc}} = 3.30$.

## 5 Application

In this section we give estimates for the cost of our attack against LWE problems from the literature. In particular, we consider NIST PQC standardized candidate KYBER [34]. We summarize in Table 1 the parameters of KYBER and outline the security level required by NIST, along with the attack complexities claimed by MATZOV. Note that MATZOV findings are not widely agreed upon in the

[7] https://github.com/kevin-carrier/CodedDualAttack/tree/main/verifyModel.

cryptographic community as the analysis is based on independence assumptions which were strongly questioned in [18].

The models C0, CC, and CN refer to different cost models for lattice reduction. These models are consistent with those presented in [6], and they can be described as follows:

**C0.** Cost estimates in the "Core-SVP" cost model [7] for Algorithm 1 using [8] as the sieving oracle. This model assumes a single SVP call suffices to reduce a lattice. It also assumes that all lower-order terms in the exponent are zero.

**CC.** Cost estimates in a classical circuit model [2,27,34] for Algorithm 1 using [8] as the sieving oracle. We derive these estimates by implementing the cost estimates from [27], those tagged "asymptotic" (cf. [28]). This is the most detailed cost estimate available in the literature. However, we caution that these estimates, too, ignore the cost of memory access and thus may significantly underestimate the true cost. That is RAM access is not "free" (cf. [28]). This cost model is called "list_decoding-classical" in [2].

**CN.** Cost estimates in a query model for Algorithm 1 using [8] as the sieving oracle. We include this cost model for completeness. This cost model is called "list_decoding-naive_classical" in [2].

These various models rely on [8] for nearest-neighbor search, using fuzzy hashing functions based on product codes. It should be added that [16] pointed out that the original analysis of [8] assumes an ideal case, underestimating the decoding cost and overlooking the suboptimal rate-distortion of product codes. Specifically, [16] estimates that for a sieving dimension of 380, the complexity of the nearest-neighbor search increases by a factor of about $2^6$. Here we kept the same way of computing the costs as in Matzov's paper [27] to keep a fair comparison with their work. Delving further into this topic and replacing for instance the simple product codes with a better approach is outside the scope of this work.

For the same reasons, we only consider the classical RAM model. Adapting our analysis to a more realistic memory access model, such as the one presented in [24], is left as future work. Furthermore, we do not compare our results with the state-of-the-art primal attacks. A fair comparison would require substantial effort, as it involves accounting for many confounding factors, such as those listed in [18, Appendix A]. Achieving a more precise estimate – down to the gate count level, as done for instance in [34] – would demand a significantly more in-depth analysis, which we leave as future work given the already considerable length of this paper. Once again, our goal here is to provide a proof of concept for dual lattice attacks and to help resolve the controversy surrounding them. In line with this objective, we deliberately chose to work with a relatively simple and likely suboptimal dual attack algorithm. There are several potential avenues for improving it, including: (i) allowing false positives and adding a verification step to filter them out, (ii) combining modulus switching with our technique, as it would enable computations in characteristic 2, thereby allowing for a much more efficient fast Fourier transform, (iii) replacing the naive product code in the sieving procedure by a better quantizer... We leave these improvements for future work, as they fall outside the scope of this paper.

**Evaluating the Complexity of Our Dual Attack.** We optimize the time complexity of Algorithm 2, as established in Theorem 4.1, under the assumptions outlined in Lemma 3.2. We assume that $1-\mu \approx 1$, and we constrain the parameters $N$ and $T$ such that $\varepsilon := R\, P_{\mathsf{wrong}}\, q^{k_{\mathsf{fft}}}$ remains close to 1; in particular, in our setting, $\eta$ is always greater than 0.62. Additionally, we select $T$ following Approximation 4.8, ensuring that $P_{\mathsf{good}} \approx \frac{1}{2}$. At the same time, we ensure that $\varepsilon$ remains close to 0. These choices guarantee that the overall success probability[8] of our algorithm is lower-bounded by approximately $0.31 - \varepsilon \approx 0.31$.

Our complexity results are summarized in the last three columns of Table 1. The associated parameters are given in the full version [12, Table C.1], and some relevant intermediate quantities are summarized in [12, Table C.2]. Note that the quantity $d_{\mathsf{lat}}$ is defined from the other parameters as in Lemma 2.8. The mean $\mu_{\mathsf{lsc}}$ of the decoding distance $d_{\mathsf{lsc}}$ and its standard deviation $\sigma_{\mathsf{lsc}}$ are computed by choosing an $[n_{\mathsf{fft}}, k_{\mathsf{fft}}]_q$ polar code and by decoding many (a thousand) random words of $\mathbb{Z}_q^{n_{\mathsf{fft}}}$. For all instances of Kyber, we used a list size of $L=1$ in the decoder (see Sect. 3.3, Lemma 3.3). This list size allows us to achieve a decoding distance close enough to the optimal decoding distance $d_{\mathrm{GV}} \triangleq \sqrt{\frac{n_{\mathsf{fft}}}{2\pi e}}\, q^{1-\frac{k_{\mathsf{fft}}}{n_{\mathsf{fft}}}}$ without incurring additional cost in the complexity. Finally, we provide in the GitHub repository[9] a file verifying that our parameters achieve the complexity claims and verify all the constraints.

**Table 1.** The LWE parameters for Kyber, the security level required by NIST, the claimed $\log_2$ complexity of MATZOV attack as given in [6, Table 2], and the $\log_2$ complexity of our dual attack Algorithm 2.

| Scheme | LWE parameters | | | Security level required by NIST | MATZOV Complexity | | | Complexity of our Algorithm 2 | | |
|---|---|---|---|---|---|---|---|---|---|---|
| | $q$ | $n$ | $\alpha$ | | C0 | CC | CN | C0 | CC | CN |
| Kyber-512 | 3329 | 512 | 3 | AES-128 (143 bits) | 115.4 | 139.2 | 134.4 | **121.8** | **139.5** | **134.5** |
| Kyber-768 | 3329 | 768 | 2 | AES-192 (207 bits) | 173.7 | 196.1 | 190.6 | **173.0** | **195.1** | **189.8** |
| Kyber-1024 | 3329 | 1024 | 2 | AES-256 (272 bits) | 241.8 | 262.4 | 256.1 | **239.0** | **259.7** | **254.6** |

[8] Note that in [27], this success probability was approximately 0.25.
[9] https://github.com/kevin-carrier/CodedDualAttack/tree/main/OptimizeCodedDualAttack.

## References

1. Lattice Attacks on NTRU and LWE: A History of Refinements, pp. 15–40. London Mathematical Society Lecture Note Series, Cambridge University Press (2021)
2. Albrecht, M.R., Gheorghiu, V., Postlethwaite, E.W., Schanck, J.M.: Estimating quantum speedups for lattice sieves. In: Moriai, S., Wang, H. (eds.) ASIACRYPT 2020, Part II. LNCS, vol. 12492, pp. 583–613. Springer, Cham (2020). https://doi.org/10.1007/978-3-030-64834-3_20
3. Albrecht, M.R.: On dual lattice attacks against small-secret LWE and parameter choices in HElib and SEAL. In: Coron, J.-S., Nielsen, J.B. (eds.) EUROCRYPT 2017, Part II. LNCS, vol. 10211, pp. 103–129. Springer, Cham (2017). https://doi.org/10.1007/978-3-319-56614-6_4
4. Albrecht, M.R., Ducas, L., Herold, G., Kirshanova, E., Postlethwaite, E.W., Stevens, M.: The general sieve kernel and new records in lattice reduction. In: Ishai, Y., Rijmen, V. (eds.) EUROCRYPT 2019. LNCS, vol. 11477, pp. 717–746. Springer, Cham (2019). https://doi.org/10.1007/978-3-030-17656-3_25
5. Albrecht, M.R., Faugère, J.C., Fitzpatrick, R., Perret, L.: modulus switching for the BKW algorithm on LWE. In: Krawczyk, H. (ed.) PKC 2014. LNCS, vol. 8383, pp. 429–445. Springer, Heidelberg (Mar (2014)
6. Albrecht, M.R., Shen, Y.: Quantum augmented dual attack. Cryptology ePrint Archive, Paper 2022/656 (2022). https://eprint.iacr.org/2022/656
7. Alkim, E., Ducas, L., Pöppelmann, T., Schwabe, P.: Post-quantum key exchange - a new hope. In: Holz, T., Savage, S. (eds.) USENIX Security 2016, pp. 327–343. USENIX Association (2016)
8. Becker, A., Ducas, L., Gama, N., Laarhoven, T.: New directions in nearest neighbor searching with applications to lattice sieving. In: Krauthgamer, R. (ed.) Proceedings of the Twenty-Seventh Annual ACM-SIAM Symposium on Discrete Algorithms, SODA 2016, Arlington, VA, USA, 10–12 January 2016, pp. 10–24. SIAM (2016).https://doi.org/10.1137/1.9781611974331.ch2
9. Brakerski, Z., Vaikuntanathan, V.: Efficient fully homomorphic encryption from (standard) LWE. In: Ostrovsky, R. (ed.) IEEE 52nd Annual Symposium on Foundations of Computer Science, FOCS 2011, Palm Springs, CA, USA, 22–25 October 2011, pp. 97–106. IEEE Computer Society (2011). https://doi.org/10.1109/FOCS.2011.12
10. Carrier, K., Debris-Alazard, T., Meyer-Hilfiger, C., Tillich, J.: Statistical decoding 2.0: reducing decoding to LPN. In: Advances in Cryptology - ASIACRYPT 2022. LNCS, Springer, Cham (2022). https://eprint.iacr.org/2022/1000
11. Carrier, K., Debris-Alazard, T., Meyer-Hilfiger, C., Tillich, J.P.: Reduction from sparse LPN to LPN, dual attack 3.0. In: Joye, M., Leander, G. (eds.) EUROCRYPT 2024, Part VI. LNCS, vol. 14656, pp. 286–315. Springer, Cham (2024). https://doi.org/10.1007/978-3-031-58754-2_11
12. Carrier, K., Meyer-Hilfiger, C., Shen, Y., Tillich, J.P.: Assessing the impact of a variant of MATZOV's attack. Cryptology ePrint Archive, Paper 2022/1750 (2025). https://eprint.iacr.org/2022/1750
13. Chen, Y.: Réduction de réseau et sécurité concrète du chiffrement complètement homomorphe (2013). https://api.semanticscholar.org/CorpusID:170791320
14. Conway, J.H., Sloane, N.J.A.: Sphere Packings, Lattices and Groups, Grundlehren der mathematischen Wissenschaften, vol. 290. Springer, Cham (1988). https://doi.org/10.1007/978-1-4757-2016-7

15. Ducas, L.: Shortest vector from lattice sieving: a few dimensions for free. In: Nielsen, J.B., Rijmen, V. (eds.) EUROCRYPT 2018. LNCS, vol. 10820, pp. 125–145. Springer, Cham (2018). https://doi.org/10.1007/978-3-319-78381-9_5
16. Ducas, L.: Estimating the hidden overheads in the BDGL lattice sieving algorithm. In: Cheon, J.H., Johansson, T. (eds.) PQCrypto 2022. LNCS, vol. 13512, pp. 480–497. Springer, Heidelberg (2022). https://doi.org/10.1007/978-3-031-17234-2_22
17. Ducas, L., Pulles, L.N.: Accurate score prediction for dual attacks. preprint (2023, preprint)
18. Ducas, L., Pulles, L.N.: Does the dual-sieve attack on learning with errors even work? In: Handschuh, H., Lysyanskaya, A. (eds.) CRYPTO 2023. LNCS, vol. 14083, pp. 37–69. Springer, Cham (2023). https://doi.org/10.1007/978-3-031-38548-3_2
19. Dudgeon, D.E., Mersereau, R.M.: Multidimensional Digital Signal Processing. Prentice Hall Professional Technical Reference (1990)
20. Espitau, T., Joux, A., Kharchenko, N.: On a dual/hybrid approach to small secret LWE. In: Bhargavan, K., Oswald, E., Prabhakaran, M. (eds.) INDOCRYPT 2020. LNCS, vol. 12578, pp. 440–462. Springer, Cham (2020). https://doi.org/10.1007/978-3-030-65277-7_20
21. Guo, Q., Johansson, T.: Faster dual lattice attacks for solving LWE with applications to CRYSTALS. In: Tibouchi, M., Wang, H. (eds.) ASIACRYPT 2021. LNCS, vol. 13093, pp. 33–62. Springer, Cham (2021). https://doi.org/10.1007/978-3-030-92068-5_2
22. Guo, Q., Johansson, T., Stankovski, P.: Coded-BKW: solving LWE using lattice codes. In: Gennaro, R., Robshaw, M. (eds.) CRYPTO 2015. LNCS, vol. 9215, pp. 23–42. Springer, Heidelberg (2015). https://doi.org/10.1007/978-3-662-47989-6_2
23. Jabri, A.A.: A statistical decoding algorithm for general linear block codes. In: Honary, B. (ed.) Cryptography and Coding 2001. LNCS, vol. 2260, pp. 1–8. Springer, Heidelberg (2001). https://doi.org/10.1007/3-540-45325-3_1
24. Jaques, S.: Memory adds no cost to lattice sieving for computers in 3 or more spatial dimensions. IACR Commun. Cryptol. (2024). https://doi.org/10.62056/ay4fbn2hd
25. Korada, S.B., Urbanke, R.: Polar codes are optimal for lossy source coding. IEEE Trans. Inform. Theory **56**(4), 1751–1768 (2010)
26. Lyubashevsky, V., Peikert, C., Regev, O.: On ideal lattices and learning with errors over rings. In: Gilbert, H. (ed.) EUROCRYPT 2010. LNCS, vol. 6110, pp. 1–23. Springer, Heidelberg (2010). https://doi.org/10.1007/978-3-642-13190-5_1
27. MATZOV: Report on the Security of LWE: Improved Dual Lattice Attack (2022). https://doi.org/10.5281/zenodo.6412487
28. Matzov, Apon, D., Bernstein, D.J., Mitchell, C., Ducas, L., Albrecht, M., Peikert, C.: Improved Dual Lattice Attack (2022). https://groups.google.com/a/list.nist.gov/g/pqc-forum/c/Fm4cDfsx65s
29. Meyer-Hilfiger, C., Tillich, J.P.: Rigorous foundations for dual attacks in coding theory. In: Theory of Cryptography Conference, TCC 2023. LNCS, vol. 14372, pp. 3–32. Springer, Cham (2023). https://eprint.iacr.org/2023/1460
30. Micciancio, D., Regev, O.: Lattice-based cryptography. In: Post-quantum Cryptography, pp. 147–191. Springer, Cham (2009)
31. Pouly, A., Shen, Y.: Provable dual attacks on learning with errors. In: Joye, M., Leander, G. (eds.) EUROCRYPT 2024, Part VI. LNCS, vol. 14656, pp. 256–285. Springer, Cham (2024). https://doi.org/10.1007/978-3-031-58754-2_10
32. Regev, O.: On lattices, learning with errors, random linear codes, and cryptography. In: Proceedings of the 37th Annual ACM Symposium on Theory of Computing, Baltimore, MD, USA, 22–24 May 2005, pp. 84–93 (2005). https://doi.org/10.1145/1060590.1060603

33. Schnorr, C.P.: Lattice reduction by random sampling and birthday methods. In: Alt, H., Habib, M. (eds.) STACS 2003. LNCS, vol. 2607, pp. 145–156. Springer, Heidelberg (2003). https://doi.org/10.1007/3-540-36494-3_14
34. Schwabe, P., et al.: CRYSTALS-KYBER. Technical report, National Institute of Standards and Technology (2020). https://csrc.nist.gov/projects/post-quantum-cryptography/round-3-submissions
35. Zamir, R., Feder, M.: On lattice quantization noise. IEEE Trans. Inform. Theory **42**(4), 1152–1159 (1996). https://doi.org/10.1109/18.508838

# Improved Lattice Blind Signatures from Recycled Entropy

Corentin Jeudy(✉) and Olivier Sanders

Orange Labs, Applied Crypto Group, Cesson-Sévigné, France
{corentin.jeudy,olivier.sanders}@orange.com

**Abstract.** Blind signatures represent a class of cryptographic primitives enabling privacy-preserving authentication with several applications such as e-cash or e-voting. It is still a very active area of research, in particular in the post-quantum setting where the history of blind signatures has been hectic. Although it started to shift very recently with the introduction of a few lattice-based constructions, all of the latter give up an important characteristic of blind signatures (size, efficiency, or security under well-known assumptions) to achieve the others. In this paper, we propose another design which revisits the link between the two main procedures of blind signatures, namely issuance and showing, demonstrating that we can significantly alleviate the second one by adapting the former. Concretely, we show that we can harmlessly inject excess randomness in the issuance phase, and then recycle the entropy surplus during showing to decrease the complexity of the zero-knowledge proof which constitutes the main component of the signature. This leads to a blind signature scheme with small sizes, low complexity, and that still relies on well-known lattice assumptions.

**Keywords:** Lattice-Based Cryptography · Blind Signature · Privacy

## 1 Introduction

Introduced by Chaum in 1982, blind signatures [21] are one of the fundamental tools of cryptography for privacy. Contrarily to standard signatures where the signer knows the message $m$ they sign and can trace the signature $s$ they generate in the process, blind signatures aim at hiding both $m$ and $s$ to the signer so as to limit traceability. More precisely, a blind signature comes with an interactive signing protocol where one can get a signature $s$ on a message $m$ such that (1) validity of $s$ can be publicly verified (as is the case with standard signatures) and (2) the signer cannot link $(s, m)$ to a specific issuance. The latter property necessarily implies that $m$ is hidden to the signer at the issuance time, hence the term "*blind signature*".

This feature might seem unwise for those who have classical signature use-cases in mind (e.g., signing a contract) but there are some other applications where blind signatures significantly improve privacy without jeopardizing security. This is typically the case of electronic cash that was introduced by Chaum


Y. Tauman Kalai and S. F. Kamara (Eds.): CRYPTO 2025, LNCS 16000, pp. 477–513, 2025.
https://doi.org/10.1007/978-3-032-01855-7_16

in his seminal work mentioned above. In this context, the signed "message" is essentially a serial number of a coin whose only purpose is to facilitate double-spending detection. For the signer (the "bank" in the e-cash terminology), the only value that matters is the number of signatures it issues as it corresponds to the number of minted coins, not their actual serial numbers. Blinding the latter is then harmless to security while being essential for privacy. Similar situations occur in other use-cases such as electronic voting [11], which led ISO/IEC to standardize blind signatures [32].

In [22], Chaum introduced a first construction which astutely leverages the RSA signing function. It defines a 2-round protocol where the user first transmits a blinded message $c = r^e \cdot \mathcal{H}(m) \bmod N$ where $N$ is the RSA modulus, $e$ is the signer's public key and $r$ is a random element of $\mathbb{Z}_N$. The signer then generates an element $s'$ such that $(s')^e = c \bmod N$ which can be unblinded by computing $s = s'/r$. Indeed, $s^e = \mathcal{H}(m) \bmod N$, meaning that $s$ is a valid RSA signature on $m$. This elegant design has however a downside as no security reduction to a standard assumption is known as of today. This led Bellare et al. [9] to introduce a tailored interactive assumption, one-more-RSA, where the adversary has access to an RSA inverse oracle. Thanks to this oracle, the reduction can easily handle all the signing queries of the EUF-CMA security experiment and then extract the "one-more" RSA inverse from the forgery. It thus allows the reduction to succeed but the security assurances such an assumption provides are arguably lower than those provided by a standard computational assumption.

Another approach, based on the celebrated Schnorr identification protocol [52], was later proposed, with several variants, some of which proven under the discrete logarithm assumption (see [50] and references therein). All these schemes inherit the 3-round approach of Schnorr's sigma protocol and thus require an additional interaction compared to [22]. While the difference might seem insignificant at a time of widespread fast communications, the sigma protocol approach introduces a very subtle issue when several signatures are generated in parallel. This problem was already detected by Pointcheval and Stern [50] who noticed that security can only be proven when a very low limit is enforced on the number of concurrent executions of the protocols. Far from being an artefact of the proof, this problem stems from a very concrete vulnerability studied by Wagner [54]. The resulting ROS attack (Random inhomogeneities in Overdetermined Solvable system of linear equations), later improved in [10] demonstrates the limits of Schnorr's blind signature and its variants. This has led cryptographers to favour two-round designs although we stress that this problem is not inherent to 3-round blind signatures, as shown for example in [26,53] which modify Schnorr's blueprint to circumvent the ROS attack.

The development of efficient zero-knowledge proof systems has led to an alternative approach in the design of blind signatures which was formalized by Fischlin [27]. It essentially consists in (1) issuing a standard signature $s$ on a hiding commitment $c$ to the message $m$ and (2) producing a zero-knowledge proof that $s$ is valid for the committed $m$. This framework actually shares many commonalities with the ones of other privacy-preserving primitives such as group signature [8,23], direct anonymous attestation [17] or anonymous credentials [18] and it is thus natural that all these mechanisms can be implemented with the same building blocks, namely zero-knowledge proofs and so-called signatures with efficient protocols (SEP) [14,19,20,49].

Unsurprisingly, the development of post-quantum blind signatures has proven to be harder. To the best of our knowledge, the first construction was proposed by Rückert [51], and was later improved in [4,15]. These schemes were based on Lyubashevsky's identification protocol [39] which can somehow be seen as the lattice counterpart of Schnorr's protocol. As a consequence, they inherit the limited number of allowed parallel issuances. Worse, these constructions were proven unsafe by Hauck et al. [30] who pointed out errors in their security proofs and even attacks for some of them. In the same paper, the authors proposed a sound construction but with poor performance as blind signatures are 7.73 MB long even when the total number of signatures is limited to 7.

In [1], the authors propose an interesting mix between the original construction of Chaum and the framework of Fischlin. Concretely, the user first generates a commitment $\mathbf{c} = \mathbf{Ar} + \mathcal{H}(m)$ which is inverted by the signer who generates a short $\mathbf{s}$ such that $\mathbf{Cs} = \mathbf{c}$ ($\mathbf{A}$ and $\mathbf{C}$ are public elements and $\mathbf{r}$ is a short random vector). A proof of knowledge of $\mathbf{s}$ is then produced, as in [27]. The first step of the protocol can thus be seen as a transposition of Chaum's approach in the lattice setting, where $\mathcal{H}(m)$ is blinded using $\mathbf{Ar}$ (instead of $r^e$) and then inverted. Unfortunately, it leads to the same problem as in [22]: the reduction is unable to answer signing queries as it does not know any trapdoor for $\mathbf{C}$ in the security game. This led [1] to resort to the same trick as in [9], namely introduce a tailored interactive assumption called one-more-ISIS. The nice performance of [1] comes thus at the cost of a heuristic security.

In [47], del Pino and Katsumata circumvent this problem by using the commitment to the message as a tag in a tag-based trapdoor system akin to [44]. Thanks to this solution, they were able to prove security of their construction under standard assumptions but at the cost of larger signatures (about 100 KB per blind signature).

Very recently, Beullens et al. [12] revisited the first part of the construction in [1] by generating the commitment $\mathbf{c}$ as $\mathbf{Ar} + \mathcal{H}(\mathcal{H}(\mathbf{r}), m)$. This apparently simple modification allows to prove security of the resulting construction under standard assumptions while offering a very attractive signature size (22 KB). Unfortunately, the issuance process requires a proof that $\mathbf{c}$ is well-formed, which is not easy to produce given its reliance on hash functions. The authors suggest to use general-purpose NIZKs but the latter are very complex to implement and are very long to generate (about 20 s per proof according to the authors' estimation), which is likely to affect users' experience.

Overall, when looking at the most advanced post-quantum blind signature schemes from the state-of-the-art, one must then choose between an efficient construction with heuristic security [1], a short and secure blind signature but with an impractical issuance process [12] and a secure construction with larger signatures [47]. As also highlighted in the context of e-cash in a project by the

Swiss national bank [31], there is a need for future research and development on post-quantum blind signatures.

### 1.1 Our Contributions

In this paper, we introduce a new lattice-based blind signature construction which is both efficient and proven secure under standard assumptions. In particular, it comes with practical issuance and verification protocols, as demonstrated by our implementation, and our signatures sizes are slightly smaller than those in [1], namely 41 KB.

Our starting point is the first step of 2-round blind signature issuance protocols. We note that, for all of them, it consists in generating some commitment $\mathbf{c}$ to the (hashed) message $\mathcal{H}(m)$ blinded with some mask depending on a random element $\mathbf{r}$. In the context of cyclic or RSA groups, this mask can usually be removed at the end of the process as illustrated by Chaum's protocol [22] or the ones we could build using some SEP schemes (e.g., [49]). In such a case, $\mathbf{r}$ does not affect the size of the blind signature and this approach therefore seems almost optimal. This is no longer true for lattice constructions [1,12,47] which must carry this randomness into the signature where it is included in the witnesses of the NIZK proof. Although the performance of lattice zero-knowledge proofs have significantly improved over the past few years, as illustrated by the powerful framework of [41], the complexity of the latter is still impacted by (1) the dimension of the witnesses vector and (2) the size of the witnesses as larger witnesses requires larger masks and in turn a larger modulus. As a consequence, the papers above naturally choose the minimal parameters for $\mathbf{r}$ so as to ensure concealment of $\mathcal{H}(m)$ (through a mask $\mathbf{Ar}$) while minimizing the impact on the proof size.

In this paper, we take the opposite view. We choose a dimension and parameters for $\mathbf{r}$ which are much larger than what is necessary to hide $\mathcal{H}(m)$ in the issuance process, but then recycle the remaining entropy to directly mask large parts of the preimage $\mathbf{s}$ so as to reduce the whole witness size in the NIZK proof. As we will explain, we can design our protocol in such a way that the negative impact of larger $\mathbf{r}$ is largely offset by the positive impact of smaller NIZK proofs.

Let us consider the following basic blind signature scheme where the user first blinds the message $\mathcal{H}(m)$ by computing a commitment $\mathbf{c} = \mathbf{Ar} + \mathbf{d}\mathcal{H}(m)$ (for some public $\mathbf{d}$) and then obtain a short $\mathbf{s}'$ from the signer such that $\mathbf{Cs}' = \mathbf{c}$ for a public matrix $\mathbf{C}$. Our first remark is that, by enforcing mild requirements on $\mathbf{C}$, one can set $\mathbf{A} = \mathbf{C}$ without jeopardizing blindness. In such a case, we usually end up with a vector $\mathbf{r}$ of higher dimension (because $\mathbf{A}$ has generally less columns than $\mathbf{C}$) but we can then merge $\mathbf{s}'$ and $\mathbf{r}$ since we now have $\mathbf{A}(\mathbf{s}' - \mathbf{r}) = \mathbf{d}\mathcal{H}(m)$. At this stage, compared to the classical approach, we thus only need a proof of knowledge of a unique vector $(\mathbf{s}' - \mathbf{r})$ instead of two vectors $\mathbf{s}'$ and $\mathbf{r}$, which already reduces the proof size.

However, when we look at the new relation $\mathbf{A}(\mathbf{s}' - \mathbf{r}) = \mathbf{d}\mathcal{H}(m)$, we can make the following comments. The first one is that the size of $\mathbf{r}$ moderately impacts the one of $\mathbf{s} = (\mathbf{s}' - \mathbf{r})$ as long as the coefficients of $\mathbf{r}$ remain smaller than those of $\mathbf{s}'$. In other words, trying to make $\mathbf{r}$ as small as possible has only very limited impacts on the resulting vector $\mathbf{s}$. The second one is that our approach leads $\mathbf{r}$ to play two roles. As in previous post-quantum blind signatures schemes, it is still the key to blind $m$. But now, it also acts as some perturbation of the preimage $\mathbf{s}'$ which is very much akin to the one used in the preimage sampling process of [44]. While we cannot use the convolution results of [46] to conclude in our case, we can still recycle a large part of the entropy of $\mathbf{r}$ to blind parts of $\mathbf{s}'$. More precisely, we show in our paper that we can fully disclose the lower part (i.e., the lower bits) of each element in $\mathbf{s}$ as they are perfectly blinded by the remaining entropy of $\mathbf{r}$. It thus only remains to hide the higher part of $\mathbf{s}$ in a zero-knowledge proof whose size is significantly smaller than the one of the classical approach where the whole vector $\mathbf{s}$ would have been hidden. Obviously the amount of bits of $\mathbf{s}$ we can safely leak directly depends on the size of $\mathbf{r}$ but, as mentioned in our first remark, we can harmlessly increase the latter as long as we remain under a reasonable threshold. In other words, we rely on the somewhat counter-intuitive reasoning: the more we increase $\mathbf{r}$, the smaller is our blind signature.

If we were to rely on an interactive argument, such as one-more-ISIS, we could prove security with only a few tweaks. Indeed, we would leverage the oracle to handle signing queries and would extract the one-more-ISIS solution from the forgery. However, as we restrict ourselves to standard assumptions we need to adapt our protocol. To handle signing queries, we will resort to tag-based pre-image sampling as in [44], which has a very important consequence for our construction. Indeed, instead of using the same matrix $\mathbf{A}$ for all issuances, we will use a matrix $\mathbf{A}_\mathfrak{t}$ which is parametrised by a tag $\mathfrak{t}$ which evolves across issuances. Fortunately, $\mathfrak{t}$ can be efficiently hidden in the zero-knowledge proof as illustrated in e.g. [5,33,42,48] but as the commitment $\mathbf{c} = \mathbf{A}_\mathfrak{t}\mathbf{r} + \mathbf{d}\mathcal{H}(m)$ now depends on it, $\mathfrak{t}$ must be either transmitted by the signer to the user in a prior flow or selected by the user. We show that both options are possible but they lead to different variants with specific features. Concretely, the first option is conceptually the simplest one and yields the shortest blind signatures but it technically makes our protocol 3-round. While this is not ideal, we stress that this does not expose us to the ROS attack due to the very different structure of our protocol. Moreover, contrarily to the Schnorr-style approach, this extra round does not require to store secret values on the signer side in preparation for the third round (as the used tag $\mathfrak{t}$ can be made public), which facilitates state management. Nevertheless, we show for completeness in the full version [34, Sec. 6] that we can make our construction 2-round using the second approach which allows the user to select his own tag. This variant obviously removes this additional round but requires to implement safeguards to prevent a malicious user from selecting the same tag twice. For example, this can be done by maintaining a set of used tags on the signer side (and rejecting new requests associated with a tag in this list) or by deriving deterministically this tag using a hash function evaluated on some public information, when available. In all cases, it requires to work with a larger tag space (to avoid incidental collisions), which in turns affects the structure of $\mathbf{A}_\mathfrak{t}$ (to limit the reduction loss) and hence the system complexity.

In all cases, our blind signature essentially consists in one vector $\mathbf{s}$ whose lower bits can be safely disclosed and whose higher bits are concealed in a zero-knowledge proof. Limiting to a minimum the size of the witness is the key to the performance of the system, leading to a blind signature size of only 41.12 KB when plugged in the framework by [5] which provides all the necessary tools (tag-based pre-image sampling and ZK proofs) for our construction. In addition to achieving such compact sizes while being based on well-known lattice assumptions, our scheme is also reasonably efficient. We provide a proof-of-concept implementation in C[1] which showcases a concrete practicality. In particular, we achieve a reasonably fast issuance proof (the most computationally intensive part of the issuance) of only 500ms with a not yet optimized implementation, which is orders of magnitude more efficient than when relying on general-purpose NIZKs as required by [12].

### 1.2 Comparison with Alternative Approaches

To better understand the rationale behind our recycling strategy and the reasons we get these concrete performance improvements in practice, we need to recall a few facts about the LNP framework [41] that has proven particularly handy for this kind of primitives. To simplify some of our explanations, let us look at the educational example of the common lattice relation $\mathbf{A}\mathbf{w} = \mathbf{u} \bmod qR$ with $\|\mathbf{w}\|_2^2 \leq B^2$. Our explanations below transfer to the (slightly) different relation of our blind signature.

One of the main interesting features of this zero-knowledge framework is its ability to prove quadratic relations modulo $q$, which, combined to approximate range proofs, can be used to prove *exact* euclidean norm bounds on the witness $\mathbf{w}$. The LNP combines a regular Schnorr-like proof (with aborts) through a masked witness $\mathbf{z} = \mathbf{y} + c\mathbf{w}$, with extra commitments and so-called all-but-one-coefficient masks (that are used to embed integer relations like the norm bound proof) to prove the norm bound exactly modulo $q$, as well as an approximate range proof to lift the norm proof to be over $\mathbb{Z}$ instead of $\mathbb{Z}_q$. The core idea of this last component is to prove that the (quadratic) norm relation over $\mathbb{Z}_q$ actually holds over $\mathbb{Z}$ because the approximate bound on the witness exclude any reduction modulo $q$. Unfortunately, this only works for sufficiently large moduli $q$, and in particular those satisfying $q > B_{\text{arp}}^2$, where $B_{\text{arp}} = \alpha B$ is an approximate (larger) bound on $\mathbf{w}$ ($\alpha$ being the slack induced by this approximate proof). As a consequence, one ends up with a modulus $q$ which can be quite large, which in turn affects the zero-knowledge proof-size (which contains commitments and all-but-one-coefficients masks that are inherently close to uniform modulo $q$).

To limit the impact on $q$, one could envision essentially two approaches. The first one consists in removing the exact norm bound requirement, and hence only retain the approximate range proof part of the LNP framework. While this does solve the problem we had with $q$ as it no longer scales with $B^2$, it implies that we can only prove an approximate bound on $\mathbf{w}$, which in turn requires working with

[1] https://github.com/latticeblindsignature/lattice-blind-signature.

much larger parameters to compensate what we lost on security. Concretely, the approximate range proof provides an element $\mathbf{z}_3 = \mathbf{y}_3 + \mathsf{R} \cdot \mathsf{coeffs}(\mathbf{w})$ over $\mathbb{Z}^{256}$, for a Gaussian mask $\mathbf{y}_3$ and a random ternary challenge matrix $\mathsf{R}$. After rejection sampling, the element $\mathbf{z}_3$ can be revealed in the proof and, using a Johnson-Lindenstrauss-like bound, can be used to infer an approximate bound on $\mathbf{w}$. The latter ensures the aforementioned bound $B_{\text{arp}}$ on $\mathbf{w}$, but with a rather large slack $\alpha \approx t \cdot \gamma_3 \cdot \sqrt{4 \cdot 337 \cdot 256/26} \approx 227.5$, where $t$ is the Gaussian tailcut for $\mathbf{z}_3$, and $\gamma_3$ is the slack linked to the rejection sampling rate (our scheme considers a rejection rate of $\sqrt{2}$ which leads to $\gamma_3 \approx 3.01$). The slack must then be taken into account in the security estimation as the extracted witness is typically used to construct an M-SIS solution. When evaluating this M-SIS assumption, one must then take the proven norm $B_{\text{arp}}$, which is bigger than the size $B$ of the original witness. This *multiplicative* slack then requires to increase the modulus $q$ by a factor of roughly $\alpha$ to preserve the same security. In our case, the blindness also requires M-LWE to be hard, whose hardness decreases as $q$ grows. The increase in $q$ must then be compensated by taking a larger lattice dimension, i.e., work over a larger ring or over the same ring but with a larger rank. In any case, it then enlarges the witness dimension, and thus the bound $B$. This snowball effect then requires taking much larger parameters than originally (if we used the exact norm proof), which deteriorates the proof size. Adopting this methodology in our construction while targetting the same security level would give a blind signature of 56.69 KB according to our estimation. This reported proof size accounts for the other steps that are still needed beyond the sole approximate range proof. In particular, one still needs to prove that $\mathbf{w}$ satisfies the correct equation (which is quadratic in our case) and that the opening $\mathbf{z}_3$ is correctly formed as $\mathbf{z}_3 = \mathbf{y}_3 + \mathsf{R} \cdot \mathsf{coeffs}(\mathbf{w})$. The possible gain in the modulus offered by the approximate range proof is then completely diluted by these other steps and the increase in parameters mentioned above, resulting in a larger blind signature.

The second approach is to keep the exact norms proof but artificially reduce the witness norm by writing $\mathbf{w}$ as $\mathbf{w}_L + b_1 \mathbf{w}_H$ for some integer $b_1$, where $\mathbf{w}_L = \mathsf{Low}(\mathbf{w}, b_1)$ and $\mathbf{w}_H = \mathsf{High}(\mathbf{w}, b_1)$ denoting the low and high-order bits respectively. This way, one trades $\mathbf{w}$ for a witness $\overline{\mathbf{w}} = [\mathbf{w}_L, \mathbf{w}_H]$ of lower norm (here $\approx \max\{b_1\sqrt{nM}, B/b_1\}$, with $M$ the dimension of $\mathbf{w}$ over the ring, which saves a factor of roughly $b_1^2$ on the modulus) but larger dimension (twice that of $\mathbf{w}$). This addresses our modulus problem but one must now hide twice as many elements. If we were to look at these components without zero-knowledge proof, the combined bit-size of $\mathbf{w}_L$ and $\mathbf{w}_H$ would equal that of the full vector $\mathbf{w}$. But the LNP proof would contain *masked* openings of these two vectors, i.e., $\mathbf{z}_1 = \mathbf{y}_1 + c\mathbf{w}_L$ and $\mathbf{z}_2 = \mathbf{y}_2 + c\mathbf{w}_H$, whose combined size is now much larger than having a single one $\mathbf{z} = \mathbf{y} + c\mathbf{w}$. Following this approach would then lead to a proof size, and thus a blind signature size, of 58.37 KB with our estimation. Therefore, this latter strategy can only be considered as a tradeoff between the modulus size and the one of masked elements, which makes overall improvements questionable.

The entropy recycling technique that we describe in our paper is an alternative approach that manages to reduce the norm of the witness (and hence $q$) without changing its dimension. The core idea is to inject excessive randomness in the blind issuance process, in anticipation of the decomposition of $\mathbf{w}$ as $\mathbf{w}_L + b_1\mathbf{w}_H$. This way, only $\mathbf{w}_H$ needs to be masked whereas $\mathbf{w}_L$ can be revealed in clear, hence our improvements.

More precisely, the blind issuance process consists in computing a short preimage $\mathbf{v}$ of $\mathbf{u}+\mathbf{c}$ by $\mathbf{A}_t$, where $\mathbf{u}$ is a public parameter (necessary for the security proof) and $\mathbf{c} = \mathbf{A}_t\mathbf{r} + \mathbf{d}\cdot\mathcal{H}(m)$ is a commitment to the (hashed) message $m$. The properties of blind signatures require $\mathbf{c}$ to be hiding but, under M-LWE, this could be achieved by taking a relatively small $\mathbf{r}$. One would then have to prove knowledge of $\mathbf{v}$ and $\mathbf{r}$ when presenting the blind signature, leading $\mathbf{v}$ and $\mathbf{r}$ to become witnesses in the LNP framework, with the problems mentioned above (in particular in the case of $\mathbf{v}$, which is rather large).

Now, if we inject additional entropy in $\mathbf{r}$, we can actually split $\mathbf{r}$ into two separate components $\mathbf{r}^{(0)}$ and $\mathbf{r}^{(1)}$ where

- $\mathbf{r}^{(0)}$ plays the same role as $\mathbf{r}$ before, namely making the commitment hiding,
- $\mathbf{r}^{(1)}$ is extra randomness, blinded by $\mathbf{r}^{(0)}$.

We can then rewrite the relation linking $\mathbf{v}$ and $\mathbf{c}$ as $\mathbf{A}_t(\mathbf{v}-\mathbf{r}^{(1)}) = \mathbf{u}+\mathbf{A}_t\mathbf{r}^{(0)}+\mathbf{d}\cdot\mathcal{H}(m)$. Focusing on $(\mathbf{v} - \mathbf{r}^{(1)})$, we can make the following two comments. First, for an appropriate choice of $\mathbf{r}^{(1)}$, $(\mathbf{v} - \mathbf{r}^{(1)})$ is only marginally larger than $\mathbf{v}$. Second, choosing an appropriate distribution on $\mathbf{r}^{(1)}$ ensures that the lower bits of $(\mathbf{v}-\mathbf{r}^{(1)})$ cannot be linked to $\mathbf{v}$ and thus can be revealed without jeopardizing privacy. If we write $\mathbf{w} = (\mathbf{v} - \mathbf{r}^{(1)})$ to make the link with the second approach described above (the one hiding both $\mathbf{w}_L$ and $\mathbf{w}_H$), we can then write $\mathbf{w}$ as $\mathbf{w}_L + b_1\mathbf{w}_H$, where only $\mathbf{w}_H$ needs to be hidden. We can indeed send $\mathbf{w}_L$ and $\mathbf{z}_2 = \mathbf{y}_2 + c\mathbf{w}_H$, instead of $\mathbf{z}_1 = \mathbf{y}_1 + c\mathbf{w}_L$ and $\mathbf{z}_2 = \mathbf{y}_2 + c\mathbf{w}_H$, hence our improvements. Finally, a careful definition of $\mathbf{r}^{(0)}$ also allows us to merge it with $\mathbf{w}_H$, thus avoiding having to increase the witness dimension, without significantly changing the norm of $\mathbf{w}_H$ ($\|\mathbf{r}^{(0)}\|_\infty \leq 1$ in our case).

Concretely, instead of a proof size of 58.37 KB for the second approach, our scheme only yields a proof size of 35.74 KB. The cost of hiding $\mathbf{w}_L$ in the zero-knowledge proof is then roughly 22.63 KB, which is to be compared to 5.38 KB when sending it in clear with our entropy recycling strategy. Our method thus yields a 4.2x improvement on the size incurred by how $\mathbf{w}_L$ is handled.

Finally, we note that our entropy recycling strategy is currently limited by a very technical point in the security reduction. Indeed, the tag-based approach that we follow to rely on classical computational assumptions leads a reduction where we need to answer a unique query without any trapdoor. This is where we use the flexibility provided by the parameter $\mathbf{u}$. It allows to manage adaptive queries by the adversary, but only to some extent which, in our case, requires to enforce some bounds on $\mathbf{r}$. It then limits the amount of extra randomness we can inject for free. We note that this constraint could be alleviated by weakening the reduction tightness or relying on somewhat interactive assumptions, but this would make security more heuristic and so does not fit our work.

### 1.3 Further Improvements

Following the preprint publication of our contribution, [35] provided a sampler similar to that of [44] which allows to truncate the gadget matrix while being compatible with advanced constructions. They apply it to our construction and show that the reduced dimension improves our blind signature size to 36.28 KB, with a communication transcript of 53.21 KB, with no impact on security. The authors only point out a very mild performance drop of around 30 ms for the sampling of the partial signature $\mathbf{s}'$, which would most likely be compensated by the improvement of the zero-knowledge proof generations and verifications due to the smaller witness dimension. We stress that our construction and performance analysis do not take this recent work into account so as to provide a fair comparison with the state-of-the-art. In particular, all the improvements we claim over existing constructions are due to our approach and not to the results of [35]. We nevertheless note that our contribution and the one in [35] are in fact complementary. We indeed focus on the core construction of blind signatures whereas [35] focuses on improving the instantiation of one of our building blocks, showing that our approach can actually lead to even shorter blind signatures.

## 2 Preliminaries

In this paper, for two integers $a \leq b$, we define $[a, b] = \{k \in \mathbb{Z} : a \leq k \leq b\}$. When $a = 1$, we simply use $[b]$ instead of $[1, b]$. Further, $q$ is a positive integer, and we define $\mathbb{Z}_q = \mathbb{Z}/q\mathbb{Z}$. We may identify the latter with the set of representatives $(-q/2, q/2] \cap \mathbb{Z}$. Vectors are written in bold lowercase letters $\mathbf{a}$ and matrices in bold uppercase letters $\mathbf{A}$. The transpose of a matrix $\mathbf{A}$ is denoted by $\mathbf{A}^T$. The identity matrix of dimension $d$ is denoted by $\mathbf{I}_d$. We use $\|\cdot\|_p$ to denote the $\ell_p$ norm of $\mathbb{R}^d$, i.e., $\|\mathbf{a}\|_p = (\sum_{i \in [d]} |a_i|^p)^{1/p}$ for any positive integer $p$, and $\|\mathbf{a}\|_\infty = \max_{i \in [d]} |a_i|$. We also define the spectral norm of a matrix $\mathbf{A}$ by $\|\mathbf{A}\|_2 = \max_{\mathbf{x} \neq \mathbf{0}} \|\mathbf{A}\mathbf{x}\|_2 / \|\mathbf{x}\|_2$.

### 2.1 Algebraic Number Theory

We now give the necessary notions in algebraic number theory. A more complete background can be found in the full version [34, App. A.1]. We present our results over a power-of-two cyclotomic ring. We take $n$ a power of two and let $R = \mathbb{Z}[x]/\langle x^n + 1\rangle$ be the power-of-two cyclotomic ring of degree $n$. We also define $R_q = \mathbb{Z}_q[x]/\langle x^n + 1\rangle$ for any modulus $q \geq 2$. We sometimes use real-valued polynomials and consider elements in $K_{\mathbb{R}} = \mathbb{R}[x]/\langle x^n + 1\rangle$.

We use $\tau$ to denote the coefficient embedding, i.e., for all $a = \sum_{i \in [0, n-1]} a_i x^i \in R$, $\tau(a) = [a_0 | \dots | a_{n-1}]^T$. We sometimes use $\tau_i(a) = a_i$ to be the projection of $\tau(a)$ onto the $i$-th component. We also denote by $M_\tau$ the multiplication matrix map, defined by the relation $\tau(ab) = M_\tau(a)\tau(b)$. In power-of-two cyclotomic fields, this corresponds to the usual nega-circulant matrix featuring the coefficients of $a$. Then, the conjugate is defined by $a^* = a(x^{-1})$. These notations are extended to vectors and matrices entry-wise, except that the conjugate of a matrix actually corresponds to the conjugate transpose. For an integer $\eta$, we define $S_\eta = \tau^{-1}([-\eta,\eta]^n)$, $\widetilde{S}_\eta = \tau^{-1}([-\eta,\eta-1]^n)$ and $T_\eta = \tau^{-1}([0,\eta]^n)$. We also define the usual vector norms $\|\cdot\|_p$ over $R$ by $\|r\|_p := \|\tau(r)\|_p$, and the spectral norm $\|\mathbf{A}\|_2$ by $\|M_\tau(\mathbf{A})\|_2$.

### 2.2 Lattices

A full-rank *lattice* $\mathcal{L}$ of rank $d$ is a discrete subgroup of $(\mathbb{R}^d,+)$. The *dual lattice* of $\mathcal{L}$ is defined by $\mathcal{L}^* = \{\mathbf{x} \in \text{Span}_{\mathbb{R}}(\mathcal{L}) : \forall \mathbf{y} \in \mathcal{L}, \mathbf{x}^T\mathbf{y} \in \mathbb{Z}\}$. A lattice over $R^d$ is identified with the lattice corresponding to its embedding into $\mathbb{R}^{nd}$. For any $\mathbf{A} \in R_q^{d\times m}$, we define the lattice $\mathcal{L}_q^\perp(\mathbf{A}) = \{\mathbf{x} \in R^m : \mathbf{A}\mathbf{x} = \mathbf{0} \bmod qR\}$, while for any $\mathbf{u} \in R_q^d$, we similarly define $\mathcal{L}_q^{\mathbf{u}}(\mathbf{A}) = \{\mathbf{x} \in R^m : \mathbf{A}\mathbf{x} = \mathbf{u} \bmod qR\}$.

### 2.3 Probabilities

For a finite set $S$, we define $|S|$ to be its cardinality, and $U(S)$ to be the uniform probability distribution over $S$. We also let $\psi_\eta$ be the centered binomial distribution of parameter $\eta \in \mathbb{N}\setminus\{0\}$ defined by the distribution of $\sum_{i\in[\eta]} a_i - b_i$ for $a_1, b_1, \ldots, a_\eta, b_\eta$ independently drawn from $U(\{0,1\})$. We then use $\mathcal{B}_\eta$ to denote the distribution over $R$ whose coefficients follow $\psi_\eta$, i.e., $\tau^{-1}(\psi_\eta^n)$. We use $x \hookleftarrow \mathcal{P}$ to note the action of sampling $x \in S$ according to the probability distribution $\mathcal{P}$. In contrast, we use $x \sim \mathcal{P}$ when the random variable $x$ follows $\mathcal{P}$.

**Probabilistic Norm Bounds.** The preimage sampler of [5], which is an instantiation of [44], requires a bound a priori on the spectral norm of the secret trapdoor $\mathbf{R}$. We use the following heuristically verified bound, used in a variety of works in the structured case, e.g. [28,41,44]. Additionally, the security proof requires bounding $\mathbf{Rm}$ but for $\mathbf{m}$ with integer coefficients. It can be seen as bound on an integer spectral norm $\|\mathbf{R}\|_{2,\mathbb{Z}} = \max_{\mathbf{x}\in R^m\setminus\{\mathbf{0}\}} \|\mathbf{R}\mathbf{x}\|_2/\|\mathbf{x}\|_2$. This quantity is implicitly defined when using this kind of bound as in [5]. We thus use the following heuristic from [5] which is empirically verified.

**Lemma 2.1** (**[5, Lem. 2.2 & 2.4]**). *Let $R = \mathbb{Z}[x]/\langle x^n+1\rangle$ with $n$ a power-of-two. Let $d, m$ be two positive integers. It (heuristically) holds that $\mathbb{P}_{\mathbf{R}\sim\mathcal{B}_1^{d\times m}}[\|\mathbf{R}\|_2 \le \frac{7}{10}(\sqrt{d}+\sqrt{m}+6)] = 1/O(1)$ (in particular non-negligible). Also, it heuristically holds that $\mathbb{P}_{\mathbf{R}\sim\mathcal{B}_1^{d\times m}}[\|\mathbf{R}\|_{2,\mathbb{Z}} \le \frac{1}{\sqrt{2}}\sqrt{nd}] = 1/C$ with $C = O(1)$ (in particular non-negligible).*

**Gaussian Measures.** For a center $\mathbf{c} \in \mathbb{R}^d$ and positive definite $\mathbf{S} \in \mathbb{R}^{d\times d}$, we define the Gaussian function $\rho_{\sqrt{\mathbf{S}},\mathbf{c}} : \mathbf{x} \in \mathbb{R}^d \mapsto \exp(-\pi(\mathbf{x}-\mathbf{c})^T\mathbf{S}^{-1}(\mathbf{x}-\mathbf{c}))$. For a countable set $A \subseteq \mathbb{R}^d$, we define the *discrete Gaussian distribution* $\mathcal{D}_{A,\sqrt{\mathbf{S}},\mathbf{c}}$ of support $A$, covariance $\mathbf{S}$ and center $\mathbf{c}$ by its density $\mathcal{D}_{A,\sqrt{\mathbf{S}},\mathbf{c}} : \mathbf{x} \in A \mapsto \rho_{\sqrt{\mathbf{S}},\mathbf{c}}(\mathbf{x})/\rho_{\sqrt{\mathbf{S}},\mathbf{c}}(A)$, where $\rho_{\sqrt{\mathbf{S}},\mathbf{c}}(A) = \sum_{\mathbf{x}\in A}\rho_{\sqrt{\mathbf{S}},\mathbf{c}}(\mathbf{x})$. When $\mathbf{c} = \mathbf{0}$, we omit it from the notations. When $\mathbf{S} = s^2\mathbf{I}_d$, we use $s$ as subscript instead of $\sqrt{\mathbf{S}}$.

For $\mathbf{c} \in K_{\mathbb{R}}^d$ and a positive definite matrix $\mathbf{S} \in \mathbb{R}^{nd \times nd}$, we define the discrete Gaussian distribution over $R^d$ by $\tau^{-1}(\mathcal{D}_{\tau(R^d),\sqrt{\mathbf{S}},\tau(\mathbf{c})})$, which we denote by $\mathcal{D}_{R,\sqrt{\mathbf{S}},\mathbf{c}}$. As coined by Micciancio and Regev [45], we define the *smoothing parameter* of a lattice $\mathcal{L}$, parameterized by $\varepsilon > 0$, by $\eta_\varepsilon(\mathcal{L}) = \inf\{s > 0 : \rho_{1/s}(\mathcal{L}^*) = 1 + \varepsilon\}$.

We first need a Gaussian regularity lemma from [29, Lem. 5.2] generalized to non-spherical distributions. We state it over rings for coherence but it also applies to the integers.

**Lemma 2.2** ([29, **Lem. 5.2**] **adapted**). *Let $d, m, q$ be positive integers, and $\overline{\mathbf{A}} \in R_q^{d \times m}$ such that $\overline{\mathbf{A}} R_q^m = R_q^d$. Then, let $\varepsilon \in (0,1)$ and $\mathbf{S} \in \mathbb{R}^{nm \times nm}$ such that $\mathbf{S} - \eta_\varepsilon(\mathcal{L}_q^\perp(\overline{\mathbf{A}}))^2 \mathbf{I}_{nm}$ is positive semi-definite. We finally define $\mathcal{P} = \overline{\mathbf{A}}\mathcal{D}_{R^m,\sqrt{\mathbf{S}}} \bmod qR$. It holds that $\forall \mathbf{x} \in R_q^d, \mathcal{P}(\mathbf{x}) \in [(1-\varepsilon)/(1+\varepsilon), 1+\varepsilon]q^{-nd}$.*

We now give the standard discrete Gaussian tail bound from [7].

**Lemma 2.3** ([7, **Lem. 1.5**]). *Let $\mathcal{L} \subset \mathbb{R}^d$ be a lattice of rank $d$, and $s > 0$. Then, for all $c > 1/\sqrt{2\pi}$, we have $\mathbb{P}_{\mathbf{x} \sim \mathcal{D}_{\mathcal{L},s}}[\|\mathbf{x}\|_2 > cs\sqrt{d}] < (c\sqrt{2\pi e}e^{-\pi c^2})^d$.*

We use $c_d$ to denote the smallest $c > 1/\sqrt{2\pi}$ such that $(c\sqrt{2\pi e}e^{-\pi c^2})^d \le 2^{-(\lambda + O(1))}$, where $\lambda$ is the implicit security parameter.

**Rejection Sampling.** Our security proof relies on a rejection sampling argument proven in [43].

**Lemma 2.4** ([43, **Lem. 3.2**]). *Let $d$ be a positive integer, and $S \subset R^d$ a set of vectors of Euclidean norm at most $T > 0$. Let $\mathscr{D}_S$ be a distribution over $S$. Let $M > 1$, $\alpha = \sqrt{\pi/\ln M}$ and $s \ge \alpha T$. We then define the following distributions.*

| | |
|---|---|
| $\mathcal{P}_1$ | *Sample $\mathbf{s} \hookleftarrow \mathscr{D}_S$, $\mathbf{y} \hookleftarrow \mathcal{D}_{R^d,s}$ and set $\mathbf{z} = \mathbf{y} + \mathbf{v}$. Then, sample $u \hookleftarrow U([0,1))$. If $\langle \tau(\mathbf{z}), \tau(\mathbf{s})\rangle < 0$ or if $u > \frac{1}{M}\exp(\pi(\|\tau(\mathbf{s})\|_2^2 - 2\langle \tau(\mathbf{z}), \tau(\mathbf{s})\rangle)/s^2)$, output $\perp$. Otherwise, output $(\mathbf{s}, \mathbf{z})$.* |
| $\mathcal{P}_2$ | *Sample $\mathbf{s} \hookleftarrow \mathscr{D}_S$, and $\mathbf{z} \hookleftarrow \mathcal{D}_{R^d,s}$. Then, sample $u \hookleftarrow U([0,1))$. If $\langle \tau(\mathbf{z}), \tau(\mathbf{s})\rangle < 0$ or if $u > \frac{1}{M}$, output $\perp$. Otherwise, output $(\mathbf{s}, \mathbf{z})$.* |

*Conditioned on not aborting, it holds that $\mathcal{P}_1$ and $\mathcal{P}_2$ are identical.*

## 2.4 High and Low Decomposition

Our blind signature scheme relies on decomposing some vectors into low order bits and high order bits, so as to only hide the high part. For that, we use the decomposition functions from [25] but tweaked to meet the requirements of our system. We consider $b$ to be a power of two. We define the following three functions.

$$\begin{aligned}\mathsf{High}(x,b) &= 2\lfloor x/2b \rfloor + 1\\ \mathsf{Low}(x,b) &= x - b \cdot \mathsf{High}(x,b)\\ \mathsf{Decompose}(x,b) &= (\mathsf{High}(x,b), \mathsf{Low}(x,b))\end{aligned}$$

where it directly holds that $\mathsf{Low}(x, b) + b \cdot \mathsf{High}(x, b) = x$. To prove the security of our scheme, we need the following two lemmas related to the low and high order distribution of a uniform variable. The proofs are provided in the full version [34, Sec. 2.4] for completeness.

**Lemma 2.5.** *Let $b$ be a power of two. It holds that* $\mathsf{Low}(U([-2b, 2b-1]), b) = U([-b, b-1])$ *and* $\mathsf{High}(U([-2b, 2b-1]), b) = U(\{-1, 1\})$. *Additionally, it holds that* $U([-b, b-1]) + b \cdot U(\{-1, 1\}) = U([-2b, 2b-1])$.

The motivation for this decomposition is to (1) minimize the size of $x$, while (2) still having independent low and high part when $x$ is uniform, and (3) still have enough entropy in the high bits. The latter two points will be essential for proving security of our construction. Another property we need from our decomposition is the invariance of the uniform distribution by shift, which we state in the following.

**Lemma 2.6.** *Let $b$ be a power of two. It holds that for any $y \in \mathbb{Z}$,* $\mathsf{Low}(y + U([-b, b-1]), b) = U([-b, b-1])$.

## 2.5 Hardness Assumptions

The security of our blind signature is based on the *Module Learning With Errors* (M-LWE) and *Module Short Integer Solution* (M-SIS) problems [37]. We consider both problems in their Hermite Normal Form.

**Definition 2.1 (M-LWE).** *Let $R = \mathbb{Z}[x]/\langle x^n + 1\rangle$ with $n$ a power-of-two. Let $d, m, k, q$ be positive integers and $\mathscr{D}_r$ a distribution on $R$. The Module Learning With Errors problem* $\text{M-LWE}^k_{n,d,m,q,\mathscr{D}_r}$ *asks to distinguish between the following distributions: (1)* $(\mathbf{A}', [\mathbf{I}_m|\mathbf{A}']\mathbf{R} \bmod qR)$, *where* $\mathbf{A}' \sim U(R_q^{m\times d})$ *and* $\mathbf{R} \sim \mathscr{D}_r^{d+m\times k}$, *and (2)* $(\mathbf{A}', \mathbf{B})$, *where* $\mathbf{A}' \sim U(R_q^{m\times d})$ *and* $\mathbf{B} \sim U(R_q^{m\times k})$. *We define* $\text{Adv}_{\text{M-LWE}}[\mathcal{A}] = |\mathbb{P}[\mathcal{A}(\mathbf{A}', [\mathbf{I}_m|\mathbf{A}']\mathbf{R}) = 1] - \mathbb{P}[\mathcal{A}(\mathbf{A}', \mathbf{B}) = 1]|$ *as the advantage of an adversary $\mathcal{A}$.*

**Definition 2.2 (M-SIS).** *Let $R = \mathbb{Z}[x]/\langle x^n + 1\rangle$ with $n$ a power-of-two. Let $d, m, q$ be positive integers and $\beta > 0$ with $m > d$. The Module Short Integer Solution problem in Hermite Normal Form* $\text{M-SIS}_{n,d,m,q,\beta}$ *asks to find* $\mathbf{x} \in \mathcal{L}_q^{\perp}([\mathbf{I}_d|\mathbf{A}'])\backslash\{\mathbf{0}\}$ *such that* $\|\mathbf{x}\|_2 \leq \beta$, *given* $\mathbf{A}' \hookleftarrow U(R_q^{d\times m-d})$. *The advantage of an adversary $\mathcal{A}$ is* $\text{Adv}_{\text{M-SIS}}[\mathcal{A}] = \mathbb{P}_{\mathbf{x}\leftarrow\mathcal{A}(\mathbf{A}')}\left[\mathbf{x} \in \mathcal{L}_q^{\perp}([\mathbf{I}_d|\mathbf{A}']) \wedge 0 < \|\mathbf{x}\|_2 \leq \beta\right]$.

When the parameters are clear from the context, we define the hardness bound of the problem $P \in \{\text{M-LWE}, \text{M-SIS}\}$ as $\varepsilon_P = \sup_{\mathcal{A}\ \mathsf{PPT}} \text{Adv}_P[\mathcal{A}]$.

## 2.6 Blind Signatures

Blind signatures extend the standard notion of digital signatures by requiring a blindness property which prevents the signer from tracing a presented signature to a specific issuance. This blindness logically affects the signing process as the signed message must be concealed but also the unforgeability notion as the signer can only keep track of the number of signed messages, not their actual content.

We use the definition and security properties from [36] that we recall below. A blind signature is a collection of three algorithms $\mathsf{Setup}$, $\mathsf{KeyGen}$, $\mathsf{Verify}$ and an interactive protocol $\mathsf{Sign}$ between a signer and a user. The $\mathsf{Setup}$ algorithm takes as input a security parameter $\lambda$ and outputs the public parameters of the system $\mathsf{pp}$. Then, the $\mathsf{KeyGen}$ algorithm uses $\mathsf{pp}$ and generates a pair of keys $(\mathsf{pk}, \mathsf{sk})$ for the signer. A user can then interact in $\mathsf{Sign}$ with a signer holding $\mathsf{sk}$ to sign a message $m$. In the end, the user gets back a signature $\mathsf{sig}$ and the signer gets no output. Finally, the $\mathsf{Verify}$ algorithm takes as input $\mathsf{pp}, \mathsf{pk}$ as well as the message-signature pair $(m, \mathsf{sig})$ and outputs 1 if the blind signature is valid, and 0 otherwise.

From the security perspective, we expect a blind signature scheme to be *correct*, i.e., honestly issued blind signatures should verify with overwhelming probability, as well as *one-more unforgeable* and *blind*. We precisely define the latter two properties here in accordance with [36]. We note that in the blindness game, the adversary may choose the keys maliciously.

**Definition 2.3 (One-More Unforgeability).** *Let* $(\mathsf{Setup}, \mathsf{KeyGen}, \mathsf{Sign}, \mathsf{Verify})$ *define a blind signature. We define the following game, where* $Q$ *is the maximal number of signature per key pair for which the scheme is proven secure.*

| ***Challenger*** $\mathcal{C}$ | | ***Adversary*** $\mathcal{A}$ |
|---|---|---|
| $\mathsf{pp} \leftarrow \mathsf{Setup}(1^\lambda)$<br>$(\mathsf{pk}, \mathsf{sk}) \leftarrow \mathsf{KeyGen}(\mathsf{pp})$ | $\mathsf{pp}, \mathsf{pk}$ $\longrightarrow$ | |
| | *$N$ **Blind Signature Queries** (with $N \leq Q$)* | |
| | $(\perp, \mathsf{sig}_i) \leftarrow \mathsf{Sign}\langle \mathcal{C}(\mathsf{pp}, \mathsf{pk}, \mathsf{sk}), \mathcal{A}(\mathsf{pp}, \mathsf{pk}, m_i)\rangle$ $\longleftrightarrow$ | *Choose* $m_i$ |
| | $(m_i^\star, \mathsf{sig}_i^\star)_{i \in [N+1]}$ $\longleftarrow$ | *Choose* $(m_i^\star, \mathsf{sig}_i^\star)_{i \in [N+1]}$ |
| $\mathcal{A}$ *wins if* $\forall i \neq j, m_i^\star \neq m_j^\star$<br>*and* $\forall i, \mathsf{Verify}(\mathsf{pk}, m_i^\star, \mathsf{sig}_i^\star, \mathsf{pp}) = 1$ | | |

*The advantage of the adversary* $\mathcal{A}$ *is* $Adv_{Blind}[\mathcal{A}] = |\mathbb{P}[\rho^\star = \rho] - 1/2|$. *We say that the blind signature satisfies blindness if the advantage of any probabilistic polynomial-time adversary* $\mathcal{A}$ *is negligible in* $\lambda$.

**Definition 2.4 (Blindness).** *Let* $(\mathsf{Setup}, \mathsf{KeyGen}, \mathsf{Sign}, \mathsf{Verify})$ *define a blind signature scheme. We define the following game.*

| *Challenger* $\mathcal{C}$ | | *Adversary* $\mathcal{A}$ |
|---|---|---|
| $\mathsf{pp} \leftarrow \mathsf{Setup}(1^\lambda)$ | $\xrightarrow{\mathsf{pp}}$ | |
| | $\xleftarrow{\mathsf{pk}, m_0, m_1}$ | *Choose* $\mathsf{pk}, \mathsf{sk}, m_0, m_1$ |
| $\rho \hookleftarrow U(\{0,1\})$ | | |
| | $(\perp, \mathsf{sig}_0) \leftarrow \mathsf{Sign}\langle \mathcal{A}(\mathsf{pp}, \mathsf{pk}, \mathsf{sk}), \mathcal{C}(\mathsf{pp}, \mathsf{pk}, m_\rho)\rangle$ $\longleftrightarrow$ | |
| | $(\perp, \mathsf{sig}_1) \leftarrow \mathsf{Sign}\langle \mathcal{A}(\mathsf{pp}, \mathsf{pk}, \mathsf{sk}), \mathcal{C}(\mathsf{pp}, \mathsf{pk}, m_{1-\rho})\rangle$ $\longleftrightarrow$ | |
| | $\xrightarrow{\mathsf{sig}_0, \mathsf{sig}_1}$ | |
| | $\xleftarrow{\rho^\star}$ | *Choose* $\rho^\star \in \{0,1\}$ |
| $\mathcal{A}$ *wins if* $\rho^\star = \rho$ | | |

*The advantage of the adversary* $\mathcal{A}$ *is* $Adv_{Blind}[\mathcal{A}] = |\mathbb{P}[\rho^\star = \rho] - 1/2|$. *We say that the blind signature satisfies blindness if the advantage of any probabilistic polynomial-time adversary* $\mathcal{A}$ *is negligible in* $\lambda$.

## 3 Blind Signature from Lattices

We now introduce our new blind signature scheme. It requires a variety of tools that we choose so as to leverage synergies, as explained below.

### 3.1 The Construction

**3.1.1 Message Space** For the sake of simplicity, we consider that all messages $m$ to be signed are elements of $T_1$, that is, elements of $R$ with binary coefficients. As we choose $R$ to be of degree $n \geq 256$, this is by no means a restriction of our scheme as one can deal with a different message space by hashing $m$ onto $T_1$ using a collision-resistant hash function.

**3.1.2 High Level Description** The first stage of our construction is the generation of the signer's key pair through the $\mathsf{KeyGen}$ algorithm. Concretely, the signer generates some short matrix $\mathbf{R}$ and publishes a public key $\mathsf{pk} = \mathbf{B} = \mathbf{AR}$ for some public matrix $\mathbf{A} = [\mathbf{I}|\mathbf{A}']$. This matrix $\mathbf{R}$ will then be used to generate short pre-images of message-dependent syndromes for matrices $\mathbf{A}_\mathfrak{t}$ parametrized by a tag $\mathfrak{t}$. In our case, we will instantiate this pre-image sampler with the elliptic sampler from [5, Alg. 4.2] (which we later call $\mathsf{SamplePre}$) where $\mathbf{A}_\mathfrak{t} = [\mathbf{A}|\mathfrak{t}\mathbf{G} - \mathbf{B}|\mathbf{A}_3]$ and $\mathfrak{t} \in \mathcal{T}_w = \{\mathfrak{t} \in T_1 : \|\mathfrak{t}\|_1 = w\}$.

Steps 1 to 4 of our $\mathsf{Sign}$ algorithm are dedicated to selection, transmission and basic verifications of the tag $\mathfrak{t}$ defining the matrix $\mathbf{A}_\mathfrak{t}$ to be used for this signature.

The goal of the user is now to get a short pre-image of a syndrome depending on $m$ while hiding it. It then computes at steps 5,6,7 and 8 a hiding commitment $\mathbf{c}$ to $m$ but with a few subtleties. Indeed, it will use the whole matrix $\mathbf{A}_\mathfrak{t}$ to hide

$m$ by generating $\mathbf{r} = [\mathbf{r}_1^T|\mathbf{r}_2^T|\mathbf{r}_3^T]^T$ and adding $\mathbf{A}_t\mathbf{r}$ to $\mathbf{d}m$ ($\mathbf{d}$ is a public vector that is necessary for our reduction to M-SIS). As explained in the introduction, this is far more entropy that what is needed to hide $m$ but the surplus will be recycled when generating the blind signature. Actually, the hiding property will only rely on the randomness of the upper bits $\mathbf{r}_{1,H}$ of $\mathbf{r}_1$, hence the separate generation of those bits.

As usual, well-formedness of $\mathbf{c}$ needs to be proven (Step 12) but here we need to introduce a few additional steps (9,10,11) to minimize the reduction loss. Indeed, one of the problems of blindly issuing signatures is that one does not know which signatures presented by the adversary are legitimate and which are forgeries. One strategy could be to systematically extract the signed messages from the proof $\pi_1$ but it will require multiple extractions, which are known to be problematic. To avoid that, we resort to a standard trick where the signed message is also encrypted under some public key $(\mathbf{A}_e, \mathbf{b}_e)$. For normal uses of the protocol, no one knows the corresponding secret key (which is enforced by the generation of $(\mathbf{A}_e, \mathbf{b}_e)$ as outputs of hash functions), which ensures blindness. Conversely, in the security proof, the reduction programs the random oracle to output public keys it controls, which enables to decrypt the ciphertext $(\mathsf{ct}_0, \mathsf{ct}_1)$ and thus to recover $m$. This way, the reduction knows, without extracting a zero-knowledge proof, which messages it has signed and is thus able to identify a forgery. More details on this part are provided in Sect. 3.2.

Once the signer has received and verified the elements transmitted by the user (Steps 13 and 14), it uses the trapdoor $\mathbf{R}$ to generate a short Gaussian pre-image $[\mathbf{v}_1^T|\mathbf{v}_2^T|\mathbf{v}_3^T]^T$ of $\mathbf{u}+\mathbf{c}$. The first vector $\mathbf{v}_1$ is then close to a Gaussian with width $s_1$, while $\mathbf{v}_2, \mathbf{v}_3$ have a smaller width $s_2$ due to the elliptic sampler of [5, Alg. 4.2]. We refer to the latter for more details. The use of the public parameter $\mathbf{u}$, together with the steps 15 to 18, are just peculiarities of the approach of [5] which are necessary to prove security of our construction.

At this stage, the user is supposed to have a short pre-image $(\mathbf{v}_1, \mathbf{v}_2, \mathbf{v}_3)$ of $\mathbf{u}+\mathbf{c}$ as it can recompute $\mathbf{v}_{1,1}$ as indicated in Step 19. If these elements are valid (verification of steps 20 and 21), this means that

$$\begin{aligned}\mathbf{A}\mathbf{v}_1 + (\mathrm{t}\mathbf{G} - \mathbf{B})\mathbf{v}_2 + \mathbf{A}_3\mathbf{v}_3 &= \mathbf{u} + \mathbf{c} \\ &= \mathbf{u} + \mathbf{A}\mathbf{r}_1 + (\mathrm{t}\mathbf{G} - \mathbf{B})\mathbf{r}_2 + \mathbf{A}_3\mathbf{r}_3 + \mathbf{d}m\end{aligned}$$

and thus that

$$\mathbf{A}(\mathbf{v}_1 - \mathbf{r}_1) + (\mathrm{t}\mathbf{G} - \mathbf{B})(\mathbf{v}_2 - \mathbf{r}_2) + \mathbf{A}_3(\mathbf{v}_3 - \mathbf{r}_3) = \mathbf{u} + \mathbf{d}m$$

The short vector $(\mathbf{v}_1 - \mathbf{r}_1, \mathbf{v}_2 - \mathbf{r}_2, \mathbf{v}_3 - \mathbf{r}_3)$ is thus a pre-image of $\mathbf{u}+\mathbf{d}m$ but it cannot be included in the blind signature because it depends on $\mathbf{v}_1, \mathbf{v}_2$ and $\mathbf{v}_3$ that are known to the signer. One could resort to zero-knowledge proofs to hide the full vector, as in previous constructions, but this would trade performance for privacy. Our construction departs from this approach by noticing that $\mathbf{r}_{1,L}$ (the lower bits of $\mathbf{r}_1$), $\mathbf{r}_2$ and $\mathbf{r}_3$ were actually hidden by $b_1\mathbf{A}\mathbf{r}_{1,H}$ in the commitment $\mathbf{c}$ and can thus, in turn, be used as perfect masks for the lower parts of $\mathbf{v}_1$, $\mathbf{v}_2$

and $\mathbf{v}_3$. This way, only the upper parts ($\mathbf{w}_{1,H}, \mathbf{w}_{2,H}$ and $\mathbf{w}_{3,H}$ in Steps 22 and 23) of $\mathbf{v}_i - \mathbf{r}_i$ need to be hidden in the zero-knowledge proof $\pi_2$ (Step 24) whereas the lower parts ($\mathbf{w}_{1,L}, \mathbf{w}_{2,L}$ and $\mathbf{w}_{3,L}$) can be revealed in clear. In particular, our scheme allows for tweaking the size of $\mathbf{r}_{1,L}, \mathbf{r}_2, \mathbf{r}_3$ to reveal more or less bits. We can then choose them so that the upper parts $\mathbf{w}_{i,H}$ all have roughly the same norms. This makes the zero-knowledge proof $\pi_2$ tighter as it "homogenizes" the witness. If we were to hide the whole vectors $\mathbf{v}_i - \mathbf{r}_i$, the first one $\mathbf{v}_1 - \mathbf{r}_1$ would be much larger than the others thus driving the proof system parameters, which is not optimal. Having small norms as well as an "homogeneous" witness in $\pi_2$ results in significant efficiency gains, which are discussed in Sect. 5.

We now give the formal description of the scheme. The bound $B_1$ and $B_2$ are the verification bounds from the standard model signature of [5]. Concretely, they are set using the Gaussian tail bound of Lemma 2.3 as $B_1 = c_{2nd} s_1 \sqrt{2nd}$ and $B_2 = c_{nk(d+1)} s_2 \sqrt{nk(d+1)}$, where $c_N$ is the tailcut parameter for dimension $N$ defined in the latter lemma.

**Algorithm 3.1: BS.Setup**

**Input:** Security parameter $1^\lambda$ (in unary encoding).

1. Choose a power-of-two $n$ based on the desired security target $\lambda$
2. Choose a positive integer $d$.
3. Choose an odd prime $q$ s.t. $q = 5 \bmod 8$.
4. Choose positive integer $w$. ▷ Hamming weight of tags
5. Choose positive integer $b$. ▷ Gadget base
6. Choose positive integers $b_1, b_2$. ▷ Decomposition bases
7. $\mathcal{T}_w \leftarrow \{\mathsf{t} \in T_1 : \|\mathsf{t}\|_1 = w\}$. ▷ Tag space
8. $k \leftarrow \lceil \log_b q \rceil$.
9. $\mathbf{G} = \mathbf{I}_d \otimes [b^0|\dots|b^{k-1}] \in R_q^{d \times dk}$. ▷ Gadget matrix
10. Choose $\varepsilon > 0$ ▷ typically $\varepsilon \approx 2^{-40}$.
11. $r \leftarrow \sqrt{\ln(2nd(2+k)(1+\varepsilon^{-1}))/\pi}$. ▷ $r \gtrsim \eta_\varepsilon(\mathbb{Z}^{nd(2+k)})$
12. $s_{\mathbf{G}} \leftarrow r\sqrt{b^2+1}$. ▷ Gadget sampling width
13. $s_1 \leftarrow \max\left(\sqrt{\frac{\pi}{\ln(2)}}(n\sqrt{d} + 2b_1\sqrt{2nd}), \sqrt{\frac{2s_{\mathbf{G}}^4}{s_{\mathbf{G}}^2-1}} \cdot \frac{7}{10}(\sqrt{2nd} + \sqrt{ndk} + 6)\right)$. ▷ Top preimage width
14. $s_2 \leftarrow \max(r\sqrt{2b^2+3}, \sqrt{\frac{\pi}{\ln(2)}} b_2 \sqrt{nk(d+1)})$. ▷ Bottom preimage width
15. $\alpha_1 \leftarrow \frac{s_1}{n\sqrt{d}+2b_1\sqrt{2nd}}$ ▷ Rejection sampling slack
16. $\alpha_2 \leftarrow \frac{s_2}{b_2\sqrt{nk(d+1)}}$
17. $M_i \leftarrow \exp(\pi/\alpha_i^2)$ for $i \in [2]$.
18. Select hash functions $\mathcal{H}_1 : \{0,1\}^{256} \to R_q^d$, $\mathcal{H}_2 : \{0,1\}^{256} \to R_q^{d \times d}$, $\mathcal{H}_3 : \{0,1\}^{256} \to R_q^{d \times k}$ and $\mathcal{H}_4 : \{0,1\}^{256} \to R_q^d$
19. $\mathsf{seed} \hookleftarrow U(\{0,1\}^{256})$
20. $\mathbf{d} \leftarrow \mathcal{H}_1(\mathsf{seed})$. ▷ follows $U(R_q^d)$
21. $\mathbf{A}' \leftarrow \mathcal{H}_2(\mathsf{seed})$. ▷ follows $U(R_q^{d \times d})$
22. $\mathbf{A}_3 \leftarrow \mathcal{H}_3(\mathsf{seed})$. ▷ follows $U(R_q^{d \times k})$
23. $\mathbf{u} \leftarrow \mathcal{H}_4(\mathsf{seed})$. ▷ follows $U(R_q^d)$
24. $\mathbf{A} \leftarrow [\mathbf{I}_d|\mathbf{A}'] \in R_q^{d \times 2d}$.

<u>Verifiable Encryption.</u>

25. Choose a prime $p \neq q$ ▷ Verifiable encryption modulus
26. Choose positive integers $m_e, d_e, \eta_e$ ▷ Verifiable encryption parameters
27. Select hash functions $\mathcal{H}_5 : \{0,1\}^{256} \to R_p^{m_e \times d_e}$ and $\mathcal{H}_6 : \{0,1\}^{256} \to R_p^{m_e}$
28. $\mathbf{A}_e \leftarrow \mathcal{H}_5(\mathsf{seed})$. ▷ follows $U(R_p^{m_e \times d_e})$
29. $\mathbf{b}_e \leftarrow \mathcal{H}_6(\mathsf{seed})$. ▷ follows $U(R_p^{m_e})$

**Output:** $\mathsf{pp} = (\lambda, n, d, q, w, b, k, r, s_{\mathbf{G}}, s_1, s_2, \alpha_1, \alpha_2, M_1, M_2, p, m_e, d_e, \eta_e, \mathsf{seed})$.

**Algorithm 3.2: BS.KeyGen**

**Input:** Public parameters $\mathsf{pp}$ as in Algorithm 3.1.

1. $\mathbf{R} \hookleftarrow \mathcal{B}_1^{2d \times dk}$ conditioned on $\|\mathbf{R}\|_2 \leq \frac{7}{10}(\sqrt{2nd} + \sqrt{ndk} + 6)$.
2. $\mathbf{B} \leftarrow \mathbf{AR} \bmod qR \in R_q^{d \times dk}$.

**Output:** $\mathsf{pk} = \mathbf{B}$, and $\mathsf{sk} = \mathbf{R}$.

**Algorithm 3.3: BS.Sign**

**Input:** Signer $S$ with $\mathsf{pp}, \mathsf{pk}, \mathsf{sk}$, state $\mathsf{st}$, and user $U$ with $\mathsf{pp}, \mathsf{pk}$ and message $m \in T_1$.

<u>Signer $S$.</u>
1. $\mathsf{t} \leftarrow F(\mathsf{st})$. ▷ $F : \{0,1\}^{256} \to \mathcal{T}_w$ from [5]
2. $\mathsf{st} \leftarrow \mathsf{st} + 1$
3. Send $\mathsf{t}$ to $U$.

<u>User $U$.</u>
4. **if** $\mathsf{t} \notin \mathcal{T}_w$, **abort**.
5. $\mathbf{r}_{1,L} \hookleftarrow U(\widetilde{S}_{b_1}^{2d})$, $\mathbf{r}_{1,H} \hookleftarrow \tau^{-1}(U(\{-1,1\}^{2nd}))$.
6. $\mathbf{r}_1 \leftarrow \mathbf{r}_{1,L} + b_1 \mathbf{r}_{1,H}$.
7. $\mathbf{r}_2 \hookleftarrow U(\widetilde{S}_{b_2}^{kd})$, $\mathbf{r}_3 \hookleftarrow U(\widetilde{S}_{b_2}^{k})$.
8. $\mathbf{c} \leftarrow \mathbf{A}\mathbf{r}_1 + (\mathsf{t}\mathbf{G} - \mathbf{B})\mathbf{r}_2 + \mathbf{A}_3\mathbf{r}_3 + \mathbf{d}m \bmod qR$.
9. $\mathbf{r}_e \hookleftarrow \mathcal{B}_{\eta_e}^{m_e}$.
10. $\mathsf{ct}_0 \leftarrow \mathbf{A}_e^T \mathbf{r}_e \bmod pR$.
11. $\mathsf{ct}_1 \leftarrow \mathbf{b}_e^T \mathbf{r}_e + \lfloor p/2 \rceil m \bmod pR$.
12. $\pi_1 \leftarrow \mathsf{Prove}_1(\mathsf{statement}_1; \mathbf{r}_1, [\mathbf{r}_2|\mathbf{r}_3], \mathbf{r}_e, m)$. ▷ $\mathsf{statement}_1$ defined in Sec. 3.3
13. Send $(\mathbf{c}, \mathsf{ct}_0, \mathsf{ct}_1, \pi_1)$ to $S$.

<u>Signer $S$.</u>
14. **if** $\mathsf{Verify}_1(\pi_1) = 0$, **abort**.
15. $\mathbf{v}_3 \hookleftarrow \mathcal{D}_{R^k, s_2}$.
16. $\mathbf{v} = [\mathbf{v}_1^T | \mathbf{v}_2^T]^T \leftarrow \mathsf{SamplePre}(\mathbf{R}, \mathbf{A}', \mathbf{u} + \mathbf{c} - \mathbf{A}_3\mathbf{v}_3, \mathsf{t}, s_1, s_2)$.
17. **if** $\|\mathbf{v}_1\|_2^2 > B_1^2$ or $\|[\mathbf{v}_2|\mathbf{v}_3]\|_2^2 > B_2^2$, go to 14.
18. Parse $\mathbf{v}_1$ into $[\mathbf{v}_{1,1}^T | \mathbf{v}_{1,2}^T]^T$ with $\mathbf{v}_{1,1}, \mathbf{v}_{1,2} \in R^d$
19. Send $(\mathbf{v}_{1,2}, \mathbf{v}_2, \mathbf{v}_3)$ to $U$.

<u>User $U$.</u>
20. $\mathbf{v}_{1,1} \leftarrow \mathbf{u} + \mathbf{c} - \mathbf{A}'\mathbf{v}_{1,2} - (\mathsf{t}\mathbf{G} - \mathbf{B})\mathbf{v}_2 - \mathbf{A}_3\mathbf{v}_3 \bmod qR$.
21. $\rho \leftarrow (\|[\mathbf{v}_{1,1}|\mathbf{v}_{1,2}]\|_2^2 \leq B_1^2) \wedge (\|[\mathbf{v}_2|\mathbf{v}_3]\|_2^2 \leq B_2^2)$.
22. **if** $\rho \neq 1$, **abort**.
23. $(\mathbf{w}_{1,H}, \mathbf{w}_{1,L}) \leftarrow \mathsf{Decompose}(\mathbf{v}_1 - \mathbf{r}_{1,L}, b_1) - (\mathbf{r}_{1,H}, \mathbf{0})$
24. $(\mathbf{w}_{i,H}, \mathbf{w}_{i,L}) \leftarrow \mathsf{Decompose}(\mathbf{v}_i - \mathbf{r}_i, b_2)$ for $i \in \{2,3\}$.

25. $\pi_2 \leftarrow \mathsf{Prove}_2(\mathsf{statement}_2; \mathsf{t}, \mathbf{w}_{1,H}, \mathbf{w}_{2,H}, \mathbf{w}_{3,H})$. ▷ $\mathsf{statement}_2$ defined in Sec. 3.3

**Output:** $S$ gets $\perp$, and $U$ gets $\mathsf{sig} = (\mathbf{w}_{1,L}, \mathbf{w}_{2,L}, \mathbf{w}_{3,L}, \pi_2)$.

**Algorithm 3.4: BS.Verify**

**Input:** Public key $\mathsf{pk}$, message $m$, blind signature $\mathsf{sig} = (\mathbf{w}_{1,L}, \mathbf{w}_{2,L}, \mathbf{w}_{3,L}, \pi_2)$, and public parameters $\mathsf{pp}$.
**Output:** $\mathsf{Verify}_2(\pi_2) \wedge (\mathbf{w}_{1,L} \in \widetilde{S}_{b_1}^{2d}) \wedge ([\mathbf{w}_{2,L}|\mathbf{w}_{3,L}] \in \widetilde{S}_{b_2}^{k(d+1)}) \wedge (m \in T_1)$.

Our protocol relies on a set of hash functions to generate the public parameters. While we treat them as distinct functions to clarify their role in our system we note that, in practice, they could be instantiated with the same extended output function, such as SHAKE256, but with different parameters and domain separators.

### 3.2 Verifiable Encryption

The well formedness of the ciphertexts (that may be generated by the adversary) is proven by the zero-knowledge proof $\pi_1$ produced at Step 12. However, the latter only enforces a certain Euclidean bound $B_{r,e}$ on $\mathbf{r}_e^\star$, not that it follows the expected distribution. We thus need to set the parameters so that $\|\mathbf{e}_e^T \mathbf{r}_e^\star\|_\infty < p/4$ based on this sole requirement in order to guarantee a correct decryption. For that, we rely on $\|\mathbf{e}_e^T \mathbf{r}_e^\star\|_\infty \leq \|\mathbf{e}_e\|_2 \cdot \|\mathbf{r}_e^\star\|_2$ and use a concentration bound for the binomial distribution to upper-bound $\|\mathbf{e}_e\|_2$ (which is selected by the challenger and thus follows the prescribed distribution). By applying Hoeffding's inequality on $\|\mathbf{e}_e\|_2^2$, we can obtain a bound of $\|\mathbf{e}_e\|_2 \leq O(\sqrt{\eta_e n m_e/2})$ with overwhelming probability where the asymptotic constant is around $t = 1.15$ for typical parameters (e.g., $n = 256$, $m_e = 7$, $\lambda = 128$, $\eta_e = 1$).

The additional requirement on the verifiable encryption is its security, through the simulation of the public key, and the simulation of ciphertexts for perfectly random keys. We later select parameters so that both can be argued by the M-LWE$_{n,d_e,m_e,p,\mathcal{B}_{\eta_e}}$ assumption, i.e., with $m_e = 2d_e + 1$.

### 3.3 Relations of Zero-Knowledge Arguments

Our blind signature requires two zero-knowledge arguments. The first one, employed in the issuance phase, aims at proving the commitment and the ciphertext are well-formed by proving knowledge of $(\mathbf{r}_1, \mathbf{r}_{23}, \mathbf{r}_e, m) \in R^{2d+k(d+1)+m_e+1}$ such that

$$\mathbf{A}\mathbf{r}_1 + [\mathsf{t}\mathbf{G} - \mathbf{B}|\mathbf{A}_3]\mathbf{r}_{23} + \mathbf{d}m = \mathbf{c} \bmod qR, \quad \|\mathbf{r}_1\|_2 \leq B_{r,1}, \|\mathbf{r}_{23}\|_2 \leq B_{r,2}, \quad m \in T_1$$
$$\mathbf{A}_e^T \mathbf{r}_e = \mathsf{ct}_0 \bmod pR, \quad \mathbf{b}_e^T \mathbf{r}_e + \lfloor p/2 \rceil m = \mathsf{ct}_1 \bmod pR, \quad \text{and} \quad \|\mathbf{r}_e\|_2 \leq B_{r,e},$$

where $B_{r,1} = 2b_1\sqrt{2nd}$, $B_{r,2} = b_2\sqrt{nk(d+1)}$, and $B_{r,e} = t\sqrt{\eta_e n m_e/2}$ and $\mathbf{r}_{23} = [\mathbf{r}_2^T|\mathbf{r}_3^T]^T$. The statement $\mathsf{statement}_1$ then contains all the public elements of the above relation, those not in red. We note here that if we were to deal with another message space and define $m = \mathcal{H}(\mathbf{m})$, there would be no need to prove correct hash evaluation. In particular, our security proofs will not make any assumption on $m$ beyond that it belongs to the set $T_1$.

The second argument is used to finalize the blind signature and proves knowledge of $(\mathbf{w}_{1,H}, \mathbf{w}_{2,H}, \mathbf{w}_{3,H}, \mathfrak{t}) \in R^{2d+k(d+1)+1}$ such that

$$b_1\mathbf{A}\mathbf{w}_{1,H} + \mathfrak{t}\mathbf{G}\mathbf{w}_{2,L} + b_2\mathfrak{t}\mathbf{G}\mathbf{w}_{2,H} - b_2\mathbf{B}\mathbf{w}_{2,H} + b_3\mathbf{A}_3\mathbf{w}_{3,H}$$
$$= \mathbf{u} + \mathbf{d}\cdot m - \mathbf{A}\mathbf{w}_{1,L} + \mathbf{B}\mathbf{w}_{2,L} - \mathbf{A}_3\mathbf{w}_{3,L} \bmod qR,$$
$$\|\mathbf{w}_{1,H}\|_2^2 \le B_1'^2, \quad \|[\mathbf{w}_{2,H}|\mathbf{w}_{3,H}]\|_2^2 \le B_2'^2, \quad \text{and} \quad \mathfrak{t} \in \mathcal{T}_w,$$

where $(\mathbf{w}_{1,L}, \mathbf{w}_{2,L}, \mathbf{w}_{3,L})$ is included in the blind signature, and $B_1' = \lfloor (B_1/b_1 + 3\sqrt{2nd})^2 \rfloor^{1/2}$, and $B_2' = \lfloor (B_2/b_2 + 2\sqrt{nk(d+1)})^2 \rfloor^{1/2}$. The statement $\mathsf{statement}_2$ then contains all the public elements of the above relation, those not in red.

The full description of these arguments is deferred to the full version [34, App. A.3 & A.4] respectively.

## 4 Security Analysis

We now prove the correctness, one-more unforgeability and blindness.

**Theorem 4.1 (Correctness).** *The blind signature of Sect. 3 is correct.*

*Proof.* First, we study the possible aborts of a legitimate signature generation. Since $F$ maps to $\mathcal{T}_w$, the user does not abort at step 4. Then, the bounds $B_{r,i}, B_{r,e}$ are set so as to ensure that the proof generation in step 12 always succeeds except if $\|\mathbf{r}_e\|_2 > B_{r,e}$, which happens with negligible probability due to our choice of binomial tailcut $t$. The verification at step 14 also goes through due to the completeness of the proof system. This holds true for the checks performed on the partial signature $(\mathbf{v}_1, \mathbf{v}_2, \mathbf{v}_3)$ thanks to the correctness of the signature scheme from [5]. Finally, we have to show that the decomposition and bounds are correct for the second argument.

First, we have $\mathbf{w}_{1,L} + b_1\mathbf{w}_{1,H} = \mathsf{Low}(\mathbf{v}_1 - \mathbf{r}_{1,L}, b_1) + b_1\mathsf{High}(\mathbf{v}_1 - \mathbf{r}_{1,L}, b_1) - b_1\mathbf{r}_{1,H} = \mathbf{v}_1 - (\mathbf{r}_{1,L} + b_1\mathbf{r}_{1,H}) = \mathbf{v}_1 - \mathbf{r}_1$. Similarly, we have $\mathbf{w}_{i,L} + b_i\mathbf{w}_{i,H} = \mathbf{v}_i - \mathbf{r}_i$ for $i \in \{2,3\}$. We thus have

$$b_1\mathbf{A}\mathbf{w}_{1,H} + \mathfrak{t}\mathbf{G}\mathbf{w}_{2,L} + b_2\mathfrak{t}\mathbf{G}\mathbf{w}_{2,H} - b_2\mathbf{B}\mathbf{w}_{2,H} + b_3\mathbf{A}_3\mathbf{w}_{3,H}$$
$$= \mathbf{u} + \mathbf{d}\cdot m - \mathbf{A}\mathbf{w}_{1,L} + \mathbf{B}\mathbf{w}_{2,L} - \mathbf{A}_3\mathbf{w}_{3,L} \bmod qR$$

Then, it holds that $\|\mathbf{w}_{1,H}\|_2 \le (B_1 + \|\mathbf{r}_1\|_2 + \|\mathbf{w}_{1,L}\|_2)/b_1 \le B_1'$, because $\mathbf{w}_{1,L}$ has entries in $\widetilde{S}_{b_1}$, and $\mathbf{r}_1$ in $\widetilde{S}_{2b_1}$. Additionally, we have $\|[\mathbf{w}_{2,H}|\mathbf{w}_{3,H}]\|_2 \le (B_2 + \|[\mathbf{r}_2|\mathbf{r}_3]\|_2 + \|[\mathbf{w}_{2,L}|\mathbf{w}_{3,L}]\|_2)/b_2 \le B_2'$, as $\mathbf{r}_i, \mathbf{w}_{i,L}$ has entries in $\widetilde{S}_{b_2}$ for $i \in \{2,3\}$. Generation and verification of the second argument then always succeeds. $\square$

**Theorem 4.2 (One-More Unforgeability).** *The blind signature of Sect. 3 is one-more unforgeable in the random oracle model, based on the hardness of* $\text{M-LWE}_{n,d_e,m_e,p,\mathcal{B}_{\eta_e}}$, $\text{M-LWE}_{n,d,d,q,\mathcal{B}_1}$, $\text{M-SIS}_{n,d,2d+2,q,\beta_{❶}}$, $\text{M-SIS}_{n,d,2d,q,\beta_{❷}}$, *and the soundness of the proof systems* ($\mathsf{Prove}_1, \mathsf{Verify}_1$) *and* ($\mathsf{Prove}_2, \mathsf{Verify}_2$). *More precisely, the advantage of* PPT *adversary in breaking the one-more unforgeability of the blind signature is upper-bounded by*

$$\begin{aligned} &Adv_{OM\text{-}UF}[\mathcal{A}] \\ &\lesssim \varepsilon^{(e)}_{\text{M-LWE}} + \varepsilon^{(2)}_{sound} + 2\max\Big(h^{\circ d}\left(C(|\mathcal{T}_w| - Q)\varepsilon^{❶}_{\text{M-SIS}} + k\varepsilon^{(1)}_{\text{M-LWE}}\right), \\ &\quad C\varepsilon^{(1)}_{\text{M-LWE}} + \frac{1+\varepsilon}{1-\varepsilon}\left(\varepsilon^{(1)}_{sound} + 4M_1M_2h^{\circ d}\left(CQ\varepsilon^{❷}_{\text{M-SIS}} + k\varepsilon^{(1)}_{\text{M-LWE}}\right)\right)\Big) \end{aligned}$$

*where* $\varepsilon^{(i)}_{sound}$ *is the soundness error of* ($\mathsf{Prove}_i, \mathsf{Verify}_i$) *from defined in the full version [34, Lem. A.2 & A.3],* $\varepsilon^{(e)}_{\text{M-LWE}}$ *and* $\varepsilon^{(1)}_{\text{M-LWE}}$ *are the respective hardness bounds of* $\text{M-LWE}_{n,d_e,m_e,p,\mathcal{B}_{\eta_e}}$ *and* $\text{M-LWE}_{n,d,d,q,\mathcal{B}_1}$, *and* $\varepsilon^{❶}_{\text{M-SIS}}$ *and* $\varepsilon^{❷}_{\text{M-SIS}}$ *are the respective hardness bounds of* $\text{M-SIS}_{n,d,2d+m+1,q,\beta_{❶}}$ *and* $\text{M-SIS}_{n,d,2d,q,\beta_{❷}}$. *The constant* $C \approx 2$ *is the one from Lemma 2.1. The function* $h^{\circ d}$ *corresponds to the* $d$*-th composition power of the function* $h$ *defined by*

$$h(x) = k\varepsilon^{(1)}_{\text{M-LWE}} + \delta\left(2k\varepsilon^{(1)}_{\text{M-LWE}} + \delta\left(k\varepsilon^{(1)}_{\text{M-LWE}} + x\right)^{\frac{2\lambda-1}{2\lambda}}\right)^{\frac{2\lambda-1}{2\lambda}},$$

*with*

$$\delta = 1 + Q(\lambda - 1/2) \cdot \left(\left(\frac{1+\varepsilon}{1-\varepsilon}\right)^{12d(n-1)+5}\left(\frac{1+\varepsilon/ndk}{1-\varepsilon/ndk}\right)^{2ndk} - 1\right)^2$$

We note that the advantage bound is rather intricate because of the $d$-th composition power of the function $h$. Fortunately, the authors of [5] provide a comprehensive bound on $h^{\circ d}$ and more explanations on why applying $h^{\circ d}$ only decreases the bit security of its input by only a few bits (typically $2d$ bits which is constant). We refer to the latter for more details on this bound, and we use the actual value of $h^{\circ d}$ when selecting parameters.

*Proof.* At a high level, the proof changes the one-more unforgeability game as follows. The challenger guesses the tag $\mathsf{t}^\star$ that will be included in one of the $Q+1$ produced signatures, hoping that it will actually correspond to a fresh adversarial signature and not a legitimately issued one. Depending on this guess, the challenger will craft the cryptographic material following either the type ❶ or type ❷ approach from [5], while also hiding a decryption key in $\mathbf{b}_e$. For each of the $Q$ emitted signatures, the challenger stores the messages $m_i'$ decrypted from the ciphertexts. Upon reception of the $Q+1$ message-signature $(m_i, \mathsf{sig}_i)_{i\in[Q+1]}$ pairs, the challenger chooses a pair $(m_i, \mathsf{sig}_i)$ such that $m_i$ does not belong to the set of decrypted messages mentioned above. Note that such an index $i$ necessarily exists as there are at most $Q$ distinct decrypted messages. It then extracts the proof included in $\mathsf{sig}_i$, which can be used to solve an M-SIS instance if the included tag is $\mathsf{t}^\star$. We now prove it formally.

We denote $G_0$ to be the original game. For each game $G$, we call $\mathrm{Adv}_G[\mathcal{A}]$ the advantage of $\mathcal{A}$ in winning the one-more unforgeability game in the modified setting of game $G$.

Game $G_1$. We first change the encryption material so that the challenger can embed a secret decryption key. More precisely, the challenger samples $\mathbf{A}_e \hookleftarrow U(R_p^{m_e \times d_e})$, $(\mathbf{s}_e, \mathbf{e}_e) \hookleftarrow \mathcal{B}_{\eta_e}^{d_e+m_e}$ and set $\mathbf{b}_e = \mathbf{A}_e\mathbf{s}_e + \mathbf{e}_e \bmod pR$. Then, when $\mathcal{A}$ queries $\mathcal{H}_5$ and $\mathcal{H}_6$ on $\mathsf{seed}$, it reprograms the random oracles and outputs $\mathbf{A}_e$ and $\mathbf{b}_e$ respectively. A distinguisher between $G_0$ and $G_1$ can then be turned into a distinguisher for $\text{M-LWE}_{n,d_e,m_e,p,\mathcal{B}_{\eta_e}}$ on the instance $(\mathbf{A}_e, \mathbf{b}_e)$. When receiving an instance $(\mathbf{A}_e, \mathbf{b}_e)$, the M-LWE distinguisher would program $\mathcal{H}_5$ and $\mathcal{H}_6$ to output $\mathbf{A}_e$ and $\mathbf{b}_e$ as above. As such, if $\mathbf{b}_e$ is uniform, it perfectly simulates $G_0$ in the random oracle model, and if $\mathbf{b}_e = \mathbf{A}_e\mathbf{s}_e + \mathbf{e}_e \bmod pR$, it simulates $G_1$. The distinguisher between $G_0$ and $G_1$ can then be used to distinguish between these two cases. As a result, we get

$$\mathrm{Adv}_{G_0}[\mathcal{A}] \leq \mathrm{Adv}_{G_1}[\mathcal{A}] + \varepsilon^{(e)}_{\text{M-LWE}},$$

where $\varepsilon^{(e)}_{\text{M-LWE}}$ is the hardness bound of $\text{M-LWE}_{n,d_e,m_e,p,\mathcal{B}_{\eta_e}}$.

Game $G_2$. We now generate all the tags $\{\mathsf{t}^{(i)}; i \in [Q]\}$ at the outset of the game instead of at each signature issuance. The challenger also uses $\mathbf{s}_e$ to decrypt the ciphertext in each of the (at most) $Q$ queries. More precisely, it computes $u^{(i)} = \mathsf{ct_1}^{(i)} - \mathbf{s}_e^T \mathsf{ct_0}^{(i)} \bmod pR$ and defines the coefficients of $m_i' \in T_1$ to be 0 if the corresponding coefficient of $u^{(i)}$ is closer to 0 than to $\lfloor p/2 \rceil$, and 1 otherwise. The challenger then stores the pairs $(m_i', \mathsf{t}^{(i)})$ in a table $\mathsf{T}$. At the end of the game, the challenger receives $((m_i, \mathbf{w}_L^{(i)}, \pi_2^{(i)}))_{i \in [Q+1]}$ from the adversary where all the proofs $\pi_2^{(i)}$ verify and all the $m_i$ are distinct. The challenger then computes $j = \min\{i \in [Q+1] : m_i \notin \mathsf{T}\}$. Then, except with the soundness error $\varepsilon^{(2)}_{\text{sound}}$ of $(\mathsf{Prove}_2, \mathsf{Verify}_2)$ stated in Lemma A.3 of the full version [34, Lem. A.3], it can extract $\pi_2^{(j)}$ and gets $(\mathbf{w}^\star_{1,H}, \mathbf{w}^\star_{2,H}, \mathbf{w}^\star_{3,H}, \mathsf{t}^\star)$ such that

$$\begin{aligned} &b_1\mathbf{A}\mathbf{w}^\star_{1,H} + \mathsf{t}^\star\mathbf{G}\mathbf{w}^{(j)}_{2,L} + b_2\mathsf{t}^\star\mathbf{G}\mathbf{w}^\star_{2,H} - b_2\mathbf{B}\mathbf{w}^\star_{2,H} + b_3\mathbf{A}_3\mathbf{w}^\star_{3,H} \\ &\quad = \mathbf{u} + \mathbf{d}\cdot m_j - \mathbf{A}\mathbf{w}^{(j)}_{1,L} + \mathbf{B}\mathbf{w}^{(j)}_{2,L} - \mathbf{A}_3\mathbf{w}^{(j)}_{3,L} \bmod qR, \\ &\|\mathbf{w}^\star_{1,H}\|_2^2 \leq B_1'^2, \quad \|[\mathbf{w}^\star_{2,H}|\mathbf{w}^\star_{3,H}]\|_2^2 \leq B_2'^2, \quad \text{and} \quad \mathsf{t}^\star \in \mathcal{T}_w. \end{aligned}$$

It then holds that

$$\mathrm{Adv}_{G_1}[\mathcal{A}] \leq \mathrm{Adv}_{G_2}[\mathcal{A}] + \varepsilon^{(2)}_{\text{sound}}.$$

Game $G_3$. We now introduce the branching of our security reduction. At the outset, the challenger samples $\rho \hookleftarrow U(\{1,2\})$. If $\rho = 1$, the challenger expects what we call a type ❶ forgery which corresponds to a one-more forgery where the extracted tag $\mathsf{t}^\star$ from $G_2$ is not in $\{\mathsf{t}^{(i)}; i \in [Q]\}$. On the other hand, if $\rho = 2$, the challenger expects a type ❷ forgery which corresponds to a one-more forgery where the extracted tag is among the emitted ones, i.e., there exists $i \in [Q]$ such that $\mathsf{t}^\star = \mathsf{t}^{(i)}$. The reduction aborts if the guess on the type of the forgery is wrong. As a result, we get

$$\mathrm{Adv}_{G_2}[\mathcal{A}] = 2\mathrm{Adv}_{G_3}[\mathcal{A}].$$

Based on the value of $\rho$ the challenger will then set the cryptographic materials and queries differently. We define $\mathrm{Adv}_G^{❶}[\mathcal{A}]$ to be the advantage of $\mathcal{A}$ in returning a type ❶ one-more forgery in game $G$, and $\mathrm{Adv}_G^{❷}[\mathcal{A}]$ for a type ❷ one-more forgery. Because in $G_3$ the type guess is correct, it holds that $\mathrm{Adv}_{G_3}[\mathcal{A}] \leq \max(\mathrm{Adv}_{G_3}^{❶}[\mathcal{A}], \mathrm{Adv}_{G_3}^{❷}[\mathcal{A}])$. We later introduce changes that may be specific to one branch only. When describing each game, we specify which branch is impacted (❶ or ❷), except if the change impacts both branches.

The first change we introduce is that after sampling $\rho$ and the set of tags, the challenger samples $\mathsf{t}^+ \hookleftarrow U(\mathcal{T}_w \setminus \{\mathsf{t}^{(i)}; i \in [Q]\})$ in branch ❶, and in branch ❷ it samples $i^+ \hookleftarrow U([Q])$ and sets $\mathsf{t}^+ = \mathsf{t}^{(i^+)}$. Because $\mathsf{t}^+$ is not used anywhere yet, it does not change the advantage. Hence, it still holds that

$$\mathrm{Adv}_{G_2}[\mathcal{A}] \leq 2\max\left(\mathrm{Adv}_{G_3}^{❶}[\mathcal{A}], \mathrm{Adv}_{G_3}^{❷}[\mathcal{A}]\right)$$

Game $G_4$ (❷). In branch ❷, the challenger hides a short relation in $\mathbf{d}$. More precisely, it samples $\mathbf{s}$ from $\mathcal{B}_1^{2d}$ such that $\|\mathbf{s}\|_{2,\mathbb{Z}} \leq \sqrt{nd}$ and defines $\mathbf{d} = \mathbf{A}\mathbf{s} \bmod qR$. It then reprograms $\mathcal{H}_1$ so as to output $\mathbf{d}$ when queried on $\mathsf{seed}$. Similarly to the change in $G_1$, we argue this change based on the $\text{M-LWE}_{n,d,d,q,\mathcal{B}_1}$ assumption. The distribution is actually $\mathcal{B}_1$ conditioned on the bound. Because the bound is verified with significant probability, the hardness is the same as that of $\text{M-LWE}_{n,d,d,q,\mathcal{B}_1}$ up to a factor $C \approx 2$. As it only impacts the branch ❷, we have

$$\mathrm{Adv}_{G_3}^{❶}[\mathcal{A}] = \mathrm{Adv}_{G_4}^{❶}[\mathcal{A}], \text{ and } \mathrm{Adv}_{G_3}^{❷}[\mathcal{A}] \leq \mathrm{Adv}_{G_4}^{❷}[\mathcal{A}] + C\varepsilon_{\text{M-LWE}}^{(1)},$$

where $\varepsilon_{\text{M-LWE}}^{(1)}$ is the hardness bound of $\text{M-LWE}_{n,d,d,q,\mathcal{B}_1}$.

Game $G_5$ (❷). We hide a short relation in $\mathbf{u}$ in branch ❷. The challenger samples $\mathbf{v}_1 \hookleftarrow \mathcal{D}_{R^{2d},s_1}$ and $[\mathbf{v}_2^T|\mathbf{v}_3^T]^T \hookleftarrow \mathcal{D}_{R^{k(d+1)},s_2}$, and computes $\mathbf{u} = \mathbf{A}\mathbf{v}_1 + (\mathsf{t}^+\mathbf{G} - \mathbf{B})\mathbf{v}_2 + \mathbf{A}_3\mathbf{v}_3 \bmod qR$. It then reprograms $\mathcal{H}_4$ so that it outputs $\mathbf{u}$ when queried on $\mathsf{seed}$. We use the same argument as from [5] by relying on the regularity lemma of [29, Lem. 5.2] recalled in Lemma 2.2. With our parameter choices, we then get that

$$\mathrm{Adv}_{G_4}^{❶}[\mathcal{A}] = \mathrm{Adv}_{G_5}^{❶}[\mathcal{A}], \text{ and } \mathrm{Adv}_{G_4}^{❷}[\mathcal{A}] \in \left[\frac{1}{1+\varepsilon}, \frac{1+\varepsilon}{1-\varepsilon}\right] \mathrm{Adv}_{G_5}^{❷}[\mathcal{A}],$$

Game $G_6$ (❷). In branch ❷, the tag $\mathsf{t}^+$ is chosen among the tags used in the signing queries. As our goal will be to hide $\mathsf{t}^+$ in the public key while still being able to answer signing queries, we need to change the query $i^+$. All other queries can be answered legitimately. Our goal is to use the hidden relation of $\mathbf{u}$ to answer the $i^+$-th query later. But it also needs to be a correct partial signature, which means we need to extract the message and commitment randomness from $\pi_1^{(i^+)}$. In this game, we thus use the extractor from the soundness property of $(\mathsf{Prove}_1, \mathsf{Verify}_1)$. It thus obtains $(\mathbf{r}_1^+, \mathbf{r}_2^+, \mathbf{r}_3^+, m^+, \mathbf{r}_e^+)$ such that

$$\mathbf{A}\mathbf{r}_1^+ + (\mathsf{t}^+\mathbf{G} - \mathbf{B})\mathbf{r}_2^+ + \mathbf{A}_3\mathbf{r}_3^+ + \mathbf{d}m^+ = \mathbf{c}^{(i^+)} \bmod qR,$$
$$\mathbf{A}_e^T\mathbf{r}_e^+ = \mathsf{ct}_0{}^{(i^+)} \bmod pR, \quad \mathbf{b}_e^T\mathbf{r}_e^+ + \lfloor p/2 \rceil m^+ = \mathsf{ct}_1{}^{(i^+)} \bmod pR,$$
$$\|\mathbf{r}_1^+\|_2 \leq B_{r,1}, \quad \|[\mathbf{r}_2^+|\mathbf{r}_3^+]\|_2 \leq B_{r,2}, \quad \|\mathbf{r}_e^+\|_2 \leq B_{r,e}, \quad m^+ \in T_1$$

except with a soundness error $\varepsilon_{\mathrm{sound}}^{(1)}$, detailed in the full version [34, Lem. A.2].

*Correct Decryption.* Notice here that the verifiable encryption proof ensures that the decrypted message $m'_{i^+}$ matches the one $(m^+)$ that is in the commitment and thus actually signed by the challenger. Indeed, when decrypting, it holds that $m'_{i^+}$ is obtained by decoding $\mathsf{ct}_1{}^{(i^+)} - \mathbf{s}_e^T\mathsf{ct}_0{}^{(i^+)} = \mathbf{e}_e^T\mathbf{r}_e^+ + \lfloor p/2 \rceil m^+ \bmod pR$. Yet, it holds that $\|\mathbf{e}_e^T\mathbf{r}_e^+\|_\infty \leq \|\mathbf{e}_e\|_2\|\mathbf{r}_e\|_2 \leq \|\mathbf{e}_e\|_2 \cdot B_{r,e}$. Then, as $\mathbf{e}_e$ is drawn from $\mathcal{B}_{\eta_e}^{m_e}$, it holds that its norm is bounded with overwhelming probability by $B_{r,e}$ as well. Because we choose $p > 4B_{r,e}^2$, we get that the decryption is correct if the tail bound on $\mathbf{e}_e$ is verified. We insist here that because $\mathbf{r}_e$ is adversarial, we can only deduce a norm bound from the proof extraction but not a particular distribution. In particular, one cannot set $p$ based on a bound on the inner product of two binomial vectors (which would be smaller) and needs to use this worst-case bound on $\mathbf{r}_e$. This correct decryption will be needed to exploit the forgery in the final game.

We then have

$$\mathrm{Adv}_{G_5}^{❶}[\mathcal{A}] = \mathrm{Adv}_{G_6}^{❶}[\mathcal{A}], \text{ and } \mathrm{Adv}_{G_5}^{❷}[\mathcal{A}] \leq \mathrm{Adv}_{G_6}^{❷}[\mathcal{A}] + \varepsilon_{\mathrm{sound}}^{(1)},$$

Game $G_7$ (❷). We further prepare the rejection sampling argument for the $i^+$-th query only. During the $i^+$-th query, the challenger samples $(\mathbf{v}_1^{(+)}, \mathbf{v}_2^{(+)}, \mathbf{v}_3^{(+)})$ legitimately using the preimage sampler, and then rejects based on the value of $(\mathbf{v}_1, \mathbf{v}_2, \mathbf{v}_3)$ which are so far independent of $(\mathbf{v}_1^{(+)}, \mathbf{v}_2^{(+)}, \mathbf{v}_3^{(+)})$. More precisely, it samples $u_1, u_2 \hookleftarrow U([0,1))$. The reduction continues only if $u_1 \leq 1/M_1$, $u_2 \leq 1/M_2$, and $\langle \mathbf{v}_1\, ,\; \mathbf{s}m^+ + \mathbf{r}_1^+ \rangle \geq 0$ and $\langle [\mathbf{v}_2|\mathbf{v}_3]\, ,\; [\mathbf{r}_2^+|\mathbf{r}_3^+] \rangle \geq 0$, otherwise the challenger aborts. We insist that if the challenger does not abort, it answers the query with $(\mathbf{v}_1^{(+)}, \mathbf{v}_2^{(+)}, \mathbf{v}_3^{(+)})$ and not the hidden relation of $\mathbf{u}$. Because the distribution of $\mathbf{v}_i$ are symmetric, the sign conditions are each verified with probability 1/2 independently of $\mathbf{s}m^+ + \mathbf{r}_1^+$ and $\mathbf{r}_j^+$. It then holds that

$$\mathrm{Adv}_{G_6}^{❶}[\mathcal{A}] = \mathrm{Adv}_{G_7}^{❶}[\mathcal{A}], \text{ and } \mathrm{Adv}_{G_6}^{❷}[\mathcal{A}] \leq 4M_1M_2\mathrm{Adv}_{G_7}^{❷}[\mathcal{A}],$$

Game $G_8$ (❷). We now use the relation hidden in $\mathbf{u}$ to answer the $i^+$-th query in branch ❷, and perform rejection sampling to ensure a correct distribution so that the adversary does not notice. After extracting $\pi_1^{(i^+)}$, the challenger samples $u_1, u_2 \hookleftarrow U([0,1))$, computes $\delta_1 = \langle \mathbf{v}_1 + \mathbf{s}m^+ + \mathbf{r}_1^+ , \ \mathbf{s}m^+ + \mathbf{r}_1^+ \rangle$ and $\delta_2 = \langle [\mathbf{v}_2 + \mathbf{r}_2^+ | \mathbf{v}_3 + \mathbf{r}_3^+] , \ [\mathbf{r}_2^+ | \mathbf{r}_3^+] \rangle$. It then aborts the reduction if

$$\delta_1 < 0, \text{ or } u_1 > \frac{1}{M_1} \exp\left(\frac{\pi}{s_1^2} \left(\|\mathbf{s}m^+ + \mathbf{r}_1^+\|_2^2 - 2\delta_1\right)\right),$$

$$\text{or } \delta_2 < 0, \text{ or } u_2 > \frac{1}{M_2} \exp\left(\frac{\pi}{s_2^2} \left(\|[\mathbf{r}_2^+ | \mathbf{r}_3^+]\|_2^2 - 2\delta_2\right)\right).$$

If the challenger did not abort, it constructs

$$\begin{bmatrix} \mathbf{v}_{1,1}^{(i^+)} \\ \mathbf{v}_{1,2}^{(i^+)} \end{bmatrix} = \mathbf{v}_1 + \mathbf{s}m^+ + \mathbf{r}_1^+, \text{ and } \mathbf{v}_2^{(i^+)} = \mathbf{v}_2 + \mathbf{r}_2^+, \mathbf{v}_3^{(i^+)} = \mathbf{v}_3 + \mathbf{r}_3^+,$$

and outputs $(\mathbf{v}_{1,2}^{(i^+)}, \mathbf{v}_2^{(i^+)}, \mathbf{v}_3^{(i^+)})$ as the partial signature in step 18 of Algorithm 3.3. Based on the bounds proven on the $\mathbf{r}_i^+$, the one enforced on $\mathbf{s}m^+$, and the way the parameters $s_1, s_2$ are set in Algorithm 3.1, the rejection sampling argument of Lemma 2.4 shows that the view of the adversary is identically distributed in $G_8$ and $G_7$.

Hybrid Games $G_{j,i}$. For both branches, we now use the hybrid argument used in [5] to hide the tag $\mathrm{t}^+$ in the public key $\mathbf{B}$. The authors rely on a specific trapdoor switching method and define hybrid games $G_{j,i}$ for $j \in [d]$ and $i \in [0,9]$. More precisely, $G_{j,0}$ is essentially $G_8$ but where $\mathbf{B} = [\mathbf{AR}_1 + \mathrm{t}^+\mathbf{G}_1 | \ldots | \mathbf{AR}_{j-1} + \mathrm{t}^+\mathbf{G}_{j-1} | \mathbf{AR}_j | \ldots | \mathbf{AR}_d]$ with $\mathbf{G}_\ell = \mathbf{e}_\ell \otimes [1|b|\ldots|b^{k-1}] \in R^{d \times k}$ where $\mathbf{e}_\ell$ is the zero vector that has a 1 at the $\ell$-th entry. In particular, we note that $G_{1,0} = G_8$. Then, $G_{j,1}$ hides a gadget in $\mathbf{A}_3$ as $\mathbf{A}_3 = \mathbf{G}_j - \mathbf{A}'_3$ for $\mathbf{A}'_3$ drawn uniformly, thus reprogramming $\mathcal{H}_3$ on input seed. In $G_{j,2}$, the challenger hides a relation in $\mathbf{A}_3$ as $\mathbf{A}_3 = \mathbf{G}_j - \mathbf{AR}'_j$ under M-LWE$^k_{n,d,d,q,\mathcal{B}_1}$. In $G_{j,3}$, the challenger uses the partial trapdoor $\mathbf{R}'_j$ instead of $\mathbf{R}_j$ to produce signatures (except for the $i^+$-th query, if $\rho = 2$, which remains unchanged), which is argued by the trapdoor switching lemma of [5, Lem. 4.1]. Then, $G_{j,4}$ simulates the partial public key $\mathbf{B}_j = \mathbf{AR}_j \bmod qR$ and instead samples $\mathbf{B}_j$ uniformly in $R_q^{d \times k}$, which is unbeknownst to $\mathcal{A}$ under M-LWE$^k_{n,d,d,q,\mathcal{B}_1}$. $G_{j,5}$ adds the tag guess as $\mathbf{B}_j = \mathbf{B}'_j + \mathrm{t}^+\mathbf{G}_j$ with $\mathbf{B}'_j$ uniform. In $G_{j,6}$, it re-introduces a partial secret key to get $\mathbf{B}_j = \mathbf{AR}_j + \mathrm{t}^+\mathbf{G}_j$ under M-LWE$^k_{n,d,d,q,\mathcal{B}_1}$. The trapdoor switching is used again in $G_{j,7}$ to use the partial trapdoor $\mathbf{R}_j$ instead of $\mathbf{R}'_j$. In $G_{j,8}$, we replace $\mathbf{AR}'_j$ by a uniform $\mathbf{A}'_3$ again under M-LWE$^k_{n,d,d,q,\mathcal{B}_1}$. Finally, $\mathbf{A}_3$ is again changed to be perfectly uniform in $G_{j,9}$ so that $G_{j,9} = G_{j+1,0}$.

The analysis of the hybrid argument is exactly the same as in [5], and it thus holds that by looping over $j \in [d]$, we have

$$\mathrm{Adv}^{❶}_{G_8}[\mathcal{A}] \lesssim h^{\circ d}\left(\mathrm{Adv}^{❶}_{G_{d,9}}[\mathcal{A}]\right), \text{ and } \mathrm{Adv}^{❷}_{G_8}[\mathcal{A}] \lesssim h^{\circ d}\left(\mathrm{Adv}^{❷}_{G_{d,9}}[\mathcal{A}]\right),$$

where $h^{\circ d}$ corresponds to the $d$-th composition power of the function $h$, which is itself defined by

$$h(x) = k\varepsilon^{(1)}_{\text{M-LWE}} + \delta\left(2k\varepsilon^{(1)}_{\text{M-LWE}} + \delta\left(k\varepsilon^{(1)}_{\text{M-LWE}} + x\right)^{\frac{2\lambda-1}{2\lambda}}\right)^{\frac{2\lambda-1}{2\lambda}},$$

with

$$\delta = 1 + Q(\lambda - 1/2)\cdot\left(\left(\frac{1+\varepsilon}{1-\varepsilon}\right)^{12d(n-1)+5}\left(\frac{1+\varepsilon/ndk}{1-\varepsilon/ndk}\right)^{2ndk} - 1\right)^2$$

Game $G_9$. For both branches, we re-introduce a short relation (without gadget) in $\mathbf{A}_3$. More precisely, it samples $\mathbf{R}'$ from $\mathcal{B}_1^{2d\times k}$ and defines $\mathbf{A}_3 = \mathbf{A}\mathbf{R}' \bmod qR$. It then reprograms the random oracle $\mathcal{H}_3$ so as to output $\mathbf{A}_3$ when queried on seed. We can again argue this change based on the M-LWE$_{n,d,d,q,\mathcal{B}_1}$ assumption. We thus get

$$\text{Adv}^{❶}_{G_{d,9}}[\mathcal{A}] \le \text{Adv}^{❶}_{G_9}[\mathcal{A}] + k\varepsilon^{(1)}_{\text{M-LWE}}, \text{ and } \text{Adv}^{❷}_{G_{d,9}}[\mathcal{A}] \le \text{Adv}^{❷}_{G_9}[\mathcal{A}] + k\varepsilon^{(1)}_{\text{M-LWE}},$$

Game $G_{10}$. In this game, the challenger aborts if the tag guess is incorrect. More precisely, in branch ❶, the adversary must return a type ❶ one-more forgery which means that $\mathsf{t}^+ \notin \{\mathsf{t}^{(i)}; i \in [Q]\}$. Because $\mathsf{t}^+$ is hidden to the view of the adversary, the guess is correct with probability $1/(|\mathcal{T}_w| - Q)$. For branch ❷, the adversary must return a type ❷ one-more forgery meaning there exists $i^\star \in [Q]$ such that $\mathsf{t}^\star = \mathsf{t}^{(i^\star)}$. The challenger thus aborts if $i^+ \neq i^\star$, meaning the guess is correct with probability $1/Q$. We thus get

$$\text{Adv}^{❶}_{G_9}[\mathcal{A}] = (|\mathcal{T}_w| - Q)\text{Adv}^{❶}_{G_{10}}[\mathcal{A}], \text{ and } \text{Adv}^{❷}_{G_9}[\mathcal{A}] = Q\text{Adv}^{❷}_{G_{10}}[\mathcal{A}],$$

Exploiting the one-more forgery. We now explain for each branch how to exploit the one-more forgery outputted by $\mathcal{A}$ to find a solution of a specific M-SIS instance. As the two branches are fairly different, we thus bound $\text{Adv}^{❶}_{G_{10}}[\mathcal{A}]$ and $\text{Adv}^{❷}_{G_{10}}[\mathcal{A}]$ separately. The challenger indeed receives two instances $\overline{\mathbf{A}} = [\mathbf{I}_d|\mathbf{A}'|\mathbf{d}|\mathbf{u}]$ and $\overline{\mathbf{A}}' = [\mathbf{I}_d|\mathbf{A}']$ of M-SIS$_{n,d,2d+2,q,\beta_❶}$ and M-SIS$_{n,d,2d,q,\beta_❷}$ respectively. The first will be used to define the material when $\rho = 1$, while the other will serve for the branch where $\rho = 2$. Depending on the value $\rho$ sampled at the outset, it discards one of these two instances and reprograms $\mathcal{H}_2$ (and $\mathcal{H}_1, \mathcal{H}_4$ when $\rho = 1$) for the relevant material[2] from the M-SIS instance. It then proceeds as in $G_{10}$ following the determined branch.

[2] Recall that in the branch ❶, all the partial signature queries are answered legitimately using the preimage sampler, and there is no hidden relation in $\mathbf{d}$ nor $\mathbf{u}$.

*Branch* ❶. We start with the easier branch to bound $\mathrm{Adv}_{G_{10}}^{❶}[\mathcal{A}]$. It holds that $\mathsf{t}^\star = \mathsf{t}^+$, which means that $\mathsf{t}^\star\mathbf{G} - \mathbf{B} = \mathsf{t}^\star\mathbf{G} - \mathbf{AR} - \mathsf{t}^+\mathbf{G} = -\mathbf{AR} \bmod qR$. We define $\mathbf{w}_1 = \mathbf{w}_{1,L}^{(j)} + b_1\mathbf{w}_{1,H}^\star$ and $\mathbf{w}_{23} = [\mathbf{w}_{2,L}^{(j)}|\mathbf{w}_{3,L}^{(j)}] + b_2[\mathbf{w}_{2,H}^\star|\mathbf{w}_{3,H}^\star]$. The challenger then aborts if $\|[-\mathbf{R}|\mathbf{R}']\mathbf{w}_{23}\|_2 > \sqrt{nd}\|\mathbf{w}_{23}\|_2$. Again, by the Johnson-Lindenstrauss-like bound of [5, Lem. 2.4] recalled in Lemma 2.1 (as $[-\mathbf{R}|\mathbf{R}']$ is indeed drawn from $\mathcal{B}_1$), the challenger continues with probability at least $1/C$ for $C \approx 2$. We then re-write the extraction equation as

$$\mathbf{A}\mathbf{w}_1 + \mathbf{A}[-\mathbf{R}|\mathbf{R}']\mathbf{w}_{23} - \mathbf{d}m_j - \mathbf{u} = \mathbf{0} \bmod qR,$$

i.e., $[\mathbf{I}_d|\mathbf{A}'|\mathbf{d}|\mathbf{u}]\mathbf{x}^\star = \mathbf{0} \bmod qR$ with $\mathbf{x}^\star = [(\mathbf{w}_1 + [-\mathbf{R}|\mathbf{R}']\mathbf{w}_{23})^T|-m_j|-1]^T$. The last coefficient is non zero which ensures $\mathbf{x}^\star \neq \mathbf{0}$. Based on the extracted value, it holds that $\|\mathbf{w}_1\|_2 \leq b_1\sqrt{2nd} + b_1B_1'$, and $\|\mathbf{w}_{23}\|_2 \leq b_2\sqrt{nk(d+1)} + b_2B_2'$. We thus have

$$\|\mathbf{x}^\star\|_2 \leq \sqrt{\left(b_1\left(\sqrt{2nd} + B_1'\right) + \sqrt{nd}\cdot b_2\left(\sqrt{nk(d+1)} + B_2'\right)\right)^2 + n + 1} = \beta_{❶},$$

thus proving that $\mathbf{x}^\star$ is a solution of $\mathrm{M\text{-}SIS}_{n,d,2d+2,q,\beta_{❶}}$. We get $\mathrm{Adv}_{\mathrm{M\text{-}SIS}}[\mathcal{A}] \geq \mathrm{Adv}_{G_{10}}^{❶}[\mathcal{A}]/C$ which leads to

$$\mathrm{Adv}_{G_{10}}^{❶}[\mathcal{A}] \leq C\varepsilon_{\mathrm{M\text{-}SIS}}^{❶}.$$

*Branch* ❷. We now bound $\mathrm{Adv}_{G_{10}}^{❷}[\mathcal{A}]$. Recall we are also in the case where $\mathsf{t}^\star = \mathsf{t}^+$ so that $\mathsf{t}^\star\mathbf{G} - \mathbf{B} = -\mathbf{AR} \bmod qR$. We define $\mathbf{w}_1$ and $\mathbf{w}_{23}$ as in the previous branch and thus obtain the same bounds on their norm from the extraction. We then define $\mathbf{\Delta w}_1 = \mathbf{w}_1 - (\mathbf{v}_1^{(i^+)} - \mathbf{r}_1^+)$ where $\mathbf{v}_1^{(i^+)}$ was part of the partial signature in the $i^+$-th query, and $\mathbf{r}_1^+$ was the randomness extracted in the $i^+$-th query. We also define

$$\mathbf{\Delta w}_{23m} = \begin{bmatrix} \mathbf{w}_{23} - \begin{bmatrix} \mathbf{v}_2^{(i^+)} - \mathbf{r}_2^+ \\ \mathbf{v}_3^{(i^+)} - \mathbf{r}_3^+ \end{bmatrix} \\ m^+ - m_j \end{bmatrix}.$$

The challenger then aborts if $\|[-\mathbf{R}|\mathbf{R}'|\mathbf{s}]\mathbf{\Delta w}_{23m}\|_2 > \sqrt{nd}\|\mathbf{\Delta w}_{23m}\|_2$ which happens with probability at most $1 - 1/C$ for $C \approx 2$ using Lemma 2.1 again. Then, it holds that $\mathbf{A}\mathbf{w}_1 + \mathbf{A}[-\mathbf{R}|\mathbf{R}']\mathbf{w}_{23} - \mathbf{A}\mathbf{s}m_j = \mathbf{u} \bmod qR$. Yet, $\mathbf{u} = \mathbf{A}\mathbf{v}_1 - \mathbf{AR}\mathbf{v}_2 + \mathbf{AR}'\mathbf{v}_3 = \mathbf{A}(\mathbf{v}_1^{(i^+)} - \mathbf{s}m^+ - \mathbf{r}_1^+) - \mathbf{AR}(\mathbf{v}_2^{(i^+)} - \mathbf{r}_2^+) + \mathbf{AR}'(\mathbf{v}_3^{(i^+)} - \mathbf{r}_3^+) \bmod qR$. We can thus rewrite the equation as

$$\mathbf{A}\left(\mathbf{\Delta w}_1 + [-\mathbf{R}|\mathbf{R}'|\mathbf{s}]\mathbf{\Delta w}_{23m}\right) = \mathbf{0} \bmod qR.$$

Because $m_j \notin \mathcal{T}$, it holds that $\mathcal{H}(m_j) \neq m'_{i^+}$. Also, based on the decryption correctness explained in Game $G_6$, it holds that $m'_{i^+} = m^+$, and as such we have $m_j \neq m^+$. Using the same unpredictability argument as in previous works, e.g., [5,33,38,41,42], the unpredictability of $\mathbf{s}$ ensures that $\mathbf{x}^\star = \mathbf{\Delta w}_1 + [-\mathbf{R}|\mathbf{R}'|\mathbf{s}]\mathbf{\Delta w}_{23m}$ is non-zero except with negligible probability. We now bound $\mathbf{x}^\star$. Because of the rejection sampling argument in game $G_8$, it holds that $\mathbf{v}_1^{(i^+)} \sim \mathcal{D}_{R^{2d},s_1}$, and $[\mathbf{v}_2^{(i^+)}|\mathbf{v}_3^{(i^+)}] \sim \mathcal{D}_{R^{k(d+1)},s_2}$. We can then derive bounds on $\mathbf{\Delta w}_1$ and $\mathbf{\Delta w}_{23m}$ using the Gaussian tail bound of Lemma 2.3, and the bounds proven on the $\mathbf{r}_i^+$, as well as the facts that $m^+$ and $m_j$ are in $T_1$. In particular, we get $\|\mathbf{\Delta w}_1\|_2 \leq b_1(\sqrt{2nd}+B_1')+B_1+2b_1\sqrt{2nd}$ ($\approx 2B_1+6b_1\sqrt{2nd}$), and similarly

$$\|\mathbf{\Delta w}_{23m}\|_2 \leq \sqrt{(b_2(B_2'+\sqrt{nk(d+1)})+B_2+b_2\sqrt{nk(d+1)})^2+n}.$$

In the end, we obtain

$$\begin{aligned}\|\mathbf{x}^\star\|_2 &\leq b_1\left(B_1'+3\sqrt{2nd}\right)+B_1+\sqrt{nd}\sqrt{\left(b_2\left(B_2'+2\sqrt{nk(d+1)}\right)+B_2\right)^2+n}\\ &= \beta_{❷},\end{aligned}$$

thus proving that $\mathbf{x}^\star$ is a solution of $\text{M-SIS}_{n,d,2d,q,\beta_{❷}}$. We obtain $\text{Adv}_{\text{M-SIS}}[\mathcal{A}] \geq \text{Adv}^{❷}_{G_{10}}[\mathcal{A}]/C - \mathsf{negl}(\lambda)$ which leads to

$$\text{Adv}^{❷}_{G_{10}}[\mathcal{A}] \leq C\varepsilon^{❷}_{\text{M-SIS}} + \mathsf{negl}(\lambda).$$

<u>Advantage Bound.</u> We can now combine all of the advantage bounds from each game hop from $G_3$, with the derived bounds on the advantages in $G_{10}$. We obtain the following equations.

$$\begin{aligned}\text{Adv}^{❶}_{G_3}[\mathcal{A}] &\lesssim h^{od}\left(C(|\mathcal{T}_w|-Q)\varepsilon^{❶}_{\text{M-SIS}}+k\varepsilon^{(1)}_{\text{M-LWE}}\right),\\ \text{Adv}^{❷}_{G_3}[\mathcal{A}] &\lesssim \varepsilon^{(1)}_{\text{M-LWE}}+\frac{1+\varepsilon}{1-\varepsilon}\left(4CM_1M_2h^{od}\left(CQ\varepsilon^{❷}_{\text{M-SIS}}+k\varepsilon^{(1)}_{\text{M-LWE}}\right)+\varepsilon^{(1)}_{\text{sound}}\right).\end{aligned}$$

Combining these inequalities with the first game hops from $G_0$ to $G_3$ gives the claimed bound on $\text{Adv}_{G_0}[\mathcal{A}]$. □

**Theorem 4.3 (Blindness).** *The blind signature of Sect. 3 is blind in the random oracle model, based on* $\text{M-LWE}_{n,d_e,m_e,p,\mathcal{B}_{\eta_e}}$, $\text{M-LWE}_{n,d,d,q,U(\widetilde{T}_1)}$, *and the zero-knowledge property of* ($\mathsf{Prove}_1, \mathsf{Verify}_1$) *and* ($\mathsf{Prove}_2, \mathsf{Verify}_2$). *More precisely, the advantage of* PPT *adversary in breaking the blindness of the blind signature is upper-bounded by*

$$Adv_{blind}[\mathcal{A}] \leq 2(\varepsilon^{(1)}_{zk}+\varepsilon^{(2)}_{zk}+\varepsilon^{(e)}_{\text{M-LWE}}+\varepsilon^{(2)}_{\text{M-LWE}}),$$

*where* $\varepsilon^{(i)}_{zk}$ *is the zero-knowledge loss of* ($\mathsf{Prove}_i, \mathsf{Verify}_i$) *defined in the full version [34, Lem. A.2 & A.3],* $\varepsilon^{(e)}_{\text{M-LWE}}$ *and* $\varepsilon^{(2)}_{\text{M-LWE}}$ *are the respective hardness bounds of* $\text{M-LWE}_{n,d_e,m_e,p,\mathcal{B}_{\eta_e}}$ *and* $\text{M-LWE}_{n,d,d,q,U(\widetilde{T}_1)}$.

*Proof.* We prove the blindness by a sequence of hybrids where we change the blindness game progressively while proving these changes can be made unbeknownst to the adversary. The game $G_0$ is the original blindness game from Definition 2.4.

Game $G_1$. In this game we first change the way hash queries are handled, especially those to derive the verifiable encryption materials. When $\mathcal{A}$ queries the random oracle $\mathcal{H}_i$ on seed, the challenger samples the matrix or vector uniformly in its space. In particular, on input seed for $\mathcal{H}_2, \mathcal{H}_5, \mathcal{H}_6$, the challenger samples $\mathbf{A}' \hookleftarrow U(R_q^{d \times d})$, $\mathbf{A}_e \hookleftarrow U(R_p^{m_e \times d_e})$ and $\mathbf{b}_e \hookleftarrow U(R_p^{m_e})$ respectively. We need to enforce it so as to embed the different M-LWE challenges. More precisely, we would need to reprogram $\mathcal{H}_5, \mathcal{H}_6$ when arguing the change in $G_3$, and $\mathcal{H}_2$ for $G_5$. In the random oracle model, $G_0$ and $G_1$ are then identical.

Game $G_2$. The challenger now simulates the zero-knowledge proofs involved in both executions of the blind signing protocols. Instead of calling $\mathsf{Prove}_1$ and $\mathsf{Prove}_2$ on the secret data, it calls the simulators $\mathcal{S}_1$ and $\mathcal{S}_2$ without resorting to the secret witnesses. Based on the zero-knowledge properties of both proof systems, Lemmas A.2 and A.3 from the full version [34] yield

$$|\mathrm{Adv}_{G_2}[\mathcal{A}] - \mathrm{Adv}_{G_1}[\mathcal{A}]| \leq 2(\varepsilon_{\mathrm{zk}}^{(1)} + \varepsilon_{\mathrm{zk}}^{(2)})$$

Game $G_3$. In this game, the challenger will further simulate the ciphertexts. For each of the two executions of the blind signature, instead of computing $\mathsf{ct}_0$ and $\mathsf{ct}_1$ legitimately, it samples $\mathbf{u}_0 \hookleftarrow U(R_p^{d_e})$ and $u_1 \hookleftarrow U(R_p)$ and define the ciphertexts as $\mathsf{ct}_0 = \mathbf{u}_0$ and $\mathsf{ct}_1 = u_1 + \lfloor p/2 \rceil m_\rho \bmod pR$ (or with $m_{1-\rho}$ for the other execution). Noticing that the randomness $\mathbf{r}_e$ is no longer used in the proof generation, this change can be argued with the M-LWE$_{n,d_e,m_e,p,\mathcal{B}_{\eta_e}}$ assumption. This argument follows the one we would use to prove the IND-CPA security of the encryption scheme. Here, we already enforced the encryption key to be uniform (i.e., so that the adversary does not have a secret key to decrypt) which results in a slightly simpler argument.

More precisely, we can use a distinguisher $\mathcal{D}$ between $G_2$ and $G_3$ to distinguish a 2-secret M-LWE$_{n,d_e,m_e,p,\mathcal{B}_{\eta_e}}$ instance

$$\begin{bmatrix} \mathbf{A}_e^T \\ \mathbf{b}_e^T \end{bmatrix} [\mathbf{r}_e^{(\rho)} | \mathbf{r}_e^{(1-\rho)}]$$

from uniform. This instance follows the Knapsack formulation of M-LWE, which is equivalent to M-LWE$_{n,d_e,m_e,p,\mathcal{B}_{\eta_e}}$ as shown for example in [16, Sec. 4.1][3]. Given a 2-secret instance $([\mathbf{u}_0^{(\rho)} | u_1^{(\rho)}], [\mathbf{u}_0^{(1-\rho)} | u_1^{(1-\rho)}])$, the distinguisher would proceed as in $G_2$ and $G_3$ except in the generation of the ciphertexts where $\mathsf{ct}_0{}^{(i)} = \mathbf{u}_0^{(i)}$ and $\mathsf{ct}_1{}^{(i)} = u_1^{(i)} + \lfloor p/2 \rceil m_i \bmod pR$. If the instance is uniform, it perfectly

[3] The loss incurred by the reduction is linked to the splitting of $p$. In our case, we can choose $p$ to split into at most $n/4$ factors to keep this loss negligible.

simulates $G_3$ and otherwise it simulates $G_2$. It then holds that

$$|\mathrm{Adv}_{G_3}[\mathcal{A}] - \mathrm{Adv}_{G_2}[\mathcal{A}]| \leq \sup_{\mathcal{D}} \mathrm{Adv}_{G_2,G_3}[\mathcal{D}] \leq 2\varepsilon^{(e)}_{\text{M-LWE}},$$

where $\varepsilon^{(e)}_{\text{M-LWE}}$ is the hardness bound of $\text{M-LWE}_{n,d_e,m_e,p,\mathcal{B}_{\eta_e}}$, and $\mathrm{Adv}_{G_2,G_3}[\mathcal{D}]$ is the advantage of $\mathcal{D}$ in distinguishing the views from $G_2$ and $G_3$.

Game $G_4$. As the messages are now masked by a perfectly random and independent value, we can have the challenger sample the ciphertexts at random directly without using the messages. So it directly samples $\mathrm{ct}_1{}^{(i)} \hookleftarrow U(R_p)$. As $u_1^{(i)}$ was chosen independently of $m_i$, the distribution stays the same and $G_3$ and $G_4$ are then identical.

Game $G_5$. We now change the way the commitment is computed by essentially relying on its hiding property. By decomposing $\mathbf{c}$ into $b_1\mathbf{A}\mathbf{r}_{1,H} + (\mathbf{A}\mathbf{r}_{1,L} + (\mathbf{t}\mathbf{G} - \mathbf{B})\mathbf{r}_2 + \mathbf{A}_3\mathbf{r}_3 + \mathbf{d}m) \bmod qR$, we replace $\mathbf{A}\mathbf{r}_{1,H}$ by a uniform vector. As $\mathbf{r}_{1,H}$ is independent from the rest, this can be done under the $\text{M-LWE}_{n,d,d,q,U(\widetilde{T}_1)}$ assumption. The reason for using only the high-order bits $\mathbf{r}_{1,H}$ and not the whole $\mathbf{r}_1$ is because $\mathbf{r}_{1,L}$ is also used in the masked part $\mathbf{w}_{1,L}$ revealed in the blind signatures. But $\mathbf{r}_{1,H}$ is used nowhere else as we simulate the second zero-knowledge proof. As a result, the challenger samples $\mathbf{t}^{(i)} \hookleftarrow U(R_q^d)$ for each execution and constructs $\mathbf{c}^{(i)} = b_1\mathbf{t}^{(i)} + (\mathbf{t}^{(i)}\mathbf{G} - \mathbf{B})\mathbf{r}_2^{(i)} + \mathbf{A}_3\mathbf{r}_3^{(i)} + \mathbf{d}m_i) \bmod qR$. Using the same reasoning as that of $G_2$-$G_3$ but for the $\text{M-LWE}_{n,d,2d,q,U(\widetilde{T}_1)}$ instance $[\mathbf{I}_d|\mathbf{A}']\mathbf{r}_{1,H} \bmod qR$, we get that

$$|\mathrm{Adv}_{G_5}[\mathcal{A}] - \mathrm{Adv}_{G_4}[\mathcal{A}]| \leq 2\varepsilon^{(2)}_{\text{M-LWE}},$$

where $\varepsilon^{(2)}_{\text{M-LWE}}$ is the hardness bound of $\text{M-LWE}_{n,d,d,q,U(\widetilde{T}_1)}$. Note that for that we need to ensure that $\mathbf{A}'$ is perfectly uniform which is the case due to our change in $G_1$. Also, notice that $\widetilde{T}_1$ does not include zero coefficients which may be unusual. Using the bijection $x \in \{0,1\} \mapsto 2x-1 \in \{-1,1\}$, a trivial reduction shows that $\text{M-LWE}_{n,d,d,q,U(\widetilde{T}_1)}$ is equivalent to $\text{M-LWE}_{n,d,d,q,U(T_1)}$, that is with binary secret/error.

Game $G_6$. We keep modifying the commitment by sampling $\mathbf{t}^{(i)} \hookleftarrow U(R_q^d)$ and computing $\mathbf{c}^{(i)} = \mathbf{t}^{(i)} + (\mathbf{t}^{(i)}\mathbf{G} - \mathbf{B})\mathbf{r}_2^{(i)} + \mathbf{A}_3\mathbf{r}_3^{(i)} + \mathbf{d}m_i) \bmod qR$. Because $b_1$ is a power-of-two less than $q$, it holds that $b_1 \in \mathbb{Z}_q^\times \subset R_q^\times$. As such, $b_1 U(R_q^d) = U(R_q^d)$ which proves that $G_5$ and $G_6$ are identically distributed.

Game $G_7$. As $\mathbf{t}^{(i)}$ is independent from the rest, we can simply sample $\mathbf{c}^{(i)}$ uniformly in $R_q^d$ without using the messages. It then holds that $G_6$ and $G_7$ are identically distributed.

Game $G_8$. Now that the randomness $\mathbf{r}_{1,L}, \mathbf{r}_2, \mathbf{r}_3$ are used nowhere else, we complete our argument by sampling the $\mathbf{w}_{j,L}$ uniformly in $\widetilde{S}_{b_j}$ without resorting to the adversarially chosen signatures $\mathbf{v}_i$. So the challenger, for each of the two blind signature executions, samples $\mathbf{w}_{j,L}^{(i)}$ uniformly with entries in $\widetilde{S}_{b_j}$.

To argue that it is identically distributed, we rely on the fact that our decomposition preserves the invariance of the uniform distribution by shift. It means that $\mathsf{Low}(y+U([-b_j,b_j-1]),b_j) = U([-b_j,b_j-1])$ for any $y \in \mathbb{Z}$ by Lemma 2.6. Applying it coefficient-wise ensures that $G_7$ and $G_8$ are identically distributed.

The final blind signatures $(\mathbf{w}_{1,L}, \mathbf{w}_{2,L}, \mathbf{w}_{3,L}, \pi_2)$, as well as the issuance transcripts, no longer depend on the messages and elements chosen by the adversary. As a result, they are independent of the bit $\rho$ which means the probability that $\mathcal{A}$ finds the correct bit is exactly $1/2$, making its advantage 0. We then have $\mathrm{Adv}_{G_8}[\mathcal{A}] = 0$. By combining the above hybrids, it then holds that $\mathrm{Adv}_{\mathsf{blind}}[\mathcal{A}] \leq 2(\varepsilon_{\mathrm{zk}}^{(1)} + \varepsilon_{\mathrm{zk}}^{(2)} + \varepsilon_{\text{M-LWE}}^{(e)} + \varepsilon_{\text{M-LWE}}^{(2)})$, as claimed. □

# 5 Performance

## 5.1 Parameter Selection

The security relies on a variety of M-SIS and M-LWE assumptions, as well as the soundness and zero-knowledge losses $\varepsilon_{\mathrm{sound}}^{(i)}$ and $\varepsilon_{\mathrm{zk}}^{(i)}$ (that also rely on some M-SIS and M-LWE assumptions identified in Lemmas A.2 and A.3 from the full version [34]). As a result, we have to estimate the hardness of each of them and compute the actual security by taking into account the reduction loss specified in Theorems 4.2 and 4.3. For the M-LWE assumptions, we use the lattice estimator [3] on the unstructured assumptions to determine the minimal BKZ block size $B$ for lattice reduction attacks. We note that algebraic attacks [2,6] or combinatorial attacks [13,54] in our case are more expensive than those based on lattice reduction. We then estimate the hardness bound with $\varepsilon_{\text{M-LWE}} = 2^{-(0.292B+16.4)}$ classically and $\varepsilon_{\text{M-LWE}} = 2^{-(0.257B+16.4)}$ quantumly. For $\text{M-SIS}_{n,d,m,q,\beta}$ assumptions, standard attacks find a smaller-dimensional lattice of dimension $N \in [nd, nm]$ that minimizes the root Hermite factor $\delta_B = \beta^{1/N} q^{-nd/N^2}$, and then we use the formula by Chen [24] to find the BKZ block size from $\delta_B$. More precisely, Chen [24] showed that under the Gaussian heuristic and the Geometric Series Assumption, the root Hermite factor $\delta_B$ of a BKZ-reduced basis with block size $B$ is $\delta_B \approx (B(\pi B)^{1/B}/2\pi e)^{1/2(B-1)}$. Then again, we estimate the hardness bound of said M-SIS instance by $\varepsilon_{\text{M-SIS}} = 2^{-(0.292B+16.4)}$ classically and $\varepsilon_{\text{M-SIS}} = 2^{-(0.257B+16.4)}$ quantumly.

We thus search for parameters $n, d, d_e, q, p$ and also the parameters of the proof systems to get the desired security when plugged into the loss functions and the plethora of assumptions considered in Theorem 4.2 and 4.3. The parameters detailed in the full version [34, App. B] lead to the hardness bounds indicated in Table 1, which still ensures 126 bits of classical security for the one-more unforgeability and 125 for the blindness, despite the reduction loss.

For these parameters, we reach blind signatures of 41.12 KB, for a total issuance transcript of 59.63 KB. We give in Table 2 the sizes in KB of each contribution. The public key of the signer is 53.94 KB but only needs to be transmitted once so we do not include it in the issuance transcript.

**Table 1.** Classical hardness bounds of the different assumptions for the signature, encryption and proof systems.

| $\varepsilon^{❶}_{\text{M-SIS}}$ | $\varepsilon^{❷}_{\text{M-SIS}}$ | $\varepsilon^{(1)}_{\text{M-LWE}}$ | $\varepsilon^{(2)}_{\text{M-LWE}}$ | $\varepsilon^{(e)}_{\text{M-LWE}}$ | $\varepsilon^{(1)}_{\text{sound}}$ | $\varepsilon^{(2)}_{\text{sound}}$ | $\varepsilon^{(1)}_{\text{zk}}$ | $\varepsilon^{(2)}_{\text{zk}}$ |
|---|---|---|---|---|---|---|---|---|
| $2^{-203.5}$ | $2^{-182.2}$ | $2^{-157.7}$ | $2^{-147.2}$ | $2^{-163.2}$ | $2^{-128.2}$ | $2^{-126.9}$ | $2^{-127.3}$ | $2^{-127}$ |

**Table 2.** Size estimates for the issuance transcript between the user and signer, and the blind signature.

| | **Issuance Transcript** | | | | | **Blind Signature** | |
|---|---|---|---|---|---|---|---|
| | $\lvert \mathbf{t} \rvert$ | $\lvert \mathbf{c} \rvert$ | $\lvert \mathbf{ct} \rvert$ | $\lvert \pi_1 \rvert$ | $\lvert \mathbf{v} \rvert$ | $\lvert \mathbf{w}_L \rvert$ | $\lvert \pi_2 \rvert$ |
| | 0.03 KB | 3.59 KB | 1.62 KB | 45.68 KB | 8.70 KB | 5.38 KB | 35.74 KB |
| **Total** | | | **59.63 KB** | | | **41.12 KB** | |

These estimates are obtained based on the parameters chosen as described above and thus depend on the reduction loss. In particular, in the case of one-more unforgeability, we need to set a bound $Q$ on the maximal number of signatures per key pair. We set $Q = 2^{32}$ which means that the tag guess loss $|\mathcal{T}_w|$ is at least $2^{32}$. In practice, the loss incurred via guessing arguments is sometimes implicitly not taken into account in the parameter selection. Actually, it is unclear whether previous papers on blind signatures account for such loss factors or not. In our case, we design our scheme so as to keep this loss acceptable and consider it when setting parameters. By discarding it, we could choose smaller parameters and end up with a transcript size of 53.19 KB and a blind signature of 36.37 KB.

### 5.2 Implementation Performance

One caveat of the blind signature in [12] is that the issuance relies on general-purpose NIZKs which are very complex and very slow in practice, even though they lead to short proofs. Our system does not need to rely on such tools which then significantly improves the issuance phase. To demonstrate the concrete practicality of our blind signature, we propose a proof-of-concept implementation in C[4]. For that, we built upon the implementation of anonymous credentials of [5] which is publicly available[5] and adapted it to our scheme and parameters. In particular, we updated the parameter-specific parts such as expansion and sampling procedures. We also implemented the encryption mechanism modulo $p$, the decomposition functions, and obviously overhaul the whole implementation of zero-knowledge proofs as our relations are different. Regarding the latter, we

4 https://github.com/latticeblindsignature/lattice-blind-signature.

5 https://github.com/Chair-for-Security-Engineering/lattice-anonymous-credentials.

point out that our scheme features the optimizations on the proof from [41, Sec. 4.4, App. A] and [40] as opposed to [5].

We benchmarked our implementation using a laptop featuring an Intel Core i7 12800H CPU running at 4.6 GHz. We used the same compilation options as [5], namely `-O3 -march=native` using `gcc 11.4.0` with `pthread` disabled when building FLINT. The timings (in milliseconds) of each main step of the blind signature can be found in Table 3.

**Table 3.** Benchmark results. Statistics over 100 executions. Where applicable, the key and message were randomized. High variance timings are due to rejection sampling.

| Round | Procedure | Reference | Time (ms) | | | |
|---|---|---|---|---|---|---|
| | | | mean | med | min | max |
| | key gen. | Alg. 3.2 | 673.873 | 498.793 | 451.248 | 1212.177 |
| ① | tag gen. | Alg. 3.3, Steps 1-2. | 0.002 | 0.002 | 0.002 | 0.014 |
| ② | tag verify | Alg. 3.3, Step 4. | 0.001 | 0.001 | 0.001 | 0.001 |
| | commit | Alg. 3.3, Steps 5-8. | 2.305 | 2.302 | 2.294 | 2.325 |
| | encrypt | Alg. 3.3, Steps 9-11. | 0.373 | 0.375 | 0.360 | 0.385 |
| | $\text{embed}_1$ | Alg. 3.3, Step 12. | 0.674 | 0.672 | 0.629 | 0.848 |
| | $\text{prove}_1$ | Alg. 3.3, Step 12. | 499.027 | 348.771 | 182.980 | 1781.727 |
| ③ | $\text{verify}_1$ | Alg. 3.3, Step 14. | 123.081 | 123.059 | 120.937 | 125.501 |
| | pre sign cmt. | Alg. 3.3, Steps 15-17. | 73.859 | 73.617 | 73.264 | 75.445 |
| | pre sig verify | Alg. 3.3, Steps 19-21. | 2.119 | 2.116 | 2.105 | 2.153 |
| | decomp. | Alg. 3.3, Steps 22-23. | 0.081 | 0.080 | 0.077 | 0.095 |
| | $\text{embed}_2$ | Alg. 3.3, Step 24. | 2.556 | 2.551 | 2.521 | 2.655 |
| | $\text{prove}_2$ | Alg. 3.3, Step 24. | 391.483 | 266.100 | 141.674 | 1864.392 |
| | $\text{verify}_2$ | | 88.116 | 88.033 | 87.289 | 90.716 |
| | verify | Alg. 3.4 | 91.034 | 90.296 | 89.544 | 95.668 |

The entire blind signature generation following Algorithm 3.3 can thus be performed in 1096 ms on average, mostly because of the generation of the two ZK proofs $\pi_1$ and $\pi_2$. Note that although $\mathsf{Prove}_2$ is part of the blind signature generation, it no longer requires the signer. The total "online" time can thus be amortized to 702 ms on average. We insist that these timings are reported by our implementation which is not yet optimized. Vast improvements could be brought for example by the use of a parameter-specific arithmetic backend (so as to rely on stack allocations rather than heap allocations which are generally much slower), parallel hashing, vectorized computations leveraging the AVX2 instruction set, etc. Additionally, as we only prove quadratic lattice relations, improvements on the zero-knowledge proof framework itself would transfer to our scheme. We leave these optimizations as future work. Nevertheless, this provides a first milestone in the implementation of lattice-based blind signatures.

### 5.3 Comparison

As discussed in the introduction, the state-of-the art of post-quantum blind signatures is limited to a few constructions, in particular since the work by Hauck et al. [30] which invalidates all previous 3-round designs. While this paper introduced a secure 3-round construction, it was essentially a proof of concept that is clearly outperformed by our scheme. We thus choose to compare our scheme to the much more competitive two-round constructions in [1,12,47]. Obviously, this comparison has some limits but we believe it remains relevant as the spirit of our construction is closer to the one of two-round designs.

In our security assessment, we opted for a more realistic lattice sieving cost model but we note that certain previous works use the Core-SVP model instead which estimate the hardness bounds as $2^{-0.292B}$ instead of $2^{-(0.292B+16.4)}$. Nevertheless, they aim for a smaller security target which means that we achieve a similar security level to these works when using the Core-SVP model. The comparison is therefore given for a target classical security of 128 bits (Table 4).

**Table 4.** Comparison of lattice-based blind signatures. The transcript size corresponds to all the messages exchanged between the signer and user. The "NIZK (iss.)" column describes the type of relations proven only in the issuance part, the proof being part of the transcript. The final generation of the blind signature includes a proof of algebraic lattice relations for all the constructions cited above.

| | Assumptions | Round | NIZK (iss.) | \|transcript\| | \|bsig\| |
|---|---|---|---|---|---|
| [1] | One-More-ISIS<br>NTRU<br>M-SIS/M-LWE | 2 | None | 1.37 KB | 45.19 KB |
| [47] | NTRU<br>M-SIS/M-LWE | 2 | Algebraic Relations | 932 KB | 102.6 KB |
| [12] | NTRU<br>M-SIS/M-LWE | 2 | General Purpose | 60 KB | 22 KB |
| Ours | M-SIS/M-LWE | 3 | Algebraic Relations | 59.63 KB | 41.12 KB |

Compared to [1], we achieve slightly smaller blind signatures at the expense of a larger transcript due to the commitment opening proof $\pi_1$. But most importantly, our construction shows that we can achieve the same level of compactness without compromising on security. Indeed, we do not need the one-more-ISIS assumption and only rely on the standard lattice assumptions M-SIS and M-LWE. Our blind signature and transcript sizes are also much smaller than the construction of [47], whose security is based on standard assumptions as well. Finally, the blind signature of [12] achieves a similar transcript size but with a blind signature that is almost twice as small as ours. However, as mentioned in the introduction, their construction requires the use of general purpose

NIZKs for the commitment opening proof which are very time-consuming. The author estimate this proof generation to be around 20 s. In our case, our issuance does not need to prove hash evaluations which means we can use efficient proof systems for algebraic lattice relations. Typically, the generation of $\pi_1$ takes on average 500 ms in our proof-of-concept implementation. As mentioned above, this timing can be vastly improved with an optimized implementation. All in all, our blind signature is competitive with the existing ones in terms of size, while providing strong security guarantees by relying solely on standard lattice assumptions, and by having a concretely efficient issuance.

**Acknowledgments.** We thank the reviewers of Crypto 2025 for their feedback and guidance.

## References

1. Agrawal, S., Kirshanova, E., Stehlé, D., Yadav, A.: Practical, round-optimal lattice-based blind signatures. In: CCS (2022). https://doi.org/10.1145/3548606.3560650
2. Albrecht, M.R., Cid, C., Faugère, J., Fitzpatrick, R., Perret, L.: Algebraic algorithms for LWE problems. ACM Commun. Comput. Algebra (2015). https://doi.org/10.1145/2815111.2815158
3. Albrecht, M.R., Player, R., Scott, S.: On the concrete hardness of learning with errors. J. Math. Cryptol. (2015)
4. Alkadri, N.A., Bansarkhani, R.E., Buchmann, J.: BLAZE: practical lattice-based blind signatures for privacy-preserving applications. In: Financial Cryptography and Data Security (2020). https://doi.org/10.1007/978-3-030-51280-4_26
5. Argo, S., Güneysu, T., Jeudy, C., Land, G., Roux-Langlois, A., Sanders, O.: Practical post-quantum signatures for privacy. In: CCS (2024). https://doi.org/10.1145/3658644.3670297
6. Arora, S., Ge, R.: New algorithms for learning in presence of errors. In: ICALP (2011). https://doi.org/10.1007/978-3-642-22006-7_34
7. Banaszczyk, W.: New bounds in some transference theorems in the geometry of numbers. Math. Ann. (1993)
8. Bellare, M., Micciancio, D., Warinschi, B.: Foundations of group signatures: formal definitions, simplified requirements, and a construction based on general assumptions. In: EUROCRYPT (2003). https://doi.org/10.1007/3-540-39200-9_38
9. Bellare, M., Namprempre, C., Pointcheval, D., Semanko, M.: The one-more-RSA-inversion problems and the security of Chaum's blind signature scheme. J. Cryptol. (2003)
10. Benhamouda, F., Lepoint, T., Loss, J., Orrù, M., Raykova, M.: On the (in)security of ROS. J. Cryptol. (2022). https://doi.org/10.1007/S00145-022-09436-0
11. Bernhard, D., Warinschi, B.: Cryptographic voting - a gentle introduction. IACR Cryptology ePrint Archive, p. 765 (2016)
12. Beullens, W., Lyubashevsky, V., Nguyen, N.K., Seiler, G.: Lattice-based blind signatures: short, efficient, and round-optimal. In: CCS (2023). https://doi.org/10.1145/3576915.3616613
13. Blum, A., Kalai, A., Wasserman, H.: Noise-tolerant learning, the parity problem, and the statistical query model. J. ACM (2003). https://doi.org/10.1145/792538.792543

14. Boneh, D., Boyen, X.: Short signatures without random oracles and the SDH assumption in bilinear groups. J. Cryptol. **21**(2), 149–177 (2007). https://doi.org/10.1007/s00145-007-9005-7
15. Bouaziz-Ermann, S., Canard, S., Eberhart, G., Kaim, G., Roux-Langlois, A., Traoré, J.: Lattice-based (partially) blind signature without restart. IACR Cryptology ePrint Archive, p. 260 (2020)
16. Boudgoust, K., Jeudy, C., Roux-Langlois, A., Wen, W.: On the hardness of module learning with errors with short distributions. J. Cryptol. (2023). https://doi.org/10.1007/s00145-022-09441-3
17. Brickell, E.F., Camenisch, J., Chen, L.: Direct anonymous attestation. In: CCS (2004). https://doi.org/10.1145/1030083.1030103
18. Camenisch, J., Lysyanskaya, A.: An efficient system for non-transferable anonymous credentials with optional anonymity revocation. In: Pfitzmann, B. (ed.) EUROCRYPT 2001. LNCS, vol. 2045, pp. 93–118. Springer, Heidelberg (2001). https://doi.org/10.1007/3-540-44987-6_7
19. Camenisch, J., Lysyanskaya, A.: A signature scheme with efficient protocols. In: Cimato, S., Persiano, G., Galdi, C. (eds.) SCN 2002. LNCS, vol. 2576, pp. 268–289. Springer, Heidelberg (2003). https://doi.org/10.1007/3-540-36413-7_20
20. Camenisch, J., Lysyanskaya, A.: Signature schemes and anonymous credentials from bilinear maps. In: Franklin, M. (ed.) CRYPTO 2004. LNCS, vol. 3152, pp. 56–72. Springer, Heidelberg (2004). https://doi.org/10.1007/978-3-540-28628-8_4
21. Chaum, D.: Blind signatures for untraceable payments. In: Chaum, D., Rivest, R.L., Sherman, A.T. (eds.) Advances in Cryptology, pp. 199–203. Springer, Boston, MA (1983). https://doi.org/10.1007/978-1-4757-0602-4_18
22. Chaum, D.: Blind signature system. In: Chaum, D. (ed.) CRYPTO. Springer, Boston (1983). https://doi.org/10.1007/978-1-4684-4730-9_14
23. Chaum, D., van Heyst, E.: Group signatures. In: Davies, D.W. (ed.) EUROCRYPT 1991. LNCS, vol. 547, pp. 257–265. Springer, Heidelberg (1991). https://doi.org/10.1007/3-540-46416-6_22
24. Chen, Y.: Réduction de Réseau et Sécurité Concrète du Chiffrement Complètement Homomorphe. Ph.D. thesis, Paris 7 (2013)
25. Cheon, J.H., et al.: HAETAE: shorter lattice-based fiat-shamir signatures. IACR Cryptology ePrint Archive, p. 624 (2023)
26. Crites, E.C., Komlo, C., Maller, M., Tessaro, S., Zhu, C.: Snowblind: a threshold blind signature in pairing-free groups. In: Handschuh, H., Lysyanskaya, A. (eds.) CRYPTO 2023. LNCS, vol. 14081, pp. 710–742. Springer, Cham (2023). https://doi.org/10.1007/978-3-031-38557-5_23
27. Fischlin, M.: Round-optimal composable blind signatures in the common reference string model. In: Dwork, C. (ed.) CRYPTO 2006. LNCS, vol. 4117, pp. 60–77. Springer, Heidelberg (2006). https://doi.org/10.1007/11818175_4
28. Genise, N., Micciancio, D., Peikert, C., Walter, M.: Improved discrete gaussian and subgaussian analysis for lattice cryptography. In: Kiayias, A., Kohlweiss, M., Wallden, P., Zikas, V. (eds.) PKC 2020. LNCS, vol. 12110, pp. 623–651. Springer, Cham (2020). https://doi.org/10.1007/978-3-030-45374-9_21
29. Gentry, C., Peikert, C., Vaikuntanathan, V.: Trapdoors for hard lattices and new cryptographic constructions. In: STOC (2008). https://doi.org/10.1145/1374376.1374407
30. Hauck, E., Kiltz, E., Loss, J., Nguyen, N.K.: Lattice-based blind signatures. Revisited. In: CRYPTO (2020). https://doi.org/10.1007/978-3-030-56880-1_18
31. Hub, B.I., Bank, S.N.: Project Tourbillon: Exploring privacy, security and scalability for CBDCs (2023). https://www.bis.org/publ/othp80.pdf

32. ISO/IEC: ISO/IEC 18370-1:2016 Information Technology—Security Techniques—Blind digital signatures (2016). https://www.iso.org/standard/62288.html
33. Jeudy, C., Roux-Langlois, A., Sanders, O.: Lattice signature with efficient protocols. Application to anonymous credentials. In: Handschuh, H., Lysyanskaya, A. (eds.) CRYPTO 2023. LNCS, vol. 14082, pp. 351–383. Springer, Cham (2023). https://doi.org/10.1007/978-3-031-38545-2_12
34. Jeudy, C., Sanders, O.: Improved lattice blind signatures from recycled entropy. IACR Cryptology ePrint Archive, p. 1289 (2024)
35. Jeudy, C., Sanders, O.: Worst-case lattice sampler with truncated gadgets and applications. IACR Cryptology ePrint Archive, p. 1952 (2024)
36. Juels, A., Luby, M., Ostrovsky, R.: Security of blind digital signatures (extended abstract). In: Kaliski, B.S. (ed.) CRYPTO 1997. LNCS, vol. 1294, pp. 150–164. Springer, Heidelberg (1997). https://doi.org/10.1007/BFB0052233
37. Langlois, A., Stehlé, D.: Worst-case to average-case reductions for module lattices. Des. Codes Crypt. **75**(3), 565–599 (2014). https://doi.org/10.1007/s10623-014-9938-4
38. Libert, B., Ling, S., Mouhartem, F., Nguyen, K., Wang, H.: Signature schemes with efficient protocols and dynamic group signatures from lattice assumptions. In: Cheon, J.H., Takagi, T. (eds.) ASIACRYPT 2016. LNCS, vol. 10032, pp. 373–403. Springer, Heidelberg (2016). https://doi.org/10.1007/978-3-662-53890-6_13
39. Lyubashevsky, V.: Lattice-based identification schemes secure under active attacks. In: Cramer, R. (ed.) PKC 2008. LNCS, vol. 4939, pp. 162–179. Springer, Heidelberg (2008). https://doi.org/10.1007/978-3-540-78440-1_10
40. Lyubashevsky, V., Nguyen, N.K.: BLOOM: bimodal lattice one-out-of-many proofs and applications. In: Agrawal, S., Lin, D. (eds.) ASIACRYPT 2022. LNCS, vol. 13794, pp. 95–125. Springer, Cham (2022). https://doi.org/10.1007/978-3-031-22972-5_4
41. Lyubashevsky, V., Nguyen, N.K., Plançon, M.: Lattice-based zero-knowledge proofs and applications: shorter, simpler, and more general. In: Dodis, Y., Shrimpton, T. (eds.) CRYPTO 2022. LNCS, vol. 13508, pp. 71–101. Springer, Cham (2022). https://doi.org/10.1007/978-3-031-15979-4_3
42. Lyubashevsky, V., Nguyen, N.K., Plancon, M., Seiler, G.: Shorter lattice-based group signatures via "Almost Free" encryption and other optimizations. In: Tibouchi, M., Wang, H. (eds.) ASIACRYPT 2021. LNCS, vol. 13093, pp. 218–248. Springer, Cham (2021). https://doi.org/10.1007/978-3-030-92068-5_8
43. Lyubashevsky, V., Nguyen, N.K., Seiler, G.: Shorter lattice-based zero-knowledge proofs via one-time commitments. In: Garay, J.A. (ed.) PKC 2021. LNCS, vol. 12710, pp. 215–241. Springer, Cham (2021). https://doi.org/10.1007/978-3-030-75245-3_9
44. Micciancio, D., Peikert, C.: Trapdoors for lattices: simpler, tighter, faster, smaller. In: Pointcheval, D., Johansson, T. (eds.) EUROCRYPT 2012. LNCS, vol. 7237, pp. 700–718. Springer, Heidelberg (2012). https://doi.org/10.1007/978-3-642-29011-4_41
45. Micciancio, D., Regev, O.: Worst-case to average-case reductions based on gaussian measures. SIAM J. Comput. (2007). https://doi.org/10.1137/S0097539705447360
46. Peikert, C.: An efficient and parallel gaussian sampler for lattices. In: Rabin, T. (ed.) CRYPTO 2010. LNCS, vol. 6223, pp. 80–97. Springer, Heidelberg (2010). https://doi.org/10.1007/978-3-642-14623-7_5
47. del Pino, R., Katsumata, S.: A new framework for more efficient round-optimal lattice-based (partially) blind signature via trapdoor sampling. In: Dodis, Y.,

Shrimpton, T. (eds.) CRYPTO 2022. LNCS, vol. 13508, pp. 36–336. Springer, Cham (2022). https://doi.org/10.1007/978-3-031-15979-4_11

48. del Pino, R., Lyubashevsky, V., Seiler, G.: Lattice-based group signatures and zero-knowledge proofs of automorphism stability. In: CCS (2018). https://doi.org/10.1145/3243734.3243852
49. Pointcheval, D., Sanders, O.: Short randomizable signatures. In: CT-RSA (2016). https://doi.org/10.1007/978-3-319-29485-8_7
50. Pointcheval, D., Stern, J.: Security arguments for digital signatures and blind signatures. J. Cryptol. (2000). https://doi.org/10.1007/S001450010003
51. Rückert, M.: Lattice-based blind signatures. In: Abe, M. (ed.) ASIACRYPT 2010. LNCS, vol. 6477, pp. 413–430. Springer, Heidelberg (2010). https://doi.org/10.1007/978-3-642-17373-8_24
52. Schnorr, C.P.: Efficient identification and signatures for smart cards. In: Brassard, G. (ed.) CRYPTO 1989. LNCS, vol. 435, pp. 239–252. Springer, New York (1990). https://doi.org/10.1007/0-387-34805-0_22
53. Tessaro, S., Zhu, C.: Short pairing-free blind signatures with exponential security. In: Dunkelman, O., Dziembowski, S. (eds.) EUROCRYPT 2022. LNCS, vol. 13276, pp. 782–811. Springer, Cham (2022). https://doi.org/10.1007/978-3-031-07085-3_27
54. Wagner, D.A.: A generalized birthday problem. In: Yung, M. (ed.) CRYPTO 2002. LNCS, vol. 2442, pp. 288–304. Springer, Heidelberg (2002). https://doi.org/10.1007/3-540-45708-9_19

# Compact Lattice Signatures via Iterative Rejection Sampling

Joel Gärtner[1,2(✉)]

[1] KTH Royal Institute of Technology, Stockholm, Sweden
jgartner@kth.se
[2] Swedish NCSA, Swedish Armed Forces, Stockholm, Sweden

**Abstract.** One of the primary approaches for constructing lattice-based signature schemes is through the "Fiat-Shamir with aborts" methodology. Schemes constructed using this approach may abort and restart during signing, corresponding to rejection sampling produced signatures in order to ensure that they follow a distribution that is independent of the secret key. This rejection sampling is only feasible when the output distribution is sufficiently wide, limiting how compact this type of signature schemes can be.

In this work, we develop a new method to construct lattice signatures with the "Fiat-Shamir with aborts" approach. By constructing signatures in a way that is influenced by the rejection condition, we can significantly lower the rejection probability. This allows our scheme to use an iterative rejection sampling to target narrower output distributions than previous methods, resulting in much more compact signatures.

In the most compact variant of our new signature scheme, the combined size of a signature and a verification key is less than half of that for ML-DSA and comparable to that of compact hash-and-sign lattice signature schemes, such as Falcon. Alternatively, by targeting a somewhat wider distribution, the rejection condition of the scheme can be securely ignored. This non-aborting variant of our scheme still retains a notable size advantage over previous lattice-based Fiat-Shamir schemes.

## 1 Introduction

As a part of their post-quantum standardization process, NIST has already standardized the signature scheme CRYSTALS-Dilithium [23] as ML-DSA and is in the process of standardizing Falcon. Both Dilithium and Falcon are lattice-based signature schemes but they are constructed using two different approaches, corresponding to the two main approaches for constructing lattice-based signature schemes. The first of these is the hash-and-sign approach of Gentry, Peikert and Vaikuntanathan [17] on which Falcon is based. The second of these, on which Dilithium is based, is the one of Lyubashevsky [21,22], which consists of an aborting variant of the Fiat-Shamir transform.

One of the primary reasons for why NIST decided to standardize Falcon in addition to Dilithium is that Falcon has significantly smaller signatures and


Y. Tauman Kalai and S. F. Kamara (Eds.): CRYPTO 2025, LNCS 16000, pp. 514–547, 2025.
https://doi.org/10.1007/978-3-032-01855-7_17

verification keys. In fact, to the best of our knowledge, there has not previously been any lattice-based Fiat-Shamir signature scheme as compact as Falcon.

A limiting factor in constructing a compact Fiat-Shamir lattice-based signature scheme is that, for its security proof, it is typically required that it produces signatures that follow some distribution which is independent of the scheme's secret. To accomplish this using the Fiat-Shamir with aborts approach, the scheme initially produces candidate signatures from a distribution that is dependent on the secret of the scheme. Only some of these signatures are actually emitted, with the scheme otherwise aborting the signing attempt and retrying. This corresponds to rejection sampling from a secret-dependent distribution to produce signatures that follow a secret-independent distribution. The rejection probability of this sampling is determined by the ratio between the size of the secret and the width of the output distribution. Because of this, unless the output distribution is sufficiently wide in relation to the size of the secret, the rejection probability is too high for it to be useable.

Altering how signatures are constructed can allow for a narrower output distribution, and thus smaller signatures, while keeping the rejection probability the same. Furthermore, the estimated security of these types of signature schemes is in large part determined by the maximal size of accepted signatures and if the scheme produces smaller signatures, we can argue for a higher security level. Alternatively, the smaller signatures allow many other parameters of the scheme to be selected differently when targeting a comparable security level. As such, an alternative signature construction that allows for better rejection sampling can influence many different aspects of the scheme.

BLISS [14] provides an example of the impact of improved rejection sampling, where rejection sampling from a bimodal Gaussian distribution allows for a significantly more compact scheme than Lyubashevsky's original approach. A more recent example is HAETAE [8,9] which relies on bimodal rejection sampling from uniform distributions over hyperballs to allow for a more compact scheme than Dilithium. It has even been shown in [11] that the approaches of BLISS and HAETAE are essentially optimal for schemes that rely on rejection sampling from bimodal distributions, and that rejection sampling from bimodal distributions is superior to similar sampling from unimodal distributions.

Very recently, the NTRU+Sign [27] signature scheme was introduced with various improvements to the BLISS signature scheme. This same work also recalibrated the parameters of the original BLISS scheme in order to ensure alignment with modern security standards.

Works have also explored the possibility of removing the rejection condition [5]. A concrete example of this is Raccoon [10], which was a submission to the first round of NIST's post-quantum standardization process for additional digital signature schemes. The Raccoon parameters are selected to ensure that rejection conditions can be securely ignored. This does, however, come at the cost of signatures that are about five times larger than those of Dilithium.

An alternative approach for constructing signatures without a rejection condition was developed for the G+G signature scheme [12]. Signatures from this scheme follow a discrete Gaussian distribution that is constructed as a convolution of two different discrete Gaussian distributions, both of which have covariance that depend on the secret key of the scheme. By carefully selecting parameters, the signatures follow a centered spherical discrete Gaussian distribution, ensuring that the signatures do not leak anything about the secret.

Even though the G+G scheme is constructed without relying on aborts, the resulting scheme is still relatively compact. The G+G scheme is, however, still far from as compact as Falcon. Additionally, due to requiring sampling from Gaussian distributions dependent on the secret key, it seems like implementing G+G securely would be non-trivial.

### 1.1 Our Contribution

In this work we present an alternative method for constructing lattice-based signatures for the Fiat-Shamir with aborts paradigm. By constructing signatures in a way that is influenced by the rejection condition, our new method allows for a rejection probability that is significantly smaller than that of previous methods. A lower rejection probability allows for greater freedom when parametrizing the scheme, allowing us to construct a signature scheme that is significantly more compact than previous lattice-based Fiat-Shamir signature schemes.

We propose concrete parametrization of a signature scheme that makes use of our new method. The signature size of the resulting scheme is approximately one third of that for ML-DSA, and the verification key size is somewhat smaller than that for ML-DSA. Additionally, the combined size of a signature and a verification key is less than half of what it is for ML-DSA and within 10% to that of Falcon.

We also consider alternative parametrization of our scheme where the rejection condition can be safely ignored. In a similar manner as for Raccoon [10], this is accomplished by using a wider output distribution. However, the penalty that we pay, in the form of increased size, is significantly smaller than for Raccoon, and our resulting scheme without aborts is still more compact than previous lattice-based Fiat-Shamir signature schemes. In particular, the combined size of a signature and a verification key for the resulting scheme is less than 60% of that for ML-DSA.

### 1.2 Technical Overview

The idea behind Lyubashevsky's signature scheme [21,22] is similar to the idea behind Schnorr signatures [26]. To sign a message with Lyubashevsky's scheme, a vector $\boldsymbol{y}$ is sampled from some relatively narrow distribution. Then, a commitment $\boldsymbol{w} = \boldsymbol{A}\boldsymbol{y} \bmod q$ is computed, where $\boldsymbol{A}$ is a matrix that is part of the verification key and $q$ is a parameter for the scheme.

Using the commitment $\boldsymbol{w}$ and the message to be signed, a challenge $\boldsymbol{c}$ is derived, with this challenge guaranteed to be a short vector. A signature is given by $(\boldsymbol{z}, \boldsymbol{c}, \boldsymbol{w})$, where $\boldsymbol{z} = \boldsymbol{y} + \boldsymbol{S}\boldsymbol{c} \bmod q$ with $\boldsymbol{S}$ the secret key of the signer. The secret key $\boldsymbol{S}$ is sampled to have short columns, and thus $\boldsymbol{Sc}$ is relatively short, ensuring that $\boldsymbol{z}$ also is a relatively short vector.

In contrast to the analogous case for typical Schnorr signatures, in the lattice setting the vector $\boldsymbol{y}$ does not perfectly mask the contribution of $\boldsymbol{Sc}$ to $\boldsymbol{z}$. This is the case as $\boldsymbol{z}$, and therefore also $\boldsymbol{y}$, must be relatively short vectors in order to ensure that signatures are hard to forge. As such, the distribution of signatures produced in this manner depend on $\boldsymbol{S}$ and may therefore leak information about the secret key of the scheme.

To ensure that the distribution of signatures does not depend on secret information, Lyubashevsky [21,22] does not output all constructed signatures. Instead, signatures are only emitted with some probability that depends on $\boldsymbol{z}$, and otherwise the signing attempt is aborted and retried with a different $\boldsymbol{y}$. By aborting with a suitable probability, it is ensured that the $\boldsymbol{z}$ vector in emitted signatures follow some secret-independent distribution. As such, emitted signatures do not leak any information about $\boldsymbol{S}$.

A variant of Lyubashevsky's scheme was later considered for the signature scheme BLISS [14]. In BLISS, valid signatures can be constructed with $\boldsymbol{z}$ either as $\boldsymbol{y} + \boldsymbol{Sc}$ or as $\boldsymbol{y} - \boldsymbol{Sc}$, with each of these two constructions for $\boldsymbol{z}$ selected with probability $1/2$. As with Lyubashevsky's original scheme, BLISS occasionally aborts and does not output the constructed $\boldsymbol{z}$.

As $\boldsymbol{y}$ is sampled from a discrete Gaussian distribution in BLISS, without rejection sampling, the distribution of BLISS signatures follows a bimodal discrete Gaussian distribution, with the two centers $\pm\boldsymbol{Sc}$. This is in contrast to the scheme of Lyubashevsky [22] where the distribution of signatures would be a unimodal Gaussian distribution with center $\boldsymbol{Sc}$ if no rejection sampling was used.

In both the unimodal and bimodal cases, a suitable rejection condition allows the output signatures to follow a centered discrete Gaussian distribution. However, the bimodal discrete Gaussian distribution is significantly more similar to the desired output distribution than a unimodal discrete Gaussian distribution centered on $\boldsymbol{Sc}$. This gives the bimodal approach of BLISS a significant advantage over the original unimodal approach of Lyubashevsky.

**Our Improved Signature Construction.** The rejection sampling in BLISS can be described through a rejection function $R(\boldsymbol{z})$, with each constructed $\boldsymbol{z}$ accepted with probability $R(\boldsymbol{z})$ and otherwise rejected. For a sampled vector $\boldsymbol{y}$, the signature is given by $\boldsymbol{z} = \boldsymbol{y} + \boldsymbol{Sc}$ with probability $R(\boldsymbol{y} + \boldsymbol{Sc})/2 = f_{\boldsymbol{Sc}}(\boldsymbol{y})$ and by $\boldsymbol{z} = \boldsymbol{y} - \boldsymbol{Sc}$ with probability $R(\boldsymbol{y} - \boldsymbol{Sc})/2 = g_{\boldsymbol{Sc}}(\boldsymbol{y})$, while it otherwise rejects the signature and tries again with a different $\boldsymbol{y}$.

With the rejection sampling formulated in this way, it is natural to consider which other choices for $f_{\boldsymbol{Sc}}$ and $g_{\boldsymbol{Sc}}$ are possible. More general functions $f_{\boldsymbol{Sc}}$ and $g_{\boldsymbol{Sc}}$ can determine both the choice of $\boldsymbol{y} \pm \boldsymbol{Sc}$ and whether or not to reject. In particular, this allows first influencing the probability of constructing $\boldsymbol{z}$ by the rejection condition for $\boldsymbol{z}$. However, note that this requires quite a bit of care as, for the output to follow the desired distribution, changing how often $\boldsymbol{z}$ is constructed must also impact the rejection probability for $\boldsymbol{z}$.

In this work, we consider such more general functions $f_{\boldsymbol{v}}$ and $g_{\boldsymbol{v}}$, with a focus on the case where the input distribution for $\boldsymbol{y}$ is a discrete Gaussian distribution while ensuring that, conditioned on $\boldsymbol{z} \neq \perp$ the emitted $\boldsymbol{z}$ follows the same distribution. By carefully crafting $f_{\boldsymbol{v}}$ and $g_{\boldsymbol{v}}$, this allows our scheme to have a significantly lower rejection probability than BLISS.

The rejection failure probability of both our new approach and the approach of BLISS depends on the norm of vectors $\boldsymbol{v}$ used to construct $\boldsymbol{z} = \boldsymbol{y} \pm \boldsymbol{v}$. In particular, it depends on the quotient $\alpha = r/\,||\boldsymbol{v}||$ between the Gaussian parameter $r$ and the norm of the vector $\boldsymbol{v}$ of maximal norm that the rejection sampling can handle. As the rejection sampling handles vectors $\boldsymbol{v} = \boldsymbol{S}\boldsymbol{c}$, the rejection probability depends on the maximal norm of $\boldsymbol{S}\boldsymbol{c}$. The signature size of the scheme essentially scales linearly with $\log(r)$ and thus also with $\log(\alpha)$. As such, if improved rejection sampling allows for a smaller $\alpha$ to be used, it allows for a more compact signature scheme.

When targeting the same rejection probability, our new approach can use a smaller $\alpha$ than previous approaches, and thus allows for smaller signatures. One could hope that this would allow our new approach to use a significantly smaller $\alpha$, and therefore enable a scheme with significantly smaller signatures. However, decreasing $\alpha$ quickly results in unacceptably large rejection probabilities for our new approach, even though it still does have an advantage over previous rejection sampling methods.

Although our new method has a noticeable advantage for small $\alpha$, its advantage is much more pronounced for larger $\alpha$. For instance, with $\alpha$ such that the old approach has a rejection probability of a bit more than 10%, our new approach has to reject less than one in a million signatures. This is a large difference in rejection probability but in practice there is only a small performance difference between rejecting 10% of the time and rejecting only very rarely. However, by additionally considering a new iterative signature construction, we can exploit this significant advantage for larger $\alpha$ to allow for much more compact signatures.

**Iterative Rejection Sampling.** Our new signature scheme is quite similar to BLISS, with an analogous relation between public and private keys, and with both $\boldsymbol{y}$ and $\boldsymbol{z}$ following a discrete Gaussian distribution. Furthermore, the space $\mathcal{C}$ of possible challenges $\mathbf{c}$ consist of vectors where all elements are either zero or one and which often are quite sparse. As noted by Ducas [13], and more recently used for the G+G signature scheme [12], this allows signatures from the scheme to be constructed as $\boldsymbol{y} + \boldsymbol{S}\boldsymbol{c}'$ for any $\boldsymbol{c}' \equiv \boldsymbol{c} \mod 2$.

For our work, we make use of this flexibility in how $\boldsymbol{c}'$ can be selected to iteratively rejection sample over the coefficients of $\boldsymbol{c}$. This consists of selecting the sign of each coefficient of $\boldsymbol{c}$ independently, corresponding to either producing $\boldsymbol{y} + \boldsymbol{v}_i$ or $\boldsymbol{y} - \boldsymbol{v}_i$ where $\boldsymbol{v}_i$ is a column of $\boldsymbol{S}$.

To construct $\boldsymbol{z}$, the iterative process is initialized with $\boldsymbol{z}_0 = \boldsymbol{y}$, and a sequence of inputs $\boldsymbol{v}_1, \ldots, \boldsymbol{v}_\kappa$ that are columns of $\boldsymbol{S}$ determined by $\boldsymbol{c}$. First, rejection sampling is performed with $\boldsymbol{z}_0$ and the input $\boldsymbol{v}_1$ to get $\boldsymbol{z}_1$ such that, conditioned on $\boldsymbol{z}_1 \neq \perp$, it follows the same distribution as $\boldsymbol{z}_0$. Repeating this leads to a sequence of vectors $\boldsymbol{y} = \boldsymbol{z}_0, \boldsymbol{z}_1, \ldots, \boldsymbol{z}_\kappa = \boldsymbol{z}$ such that, for every $i \in \{1, \ldots, \kappa\}$ and conditioned on $\boldsymbol{z}_i \neq \perp$, $\boldsymbol{z}_i$ follows the same distribution as $\boldsymbol{y}$. Thus, the output $\boldsymbol{z}$ follows the desired distribution and there are $a_i \in \{0, 1\}$ such that

$$\boldsymbol{z} = \boldsymbol{y} + \sum_{i=1}^{\kappa} (-1)^{a_i} \boldsymbol{v}_i = \boldsymbol{y} + \boldsymbol{S}\boldsymbol{c}'$$

for some $\boldsymbol{c}' \equiv \boldsymbol{c} \mod 2$.

Each vector $\boldsymbol{v}_i$ added in the iterative steps is a column of $\boldsymbol{S}$ and is therefore expected to be significantly shorter than $\boldsymbol{S}\boldsymbol{c}$. Each rejection sampling step thus handles shorter vectors $\boldsymbol{v}_i$ than a single-step construction of $\boldsymbol{z}$ would have to handle. Although this iterative construction requires multiple steps succeeding, it does allow a larger $\alpha$ to be used for each of the rejection sampling steps. With our new rejection sampling, the larger $\alpha$ more than makes up for multiple steps having to succeed, allowing our scheme to target a significantly narrower output distribution than previous schemes.

### 1.3 Concrete Signature Scheme

For efficiency and compactness, we use structured lattices as the basis for our signature scheme. In particular, we work with elements in the ring $\mathcal{R} = \mathbb{Z}[x]/(x^n + 1)$. We additionally limit ourself to $n$ that are powers of two to enable efficient computations through the Number Theoretic Transform (NTT), with a particular focus on $n = 256$.

For our scheme, we let the challenge space $\mathcal{C}$ be a subset of $\mathcal{R}$, selected to only contain ring elements with at most $\kappa$ non-zero coefficients, with all non-zero elements equal to 1. Furthermore, the secret $\boldsymbol{S}$ of our scheme is a short vector $\boldsymbol{s} \in \mathcal{R}^k$, where $k$ is a relatively small integer typically not larger than 10. Similar to BLISS [14], HAETAE [8,9] and G+G [12], keys are generated such that $\boldsymbol{A}\boldsymbol{s} = q\boldsymbol{j} \mod 2q$ where $\boldsymbol{A} \in \mathcal{R}^{m \times k}$ is the verification key with $2m \approx k$ and $\boldsymbol{j} = [1, 0, \ldots, 0]^T$ the first unit vector.

A signature for the message $\mu$ from the scheme consist of $(\boldsymbol{z}, c)$ where $c \in \mathcal{C}$ and $\boldsymbol{z}$ is a relatively short vector such that

$$\mathcal{H}(\boldsymbol{A}\boldsymbol{z} - qc\boldsymbol{j} \mod 2q, \mu) = c$$

for $\mathcal{H}$ some cryptographic hash function with output in $\mathcal{C}$. To construct such a signature, the signer samples $\boldsymbol{y}$ from a relatively narrow discrete Gaussian distribution. From this $\boldsymbol{y}$, the signer computes $\boldsymbol{w} = \boldsymbol{A}\boldsymbol{y} \mod 2q$ and lets $c = \mathcal{H}(\boldsymbol{w}, \mu)$.

Next, the vector $\boldsymbol{z}$ is constructed using the previously mentioned iterative rejection sampling. If the rejection sampling fails by producing $\boldsymbol{z} = \perp$, the process is restarted by sampling a new $\boldsymbol{y}$. Otherwise, $\boldsymbol{z} = \boldsymbol{y} + \boldsymbol{s}c'$ for some

$c' \equiv c \mod 2$ and $\boldsymbol{z}$ follows a relatively narrow discrete Gaussian distribution. Therefore, $\boldsymbol{z}$ is expected to be relatively short and since $\boldsymbol{As} \equiv q\boldsymbol{j} \mod 2q$

$$\mathcal{H}(\boldsymbol{Az} - qc\boldsymbol{j} \bmod 2q, \mu) = \mathcal{H}(\boldsymbol{w} + qc'\boldsymbol{j} - qc\boldsymbol{j} \bmod 2q, \mu) = \mathcal{H}(\boldsymbol{w}, \mu) = c$$

showing that $(\boldsymbol{z}, c)$ is a valid signature.

Due to our definition of $\mathcal{C}$, $\boldsymbol{s}c$ is equal to the sum of at most $\kappa$ terms of the form $x^j\boldsymbol{s}$, and the iterative rejection sampling selects the sign for each of these terms individually. Each of these terms have the same length, namely $||\boldsymbol{s}||$, and our rejection probability depends on this norm.

For simplicity we ensure that all secret keys of our scheme have the same rejection probability, which is determined by the maximal value of $||\boldsymbol{s}||$ over all possible secrets. The secret keys for our scheme are therefore sampled with a length bound $B$, guaranteeing that $||\boldsymbol{s}|| \leq B$.

The bound $B$ on the length of the secret key indirectly impacts the size of signatures from the scheme. With the distributions that $\boldsymbol{y}$ and $\boldsymbol{z}$ follow left unchanged, increasing the bound $B$ results in a larger rejection probability. To increase $B$ without altering the rejection probability, $\boldsymbol{y}$ and $\boldsymbol{z}$ must follow wider distributions, leading to larger signatures.

**Security.** The security of our scheme follows from standard arguments in basically the same way as for BLISS.

To argue that it is hard to forge signatures, we assume that the $\boldsymbol{A}$ matrix is constructed from elements that are computationally hard to distinguish from uniformly random. In the random oracle model, it can then be proven that an efficient algorithm for forging signatures implies that the Module Short Integer Solutions (MSIS) problem is easy. Thus, our scheme's security against forgeries can be based upon the assumed hardness of the MSIS problem.

For the MSIS problem, a matrix $\boldsymbol{A}$ is sampled uniformly at random modulo $q$ and the task is to recover a non-zero vector $\boldsymbol{x}$ such that $\boldsymbol{Ax} \equiv \boldsymbol{0} \mod q$ with $||\boldsymbol{x}|| \leq B$ for some length bound $B$. The concrete hardness of the MSIS problem is in large part determined by this length bound $B$. Furthermore, for certain parameter choices, the MSIS problem is at least as hard as standard lattice problems restricted to module lattices [20].

Given an efficient algorithm for forging signatures, the security reduction for the signature scheme can be used to produce short vectors $\boldsymbol{x}$ such that $\boldsymbol{Ax} \equiv \boldsymbol{0} \mod q$. The length of the produced $\boldsymbol{x}$ vector is directly related to the length of the $\boldsymbol{z}$ vector in the forged signatures. If $\boldsymbol{z}$ follows a narrower distribution, the reduction produces shorter vectors and thus solves a harder instance of the MSIS problem.

Besides the width of the distribution of $\boldsymbol{z}$, the hardness of the underlying MSIS problem also depends on the dimension of $\boldsymbol{A} \in \mathcal{R}^{m \times k}$, with a larger $m$ leading to a harder problem. The value of $k$ also has some effect on the hardness of the MSIS problem, with a larger $k$ sometimes making the problem easier. However, a more significant reason to prefer a smaller $k$ is that $\boldsymbol{z}$ is a $k$-dimensional vector, and the size of signatures therefore directly depend on $k$.

As mentioned above, we assume that the public key is constructed from elements that are hard to distinguish from uniformly random. There are multiple alternatives for how to sample the secret vector $\boldsymbol{s}$ and the verification key $\boldsymbol{A}$ to achieve this. In particular, there are natural ways to construct such keys based on the assumed hardness of the Module Learning With Errors (MLWE) [20] and NTRU [19] problems. Another alternative is to create keys based on the assumed hardness of the NTWE problem that was recently introduced by Gärtner [16][1]. There are different benefits for the choice of problem to base the scheme on, and next we describe some of the tradeoffs.

**Choice of Structure.** A natural choice is to base the scheme on the MLWE problem, as done in for instance HAETAE [8,9] and G+G [12]. In such a scheme, small $\boldsymbol{s}_0 \in \mathcal{R}^\ell$ and $\boldsymbol{e} \in \mathcal{R}^m$ are sampled as the secret of the scheme and $\boldsymbol{A}_0 \in \mathcal{R}^{m\times\ell}$ is sampled uniformly at random modulo $q$. The verification key is then given by $\boldsymbol{A}_0, \boldsymbol{b}$ where $\boldsymbol{b} = \boldsymbol{A}_0\boldsymbol{s}_0 + \boldsymbol{e} \mod q$, and the public matrix $\boldsymbol{A}$ and secret vector $\boldsymbol{s}$ are given as

$$\boldsymbol{A} = [q\boldsymbol{j} - 2\boldsymbol{b}, 2\boldsymbol{A}_0, 2\boldsymbol{I}_m] \text{ and } \boldsymbol{s} = [1, \boldsymbol{s}_0^T, \boldsymbol{e}^T]^T.$$

As this results in $\boldsymbol{s} \in \mathcal{R}^{\ell+m+1}$, the $\boldsymbol{z}$ part of signatures is also an $(\ell+m+1)$-dimensional vector over $\mathcal{R}$. Thus, $\boldsymbol{z}$ can be represented by $(\ell+m+1)n$ coefficients, all of which are relatively small integers.

For a more compact scheme, we could instead base the scheme on the NTRU problem, similar to for instance BLISS [14] and NTRU+Sign [27]. To target a similar security level, the ring $\mathcal{R}' = \mathbb{Z}[x]/(x^{n'}+1)$, with $n' = \ell n$ would have to be used. With the original approach of BLISS, the key generation samples small $f, g \in \mathcal{R}'$ as the private key and computes $h = (2g+1)f^{-1} \mod q$ as the public key. The public matrix $\boldsymbol{A}$ and secret vector $\boldsymbol{s}$ are then given by

$$\boldsymbol{A} = [2h, q-2] \text{ and } \boldsymbol{s} = [f, 2g+1]^T$$

and, as detailed in [14], this leads to $\boldsymbol{A}\boldsymbol{s} = q \mod 2q$.

For such an NTRU-based scheme, $\boldsymbol{z}$ has $2n' = 2\ell n$ coefficients. Meanwhile, parametrizing an MLWE-based version of the scheme with $m = \ell$ results in $\boldsymbol{z}$ having $(2\ell+1)n$ coefficients. When targeting similar rejection probability, the coefficients of $\boldsymbol{z}$ for the NTRU-based scheme have similar size as those for an MLWE-based version. As such, signatures of an NTRU-based version of the scheme are somewhat smaller than those of a comparable MLWE-based scheme. However, the NTRU structure limits the flexibility of parameter selection as, in contrast to an MLWE-based scheme, it is not directly possible to select $\ell$ and $m$ independently from each other. Additionally, for the most efficient NTT

[1] This same problem was first implicitly used for the signature scheme of [2], although without being formally defined. Followup work from this led to a later independent reintroduction of the NTWE problem under the name v-MNTRU [4].

calculations $n'$ is limited to powers of two, further limiting the flexibility of parameter selection.

To get the compact signatures of an NTRU-based scheme with the flexibility of an MLWE-based scheme, we instead rely on the NTWE problem. The secret key of such an NTWE-based scheme consists of $\boldsymbol{s}_0 \in \mathcal{R}^{\ell'}$, $\boldsymbol{e} \in \mathcal{R}^m$ and $f \in \mathcal{R}$, where $f = 2f_0 + 1$ with the elements of $\boldsymbol{s}_0, \boldsymbol{e}$ and $f_0$ sampled from some narrow distribution. The verification key of such a scheme consists of $(\boldsymbol{A}_0, \boldsymbol{b})$ where $\boldsymbol{A}_0 \in \mathcal{R}^{m \times \ell'}$ is sampled with elements uniformly at random modulo $q$ and

$$\boldsymbol{b} = (\boldsymbol{A}_0 \boldsymbol{s}_0 + \boldsymbol{e}) f^{-1} \bmod q.$$

The public matrix and private vector are then given by

$$\boldsymbol{A} = [q\boldsymbol{j} - 2\boldsymbol{b}, 2\boldsymbol{A}_0, 2\boldsymbol{I}_m] \bmod 2q \text{ and } \boldsymbol{s} = [f, \boldsymbol{s}^T, \boldsymbol{e}^T]^T$$

which ensures that $\boldsymbol{A}\boldsymbol{s} = q\boldsymbol{j} \bmod 2q$, as desired.

To target a comparable security level, this NTWE-based version can be parametrized with $\ell' = \ell - 1$ with the coefficients of $\boldsymbol{z}$ still having similar sizes as the ones in the MLWE and NTRU-based versions. Thus, $\boldsymbol{z}$ can be represented by $n(\ell' + m + 1) = n\ell + nm$ relatively small integers and, with $m = \ell$, the size of $\boldsymbol{z}$ is thus essentially the same for this NTWE-based version and for the NTRU-based version. Furthermore, as with the MLWE-based version, we can keep $n$ fixed to some power of two and freely change $\ell'$ and $m$ in order to alter the targeted security level. As such, this NTWE-based scheme provides the flexibility of an MLWE-based scheme with the compactness of an NTRU-based scheme and it is therefore the focus of this work.

## 2 Preliminaries

### 2.1 Notation

We denote matrices by bold upper case letters and vectors by bold lower case letters. We use $\boldsymbol{j} = [1, 0, \ldots, 0]^T$ to denote the first unit vector, with its dimension implicit from the context. The uniform distribution over a set $\mathcal{S}$ we denote by $\mathcal{U}(\mathcal{S})$ and taking a sample $x$ from a distribution $\mathcal{D}$ we denote by $x \leftarrow \mathcal{D}$.

We primarily make use of the Euclidean $\ell_2$ norm, which we denote by $||\cdot||$. We additionally use the infinity norm and $\ell_1$ norm which we denote by $||\cdot||_\infty$ and $||\cdot||_1$ respectively.

Our signature scheme works in the ring $\mathcal{R} = \mathbb{Z}[x]/(x^n + 1)$ where $n$ is a power of two. To each element in $\mathcal{R}$ we associate an $n$-dimensional coefficient vector. Vectors in $\mathcal{R}^k$ can thus be associated with an $nk$-dimensional vector consisting of the coefficients of the $k$ ring elements. We let the norm $||\boldsymbol{v}||$ of a vector $\boldsymbol{v} \in \mathcal{R}^k$ be the norm of this coefficient vector.

We use the standard modular reduction $y = x \bmod p$ such that $y$ is the unique value in $[0, p)$ that satisfies $y = x + kp$ for some integer $k$. Additionally we use the centered modular reduction $y = x \bmod^{\pm} p$ with $y$ the unique value in $[-p/2, p/2)$ such that $y = x + kp$ for some integer $k$. We also denote by $\mathrm{LSB}(x)$

the least significant bit of $x$. All of these functions are naturally extended to vectors, to elements of $\mathcal{R}$ through their coefficient vectors, and to vectors over $\mathcal{R}$.

For a function $f$ and a set $\mathcal{S}$, we let

$$f(\mathcal{S}) = \sum_{x \in \mathcal{S}} f(x).$$

### 2.2 Signature Schemes

A signature scheme consist of three algorithms (KeyGen, Sign, Verify). The KeyGen algorithm outputs a verification key $\mathsf{vk}$ and a signing key $\mathsf{sk}$. The signing key $\mathsf{sk}$ can be used to sign a message $\mu$ via $\mathsf{Sig} \leftarrow \mathrm{Sign}(\mathsf{sk}, \mu)$ and the signature can be verified via $\mathrm{Verify}(\mathsf{Sig}, \mathsf{vk}, \mu)$. With the signature scheme we consider, for valid keys $(\mathsf{vk}, \mathsf{sk}) \leftarrow \mathrm{KeyGen}$, signatures produced via $\mathsf{Sig} \leftarrow \mathrm{Sign}(\mathsf{sk}, \mu)$ always pass verification, as indicated by $\mathrm{Verify}(\mathsf{Sig}, \mathsf{vk}, \mu)$ outputting 1.

For the scheme to be considered secure, it must be hard to forge a signature that passes verification. Three different security notions are relevant for our signature scheme and the proof of its security.

The weakest of the security notions that we consider, which is only used in proving the stronger security properties, is unforgeability under no message attacks (UF-NMA). The advantage of an adversary $\mathcal{A}$ in the UF-NMA security game is given by

$$\Pr\left[\mathrm{Verify}(\mathsf{Sig}, \mathsf{vk}, \mu) = 1 \mid (\mathsf{Sig}, \mu) \leftarrow \mathcal{A}(\mathsf{vk})\right]$$

where $\mathsf{vk}$ is a verification key given by KeyGen.

A stronger security notion is unforgeability under chosen message attacks (UF-CMA). The advantage of an adversary in this security game is similar to that of the UF-NMA game, but the adversary is additionally given access to an oracle that signs any message chosen by the adversary. However, the adversary is required to provide a forgery for a message for which the oracle has not provided a signature.

The strongest security notion we consider is strong unforgeability under chosen message attacks (sUF-CMA). The advantage of an adversary in this security game is defined almost the same as for the UF-CMA game, but the adversary is now successful as long as it provides a valid signature which it has not received from the oracle, even if the forgery is for a message which the oracle has provided a different signature for.

### 2.3 Lattice Assumptions

The security of our scheme can be based on the assumed hardness of the decision NTWE problem and the MSIS problem. The decision NTWE problem and normal form MSIS problem that we rely upon are given by the following definitions.

**Definition 1 (NTWE distribution).** *Let $q$ be a prime, $m$ and $\ell$ be positive integers and $\mathcal{D}$ be some distribution over $\mathcal{R}$. Furthermore, let $\boldsymbol{s}$ be a vector in $\mathcal{R}^\ell$ and $f$ be an invertible element of $\mathcal{R}_q$. Then, a sample from the NTWE distribution $\mathcal{W}^m_{s,f,\mathcal{D}}$ is given by $(\boldsymbol{A}, \boldsymbol{b})$ for $\boldsymbol{A} \leftarrow \mathcal{U}(\mathcal{R}_q^{m\times\ell})$ and $\boldsymbol{b} = (\boldsymbol{As} + \boldsymbol{e})f^{-1} \bmod q$ where $\boldsymbol{e} \leftarrow \mathcal{D}^m$.*

**Definition 2 (Decision NTWE problem).** *The advantage of an adversary $\mathcal{A}$ against the NTWE$_{q,m,\ell,\mathcal{D}}$ problem is given by*

$$\left| \begin{array}{c} \Pr\left[\mathcal{A}(\boldsymbol{A}, \boldsymbol{b}) = 1 \mid \boldsymbol{A} \leftarrow \mathcal{R}_q^{m\times\ell}, \boldsymbol{b} \leftarrow \mathcal{R}_q^m\right] - \\ \Pr\left[\mathcal{A}(\boldsymbol{A}, \boldsymbol{b}) = 1 \mid (\boldsymbol{A}, \boldsymbol{b}) \leftarrow \mathcal{W}^m_{s,f,\mathcal{D}}\right] \end{array} \right|$$

*where $\boldsymbol{s}$ is sampled from $\mathcal{D}^\ell$ and $f = 2f_0+1$ with $f_0$ sampled from $\mathcal{D}$ conditioned on $f$ being invertible in $\mathcal{R}_q$.*

**Definition 3 (Normal form MSIS problem).** *Let $q$ be a prime, $m$ and $k$ be positive integers and $B > 0$ be some bound. The advantage of an adversary $\mathcal{A}$ against the MSIS$_{q,m,k,B}$ problem is given by*

$$\Pr\left[0 < ||\boldsymbol{y}|| < B \wedge [\boldsymbol{A}, \boldsymbol{I}_m] \cdot \boldsymbol{y} \equiv 0 \mod q \mid \boldsymbol{A} \leftarrow \mathcal{R}_q^{m\times k}, \boldsymbol{y} \leftarrow \mathcal{A}(\boldsymbol{A})\right].$$

The security of our scheme in the random oracle model can be based on the assumed hardness of the MSIS problem by making use of the forking lemma. However, to construct a more efficient scheme, we instead rely on a special self-target variant of the MSIS problem. This same approach is taken by most other similar lattice-based signature schemes that are constructed using the Fiat-Shamir paradigm.

Such a self-target variant of the MSIS problem could potentially be easier than the ordinary MSIS problem with the same parameters. However, as in previous works, we assume that the self-target MSIS problem actually is as hard as the corresponding MSIS problem. This is motivated by the fact that the only known way to solve this self-target MSIS problem is through solving the corresponding MSIS problem. More specifically, we rely on a bimodal self target MSIS problem defined below, which is the same problem that HAETAE [8,9] relies on.

This BimodalSelfTargetMSIS problem is parametrized by a size bound $B > 0$ and integers $q, m, \ell > 0$. Furthermore, it depends on a hash function $\mathcal{H}$ from $\mathcal{R}_{2q}^m \times \mathcal{M}$ to $\mathcal{C}$ where $\mathcal{M} \subset \{0,1\}^*$ is a message space and $\mathcal{C} \subseteq \mathcal{R}_2$ is a challenge space.

**Definition 4 (BimodalSelfTargetMSIS$_{\mathcal{H},q,m,\ell,B}$problem).** *An adversary $\mathcal{A}$ against the BimodalSelfTargetMSIS$_{\mathcal{H},q,m,\ell,B}$ problem is given $\boldsymbol{A}_0 \in \mathcal{R}^{m\times\ell}$ and $\boldsymbol{b} \in \mathcal{R}^m$ with elements sampled uniformly at random in $\mathcal{R}_q$. The adversary is to produce $(\boldsymbol{z}, c, \mu) \in (\mathcal{R}^{m+\ell+1}, \mathcal{C}, \mathcal{M})$ such that $\boldsymbol{z} \neq \boldsymbol{0}$, $||\boldsymbol{z}|| < B$ and*

$$\mathcal{H}(\boldsymbol{Az} - qc\boldsymbol{j} \bmod 2q, \mu) = c$$

*where $\boldsymbol{A} = [q\boldsymbol{j} - 2\boldsymbol{b}, 2\boldsymbol{A}_0, 2\boldsymbol{I}] \bmod 2q$.*

### 2.4 Discrete Gaussian Distributions

We use $\rho_r(\boldsymbol{v})$ to denote the Gaussian function $\exp(-\|\boldsymbol{v}\|^2/(2r^2))$, and let $\rho(\boldsymbol{v}) = \rho_1(\boldsymbol{v})$. The discrete Gaussian distribution $\mathcal{D}_{\mathcal{L},r}$ with parameter $r$ over a lattice $\mathcal{L}$ is the distribution where the probability of a vector $\boldsymbol{v} \in \mathcal{L}$ is given by

$$\frac{\rho_r(\boldsymbol{v})}{\sum_{\boldsymbol{w}\in\mathcal{L}} \rho_r(\boldsymbol{w})} = \frac{\rho_r(\boldsymbol{v})}{\rho_r(\mathcal{L})}$$

and the probability of $\boldsymbol{v} \notin \mathcal{L}$ is 0. We also consider discrete Gaussian distributions over the ring $\mathcal{R} = \mathbb{Z}[x]/(x^n + 1)$, where we sample the coefficient vector of an element in $\mathcal{R}$. This also naturally extends to sampling vectors over $\mathcal{R}$.

## 3 Our New Rejection Sampling Method

In this section we describe our new rejection sampling method and its advantages over previous methods. Given a sample $\boldsymbol{y}$ from some distribution and some vector $\boldsymbol{v}$ with limited norm, the rejection sampling should either abort and output $\perp$ or output a vector $\boldsymbol{z}$ such that $\boldsymbol{z} = \boldsymbol{y} + k\boldsymbol{v}$ for some odd integer $k$. Additionally, conditioned on $\boldsymbol{z} \neq \perp$, the output from the rejection sampling should follow some distribution that is independent of $\boldsymbol{v}$. Quite similar to bimodal rejection sampling, unless it aborts, our sampling outputs either $\boldsymbol{y} + \boldsymbol{v}$ or $\boldsymbol{y} - \boldsymbol{v}$.

The novelty of our new method is that the rejection sampling is given more freedom in selecting whether to output $\boldsymbol{y} + \boldsymbol{v}$ or $\boldsymbol{y} - \boldsymbol{v}$. Previous methods for rejection sampling from bimodal distributions first randomly select $\boldsymbol{y}+\boldsymbol{v}$ or $\boldsymbol{y}-\boldsymbol{v}$ with equal probability and then either rejects or outputs the result. We instead select the output via the procedure $R_{\boldsymbol{v}}(\boldsymbol{y})$ in Fig. 1 for more general functions $f_{\boldsymbol{v}}$ and $g_{\boldsymbol{v}}$.

$R_{\boldsymbol{v}}(\boldsymbol{y})$

$(a, b) = (f_{\boldsymbol{v}}(\boldsymbol{y}), g_{\boldsymbol{v}}(\boldsymbol{y}))$
$r \leftarrow \mathcal{U}([0, 1))$
**if** $r < a$
  **return** $\boldsymbol{y} - \boldsymbol{v}$
**if** $r < a + b$
  **return** $\boldsymbol{y} + \boldsymbol{v}$
**return** $\perp$

**Fig. 1.** New method for rejection sampling, dependent on functions $f_{\boldsymbol{v}}$ and $g_{\boldsymbol{v}}$.

For the output of our new rejection sampling, conditioned on it not being $\perp$, to be independent of the vector $\boldsymbol{v}$, the functions $f_{\boldsymbol{v}}$ and $g_{\boldsymbol{v}}$ must satisfy certain properties. The following lemma details conditions on these functions under which the output of $R_{\boldsymbol{v}}(\boldsymbol{y})$ follows some given distribution $\mathcal{Z}$.

**Lemma 1.** *Let $\mathcal{Y}, \mathcal{Z}$ be some distributions with $p_y(\boldsymbol{y})$ the probability of $\boldsymbol{y} \leftarrow \mathcal{Y}$ and $p_z(\boldsymbol{z})$ the probability of $\boldsymbol{z} \leftarrow \mathcal{Z}$ and let $\boldsymbol{v}$ be some non-zero vector. Furthermore, let $f_v(\boldsymbol{z})$ and $g_v(\boldsymbol{z})$ be functions and $M \geq 1$ be a parameter such that*

$$f_v(\boldsymbol{z}) + g_v(\boldsymbol{z}) \leq 1 \tag{1}$$

$$f_v(\boldsymbol{z}) \geq 0, \quad g_v(\boldsymbol{z}) \geq 0 \tag{2}$$

$$p_y(\boldsymbol{z}+\boldsymbol{v})f_v(\boldsymbol{z}+\boldsymbol{v}) + p_y(\boldsymbol{z}-\boldsymbol{v})g_v(\boldsymbol{z}-\boldsymbol{v}) = \frac{p_z(\boldsymbol{z})}{M} \tag{3}$$

*for all $\boldsymbol{z}$. Then, the distribution of $\boldsymbol{z} \leftarrow R_v(\boldsymbol{y})$ conditioned on $\boldsymbol{z} \neq \perp$ is $\mathcal{Z}$ and the probability that $\boldsymbol{z} = \perp$ is $1 - 1/M$.*

*Proof.* Based on the properties of $f_v$ and $g_v$ we are guaranteed that $R_v(\boldsymbol{y})$ returns $\boldsymbol{y} - \boldsymbol{v}$ with probability $f_v(\boldsymbol{y})$ and $\boldsymbol{y} + \boldsymbol{v}$ with probability $g_v(\boldsymbol{y})$. The probability of an input $\boldsymbol{y}$ is $p_y(\boldsymbol{y})$, and the probability of an output $\boldsymbol{z}$ is therefore

$$p_y(\boldsymbol{z}+\boldsymbol{v})f_v(\boldsymbol{z}+\boldsymbol{v}) + p_y(\boldsymbol{z}-\boldsymbol{v})g_v(\boldsymbol{z}-\boldsymbol{v}),$$

which via (3) is equal to $p_z(\boldsymbol{z})/M$. As this is a scaling of the desired output probability distribution, this gives that conditioned on $\boldsymbol{z} \neq \perp$, the output is distributed as if from $\mathcal{Z}$.

The probability that the procedure does not output $\perp$ is given by the sum of $p_z(\boldsymbol{z})/M$ over all $\boldsymbol{z} \neq \perp$. As $p_z$ is a probability distribution and thus sums to 1, the probability over $\boldsymbol{y}$ that $R_v(\boldsymbol{y})$ outputs something other than $\perp$ is $1/M$ and the probability of $\boldsymbol{z} = \perp$ is thus $1 - 1/M$. □

In the following subsections we detail how we construct functions $f_v$ and $g_v$ that fulfill the properties of Lemma 1.

First, in Sect. 3.1, we consider requirements of such functions when the input and output distributions are the same distribution and when we attempt to target zero rejection probability via setting $M = 1$. In this relatively general setting, we are unable to construct $f_v$ and $g_v$ that are guaranteed to fulfill the properties of Lemma 1.

In Sect. 3.2, we allow for $M > 1$ in a more specialized setting where we adapt the construction of $f_v$ and $g_v$ from Sect. 3.1 to get functions that are guaranteed to fulfill all the properties of Lemma 1. In this more specialized setting, an outcome $\boldsymbol{x}$ of the relevant distribution only depends on $||\boldsymbol{x}||$, with the probability of $\boldsymbol{x}$ decreasing as $||\boldsymbol{x}||$ increases.

For our signature scheme, we rely on these functions $f_v$ and $g_v$ for the specific case when the relevant distribution is a discrete Gaussian distribution. In Sect. 3.3, we further analyze the resulting functions $f_v$ and $g_v$ in this setting. In particular, for this setting we somewhat simplify the definition of these functions $f_v$ and $g_v$ and show that they can be efficiently computed to sufficient precision.

Finally, in Sect. 3.4 we detail the concrete advantage of our new rejection sampling compared to previous rejection sampling methods. In particular, we focus on a comparison to rejection sampling from bimodal Gaussian distributions, as used with BLISS, since this seems like the most relevant comparison.

### 3.1 Same Input and Output Distributions

For our analysis, we limit ourself to the case where $\mathcal{Z} = \mathcal{Y}$, and thus $p_y(\boldsymbol{x}) = p_z(\boldsymbol{x}) = p(\boldsymbol{x})$ for every $\boldsymbol{x}$. Functions $f_v$ and $g_v$ that satisfy the requirements of Lemma 1 must thus satisfy that

$$\frac{p(\boldsymbol{z})}{M} = p(\boldsymbol{z}+\boldsymbol{v})f_v(\boldsymbol{z}+\boldsymbol{v}) + p(\boldsymbol{z}-\boldsymbol{v})g_v(\boldsymbol{z}-\boldsymbol{v}). \tag{4}$$

This can be seen as $f_v$ and $g_v$ redistributing part of the input probability on the points $\boldsymbol{z}+\boldsymbol{v}$ and $\boldsymbol{z}-\boldsymbol{v}$ to ensure the correct probability for the output $\boldsymbol{z}$.

The functions $f_v$ and $g_v$ also influence the probability of other outputs. In particular, the function $g_v$ also distribute part of the probability of the input $\boldsymbol{z}+\boldsymbol{v}$ to ensure that the probability for the output $\boldsymbol{z}+2\boldsymbol{v}$ is correct. Similarly, the function $f_v$ distribute part of the probability of the input $\boldsymbol{z}-\boldsymbol{v}$ to ensure the correct probability for the output $\boldsymbol{z}-2\boldsymbol{v}$. The dependence on other inputs cascades, and the functions $f_v$ and $g_v$ thus redistribute the probability of inputs that are an odd multiple of $\boldsymbol{v}$ away from $\boldsymbol{z}$ to ensure the correct probability of outputs that are even multiples of $\boldsymbol{v}$ away from $\boldsymbol{z}$.

For the procedure $R_v$ to never reject, the functions $f_v$ and $g_v$ must satisfy the properties of Lemma 1 with $M = 1$. For this to be possible for all points related to any given $\boldsymbol{z}$, the probability weight on inputs must equal the probability weight on outputs. This corresponds to the requirement that

$$\sum_{k\in\mathbb{Z}} p(\boldsymbol{z}+2k\boldsymbol{v}) = \sum_{k\in\mathbb{Z}} p(\boldsymbol{z}+(2k+1)\boldsymbol{v})$$

or equivalently that

$$\sum_{k\in\mathbb{Z}} (-1)^k p(\boldsymbol{z}+k\boldsymbol{v}) = 0. \tag{5}$$

However, note that although this requirement is necessary, it is not sufficient for $M = 1$ to be possible. For instance, it is impossible to construct valid functions $f_v$ and $g_v$ if $p(\boldsymbol{z}) = t \neq 0$ and $p(\boldsymbol{z}+3\boldsymbol{v}) = t$ while $p(\boldsymbol{z}+k\boldsymbol{v}) = 0$ for all other $k$.

If (5) holds, there is a natural description of $f_v$ and $g_v$ that may satisfy the properties of Lemma 1 with $M = 1$. This pair of functions is determined by considering the consequences of (4) being satisfied for $\boldsymbol{z}' = \boldsymbol{z}+2k\boldsymbol{v}$ for every integer $k \neq 0$. With (4) satisfied for every other related output, the probability weight left for $f_v(\boldsymbol{z}+\boldsymbol{v})$ and $g_v(\boldsymbol{z}-\boldsymbol{v})$ can be determined, and this gives our definition for these functions.

In order for (4) to be satisfied for every output of the form $\boldsymbol{z}+2k\boldsymbol{v}$ with $k > 0$, the remaining probability weight on input $\boldsymbol{z}+\boldsymbol{v}$ is

$$p(\boldsymbol{z}+\boldsymbol{v}) - \sum_{k=2}^{\infty} (-1)^k p(\boldsymbol{z}+k\boldsymbol{v}).$$

Letting $f_v$ distribute the remaining probability weight to the output $\boldsymbol{z}$ gives that

$$f_v(\boldsymbol{z}+\boldsymbol{v}) = \sum_{k=0}^{\infty} (-1)^k \frac{p(\boldsymbol{z}+(k+1)\boldsymbol{v})}{p(\boldsymbol{z}+\boldsymbol{v})}$$

or equivalently

$$f_{\boldsymbol{v}}(\boldsymbol{y}) = \sum_{k=0}^{\infty}(-1)^k \frac{p(\boldsymbol{y}+k\boldsymbol{v})}{p(\boldsymbol{y})}.$$

Similarly, letting the remaining probability weight on the input $\boldsymbol{z}-\boldsymbol{v}$ be distributed by $g_{\boldsymbol{v}}$ to $p(\boldsymbol{z})$ gives that

$$g_{\boldsymbol{v}}(\boldsymbol{y}) = \sum_{k=0}^{\infty}(-1)^k \frac{p(\boldsymbol{y}-k\boldsymbol{v})}{p(\boldsymbol{y})}.$$

These functions fulfill

$$\begin{aligned} f_{\boldsymbol{v}}(\boldsymbol{z}+\boldsymbol{v})p(\boldsymbol{z}+\boldsymbol{v}) + g_{\boldsymbol{v}}(\boldsymbol{z}-\boldsymbol{v})p(\boldsymbol{z}-\boldsymbol{v}) \\ &= \sum_{k=0}^{\infty}(-1)^k(p(\boldsymbol{z}+(k+1)\boldsymbol{v}) + (p(\boldsymbol{z}-(k+1)\boldsymbol{v})) \\ &= p(\boldsymbol{z}) - \sum_{k\in\mathbb{Z}}(-1)^k p(\boldsymbol{z}+k\boldsymbol{v}) = p(\boldsymbol{z}) \end{aligned}$$

with final equality as (5) holds.

For our signature scheme, we can not directly apply this approach as (5) does not hold for every $\boldsymbol{z}$. Furthermore, even with (5) satisfied, these definitions do not guarantee that $f_{\boldsymbol{v}}(\boldsymbol{z}) \geq 0$ and $g_{\boldsymbol{v}}(\boldsymbol{z}) \geq 0$ for every $\boldsymbol{z}$. In the next section, we add some additional requirements on $p(\boldsymbol{z})$ and allow for $M > 1$. This allows us to alter the definitions of $f_{\boldsymbol{v}}$ and $g_{\boldsymbol{v}}$ so that they do fulfill all the properties of Lemma 1. As we consider $M > 1$, these altered definitions work even if (5) does not hold.

### 3.2 Norm-Dependent Distribution

In this section, we limit ourself to $p(\boldsymbol{z})$ that depend only on the norm of $\boldsymbol{z}$ and decrease with increasing norm. This is for instance the case for Gaussian distributions, which is the distribution we use for our signature scheme. With such a limitation on $p(\boldsymbol{z})$, we can find a suitable definition for $f_{\boldsymbol{v}}$ and $g_{\boldsymbol{v}}$ that satisfy all requirements of Lemma 1.

For this analysis, we define the function

$$S_{\boldsymbol{v}}(\boldsymbol{y}) = \sum_{k=0}^{\infty}(-1)^k \frac{p(\boldsymbol{y}+k\boldsymbol{v})}{p(\boldsymbol{y})}$$

which is the definition of $f_{\boldsymbol{v}}(\boldsymbol{y})$ from the previous section. Furthermore, as $p(\boldsymbol{y})$ is only determined by the norm of $\boldsymbol{y}$, we have that

$$S_{\boldsymbol{v}}(-\boldsymbol{y}) = \sum_{k=0}^{\infty}(-1)^k \frac{p(-\boldsymbol{y}+k\boldsymbol{v})}{p(-\boldsymbol{y})} = \sum_{k=0}^{\infty}(-1)^k \frac{p(\boldsymbol{y}-k\boldsymbol{v})}{p(\boldsymbol{y})}$$

which is the definition of $g_{\boldsymbol{v}}(\boldsymbol{y})$ from the previous section.

We are guaranteed that either

$$||\boldsymbol{y} + (k+1)\boldsymbol{v}||^2 \geq ||\boldsymbol{y} + k\boldsymbol{v}||^2 \text{ or } ||\boldsymbol{y} - (k+1)\boldsymbol{v}||^2 \geq ||\boldsymbol{y} - k\boldsymbol{v}||^2$$

for every $k \geq 0$ and we know that $p(\boldsymbol{x})$ is decreasing with increasing $||\boldsymbol{x}||$. From this it follows that either $S_{\boldsymbol{v}}(\boldsymbol{y}) \geq 0$ or $S_{\boldsymbol{v}}(-\boldsymbol{y}) \geq 0$, since for at least one of these functions, the absolute values of terms in the sum are strictly decreasing. The idea is to define both $f_{\boldsymbol{v}}(\boldsymbol{y})$ and $g_{\boldsymbol{v}}(\boldsymbol{y})$ based on the one of $S_{\boldsymbol{v}}(\boldsymbol{y})$ and $S_{\boldsymbol{v}}(-\boldsymbol{y})$ that is guaranteed to be positive. This corresponds to deciding whether to sum up positive or negative multiples of $\boldsymbol{v}$ based on which choice moves the sum away from $\mathbf{0}$.

In particular, if $\langle \boldsymbol{y}, \boldsymbol{v}\rangle \geq ||\boldsymbol{v}||^2$, then we let $f_{\boldsymbol{v}}(\boldsymbol{y}) = S_{\boldsymbol{v}}(\boldsymbol{y})/M \geq 0$ for some $M \geq 1$. In order for (4) to be fulfilled for $\boldsymbol{z} = \boldsymbol{y} - \boldsymbol{v}$, we then require that

$$g_{\boldsymbol{v}}(\boldsymbol{y} - 2\boldsymbol{v}) = \frac{p(\boldsymbol{y} - \boldsymbol{v}) - S_{\boldsymbol{v}}(\boldsymbol{y})p(\boldsymbol{y})}{Mp(\boldsymbol{y} - 2\boldsymbol{v})} = \frac{1 - S_{\boldsymbol{v}}(\boldsymbol{y} - 2\boldsymbol{v})}{M}.$$

Similarly, if $\langle \boldsymbol{y}, \boldsymbol{v}\rangle < ||\boldsymbol{v}||^2$, we instead let $f_{\boldsymbol{v}}(\boldsymbol{y}) = (1 - S_{\boldsymbol{v}}(-\boldsymbol{y}))/M$ which leads to the requirement that

$$g_{\boldsymbol{v}}(\boldsymbol{y} - 2\boldsymbol{v}) = \frac{p(-\boldsymbol{y} + \boldsymbol{v}) + (S_{\boldsymbol{v}}(-\boldsymbol{y}) - 1)p(\boldsymbol{y})}{Mp(-\boldsymbol{y} + 2\boldsymbol{v})} = \frac{S_{\boldsymbol{v}}(-\boldsymbol{y} + 2\boldsymbol{v})}{M}.$$

in order for (4) to be fulfilled for $\boldsymbol{z} = \boldsymbol{y} - \boldsymbol{v}$.

These definitions for $f_{\boldsymbol{v}}$ and $g_{\boldsymbol{v}}$ are detailed in the theorem below, where we prove that, for a suitable $M$, these functions fulfill all requirements of Lemma 1. Note that if (5) is fulfilled for all relevant $\boldsymbol{y}$, then these functions satisfy the requirements of Lemma 1 with $M = 1$ and we recover the same functions as considered in the previous section.

**Theorem 1.** *Let $\mathcal{K}_{\boldsymbol{v}}$ be the set of $\boldsymbol{y}$ such that $|\langle \boldsymbol{y}, \boldsymbol{v}\rangle| \leq ||\boldsymbol{v}||^2$ and let $M \geq 1$ be such that*

$$M \geq \max_{\boldsymbol{y} \in \mathcal{K}_{\boldsymbol{v}}} 1 - \sum_{k \in \mathbb{Z}} (-1)^k \frac{p(\boldsymbol{y} + k\boldsymbol{v})}{p(\boldsymbol{y})}.$$

*Then, the functions*

$$f_{\boldsymbol{v}}(\boldsymbol{y}) = \begin{cases} \dfrac{S_{\boldsymbol{v}}(\boldsymbol{y})}{M} & If \langle \boldsymbol{y}, \boldsymbol{v}\rangle \geq ||\boldsymbol{v}||^2 \\ \dfrac{1 - S_{\boldsymbol{v}}(-\boldsymbol{y})}{M} & If \langle \boldsymbol{y}, \boldsymbol{v}\rangle < ||\boldsymbol{v}||^2 \end{cases}$$

*and*

$$g_{\boldsymbol{v}}(\boldsymbol{y}) = \begin{cases} \dfrac{1 - S_{\boldsymbol{v}}(\boldsymbol{y})}{M} & If \langle \boldsymbol{y}, \boldsymbol{v}\rangle \geq -||\boldsymbol{v}||^2 \\ \dfrac{S_{\boldsymbol{v}}(-\boldsymbol{y})}{M} & If \langle \boldsymbol{y}, \boldsymbol{v}\rangle < -||\boldsymbol{v}||^2 \end{cases}$$

*fulfill all the requirements of Lemma 1.*

*Proof.* We begin by showing that (3) holds for these definitions of $f_v$ and $g_v$. For $z$ such that $\langle z, v\rangle \geq 0$, we have $\langle z-v, v\rangle \geq -\left|\left|v^2\right|\right|$ and $\langle z+v, v\rangle \geq \left|\left|v^2\right|\right|$. As such, we have

$$\begin{aligned} p(z+v)f_v(z+v) &+ p(z-v)g_v(z-v) \\ &= \frac{S_v(z+v)p(z+v) + (1-S_v(z-v))p(z-v)}{M} \\ &= \frac{p(z-v)}{M} + \sum_{k=0}^{\infty}(-1)^k \frac{p(z+(k+1)v) - p(z+(k-1)v)}{M} \\ &= \frac{p(z)}{M} \end{aligned}$$

as expected. Furthermore, when $\langle z, v\rangle < 0$, we have $\langle z-v, v\rangle < -\left|\left|v^2\right|\right|$ and $\langle z+v, v\rangle < \left|\left|v^2\right|\right|$ and thus

$$\begin{aligned} p(z+v)f_v(z+v) &+ p(z-v)g_v(z-v) \\ &= \frac{(1-S_v(-z-v))p(z+v) + S_v(-z+v)p(z-v)}{M} \\ &= \frac{p(z+v)}{M} + \sum_{k=0}^{\infty}(-1)^k \frac{p(z-(k-1)v) - p(z-(k+1)v)}{M} \\ &= \frac{p(z)}{M} \end{aligned}$$

as expected.

Next, we show that $f_v(y) \geq 0$ and $g_v(y) \geq 0$ for every $y$. This follows from showing that, when $\langle y, v\rangle \geq -||v||^2$ then $S_v(y) \leq 1$ and when $\langle y, v\rangle \geq ||v||^2$ then $S_v(y) \geq 0$. To this end, we first note that

$$||y+kv||^2 = ||y||^2 + 2k\langle y, v\rangle + k^2\,||v||^2$$

and see that if $\langle y, v\rangle \geq 0$, then $||y+kv||$ is greater than $||y+(k-1)v||$ for every $k \geq 1$.

When $\langle y, v\rangle \geq 0$, and thus also when $\langle y, v\rangle \geq ||v||^2$, we have

$$S_v(y) = \sum_{k=0}^{\infty}(-1)^k \frac{p(y+kv)}{p(y)} = \sum_{k=0}^{\infty} \frac{p(y+2kv) - p(y+(2k+1)v)}{p(y)} \geq 0$$

as every term in the second sum is non-negative. Furthermore, when $\langle y, v\rangle \geq -||v||^2$, we have

$$\begin{aligned} S_v(y) = \sum_{k=0}^{\infty}(-1)^k \frac{p(y+kv)}{p(y)} &= 1 - \sum_{k=1}^{\infty}(-1)^{k+1} \frac{p(y+kv)}{p(y)} \\ &= 1 - S_v(y+v) \cdot \frac{p(y+v)}{p(y)} \end{aligned}$$

and this is upper bounded by 1 as $S_v(y+v) \geq 0$ since $\langle y+v, v\rangle \geq 0$.

Finally, left to show is only that $f_v(\boldsymbol{y}) + g_v(\boldsymbol{y}) \leq 1$ for every $\boldsymbol{y}$. To this end, we first note that when $|\langle \boldsymbol{y}, \boldsymbol{v}\rangle| > ||\boldsymbol{v}||^2$ this is trivially true as

$$f_v(\boldsymbol{y}) + g_v(\boldsymbol{y}) = \begin{cases} \dfrac{S_v(\boldsymbol{y}) + 1 - S_v(\boldsymbol{y})}{M} & If \langle \boldsymbol{y}, \boldsymbol{v}\rangle > ||\boldsymbol{v}||^2 \\ \dfrac{S_v(-\boldsymbol{y}) + 1 - S_v(-\boldsymbol{y})}{M} & If \langle \boldsymbol{y}, \boldsymbol{v}\rangle < -||\boldsymbol{v}||^2 \end{cases} = \frac{1}{M}.$$

Meanwhile, when $|\langle \boldsymbol{y}, \boldsymbol{v}\rangle| \leq ||\boldsymbol{v}||^2$, we have that

$$\begin{aligned} f_v(\boldsymbol{y}) + g_v(\boldsymbol{y}) &= \frac{2 - S_v(\boldsymbol{y}) - S_v(-\boldsymbol{y})}{M} \\ &= \frac{1}{M}\left(1 - \sum_{k \in \mathbb{Z}} (-1)^k \frac{p(\boldsymbol{y} + k\boldsymbol{v})}{p(\boldsymbol{y})}\right) \leq 1. \end{aligned}$$

with final inequality due to the definition of $M$ in the theorem statement. □

### 3.3 Discrete Gaussian Distributions

To actually make use of the definitions of $f_v(\boldsymbol{y})$ and $g_v(\boldsymbol{y})$ in Theorem 1 we must be able to efficiently compute $S_v(\boldsymbol{y})$ with sufficiently high precision. In this section, we show that this is possible when we work with a discrete Gaussian distribution, which is the case we focus on in this work.

When considering a discrete Gaussian distribution, $p(\boldsymbol{y})$ is proportional to $\rho_r(\boldsymbol{y})$ for some Gaussian parameter $r$. As such, we have that

$$S_v(\boldsymbol{y}) = \sum_{k \geq 0} (-1)^k \frac{\rho_r(\boldsymbol{y} + k\boldsymbol{v})}{\rho_r(\boldsymbol{y})}$$

and we want to efficiently compute a sufficiently good approximation of this $S_v(\boldsymbol{y})$. The following lemma bounds the error incurred by only including the $t$ first terms of the infinite sum in the expression for $S_v(\boldsymbol{y})$, in the regime where its value is relevant to us. This shows that only accounting for a few terms of this sum provides a sufficiently good approximation of $S_v(\boldsymbol{y})$. In particular, only including the first 20 terms of the sum results in a value that differs significantly less than $2^{-256}$ from the true value of the infinite sum, even for the worst case[2] where $||\boldsymbol{v}|| = 1$. Since the lemma follows from simple calculations, we omit the proof from here and instead include it in a full version of this work [18].

**Lemma 2.** *The function $S_v(\boldsymbol{y})$ only depends on $\langle \boldsymbol{y}, \boldsymbol{v}\rangle$ and $||\boldsymbol{v}||^2$. Furthermore, for arbitrary $t \geq 1$, fixed $\boldsymbol{v}$ and with $\langle \boldsymbol{y}, \boldsymbol{v}\rangle \geq -||\boldsymbol{v}||^2$ then*

$$\left| S_v(\boldsymbol{y}) - \sum_{k=0}^{t} (-1)^k \frac{\rho_r(\boldsymbol{y} + k\boldsymbol{v})}{\rho_r(\boldsymbol{y})} \right| \leq \frac{\rho_r(t\boldsymbol{v})}{\rho_r(\boldsymbol{v}) - \rho_r(2\boldsymbol{v})}$$

[2] The special case $\boldsymbol{v} = \boldsymbol{0}$ is never relevant for our rejection sampling.

To actually compute $f_v$ and $g_v$, we must also have an efficient way to compute a value for $M$. The value of $M$ must be no smaller than the infinite sum in Theorem 1 and we determine a simple expression that satisfy this in Lemma 3 below. This bound is very tight for relevant parameters, and there is therefore no significant downside to using this expression for $M$. However, note that the main purpose of this is to simplify the expression for $M$. We therefore do not include the proof here, instead including it in a full version of this paper [18].

**Lemma 3.** *Let $\mathcal{K}_v$ be the set of $\boldsymbol{y}$ such that $|\langle \boldsymbol{y}, \boldsymbol{v}\rangle| \leq ||\boldsymbol{v}||^2$ and let $\alpha = r/\,||\boldsymbol{v}||$. Then*

$$\max_{\boldsymbol{y}\in\mathcal{K}_v} 1 - \sum_{k\in\mathbb{Z}}(-1)^k \frac{\rho_r(\boldsymbol{y}+k\boldsymbol{v})}{\rho_r(\boldsymbol{y})} \leq 1 + \frac{2\alpha\sqrt{2\pi}\rho(\pi\alpha)}{\rho_\alpha(1)\cdot(1-\rho_1(2\pi\alpha))} = M_\alpha$$

*and $M_\alpha$ is strictly decreasing with $\alpha$.*

This finally gives the expression for the functions $f_v$ and $g_v$ that we use for the rejection sampling via $R_v$ for our signature scheme. These definitions for $f_v$ and $g_v$ are given in Corollary 1 below, which follows from combining Theorem 1 with Lemma 3.

**Corollary 1.** *Let $\alpha > 0$ and let*

$$M = M_\alpha = 1 + \frac{2\alpha\sqrt{2\pi}\rho(\pi\alpha)}{\rho_\alpha(1)\cdot(1-\rho(2\pi\alpha))}.$$

*For every vector $\boldsymbol{v}$ such that $\alpha \leq r/\,||\boldsymbol{v}||$, the functions $f_v$ and $g_v$ defined via*

$$f_v(\boldsymbol{y}) = \begin{cases} \frac{S_v(\boldsymbol{y})}{M} & If \langle \boldsymbol{y}, \boldsymbol{v}\rangle \geq ||\boldsymbol{v}||^2 \\ \frac{1-S_v(-\boldsymbol{y})}{M} & If \langle \boldsymbol{y}, \boldsymbol{v}\rangle < ||\boldsymbol{v}||^2 \end{cases}$$

*and*

$$g_v(\boldsymbol{y}) = \begin{cases} \frac{1-S_v(\boldsymbol{y})}{M} & If \langle \boldsymbol{y}, \boldsymbol{v}\rangle \geq -||\boldsymbol{v}||^2 \\ \frac{S_v(-\boldsymbol{y})}{M} & If \langle \boldsymbol{y}, \boldsymbol{v}\rangle < -||\boldsymbol{v}||^2 \end{cases}$$

*fulfill all the requirements of Lemma 1.*

### 3.4 Benefit of Our Method

Using the functions $f_v$ and $g_v$, as given by Corollary 1 to rejection sample with $R_v$ leads to a repetition rate of $M$. We want to compare this $M$ with the repetition rate of previous works for lattice-based signatures constructed using the Fiat-Shamir with aborts methodology. In particular, we compare our repetition rate to that of schemes relying on rejection sampling from bimodal Gaussian distributions.

For this comparison, we define the set $\mathcal{V}$ to contain all possible vectors $\boldsymbol{v}$ that we want the functions $f_{\boldsymbol{v}}$ and $g_{\boldsymbol{v}}$ given by Corollary 1 to handle. The rejection rate of both our approach and previous ones is dependent on $\alpha = r/\|\boldsymbol{w}\|$, where $\boldsymbol{w}$ is the element of $\mathcal{V}$ of maximal norm. In this setting, bimodal Gaussian schemes such as BLISS [14], have a repetition rate of $\exp(1/(2\alpha^2)) = 1/\rho_\alpha(1)$, and the expected number of rejections is thus $1/\rho_\alpha(1) - 1$.

In order to illustrate the benefit of our new method, we provide a plot in Fig. 2 with the logarithm of the expected number of rejections for our new method compared to the same value for BLISS. For the parametrizations in BLISS, a value of $\alpha$ between 0.5 and 1 is used. As can be seen from the plot in Fig. 2, our new method has a noticeable advantage in the rejection rate for the values of $\alpha$ used for BLISS. From this it also follows that, with the same rejection rate, our new method allows for a parametrization with somewhat smaller $\alpha$, leading to somewhat smaller signatures.

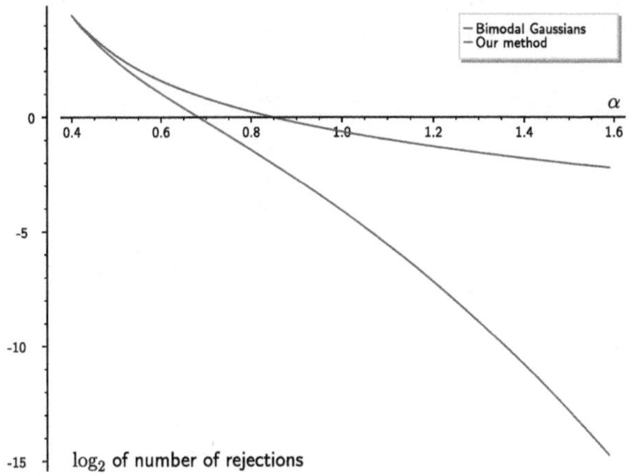


**Fig. 2.** Base two logarithm of the expected number of rejections for each signature with normal bimodal Gaussian rejection sampling and with our new method.

Note that the advantage in terms of rejection rate of our method increase as $\alpha$ increase. For relatively large $\alpha$ the ordinary bimodal Gaussian rejection sampling method still has to reject relatively frequently, whereas the rejection rate for our new method quickly approaches 0 with larger $\alpha$. By itself, this does not provide a significant advantage as, from a performance perspective, there is not that big of a difference between rejecting one out of ten signatures compared to rejecting signatures only very rarely.

The low rejection rate for larger $\alpha$ can, however, be used to ensure that even if the sampling is repeated multiple times, there is still a high probability that all repetitions succeed. This allows our new method to gain a significant advantage over previous methods, as it enables an iterative construction of $\boldsymbol{z}$. As described in Sect. 1.2, this is accomplished by iteratively performing rejection sampling over each of the coefficients of $\boldsymbol{c}$. This iterative process is initialised with $\boldsymbol{z}_0 = \boldsymbol{y}$ and $k \leq \kappa$ vectors $\boldsymbol{c}_i$ such that $\boldsymbol{c} = \sum_i \boldsymbol{c}_i$ while each $\boldsymbol{c}_i$ consists of zeroes and a single 1. The iterative process then constructs $\boldsymbol{z}_i = \boldsymbol{z}_{i-1} \pm \boldsymbol{S}\boldsymbol{c}_i$ for each $i \in 1, \ldots, k$, with the final output of the rejection sampling given by $\boldsymbol{z} = \boldsymbol{z}_k$.

Similar to without the iterative approach, the functions $f_{\boldsymbol{v}}$ and $g_{\boldsymbol{v}}$ used for the iterative rejection sampling are defined via Corollary 1. However, compared to the non-iterative approach, the set $\mathcal{V}$ that the functions has to handle vectors $\boldsymbol{v}$ from is different. With the iterative rejection sampling $\mathcal{V}$ consists of all possible columns of $\boldsymbol{S}$, whereas without it, the set consists of all possible values of $\boldsymbol{S}\boldsymbol{c}$. As the longest column of $\boldsymbol{S}$ is significantly shorter than the longest vector of the form $\boldsymbol{S}\boldsymbol{c}$, this allows the functions $f_{\boldsymbol{v}}$ and $g_{\boldsymbol{v}}$ to be defined with $M = M_\alpha$ for a significantly larger $\alpha$.

Another benefit of our new method for rejection sampling is that the rejection probability decrease exponentially with increasing $\alpha$. As such, it is easy to select parameters that target a negligible rejection probability and therefore allow the rejection condition to be safely ignored. To quantify this, we note that the rejection probability is given by

$$\begin{aligned} 1 - \frac{1}{M} &= \frac{2\alpha\sqrt{2\pi}\rho(\pi\alpha)}{\rho_\alpha(1) \cdot (1 - \rho(2\pi\alpha)) + 2\alpha\sqrt{2\pi}\rho(\pi\alpha)} \\ &\leq \frac{2\alpha\sqrt{2\pi}\rho(\pi\alpha)}{\rho_\alpha(1) \cdot (1 - \rho(2\pi\alpha))} < 4\alpha\sqrt{2\pi}\rho(\pi\alpha) \end{aligned}$$

with the final inequality holding when $\alpha \geq 1$. From this, it follows that

$$\log\left(1 - \frac{1}{M}\right) = \log(4\alpha\sqrt{2\pi}) - \log(e)\pi^2\alpha^2/2 \tag{6}$$

from which we can see that $\alpha \geq 4$ leads to a rejection probability that is smaller than $2^{-108}$.

A signature scheme parametrized with $\alpha \geq 4$ could thus quite likely be used to sign on the order of $2^{100}$ messages without ever triggering the rejection condition. Furthermore, only a little information about the secret is leaked if a single signature that should have been rejected is emitted by the signature scheme. As such, a scheme parametrized with $\alpha \geq 4$ can be implemented while ignoring the rejection condition, without this significantly impacting the security of the scheme.

## 4 Signature Scheme

The high-level construction of our signature scheme is the same as that of BLISS. However, our scheme differs from BLISS by using our new method for rejection sampling in an iterative manner to construct the signatures. Additionally, the public key of our scheme is constructed based on the NTWE problem whereas BLISS is based on the NTRU problem.

Due to the iterative construction of our signatures, there are several separate chances for rejection, once for each of the at most $\kappa$ non-zero coefficient of $c$. However, the iterative construction also allows for a larger $\alpha$ to be used and therefore results in a lower rejection probability. Although having to repeat the sampling $\kappa$ times increases the total rejection probability, when using our new rejection sampling, this is more than compensated for by the iterative construction enabling a larger $\alpha$ to be used. As such, when targeting a similar total rejection probability, the iterative construction allows our scheme to be parametrized with significantly smaller parameters, resulting in a more compact scheme.

Note that our iterative construction of signatures could also be used with previous rejection sampling methods to enable a larger $\alpha$. However, for previous methods, the larger $\alpha$ typically does not compensate for the increase to total rejection probability due to having to repeat the sampling $\kappa$ times. Thus, although a similar iterative construction of signatures is possible also with previous rejection sampling methods, it would not be beneficial.

Our signature scheme makes use of the functions $f_v$ and $g_v$ from Corollary 1 to implement the rejection sampling procedure $R_v(\boldsymbol{y})$ described in Fig. 1. For the definition of these functions, we let $\mathcal{V}$ be the set of all possible secret vectors $\boldsymbol{s}$, ensuring that the scheme has the same rejection probability for all possible secrets. We furthermore ensure that only keys with $||\boldsymbol{s}|| \leq B_\mathrm{k}$ are generated, and thus $\alpha = r/B_\mathrm{k}$ is used to determine the value of $M = M_\alpha$.

To illustrate the high level structure of the scheme, we present an uncompressed version of our scheme in Fig. 3 and briefly describe it in the next section. As described in Sect. 4.2, significantly more compact signatures are possible through utilizing compression techniques similar to those utilized in many previous works [3,8,12,23]. Although this compression somewhat complicates the description of the scheme, it is relatively standard and is very similar to that of previous schemes. Because of this, most details of the compression are left to the full version of this work [18].

### 4.1 Uncompressed Signature Scheme

For the key-generation $\boldsymbol{A}_0$ and $\boldsymbol{b}$ are generated as an NTWE instance, and, assuming the hardness of the decision NTWE problem, the pair $(\boldsymbol{A}_0, \boldsymbol{b})$ are computationally indistinguishable from uniformly random. The verification key $\boldsymbol{A}$ is constructed from $\boldsymbol{A}_0$ and $\boldsymbol{b}$ whereas the secret key $\boldsymbol{s}$ is constructed from the secret of the NTWE instance, with these keys constructed to fulfill that $\boldsymbol{A}\boldsymbol{s} \equiv q\boldsymbol{j} \mod 2q$.

For signing a message, a relatively short vector $\boldsymbol{y}$ is sampled and a commitment $\boldsymbol{w} = \boldsymbol{A}\boldsymbol{y} \bmod 2q$ is computed. From this, and the message to be signed, a challenge $c$ is derived using a random oracle $\mathcal{H} : \mathcal{R}_q^m \times \mathcal{M} \to \mathcal{C}$ where $\mathcal{M}$ is the message space and $\mathcal{C}$ is some challenge space. In practice this random oracle is instantiated from a secure hash function combined with a way to sample from the challenge space, in the same way as for HAETAE.

A signature consist of this challenge, and a short vector $\boldsymbol{z}$ such that

$$\boldsymbol{Az} \equiv \boldsymbol{w} + qc\boldsymbol{j} \mod 2q. \tag{7}$$

To construct $\boldsymbol{z}$, the rejection sampling procedure $R_{\boldsymbol{v}}$ in Fig. 1 is used with the functions $f_{\boldsymbol{v}}$ and $g_{\boldsymbol{v}}$ from Corollary 1. The vectors $\boldsymbol{v}$ that are used are given by $\boldsymbol{s}x^j$, for each monomial $x^j$ in $c$. The end result is $\boldsymbol{z} = \boldsymbol{y} + \boldsymbol{s}c'$ for some ternary $c' \equiv c \mod 2$ which ensures that (7) holds.

Verification verifies that $\boldsymbol{z}$ is sufficiently short, and implicitly verifies that (7) holds by checking that

$$\mathcal{H}(\boldsymbol{Az} - qc\boldsymbol{j} \bmod 2q, \mu) = \mathcal{H}(\boldsymbol{w}, \mu) = c.$$

**KeyGen**

1: $A_0 \leftarrow \mathcal{U}(\mathcal{R}_q)^{m\times\ell}$
2: $\boldsymbol{s}_0 \leftarrow \mathcal{D}^{\ell}_{\mathcal{R},\sigma}$
3: $\boldsymbol{e} \leftarrow \mathcal{D}^{m}_{\mathcal{R},\sigma}$
4: $f_0 \leftarrow \mathcal{D}_{\mathcal{R},\sigma}$
5: $f = 2f_0 + 1$
6: **if** $f$ is not invertible in $\mathcal{R}_q$
7: Goto line 4
8: $\boldsymbol{b} = (\boldsymbol{A}_0\boldsymbol{s}_0 + \boldsymbol{e})/f \bmod q$
9: $\boldsymbol{A} = [q\boldsymbol{j} - 2\boldsymbol{b}, 2\boldsymbol{A}_0, 2\boldsymbol{I}_m]$
10: $\boldsymbol{s} = [f, \boldsymbol{s}_0, \boldsymbol{e}]$
11: **if** $\|\boldsymbol{s}\| \geq B_{\mathrm{k}}$
12: Goto line 2
13: **return** $vk = \boldsymbol{A}, sk = \boldsymbol{s}$

**Verify**$((\boldsymbol{z}, c), \boldsymbol{A}, \mu)$

1: Reject if $\|\boldsymbol{z}\| > B_{\mathrm{s}}$
2: Accept if $\mathcal{H}(\boldsymbol{Az} - qc\boldsymbol{j} \bmod 2q, \mu) = c$

**Sign**$(\boldsymbol{A}, \boldsymbol{s}, \mu)$

1: $\boldsymbol{y} \leftarrow \mathcal{D}^{\ell+m+1}_{\mathcal{R},r}$
2: $\boldsymbol{w} = \boldsymbol{Ay} \bmod 2q$
3: $c = \mathcal{H}(\boldsymbol{w}, \mu)$
4: $\boldsymbol{z} = \mathrm{RejectSample}(\boldsymbol{y}, c)$
5: **if** $\boldsymbol{z} = \perp$ or $\|\boldsymbol{z}\| > B_{\mathrm{s}}$
6: Goto line 1
7: **return** $(\boldsymbol{z}, c)$

**RejectSample**$(\boldsymbol{z}_0, c)$

1: $k = 0$
2: **for** Each monomial $x^j$ in $c$
3: $k = k + 1$
4: $\boldsymbol{z}_k = R_{\boldsymbol{s}x^j}(\boldsymbol{z}_{k-1})$
5: **if** $\boldsymbol{z}_k = \perp$
6: **return** $\perp$
7: $r \leftarrow \mathcal{U}([0, 1))$
8: **if** $r > M^{k-\kappa}$
9: **return** $\perp$
10: **return** $\boldsymbol{z}_k$

**Fig. 3.** Key-generation, signing and verification for an uncompressed version of our new scheme with an auxiliary function for rejection sampling.

**Challenge Space.** The challenge space $\mathcal{C}$ of our signature scheme contains elements in $\mathcal{R}$ with at most $\kappa$ non-zero coefficients, and with $\mathcal{C}$ that contains a sufficiently large number of possible challenges. For most parametrizations, $\mathcal{C}$ consist of elements with exactly $\kappa$ coefficients equal to one and the remaining coefficients equal to zero.

For the parametrizations which target the highest security level, the challenge space $\mathcal{C}$ is selected somewhat differently in order to increase its size. As with HAETAE [8,9], for these parametrizations $\mathcal{C}$ instead consist of exactly half of all possible degree $n-1$ polynomials with only 0 and 1 coefficients. Furthermore, the challenge polynomials all contain at most $n/2$ non-zero coefficients. In this case, the challenge space thus contains $2^{n-1}$ different elements. For details on exactly which polynomials are included, and how to sample from this challenge space, we refer to Sect. 2.4 of [9].

In order to ensure that the rejection sampling does not influence the distribution of challenges $c$ in signatures that are output, we ensure that every challenge $c$ has the same rejection probability. Over a random $\boldsymbol{y}$, the function $R_{\boldsymbol{v}}(\boldsymbol{y})$ has the same rejection rate for every $\boldsymbol{v}$, and thus the rejection rate for a challenge $c$ is influenced only by the number of non-zero coefficients in $c$.

As mentioned above, for the highest security level, the number of non-zero coefficients vary and challenges with fewer non-zero coefficients require fewer iterative steps for the rejection sampling. As each iterative step has the same rejection rate, if not handled separately, challenges with fewer non-zero coefficients would be more likely in output signatures. To ensure that every challenge $c$ is equally likely, signatures that have fewer than $\kappa$ non-zero coefficients are therefore rejected with a suitable probability.

**Bounds.** For our scheme, a discrete Gaussian distribution $\mathcal{D}_{\mathcal{R},\sigma}$ with parameter $\sigma$ is used for sampling secrets. To bound the rejection probability, we ensure that $||\boldsymbol{s}|| < B_{\mathrm{k}}$ by rejecting secret keys with norm larger than this. We select $B_{\mathrm{k}}$ as $\sigma\sqrt{n(m+\ell+4)}$, resulting in approximately half of the secret keys being rejected.

Limiting the norm of the secret key by $B_{\mathrm{k}}$ results in secrets sampled from a narrower distribution, and should somewhat decrease the security of the scheme. However, as around half of the secret keys are still accepted, the security against lattice attacks should not decrease by significantly more than 1 bit. For simplicity, we do not account for this small security loss in our security estimates.

As $\boldsymbol{z}$ follows a discrete Gaussian distribution, there is no upper bound on $||\boldsymbol{z}||$. However, in order to ensure that signature forgery is hard, only sufficiently short $\boldsymbol{z}$ can be accepted as valid signatures. As such, only signatures that satisfy $||\boldsymbol{z}|| \leq B_{\mathrm{s}}$ are emitted. If a $\boldsymbol{z}$ with larger norm is generated during a signing attempt, the signature is rejected and the signing of the message is retried.

The bound $B_{\mathrm{s}}$ must be set to not result in too many signature rejections, while still only accepting relatively short $\boldsymbol{z}$. We therefore set $B_{\mathrm{s}} = \left\lceil 1.02r\sqrt{n(\ell+m+1)} \right\rceil$, which from testing results in rejecting around 20% of constructed signatures. For the parametrizations targeting higher security levels, this rejection probability is somewhat lower. Note that this rejection of $\boldsymbol{z}$ with too large norm only applies to the final signature, and not to the intermediate $\boldsymbol{z}_i$ during the iterative rejection sampling.

### 4.2 More Compact Signatures

Compressing the signatures and encoding them in a compact way leads to significantly smaller signatures. The compression and encoding we use is very similar to that used for HAETAE, which in turn is similar to what many other lattice-based signature schemes use.

In particular, as with several recent schemes such as HAETAE and G+G, we make use of the rANS encoding of Duda [15] to encode our signatures. This results in signature sizes that are close to the entropy of the distribution that the signatures follow.

Additionally, we do not include the last $m$ coordinates of the $\boldsymbol{z}$ vector in the signature, instead replacing them with a hint vector. This is similar to several other Fiat-Shamir signature schemes, including Dilithium [23]. Compressing the signatures in this way is enabled by not committing to the full $\boldsymbol{w}$ vector during signing, instead only committing to higher order bits of this vector by rounding the coefficients of $\boldsymbol{w}$ to the nearest multiple of some parameter $\tau$. With a larger $\tau$, the compressed signature becomes smaller.

A downside to using a larger compression parameter $\tau$ is that the security of the scheme is based on the assumed hardness of the MSIS problem with a larger bound $B_{\mathrm{v}} > B_{\mathrm{s}}$. Analysis of the signature compression is relatively standard and we therefore omit this analysis from here and instead include it in the full version of this work [18]. The full version also explains relevant details of the rANS encoding used.

An additional size optimization that is almost always used for lattice-based cryptosystems is to pseudorandomly derive uniformly random values from a short seed. In our case, this allows the verification key to be represented by $\boldsymbol{b}$ and a short seed from which $\boldsymbol{A}_0$ is derived. For the concrete verification key sizes we present, we therefore account for the size of $\boldsymbol{A}_0$ only as a 32-byte seed.

### 4.3 Security

The theoretical security of our signature scheme is given by Theorem 2 and follows from relatively standard arguments based on the Fiat-Shamir transform. In particular, the proof makes use of the fact that the produced signatures follow a distribution that is independent of the secret key of the scheme. As the proof follows the same structure as the one for HAETAE [8,9] without much novelty, we omit it from here and instead include it in the full version of this work [18].

**Theorem 2.** *Let $\gamma$ be the commitment min-entropy of our signature scheme and $\beta$ the probability that it restarts during signing. Furthermore, let $\mathcal{A}$ be a UF-CMA attacker against our signature scheme that makes $q_S$ queries to the signing oracle and $q_H$ queries to the random oracle $\mathcal{H}$.*

*Then there are adversaries $\mathcal{B}$ and $\mathcal{B}'$ with essentially the same running time as $\mathcal{A}$ such that*

$$\mathsf{Adv}^{UF\text{-}CMA}(\mathcal{A}) \leq \mathsf{Adv}^{NTWE}_{q,m,\ell,\mathcal{D}_{\mathcal{R},\sigma}}(\mathcal{B}) + \mathsf{Adv}^{BimodalSelfTargetMSIS}_{\mathcal{H},q,m,\ell,B_v}(\mathcal{B}') + \frac{2q_S 2^{-\gamma/2}}{1-\beta}\sqrt{q_H + 1 + \frac{q_S}{1-\beta}} + 2^{-\gamma/2+1}(q_H+1)\sqrt{\frac{q_S}{1-\beta}}.$$

*Additionally, let $\mathcal{A}'$ be an adversary against the sUF-CMA security of our signature scheme that makes $q'_S$ queries to the signing oracle and $q'_H$ queries to the random oracle $\mathcal{H}$. Then there are adversaries $\mathcal{F}, \mathcal{F}', \mathcal{F}''$ with essentially the same running time as $\mathcal{A}$ such that*

$$\mathsf{Adv}^{sUF\text{-}CMA}(\mathcal{A}') \leq 2\mathsf{Adv}^{NTWE}_{q,m,\ell,\mathcal{D}_{\mathcal{R},\sigma}}(\mathcal{F}) + \mathsf{Adv}^{BimodalSelfTargetMSIS}_{\mathcal{H},q,m,\ell,B_v}(\mathcal{F}') + \mathsf{Adv}^{MSIS}_{q,m,\ell,2B_v}(\mathcal{F}'') + \frac{2q'_S 2^{-\gamma/2}}{1-\beta}\sqrt{q'_H + 1 + \frac{q'_S}{1-\beta}} + 2^{-\gamma/2+1}(q'_H+1)\sqrt{\frac{q'_S}{1-\beta}}.$$

## 5 Concrete Parameters

In Table 1 we present some suggested parametrizations of our scheme which have a noticeable, but acceptable, rejection probability. Additionally, in Table 2 we present some parametrizations with negligible rejection probability. By applying some additional restrictions to the scheme, all rejection conditions of these parametrizations can be securely ignored. These additional restrictions are compatible with the parametrizations in Table 2 and are further described in the full version of this work [18]. We also provide a comparison of the verification key and signature sizes of our scheme to that of alternative schemes in Table 3.

The public key size presented in the tables is

$$\left\lceil \frac{nm\lceil \log(q) \rceil}{8} \right\rceil + 32$$

bytes. This corresponds to representing each coefficient of $\boldsymbol{b}$ as a $\lceil \log(q) \rceil$ bit integer, while $\boldsymbol{A}_0$ is represented by a 32-byte seed. The concrete signature size we provide for our scheme is an approximation of the entropy for the distributions of compressed signatures plus 64 bytes. This includes 32 bytes for the representation of $c$ and 32 additional bytes as leeway for padding to ensure a fixed signature size. Additional details on how signature size is estimated are included in the full version of this work [18].

We have not extensively investigated the probability that constructed signatures can be encoded into the size we present in the tables. However, from testing we have determined that at least a large majority of all signatures can be encoded to the presented size for all parametrizations that we consider.

### 5.1 Selecting Parameters

The security estimates of our proposed parametrizations presented in Tables 1 and 2 are computed with the lattice estimator [1]. The security estimates are given via the

`*.estimate.rough`

functions, providing an approximation of the core-SVP security.

The security of our scheme follows from Theorem 2 and our security estimates follows from estimating the concrete hardness of the relevant variants of the BimodalSelfTargetMSIS and NTWE problems. For both of these underlying problems, we make the assumption that the structure present in $\mathcal{R}$ can not be efficiently exploited, and that the structured lattice problems are as hard as unstructured counterparts. Additionally, for the concrete security of the scheme, similar to HAETAE, we assume that the min-entropy of the scheme is large enough for us to safely ignore the contribution of these terms in Theorem 2.

The concrete parameters proposed in Tables 1 and 2 have been selected such that the estimated core-SVP security closely corresponds to the desired security levels. Additionally, the parameters are selected to have an acceptable rejection probability and in an attempt to minimize the combined size of a verification key and a signature.

**MSIS Security.** A classical reduction in the random oracle model shows that an algorithm solving the $\text{BimodalSelfTargetMSIS}_{\mathcal{H},q,m,\ell,B_\text{v}}$ problem efficiently can be used to efficiently solve the $\text{MSIS}_{q,m,\ell,2B_\text{v}}$ problem. However, this reduction is not tight and, as it makes use of rewinding and the forking lemma, it can not easily be translated to a reduction in the quantum random oracle model.

Instead of using this reduction to argue for the security of our scheme, we heuristically assume that the $\text{BimodalSelfTargetMSIS}_{\mathcal{H},q,m,\ell,B_\text{v}}$ problem is as hard as the $\text{MSIS}_{q,m,\ell,B_\text{v}}$ problem. Motivation for this approach is that the only way to solve this BimodalSelfTargetMSIS problem seems to be to to solve this corresponding MSIS problem. This same approach is also used in several previous works, such as Dilithium [23] and HAETAE [8,9].

**NTWE Security.** We estimate the hardness of the NTWE problem in the same way as in [16]. This assumes that the NTWE problem with $\boldsymbol{A} \in \mathcal{R}^{m\times\ell}$ is essentially as hard as the rank $\ell+1$ module-LWE problem.

More specifically, the $\text{NTWE}_{q,m,\ell,\mathcal{D}_{\mathcal{R},\sigma}}$ problem is estimated to be as hard to solve as the unstructured LWE problem with $\boldsymbol{A} \in \mathbb{Z}_q^{m'\times\ell'}$ where $m' = mn$ and $\ell' = (\ell+1)n - 1$. Furthermore, for the unstructured LWE problem, it is assumed that all elements of the secret are sampled from $\mathcal{D}_{\mathbb{Z},\sigma}$. With this estimate, as $f = 2f_0 + 1$ is deterministically constructed from $f_0 \leftarrow \mathcal{D}_{\mathcal{R},\sigma}$, we do not account for the fact that $f$ is larger than if directly sampled from $\mathcal{D}_{\mathcal{R},\sigma}$. For our proposed parameters, the concrete estimated NTWE hardness is given by the estimated core-SVP hardness of solving such a search LWE problem.

**Table 1.** Proposed parametrizations of our signature scheme. The reported rejection rates only accounts for the probability that $\boldsymbol{z} = \perp$ is produced by RejectSample$(\boldsymbol{y}, c)$ and not the probability that $||\boldsymbol{z}|| > B_{\mathrm{s}}$.

| Security | 120 | 180 | 260 |
|---|---|---|---|
| $q$ | 12289 | 50177 | 50177 |
| $\ell$ | 1 | 3 | 4 |
| $m$ | 2 | 2 | 3 |
| $\sigma$ | 2.60 | 1.00 | 1.50 |
| $r$ | 128 | 55 | 95 |
| $\kappa$ | 58 | 80 | 128 |
| $\tau$ | 256 | 128 | 128 |
| $B_{\mathrm{k}}$ | 110.07 | 48.00 | 79.60 |
| $B_{\mathrm{s}}$ | 4178 | 2199 | 4386 |
| $B_{\mathrm{v}}$ | 5649 | 2946 | 5300 |
| Rejection rate | 0.460 | 0.642 | 0.617 |
| Rejection rate per coefficient | 0.0106 | 0.0127 | 0.0075 |
| Verification Key Size (bytes) | 928 | 1056 | 1568 |
| Signature Size (bytes) | 775 | 1184 | 1694 |
| Combined (bytes) | 1703 | 2240 | 3262 |
| BKZ block size to break SIS (Strong UF) | 420 (332) | 629 (500) | 899 (730) |
| Core-SVP cost | 122 (96) | 183 (146) | 262 (213) |
| BKZ block size to break NTWE | 414 | 618 | 881 |
| Core-SVP cost | 120 | 180 | 257 |

### 5.2 Comparison to Other Schemes

**Compactness.** In Table 3 we present the sizes of verification keys and signatures for our scheme and for other lattice-based signature schemes. Out of the presented signature schemes, only Falcon [25] and HAWK [6] have comparable sizes to our new system. Both HAWK and Falcon are based on the hash-and-sign paradigm using NTRU lattices. Meanwhile, the other schemes in the comparison are based on some variant of the Fiat-Shamir transform.

As can be seen in Table 3, our scheme is significantly more compact than all other Fiat-Shamir-based schemes in the comparison. Furthermore, even when parametrized to have negligible rejection probability, our scheme is still more compact than previous Fiat-Shamir-based schemes. The smaller verification keys and signatures are the main advantage of our new signature scheme compared to other Fiat-Shamir-based schemes.

**Secure Implementation.** The more compact hash-and-sign-based schemes Falcon and HAWK have some downsides compared to the Fiat-Shamir-based schemes, and our scheme also has similar downsides. Compared to Dilithium,

**Table 2.** Alternative parametrizations of our signature scheme which have a negligible rejection probability, allowing producing signatures without rejection.

| Security | 120 | 180 | 260 |
|---|---|---|---|
| $q$ | 50177 | 50177 | 50177 |
| $\ell$ | 2 | 3 | 4 |
| $m$ | 2 | 3 | 4 |
| $\sigma$ | 0.90 | 1.00 | 1.45 |
| $r$ | 165 | 205 | 325 |
| $\kappa$ | 58 | 80 | 128 |
| $\tau$ | 512 | 512 | 256 |
| $B_{\mathrm{k}}$ | 40.73 | 50.60 | 80.37 |
| $B_{\mathrm{s}}$ | 7541 | 10679 | 18769 |
| $B_{\mathrm{v}}$ | 10460 | 14254 | 20849 |
| Rejection rate | $2^{-111}$ | $2^{-112}$ | $2^{-111}$ |
| Verification Key Size (bytes) | 1056 | 1568 | 2080 |
| Signature Size (bytes) | 1059 | 1475 | 2161 |
| Combined (bytes) | 2115 | 3043 | 4241 |
| BKZ block size to break SIS (Strong UF) | 416 (337) | 670 (552) | 889 (742) |
| Core-SVP cost | 121 (98) | 195 (161) | 259 (216) |
| BKZ block size to break NTWE | 422 | 618 | 874 |
| Core-SVP cost | 123 | 180 | 255 |

Falcon has the downside of implementations requiring floating point operations, which can be hard to implement in a side-channel secure manner.

Our scheme may also be hard to implement in a side-channel secure manner, as it has previously been observed that implementations of rejection sampling from Gaussian distributions may be vulnerable to side-channel attacks [7,24]. Furthermore, our new more advanced rejection sampling may further complicate developing side-channel secure implementations. Although developing a secure implementation for our scheme almost certainly is harder than for schemes such as Dilithium and HAETAE, it is not directly clear how this aspect of our scheme compares to Falcon.

**Hardness Assumptions.** Compared to other lattice-based schemes, HAWK has the downside of relying on the assumed hardness of a problem that is not as well studied as other lattice problems. Our scheme has the similar downside on relying on the relatively new NTWE problem. However, as the NTWE problem can be seen as a natural combination of the NTRU and LWE problems, it can be argued to be better understood than the lattice isomorphism problem upon which HAWK is based.

Furthermore, as explained in Sect. 1.3, our scheme could also have been based on NTRU or MLWE lattices. An NTRU-based variant of our scheme would have similar sizes as the one we propose, but with less flexibility in how parameters can be selected. Meanwhile, an MLWE-based variant of our scheme would have the same flexibility in parameter choices, but with somewhat larger sizes. Our NTWE-based parametrization can be directly transferred to an MLWE-based variant of the scheme, leading to a scheme with similar security that has the same verification key sizes but with signatures that are 250–300 bytes larger for all targeted security levels. Thus, an MLWE-based variant of our scheme would still be significantly more compact than previous lattice-based Fiat-Shamir signature schemes.

**Efficiency.** Another point of comparison is how long it takes to sign a message. Due to the more advanced rejection sampling of our scheme, signing may be somewhat slower with our scheme than with previous Fiat-Shamir-based signature schemes. Additionally, our signing must repeat the rejection sampling multiple times in an iterative manner in order to actually produce a signature, increasing the runtime of signing.

We do, however, believe that each iterative step of the rejection sampling should have a cost comparable to that of previous approaches. Although the functions that should be computed are expressed as an infinite sum, Lemma 2 shows that it is sufficient to account only for a few terms of the sum. Additionally, the lemma shows that the sum only depends on the two integers $\langle \boldsymbol{y}, \boldsymbol{v} \rangle$ and $||\boldsymbol{v}||^2$ and only minimal computations that handle high dimensional vectors are thus required to compute the sum.

As we have not developed an optimized implementation of our scheme, we can not fairly compare the execution time of our scheme to that of previous schemes. However, we believe that in many contexts, the smaller signatures and verification keys of our scheme more than make up for the somewhat longer signing time.

## 6 Conclusion

Thanks to our new rejection sampling, we are able to construct a signature scheme that is significantly more compact than previous lattice-based Fiat-Shamir signature schemes. There are, however, downsides to our new scheme and still potential for it to be further improved.

A notable downside with our new sampling is its reliance on discrete Gaussian distributions which may be hard to implement in a side-channel secure manner. Meanwhile, uniformly random distributions over hypercubes and hyperballs can be sampled from relatively easily, motivating their use for Dilithium and HAETAE respectively. It may therefore be interesting if our new approach to rejection sampling could be adapted to distributions that are easier to sample from.

**Table 3.** Signature sizes in bytes for different lattice-based signature schemes.The sizes for BLISS are based on the updated analysis of [27]. Security level presented for HAWK is based directly on target NIST security category.

| Scheme | Security Level | VK Size | Signature Size | Total |
|---|---|---|---|---|
| NTRU+Sign-512 | 93 | 768 | 751 | 1519 |
| Falcon-512 | 120 | 897 | 666 | 1563 |
| HAWK-512 | 120 | 1024 | 555 | 1579 |
| Ours with rejection | 120 | 928 | 775 | 1703 |
| BLISS-512 | 87 | 896 | 831 | 1727 |
| NTRU G+G-512 | 85 | 1021 | 992 | 2013 |
| Ours without rejection | 121 | 1056 | 1059 | 2115 |
| HAETAE-120 | 119 | 992 | 1474 | 2466 |
| G+G-120 | 121 | 1472 | 1677 | 3149 |
| Dilithium-2 | 123 | 1312 | 2420 | 3732 |
| Ours with rejection | 180 | 1056 | 1184 | 2240 |
| Ours without rejection | 180 | 1568 | 1475 | 3043 |
| NTRU+Sign-1024 | 211 | 1664 | 1551 | 3215 |
| BLISS-1024 | 178 | 1792 | 1836 | 3628 |
| HAETAE-180 | 180 | 1472 | 2349 | 3821 |
| NTRU G+G-180 | 178 | 2080 | 1769 | 3849 |
| G+G-180 | 178 | 1952 | 2143 | 4095 |
| Dilithium-3 | 183 | 1952 | 3293 | 5245 |
| Falcon-1024 | 273 | 1793 | 1280 | 3073 |
| Ours with rejection | 257 | 1568 | 1694 | 3262 |
| HAWK-1024 | 260 | 2440 | 1221 | 3661 |
| Ours without rejection | 255 | 2080 | 2161 | 4241 |
| HAETAE-260 | 256 | 2080 | 2948 | 5028 |
| G+G-260 | 260 | 2336 | 2804 | 5140 |
| Dilithium-5 | 252 | 2592 | 4595 | 7187 |

Improvements of our rejection sampling may also be possible by further using the available flexibility in how the $\boldsymbol{z}$ vector in signatures can be constructed. In the same way as for the G+G signature scheme, $\boldsymbol{z}$ can be constructed as $\boldsymbol{y} + \boldsymbol{s}c + 2\boldsymbol{s}k$ for arbitrary $k \in \mathcal{R}$. We only use this flexibility to iteratively select the sign of coefficients of $c$, but further improvements may be possible by not imposing this limitation in how $k$ is selected. However, selecting $k$ more freely would complicate the analysis needed to ensure that the sampling produces the correct output distribution.

Finally, techniques used for NTRU+Sign [27] may also be beneficial for our scheme in order to further decrease the signature sizes. In particular, by constructing the public key somewhat differently in NTRU+Sign, the bimodal rejection sampling can be performed modulo $q$ instead of modulo $2q$ and a similar optimization may be possible with our scheme.

**Acknowledgments.** This research has been supported in part by the Swedish Armed Forces and was conducted at KTH Center for Cyber Defense and Information Security (CDIS). The author would like to thank Johan Håstad for extensive comments and useful discussions on early versions of this manuscript. The author also thanks Martin Ekerå for helpful feedback and comments.

## References

1. Albrecht, M.R., Player, R., Scott, S.: On the concrete hardness of learning with errors. J. Math. Cryptol. **9**(3), 169–203 (2015). https://doi.org/10.1515/jmc-2015-0016
2. Bai, S., Beard, A., Johnson, F., Vidhanalage, S.K.B., Ngo, T.: Fiat-shamir signatures based on module-NTRU. In: Nguyen, K., Yang, G., Guo, F., Susilo, W. (eds.) ACISP 22: 27th Australasian Conference on Information Security and Privacy. Lecture Notes in Computer Science, vol. 13494, pp. 289–308. Springer, Cham, Switzerland, Wollongong, NSW, Australia (2022). https://doi.org/10.1007/978-3-031-22301-3_15
3. Bai, S., Galbraith, S.D.: An improved compression technique for signatures based on learning with errors. In: Benaloh, J. (ed.) Topics in Cryptology –CT-RSA 2014. Lecture Notes in Computer Science, vol. 8366, pp. 28–47. Springer, Cham, Switzerland, San Francisco, CA, USA (2014). https://doi.org/10.1007/978-3-319-04852-9_2
4. Bai, S., Jangir, H., Lin, H., Ngo, T., Wen, W., Zheng, J.: Compact encryption based on module-NTRU problems. In: Saarinen, M.J., Smith-Tone, D. (eds.) Post-Quantum Cryptography - 15th International Workshop, PQCrypto 2024, Part I, pp. 371–405. Springer, Cham, Switzerland, Oxford, UK (2024).https://doi.org/10.1007/978-3-031-62743-9_13
5. Behnia, R., Chen, Y., Masny, D.: On removing rejection conditions in practical lattice-based signatures. In: Cheon, J.H., Tillich, J.-P. (eds.) PQCrypto 2021 2021. LNCS, vol. 12841, pp. 380–398. Springer, Cham (2021). https://doi.org/10.1007/978-3-030-81293-5_20
6. Bos, J.W., et al.: HAWK. Tech. rep., National Institute of Standards and Technology (2023). https://csrc.nist.gov/Projects/pqc-dig-sig/round-1-additional-signatures
7. Bruinderink, L.G., Hülsing, A., Lange, T., Yarom, Y.: Flush, gauss, and reload - a cache attack on the BLISS lattice-based signature scheme. In: Gierlichs, B., Poschmann, A.Y. (eds.) Cryptographic Hardware and Embedded Systems – CHES 2016. Lecture Notes in Computer Science, vol. 9813, pp. 323–345. Springer Berlin Heidelberg, Germany, Santa Barbara, CA, USA (2016). https://doi.org/10.1007/978-3-662-53140-2_16
8. Cheon, J.H., et al.: HAETAE. Tech. rep., National Institute of Standards and Technology (2023). https://csrc.nist.gov/Projects/pqc-dig-sig/round-1-additional-signatures

9. Cheon, J.H., et al.: HAETAE: shorter lattice-based fiat-shamir signatures. IACR Trans. Cryptographic Hardware Embedded Syst. **2024**(3), 25–75 (2024). https://doi.org/10.46586/tches.v2024.i3.25-75, https://tches.iacr.org/index.php/TCHES/article/view/11669
10. del Pino, R., Espitau, T., et al.: Raccoon. Tech. rep., National Institute of Standards and Technology (2023). https://csrc.nist.gov/Projects/pqc-dig-sig/round-1-additional-signatures
11. Devevey, J., Fawzi, O., Passelègue, A., Stehlé, D.: On rejection sampling in Lyubashevsky's signature scheme. In: Agrawal, S., Lin, D. (eds.) Advances in Cryptology – ASIACRYPT 2022, Part IV. Lecture Notes in Computer Science, vol. 13794, pp. 34–64. Springer, Cham, Switzerland, Taipei, Taiwan (2022). https://doi.org/10.1007/978-3-031-22972-5_2
12. Devevey, J., Passelègue, A., Stehlé, D.: G+G: A fiat-shamir lattice signature based on convolved gaussians. In: Guo, J., Steinfeld, R. (eds.) Advances in Cryptology – ASIACRYPT 2023, Part VII. Lecture Notes in Computer Science, vol. 14444, pp. 37–64. Springer, Singapore, Singapore, Guangzhou, China (2023). https://doi.org/10.1007/978-981-99-8739-9_2
13. Ducas, L.: Accelerating bliss: the geometry of ternary polynomials. Cryptology ePrint Archive, Report 2014/874 (2014). https://eprint.iacr.org/2014/874
14. Ducas, L., Durmus, A., Lepoint, T., Lyubashevsky, V.: Lattice signatures and bimodal Gaussians. In: Canetti, R., Garay, J.A. (eds.) Advances in Cryptology – CRYPTO 2013, Part I. Lecture Notes in Computer Science, vol. 8042, pp. 40–56. Springer Berlin Heidelberg, Germany, Santa Barbara, CA, USA (2013). https://doi.org/10.1007/978-3-642-40041-4_3
15. Duda, J.: Asymmetric numeral systems: entropy coding combining speed of Huffman coding with compression rate of arithmetic coding (2014). https://arxiv.org/abs/1311.2540
16. Gärtner, J.: NTWE: a natural combination of NTRU and LWE. In: Johansson, T., Smith-Tone, D. (eds.) Post-Quantum Cryptography - 14th International Workshop, PQCrypto 2023, pp. 321–353. Springer, Cham, Switzerland, College Park, USA (2023). https://doi.org/10.1007/978-3-031-40003-2_12
17. Gentry, C., Peikert, C., Vaikuntanathan, V.: Trapdoors for hard lattices and new cryptographic constructions. In: Ladner, R.E., Dwork, C. (eds.) 40th Annual ACM Symposium on Theory of Computing, pp. 197–206. ACM Press, Victoria, BC, Canada (2008). https://doi.org/10.1145/1374376.1374407
18. Gärtner, J.: Compact lattice signatures via iterative rejection sampling. Cryptology ePrint Archive, Paper 2024/2052 (2024). https://eprint.iacr.org/2024/2052
19. Hoffstein, J., Pipher, J., Silverman, J.H.: NTRU: a ring-based public key cryptosystem. In: Buhler, J.P. (eds) Third Algorithmic Number Theory Symposium (ANTS). Lecture Notes in Computer Science, vol. 1423, pp. 267–288. Springer, Berlin, Heidelberg (1998). https://doi.org/10.1007/BFb0054868
20. Langlois, A., Stehlé, D.: Worst-case to average-case reductions for module lattices. Des. Codes Crypt. **75**(3), 565–599 (2015). https://doi.org/10.1007/s10623-014-9938-4
21. Lyubashevsky, V.: Fiat-Shamir with aborts: applications to lattice and factoring-based signatures. In: Matsui, M. (ed.) ASIACRYPT 2009. LNCS, vol. 5912, pp. 598–616. Springer, Heidelberg (2009). https://doi.org/10.1007/978-3-642-10366-7_35

22. Lyubashevsky, V.: Lattice signatures without trapdoors. In: Pointcheval, D., Johansson, T. (eds.) Advances in Cryptology – EUROCRYPT 2012. Lecture Notes in Computer Science, vol. 7237, pp. 738–755. Springer Berlin Heidelberg, Germany, Cambridge, UK (2012). https://doi.org/10.1007/978-3-642-29011-4_43
23. Lyubashevsky, V., Ducas, L., Kiltz, E., Lepoint, T., Schwabe, P., Seiler, G., Stehlé, D., Bai, S.: CRYSTALS-DILITHIUM. Tech. rep., National Institute of Standards and Technology (2022). https://csrc.nist.gov/Projects/post-quantum-cryptography/selected-algorithms-2022
24. Pessl, P.: Analyzing the shuffling side-channel countermeasure for lattice-based signatures. In: Dunkelman, O., Sanadhya, S.K. (eds.) Progress in Cryptology - INDOCRYPT 2016: 17th International Conference in Cryptology in India. Lecture Notes in Computer Science, vol. 10095, pp. 153–170. Springer, Cham, Switzerland, Kolkata, India (2016). https://doi.org/10.1007/978-3-319-49890-4_9
25. Prest, T., et al.: FALCON. Tech. rep., National Institute of Standards and Technology (2022). https://csrc.nist.gov/Projects/post-quantum-cryptography/selected-algorithms-2022
26. Schnorr, C.P.: Efficient signature generation by smart cards. J. Cryptol. **4**(3), 161–174 (1991). https://doi.org/10.1007/BF00196725
27. Woo, J., et al.: NTRU+sign: compact NTRU-based signatures using bimodal distributions. Cryptology ePrint Archive, Paper 2025/106 (2025). https://eprint.iacr.org/2025/106

# The Algebraic One-More MISIS Problem and Applications to Threshold Signatures

Chenzhi Zhu(✉) and Stefano Tessaro

Paul G. Allen School of Computer Science & Engineering, University of Washington, Seattle, USA
{zhucz20,tessaro}@cs.washington.edu

**Abstract.** This paper introduces a new one-more computational problem for lattice-based cryptography, which we refer to as the *Algebraic One-More MISIS* problem, or AOM-MISIS for short. It is a modification of the AOM-MLWE problem recently introduced by Espitau et al. (CRYPTO '24) to prove security of new two-round threshold signatures.

Our first main result establishes that the hardness of AOM-MISIS is implied by the hardness of MSIS and MLWE (with suitable parameters), both of which are standard assumptions for efficient lattice-based cryptography. We prove this result via a new generalization of a technique by Tessaro and Zhu (EUROCRYPT '23) used to prove hardness of a one-more problem for linear hash functions assuming their collision resistance, for which no clear lattice analogue was known. Since the hardness of AOM-MISIS implies the hardness of AOM-MLWE, our result resolves the main open question from the work of Espitau et al., who only provided a similar result for AOM-MLWE restricted to *selective* adversaries, a class which does not cover the use for threshold signatures.

Furthermore, we show that our novel formulation of AOM-MISIS offers a better interface to develop tighter security bounds for state-of-the-art two-round threshold signatures. We exemplify this by providing new proofs of security, assuming the hardness of MLWE and MSIS, for two threshold signatures, the one proposed in the same work by Espitau et al., as well as a recent construction by Chairattana-Apirom et al. (ASIACRYPT 2024). For the former scheme, we also show that it satisfies the strongest security notion (TS-UF-4) in the security hierarchy of Bellare et al. (CRYPTO '22), as a result of independent interest.

## 1 Introduction

*One-more* assumptions enable proofs of security for several interactive protocols, most notably identification schemes, threshold signatures, multi-signatures, and blind signatures. The perhaps most prominent example is the *one-more discrete logarithm assumption* (OMDL) [7], which requires the hardness of computing $Q$ discrete logarithm instances given access to an oracle that allows the adversary to compute $Q-1$ discrete logarithms of *arbitrary* group elements. It has been used throughout several security proofs (e.g., cf. [6,7,22,36]), where the oracle


Y. Tauman Kalai and S. F. Kamara (Eds.): CRYPTO 2025, LNCS 16000, pp. 548–581, 2025.
https://doi.org/10.1007/978-3-032-01855-7_18

allows the reduction to simulate secret-key dependent behavior of honest parties without knowing the secret key. This notwithstanding, the main point of controversy is that an assumption such as OMDL is very strong–for instance, Koblitz and Menezes [28] point out that in certain groups, it is easier to break OMDL than to solve the standard discrete logarithm problem. The only available route justifying its plausible hardness on standard elliptic curves is a proof [5] in the generic-group model (GGM) [34,40].

PROVABLY-HARD ONE-MORE PROBLEMS. A few recent works [4,42] follow a different path: While they still leverage the power of one-more problems as an intermediate *interface* to design modular security proofs, they also instantiate the underlying mathematical structure to support a proof that the one-more problem is indeed hard based on more standard assumptions, such as the hardness of (standard) discrete log/RSA (in [42]) or of DDH (in [4]).

This is the angle pursued by this paper—we seek one-more problems which are sufficiently *expressive* to enable useful security proofs, while also enjoying *provable* hardness from standard assumptions. This paper deals specifically with *lattice-based cryptography.* Espitau, Katsumata, and Takemure (EKT) [20] recently introduced a one-more problem they refer to as *algebraic one-more MLWE (AOM-MLWE)* and show that its hardness yields the security of a two-round threshold signature. They also establish the *selective* hardness of AOM-MLWE from the standard MLWE and MSIS assumptions, which is however unfortunately not sufficient to support their application to threshold signatures. Another example—less relevant for this work, however—is the one-more ISIS problem [2], used in the construction of lattice-based blind signatures, which has also only been validated via cryptanalysis.

OUR CONTRIBUTIONS, IN A NUTSHELL. We introduce a new variant of AOM-MLWE which we refer to as *Algebraic One-More MISIS* (AOM-MISIS, for short),[1] and for which we show two different types of results:

- ***Provability.*** We show that the hardness of AOM-MISIS follows from the hardness of MSIS and MLWE, with suitable parameters. In fact, the hardness of AOM-MISIS *implies* the hardness of AOM-MLWE, and thus our result carries over to AOM-MLWE, providing the first reduction of AOM-MLWE to standard assumptions, which was left as a main open question in [20].
- ***Expressivity.*** We show the security of the EKT threshold signature scheme from [20], as well as of the recent scheme by Chairattana-Apirom, Tessaro, and Zhu [13], assuming the hardness of AOM-MISIS. In turn, this establishes the security of these schemes from MSIS and MLWE. We obtain either better concrete security bounds compared to [13], or proofs under weaker assumptions compared to [20] for slightly larger concrete parameter sets. We also give a proof that the EKT scheme satisfies the strongest notion of security in the hierarchy of Bellare *et al.* [6].

[1] Our naming is due to the fact that we prefer to think of our problem as a one-more version of Inhomogenous SIS (SIS), rather than of LWE.

ALGEBRAIC ONE-MORE MISIS. The definition of AOM-MISIS relies on the cyclotomic ring $R = \mathbb{Z}[X]/(X^N + 1)$, where $N$ is a power of two, as well as the associated ring $R_q = R/qR \cong \mathbb{Z}_q[X]/(X^N + 1)$ for an odd prime $q$. The problem is defined via the following game:

- **Input.** The adversary is initially given a matrix $A = [\overline{A}|\mathbb{I}_k] \in R_q^{k \times m}$, where $\overline{A} \leftarrow_\$ R_q^{k \times (m-k)}$, as well as $Q$ instances $\boldsymbol{t}_i \leftarrow A\boldsymbol{s}_i$, for $i \in [Q]$, where $\boldsymbol{s}_i \leftarrow_\$ \mathscr{D}_{\sigma_i}^m$ is "small", and sampled from an $m$-dimensional discrete Gaussian with parameter $\sigma_i$. The instance number $Q$ is a parameter of the game.
- **Oracle access.** The adversary can also (adaptively) query an oracle PI which takes as input a $Q$-dimensional vector $\boldsymbol{b} \in R^Q$, and returns $\sum_{i \in [Q]} b_i \boldsymbol{s}_i$.

To win, the adversary needs to output both $\hat{\boldsymbol{b}} = (\hat{b}_1, \ldots, \hat{b}_Q) \in R^Q$ and a "short" solution $\hat{\boldsymbol{s}} \in R^m$ such that

$$\sum_{i \in [Q]} \hat{b}_i \boldsymbol{t}_i = A\hat{\boldsymbol{s}} \, .$$

To exclude trivial winning strategies, $\hat{\boldsymbol{b}}$ must however not be in the span of the vectors $\boldsymbol{b}_1, \boldsymbol{b}_2, \ldots$ queried to PI. We in fact require something stronger, namely that in order to win, the adversary also needs to additionally output $\boldsymbol{u} \in R^Q$, along with $\hat{\boldsymbol{b}}$ and $\hat{\boldsymbol{s}}$, and the following two properties need to be satisfied:

- The vector $\boldsymbol{u}$ is orthogonal to all vectors $\boldsymbol{b}_1, \boldsymbol{b}_2, \ldots$ queried to PI, but not to $\hat{\boldsymbol{b}}$, i.e., $\boldsymbol{b}_i^\top \boldsymbol{u} = 0$, but $\hat{\boldsymbol{b}}^\top \boldsymbol{u} \neq 0$. Here, orthogonality is defined with respect to the ring $R$.
- Both vectors $(\hat{b}_1 \cdot \sigma_1, \ldots, \hat{b}_Q \cdot \sigma_Q)$ and $(u_1/\sigma_1, \ldots, u_Q/\sigma_Q)$ are appropriately small, when interpreted as real vectors. Both conditions are necessary, as otherwise a simple attack exists.

Our main result is a concrete reduction showing that the AOM-MISIS problem is indeed hard if the Module LWE (MLWE) and Module SIS (MSIS) assumptions also hold with suitable parameters, related to the parameters of the above game. Our proof relies on a novel *generalization* of the technique by Tessaro and Zhu [42], which was originally used to obtain hard one-more problems based on linear hash functions. The origin of this technique goes back to the analysis of Okamoto signatures [37], and was used also in [25]. Some prior works [26,42] can be interpreted as attempts to adapt this approach to the lattice setting in limited ways, but in our context, they would lead to worse parameters and restrictions on the generality of our game. We discuss further details in Sect. 2 below.

We note that the hardness of AOM-MISIS implies the hardness of AOM-MLWE, and thus we resolve the main open problem from [20], which only provided an analysis for *selective* adversaries issuing their oracle queries beforehand. In fact, the main difference between AOM-MISIS and AOM-MLWE is the winning condition. We require outputting a single short solution for a suitable non-trivial linear combination of the challenges, whereas AOM-MLWE requires outputting $Q$ short solutions for all challenges, given $Q - 1$ access to a similar oracle, although with different conditions on the queries. These changes are what in part enables simpler reductions for threshold signatures. A more detailed discussion is provided in Sect. 4.2.

APPLICATIONS TO THRESHOLD SIGNATURES. We first recall that in a *t-out-of-n threshold signature scheme* [18,19], $n$ potential signers each hold a secret share of a secret signing key, with an associated public verification key. Any subset of (at least) $t$ of these signers is able to jointly produce a signature, via interaction, whereas an adversary that controls fewer than $t$ signers should not be able, on its own, to come up with a valid signature.

We leverage AOM-MISIS to obtain tighter analyses for state-of-the-art *two-round* lattice-based threshold signatures, based on the MSIS/MLWE assumptions, and without assuming the hardness of any ad-hoc one-more problem. We focus on two threshold signatures, which we refer to as CTZ [13] and EKT [20]. There are several small differences between the two constructions, despite the fact that they instantiate similar ideas. Both can be seen as a natural threshold version of the Fiat-Shamir-with-abort paradigm [31] that also underlies DILITHIUM [33], albeit dispensing with the actual abort, and using a sufficiently large modulus instead. In particular, EKT is a threshold version of Raccoon [38], submitted to the additional NIST call for post-quantum signatures [35]. They are natural lattice analogues of FROST [6,15,29], a very lightweight threshold Schnorr signature.

Taking some liberty from their formal description, in both schemes, as a result of the second round, the $i$-th signer produces an affine signature share

$$\boldsymbol{z}_i = \boldsymbol{r}_i + c \cdot \lambda_i \mathsf{ss}_i ,$$

in a suitable algebraic structure, where $\mathsf{ss}_i$ is the $i$-th signer's key share, $c$ is a hash value associated with the signature, and $\lambda_i$ is a linear reconstruction coefficient associated with the secret sharing scheme. With $S$ being the set of signers, the final signature has format $(\boldsymbol{R}, \boldsymbol{z})$, where $\boldsymbol{R} = A \sum_{i \in S} \boldsymbol{r}_i$, ($A$ is a public matrix) and $\boldsymbol{z} = \sum_{i \in S} \boldsymbol{z}_i$. However, the two schemes differ in the following aspects:

- In CTZ, to avoid leakage of the secret shares, $\lambda_i \mathsf{ss}_i$ needs to remain sufficiently small and thus a secret sharing scheme with small reconstruction coefficients is needed. This incurs a significant cost due to the larger share size when compared to Shamir secret sharing. The security proof in [13] is fairly involved, and gives a direct reduction to MSIS.
- To enable the use of Shamir secret sharing, EKT changes the initial setup to ensure that any pair of signers shares a secret key, and these keys are used, in each execution of the signing protocol, to generates (pseudo)random masks $(\mathsf{msk}_i)_{i \in S}$ such that $\sum_{i \in S} \mathsf{msk}_i = 0$. The $i$-th signer then sends $\boldsymbol{z}_i + \mathsf{msk}_i$ in the second round instead of $\boldsymbol{z}_i$, and this ensures that only the *sum* of the $\boldsymbol{z}_i$'s is leaked. The security proof in [20] relies on the direct use of the AOM-MLWE assumption, and since the constructed adversary is inherently not selective, they need to rely on a conjecture about the hardness of AOM-MLWE.

In Sects. 5 and 6, we give new security analyses for both schemes based on direct reductions from AOM-MISIS, which in turn yield concrete security proofs from MLWE and MSIS. Our result for CTZ yields better parameters than the analysis of [13]. The result about EKT, in addition to now basing security on MLWE/MSIS alone, also shows a strong security property for this scheme, namely TS-UF-4 in the hierarchy of Bellare et al. [6]. The concrete efficiency numbers derived from our bounds are somewhat worse than those from EKT, but their concrete analysis relies on their own cryptanalysis of AOM-MLWE, whereas we use standard parameters for MLWE and MSIS. Closing the gap between the cryptoanalysis-driven parameter choices and those derived from our security reduction remains an interesting open problem.

The recent work on Ringtail [11] also proposes a threshold signature scheme similar in spirit to EKT and with a proof of security under MLWE. In Ringtail, unlike EKT, signers need to know already in the first round the set of involved signers $S$, and thus, unlike EKT and CTZ, Ringtail is not partially non-interactive in the sense of Bellare *et al.* [6]. Ringtail also needs to authenticate first-round messages. The authors of Ringtail mention removing these restrictions, while preserving comparable efficiency and provability from MLWE/MSIS, is an open problem, which we resolve here based on the EKT scheme.

Ringtail's security bound degrades with the number of random oracle queries, whereas ours degrades with the number of signing sessions. We note that the latter is a system parameter that can be enforced, whereas the former scales with the running time of the adversary.

<u>Remarks on CTZ.</u> While the concrete efficiency of CTZ is significantly worse than that of EKT, we see value in the CTZ construction because it does not rely on pairwise masks. CTZ closely resembles the structure of the original FROST protocol, making it a promising starting point for achieving identifiable aborts (constructing efficient partially non-interactive lattice-based threshold signatures with identifiable aborts is a big open problem in the field). In contrast, achieving identifiable aborts in EKT seems less likely without relying on heavyweight NIZK proofs, due to its reliance on pairwise masks.

Also, the security argument of CTZ works for a class of linear secret sharing schemes rather than a specific scheme. Its main source of inefficiency stems from the underlying secret sharing scheme, and its efficiency could be significantly improved if better instantiations of the underlying secret sharing scheme are proposed.

<u>Other related work.</u> We note here that there are other approaches to threshold signatures. First off, *Fully-Homomorphic Encryption* (FHE) generically yields round-optimal threshold signatures [3,9,10]. These require however the homomorphic evaluation of the signing algorithm, and thus come with a substantial computational overhead. Earlier works [14,16] proposed two-round $n$-out-of-$n$ threshold signatures derived from constructions for the related notion of multi-signatures. Gur *et al.* [24] proposed two-round construction based on linearly homomorphic encryption (LHE) which supports arbitrary thresholds. Both rounds are message-dependent. More recently, Pino *et al.* [17] propose a more efficient lattice-based threshold signature scheme that does not rely on FHE or the aforementioned heavy primitives, but the drawback is that the protocol has

three message-dependent rounds. Recent work [27] also gives a five-round threshold signature with adaptive security based on MLWE/MSIS, whereas a threshold version of Falcon [39] was presented in [21]. The latter scheme is designed for robustness but requires four message-dependent rounds and incurs quadratic communication complexity in the threshold.

## 2 Technical Overview

The main goal of this section is to provide a detailed overview of our main result establishing the hardness of AOM-MISIS based on MSIS and MLWE. We stress that our reduction will involve concrete parameters, but we keep the discussion in this section somewhat qualitative on this front.

At a technical level, it helps to see AOM-MISIS as a lattice-based analogue of the AOMPR framework proposed by Tessaro and Zhu (TZ) [42] to define one-more problems for linear hash functions. Their framework does not cover lattice problems, however—we aim to adapt it to lattices, and this presents a number of challenges, which we explain in this section. We will also discuss how prior works have already tried to overcome such challenges, how those approaches are not sufficient for our purposes, and what we do instead.

We focus first on a variant of AOM-MISIS we denote as wAOM-MISIS, where the adversary does not output the relaxation vector $\hat{\boldsymbol{b}}$ and is instead asked to output $Q$ solutions $\hat{\boldsymbol{s}}_1, \ldots, \hat{\boldsymbol{s}}_Q$ with small norm (instead of a single solution) such that $\boldsymbol{t}_i = A\hat{\boldsymbol{s}}_i$ for all $i \in [Q]$. Also, the constraint $\hat{\boldsymbol{b}}^T \boldsymbol{u} \neq 0$ is now changed to $\boldsymbol{u} \neq 0$ instead, while $\boldsymbol{b}_i^T \boldsymbol{u} = 0$ still must hold for the queries to PI.

This problem is not easier than AOM-MISIS: If the adversary wins the wAOM-MISIS game, there exists an index $i \in [Q]$ such that $u_i \neq 0$, and thus the adversary can win the original game by outputting $(\hat{\boldsymbol{s}}_i, \boldsymbol{e}_i, \boldsymbol{u})$, where $\boldsymbol{e}_i$ is the $i$-th unit vector. This is also the idea underlying the proof that AOM-MISIS hardness implies the hardness of AOM-MLWE in Sect. 4.2.

**Reduction ideas from** [42]**.** We now provide a self-contained review of TZ's proof framework in the context of wAOM-MISIS, and explain where it fails. In particular, given an adversary $\mathcal{A}$ for the wAOM-MISIS game, we build a simple MSIS adversary $\mathcal{B}$ that takes a random matrix $A \in R_q^{k \times m}$ as input and outputs a vector $\boldsymbol{z}$ with small norm such that $A\boldsymbol{z} = 0$. To start with, $\mathcal{B}$ runs $\mathcal{A}$ by simulating the wAOM-MISIS game faithfully using the matrix $A$ and sampling $\boldsymbol{s}_i$ by itself. After receiving $(\hat{\boldsymbol{s}}_1, \ldots, \hat{\boldsymbol{s}}_Q, \boldsymbol{u})$, if $\mathcal{A}$ wins, $\mathcal{B}$ finds an index $i \in [Q]$ such that $\hat{\boldsymbol{s}}_i \neq \boldsymbol{s}_i$ and outputs $\boldsymbol{z} \leftarrow \hat{\boldsymbol{s}}_i - \boldsymbol{s}_i$. Otherwise, $\mathcal{B}$ aborts.

<u>ANALYSIS OF $\mathcal{B}$.</u> It is not hard to see that $\mathcal{B}$ wins the MSIS game if such an index $i$ indeed exists, since $A\boldsymbol{z} = A\hat{\boldsymbol{s}}_i - A\boldsymbol{s}_i = 0$ and $\|\boldsymbol{z}\| \leqslant \|\boldsymbol{s}_i\| + \|\hat{\boldsymbol{s}}_i\|$ is bounded given both $\|\boldsymbol{s}_i\|$ and $\|\hat{\boldsymbol{s}}_i\|$ are bounded. Here $\|\cdot\|$ denotes the $\ell_2$-norm. The hard part is to show that such $i$ exists w.h.p. under the assumption that $\mathcal{A}$ wins w.h.p., and this is what we discuss next.

Following the same lines as TZ, we can assume w.l.o.g. that $\mathcal{A}$ is deterministic, and thus the view $\text{View}_{\mathcal{A}}(\boldsymbol{s}_1, \ldots, \boldsymbol{s}_Q)$ of $\mathcal{A}$ (assuming the matrix $A$ is fixed) is completely determined by the challenge secrets $(\boldsymbol{s}_1, \ldots, \boldsymbol{s}_Q)$. Also, we denote by $\mathbf{D}$ the set of secrets $(\boldsymbol{s}_1, \ldots, \boldsymbol{s}_Q)$ such that $\mathcal{A}$ wins the wAOM-MISIS game.

While this is not the case for us, suppose for now that $\mathbf{D}$ is finite and each $(\boldsymbol{s}_1, \ldots, \boldsymbol{s}_Q)$ is sampled uniformly from $\mathbf{D}$. The first step is to find a *derangement* $\Phi$ of $\mathbf{D}$, i.e., a permutation of $\mathbf{D}$ without fixed points, such that for any $(\boldsymbol{s}_1, \ldots, \boldsymbol{s}_Q) \in \mathbf{D}$, $\text{View}_{\mathcal{A}}(\boldsymbol{s}_1, \ldots, \boldsymbol{s}_Q) = \text{View}_{\mathcal{A}}(\boldsymbol{s}'_1, \ldots, \boldsymbol{s}'_Q)$ with $(\boldsymbol{s}'_1, \ldots, \boldsymbol{s}'_Q) = \Phi(\boldsymbol{s}_1, \ldots, \boldsymbol{s}_Q)$. Therefore, $\mathcal{A}$ also produces the same output $(\hat{\boldsymbol{s}_1}, \ldots, \hat{\boldsymbol{s}_n}, \boldsymbol{u})$ in both cases. Since $(\boldsymbol{s}_1, \ldots, \boldsymbol{s}_Q) \neq (\boldsymbol{s}'_1, \ldots, \boldsymbol{s}_Q)$, there exists an index $i \in [Q]$ such that $\boldsymbol{s}_i \neq \boldsymbol{s}'_i$ and thus either $\boldsymbol{s}_i \neq \hat{\boldsymbol{s}}_i$ or $\boldsymbol{s}'_i \neq \hat{\boldsymbol{s}}_i$, which means $\mathcal{B}$ wins the MSIS game in at least one of the cases. Since $\Phi$ is a permutation of $\mathbf{D}$, for at least half of elements in $\mathbf{D}$ lead to $\mathcal{B}$ winning. Therefore, $\mathcal{B}$ wins with at least half of the probability that $\mathcal{A}$ wins. Crucially, note that $\Phi$ does not need to be efficient for this argument to succeed, as the algorithm $\mathcal{B}$ described above is the actual reduction.

<u>CONSTRUCTING $\Phi$.</u> The first idea is to define $\Phi$ such that

$$\Phi(\boldsymbol{s}_1, \ldots, \boldsymbol{s}_Q) := (\boldsymbol{s}_1 + u_1 \cdot \Delta, \ldots, \boldsymbol{s}_Q + u_Q \cdot \Delta) \ , \tag{1}$$

where $\Delta \in R^m$ is a non-zero vector such that $A\Delta = 0$ (we will discuss below how to ensure such $\Delta$ exists), and $\boldsymbol{u}$ is the vector output by $\mathcal{A}$ in an execution with the secret value $(\boldsymbol{s}_1, \ldots, \boldsymbol{s}_Q)$. It is not hard to check that $(\boldsymbol{s}_1, \ldots, \boldsymbol{s}_Q)$ and $\Phi(\boldsymbol{s}_1, \ldots, \boldsymbol{s}_Q)$ produce the same view. First off, since $A(\boldsymbol{s}_i + u_i \cdot \Delta) = A\boldsymbol{s}_i + u_i \cdot (A\Delta) = A\boldsymbol{s}_i$, the input of $\mathcal{A}$ is identical in both cases. Further, for each PI query $\boldsymbol{b}$ made by $\mathcal{A}$, since $\boldsymbol{u}$ is a non-zero vector satisfying $\sum_{i\in[Q]} u_i b_i = 0$, we have $\sum_{i\in[Q]} b_i(\boldsymbol{s}_i + u_i \cdot \Delta) = \sum_{i\in[Q]} b_i \boldsymbol{s}_i + (\sum_{i\in[Q]} b_i u_i) \cdot \Delta = \sum_{i\in[Q]} b_i \boldsymbol{s}_i$, which means the response received by $\mathcal{A}$ is identical in both cases.

<u>ISSUES AND PRIOR APPROACHES.</u> The issue with the above approach is that in our setting the secrets are not sampled uniformly from a set. Two prior works [26, 42] have overcome this issue by sampling $\boldsymbol{s}_i$ uniformly from a bounded box $\mathscr{B}^m_{\beta_i} := \{\boldsymbol{x} \in R^m | \, \|\boldsymbol{x}\| \leqslant \beta_i\}$. Still, the challenge now is that $\Phi$ is no longer a permutation over a subset of $\mathscr{B}^m_{\beta_1} \times \cdots \times \mathscr{B}^m_{\beta_Q}$, since $\|\boldsymbol{s}_i + u_i \cdot \Delta\|$ can be larger than $\beta_i$ even though $\|\boldsymbol{s}_i\| \leqslant \beta_i$.

To overcome this issue, Hauck *et al.* [26][2] proposed to set $\beta_i$ to be very large such that the total faction of $\boldsymbol{s}_i \in \mathscr{B}^m_{\sigma_i}$ such that $\boldsymbol{s}_i + u_i \cdot \Delta$ falls outside $\mathscr{B}^m_{\sigma_i}$ is negligible in the security parameter $\kappa$. Then, one can still show $\mathcal{B}$ wins with nearly at least half of the winning probability of $\mathcal{A}$. However, this requires $\sigma_i = \Omega(2^\kappa \|u_i \Delta\|)$, which results in very inefficient constructions using this approach.

Chairattana-Apirom et al. [13] overcame the $2^\kappa$ barrier with a different approach. They let $\boldsymbol{s}_1$ be sampled from $\mathscr{B}^m_{\beta_1}$, whereas $\boldsymbol{s}_i$ is sampled from $\mathscr{D}^m_{\sigma_i}$. They use this in the security proof of their threshold signature scheme based on the MSIS assumption, but their technique can be massaged into a reduction from MSIS to a restricted version of the wAOM-MISIS game, where the PI queries are restricted, but still sufficient for their application.

[2] We note that [26] precedes [42], but deals with a lattice-analogue of a linear-hash function based framework introduced by [25] similar in spirit to that of [42].

Their proof is in some sense a probabilistic relaxation of TZ's, in that for any $s_1 \in R^m$, they consider a *random variable* $\text{View}_{\mathcal{A}}(s_1)$ which represents the view of $\mathcal{A}$ given the first secret is $s_1$, whereas the remaining secrets are sampled afresh from discrete Gaussian distributions. If for any $s_1 \neq s_1' \in R^m$, such that $As_1 = As_1'$, we can show that $\text{View}_{\mathcal{A}}(s_1)$ and $\text{View}_{\mathcal{A}}(s_1')$ are identically distributed, then we can once again carry out the same argument as above. They in fact generalize this argument by showing that if the Rényi divergence of $\text{View}_{\mathcal{A}}(s_1)$ from $\text{View}_{\mathcal{A}}(s_1')$ is small, one can still show that the winning probabilities of $\mathcal{B}$ and $\mathcal{A}$ are sufficiently related. Finally, they show the Rényi divergence is indeed bounded for the special types of queries they consider. Doing so, they ensure that $\sigma_i$ depends linearly on $\sqrt{Q}$ instead of $2^\kappa$.

Still, their reduction fails if $\mathcal{A}$ issues general PI queries, and this is because the Rényi divergence of $\text{View}_{\mathcal{A}}(s_1)$ from $\text{View}_{\mathcal{A}}(s_1')$ is no longer bounded. For example, the first secret (either $s_1$ or $s_1'$) can be recovered from an PI query with input $(1, 0, \ldots, 0)$. Moreover, they need to ensure that almost all $s_1$'s have one partner $s_i' \neq s_i \in \mathscr{B}_{\beta_1}^m$ such that $As_1 = As_1'$, and this requires $\beta_1 \geqslant 2^{\kappa/N} q^{k/m}$,[3] which leads to inefficient parameters in their threshold signature.

## 2.1 Step 1: Generalizing TZ's Argument

Our goal is to provide a reduction that supports an adversary $\mathcal{A}$ without any extra restrictions on its queries to PI, and furthermore that ensures hardness even for sufficiently small parameter choices in wAOM-MISIS. For this reason, we take a different route and generalize TZ's argument to a setting where each $s_i$ is sampled (independently) from an arbitrary distribution $\mathcal{P}_i$, rather than uniformly from a finite set.

Let $\mathcal{P} = \mathcal{P}_1 \times \cdots \times \mathcal{P}_Q$ be the joint distribution of $(s_1, \ldots, s_Q)$. Then, instead of requiring $\Phi$ to be a permutation of $\mathbf{D}$ (recalling that $\mathbf{D}$ is the set of secrets $(s_1, \ldots, s_Q)$ that make $\mathcal{A}$ win the wAOM-MISIS game), we require that the distribution of $(s_1, \ldots, s_Q)$ conditioned on $(s_1, \ldots, s_Q) \in \mathbf{D}$ (denoted as $\mathcal{P}_{|\mathbf{D}}$) is identical to that of $\Phi(s_1, \ldots, s_Q)$ conditioned on $(s_1, \ldots, s_Q) \in \mathbf{D}$ (denoted as $\Phi(\mathcal{P}_{|\mathbf{D}})$). The original TZ approach corresponds to the case when $\mathcal{P}$ is a uniform distribution over $\mathbf{D}$. Here, since arbitrary distributions over $\mathbf{D}$ are allowed, we no longer require $\mathbf{D}$ to be a finite set. The two other requirements for $\Phi$ remain the same, i.e., $\Phi$ has no fixed point over $\mathbf{D}$ and $\text{View}_{\mathcal{A}}(s_1, \ldots, s_Q) = \text{View}_{\mathcal{A}}(\Phi(s_1, \ldots, s_Q))$.

Our key observation here is that the previous argument to lower bound the success probability of $\mathcal{B}$ still applies. To see this, it helps us to extend $\Phi$ to the space of all potential secrets (not only those in $\mathbf{D}$) by defining $\Phi(s_1, \ldots, s_Q) := (s_1, \ldots, s_Q)$ for all $(s_1, \ldots, s_Q) \in R^m \backslash \mathbf{D}$. Then, consider the following two adversaries $\mathcal{B}'$ and $\mathcal{B}''$.

- $\mathcal{B}'$ is the same as $\mathcal{B}$ except that $\mathcal{B}'$ samples $(s_1, \ldots, s_Q)$ from $\Phi(\mathcal{P})$.

[3] Since $N$ is usually set to 512 or 1024, the leading term here is $q^{k/m}$.

- $\mathcal{B}''$ is the same as $\mathcal{B}$ except that 1. $\mathcal{B}''$ samples $(\boldsymbol{r}_1, \ldots, \boldsymbol{r}_Q) \leftarrow_{\$} \mathcal{P}$ and computes secrets as $(\boldsymbol{s}_1, \ldots, \boldsymbol{s}_Q) \leftarrow \Phi(\boldsymbol{r}_1, \ldots, \boldsymbol{r}_Q)$; 2. after $\mathcal{A}$ returns, $\mathcal{B}''$ outputs $\hat{\boldsymbol{s}}_i - \boldsymbol{r}_i$ if there exists $\boldsymbol{r}_i \neq \hat{\boldsymbol{s}}_i$.

We note that $\mathcal{B}'$ and $\mathcal{B}''$ do not need to be efficient. They are only used to compute the winning probability of the (efficient) adversary $\mathcal{B}$.

Denote now by $\mathsf{PWin}_{\mathcal{X}}$ the winning probability of $\mathcal{X} \in \{\mathcal{A}, \mathcal{B}, \mathcal{B}', \mathcal{B}''\}$. Then, the conclusion that $\mathsf{PWin}_{\mathcal{B}} \geqslant 1/2\mathsf{PWin}_{\mathcal{A}}$ is a straightforward corollary of the following three facts.

**Fact 1.** $\mathsf{PWin}_{\mathcal{B}} = \mathsf{PWin}_{\mathcal{B}'}$;
**Fact 2.** $\mathsf{PWin}_{\mathcal{B}} = \mathsf{PWin}_{\mathcal{B}''}$;
**Fact 3.** $\mathsf{PWin}_{\mathcal{B}'} + \mathsf{PWin}_{\mathcal{B}''} \geqslant \mathsf{PWin}_{\mathcal{A}}$.

Fact 1 is straightforward since $\mathcal{P}$ is identical to $\Phi(\mathcal{P})$, which means $\mathcal{B}$ and $\mathcal{B}'$ behave the same. Fact 2 is also not hard to see. Since $\mathrm{View}_A(\boldsymbol{r}_1, \ldots, \boldsymbol{r}_Q) = \mathrm{View}_A(\Phi(\boldsymbol{r}_1, \ldots, \boldsymbol{r}_Q)) = \mathrm{View}_A(\boldsymbol{s}_1, \ldots, \boldsymbol{s}_Q)$, even if $\mathcal{B}''$ sets the secrets to $(\boldsymbol{r}_1, \ldots, \boldsymbol{r}_Q)$ instead of $\boldsymbol{s}_1, \ldots, \boldsymbol{s}_Q$, the output of $\mathcal{B}''$ remain the same. However, then, $\mathcal{B}''$ is identical to $\mathcal{B}$, which implies the second fact.

Finally, to prove the third fact, we can interpret the sampling process of $\mathcal{B}'$ as first sampling $(\boldsymbol{r}_1, \ldots, \boldsymbol{r}_Q)$ from $\mathcal{P}$ and then set $(\boldsymbol{s}_1, \ldots, \boldsymbol{s}_Q) \leftarrow \Phi(\boldsymbol{r}_1, \ldots, \boldsymbol{r}_Q)$. Then, the only difference between $\mathcal{B}'$ and $\mathcal{B}''$ is that $\mathcal{B}'$ check whether there exists $\boldsymbol{s}_i \neq \hat{\boldsymbol{s}}_i$, while $\mathcal{B}''$ check whether there exists $\boldsymbol{r}_i \neq \hat{\boldsymbol{s}}_i$. Since $\Phi$ has no fixed point over $\mathbf{D}$, we know $(\boldsymbol{r}_1, \ldots, \boldsymbol{r}_Q) \neq (\boldsymbol{s}_1, \ldots, \boldsymbol{s}_Q)$ if $(\boldsymbol{r}_1, \ldots, \boldsymbol{r}_Q) \in \mathbf{D}$. Therefore, for each $(\boldsymbol{r}_1, \ldots, \boldsymbol{r}_Q) \in \mathbf{D}$, at least one of $\mathcal{B}'$ and $\mathcal{B}''$ wins, which implies Fact 3.

However, if we use $\Phi$ from Eq. 1, this extended argument does not give us any benefit. Indeed, $\Phi$ as define is a bijection over $\mathbf{D}$, and therefore, the relaxed condition $\mathcal{P}_{|\mathbf{D}} = \Phi(\mathcal{P}_{|\mathbf{D}})$ still requires $\mathcal{P}$ to be a uniform distribution over $\mathbf{D}$. Also, it is unclear whether there are other ways to construct such $\Phi$.

<u>FURTHER RELAXATION ON THE REQUIREMENTS OF $\Phi$.</u> The way out from the above situation is that the two distributions do not need to be exactly identical. In fact, this condition is only needed by Fact 1. Concretely, we relax the condition that $\mathcal{P}_{|\mathbf{D}} = \Phi(\mathcal{P}_{|\mathbf{D}})$ to requiring that the Rényi divergence of $\mathcal{P}_{|\mathbf{D}}$ from $\Phi(\mathcal{P}_{|\mathbf{D}})$ is small, denoted as $R_\alpha\left(\Phi(\mathcal{P}_{|\mathbf{D}}) \| \mathcal{P}_{|\mathbf{D}}\right)$, where $\alpha > 1$ is a parameter we can choose. Then, due to the property of Rényi divergence (formally see Lemma 4),

$$\mathsf{PWin}_{\mathcal{B}'} \leqslant \left(R_\alpha\left(\Phi(\mathcal{P}_{|\mathbf{D}}) \| \mathcal{P}_{|\mathbf{D}}\right) \cdot \mathsf{PWin}_{\mathcal{B}}\right)^{(\alpha-1)/\alpha} .$$

Combining with Fact 2 and 3, it gives

$$\mathsf{PWin}_{\mathcal{A}} \leqslant \mathsf{PWin}_{\mathcal{B}} + \left(R_\alpha\left(\Phi(\mathcal{P}_{|\mathbf{D}}) \| \mathcal{P}_{|\mathbf{D}}\right) \cdot \mathsf{PWin}_{\mathcal{B}}\right)^{(\alpha-1)/\alpha} ,$$

which upper bounds the winning probability of $\mathcal{A}$ by the advantage of solving the MSIS problem. We note that it is possible to get analogous statements using other distance measures, but they fail to give equally good parameters in our application scenarios.

Also, we emphasize that although both our work and [13] use Rényi divergence, the latter work bounds Rényi divergence between the *views* of $\mathcal{A}$, when run with different secrets, whereas we bound the Rényi divergence between distributions of *secrets* before and after applying the $\Phi$ map. The context where we use Rényi divergence is also very different from that of other works in lattice-based cryptography.

### 2.2 Step 2: Upper Bounding $R_\alpha\left(\Phi(\mathcal{P}_{|\mathbf{D}})\|\mathcal{P}_{|\mathbf{D}}\right)$

It is left to show that $R_\alpha\left(\Phi(\mathcal{P}_{|\mathbf{D}})\|\mathcal{P}_{|\mathbf{D}}\right)$ is bounded, for the specific construction of $\Phi$ given in Eq. 1, and again assuming a suitable $\Delta$ exists. The intuition that the two distributions should be close is that $\Phi$ is local in the sense that it maps each element to a nearby one given $\|(u_1\Delta, \dots, u_Q\Delta)\|$ is small. Since each secret is sampled from a discrete Gaussian distribution, elements that are close in distance have similar probabilities of being sampled. However, turning this idea into a proof is still challenging, as both $\mathcal{P}_{|\mathbf{D}}$ and $\Phi(\mathcal{P}_{|\mathbf{D}})$ are not "well-structured" distributions, since both the set $\mathbf{D}$ and $\boldsymbol{u}$ can be arbitrarily determined by $\mathcal{A}$.

Our key insight here is that $\mathbf{D}$ can be decomposed into several disjoint sets such that the distributions conditioned on each set is a one-dimensional discrete Gaussian. Then, we can upper bound the Rényi divergence of the distributions conditioned on each set, which implies an upper bound on $R_\alpha\left(\Phi(\mathcal{P}_{|\mathbf{D}})\|\mathcal{P}_{|\mathbf{D}}\right)$.

More precisely, for each $(\boldsymbol{s}_1, \dots, \boldsymbol{s}_Q) \in \mathbf{D}$, our definition of $\Phi$ in Eq. 1 also ensures that $\mathrm{View}_{\mathcal{A}}(\boldsymbol{s}_1, \dots, \boldsymbol{s}_Q)$ is identical to $\mathrm{View}_{\mathcal{A}}(\boldsymbol{s}_1 + ku_1 \cdot \Delta, \dots, \boldsymbol{s}_Q + ku_Q \cdot \Delta)$ for any $k \in \mathbb{Z}$, where $\boldsymbol{u}$ is the vector output by $\mathcal{A}$ given secrets being $(\boldsymbol{s}_1, \dots, \boldsymbol{s}_Q)$. Denote $\mathcal{S}_{\mathsf{W}}[\boldsymbol{s}_1, \dots, \boldsymbol{s}_Q] := \{(\boldsymbol{s}_1 + ku_1 \cdot \Delta, \dots, \boldsymbol{s}_Q + ku_Q \cdot \Delta) | k \in \mathbb{Z}\}$. We can show that $\Phi$ is a bijection over $\mathcal{S}_{\mathsf{W}}[\boldsymbol{s}_1, \dots, \boldsymbol{s}_Q]$, and all the $\mathcal{S}_{\mathsf{W}}[\boldsymbol{s}_1, \dots, \boldsymbol{s}_Q]$ sets are either the same or disjoint with each other. Therefore, we just need to bound

$$R_\alpha\left(\Phi(\mathcal{P}_{|\mathcal{S}_{\mathsf{W}}[\boldsymbol{s}_1,\dots,\boldsymbol{s}_Q]})\|\mathcal{P}_{|\mathcal{S}_{\mathsf{W}}[\boldsymbol{s}_1,\dots,\boldsymbol{s}_Q]}\right)$$

for each $(\boldsymbol{s}_1, \dots, \boldsymbol{s}_Q) \in \mathbf{D}$.

Now the problem is much easier since $\mathcal{P}_{|\mathcal{S}_{\mathsf{W}}[\boldsymbol{s}_1,\dots,\boldsymbol{s}_Q]}$ is well structured: each $\mathcal{P}$ is a discrete Gaussian distribution over $R^{Qm}$, and $\mathcal{S}_{\mathsf{W}}[\boldsymbol{s}_1, \dots, \boldsymbol{s}_Q]$ is a one-dimensional lattice over $R^{Qm}$. In fact, we can transform $\mathcal{P}_{|\mathcal{S}_{\mathsf{W}}[\boldsymbol{s}_1,\dots,\boldsymbol{s}_Q]}$ into a discrete Gaussian over $\mathbb{Z}$ with standard deviation $\|(u_1/\sigma_1 \cdot \Delta, \dots, u_Q/\sigma_Q \cdot \Delta))\|^{-1}$,[4] while $\Phi(\mathcal{P}_{|\mathcal{S}_{\mathsf{W}}[\boldsymbol{s}_1,\dots,\boldsymbol{s}_Q]})$ is exactly the same distribution shifted by 1. Therefore, we can use the upper bound from [41] (see also Lemma 6) of the Rényi divergence.

We refer to Sect. 4.3 for the proof details.

**Further optimizations.** We explain in this subsection two further optimizations we do to the reduction, which give us better parameters.

<u>Outputting only one solution.</u> We observe that the reduction $\mathcal{B}$ uses only one of the solutions output by $\mathcal{A}$, which means most of the solutions are actually redundant. In fact, the reduction still works if $\mathcal{A}$ outputs a single solution $(i, \hat{\boldsymbol{s}})$

[4] This is the reason why we bound $\|u_1/\sigma_1, \dots, u_Q/\sigma_Q\|$ in the winning condition.

for the $i$-th challenge satisfying $u_i \neq 0$ and $\mathcal{B}$ just outputs $\hat{\boldsymbol{s}} - \boldsymbol{s}_i$ if $\hat{\boldsymbol{s}} \neq \boldsymbol{s}_i$. This is because for each $(\boldsymbol{s}_1, \ldots, \boldsymbol{s}_Q) \in \mathbf{D}$ and $(\boldsymbol{s}'_1, \ldots, \boldsymbol{s}'_Q) = \Phi(\boldsymbol{s}_1, \ldots, \boldsymbol{s}_Q)$, we have $\boldsymbol{s}_i \neq \boldsymbol{s}_i + u_i \cdot \Delta = \boldsymbol{s}'_i$ if $u_i \neq 0$, and thus $\mathcal{B}$ wins in at least one of the cases if $\mathcal{A}$ outputs a solution for the $i$-th challenge. This leads us to define our AOM-MISIS problem, where $\mathcal{A}$ is only required to output a single solution $\hat{\boldsymbol{s}}$ together with a relaxation vector $\hat{\boldsymbol{b}}$ such that $\sum_{i \in [Q]} \hat{b}_i \boldsymbol{t}_i = A\hat{\boldsymbol{s}}$. Similarly, the requirement on the special solution becomes $\sum_{i \in [Q]} u_i \hat{b}_i \neq 0$. The relaxation vector $\hat{\boldsymbol{b}}$ is needed when reducing the security of the threshold signatures to the hardness of AOM-MISIS.

<u>Reducing the Norm of $\Delta$.</u> One question we do not answer in the above discussion is how to guarantee the existence of a small non-zero vector $\Delta \in R^m$ such that $A\Delta = 0$. Such $\Delta$ must exist in $\mathscr{B}^m_\beta$ if $|\mathscr{B}^m_{\beta/2}| > q^{kN}$, which implies $\beta = \Omega(q^{k/m})$. However, this results in a large $\|\Delta\|$ negatively impacting both the Rényi divergence bound and $\sigma_i$, which depends linearly on $\|\Delta\|$.

We can get a smaller $\|\Delta\|$ by relying on the MLWE assumption to embed a small $\Delta$ into $A$ as a (very minimal) trapdoor. We sample $A$ as $[\boldsymbol{d}|D|\mathbb{I}_k]$, where $D \leftarrow_\$ R_q^{(m-k-1)\times k}$ and $\boldsymbol{d} = D\boldsymbol{a} + \boldsymbol{e}$ with $\boldsymbol{a} \leftarrow_\$ \mathscr{B}^{m-k-1}_{\beta_{\mathsf{lwe}}}$ and $\boldsymbol{e} \leftarrow_\$ \mathscr{B}^k_{\beta_{\mathsf{lwe}}}$. Then, we can let $\Delta = (1, -\boldsymbol{a}, -\boldsymbol{e})$, which satisfies $A\Delta = 0$, and $\|\Delta\| \leqslant \sqrt{m}\beta_{\mathsf{lwe}}$, which is much smaller than $q^{k/m}$. By the MLWE assumption, $[\boldsymbol{d}|D]$ is computationally indistinguishable from a matrix uniformly sampled from $R_q^{(m-k)\times k}$.

Two remarks are in order. The first is that this trick would not have worked to improve the parameters of [13] directly, as they need something stronger than the existence of a small $\Delta$. Second, the way we use MLWE here is different than its use to improve parameters in prior works on lattice-based signatures and threshold signatures (e.g. [12,17,32]). It is really tailored at supporting our tighter analysis of the reduction via the embedding of a small enough $\Delta$.

# 3 Preliminaries

## 3.1 Notation

For any positive integers $k < n$, $[n]$ denotes $\{1, \ldots, n\}$, and $[k..n]$ denotes $\{k, \ldots, n\}$. We use $\kappa$ to denote the security parameter. For a sequence of variables $x_1, \ldots, x_\ell$, we use $x_{[i]}$ to denote $(x_1, \ldots, x_j)$ and $x_{[i..j]}$ to denote $(x_i, \ldots, x_j)$.

For a finite set $S$, $|S|$ denotes the size of $S$, and $x \leftarrow_\$ S$ denotes sampling an element uniformly from $S$ and assigning it to $x$. For a distribution $\mathcal{D}$, denote $\mathrm{Supp}(\mathcal{D})$ as the support of $\mathcal{D}$, and $x \leftarrow_\$ \mathcal{D}$ denotes sampling $x$ according to $\mathcal{D}$. For any $y \in \mathrm{Supp}(\mathcal{D})$, denote $\mathcal{D}(y) := \mathsf{Pr}_{x \leftarrow_\$ \mathcal{D}}[x = y]$, and for $S \subseteq \mathrm{Supp}(\mathcal{D})$, denote $\mathcal{D}(S) := \mathsf{Pr}_{x \leftarrow_\$ \mathcal{D}}[x \in S]$. For any set $T$ and any function $F : \mathrm{Supp}(\mathcal{D}) \to T$, denote $F(\mathcal{D})$ as the distribution of $F(x)$ for $x$ sampled from $\mathcal{D}$.

For any vector space $V$ over a field $F$ and a set $S \in V$, we denote $\mathsf{Span}_F(S)$ as the $F$-span of $S$, which is the smallest $F$-subspace of $V$ that contains $S$. In particular, we omit $F$ from the subscript if $F = \mathbb{R}$. For a finite set $S = \{v_1, \ldots, v_n\} \subseteq V$, we say $S$ is $F$-linearly independent if and only if for any non-zero $(a_1, \ldots, a_n) \in F^n$, $\sum_{i \in [n]} a_i v_i \neq 0$. We say $S$ is a $F$-basis of $V$ if and only if $S$ is $F$-linearly independent and $\mathsf{Span}_F(S) = V$. When $F$ is not specified, we assume $F = \mathbb{R}$. The dimension of $V$ is equal to the size of $S$.

For any integer $p > 0$ and any $x \in \mathbb{Z}_p$, denote $\bar{x} \in \mathbb{Z}$ to be the lift of $x$ such that $\bar{x} \in [0..p-1]$ and $\bar{x} = x \mod p$. We use $\lfloor \cdot \rceil : \mathbb{R} \to \mathbb{Z}$ to denote the rounding operator that maps any $x \in \mathbb{R}$ to $\lfloor x + 1/2 \rfloor$. For any integers $v > 0$ and $q > 2^v$, denote $q_v = \lfloor q/2^v \rfloor$ and denote $\lfloor \cdot \rceil_v : \mathbb{Z}_q \to \mathbb{Z}_{q_v}$ a function that maps $x \in \mathbb{Z}_q$ to $\lfloor \bar{x}/2^v \rceil \in \mathbb{Z}_{q_v}$. These operations can be extended an element $x$ in $R$ or $R_q$ by applying them to each coefficient of $x$.

## 3.2 Polynomial Rings

Let $q$ be an odd prime and $N$ be a power of 2. We denote the ring $R := \mathbb{Z}[X]/(X^N + 1)$, contained in the cyclotomic field $K := \mathbb{Q}[X]/(X^N + 1)$, and let $R_q := R/qR \cong \mathbb{Z}_q[X]/(X^N + 1)$. Denote $K_{\mathbb{R}} := \mathbb{R} \otimes K \cong \mathbb{R}[X]/(X^N + 1)$. For an element $v \in K_{\mathbb{R}}$, where $v = \sum_{i=0}^{N-1} v_i X^i$, we denote its conjugate as $v^* = \sum_{i=0}^{N-1} -v_i X^{N-i}$. We use $\phi$ to denote the coefficient embedding that embeds $K_{\mathbb{R}}$ in $\mathbb{R}^N$, and $\phi$ maps $v$ to vector $(v_0, \ldots, v_{N-1}) \in \mathbb{R}^N$. When applying $\phi$ to a vector $\boldsymbol{v} \in K_{\mathbb{R}}^m$, $\phi$ maps $\boldsymbol{v}$ to a vector in $\mathbb{R}^{mN}$ by applying $\phi$ to each entry of $\boldsymbol{v}$. The map $\phi$ is a bijection, and we denote its inverse by $\phi^{-1}$. An $\ell_p$-norm of $\boldsymbol{v} \in K_{\mathbb{R}}^m$ is given by $\|\boldsymbol{v}\|_p := \|\phi(\boldsymbol{v})\|_p = \left(\sum_{i=1}^{m} \sum_{j=0}^{N-1} |v_{i,j}|^p\right)^{\frac{1}{p}}$, where $v_{i,j}$ denotes the coefficient of $X^j$ of the $i$-th entry of $\boldsymbol{v}$. Additionally, the $\ell_\infty$-norm of $\boldsymbol{v}$ is defined as $\|\boldsymbol{v}\|_\infty := \max_{i \in [m], j \in [0..N-1]} |v_{i,j}|$. For the $\ell_2$-norm, we omit the subscript and denote $\|\boldsymbol{v}\|$ as the $\ell_2$-norm of $\boldsymbol{v}$. Denote the conjugate transpose of $\boldsymbol{v} \in K_{\mathbb{R}}^m$ as $\boldsymbol{v}^\dagger := (\boldsymbol{v}^*)^T$. We define the inner product of two vectors $\boldsymbol{v}, \boldsymbol{v}' \in K_{\mathbb{R}}^m$ as $\langle \boldsymbol{v}, \boldsymbol{v}' \rangle := \phi(\boldsymbol{v})^T \phi(\boldsymbol{v}') = \langle \phi(\boldsymbol{v}), \phi(\boldsymbol{v}') \rangle$. We have $\|\boldsymbol{v}\| = \langle \boldsymbol{v}, \boldsymbol{v} \rangle$. We say $\boldsymbol{v}$ is a unit vector if $\|\boldsymbol{v}\| = 1$.

Also, we define a map $\phi_{\mathsf{M}}$ that maps each element in $K_{\mathbb{R}}$ to a matrix in $\mathbb{R}^{N \times N}$ as follows. Let $M_X := \begin{pmatrix} \mathbf{0} & -1 \\ \mathbb{I}_{N-1} & \mathbf{0} \end{pmatrix} \in \mathbb{R}^N$, where $I_{N-1}$ is the identity matrix in $\mathbb{R}^{N-1}$. For each $v \in K_{\mathbb{R}}$, $\phi_{\mathsf{M}}(v) := \sum_{i=0}^{N-1} v_i M_X^i$, which can be viewed as the matrix representation of $v$. In particular, for $\phi$ and $\phi_{\mathsf{M}}$, the following properties hold: for any $v, v' \in K_{\mathbb{R}}$, $\phi_{\mathsf{M}}(v^*) = \phi_{\mathsf{M}}(v)^T$, $\phi_{\mathsf{M}}(vv') = \phi_{\mathsf{M}}(v)\phi_{\mathsf{M}}(v')$ and $\phi_{\mathsf{M}}(v)\phi(v') = \phi(vv')$. We extend the above definitions to $R_q$ by representing each $v \in R_q$ as $v = \sum_{i=0}^{N-1} v_i X^i$, where $v_i \in \{-(q-1)/2, \ldots, (q-1)/2\}$.

For a matrix $M \in K_{\mathbb{R}}^{m \times m}$, we denote its conjugate transpose as $M^\dagger = (M^*)^T$, and we say $M$ is *hermitian* if $M = M^\dagger$. We say $M$ is *positive definite* if and only if $M$ is hermitian and for all $\boldsymbol{x} \in K_{\mathbb{R}}^m \backslash \{\mathbf{0}\}$, $\langle \boldsymbol{x}, M\boldsymbol{x} \rangle > 0$, or equivalently, $\phi_{\mathsf{M}}(M)$ is positive definite. Also, denote $\sigma_{\min}(M) := \inf_{\boldsymbol{x} \in K_{\mathbb{R}}^m, \|\boldsymbol{x}\|=1} \langle \boldsymbol{x}, M\boldsymbol{x} \rangle$ as the smallest singular value of $M$ and $\sigma_{\max}(M) := \sup_{\boldsymbol{x} \in K_{\mathbb{R}}^m, \|\boldsymbol{x}\|=1} \langle \boldsymbol{x}, M\boldsymbol{x} \rangle$ as the largest singular value of $M$.

We borrow the following lemma from [8], which establishes the property of the set of signed monomials $\mathcal{S}_{\mathsf{b}} := \{\pm 1, \ldots, \pm X^{N-1}\} \subseteq R_q$.

**Lemma 1 (Lemma 3.1 of [8]).** *Let* $\mathcal{S}_{\mathsf{b}} := \{\pm 1, \ldots, \pm X^{N-1}\} \subseteq R_q$*. For any* $b, \bar{b} \in \mathcal{S}_{\mathsf{b}}$ *such that* $b \neq \bar{b}$*, there exists* $\gamma \in R$ *such that* $(b - \bar{b})\gamma = 2 \mod q$ *and* $\gamma$ *is a polynomial with coefficients only in* $\{-1, 0, 1\}$.

### 3.3 Lattices and Discrete Gaussian Distributions

In this subsection, we give definitions for lattices and discrete Gaussian distributions over $\mathbb{R}$ and $K_{\mathbb{R}}$. An $m$-dimensional lattice $\Lambda$ over $\mathbb{Z}$ (resp. $R$) is a discrete additive subgroup of $\mathbb{Z}$ (resp. $R$). Equivalently, $\Lambda = \mathcal{L}(\{\boldsymbol{b}_1, \ldots, \boldsymbol{b}_k\}) := \{\sum_{i \in [k]} x_i \boldsymbol{b}_i : x_i \in \mathbb{Z}\}$ for a set of linearly independent vectors $\boldsymbol{b}_1, \ldots, \boldsymbol{b}_k \in \mathbb{Z}^m$ (resp. $R^m$), which is referred to as a basis of $\Lambda$. The size $k$ is the *rank* of the lattice $\Lambda$. We say $\Lambda$ is a *full rank* lattice if $k = m$ (resp. $k = mN$ for $\Lambda$ over $R$). For any $a \in \mathbb{Z}^m$ (resp. $R^m$), $\Lambda + a$ is a *coset* of $\Lambda$. The *dual lattice* of $\Lambda$ is denoted as $\Lambda^* = \{\boldsymbol{x} \in \mathsf{Span}(\Lambda) : \forall\, \boldsymbol{y} \in \Lambda, \langle \boldsymbol{x}, \boldsymbol{y} \rangle \in \mathbb{Z}\}$. A $\Lambda$-subspace is the linear span of some subset of $\Lambda$, i.e., a subspace $S$ such that $S = \mathsf{Span}(S \cap \Lambda)$.

For a matrix $A \in R_q^{k \times m}$, we define the $R$-lattice $\Lambda_q^{\perp}(A) \subseteq R^m$ as $\Lambda_q^{\perp}(A) := \{\boldsymbol{x} \in R^m : A\boldsymbol{x} = 0 \bmod q\}$, which is full-rank since $qR^m \subseteq \Lambda_q^{\perp}(A)$.

For a positive definite matrix $\Sigma \in \mathbb{R}^{m \times m}$ (resp. an invertible positive definite matrix $\Sigma \in K_{\mathbb{R}}^{m \times m}$) and a vector $\boldsymbol{c} \in \mathbb{R}^n$ (resp. $K_{\mathbb{R}}^m$), we define the function $\rho_{\Sigma,\boldsymbol{c}}$ over $\mathbb{R}^m$ (resp. $K_{\mathbb{R}}^m$) as $\rho_{\Sigma,\boldsymbol{c}}(\boldsymbol{x}) := \exp\left(-\pi \langle \boldsymbol{x} - \boldsymbol{c}, \Sigma^{-1}(\boldsymbol{x} - \boldsymbol{c}) \rangle\right)$. Then, we denote $\mathscr{D}^m_{\Lambda+\boldsymbol{a},\Sigma,\boldsymbol{c}}$ as the discrete Gaussian distribution over a lattice coset $\Lambda + \boldsymbol{a} \subseteq \mathbb{Z}^m$ (resp. $R^m$) with covariance matrix $\Sigma$, centered at $\boldsymbol{c} \in \mathbb{R}^m$, where for $\boldsymbol{x} \in \Lambda + \boldsymbol{a}$, we define

$$\mathscr{D}^m_{\Lambda+\boldsymbol{a},\Sigma,\boldsymbol{c}}(\boldsymbol{x}) := \mathsf{Pr}[\boldsymbol{x} \leftarrow_{\$} \mathscr{D}^m_{\Lambda+\boldsymbol{a},\Sigma,\boldsymbol{c}}] = \rho_{\Sigma,\boldsymbol{c}}(\boldsymbol{x}) / \rho_{\Sigma,\boldsymbol{c}}(\Lambda + \boldsymbol{a})$$

where $\rho_{\Sigma,\boldsymbol{c}}(\Lambda + \boldsymbol{a}) = \sum_{\boldsymbol{x} \in \Lambda + \boldsymbol{a}} \rho_{\Sigma,\boldsymbol{c}}(\boldsymbol{x})$. For $\Lambda + \boldsymbol{a} \subseteq R^m$, we denote $\mathscr{D}^{m, \bmod q}_{\Lambda+\boldsymbol{a},\Sigma,\boldsymbol{c}}(\boldsymbol{x})$ as the distribution of $(\boldsymbol{x} \bmod q) \in R_q^m$ for $\boldsymbol{x}$ sampled from $\mathscr{D}^m_{\Lambda+\boldsymbol{a},\Sigma,\boldsymbol{c}}$.

Also, we make some remarks about the notations we will use throughout the paper. When $\Sigma = \sigma^2 \mathbb{I}_m$ for $\sigma \in \mathbb{R}$, we will use $\rho_{\sigma,\boldsymbol{c}}$ and $\mathscr{D}^m_{\Lambda+\boldsymbol{a},\sigma,\boldsymbol{c}}$ as $\rho_{\Sigma,\boldsymbol{c}}$ and $\mathscr{D}^m_{\Lambda+\boldsymbol{a},\Sigma,\boldsymbol{c}}$, respectively. If the center $\boldsymbol{c} = 0$, then we omit the subscript $\boldsymbol{c}$ from $\rho_{\Sigma,\boldsymbol{c}}$ and $\mathscr{D}^m_{\Lambda+\boldsymbol{a},\Sigma,\boldsymbol{c}}$. Moreover, when $\Lambda + \boldsymbol{a} = \mathbb{Z}^m$ (resp. $\Lambda + \boldsymbol{a} = R^m$), we omit $\Lambda + \boldsymbol{a}$ from the subscript of $\mathscr{D}^m_{\Lambda+\boldsymbol{a},\Sigma,\boldsymbol{c}}$.

The smoothing parameter of a lattice $\Lambda$ with respect to $\varepsilon > 0$, denoted by $\eta_\varepsilon(\Lambda)$, is the smallest $s > 0$ such that $\rho_{1/s}(\Lambda^* \backslash \{0\}) \leqslant \varepsilon$. Throughout the paper, we set $\varepsilon = 2^{-2\kappa}$.

We borrow the following lemma from [1] that bounds the $\ell_2$-norm of discrete Gaussian random variables and adapt it to lattices over $K_{\mathbb{R}}$.

**Lemma 2 (Lemma 3 of [1] adapted to $K_{\mathbb{R}}$).** *For any* $\varepsilon \in (0, 1)$*, a lattice* $\Lambda \subseteq R^m$*,* $\boldsymbol{c} \in K_{\mathbb{R}}^m$*, and* $\sigma \geqslant \eta_\varepsilon(\Lambda)$*, then* $\mathsf{Pr}[\|\boldsymbol{x} - \boldsymbol{c}\| \geqslant \sigma\sqrt{mN} : \boldsymbol{x} \leftarrow_{\$} \mathscr{D}_{\Lambda,\sigma,\boldsymbol{c}}] \leqslant \frac{1+\varepsilon}{1-\varepsilon} \cdot 2^{-mN}$.

We also borrow the following lemma from [23] that show upper bounds of smoothing parameters for general lattices.

| Game $\text{MSIS}^{\mathcal{A}}_{q,N,k,m,\beta}$ : | Game $\text{MLWE}^{\mathcal{A}}_{q,N,k,m,\beta}$ : |
|---|---|
| $\overline{A} \leftarrow_{\$} R_q^{k\times(m-k)}$<br>$A \leftarrow [\overline{A}\|\mathbb{I}_k]$<br>$\boldsymbol{x} \leftarrow \mathcal{A}(A)$<br>Return $(\|\boldsymbol{x}\| \leqslant \beta \wedge A\boldsymbol{x} = 0)$ | $\overline{A} \leftarrow_{\$} R_q^{k\times(m-k)}$ ; $A \leftarrow [\overline{A}\|\mathbb{I}_k]$<br>$\boldsymbol{s} \leftarrow_{\$} \mathscr{B}_\beta^m$ ; $\boldsymbol{t}_0 \leftarrow A\boldsymbol{s}$ ; $\boldsymbol{t}_1 \leftarrow_{\$} R_q^k$<br>$b \leftarrow_{\$} \{0,1\}$<br>$\hat{b} \leftarrow \mathcal{A}(A, t_b)$<br>Return $(\hat{b} = b)$ |

**Fig. 1.** The module-SIS and module-LWE problems, where $R := \mathbb{Z}[X]/(X^N+1)$, $R_q := R/qR$ and $\mathscr{B}^m_{\beta_{\mathsf{lwe}}} := \{\boldsymbol{x} \in R^m \mid \|\boldsymbol{x}\|_\infty \leqslant \beta_{\mathsf{lwe}}\}$.

---

**Lemma 3 (Lemma 2.6 of [23]).** *For any full-rank lattice $\Lambda$ in $\mathbb{R}^m$ and $\varepsilon > 0$, $\eta_\varepsilon(\Lambda) \leqslant \frac{\sqrt{\log(2m(1+1/\varepsilon))/\pi}}{\lambda_1^\infty(\Lambda^*)}$, where $\lambda_1^\infty(\Lambda^*)$ denotes the $\ell_2$ norm of the shortest non-zero vector in the $\ell_\infty$ norm in the dual lattice $\Lambda^*$.*

### 3.4 Assumptions

We recall the module short integer solution (MSIS) problem and the module learning with error (MLWE) problem (defined in Fig. 1). The advantage of $\mathcal{A}$ for the MSIS problem is defined as $\mathsf{Adv}^{\text{msis}}_{q,N,k,m,\beta}(\mathcal{A}) := \Pr\left[\text{MSIS}^{\mathcal{A}}_{q,N,k,m,\beta} = 1\right]$. The advantage of $\mathcal{A}$ for the MLWE problem is defined as $\mathsf{Adv}^{\text{mlwe}}_{q,N,k,m,\beta}(\mathcal{A}) := \Pr\left[\text{MLWE}^{\mathcal{A}}_{q,N,k,m,\beta} = 1\right]$.

### 3.5 Rényi Divergence

We define the notion of Rényi Divergence between two distributions $P, Q$ which we will use in our analysis of the scheme.

**Definition 1 (Rényi Divergence).** *Let $P, Q$ be two discrete probability distributions such that $\text{Supp}(P) \subseteq \text{Supp}(Q)$. We define the Rényi Divergence of order $\alpha$, for $\alpha \in (1, \infty)$ as $R_\alpha(P\|Q) := \left(\sum_{x\in Supp(P)} \frac{P(x)^\alpha}{Q(x)^{\alpha-1}}\right)^{\frac{1}{\alpha-1}}$.*

The following lemma gives basic properties of the Rényi Divergence.

**Lemma 4 (Lemma 4.1 of [30]).** *Let $\alpha \in (1,\infty)$ and $P$, $Q$ be discrete probability distributions with $\text{Supp}(P) \subseteq \text{Supp}(Q)$. Then, the following properties hold:*

- ***Data Processing Inequality:*** *$R_\alpha(P^f\|Q^f) \leqslant R_\alpha(P\|Q)$ for any function $f$, where $P^f$ (and $Q^f$) denotes the distribution which samples $x \leftarrow_{\$} P$ ($x \leftarrow_{\$} Q$) and outputs $f(x)$.*
- ***Probability Preservation:*** *Let $E \subseteq \text{Supp}(Q)$ be an arbitrary event. Then, for $\alpha \in (1,\infty)$, $\Pr_{x \leftarrow_{\$} P}[E] \leqslant (\Pr_{x \leftarrow_{\$} Q}[E] R_\alpha(P\|Q))^{(\alpha-1)/\alpha}$.*

Also, we show the following property. The proof is provided in the full version of the paper.

**Lemma 5.** *Let $P$ and $Q$ denote two distributions over the union of a countable number of disjoint sets $\{S_i\}_{i\in U}$ such that $P(S_i) = Q(S_i)$ for any $i \in U$. Then, for any $\alpha > 1$, if there exists $\delta$ such that $R_\alpha\left(P_{|S_i}\|Q_{|S_i}\right) \leqslant \delta$ for any $i \in U$, then $R_\alpha(P\|Q) \leqslant \delta$.*

We borrow the following lemma from [41], which upperbounds the Rényi Divergence between two discrete Gaussian distributions with different centers.

**Lemma 6 (Lemma 5 of [41]).** *For any $m$-dimensional lattice $\Lambda \subseteq \mathbb{R}^m$, $\sigma > 0$, and two vectors $\mathbf{c}, \mathbf{c}' \in \mathbb{R}^m$, let $P = \mathscr{D}^m_{\Lambda,\sigma,\mathbf{c}}$ and $Q = \mathscr{D}^m_{\Lambda,\sigma,\mathbf{c}'}$. If $\mathbf{c}, \mathbf{c}' \in \Lambda$, set $\varepsilon = 0$. Otherwise, fix $\varepsilon \in (0,1)$ and assume $\sigma \geqslant \eta_\varepsilon(\Lambda)$. Then, $R_\alpha(P\|Q) \leqslant \left(\frac{1+\varepsilon}{1-\varepsilon}\right)^{\frac{\alpha}{\alpha-1}} \exp\left(\alpha\pi\frac{\|\mathbf{c}-\mathbf{c}'\|^2}{\sigma^2}\right)$.*

### 3.6 Threshold Signatures

We use the formalization proposed by Bellare et al. [6], which is also used in [13, 42].

<u>Syntax.</u> A (partially) non-interactive threshold signature schemes for $n$ signers and threshold $t$ is a tuple of efficient (randomized) algorithms $\mathsf{TS} = (\mathsf{Setup}, \mathsf{KeyGen}, \mathsf{SPP}, \mathsf{LPP}, \mathsf{LR}, \mathsf{PS}, \mathsf{Agg}, \mathsf{Vf})$ that behave as follows. An execution of the scheme involves a leader as well as $n$ signers. The setup algorithm $\mathsf{Setup}(1^\kappa)$ initializes the state $\mathsf{st}_i$ for each signer $i \in [n]$, as well as the state $\mathsf{st}_0$ for the leader, and additionally a public parameter *par*. (We assume *par* is given as implicit input to all other algorithms.) The key generation algorithm $\mathsf{KeyGen}()$ returns a public verification key $\mathsf{pk}$, and a secret key $\mathsf{sk}_i$ for each signer $i$. (This means in particular that we assume ideal key generation, and as in prior works, do not model distributed key generation.)

The signing protocol proceeds in two rounds: In a first, message-independent offline round, any signer $i$ can run $\mathsf{SPP}(\mathsf{st}_i)$ to generate a *pre-processing token* $pp$, which is sent to the leader, and the leader runs $\mathsf{LPP}(i, pp, \mathsf{st}_0)$ to update its state $\mathsf{st}_0$ to incorporate token $pp$. In the second, online, round, for a signer set $SS \subseteq [n]$ with size $t$ and message $\mu \in \{0,1\}^*$, the leader runs $\mathsf{LR}(\mu, SS, \mathsf{st}_0)$ to generate a leader request $lr$ with $lr.\mathsf{msg} = \mu$ and $lr.\mathsf{SS} = SS$ and sends $lr$ to each signer $i \in SS$. Then, each signer $i$ runs $\mathsf{PS}(lr, i, \mathsf{st}_i)$ to generate its partial signature $psig_i$. Finally, the leader computes a signature $sig$ for $\mu$ by running $\mathsf{Agg}(\{psig_i\}_{i\in SS})$. The (deterministic) verification algorithm $\mathsf{Vf}(\mathsf{pk}, \mu, sig)$ outputs a bit that indicates whether $sig$ is valid for $(\mathsf{pk}, \mu)$.

An honest execution of the signing protocol to sign a message $\mu \in \{0,1\}^*$ is represented in the correctness game TS-COR (defined in Fig. 2). We say that $\mathsf{TS}$ is *correct* with correctness error $\varepsilon_{\mathsf{cor}}$ if for $\mu \in \{0,1\}^*$ and $SS \subseteq [n]$ with $|SS| \geqslant t$, we have $\mathsf{Pr}[\text{TS-COR}_{\mathsf{TS}}(\kappa, \mu, SS) = 1] \leqslant \varepsilon_{\mathsf{cor}}$.

Game $\text{TS-COR}_{\text{TS}}^{\mathcal{A}}(\kappa, \mu, SS)$ :
$par \leftarrow \mathsf{Setup}(1^\kappa)$ ; $(\mathsf{pk}, \{\mathsf{sk}_i\}_{i\in[n]}) \leftarrow \mathsf{KeyGen}()$
For $i \in [n]$ do $\mathsf{st}_i.\mathsf{sk} \leftarrow \mathsf{sk}_i$ ; $\mathsf{st}_i.\mathsf{pk} \leftarrow \mathsf{pk}$
For $i \in SS$ do
  $(pp_i, \mathsf{st}_i) \leftarrow \mathsf{SPP}(\mathsf{st}_i)$ ; $\mathsf{st}_0 \leftarrow \mathsf{LPP}(i, pp_i, \mathsf{st}_0)$
$(lr, \mathsf{st}_0) \leftarrow \mathsf{LR}(\mu, SS, \mathsf{st}_0)$
For $i \in SS$ do $(psig_i, \mathsf{st}_i) \leftarrow \mathsf{PS}(lr, i, \mathsf{st}_i)$
$sig \leftarrow \mathsf{Agg}(\{psig_i\}_{i\in SS})$
Return $\mathsf{Vf}(\mathsf{pk}, \mu, sig) = 0$

**Fig. 2.** The TS-COR game for a threshold signature scheme TS for $n$ signers and threshold $t$.

SECURITY. Roughly speaking, unforgeability ensures that an adversary cannot forge a signature for a message that has not been considered as signed, considering the corruption status and the adversary's interactions with honest parties. A hierarchy for unforgeability of threshold signatures is proposed in [6]. In this paper, we consider TS-UF-0 and TS-UF-4, which differ only in how they define when a message is considered as signed. In particular, for TS-UF-0, a message is considered as signed only if the adversary received a partial signature from at least one honest signer for $\mu$, and for TS-UF-4, the condition is much stronger - a message is considered as signed only if there exists a leader request $lr$ for $\mu$ such that the adversary received partial signatures from all honest parties in $lr.\mathsf{SS}$ for that leader request $lr$. Formally, the TS-UF-0 and TS-UF-4 games are defined in Fig. 3, where TS.HF denotes the space of the hash functions used in TS from which the random oracle is drawn. The advantage of $\mathcal{A}$ for the TS-UF-X game is defined as $\mathsf{Adv}_{\mathsf{TS}}^{\text{ts-uf-X}}(\mathcal{A}, \kappa) := \Pr\left[\text{TS-UF-X}_{\mathsf{TS}}^{\mathcal{A}}(\kappa) = 1\right]$ for $\mathsf{X} \in \{0, 4\}$.

# 4 Algebraic One-More MISIS Problem

In this section, we first formally define the algebraic one-more MISIS (AOM-MISIS) problem, then provide a comparison with the AOM-MLWE problem, and finally present a formal reduction from standard lattice problems to AOM-MISIS.

## 4.1 Definition of AOM-MISIS

The algebraic one-more MISIS game is defined in Fig. 4. The game is defined implicitly over the cyclotomic ring $R = \mathbb{Z}[X]/(X^N + 1)$, where $N$ is a power of two, as well as the associated ring $R_q = R/qR \cong \mathbb{Z}_q[X]/(X^N + 1)$ for an odd prime $q$. The adversary $\mathcal{A}$ is given $Q$ MISIS challenges $\boldsymbol{t}_1, \ldots, \boldsymbol{t}_Q$ and the goal is to output a short solution $\hat{\boldsymbol{s}}$ for a linear combination of the challenges $\sum_{i\in[Q]} \hat{b}_i \boldsymbol{t}_i$, where the norm of $\hat{\boldsymbol{b}}$ is suitably bounded. The adversary can also issue queries

| Game $\boxed{\text{TS-UF-0}^{\mathcal{A}}_{\mathsf{TS}}(\kappa)}$, $\text{TS-UF-4}^{\mathcal{A}}_{\mathsf{TS}}(\kappa)$ : | Oracle $\text{PPO}(i)$ : |
|---|---|
| $par \leftarrow \mathsf{Setup}(1^\kappa)$ ; $\mathrm{H} \leftarrow\!\!\$\ \mathsf{TS.HF}$ ; $\mathrm{S} \leftarrow \varnothing$<br>$\mathrm{curSS} \leftarrow ()$<br>$(\mu, sig) \leftarrow \mathcal{A}^{\text{INIT},\text{PPO},\text{PSIGNO},\text{RO}}(par)$<br>Return $(\mu \notin \mathrm{S} \wedge \mathsf{Vf}(\mathsf{pk}, \mu, sig) = 1)$<br><br>Oracle $\text{INIT}(\mathsf{CS})$ :<br>Require: $CS \subseteq [n]$ and $\lvert CS \rvert < t$<br>$\mathsf{HS} \leftarrow [n] \backslash \mathsf{CS}$<br>$(\mathsf{pk}, \mathsf{sk}_1, \ldots, \mathsf{sk}_n) \leftarrow \mathsf{KeyGen}()$<br>For $i \in \mathsf{HS}$ do $\mathsf{st}_i.\mathsf{sk} \leftarrow \mathsf{sk}_i$ ; $\mathsf{st}_i.\mathsf{pk} \leftarrow \mathsf{pk}$<br>Return $(\mathsf{pk}, \{\mathsf{sk}_i\}_{i \in \mathsf{CS}})$<br><br>Oracle $\text{RO}(x)$ :<br>Return $\mathrm{H}(x)$ | Require: $i \in \mathsf{HS}$<br>$(pp, \mathsf{st}_i) \leftarrow\!\!\$\ \mathsf{SPP}(\mathsf{st}_i)$<br>$\mathrm{PP}_i \leftarrow \mathrm{PP}_i \cup \{pp\}$<br>Return $pp$<br><br>Oracle $\text{PSIGNO}(i, lr)$ :<br>Require: $lr.\mathsf{SS} \subseteq [n]$ and $i \in \mathsf{HS} \cap lr.\mathsf{SS}$<br>$(psig, \mathsf{st}_i') \leftarrow\!\!\$\ \mathsf{PS}(lr, i, \mathsf{st}_i)$<br>If $psig = \bot$ then return $\bot$<br>$\mu \leftarrow lr.\mathsf{msg}$<br>$\boxed{\mathrm{S} \leftarrow \mathrm{S} \cup \{\mu\}}$<br>If $\mathrm{curSS}(lr) = \bot$ then<br>  $\mathrm{curSS}(lr) \leftarrow \{i\}$<br>Else $\mathrm{curSS}(lr) \leftarrow \mathrm{curSS}(lr) \cup \{i\}$<br>If $\mathrm{curSS}(lr) = lr.\mathsf{SS} \cap \mathsf{HS}$ then<br>  $\mathrm{S} \leftarrow \mathrm{S} \cup \{\mu\}$<br>Return $psig$ |

**Fig. 3.** The game TS-UF-0 and the game TS-UF-4 for a threshold signature scheme $\mathsf{TS}$ for $n$ signers and threshold $t$, where TS-UF-0 contains all but the highlight boxes and TS-UF-4 contains all but the dashed boxes. In particular, in TS-UF-4, a table curSS is maintained to record, for each $lr$, the set of signers that have received a partial signing query on $lr$. A message $\mu$ is considered signed if and only if $\mathrm{curSS}(lr)$ contains the set of honest parties in $lr.\mathsf{SS}$.

to the oracle PI which reveal linear combinations of the secrets. To win, the adversary also needs to output an additional vector $\boldsymbol{u}$ which is orthogonal to all queries to PI, but not to the vector $\hat{\boldsymbol{b}}$. We can also view the existence of such $\boldsymbol{u}$ as a constraint on the PI queries. We refer the reader to the introduction for some additional intuition. Here, for $\mathsf{par} = (q, N, k, m, Q, (\sigma_i)_{i \in [Q]}, \beta_{\mathsf{s}}, \beta_{\mathsf{b}}, \beta_{\mathsf{u}})$, we define the *advantage* of an adversary $\mathcal{A}$ as

$$\mathsf{Adv}^{\text{aom-misis}}_{\mathsf{par}}(\mathcal{A}, \kappa) = \mathsf{Pr}\left[\text{AOM-MISIS}^{\mathcal{A}}_{\mathsf{par}}(\kappa) = 1\right] . \tag{2}$$

We note that we slightly abuse notation in the asymptotic definition of the game, since it is understood that all parameters grow with $\kappa$, including $Q$, and thus the notation $(\sigma_i)_{i \in Q}$ is not entirely well-defined. This will not be an issue in actual use cases, and we dispense with a more rigorous definition.

*Remark 1.* We note that for each $i \in [Q]$, it is equivalent to sample $\boldsymbol{s}_i$ from $\mathscr{D}^{m, \text{mod } q}_{\sigma_i}$ instead of $\mathscr{D}^{m}_{\sigma_i}$, since the view of $\mathcal{A}$ remains unchanged. With this insight, it is natural to allow $\sigma_i$ to be $\infty$, in which case $\boldsymbol{s}_i$ is sampled uniformly from $R_q^m$, $1/\sigma_i = 0$, and we require $\hat{b}_i = 0$ in the winning condition (since, o.w.,

Game $\text{AOM-MISIS}^{\mathcal{A}}_{q,N,k,m,Q,(\sigma_i)_{i\in[Q]},\beta_{\mathsf{s}},\beta_{\mathsf{b}},\beta_{\mathsf{u}}}(\kappa)$ :

$B \leftarrow \varnothing$
$\overline{A} \leftarrow_\$ R_q^{k\times(m-k)}$ ; $A \leftarrow [\overline{A}|\mathbb{I}_k]$
For $i \in [Q]$,
  $\boldsymbol{s}_i \leftarrow \mathscr{D}^m_{\sigma_i}$ ; $\boldsymbol{t}_i \leftarrow A\boldsymbol{s}_i \bmod q$
$(\hat{\boldsymbol{s}}, \hat{\boldsymbol{b}}, \boldsymbol{u}) \leftarrow \mathcal{A}^{\mathrm{PI}}(A, \{\boldsymbol{t}_i\}_{i\in[Q]})$ // $\hat{\boldsymbol{s}} \in R^m, \hat{\boldsymbol{b}}, \boldsymbol{u} \in R^Q$
Return $(\forall \boldsymbol{b} \in B : \boldsymbol{b}^T\boldsymbol{u} = 0 \mod q) \wedge \hat{\boldsymbol{b}}^T\boldsymbol{u} \neq 0 \wedge$
  $\|(u_1/\sigma_1, \ldots, u_Q/\sigma_Q)\|_2 \leqslant \beta_{\mathsf{u}} \wedge$
  $\|\hat{\boldsymbol{s}}\|_2 \leqslant \beta_{\mathsf{s}} \wedge \left\|(\hat{b}_1 \cdot \sigma_1, \ldots, \hat{b}_Q \cdot \sigma_Q)\right\|_1 \leqslant \beta_{\mathsf{b}} \wedge$
  $\sum_{i\in[Q]} \hat{b}_i\boldsymbol{t}_i = A\hat{\boldsymbol{s}} \mod q$

Oracle $\mathrm{PI}(\boldsymbol{b} \in R^Q)$ :

$B \leftarrow B \cup \{\boldsymbol{b}\}$
Return $\sum_{i\in[Q]} b_i\boldsymbol{s}_i \mod q \ (\in R_q^m)$

**Fig. 4.** The AOM-MISIS game, where $R := \mathbb{Z}[X]/(X^N + 1)$ and $R_q := R/qR$.

$\left\|\hat{b}_i \cdot \sigma_i\right\|_1$ is $\infty$). This extension is used, in particular, in our security reduction of the CTZ construction (see Sect. 5.1), where the random values for generating the key shares are sampled uniformly from $R_q^m$.

## 4.2 Comparison with Prior Work

We present in Fig. 5 the AOM-MLWE problem proposed by Espitau et al. [20]. In our formulation, the PI oracle corresponds to the $\mathcal{O}_{\mathsf{solve}}$ oracle in their notation, and the constraints on PI queries are explicitly stated within the game. More precisely, the constraints are:

- The number of PI queries is exactly $Q - 1$.
- Denote $\begin{pmatrix} \boldsymbol{v}^T \\ \underline{D} \end{pmatrix} = [\boldsymbol{d}_1|\cdots|\boldsymbol{d}_{Q-1}]$, where $\boldsymbol{d}_i$ denotes the $i$-th PI query. $\underline{D}$ is an invertible matrix.
- Let $\boldsymbol{w} \leftarrow (\boldsymbol{v}^T\underline{D}^{-1})^T$. The $\ell_2$-norm of each entry of $\boldsymbol{w}$ is bounded by $\beta_{\mathsf{d}}$.

We also define, for $\mathsf{par} = (q, N, k, m, Q, (\sigma_i)_{i\in[Q]}, \beta_{\mathsf{s}}, \beta_{\mathsf{e}}, \beta_{\mathsf{b}}, \beta_{\mathsf{d}})$, the corresponding advantage $\mathsf{Adv}^{\text{aom-mlwe}}_{\mathsf{par}}(\mathcal{A}, \kappa) = \Pr\left[\text{AOM-MLWE}^{\mathcal{A}}_{\mathsf{par}}(\kappa) = 1\right]$.

Compared with the AOM-MLWE problem, our problem differs in the following key aspects:

1. Our problem only asks the adversary to output one special solution $\hat{\boldsymbol{s}}$ for a linear combination of the challenges, while the AOM-MLWE problem demands one solution for each challenge. This makes our problem inherently easier to solve, as noted at the beginning of Sect. 2. Moreover, this relaxation simplifies the security reduction, as it only needs to extract one solution rather than

Game $\text{AOM-MLWE}^{\mathcal{A}}_{q,k,m,Q,(\sigma_i)_{i\in[Q]},\beta_s,\beta_e,\beta_b,\beta_d}(\kappa)$ :

$\mathsf{cnt} \leftarrow 0$
$\overline{A} \leftarrow_\$ R_q^{k\times(m-k)}$ ; $A \leftarrow [\overline{A}|\mathbb{I}_k]$
For $i \in [Q]$,
  $\boldsymbol{s}_i \leftarrow \mathscr{D}^m_{\sigma_i}$ ; $\boldsymbol{t}_i \leftarrow A\boldsymbol{s}_i \bmod q$
$(\hat{\boldsymbol{b}}, \hat{\boldsymbol{s}}_1, \ldots, \hat{\boldsymbol{s}}_Q) \leftarrow \mathcal{A}^{\mathrm{PI}}(A, \{\boldsymbol{t}_i\}_{i\in[Q]})$ // $\hat{\boldsymbol{s}} \in R^m, \hat{\boldsymbol{b}}$
If $\mathsf{cnt} \neq Q-1$ then return 0
Parse $\begin{pmatrix} \boldsymbol{v}^T \\ \underline{D} \end{pmatrix} \leftarrow [\boldsymbol{d}_1|\cdots|\boldsymbol{d}_{Q-1}]$
If $\underline{D}^{-1}$ does not exist then return 0
$\boldsymbol{w} \leftarrow (\boldsymbol{v}^T\underline{D}^{-1})^T$
Return $(\forall i \in [Q-1] : \|w_i\| \leqslant \beta_d) \wedge$
  $\left\|(\hat{s}_{1,[m-k]}, \ldots, \hat{s}_{Q,[m-k]})\right\|_2 \leqslant \beta_s \wedge$
  $\left\|(\hat{s}_{1,[(m-k+1)..m]}, \ldots, \hat{s}_{Q,[(m-k+1)..m]})\right\|_2 \leqslant \beta_e \wedge$
  $(\forall i \in [Q] : b_i \neq 0 \wedge \|b_i\| \leqslant \beta_b \wedge \hat{b}_i\boldsymbol{t}_i = A\hat{\boldsymbol{s}}_i \bmod q)$

Oracle $\mathrm{PI}(\boldsymbol{b} \in R^Q)$ :

$\mathsf{cnt} \leftarrow \mathsf{cnt} + 1$
$\boldsymbol{d}_{\mathsf{cnt}} \leftarrow \boldsymbol{b}$
Return $\sum_{i\in[Q]} b_i \boldsymbol{s}_i$

**Fig. 5.** The AOM-MLWE game.

multiple, making it easier to reduce from our assumption. Additionally, it enables better parameter selections, since the norm bound applies to a single solution instead of $n$ solutions.

2. The constraints on the PI queries differ between AOM-MLWE and our problem. In particular, their constraints are a special case of ours: given the PI queries satisfying their constraints, we can verify that these queries also satisfy our constraints by setting $\boldsymbol{u} = (1, -\boldsymbol{w})$, since $\boldsymbol{u}\begin{pmatrix} \boldsymbol{v}^T \\ \underline{D} \end{pmatrix} = 0$. We will show this formally later in this section.
3. The norm bounding approach is different. In AOM-MLWE, the norm of each entry of $\hat{\boldsymbol{b}}$ and $\hat{\boldsymbol{w}}$ is bounded individually. In contrast, we bound the norm of the entire vectors $\hat{\boldsymbol{b}}$ and $\hat{\boldsymbol{u}}$, with each entry weighted by the standard deviation of the corresponding challenge. This adjustment leads to better parameter selections.

In short, our problem is easier to reduce from and enables better parameter selections. In Lemma 7, we formally show that the hardness of our problem implies the hardness of theirs, and we discuss the improvement in the parameter selections in Sect. 6.1, Remark 3.

*Remark 2.* We note that Espitau et al. [20] propose an alternative way of defining constraints, which, like ours, requires the existence of a nonzero vector $\boldsymbol{u}$ that is orthogonal to all PI queries. The key difference is that they impose a bound on the norm of each entry of $\boldsymbol{u}$. We can show that the hardness of our problem also implies the hardness of theirs under these constraints. However, we omit a formal analysis here, as the proof idea is very similar, and this alternative version is not used to establish the security of their threshold signature scheme.

**Lemma 7.** *For any* $\mathsf{par} = (q, N, k, m, Q, (\sigma_i)_{i\in[Q]}, \beta_\mathsf{s}, \beta_\mathsf{e}, \beta_\mathsf{b}, \beta_\mathsf{d})$ *and any adversary $\mathcal{A}$ playing the game* AOM-MLWE$^{\mathcal{A}}_{\mathsf{par}}$*, there exists an* AOM-MISIS *adversary $\mathcal{B}$ running in time roughly the same as $\mathcal{A}$ such that*

$$\mathsf{Adv}^{\text{aom-mlwe}}_{\mathsf{par}}(\mathcal{A}, \kappa) \leqslant \mathsf{Adv}^{\text{aom-misis}}_{\mathsf{par}'}(\mathcal{B}, \kappa) ,$$

*where* $\mathsf{par}' = (q, N, k, m, Q, (\sigma_i)_{i\in[Q]}, \beta'_\mathsf{s} = \beta_\mathsf{s} + \beta_\mathsf{e}, \beta'_\mathsf{b} = \sqrt{N}\beta_\mathsf{b}\sigma_1, \beta_\mathsf{u} = 1/\sigma_1 + \beta_\mathsf{d}\sqrt{Q}/(\min_{i\in[2..Q]} \sigma_i))$.

Roughly, the proof idea is that for an adversary $\mathcal{A}$ that wins the game AOM-MLWE, $\mathcal{A}$ can win the game AOM-MISIS by outputting only the solution to the first challenge (i.e., outputting $\hat{s}_1$ and $(\hat{b}_1, 0, \ldots, 0)$) and outputting $\boldsymbol{u} \leftarrow (1, -\boldsymbol{v}^T\underline{D}^{-1})$. It is not hard to check $\boldsymbol{u}$ satisfies the constraints of the game AOM-MISIS. The formal proof is provided in the full version of the paper.

### 4.3 Reduction from MSIS and MLWE

This section shows our main result establishing hardness of AOM-MISIS from the hardness of MLWE and MSIS. (We remind the reader that we also provided a detailed overview of this proof in Sect. 2 above.)

**Theorem 1.** *For any $\varepsilon \in (0, 1)$, $\alpha > 1$, any* $\mathsf{par} = (q, N, k, m, Q, (\sigma_i)_{i\in[Q]}, \beta_\mathsf{s}, \beta_\mathsf{b}, \beta_\mathsf{u})$ *such that $mN \geqslant 2\kappa$ and $\sigma_i \geqslant \sqrt{\log(6mN)/\pi}$, and any* AOM-MISIS *adversary $\mathcal{A}$, there exist a* MSIS *adversary $\mathcal{B}$ and two* MLWE *adversaries $\mathcal{C}$ and $\mathcal{D}$, such that*

$$\mathsf{Adv}^{\text{aom-misis}}_{\mathsf{par}}(\mathcal{A}, \kappa) \leqslant 2\delta_\alpha \left(\mathsf{Adv}^{\text{msis}}_{q,k,m,\beta_\mathsf{sis}}(\mathcal{B}, \kappa) + \mathsf{Adv}^{\text{mlwe}}_{q,k,m-1,\beta_\mathsf{lwe}}(\mathcal{D}, \kappa)\right)^{\frac{\alpha}{\alpha-1}} + \mathsf{Adv}^{\text{mlwe}}_{q,k,m-1,\beta_\mathsf{lwe}}(\mathcal{C}, \kappa) + Q \cdot 2^{-2\kappa+2} ,$$

*where* $\delta_\alpha = \frac{1+\varepsilon}{1-\varepsilon} \cdot \exp\left((\alpha-1)\pi^2/\log(2(1+1/\varepsilon))\right)$, $\beta_\mathsf{sis} = \beta_\mathsf{s} + \sqrt{mN}\beta_\mathsf{b}$, *and* $\beta_\mathsf{lwe} = 1/(\beta_\mathsf{u}\sqrt{mN\log(2(1+1/\varepsilon))/\pi})$. *The three adversaries have, roughly the same running time as that of $\mathcal{A}$.*

*Proof.* We prove the theorem via the following series of games.

- $\mathbf{G}_0$**:** Same as the AOM-MISIS game.
- $\mathbf{G}_1$**:** Same as $\mathbf{G}_0$ except that $A$ is sampled with a short solution embedded, i.e., $A \leftarrow [D\boldsymbol{a} + \boldsymbol{e}|D|\mathbb{I}_k]$ for $(\boldsymbol{a}, \boldsymbol{e}) \leftarrow_\$ \mathscr{B}^{m-1}_{\beta_\mathsf{lwe}}$, where $\mathscr{B}^{m-1}_{\beta_\mathsf{lwe}} := \{\boldsymbol{x} \in R^{m-1} | \|\boldsymbol{x}\|_\infty \leqslant \beta_\mathsf{lwe}\}$, and $D \leftarrow_\$ R_q^{k\times(m-k-1)}$. Since the only difference between $\mathbf{G}_0$ and $\mathbf{G}_1$ is that $\overline{A}$ is replaced with a MLWE challenge, there exists a MLWE adversary $\mathcal{C}$ such that

$$\mathsf{Adv}^{\mathbf{G}_0}(\mathcal{A}, \kappa) \leqslant \mathsf{Adv}^{\mathbf{G}_1}(\mathcal{A}, \kappa) + \mathsf{Adv}^{\text{mlwe}}_{q,k,m-1,\beta_\mathsf{lwe}}(\mathcal{C}, \kappa) . \quad (3)$$

$\mathbf{G}_2$: Same as $\mathbf{G}_1$ except that the game aborts if there exists $i \in [Q]$ such that $\|\boldsymbol{s}_i\| > \sigma_i\sqrt{mN}$. To bound $\Pr[\mathbf{G}_2 \text{ aborts}]$, since $\boldsymbol{s}_i$ is sampled from $\mathscr{D}_{\sigma_i}^m$ and $\sigma_i \geqslant \sqrt{\log(6mN)/\pi} = \eta_{\varepsilon'}(R^m)$ with $\varepsilon' = 1/2$, by Lemma 2, $\Pr[\|\boldsymbol{s}_i\| > \sigma_i\sqrt{mN}] \leqslant 3 \cdot 2^{-mN} \leqslant 2^{-2\kappa+2}$. By the Union Bound, $\Pr[\mathbf{G}_2 \text{ aborts}] \leqslant \sum_{i\in[Q]} \Pr[\|\boldsymbol{s}_i\| > \sigma_i\sqrt{mN}] \leqslant Q \cdot 2^{-2\kappa+2}$. Therefore,

$$\mathsf{Adv}^{\mathbf{G}_1}(\mathcal{A}, \kappa) \leqslant \mathsf{Adv}^{\mathbf{G}_2}(\mathcal{A}, \kappa) + Q \cdot 2^{-2\kappa+2} . \tag{4}$$

Consider a variant of the MSIS game, where $A$ is sampled with a short solution embedded (same as the above $\mathbf{G}_1$), i.e., $A \leftarrow [D\boldsymbol{a} + \boldsymbol{e}|D|\mathbb{I}_k]$ for $(\boldsymbol{a}, \boldsymbol{e}) \leftarrow_\$ \mathscr{B}_{\beta_{\mathsf{lwe}}}^{m-1}$, where $\mathscr{B}_{\beta_{\mathsf{lwe}}}^{m-1} := \{\boldsymbol{x} \in R^{m-1} | \|\boldsymbol{x}\|_\infty \leqslant \beta_{\mathsf{lwe}}\}$, and $D \leftarrow_\$ R_q^{k\times(m-k-1)}$. We refer to the game as td-MSIS. We construct $\mathcal{B}$ playing the td-MSIS game as follows. Given the td-MSIS challenge $A' \in R_q^{k\times(m-k)}$, $\mathcal{B}$ runs $\mathcal{A}$ by simulating the game $\mathbf{G}_2$ with $\mathcal{A}$ faithfully except that $\mathcal{B}$ sets $A \leftarrow A'$ instead of sampling $A$ by itself. After receiving the output $(\hat{\boldsymbol{s}}, \hat{\boldsymbol{b}}, \boldsymbol{u})$ from $\mathcal{A}$, if $\mathcal{A}$ wins the game $\mathbf{G}_2$ simulated by $\mathcal{B}$, $\mathcal{B}$ outputs $\boldsymbol{x} \leftarrow \hat{\boldsymbol{s}} - \sum_{i\in[Q]} \hat{b}_i\boldsymbol{s}_i$. Otherwise, $\mathcal{B}$ aborts.

<u>ANALYSIS OF $\mathcal{B}$.</u> Similar to the hybrid between $\mathbf{G}_0$ and $\mathbf{G}_1$, the td-MSIS game is computationally indistinguishable from the MSIS game under the MLWE assumption. Therefore, there exists a MLWE adversary $\mathcal{D}$ such that

$$\mathsf{Adv}^{\text{td-msis}}_{q,k,m-1,\beta_{\mathsf{sis}}}(\mathcal{B}, \kappa) \leqslant \mathsf{Adv}^{\text{msis}}_{q,k,m-1,\beta_{\mathsf{sis}}}(\mathcal{B}, \kappa) + \mathsf{Adv}^{\text{mlwe}}_{q,k,m-1,\beta_{\mathsf{lwe}}}(\mathcal{D}, \kappa) . \tag{5}$$

*Claim.* $\mathsf{Adv}^{\mathbf{G}_2}(\mathcal{A}, \kappa) \leqslant 2\delta_\alpha \mathsf{Adv}^{\text{td-msis}}_{q,k,m-1,\beta_{\mathsf{sis}}}(\mathcal{B}, \kappa)^{(\alpha-1)/\alpha}$ .

We can conclude the proof since

$$\begin{aligned}\mathsf{Adv}^{\text{aom-misis}}_{\mathsf{par}}(\mathcal{A}, \kappa) &\leqslant \mathsf{Adv}^{\mathbf{G}_2}(\mathcal{A}, \kappa) + \mathsf{Adv}^{\text{mlwe}}_{q,k,m-1,\beta_{\mathsf{lwe}}}(\mathcal{C}, \kappa) + Q \cdot 2^{-2\kappa+2} \\ &\leqslant 2\delta_\alpha \mathsf{Adv}^{\text{td-msis}}_{q,k,m-1,\beta_{\mathsf{sis}}}(\mathcal{B}, \kappa)^{(\alpha-1)/\alpha} + \mathsf{Adv}^{\text{mlwe}}_{q,k,m-1,\beta_{\mathsf{lwe}}}(\mathcal{C}, \kappa) + Q \cdot 2^{-2\kappa+2} \\ &\leqslant 2\delta_\alpha \left(\mathsf{Adv}^{\text{msis}}_{q,k,m,\beta_{\mathsf{sis}}}(\mathcal{B}, \kappa) + \mathsf{Adv}^{\text{mlwe}}_{q,k,m-1,\beta_{\mathsf{lwe}}}(\mathcal{D}, \kappa)\right)^{\frac{\alpha}{\alpha-1}} \\ &\quad + \mathsf{Adv}^{\text{mlwe}}_{q,k,m-1,\beta_{\mathsf{lwe}}}(\mathcal{C}, \kappa) + Q \cdot 2^{-2\kappa+2} ,\end{aligned}$$

where the first inequality follows from Equations (3) and (4), the second inequality follows from the claim, and the third inequality follows from Equation (5). □

We now prove the above claim.

*Proof.* Consider a fixed randomness $(\boldsymbol{a}, \boldsymbol{e}, D)$ of td-MSIS. Also, w.l.o.g. assume $\mathcal{A}$ is deterministic. Then, the execution of $\mathcal{B}$ is determined by $\boldsymbol{s}_1, \ldots, \boldsymbol{s}_Q$. We define a map $\Phi_{\boldsymbol{a},\boldsymbol{e},D,\mathcal{A}} : R^{Qm} \to R^{Qm}$ as follows such that the view of $\mathcal{A}$ given $(\boldsymbol{s}_1, \ldots, \boldsymbol{s}_Q)$ is exactly the same as that given $\Phi_{\boldsymbol{a},\boldsymbol{e},D,\mathcal{A}}(\boldsymbol{s}_1, \ldots, \boldsymbol{s}_Q)$. Consider the execution given $(\boldsymbol{s}_1, \ldots, \boldsymbol{s}_Q)$. To simplify notation, we omit the subscript of $\Phi$ for the rest of the proof. If $\mathcal{A}$ does not win the $\mathbf{G}_2$ simulated by $\mathcal{B}$, we set $\Phi(\boldsymbol{s}_1,\dots,\boldsymbol{s}_Q) = (\boldsymbol{s}_1,\dots,\boldsymbol{s}_Q)$. Otherwise, we set $\Phi(\boldsymbol{s}_1,\dots,\boldsymbol{s}_Q) = (\boldsymbol{s}_1 + u_1\Delta,\dots,\boldsymbol{s}_Q + u_Q\Delta)$, where $\boldsymbol{u} \in R^Q$ is output by $\mathcal{A}$ and $\Delta = (1, -\boldsymbol{a}, -\boldsymbol{e}) \in R^m$.

It is not hard to see that the view of $\mathcal{A}$ given $(\boldsymbol{s}_1,\dots,\boldsymbol{s}_Q)$ is identical to that given $\Phi(\boldsymbol{s}_1,\dots,\boldsymbol{s}_Q)$. In particular, in the case that $\mathsf{AWin}$ occurs, $\Phi(\boldsymbol{s}_1,\dots,\boldsymbol{s}_Q)$ leads to the same view since $\sum_{i\in[Q]} b_i(\boldsymbol{s}_i + u_i\Delta) = \sum_{i\in[Q]} b_i\boldsymbol{s}_i + \Delta\sum_{i\in[Q]} b_i u_i = \sum_{i\in[Q]} b_i\boldsymbol{s}_i$ for any $(b_1,\dots,b_Q) \in B$ and $A(\boldsymbol{s}_i + u_i\Delta) = A\boldsymbol{s}_i$ for any $i \in [Q]$ due to the fact that $A\cdot\Delta = [D\boldsymbol{a} + \boldsymbol{e}|D|\mathbb{I}_k]\cdot(1, -\boldsymbol{a}, -\boldsymbol{e})^T = \boldsymbol{0}$.

Also, it is not hard to see that $\Phi$ is a bijection. For $(\boldsymbol{s}_1,\dots,\boldsymbol{s}_Q) \in R^{mQ}$, suppose $\Phi(\boldsymbol{s}'_1,\dots,\boldsymbol{s}'_Q) = (\boldsymbol{s}_1,\dots,\boldsymbol{s}_Q)$. Since $(\boldsymbol{s}'_1,\dots,\boldsymbol{s}'_Q)$ leads to the same view of $\mathcal{A}$ as $(\boldsymbol{s}_1,\dots,\boldsymbol{s}_Q)$, we have either $(\boldsymbol{s}'_1,\dots,\boldsymbol{s}'_Q) = (\boldsymbol{s}_1,\dots,\boldsymbol{s}_Q)$ in case that $\mathsf{AWin}$ does not occur, or $(\boldsymbol{s}'_1,\dots,\boldsymbol{s}'_Q) = (\boldsymbol{s}_1 - u_1\Delta,\dots,\boldsymbol{s}_Q - u_Q\Delta)$ in case that $\mathsf{AWin}$ occurs and $\mathcal{A}$ outputs $\boldsymbol{u}$ given $(\boldsymbol{s}_1,\dots,\boldsymbol{s}_Q)$. Also, it also shows that such $(\boldsymbol{s}'_1,\dots,\boldsymbol{s}'_Q)$ always exists, which means $\Phi$ is a bijection.

In the game $\mathbf{G}_2$, the distribution of $(\boldsymbol{s}_1,\dots,\boldsymbol{s}_Q)$ is $\mathscr{D}_\Sigma^{mQ}$, where $\Sigma = \mathbb{I}_m \otimes \mathrm{diag}(\sigma_1^2,\dots,\sigma_Q^2)$. Denote $P = \Phi(\mathscr{D}_\Sigma^{mQ})$. Following the idea described in Sect. 2.1, consider the following two adversaries $\mathcal{B}'$ and $\mathcal{B}''$.

- $\mathcal{B}'$ is the same as $\mathcal{B}$ except that $\mathcal{B}'$ samples $(\boldsymbol{s}_1,\dots,\boldsymbol{s}_Q)$ from $P$.
- $\mathcal{B}''$ is the same as $\mathcal{B}$ except that 1. $\mathcal{B}''$ samples $(\boldsymbol{r}_1,\dots,\boldsymbol{r}_Q) \leftarrow\!\!\$\ \mathscr{D}_\Sigma^{mQ}$ and computes secrets as $(\boldsymbol{s}_1,\dots,\boldsymbol{s}_Q) \leftarrow \Phi(\boldsymbol{r}_1,\dots,\boldsymbol{r}_Q)$; 2. after $\mathcal{A}$ returns, $\mathcal{B}''$ outputs $\hat{\boldsymbol{s}}_i - \boldsymbol{r}_i$ if there exists $\boldsymbol{r}_i \neq \hat{\boldsymbol{s}}_i$.

We note that $\mathcal{B}'$ and $\mathcal{B}''$ do not need to be efficient. They are only used to compute the winning probability of the (efficient) adversary $\mathcal{B}$.

Denote now by $\mathsf{PWin}_{\mathcal{X}}$ the winning probability of $\mathcal{X} \in \{\mathcal{A},\mathcal{B},\mathcal{B}',\mathcal{B}''\}$. Then, we will show the following three facts.

**Fact 1.** $\mathsf{PWin}_{\mathcal{B}'} \leqslant \delta_\alpha \mathsf{PWin}_{\mathcal{B}}^{(\alpha-1)/\alpha}$;
**Fact 2.** $\mathsf{PWin}_{\mathcal{B}} = \mathsf{PWin}_{\mathcal{B}''}$;
**Fact 3.** $\mathsf{PWin}_{\mathcal{B}'} + \mathsf{PWin}_{\mathcal{B}''} \geqslant \mathsf{PWin}_{\mathcal{A}}$.

We can conclude the proof from the facts since

$$\begin{aligned}\mathsf{Adv}^{\mathbf{G}_2}(\mathcal{A},\kappa) &= \mathsf{PWin}_{\mathcal{A}} \leqslant \mathsf{PWin}_{\mathcal{B}'} + \mathsf{PWin}_{\mathcal{B}''} \leqslant \delta_\alpha \mathsf{PWin}_{\mathcal{B}}^{(\alpha-1)/\alpha} + \mathsf{PWin}_{\mathcal{B}} \\ &\leqslant 2\delta_\alpha \mathsf{PWin}_{\mathcal{B}}^{(\alpha-1)/\alpha} = 2\delta_\alpha \mathsf{Adv}_{q,k,m-1,\beta_{\mathsf{sis}}}^{\text{td-msis}}(\mathcal{B},\kappa)^{(\alpha-1)/\alpha},\end{aligned}$$

where the last inequality is due to the fact that $\delta_\alpha \geqslant 1$ and $(\alpha-1)/\alpha < 1$.

We now show the above three facts. For Fact 1, since the only difference between $\mathcal{B}$ and $\mathcal{B}'$ is the distribution of $(\boldsymbol{s}_1,\dots,\boldsymbol{s}_Q)$, by Lemma 4,

$$\mathsf{PWin}_{\mathcal{B}'} \leqslant \left(\mathsf{PWin}_{\mathcal{B}} \cdot R_\alpha\left(P\|\mathscr{D}_\Sigma^{mQ}\right)\right)^{(\alpha-1)/\alpha}.$$

Therefore, Fact 1 follows from the following lemma, which we prove in the full version of the paper.

**Lemma 8.** *For the discrete Gaussian distribution $\mathscr{D}_{\Sigma}^{mQ}$ (defined in Sect. 3.3), where $\Sigma = \mathbb{I}_m \otimes \mathrm{diag}(\sigma_1^2, \ldots, \sigma_Q^2)$, and the distribution $P = \Phi(\mathscr{D}_{\Sigma}^{mQ})$,*

$$R_\alpha \left(P \| \mathscr{D}_{\Sigma}^{mQ}\right) \leqslant \left(\frac{1+\varepsilon}{1-\varepsilon}\right)^{\frac{\alpha}{\alpha-1}} \cdot \exp\left(\alpha\pi^2 / \log(2(1+1/\varepsilon))\right) .$$

The arguments for Facts 2 and 3 follow exactly as in Sect. 2.1. We repeat here for completeness. For Fact 2, since $\mathrm{View}_A(\boldsymbol{r}_1, \ldots, \boldsymbol{r}_Q) = \mathrm{View}_A(\Phi(\boldsymbol{r}_1, \ldots, \boldsymbol{r}_Q)) = \mathrm{View}_A(\boldsymbol{s}_1, \ldots, \boldsymbol{s}_Q)$, even if $\mathcal{B}''$ sets the secrets to $(\boldsymbol{r}_1, \ldots, \boldsymbol{r}_Q)$ instead of $\boldsymbol{s}_1, \ldots, \boldsymbol{s}_Q$, the output of $\mathcal{B}''$ remain the same. However, then, $\mathcal{B}''$ is identical to $\mathcal{B}$, which implies the second fact.

Finally, to prove the third fact, we can interpret the sampling process of $\mathcal{B}'$ as first sampling $(\boldsymbol{r}_1, \ldots, \boldsymbol{r}_Q)$ from $\mathcal{P}$ and then setting $(\boldsymbol{s}_1, \ldots, \boldsymbol{s}_Q) \leftarrow \Phi(\boldsymbol{r}_1, \ldots, \boldsymbol{r}_Q)$. Then, the only difference between $\mathcal{B}'$ and $\mathcal{B}''$ is that $\mathcal{B}'$ check whether there exists $\boldsymbol{s}_i \neq \hat{\boldsymbol{s}}_i$, while $\mathcal{B}''$ check whether there exists $\boldsymbol{r}_i \neq \hat{\boldsymbol{s}}_i$. If $\mathcal{A}$ wins the game $\mathbf{G}_2$ simulated by $\mathcal{B}'$ or $\mathcal{B}''$, we know $(\boldsymbol{r}_1, \ldots, \boldsymbol{r}_Q) \neq \Phi(\boldsymbol{r}_1, \ldots, \boldsymbol{r}_Q) = (\boldsymbol{s}_1, \ldots, \boldsymbol{s}_Q)$ by the definition of $\Phi$, and thus, at least one of $\mathcal{B}'$ and $\mathcal{B}''$ wins, which implies Fact 3. □

## 5 Analysis of the CTZ Construction

As our first application to threshold signatures, this section applies AOM-MISIS to the analysis of the CTZ construction [13].

### 5.1 Construction and Main Security Theorem

We present the scheme $\mathsf{CTZ}[\mathsf{SecSha}]$ in Fig. 6, where $\mathsf{SecSha} = \mathsf{SecSha}_{t,n,B_{\mathsf{ss}}}$ is a linear threshold secret sharing scheme with small coefficients. The definition of linear threshold secret sharing schemes is provided in the full version of the paper. In Fig. 7, we give the description of the parameters used in the protocol. One small change here is that the signing key is sampled from a discrete Gaussian distribution with standard deviation $\sigma_{\mathsf{sk}}$ instead of a uniform distribution over the set of vectors with $\ell_\infty$-norm bounded by $\sigma_{\mathsf{sk}}$. We note that this does not affect the correctness of the scheme, as the $\ell_2$-norm of $\widehat{\mathsf{sk}}$ remains bounded by $\sqrt{mN}\sigma_{\mathsf{sk}}$ except for a negligible probability, which is the exact property needed in the correctness proof.

For unforgeability, we show that TS-UF-0 security of $\mathsf{CTZ}$ is implied by the hardness of the AOM-MISIS problem in the random oracle model, which is formally stated in the following theorem. In particular, we consider an extension of AOM-MISIS (See Remark 1 for details) in which some $\sigma_i$ can be $\infty$. The full proof of Theorem 2 is provided in the full version of the paper.

**Theorem 2** (TS-UF-0 **of** $\mathsf{CTZ}$). *For any integers $q = q(\kappa), k = k(\kappa), m = m(\kappa)$, any linear threshold secret sharing scheme $\mathsf{SecSha} = \mathsf{SecSha}_{t,n,B_{\mathsf{ss}}}$ with small coefficients, and any* TS-UF-0 *adversary $\mathcal{A}$ making at most $\mathsf{q}_s = \mathsf{q}_s(\kappa)$*

$\underline{\mathsf{Setup}(1^\kappa):}$
$\overline{A} \leftarrow_\$ R_q^{k\times(m-k)}$ ; $A \leftarrow [\overline{A} | \mathbb{I}_k]$
$par \leftarrow A$
For $i \in [n]$ do
  $\mathsf{st}_0.\mathrm{curPP}_i \leftarrow \varnothing$
  $\mathsf{st}_i.\mathrm{mapPP} \leftarrow ()$
Return $par$

$\underline{\mathsf{KeyGen}():}$
$\widehat{\mathsf{sk}} \leftarrow_\$ \mathscr{D}^m_{\sigma_{\mathsf{sk}}}$ ; $\mathsf{pk} \leftarrow A\widehat{\mathsf{sk}} \bmod q$
$\boldsymbol{\rho}_1, \ldots, \boldsymbol{\rho}_K \leftarrow_\$ R_q^m$
$(\mathsf{ss}_1, \ldots, \mathsf{ss}_L)^T \leftarrow$
  $M \cdot (\widehat{\mathsf{sk}}, \boldsymbol{\rho}_1, \ldots, \boldsymbol{\rho}_K)^T$
For $i \in [n]$ do $\mathsf{sk}_i \leftarrow (\mathsf{ss}_j)_{j\in T_i}$
Return $(\mathsf{pk}, (\mathsf{sk}_i)_{i\in[n]})$

$\underline{\mathsf{SPP}(\mathsf{st}_i):}$
For $j \in [0..\ell]$ do $\boldsymbol{r}_j \leftarrow_\$ \mathscr{D}^m_{\sigma_r}$
For $j \in [0..\ell]$ do $\boldsymbol{R}_j \leftarrow A\boldsymbol{r}_j \bmod q$
$pp \leftarrow (\boldsymbol{R}_j)_{j\in[0..\ell]}$
$\mathsf{st}_i.\mathrm{mapPP}(pp) \leftarrow (\boldsymbol{r}_j)_{j\in[0..\ell]}$
Return $(pp, \mathsf{st}_i)$

$\underline{\mathsf{LPP}(i, pp, \mathsf{st}_0):}$
$\mathsf{st}_0.\mathrm{curPP}_i \leftarrow \mathsf{st}_0.\mathrm{curPP}_i \cup \{pp\}$
Return $\mathsf{st}_0$

$\underline{\mathsf{LR}(\mu, SS, \mathsf{st}_0):}$
If $\exists\, i \in SS : \mathsf{st}_0.\mathrm{curPP}_i = \varnothing$ then
  Return $\perp$
$lr.\mathsf{msg} \leftarrow \mu$ ; $lr.\mathsf{SS} \leftarrow SS$
For $i \in SS$ do
  Pick $pp_i$ from $\mathsf{st}_0.\mathrm{curPP}_i$
  $lr.\mathsf{PP}(i) \leftarrow pp_i$
  $\mathsf{st}_0.\mathrm{curPP}_i \leftarrow \mathsf{st}_0.\mathrm{curPP}_i \backslash \{pp_i\}$
Return $(lr, \mathsf{st}_0)$

$\underline{\mathsf{CompPar}(\mathsf{pk}, lr):}$
$\mu \leftarrow lr.\mathsf{msg}$
For $i \in lr.\mathsf{SS}$ do
  $(b_j)_{j\in[\ell]} \leftarrow \mathrm{H}_1(\mathsf{pk}, lr)$
  $(\boldsymbol{R}_{i,j})_{j\in[0..\ell]} \leftarrow lr.\mathsf{PP}(i)$
$\boldsymbol{R} \leftarrow \sum_{i\in lr.\mathsf{SS}} \left(\boldsymbol{R}_{i,0} + \sum_{j\in[\ell]} b_j \boldsymbol{R}_{i,j}\right)$
$c \leftarrow \mathrm{H}_2(\mathsf{pk}, \mu, \boldsymbol{R})$
Return $(\boldsymbol{R}, c, (b_j)_{j\in[\ell]})$

$\underline{\mathsf{PS}(lr, i, \mathsf{st}_i):}$
$pp_i \leftarrow lr.\mathsf{PP}(i)$
If $\mathsf{st}_i.\mathrm{mapPP}(pp_i) = \perp$ then return $(\perp, \mathsf{st}_i)$
$(\boldsymbol{r}_j)_{j\in[0..\ell]} \leftarrow \mathsf{st}_i.\mathrm{mapPP}(pp_i)$
$\mathsf{st}_i.\mathrm{mapPP}(pp_i) \leftarrow \perp$
$(\boldsymbol{R}, c, (b_j)_{j\in[\ell]}) \leftarrow \mathsf{CompPar}(\mathsf{st}_i.\mathsf{pk}, lr)$
$(\mathsf{ss}_j)_{j\in T_i} \leftarrow \mathsf{st}_i.\mathsf{sk}$
$\boldsymbol{z} \leftarrow \boldsymbol{r}_0 + \sum_{j\in[\ell]} b_j \cdot \boldsymbol{r}_j$
  $+2c \cdot \sum_{j\in T_i} \lambda_j^{lr.\mathsf{SS}} \mathsf{ss}_j \bmod q$
Return $((\boldsymbol{R}, \boldsymbol{z}), \mathsf{st}_i)$

$\underline{\mathsf{Agg}(\mathrm{PS}, \mathsf{st}_0):}$
$\boldsymbol{R} \leftarrow \perp$ ; $\boldsymbol{z} \leftarrow 0$
For $(\boldsymbol{R}', \boldsymbol{z}') \in \mathrm{PS}$ do
  If $\boldsymbol{R} = \perp$ then $\boldsymbol{R} \leftarrow \boldsymbol{R}'$
  If $\boldsymbol{R} \neq \boldsymbol{R}'$ then return $(\perp, \mathsf{st}_0)$
  $\boldsymbol{z} \leftarrow \boldsymbol{z} + \boldsymbol{z}'$
Return $((\boldsymbol{R}, \boldsymbol{z}), \mathsf{st}_0)$

$\underline{\mathsf{Vf}(\mathsf{pk}, \mu, sig):}$
$(\boldsymbol{R}, \boldsymbol{z}) \leftarrow sig$
If $\|\boldsymbol{z}\| > \beta_z$ then return 0
$c \leftarrow \mathrm{H}_2(\mathsf{pk}, \mu, \boldsymbol{R})$
Return $(A\boldsymbol{z} = \boldsymbol{R} + 2c \cdot \mathsf{pk} \bmod q)$

**Fig. 6.** Lattice-based $t$-out-of-$n$ threshold signatures $\mathsf{CTZ}[\mathsf{SecSha}]$, where $\mathsf{SecSha} = \mathsf{SecSha}_{t,n,B_{\mathsf{ss}}}$ is $t$-out-of-$n$ a linear secret sharing scheme with small coefficients. In particular, $K$ denotes the randomness size of $\mathsf{SecSha}$, $L$ denotes the total share size, $M$ denotes the sharing matrix, $T_i$ denotes the set of shares of party $i$, and $\lambda_j^{lr.\mathsf{SS}}$ denotes the reconstruction coefficient. Also, $\mathrm{H}_1 : \{0,1\}^* \to \mathcal{S}_{\mathsf{b}}^\ell$ and $\mathrm{H}_2 : \{0,1\}^* \to \mathcal{S}_{\mathsf{c}}$. We remark that, as stated earlier, the public parameter $par$ is implicitly given to all algorithms except $\mathsf{Setup}$.

---

*queries to* PPO *and* $\mathsf{q}_h = \mathsf{q}_h(\kappa)$ *queries to* RO, *there exists an* AOM-MISIS

| Parameters | Description |
|---|---|
| $\kappa$ | Security parameter |
| $n$ | Number of signers |
| $t$ | Threshold for signing |
| $N$ | $N \geqslant 2\kappa$, power of two defining the ring $R$ |
| $q$ | Prime modulus |
| $k$ | Number of rows of $A$ |
| $m$ | $m > k$, number of columns of $A$, |
| $\ell + 1$ | $\ell = 2\kappa/\log(2N)$, number of nonces for each signer |
| $\mathcal{S}_{\mathsf{b}}$ | $\mathcal{S}_{\mathsf{b}} = \{\pm 1, \pm X, \ldots, \pm X^{N-1}\}$, set for the aggregating coefficients $b_j$ |
| $\beta_{\mathsf{c}}$ | Satisfying $2^{\beta_{\mathsf{c}}}\binom{N}{\beta_{\mathsf{c}}} \geqslant 2^{2\kappa}$, the $\ell_1$-norm of the challenge $c$, |
| $\mathcal{S}_{\mathsf{c}}$ | $\mathcal{S}_{\mathsf{c}} = \{c \in R : \|c\|_\infty = 1, \|c\|_1 = \beta_{\mathsf{c}}\}$, set of the challenges $c$ |
| $\sigma_{\mathsf{sk}}$ | Standard deviation of the signing key $\mathsf{sk}$ |
| $\sigma_{\mathsf{r}}$ | Standard deviation of the nonces $\boldsymbol{r}_i$ |
| $\nu_{\mathsf{pk}}$ | Only for EKT: satisfying $\lfloor q/2^{\nu_{\mathsf{pk}}} \rfloor = \lfloor q/2^{\nu_{\mathsf{pk}}} \rceil$, number of bits saved on $\mathsf{pk}$ |
| $\nu_{\mathsf{r}}$ | Only for EKT: satisfying $\lfloor q/2^{\nu_{\mathsf{r}}} \rfloor = \lfloor q/2^{\nu_{\mathsf{r}}} \rceil$, number of bits saved on $\boldsymbol{h}$ |
| $q_{\nu_{\mathsf{pk}}}, q_{\nu_{\mathsf{r}}}$ | Only for EKT: $(q_{\nu_{\mathsf{pk}}}, q_{\nu_{\mathsf{r}}}) = (\lfloor q/2^{\nu_{\mathsf{pk}}} \rfloor, \lfloor q/2^{\nu_{\mathsf{r}}} \rfloor)$ the rounded moduli |
| $\beta_{\mathsf{z}}$ | $\ell_2$-norm bound of a valid signature vector $\boldsymbol{z}$ (or $(\boldsymbol{z}, 2^{\nu_{\mathsf{pk}}}\boldsymbol{h})$ for EKT) |

**Fig. 7.** Parameters for CTZ and EKT. Some parameters only apply to EKT.

*adversary $\mathcal{B}$ running in time roughly two times that of $\mathcal{A}$ such that*

$$\mathsf{Adv}_{\mathsf{CTZ}}^{\text{ts-uf-0}}(\mathcal{A}, \kappa) \leqslant \sqrt{\mathsf{q}\mathsf{Adv}_{\mathsf{par}}^{\text{aom-misis}}(\mathcal{B}, \kappa) + 8\mathsf{q}^3 2^{-2\kappa}}\ .$$

*where* $\mathsf{q} = \mathsf{q}_h + \mathsf{q}_s + 1$ *and* $\mathsf{par} = (q, k, m, Q = 1 + K + \mathsf{q}_s(1+\ell), (\sigma_i)_{i\in[Q]}, \beta_{\mathsf{s}} = 2\beta_{\mathsf{z}}, \beta_{\mathsf{b}} = 4\sigma_{\mathsf{sk}}\beta_{\mathsf{c}}, \beta_{\mathsf{u}} = 1/\sigma_{\mathsf{sk}} + \beta_{\mathsf{c}}B_{\mathsf{ss}}\sqrt{8N\mathsf{q}_s}/\sigma_{\mathsf{r}})$ *with* $\sigma_1 = \sigma_{\mathsf{sk}}$, $\sigma_{1+i} = \infty$ *for* $i \in [K]$, $\sigma_{1+K+i} = \sigma_{\mathsf{r}}$ *for* $i \in [\mathsf{q}_s(\ell+1)]$.

For completeness, we recall the correctness theorem from [13], which is needed for parameter selections later.

**Theorem 3 (Correctness of CTZ [13]).** *For any integers $1 < t \leqslant n$, any linear threshold secret sharing scheme* SecSha = $\mathsf{SecSha}_{t,n,B_{\mathsf{ss}}}$ *with small coefficients, given* $\sigma_{\mathsf{r}} \geqslant 2\sqrt{6mN\log(2mN)\kappa/\pi}$ *and* $\beta_{\mathsf{z}} \geqslant \sqrt{mN}(2\beta_{\mathsf{c}}\sigma_{\mathsf{sk}} + \sigma_{\mathsf{r}}\sqrt{n(1+\ell)})$, *the threshold signature scheme* CTZ[SecSha] *is correct with correctness error* $\varepsilon_{\mathsf{cor}} \leqslant (2 + 4n(\ell+1)) \cdot 2^{-2\kappa}$.

### 5.2 Parameter Selection

In this section, we first discuss the asymptotic parameters selection derived from the security theorems and the hardness of AOM-MISIS, then compare these parameters with those proposed in [13], and finally estimate the concrete efficiency based on the parameter selections.

| | $\log_2(q)$ | $k$ | $m$ | $\sigma_{\mathsf{sk}}$ | $\sigma_{\mathsf{r}}$ | $\beta_{\mathsf{z}}$ | $\lvert\mathsf{pk}\rvert$ | $\lvert sig\rvert$ | Comm. |
|---|---|---|---|---|---|---|---|---|---|
| [13] | 119 | 8 | 50 | $2^{18}$ | $2^{105.06}$ | $2^{117.25}$ | 60.73KB | 440.32KB | 2.02MB |
| This work | 94.1 | 7 | 17 | $2^{9.1}$ | $2^{80.5}$ | $2^{91.96}$ | 42.14KB | 144.47KB | 1.24MB |

**Fig. 8.** The concrete parameters and estimated efficiency for $\kappa = 128$ and $n = 32$ in [13] and this work. We set $(N, \ell, \beta_{\mathsf{c}}) = (512, 26, 64)$. The last second column denotes the communication complexity per signer.

ASYMPTOTIC PARAMETER SELECTIONS. Denote $\beta_{\mathsf{lwe}}$ as the norm of the underlying MLWE assumption. Initially, we select $N, m, k, \beta_{\mathsf{lwe}}$ such that $N$ is a power of $N \geqslant 2\kappa$, $m, k = \mathsf{poly}(\kappa)$, and $\beta_{\mathsf{lwe}} \geqslant m\log(N)$.[5] (We note that when estimating the concrete efficiency, we will enumerate through plausible $(N, m, k, \beta_{\mathsf{lwe}})$ tuples and pick the one that yields the best efficiency.) Then, we set other parameters as follows.

- Set $\beta_{\mathsf{c}}$ as the smallest integer such that $2^{\beta_{\mathsf{c}}}\binom{N}{\beta_{\mathsf{c}}} \geqslant 2^{2\kappa}$.
- $\sigma_{\mathsf{sk}} = \max\{2\beta_{\mathsf{lwe}}\sqrt{mN}, \sqrt{\log(6mN)/\pi}\}$. The first term is usually the leading term.
- $\sigma_{\mathsf{r}} = \max\{\sigma_{\mathsf{sk}}\beta_{\mathsf{c}}B_{\mathsf{ss}}\sqrt{8N\mathsf{q}_s}, 2\sqrt{6mN\log(2mN)\kappa/\pi}\}$. The first term is usually the leading term.
- $\beta_{\mathsf{z}} = \sqrt{mN}(2\beta_{\mathsf{c}}\sigma_{\mathsf{sk}} + \sigma_{\mathsf{r}}\sqrt{n(1+\ell)})$
- Denote $\beta_{\mathsf{sis}} = 2\beta_{\mathsf{z}} + 4\sigma_{\mathsf{sk}}\beta_{\mathsf{c}}\sqrt{mN}$.
- Select $q$ such that the problem $\mathrm{MSIS}_{q,k,m,\beta_{\mathsf{sis}}}$ and the problem $\mathrm{MLWE}_{q,N,k,m,\beta_{\mathsf{lwe}}}$ are assumed to be exponentially hard in $\kappa$.

By Theorem 2 and Theorem 1 with $\varepsilon = 1/2$ and $\alpha = 2$ (we can further optimize the concrete bound by adjusting $\alpha$), TS-UF-0 of $\mathsf{CTZ}$ is implied by the hardness of $\mathrm{MSIS}_{q,k,m,\beta_{\mathsf{sis}}}$ and $\mathrm{MLWE}_{q,N,k,m,\beta_{\mathsf{lwe}}}$.

COMPARED WITH [13] The differences of the parameter selections between [13] and ours shows in the selections of $\sigma_{\mathsf{sk}}$ and $\sigma_{\mathsf{r}}$. In particular, the prior work requires

- $\sigma_{\mathsf{sk}} = q^{k/m}2^{2\kappa/(Nm)}$.
- $\sigma_{\mathsf{r}} = \max\{N\beta_{\mathsf{c}}B_{\mathsf{ss}}\sigma_{\mathsf{sk}}\sqrt{32\pi\mathsf{q}_s mN}, \frac{16N\sqrt{3m}}{\sqrt{\pi}}q^{\frac{k}{m}}\sqrt{N(\log(2mN)+2\kappa)}\}$. The first term is usually the leading term.

For $\sigma_{\mathsf{sk}}$, $q^{k/m}$ is significantly larger than $2\beta_{\mathsf{lwe}}\sqrt{mN}$, which influences the choice of $k$ and $m$. In particular, one needs to set $m$ to be several times larger than $k$ to ensure $\sigma_{\mathsf{sk}}$ does not cause the parameters to grow excessively. For $\sigma_{\mathsf{r}}$, we can see a factor of $N\sqrt{m}$ improvement by comparing the first term inside the maximization.

[5] This is for guaranteeing the underlying MLWE is hard.

<u>CONCRETE EFFICIENCY.</u> We show a set of concrete parameters and estimated efficiency for $\kappa = 128$ and $n = 32$, and compare them with those from [13] in Fig. 8, where we can see improvements in both signature sizes and communication complexity. We derive the parameters following our parameter selections mentioned above. To estimate the concrete hardness of MSIS and MLWE, we use the state-of-art tool, lattice estimator,[6] which is also used in other prior works [11,17,20].

## 6 Analysis of the EKT Construction

We apply AOM-MISIS to the analysis of the EKT construction and discuss the parameter selections in this section.

### 6.1 Construction and Main Security Theorem

We recall the EKT construction from [20] in Fig. 9. A summary of the parameters used by the scheme is provided in Fig. 7. The scheme also depends on a pseudorandom function PRF with suitable domain and range. The Lagrange coefficient $L_{U,j} \in \mathbb{Z}_q$ for any subset $U \subseteq [n]$ and $j \in U$ is defined as $L_{U,j} := \prod_{i \in U \setminus \{j\}} \frac{-i}{j-i}$.

The following theorem establishes TS-UF-4 security for EKT from the hardness of AOM-MISIS. In the theorem statement, $\mathsf{Adv}^{\mathsf{prf}}_{\mathsf{PRF}}(\mathcal{C}, \kappa)$ refers to the standard PRF advantage of an adversary $\mathcal{C}$. The full proof of Theorem 4 is provided in the full version of the paper.

**Theorem 4 (TS-UF-4 of EKT).** *For any integers $q = q(\kappa), k = k(\kappa), m = m(\kappa)$, any pseudorandom function* PRF, *and any* TS-UF-4 *adversary $\mathcal{A}$ making at most $\mathsf{q}_s = \mathsf{q}_s(\kappa)$ queries to* PPO *and $\mathsf{q}_h = \mathsf{q}_h(\kappa)$ queries to* RO, *given $\sigma_{\mathsf{r}} > 2N \cdot q^{\frac{1}{m} + \frac{1}{N(m-k)}}$, there exist an* AOM-MISIS *adversary $\mathcal{B}$ and a* PRF *adversary $\mathcal{C}$ running in time roughly two times that of $\mathcal{A}$ such that*

$$\mathsf{Adv}^{\mathsf{ts\text{-}uf\text{-}4}}_{\mathsf{EKT[PRF]}}(\mathcal{A}, \kappa) \leqslant \sqrt{\mathsf{q}\mathsf{Adv}^{\mathsf{aom\text{-}misis}}_{\mathsf{par}}(\mathcal{B}, \kappa) + 8\mathsf{q}^3 2^{-2\kappa}} + n^2 \cdot \mathsf{Adv}^{\mathsf{prf}}_{\mathsf{PRF}}(\mathcal{C}, \kappa) + \mathsf{q}_s^2 \cdot 2^{-2\kappa+1} \; .$$

*where $\mathsf{q} = \mathsf{q}_h + \mathsf{q}_s + 1$ and $\mathsf{par} = (q, k, m, Q = 1 + \mathsf{q}_s(1 + \ell), (\sigma_i)_{i \in [Q]}, \beta_{\mathsf{s}} = (2^{\nu_{\mathsf{r}}+2} + \beta_{\mathsf{c}} \cdot 2^{\nu_{\mathsf{pk}}+1}) \cdot \sqrt{Nk} + 4\beta_{\mathsf{z}}, \beta_{\mathsf{b}} = 4\sigma_{\mathsf{sk}}\beta_{\mathsf{c}}, \beta_{\mathsf{u}} = 1/\sigma_{\mathsf{sk}} + \beta_{\mathsf{c}}\sqrt{8N\mathsf{q}_s}/\sigma_{\mathsf{r}})$ with $\sigma_1 = \sigma_{\mathsf{sk}}$, $\sigma_{1+i} = \sigma_{\mathsf{r}}$ for $i \in [\mathsf{q}_s(\ell + 1)]$.*

*Remark 3.* We note that we can directly establish TS-UF-0 security of EKT from AOM-MISIS by applying the unforgeability theorem from [20] and Lemma 7. However, the resulting parameters are worse than those in Theorem 4. Specifically, $\beta_{\mathsf{u}}$ becomes $1/\sigma_{\mathsf{sk}} + 2\beta_{\mathsf{c}}\sqrt{\ell N \mathsf{q}_s}/\sigma_{\mathsf{r}}$, and $\beta_{\mathsf{b}}$ becomes $4\sigma_{\mathsf{sk}}\sqrt{\beta_{\mathsf{c}} N}$.

Also, we recall the correctness theorem from [20], which is needed for parameter selection later.

**Theorem 5 (Correctness of EKT [20]).** *For any integers $1 < t \leqslant n$, any pseudorandom function* PRF, *given $\sigma_{\mathsf{r}} \geqslant \sqrt{(\log(2Nm) + \kappa)/\pi}$ and $\beta_{\mathsf{z}} \geqslant (\beta_{\mathsf{c}} 2^{\nu_{\mathsf{pk}}} + 2^{\nu_{\mathsf{r}}})\sqrt{mN} + e^{1/4}(2\beta_{\mathsf{c}}\sigma_{\mathsf{sk}} + \sigma_{\mathsf{r}}\sqrt{n(1+\ell)})\sqrt{N}(\sqrt{k} + \sqrt{m-k})$, the threshold signature scheme* EKT[PRF] *is correct with correctness error negligible in $\kappa$.*

[6] https://github.com/malb/lattice-estimator.

**Setup($1^\kappa$):**

$\widehat{A} \leftarrow\!\!\$\ R_q^{k\times(m-k)}$ ; $A \leftarrow [\widehat{A}|\mathbb{I}_k]$
$par \leftarrow A$
For $i \in [n]$ do
  $\mathsf{st}_0.\mathrm{curPP}_i \leftarrow \varnothing$
  $\mathsf{st}_i.\mathrm{mapPP} \leftarrow ()$
Return $par$

**KeyGen():**

$\widehat{\mathsf{sk}} \leftarrow\!\!\$\ \mathscr{D}^m_{\sigma_{\mathsf{sk}}}$
$\mathsf{pk} \leftarrow \left\lfloor 2A \cdot \widehat{\mathsf{sk}} \right\rceil_{\nu_{\mathsf{pk}}}$ // $\mathsf{pk} \in R^k_{q_{\nu_{\mathsf{pk}}}}$
For $(i,j) \in [n] \times [n]$ do
  $\mathsf{seed}_{i,j} \leftarrow \{0,1\}^\kappa$
$\boldsymbol{a}_1, \ldots, \boldsymbol{a}_{t-1} \leftarrow\!\!\$\ R_q^{m-k}$
For $i \in [n]$ do
  $\boldsymbol{s}_i \leftarrow \widehat{\mathsf{sk}}_{[m-k]} + \sum_{j=1}^{t-1} \boldsymbol{a}_j i^j$
  $\mathsf{sk}_i \leftarrow (\boldsymbol{s}_i, (\mathsf{seed}_{i,j}, \mathsf{seed}_{j,i})_{j\in[n]})$
Return $(\mathsf{pk}, (\mathsf{sk}_i)_{i\in[n]})$

**SPP($\mathsf{st}_i$):**

For $j \in [0..\ell]$ do $\boldsymbol{r}_j \leftarrow\!\!\$\ \mathscr{D}^m_{\sigma_{\mathsf{r}}}$
For $j \in [0..\ell]$ do $\boldsymbol{R}_j \leftarrow A \cdot \boldsymbol{r}_j$
$pp \leftarrow (\boldsymbol{R}_j)_{j\in[0..\ell]}$
$\mathsf{st}_i.\mathrm{mapPP}(pp) \leftarrow (\boldsymbol{r}_j)_{j\in[0..\ell]}$
Return $(pp, \mathsf{st}_i)$

**LPP($i, pp, \mathsf{st}_0$):**

$\mathsf{st}_0.\mathrm{curPP}_i \leftarrow \mathsf{st}_0.\mathrm{curPP}_i \cup \{pp\}$
Return $\mathsf{st}_0$

**LR($\mu, SS, \mathsf{st}_0$):**

If $\exists\, i \in SS : \mathsf{st}_0.\mathrm{curPP}_i = \varnothing$ then
  Return $\perp$
$lr.\mathsf{msg} \leftarrow \mu$ ; $lr.\mathsf{SS} \leftarrow SS$
For $i \in SS$ do
  Pick $pp_i$ from $\mathsf{st}_0.\mathrm{curPP}_i$
  $lr.\mathsf{PP}(i) \leftarrow pp_i$
  $\mathsf{st}_0.\mathrm{curPP}_i \leftarrow \mathsf{st}_0.\mathrm{curPP}_i \backslash \{pp_i\}$
Return $(lr, \mathsf{st}_0)$

**CompPar($\mathsf{pk}, lr$):**

$\mu \leftarrow lr.\mathsf{msg}$
For $i \in lr.\mathsf{SS}$ do
  $(b_j)_{j\in[\ell]} \leftarrow \mathrm{H}_1(\mathsf{pk}, lr)$
  $(\boldsymbol{R}_{i,j})_{j\in[0..\ell]} \leftarrow lr.\mathsf{PP}(i)$
$\boldsymbol{R} \leftarrow \left\lfloor \sum_{i\in lr.\mathsf{SS}} \left( \boldsymbol{R}_{i,0} + \sum_{j\in[\ell]} b_j \boldsymbol{R}_{i,j} \right) \right\rceil_{\nu_{\mathsf{r}}}$
$c \leftarrow \mathrm{H}_2(\mathsf{pk}, \mu, \boldsymbol{R})$
Return $(\boldsymbol{R}, c, (b_j)_{j\in[\ell]})$

**PS($lr, i, \mathsf{st}_i$):**

$pp_i \leftarrow lr.\mathsf{PP}(i)$
If $\mathsf{st}_i.\mathrm{mapPP}(pp_i) = \perp$ then return $(\perp, \mathsf{st}_i)$
$(\boldsymbol{r}_j)_{j\in[0..\ell]} \leftarrow \mathsf{st}_i.\mathrm{mapPP}(pp_i)$
$\mathsf{st}_i.\mathrm{mapPP}(pp_i) \leftarrow \perp$
$(\boldsymbol{R}, c, (b_j)_{j\in[\ell]})) \leftarrow \mathsf{CompPar}(\mathsf{st}_i.\mathsf{pk}, lr)$
$(\boldsymbol{s}_i, (\mathsf{seed}_{i,j}, \mathsf{seed}_{j,i})_{j\in[n]}) \leftarrow \mathsf{st}_i.\mathsf{sk}$
$\mathsf{mask} \leftarrow \sum_{j\in lr.SS} \mathsf{PRF}(\mathsf{seed}_{i,j}, (\mathsf{pk}, lr))$
$\mathsf{mask}' \leftarrow \sum_{j\in lr.SS} \mathsf{PRF}(\mathsf{seed}_{j,i}, (\mathsf{pk}, lr))$
$\boldsymbol{z} \leftarrow \boldsymbol{r}_{0,[m-k]} + \sum_{j\in[\ell]} b_j \cdot \boldsymbol{r}_{j,[m-k]}$
  $+ 2c \cdot L_{lr.\mathsf{SS},j} \cdot \boldsymbol{s}_j + \mathsf{mask} - \mathsf{mask}' \bmod q$
Return $((\boldsymbol{R}, \boldsymbol{z}), \mathsf{st}_i)$

**Agg(PS, $\mathsf{st}_0$):**

$\boldsymbol{R} \leftarrow \perp$ ; $\boldsymbol{z} \leftarrow 0$
For $(\boldsymbol{R}', \boldsymbol{z}') \in \mathrm{PS}$ do
  If $\boldsymbol{R} = \perp$ then $\boldsymbol{R} \leftarrow \boldsymbol{R}'$
  If $\boldsymbol{R} \neq \boldsymbol{R}'$ then return $(\perp, \mathsf{st}_0)$
  $\boldsymbol{z} \leftarrow \boldsymbol{z} + \boldsymbol{z}'$
$c \leftarrow \mathrm{H}_2(\mathsf{pk}, \mu, \boldsymbol{R})$
$\boldsymbol{h} \leftarrow \boldsymbol{R} - \left\lfloor \widehat{A}\boldsymbol{z} - 2^{\nu_{\mathsf{pk}}} \cdot c \cdot \overline{\mathsf{pk}} \right\rceil_{\nu_{\mathsf{r}}}$ // $\boldsymbol{h} \in R^k_{q_{\nu_{\mathsf{r}}}}$
Return $((c, \boldsymbol{z}, \boldsymbol{h}), \mathsf{st}_0)$

**Vf($\mathsf{pk}, \mu, sig$):**

$(c, \boldsymbol{z}, \boldsymbol{h}) \leftarrow sig$
If $\left\|(\boldsymbol{z}, 2^{\nu_{\mathsf{r}}}\overline{\boldsymbol{h}} \bmod q)\right\|_2 > \beta_{\mathsf{z}}$ then return 0
$c' \leftarrow \mathrm{H}_2(\mathsf{pk}, \mu, \left\lfloor \widehat{A}\boldsymbol{z} - 2^{\nu_{\mathsf{pk}}} \cdot c \cdot \overline{\mathsf{pk}} \right\rceil_{\nu_{\mathsf{r}}} + \boldsymbol{h})$
Return $(c' = c)$

**Fig. 9.** Lattice-based $t$-out-of-$n$ threshold signatures $\mathsf{EKT}[\mathsf{PRF}]$, where $\mathsf{PRF}$ is a pseudorandom function. Here, $\mathrm{H}_1 : \{0,1\}^* \to \mathcal{S}_{\mathsf{b}}^\ell$ and $\mathrm{H}_2 : \{0,1\}^* \to \mathcal{S}_{\mathsf{c}}$. Also, $L_{lr.\mathsf{SS},j}$ denotes the Lagrange coefficient, and $\overline{\mathsf{pk}}, \overline{\boldsymbol{h}} \in R^k$ denote the lift (see Section 3.1 for more details) of $\mathsf{pk}$ and $\boldsymbol{h}$ respectively. Also, we remark that, as stated earlier, the public parameter $par$ is implicitly given to all algorithms except $\mathsf{Setup}$.

### 6.2 Parameter Selection

In this section, we first discuss the asymptotic parameters selection derived from the security theorems and the hardness of AOM-MISIS, then compare these parameters with those proposed in [20], and finally estimate the concrete efficiency based on the parameter selections. We also discuss how our parameters are compared to the parameters of Ringtail [11].

ASYMPTOTIC PARAMETER SELECTIONS. Denote $\beta_{\mathsf{lwe}}$ as the norm of the underlying MLWE assumption. Initially, we select $N, m, k, \beta_{\mathsf{lwe}}$ such that $N$ is a power of $N \geqslant 2\kappa$, $m, k = \mathsf{poly}(\kappa)$, and $\beta_{\mathsf{lwe}} \geqslant m \log(N)$.[7] (We note that when estimating the concrete efficiency, we will enumerate through plausible $(N, m, k, \beta_{\mathsf{lwe}})$ tuples and pick the one that yields the best efficiency.) Then, we set other parameters as follows.

- Set $\beta_{\mathsf{c}}$ as the smallest integer such that $2^{\beta_{\mathsf{c}}}\binom{N}{\beta_{\mathsf{c}}} \geqslant 2^{2\kappa}$.
- $\sigma_{\mathsf{sk}} = \max\{2\beta_{\mathsf{lwe}}\sqrt{mN}, \sqrt{\log(6mN)/\pi}\}$. The first term is usually the leading term.
- $\sigma_{\mathsf{r}} = \max\{\sigma_{\mathsf{sk}}\beta_{\mathsf{c}}\sqrt{8N\mathsf{q}_s}, \sqrt{(\log(2Nm) + \kappa)/\pi}, 2N \cdot q^{\frac{1}{m} + \frac{1}{N(m-k)}}\}$. The first term is usually the leading term.
- $\nu_{\mathsf{pk}} = \log_2(\sigma_{\mathsf{r}}/\beta_{\mathsf{c}})$ and $\nu_{\mathsf{r}} = \log_2(\sigma_{\mathsf{r}})$.
- $\beta_{\mathsf{z}}$ is set as shown in Theorem 5
- Denote $\beta_{\mathsf{sis}} = 2\beta_{\mathsf{z}} + 4\sigma_{\mathsf{sk}}\beta_{\mathsf{c}}\sqrt{mN}$.
- Select $q$ such that the problem $\mathrm{MSIS}_{q,k,m,\beta_{\mathsf{sis}}}$ and the problem $\mathrm{MLWE}_{q,N,k,m,\beta_{\mathsf{lwe}}}$ are assumed to be exponentially hard in $\kappa$.

By Theorem 4 and Theorem 1 with $\varepsilon = 1/2$ and $\alpha = 2$ (we can further optimize the concrete bound by adjusting $\alpha$), TS-UF-4 of $\mathsf{EKT}$ is implied by the hardness of $\mathrm{MSIS}_{q,k,m,\beta_{\mathsf{sis}}}$ and $\mathrm{MLWE}_{q,N,k,m,\beta_{\mathsf{lwe}}}$.

COMPARISON WITH [20]. Although the prior work does not give a security reduction to standard lattice assumptions, they provide candidate asymptotic parameters based on the heuristic assumption that the selective version of AOM-MLWE is as hard as the adaptive version. Still, our asymptotic parameters are slightly better than their candidate asymptotic parameters provided in [20]. The key difference lies in the choice of $\sigma_{\mathsf{r}}$, which significantly impacts efficiency. In particular, the prior work requires $\sigma_{\mathsf{r}} = \Omega(\beta_{\mathsf{c}}\beta_{\mathsf{lwe}}N\sqrt{\mathsf{q}_s Nk})$, while we require $\sigma_{\mathsf{r}} = \Omega(\beta_{\mathsf{c}}\beta_{\mathsf{lwe}}N\sqrt{\mathsf{q}_s m})$. Therefore, there is roughly a factor of $\sqrt{N}$ improvement.

COMPARISON WITH RINGTAIL [11]. Ringtail is very close to EKT. The main differences are that the output space of hash function $\mathrm{H}_1$ changes and the nonces $\boldsymbol{r}_j$ are sampled from unbalanced discrete Gaussian distributions. In particular, in Ringtail, the first $m-k$ entries of each nonce $\boldsymbol{r}_{j,[m-k]}$ is sampled from $\mathscr{D}_{\sigma_{\mathsf{r}}}^{m-k}$, while the rest $\boldsymbol{r}_{j,[(m-k+1)..m]}$ is sampled from $\mathscr{D}_{\sigma_{\mathsf{r}}'}^{k}$ with $\sigma_{\mathsf{r}}' \neq \sigma_{\mathsf{r}}$. Therefore, it is possible to compare the parameter selections directly.

[7] This is for guaranteeing the underlying MLWE is hard.

| $\kappa$ | $\log_2(q)$ | $k$ | $m$ | $\sigma_{\mathsf{sk}}$ | $\sigma_{\mathsf{r}}$ | $\beta_{\mathsf{z}}$ | $\lvert\mathsf{pk}\rvert$ | $\lvert sig\rvert$ | Comm. |
|---|---|---|---|---|---|---|---|---|---|
| 128 | 69.3 | 6 | 11 | $2^{10.6}$ | $2^{52.6}$ | $2^{66.2}$ | 8.72KB | 30.88KB | 766.83KB |
| 192 | 69.6 | 8 | 15 | $2^{10.6}$ | $2^{52.6}$ | $2^{66.5}$ | 11.74KB | 42.90KB | 1.01MB |
| 256 | 70.2 | 10 | 18 | $2^{11.17}$ | $2^{53.2}$ | $2^{67.1}$ | 14.76KB | 50.72KB | 1.29MB |

**Fig. 10.** The concrete parameters and estimated efficiency of the EKT scheme for $\kappa = 128, 192, 256$ and $n = 1024$. We set $(N, \ell, \beta_{\mathsf{c}}) = (512, 26, 64)$. The last second column denotes the communication complexity per signer.

The key difference still lies in the choice of $\sigma_{\mathsf{r}}$. In particular, Ringtail requires $\sigma_{\mathsf{r}} = \Omega(\beta_{\mathsf{c}}\sqrt{\mathsf{q}_h})$, where $\mathsf{q}_h$ denotes the number of random oracle queries. Here we offer different trade-offs. A key drawback of their parameters is that $\sigma_{\mathsf{r}}$ depends on $\mathsf{q}_h$, which is typically assumed to be much larger than $\mathsf{q}_s$. This is because $\mathsf{q}_s$ refers to the number of online signing queries and is a system parameter that can be enforced, while $\mathsf{q}_h$ scales with the offline computational power of the adversary. However, if we set $\mathsf{q}_h = \mathsf{q}_s$, their $\sigma_{\mathsf{r}}$ is smaller than ours roughly by a factor of $\beta_{\mathsf{lwe}} N\sqrt{m}$.

<u>CONCRETE EFFICIENCY.</u> We show a set of concrete parameters and estimated efficiency for $\kappa \in \{128, 192, 256\}$ and $n = 1024$ in Fig. 10. We derive the parameters following our parameter selections mentioned above, and similar to the CTZ scheme, we estimate the concrete hardness of MSIS and MLWE using the lattice estimator. We note that our concrete parameters are worse than those given in [20], although in a similar ballpark. However, worse parameters are to be expected. This is because their parameter selection is based on their direct cryptanalysis of AOM-MLWE, whereas we rely on a reduction from two standard lattice assumptions. In a similar spirit, our parameters are worse than those claimed for Ringtail in [11], however this is to be expected, too, as they heuristically assume $\mathsf{q}_h = \mathsf{q}_s$ (also see the above discussion) to set parameters. In practice, however, we expect $\mathsf{q}_h$ to be best approximated conservatively by the running time of the adversary, and this can be as high as $2^{256}$, whereas $\mathsf{q}_s$ could typically be $2^{60}$. The authors of Ringtail were aware of this fact, and their choice was motivated by their conjecture that a better dependency would be possible. We confirm their conjecture for the case of EKT.

**Acknowledgments.** This research was partially supported by NSF grants CNS-2026774, CNS-2154174, CNS-2426905, a gift from Microsoft, and a Stellar Development Foundation Academic Research Award.

## References

1. Agrawal, S., Gentry, C., Halevi, S., Sahai, A.: Discrete Gaussian leftover hash lemma over infinite domains. In: Sako, K., Sarkar, P. (eds.) ASIACRYPT 2013, Part I. LNCS, vol. 8269, pp. 97–116. Springer, Berlin, Heidelberg (2013). https://doi.org/10.1007/978-3-642-42033-7_6
2. Agrawal, S., Kirshanova, E., Stehlé, D., Yadav, A.: Practical, round-optimal lattice-based blind signatures. In: Yin, H., Stavrou, A., Cremers, C., Shi, E. (eds.) ACM CCS 2022, pp. 39–53. ACM Press (Nov 2022). https://doi.org/10.1145/3548606.3560650
3. Agrawal, S., Stehlé, D., Yadav, A.: Round-optimal lattice-based threshold signatures, revisited. In: Bojanczyk, M., Merelli, E., Woodruff, D.P. (eds.) ICALP 2022. LIPIcs, vol. 229, pp. 8:1–8:20. Schloss Dagstuhl (2022). https://doi.org/10.4230/LIPIcs.ICALP.2022.8
4. Bacho, R., Loss, J., Tessaro, S., Wagner, B., Zhu, C.: Twinkle: Threshold signatures from DDH with full adaptive security. In: Joye, M., Leander, G. (eds.) EUROCRYPT 2024, Part I. LNCS, vol. 14651, pp. 429–459. Springer, Cham (2024). https://doi.org/10.1007/978-3-031-58716-0_15
5. Bauer, B., Fuchsbauer, G., Plouviez, A.: The one-more discrete logarithm assumption in the generic group model. In: Tibouchi, M., Wang, H. (eds.) ASIACRYPT 2021, Part IV. LNCS, vol. 13093, pp. 587–617. Springer, Cham (2021). https://doi.org/10.1007/978-3-030-92068-5_20
6. Bellare, M., Crites, E.C., Komlo, C., Maller, M., Tessaro, S., Zhu, C.: Better than advertised security for non-interactive threshold signatures. In: Dodis, Y., Shrimpton, T. (eds.) CRYPTO 2022, Part IV. LNCS, vol. 13510, pp. 517–550. Springer, Cham (2022). https://doi.org/10.1007/978-3-031-15985-5_18
7. Bellare, M., Namprempre, C., Pointcheval, D., Semanko, M.: The one-more-RSA-inversion problems and the security of Chaum's blind signature scheme. J. Cryptol. **16**(3), 185–215 (2003). https://doi.org/10.1007/s00145-002-0120-1
8. Benhamouda, F., Camenisch, J., Krenn, S., Lyubashevsky, V., Neven, G.: Better zero-knowledge proofs for lattice encryption and their application to group signatures. In: Sarkar, P., Iwata, T. (eds.) ASIACRYPT 2014, Part I. LNCS, vol. 8873, pp. 551–572. Springer, Berlin, Heidelberg (2014). https://doi.org/10.1007/978-3-662-45611-8_29
9. Boneh, D., Gennaro, R., Goldfeder, S., Jain, A., Kim, S., Rasmussen, P.M.R., Sahai, A.: Threshold cryptosystems from threshold fully homomorphic encryption. In: Shacham, H., Boldyreva, A. (eds.) CRYPTO 2018, Part I. LNCS, vol. 10991, pp. 565–596. Springer, Cham (2018). https://doi.org/10.1007/978-3-319-96884-1_19
10. Boneh, D., Gennaro, R., Goldfeder, S., Kim, S.: A lattice-based universal thresholdizer for cryptographic systems. Cryptology ePrint Archive, Report 2017/251 (2017). https://eprint.iacr.org/2017/251
11. Boschini, C., Kaviani, D., Lai, R.W.F., Malavolta, G., Takahashi, A., Tibouchi, M.: Ringtail: practical two-round threshold signatures from learning with errors. Cryptology ePrint Archive, Paper 2024/1113 (2024). https://doi.org/10.1109/SP61157.2025.00070, https://eprint.iacr.org/2024/1113
12. Boschini, C., Takahashi, A., Tibouchi, M.: MuSig-L: lattice-based multi-signature with single-round online phase. In: Dodis, Y., Shrimpton, T. (eds.) CRYPTO 2022, Part II. LNCS, vol. 13508, pp. 276–305. Springer, Cham (2022). https://doi.org/10.1007/978-3-031-15979-4_10

13. Chairattana-Apirom, R., Tessaro, S., Zhu, C.: Partially non-interactive two-round lattice-based threshold signatures. In: Chung, K.M., Sasaki, Y. (eds.) ASIACRYPT 2024, Part IV. LNCS, vol. 15487, pp. 268–302. Springer, Singapore (2024). https://doi.org/10.1007/978-981-96-0894-2_9
14. Chen, Y.: DualMS: efficient lattice-based two-round multi-signature with trapdoor-free simulation. In: Handschuh, H., Lysyanskaya, A. (eds.) CRYPTO 2023, Part V. LNCS, vol. 14085, pp. 716–747. Springer, Cham (2023). https://doi.org/10.1007/978-3-031-38554-4_23
15. Connolly, D., Komlo, C., Goldberg, I., Wood, C.A.: Two-Round Threshold Schnorr Signatures with FROST. Internet-Draft draft-irtf-cfrg-frost-10, Internet Engineering Task Force (2022). https://datatracker.ietf.org/doc/draft-irtf-cfrg-frost/10/, work in Progress
16. Damgård, I., Orlandi, C., Takahashi, A., Tibouchi, M.: Two-round n-out-of-n and multi-signatures and trapdoor commitment from lattices. In: Garay, J. (ed.) PKC 2021, Part I. LNCS, vol. 12710, pp. 99–130. Springer, Cham (2021). https://doi.org/10.1007/978-3-030-75245-3_5
17. Del Pino, R., Katsumata, S., Maller, M., Mouhartem, F., Prest, T., Saarinen, M.J.O.: Threshold Raccoon: practical threshold signatures from standard lattice assumptions. In: Joye, M., Leander, G. (eds.) EUROCRYPT 2024, Part II. LNCS, vol. 14652, pp. 219–248. Springer, Cham (2024). https://doi.org/10.1007/978-3-031-58723-8_8
18. Desmedt, Y.: Society and group oriented cryptography: a new concept. In: Pomerance, C. (ed.) CRYPTO'87. LNCS, vol. 293, pp. 120–127. Springer, Berlin, Heidelberg (1988). https://doi.org/10.1007/3-540-48184-2_8
19. Desmedt, Y., Frankel, Y.: Threshold cryptosystems. In: Brassard, G. (ed.) CRYPTO'89. LNCS, vol. 435, pp. 307–315. Springer, New York (1990). https://doi.org/10.1007/0-387-34805-0_28
20. Espitau, T., Katsumata, S., Takemure, K.: Two-round threshold signature from algebraic one-more learning with errors. In: Reyzin, L., Stebila, D. (eds.) CRYPTO 2024, Part VII. LNCS, vol. 14926, pp. 387–424. Springer, Cham (2024). https://doi.org/10.1007/978-3-031-68394-7_13
21. Espitau, T., Niot, G., Prest, T.: Flood and Submerse: distributed key generation and robust threshold signature from lattices. In: Reyzin, L., Stebila, D. (eds.) CRYPTO 2024, Part VII. LNCS, vol. 14926, pp. 425–458. Springer, Cham (2024). https://doi.org/10.1007/978-3-031-68394-7_14
22. Fuchsbauer, G., Plouviez, A., Seurin, Y.: Blind Schnorr signatures and signed ElGamal encryption in the algebraic group model. In: Canteaut, A., Ishai, Y. (eds.) EUROCRYPT 2020, Part II. LNCS, vol. 12106, pp. 63–95. Springer, Cham (2020). https://doi.org/10.1007/978-3-030-45724-2_3
23. Gentry, C., Peikert, C., Vaikuntanathan, V.: Trapdoors for hard lattices and new cryptographic constructions. In: Ladner, R.E., Dwork, C. (eds.) 40th ACM STOC. pp. 197–206. ACM Press (2008). https://doi.org/10.1145/1374376.1374407
24. Gur, K.D., Katz, J., Silde, T.: Two-round threshold lattice signatures from threshold homomorphic encryption. Cryptology ePrint Archive, Paper 2023/1318 (2023). https://eprint.iacr.org/2023/1318, https://eprint.iacr.org/2023/1318
25. Hauck, E., Kiltz, E., Loss, J.: A modular treatment of blind signatures from identification schemes. In: Ishai, Y., Rijmen, V. (eds.) EUROCRYPT 2019, Part III. LNCS, vol. 11478, pp. 345–375. Springer, Cham (2019). https://doi.org/10.1007/978-3-030-17659-4_12

26. Hauck, E., Kiltz, E., Loss, J., Nguyen, N.K.: Lattice-based blind signatures, revisited. In: Micciancio, D., Ristenpart, T. (eds.) CRYPTO 2020, Part II. LNCS, vol. 12171, pp. 500–529. Springer, Cham (2020). https://doi.org/10.1007/978-3-030-56880-1_18
27. Katsumata, S., Reichle, M., Takemure, K.: Adaptively secure 5 round threshold signatures from MLWE/MSIS and DL with rewinding. In: Reyzin, L., Stebila, D. (eds.) CRYPTO 2024, Part VII. LNCS, vol. 14926, pp. 459–491. Springer, Cham (2024). https://doi.org/10.1007/978-3-031-68394-7_15
28. Koblitz, N., Menezes, A.: Another look at non-standard discrete log and Diffie-Hellman problems. J. Math. Cryptol. **2**(4), 311–326 (2008). https://doi.org/10.1515/JMC.2008.014
29. Komlo, C., Goldberg, I.: FROST: flexible round-optimized Schnorr threshold signatures. In: Dunkelman, O., Jacobson, Jr., M.J., O'Flynn, C. (eds.) SAC 2020. LNCS, vol. 12804, pp. 34–65. Springer, Cham (2020). https://doi.org/10.1007/978-3-030-81652-0_2
30. Langlois, A., Stehlé, D., Steinfeld, R.: GGHLite: more efficient multilinear maps from ideal lattices. In: Nguyen, P.Q., Oswald, E. (eds.) EUROCRYPT 2014. LNCS, vol. 8441, pp. 239–256. Springer, Berlin, Heidelberg (2014). https://doi.org/10.1007/978-3-642-55220-5_14
31. Lyubashevsky, V.: Fiat-Shamir with aborts: applications to lattice and factoring-based signatures. In: Matsui, M. (ed.) ASIACRYPT 2009. LNCS, vol. 5912, pp. 598–616. Springer, Berlin, Heidelberg (2009). https://doi.org/10.1007/978-3-642-10366-7_35
32. Lyubashevsky, V.: Lattice signatures without trapdoors. In: Pointcheval, D., Johansson, T. (eds.) EUROCRYPT 2012. LNCS, vol. 7237, pp. 738–755. Springer, Berlin, Heidelberg (2012). https://doi.org/10.1007/978-3-642-29011-4_43
33. Lyubashevsky, V., .: CRYSTALS-DILITHIUM. Tech. rep., National Institute of Standards and Technology (2022). https://csrc.nist.gov/Projects/post-quantum-cryptography/selected-algorithms-2022
34. Maurer, U.M.: Abstract models of computation in cryptography (invited paper). In: Smart, N.P. (ed.) 10th IMA International Conference on Cryptography and Coding. LNCS, vol. 3796, pp. 1–12. Springer, Berlin, Heidelberg (2005). https://doi.org/10.1007/11586821_1
35. National Institute of Standards and Technology: Post-Quantum Cryptography: Additional Digital Signature Schemes (2022–Present). https://csrc.nist.gov/projects/pqc-dig-sig
36. Nick, J., Ruffing, T., Seurin, Y.: MuSig2: simple two-round Schnorr multi-signatures. In: Malkin, T., Peikert, C. (eds.) CRYPTO 2021, Part I. LNCS, vol. 12825, pp. 189–221. Springer, Cham, Virtual Event (2021). https://doi.org/10.1007/978-3-030-84242-0_8
37. Okamoto, T.: Provably secure and practical identification schemes and corresponding signature schemes. In: Brickell, E.F. (ed.) CRYPTO'92. LNCS, vol. 740, pp. 31–53. Springer, Berlin, Heidelberg (1993). https://doi.org/10.1007/3-540-48071-4_3
38. del Pino, R., Katsumata, S., Prest, T., Rossi, M.: Raccoon: a masking-friendly signature proven in the probing model. In: Reyzin, L., Stebila, D. (eds.) CRYPTO 2024, Part I. LNCS, vol. 14920, pp. 409–444. Springer, Cham (2024). https://doi.org/10.1007/978-3-031-68376-3_13
39. Prest, T., et al.: FALCON. Tech. rep., National Institute of Standards and Technology (2022). https://csrc.nist.gov/Projects/post-quantum-cryptography/selected-algorithms-2022

40. Shoup, V.: Lower bounds for discrete logarithms and related problems. In: Fumy, W. (ed.) EUROCRYPT'97. LNCS, vol. 1233, pp. 256–266. Springer, Berlin, Heidelberg (1997). https://doi.org/10.1007/3-540-69053-0_18
41. Takashima, K., Takayasu, A.: Tighter security for efficient lattice cryptography via the Rényi divergence of optimized orders. In: Au, M.H., Miyaji, A. (eds.) ProvSec 2015. LNCS, vol. 9451, pp. 412–431. Springer, Cham (2015). https://doi.org/10.1007/978-3-319-26059-4_23
42. Tessaro, S., Zhu, C.: Threshold and multi-signature schemes from linear hash functions. In: Hazay, C., Stam, M. (eds.) EUROCRYPT 2023, Part V. LNCS, vol. 14008, pp. 628–658. Springer, Cham (2023). https://doi.org/10.1007/978-3-031-30589-4_22

# Complexity-Theoretic Foundations

# Uniform Black-Box Separations via Non-malleable Extractors

Marshall Ball[1(✉)] and Dana Dachman-Soled[2]

[1] New York University, New York, USA
marshall@cs.nyu.edu
[2] University of Maryland, College Park, USA
danadach@umd.edu

**Abstract.** We construct $t$-non-malleable extractors—which allow an attacker to tamper with a source $t$ times—for high min-entropy sources samplable by poly-time hierarchy circuits and for tampering classes corresponding to poly-time hierarchy functions from derandomization-type assumptions.

We then show an application of this new object to ruling out constructions of succinct, non-interactive, arguments (SNARGs) secure against *uniform* adversaries from *uniform* falsifiable assumptions via a class of black-box reductions that has not been previously considered in the literature. This class of black-box reductions allows the reduction to arbitrarily set the *coins*, as well as the input, of the uniform adversary it interacts with. The class of reductions we consider is restricted in allowing only non-adaptive queries to the adversary.

## 1 Introduction

(Seedless) randomness extractors are deterministic functions that transform an adversarial, unpredictable source into something statistically close to uniformly random bits. An $n$-bit source, $X$, is said to have *min-entropy* $k$ if for all $x$, $\Pr[X = x] \leq 2^{-k}$. Regrettably, deterministic or seedless randomness extractors do not exist for arbitrary $n$-bit sources, even those with min-entropy $n-1$. However, such randomness extractors *do* exist for more structured source classes: sources formed by concatenating shorter, independent, unpredictable sources [13]; sources samplable by small circuits [50]; etc.

(Seedless) non-malleable extractors, introduced by Cherangchi and Guruswami [12], are randomness extractors with a very strong property that resembles limited independence. Namely, the output of the randomness extractor should be statistically-close to uniform, even if one sees the extractor evaluated on strings related to the source.

In particular, we say a deterministic function NMExt is a (relaxed, seedless) *t-non-malleable extractor* for a class of sources, $\mathcal{X}$, and a class of tampering

M. Ball—Supported in part by NSF grant CCF-2443735 and the Simons Foundation.
D. Dachman-Soled—Supported in part by NSF grants CNS-2154705 and CNS-1933033.


Y. Tauman Kalai and S. F. Kamara (Eds.): CRYPTO 2025, LNCS 16000, pp. 585–616, 2025.
https://doi.org/10.1007/978-3-032-01855-7_19

functions, $\mathcal{F}$, if for any source $X \in \mathcal{X}$ and any sequence of $t$ functions $f_1, \ldots, f_t \in \mathcal{F}$ without fixed points[1], the output

$$[(\mathrm{NMExt}(X), \mathrm{NMExt}(f_1(X)), \ldots, \mathrm{NMExt}(f_t(X)) \\ \approx (\mathcal{U}, \mathrm{NMExt}(f_1(X)), \ldots, \mathrm{NMExt}(f_t(X)).$$

Since their introduction, there has been a concerted effort in constructing *explicit* (seedless) non-malleable extractors for various combinations of source classes and tampering classes. Central to this study has been *non-malleable two-source extractors*: non-malleable extractors for the class of sources that are the concatenation of two independent high min-entropy sources, $(X, Y)$, and the class of tampering functions that may independently tamper each half of the source independently, $(X, Y) \mapsto (f(X), g(Y))$ for any $f, g$.

Part of the reason for this focus is that non-malleable two-source extractors have found a variety of powerful applications:

1. Generic-compilers for *tamper and leakage resilient key-derivation* when an attacker, perhaps due to physical constraints, can only independently leak and tamper on each half of a key at rest.
2. *Split-state non-malleable codes* [12]: means of *encoding* information such that tampering independently with the left and right halves of the codeword either does not change the encoded information or decodes something completely unrelated.
3. *Two-source extractors* [30,36], particularly in the low min-entropy regime. Perhaps most surprisingly, non-malleable two-source extractors with low error have been central to recent breakthroughs in explicitly constructing two-source extractors (and hence other downstream applications such as Ramsey graphs).
4. *Non-malleable extractors* [5] for other classes of sources and tampering functions.

This last application is perhaps most relevant to the kind of non-malleable extractor studied in this work: non-malleable extractors for *bounded polynomial-size post-selecting sources and tampering functions.*

A size $s$ *post-selecting source*, introduced by Ball et al. [6], is a generalization of size $s$ samplable sources [50] (sources samplable by a size $s$ circuit with uniformly random input bits) and size $s$ recognizable sources [46] (sources uniform over the witness set of a size $s$ circuit). A post-selecting source $X$ is associated with (at least one) size $s$ circuit $C$ with two outputs, an $n$-bit output $x = C_1(r)$ and a special flag $\phi = C_2(r)$, such that the source is sampled by the circuit on a random input *conditioned* on the flag being set to 1:

$$X \equiv (C_1(\mathcal{U}) | C_2(U) = 1).$$

[1] The general notion of a (seedless) non-malleable extractor does not require the fixed point restriction, but is more complicated to state. (Note that if $f_i(X) = X$ then the output of the extractor will be the same. This is resolved in the usual manner, by defining a simulator that outputs unrelated strings and locations where the tampered extractor outputs are the same as the source. The two notions are equivalent up to a small loss in parameters for many natural source/tampering classes.

Perhaps most importantly, these sources capture samplable sources after conditioning on efficiently computable leakage on the source.[2] Given this, such extractors naturally have applications in tamper and leakage-resilient key-derivation against a large natural class of sources, leakage, and tampering (where all 3 correspond polynomial time procedures).

The primary focus of this work is yet another surprising application of explicit non-malleable extractors: the impossibility of certain kinds of *uniform black-box reductions.*

By uniform BB reductions we mean the following: The underlying primitive is assumed to be secure against uniform adversaries and the constructed primitive is proven secure against uniform adversaries. The reduction used in the proof of security is itself uniform. The reduction interacts with the uniform adversary and uses it to break the underlying primitive.

In this work, we further consider "generalized black-box reductions", where the reduction is allowed to arbitrarily fix the random tape of the adversary. Previous impossibility results for uniform black-box reductions did not allow the reduction to access the random tape of the adversary. The difficulty in our setting lies in the fact that the uniform adversary (with a constant size description) has *no other source of randomness* other than the arbitrarily set random tape provided by the reduction.

*The Case of SNARGs.* Succinct non-interactive arguments (SNARGs) are proof systems for languagues in $\mathsf{NP}$ with proofs $\pi$ whose lengths are much smaller than the witness $w$. Although SNARGs are widely used in practice [44], Gentry and Wichs [20] showed that, under a natural assumption, it is impossible to prove the adaptive soundness of a SNARG via a reduction from a *falsifiable assumption* [39] when the reduction treats the adversary as a black-box. More precisely, they showed that either a black-box reduction that does not access the coins of the adversary does not exist, or that the underlying falsifiable assumption can be broken by a poly-size non-uniform adversary.

*The Gentry-Wichs Meta-Reduction.* We briefly recap the Gentry-Wichs impossibility proof. Assuming the existence of a polynomial-time, black-box reduction $R$, they show the existence of an inefficient SNARG adversary $A$ that, given an input $\mathsf{crs}$, breaks soundness by producing proofs $\pi_{no}$ that verify correctly for statements $x_{no} \notin L$. By assumption, the reduction $R$ with black-box access to $A$ must break the falsifiable assumption when interacting with this adversary. Next, they show the existence of an efficient simulator $\mathsf{Sim}$ for $A$ that fools any polynomial-time distinguisher. This implies that $R^{\mathsf{Sim}}$ must also break the falsifiable assumption (otherwise one can distinguish between $A$ and $\mathsf{Sim}$). Finally, since $R^{\mathsf{Sim}}$ is an efficient algorithm that breaks the falsifiable assumption, it implies that if a black-box reduction exists, the falsifiable assumption can be broken by poly-time adversaries.

To obtain the SNARG adversary $A$ that breaks soundness, Gentry and Wichs prove a "leakage lemma", stating that if distributions $\mathcal{L}$ and $\bar{\mathcal{L}}$ (over $L$ and $\bar{L}$

[2] It should be noted this class also captures samplable sources that are conditioned on leakage on the *intermediate* values of the sampling process.

resp.) are indistinguishable, then for short leakage $\pi_{yes}$, there exists a distribution over leakage $\pi_{no}$ such that $\{(x_{yes}, \pi_{yes}) : x_{yes} \leftarrow \mathcal{L}\}$ is indistinguishable from $\{(x_{no}, \pi_{no}) : x_{no} \leftarrow \bar{\mathcal{L}}\}$. Gentry-Wichs instantiate their leakage lemma as follows: $\mathcal{L}$ is a distribution on yes-instances of $\mathcal{L}$, $\bar{\mathcal{L}}$ is a distribution on no-instances, and $\pi$ is the SNARG proof for $x$. The lemma then yields, for every CRS $\mathsf{crs}$, an augmented no-distribution $(x_{no}, \pi_{no}) \leftarrow \bar{\mathcal{L}}^*_{\mathsf{crs}}$ that is indistinguishable from the SNARG yes-distribution $(x_{yes}, \pi_{yes} \leftarrow \mathcal{L}^*_{\mathsf{crs}}$. Thus, $A(\mathsf{crs})$ is defined to output samples from $\bar{\mathcal{L}}^*_{\mathsf{crs}}$ while $\mathsf{Sim}(\mathsf{crs})$ outputs samples from $\mathcal{L}^*_{\mathsf{crs}}$. Follow-up work of Jetchev and Pietrzak [27] gave a constructive proof of the leakage lemma, bounding the size of the randomized circuit needed to generate the fake proof $\pi_{no}$, given the sample $x_{no} \sim \bar{\mathcal{L}}$.

The original Gentry/Wichs proof assumed that the reduction does not access the random coins of the adversary and therefore, upon submitting a $\mathsf{crs}$, only sees random draws from the $\mathcal{L}^*_{\mathsf{crs}}$ or $\bar{\mathcal{L}}^*_{\mathsf{crs}}$ distribution. They did not give a constructive $\bar{\mathcal{L}}^*_{\mathsf{crs}}$ distribution, but just showed its existence. Further, their final simulator (for the non-security parameter preserving case) is non-uniform, since it holds an internal table with draws from the $\bar{\mathcal{L}}^*_{\mathsf{crs}}$ distribution for all security parameters below some threshold. In follow-up work, Vadhan and Zheng [51] used the uniform min-max theorem to remove these last two restrictions: They gave a uniform and constructive $\bar{\mathcal{L}}^*_{\mathsf{crs}}$ distribution and showed, using this, that the real adversary and the simulated adversary could both be made uniform. However, they still assumed that the reduction does not access the random coins of the adversary. In another work of Chung et al. [14], it was shown that one could remove the restriction that the reduction does not access the coins of the adversary by considering a non-uniform, deterministic, adversary that applies an internally hard-wired random oracle to the submitted $\mathsf{crs}$ to obtain the random coins for sampling the distributions. Our goal, on the other hand, is to construct a uniform adversary and a uniform simulator, in order to show that even if attempting to construct a SNARG that is secure against uniform adversaries then either (1) no black-box reduction exists (even one that can arbitrarily set the random coins of the adversary) or (2) the underlying assumption is insecure even against *uniform* poly-time adversaries.

### 1.1 Our Results

Before we begin describing our results, we first make some brief remarks about our assumptions. All our results follow from the existence of strong circuit lower bounds of the form "$\mathsf{E} = \mathsf{DTIME}(2^{O(n)})$ requires exponential-size $X$-circuits" for some $X \in \{$nondeterministic, $\Sigma_2\}$. These types arose in the derandomization literature. Impagliazzo and Wigderson [25] famously showed that "$\mathsf{E}$ requires exponential size circuits" implies $\mathsf{BPP} = \mathsf{P}$. Impagliazzo and Wigderson's assumption effectively says that non-uniformity does not always significantly speed up computation. Strengthenings of this assumption to exponential size nondeterministic circuits (circuits that take witnesses in addition to their input) or $\Sigma_i$-circuits (circuits with gates that compute a $\Sigma_i$-complete function) and related classes were first introduced in the context of derandomizing nondeterminstic complexity classes (e.g. showing sufficient conditions for $\mathsf{AM} = \mathsf{NP}$), and have since seen extensive use in the context of derandomization [7,16,19,22,24,29,38,47–50].

*Improved Non-malleable Extractors for Efficient Sources and Tampering.* Prior work by Ball, Dachman-Soled, and Loss [5] constructed non-malleable extractors for sources samplable or recognizable by polynomial-size circuits and tampered by polynomial-size circuits under a circuit lower bound assumption from the derandomization community. We improve the state of the art for non-malleable extractors in the setting of efficiently samplable sources and efficiently computable sources in 3 dimensions:

1. Many tamperings: our extractors are resilient to $t$-tamperings where $t$ is slightly less than the min-entropy of the source.[3] Prior work only considered the special case of $t = 1$.
2. Wider source class: our extractors work for post-selecting sources. This is a superset of the class of samplable and recognizable sources considered by prior work.
3. Improved assumptions: our extractors are secure under the assumption that $\mathsf{E} = \mathsf{DTIME}(2^{O(n)})$ is hard for exponential-size nondeterministic circuits. Prior work assumed that $\mathsf{E}$ was hard for exponential-size $\Sigma_2$-circuits.[4] Comparable to the polynomial hierarchy, it is consistent with current knowledge that functions computable by exponential size nondeterministic circuits form a strict subset of those functions computed by exponential size $\Sigma_2$-circuits. This assumption matches the best assumptions currently known for such extractors *without any non-malleability property* [6].

**Theorem 1 (Informal).** *Let $s(n) = \mathsf{poly}(n)$. Assuming $\mathsf{E} = \mathsf{DTIME}(2^{O(n)})$ requires exponential-size nondeterministic circuits, there exists a constant $c$ and an efficiently computable $\tilde{O}(n)$-non-malleable extractor with error $n^{-\Omega(1)}$, $\mathsf{NMExt}_s : \{0,1\}^n \to \{0,1\}^m$ where $m = \tilde{\Omega}(n)$, for the class of size $s(n)$ post-selecting sources on $n$-bits with min-entropy $k \geq c \cdot n$ and the class of size $s(n)$-tampering functions.*

*Moreover, this result relativizes: for any oracle $O$, if $\mathsf{E}$ is hard for exponential-size nondeterministic $O$-oracle circuits, the above holds with respect to the class of sources samplable by post-selecting size $s(n)$ $O$-oracle circuits and size $s(n)$ $O$-oracle tampering functions.*

[3] Min-entropy is always an upper-bound on the number of tamperings. Let $E : \{0,1\}^n \to \{0,1\}$ be any function and fix any strings $c_0, c_1$ such that $E(c_0) = 0$ and $E(c_1) = 1$. Consider $X$ uniform on the first $k$ bits and 0 elsewhere. Consider the tampering functions $f_i : x \mapsto c_{x_i}$. Finally, notice that $X$ (and hence $E(X)$) is fully determined by $E(f_1(X)), \dots, E(f_k(X))$.

[4] Ball et al.'s stated assumptions require hardness against either $\Sigma_3$ or $\Sigma_4$ circuits, depending on the source class. But hardness against $\Sigma_2$-circuits is a corollary of their technical lemmas and subsequent improvements in "vanilla" randomness extractors for these source classes [6].

A downside of this result is $n^{-\Omega(1)}$ statistical error. Unfortunately, as shown by Applebaum et al. [3], this is inherent in any randomness extractor built from these assumptions in a black-box way. While this does not suffice for many cryptographic applications, it is sufficient for the flagship application of this paper.

*Application: New Impossibility Results for SNARGs.* We consider reductions $R$ that are "black-box" in the adversary–i.e. the reduction accesses the adversary via oracle queries. Further, we consider non-adaptive reductions in which all oracle queries are made simultaneously. Importantly, our oracle allows the reduction $R$ to select the coins of $A$ arbitrarily. In particular, it does not need to sample them uniformly at random.

However, we do restrict the reduction in the following ways:

- There is a fixed constant $c$ such that on input security parameter $\lambda$, $R$ only queries $A$ on security parameters $\lambda' \geq \lambda^{1/c}$.
- The number of queries that the reduction makes, $t = \mathsf{poly}(\lambda)$, is a fixed polynomial in the security parameter

Following Pass [43], we consider both restrictions above to fall under the definition of "security-preserving" reductions.

We therefore call the class of reductions that we consider *security-preserving, non-adaptive query, generalized black-box reductions* or *SPNA-generalized black-box reductions.*

We prove the following theorem:

**Theorem 2 (Informal).** *Assume that an* NP *language* $\mathcal{L}$ *has a sub-exponentially hard subset-membership problem and that* E *requires exponential-size* $\Sigma_2$*-circuits. Let* $\Pi$ *be a candidate SNARG for* $\mathcal{L}$*. Then, for any uniform, falsifiable assumption one of the following must hold:*

- *There is a uniform, poly-time adversary that breaks the falsifiable assumption.*
- *There is no SPNA-generalized black-box reduction showing the uniform soundness of* $\Pi$ *based on the falsifiable assumption.*

We believe that our techniques extend to other cases where meta-reductions have been used to rule out constructions of non-interactive primitives from falsifiable assumptions, such as the impossibility result of Pass for perfect non-interactive zero knowledge (NIZK) [42]. A main remaining open question is whether our results can be extended to rule out *adaptive*, generalized black-box reductions as well.

### 1.2 Related Work

*Non-malleable Extractors.* There is a long line of research on non-malleable extractors (NME) [12,15] resilient against various classes of tampering [5,11,31–35], with particular attention focused on the case of two-source non-malleable extractors and split-state tampering [31,34,35]. There has also been significant work on variants of NME—and the closely related primitive of non-malleable codes [17]—that extend the definitions to various forms of many-time tampering [2,10,18,41].

*Seedless Extractors for Samplable and Recognizable Sources.* Trevisan and Vadhan [50] considered seedless extractors for the class of distributions samplable by bounded polynomial sized circuits. Under the assumption that $\mathsf{E}$ requires exponential size $\Sigma_4$ circuits, they presented constructions of seedless extractors for linear min-entropy, samplable sources over $n$ bits, that output $\Omega(n)$ bits that are $1/\mathsf{poly}$-close to uniform. Applebaum et al. [3] showed that the $1/\mathsf{poly}$ error is somewhat inherent by ruling out black-box reductions in this setting. They introduced a notion of *relative-error* extractors and showed that if the output of the extractor is $1/\mathsf{poly}$-close to uniform with relative error, then every event occurs w.r.t. the output distribution with probability at most $(1 + 1/\mathsf{poly})$ times the probability it occurs w.r.t. the uniform distribution. In particular, events that are negligible under the uniform distributions cannot become noticeable under the distribution outputted by the extractor. Under the assumption that $\mathsf{E}$ requires exponential size $\Sigma_4$ circuits, they constructed relative-error seedless extractors whose outputs are $1/\mathsf{poly}$-close to uniform with relative error for linear min-entropy, samplable sources. Under the assumption that $\mathsf{E}$ requires exponential size $\Sigma_3$ circuits, they constructed relative-error seedless extractors whose outputs are $1/\mathsf{poly}$-close to uniform with relative error for linear min-entropy, recognizable sources.

The meta reduction technique has been used in various works to rule out (among others) the construction of non-interactive primitives—such as perfect non-interactive zero-knowledge (NIZK)—from all falsifiable assumptions [9,42]. To the best of our knowledge, all of these results construct an inefficient adversary that samples responses from some distribution and they do not allow the reduction to access the random coins of the adversary. As mentioned above, Chung et al. [14] extended the technique to remove this restriction, but at the cost of hardwiring a random oracle into the inefficient adversary, and then considering the behavior of the reduction relative to a draw from a distribution over non-uniform adversaries.

A recent line of work has managed to almost fully circumvent the Gentry-Wichs impossibility result and obtain adaptive SNARGs (for $\mathsf{NP}$ and $\mathsf{UP}$) from falsifiable assumptions [37,52–54]. The reason these results do not contradict the Gentry-Wichs impossibility is that their notion of adaptivity is slightly weaker. Specifically, in the recent results, the circuit computing the $\mathsf{NP}$-relation, and hence the length of the statement itself, must be fixed in advance, before the $\mathsf{crs}$ is published. Then, the adversary breaking soundness can choose a statement that depends on the $\mathsf{crs}$, but whose length is upper-bounded by the circuit's input length. On the other hand, in the Gentry-Wichs impossibility result, it is crucial for the construction of the attacker that the length of the $\mathsf{crs}$ is fixed *first*, then an $\mathsf{NP}$-language that is at least $2^{|\mathsf{crs}|}$-hard, and a corresponding statement, is chosen.

In the case of security-parameter preserving reductions for SNARGs, Campanelli et al. [9] ruled out even the weaker form of adaptive soundness described above (where the $\mathsf{crs}$ size can grow with the length of the statement size). However, that result also does not rule out reductions that access the random coins of the adversary. Thus, one implication of our result is extending their impossibility result even to the case where the reduction accesses the random coins of the adversary but is non-adaptive.

## 2 Technical Overview

Before we begin explaining our results, we need to introduce a critical ingredient in both constructions: *seed-extending pseudorandom generators* [28]. A seed-extending PRG, introduced by Kinne, Van Melkebeek, and Shaltiel, for a class $\mathcal{C}$ is a PRG whose output contains the seed as a prefix, $G(s) = (s, y)$ for some $y$, and fools any $C \in \mathcal{C}$. Observe that "cryptographic" seed-extending PRGs, by which we mean fixed polytime-computable and PPT-secure seed-extending PRGs, are impossible: one can always distinguish by evaluating $G$. Thus, such PRGs are only possible in the "complexity-theoretic" or "derandomization" regime where $G$ is not computable in the adversarial class $\mathcal{C}$. Kinne et al. [28] observed that the standard presentation of Nisan and Wigderson's generator [40] is indeed seed-extending and hence follows from standard derandomization assumptions, such as those used in this work.

### 2.1 Our $t$-$\mathsf{NMExt}$ Construction

We begin by recapping the $\mathsf{NMExt}$ constructon of Ball et al. [5] for single-time tampering for the class of bounded polynomial-size circuits. Our goal is to extend this construction to $t$-time tampering (and to tampering circuits in higher complexity classes). The $\mathsf{NMExt}$ of [5] is simple: On input $x$, the non-malleable extractor applies a deterministic extractor $\mathsf{Ext}$ for samplable sources to obtain $\sigma$, then applies a seed extending PRG to $\sigma$ to obtain $G(\sigma) = (\sigma||y)$, and finally applies a two-source non-malleable extractor $2\text{NMExt}((\sigma||y), x)$ to obtain the final output.

Our $t$-$\mathsf{NMExt}$ construction is nearly identical, except we replace the two-source non-malleable extractor with a two-source $t$-non-malleable extractor. We first recall the security proof of Ball et al. and then point out the key differences.

The security proof for the non-malleable extractor proceeds by a proof by contradiction: Assume $\mathsf{NMExt}$ does not achieve non-malleability against tampering functions $f \in \mathcal{F}$. Using the definition of relaxed non-malleability, this means that, for some $f \in \mathcal{F}$, the statistical distance between the distributions $\{(\mathsf{NMExt}(X), \mathsf{NMExt}(f(X))\}$ and $\{(U, \mathsf{NMExt}(f(X))\}$ is at least $1/\mathsf{poly}$. Now, we use this fact to construct a constant-round private-coin interactive proof for proving (roughly) that $G(\sigma) = (\sigma||y)$, from which we will derive a contradiction to the security of PRG $G$ against non-deterministic distinguishers. This follows by applying classical results to convert the $\mathsf{IP}$ to a nondeterministic circuit via (a) emulating with a public coin protocol [23], (b) collapsing the rounds of result to an $\mathsf{AM}$ protocol [4], and (c) derandomizing the $\mathsf{AM}$ protocol with non-uniformity [1]. So in short, it suffices to construct a constant-round $\mathsf{IP}$.

In the $\mathsf{IP}$ protocol, both parties receive as input $(\sigma, y)$, where $y$ is either equal to $G(\sigma)$ or is chosen uniformly at random and independently of $\sigma$.

Arthur pre-samples $x$ such that $\mathsf{Ext}(x) = \sigma$. Then Arthur computes $\tilde{\sigma} = \mathsf{Ext}(f(x))$ and sends it to Merlin. Merlin is supposed to compute $(\tilde{\sigma}||\tilde{y}) = G(\tilde{\sigma})$ and send $\tilde{y}$ back to Arthur. Arthur then computes $\tilde{z} = \text{2NMExt}((\tilde{\sigma}, \tilde{y}), \tilde{x})$ and computes $z$ to be either $\text{2NMExt}((\sigma, y), z)$ or to be uniform random. Arthur sends $(z, \tilde{z})$ to Merlin and asks Merlin to guess whether $z$ was chosen as the output of 2NMExt or uniformly at random. If Merlin guesses correctly, Arthur guesses that $(\sigma||y) = G(\sigma)$. Otherwise, Arthur guesses that $y$ is uniform random.

Completeness of the $\mathsf{IP}$ protocol follows immediately from the assumption that $\mathsf{NMExt}$ does not achieve relaxed non-malleability, and hence the two distributions are distinguishable by Merlin.

To argue soundness, one can show that due to the security of the 2NMExt, regardless of the $\tilde{y}$ returned by (a dishonest) Merlin, the output of the 2NMExt is statistically close to uniform. They argue this by showing that the 2NMExt is actually also a *strong* 2NMExt–i.e. indistinguishability of the distributions holds even given one of the inputs to the 2NMExt. In our case, Merlin knows the entire $(\sigma, y)$ since it is part of the input. However, the $\tilde{y}$ that is returned by Merlin is *independent of* $x$*, conditioned on* $\sigma = \mathsf{Ext}(x)$*, and* $\tilde{\sigma} = \mathsf{Ext}(f(x))$. Thus, by making the length of $x$ sufficiently longer than the sum of the lengths of $\sigma$ and $\tilde{\sigma}$, one can ensure that $x$ still has sufficiently high min-entropy conditioned on $\sigma, \tilde{\sigma}$. Therefore, due to the security guarantee of the 2NMExt, Merlin cannot distinguish the two distributions with high probability.

In the $t$-tampering setting, Arthur simply computes all $t$ tampered seeds $\tilde{\sigma}_1, \ldots, \tilde{\sigma}_t$ and sends all of them over to Merlin to expand. Note that any malicious Merlin can now be recast as a $t$-tampering strategy on the left source. The rest of the proof proceeds similarly.

One missing piece from the proof sketch above is how Arthur can efficiently sample the source conditioned on the output of extractor being correct (or even sample a post-selecting source at all, given that output is only produced when the flag $\phi = 1$). Previously, this was accomplished by equipping Arthur with an $\mathsf{NP}$-oracle and running classical uniform witness sampling algorithms. However, equipping Arthur with such an oracle ultimately yields a $\Sigma_2$-circuit breaking the PRG.

Here, we instead observe that a careful inspection of Goldwasser and Sipser's public coin emulation [23] (see also parametric improvement and modern presentation by Goldreich and Leshkowitz [21]) reveals that only a significant (multiplicative) gap between the completeness and soundness parameters is required to convert an $\mathsf{IP}$ to an $\mathsf{AM}$ protocol. This is because this emulation simply proves an (approximate) bound on the number of accepting coins that Arthur could have. Critically, this means that it is not necessary that Arthur ever actually accept with non-negligible probability when designing an IP! Instead we can design a non-functional IP with a completeness/soundness gap and simply compile the result to get a functional public coin protocol.

Concretely, in our IP we have Arthur simply give up and reject whenever the sampling fails, which almost always happens. However, because we are conditioning on the output of an *extractor* taking a certain value (and recall that an extractor's output is statistically close to uniform), we can (with a little work) get fine-grained bounds on the exponentially-small probability of successfully sampling and, thus, ultimately control the relative gap between completeness and soundness.

Prior work constructed non-malleable extractors for samplable sources assuming E is hard for exponential-size $\Sigma_2$-circuits and samplable source extractors. The upshot of this new analytical approach is that to construct non-malleable extractors for post-selecting sources one need not invoke any additional assumption beyond those known to yield extractors for post-selecting sources: E is hard for exponential-size *nondeterminisitic* circuits.

Finally, we note that both this proof and Ball et al.'s extractor result [6] relativize. So, by giving Arthur access to an oracle $O$ we can "lift" this technique to handle sources sampled via post-selecting $O$-oracle circuits[5] of polynomial size and $O$-oracle tampering circuits of polynomial size, at the expense of assuming E is hard for exponential-size nondeterministic $O$-oracle circuits.

### 2.2 Application: Ruling Out Falsifiable Reductions to SNARGs

As a first attempt, we consider an adversary $A$ that depends on the reduction $R$ and which responds with $\perp$ if the query it is given, $(\mathsf{crs}, r)$, occurs too frequently with respect to the output distribution of $R$. (Specifically, conditioned on $(\mathsf{crs}, r)$ *not* having the above property, the marginal distribution produced by the reduction interacting with the external challenger will have high min-entropy). Since $r$ is uniformly distributed in the real security game, and since there is a relatively small number of such pairs $(\mathsf{crs}, r)$, $A$ will refuse to respond with only negligible probability in the real security game, and thus will still be a legitimate SNARG adversary. On the other hand, if the individual query does not occur too frequently, $A$ will apply a seedless, deterministic extractor[6] to the query (since conditioned on this event, the marginal distribution on the query has sufficiently high min-entropy) to obtain $v$, and then a seed-extending PRG to $v$ to obtain $(v||w)$. Finally, the adversary will use the $w$ outputted by the PRG to sample $(x_{no}, \pi_{no})$ from the augmented "no" distribution $\bar{\mathcal{L}}^*_{\mathsf{crs}}$ discussed above, and will return $(x_{no}, \pi_{no})$. The goal, as in Gentry-Wichs, is to switch to an efficient adversary, who computes $w$ but then returns $(x_{yes}, \pi_{yes})$ sampled from the augmented "yes" distribution $\mathcal{L}^*_{\mathsf{crs}}$ discussed above.

There are three problems with this initial approach:

---

[5] These are circuits with $O$-gates in addition to the standard basis, $\{\wedge, \vee, \neg\}$.

[6] See for example, [6,50].

- The biggest problem is that the adversary we design must be *stateless*, so it can only extract entropy from an individual query $(\mathsf{crs}, r)$ in order to sample $(x_{no}, \pi_{no})$, as sketched above. On the other hand, the reduction's view includes the entire set of queries and responses, and the reduction may choose queries that are correlated and inter-dependent. However, if the queries are correlated, the randomness $w$ extracted from the queries may also be correlated. It is therefore not clear how we can argue that the reduction cannot distinguish the joint distribution of correlated draws from $\bar{\mathcal{L}}^*_{\mathsf{crs}}$ from correlated draws from $\mathcal{L}^*_{\mathsf{crs}}$. For example, when using correlated randomness to sample, we cannot rule out a case where the correlated draws from the augmented "yes" distribution, $\mathcal{L}^*_{\mathsf{crs}}$, reveal the witness, whereas in the case of the augmented "no" distribution, $\bar{\mathcal{L}}^*_{\mathsf{crs}}$, no witness exists.
- The second main problem is that in the meta-reduction proof strategy, we must ultimately switch to the efficient adversary, $\mathsf{Sim}$, without the reduction detecting it. However, an efficient $\mathsf{Sim}$ cannot check whether a submitted query $(\mathsf{crs}, r)$ occurs frequently or not, since checking this requires (approximately) counting the number of pre-images of a given output. This means that the simulator must be indistinguishable from the real adversary, while also behaving identically in the case that an indiviudal query occurs frequently or not.
- The final problem arises in the proof of indistinguishability of the real adversary and $\mathsf{Sim}$: When we switch from the true output of the seed-extending PRG to a random output, we still need to be able to sample from the augmented "no" distribution, $\bar{\mathcal{L}}^*_{\mathsf{crs}}$, in order to simulate the hybrid distribution. This sampling process is computationally bounded, but not poly-time. This means that we require the seed-extending PRG to be hard even against distinguishers who can sample from $\bar{\mathcal{L}}^*_{\mathsf{crs}}$. But since sampling from $\bar{\mathcal{L}}^*_{\mathsf{crs}}$ is inefficient, such a seed-extending PRG cannot be poly-time computable.

To solve the first problem, we use $(t-1)$-*non-malleable extractors* against $\mathsf{NP}$-tampering functions. The main observation is that, since the reduction is non-adaptive, for any $i \in [t]$, and $j \neq i$, we can view the $j$-th query $(\mathsf{crs}_j, r_j)$ as the output of an $\mathsf{NP}$-tampering function applied to the $i$-th output $(\mathsf{crs}_i, r_i)$. More precisely, given input $(\mathsf{crs}_i, r_i)$, the $j$-th tampering function uses its $\mathsf{NP}$ powers to pre-sample randomness $U$ for the reduction/challenger (see Theorem 5), and runs the reduction/challenger forwards on $U$ to compute the $j$-th query.

To solve the second problem, in the case where an individual query occurs frequently, the *real* adversary will actually sample $(x_{yes}, \pi_{yes})$ from $\mathcal{L}^*_{\mathsf{crs}}$, instead of outputting $\perp$. Ultimately, we will switch from an inefficient adversary that samples from $\bar{\mathcal{L}}^*_{\mathsf{crs}}$ in the case of low frequency, to a poly-time simulator that always samples from $\mathcal{L}^*_{\mathsf{crs}}$. Thus, the simulator ultimately does not have to check whether a query occurs frequently or not, since it will always apply a poly-time computable PRG (which is hard for the reduction to compute, but still poly-time), and then use the randomness to sample from $\mathcal{L}^*_{\mathsf{crs}}$.

To resolve the third problem, we modify the real adversary to use *two* different PRG's: $G_{hard}$ and $G_{easy}$. $G_{hard}$ is hard even for distinguishers who can sample from $\bar{\mathcal{L}}^*_{\mathsf{crs}}$, whereas $G_{easy}$ is only hard for bounded poly-time distinguishers (such as the reduction itself). $G_{hard}$ will be applied in the case that an individual query has low frequency, whereas $G_{easy}$ will be applied in the case that an individual query has high frequency. When we switch from the inefficient adversary who samples from $\bar{\mathcal{L}}^*_{\mathsf{crs}}$ to the efficient adversary who samples from $\mathcal{L}^*_{\mathsf{crs}}$, we will also switch the PRG from $G_{hard}$ to $G_{easy}$, using a careful sequence of hybrids. Thus, the final simulator always does the following, regardless of the frequency of the individual query $(\mathsf{crs}, r)$ (1) applies the $(t-1)$-non-malleable extractor to obtain $v$; (2) applies the seed-extending PRG $G_{easy}$ to $v$ to obtain $(v||w)$; (3) uses the resulting random coins $w$ to sample $(x_{yes}, \pi_{yes})$ from $\mathcal{L}^*_{\mathsf{crs}}$ and (4) outputs $(x_{yes}, \pi_{yes})$ to the reduction. Note that the final simulator is now a uniform, polynomial time algorithm.

# 3 Preliminaries

## 3.1 Notation

For a distribution $\mathcal{D}$, we denote by $\mathcal{D}(u)$ a draw from $\mathcal{D}$ using coins $u$.

We denote by $U_k$ a uniform random variable over $k$ bits. When the number of bits, $k$, is clear from context or implicit, we use $U$ for simplified notation.

For $S \subseteq N$, where $S = \{i_1, \ldots, i_\ell : i_1 < \cdots < i_\ell\}$ and any $n$-ary string of values $x_1, \ldots, x_n$, let $x_S$ denote the string $(x_{i_1}, \ldots, x_{i_\ell})$. For random variables $X, Y$, we write $\Delta(X;Y) \leq \epsilon$ or $X \approx_\epsilon Y$ if the total variation distance between their distributions is at most $\epsilon$.

## 3.2 Complexity Classes and Assumptions

We take $\mathsf{E}$ to denote $\mathsf{DTIME}[2^{O(n)}]$ the class of languages decidable by deterministic Turing machines in $2^{cn}$-time for some constant $c$. We take circuits to denote circuits over the standard basis $\{\vee, \wedge, \neg\}$. For any language $O$, an $O$-oracle aided circuit is a circuit that has special gates that decide $O$, in addition to the standard-basis. For any circuit, we say it has size $s$ if it contains at most $s$ gates. We say it has depth $d$ if the longest path from any input to any output gate is of size $d$. A circuit family, $\{C_n\}_{n \in \mathbb{N}}$, is a collection of circuits such that $C_n$ takes inputs of length $n$. We take the $\mathsf{SIZE}[s(n)]$ to denote the function families computable by a circuit family $\{C_n\}_{n \in \mathbb{N}}$ such that $C_n$ has size at most $s(n)$, for large enough $n$. Similarly, we take $\mathsf{SIZE}^O[s(n)]$ to denote the function families computable by an $O$-oracle aided circuit family $\{C_n\}_{n \in \mathbb{N}}$ such that $C_n$ has size at most $s(n)$, for sufficiently large $n$.

## 3.3 Seedless $t$-Non-malleable Extractors

**Definition 1 (Tampering functions).** *For any $n > 0$, let $\mathcal{H}_n$ denote the set of all functions $h : \{0,1\}^n \to \{0,1\}^n$. Any subset $\mathcal{G} \subseteq \mathcal{H}_n$ is a family of tampering functions. For any class of boolean functions $\mathcal{F} = \{f : \{0,1\}^n \to \{0,1\}\}$, we take $\mathcal{F}^n$ to denote the class of $n$-output functions where each output is computed by* *some function in* $\mathcal{F}$, *i.e.* $\mathcal{F}^n = \{f_{i_1,\ldots,i_n} : x \mapsto f_{i_1}(x), \ldots, f_{i_n}(x) \mid f_{i_1}, \ldots, f_{i_n} \in \mathcal{F}\}$.

The particular classes of tampering functions we consider in this work:

- Tampering where each output is computable by an $s(n)$-size circuit, $\mathsf{SIZE}[s(n)]$.
- Tampering where each output is computable by an $s(n)$-size circuit with $O$-oracle gates, $\mathsf{SIZE}^O[s(n)]$.
- Split-state tampering where two halves of an input are tampered indepen dently and arbitrarily: $\{(\tau_L, \tau_R) : x_1, \ldots, x_{2n} \mapsto \tau_L(x_1, \ldots, x_n), \tau_R(x_{n+1}, \ldots, x_{2n}) | \tau_L, \tau_R \in \mathcal{H}_n\}$.

**Definition 2 (Relaxed Seedless $t$-non-malleable extractor).** *Let $\mathcal{X}$ be a family of sources on $\{0,1\}^n$ and $\mathcal{F}$ be a class of tampering functions acting on $\{0,1\}^n$. Further assume that all $f \in \mathcal{F}$ does not have any fixed points. A function* NMExt : $\{0,1\}^n \to \{0,1\}^m$ *is defined to be a relaxed $(\epsilon, t)$-non-malleable extractor with respect to $\mathcal{X}$ and $\mathcal{F}$ if the following hold: for any $X \in \mathcal{X}$ and any set $\{f_1, \ldots, f_t\}$, such that for all $i \in [t]$, $f_i \in \mathcal{F}$, we have*

$$\Delta\Big((\mathrm{NMExt}(X), \mathrm{NMExt}(f_1(X)), \ldots, \mathrm{NMExt}(f_t(X)));$$
$$(\mathcal{U}_m, \mathrm{NMExt}(f_1(X)), \ldots, \mathrm{NMExt}(f_t(X))\Big) \leq \epsilon.$$

### 3.4 Seed-Extending Pseudorandom Generators

**Definition 3** ([28]). *A function $G : \{0,1\}^\ell \to \{0,1\}^n$ is said to be an $\epsilon$-*pseudorandom generator (PRG) *for a class $\mathcal{C}$, if for all $C \in \mathcal{C}$,*

$$\Delta(C(G(\mathcal{U}_\ell)); C(\mathcal{U}_n)) \leq \epsilon$$

*A PRG, $G$, is said to be* seed-extending *if the prefix of its output is its input, i.e. $G(\sigma) = \sigma, G'(\sigma)$ for some function $G' : \{0,1\}^\ell \to \{0,1\}^{n-\ell}$.*

We are principally concerned with seed-extending PRGs against various types of circuits of a given size: non-deterministic circuits, non-deterministic $\mathsf{NP}$-circuits, etc. Throughout this paper, we take a PRG for a class of circuits of size $s$ to mean a $1/s$-PRG for that class of circuits. Note that because we are interested in both seed-extending PRGs, as well as PRGs for non-deterministic circuits, so-called "cryptographic" PRGs which can be easily evaluated by the classes they are constructed to fool do not suffice: a distinguisher given the seed, or nondeterminism, can easily determine if a string is in the PRG's image. Thankfully, as observed by Kinne et al. [28], Nisan and Wigderson's seminal construction yields a seed extending PRG, provided one starts with an appropriately hard function. We conclude with the formal theorem statement.

**Theorem 3** ([3,25,28,29,47,48]). *If* $\mathsf{E}$ *requires exponential size circuits of type* $X \in \{$*deterministic, nondeterministic*, $\mathsf{NP}, \Sigma_i\}$, *then for every constant* $c > 1$ *there exists a constant* $\alpha > 1$ *such that for every sufficiently large* $n$, *and every* $r$ *such that* $\alpha \log n \leq \ell \leq n$ *there is a seed-extending PRG,* $\mathsf{G} : \{0,1\}^\ell \to \{0,1\}^n$, *for size* $n^c$ *circuits of type* $X \in \{$*deterministic, nondeterministic*, $\mathsf{NP}, \Sigma_i\}$.

### 3.5 Witness Sampling

We also require the following classical, relativizing results on approximate counting and sampling NP-witnesses.

**Theorem 4 (Approximate Counting with an NP-oracle** [26]**).** *For every* $i \geq 0$, *every sufficiently large* $s$ *and every* $\epsilon > 0$, *there is a* $\Sigma_{i+1}$*-circuit* $A$ *of size* $\mathsf{poly}(s/\epsilon)$ *that given a* $\Sigma_i$*-circuit* $C : \{0,1\}^n \to \{0,1\}$ *of size* $s$ *outputs a value* $\widehat{M}$ *such that*

$$\widehat{M} \in (1 \pm \epsilon)|\{x : C(x) = 1\}|$$

**Theorem 5 (Sampling Witnesses with an NP-oracle** [8,26]**).** *For every* $i \geq 0$, *every sufficiently large* $s$ *and every* $\delta > 0$, *there is a randomized* $\Sigma_{i+1}$*-circuit* $A$ *of size* $\mathsf{poly}(s/\log(1/\delta))$ *that given a* $\Sigma_i$*-circuit* $C : \{0,1\}^n \to \{0,1\}$ *of size* $s$ *outputs a value in* $\{0,1\}^n \cup \bot$ *such that for every size* $s$ $\Sigma_i$*-circuit,* $\Pr[A(C) = \bot] \leq \delta$ *and the distribution* $(A(C)|A(C) \neq \bot)$ *is uniform over* $\{x : C(x) = 1\}$.

### 3.6 SNARGs and Black-Box Reductions

Our work is concerned with provable security for SNARGs, defined below. Note that we require *adaptive* soundness, i.e., soundness even against adversaries that are allowed to select their instance after seeing the common reference string.

**Definition 4 (Uniform Succinct Non-Interactive Arguments for NP).** *A SNARG system* $\Pi$ *consists of three polynomial-time algorithms* $\Pi = (\mathsf{G}, \mathsf{P}, \mathsf{V})$*:*

- $(\mathsf{crs}, \mathsf{priv}) \leftarrow \mathsf{G}(1^\lambda)$*: The generation algorithm takes as input the security parameter* $\lambda$ *and outputs a common reference string* $\mathsf{crs}$ *as well as private verification information* $\mathsf{priv}$.
- $\pi \leftarrow \mathsf{P}(\mathsf{crs}, x, w)$*: The prove algorithm takes in the* $\mathsf{crs}$, *a statement* $x$, *and a witness* $w$, *and outputs a proof* $\pi$.
- $b \leftarrow \mathsf{V}(\mathsf{priv}, x, \pi)$*: the verification algorithm takes as input* $\mathsf{priv}$, *a statement* $x$, *and a proof* $\pi$, *and outputs a bit* $b$ *(1 denotes acceptance, 0 denotes rejection).*

*We say that* $\Pi$ *is a succinct non-interactive argument (SNARG) for a language* $L$ *in* $\mathcal{NP}$ *with corresponding relation* $\mathcal{R}$ *if it satisfies the following three properties:*

**Completeness:** *For all* $(x, w) \in \mathcal{R}$,

$$\Pr\left[\mathsf{V}(\mathsf{priv}, x, \pi) = 0 \,\middle|\, \begin{array}{c}(\mathsf{crs}, \mathsf{priv}) \leftarrow \mathsf{G}(1^\lambda) \\ \pi \leftarrow \mathsf{P}(\mathsf{crs}, x, w)\end{array}\right] = \mathsf{negl}(\lambda)\,. \tag{1}$$

**Uniform Adaptive Soundness:** *For all uniform, PPT* $\bar{\mathsf{P}}$,

$$\Pr\left[\mathsf{V}(\mathsf{priv}, x, \pi) = 1 \wedge x \notin L \,\middle|\, \begin{array}{c}(\mathsf{crs}, \mathsf{priv}) \leftarrow \mathsf{G}(1^\lambda) \\ (x, \pi) \leftarrow \bar{\mathsf{P}}(\mathsf{crs})\end{array}\right] = \mathsf{negl}(\lambda)\,. \tag{2}$$

**Succinctness:** *All proofs* $\pi$ *produced by* $\mathsf{P}$ *satisfy* $|\pi| = \mathsf{poly}(\lambda)(|x| + |w|)^{o(1)}$.

We say that a PPT $\bar{\mathsf{P}}$ breaks a SNARG system $\Pi = (\mathsf{G}, \mathsf{P}, \mathsf{V})$ if the probability that $\mathsf{V}$ outputs 1 in the soundness experiment with $\bar{\mathsf{P}}$ exceeds $1/p(\lambda)$ for some polynomial $p$ and infinitely many $\lambda$.

**Definition 5 (Uniform Falsifiable Assumption).** *A uniform falsifiable assumption is a pair* $(\mathsf{M}, c)$ *where* $\mathsf{M}$ *is an interactive uniform poly-time algorithm ("the challenger") and* $c$ *is a constant ("the guessing probability"). The output of* $\mathsf{M}$ *is a single bit; we let the output* 1 *mean* **win**.

*Such an assumption* $(\mathsf{M}, c)$ *is said to be true if, for every uniform, PPT* $A$,

$$\Pr[\langle \mathsf{M}, A\rangle(1^\lambda) = \mathbf{win}] \leq c + \mathsf{negl}(\lambda)\,, \tag{3}$$

*where the probability is taken over the coins of* $\mathsf{M}$ *and* $A$.

We say that a uniform, PPT $A$ breaks the assumption $(\mathsf{M}, c)$ if the probability that it wins the security experiment $\langle \mathsf{M}, A\rangle$ exceeds $c + 1/p(\lambda)$ for some polynomial $p$ and infinitely many $\lambda$.

**Definition 6 (Non-Adaptive Black-Box Reduction for SNARGs).** *Let* $\Pi$ *be a SNARG and* $(\mathsf{M}, c)$ *a falsifiable assumption. A non-adaptive, black-box reduction (establishing the soundness of* $\Pi$*, based on the assumption* $(\mathsf{M}, c)$*) is an interactive PPT oracle algorithm* $R$ *such that for every uniform adversary* $A$ *that breaks the SNARG system* $\Pi$*,* $R^A$ *breaks the assumption* $(\mathsf{M}, c)$*. Further, all of* $R$*'s quries to* $A$ *must be submitted simultaneously.*

Note that the oracle in the above definition allows the reduction $R$ to select the coins of $A$ in any manner at all. In particular, it need not sample them uniformly at random.

However we do restrict the reduction in the following ways:

- There is a fixed constant $c$ such that on input security parameter $\lambda$, $R$ only queries $A$ on security parameters $\lambda' \geq \lambda^{1/c}$.
- The number of queries the reduction makes, $t = \mathsf{poly}(\lambda)$, is a fixed polynomial in the security parameter (and in particular is independent of the length of the random tape of the adversary).

Following Pass [43], we consider both restrictions above to fall under the definition of "security-preserving" reductions.

We call the class of non-adaptive, black-box reductions that can arbitrarily set the adversary's random tape, but have the above two restrictions *security-preserving, non-adaptive query, generalized black-box reductions* or *SPNA-generalized black-box reductions.*

## 4 Main Application

In this section, we use our construction of $(t-1)$-non-malleable extractors as a building block to obtain the following result:

**Theorem 6.** *Assume that an* $\mathsf{NP}$ *language* $\mathcal{L}$ *has a sub-exponentially hard subset-membership problem and that* $\mathsf{E}$ *requires exponential-size* $\Sigma_2$*-circuits. Let* $\Pi = (\mathsf{G}, \mathsf{P}, \mathsf{V})$ *be a candidate SNARG for* $\mathcal{L}$*, satisfying the completeness and succinctness properties. Then, for any uniform, falsifiable assumption* $(\mathsf{M}, c)$*, one of the following must hold:*

- *There is a uniform, poly-time adversary that breaks* $(\mathsf{M}, c)$.
- *There is no SPNA-generalized black-box reduction showing the uniform soundness of* $\Pi$ *based on the assumption* $(\mathsf{M}, c)$.

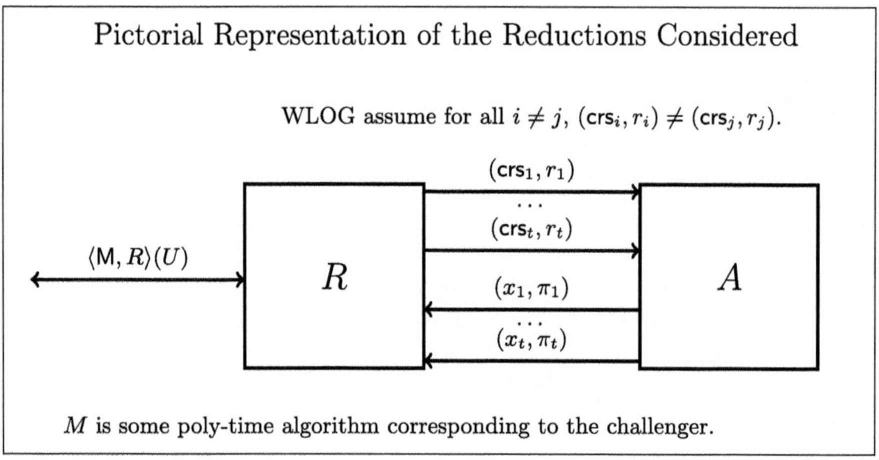


**Fig. 1.** A SPNA-generalized black-box reduction from a uniform, falsifiable assumption to uniform SNARGs.

Towards proving the theorem, we assume the existence of a SPNA-generalized black-box reduction $R$ making $t := t(\lambda)$ queries on security parameter $\lambda$. See Fig. 1 for a pictorial representation. We next describe certain building-blocks that will be used to define our SNARG adversary $A$.

### 4.1 Hard Languages and Leakage Simulation Theorem

We assume existence of an NP-language $L$ and distributions $\mathcal{L}^+$, $\bar{\mathcal{L}}$ where $\mathcal{L}^+$ is a distribution over statement, witness pairs $(x, w)$, where in $x \in L$, and $\bar{\mathcal{L}}$ is a distribution over no instances. The distribution over the first output of $\mathcal{L}^+$ is denoted as $\mathcal{L}$. We require that $\mathcal{L}$ and $\bar{\mathcal{L}}$ should be indistinguishable against non-uniform adversaries of size $\mathsf{poly}(2^{\lambda_{pi}})$.

For a fixed $\mathsf{crs}$, let $\mathcal{L}^*_{\mathsf{crs}}$ denote the joint distribution $(x, \pi)$ of statements $x \sim \mathcal{L}$ and corresponding proofs $\pi$ with respect to $\mathsf{crs}$. We can efficiently sample from $\mathcal{L}^*_{\mathsf{crs}}$ by sampling $(x, w) \sim \mathcal{L}^+$ and honestly computing the proof $\pi$ using $w$ w.r.t $\mathsf{crs}$. Assume the length of $\pi$ is $\lambda_\pi$.

We have the following theorem by Jetchev and Pietrzak [27]:

**Theorem 7** ([27]). *For every* $\mathsf{crs}$*, there exists a* $\mathsf{poly}(2^{\lambda_\pi})$*-size randomized circuit* $C_{\mathsf{crs}}$ *such that for all* $\mathsf{poly}(\lambda)$*-sized distinguishers* $D$

$$\left| \Pr_{(x,\pi)\sim\mathcal{L}^*_{\mathsf{crs}}}[D(x,\pi)=1] - \Pr_{x\sim\mathcal{L},\rho\sim\{0,1\}^{p(\lambda)}}[D(x, C_{\mathsf{crs}}(x;\rho))=1] \right| \le \frac{1}{\mathsf{poly}(\lambda)}.$$

We now define the distribution used by the SNARG adversary to sample false statements and proofs. For every fixed $\mathsf{crs}$, let $\bar{\mathcal{L}}^*_{\mathsf{crs}}$ be the following distribution:

- Sample $x \sim \bar{\mathcal{L}}$
- Sample $\pi \sim C_{\mathsf{crs}}(x; U)$, where $U$ is a uniform random variable, and $C_{\mathsf{crs}}$ is the lexicographically first randomized circuit of size $\mathsf{poly}(2^{\lambda_\pi})$ guaranteed by Theorem 7.

Using the hardness of distinguishing $\mathcal{L}$ and $\bar{\mathcal{L}}$ we obtain the following corollary:

**Corollary 1.** *For every* $\mathsf{crs}$ *and for all* $\mathsf{poly}(\lambda)$*-sized distinguishers* $D$*,*

$$\left| \Pr_{(x,\pi)\sim\mathcal{L}^*_{\mathsf{crs}}}[D(x,\pi)=1] - \Pr_{(x,\pi)\sim\bar{\mathcal{L}}^*_{\mathsf{crs}}}[D(x,\pi)=1] \right| \le \frac{1}{\mathsf{poly}(\lambda)}.$$

### 4.2 $(t-1)$-Non-malleable Extractor

We require a relaxed $(t-1, 1/\mathsf{poly})$-non-malleable extractor $\mathsf{NMExt}$ that is computable in uniform polynomial-time for high-min-entropy sources $Z$ sampled by bounded $\mathsf{poly}(\lambda)$-size $\Sigma_2$-circuits. $\mathsf{NMExt}$ must be secure against the class $\mathcal{F}$ of tampering functions $f$ consisting of bounded $\mathsf{poly}(\lambda)$-size $\mathsf{NP}$-circuits. In the full version of this paper we show that such non-malleable extractors can be constructed under the assumption that $\mathsf{E}$ requires exponential-size $\Sigma_2$-circuits.

### 4.3 Seed-Extending PRG's

We need two types of seed-extending PRG's:

- $G_{hard}$ takes as input a seed of length security parameter $\lambda$. $G_{hard}$ can take even time exponential in $\lambda$ to compute, but it must be *uniform*. $G_{hard}$ is secure against bounded $\mathsf{poly}(\lambda)$-size $\Sigma_2$-circuits and is also secure against $\mathsf{poly}(2^{\lambda_\pi})$-size (regular) circuits.
- $G_{easy}$ takes as input a seed of length security parameter $\lambda$. $G_{easy}$ must be computable in *uniform* polynomial-time. $G_{easy}$ must be secure against bounded $\mathsf{poly}(\lambda)$-size $\Sigma_2$-circuits.

Theorem 3 implies that such seed-extending PRG's can be constructed under the assumption that $\mathsf{E}$ requires exponential-size $\Sigma_2$-circuits.

### 4.4 Distributions We Consider

We next define several distributions and the tampering functions that will be used inf the definition of the real adversary $A$, as well as in the Hybrid argument used in our proof, where we switch from the inefficient adversary $A$ to an efficient simulator.

*Distribution over R's queries:* Let $\mathcal{D}$ be the following poly-samplable distribution:
On input $u \sim U$:

1. Run $\langle \mathsf{M}, R\rangle(u)$ to obtain $(\mathsf{crs}_1, r_1), \ldots, (\mathsf{crs}_t, r_t)$.
2. Output $(\overrightarrow{\mathsf{crs}}, \overrightarrow{r}) := (\mathsf{crs}_1, r_1), \ldots, (\mathsf{crs}_t, r_t)$.

For $i \in [t]$, we denote by $\mathcal{D}[i][1]$ the output $\mathsf{crs}_i$.
For $i \in [t]$, let $\mathcal{D}_i$ be the distribution over the $i$-th $(\mathsf{crs}_i, r_i)$ pair outputted by $\mathcal{D}$. We further let $\mathcal{D}_i[1]$ or $\mathcal{D}_i(u)[1]$ indicate the crs part of the output, whereas $\mathcal{D}_i[2]$ or $\mathcal{D}_i(u)[2]$ indicate the randomness part of the output.

*Set of "infrequent" queries made by R.* Let $\mathcal{S}$ be the set

$$\left\{ r : \forall i \in [t], \Pr_{\mathcal{D}_i[2]}[r] \leq \frac{2^{\log^2(\lambda)}}{2^{|r|}} \right\}.$$

*Probability a query is "infrequent."* For $i \in [t]$, let $p_i$ be the probability $\Pr_{r_i \sim \mathcal{D}_i[2]}[r_i \in \mathcal{S}]$.

*Distributions over R's queries, conditioned on the query being "infrequent."*

- For $i \in [t]$, let $Z_i$ be the distribution $(\mathsf{crs}_i, r_i) \sim \mathcal{D}_i \mid (r_i \in \mathcal{S})$.
- For $i \in [t]$, let $C_i$ be the distribution $(\overrightarrow{\mathsf{crs}}, \overrightarrow{r}) = ((\mathsf{crs}_1, r_1), \ldots, (\mathsf{crs}_t, r_t)) \sim \mathcal{D} | r_i \in \mathcal{S}$.

*Distribution over i-th Reduction query, conditioned on all queried* $\mathsf{crs}$*'s.* For $i \in [t]$, let $Z_i(\overrightarrow{\mathsf{crs}})$ be the distribution $\mathcal{D}_i(u)$, where $u$ is chosen uniformly at random from the set $\{u : \mathcal{D}_i(u)[2] \in \mathcal{S} \wedge \mathcal{D}_1(u)[1] = \mathsf{crs}_1 \wedge \cdots \wedge \mathcal{D}_t(u)[1] = \mathsf{crs}_t)\}$.

Note that

- If $p_i \geq \frac{1}{2^{\log^2(\lambda)}}$ then with all but negligible probability over choice of $\overrightarrow{\mathsf{crs}} \sim C_i$, the min entropy of $Z_i(\overrightarrow{\mathsf{crs}})$ is at least $|r| - t|\mathsf{crs}| - 3\log^2(\lambda)$. This is a sufficiently high fraction for extraction w.r.t. $|\mathsf{crs}| + |r|$ when $|r| \gg t|\mathsf{crs}|$.
- At most $\frac{t \cdot 2^{|r|}}{2^{\log^2(\lambda)}}$ number of random tapes do not fall into the set $\mathcal{S}$. Therefore

$$\Pr_{r \sim U}[r \notin \mathcal{S}] \leq \mathsf{negl}(\lambda).$$

The second bullet will imply that our real adversary $A$ is a valid SNARG adversary even though it does not break the soundness of the SNARG (it will return a proof of a true statement) when $r \notin \mathcal{S}$.

*Complexity of Sampling.* As written above, sampling from $Z_i(\overrightarrow{\mathsf{crs}})$ requires access to a #P oracle, since checking membership of $r \in \mathcal{S}$ requires computing the exact number of pre-images $u$ such that $\mathcal{D}_i(u)[2] = r$. We chose to define $\mathcal{S}$ in this way for conceptual simplicity. In the following, we describe an alternate definition of $\mathcal{S}$ that allows for more efficient sampling.

Existence of a *relative error approximator* that can be deterministically computed using a uniform NP circuit follows from an assumption we already require (that E requires exponential-size non-deterministic circuits) [45]. On input $r$, the relative error approximator outputs a value $\rho(r)$ such that for all $r$,

$$(1-\epsilon) \cdot \Pr_{r \sim \mathcal{D}_i[2]}[r] \leq \rho(r) \leq \Pr_{r \sim \mathcal{D}_i[2]}[r].$$

We therefore re-define the set $\mathcal{S} := \{r : \rho(r) \leq (1-\epsilon) \cdot \frac{2^{\log^2(\lambda)}}{2^{|r|}}\}$. Note that if $r \in \mathcal{S}$ then $\Pr_{r \sim \mathcal{D}_i[2]}[r] \leq \frac{2^{\log^2(\lambda)}}{2^{|r|}}$. This means that the min-entropy conditioned on being in $\mathcal{S}$ remains the same as in our previous definition of $\mathcal{S}$. On the other hand, if $r \notin \mathcal{S}$, then $\Pr_{r \sim \mathcal{D}_i[2]}[r] \geq (1-\epsilon)\frac{2^{\log^2(\lambda)}}{2^{|r|}}$. This implies that the fraction of random tapes that do not fall into the set $\mathcal{S}$ will still be negligibly small and so $A$ is still a valid SNARG adversary. Further, using this alternate definition of $\mathcal{S}$, the distribution $Z_i(\overrightarrow{crs})$ itself can be sampled by $\Sigma_2$-circuits.

## 4.5 Tampering Functions

For $i, j \in [t]$, fixed $\overrightarrow{\mathsf{crs}}$, and fixed random coins $\rho$, let $f^i_{j,\overrightarrow{\mathsf{crs}},\rho}$ be the tampering function that uses $\rho$ to sample a pre-image $u$ uniformly at random from the set: $\{u : \mathcal{D}_i(u)[2] = r_i \wedge \mathcal{D}_1(u)[1] = \mathsf{crs}_1 \wedge \cdots \wedge \mathcal{D}_t(u)[1] = \mathsf{crs}_t\}$. Then $f^i_{j,\overrightarrow{\mathsf{crs}},\rho}$ outputs $D_j(u)$. Such a tampering function can be implemented using a polynomial-size NP circuit. See Theorem 5 for more details.

Note that our tampering functions have *no fixed points* since the reduction never outputs the same query twice (in such a case the reduction could simply respond to its own query by copying the previous output).

Since $Z_i(\overrightarrow{\mathsf{crs}})$ has high min-entropy with all but negligible probability over choice of $\overrightarrow{\mathsf{crs}} \sim C_i$, by relaxed $(t-1)$-non-malleability, we have that for $i \in [t]$, and for every $\rho$, with all but negligible probability over $\vec{\mathsf{crs}} \sim C_i$:

$$\begin{aligned}&\left(\mathsf{NMExt}(Z_i(\vec{\mathsf{crs}})), [\mathsf{NMExt}(f^i_{j,\vec{\mathsf{crs}},\rho}(Z_i(\vec{\mathsf{crs}})))]_{j\in[t]\setminus\{i\}}\right)\\ &\overset{s}{\approx} \left(U, [\mathsf{NMExt}(f^i_{j,\vec{\mathsf{crs}},\rho}(Z_i(\vec{\mathsf{crs}})))]_{j\in[t]\setminus\{i\}}\right).\end{aligned} \tag{4}$$

## 4.6 The Real Adversary $A$

We now define the real, inefficient, uniform SNARG adversary $A$:

*The Real Adversary A.* On input $(\mathsf{crs}, r)$:

1. Using brute-force search, find the lexicographically first circuit $C_{\mathsf{crs}}$ of size $\mathsf{poly}(2^{\lambda_\pi})$ guaranteed by Theorem 7.
2. Compute $v = \mathsf{NMExt}(\mathsf{crs}, r)$.
3. If $(\mathsf{crs}, r) \in \mathcal{S}$
   (a) Compute $(v, w) = G_{hard}(v)$. Note that $G_{hard}$ takes superpolynomial time to compute. Let $w = w^1||w^2$.
   (b) Set $x = \bar{\mathcal{L}}(w^1)$
   (c) Set $\pi = C_{\mathsf{crs}}(x; w^2)$.
   (d) Output $(x, \pi)$
4. If $(\mathsf{crs}, r) \notin \mathcal{S}$
   (a) Compute $(v, w) = G_{easy}(v)$. Note that $G_{easy}$ takes polynomial time to compute.
   (b) Compute $(x, \pi) = \mathcal{L}^*_{\mathsf{crs}}(w)$ in polynomial time.
   (c) Output $(x, \pi)$.

We consider the augmented view of $\langle \mathsf{M}, R\rangle$ that includes the entire random string $u$ that the challenger $\mathsf{M}$ and reduction $R$ use during their interaction (this allows full reconstruction of the joint view of $R$ and the challenger corresponding to the falsifiable assumption.). In particular, the views of both $R$ and $\mathsf{M}$ can be fully recovered given the augmented view.

$$\mathsf{View}^{Real}_{\mathsf{aug}} = (u, (x_1, \pi_1), (x_2, \pi_2)).$$

## 4.7 The Uniform PPT Simulator

*The simulator* $\mathsf{Sim}$. On input $(\mathsf{crs}, r)$:

1. Compute $v = \mathsf{NMExt}(\mathsf{crs}, r)$.
2. Compute $(v, w) = G_{easy}(v)$. Note that $G_{easy}$ takes polynomial time to compute.
3. Compute $(x, \pi) = \mathcal{L}^*_{\mathsf{crs}}(w)$ in polynomial time.
4. Output $(x, \pi)$.

### 4.8 Hybrid Argument for $t$ Parallel Queries

We will now argue–via a sequence of hybrids–that the real, inefficient, adversary $A$ can be simulated by the uniform, PPT simulator Sim given in the previous section. Specifically, the real experiment generates a distribution over augmented views that is identical to the distribution in Hybrid $H_{1,0}$, whereas the simulator generates a distribution over augmented views that is identical to the distribution in Hybrid $H_{t,5}$. We will argue that each pair of consecutive hybrids is either perfectly, statistically, or computationally indistinguishable with distinguishing probability $1/\mathsf{poly}$ for some poly. Since it can be checked in polynomial time that the augmented view of the real experiment consists of a "break" of the underlying falsifiable assumption, it must therefore also be the case that the efficiently generated simulated distribution consists of a "break" of the underlying falsifiable assumption with $1/\mathsf{poly}$ probability.

For $i \in [1,\ldots,t]$, we define the following sequence of hybrids: $H_{1,0}, H_{1,1}, \ldots, H_{1,5}, H_{2,0}, H_{2,1}, \ldots, H_{t,5}$.

*Hybrid* $H_{i,0}$. In this Hybrid, we switch the order of sampling. Specifically, letting $p_i$ be the probability that the $i$-th query is not a "frequent query," with probability $p_i$, we first sample the $t$ values of the crs, we then sample the $t$ outputs of NMExt and the derived coins of the adversary, we then *pre-sample* the randomness $u$ of the reduction and challenger and re-compute the entire augmented view, where the responses of the adversary for the first $i-1$ queries are chosen from the "yes" distribution, whereas the responses for the last $t-i+1$ queries are chosen from the "no" distribution. With probability $1-p_i$, we do not change the distribution of this Hybird, and we sample the view by running experiment $H_{i-1,5}$, conditioned on the $i$-th query being a "frequent query." The formal description of the hybrid follows:

Let $p_i := \Pr_{r_i \sim \mathcal{D}_i[2]}[r_i \in \mathcal{S}]$. With probability $p_i$ do the following:

1. Sample $u$ uniformly at random from the set $\{u : \mathcal{D}_i(u)[2] \in \mathcal{S}\}$. Fix $\mathsf{crs}_i = \mathcal{D}_i(u)[1]$, and fix $\rho$ uniformly at random. For $j \in [t] \setminus \{i\}$, fix $\mathsf{crs}_j = D_j(u)[1]$ and $v_j = \mathsf{NMExt}(f_{\mathsf{crs}_j}(\mathcal{D}_i(u)))$. Note that the distribution over $\overrightarrow{\mathsf{crs}} := (\mathsf{crs}_1, \ldots, \mathsf{crs}_t)$ is identical to a draw from $C_1$. Further, $\mathcal{D}_i(u)$ conditioned on $\overrightarrow{\mathsf{crs}}$ is identical to the distribution $Z_i(\overrightarrow{\mathsf{crs}})$.
2. For $j \geq i$, fix the circuits $C_{\mathsf{crs}_j}$, each of size $\mathsf{poly}(2^{\lambda_\pi})$.
3. For $j > i$, compute $v_j || w_{j,hard} = G_{hard}(v_j)$. Let $w_{j,hard} = w^1_{j,hard} || w^2_{j,hard}$. Set $x_{j,no} = \bar{\mathcal{L}}(w^1_{j,hard}), \pi_{j,no} = C_{\mathsf{crs}_j}(x_{j,no}; w^2_{j,hard})$.
4. For $j \in [t] \setminus \{i\}$, compute $v_j || w_{j,easy} = G_{easy}(v_j)$, Set $(x_{j,yes}, \pi_{j,yes}) = \mathcal{L}^*_{\mathsf{crs}_j}(w_{j,easy})$.
5. Sample $v_i = \mathsf{NMExt}(Z_i(\overrightarrow{\mathsf{crs}}))$, conditioned on $v_j = \mathsf{NMExt}(f^i_{j,\overrightarrow{\mathsf{crs}},\rho})(Z_i(\overrightarrow{\mathsf{crs}})))$ for $j \in [t] \setminus \{i\}$.
6. Compute $v_i || w_i = G_{hard}(v_i)$. Let $w_i = w^1_i || w^2_i$.
7. Pre-sample $u$ uniformly at random from the set

$$\{u : \mathcal{D}_i(u)[2] \in \mathcal{S} \wedge \mathcal{D}_1(u)[1] = \mathsf{crs}_1 \cdots \wedge \mathcal{D}_t(u)[1] = \mathsf{crs}_t \wedge \text{ for } j \in [t] \setminus \{i\}, \mathsf{NMExt}(f^i_{j,\overrightarrow{\mathsf{crs}},\rho}(\mathcal{D}_i(u))) = v_j \wedge \mathsf{NMExt}(\mathcal{D}_i(u)) = v_i\}.$$

8. Using $u$, $(\vec{\mathsf{crs}}, \vec{r}) = (\mathsf{crs}_1, r_1), \ldots, (\mathsf{crs}_t, r_t)$ can be efficiently computed.
9. For $j < i$, set $(x_j, \pi_j) = (x_{j,yes}, \pi_{j,yes})$.
10. For $j > i$, if $(\mathsf{crs}_j, r_j) \in \mathcal{S}$ set $(x_j, \pi_j) = (x_{j,no}, \pi_{j,no})$ and if $(\mathsf{crs}_j, r_j) \notin \mathcal{S}$ set $(x_j, \pi_j) = (x_{j,yes}, \pi_{j,yes})$.
11. Set $x_i = \bar{\mathcal{L}}(w_i^1)$
12. Set $\pi_i = C_{\mathsf{crs}_i}(x_i; w_i^2)$.

With probability $1 - p_i$, run experiment $H_{i-1,5}$, conditioned on $(\mathsf{crs}_i, r_i) \notin \mathcal{S}$. We denote the augmented view in this hybrid as

$$\mathsf{View}_{\mathsf{aug}}^{H_{i,0}} = (u, (x_1, \pi_1), \ldots, (x_t, \pi_2)) .$$

Note that hybrid $H_{1,0}$ is identical to the real experiment the only difference is the order of sampling.

*Hybrid* $H_{i,1}$. In this Hybrid, we replace the sampled output of the non-malleable extractor on the $i$-th query $(v_i)$ with a uniform random value. To allow for the switch, we rely on the statistical properties of the $(t-1)$-non-malleable extractor against the distribution $Z_i(\vec{\mathsf{crs}})$ (which we have argued has min-entropy and is samplable by bounded $\mathsf{poly}(\lambda)$-size $\Sigma_2$-circuits in Sect. 4.4, and the tampering functions $f^i_{j,\vec{\mathsf{crs}},\rho}$, which we have argued can be computed by $\mathsf{poly}(\lambda)$-size $\Sigma_2$-circuits in Sect. 4.5. The formal description of the hybrid follows:

Let $p_i := \Pr_{r_i \sim \mathcal{D}_i[2]}[r_i \in \mathcal{S}]$. With probability $p_i$ do the following:

1. Sample $u$ uniformly at random from the set $\{u : \mathcal{D}_i(u)[2] \in \mathcal{S}\}$. Fix $\mathsf{crs}_i = \mathcal{D}_i(u)[1]$ and fix $\rho$ at random. For $j \in [t] \setminus \{i\}$, fix $\mathsf{crs}_j = D_j(u)[1]$ and $v_j = \mathsf{NMExt}(f^i_{j,\vec{\mathsf{crs}},\rho}(\mathcal{D}_i(u)))$. Note that the distribution over $\vec{\mathsf{crs}} := (\mathsf{crs}_1, \ldots, \mathsf{crs}_t)$ is identical to a draw from $C_1$. Further, $\mathcal{D}_i(u)$ conditioned on $\vec{\mathsf{crs}}$ is identical to the distribution $Z_i(\vec{\mathsf{crs}})$.
2. Fix the circuits $C_{\mathsf{crs}_1}, \ldots, C_{\mathsf{crs}_t}$, each of size $\mathsf{poly}(2^{\lambda_\pi})$.
3. For $j > i$, compute $v_j || w_{j,hard} = G_{hard}(v_j)$. Let $w_{j,hard} = w^1_{j,hard} || w^2_{j,hard}$. Set $x_{j,no} = \bar{\mathcal{L}}(w^1_{j,hard})$, $\pi_{j,no} = C_{\mathsf{crs}_j}(x_{j,no}; w^2_{j,hard})$.
4. For $j \in [t] \setminus \{i\}$, compute $v_j || w_{j,easy} = G_{easy}(v_j)$, Set $(x_{j,yes}, \pi_{j,yes}) = \mathcal{L}^*_{\mathsf{crs}_j}(w_{j,easy})$.
5. Sample $v_i$ uniformly at random.
6. Compute $v_i || w_i = G_{hard}(v_i)$. Let $w_i = w_i^1 || w_i^2$.
7. Pre-sample $u$ uniformly at random from the set

$$\{u : \mathcal{D}_i(u)[2] \in \mathcal{S} \wedge \mathcal{D}_1(u)[1] = \mathsf{crs}_1 \cdots \wedge \mathcal{D}_t(u)[1] = \mathsf{crs}_t \wedge \\ \text{for } j \in [t] \setminus \{i\}, \mathsf{NMExt}(f^i_{j,\vec{\mathsf{crs}},\rho}(\mathcal{D}_i(u))) = v_j \wedge \mathsf{NMExt}(\mathcal{D}_i(u)) = v_i\}.$$

8. Using $u$, $(\vec{\mathsf{crs}}, \vec{r}) = (\mathsf{crs}_1, r_1), \ldots, (\mathsf{crs}_t, r_t)$ can be efficiently computed.
9. For $j < i$, set $(x_j, \pi_j) = (x_{j,yes}, \pi_{j,yes})$.
10. For $j > i$, if $(\mathsf{crs}_j, r_j) \in \mathcal{S}$ set $(x_j, \pi_j) = (x_{j,no}, \pi_{j,no})$ and if $(\mathsf{crs}_j, r_j) \notin \mathcal{S}$ set $(x_j, \pi_j) = (x_{j,yes}, \pi_{j,yes})$.
11. Set $x_i = \bar{\mathcal{L}}(w_i^1)$

12. Set $\pi_i = C_{\mathsf{crs}_i}(x_i; w_i^2)$.

With probability $1 - p_i$, run experiment $H_{i-1,5}$, conditioned on $(\mathsf{crs}_i, r_i) \notin \mathcal{S}$.

*Claim.*

$$\mathsf{View}_{\mathsf{aug}}^{H_{i,0}} \overset{s}{\approx} \mathsf{View}_{\mathsf{aug}}^{H_{i,1}}$$

*Proof.* If $p_i$ is negligible, then $H_{i,0}$ and $H_{i,1}$ are both statistically close to the distribution $H_{i-1,5}$, conditioned on $(\mathsf{crs}_i, r_i) \notin \mathcal{S}$ (and hence to each other). On the other hand, if $p_i \geq \frac{1}{2^{\log^2(\lambda)}}$, then the distribution $Z_i(\overrightarrow{\mathsf{crs}})$ has high min-entropy and can be sampled by bounded $\mathsf{poly}(\lambda)$-size $\Sigma_2$-circuits (as shown in Sect. 4.4), and the tampering functions $f^i_{j,\overrightarrow{\mathsf{crs}},\rho}$ can also be computed by $\mathsf{poly}(\lambda)$-size $\Sigma_2$-circuits (as shown in Sect. 4.5). Therefore, due to the relaxed $(t-1)$-non-malleability of NMExt (Def 2), $\mathsf{View}_{\mathsf{aug}}^{H_{i,0}}$ and $\mathsf{View}_{\mathsf{aug}}^{H_{i,1}}$ are 1/poly-statistically close.

*Hybrid* $H_{i,2}$. In this Hybrid, we replace the output of the "hard" PRG $G_{hard}(v_i)$ with a random string $w_i$. Note that this PRG is sufficiently hard that we can compute the remainder of the hybrid distribution (which includes pre-sampling the coins $u$ of the reduction and challenger and computing the fake proof $\pi_i = C_{\mathsf{crs}_i}(x_i; w_i^2)$) without breaking the security of the PRG (See Sect. 4.3). Thus, indistinguishability of the hybrids will follow from the security of the PRG. The formal description of the hybrid follows:

Let $p_i := \Pr_{r_i \sim \mathcal{D}_i[2]}[r_i \in \mathcal{S}]$. With probability $p_i$ do the following:

1. Sample $u$ uniformly at random from the set $\{u : \mathcal{D}_i(u)[2] \in \mathcal{S}\}$. Fix $\mathsf{crs}_i = \mathcal{D}_i(u)[1]$ and fix $\rho$ at random. For $j \in [t] \setminus \{i\}$, fix $\mathsf{crs}_j = D_j(u)[1]$ and $v_j = \mathsf{NMExt}(f^i_{j,\overrightarrow{\mathsf{crs}},\rho}(\mathcal{D}_i(u)))$. Note that the distribution over $\overrightarrow{\mathsf{crs}} := (\mathsf{crs}_1, \ldots, \mathsf{crs}_t)$ is identical to a draw from $C_1$. Further, $\mathcal{D}_i(u)$ conditioned on $\overrightarrow{\mathsf{crs}}$ is identical to the distribution $Z_i(\overrightarrow{\mathsf{crs}})$.
2. Fix the circuits $C_{\mathsf{crs}_1}, \ldots, C_{\mathsf{crs}_t}$, each of size $\mathsf{poly}(2^{\lambda_\pi})$.
3. For $j > i$, compute $v_j || w_{j,hard} = G_{hard}(v_j)$. Let $w_{j,hard} = w^1_{j,hard} || w^2_{j,hard}$. Set $x_{j,no} = \bar{\mathcal{L}}(w^1_{j,hard})$, $\pi_{j,no} = C_{\mathsf{crs}_j}(x_{j,no}; w^2_{j,hard})$.
4. For $j \in [t] \setminus \{i\}$, compute $v_j || w_{j,easy} = G_{easy}(v_j)$, Set $(x_{j,yes}, \pi_{j,yes}) = \mathcal{L}^*_{\mathsf{crs}_j}(w_{j,easy})$.
5. Sample $v_i$ uniformly at random.
6. Sample $w_i$ uniformly at random. Let $w_i = w_i^1 || w_i^2$.
7. Pre-sample $u$ uniformly at random from the set

$$\{u : \mathcal{D}_i(u)[2] \in \mathcal{S} \wedge \mathcal{D}_1(u)[1] = \mathsf{crs}_1 \cdots \wedge \mathcal{D}_t(u)[1] = \mathsf{crs}_t \wedge$$
$$\text{for } j \in [t] \setminus \{i\},\ \mathsf{NMExt}(f^i_{j,\overrightarrow{\mathsf{crs}},\rho}(\mathcal{D}_i(u))) = v_j \wedge \mathsf{NMExt}(\mathcal{D}_i(u)) = v_i\}.$$

8. Using $u$, $(\overrightarrow{\mathsf{crs}}, \vec{r}) = (\mathsf{crs}_1, r_1), \ldots, (\mathsf{crs}_t, r_t)$ can be efficiently computed.
9. For $j < i$, set $(x_j, \pi_j) = (x_{j,yes}, \pi_{j,yes})$.
10. For $j > i$, if $(\mathsf{crs}_j, r_j) \in \mathcal{S}$ set $(x_j, \pi_j) = (x_{j,no}, \pi_{j,no})$ and if $(\mathsf{crs}_j, r_j) \notin \mathcal{S}$ set $(x_j, \pi_j) = (x_{j,yes}, \pi_{j,yes})$.

11. Set $x_i = \bar{\mathcal{L}}(w_i^1)$
12. Set $\pi_i = C_{\mathsf{crs}_i}(x_i; w_i^2)$.

With probability $1 - p_i$, run experiment $H_{i-1,5}$, conditioned on $(\mathsf{crs}_i, r_i) \notin \mathcal{S}$.

*Claim.*

$$\mathsf{View}_{\mathsf{aug}}^{H_{i,1}} \overset{c}{\approx} \mathsf{View}_{\mathsf{aug}}^{H_{i,2}}$$

*Proof.* Consider the following distribution over circuits:

*Non-uniform advice.*

1. Sample $u$ uniformly at random from the set $\{u : \mathcal{D}_i(u)[2] \in \mathcal{S}\}$. Fix $\mathsf{crs}_i = \mathcal{D}_i(u)[1]$ and fix $\rho$ at random. For $j \in [t] \setminus \{i\}$, fix $\mathsf{crs}_j = D_j(u)[1]$ and $v_j = \mathsf{NMExt}(f^i_{j,\overrightarrow{\mathsf{crs}},\rho}(\mathcal{D}_i(u)))$.
2. Fix the circuits $C_{\mathsf{crs}_j}, j \geq i$, each of size $\mathsf{poly}(2^{\lambda_\pi})$.
3. For $j \in [t] \setminus \{i\}$, compute $v_j||w_{j,easy} = G_{easy}(v_j)$, Set $(x_{j,yes}, \pi_{j,yes}) = \mathcal{L}^*_{\mathsf{crs}_j}(w_{j,easy})$.
4. For $j > i$, $v_j||w_{j,hard} = G_{hard}(v_j)$. Let $w_{j,hard} = w^1_{j,hard}||w^2_{j,hard}$. Set $x_{j,no} = \bar{\mathcal{L}}(w^1_{j,hard})$, $\pi_{j,no} = C_{\mathsf{crs}_2}(x_{j,no}; w^2_{j,hard})$.

Given an input $v_i||w_i$, where $w_i = w_i^1||w_i^2$ the circuit does as follows:

1. Pre-sample $u$ uniformly at random from the set

$$\{u : \mathcal{D}_i(u)[2] \in \mathcal{S} \wedge \mathcal{D}_1(u)[1] = \mathsf{crs}_1 \cdots \wedge \mathcal{D}_t(u)[1] = \mathsf{crs}_t \wedge \\ \text{for } j \in [t] \setminus \{i\}, \mathsf{NMExt}(f^i_{j,\overrightarrow{\mathsf{crs}},\rho}(\mathcal{D}_i(u))) = v_j \wedge \mathsf{NMExt}(\mathcal{D}_i(u)) = v_i\}.$$

2. Using $u$, $(\mathsf{crs}_1, r_1), \ldots, (\mathsf{crs}_t, r_t)$ can be efficiently computed.
3. For $j < i$, set $(x_j, \pi_j) = (x_{j,yes}, \pi_{j,yes})$.
4. For $j > i$, if $(\mathsf{crs}_j, r_j) \in \mathcal{S}$ set $(x_j, \pi_j) = (x_{j,no}, \pi_{j,no})$ and if $(\mathsf{crs}_j, r_j) \notin \mathcal{S}$ set $(x_j, \pi_j) = (x_{j,yes}, \pi_{j,yes})$.
5. Set $x_i = \bar{\mathcal{L}}(w_i^1)$
6. Set $\pi_i = C_{\mathsf{crs}_i}(x_i; w_i^2)$.

Assume $(v_i||w_i)$ is either random or the output of a PRG $G_{hard}(v_i)$ that is computed in time $2^{\mathsf{poly}(\lambda)}$ and is secure against $\Sigma_2$-circuits of polynomial size $p_1(\lambda)$ (needed to pre-sample $u$, and check whether $(crs_j, r_j) \in \mathcal{S}$), and (regular) circuits of size $\mathsf{poly}(2^{\lambda_\pi})$ (needed to compute the circuit $C_{crs_i}(x_i; w_i^2)$.

If $(v_i||w_i)$ is the output of $G_{hard}$, then we exactly obtain the Hybrid 1 distribution, whereas if $(v_i||w_i)$ is random, we exactly obtain the Hybrid 2 distribution. By the security of the PRG $G_{hard}$ against this complexity class, Hybrid 1 and Hybrid 2 are indistinguishable.

*Hybrid* $H_{i,3}$ In this Hybrid, we replace the "no" instance $x_i = \overline{\mathcal{L}}(w_i^1), \pi_i = C_{\mathsf{crs}_i}(x_i; w_i^2)$ with a "yes" instance $(x_i, \pi_i) = \mathcal{L}^*_{\mathsf{crs}_i}(w_i)$. Since the value of $w_i$ is independent of all other random variables in the experiment, we can performs all the inefficient parts of the experiment in a pre-processing stage. In the online stage, all that must be done is plugging in $(x_i, \pi_i)$ as the $i$-th response of the oracle and using the pre-sampled random coins $u$ (given as non-uniform advice) to complete the experiment. The formal description of the hybrid follows:

Let $p_i := \Pr_{r_i \sim \mathcal{D}_i[2]}[r_i \in \mathcal{S}]$. With probability $p_i$ do the following:

1. Sample $u$ uniformly at random from the set $\{u : \mathcal{D}_i(u)[2] \in \mathcal{S}\}$. Fix $\mathsf{crs}_i = \mathcal{D}_i(u)[1]$ and fix $\rho$ at random. For $j \in [t] \setminus \{i\}$, fix $\mathsf{crs}_j = D_j(u)[1]$ and $v_j = \mathsf{NMExt}(f^i_{j,\vec{\mathsf{crs}},\rho}(\mathcal{D}_i(u)))$. Note that the distribution over $\vec{\mathsf{crs}} := (\mathsf{crs}_1, \ldots, \mathsf{crs}_t)$ is identical to a draw from $C_1$. Further, $\mathcal{D}_i(u)$ conditioned on $\vec{\mathsf{crs}}$ is identical to the distribution $Z_i(\vec{\mathsf{crs}})$.
2. Fix the circuits $C_{\mathsf{crs}_1}, \ldots, C_{\mathsf{crs}_t}$, each of size $\mathsf{poly}(2^{\lambda_\pi})$.
3. For $j > i$, compute $v_j || w_{j,hard} = G_{hard}(v_j)$. Let $w_{j,hard} = w^1_{j,hard} || w^2_{j,hard}$. Set $x_{j,no} = \bar{\mathcal{L}}(w^1_{j,hard}), \pi_{j,no} = C_{\mathsf{crs}_j}(x_{j,no}; w^2_{j,hard})$.
4. For $j \in [t] \setminus \{i\}$, compute $v_j || w_{j,easy} = G_{easy}(v_j)$, Set $(x_{j,yes}, \pi_{j,yes}) = \mathcal{L}^*_{\mathsf{crs}_j}(w_{j,easy})$.
5. Sample $v_i$ uniformly at random.
6. Sample $w_i$ uniformly at random.
7. Pre-sample $u$ uniformly at random from the set

$$\{u : \mathcal{D}_i(u)[2] \in \mathcal{S} \wedge \mathcal{D}_1(u)[1] = \mathsf{crs}_1 \cdots \wedge \mathcal{D}_t(u)[1] = \mathsf{crs}_t \wedge \\ \text{for } j \in [t] \setminus \{i\},\ \mathsf{NMExt}(f^i_{j,\vec{\mathsf{crs}},\rho}(\mathcal{D}_i(u))) = v_j \wedge \mathsf{NMExt}(\mathcal{D}_i(u)) = v_i\}.$$

8. Using $u$, $(\vec{\mathsf{crs}}, \vec{r}) = (\mathsf{crs}_1, r_1), \ldots, (\mathsf{crs}_t, r_t)$ can be efficiently computed.
9. For $j < i$, set $(x_j, \pi_j) = (x_{j,yes}, \pi_{j,yes})$.
10. For $j > i$, if $(\mathsf{crs}_j, r_j) \in \mathcal{S}$ set $(x_j, \pi_j) = (x_{j,no}, \pi_{j,no})$ and if $(\mathsf{crs}_j, r_j) \notin \mathcal{S}$ set $(x_j, \pi_j) = (x_{j,yes}, \pi_{j,yes})$.
11. Set $(x_i, \pi_i) = \mathcal{L}^*_{\mathsf{crs}_i}(w_i)$.

With probability $1 - p_i$, run experiment $H_{i-1,5}$, conditioned on $(\mathsf{crs}_i, r_i) \notin \mathcal{S}$.

*Claim.*

$$\mathsf{View}^{H_{i,2}}_{\mathsf{aug}} \stackrel{c}{\approx} \mathsf{View}^{H_{i,3}}_{\mathsf{aug}}$$

*Proof.* Since $w_i$ is independent of all other random variables in the experiment, we will use the non-uniform advice to pre-sample a view missing only $(x_i, \pi_i)$, which are both computed from $w_i = w_i^1 || w_i^2$.

Specifically, we sample $(u, [(x_j, \pi_j)]_{j \in [t] \setminus \{i\}})$ and note that $(\vec{\mathsf{crs}}, \vec{r}) = (\mathsf{crs}_1, r_1), \ldots, (\mathsf{crs}_t, r_t)$ can be computed in polynomial time given $u$. These are hardwired into the circuit as non-uniform advice.

The circuit then receives $(x_i, \pi_i)$, where either $(x_i, \pi_i) \sim \mathcal{D}^*_{yes,\mathsf{crs}_i}$ or $(x_i, \pi_i) \sim \mathcal{D}^*_{no,\mathsf{crs}_i}$. The circuit returns the view $(u, (x_1, \pi_1), \ldots, (x_t, \pi_t))$ to the adversary and outputs whatever the adversary does.

Note that if $(x_i, \pi_i) \sim \mathcal{D}^*_{no,\mathsf{crs}_i}$ then the view of the adversary is identical to Hybrid $H_{i,3}$, whereas if $(x_i, \pi_i) \sim \mathcal{D}^*_{yes,\mathsf{crs}_i}$ the view of the adversary is identical to Hybrid $H_{i,4}$. Thus, a distinguishing adversary implies a contradiction to Corollary 1.

*Hybrid* $H_{i,4}$ In this Hybrid, we switch back from $w_i$ being chosen uniformly at random, to $w_i$ being computed using a PRG. However, this time we use $(v_i||w_i) = G_{easy}$ instead of $G_{hard}$. Note that at this stage, the only inefficient parts of the hybrid experiment are the pre-sampling of $u$ conditioned on fixing certain random variables in the experiment. Since we chose $G_{easy}$ to be a poly-time computable PRG that is secure against NP-circuits of polynomial size, this pre-sampling step can be done without breaking the security of $G_{easy}$ (see Sect. 4.3). Thus, indistinguishability of the hybrids will follow from the security of the PRG. The formal description of the hybrid follows:

Let $p_i := \Pr_{r_i \sim \mathcal{D}_i[2]}[r_i \in \mathcal{S}]$. With probability $p_i$ do the following:

1. Sample $u$ uniformly at random from the set $\{u : \mathcal{D}_i(u)[2] \in \mathcal{S}\}$. Fix $\mathsf{crs}_i = \mathcal{D}_i(u)[1]$ and fix $\rho$ at random. For $j \in [t] \setminus \{i\}$, fix $\mathsf{crs}_j = D_j(u)[1]$ and $v_j = \mathsf{NMExt}(f^i_{j,\overrightarrow{\mathsf{crs}},\rho}(\mathcal{D}_i(u)))$. Note that the distribution over $\overrightarrow{\mathsf{crs}} := (\mathsf{crs}_1, \ldots, \mathsf{crs}_t)$ is identical to a draw from $C_1$. Further, $\mathcal{D}_i(u)$ conditioned on $\overrightarrow{\mathsf{crs}}$ is identical to the distribution $Z_i(\overrightarrow{\mathsf{crs}})$.
2. Fix the circuits $C_{\mathsf{crs}_1}, \ldots, C_{\mathsf{crs}_t}$, each of size $\mathsf{poly}(2^{\lambda_\pi})$.
3. For $j > i$, compute $v_j||w_{j,hard} = G_{hard}(v_j)$. Let $w_{j,hard} = w^1_{j,hard}||w^2_{j,hard}$. Set $x_{j,no} = \bar{\mathcal{L}}(w^1_{j,hard}), \pi_{j,no} = C_{\mathsf{crs}_j}(x_{j,no}; w^2_{j,hard})$.
4. For $j \in [t] \setminus \{i\}$, compute $v_j||w_{j,easy} = G_{easy}(v_j)$, Set $(x_{j,yes}, \pi_{j,yes}) = \mathcal{L}^*_{\mathsf{crs}_j}(w_{j,easy})$.
5. Sample $v_i$ uniformly at random.
6. Set $(v_i||w_i) = G_{easy}(v_i)$.
7. Pre-sample $u$ uniformly at random from the set

$$\{u : \mathcal{D}_i(u)[2] \in \mathcal{S} \wedge \mathcal{D}_1(u)[1] = \mathsf{crs}_1 \cdots \wedge \mathcal{D}_t(u)[1] = \mathsf{crs}_t \wedge$$
$$\text{for } j \in [t] \setminus \{i\},\ \mathsf{NMExt}(f^i_{j,\overrightarrow{\mathsf{crs}},\rho}(\mathcal{D}_i(u))) = v_j \wedge \mathsf{NMExt}(\mathcal{D}_i(u)) = v_i\}.$$

8. Using $u$, $(\overrightarrow{\mathsf{crs}}, \vec{r}) = (\mathsf{crs}_1, r_1), \ldots, (\mathsf{crs}_t, r_t)$ can be efficiently computed.
9. For $j < i$, set $(x_j, \pi_j) = (x_{j,yes}, \pi_{j,yes})$.
10. For $j > i$, if $(\mathsf{crs}_j, r_j) \in \mathcal{S}$ set $(x_j, \pi_j) = (x_{j,no}, \pi_{j,no})$ and if $(\mathsf{crs}_j, r_j) \notin \mathcal{S}$ set $(x_j, \pi_j) = (x_{j,yes}, \pi_{j,yes})$.
11. Set $(x_i, \pi_i) = \mathcal{L}^*_{\mathsf{crs}_i}(w_i)$.

With probability $1 - p_i$, run experiment $H_{i-1,5}$, conditioned on $(\mathsf{crs}_i, r_i) \notin \mathcal{S}$.

*Claim.*

$$\mathsf{View}^{H_{i,3}}_{\mathsf{aug}} \stackrel{c}{\approx} \mathsf{View}^{H_{i,4}}_{\mathsf{aug}}$$

*Proof.* Consider the following distribution over circuits:

*Non-uniform advice.*

1. Sample $u$ uniformly at random from the set $\{u : \mathcal{D}_i(u)[2] \in \mathcal{S}\}$. Fix $\mathsf{crs}_i = \mathcal{D}_i(u)[1]$ and fix $\rho$ at random. For $j \in [t] \setminus \{i\}$, fix $\mathsf{crs}_j = D_j(u)[1]$ and $v_j = \mathsf{NMExt}(f^i_{j,\vec{\mathsf{crs}},\rho}(\mathcal{D}_i(u)))$.
2. Fix the circuits $C_{\mathsf{crs}_j}, j \geq i$, each of size $\mathsf{poly}(2^{\lambda_\pi})$.
3. For $j > i$, compute $v_j||w_{j,hard} = G_{hard}(v_j)$. Let $w_{j,hard} = w^1_{j,hard}||w^2_{j,hard}$. Set $x_{j,no} = \bar{\mathcal{L}}(w^1_{j,hard}), \pi_{j,no} = C_{\mathsf{crs}_j}(x_{j,no}; w^2_{j,hard})$.
4. For $j \in [t] \setminus \{i\}$, compute $v_j||w_{j,easy} = G_{easy}(v_j)$, Set $(x_{j,yes}, \pi_{j,yes}) = \mathcal{L}^*_{\mathsf{crs}_j}(w_{j,easy})$.

Given an input $v_i||w_i$, the circuit does as follows:

1. Pre-sample $u$ uniformly at random from the set

$$\{u : \mathcal{D}_i(u)[2] \in \mathcal{S} \wedge \mathcal{D}_1(u)[1] = \mathsf{crs}_1 \cdots \wedge \mathcal{D}_t(u)[1] = \mathsf{crs}_t \wedge \\ \text{for } j \in [t] \setminus \{i\},\ \mathsf{NMExt}(f^i_{j,\vec{\mathsf{crs}},\rho}(\mathcal{D}_i(u))) = v_j \wedge \mathsf{NMExt}(\mathcal{D}_i(u)) = v_i\}.$$

2. Using $u$, $(\vec{\mathsf{crs}}, \vec{r}) = (\mathsf{crs}_1, r_1), \ldots, (\mathsf{crs}_t, r_t)$ can be efficiently computed.
3. For $j < i$, set $(x_j, \pi_j) = (x_{j,yes}, \pi_{j,yes})$.
4. For $j > i$, if $(\mathsf{crs}_j, r_j) \in \mathcal{S}$ set $(x_j, \pi_j) = (x_{j,no}, \pi_{j,no})$ and if $(\mathsf{crs}_j, r_j) \notin \mathcal{S}$ set $(x_j, \pi_j) = (x_{j,yes}, \pi_{j,yes})$.
5. Set $(x_i, \pi_i) = \mathcal{L}^*_{\mathsf{crs}_i}(w_i)$.

Assume $(v_i||w_i)$ is either random or the output of a PRG $G_{easy}(v_i)$ that is computed in polynomial time and is secure against NP-circuits of polynomial size $p_1(\lambda)$ (needed to pre-sample $u$, and check whether $(crs_j, r_j) \in \mathcal{S}$).

If $(v_i||w_i)$ is the output of $G_{easy}$, then we exactly obtain the Hybrid $H_{i,4}$ distribution, whereas if $(v_i||w_i)$ is random, we exactly obtain the Hybrid $H_{i,3}$ distribution. By the security of the PRG $G_{easy}$ against this complexity class, Hybrid $H_{i,3}$ and Hybrid $H_{i,4}$ are indistinguishable.

*Hybrid $H_{i,5}$* In this Hybrid, we go back to sampling $v_i = \mathsf{NMExt}(Z_i(\vec{\mathsf{crs}})$ from the correct distribution, instead of choosing it uniformly at random. Again, indistinguishability follows from the statistical properties of the $(t-1)$-non-malleable extractor. The formal description of the hybrid follows:

Let $p_i := \Pr_{r_i \sim \mathcal{D}_i[2]}[r_i \in \mathcal{S}]$. With probability $p_i$ do the following:

1. Sample $u$ uniformly at random from the set $\{u : \mathcal{D}_i(u)[2] \in \mathcal{S}\}$. Fix $\mathsf{crs}_i = \mathcal{D}_i(u)[1]$ and fix $\rho$ at random. For $j \in [t] \setminus \{i\}$, fix $\mathsf{crs}_j = D_j(u)[1]$ and $v_j = \mathsf{NMExt}(f^i_{j,\vec{\mathsf{crs}},\rho}(\mathcal{D}_i(u)))$. Note that the distribution over $\vec{\mathsf{crs}} := (\mathsf{crs}_1, \ldots, \mathsf{crs}_t)$ is identical to a draw from $C_1$. Further, $\mathcal{D}_i(u)$ conditioned on $\vec{\mathsf{crs}}$ is identical to the distribution $Z_i(\vec{\mathsf{crs}})$.
2. Fix the circuits $C_{\mathsf{crs}_1}, \ldots, C_{\mathsf{crs}_t}$, each of size $\mathsf{poly}(2^{\lambda_\pi})$.
3. For $j > i$, compute $v_j||w_{j,hard} = G_{hard}(v_j)$. Let $w_{j,hard} = w^1_{j,hard}||w^2_{j,hard}$. Set $x_{j,no} = \bar{\mathcal{L}}(w^1_{j,hard}), \pi_{j,no} = C_{\mathsf{crs}_j}(x_{j,no}; w^2_{j,hard})$.

4. For $j \in [t] \setminus \{i\}$, compute $v_j||w_{j,easy} = G_{easy}(v_j)$, Set $(x_{j,yes}, \pi_{j,yes}) = \mathcal{L}^*_{\mathsf{crs}_j}(w_{j,easy})$.
5. Sample $v_i = \mathsf{NMExt}(Z_i(\vec{\mathsf{crs}}))$, conditioned on $v_j = \mathsf{NMExt}(f_j(Z_i(\vec{\mathsf{crs}}))), j \in [t] \setminus \{i\}$.
6. Set $(v_i||w_i) = G_{easy}(v_i)$.
7. Pre-sample $u$ uniformly at random from the set

$$\{u : \mathcal{D}_i(u)[2] \in \mathcal{S} \wedge \mathcal{D}_1(u)[1] = \mathsf{crs}_1 \cdots \wedge \mathcal{D}_t(u)[1] = \mathsf{crs}_t \wedge \\ \text{for } j \in [t] \setminus \{i\}, \mathsf{NMExt}(f^i_{j,\vec{\mathsf{crs}},\rho}(\mathcal{D}_i(u))) = v_j \wedge \mathsf{NMExt}(\mathcal{D}_i(u)) = v_i\}.$$

8. Using $u$, $(\vec{\mathsf{crs}}, \vec{r}) = (\mathsf{crs}_1, r_1), \ldots, (\mathsf{crs}_t, r_t)$ can be efficiently computed.
9. For $j < i$, set $(x_j, \pi_j) = (x_{j,yes}, \pi_{j,yes})$.
10. For $j > i$, if $(\mathsf{crs}_j, r_j) \in \mathcal{S}$ set $(x_j, \pi_j) = (x_{j,no}, \pi_{j,no})$ and if $(\mathsf{crs}_j, r_j) \notin \mathcal{S}$ set $(x_j, \pi_j) = (x_{j,yes}, \pi_{j,yes})$.
11. Set $(x_i, \pi_i) = \mathcal{L}^*_{\mathsf{crs}_i}(w_i)$.

With probability $1 - p_i$, run experiment $H_{i-1,5}$, conditioned on $(\mathsf{crs}_i, r_i) \notin \mathcal{S}$.

*Claim.*

$$\mathsf{View}^{H_{i,4}}_{\mathsf{aug}} \overset{s}{\approx} \mathsf{View}^{H_{i,5}}_{\mathsf{aug}}$$

*Proof.* If $p_i$ is negligible, then $H_{i,4}$ and $H_{i,5}$ are both statistically close to the distribution $H_{i-1,5}$, conditioned on $(\mathsf{crs}_i, r_i) \notin \mathcal{S}$ (and hence to each other). On the other hand, if $p_i \geq \frac{1}{2^{\log^2(\lambda)}}$, then the distribution $Z_i(\vec{\mathsf{crs}})$ has high min-entropy and can be sampled by bounded $\mathsf{poly}(\lambda)$-size $\Sigma_2$-circuits (as shown in Sect. 4.4), and the tampering functions $f^i_{j,\vec{\mathsf{crs}},\rho}$ can also be computed by $\mathsf{poly}(\lambda)$-size $\mathsf{NP}$-circuits (as shown in Sect. 4.5). Therefore, due to the relaxed $(t-1)$-non-malleability of $\mathsf{NMExt}$ (Def 2), $\mathsf{View}^{H_{i,4}}_{\mathsf{aug}}$ and $\mathsf{View}^{H_{i,5}}_{\mathsf{aug}}$ are $1/\mathsf{poly}$-statistically close.

We claim that Hybrid $H_{i,5}$ is identical to the following hybrid, we simply re-arrange the order of sampling. Specifically, in this Hybrid, we first sample the coins of the reduction and challenger, run the experiment forward. Given all the queries, $(\vec{\mathsf{crs}}, \vec{r})$, we run the non-malleable extractor to obtain $v_1, \ldots, v_t$. For $j \leq i$, we run $(v_j, w_j) = G_{easy}(v_j)$ and sample $(x_j, \pi_j) = \mathcal{L}^*_{\mathsf{crs}_j}(w_j)$ from the "yes" distribution. For $j > i$, if the query $(\mathsf{crs}_j, r_j)$ is not "frequent", we run $(v_j, w_j) = G_{hard}(v_j)$ and sample $x_j = \overline{\mathcal{L}}(w^1_j)$, $\pi_j = C_{\mathsf{crs}_j}(x_j; w^2_j)$ from the "no" distribution. Otherwise, if the query $(\mathsf{crs}_j, r_j)$ is "frequent", we run $(v_j, w_j) = G_{easy}(v_j)$ and sample $(x_j, \pi_j) = \mathcal{L}^*_{\mathsf{crs}_j}(w_j)$ from the "yes" distribution.

*Hybrid $H_{i,5}$*

1. Sample $u$ uniformly at random and fix $u$.
2. Using $u$, $(\vec{\mathsf{crs}}, \vec{r}) = (\mathsf{crs}_1, r_1), \ldots, (\mathsf{crs}_2, r_2)$ can be efficiently computed.
3. For $j > i$, fix the circuits $C_{\mathsf{crs}_j}$ of size $\mathsf{poly}(2^{\lambda_\pi})$.
4. For $j \in [t]$, set $v_j = \mathsf{NMExt}(\mathsf{crs}_j, r_j)$.
5. For $j \leq i$, set $v_j||w_j = G_{easy}(v_j)$ and set $(x_j, \pi_j) = \mathcal{L}^*_{\mathsf{crs}_j}(w_j)$.
6. For $j > i$, if $(\mathsf{crs}_j, r_j) \in \mathcal{S}$

(a) Compute $(v_j, w_j) = G_{hard}(v_j)$. Let $w_j = w_j^1 || w_j^2$.
(b) Set $x_j = \bar{\mathcal{L}}(w_j^1)$
(c) Set $\pi_j = C_{\mathsf{crs}_j}(x_j; w_j^2)$.

7. For $j > i$, if $(\mathsf{crs}_j, r_j) \notin \mathcal{S}$
   (a) Compute $(v_j, w_j) = G_{easy}(v_j)$. Note that $G_{easy}$ takes polynomial time to compute.
   (b) Set $(x_j, \pi_j) = \mathcal{L}^*_{\mathsf{crs}_j}(w_2)$.

Note that the distribution produced by $H_{-1,5}$ is identical to the one produced by the interaction of $R$ with the real adversary $A$. Looking at the definition of the distribution in Hybrid $H_{i,0}$, we further claim that for $i \in \{-1, \ldots, t-1\}$, $H_{i,5}$ is identical to $H_{i+1,0}$, with only the order of sampling changed.

Finally, we note that $H_{t,5}$ is a polynomial-time algorithm that produces a distribution over views identical to the one produced by the interaction of $R$ with Sim.

This concludes the proof of Theorem 6.

## References


1. Adleman, L.M.: Two theorems on random polynomial time. In: FOCS, pp. 75–83. IEEE Computer Society (1978)
2. Aggarwal, D., Döttling, N., Nielsen, J.B., Obremski, M., Purwanto, E.: Continuous non-malleable codes in the 8-split-state model. In: Ishai, Y., Rijmen, V. (eds.) EUROCRYPT 2019. Part I, volume 11476 of LNCS, pp. 531–561. Springer, Cham (2019). https://doi.org/10.1007/978-3-030-17653-2_18
3. Applebaum, B., Artemenko, S., Shaltiel, R., Yang, G.: Incompressible functions, relative-error extractors, and the power of nondeterministic reductions. Comput. Complex. **25**(2), 349–418 (2016)
4. Babai, L., Moran, S.: Arthur-merlin games: a randomized proof system, and a hierarchy of complexity classes. J. Comput. Syst. Sci. **36**(2), 254–276 (1988)
5. Ball, M., Dachman-Soled, D., Loss, J.: (Nondeterministic) hardness vs. non-malleability. In: Dodis, Y., Shrimpton, T. (eds.) CRYPTO 2022. Part I, volume 13507 of LNCS, pp. 148–177. Springer, Cham (2022). https://doi.org/10.1007/978-3-031-15802-5_6
6. Ball, M., Goldin, E., Dachman-Soled, D., Mutreja, S.: Extracting randomness from samplable distributions, revisited. In: 64th FOCS, pp. 1505–1514. IEEE Computer Society Press (2023)
7. Barak, B., Ong, S.J., Vadhan, S.P.: Derandomization in cryptography. In: Boneh, D. (ed.) CRYPTO 2003. LNCS, vol. 2729, pp. 299–315. Springer, Berlin, Heidelberg (2003). https://doi.org/10.1007/978-3-540-45146-4_18
8. Bellare, M., Goldreich, O., Petrank, E.: Uniform generation of np-witnesses using an np-oracle. Inf. Comput. **163**(2), 510–526 (2000)
9. Campanelli, M., Ganesh, C., Khoshakhlagh, H., Siim, J.: Impossibilities in succinct arguments: Black-box extraction and more. In: El Mrabet, N., De Feo, L., Duquesne, S. (eds.) AFRICACRYPT 23. LNCS, vol. 14064, pp. 465–489. Springer, Cham (2023). https://doi.org/10.1007/978-3-031-37679-5_20

10. Chattopadhyay, E., Goyal, V., Li, X.: Non-malleable extractors and codes, with their many tampered extensions. In: Wichs, D., Mansour, Y., editors 48th ACM STOC, pp. 285–298. ACM Press (2016)
11. Chattopadhyay, E., Li, X.: Non-malleable codes and extractors for small-depth circuits, and affine functions. In: Hatami, H., McKenzie, P., King, V., (eds) 49th ACM STOC, pp. 1171–1184. ACM Press (2017)
12. Cheraghchi, M., Guruswami, V.: Non-malleable coding against bit-wise and split-state tampering. In: Lindell, Y. (ed.) TCC 2014. LNCS, vol. 8349, pp. 440–464. Springer, Berlin, Heidelberg (2014). https://doi.org/10.1007/s00145-015-9219-z
13. Chor, B., Goldreich, O.: Unbiased bits from sources of weak randomness and probabilistic communication complexity (extended abstract). In: 26th FOCS, pp. 429–442. IEEE Computer Society Press (1985)
14. Chung, K.-M., Lin, H., Mahmoody, M., Pass, R.: On the power of nonuniformity in proofs of security. In: Kleinberg, R.D. ed. ITCS 2013, pp. 389–400. ACM (2013)
15. Dodis, Y., Wichs, D.: Non-malleable extractors and symmetric key cryptography from weak secrets. In: Mitzenmacher, M., editor 41st ACM STOC, pp. 601–610. ACM Press (2009)
16. Drucker, A.: Nondeterministic direct product reductions and the success probability of SAT solvers. In: 54th FOCS, pp. 736–745. IEEE Computer Society Press (2013)
17. Dziembowski, S., Pietrzak, K., Wichs, D.: Non-malleable codes. In: Yao, editor, ICS 2010, pp. 434–452. Tsinghua University Press (2010)
18. Faust, S., Mukherjee, P., Nielsen, J.B., Venturi, D.: Continuous non-malleable codes. In: Lindell, Y. (ed.) TCC 2014. LNCS, vol. 8349, pp. 465–488. Springer, Berlin, Heidelberg (2014). https://doi.org/10.1007/978-3-642-54242-8_20
19. Feige, U., Lund, C.: On the hardness of computing the permanent of random matrices. Comput. Complex. **6**(2), 101–132 (1997)
20. Gentry, C., Wichs, D.: Separating succinct non-interactive arguments from all falsifiable assumptions. In: Fortno, L., Vadhan, editors, 43rd ACM STOC, pp. 99–108. ACM Press (2011)
21. Goldreich, O., Leshkowitz, M.: On emulating interactive proofs with public coins. In: Goldreich, O., editor, Computational Complexity and Property Testing - On the Interplay Between Randomness and Computation, volume 12050 of Lecture Notes in Computer Science, pp. 178–198. Springer, Cham (2020). https://doi.org/10.1007/978-3-030-43662-9_12
22. Goldreich, O., Wigderson, A.: Derandomization that is rarely wrong from short advice that is typically good. In: RANDOM, volume 2483 of Lecture Notes in Computer Science, pp. 209–223. Springer, Berlin, Heidelberg (2002). https://doi.org/10.1007/3-540-45726-7_17
23. Goldwasser, S., Sipser, M.: Private coins versus public coins in interactive proof systems. In: 18th ACM STOC, pp. 59–68. ACM Press (1986)
24. Gutfreund, D., Shaltiel, R., Ta-Shma, A.: Uniform hardness versus randomness tradeoffs for Arthur-Merlin games. Comput. Complex. **12**(3–4), 85–130 (2003)
25. Impagliazzo, R., Wigderson, A.: P = BPP if E requires exponential circuits: derandomizing the XOR lemma. In: 29th ACM STOC, pp. 220–229. ACM Press (1997)
26. Jerrum, M., Valiant, L.G., Vazirani, V.V.: Random generation of combinatorial structures from a uniform distribution. Theor. Comput. Sci. **43**, 169–188 (1986)
27. Jetchev, D., Pietrzak, K.: How to fake auxiliary input. In: Lindell, Y. (ed.) TCC 2014. LNCS, vol. 8349, pp. 566–590. Springer, Berlin, Heidelberg (2014). https://doi.org/10.1007/978-3-642-54242-8_24

28. Kinne, J., van Melkebeek, D., Shaltiel, R.: Pseudorandom generators, typically-correct derandomization, and circuit lower bounds. Comput. Complex. **21**(1), 3–61 (2012)
29. Klivans, A.R., van Melkebeek, D.: Graph nonisomorphism has subexponential size proofs unless the polynomial-time hierarchy collapses. SIAM J. Comput. **31**(5), 1501–1526 (2002)
30. Li, S.: Scheduling to minimize total weighted completion time via time-indexed linear programming relaxations. In: Umans, C., ed., 58th FOCS, pp. 283–294. IEEE Computer Society Press (2017)
31. Li, X.: Non-malleable extractors, two-source extractors and privacy amplification. In: 53rd FOCS, pp. 688–697. IEEE Computer Society Press (2012)
32. Li, X.: New independent source extractors with exponential improvement. In: Boneh, D., Roughgarden, T., Feigenbaum, J., eds, 45th ACM STOC, pp. 783–792. ACM Press, June 2013
33. Li, X.: Three-source extractors for polylogarithmic min-entropy. In: Guruswami, V., ed., 56th FOCS, pp. 863–882. IEEE Computer Society Press (2015)
34. Li, X.: Improved non-malleable extractors, non-malleable codes and independent source extractors. In: Hatami, H., McKenzie, P., King, V., eds. 49th ACM STOC, pp. 1144–1156. ACM Press (2017)
35. Li, X.: Non-malleable extractors and non-malleable codes: Partially optimal constructions. In: 34th Computational Complexity Conference, CCC 2019, July 18-20, 2019, New Brunswick, NJ, USA, pp. 28:1–28:49 (2019)
36. Li, X.: Two source extractors for asymptotically optimal entropy, and (many) more. In: 64th FOCS, pp. 1271–1281. IEEE Computer Society Press (2023)
37. Mathialagan, S., Peters, S., Vaikuntanathan, V.: Adaptively sound zero-knowledge SNARKs for UP. Cryptology ePrint Archive, Paper 2024/227 (2024). https://eprint.iacr.org/2024/227
38. Miltersen, P.B., Vinodchandran, N.V.: Derandomizing Arthur-Merlin games using hitting sets. Comput. Complex. **14**(3), 256–279 (2005)
39. Naor, M.: On cryptographic assumptions and challenges. In: Annual International Cryptology Conference, pp. 96–109. Springer, Berlin, Heidelberg (2003). https://doi.org/10.1007/978-3-540-45146-4_6
40. Nisan, N., Wigderson, A.:. Hardness vs. randomness (extended abstract). In: 29th FOCS, pp. 2–11. IEEE Computer Society Press (1988)
41. Ostrovsky, R., Persiano, G., Venturi, D., Visconti, I.: Continuously non-malleable codes in the split-state model from minimal assumptions. In: Shacham, H., Boldyreva, A. (eds.) CRYPTO 2018. Part III, volume 10993 of LNCS, pp. 608–639. Springer, Cham (2018). https://doi.org/10.1007/s00145-020-09362-z
42. Pass, R.: Unprovable security of perfect NIZK and non-interactive non-malleable commitments. In: Sahai, A. (ed.) TCC 2013. LNCS, vol. 7785, pp. 334–354. Springer, Berlin, Heidelberg (2013). https://doi.org/10.1007/978-3-642-36594-2_19
43. Pass, R.: Unprovable security of perfect nizk and non-interactive non-malleable commitments (2017). https://www.cs.cornell.edu/~rafael/papers/limits2new.pdf. Accessed 10 Feb 2025
44. Sasson, E.B., et al.: Zerocash: Decentralized anonymous payments from bitcoin. In: 2014 IEEE Symposium on Security and Privacy, pp. 459–474. IEEE (2014)
45. Shaltiel, R., Umans, C.: Pseudorandomness for approximate counting and sampling. In: 20th Annual IEEE Conference on Computational Complexity (CCC'05), pp. 212–226 (2005)

46. Shaltiel, R.: Weak derandomization of weak algorithms: Explicit versions of yao's lemma. Comput. Complex. **20**(1), 87–143 (2011)
47. Shaltiel, R., Umans, C.: Simple extractors for all min-entropies and a new pseudorandom generator. J. ACM **52**(2), 172–216 (2005)
48. Shaltiel, R., Umans, C.: Pseudorandomness for approximate counting and sampling. Comput. Complex. **15**(4), 298–341 (2006)
49. Shaltiel, R., Umans, C.: Low-end uniform hardness versus randomness tradeoffs for AM. SIAM J. Comput. **39**(3), 1006–1037 (2009)
50. Trevisan, L., Vadhan, S.P.: Extracting randomness from samplable distributions. In: 41st FOCS, pp. 32–42. IEEE Computer Society Press (2000)
51. Vadhan, S., Zheng, C.J.: A uniform min-max theorem with applications in cryptography. In: Canetti, R., Garay, J.A. (eds.) CRYPTO 2013. LNCS, vol. 8042, pp. 93–110. Springer, Heidelberg (2013). https://doi.org/10.1007/978-3-642-40041-4_6
52. Waters, B., Wu, D.J.: Adaptively-sound succinct arguments for NP from indistinguishability obfuscation. Cryptology ePrint Archive, Paper 2024/165 (2024). https://eprint.iacr.org/2024/165
53. Waters, B., Wu, D.J.: A pure indistinguishability obfuscation approach to adaptively-sound SNARGs for NP. Cryptology ePrint Archive, Paper 2024/933 (2024). https://eprint.iacr.org/2024/933
54. Waters, B., Zhandry, M.: Adaptive security in SNARGs via iO and lossy functions. Cryptology ePrint Archive, Paper 2024/254 (2024). https://eprint.iacr.org/2024/254

# Hardness Along the Boundary: Towards One-Way Functions from the Worst-Case Hardness of Time-Bounded Kolmogorov Complexity

Yanyi Liu[1(✉)] and Rafael Pass[2]

[1] Cornell Tech, New York, USA
yl2866@cornell.edu

[2] Cornell Tech, Technion and TAU, New York, USA
rafael@cs.cornell.edu

**Abstract.** We consider the question of whether worst-case hardness of the time-bounded Kolmogorov complexity problem, $\mathsf{MINK}^{\mathsf{poly}}$—that is, determining whether a string is time-bounded Kolmogorov random ($K^t$-random) or not—suffices to imply the existence of one-way functions (OWF).

Roughly speaking, our main result shows that under a natural strengthening of standard-type derandomization assumptions, worst-case hardness of the *boundary* version of this classic problem characterizes OWFs. In more detail, let $\mathsf{boundary\text{-}MINK}^{t_1,t_2}$ denote the problem of, given an instance $x$, deciding whether (a) $K^{t_2}(x) \geq n-1$, or (b) $K^{t_1}(x) < n-1$ *but* $K^{t_2} > n - \log n$; that is, deciding whether $x$ is $K^t$-random, or just "near" $K^t$-random. We say that $\mathsf{boundary\text{-}MINK}^{\mathsf{poly}} \notin \mathsf{ioBPP}$ if $\mathsf{boundary\text{-}MINK}^{\mathsf{poly}} \notin \mathsf{ioBPP}$ for all polynomials $t_1, t_2$.

We show that under a natural strengthening of standard derandomization assumptions (namely, there exists a constant $\varepsilon > 0$ such that $\mathsf{E} \not\subseteq \mathsf{ioNTIME}[2^{kn}]/2^{\varepsilon n}$ for every $k \in \mathbb{N}$), OWF exist iff $\mathsf{boundary\text{-}MINK}^{\mathsf{poly}} \notin \mathsf{ioBPP}$. Along the way, we also demonstrate that if we consider the probabilistic version of Kolmogorov complexity (referred to as $pK^t$) instead, then the characterization holds unconditionally.

We finally observe that for most standard optimization problems, hardness "along boundary" is equivalent to "plain" worst-case hardness, indicating that assuming hardness along the boundary may be WLOG.

Research partly supported by NSF CNS-2149305.
Supported in part by NSF Award CNS 2149305, AFOSR Award FA9550-23-1-0387, AFOSR Award FA9550-23-1-0312, AFOSR Award FA9550-24-1-0267, ISF Award 2338/23 and ERC Advanced Grant KolmoCrypt - 101142322. Any opinions, findings and conclusions or recommendations expressed in this material are those of the author(s) and do not necessarily reflect the views of the United States Government, the AFOSR, the European Union or the European Research Council Executive Agency.


Y. Tauman Kalai and S. F. Kamara (Eds.): CRYPTO 2025, LNCS 16000, pp. 617–650, 2025.
https://doi.org/10.1007/978-3-032-01855-7_20

# 1 Introduction

A *one-way function* [DH76] (OWF) is a function $f$ that can be efficiently computed (in polynomial time), yet no probabilistic polynomial-time (PPT) algorithm can invert $f$ with inverse polynomial probability for infinitely many input lengths $n$. Whether one-way functions exist is unequivocally the most important open problem in Cryptography (and arguably the most important open problem in the theory of computation, see e.g., [Lev03]): OWFs are both necessary [IL89] and sufficient for many of the most central cryptographic primitives and protocols (e.g., pseudorandom generators [BM84,HILL99], pseudorandom functions [GGM84], private-key encryption [GM84], digital signatures [Rom90], commitment schemes [Nao91], identification protocols [FS90], coin-flipping protocols [Blu82], and more). These primitives and protocols are often referred to as *private-key primitives*, or "Minicrypt" primitives [Imp95] as they exclude the notable task of public-key encryption [DH76,RSA83]. Additionally, as observed by Impagliazzo [Gur89,Imp95], the existence of a OWF is equivalent to the existence of polynomial-time method for sampling hard *solved* instances for an NP language (i.e., hard instances together with their witnesses).

**Complexity-Theoretic Characterizations of OWFs: Kolmogorov Complexity.** We here focus on the question of whether there exists some "simple" complexity-theoretic characterizations of the existence of OWFs. Recently, [LP20] presented an *average-case* characterization of OWFs through a natural computational problem—the *time-bounded Kolmogorov complexity problem* [Kol68,Sip83,Ko86,Har83]: Let the Kolmogorov complexity of a string $x$, denoted $K(x)$, be defined as the length of the shortest program that outputs $x$, and the $t(\cdot)$-bounded version, $K^t(x)$, be defined as the length of the shortest program that outputs the string $x$ within time $t(|x|)$. While determining (or deciding for some particular threshold $s(\cdot)$) the Kolmogorov complexity of a string $x$ is uncomputable, as surveyed by Trakhtenbrot [Tra84], the problem of efficiently computing/deciding $K^t$-complexity (when $t$ is a polynomial) predates the theory of NP-completeness and was studied in the Soviet Union since the 60s as a candidate for a problem that requires "brute-force search". Indeed, so far no non-trivial attacks are known in the uniform setting (and only very recently a non-trivial attack of circuit size roughly $2^{4n/5}$ was presented in the non-uniform setting [MP23,HIW24]).

The work of [LP20] showed that mild average-case hardness of computing $K^t$ (or simply deciding whether it is large or small) w.r.t. the *uniform* distribution over instances, characterizes the existence of OWF. [LP23b], furthermore, show that if we consider a probabilistic analog of $K^t$, referred to as *probabilistic* $K^t$ or $pK^t$ [GKLO22]—where for some constant $\delta$ (think of $\delta = 2/3$), $pK^t_\delta(x)$ is defined as the smallest $\omega$ such that with probability $\delta$ over the choice of a random string $r$, there exists a program of length at most $\omega$ that generates $x$ if being provided $r$—then mild average-case hardness with respect to *any* a-priori polynomially time-bounded sampler over instances also characterizes OWFs (i.e., not just the uniform distribution), and this results also extends to $K^t$ under standard derandomization assumptions.

**Does Just *Worst-case* Hardness of $K^t$ Suffice?** These above results, however, only apply in the setting of *average-case hardness*. We are here interested in the question of whether simply *worst-case hardness* of computing/deciding $K^t$ suffices to characterize or even just obtain OWFs.

> *Does worst-case hardness of deciding $K^t(x) > s$ imply the existence of OWFs?*

Beyond being interesting in its own right, this question is motivated by the fact that in recent years, there has been great progress (see e.g. [Ila20,ILO20,Ila21] [Ila22,LP22b,Hir22,Ila23]) towards showing that the decisional $K^t$ problem is NP-complete; in particular, the very recent work by Ilango [Ila23] shows NP-completeness in the random oracle model (and thus giving a heuristic NP-completeness reduction). Notably, if OWF can be based on the worst-case hardness of this problem, and the problem can be shown to be NP-complete, then we would base OWF on just the assumption that $\mathsf{NP} \not\subseteq \mathsf{BPP}$.

Intriguingly, a result by Hirahara [Hir18] shows that if we were to consider a "gap" version of the $K^t$ problem, where the goal is to distinguish between $x$ such that $K^{t_1}(x) < s$ and $K^{t_2}(x) > s + n^{\epsilon}$, for all $t_2 = \mathsf{poly}(t_1)$, then worst-case hardness of this problem implies what is referred to as *errorless* average-case hardness (w.r.t. deterministic algorithm).[1] Unfortunately, to apply the result of [LP20], we require the more standard notion of *two-sided* error average-case hardness.

Recently, however, worst-case characterizations of OWF were also obtained [LP23a,HN23], considering some variants of the time-bounded Kolmogorov complexity problem. In particular, [LP23a] characterize OWFs through the problem of determining whether $K^t(x)$ is large or small, but restricting attention to instances $x$ with very large *unbounded* Kolmogorov complexity (i.e., $K(x) > n - O(\log n)$), or alternatively to strings $x$ whose so-called "computational depth", $cd^t(x) = K^t(x) - K(x) < O(\log n)$, is small (whereby "restricting attention" means that we consider worst-case hardness of a promise problem that only considers those instances; that is, any efficient algorithm must fail on one of those instances in the promise). [HN23], in turn, provide a worst-case characterization of a variant of OWFs, referred to as infinitely-often OWF through the problem of "estimating the probability that a random time-bounded program outputs a certain string" (which can be shown to be related to the notion of

---

[1] Roughly speaking, *errorless* average-case hardness refers to average-case hardness w.r.t. algorithms that either provide the right answer or $\perp$ (and $\perp$ should only be output with small probability). In other words, hardness holds w.r.t. algorithms that "know" when they fail. This is in contrast to the notion of *two-sided* error hardness where we allow the attacker to fail (without knowing it) on some small set of inputs.

probabilistic $K^t$), while restricting attention to instances satisfying an analog of small computational depth (with respect to this complexity notion).[2]

The unappealing aspect of the above characterizations is that once we add the "conditioning", it becomes less clear what the intuitive interpretation of the problems is. On a technical level, the property that we condition on (i.e., computational depth being small, or Kolmogorov complexity being large) is not *decidable.* While it is not hard to modify the condition to become decidable in exponential-time (by considering $K^{\mathsf{EXP}}$ instead of $K$), we still end up with a promise problem where the promise is outside of the polynomial hierarchy, so while "syntactically close" to the original $K^t$ problem, in terms of computational complexity, the problems appear very different.

**Our Results in a Nutshell: Boundary Hardness Characterizes OWFs.** Roughly speaking, the main result of this paper will be that under standard derandomization assumptions, it will suffice to condition on instances having "not too small" *time-bounded* Kolmogorov complexity (as opposed to them having high Kolmogorov complexity). Doing so enables us to obtain the following natural statement: under appropriate derandomization assumptions, worst-case hardness of the problem of deciding whether the time-bounded Kolmogorov complexity of a string $x$ is "very large" or "intermediate" implies, and in fact, characterizes OWFs. We will refer to this as the *boundary time-bounded Kolmogorov complexity problem.* Furthermore, the same characterization holds *unconditionally* once we consider $pK^t$ instead of $K^t$.

### 1.1 Statement of Results

To state our results more formally, let us first recall the standard $\mathsf{MINK}^{\mathsf{poly}}$ problem; the probabilistic version of the problem, $\mathsf{MINpK}^{\mathsf{poly}}$, is defined analogously (see Sect. 3.1). For any polynomials $t_1 < t_2$, let $\mathsf{MINK}^{t_1,t_2}$ denote the promise problem consisting of:

- YES: $x \in \{0,1\}^n$, $K^{t_1}(x) \leq n-2$.
- NO: $x \in \{0,1\}^n$, $K^{t_2}(x) \geq n-1$,

In essence, the goal is to distinguish between so-called *time-bounded Kolmogorov-random strings* (i.e., $x$ s.t. $K^t(x) \geq n-1$) and those that are not. We say that $\mathsf{MINK}^{\mathsf{poly}} \notin \mathsf{ioBPP}$ if for all polynomials $t_1, t_2$, $t_2(n) \geq t_1(n) \geq 2n$, $\mathsf{MINK}^{t_1,t_2} \notin \mathsf{ioBPP}$.[3]

[2] An alternative type of worst-case characterization of OWFs was also obtained in [HN23], where it is shown that OWFs exists iff $\mathsf{NP} \not\subseteq \mathsf{BPP}$ and a certain "distributional"-$K^t$ problem is $\mathsf{NP}$-complete w.r.t. a certain type of (restricted) reductions. Note that simply worst-case hardness of the distributional $K^t$ problem alone is not sufficient to get OWFs Rather the characterization is in terms both a hardness assumption ($\mathsf{NP} \not\subseteq \mathsf{BPP}$) combined with an feasibility assumption (the existence of a certain type of $\mathsf{NP}$-completeness reduction).

[3] Recall that $\mathsf{ioBPP}$ denotes the class of promise problems that admit a probabilistic polynomial time algorithm on infinitely many input lengths.

The *boundary* version (denoted by boundary-$\mathsf{MINK}^{t_1,t_2}$) is defined as the promise problem consisting of:

- YES: $x \in \{0,1\}^n$, $K^{t_1}(x) \leq n-2$ and $K^{t_2}(x) > n - \log n$.
- NO: $x \in \{0,1\}^n$, $K^{t_2}(x) \geq n-1$.

and boundary-$\mathsf{MINK}^{\mathsf{poly}}$ is analogously defined. In other words, the problem requires:

*Deciding whether a string $x$ is* **(a)** *time-bounded Kolmogorov random, or* **(b)** *just "near" time-bounded Kolmogorov random (i.e., having "intermediate" time-bounded Kolmogorov complexity.)*

Let Derand denote the following derandomization assumptions (which is a stronger version of commonly used derandomization assumption: there exists a constant $\varepsilon > 0$ such that $\mathsf{E} \not\subseteq \mathsf{ioNTIME}[2^{kn}]/2^{\varepsilon n}$ for every $k \in \mathbb{N}$. We are now ready to state our main theorem:

**Theorem 1.** *Assuming* Derand, *OWFs exist if and only if* boundary-$\mathsf{MINK}^{\mathsf{poly}} \notin$ ioBPP.

As a warm-up and stepping stone towards this result, we show an *unconditional* characterization of OWF through the worst-case hardness of boundary-$\mathsf{MINpK}^{\mathsf{poly}}$.

**Theorem 2.** *OWFs exist if and only if* boundary-$\mathsf{MINpK}^{\mathsf{poly}} \notin$ ioBPP.

**A Note on the Derandomization Assumption:** Let us provide some context for our new derandomization assumption. The most classic derandomization assumptions in the literature assert the existence of a function $f\colon \{0,1\}^n \to \{0,1\}$ computable in $2^{100n}$ time that cannot be computed by deterministic [IW97], or non-deterministic [KvM02,MV05,SU05], $2^{0.01n}$-time algorithms with $2^{0.01n}$ advice.[4] (Prior works on the coding theorem—as we shall discuss shortly, this will be a key building block for us—rely on the non-deterministic version (i.e., [GKLO22,LP23b]).)

Our Derand assumption is a natural *strengthening* of the assumption of [KvM02] where, in essence, we require for every $k$, the existence of a function running in time $2^{100kn}$ that is secure against attackers with running time $2^{0.01kn}$ (but still only $2^{0.01n}$ advice). In other words, we allow the attacker to run in time $> 2^n$, but the hard function can be computed in time $\gg 2^n$. (Note that, just as for [IW97,KvM02], for each $k$, there is a $\mathsf{poly}(n)2^{kn}$-time complete hard function.) As for intuition, Derand relies on exactly the same intuition as [IW97,KvM02]: non-determinism and short advice should not enable polynomial speed-up for computations (and this should hold equally for $2^n$ [IW97,KvM02] as $2^{kn}$ time (this paper) computations).

[4] There is nothing special about 100 and 0.01, they could be any constant; we just wrote 100 to make the assumption more concrete, and to enable easier comparing the assumptions with other ones.

As far as we know this assumption is new, but the idea of considering attackers with running time $> 2^n$ was recently introduced by Chen and Tell [CT21] where a quantitatively stronger version is used: for every $k \geq 1$, exist a function computable in time $2^{100kn}$ that cannot be computed by $2^{99kn}$-time algorithms with $2^{0.99n}$ advice (i.e., they consider an almost-optimal hardness version). On the other hand, [CT21] only make this assumption w.r.t. deterministic attackers, whereas we need it w.r.t. non-deterministic ones. [CT23] considers a non-deterministic version of [CT21], but theirs is again incomparable since they allow the function to be computable by a *non-deterministic* $2^{100kn}$ algorithm.

### 1.2 Is Hardness Along the Boundary WLOG?

A natural question is whether the boundary-$\mathsf{MINK}^{\mathsf{poly}}$ problem is equivalent to the $\mathsf{MINK}^{\mathsf{poly}}$ problem (which would resolve the above central question of whether worst-case hardness of $\mathsf{MINK}^{\mathsf{poly}}$ suffices to get OWFs, at least under derandomization assumption). Intuitively, instances on the "boundary" seem to be the hardest to deal with (exactly because they are on the boundary) so one would expect this to be the case. While we cannot prove this formally, we note that for most natural optimization problems, hardness along the boundary is equivalent to simply standard hardness.

For simplicity, consider $3SAT$: Is the "boundary-$3SAT$" problem easier than simply $3SAT$, where in boundary-$3SAT$ you only need to distinguish between (a) fully satisfiable instances, and (b) unsatisfiable instances where we are guaranteed that at least $n - \log n$ clauses can be satisfied (i.e., close to satisfiable clauses)? Indeed, as pointed out to us by Johan Håstad, the answer is no. To solve $3SAT$ using a boundary-$3SAT$ oracle, simply run the decider for the boundary problem; if it answers NO, output NO. Otherwise, iteratively replaces the last (non-dummy) clause with a dummy clause that always is true, and again query the boundary oracle. Note that if we are given a NO instance, this procedure will make sure that we eventually end up in the boundary region and the decider will output NO. And if we are given a YES-instance, the decider will always output YES.

More generally, the above approach works for any optimization problem where we can "smoothly" transform an instance $x$ into an instance $x'$ whose value will eventually increase, but never more than $O(1)$, or even just $O(\log n)$ in any one step. As far as we know, most natural optimization problems indeed satisfy this property and as such their worst-case hardness of their boundary versions is equivalent to worst-case hardness of their standard version.[5] Indeed, this even is the case for the boundary-$\mathsf{MINK}^{t_1,t_2}$ problem when restricting to the case that $t_1 = t_2$ (at least under appropriate derandomization assumptions). The reason for this is that we can smoothly increase the $K^t$-complexity of a string $x$ by replacing the last bit of it by a random string[6] and we will finally end up

[5] Most but not all: as pointed out to us by Per Austrin, this may not be the case for the *longest path problem.*

[6] Arguing that this does not *decrease* the $K^t$ complexity non-trivial and requires using a so-called a computational "weak" symmetry-of-information theorem [Ila23], which

with a string that is required to have $K^t$-complexity $n - O(\log n)$ (with high probability).

Unfortunately, this argument does not work when we allow $t_2 > t_1$ (as we require for our result). The issue is that there may be a gap between $K^{t_1}(x)$ and $K^{t_2}(x)$ so when we are gradually increasing $K^{t_2}(x)$ to end up in the promise (i.e., in the "boundary region"), we may have accidentally pushed $K^{t_1}(x)$ to become $\geq n-1$ and inadvertently transformed a YES-instance to a NO-instance!

Perhaps intriguingly, in the average-case characterization of OWF of [LP20] it actually suffices to require hardness of the $\mathsf{MINK}^{t_1,t_2}$ for the case that $t_1 = t_2$ (i.e., deciding whether $K^t(x)$ is small or large). In contrast, as we shall discuss in more detail later on, our analysis is non-black box in the attacker, and the parameter $t_2$ needs to be larger than the running-time of the attacker, which is why we require hardness w.r.t. any $t_2 = \mathsf{poly}(t_1)$; this is similar to the worst-case to errorless average-case reduction of Hirahara [Hir18].

## 1.3 Proof Overview

We proceed to a proof outline of our results. We focus on explaining how we obtain a OWF from the worst-case hardness of boundary-$\mathsf{MINK}^{\mathsf{poly}}$ (i.e., the "if"' direction of Theorem 1). The converse direction will follow mostly using the techniques from [LP23a], which passed through the notion of an "entropy-preserving PRG" constructed in [LP20] (and later improved in [LP23a]).

Towards this, it is instructive to briefly review the worst-case characterization of OWFs in [LP23a] (and how it is proved).

**Earlier Approaches and the Key Obstacle.** As mentioned in the introduction, [LP23a] obtained an initial worst-case characterization of OWFs: they showed that the worst-case hardness of distinguishing whether $K^t$ of an input $x \in \{0,1\}^n$ is at most $n-2$, given that the instance has *time unbounded* Kolmogorov complexity at least $n - \log n$, implies OWFs. (As mentioned before, a related result, relying on similar intuitions, is also proved by [HN23], but for our purposes, the approach in [LP23a] is more relevant.) Roughly speaking, the results of [LP23a] first rely on the result of [LP20] showing that average-case hardness of $\mathsf{MINK}^{\mathsf{poly}}$ implies the existence of OWFs. In more detail, [LP20] presents a reduction for solving $\mathsf{MINK}^{\mathsf{poly}}$ given a OWF inverter (for their specific OWF). [LP23a] showed that this reduction, in fact, also solves the worst-case problem on all instances with high *unbounded* Kolmogorov complexity. This follows from the simple observation that since the average-case reduction fails only with small probability on the uniform distribution, the strings on which it fails must have small (unbounded) Kolmogorov complexity, as they can be enumerated (so we can encode each such string as the index in the enumeration).

We plan to rely on exactly the same reduction. However, to make it work in our setting, we need to argue that if the reduction fails on some instance $x$, then the *time-bounded* Kolmogorov complexity of $x$ is small—in other words,

holds unconditionally for $pK^t$ and also for $K^t$ under appropriate derandomization assumptions [Ila23].

we require so-called *language compression with efficient decompression* [Sip83, GS85] [BLM00, BLM05, Hir21] for the set of instances $x$ on which the reduction fails. In fact, for our purposes, it will suffice to require an efficient decompression algorithm having access to a OWF inverter oracle (as our goal is to establish the existence of OWFs).

Unfortunately, it is an open problem to obtain language compression with efficient decompression for languages in $\mathsf{NP}$ (even relative to a OWF inverter). A step towards such language compression was recently taken by Hirahara et al. [HIL+23], which shows that a notion of "average-case language compression" can be achieved using a OWF inverter; this, notion, however, will not suffice for us—we require all-input compression.

**Our Approach: Language-Specific Instance Compression.** Rather than generically solving the language compression problem, we will show that for the *specific* language of interest to us (i.e., the set of strings for which the decider fails), we can obtain a short representation of all instances, that can be efficiently decompressed (i.e., their $K^{\mathsf{poly}}$-complexity) is (relatively) small—in more details $K^{\mathsf{poly}}(x) < n - \log n$. This will suffice to show that if the decider fails on some instance $x$, then $K^{\mathsf{poly}}(x) < n - \log n$, so the instance is not part of the promise of the boundary problem.

On a high-level, we prove the above through the following two steps:

- **Step 1:** Showing that elements on which the decider fails can be sampled with probability $\geq n^c/2^n$ for any $c$, by an algorithm running in time $T = \mathsf{poly}(n^c)$.
- **Step 2:** Relying on/Proving a so-called "Coding Theorem"' [LOZ22] bounding the $K^t$ (or $pK^t$) complexity of an element by, roughly, the *logarithm* of the inverse of the probability by which it can be sampled.

Taken together, we get that elements on which the decider fails must have $K^{\mathsf{poly}}$-complexity (resp. $pK^{\mathsf{poly}}$-complexity) at most (roughly) $\log(2^n/n^c) = n - c\log n$.

To prove Theorem 2 (i.e., the characterization in terms of $pK^{\mathsf{poly}}$), it will suffice to demonstrate Step 2 w.r.t. $pK^{\mathsf{poly}}$, and such a Coding Theorem is already known [LOZ22, San23]. (And as such, the result on $pK^{\mathsf{poly}}$ can be viewed as a warm-up case for our result for $K^{\mathsf{poly}}$). In fact, [LOZ22, GKLO22] also provide a Coding Theorem for $K^{\mathsf{poly}}$ based on derandomization assumptions, but this Coding Theorem loses $O(\log T)$ in the bound where $T$ is the running time of the sampler, and consequently combined with Step 1 we do not get any non-trivial compressions. As an independent technical contribution, we show how to get a tight Coding Theorem for $K^{\mathsf{poly}}$ based on a derandomization assumption; we note, however, that the derandomization assumption that we rely on is a stronger than the one used in [LOZ22, GKLO22] (to prove the non-tight Coding Theorem), but of a similar spirit.

We proceed to provide a more detailed outline of Steps 1 and 2.

**Step 1:** Recall that our goal is to show that elements on which the [LP20] decider fails can be sampled with probability $\geq n^c/2^n$ for any $c$, by an algorithm running in time $T = \mathsf{poly}(n^c)$. Towards showing this, we proceed in two steps, letting $\mathsf{bad}$, denote the set of instances on which the reductions from [LP20] fail.

- **Hitting $\mathsf{bad}$ through** [LP20] **Sampling:** In the first step, we show that by the [LP20] construction/reduction, it follows that there exists an efficient way to sample instances in $L$. Roughly speaking, the OWF construction samples strings $x$ together with their $K^t$ witness; furthermore, for those instances $x$ we can check whether the reduction fails (since the reduction actually provides a witness when it succeeds).
  Additionally, the one-way function distribution is point-wise multiplicatively close to the uniform distribution (i.e., it dominates the uniform distribution) so each $x \in \{0,1\}^n$ is sampled with probability at least $2^{-n}/O(n)$ by the OWF construction. More precisely,
  - Each string $x \in \{0,1\}^n$ is sampled with probability at least $\frac{1}{O(n)} \cdot 2^{-n}$.
  - The reduction fails (on instance $x$) only when the inverter fails to invert the [LP20] OWF on $x$ (which thus is efficiently checkable). Consequently, the probability we sample an element on which the reduction fails is $\epsilon$, where $\epsilon$ is the failure probability of the OWF inverter.

  It is important to note here that by Yao's hardness amplification theorem [Yao82] (already employed in [LP20]), $\epsilon$ can be made into an arbitrarily small polynomial—this point will be crucial to us shortly.
  As a consequence of the above two points, we have that the OWF sampler in this first step samples elements in $\mathsf{bad}$ with probability at least $2^{-n}/O(n)$, but the total weight of those elements is $\epsilon$.
- **Boosting the Probabilities through Rejection Sampling:** In the second step, we show how to "boost" the probability of elements in $\mathsf{bad}$. The idea is simple: As the algorithm in step 1 enables checking whether the reduction failed (simply to find the appropriate length $K^t$ witness), we can just repeatedly run the sampler until we find an element on which the reduction fails. Since the total weight of elements in $\mathsf{bad}$ is $\epsilon$, we have that sampling conditioned on ending up in $\mathsf{bad}$, the probability of each element in bad is $2^{-n}/O(n) \times 1/\epsilon$, which can be lowerbounded by $n^c/2^n$ for any choice of $c$ by choosing an appropriately small $\epsilon$ (which as mentioned above can be achieved by using Yao's hardness amplification [Yao82]). Of course the issue is that this sampler only runs in expected polynomial time and not strict polynomial time, but by appropriately cutting off its running time we can make sure to not lose too much in the probabilities (essentially by a union bound).

This concludes the argument that elements on which the decider fails can be sampled with high probability.

**Step 2: An Improved Coding Theorem for $K^{\mathsf{poly}}$.** We turn to discussing how all such element (i.e., those on which the decider fails, and consequently by Step 1, that can be sampled with high probability) can be compressed into $n - \log n$ bits (with efficient decompression). As previously discussed, towards this, we will rely on a so-called Coding Theorem. As mentioned above, to prove Theorem 2 (i.e., to upperbound $pK^{\mathsf{poly}}$), we can directly combine Step 1 with the known Coding Theorem of [LOZ22,San23], that shows exactly the desired *probabilistic* compression for elements sampled with high probability.

**Theorem 3.** **(Coding Theorem for $pK^{\mathsf{poly}}$ [LOZ22, San23])** *There exists a (universal) constant $d$ such that for any (efficiently) samplable distribution ensemble $\mathcal{D} = \{\mathcal{D}_n\}_{n\in\mathbb{N}}$, there exists a polynomial $t(n)$ such that for all sufficiently large $n \in \mathbb{N}$, all $x \in \mathsf{supp}(\mathcal{D}_n)$,*

$$pK^t(x) \leq \lceil \log 1/p_x \rceil + d \log n$$

*where $p_x = \Pr[\mathcal{D}_n = x]$.*

Additionally, as mentioned, [LOZ22, GKLO22] also provide a Coding Theorem for $K^{\mathsf{poly}}$ based on derandomization assumptions, but this Coding Theorem loses $O(\log T)$ in the bound where $T$ is the running time of the sampler; this Coding Theorem will not suffice for us (since whatever gain we get from Step 1 in terms of sampling probability, gets "eaten up" by the overhead in running-time due to the rejection sampling condition on the event $\mathsf{bad}$).

As an independent technical contribution (which we hope may be of independent interest), we show how to get a tight Coding Theorem for $K^t$ based on $\mathsf{Derand}$:

**Theorem 4.** **((Improved) Coding Theorem for $K^{\mathsf{poly}}$)** *Assuming* $\mathsf{Derand}$, *there exists a (universal) constant $d$ such that for any (efficiently) samplable distribution ensemble $\mathcal{D} = \{\mathcal{D}_n\}_{n\in\mathbb{N}}$, there exists a polynomial $t(n)$ such that for all sufficiently large $n \in \mathbb{N}$, all $x \in \mathsf{supp}(\mathcal{D}_n)$,*

$$K^t(x) \leq \lceil \log 1/p_x \rceil + d \log n$$

*where $p_x = \Pr[\mathcal{D}_n = x]$.*

We emphasize that compared to the existing Coding Theorem [LOZ22, GKLO22], the above theorem only has a logarithmic overhead in terms of $n$, whereas in the earlier Coding Theorem, the compression overhead is logarithmic in the runtime of the distribution $\mathcal{D}$. (On the other hand, as mentioned, we are using a slightly stronger derandomization assumption).

Towards proving Theorem 4, we will rely on the same approach as [LOZ22]; we rely on the Coding Theorem for $pK^{\mathsf{poly}}$ (i.e., Theorem 3 above), and next show that, under derandomization assumptions, $K^{\mathsf{poly}}$ is no more than $pK^{\mathsf{poly}}$ with an additive logarithmic term. Our contribution will be showing a tighter derandomization result (i.e. a tighter correspondence between $K^{\mathsf{poly}}$ and $pK^{\mathsf{poly}}$) under a stronger derandomization assumption. We now proceed to show how this is done.

Recall that for any polynomial $t$, any $x \in \{0,1\}^*$, $pK^t(x)$ is defined to be the smallest $\omega$ such that for a $2/3$ fraction of the choice of a random string $r \in \{0,1\}^{t(n)}$, there exists a program $M$ of length $\leq \omega$ that produces $x$ given $r$ within time $t(n)$. In order to "derandomize" $pK^{\mathsf{poly}}$ into $K^{\mathsf{poly}}$, it suffices to find a succinct description to any such string $r$, which together with the program $M$ (that exists for $r$) produces a $K^{\mathsf{poly}}$-witness for $x$. As observed by [GKLO22], we can obtain such a succinct description of $r$ by relying on a (complexity-theoretic) PRG (with a small seed length) that fools the following non-deterministic circuit

$C_{x,\omega}$: $C_{x,\omega}$ takes a random-tape $r \in \{0,1\}^{t(n)}$ as input, guesses a program $M$ of size $\omega$, outputs 1 if $M(r)$ generates $x$ within $t(n)$ steps (and 0 otherwise).[7] We can use a seed of the PRG (that leads $C_{x,\omega}$ to output 1) as the succinct description we need (and thus the seed itself will be our overhead).

Following the *Hardness vs. Randomness paradigm* [NW94], there has been an elegant line of research [KvM02, MV05, SU05] on constructing such PRGs (in particular, those that enable the derandomization of $\mathsf{AM}$ to $\mathsf{NP}$). These constructions, however, have seed length that is at least $O(\log t(n))$ when derandomizing circuits of input size $t(n)$ (which is the case for $C_{x,\omega}$). This causes an overhead of $O(\log t(n))$ (as opposed to $d \log n$ for a universal constant $d$), and indeed, this is why the Coding Theorem of [LOZ22, GKLO22] loses a term of $O(\log t(n))$. We overcome this issue by constructing a new PRG with *near-optimal seed length* (which also may be of independent interest).

**(Non-Black-Box) PRGs with Near-Optimal Seed Length.** Thus, the question is whether we can improve the seed length in these PRG constructions from $O(\log t(n))$ to $d \log n$. Unfortunately, as noted in [SU05], constructions following the standard Hardness vs. Randomness paradigm cannot have a seed length of $o(\log t(n))$! (Roughly speaking, any "black-box" PRG construction from a hard function can be viewed as an extractor [Tre01] and the above bound follows from bounds on the seed length of extractors [NZ96, RTS00].)

This barrier was very recently broken using a non-black-box approach in the work of Chen and Tell [CT21], and is closely related to the question of whether "super-efficient derandomization" [DMOZ22] is possible, but their work relies on the existence of OWF and thus is of little help to us.[8]

We here present an alternative approach to overcome this barrier without the use of OWFs. While the seed-length of our PRG will be small, its running-time will still be large, so it will not solve the question of whether super-efficient derandomization is possible without OWFs, but it will suffice for our purposes of derandomizing $pK^{\mathsf{poly}}$.

We proceed to explain our approach. Towards this, let us first recall the standard NW paradigm [NW94]: It provides a PRG construction $G$ that transforms a hard-to-compute function $f \in \{0,1\}^{\ell}$ (i.e., the truth table of a hard function) into a PRG with output length $m$. The security reduction shows how to use any attacker distinguishing $G^f$ from random to compute $f$ using $\mathsf{poly}(m)$ bits of (non-uniform) advice.

To get a PRG with small seed length, our idea is to compose two NW-style PRGs: $G(\cdot) = G_1(G_2(\cdot))$ where $G_2 : \{0,1\}^{c_1 \cdot \log n} \to \{0,1\}^{c_2 \cdot \log t(n)}$, $G_1 : \{0,1\}^{c_2 \cdot \log t(n)} \to \{0,1\}^{t(n)}$ (where $c_1$ and $c_2$ are universal constants independent of $t$). (In other words, use one PRG to expand the seed from $O(\log n)$ to $O(\log t(n))$, and next use another PRG on top of this "large" seed.) The key observation is that while the security reduction of the outer PRG $G_1$ requires

[7] We remark that $C_{x,\omega}$ has input length $t(n)$ because the "probabilistic" program $M$ runs in time $t(n)$ and can use up to $t(n)$ bits of randomness.

[8] Roughly speaking, a PRG with a small seed enables small simulation overhead when performing derandomization since we have less seed that we need to go over.

$\Omega(t(n))$ bits of advice, the advice will *not* appear in the security game for the inner PRG $G_2$; in fact, as we shall see, $G_2$ only needs to handle attackers with $n + O(\log n)$ bits of advice (as opposed to $t(n)$).

To see why this is the case, note that to prove that $G$ is secure in the eyes of $C_{x,\omega}$, we proceed by a hybrid argument showing that (a) $G_1(\mathcal{U}_{c_2 \log t(n)})$ and $\mathcal{U}_{t(n)}$ are indistinguishable in the eyes of $C_{x,\omega}(\cdot)$; and that (b) $G_2(\mathcal{U}_{c_1 \log n})$ and $\mathcal{U}_{c_2 \log t(n)}$ are indistinguishable in the eyes of $C_{x,\omega}(G_1(\cdot))$. The existence of $G_1$ satisfying (a) follows from the standard Hardness vs. Randomness paradigm (under standard derandomization assumptions, and in particular those implied by $\mathsf{Derand}$) since the seed of $G_1$ is long enough. On the other hand, in (b), $G_2$ only needs to fool $C_{x,\omega}(G_1(\cdot))$, which has advice size $|x| + |\omega| \leq n + \log n$ and input length $c_2 \log t(n)$; so the seed length only needs to depend logarithmically on $n$ and $\log t(n)$ (which is tiny). The problem, however, is that the runtime of $G_1$ does contribute to the runtime of the attacker in the security game for $G_2$ (which leads to an attacker that runs in time polynomial in $t(n)$). This means that the hard function employed in $G_2$, denoted by $f$, needs to be hard against algorithms with advice size $O(n, \mathsf{poly}\log t(n))$, but *running time* $\mathsf{poly}(t(n))$, which follows from our derandomization assumption $\mathsf{Derand}$.[9]

**A Note on the Non-black-box Nature of the Proof:** Let us emphasize that the above use of the Coding Theorem makes our security analysis non-black-box in the attacker, and furthermore only works if the attacker is a *uniform* probabilistic polynomial-time algorithm. In more detail, to apply the Coding Theorem (to compress the inputs $x$ on which the decider fails), we require the input $x$ to be samplable in *uniform* polynomial time; as we described above in Step 1, this is shown by applying rejection sampling on the attacker, so if the attacker is non-uniform then we can only sample from the distribution in non-uniform polynomial time and we can no longer apply Step 2.

### 1.4 Overview of the Paper

In Sect. 2, we recall some standard definitions; Sect. 3 contains the formalization of problems we consider and the statement of our main results. Section 4 considers Coding Theorems and additionally abstracts out a more general version of them (including the above rejection sampling step). Section 5 proves the forward direction of the main theorems, and Sect. 6 proves the backward direction. Finally, in Sect. 7 we prove the new tighter correspondence between $pK^t$ and $K^t$ (which is used in Sect. 4); this section also includes the construction of our near-optimal seed-length PRG.

---

[9] In the literature, a padding trick is typically used to resolve this type of issues (i.e., running $f$ on a larger input length), but this will blow up the seed length by too much for us. To overcome this issue, we here instead rely on a stronger hardness assumption (namely, $\mathsf{Derand}$), in which we decouple the advice size of the attacker from its running time; that is, we assume that there exists $\varepsilon > 0$ such that $\mathsf{E} \not\subseteq \mathsf{ioNTIME}[2^{kn}]/2^{\varepsilon n}$ for *every* $k$.

### 1.5 Open Problems

We briefly note a few open problems.

- **Dealing with non-uniform attackers:** As mentioned above, our results only characterize OWFs secure w.r.t. uniform (i.e., PPT) attackers. While typically security w.r.t. uniform attackers directly yield security w.r.t. non-uniform attacker (one we make non-uniform security assumptions), this does not follow in our setting since our proof is non-black-box in the attacker. We leave open the question of finding a natural problem characterizing OWFs secure also w.r.t. non-uniform PPT attacker. (We note that the problem in [LP23a] works in both the uniform and the non-uniform setting).
- **Basing Security on a Search Problem:** We note that in the average-case setting, the construction of [LP20] can also be based on average-case hardness of the *search* version of $K^t$ complexity problem. Our reduction can also be modified to provide a witness for YES-instances inside the promise (i.e., $K^t$ is "intermediate"), but when $K^t$ is "small" we may no longer efficiently find the witness (we just prove that one exists); if one could prove a Coding Theorem that also enables to efficiently perform the compression (as opposed to just guaranteeing that it exists), then this issue would be resolved and one would have based security on the general (i.e., non-boundary) version of the $K^t$ problem (i.e., $\mathsf{MK}^t\mathsf{P}$).
- **Improving the "width" of the boundary:** Our notion of a boundary problem considers a boundary of width $O(\log n)$. We note that if the width would be improved to $O(n/\log n)$, that would yield a construction of OWFs starting from the worst-case hardness of the standard $\mathsf{MK}^t\mathsf{P}$ problem w.r.t. adversaries running in time $2^{O(n/\log n)}$ (and $t = 2^{O(n/\log n)}$) (i.e., assuming the uniform Perebor conjecture).
- **Relativization barriers:** We mention that while our proof is non-black-box in terms of the attacker, the analysis relativizes and therefore is subject to the barriers in [Imp11, HN22a, HN22b]. We leave open the problem of developing non-relativizing techniques that can go beyond that barrier.

## 2 Preliminaries

For any circuit $C : \{0,1\}^m \to \{0,1\}^n$, we abuse the notation to let $C$ also denote the random variable $C(\mathcal{U}_m)$.

### 2.1 One-Way Functions

We recall the definition of one-way functions [DH76]. Roughly speaking, a function $f$ is one-way if it is polynomial-time computable, but hard to invert for $\mathsf{PPT}$ attackers.

**Definition 5.** *Let $f : \{0,1\}^* \to \{0,1\}^*$ be a polynomial-time computable function. $f$ is said to be a* one-way function (OWF) *if for every* PPT *algorithm $\mathcal{A}$, there exists a negligible function $\mu$ such that for all $n \in \mathbb{N}$,*

$$\Pr[x \leftarrow \{0,1\}^n; y = f(x) : \mathcal{A}(1^n, y) \in f^{-1}(f(x))] \leq \mu(n)$$

We may also consider a weaker notion of a *weak one-way function* [Yao82], where we only require all PPT attackers to fail with probability noticeably bounded away from 1:

**Definition 6.** *Let $f : \{0,1\}^* \to \{0,1\}^*$ be a polynomial-time computable function. $f$ is said to be an* $\alpha$-weak one-way function ($\alpha$-weak OWF) *if for every* PPT *algorithm $\mathcal{A}$, for all sufficiently large $n \in N$,*

$$\Pr[x \leftarrow \{0,1\}^n; y = f(x) : \mathcal{A}(1^n, y) \in f^{-1}(f(x))] < 1 - \alpha(n)$$

*We say that $f$ is simply a* weak one-way function (weak OWF) *if there exists some polynomial $q > 0$ such that $f$ is a $\frac{1}{q(\cdot)}$-weak OWF.*

Yao's hardness amplification theorem [Yao82] shows that any weak OWF can be turned into a (strong) OWF.

**Theorem 7.** ([Yao82]) *Assume there exists a weak one-way function. Then there exists a one-way function.*

### 2.2 Time-Bounded Kolmogorov Complexity

We introduce the notion of time-bounded conditional Kolmogorov complexity. Roughly speaking, the *t-time-bounded Kolmogorov complexity*, $K^t(x \mid z)$, of a string $x \in \{0,1\}^*$ conditioned on a string $z \in \{0,1\}^*$ is the length of the shortest program $\Pi = (M, y)$ such that $\Pi(z)$ outputs $x$ in $t(|x|)$ steps.

Formally, fix some universal RAM machine $U$ (with only polynomial overhead), and let $t(\cdot)$ be a running time bound. For any string $x, z \in \{0,1\}^*$, we define

$$K^t(x \mid z) = \min\{w \in \mathbb{N} \mid \exists \Pi \in \{0,1\}^w, U(\Pi(z), 1^{t(|x|)}) = x\}$$

When $z$ is an empty string, we simply denote the quantity by $K^t(x)$. We consider RAM machines (as in [LP22b, GKLO22]) since it allows $z$ to be as long as the running time of the machine $\Pi$ (or even longer).

Very recently, Goldberg et al. [GKLO22] introduced a probabilistic variant of time-bounded Kolmogorov complexity, denoted as $pK^t$. Let us recall the notion here. Roughly speaking, in the probabilistic version, the program is allowed to be picked after a uniform random string. And a string will have small $pK^t$-complexity if a short program exists over a large fraction of random strings. We proceed to the formal definition. Let $\delta(n)$ be a probability threshold function.

For any string $x \in \{0,1\}^*$, the $\delta$-probabilistic $t$-bounded Kolmogorov complexity of $x$ [GKLO22], $pK^t_\delta(x)$, is defined to be

$$pK^t_\delta(x) = \min\{w \in \mathbb{N} \mid \Pr[r \leftarrow \{0,1\}^{t(|x|)} : K^t(x \mid r) \leq w] \geq \delta(n)\}$$

The constant $\delta$ will be usually considered as being 2/3. We omit the subscript $\delta$ if $\delta = 2/3$.

We refer the reader to Sect. 3.1 for the definitions of computational problems involving $K^{\mathsf{poly}}$ and $pK^{\mathsf{poly}}$ we needed in this work.

### 2.3 Distributions, Random Variables, and Entropy

Let $\mathcal{D}$ be a distribution. We let $\mathsf{supp}(\mathcal{D})$ denote the support of $\mathcal{D}$. We say that $\mathcal{D} = \{\mathcal{D}_n\}_{n\in\mathbb{N}}$ is an *ensemble* if for all $n \in \mathbb{N}$, $D_n$ is a probability distribution over $\{0,1\}^n$. We say that an ensemble $\mathcal{D} = \{D_n\}_{n\in\mathbb{N}}$ is (efficiently) *samplable* if there exists a probabilistic polynomial-time Turing machine $S$ such that $S(1^n)$ samples $D_n$.

For any two random variables $X$ and $Y$ defined over some set $\mathcal{V}$, we let $\mathsf{SD}(X,Y) = \frac{1}{2}\sum_{v\in\mathcal{V}} |\Pr[X = v] - \Pr[Y = v]|$ denote the *statistical distance* between $X$ and $Y$.

For a random variable $X$, let $H(X) = \mathsf{E}[\log \frac{1}{\Pr[X=x]}]$ denote the (Shannon) entropy of $X$, and let $H_\infty(X) = \min_{x\in\mathsf{Supp}(X)} \log \frac{1}{\Pr[X=x]}$ denote the *min-entropy* of $X$.

The following lemma/fact will be useful for us.

**Lemma 8.** ([LP23a, **Lemma 2.6**]) *Let $X$ be a random variable distributed over $S \subseteq \{0,1\}^n$, $E$ be an set $\subseteq S$. It holds that*

$$\Pr[x \leftarrow X : x \in E] \leq \frac{\log|S| + 1 - H(X)}{\log|S| - \log|E|}$$

## 3 Main Results

Before presenting the main results in this work, let us formally define the computational problems needed in our results.

### 3.1 Problem Definitions

**The $K^{\mathsf{poly}}$ Problem and Its Boundary Version.** For any polynomials $t_1, t_2$, $t_1(n) \leq t_2(n)$, define the time-bounded Kolmogorov complexity problem (denoted by $\mathsf{MINK}^{t_1,t_2}$) as the promise problem consisting of

- $\mathsf{YES}$: strings $x \in \{0,1\}^n$, $K^{t_1}(x) \leq n-2$.
- $\mathsf{NO}$: strings $x \in \{0,1\}^n$, $K^{t_2}(x) \geq n-1$.

In addition, we can define its boundary version (denoted by $\mathsf{boundary}\text{-}\mathsf{MINK}^{t_1,t_2}$) as

- YES: strings $x \in \{0,1\}^n$, $K^{t_1}(x) \leq n-2$ and $K^{t_2}(x) > n - \log n$.
- NO: strings $x \in \{0,1\}^n$, $K^{t_2}(x) \geq n-1$.

**$pK^{\mathsf{poly}}$ Problem and Its Boundary Version.** For any polynomials $t_1, t_2$, $t_1(n) \leq t_2(n)$, and a parameter $\delta(n) > 0$, define the time-bounded probabilistic Kolmogorov complexity problem (denoted by $\mathsf{MINpK}_\delta^{t_1,t_2}$) as the promise problem consisting of

- YES: strings $x \in \{0,1\}^n$, $pK_\delta^{t_1}(x) \leq n - \lceil \log(1/(1-\delta)) \rceil - 2$.
- NO: strings $x \in \{0,1\}^n$, $pK_{1-\delta}^{t_2}(x) \geq n - \lceil \log(1/(1-\delta)) \rceil - 1$.

We remark that the threshold (compared with the threshold in $\mathsf{MINK}^{t_1,t_2}$) is shifted from $n-2$ to $n - \lceil \log(1/(1-\delta)) \rceil - 2$ to ensure that the NO instance set is not empty.

Analogously, we can also define the boundary version (denoted by $\mathsf{boundary\text{-}MINpK}_\delta^{t_1,t_2}$) as

- YES: strings $x \in \{0,1\}^n$, $pK_\delta^{t_1}(x) \leq n - \lceil \log(1/(1-\delta)) \rceil - 2$ and $pK_{1-\delta}^{t_2}(x) > n - \log n$.
- NO: strings $x \in \{0,1\}^n$, $pK_{1-\delta}^{t_2}(x) \geq n - \lceil \log(1/(1-\delta)) \rceil - 1$.

We will consider $\delta = \frac{2}{3}$ and simply denote $\mathsf{MINpK}_\delta^{t_1,t_2}$ (resp $\mathsf{boundary\text{-}MINpK}_\delta^{t_1,t_2}$) by $\mathsf{MINpK}^{t_1,t_2}$ (resp $\mathsf{boundary\text{-}MINpK}^{t_1,t_2}$) where $\delta = \frac{2}{3}$.

Finally, for $K^{\mathsf{poly}}$ (resp $pK^{\mathsf{poly}}$), we say that $\mathsf{MINK}^{\mathsf{poly}} \notin \mathsf{ioBPP}$ (resp $\mathsf{MINpK}^{\mathsf{poly}} \notin \mathsf{ioBPP}$) if for all polynomials $t_1, t_2$, $t_2(n) \geq t_1(n) \geq 2n$, $\mathsf{MINK}^{t_1,t_2} \notin \mathsf{ioBPP}$ (resp $\mathsf{MINpK}^{t_1,t_2} \notin \mathsf{ioBPP}$).

## 3.2 Main Theorems

We are ready to describe the main results in this work. Our first (and warm-up) result shows that the existence of OWFs is equivalent to the worst-case hardness of the boundary version of $\mathsf{MINpK}^{\mathsf{poly}}$.

**Theorem 9.** *OWFs exist if and only if* $\mathsf{boundary\text{-}MINpK}^{\mathsf{poly}} \notin \mathsf{ioBPP}$.

**Proof:** The theorem follows from (the first bullet of) Theorem 16 (which proves the "if" direction), and Theorem 21 and Lemma 23 (that together prove the "only if" direction). ∎

Our main result extends this theorem to obtain a characterization of OWFs based on the worst-case hardness of the boundary version of $\mathsf{MINK}^{\mathsf{poly}}$; this time, however, we will rely on a standard derandomization assumption.

**Theorem 10.** *Assume that there exists a constant $\varepsilon > 0$ such that $\mathsf{E} \not\subseteq \mathsf{ioNTIME}[2^{kn}]/2^{\varepsilon n}$ for every $k \in \mathbb{N}$. Then, OWFs exist if and only if* $\mathsf{boundary\text{-}MINK}^{\mathsf{poly}} \notin \mathsf{ioBPP}$.

**Proof:** The equivalence follows from (the second bullet of) Theorem 16 (which proves the "if" direction), and Theorem 21 and Lemma 22 (that together prove the "only if" direction). ∎

## 4 Source Coding Theorems

In this section, we start by recall the Time-Bounded Coding Theorem for $pK^t$ of [LOZ22] (which in turn is an efficient version of the classic Coding Theorem for unbounded Kolmogorov Complexity). We next present a useful rejection sampling lemma which may be viewed as a generalization of the Coding Theorem.

Finally, we show how to use appropriate PRGs (constructed in Sect. 7) to also establish a tight Coding Theorem for $K^t$, and also establish the generalized version. We start by reviewing the Coding Theorem for $pK^{\mathsf{poly}}$, introduced in [LOZ22].[10]

**Theorem 11 (Source Coding Theorem for $pK^{\mathsf{poly}}$ [LOZ22,San23].)** *For any (efficiently) samplable distribution ensemble $\mathcal{D} = \{\mathcal{D}_n\}_{n\in\mathbb{N}}$, there exists a polynomial $t(n)$ such that for all sufficiently large $n \in \mathbb{N}$, all $x \in \mathsf{supp}(\mathcal{D}_n)$,*

$$pK^t(x) \leq \log 1/p_x + 4\log n$$

*where $p_x = \Pr[\mathcal{D}_n = x]$.*

We turn to proving the following generalized version of the Coding Theorem obtained by relying on rejection sampling.

**Lemma 12.** *For any samplable distribution ensemble $\mathcal{D} = \{\mathcal{D}_n\}_{n\in\mathbb{N}}$, any polynomial $q(n)$, there exists a polynomial $t(n)$ such that for any sufficiently large $n \in \mathbb{N}$, if*

$$\Pr[\mathcal{D}_n = \bot] \geq 1 - \frac{1}{q(n)}$$

*then, for every $x \in \mathsf{supp}(\mathcal{D}_n)$ such that $x \neq \bot$, it holds that*

$$pK^t(x) \leq \log 1/p_x - \log(q(n)/4) + 4\log n$$

*where $p_x = \Pr[\mathcal{D}_n = x]$.*

**Proof:** Consider the distribution ensemble $\mathcal{D}' = \{\mathcal{D}'_n\}_{n\in\mathbb{N}}$ sampled by the following algorithm. For each $n \in \mathbb{N}$, $\mathcal{D}'_n$ draws $q(n)/2$ i.i.d. samples $x_1, \ldots, x_{q(n)/2}$ from $\mathcal{D}_n$. $\mathcal{D}'_n$ simply output $x_i$ with the smallest index $i$ for which $x_i \neq \bot$. If all of $x_i$ are $\bot$, $\mathcal{D}'_n$ outputs $\bot$.

We claim that for all sufficiently large $n$ satisfying

$$\Pr[x \leftarrow \mathcal{D}_n : \mathcal{D}_n \neq \bot] \leq \frac{1}{q(n)}$$

and for any $x \in \mathsf{supp}(\mathcal{D}_n)$, $x \neq \bot$, it holds that

$$p'_x \geq p_x \cdot q(n)/4$$

[10] The original statement of this coding theorem has a slightly worse bound but the proof actually proved this stronger statement. This was observed in [San23].

where $p'_x = \Pr[\mathcal{D}'_n = x]$ and $p_x = \Pr[\mathcal{D}_n = x]$. Let $\delta$ denote the probability that $\mathcal{D}_n$ does not output $\perp$. Recall that due to our assumption, $\delta \leq \frac{1}{q(n)}$. It follows from our construction of $\mathcal{D}'_n$ that

$$\begin{aligned} p'_x &= \sum_{i=1}^{q(n)/2} \Pr_{x_1,\ldots,x_{i-1}\leftarrow\mathcal{D}_n}[x_1 = \perp \wedge \ldots \wedge x_{i-1} = \perp] \cdot \Pr_{x_i\leftarrow\mathcal{D}_n}[x_i = x] \\ &= \sum_{i=1}^{q(n)/2} (1-\delta)^{i-1} \cdot p_x \\ &\geq \sum_{i=1}^{q(n)/2} (1-\delta)^{q(n)/2} \cdot p_x \\ &\geq q(n)/2 \cdot (1 - q(n)\delta/2) \cdot p_x \\ &\geq p_x \cdot q(n)/4 \end{aligned}$$

Finally, notice that the distribution ensemble $\mathcal{D}'$ is efficiently samplable if the ensemble $\mathcal{D}$ is. Thus, by applying Theorem 11 to the distribution $D'$ (and letting $t$ be the polynomial guaranteed to exist by Theorem 11), it follows that

$$\begin{aligned} pK^t(x) &\leq \log 1/p'_x + 4\log n \\ &\leq \log 1/p_x - \log(q(n)/4) + 4\log n \end{aligned}$$

which concludes our proof. ■

We next show how to extend the above to also apply to $K^t$. We do this by relying on the following tighter connection between $pK^t$ and $K^t$, the proof of which is postponed to Sect. 7:

**Lemma 13. (Derandomizing $pK^{\mathsf{poly}}$).** *Assume that there exists a constant $\varepsilon > 0$ such that $\mathsf{E} \not\subseteq \mathsf{ioNTIME}[2^{kn}]/2^{\varepsilon n}$ for every $k \in \mathbb{N}$. There exists a constant $d$ such that the following holds. For every polynomial $t$, there exists a polynomial $t'$ such that for every sufficiently long $x \in \{0,1\}^*$,*

$$K^{t'}(x) \leq pK^t(x) + d\log|x|$$

Armed with this wemma, we show that Theorem 11 and Lemma 12 also hold for $K^{\mathsf{poly}}$ under the assumption $\mathsf{Derand}$.

**Theorem 14. (Source Coding Theorem for $K^{\mathsf{poly}}$).** *Assume that there exists a constant $\varepsilon > 0$ such that $\mathsf{E} \not\subseteq \mathsf{ioNTIME}[2^{kn}]/2^{\varepsilon n}$ for every $k \in \mathbb{N}$. There exists a constant $d$ such that the following holds.*

*For any (efficiently) sampleable distribution ensemble $\mathcal{D} = \{\mathcal{D}_n\}_{n\in\mathbb{N}}$, there exists a polynomial $t(n)$ such that for all sufficiently large $n \in \mathbb{N}$, all $x \in \mathsf{supp}(\mathcal{D}_n)$,*

$$K^t(x) \leq \log 1/p_x + (d+4)\log n$$

*where $p_x = \Pr[\mathcal{D}_n = x]$.*

**Proof:** This Theorem directly follows from Lemma 13 and Theorem 11. ■

**Lemma 15.** *Assume that there exists a constant* $\varepsilon > 0$ *such that* $\mathsf{E} \not\subseteq \mathsf{ioNTIME}[2^{kn}]/2^{\varepsilon n}$ *for every* $k \in \mathbb{N}$. *There exists a constant* $d$ *such that the following holds.*

*For any samplable distribution ensemble* $\mathcal{D} = \{\mathcal{D}_n\}_{n\in\mathbb{N}}$, *any polynomial* $q(n)$, *there exists a polynomial* $t(n)$ *such that for any sufficiently large* $n \in \mathbb{N}$, *if*

$$\Pr[\mathcal{D}_n = \bot] \geq 1 - \frac{1}{q(n)}$$

*then, for every* $x \in \mathsf{supp}(\mathcal{D}_n)$ *such that* $x \neq \bot$, *it holds that*

$$K^t(x) \leq \log 1/p_x - \log(q(n)/4) + (d+4)\log n$$

*where* $p_x = \Pr[\mathcal{D}_n = x]$.

**Proof:** This Lemma follows from the proof of Lemma 12 by replacing the use of Theorem 11 by Theorem 14. ■

## 5 OWFs from Hardness of boundary-MINpK$^{\mathsf{poly}}$

We turn to proving the forward direction of our main theorems.

**Theorem 16.** *The following statements hold:*

- *If for all polynomials* $t_1, t_2$, $t_1(n) \leq t_2(n)$,

$$\text{boundary-MINpK}^{t_1,t_2} \notin \text{ioBPP}$$

  *Then, OWFs exist.*
- *Assume that* $\mathsf{E} \not\subseteq \mathsf{ioNTIME}[2^{kn}]/2^{\Omega(n)}$ *for every* $k \in \mathbb{N}$. *If for all polynomials* $t_1, t_2$, $t_1(n) \leq t_2(n)$,

$$\text{boundary-MINK}^{t_1,t_2} \notin \text{ioBPP}$$

  *Then, OWFs exist.*

**Proof:** The first bullet follows by Lemma 17 and Theorem 18 (proven below), and Theorem 7. The second bullet follows by Lemma 17 and Theorem 19 (proven below), and Theorem 7. ■

In fact, we will prove a slightly more general result from which the above theorem follows. Towards this, we will introduce new promise problems regarding $pK^{\mathsf{poly}}$ (and $K^{\mathsf{poly}}$).

For any polynomials $t_1(n), t_2(n), t_1(n) \leq t_2(n)$, any threshold function $s(n) > 0$, and any constant $\beta > 0$, define the promise problem $\Pi^{t_1,t_2}_{pK,\beta}[s]$ (for $pK^{\mathsf{poly}}$) as

- YES instances: $x \in \{0,1\}^*$, $pK^{t_1}_{2/3}(x) \leq s(|x|)$, $pK^{t_2}_{1/3}(x) > pK^{t_1}_{2/3}(x) - \beta \log |x|$.
- NO instances: $x \in \{0,1\}^*$, $pK^{t_1}_{1/3}(x) > s(|x|)$.

We will also define $\Pi^{t_1,t_2}_{K,\beta}[s]$ for $K^{\mathsf{poly}}$, by replacing $pK$ with $K$ in the above definition (and simply ignoring the threshold for $pK$). Roughly speaking, the problem $\Pi^{t_1,t_2}_{K,\beta}[s]$ (resp $\Pi^{t_1,t_2}_{pK,\beta}[s]$) generalizes $\mathsf{boundary\text{-}MINK}^{t_1,t_2}$ (resp $\mathsf{boundary\text{-}MINpK}^{t_1,t_2}$) in the following ways: (1) it considers an arbitrary threshold function $s$ (as opposed to being fixed to $n-2$); (2) the "boundary" could be potentially wider ($\beta \log |x|$ against $\log |x|$); (3) the (Kolmogorov complexity) time bound for NO instances is $t_1$ (as opposed to $t_2$) (which allows the promise problem to consider more instances).

Thus, as it is a generalization of the boundary problem, the hardness of $\mathsf{boundary\text{-}MINpK}^{t_1,t_2}$ will imply the hardness of $\Pi^{t_1,t_2}_{pK,\beta}[s]$ for $\beta = 1$ and $s(n) = n - \lceil \log 3 \rceil - 2$. (The same statement (but replacing $s(n)$ with $n-2$) also holds for $K^{\mathsf{poly}}$.)

**Lemma 17.** *For any $t_1(n), t_2(n), t_1(n) \leq t_2(n)$. Let threshold $s(n) = n - \lceil \log 3 \rceil - 2$, $\beta = 1$,*

$$\mathsf{boundary\text{-}MINpK}^{t_1,t_2} \notin \mathsf{ioBPP} \Rightarrow \Pi^{t_1,t_2}_{pK,\beta}[s] \notin \mathsf{ioBPP}$$

*In addition, the same statement also holds when $pK$ is replaced by $K$ and $s(n)$ by $s(n) = n - 2$.*

**Proof:** Let $\Pi_{\mathsf{YES}}$ (resp $\Pi_{\mathsf{NO}}$) denote the set of YES instances (resp NO instances) of the promise problem $\Pi^{t_1,t_2}_{pK,\beta}[s]$. We first show that $\mathsf{boundary\text{-}MINpK}^{t_1,t_2}_{\mathsf{YES}} \subseteq \Pi_{\mathsf{YES}}$. For any $x \in \mathsf{boundary\text{-}MINpK}^{t_1,t_2}_{\mathsf{YES}}$, it holds that

$$pK^{t_1}_{2/3}(x) \leq n - \lceil \log 3 \rceil - 2 = s(n), \; pK^{t_2}_{1/3}(x) > s(n) - \log n \geq pK^{t}_{2/3}(x) - \beta \log n$$

Thus, $x \in \Pi_{\mathsf{YES}}$. In addition, we claim that $\mathsf{boundary\text{-}MINpK}^{t_1,t_2}_{\mathsf{NO}} \subseteq \Pi_{\mathsf{NO}}$. This follows from the fact that for any $x \in \mathsf{boundary\text{-}MINpK}^{t_1,t_2}_{\mathsf{NO}}$,

$$pK^{t_1}_{1/3}(x) \geq pK^{t_2}_{1/3}(x) > n - \lceil \log 3 \rceil - 2 = s(n)$$

since $t_1(n) \leq t_2(n)$. Finally, we remark that all the above still holds if we replace $pK$ with $K$ (and $s(n)$ by $s(n) = n - 2$). ■

We turn to proving that $\Pi^{t_1,t_2}_{pK,\beta}[s] \notin \mathsf{ioBPP}$ implies OWFs.

**Theorem 18.** *Assume that there exist a polynomial $t_1(n)$, a threshold $0 < s(n) < n - 1$, and a constant $\beta > 0$ such that for all sufficiently large polynomials $t_2(n)$, $\Pi^{t_1,t_2}_{pK,\beta}[s] \notin \mathsf{ioBPP}$. Then, weak one-way functions exist.*

**Proof:** Consider any polynomial $t_1(n)$, any threshold $s(n)$, and any constant $\beta$. We consider the function $f : \{0,1\}^{\lceil \log(n) \rceil + n + t_1(n)} \to \{0,1\}^*$, which takes an input $\ell || \Pi' || r$ where $|\ell| = \lceil \log(n) \rceil$, $|\Pi'| = n$ and $|r| = t_1(n)$, outputs

$$f(\ell || \Pi' || r) = \ell || U(\Pi(r), 1^{t_1(n)}) || r$$

where $\Pi$ is a prefix of $\Pi'$ and $\Pi$ is of length $\ell$ (where the bit-string $\ell$ is interpreted as an integer $\in [n]$).

This function is only defined over some input lengths, but by an easy padding trick, it can be transformed into a function $f'$ defined over all input lengths, such that if $f$ is weakly one-way (over the restricted input lengths), then $f'$ will be weakly one-way (over all input lengths): $f'(x')$ simply truncates its input $x'$ (as little as possible) so that the (truncated) input $x$ now becomes of length $n' = \lceil \log(n) \rceil + n + t_1(n)$ for some $n$ and outputs $f(x)$. This will decrease the input length by a polynomial factor (since $t_1$ is a polynomial) so the padding trick can be applied here.

We now show that $f$ is a weak OWF (over the restricted input length). Let $q(n) = 90n^{5+2\beta}$. We assume for contradiction that $f$ is not $\frac{1}{q}$-weak one-way. (In the proof below, although the input length of $f$ we consider is $m = \lceil \log(n) \rceil + n + t_1(n)$ for some $n$, we will view $n$ as the "security parameter" and analyze the one-wayness of $f$ on input length $m = m(n)$ (but computing the running time and the inversion probability in terms of the security parameter $n$). Since $n$ and $m$ are polynomially related, we can still conclude that $f$ is weak one-way.) Then, there exists a $\mathsf{PPT}$ attacker $\mathcal{A}$ that inverts $f$ with probability at least $1 - \frac{1}{q(n)}$ for infinitely many $n$.

We will consider the distribution $\mathcal{D} = \{\mathcal{D}_n\}_{n \in \mathbb{N}}$, which helps us compress the instances on which $\mathcal{A}$ fails to invert $f$. $\mathcal{D}$ proceeds as follows: for each $n \in \mathbb{N}$, runs the function $f$ on uniformly sampled input $\leftarrow \mathcal{U}_{\lceil \log(n) \rceil + n + t_1(n)}$. Denote the output of $f$ by $(\ell, y, r)$. Next, the distribution feeds the output of $f$ to the attacker $\mathcal{A}$ and checks whether $\mathcal{A}$ succeeds in inverting $(\ell, y, r)$. If $\mathcal{A}$ succeeds, it simply outputs $\perp$. If $\mathcal{A}$ does not succeed, it will output the string $y$.

Notice that $\mathcal{D}$ will mostly output $\perp$, and will output $\perp$ with probability $\geq 1 - \frac{1}{q(n)}$ on "security parameter" $n$ for which $\mathcal{A}$ succeeds in inverting $f$. In addition, the ensemble $\mathcal{D}$ can be efficiently sampled (since both $f$ and $\mathcal{A}$ are efficient). Let $t_2$ be the polynomial we obtain from Lemma 12 when plugging in the distribution $\mathcal{D}$ and the polynomial $q$.

We turn to constructing a $\mathsf{PPT}$ algorithm $M$ to decide the promise problem $\Pi_{pK,\beta}^{t_1,t_2}[s]$. Our algorithm $M$, on input $z$, samples a random string $r \in \{0,1\}^{t_1(n)}$. Then, it runs $\mathcal{A}(i || z || r)$ for every $i \in [n]$ where $i$ is represented as a $\lceil \log(n) \rceil$-bit string, and outputs 1 if and only if the length of the shortest program $\Pi$ output by $\mathcal{A}$, which on input $r$ produces the string $z$ within $t_1(n)$ steps, is at most $s(n)$. Since $\mathcal{A}$ runs in polynomial time, our algorithm will also terminate in polynomial time.

We next show that $M$ is a worst-case algorithm (that succeeds infinitely often) for $\Pi_{pK,\beta}^{t_1,t_2}[s]$ (which will be a contradiction and concludes the proof). Fix any sufficiently large $n$ on which $\mathcal{A}$ succeeds in inverting $f$.

We first show that $M$ will output 1 with probability at least 3/5 on any YES instance of $\Pi^{t_1,t_2}_{pK,\beta}[s]$. Assume for contradiction that $M$ on input some YES instance of $\Pi^{t_1,t_2}_{pK,\beta}[s]$, $z$, outputs 1 with probability $< 3/5$. Notice that since $z$ is a YES instance, we have that

$$pK^{t_1}_{2/3}(z) \leq s(n) \text{ and } pK^{t_2}_{1/3}(z) > pK^{t_1}_{2/3}(z) - \beta \log n \quad (1)$$

Let $w = pK^{t_1}_{2/3}(z)$. It follows that for at least a 2/3 fraction of randomness $r \in \{0,1\}^{t_1(n)}$, the length of the shortest program that on input $r$ produces the string $z$, $w_r$, will be at most $w$. We refer to such $r$ as being "good", and let $G$ denote the set of good randomness for $z$. Consider the set $S = \{(w_r, z, r) : r \in G\}$. Since $M$ outputs 1 with probability $< 3/5$, $\mathcal{A}$ must fail to invert $f$ with probability at least

$$\frac{2}{3} - \frac{3}{5} \geq \frac{1}{15}$$

on uniformly random element $\in S$. However, each element in $S$ will be sampled with probability at least

$$\frac{1}{n} \cdot \frac{1}{2^{w_r}} \cdot \frac{1}{2^{|r|}} \geq \frac{1}{n} 2^{-w-t_1(n)}$$

in the one-way function experiment. Thus, the probability that distribution $\mathcal{D}_n$ samples the string $z$, $p_z$, will be at least

$$\frac{1}{n} 2^{-w-t(n)} \cdot |S| \cdot \frac{1}{15} \geq \frac{2}{45n} 2^{-w}$$

Now we can apply Lemma 12 to conclude that the $pK^{t_2}_{1/3}$-complexity of $z$ is at most

$$\begin{aligned} pK^{t_2}_{1/3}(z) \leq pK^{t_2}_{2/3}(z) &\leq \log 1/p_z - \log(q(n)/4) + 4 \log n \\ &\leq w - \log(q(n)/(90n^5)) \\ &= pK^{t_1}_{2/3}(z) - 2\beta \log n \end{aligned}$$

which contradicts to Eq. 1.

It remains to show that if $z \in \{0,1\}^n$ is a NO instance, then $M(z)$ will output 1 with probability $< 2/5$. Notice that since $z$ is a NO instance, $pK^{t_1}_{1/3} > s(n)$. Therefore, there exists no more than 1/3 fraction of random tapes $r$ for which there is a program of length $\leq s(n)$ that taking $r$ as input produces $z$. Finally, note that $M$ will output 1 only when it finds such a program. It follows that $M(z)$ outputs 1 with probability at most $1/3 < 2/5$. ■

Finally, we show that the implication also holds if we consider $K^{\mathsf{poly}}$ (instead of $pK^{\mathsf{poly}}$). This is not a direct consequence of Theorem 18 and Lemma 13 (which would prove a gap version of the result). Nevertheless, it essentially follows from similar ideas, and we here provide a proof.

**Theorem 19.** *Assume that there exists a constant* $\varepsilon > 0$ *such that* $\mathsf{E} \not\subseteq \mathsf{ioNTIME}[2^{kn}]/2^{\varepsilon n}$ *for every* $k \in \mathbb{N}$.

*If there exist a polynomial* $t_1(n)$, *a threshold* $0 < s(n) < n-1$, *and a constant* $\beta > 0$ *such that for all sufficiently large polynomials* $t_2(n)$, $\Pi_{K,\beta}^{t_1,t_2}[s] \notin \mathsf{ioBPP}$, *then, weak one-way functions exist.*

**Proof:** Consider the function $f : \{0,1\}^{n+\lceil \log(n) \rceil} \to \{0,1\}^*$, which given an input $\ell || \Pi'$ where $|\ell| = \lceil \log(n) \rceil$ and $|\Pi'| = n$, outputs

$$\ell || U(\Pi, 1^{t_1(n)})$$

where $\Pi$ is the $\ell$-bit prefix of $\Pi'$. Note that $U$ only has polynomial overhead, so $f$ can be computed in polynomial time.

This function is only defined over some input lengths, but by an easy padding trick, it can be transformed into a function $f'$ defined over all input lengths, such that if $f$ is weak one-way (over the restricted input lengths), then $f'$ will be weak one-way (over all input lengths): $f'(x')$ simply truncates its input $x'$ (as little as possible) so that the (truncated) input $x$ now becomes of length $n' = n + \lceil \log(n) \rceil$ for some $n$ and outputs $f(x)$.

Assume for contradiction that $f$ is not $\frac{1}{q(n)}$-weak one-way where $q(n) = 12n^{5+2\beta+d}$ (where $d$ is the universal constant in Lemma 15). Then, there exists $\mathsf{PPT}$ attacker $\mathcal{A}$ such that the attacker $\mathcal{A}$ inverts the function $f$ with probability at least $1 - \frac{1}{q(n)}$ for infinitely many $n$. We will consider the distribution $\mathcal{D} = \{\mathcal{D}_n\}_{n\in\mathbb{N}}$ (that helps us compress instances on which the inverter $\mathcal{A}$ fails): For each $n \in \mathbb{N}$, $\mathcal{D}_n$ runs the function $f$ on uniformly sampled input $\leftarrow \mathcal{U}_{n+\lceil \log(n) \rceil}$. Denote the output of $f$ by $(\ell, y)$. Next, $\mathcal{D}_n$ feeds the output of $f$ to the attacker $\mathcal{A}$ and checks whether $\mathcal{A}$ succeeds in inverting $(\ell, y)$. If $\mathcal{A}$ succeeds, $\mathcal{D}_n$ simply outputs $\perp$. If $\mathcal{A}$ does not succeed, $\mathcal{D}_n$ will output the string $y$.

Notice that $\mathcal{D}_n$ will mostly output $\perp$, and will not output $\perp$ with probability $\leq \frac{1}{q(n)}$ on input length $n$ for which $\mathcal{A}$ succeeds in inverting $f$. In addition, the ensemble $\mathcal{D}$ can be efficiently sampled (since both $f$ and $\mathcal{A}$ are efficient). Let $t_2$ be the polynomial we obtain from Lemma 15 when plugging in the distribution $\mathcal{D}$ and the polynomial $q$.

We turn to constructing a $\mathsf{PPT}$ algorithm $M$ to decide $\Pi_{K,\beta}^{t_1,t_2}[s]$ infinitely often. Our algorithm $M$, on input $z$, runs $\mathcal{A}(i||z)$ for every $i \in [n]$ where $i$ is represented as a $\lceil \log(n) \rceil$-bit string, and outputs 1 if and only if the length of the shortest program $\Pi$ output by $\mathcal{A}$, which produces the string $z$ within $t_1(n)$ steps, is at most $s(n)$. Since $\mathcal{A}$ runs in polynomial time, our algorithm will also terminate in polynomial time. Fix some sufficiently large $n$ on which the inverter $\mathcal{A}$ succeeds in inverting $f$.

We next show that our algorithm will output 1 with probability at least 2/3 on input YES instances of $\Pi_{K,\beta}^{t_1,t_2}[s]$ of length $n$. Assume for contradiction that $M$ outputs 1 with probability $< 2/3$ on some YES instances $z \in \{0,1\}^n$. We have that

$$K^{t_1}(z) \leq s(n) \text{ and } K^{t_2}(z) > K^{t_1}(z) - \beta \log n \quad (2)$$

Let $w = K^{t_1}(z)$. Note that there must exist a program of size $w$ such that the program outputs $z$ in time $t_1(n)$. Therefore, $(w, z)$ will be sampled with probability

$$\frac{1}{n}2^{-w}$$

in the one-way function experiment. In addition, since $\Pr[M(z) = 1] < 2/3$, $\mathcal{A}$ must fail to invert $f$ on input $(w||z)$ with probability at least 1/3. So, the probability that $\mathcal{D}_n$ samples the string $z$, $p_z$, is at least

$$\frac{1}{3n}2^{-w}$$

It follows from Lemma 15 that the $K^{t_2}$ complexity of $z$ is at most

$$\begin{aligned}
&\log 1/p_z - \log(q(n)/4) + (d+4)\log n \\
&\leq w + \log(3n) - \log(q(n)/4) + (d+4)\log n \\
&= K^{t_1}(z) - \log(q(n)/(12n^{d+5})) \\
&= K^{t_1}(z) - 2\beta \log n
\end{aligned}$$

which contradicts to Eq. 2.

We finally prove that if $z$ is a NO instance (and thus $K^{t_1}(z) > s(n)$), $M(z)$ will never output 1. Note that $M(z)$ will output 1 only when it finds a $K^{t_1}$-witness of $z$ with length no more than $s(n)$, and there is no such witness if $K^{t_1}(z) > s(n)$, which proves our claim and concludes the proof. ■

## 6 Hardness of boundary-MINK$^{\mathsf{poly}}$ from OWFs

We here prove the worst-case hardness of boundary-MINK$^{\mathsf{poly}}$ from the existence of OWFs. The proof is very similar in nature to the proof from [LP20] (with some strengthenings from [LP23a]).

We start by recalling the notion of a conditionally-secure entropy-preserving pseudorandom generator [LP20] (and its strengthened version in [LP23a]), which will be an important tool in our proof.

**Definition 20.** *An efficiently computable function $g : \{0,1\}^n \times \{0,1\}^{m(n)} \rightarrow \{0,1\}$ is a* $\varepsilon(\cdot)$-conditionally-secure $\alpha$-entropy-preserving pseudorandom generator ($\varepsilon$-cond $\alpha$-EP-PRG) *if there exist a sequence of events $= \{E_n\}_{n\in\mathbb{N}}$ such that the following conditions hold:*

- **(pseudorandomness):** *For every* PPT *attacker $\mathcal{A}$ and sufficiently large $n \in \mathbb{N}$,*

$$|\Pr[s\leftarrow\{0,1\}^n : \mathcal{A}(1^n, g(\mathcal{U}_n))=1 \mid E_n] - \Pr[r\leftarrow\{0,1\}^{m(n)} : \mathcal{A}(1^n, \mathcal{U}_m)=1]| < \varepsilon(n), \tag{3}$$

- **(entropy-preserving):** *For all sufficiently large $n \in \mathbb{N}$, $H([g(\mathcal{U}_n \mid E_n)]_n) \geq n - \alpha \log n$ (where $[x]_n$ denotes the $n$-bit prefix of the string $x$).*

*We refer to the constant* $\alpha$ *as the* entropy-loss constant.

We say that $g : \{0,1\}^n \times \{0,1\}^{m(n)} \to \{0,1\}$ has rate-1 efficiency if its running time on input length $n$ is at most $m + O(m^{\varepsilon})$ for some constant $\varepsilon < 1$. Recall that a rate-1 efficient cond EP-PRG can be constructed from OWFs [LP20,LP23a].

**Theorem 21 (Cond EP-PRG from OWFs** [LP21,LP23a]**).** *Assume that OWFs exist. Then, for any constant* $\alpha > 0, \gamma > 0$, *there exists a rate-1 efficient* 0.1*-cond* $\alpha$*-EP-PRG* $g : \{0,1\}^n \to \{0,1\}^{n+\gamma \log n}$.

We remark that in [LP20], they only obtain a cond EP-PRG with entropy loss constant $\alpha$ for some constant $\alpha$. Nevertheless, [LP23a] improve the construction and prove that there exists a cond EP-PRG for every constant $\alpha > 0$.

The next two lemmas show that cond EP-PRG implies the worst case hardness of $\mathsf{boundary\text{-}MINK}^{\mathsf{poly}}$, and the implication also holds for $pK^{\mathsf{poly}}$. The lemmas follow from similar lines in [LP20,LP23a], and their proofs are deferred to the full version.

**Lemma 22.** *Assume that there exists a rate-1 efficient* $\varepsilon$*-cond* $\alpha$*-EP-PRG* $g : \{0,1\}^n \to \{0,1\}^{n+\gamma \log n}$ *for* $\varepsilon = \alpha = \gamma = 0.1$*. Then, for all polynomials* $t_1, t_2$, $t_2(n) \geq t_1(n) \geq 2n$, $\mathsf{boundary\text{-}MINK}^{t_1,t_2} \notin \mathsf{ioBPP}$.

**Lemma 23.** *Assume that there exists a rate-1 efficient* $\varepsilon$*-cond* $\alpha$*-EP-PRG* $g : \{0,1\}^n \to \{0,1\}^{n+\gamma \log n}$ *for* $\varepsilon = \alpha = \gamma = 0.1$*. Then, for all polynomials* $t_1, t_2$, $t_2(n) \geq t_1(n) \geq 2n$, $\mathsf{boundary\text{-}MINpK}^{t_1,t_2} \notin \mathsf{ioBPP}$.

## 7 Derandomizing $pK^{\mathsf{poly}}$ and a (Near) Seed-Optimal PRG

In this section, provide a proof of Lemma 13; that is, we show how to upperbound $K^{\mathsf{poly}}$ by $pK^{\mathsf{poly}}$ plus an additive logarithmic term, assuming derandomization assumptions. As described in the introduction, we achieve this result by presenting a new construction of a PRG against non-deterministic programs with near-optimal seed length.

### 7.1 Complexity-Theoretic PRGs and Non-uniform Programs

Towards derandomizing $pK^{\mathsf{poly}}$, let us recall the notion of a complexity-theoretic PRGs.

**Definition 24 (Complexity-theoretic PRG).** *Let* $g : \{0,1\}^{\ell(m)} \to \{0,1\}^m$ *be a function computable in polynomial time in its output length. We say that* $g$ *is a* complexity $\varepsilon(\cdot)$-pseudorandom generator (complexity $\varepsilon$-PRG) against complexity class $\mathcal{C}$ *if for any distinguisher* $D \in \mathcal{C}$, *all* $m \in \mathbb{N}$,

$$|\Pr[D(g(\mathcal{U}_{\ell(m)})) = 1] - \Pr[D(\mathcal{U}_m) = 1]| < \varepsilon(m)$$

*We refer to* $\varepsilon$ *as* distinguishing gap. *We simply say that* $g$ *is a* complexity-theoretic PRG *if* $g$ *is a* $\varepsilon$*-PRG for* $\varepsilon = \frac{1}{6}$.

We will consider complexity-theoretic PRGs that fool non-adaptive non-uniform $D$-oracle programs, which we introduce here.

**Definition 25 ((Non-adaptive) Non-uniform Programs).** *A non-adaptive non-uniform D-oracle program A on n-bit inputs consists of a pair of non-uniform programs* $A_{\mathsf{pre}}$ *and* $A_{\mathsf{post}}$*. The program* $A_{\mathsf{pre}}$ *on input* $x \in \{0,1\}^n$ *outputs queries* $q_1, \ldots, q_k$*. The program* $A_{\mathsf{post}}$ *receives* $x$ *together with* $a_1, \ldots, a_k$ *(where* $a_i = 1$ *if and only if* $q_i \in D$*), and it outputs a single bit.*

*The running time (resp advice complexity) of A is defined to be the sum of the running time (resp advice complexity) of* $A_{\mathsf{pre}}$ *and* $A_{\mathsf{post}}$*. We refer to k as the query complexity of A.*

## 7.2 Constructing Complexity-Theoretic PRG with Seed Length $O(\log n)$

Our start point is the "standard" complexity-theoretic PRG that can be used to derandomize $\mathsf{AM}$.

**Theorem 26** ([SU05])**.** *Assume that* $\mathsf{E} \not\subseteq \mathsf{ioNSIZE}[2^{\Omega(n)}]$*, there exists a complexity-theoretic PRG* $g : \{0,1\}^{O(\log n)} \to \{0,1\}^n$ *against* $\mathsf{NSIZE}[O(n)]$.

However, the above PRG falls short in its seed lengt: if we use it to directly derandomize $pK^t$, it incurs an $O(\log t(|x|))$ overhead. Towards building the PRG we need, we first call the following result from [SU06], which enables us to transform nondeterministic hardness to $\mathsf{SAT}$-oracle hardness.

**Theorem 27** ([SU06] **(c.f.** [CT23, **Theorem 5.11**]))**.** *There exists a universal constant* $c_{\mathsf{RC}}$ *such that the following holds. For any integer* $k \geq 1$*, constant* $0 < \varepsilon < 1/200$*, if* $\mathsf{E} \not\subseteq \mathsf{ioNTIME}[2^{2kn+2\varepsilon c_{\mathsf{RC}} n}]/2^{2\varepsilon n}$*, then* $\mathsf{E}$ *does not have an (infinitely-often) non-adaptive non-uniform* $\mathsf{SAT}$*-oracle program with running time* $2^{kn}$*, advice complexity* $2^{\varepsilon n}$*, and query complexity* $2^{\varepsilon n}$*.*

**Proof:** This Theorem is obtained by taking $\varepsilon' = 1/2, k' = 2^{2\varepsilon n}, T = 2^{2kn+2\varepsilon c_{\mathsf{RC}} n}, \alpha = 2^{2\varepsilon n}$ into [CT23, Theorem 5.11] (and due to collisions in the notations, we denote $k$ (resp $\varepsilon$) in [CT23, Theorem 5.11] by $k'$ (resp $\varepsilon'$)). Also notice that $E \notin \mathsf{ioNTIME}[T]/k'$ implies that $E$ does not have single-value non-deterministic program with advice complexity $k'$ and running time $T$. ■

We rely on the notion of *black-box PRG construction from a worst-case hard function f* [STV01, Vad12]. Roughly speaking, this notion of black-box PRG from a function $f$ requires the existence of an efficient oracle algorithm that given (a) some fixed advice string, and (b) black-box access to any distinguisher for the PRG, is able to compute function $f$. We remark that we here only consider deterministic reductions $R$ that reconstruct each bit of $f$ with probability 1 (whereas [Vad12] considered probabilistic reductions). Notice that probabilistic reductions can be made to be deterministic at the price of requiring a longer advice string.

**Definition 28 (Reconstructive PRG (c.f. [Vad12, Definition 7.65])).** *Let $g : 1^n \times 1^m \times \{0,1\}^d \to \{0,1\}^m$ be a (deterministic) oracle algorithm, and let $k(\cdot)$ be functions. We say that $g$ is a k*-reconstructive PRG construction *if there exist a (deterministic) algorithm $R$ such that for every $f : [n] \to \{0,1\}$ and $T : \{0,1\}^m \to \{0,1\}$, if*

$$|\Pr[T(g^f(1^n, 1^m, \mathcal{U}_d)) = 1] - \Pr[T(\mathcal{U}_m) = 1]| \geq \frac{1}{6}$$

*then there exists a string $z \in \{0,1\}^{k(n,m)}$ such that for all $i \in [n]$,*

$$R^T(z, i) = f(i)$$

We next observe that the Sudan-Trevisan-Vadhan PRG [STV01] obtain by combining a locally list-decodable error correcting code [STV01] and the Nisan-Wigderson PRG construction [NW94] yields a strongly black-box construction of a PRG (as argued in [Vad12]).

**Theorem 29 ([STV01]; see also [Vad12, Theorem 7.67.] [LP22a, Theorem 3.11]).** *There exists a k-reconstructive PRG construction $g : 1^n \times 1^m \times \{0,1\}^d \to \{0,1\}^m$ such that for every $m \in \mathbb{N}$, $n \geq m$, $f : [n] \to \{0,1\}$ the following conditions are satisfied:*

1. *Explicitness: $g^f$ is computable in uniform time* $\mathsf{poly}(m, n)$.
2. *Seed length: $d(n, m) = O(\log^2 n / \log m)$.*
3. *Reduction running time: $t(n, m) = \mathsf{poly}(m, \log n)$.*
4. *Reduction advice complexity: $k(n, m) \leq t(n, m)$.*

*In addition, the reduction $R$ only makes non-adaptive queries.*

Now we are ready to construct the complexity-theoretic PRG we need.

**Theorem 30.** *Assume that there exists a constant $\varepsilon > 0$ such that $\mathsf{E} \not\subseteq \mathsf{ioNTIME}[2^{kn}]/2^{\varepsilon n}$ for every $k \in \mathbb{N}$. There exists an constant $c$ such that the following holds. For every polynomial $t$, there exists a complexity-theoretic PRG $G : \{0,1\}^{c \log n} \to \{0,1\}^n$ against $\mathsf{NTIME}[t(n)]/n$.*

**Proof:** Notice that we start with the hardness of $\mathsf{E}$ against non-uniform nondeterministic programs, whereas to use the reconstructive PRG construction, we need to rely on hardness against non-adaptive non-uniform $\mathsf{SAT}$-oracle programs. Thus, we first apply Theorem 27 to transform hardness. Let $\varepsilon' = \min\{\varepsilon, 1/200\}$. And it follows that for every $k \geq 1$, $\mathsf{E}$ does not have an (infinitely often) non-adaptive non-uniform $\mathsf{SAT}$-oracle program with running time $2^{kn}$, advice complexity and query complexity $2^{\varepsilon' \cdot n}$.

Given the hardness assumption, we will be needing a (standard) padding argument (that works for every $k \geq 1$). Let $\theta \leq \varepsilon'/c_0$ be a sufficiently small constant (where $c_0$ is a universal constant that will be fixed later). We will use (the truth table of) a hard function $\in \mathsf{E}$ on input $\log n$ to construct a PRG with output length $m = n^\theta$.

Consider any polynomial $t(m)$. We proceed to building our complexity-theoretic PRG secure against $\mathsf{NTIME}[t(m)]/m$. Let $k$ be a (large enough) integer such that $m^{k/4} \geq t(m)$. By the argument above, there exists a language $L_k \in \mathsf{E}$ such that $L_k$ does not have an (infinitely often) non-adaptive non-uniform $\mathsf{SAT}$-oracle programs with running time $2^{kn}$, advice complexity and query complexity $2^{\varepsilon' \cdot n}$. Let $f_{k,\ell} \in \{0,1\}^{2^\ell}$ denote the truth table of $L_k$ on input length $\ell$. For any output length $m \in \mathbb{N}$, let $n = m^{1/\theta}$, and our PRG $G_k$ is defined as

$$G_k \stackrel{\text{def}}{=} g^{f_{k,\log n}}(1^n, 1^m) : \{0,1\}^d \to \{0,1\}^m$$

where $g$ is the reconstructive PRG construction in Theorem 29.

Notice that $g^{f_{k,\log n}}$ can be computed in time polynomial in $m$ since both the truth table $f_{k,\log n}$ and the oracle machine $g$ have running time $\mathsf{poly}(n, m) = \mathsf{poly}(m)$. In addition, the seed length $d = d(n, m) = O(\log^2 n/\log m) = O((1/\theta)^2 \log m)$. Let $c$ be a constant such that $d(n, m) \leq c \log m$ and we conclude that $G_k$ has seed length $c \log m$.

We turn to arguing the security of $G_k$. Assume (for contradiction) that for some $m \in \mathbb{N}$, there exists a nondeterministic non-uniform program $D \in \mathsf{NTIME}[t(m)]/m$ such that

$$|\Pr[D(G_k(\mathcal{U}_d)) = 1] - \Pr[D(\mathcal{U}_m) = 1]| \geq \frac{1}{6}$$

Let $R$ be the deterministic reduction for $g$ as in Theorem 29, and let $t_R(n, m)$ be the running time of $R$. Note that $t_R(n, m) = \mathsf{poly}(m, \log n) \leq \mathsf{poly}(m)$ and $R$ also has advice complexity $t_R(n, m)$. By the reconstructive property of $g$, it follows that there exists an advice string $z_R \in \{0,1\}^{t_R(n,m)}$ such that for all $i \in [n]$,

$$R^D(z_R, i) = f(i)$$

Therefore, $R^D$ with advice $z_R$ decides the hard language $L_k$ on input length $\ell = \log n$.

In order to reach a contradiction, it remains to argue that $R^D(z_R, \cdot)$ can be implemented by a non-adaptive non-uniform $\mathsf{SAT}$-oracle program. Recall that $D$ is a nondeterministic non-uniform program with running time $t(m)$ and advice complexity $m$. Let $z_D$ denote the advice string that $D$ receives. Consider the following two programs $A_{\mathsf{pre}}, A_{\mathsf{post}}$ that act as follows.

- $A_{\mathsf{pre}}$ receives $z_R$ and $z_D$ as advice. On input $y \in [n]$, it uses $z_R$ to simulate the reduction $R$ on input $y$ and obtains the queries $x_1, \ldots, x_{t_R}$ that $R$ makes to $D$. (Note that since $R$ is also non-adaptive, we can obtain those queries.) For each $x_i$, notice that $D(x_i)$ can be transformed to a $\mathsf{SAT}$ formula $\phi_i$ of length $t(m) \log t(m)$ such that $\phi_i \in \mathsf{SAT}$ iff $D(x_i) = 1$ in time $t(m)^2$ (using the advice $z_D$ for $D$). Finally, $A_{\mathsf{pre}}$ outputs $\phi_1, \ldots, \phi_{t_R}$.
- $A_{\mathsf{pre}}$ receives $z_R$ as advice. On input $y \in [n]$ together with $a_1, \ldots, a_{t_R}$, it simply simulates $R^D(z_R, y)$ but replacing the $i$-th answer obtained from $D$ with $a_i$, and outputs what the reduction outputs.

Notice that the attacker $A = (A_{\mathsf{pre}}, A_{\mathsf{post}})$ decides $L_k$ on input length $\ell$, and it has advice complexity

$$2|z_R| + |z_D| \leq 2t_R(n,m) + m \leq \mathsf{poly}(m, \log n) \leq n^{O(1)\theta} = 2^{O(1)\theta\cdot\ell}$$

running time

$$t_R(n,m)\cdot t(m)^2 + t_R(n,m) \leq 2^{O(1)\theta\cdot\ell}\cdot t(m)^2 \leq 2^{O(1)\theta\cdot\ell}m^{k/2} \leq 2^{k\cdot\ell}$$

and query complexity

$$t_R(n,m) \leq 2^{O(1)\theta\cdot\ell}$$

By picking $\theta < \varepsilon'/c_0$ for some sufficiently large constant $c_0$, we have that both the advice complexity and the query complexity are $\leq 2^{\varepsilon'\cdot\ell}$. ■

### 7.3 Derandomizing $pK^{\mathsf{poly}}$

We are not ready to use the above constructed PRG to derandomize $pK^t$.

**Lemma 31 (Derandomizing $pK^{\mathsf{poly}}$, Lemma 13 Restated).** *Assume that there exists a constant $\varepsilon > 0$ such that $\mathsf{E} \not\subseteq \mathsf{ioNTIME}[2^{kn}]/2^{\varepsilon n}$ for every $k \in \mathbb{N}$. There exists a constant $d$ such that the following holds. For every polynomial $t$, there exists a polynomial $t'$ such that for every sufficiently long $x \in \{0,1\}^*$,*

$$K^{t'}(x) \leq pK^t(x) + d\log|x|$$

**Proof:** Consider any polynomial $t$, and some sufficiently long string $x \in \{0,1\}^n$. Let $w$ denote the $pK^t$-complexity of $x$. Let $g$ be the complexity-theoretic PRG guaranteed to exist in Theorem 26 (since that the assumption we make in this Lemma trivially implies the assumption needed in Theorem 26). Also let $c$ be the constant in Theorem 30.

We start with the nondeterministic non-uniform program $D_1$ defined as follows. $D_1$ takes a "random tape" $r \in \{0,1\}^{t(n)}$ as input, and guesses a $pK^t$-witness $\Pi$ of $x$ (with respect to the random tape $r$) of length no more than $w$. Finally, $D_1$ outputs 1 if $\Pi$ on input $r$ produces the string $x$. (Let $T(n)$ be the polynomial that bounds the running time of $D_1$.) Notice that the running time of $D_1$, $T = T(n)$, is at most $O(t(n)\log t(n))$, and the advice complexity of $D_1$, $\ell$, is $|x| + |w|$. It follows from Theorem 26 that $D_1$ cannot distinguish the output of $g$ on a seed of length $O(\log T)$ from the uniform distribution with advantage 1/6.

However, the seed length of $g$, $O(\log T)$, is still too long, and we need to apply another complexity-theoretic PRG to further reduce the seed length. We next consider the nondeterministic non-uniform program $D_2$, which on input $\in \{0,1\}^\ell$, uses its first $O(\log T)$ bits (denote the string by $v$), and computes $r = g(v)$. Finally, $D_2$ outputs 1 if $D_1(r)$ outputs 1. Observe that $D_2$ runs in time $T(n) \leq T(\ell)$ and uses $\leq \ell$ bits of advice. Let $G$ be the complexity-theoretic PRG for the polynomial $T$ guaranteed to exists by Theorem 30. It follows that

$D_2$ cannot distinguish the output of $G$ on seed length $c \log \ell$ from the uniform distribution with advantage 1/6.

Lastly, by the above argument, it holds that

$$\Pr[D_2(G(\mathcal{U}_{c \log \ell})) = 1] \geq \Pr[D_2(\mathcal{U}_\ell) = 1] - \frac{1}{6}$$
$$= \Pr[D_1(g(\mathcal{U}_{O(\log T)})) = 1] - \frac{1}{6} \geq \Pr[D_1(\mathcal{U}_{t(n)}) = 1] - \frac{1}{3}$$

In addition, it follows from the definition of $D_1$ (together with $pK^t(x) = w$) that $D_1$ will output 1 with probability at least 2/3 on the uniform distribution. Thus,

$$\Pr[D_2(G(\mathcal{U}_{c \log \ell})) = 1] \geq \frac{1}{3}$$

Now we are ready to show that $x$ also has small $K^{t'}$-complexity for some polynomial $t'$. Let $s$ be a seed of length $c \log \ell$ such that $D_2(G(s)) = 1$. Let $r$ be the random tape obtained by running $g$ on the first $O(\log T)$-bit of $G(s)$. Since $D_2(G(s)) = 1$, there exists a program $\Pi$ such that $\Pi$ on input $r$ will output $x$ in time $t(n)$. Consider the program $M$ with the polynomial $t$, code of $g$ and $G$, the integer $n$, the seed $s$ (of length $\leq 2c \log n$), and the program $\Pi$ (of length $\leq w$) hardcoded. $M$ uses $s$ to obtain the string $r$ and output the string obtained by running $\Pi$ on $r$. Notice that the PRG $G$, $g$, and the program $\Pi$ all run in polynomial time in $n$, and let $t'(n)$ be the polynomial such that $M$ runs in time $t'(n)$. In addition, the program $M$ has description length

$$\log n + 2 \log n + 4c \log n + w \leq pK^t(x) + d \log n$$

for some constant $d$ (that does not depend on $t$). Thus, we conclude that

$$K^{t'}(x) \leq pK^t(x) + d \log n$$

■

**Acknowledgements.** We are very grateful to Johan Håstad, Per Austrin and Noam Mazor for helpful conversations. In particular, we are grateful to Johan Håstad for pointing out that the border version of SAT (and 3SAT) is equivalent to the standard (i.e., non-border) version (and with his permission, we have included his proofs of these observations in the paper). Thanks so much!

## References

BLM00. Buhrman, H., Laplante, S., Miltersen, P.B.: New bounds for the language compression problem. In: Proceedings 15th Annual IEEE Conference on Computational Complexity, pp. 126–130. IEEE (2000)

BLM05. Buhrman, H., Lee, T., van Melkebeek, D.: Language compression and pseudorandom generators. Comput. complexity **14**(3), 228–255 (2005)

Blu82. Blum, M.: Coin flipping by telephone - a protocol for solving impossible problems. In: COMPCON'82, Digest of Papers, Twenty-Fourth IEEE Computer Society International Conference, San Francisco, California, USA, 22-25 February 1982, pp. 133–137. IEEE Computer Society (1982)

BM84. Blum, M., Micali, S.: How to generate cryptographically strong sequences of pseudo-random bits. SIAM J. Comput. **13**(4), 850–864 (1984)

CT21. Chen, L., Tell, R.: Simple and fast derandomization from very hard functions: eliminating randomness at almost no cost. In: Proceedings of the 53rd Annual ACM SIGACT Symposium on Theory of Computing, pp. 283–291 (2021)

CT23. Chen, L., Tell, R.: When arthur has neither random coins nor time to spare: Superfast derandomization of proof systems. In: Proceedings of the 55th Annual ACM Symposium on Theory of Computing, pp. 60–69 (2023)

DH76. Diffie, W., Hellman, M.: New directions in cryptography. IEEE Trans. Inf. Theory **22**(6), 644–654 (1976)

DMOZ22. Doron, D., Moshkovitz, D., Justin, O., Zuckerman, D.: Nearly optimal pseudorandomness from hardness. J. ACM **69**(6), 1–55 (2022)

FS90. Feige, U., Shamir, A.: Witness indistinguishable and witness hiding protocols. In: STOC 1990, pp. 416–426 (1990)

GGM84. Goldreich, O., Goldwasser, S., Micali, S.: How to construct random functions. In: FOCS (1984)

GKLO22. Goldberg, H., Kabanets, V., Lu, Z., Oliveira, I.C.: Probabilistic kolmogorov complexity with applications to average-case complexity. In: 37th Computational Complexity Conference (CCC 2022). Schloss Dagstuhl-Leibniz-Zentrum für Informatik (2022)

GM84. Goldwasser, S., Micali, S.: Probabilistic encryption. J. Comput. Syst. Sci. **28**(2), 270–299 (1984)

GS85. Goldberg, A., Sipser, M.: Compression and ranking. In: Proceedings of the seventeenth annual ACM Symposium on Theory of Computing, pp. 440–448 (1985)

Gur89. Gurevich, Y.: The challenger-solver game: variations on the theme of p=np. In: Logic in Computer Science Column, The Bulletin of EATCS (1989)

Har83. Hartmanis,J.: Generalized kolmogorov complexity and the structure of feasible computations. In: 24th Annual Symposium on Foundations of Computer Science (sfcs 1983), pp. 439–445 (Nov 1983)

HIL+23. Hirahara, S., Ilango, R., Lu, Z., Nanashima, M., Oliveira, I.C.: A duality between one-way functions and average-case symmetry of information. Cryptology ePrint Archive (2023)

HILL99. Håstad, J., Impagliazzo, R., Levin, L.A., Luby, M.: A pseudorandom generator from any one-way function. SIAM J. Comput. **28**(4), 1364–1396 (1999)

Hir18. Hirahara, S.: Non-black-box worst-case to average-case reductions within NP. In: 59th IEEE Annual Symposium on Foundations of Computer Science, FOCS 2018, pp. 247–258 (2018)

Hir21. Hirahara, S.: Average-case hardness of np from exponential worst-case hardness assumptions. In: Proceedings of the 53rd Annual ACM SIGACT Symposium on Theory of Computing, pp. 292–302 (2021)

Hir22. Hirahara, S.: Np-hardness of learning programs and partial mcsp. In: 2022 IEEE 63rd Annual Symposium on Foundations of Computer Science (FOCS), pp. 968–979. IEEE (2022)

HIW24. Hirahara, S., Ilango, R., Williams, R.: Beating brute force for compression problems. Electronic Colloquium on Computational Complexity (2024). https://eccc.weizmann.ac.il/report/2023/171/

HN22a. Hirahara, S., Nanashima, M.: Finding errorless pessiland in error-prone heuristica. In: 37th Computational Complexity Conference (CCC 2022). Schloss-Dagstuhl-Leibniz Zentrum für Informatik (2022)

HN22b. Hirahara, S., Nanashima, M.:On worst-case learning in relativized heuristica. In: 2021 IEEE 62nd Annual Symposium on Foundations of Computer Science (FOCS), pp. 751–758. IEEE (2022)

HN23. Hirahara, S., Nanashima, M.: Learning in pessil and via inductive inference (2023)

IL89. Impagliazzo, R., Luby, M.: One-way functions are essential for complexity based cryptography (extended abstract). In: 30th Annual Symposium on Foundations of Computer Science, Research Triangle Park, North Carolina, USA, 30 October - 1 November 1989, pp. 230–235 (1989)

Ila20. Ilango, R.:Approaching MCSP from above and below: Hardness for a conditional variant and AC0[p]. In: 11th Innovations in Theoretical Computer Science Conference, ITCS 2020, pp. 34:1–34:26 (2020)

Ila21. Ilango, R.: The minimum formula size problem is (eth) hard. In: 2021 IEEE 62nd Annual Symposium on Foundations of Computer Science (FOCS), pp. 427–432. IEEE (2021)

Ila22. Ilango, R.: Constant depth formula and partial function versions of mcsp are hard. SIAM J. Comput. FOCS20–317 (2022)

Ila23. Ilango, R.: Sat reduces to the minimum circuit size problem with a random oracle. In: 2023 IEEE 64th Annual Symposium on Foundations of Computer Science (FOCS), pp. 733–742 (2023)

ILO20. Ilango, R., Loff, B., Oliveira, I.C.: NP-hardness of circuit minimization for multi-output functions. In: 35th Computational Complexity Conference, CCC 2020, pp. 22:1–22:36 (2020)

Imp95. Impagliazzo, r.: A personal view of average-case complexity. In: Structure in Complexity Theory 1995, pp. 134–147 (1995)

Imp11. Impagliazzo, R.: Relativized separations of worst-case and average-case complexities for np. In: 2011 IEEE 26th Annual Conference on Computational Complexity, pp. 104–114. IEEE (2011)

IW97. Impagliazzo, R., Wigderson, A.: P = BPP if $e$ requires exponential circuits: derandomizing the xor lemma. In: STOC 1997, pp. 220–229 (1997)

Ko86. Ko, K.-I.: On the notion of infinite pseudorandom sequences. Theor. Comput. Sci. **48**(3), 9–33 (1986)

Kol68. Kolmogorov, A.N.: Three approaches to the quantitative definition of information. Int. J. Comput. Math. **2**(1–4), 157–168 (1968)

KvM02. Klivans, A.R., van Melkebeek, D.: Graph nonisomorphism has subexponential size proofs unless the polynomial-time hierarchy collapses. SIAM J. Comput. **31**(5), 1501–1526 (2002)

Lev03. Levin, L.A.: The tale of one-way functions. Probl. Inf. Transm. **39**(1), 92–103 (2003)

LOZ22. Lu, Z., Oliveira, I.C., Zimand, M.: Optimal coding theorems in time-bounded kolmogorov complexity. In: 49th International Colloquium on Automata, Languages, and Programming (ICALP 2022). SchlossDagstuhl-Leibniz-Zentrum fur Informatik (2022)

LP20. Liu, Y., Pass, R.:On one-way functions and Kolmogorov complexity. In: 61st IEEE Annual Symposium on Foundations of Computer Science, FOCS 2020, Durham, NC, USA, 16-19 November 2020, pp. 1243–1254. IEEE (2020)

LP21. Liu, Y., Pass, R.: Cryptography from sublinear time hardness of time-bounded kolmogorov complexity. In: STOC (2021)

LP22a. Liu, Y., Pass, R.: Leakage-resilient hardness vs randomness. Electronic Colloquium Comput. Complex. (2022). https://eccc.weizmann.ac.il/report/2022/113/

LP22b. Liu, Y., Pass, R.: On one-way functions from np-complete problems. In: Proceedings of the 37th Computational Complexity Conference, pp. 1–24 (2022)

LP23a. Liu, Y., Pass, R.: On one-way functions and the worst-case hardness of time-bounded kolmogorov complexity. Cryptology ePrint Archive, 1086 (2023)

LP23b. Liu, Y., Pass, R.: One-way functions and the hardness of (probabilistic) time-bounded kolmogorov complexity w.r.t. samplable distributions. In: CRYPTO 2023 (2023)

MP23. Mazor, N., Pass, R.: The non-uniform perebor conjecture for time-bounded kolmogorov complexity is false. Cryptology ePrint Archive (2023)

MV05. Miltersen, P.B., Vinodchandran, N.V.: Derandomizing arthur-merlin games using hitting sets. Comput. Complexity **14**(3), 256–279 (2005)

Nao91. Naor, M.: Bit commitment using pseudorandomness. J. Cryptol. **4**(2), 151–158 (1991). https://doi.org/10.1007/BF00196774

NW94. Nisan, N., Wigderson, A.: Hardness vs randomness. J. Comput. Syst. Sci. **49**(2), 149–167 (1994)

NZ96. Nisan, N., Zuckerman, D.: Randomness is linear in space. J. Comput. Syst. Sci. **52**(1), 43–52 (1996)

Rom90. Rompel, J.: One-way functions are necessary and sufficient for secure signatures. In: STOC, pp. 387–394 (1990)

RSA83. Rivest, R.L., Shamir, A., Adleman, L.M.: A method for obtaining digital signatures and public-key cryptosystems (reprint). Commun. ACM **26**(1), 96–99 (1983)

RTS00. Radhakrishnan, J., Ta-Shma, A.: Bounds for dispersers, extractors, and depth-two superconcentrators. SIAM J. Discret. Math. **13**(1), 2–24 (2000)

San23. Santhanam, R.: An algorithmic approach to uniform lower bounds. In: 38th Computational Complexity Conference (CCC 2023). Schloss-Dagstuhl-Leibniz Zentrum für Informatik (2023)

Sip83. Sipser, M.: A complexity theoretic approach to randomness. In: Proceedings of the 15th Annual ACM Symposium on Theory of Computing, 25-27 April, 1983, Boston, Massachusetts, USA, pp. 330–335. ACM (1983)

STV01. Sudan, M., Trevisan, L., Vadhan, S.: Pseudorandom generators without the xor lemma. J. Comput. Syst. Sci. **62**(2), 236–266 (2001)

SU05. Shaltiel, R., Umans, C.: Simple extractors for all min-entropies and a new pseudorandom generator. J. ACM (JACM) **52**(2), 172–216 (2005)

SU06. Shaltiel, R., Umans, C.: Pseudorandomness for approximate counting and sampling. Comput. Complexity **15**(4), 298–341 (2006)

Tra84. Trakhtenbrot, B.A.: A survey of Russian approaches to perebor (brute-force searches) algorithms. Annals History Comput. **6**(4), 384–400 (1984)

Tre01. Trevisan, L.: Extractors and pseudorandom generators. J. ACM **48**(4), 860–879 (2001)

Vad12. Vadhan, S.P.: Pseudorandomness. Foundations and Trends® in Theoretical Computer Sci. **7**(1–3):1–336 (2012)

Yao82. Yao, A.C.-C.: Theory and applications of trapdoor functions (extended abstract). In: 23rd Annual Symposium on Foundations of Computer Science, 3-5 November 1982, Chicago, Illinois, USA, pp. 80–91 (1982)

# Pseudorandomness Properties of Random Reversible Circuits

William Gay(✉), William He, Nicholas Kocurek, and Ryan O'Donnell

Carnegie Mellon University, Pittsburgh, USA
{wgay,nkocurek}@andrew.cmu.edu, {wrhe,odonnell}@cs.cmu.edu

**Abstract.** Motivated by practical concerns in cryptography, we study pseudorandomness properties of permutations on $\{0,1\}^n$ computed by random circuits made from reversible 3-bit gates (permutations on $\{0,1\}^3$). Our main result is that a random circuit of depth $\sqrt{n} \cdot \widetilde{O}(k^3)$, with each layer consisting of $\Theta(n)$ random gates in a fixed two-dimensional nearest-neighbor architecture, yields approximate $k$-wise independent permutations.

Our result can be seen as a particularly simple/practical block cipher construction that gives provable statistical security against attackers with access to $k$ input-output pairs within few rounds.

The main technical component of our proof consists of two parts:

1. We show that the Markov chain on $k$-tuples of $n$-bit strings induced by a single random 3-bit one-dimensional nearest-neighbor gate has spectral gap at least $1/n \cdot \widetilde{O}(k)$. Then we infer that a random circuit with layers of random gates in a (nearly) fixed *one-dimensional* gate architecture yields approximate $k$-wise independent permutations of $\{0,1\}^n$ in depth $n \cdot \widetilde{O}(k^2)$.
2. We show that if the $n$ wires are layed out on a *two-dimensional* lattice of bits, then repeatedly alternating applications of approximate $k$-wise independent permutations of $\{0,1\}^{\sqrt{n}}$ to the rows and columns of the lattice yields an approximate $k$-wise independent permutation of $\{0,1\}^n$ in small depth.

Our work improves on the original work of Gowers [8], who showed a gap of $1/\text{poly}(n,k)$ for one random gate (with non-neighboring inputs); and, on subsequent work [3,14] improving the gap to $\Omega(1/n^2k)$ in the same setting.

**Keywords:** block ciphers · Markov chains · information-theoretic security

## 1 Introduction

Motivated by questions in the analysis of practical cryptosystems (block ciphers), we study pseudorandomness properties of random reversible circuits. That is, we study the indistinguishability of truly random permutations of $\{0,1\}^n$ versus permutations computed by small, randomly chosen reversible circuits.


Y. Tauman Kalai and S. F. Kamara (Eds.): CRYPTO 2025, LNCS 16000, pp. 651–678, 2025.
https://doi.org/10.1007/978-3-032-01855-7_21

Our main results concern the extent to which small random reversible circuits compute *approximate k-wise independent* permutations. This corresponds to *statistical security* against adversaries that get $k$ input-output pairs from the permutation.

### 1.1 Cryptographic Considerations

Block ciphers lie at the core of many practical implementations of cryptography. Constructions such as the Advanced Encryption Standard (AES) and Data Encryption Standard (DES) are commonly implemented in hardware on computers as instantiations of pseudorandom permutations, and much is demanded of both their security and efficiency. The need for simple and efficient hardware implementations is often in tension with the hope that these block ciphers are secure against cryptanalysis.

Short of showing unconditional security of a particular block cipher against general polynomial-time adversaries, one might hope to show that random reversible circuits are secure against certain classes of cryptographic attacks. Examples of known attacks against block ciphers include linear cryptanalysis, differential cryptanalysis, higher-order attacks, algebraic attacks, integral cryptanalysis, and more. See, for example, [19,20] and the references therein.

We study a pseudorandomness property that implies security against many of these known classes of attacks:

**Definition 1.** *A distribution $\mathcal{P}$ on permutations of $\{0,1\}^n$ is said to be $\varepsilon$-*approximate $k$-wise independent *if for all distinct $x^{(1)}, \dots, x^{(k)} \in \{0,1\}^n$, the distribution of $(\boldsymbol{g}(x^{(1)}), \dots, \boldsymbol{g}(x^{(k)}))$ for $\boldsymbol{g} \sim \mathcal{P}$ has total variation distance at most $\varepsilon$ from the uniform distribution on $k$-tuples of distinct strings from $\{0,1\}^n$.*

By definition, such distributions are statistically secure (up to advantage $\varepsilon$) against an adversary that gets access to any $k$ input-output pairs, chosen non-adaptively. For example, approximate 2-wise independence implies security against linear and differential attacks, and approximate $k$-wise independence for larger $k$ implies security against higher-order differential attacks. Moreover, Maurer and Pietrzak [22] have shown that this can easily be upgraded to security against *adaptive* queries by composing two draws from the pseudorandom permutation (the second inverted).

One might be more interested in the security of $\mathcal{P}$ against any polynomial-time adversary though. Such adversaries can make any polynomial number of queries to the permutation, so to use the security guarantee of approximate $k$-wise independence to infer computational security, one would need to set $k$ to be superpolynomial. A simple argument shows that such permutations require superpolynomial circuit complexity.

However, all known computationally efficient attacks against block ciphers fail as soon as approximate 4-wise independence holds. That is, we know of no approximate 4-wise independent permutation generated as the composition of many local permutations (gates) that is efficiently distinguishable from a completely random permutation of the set of $n$-bit strings. To highlight this fact, it was conjectured in [14] (Sect. 6) that any $\exp(-n)$-approximate 4-wise independent permutation which is obtained by composing some number of reversible gates forms a pseudorandom permutation. This provides further motivation for the study of approximate $k$-wise independence.

In addition to providing security guarantees, much focus is put on designing simple and efficient block ciphers. Recall that a random reversible circuit takes as input some $n$-bit string and computes a permutation by letting a sequence of random gates on 3 bits[1] act on the $n$-bit strings. In this paper we study a natural class of very efficiently implementable circuits, known as brickwork circuits. A brickwork circuit is formed by organizing the bits (also called wires of the circuit) into a low-dimensional lattice and applying layers of gates acting on nearest-neighbors in this lattice at a time. See Fig. 1 for an illustration of this architecture.

The natural efficiency-related question to then ask is how much depth is required for these brickwork circuits to become pseudorandom. In other words, we hope for a class of random reversible circuits that has the following desirable properties:

- The gate architecture is fixed and all gates in the circuit act on nearest-neighbor wires in a low-dimensional Euclidean geometry.
- The circuits become approximate $k$-wise independent in very low depth.
- The circuit yields a straightforward implementation of its inverse.

The first item in this list are especially important for implementations in hardware. The second item shows that they can be run for a short amount of time to achieve pseudorandomness, since circuit depth in this setting corresponds to "wall clock time." Finally, the third item is relevant to efficient decryption.

In this paper we introduce a construction of a candidate block cipher/pseudorandom permutation from random local circuits that could yield straightforward and efficient implementations in hardware, and our main result shows that this class of random reversible circuits satisfies these desirable properties:

**Theorem 1.** *For $k \leq 2^{O(\sqrt{n})}$, there is a class of random reversible circuits with a fixed[2] gate architecture on a two-dimensional lattice (Fig. 1) computing permutations that are $2^{-\sqrt{n}k}$-approximate k-wise independent at depth $\sqrt{n} \cdot \widetilde{O}(k^3)$.*[3]

This result shows that our candidate block cipher becomes secure against a wide class of attacks in very low depth, by setting $k$ to be various small values.

---

[1] Note that gates that act on three wires are necessary, since the set of gates acting on two wires at a time can generate only $\mathbb{F}_2$-affine permutations of the hypercube. Such permutations do not exhibit nontrivial types of pseudorandomness.

[2] Each layer consists of a single layer of $\Theta(n)$ disjoint gates that are either in an "even" or "odd" configuration.

[3] Our result holds even when every gate is assumed to be a DES[2] gate. A gate of type DES[2] if (up to ordering the $c$ bits) it is of the form $(x, b) \mapsto (x, b \oplus f(x))$ for some $f : \{0,1\}^2 \to \{0,1\}$.

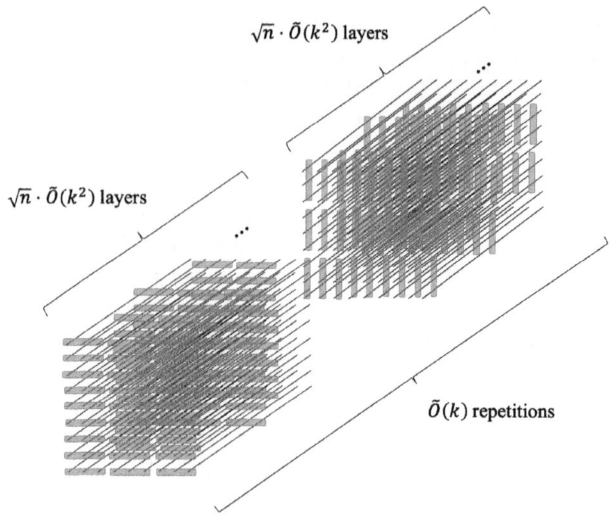


**Fig. 1.** Our two-dimensional brickwork circuit architecture. Each green bar represents a single random 3-bit gate. Theorem 1 states that with the stated number of layers of random gates, the permutation becomes $2^{-\sqrt{n}k}$-approximate $k$-wise independent.

If the conjecture from [14] were to hold, then by setting $k = 4$, Theorem 1 would imply that random brickwork circuits of *sublinear* depth form computationally secure pseudorandom permutations.

Our construction is a variant of the random reversible circuits introduced by Gowers [8]. In this initial work, Gowers also analyzed the approximate $k$-wise independence of random reversible circuits. However, we emphasize that this analysis is a departure from the previous literature on approximate $k$-wise independent permutations from random reversible circuits, which has focused on circuits with non-nearest-neighbor gates without fixed architectures. Our main contribution is showing that even with such desirable properties (fixed gate architecture, geometric locality of gates), circuits still exhibit pseudorandomness properties with small size/depth. Note that the AES block cipher also exhibits a similar 2D-lattice-based structure. A natural continuation of this work would be to apply similar mixing time arguments to prove similar results about AES, which feature some additional gates to promote "confusion-diffusion" and seem to exhibit mixing in even smaller depth.

The construction of these structured circuits are partially inspired by the study of *unitary designs* in quantum physics, in particular [2,12], but the resulting analysis for our case of permutations differs significantly.

Theorem 1 follows from the following two results. First we show that random reversible circuits with fixed *one-dimensional* gate architectures become approximate $k$-wise independent in small depth.

**Theorem 2.** *A random one-dimensional brickwork circuit (Fig. 2) of depth* $n \cdot \widetilde{O}(k^2)$ *computes a permutation that is* $2^{-nk}$*-approximate* $k$*-wise independent.*

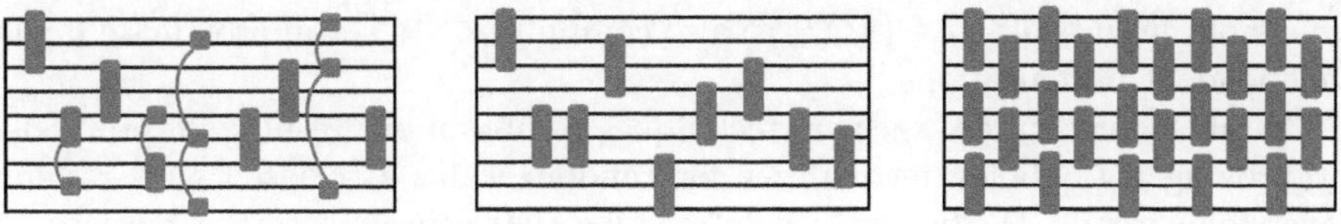

**Fig. 2.** The first circuit is an example of a circuit with generic 3-bit gates. The second is an example of a circuit with 1D nearest-neighbor 3-bit gates. The third is an example of a 1D brickwork circuit with five layers.

Then, we show that instantiating a certain construction of two-dimensional random reversible circuits with the one-dimensional reversible circuits from Theorem 2 maintains approximate $k$-wise independence:

**Theorem 3.** *Suppose there exists a random reversible circuit with a one-dimensional gate architecture that is $2^{-nk}$-approximate $k$-wise independent. Then there exists a class of random reversible circuits with a gate architecture on a two-dimensional lattice computing permutations that are $2^{-\sqrt{n}k}$-approximate $k$-wise independent at depth $\sqrt{n} \cdot \widetilde{O}(k^3)$.*

We prove Theorem 2 with a more general quantitative guarantee, which follows immediately from Theorem 8: that a random brickwork circuit of depth $(nk + \log(1/\varepsilon)) \cdot \widetilde{O}(k)$ computes an $\varepsilon$-approximate $k$-wise independent permutation of $\{0,1\}^n$. Note that Theorem 2 follows by setting $\varepsilon = 2^{-nk}$.

We also obtain a generalization of Theorem 1 by generalizing Theorem 3 to higher-dimensional lattices:

**Theorem 4.** *For all $3 \leq D \leq O\left(\frac{\log n}{\log\log n}\right)$ a random reversible circuit with a certain $D$-dimensional gate architecture computes permutations that are $2^{-n^{1/D}}$-approximate $k$-wise independent permutations of $\{0,1\}^n$ with depth $\exp(D) \cdot n^{1/D} \cdot \widetilde{O}(k^3)$, given that $k \log k \leq O(n^{1/3})$ and $n$ is large enough.*

*Optimal dependence on $n$.* Note that the dependencies on $n$ in Theorem 1, Theorem 2, and Theorem 4 are all tight for the specific gate architectures mentioned in each respective result. This can be seen by a light-cone argument: even approximate 2-wise independence is not possible if there are two wires that cannot influence each other.

*On circuit size.* While the parameter we emphasize in our results is depth, it is interesting to note that our high-dimensional circuit achieves a size vs. $\varepsilon$ tradeoff comparable to that of [9]. To illustrate this, we set $k = O(1)$. However, we note that our tradeoffs hold for growing $k$ as well; we make this simplification for ease of exposition.

In our general Theorem 4 we show that (given $D = O(\log n/\log\log n)$) a class of random reversible circuits of size $n^{1+1/D} \cdot \exp(D)$ compute $2^{-\Theta(n^{1/D})}$-approximate $k$-wise independent permutations. The tradeoff in [9] is that random reversible circuits of size $\widetilde{O}(n^{1+1/D})$ also compute $2^{-\Theta(n^{1/D})}$-approximate $k$-wise independent permutations.

While we use purely spectral techniques to obtain our results, [9] proceeded by proving log-Sobolev inequalities for random walks associated with random reversible circuits. We believe it is interesting that using spectral techniques, we recover similar mixing time results as those obtained from log-Sobolev inequalities.

### 1.2 Related Topics in Pseudorandomness

*Unitary designs.* The definition of approximate $k$-wise independence can be framed in terms of approximating a truly random $2^n$-by-$2^n$ permutation matrix by a pseudorandom one up to $k$th moments. If one replaces permutation matrices with general unitary matrices, then one arrives at the definition of an (approximate) unitary $k$-design. An (approximate) unitary $k$-design is a distribution $\mathcal{P}$ on the unitary group that resembles the Haar random measure on the unitary group up to $k$th moments.

Among various motivations for constructing (approximate) unitary $k$-designs are derandomization of quantum algorithms, modeling of black holes, and the study of topological order. See, for example, [2,6,13,15,28]. Often, the goal is to obtain more efficient implementations of unitary designs using small quantum circuits; this goal is similar to the goal of this paper [2,4,5,10–12,16,21,23].

Recently there has been work on reducing the design of approximate unitary $k$-designs to the design of approximate $k$-wise independent permutations. For example, [4,23] provides constructions of approximate unitary $k$-designs from approximate $k$-wise independent permutations in a black-box way. These constructions provide further motivation for the study of efficiently generated $k$-wise independent permutations.

*Derandomization.* Approximate $k$-wise independent permutation distributions $\mathcal{P}$ have many applications outside of cryptography; derandomization, for example [24]. In such applications, another important parameter is the number of truly random "seed" bits needed to generate a draw from $\mathcal{P}$. By using techniques such as derandomized squaring, one can generally reduce the seed length to $O(nk)$ for any construction; see [17]. This is true for the results in our paper, and we don't discuss this angle further. We are generally focused on the circuit complexity of our permutations.

### 1.3 Techniques and Comparison with Previous Work

Recall that our main result Theorem 1 is about the approximate $k$-wise independence of brickwork circuits of small depth. We arrive at our result via two steps: proving Theorem 2 and proving Theorem 3. We first discuss the proof of Theorem 2.

**Spectral Gaps of Structured Random Reversible Circuits.** We prove Theorem 2 by lower bounding the spectral gap of the random walk on the set of $k$-tuples of $n$-bit strings associated with a random one-dimensional brickwork circuits. The only prior work on brickwork or nearest-neighbor gates for implementing permutations is work of [7], but their results are quantitatively weaker.

Prior work in this area, which deals with non-nearest-neighbor random gates, proceeded by bounding the spectral gap of the random walk on $k$-tuples induced by a single random DES[2] gate.

These earlier works bounded the spectral gap using the canonical paths method ( [8,14]) or multicommodity flows and the comparison method ( [3]). We depart from these methods and use techniques from the physics literature concerned with the extent to which random *quantum* circuits are *unitary* $k$-designs. Specifically, for Theorem 9 we use the induction-on-$n$ technique developed in [10], and for our main Theorem 7 we employ the more sophisticated Nachtergaele method [25] as in the work of Brandão, Harrow, and Horodecki [2]. In fact, it was posed as a question in [2] whether their techniques could be extended to construct approximate $k$-wise independent permutations. We answer this question in the affirmative. Our analyses use Fourier and spectral graph theory methods. In both cases, the inductive technique only begins to work for $n \geq \Theta(\log k)$, and for smaller $n$ we need to base our argument on [3]; in the case of nearest-neighbor gates, this requires a further comparison-method based argument.

One can also interpret our result as the construction of a Cayley graph on $\mathfrak{A}_{2^n}$ with spectral gap $\Omega(1/n2^n)$ and degree $O(n)$. Previous work on this by Kassabov [18] constructed constant-degree expanders out of Cayley graphs on $\mathfrak{A}_{2^n}$, but it is not clear if this random walk can be implemented by short circuits. Especially for the cryptographic applications of this work, it is important that our random walks have low circuit complexity.

In the context of non-nearest-neighbor random gates, the best prior result was the following theorem of Brodsky and Hoory for general (non-nearest-neighbor) reversible architecture:

**Theorem 5.** *( [3].) Consider the permutation on* $\{0,1\}^n$ *computed by a reversible circuit of* $O(n^3k^2)$ *randomly chosen* DES[2]*-gates (meaning in particular that each gate's* 3 *fan-in wires are randomly chosen). This is* $2^{-O(nk)}$*-approximate* $k$*-wise independent. More generally, such circuits of size* $O(n^2k) \cdot (nk + \log(1/\varepsilon))$ *suffices for* $\varepsilon$*-approximate* $k$*-wise independence.*

There is a simple reduction from general gates to nearest-neighbor gates that incurs factor-$\Omega(n)$ size blowup. Plugging this into Theorem 5 would yield $2^{-O(nk)}$-approximate $k$-wise independent permutations formed from nearest-neighbor reversible circuits of size $O(n^4k^2)$. Besides being non-brickwork, this is worse than our Theorem 2 by a factor of about $n^2$. We should note that Brodsky and Hoory also prove the following:

**Theorem 6.** *( [3].) If* $k \leq 2^{n/50}$*, then Theorem 5 also holds for random reversible circuits of size* $\widetilde{O}(n^2k^2 \log(1/\varepsilon))$.

The improved dependence on $n$ in this theorem, namely $\widetilde{O}(n^2)$, is good, but one should caution that the dependence on $\log(1/\varepsilon)$ is *multiplicative.* Thus except in the rather weak case when $\varepsilon \gg 2^{-nk}$, this term introduces a factor of at least $nk$ back into the bound, making it worse than Theorem 5.

All of the difficulty in our main result Theorem 2 comes from analyzing the *spectral gap* of the natural random walk on $k$-tuples of strings arising from picking *one* random nearest-neighbor gate. Note that by spectral gap we actually mean the gap between the top eigenvalue and the next largest eigenvalue, since the chains we work with often are disconnected. We prove:

**Theorem 7.** *Let $P$ be the transition matrix for the random walk on $\{0,1\}^{nk}$ corresponding to one random nearest-neighbor* DES[2] *gate. Then $P$ has a spectral gap of $1/(n \cdot \widetilde{O}(k))$.*

Given this result, Theorem 2 follows almost directly by using the *detectability lemma* from Hamiltonian complexity theory [1], as in analogous results for unitary designs due to [2]. The intermediate step is again proving the one-step spectral gap lower bound.

**Theorem 8.** *Let $P$ be the transition matrix for the random walk on $\{0,1\}^{nk}$ corresponding to one layer of brickwork gates. Then $P$ has a spectral gap of $\eta \geq 1/\widetilde{O}(k)$.*

Note that Theorem 8 directly implies Theorem 2 by the standard Markov chain mixing time bound using spectral gaps.

We also prove an analogous result to Theorem 7 in the case of non-nearest-neighbor gates:

**Theorem 9.** *Let $P$ be the transition matrix for the random walk on $\{0,1\}^{nk}$ corresponding to one random* DES[2] *gate. Then $P$ has a spectral gap of $\Omega(1/(nk \cdot \log k))$.*

Although it may look like this result is conceptually dominated by Theorem 7, we include it as it has improved $\log k$ factors, and its proof reveals some of the ideas we use in our proof of Theorem 7.

*Proof ideas.* The idea that underlies the proofs of all of these theorems is to compare the random walks induced by applying random local permutations to $k$-tuples of strings to the random walks induced by completely resampling subsets of bits in every element of a $k$-tuple of strings. The difference between these two operations is essentially the difference between sampling with replacement and sampling without replacement. To illustrate, given a tuple $(x^1, \ldots, x^k)$ of strings, let $\boldsymbol{F}_S(x^1, \ldots, x^k) = (\boldsymbol{y}^1, \ldots, \boldsymbol{y}^k)$ be a random tuple of strings where for all $a \notin S$ we have $\boldsymbol{y}^i_a = x^i_a$, but where each $\boldsymbol{y}^i_a$ for $a \in S$ is an independent completely random element of $\{\pm 1\}$. From this, it is clear that if $S \cup T = [n]$ then $\boldsymbol{F}_T \circ \boldsymbol{F}_S(x^1, \ldots, x^k)$ is a completely random tuple of strings.

Much of the work in our proofs is showing that in fact, this intuition still approximately holds when $\boldsymbol{F}_S$ is replaced with a random local permutation $\boldsymbol{\pi}_S$

that only acts on bits in $S$, applied to each element of the tuple, when $S$ is a large enough set. Note that if $(x^1,\dots,x^k)$ is a tuple of strings, then to sample $(\boldsymbol{y}^1,\dots,\boldsymbol{y}^k) = (\boldsymbol{\pi}_S(x^1),\dots,\boldsymbol{\pi}_S(x^k))$ one can equivalently carry out the following process. Consider the substrings $(x^1|_S,\dots,x^k|_S)$. Then, for every $i \in [k]$, resample $\boldsymbol{y}^i|_S$ from $\{\pm1\}^S$ at random from the remaining available strings (noting that the $\boldsymbol{y}^i|_S$ must be distinct for distinct $x^i|_S$. If $S$ is a large enough set, and the strings $x^1|_S,\dots,x^k|_S$ were all distinct, then this process strongly resembles the process of drawing each $\boldsymbol{y}^i|_S$ independently. In this sense, for such tuples $(x^1,\dots,x^k)$, we have the following resemblance in distributions:

$$(\boldsymbol{\pi}_S(x^1),\dots,\boldsymbol{\pi}_S(x^k)) \approx \boldsymbol{F}_S(x^1,\dots,x^k). \tag{1}$$

On the other hand, if the $x^1|_S,\dots,x^k|_S$ were not distinct, then we use a simple argument based on escape probabilities to show that such tuples also exhibit good expansion.

Equipped with this comparison, we are able to prove statements of the form

$$(\boldsymbol{\pi}_T\boldsymbol{\pi}_S(x^1),\dots,\boldsymbol{\pi}_T\boldsymbol{\pi}_S(x^k)) \approx \boldsymbol{F}_T\boldsymbol{F}_S(x^1,\dots,x^k)$$

when $S$ and $T$ satisfy certain properties, such as having sufficiently large overlap. When $S \cup T = [n]$ it turns out that the distribution on the right-hand side is equal to a completely random $k$-tuple of $n$-bit strings. Via a lemma of Nachtergaele [25] from quantum physics, a linear-algebraic formalization of this approximation results in a large spectral gap for the spectral gaps associated with geometrically-local random reversible circuits.

**Two-Dimensional Construction.** To obtain the reduction Theorem 3 we use a technique inspired by [12], which obtained a similar reduction in setting of constructing unitary $k$-designs using random quantum circuits. However, there are some complications that arise when working with permutations rather than general unitaries, so our approach departs significantly from that of [12].

Our construction, however, is essentially identical to that of [12]. Let $\mathcal{B}$ be a distribution on circuits computing an approximately $k$-wise independent permutation of $\{0,1\}^{\sqrt{n}}$. Let $X \in \{\pm1\}^{\sqrt{n}\times\sqrt{n}}$ be input to our circuit in the form of a two-dimensional lattice, a grid.

1. For each row in $X$, we sample independent circuits from $\mathcal{B}$ and apply in parallel.
2. For each column in $X$, we sample independent circuits from $\mathcal{B}$ and apply in parallel.
3. We repeat steps and 1 and 2 a total of $O(k \log k)$ times, and finally step 1 exactly once more.

What we get as a result is a circuit of $2t+1$ "layers", with each layer consisting of $\sqrt{n}$ parallel circuits from the family $\mathcal{B}$ all in one of two directions in our lattice. If the circuits in $\mathcal{B}$ have depth $d$ then the depth of our circuit is $O(k \log k) \cdot d$.

We show that the circuit construction above computes permutations that are $\varepsilon$-approximate $k$-wise independent.

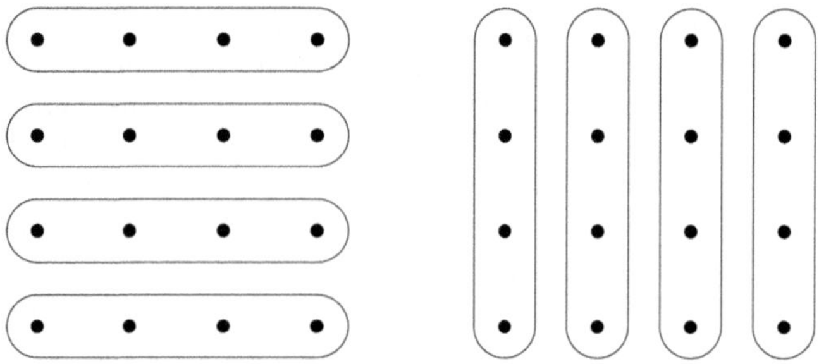

**Fig. 3.** Step 1 applies parallel circuits from $\mathcal{B}$ to the rows, while Step 2 applies to the columns. Our circuit alternates between layers of the two.

*Proof ideas.* As in the 1D case, we reduce analyzing $k$-wise independence of our random reversible circuits to the analyzing the natural induced Markov chain on $\{0,1\}^{nk}$. The induced circuit distribution being approximately uniform then corresponds to mixing in the Markov chain which can be accomplished via establishing a spectral gap or a log-Sobolev inequality.

Our proof does not rely on log-Sobolev inequalities, but rather proceeds entirely through spectral arguments about the random walk operators. However, for sublinear-in-$n$ mixing time (corresponding to circuit depth), it does not suffice to prove a simple spectral gap for our random walk. The reason for this is that naively bounding the mixing time using the spectral gap immediately results in a mixing time at least $\Theta(\log(2^{nk})) = \Theta(nk)$. Thus, we need to proceed more carefully by expressing the total variation distance (which is an $\ell_1$ distance) of the distributions induced by running the Markov chain for some number of steps more directly in terms of the spectral properties of the transition matrices.

In particular, we derive approximations that resemble those of the type in Eq. 1, but now the quality of the approximation depends on how many substring collisions the tuple $(x^1, \ldots, x^k)$ has. To formalize this quantitatively, we assign each tuple $(x^1, \ldots, x^k)$ to a certain group of tuples based on the collision pattern it experiences. By bounding the contribution to the total variation distance of each group of tuples and analyzing the transition probabilities between these groups, we can directly analyze the mixing time without directly exhibiting a functional inequality for the corresponding Markov chain.

### 1.4 Comparison with Subsequent Work

Since the release of the first version of this work, there have been a number of subsequent works on approximate $k$-wise independent permutations and unitary $k$-designs. Of these, perhaps the most relevant to this work are the recent results in [5,9]:

**Theorem 10** **([9], Theorem 2).** *For any $n$ and $k \leq 2^{n/50}$, a random reversible circuit with $\widetilde{O}(nk \cdot \log(1/\varepsilon))$ DES[2] gates computes an $\varepsilon$-approximate $k$-wise independent permutation.*

**Theorem 11** **([5], Corollary 1.3).** *For any* $n \geq 4$ *and* $k \leq \Theta(2^{n/6.1})$*, a random reversible circuit with* $\widetilde{O}(n(nk + \log(1/\varepsilon)))$ DES[2] *gates computes an* $\varepsilon$*-approximate* $k$*-wise independent permutation.*

It is worth noting the ways in which our results, Theorem 10, and Theorem 11 supersede each other and are incomparable. We first note that the size bound of $\widetilde{O}(nk(nk+\log(1/\varepsilon))$ implied by Theorem 9 is immediately superseded by both Theorem 10 and Theorem 11.[4]

However, the main results of this paper on random reversible circuits with nearest-neighbor gates (Theorem 7) and random brickwork circuits (Theorem 2) are still the state-of-the-art. Subsequent works [5,9] say nothing more about reversible circuits with such structured gates than what can be deduced by an application of the comparison method as in Lemma 11. Such an application immediately incurs a poly$(n)$ blow-up in the size of the circuits.

[5] claims that it is likely that their techniques can be adapted to show a $\widetilde{O}(1/n)$ bound on the spectral gap of the random walk induced by one layer of a random brickwork circuit. On the other hand, our spectral gap is $\widetilde{O}(1/k)$. Thus, if such a result were to be proved, it would be an improvement only if $k$ exceeds $n$. We emphasize that for many purposes one might be interested in the case where $k$ is a constant and $n$ grows. See, for example, the discussion in Sect. 1.1 on a conjecture of [14].

## 2 Proof Overview

### 2.1 One-Dimensional Circuits

Recall that the main technical content behind the proof of Theorem 2 is to exhibit a spectral gap for the random walk matrix induced by applying a single brickwork layer of fixed random gates. The first step to exhibit this spectral gap is to show that a *single* random geometrically local gate also exhibits a large spectral gap, and the result about a single brickwork layer follows by the detectability lemma of Aharonov et al. [1].

To bound the spectral gap induced by a single random geometrically local gate, we note that the corresponding Laplacian is of the form

$$L = \mathop{\mathbf{E}}_{a\in\{1,\dots,n-2\}}[L_{\boldsymbol{a}}],$$

where each $L_{\boldsymbol{a}}$ corresponds to the application of a single random gate to the bits $\boldsymbol{a}, \boldsymbol{a}+1, \boldsymbol{a}+2$. This type of operator can also be viewed as the Hamiltonian of a physical system consisting of $n$ particles on a one-dimensional lattice with nearest-neighbor interactions. To analyze the spectral gap of this operator, we use tools from quantum many-body physics.

In particular, a result of Nachtergaele [25] shows how to reduce exhibiting a spectral gap for this $n$-particle system to exhibiting a spectral gap for a smaller

---

[4] In this discussion we ignore factors logarithmic in $n$ and $k$.

system. Previous results allow us to bound the spectral gap for this smaller system, but the main technical content in the proof of Theorem 2 is to show that the hypotheses of this result of [25] are satisfied by the operators we are interested in.

As alluded to before, showing that these hypotheses are satisfied involves proving statements such as

$$(\boldsymbol{\pi}_T\boldsymbol{\pi}_S(x^1), \ldots, \boldsymbol{\pi}_T\boldsymbol{\pi}_S(x^k)) \approx \boldsymbol{F}_T\boldsymbol{F}_S(x^1, \ldots, x^k).$$

Recall that to show comparisons of the above form, the plan is to compare the processes of sampling with replacement and sampling without replacement in the setting where not too many elements are being resampled, relative to the total number of elements. To see why this comparison is relevant, note that applying a random permutation to each element in a $k$-tuple of strings is almost equivalent to sampling $k$ elements from a set of strings with replacement.

Combinatorially, directly analyzing probabilities allows us to bound the distance between resampling with replacement and resampling without replacement. To relate this combinatorial bound to a linear-algebraic quantity, we use Lemma 6.

An issue arises when we try to apply this comparison: the comparison does not hold on a small subset of $k$-tuples of $n$-bit strings. However, we show that this set exhibits good expansion already, or that the probability of a random walk escaping from this region is already large. Formally, Lemma 8 relates the escape probabilities from a region of the Markov chain to the quadratic form induced by its transition operator.

### 2.2 Two-Dimensional Circuits

The proof of Theorem 1 proceeds by instantiating the lattice construction in Theorem 3 with the one-dimensional construction in Theorem 2. We now overview the proof of Theorem 3.

Recall that in the 1D case we related our circuit construction to an induced Markov chain on the set of $k$-tuples of $n$-bit strings and exhibited a spectral gap for this Markov chain to deduce fast mixing. We will start by showing why this argument does not suffice for a sublinear-in-$n$ dependence on $n$ in the mixing time.

Recall that the standard spectral argument states that given spectral gap $\lambda$ for a reversible Markov chain on state space $S$ the time to mix is bounded above by

$$\frac{1}{\lambda} \cdot (\log |S| + \log(1/\varepsilon)).$$

However, note that the state space $S$ in our context consists of the set of $k$-tuples of distinct $n$-bit strings, and therefore $\log(||S||) \approx nk$. Therefore, since $\lambda$ is always bounded above by 1, the best mixing time one could hope for via this naive analysis would already have a linear dependence in $n$.

Therefore, we need to develop a more refined argument, which deals more directly with total variation distance. We now describe this approach. Recall that our 2D circuit construction involves alternating layers of row and column-oriented 1D circuits. As such, the Markov operator $T_P$ for the circuit can be expressed as $T_P = T_{P_R}(T_{P_C}T_{P_R})^t$ where $T_{P_R}$ and $T_{P_C}$ are the induced operators corresponding to individual row and column-oriented layers.

We can now express the TV distance between relevant distributions as follows. Let $X \in \{\pm 1\}^{nk}$ be a $k$-tuple of unique $n$-bit strings (we will call the set of such $k$-tuples $\mathscr{D}$), which corresponds to a single state in our Markov chain. Then the TV distance between the uniform distribution on $\mathscr{D}$ and the output of a random circuit from our construction on $X$ can be expressed as

$$\sum_{Y \in \mathscr{D}} \left| \mathbf{Pr}[X \to_{T_P} Y] - \frac{1}{|\mathscr{D}|} \right| = \sum_{Y \in \mathscr{D}} |\langle e_X, (T_P - T_G)e_Y \rangle|.$$

where $\mathbf{Pr}[X \to_{T_P} Y]$ specifies the probability that our sampled circuit outputs $Y$ on the inputs in $X$ and $e_X$ represents the point mass on $X$ vector. This linear algebraic view turns out to be useful in providing bounds, since it allows us to use spectral techniques.

First, we introduce as an intermediate for analysis a *fully idealized* row-column operator $T_{G_R}(T_{G_C}T_{G_R})^t$ which is analogous to the circuit operator $T_{P_R}(T_{P_C}T_{P_R})$ but with each 1D circuit replaced by a fully random permutation. By the approximate $k$-wise independence of the row and column permutations, replacing $T_P$ by this operator does not change the TV distance much.

We then look at the quantity

$$\sum_{Y \in \mathscr{D}} \left| \langle e_X, (T_{G_R}(T_{G_C}T_{G_R})^t - T_G)e_Y \rangle \right|.$$

Each term in this sum can be bound using spectral techniques. Here, we reuse the idea of providing an orthogonal decomposition of the space $\mathbb{R}^{\{\pm 1\}^{nk}}$ by partitioning $\{\pm 1\}^{nk}$ and doing casework on how these random permutations act on particular tuples in $\{\pm 1\}^{nk}$. For example, if a $k$-tuple of grids $X$ has that all rows across the tuple are distinct, then the action of $G_R$ on $X$ is actually very close to the action of $G$ already. To see this, observe that $G_R$ applies a uniform permutation on each row, which can be seen as sampling distinct rows across the tuple. Conversely, $G$ samples distinct grids. Compare this to the operators $H_R$ and $H$, which do the same sampling completely uniformly. While $G_R$ and $G$ are different, $H_R$ and $H$ are exactly the same. In the regime $k \ll 2^{n/2}$, the classic birthday bound tells us that these processes then look very similar.

These regions where $G_R$ looks like $G$ end up being quite large. However, there exist small regions of the graph on which $G_R$ and $G$ act very differently, and indeed it is this fact that causes the operator norm of $T_{G_R} - T_G$ to be large. For example, it can be the case that $X$ is such that all but one row is completely uniform on all elements in a $k$-tuple of $\sqrt{n}$-by-$\sqrt{n}$ grids. Then $G_R X$ must have the same property.

However, in such regions, $G_C$ must then act somewhat similarly to a completely random permutation $G$. More specifically, we will be able to show that by applying $G_C$ in between applications of $G_R$, we are able to "escape" the bad regions where $G_R$ does not look like $G$ and show that the end result operator is comparable. We end up with a spectral bound along the lines of:

$$\|T_{G_C}T_{G_R} - T_G\|_2 \ll \frac{1}{2\sqrt{n}}.$$

Powering (which corresponds to repeating the construction sequentially) allows us to improve this bound exponentially. There is one slight problem that arises here: black box converting this to the statement on the TV distance as above suffers from a blow up on the order $2^{nk}$, similar to the reason we cannot apply a naive spectral norm bound to mixing time argument in the first place.

We get around this by observing that in our setting the Markov chain is actually "warm-started" by the first application of $G_R$, in that, $\|T_{G_R}e_X\|_2$ is small already. This does not quite work as is: the bad regions of $\{\pm 1\}^{nk}$ still have that $\|T_{G_R}e_X\|_2$ is too large. We supplement by showing that in this case $G_C$ helps us escape the bad region with good probability. This argument breaks in our favor: viewed this way the warm-start brings the blow up from $2^{nk}$ to $2^{\sqrt{n}\cdot\tilde{O}(k)}$.

See the full version of this paper for the full proof of Theorem 3.

## 3 Preliminaries

### 3.1 Some Linear Operators

*Notation.* We switch from $\{0,1\}$ notation to $\{\pm 1\}$ notation to facilitate later Fourier analysis. We will regard elements of $\{\pm 1\}^{nk}$ as tuples $(X^1, \ldots, X^k)$, where each $X^i \in \{\pm 1\}^n$. If $X^i \in \{\pm 1\}^n$, let $X^i_S$ denote the vector $X^i$ restricted to indices in $S$, so that if $S = \{a_1, \ldots, a_{|S|}\}$ with $a_1 < \cdots < a_{|S|}$ then $X^i_S = (X^i_{a_1}, \ldots, X^i_{a_{|S|}})$. For two vectors $x, y \in \{\pm 1\}^n$, define $\Delta(x, y) = \{a \in [n] : x_a \neq y_a\}$. Unless otherwise specified, log is $\log_2$. For positive integers $a \leq b$ denote $[a, b] = \{a, a+1, \cdots, b-1, b\}$ and let $[a] = [1, a]$. Let $\mathbf{1}$ be the all 1s vector, with length determined by context. When $L$ is a self-adjoint operator let $\lambda_2(L)$ be its second-smallest distinct eigenvalue. If $g \in \mathfrak{S}_{\{0,1\}^\gamma}$ is a permutation and $S \subseteq [n]$ has $|S| = \gamma$ then define $g^S \in \mathfrak{S}_{\{0,1\}^n}$ by setting $(g^S x)_S = g(x_S)$, where coordinates are interpreted to be in lexicographic order, and $(g^S x)_{[n]\setminus S} = x_{[n]\setminus S}$.

When $\mathcal{U}$ is a set, we let $\mathbb{R}^{\mathcal{U}}$ denote the vector space of all functions $\mathcal{U} \to \mathbb{R}$. We equip this space with the inner product $\langle \cdot, \cdot \rangle$ given by

$$\langle f, g \rangle = \sum_{x \in \mathcal{U}} f(x) g(x)$$

for $f, g : \mathcal{U} \to \mathbb{R}$. Also define the norm by $\|f\|_2 = \sqrt{\langle f, f \rangle}$.

*Random walk operators.* Suppose $R$ is a random walk operator corresponding to drawing the next state from the distribution $\mathcal{D}_X$, where $X$ is the current state. For $S \subseteq \mathcal{U}$ we will often write $\mathbf{Pr}_{Y \sim \mathcal{D}_x}[\mathbf{Y} \in S]$ as $\mathbf{Pr}[X \to_{T_\mathcal{D}} S]$. When $S = \{Y\}$ is a singleton we use write $\mathbf{Pr}[X \to_{T_\mathcal{D}} S] = \mathbf{Pr}[X \to_{T_\mathcal{D}} Y]$.

**Lemma 1.** *For* $X, Y \in \{\pm 1\}^{nk}$, $\langle e_X, Re_Y \rangle = \boldsymbol{Pr}[X \to_R Y]$.

This above lemma is especially useful as it can be extended across sequential distributions:

**Lemma 2.** *For* $X, Y \in \{\pm 1\}^{nk}$, $\langle e_X, R_1 R_2 e_Y \rangle = \boldsymbol{Pr}[X \to_{R_2 R_1} Y]$.

It is worth pointing out the order of the operators on the bottom is written interpreting $R_1$ and $R_2$ as matrices. The order of application effectively flips under the composition here from how it is written above, so it is important to keep track of orientation.

Throughout the proof of Theorem 2, we use the following notation:

**Definition 2.** *Let $n$ be fixed. Define the distribution $\mathcal{D}_X^{m,S,k}$ to be the law of $\mathbf{Y}$, where to draw $\mathbf{Y}$ first one draws $\boldsymbol{\sigma}' \in \mathfrak{S}_{\{\pm 1\}^{|S|}}$ and then defines* $\mathbf{Y} = \left((\boldsymbol{\sigma}' x_S^1, x_{\overline{S}}^1), \ldots, (\boldsymbol{\sigma}' x_S^k, x_{\overline{S}}^k)\right)$. *The following is the corresponding random walk operator.*

$$(R_{n,S,k} f)(X) = \mathop{\mathbf{E}}_{\mathbf{Y} \sim \mathcal{D}_X^{m,S,k}} [f(\mathbf{Y})].$$

**Lemma 3.** *For any $n, S, k$ we have that $R_{n,S,k}$ is self-adjoint.*

**Lemma 4.** *For any $S \subseteq [n]$ we have $R_{n,S,k}\mathbf{1} = \mathbf{1}$.*

In some contexts it is easier to work with the Laplacians of these operators:

**Definition 3.** *For any operator $R$ on a vector space $V$ let $L(R)$ denote its Laplacian* $\mathrm{Id}_V - R$.

### 3.2 Fourier Analysis of Boolean Functions

**Definition 4.** *Let $S_1, \ldots, S_k \subseteq [n]$. Then define the function $\chi_{S_1,\ldots,S_k}$ by defining for $X \in \{\pm 1\}^{nk}$,*

$$\chi_{S_1,\ldots,S_k}(X) = \prod_{i \in [k]} \prod_{a \in S_i} X_a^i.$$

**Lemma 5** ([26]). *The functions $\chi_{S_1,\ldots,S_k}$ for $S_1, \ldots, S_k \subseteq [n]$ form an orthogonal basis of* $\mathbb{R}^{\{\pm 1\}^{nk}}$.

### 3.3 Comparison Bounds

Recall that our main idea is to approximate one random walk by a simpler random walk. The following Lemma 6 formalizes this linear algebraically.

**Lemma 6.** *Suppose $A$ and $B$ are self-adjoint random walk matrices on a domain $\mathcal{U}$. Let* Supp $\subseteq \mathcal{U}$. *Then for any $f, g : \mathcal{U} \to \mathbb{R}$ with* $\text{Supp}(f) = \text{Supp}(g) = \text{Supp}$ *we have*

$$|\langle f, (A-B)g\rangle| \leq \sqrt{\sum_{X\in\text{Supp}} f(X)^2 \sum_{Y\in\text{Supp}} |\boldsymbol{Pr}[X \to_A Y] - \boldsymbol{Pr}[X \to_B Y]|} \cdot \sqrt{\sum_{X\in\text{Supp}} g(X)^2 \sum_{Y\in\text{Supp}} |\boldsymbol{Pr}[X \to_A Y] - \boldsymbol{Pr}[X \to_B Y]|}.$$

*In particular, when $f = g$ we get*

$$|\langle f, (A-B)f\rangle| \leq \sum_{X\in\text{Supp}(f)} f(X)^2 \sum_{Y\in\text{Supp}(f)} |\boldsymbol{Pr}[X \to_A Y] - \boldsymbol{Pr}[X \to_B Y]|,$$

*Proof.* We directly compute

$$\begin{aligned}|\langle f, (A-B)g\rangle| &= \left|\sum_{X\in\mathcal{U}} f(X)((Ag)(X) - (Bg)(X))\right| \\ &= \left|\sum_{X\in\mathcal{U}} f(X) \sum_{Y\in\mathcal{U}} g(Y)(\mathbf{Pr}[X \to_A Y] - \mathbf{Pr}[X \to_B Y])\right|.\end{aligned}$$

By assumption on the support of $f$ and $g$, we have that the above is bounded from above by

$$\begin{aligned}&\sum_{X,Y\in\text{Supp}} |f(X)||g(Y)||\mathbf{Pr}[X \to_A Y] - \mathbf{Pr}[X \to_B Y]| \\ &\leq \sqrt{\sum_{X,Y\in\text{Supp}} f(X)^2|\mathbf{Pr}[X \to_A Y] - \mathbf{Pr}[X \to_B Y]|} \cdot \sqrt{\sum_{X,Y\in\text{Supp}} g(Y)^2|\mathbf{Pr}[X \to_A Y] - \mathbf{Pr}[X \to_B Y]|} \\ &= \sqrt{\sum_{X,Y\in\text{Supp}} f(X)^2|\mathbf{Pr}[X \to_A Y] - \mathbf{Pr}[X \to_B Y]|} \cdot \sqrt{\sum_{X,Y\in\text{Supp}} g(Y)^2|\mathbf{Pr}[Y \to_A X] - \mathbf{Pr}[Y \to_B X]|} \\ &\qquad\qquad \text{(Self-adjointness of } A \text{ and } B) \\ &= \sqrt{\sum_{X\in\text{Supp}} f(X)^2 \sum_{Y\in\text{Supp}} |\mathbf{Pr}[X \to_A Y] - \mathbf{Pr}[X \to_B Y]|}\end{aligned}$$

$$\cdot \sqrt{\sum_{X \in \text{Supp}} g(X)^2 \sum_{Y \in \text{Supp}} |\mathbf{Pr}[X \to_A Y] - \mathbf{Pr}[X \to_B Y]|}.$$

This Lemma 6 will be frequently used in conjunction with the following bound relating sampling with replacement and sampling without replacement:

**Lemma 7.** *If $k \leq \sqrt{N}$ then*

$$\prod_{i=0}^{k-1} \frac{N}{N-i} \leq 1 + \frac{k^2}{N}.$$

*Proof.* We prove by induction on $i$. If $i = 0$ then the result is trivially true. Now assume that $\prod_{i=0}^{k-2} \frac{N}{N-i} \leq 1 + \frac{(k-1)^2}{N}$. Then

$$\prod_{i=0}^{k-1} \frac{N}{N-i} \leq \left(1 + \frac{(k-1)^2}{N}\right)\left(1 + \frac{k-1}{N-k+1}\right)$$
$$\leq \left(1 + \frac{(k-1)^2}{N}\right)\left(1 + \frac{k}{N}\right) \leq \left(1 + \frac{k^2}{N}\right).$$

The inequalities follow because $k \leq \sqrt{N}$.

### 3.4 Escape Probabilities

Another idea that is key to our spectral gap proofs is to bound the contribution to spectra of "badly-behaved regions" of the state spaces of random walks by showing that these sets exhibit probable escape. This Lemma 8 formalizes this linear algebraically.

**Lemma 8.** *Suppose $A$ is a random walk matrix on a domain $\mathcal{U}$ such that the uniform distribution on $\mathcal{U}$ is a stationary distribution for $A$. Let $f, g : \mathcal{U} \to \mathbb{R}$ be such that for any $X \in \text{Supp}(f)$,*

$$\boldsymbol{Pr}[X \to_A \text{Supp}(g)] \leq \varepsilon.$$

*Then*

$$|\langle f, Ag \rangle| \leq \sqrt{\varepsilon}\, \|f\|_2\, \|g\|_2\,.$$

*Proof.* We directly compute:

$$|\langle f, Ag \rangle|$$
$$= \left| \sum_{X \in \mathcal{U}} f(X) \mathbf{1}[X \in \text{Supp}(f)] \underset{\mathbf{Y} \sim \mathcal{D}_X}{\mathbf{E}} [g(\mathbf{Y}) \mathbf{1}[\mathbf{Y} \in \text{Supp}(g)]] \right|$$

$$\leq \|f\|_2 \sqrt{\sum_{X \in \mathcal{U}} \mathbf{1}[X \in \text{Supp}(f)]^2 \mathop{\mathbf{E}}_{\mathbf{Y} \sim \mathcal{D}_X} [g(\mathbf{Y})\mathbf{1}[\mathbf{Y} \in \text{Supp}(g)]]^2}$$

(Cauchy-Schwarz)

$$\leq \|f\|_2 \sqrt{\sum_{X \in \mathcal{U}} \mathbf{1}[X \in \text{Supp}(f)] \left( \sqrt{\mathop{\mathbf{E}}_{\mathbf{Y} \sim \mathcal{D}_X} [g(\mathbf{Y})^2] \mathop{\mathbf{E}}_{\mathbf{Y} \sim \mathcal{D}_X} \left[ \mathbf{1}[\mathbf{Y} \in \text{Supp}(g)]^2 \right]} \right)^2}$$

(Cauchy-Schwarz)

$$= \|f\|_2 \sqrt{\sum_{X \in \mathcal{U}} \mathbf{1}[X \in \text{Supp}(f)] \mathop{\mathbf{E}}_{\mathbf{Y} \sim \mathcal{D}_X} [g(\mathbf{Y})^2] \mathop{\mathbf{E}}_{\mathbf{Y} \sim \mathcal{D}_X} [\mathbf{1}[\mathbf{Y} \in \text{Supp}(g)]]}$$

$$= \|f\|_2 \sqrt{\sum_{X \in \mathcal{U}} \mathbf{1}[X \in \text{Supp}(f)] \mathop{\mathbf{E}}_{\mathbf{Y} \sim \mathcal{D}_X} [g(\mathbf{Y})^2] \mathbf{Pr}[X \to_A \text{Supp}(g)]}.$$

Now, consider each possible value that $X$ may take. If $X \in \text{Supp}(f)$ then by the assumption, we have that $\mathbf{Pr}[X \to_A \text{Supp}(g)] \leq \varepsilon$. Otherwise if $X \notin \text{Supp}(f)$ we have that $\mathbf{1}[X \in \text{Supp}(f)] = 0$. In both cases, $\mathbf{1}[X \in \text{Supp}(f)]\mathbf{Pr}[X \to_A \text{Supp}(g)] \leq \varepsilon$. Continuing with our calculation, we find that:

$$\begin{aligned} |\langle f, Ag \rangle| &\leq \|f\|_2 \left| \sqrt{|\mathcal{U}| \mathop{\mathbf{E}}_{\mathbf{X} \sim \mathcal{U}} \left[ \varepsilon \mathop{\mathbf{E}}_{\mathbf{Y} \sim \mathcal{D}_\mathbf{X}} [g(\mathbf{Y})^2] \right]} \right| \\ &= \sqrt{\varepsilon} \|f\|_2 \left| \sqrt{|\mathcal{U}| \mathop{\mathbf{E}}_{\mathbf{X} \sim \mathcal{U}} \left[ \mathop{\mathbf{E}}_{\mathbf{Y} \sim \mathcal{D}_\mathbf{X}} [g(\mathbf{Y})^2] \right]} \right|. \end{aligned}$$

At this point, we note that sampling $\mathbf{X}$ uniformly at random and then sampling $\mathbf{Y} \sim \mathcal{D}_\mathbf{X}$ gives the same distribution as sampling $\mathbf{Y}$ uniformly by stationarity of the uniform distribution. This completes the proof by the following:

$$|\langle f, Ag \rangle| \leq \sqrt{\varepsilon} \|f\|_2 \left| \sqrt{|\mathcal{U}| \mathop{\mathbf{E}}_{\mathbf{X} \in \mathcal{U}} [g(\mathbf{X})^2]} \right| = \sqrt{\varepsilon} \|f\|_2 \|g\|_2 .$$

# 4 Spectral Gaps

## 4.1 Fully Random Gates

Throughout this section let $n$ be a fixed positive integer. Recalling Definition 2, the operators in focus in this section are operators of the following form for $m \leq n$:

$$R_{n,m,k} = \frac{1}{\binom{n}{m}} \sum_{S \in \binom{[n]}{m}} R_{n,S,k}.$$

Also define the Laplacian $L_{n,m,k} = L(R_{n,m,k})$.

In this section we prove Theorem 9 by building on the previously-mentioned following result of Brodsky and Hoory:

**Theorem 12** **([3], Theorem 2).** *For any $m$ and $f : \{\pm 1\}^{mk} \to \mathbb{R}$ and $k \le 2^m - 2$, we have that*[5]

$$|\langle f, (R_{m,3,k} - R_{m,m,k})f\rangle| \le 1 - \Omega\left(\frac{1}{m^2 k}\right)\langle f, f\rangle.$$

Our main contribution is a finer analysis in the case when $k$ is small relative to $m$, which results in the following theorem.

**Theorem 13.** *Assume that $m \ge 100$ and $k \le 2^{m/10}$. Given $f : \{\pm 1\}^{mk} \to \mathbb{R}$, we have*

$$|\langle f, (R_{m,m-1,k} - R_{m,m,k})f\rangle| \le \left(\frac{1}{m} + \frac{k^2}{2^{m/4}}\right)\langle f, f\rangle.$$

Theorem 13 is proven in the full version of this paper.

The following lemma allows us to combine Theorem 13 with the previously-known Theorem 12 to bring the quadratic dependence on the number of wires ($n$) to linear.

**Lemma 9** **([27], Lemma 3.2).** *Fix a positive integer $n_0 \ge 4$. For each $k$ and $m_1 \ge m_2$ let $\tau_{m_1,m_2,k}$ be some real number such that*[6]

$$L_{m_1,m_2,k} \ge \tau_{m_1,m_2,k} L_{m_1,m_1,k}.$$

*Then for any sequence $n_0 = m_0 \le m_1 \le \cdots \le m_{t-1} \le m_t = n$ we have*

$$L_{n,n_0,k} \ge \left(\prod_{i\in[t-1]} \tau_{m_i,m_{i-1},k}\right) L_{n,n,k}.$$

Together, Theorem 12, Theorem 13, and Lemma 9 yield the following initial spectral gap.

**Corollary 1.** *For any $n$ and $k \le 2^{n/3}$, we have*

$$L_{n,3,k} \ge \Omega\left(\frac{1}{nk \cdot \log k}\right) L_{n,n,k}.$$

*Proof.* Theorem 13 shows that for all $m \ge 20 \log k$ we have $\tau_{m,m-1,k} \ge 1 - \frac{1}{m} - \frac{k^2}{2^{m/3}}$. Theorem 12 shows that

$$L_{20\log k,3,k} \ge \Omega\left(\frac{1}{k \cdot \log^2 k}\right) L_{20\log k,20\log k,k},$$

---

[5] [3] actually proves this inequality for the operator $R^{\mathrm{DES}[2]}_{m,3,k}$ in place of $R_{m,3,k}$, which is the random walk operator induced by placing a random width-2 permutation (which acts on 3 bits). However, a standard comparison of Markov chains shows that our statement of the result easily follows. See Sect. 4.3.

[6] All inequalities between operators in this paper are in the PSD order.

or equivalently $\tau_{20\log k,3,k} \geq \Omega\left(\frac{1}{k\log^2 k}\right)$.

Combining these using Lemma 9 we have for large enough $k$ that

$$\begin{aligned} L_{n,3,k} \geq& \Omega\left(\frac{1}{k\log^2 k}\right) \prod_{m=20\log k}^{n} \left(1-\frac{1}{m}-\frac{k^2}{2^{m/4}}\right) L_{n,n,k} \\ \geq& \Omega\left(\frac{1}{k\log^2 k}\right) \frac{20\log k}{n} \prod_{m=20\log k}^{n} \left(1-\frac{k^2}{2^{m/4-1}}\right) \cdot L_{n,n,k} \\ \geq& \Omega\left(\frac{1}{nk\cdot\log k}\right) \cdot \left(1-\sum_{m=20\log k}^{n} \frac{k^2}{2^{m/4-1}}\right) \cdot L_{n,n,k} \geq \Omega\left(\frac{1}{nk\cdot\log k}\right) \cdot L_{n,n,k}. \end{aligned}$$

We leverage the initial spectral gap from Corollary 1 to produce our designs by sequentially composing many copies of this pseudorandom permutation. This is akin to showing that the second largest eigenvalue of the square of a graph is quadratically smaller than that of the original graph.

Theorem 9 follows directly from Sect. 4.3 with standard spectral-gap to mixing time bounds.

### 4.2 Nearest-Neighbor Random Gates

**Reduction to the Large $k$ Case.** One step in a random reversible circuit with 1D-nearest-neighbor gates is described by the operator $R^{3\text{-NN}}_{n,[n-2],k}$. Note that we can write[7]

$$R^{3\text{-NN}}_{n,[n-2],k} = \mathop{\mathbf{E}}_{\mathbf{a}\in[n-2]} \left[R_{n,\{\mathbf{a},\mathbf{a+1},\mathbf{a+2}\},k}\right].$$

Define the corresponding Laplacian $L^{\gamma\text{-NN}}_{n,I,k} = L(R^{\gamma\text{-NN}}_{n,I,k})$.

Because the local terms $R_{n,\{\mathbf{a},\mathbf{a+1},\mathbf{a+2}\},k}$ are projectors, to analyze such an operator we can use the following theorem of Nachtergaele.

**Theorem 14 ([25], Theorem 3).** *Let $\{h_{a,a+1,a+2}\}_{a\in[n-2]}$ be projectors acting on $(\mathbb{R}^2)^{\otimes d}$ such that each $h_{\{a,a+1,a+2\}}$ only acts on the $a, a+1, a+2$th tensor factor. For $I = [a,b] \subseteq [n]$ define the subspace*

$$\mathcal{G}_I = \left\{ f \in (\mathbb{R}^2)^{\otimes d} : \sum_{a'\in[a,b-2]} h_{a',a'+1,a'+2} f = 0 \right\}.$$

*Let $G_I$ be the projector to $\mathcal{G}_I$.*

*Now suppose there exists $\ell$ and $n_\ell$ and $\varepsilon_\ell \leq \frac{1}{\sqrt{\ell}}$ such that for all $n_\ell \leq m \leq n$,*

$$\left\|G_{[m-\ell-1,m]}\left(G_{[m-1]} - G_{[m]}\right)\right\|_{\text{op}} \leq \varepsilon_\ell.$$

[7] More generally, we write $R^{\gamma\text{-NN}}_{n,S,k}$ to denote $\mathbf{E}_{a\in S}\left[R_{n,\{\mathbf{a},\dots,\mathbf{a}+\gamma-1\},k}\right]$.

*Then*

$$\lambda_2\left(\sum_{a\in[n-2]} h_{\{a,a+1,a+2\}}\right) \geq \frac{\left(1-\varepsilon_\ell\sqrt{\ell}\right)^2}{\ell-3}\lambda_2\left(\sum_{a\in[\ell]} h_{\{a,a+1,a+2\}}\right).$$

*Recall $\lambda_2(h)$ denotes the second-smallest distinct eigenvalue of the operator $h$.*

**Theorem 15.** *Fix any $m \geq 100$ and $k \leq 2^m - 2$ and set $\ell = 10\log k$. Then we have*

$$\left\|R_{m,[m-\ell-1,m],k}\left(R_{m,[m-1],k} - R_{m,[m],k}\right)\right\|_{\text{op}} \leq \frac{1}{\ell}.$$

Theorem 15 is established in the full version of this paper.

**Corollary 2.** *We have for $k \geq 3$ that*

$$\lambda_2\left(L^{3\text{-}NN}_{n,[n-2],k}\right) \geq \frac{1}{2n}\lambda_2\left(L^{3\text{-}NN}_{10\log k+2,[10\log k-2],k}\right)$$

*Proof.* Setting $h_{a,a+1,a+2} = \text{Id} - R_{n,\{a,a+1,a+2\},k}$ for each $a \in [n]$, we see that the projections $G$ (as in the statement of Theorem 14) are given by $G_{[a]} = R_{n,[\min\{n,a+2\}],k}$ for any $a \in [n]$. To see this, note first that $R_{n,[\min\{n,a+2\}],k}$ is indeed a projection. Now let $f$ be such that $R_{n,[\min\{n,a+2\}],k}f = f$. For every $\sigma \in \mathfrak{S}_{\{\pm1\}^n}$ define $f^\sigma$ by $f^\sigma(X) = f(\sigma X)$ for all $X \in \{\pm1\}^{nk}$. Then by invariance of $R_{n,[\min\{n,a+2\}],k}$ under a permutation applied to bits in $[\min\{n, a+2\}]$ we have

$$f^\sigma = R_{n,[\min\{n,a+2\}],k}f^\sigma = R_{n,[\min\{n,a+2\}],k}f = f.$$

for any $\sigma \in \mathfrak{S}_{\{\pm1\}^{[\min\{n,a+2\}]}}$. The converse of this holds as well by a similar argument. Therefore, $f^{\sigma^{\{a',a'+1,a'+2\}}} = f$ for any $\sigma \in \mathfrak{S}_{\{0,1\}^8}$ for $a' \leq a$, proving that such an $f$ is truly in the ground space of $R_{n,\{a',a'+1,a'+2\},k}$ for any $a' \leq a$. The converse of this holds as well, because the permutations of the form $\sigma^{\{a',a'+1,a'+2\}}$ with $a' \leq a$ generate the group of permutations of the form $\rho^{\{a,b,c\}}$ for $\{a,b,c\} \in \binom{[\min\{n,a+2\}]}{3}$. Such an argument also proves the converse, so the $R$ operators serve as the projections from Theorem 14.

Therefore, by Theorem 15 we have that the hypotheses of Theorem 14 are satisfied with $\ell = 10\log k$ and $\varepsilon_\ell = \frac{1}{\ell}$. That is, for any $m \leq n$ we have

$$\left\|G_{[m-\ell-1,m]}\left(G_{[m-1]} - G_{[m]}\right)\right\|_{\text{op}} = \left\|R_{n,[m-\ell-1,m],k}\left(R_{n,[m-1],k} - R_{n,[m],k}\right)\right\|_{\text{op}}$$
$$= \left\|\left(R_{m,[m-\ell-1,m],k}\left(R_{m,[m-1],k} - R_{m,[m],k}\right)\right) \otimes \text{Id}_{[m+1,n]}\right\|_{\text{op}} \leq \frac{1}{\ell}.$$

Therefore the conclusion of Theorem 14 is that

$$\lambda_2\left((n-2)L^{3\text{-NN}}_{n,[n-2],k}\right) \geq \frac{\left(1-\frac{1}{\sqrt{\ell}}\right)^2}{\ell-2}\lambda_2\left(\ell L^{3\text{-NN}}_{\ell+2,[\ell-2],k}\right) \geq \frac{1}{2}\lambda_2\left(L^{3\text{-NN}}_{\ell+2,[\ell-2],k}\right).$$

Recalling our setting of $\ell$ completes the proof.

**Comparison Method for the Large $k$ Case.** We can use the spectral gap proved in Theorem 12 for the random walk induced by completely random 3-bit gates to show a spectral gap for the random walk induced by random 3-bit gates, where the three bits on which the gate acts on are $a, a+1, a+2$ for some $a \in [n]$. Our proof is a simple application of the comparison method applied to random walks on multigraphs.

We take the following definition of (multi)graphs. A graph is a pair of sets $(V, E)$ such that there is a partition $E = \bigcup_{(x,y)\in V^2} E_{x,y}$. If $e \in E_{x,y}$ then we say that $e$ *connects* the vertex $x$ to the vertex $y$, and we define $u(e) = x$ and $v(e) = y$. The degree $\deg(x)$ of a vertex $x \in V$ is the number of edges originating at $e$, or $\sum_{y\in V} |E_{x,y}|$. We say that a graph is regular if $\deg(x) = \deg(y)$ for all $x, y \in V$.

The *random walk* on a graph $(V, E)$ beginning at a vertex $x \in V$ consists of the Markov chain $\{\boldsymbol{x}_i\}_{i\geq 0}$ on state space $V$ such that $\boldsymbol{x}_0 = x$ with probability 1, and to draw $\boldsymbol{x}_{i+1}$ given $\boldsymbol{x}_i$ we sample a uniform random edge $\boldsymbol{e}$ from $\bigcup_{y\in V} E_{x,y}$. We set $\boldsymbol{x}_{i+1}$ equal to the unique $y \in V$ such that $\boldsymbol{e} \in E_{x,y}$.

A *Schreier graph* is a graph with vertices $V$ such that some group $\mathfrak{G}$ acts on $V$. Let $S \subseteq \mathfrak{G}$ be some subset of group elements. The edge set consists of elements of the form $(X, \sigma)$ $(\sigma \in S)$, so that $(X, \sigma) \in E_{X,\sigma X}$. We call the resulting graph $\mathrm{Sch}(V, S)$.

**Definition 5.** *Let $S$ and $\widetilde{S}$ be subsets of a group acting on a set $V$. For each $\sigma \in S$ let $\Gamma(\sigma)$ be a sequence $(\widetilde{\sigma}_1, \ldots, \widetilde{\sigma}_t)$ of elements of $\widetilde{S}$ such that $\sigma v = \widetilde{\sigma}_t \ldots \widetilde{\sigma}_1 v$ for all $v \in V$, so we regard $\Gamma$ as a map from $S$ to sets of paths using edges in $\widetilde{S}$. Define the congestion ratio of $\Gamma$ to be*

$$B(\Gamma) = \max_{\widetilde{\sigma}\in\widetilde{S}} \left\{ |\widetilde{S}| \mathop{\mathbf{E}}_{\sigma\in S} [N(\widetilde{\sigma}, \Gamma(\sigma)) |\Gamma(\sigma)|] \right\},$$

*where $N(\widetilde{\sigma}, \Gamma(\sigma))$ is the number of times $\widetilde{\sigma}$ appears in the sequence $\Gamma(\sigma)$.*

**Lemma 10.** *Let $G = \mathrm{Sch}(V, S)$ and $\widetilde{G} = \mathrm{Sch}(V, \widetilde{S})$ be the connected Schreier graphs of the action of a group. Let $L$ and $\widetilde{L}$ be the Laplacian operators for the non-lazy random walks on $G$ and $\widetilde{G}$, respectively. Suppose there exists a $\Gamma$ as in Definition 5. Then*

$$\lambda_2(L) \geq \left( \max_{v\in V} \frac{\pi(v)}{\widetilde{\pi}(v)} \right) B(\Gamma) \lambda_2(\widetilde{L}).$$

*Here $\pi$ and $\widetilde{\pi}$ are the stationary distributions for $G$ and $\widetilde{G}$, respectively.*

We prove this in the full version of this paper. It is essentially a reformulation of a standard result about comparisons on general Markov chains in [29].

**Lemma 11.** *For any $n, k$ we have*

$$\lambda_2\left(L^{3\text{-}NN}_{n,[n-2],k}\right) \geq \frac{1}{100000 n^3} \lambda_2(L_{n,3,k}).$$

*Proof.* Note that $L_{n,3,k}$ and $L^{\text{3-NN}}_{n,[n-2],k}$ are simply the Laplacians of random walks on Schreier graphs with $\mathfrak{S}_{\{\pm1\}^n}$ acting on $\{\pm1\}^{nk}$ by $e(X^1,\ldots,X^k) = (eX^1,\ldots,eX^k)$. In the case of $L_{n,3,k}$ the edges are given by elements of the form $h^{\{a,b,c\}}$ for $h \in \mathfrak{S}_{\{\pm1\}^3}$ and $\{a,b,c\} \in \binom{[n]}{3}$. In the case of $L^{\text{3-NN}}_{n,[n-3],k}$ the edges are given by elements of the form $g^{\{a,a+1,a+2\}}$ for $g \in \mathfrak{S}_{\{\pm1\}^3}$ and $a \in [n-2]$. We deal with each connected component separately. Note that every connected component is isomorphic to $\{(X^1,\ldots,X^{k'}) : X^i \neq X^j \iff i \neq j\}$ for $k' \leq k$, so we bound the spectral gap for the walk on $\{(X^1,\ldots,X^k) : X^i \neq X^j \iff i \neq j\}$.

We provide a map $\Gamma$ from $\{h^{\{a,b,c\}} : h \in \mathfrak{S}_{\{0,1\}^3}, a,b,c \in [n]\}$ to sequences of elements of the form $g^{\{a,a+1,a+2\}}$ for $a \in [n-2]$ such that for any $h^{\{a,b,c\}}$ the sequence $\Gamma(h^{\{a,b,c\}}) = (g_1^{\{a_1,a_1+1,a_1+2\}},\ldots,g_t^{\{a_t,a_t+1,a_t+2\}})$ satisfies $h^{\{a,b,c\}} = g_t^{\{a_t,a_t+1,a_t+2\}} \cdots g_1^{\{a_1,a_1+1,a_1+2\}}$.

The hope is to construct $\Gamma$ such that $B(\Gamma)$ is small and then to apply Lemma 10. To this end we define $\Gamma$ as follows. Assume $a < b < c$. Fix $h \in \mathfrak{S}_8, a \in [n-2]$. Let $d \in [n-2]$ be arbitrary. Then write

$$h^{\{a,b,c\}} = \mathsf{Sort}^{-1} \cdot g^{\{d,d+1,d+2\}} \cdot \mathsf{Sort},$$

Here $\mathsf{Sort}$ sends the $a$th coordinate to the $d$th coordinate, the $b$th to the $d+1$th, and the $c$th to the $d+2$th. The permutations $\mathsf{Sort}$ and $\mathsf{Sort}^{-1}$ can each be implemented using at most $3n$ gates of the form $g^{\{a'-1,a',a'+1\}}$ and $g^{\{a'+1,a'+2,a'+3\}}$ where each $g$ swaps coordinates; this is just by a standard partial sorting algorithm. Write $\mathsf{Sort} = g_{3n}^{\{a_{3n},a_{3n}+1,a_{3n}+2\}} \cdots g_1^{\{a_1,a_1+1,a_1+2\}}$. Then set

$$\Gamma(h^{\{a,b,c\}}) = \left(g_1^{\{a_1,a_1+1,a_1+2\}},\ldots,g_{3n}^{\{a_{3n},a_{3n}+1,a_{3n}+2\}}, h^{(d,d+1,d+2)},\ldots,\left(g_1^{\{a_1,a_1+1,a_1+2\}}\right)^{-1}\right).$$

We have $B(\Gamma) \leq 100000n^3$ trivially, so we have proved the result by applying Lemma 10 and the fact that the stationary distributions for both chains are uniform.

**Corollary 3.** *For any $n,k$ we have*

$$\lambda_2\left(L^{\text{3-NN}}_{n,[n-2],k}\right) \geq \Omega\left(\frac{1}{nk \cdot \log^5(k)}\right).$$

*Proof.* Lemma 11 shows that $\lambda_2\left(L^{\text{3-NN}}_{\ell+2,[\ell],k'}\right) \geq \frac{1}{\ell^3}\lambda_2(L_{\ell+2,3,k'})$ for all $\ell$ and $k'$. Theorem 12 states that $\lambda_2(L_{\ell+2,3,k'}) \geq \frac{1}{(\ell+2)^2 k'}$ for all $\ell$ and $k'$. If we set $\ell = 10\log k$ and use Corollary 2 then we get

$$\lambda_2\left(L^{\text{3-NN}}_{n,[n-2],k}\right) \geq \frac{1}{2n} \cdot \lambda_2\left(L^{\text{3-NN}}_{10\log k+2,[10\log k],k}\right) \geq \frac{1}{2n} \cdot \frac{1}{100000k\log^5(k)}.$$

This implies the result.

As in the case for fully random gates, Theorem 7 follows from Corollary 3 and Sect. 4.3.

### 4.3 Restricting the Gate Set

So far all of our results have dealt with random circuits with arbitrary gates acting on 3 bits. However, for practical applications we are often in further restricting the type of 3-bit gates. However, as long as the arbitrary gate set is universal on 3 bits, we lose just a constant factor in the mixing time when we restrict our random circuits to use that gate set, by a standard application of the comparison method. We prove that we can perform this conversion before proving our results about brickwork circuits in Sect. 4.4 because it is somewhat easier to prove for the case of single gates acting at a time.

**Lemma 12.** *We have*

$$\lambda_2\left(L_{n,[n-2],k}^{3\text{-}NN,\mathrm{DES}[2]}\right) \geq \Omega\left(\lambda_2\left(L_{n,[n-2],k}^{3\text{-}NN}\right)\right)$$

*Proof.* We compare the Markov chains given by these two Laplacians by providing a way to write edges in the one induced by arbitrary 3-bit nearest-neighbor gates as paths in the one induced by 3-bit nearest-neighbor gates with generators $\mathcal{G}$. Again we focus on the connected component $\{(X^1, \ldots, X^k) : X^i \neq X^j \iff i \neq j\}$.

For each $g^S$ for $g \in \mathfrak{S}_8$ and $S \in \binom{[n]}{3}$ let $\Gamma(g^S) = (g_{i_1}^S, \ldots, g_{i_{8!}}^S)$ where we have fixed an arbitrary expansion of $g = g_{i_1} \cdots g_{i_{8!}}$, and each $g_{i_j}$ is of type DES[2]. Then in the notation of Lemma 10 we have that

$$\begin{aligned}
B(\Gamma) = & \max_{g\in\mathcal{G}, a\in[n-2]} \Bigg\{ |\mathcal{G}|(n-2) \\
& \cdot \mathop{\mathbf{E}}_{\mathbf{g}\in\mathfrak{S}_8, \mathbf{a}\in[n-2]} \left[ N\left(g^{\{a,a+1,a+2\}}, \Gamma(\mathbf{g}^{\{\mathbf{a},\mathbf{a}+1,\mathbf{a}+2\}})\right) \left|\Gamma(\mathbf{g}^{\{\mathbf{a},\mathbf{a}+1,\mathbf{a}+2\}})\right| \right] \Bigg\} \\
\leq & \max_{g\in\mathcal{G}, a\in[n-2]} \left\{ 8!n \mathop{\mathbf{E}}_{\mathbf{g}\in\mathfrak{S}_8, \mathbf{a}\in[n-2]} \left[ 8!N\left(g^{\{a,a+1,a+2\}}, \Gamma(\mathbf{g}^{\{\mathbf{a},\mathbf{a}+1,\mathbf{a}+2\}})\right) \right] \right\} \\
\leq & \max_{g\in\mathcal{G}, a\in[n-2]} \left\{ (8!)^3 n \mathbf{Pr}_{\mathbf{g}\in\mathfrak{S}_8, \mathbf{a}\in[n-2]} \left[ g^{\{a,a+1,a+2\}} \in \Gamma(\mathbf{g}^{\{\mathbf{a},\mathbf{a}+1,\mathbf{a}+2\}}) \right] \right\} \\
\leq & \max_{g\in\mathcal{G}, a\in[n-2]} \left\{ (8!)^3 n \mathbf{Pr}_{\mathbf{g}\in\mathfrak{S}_8, \mathbf{a}\in[n-2]} [a = \mathbf{a}] \right\} \\
\leq & (8!)^3.
\end{aligned}$$

Applying Lemma 10 completes the proof.

This shows that the random walk given by applying random gates on 3 bits of type DES[2] has spectral gap $\widetilde{\Omega}(1/nk)$, by combining with Corollary 3. A similar proof essentially shows the same result for the random circuit models where gates on arbitrary sets of 3 bits.

### 4.4 Brickwork Circuits

The spectral gap for brickwork circuits follows almost directly from the spectral gap for circuits with nearest-neighbor gates (Corollary 3), as in [2]. First we show that the random walk induced by 3-bit nearest neighbor DES[2] gates, where the 3 bits on which gates act on are of the form $\{a, a+1, a+2\}$ for any $a \in [n-2]$, has approximately the same spectral gap as that in which the random gates are of the form $\{a, a+1, a+2\}$ for $a \in [n-2]$ but with the restriction that $a \neq 0 \bmod 3$. Use the notation $L^{\text{3-NN,DES[2]}}_{n,[n-2],k}$ and $L^{\text{3-NN,DES[2]}}_{n,\{a \in [n-2], a=1,2 \bmod 3\},k}$ for the Laplacians of these random walks. Assume that $n = 0 \bmod 3$; the other cases follow similarly.

**Lemma 13.** *For any $n, k$ we have*

$$\lambda_2\Big(L^{\textit{3-NN},\text{DES[2]}}_{n,\{a\in[n-2],a=1,2 \textit{ mod } 3\},k}\Big) \geq \Omega\Big(\lambda_2\Big(L^{\textit{3-NN}}_{n,[n-2],k}\Big)\Big).$$

*Proof.* By Lemma 12, it suffices to show

$$\lambda_2\Big(L^{\text{3-NN,DES[2]}}_{n,\{a\in[n-2],a=1,2 \bmod 3\},k}\Big) \geq \Omega\Big(\lambda_2\Big(L^{\text{3-NN,DES[2]}}_{n,[n-2],k}\Big)\Big).$$

We use the comparison method. Again we focus on the connected component $\{(X^1, \ldots, X^k) : X^i \neq X^j \iff i \neq j\}$. For each $g \in \mathfrak{S}_{\{0,1\}^3} \cong \mathfrak{S}_8$ of type DES[2] and $a \in [n-2]$ we provide a sequence $\Gamma(g^{\{a,a+1,a+2\}})$ of permutations multiplying to $g^{\{a,a+1,a+2\}}$ using only permutations of the form $h^{\{b,b+1,b+2\}}$ with $b \neq 0 \bmod 3$ such that the resulting congestion $B(\Gamma)$ is small.

We define $\Gamma$ as follows. Fix $g \in \mathfrak{S}_8, a \in [n-2]$ where $g$ is of type DES[2]. If $a \neq 0 \bmod 3$ then simply set $\Gamma(g^{\{a,a+1,a+2\}}) = (g^{\{a,a+1,a+2\}})$. Otherwise $a = 0 \bmod 3$. Then there exists a sequence of 64! permutations of the form $g_i^{\{b_i,b_i+1,b_i+2\}}$ with each $b_i \in \{a-1, a+1\}$ such that $g = g_1^{\{b_1,b_1+1,b_1+2\}} \cdots g_1^{\{b_{64!},\ldots,b_{64!}+1,\ldots,b_{64!}+2\}}$. This is because we can implement the gate $g^{\{a,a+1,a+2\}}$ as

$$g^{\{a,a+1,a+2\}} = \mathsf{Sort}^{-1} \cdot g^{\{a-1,a,a+1\}} \cdot \mathsf{Sort},$$

where $\mathsf{Sort}$ sends the string $(x_1, \ldots, x_{a-1}, x_a, x_{a+1}, x_{a+2}, \ldots, x_n)$ to the string $(x_1, \ldots, x_a, x_{a+1}, x_{a+2}, x_{a-1}, \ldots, x_n)$. The permutations $\mathsf{Sort}$ and $\mathsf{Sort}^{-1}$ can each be implemented as the product of at most 32! permutations of the form $h^{\{a-1,a,a+1\}}$ and $h^{\{a+1,a+2,a+3\}}$ where each $h$ is of type DES[2]. This gives the implementation of $g^{\{a,a+1,a+2\}}$ as the product of at most 64! elements of the form $g^{\{a-1,a,a+1\}}$ or $g^{\{a,a+1,a+2\}}$, and this defines $\Gamma(g^{\{a,a+1,a+2\}})$ for such $g$ and $a$.

In the notation of Lemma 10, the congestion of $\Gamma$ is bounded:

$$\begin{aligned} B(\Gamma) \leq & \max_{g\in\mathcal{G},a=1,2 \bmod 3} \Bigg\{ \frac{8! \cdot 2n}{3} \\ & \cdot \mathop{\mathbf{E}}_{\mathbf{g}\in\mathfrak{S}_8,\mathbf{a}\in[n-2]} \Big[ N\Big(g^{\{a,a+1,a+2\}}, \Gamma(\mathbf{g}^{\{\mathbf{a},\mathbf{a}+1,\mathbf{a}+2\}})\Big) \Big| \Gamma(\mathbf{g}^{\{\mathbf{a},\mathbf{a}+1,\mathbf{a}+2\}}) \Big| \Big] \Bigg\} \\ \leq & 70! \max_{g\in\mathcal{G},a=1,2 \bmod 3} \Bigg\{ n \mathop{\mathbf{E}}_{\mathbf{g}\in\mathfrak{S}_8,\mathbf{a}\in[n-2]} \Big[ N\Big(g^{\{a,a+1,a+2\}}, \Gamma(\mathbf{g}^{\{\mathbf{a},\mathbf{a}+1,\mathbf{a}+2\}})\Big) \Big] \Bigg\} \end{aligned}$$

$$\leq 70! \max_{g\in\mathcal{G},a=1,2 \bmod 3} \left\{ n\mathbf{Pr}_{\mathbf{g}\in\mathfrak{S}_8,\mathbf{a}\in[n-2]} \left[ g^{\{a,a+1,a+2\}} \in \Gamma(\mathbf{g}^{\{\mathbf{a},\mathbf{a+1},\mathbf{a+2}\}}) \right] \right\}$$
$$\leq 70! \max_{g\in\mathcal{G},a=1,2 \bmod 3} \left\{ n\mathbf{Pr}_{\mathbf{g}\in\mathfrak{S}_8,\mathbf{a}\in[n-2]} [a \in \{\mathbf{a}-1,\mathbf{a},\mathbf{a}+1\}] \right\}$$
$$\leq 71!.$$

Here we used that $\left|\Gamma(g^{\{a,a+1,a+2\}})\right| \leq 64!$ always. Applying Lemma 10 completes the proof.

Given this restriction to DES[2] gates, the idea to prove the spectral gap for the random walk corresponding to a random brickwork circuit is to write the transition operator corresponding to one layer of brickwork gates as

$$R_{n,k}^{\text{brickwork,DES[2]}} = \frac{1}{2} R_{n,\{1,2,3\},k}^{\text{DES[2]}} R_{n,\{4,5,6\},k}^{\text{DES[2]}} \cdots R_{n,\{n-2,n-1,n\},k}^{\text{DES[2]}} + \frac{1}{2} R_{n,\{2,3,4\},k}^{\text{DES[2]}} R_{n,\{5,6,7\},k}^{\text{DES[2]}} \cdots R_{n,\{n-4,n-3,n-2\},k}^{\text{DES[2]}}.$$

Here the operator $R_{n,S,k}^{\text{DES[2]}}$ is the transition operator for the Markov chain that is similar to $R_{n,S,k}$ but with the restriction that each step is induced by a gate of type DES[2]. Then we note that each individual factor in each of the two products all commute, and every factor commutes with all but at most 7 other factors. The detectability lemma [1] bounds the spectral gap of this operator.

**Lemma 14** **([2], Sect. 4.A).** *For any $n, k$ we have*

$$\lambda_2\left(L_{n,k}^{\text{brickwork,DES[2]}}\right) \geq n\Omega\left(\lambda_2\left(L_{n,\{a\in[n-2],a=1,2 \ mod \ 3\},k}^{3\text{-}NN,\text{DES[2]}}\right)\right).$$

**Corollary 4.** *For any $n, k$ we have*

$$\lambda_2\left(L_{n,k}^{\text{brickwork,DES[2]}}\right) \geq \Omega\left(\frac{1}{k \cdot \text{polylog}(k)}\right).$$

As in the case for fully random gates and nearest-neighbor random gates, Theorem 8 follows from Corollary 4.

## References


1. Aharonov, D., Arad, I., Landau, Z., Vazirani, U.: The Detectability Lemma and Quantum Gap Amplification. In: Proceedings of the Forty-First Annual ACM Symposium on Theory of Computing. pp. 417–426 (2009)
2. Brandao, F.G., Harrow, A.W., Horodecki, M.: Local random quantum circuits are approximate polynomial-designs. Commun. Math. Phys. **346**, 397–434 (2016)
3. Brodsky, A., Hoory, S.: Simple permutations mix even better. Random Struct. Algorithms **32**(3), 274–289 (2008)
4. Chen, C.F., Docter, J., Xu, M., Bouland, A., Hayden, P.: Efficient Unitary T-designs from Random Sums. arXiv preprint arXiv:2402.09335 (2024)
5. Chen, C.F., Haah, J., Haferkamp, J., Liu, Y., Metger, T., Tan, X.: Incompressibility and spectral gaps of random circuits. arXiv preprint arXiv:2406.07478 (2024)

6. Dankert, C., Cleve, R., Emerson, J., Livine, E.: Exact and approximate unitary 2-designs and their application to fidelity estimation. Phys. Rev. A-Atomic, Molecul. Opt. Phys. **80**(1), 012304 (2009)
7. Feng, X., Ippoliti, M.: Dynamics of pseudoentanglement. arXiv preprint arXiv:2403.09619 (2024)
8. Gowers, W.: An almost m-wise independent random permutation of the cube. Combinatorics, Probability Comput. **5**(2), 119–130 (1996)
9. Gretta, L., He, W., Pelecanos, A.: More efficient approximate $k$-wise independent permutations from random reversible circuits via log-sobolev inequalities. Cryptology ePrint Archive (2024)
10. Haferkamp, J., Hunter-Jones, N.: Improved spectral gaps for random quantum circuits: large local dimensions and all-to-all interactions. Phys. Rev. A **104**(2), 022417 (2021)
11. Haferkamp, J., Montealegre-Mora, F., Heinrich, M., Eisert, J., Gross, D., Roth, I.: Efficient unitary designs with a system-size independent number of non-clifford gates. Commun. Math. Phys. **397**(3), 995–1041 (2023)
12. Harrow, A.W., Mehraban, S.: Approximate unitary t-designs by short random quantum circuits using nearest-neighbor and long-range gates. Commun. Math. Phys. **401**(2), 1531–1626 (2023)
13. Hayden, P., Preskill, J.: Black holes as mirrors: quantum information in random subsystems. J. High Energy Phys. **2007**(09), 120 (2007)
14. Hoory, S., Magen, A., Myers, S., Rackoff, C.: Simple permutations mix well. Theoret. Comput. Sci. **348**(2–3), 251–261 (2005)
15. Huang, H.Y., Kueng, R., Preskill, J.: Predicting many properties of a quantum system from very few measurements. Nat. Phys. **16**(10), 1050–1057 (2020)
16. Hunter-Jones, N.: Unitary Designs from Statistical Mechanics in Random Quantum Circuits. arXiv preprint arXiv:1905.12053 (2019)
17. Kaplan, E., Naor, M., Reingold, O.: Derandomized constructions of k-wise (almost) independent permutations. Algorithmica **55**(1), 113–133 (2009)
18. Kassabov, M.: Symmetric groups and expander graphs. Invent. Math. **170**(2), 327–354 (2007)
19. Liu, T., Pelecanos, A., Tessaro, S., Vaikuntanathan, V.: Layout graphs, random walks and the t-wise independence of SPN block ciphers. In: Annual International Cryptology Conference, pp. 694–726. Springer (2023)
20. Liu, T., Tessaro, S., Vaikuntanathan, V.: The $t$-wise independence of substitution-permutation networks. In: Malkin, T., Peikert, C. (eds.) CRYPTO 2021. LNCS, vol. 12828, pp. 454–483. Springer, Cham (2021). https://doi.org/10.1007/978-3-030-84259-8_16
21. Ma, F., Huang, H.Y.: How to construct random unitaries. arXiv preprint arXiv:2410.10116 (2024)
22. Maurer, U., Pietrzak, K.: Composition of random systems: when two weak make one strong. In: Naor, M. (ed.) TCC 2004. LNCS, vol. 2951, pp. 410–427. Springer, Heidelberg (2004). https://doi.org/10.1007/978-3-540-24638-1_23
23. Metger, T., Poremba, A., Sinha, M., Yuen, H.: Simple constructions of linear-depth t-designs and pseudorandom unitaries. arXiv preprint arXiv:2404.12647 (2024)
24. Mohanty, S., O'Donnell, R., Paredes, P.: Explicit near-ramanujan graphs of every degree. In: Proceedings of the 52nd Annual ACM SIGACT Symposium on Theory of Computing, pp. 510–523 (2020)
25. Nachtergaele, B.: The spectral gap for some spin chains with discrete symmetry breaking. Commun. Math. Phys. **175**, 565–606 (1996)

26. O'Donnell, R.: Analysis of Boolean Functions. Cambridge University Press (2014)
27. O'Donnell, R., Servedio, R.A., Paredes, P.: Explicit orthogonal and unitary designs. In: 2023 IEEE 64th Annual Symposium on Foundations of Computer Science (FOCS), pp. 1240–1260. IEEE (2023)
28. Scott, A.J.: Optimizing quantum process tomography with unitary 2-designs. J. Phys. A: Math. Theoret. **41**(5), 055308 (2008)
29. Wilmer, E., Levin, D.A., Peres, Y.: Markov Chains and Mixing Times. American Mathematical Soc., Providence (2009)

# Efficient Randomized Strong 2-Source Non-malleable Extractor for Any Linear Min-Entropy

Divesh Aggarwal[1(✉)], Pranjal Dutta[2], Saswata Mukherjee[2], Satyajeet Nagargoje[3], and Maciej Obremski[2]

[1] Center for Quantum Technologies and Department of Computer Science, National University of Singapore, Singapore, Singapore
divesh@comp.nus.edu.sg

[2] National University of Singapore, Singapore, Singapore

[3] Georgetown University, Washington, D.C., USA

**Abstract.** Randomness is a fundamental requirement in cryptographic systems, enabling secure encryption, commitments, and zero-knowledge proofs. However, real-world randomness sources often suffer from weaknesses that adversaries can exploit, leading to significant security vulnerabilities. While deterministic randomness extraction from a single min-entropy source is impossible, two-source extractors provide a robust solution by generating nearly uniform randomness from two independent weak sources. Moreover, cryptographic systems must also be resilient to leakage and tampering attacks, necessitating the development of non-malleable two-source extractors.

In this work, we construct a two-source non-malleable extractor in the Common Reference String (CRS) model, where a random low-degree polynomial is sampled once and made accessible to independent random sources, the distinguisher, and the tamperer. Our extractor requires only linear min-entropy in both sources and doesn't rely on strong computational assumptions, in contrast to prior constructions requiring computational assumptions such as sub-exponential hardness of the Decisional Diffie-Hellman (DDH) problem. Notably, our construction builds upon and relies on the recent breakthrough proof of the polynomial Freiman-Ruzsa conjecture. A connection of the Freiman-Ruzsa conjecture with two-source extractors was considered in prior work [ZBS11, AGMR24], but their construction did not achieve non-malleability.

Our results advance the state of non-malleable cryptographic primitives, with applications in secure storage, leakage-resilient cryptography, and privacy amplification. By eliminating the need for strong computational hardness assumptions, our techniques provide a more foundational and widely applicable method for randomness extraction.

We also show, that the requirements on CRS for our application are so mild that the CRS can be sampled with 2 party computation even when one of the parties is malicious (setting in which establishing unbiased coins is impossible).


Y. Tauman Kalai and S. F. Kamara (Eds.): CRYPTO 2025, LNCS 16000, pp. 679–713, 2025.
https://doi.org/10.1007/978-3-032-01855-7_22

**Keywords:** Randomness Extraction · Tamper-resilient cryptography · Leakage-resilient cryptography

## 1 Introduction

*Cryptography with weak randomness.* Randomness is a fundamental requirement in cryptography. Many core cryptographic primitives, including semantically secure encryption, commitments, and zero-knowledge proofs rely on it. Dodis, Ong, Prabhakaran, and Sahai [DOPS04] established that these primitives cannot be securely implemented using weak randomness sources, even those with high min-entropy, and instead require truly random inputs.

Despite its necessity, obtaining perfect randomness in real-world applications is highly challenging. Numerous cryptographic attacks exploit flaws in randomness generation. For instance, Breitner and Heninger [BH19] demonstrated how weak randomness in key generation allowed them to recover hundreds of Bitcoin private keys. Similar vulnerabilities have been reported in other cryptographic contexts [HDWH12, BCC+13].

Real-world randomness often originates from physical processes, such as electronic noise or user activity, which contain entropy but rarely produce uniformly random outputs. Additionally, adversaries may gain partial insight into the randomness generation process, further compromising its quality. The difficulty arises not only from the lack of uniformity of the source but also from the uncertainty about the exact distribution.

The best one can hope for is to deterministically extract a nearly perfect random string for direct usage in the desired application. While there are source models which allow for deterministic randomness extraction, such as von Neumann sources [VN51], affine sources [Bou07], and other efficiently generated or recognizable sources [Blu86, SV86, TV00, DGW09, KRVZ06, Dvi12, BGLZ15, CL16], all these models make strong assumptions about the structure of the source.

One can at best assume that they satisfy some minimal property, for example, that none of the outcomes is highly likely. This is the most natural, flexible, and well-studied source model and it is captured by the notion of min-entropy. The situation is complicated even further by the presence of leakage and tampering attacks.

*Leakage and Tampering Attacks.* In modern cryptographic systems, ensuring security against adversaries who may gain partial knowledge of secret information is critical. This is where leakage-resilient cryptography plays a vital role. Traditional cryptographic models assume that secret keys remain entirely hidden from attackers, but in reality, side-channel attacks, memory leakage, and hardware vulnerabilities can expose portions of the secret state. Leakage-resilient cryptography is designed to withstand such threats by ensuring that security is preserved even when an adversary obtains partial information about the secret. These techniques are particularly crucial in embedded systems, smart cards, and cloud computing, where attackers may exploit unintended information leaks, such as power consumption, timing variations, or electromagnetic emissions. So, even if we have uniform randomness, it is essential for applications that the source remains uniform conditioned on the view of an adversary, who potentially can obtain leakage about the source. For example, this problem was considered for partial key exposure by [CDH+00, DSS01]and later generalized to memory leakage by [Dzi06, DCLW06, AGV09].

Equally important is non-malleable cryptography, which prevents adversaries from tampering with encrypted and signed messages or even worse with the secret keys in a meaningful way. In many real-world scenarios, attackers not only aim to learn secret information but also to modify data in a controlled manner to deceive or manipulate the system. An example of this is a related key attack where the adversary can tamper with the secret key, and observe the outputs of the cryptographic algorithms on those related keys [GLM+04, BDK08, FKOS22]. Non-malleability ensures that any modification/tampering results in an output that is either completely unusable or unrelated to the original message. Together, leakage-resilience and non-malleability strengthen cryptographic foundations, ensuring robust security even in the presence of sophisticated and resourceful adversaries.

*Two-source extractors.* Sadly, assuming a lower bound on the min-entropy of the source does not allow deterministic extraction of even 1 almost uniformly random bit [CG88]. This holds even in the highly optimistic case where the source is supported on $\{0,1\}^d$ and has min-entropy $d-1$. Fortunately, [CG88] showed that if we are given two independent min-entropy sources, then we can produce uniform randomness via what is called a two-source extractor.

The problem of constructing explicit low-error two-source extractors for low min-entropy sources was an important focus of research in pseudorandomness over more than 30 years, with fundamental connections to combinatorics and many applications in computer science. The first non-trivial explicit construction was given by Chor and Goldreich [CG88], who showed that the inner product function is a low-error two-source extractor for $n$-bit sources with min-entropy $(1/2+\gamma)n$, where $\gamma > 0$ is an arbitrarily small constant. A standard application of the probabilistic method shows that (inefficient) low-error two-source extractors exist for polylogarithmic min-entropy. Although several attempts were made to improve the construction of [CG88] to allow sources with smaller min-entropy, the major breakthrough results were obtained after almost two decades. Raz [Raz05] gave an explicit low-error two-source extractor where one of the sources must have min-entropy $(1/2+\gamma)n$ for an arbitrarily small constant $\gamma > 0$, while the other source is allowed to have logarithmic min-entropy. In an incomparable result, Bourgain [Bou05] gave an explicit low-error two-source extractor for sources with min-entropy $(1/2-\gamma)n$, where $\gamma > 0$ is a small constant. Recently, an improved analysis by Lewko [Lew19] showed that Bourgain's extractor can handle sources with min-entropy $4n/9$. In another line of work, Chattopadhyay and Zuckerman [CZ19] succeeded in constructing explicit 1-bit two-source extractors for polylogarithmic min-entropy with polynomially small error (this was quickly improved to larger output length [Li16] and near-logarithmic min-entropy [BADTS17, Coh17, Li17], with the state-of-the-art currently found in [Li23].

The applications for two-source extractors in cryptography goes beyond just extracting randomness from sources with small min-entropy. Two-source extractors play a crucial role in leakage-resilient cryptography by enabling the generation of uniform randomness even when individual sources may be partially compromised. For example, Davi, Dziembowski, and Venturi [DDV10] used two-source extractors to build a leakage-resilient storage scheme in the model where the physical memory may leak some side-channel information.

*Non-malleable extractors.* In a breakthrough result, Dodis and Wichs [DW09] introduced the notion of seeded non-malleable extractors as a natural tool for applications in tamper-resilient cryptography. Their main goal was towards achieving privacy amplification against active adversaries [MW97] with an optimal number of rounds and small entropy loss. Roughly speaking, the output of a seeded non-malleable extractor with a uniformly random seed and a source X with some min-entropy should look uniformly random to an adversary who can tamper the seed and obtain the output of the non-malleable extractor on a tampered seed. A natural strengthening of both seeded non-malleable extractors, and two-source extractors are two-source *non-malleable* extractors (also known as seedless non-malleable extractors). Two-source non-malleable extractors were introduced by Cheraghchi and Guruswami [CG14] [CG17] in the single-tampering setting and by Chattopadhyay, Goyal, and Li [CGL16] in the multi-tampering setting. Roughly speaking, a function $\mathrm{nmExt} : \{0,1\}^n \times \{0,1\}^n \to \{0,1\}^m$ is said to be a non-malleable extractor if the output of the extractor remains close to uniform (in statistical distance), even conditioned on the output of the extractor on an input correlated with the original source. In other words, we require that

$$\mathrm{nmExt}(X,Y), \mathrm{nmExt}(f(X),g(Y)) \approx_\varepsilon U_m, \mathrm{nmExt}(f(X),g(Y)),$$

where $X$ and $Y$ are independent sources with enough min-entropy, $f, g : \{0,1\}^n \to \{0,1\}^n$ are arbitrary tampering functions such that $(f,g)$ has no fixed points, $U_m$ is uniform over $\{0,1\}^m$ and independent of the rest, and $\approx_\varepsilon$ means the two distributions are $\varepsilon$-close in statistical distance (for small $\varepsilon$). The original motivation for studying efficient two-source non-malleable extractors stems from the fact that they directly yield efficient split-state non-malleable codes [DPW18] (provided the extractor also supports efficient preimage sampling).

The initial constructions of non-malleable codes [DKO13, ADL14] were largely based on the (limited) non-malleability of the inner-product two-source extractor. Later, improved constructions of non-malleable codes in the split-state model can be broadly classified as: those that made use of both the inner-product two-source extractor [ADKO15, AO20, AKO+22] and more sophisticated constructions of two-source non-malleable extractors [CGL16, Li17, Li19, ACO23, Li23] that required alternating extractors. This topic has been extensively explored in the literature; for a more comprehensive list of works on non-malleable codes in the split-state model, see [Li23] and the references therein. Non-malleable codes and two-source non-malleable extractors have since been applied to other areas, including non-malleable secret sharing [GK18a, GK18b, BS19, ADN+19], randomness extraction from adversarial sources [CGGL19], network extraction protocols [GSZ21], non-malleable commitments [GPR16], and privacy amplification [CKOS19, AOR+22].

In particular, in [AOR+22], the authors present an extension of privacy amplification (PA) against active adversaries, where Eve, as an active adversary, is further allowed to *fully corrupt* the internal memory of one of the honest parties, Alice or Bob, before the protocol execution. Their construction required two-source non-malleable extractors where one source has a small entropy rate $\delta$ (where $\delta$ is a constant close to 0). Such non-malleable two-source extractors were constructed in [ACO23, Li23].

*(Non-malleable) Extractors in the CRS Model were introduced by* [GKK20]. The Common Reference String (CRS) model, introduced by Garg, Kalai, and Khurana [GKK20], provides a computational framework for constructing non-malleable extractors. In this model, a CRS is sampled once and for all, and three adversaries have full access to it: the sampler, which samples independent randomness sources with sufficient min-entropy; the tamperer, which is allowed to tamper with these source samples; and the distinguisher, which attempts to distinguish the extractor's output from a uniform distribution, given access to outputs on tampered versions. Their work constructed a one-source non-malleable extractor in this model under the DDH assumption, but only handled one-sided tampering. In a follow-up work, [AOR+22] extended this approach to two-source non-malleable extractors, achieving significantly improved parameters while handling both-sided tampering. Their construction remains secure against an unbounded distinguisher under the existence of nearly optimal collision-resistant hash functions. Furthermore, under the quasi-polynomial hardness of the DDH assumption, their extractor requires much lower min-entropy and handles a broader class of tampering functions, significantly improving upon previous constructions.

In [AGMR24] Alrabiah, Goodman, Mosheiff, and Ribeiro explored the properties of random low-degree multivariate polynomials over $\mathbb{F}_2$, they show that such polynomials are good extractors for sumset sources and any small families of sources. Most relevant to our context, they give the construction of a two-source extractor for small min-entropy in the CRS model. Their construction obtains negligible error relevant in cryptographic setting.

### 1.1 Our Contributions

Our main result is a two-source non-malleable extractor construction in the CRS model, where a random *low* degree polynomial needs to be sampled once and for all, and then the independent random sources, the distinguisher and the tamperer are allowed arbitrary access to this polynomial. The informal theorem statement is as below.

**Theorem 1 (Informal).**

1. *For all* $n$*, constant* $\rho > 0$ *there are constants* $\mu, \gamma > 0$ *so that there is an efficiently sampleable polynomial* $p$ *and the efficiently computable function* $\mathrm{nmExt}_p : \{0,1\}^n \times \{0,1\}^n \to \{0,1\}^m$*, that depends on* $p$*, is with probability* $1 - 2^{-\Omega(n^2)}$ *over the randomness of* $p$*, an* $(n, m, \rho n, 2^{-\gamma n})$ *2-source non-malleable extractor, where* $m = \mu n$*.*
2. *For all* $n$*, there are constants* $C_0 > 0$ *and* $\sigma, \nu > 0$ *so that there is an efficiently sampleable polynomial* $p$ *and the efficiently computable function* $\mathrm{nmExt}_p : \{0,1\}^n \times \{0,1\}^n \to \{0,1\}^m$*, that depends on* $p$*, is with probability* $1 - 2^{-\Omega(n^2)}$ *over the randomness of* $p$*, an* $\left(n, m, \frac{C_0 n}{\log n}, 2^{-\sigma\sqrt{n}}\right)$ *2-source non-malleable extractor, where* $m = \nu\sqrt{n}$*.*

This should in particular be contrasted with [GKK20, AOR+22] which required very strong computational assumptions in addition to the common reference string, for the construction of a two-source non-malleable extractor. Our construction on the other hand does not require any additional assumption.

Our work is heavily inspired from [ZBS11] that showed a connection between a two-source extractor and the polynomial Freiman-Ruzsa conjecture.

Notice that a non-malleable two-source extractor is also, by default, a two-source extractor. Alrabiah, Goodman, Mosheiff, and Ribeiro [AGMR24] also gave a construction of two-source extractors for small min-entropy in the CRS model, but it doesn't seem easy to extend their construction to give a two-source non-malleable extractor.

It should also be noted that in the absence of CRS our polynomial can even be sampled by two parties that mutually distrust each other. See Sect. 4, Sect. 5.

### 1.2 Technical Overview

In this exposition we focus on extractors with 1 bit output. With a bit of care and handling technical issues, we are able to obtain large output extractors with similar methods.

As a warm-up, let's build two source extractor first. It is well known that if $A$ and $B$ are two subsets of $\{0,1\}^n$ such that $\log|A| + \log|B| > n+1$ then if we sample $a \leftarrow A$ and $b \leftarrow B$ independently and uniformly at random and evaluate inner product $\langle a, b\rangle$ the output distribution will be statistically close to uniform. In the language of random variables this translates to $\langle X, Y\rangle$ is statistically close to uniform if $X, Y$ are independent random variables over $\{0,1\}^n$ such that $H_\infty(X) + H_\infty(Y) > n+1$. The equivalence of these two views comes from a standard observation that every random variable with min-entropy $k$ can be decomposed into a convex combination of distributions that are uniform over sets of size $2^k$ (i.e. flat sources).

Recent progress in additive combinatorics gives us a much stronger statement to work with: if $\dim_{\mathbb{F}_2}(A) + \dim_{\mathbb{F}_2}(B) > n+1$ (where $\dim_{\mathbb{F}_2}$ stands from dimension of the span of the set, see Definition 7), then the inner-product $\langle a, b\rangle$

of independent uniform samples $a \leftarrow A$ and $b \leftarrow B$ will be distributed uniformly at random.

The idea behind two-source extractor is therefore simple – given two random sources $X$ and $Y$ over $\{0,1\}^n$ that fulfil some minimal lower bound on min-entropy $H_\infty(X), H_\infty(Y) > \rho \cdot n$, if we could deterministically encode $X \to \psi(X)$ and $Y \to \psi(Y)$, such that $\psi(\mathrm{Supp}(X))$ has large dimension (specifically, for every random variables with min-entropy at least $\rho \cdot n$ we need $\dim_{\mathbb{F}_2}(\psi(\mathrm{Supp}(X))) > \frac{n+1}{2}$), then we could simply apply inner-product

$$(X, Y) \to \langle \psi(X), \psi(Y) \rangle$$

and know that the output is uniform since

$$\dim_{\mathbb{F}_2}(\psi(\mathrm{Supp}(X))) + \dim_{\mathbb{F}_2}(\psi(\mathrm{Supp}(Y))) > n + 1\,.$$

There are some technical limitations to this approach like the size of the output of $\psi$ has to be linear in the size of the input but for the purpose of this overview, we don't get into those technical details.

So, it suffices to find an appropriate $\psi$. Let us begin by picking $\psi$ as a random degree $t = O(n)$ polynomial over $\mathbb{F}_{2^n}$, i.e. $\psi : \mathbb{F}_{2^n} \to \mathbb{F}_{2^n}$. Notice that randomness complexity (or description) of such polynomial is $(t+1) \cdot n$ which is efficient to express and work with.

Now we need to show that for any $X$ random variable with $H_\infty(X) \geq \rho \cdot n$, we have $\dim(\psi(\mathrm{Supp}(X))) > 0.51 \cdot n$ (where 0.51 is a placeholder for "slightly more than half"). Again, it is sufficient to talk about $X$, a flat distribution over a set of the size $2^{\rho \cdot n}$. This task can be viewed as a *matrix problem*: Find a matrix with rows iterated by all $2^n$ strings representing all possible values of $x \in \{0,1\}^n$, and let $i$-th row be filled with $\psi(i) \in \{0,1\}^n$, this means our matrix has $2^n$ rows and $n$ columns. To show that for any random variable $X$ with $H_\infty(X) > \rho \cdot n$ we have $\dim_{\mathbb{F}_2}(\mathrm{Supp}(X)) > 0.51 \cdot n$, all we need to show is that any $2^{\rho \cdot n}$ rows of our matrix span space of dimension at least $0.51 \cdot n$. We will focus on fixed set of rows and then union-bound over all possible choices of $2^{\rho \cdot n}$ rows.

First, notice that $\psi$ is a random polynomial of degree $t$, which means that all $t$ rows in our matrix are independent and uniformly random. So clearly probability that the fixed $2^{\rho \cdot n}$ rows of our matrix are spanning a large dimension space is very high, it's as high as the probability that $t$ uniformly random vectors span a high dimensional space. But we have the order of quantifiers wrong, we fixed the choice of rows and said it's very likely they are of high dimension, what we need to show is that every choice of rows gives a high dimensional space. This can be done via union bound over $\binom{2^n}{2^{\rho \cdot n}}$ possible sources. Let's get some optimistic bound on the failure probability i.e. probability that $t$ uniformly random vectors do not span space of dimension at least $0.51 \cdot n$, such probability is clearly smaller than $2^{0.51 \cdot n \cdot t}$, this follows from picking a subspace of dimension $0.49 \cdot n$, each vector falls into this space with probability $2^{0.51 \cdot n}$. Even this extremely optimistic bound on the failure probability $2^{0.51 \cdot n \cdot t}$ can not withstand the union bound $\binom{2^n}{2^{\rho \cdot n}}$.

*First idea:* Notice that we don't have to union bound over $\binom{2^n}{2^{\rho \cdot n}}$ sources. Instead, it is actually sufficient to bound over all choices of $t$ rows as it is sufficient to show that every $t$ rows span a sufficiently large space, as every source of high entropy contains some $t$ possible values/rows (since $t < 2^{\rho \cdot n}$). But our optimistic failure probability of $2^{0.51 \cdot n}$ still can't withstand a union bound of $\binom{2^n}{t} \approx 2^{n \cdot t}$.

*Second idea:* We have to boost the probability that each of $t$ rows have a large span. This can be done by picking larger $t$. However, this will also increase the union-bound penalty and leads nowhere (at least if we want to keep $t$ reasonably small). Let us increase the size of each row then: $\psi : \{0,1\}^n \rightarrow \{0,1\}^{10n}$ while maintaining the $t-$wise independence. Now our $t$ random vectors are much longer and span space of dimension $0.51 \cdot 10 \cdot n$ with much higher probability that can withstand $2^{n \cdot t}$ union-bound penalty. Sampling such function $\psi$ is also easy: pick a random polynomial $p : \mathbb{F}_{2^{10n}} \rightarrow \mathbb{F}_{2^{10n}}$ of degree $t$, and let $\psi(x) = p(0^{9n} \circ x)$. Notice that because of the union bound we get that almost every polynomial $p$ gives us a matrix such that each $t$ rows of this matrix span large dimensional space. Thus we are done:

$$(X, Y) \rightarrow \langle p(0^{9n} \circ X), p(0^{9n} \circ Y) \rangle ,$$

is a good extractor for sources with min-entropy[1] at least $\rho \cdot n$.

*Building non-malleable extractor:* Now that the warm-up is concluded and we have constructed a two-source extractor we can proceed with the construction of a non-malleable two-source extractor. The construction will be basically the same,

$$(X, Y) \rightarrow \langle p(0^{9n} \circ X), p(0^{9n} \circ Y) \rangle .$$

It is just that the polynomial $p$ will have to be of slightly higher (but still linear) degree.

To show that $\mathrm{nmExt}(X, Y), \mathrm{nmExt}(f(X), g(Y))$ is close to $U, \mathrm{nmExt}(f(X), g(Y))$ by XOR lemma, all we need to show is that both $\mathrm{nmExt}(X, Y)$ is close to uniform and $\mathrm{nmExt}(X, Y) + \mathrm{nmExt}(f(X), g(Y))$ is also close to uniform.

First statement is already done – that is simply the extractor statement from the warm-up part of this exposition. Let us focus on proving that $\mathrm{nmExt}(X, Y)+$ $\mathrm{nmExt}(f(X), g(Y))$ is uniform. Notice:

$$\begin{aligned} &\mathrm{nmExt}(X, Y) + \mathrm{nmExt}(f(X), g(Y)) = \\ &= \langle p(0^{9n} \circ X), p(0^{9n} \circ Y) \rangle + \langle p(0^{9n} \circ f(X)), p(0^{9n} \circ g(Y)) \rangle = \\ &= \langle p(0^{9n} \circ X) \circ p(0^{9n} \circ f(X)), p(0^{9n} \circ Y) \circ p(0^{9n} \circ g(Y)) \rangle \end{aligned}$$

Consider our matrix again, with $2^n$ rows, with $i$'th row equal $p(0^{9n} \circ i) \circ$ $p(0^{9n} \circ f(i))$, now each row is $20 \cdot n$ bits long. If we could show again that every

[1] Above we only really required that $t \leq 2^{\rho \cdot n}$, so one can ask a fair question why not require entropy $\log t$? Unfortunately this is a result of our proof approach via additive combinatorics that require us to have entropy linear in $n$.

$t$-rows form a high dimension subspace (say, dimension $0.51 \cdot 20 \cdot n$) we would be done. Sadly, this is not quite true. If $f$ is a constant function then the dimension spanned by any $t$ rows is at best $10 \cdot n$ which is not enough.

At this point we identify, that $f$−close to constant is the only barrier standing between us and the proof. But notice that if $f$ is close to constant then $\text{nmExt}(f(X), g(Y))$ is basically a deterministic function of $Y$, and by a strong extraction property $\text{nmExt}(X,Y) = \langle p(0^{9n} \circ X), p(0^{9n} \circ Y)\rangle$ is close to uniform even given $Y$, which means $\text{nmExt}(X,Y)$ is close to uniform even given $\text{nmExt}(f(X), g(Y))$. So in the case of close to constant $f$ we are done.

What happens when $f$ is far from constant i.e. almost bijective? Then look at the rows of our matrix $p(0^{9n} \circ i) \circ p(0^{9n} \circ f(i))$, if $f$ is close to bijection than for any large enough set of rows (remember $t << 2^{\rho \cdot n}$ so we have plenty of rows to play with) we can find subset of $t$ rows that $x_1, ..., x_t, f(x_1), ..., f(x_t)$ are all $2t$ *distinct* values, and thus all $t$ vectors $p(0^{9n} \circ x_i) \circ p(0^{9n} \circ f(x_i))$ are uniform and independent. Thus, we can show that every such $t$ row spans large dimension subspace with an overwhelming probability that can withstand a union bound.

Notice that there are plenty of functions that are neither close to constant nor far from constant: function can be constant on some part of domain and bijective on the rest. This is formally handled by splitting domain into subsets: part of domain where $f$ is constant and part of domain where $f$ is not constant. We prove that our extractor is good on each partition(which follows exactly the ideas highlighted above) and then combine it all together.

*Two-party setting.* To sample the polynomial in two-party setting Alice and Bob can proceed as follows: Alice will come up with polynomial $q$ of degree $10 \cdot 30 \cdot n$, in response Bob will generate a polynomial $r$ of degree $30 \cdot n$, the combined polynomial is degree $10 \cdot 30 \cdot n$ and is equal to $q + r$. Notice that we need $30 \cdot n$-wise independent function, and if Bob was honest that is trivially guaranteed by the uniformity of $r$. If Alice was honest then we can guarantee that the polynomial $q + r$ has been sampled from the source of min-entropy at least $9 \cdot 30 \cdot n^2$ (i.e. the entropy rate of the source was at least $\approx 0.9$) which is sufficient by Remark 21. We also note that this can be generalized to multiple parties where each party publishes shorter and shorter polynomials and last one picks polynomial degree $30 \cdot n$. For formal proof one can look at Sect. 5. This also means that if malicious Bob decides not to publish his polynomial (abort), Alice can safely reset and engage in the selection process again, and again, polynomial number of times, and as long as at least one of reruns terminates Alice is guaranteed that the generated polynomial is good.

This result is impressive because it demonstrates that the common reference string (CRS) required for the extractor is so weak that it can be securely sampled even in the presence of a malicious party using a two-party computation protocol. In contrast, as shown by Cleve [Cle86], it is impossible to sample uniform random coins with guaranteed fairness in the presence of a single malicious participant—one party can always bias the protocol. Therefore, our construction circumvents this barrier by requiring only a highly relaxed form of the CRS, significantly lowering the trust and setup assumptions compared to traditional approaches that demand strong, unbiased randomness. This advances both the practicality and the robustness of protocols in the CRS model.

This protocol can be expanded to larger number of parties where each subsequent party samples smaller and smaller polynomials - albeit this becomes impractical with larger number of parties.

## 2 Preliminaries

For a positive integer $n$, we denote $[n] := \{1, \cdots, n\}$. For strings $x, y$, we denote $x \circ y$ to be the concatenation of the strings $x, y$. If $M$ be a $n \times n$ matrix with entries from $\mathbb{F}_2$ and $S$ be a set $\{v_1, \cdots, v_t\} \subseteq \mathbb{F}_2^n$, we denote $M \cdot S = \{M.v_1, \cdots, M \cdot v_t\}$. For any set $S$, we use $\mathbf{X} \sim S$ to denote that $\mathbf{X}$ is a distribution over the set $S$. And for any positive integer $n$, we use the notation $\mathcal{U}_n$ to denote the uniform distribution over $\{0,1\}^n$. We define the support and min-entropy of a random variable as follows.

**Definition 1 (Support).** *For a random variable* $\mathbf{X} \sim \{0,1\}^n$, *we say support of* $\mathbf{X}$,

$$\text{Supp}(\mathbf{X}) := \{x \in \{0,1\}^n : \Pr[\mathbf{X} = x] \neq 0\}.$$

**Definition 2 (Min-entropy).** *For a random source* $\mathbf{X} \sim \{0,1\}^n$, *we say* $\mathbf{X}$ *has min-entropy (denote it as* $H_\infty(\mathbf{X})$*) at least* $k$ *if, for all* $x \in \{0,1\}^n$,

$$\Pr[\mathbf{X} = x] \leq 2^{-k}.$$

*We say* $\mathbf{X}$ *is an* $(n,k)$ *source if* $\mathbf{X} \sim \{0,1\}^n$ *and* $H_\infty(\mathbf{X}) \geq k$.

**Fact 2.** *For any two distributions* $\mathbf{X}, \mathbf{Y} \sim \{0,1\}^n$, *we have* $H_\infty((\mathbf{X}, \mathbf{Y})) \geq H_\infty(\mathbf{X})$, *where* $(\mathbf{X}, \mathbf{Y})$ *is the joint distribution of* $\mathbf{X}, \mathbf{Y}$.

Flat sources are a special class of $(n,k)$ sources defined as follows.

**Definition 3 (Flat sources).** *For any random variable* $\mathbf{X}$ *over* $\{0,1\}^n$, *we call it a flat-*$k$ *source if there is* $S \subseteq \{0,1\}^n$ *so that* $|S| = 2^k$ *and* $\mathbf{X}$ *is uniform over* $S$.

The following lemma gives a relation between min-entropy $k$ sources and flat-$k$ sources.

**Lemma 1 ([Vad12, Lemma 6.10]).** *Any* $(n,k)$*-source* $\mathbf{X}$ *is a convex combination of flat-*$k$ *sources, i.e.,* $\mathbf{X} = \sum_i p_i \mathbf{X}_i$ *where for all* $i$, $p_i \geq 0$, $\sum_i p_i = 1$ *and each* $\mathbf{X}_i$ *is a flat-*$k$ *source.*

A 2-source disperser (with one-bit output) is a deterministic function that takes two entropy sources, and outputs a non-constant bit.

**Definition 4 (2-Source Dispersers).** *A function* $f : \{0,1\}^n \times \{0,1\}^n \to \{0,1\}$ *is an* $(n,k)$ *2-source disperser if for all sources* $\mathbf{X} \sim \{0,1\}^n, \mathbf{Y} \sim \{0,1\}^n$ *with* $H_\infty(\mathbf{X}) \geq k$, $H_\infty(\mathbf{Y}) \geq k$, $\text{Supp}(f(\mathbf{X}, \mathbf{Y})) = \{0,1\}$.

The statistical distance is a standard measure for the proximity of two random variables sampled from the same set.

**Definition 5 (Statistical Distance).** *Given two random variables* $A, B \sim \Omega$, *we define the statistical distance as*

$$\Delta(A; B) := \frac{1}{2} \sum_{\omega \in \Omega} |\Pr[A = \omega] - \Pr[B = \omega]|.$$

The following inequality states that if $\mathbf{X}, \mathbf{Y}$ are statistically close, then $f(\mathbf{X}), f(\mathbf{Y})$ are also statistically close.

**Lemma 2 (Data processing inequality** [Vad12, **Lemma 6.3**]**).** *For any possibly randomized function* $f : \{0,1\}^n \to \{0,1\}^*$, *and random sources* $\mathbf{X}, \mathbf{Y} \sim \{0,1\}^n$, $\Delta(f(\mathbf{X}); f(\mathbf{Y})) \leq \Delta(\mathbf{X}; \mathbf{Y})$.

A 2-source extractor is a deterministic function that takes as input two entropy sources, and outputs a random variable that is statistically close to uniform.

**Definition 6 (2-source extractors).** *A function* $\mathrm{Ext} : \{0,1\}^n \times \{0,1\}^n \to \{0,1\}^m$ *is an* $(n, m, k, \varepsilon)$ *2-source extractor if for all independent sources* $\mathbf{X} \sim \{0,1\}^n$, $\mathbf{Y} \sim \{0,1\}^n$ *with* $H_\infty(\mathbf{X}), H_\infty(\mathbf{Y}) \geq k$ *we have*

$$\Delta(\mathrm{Ext}(\mathbf{X}, \mathbf{Y}); \mathcal{U}_m) \leq \varepsilon\,.$$

*The extractor is said to be an* $(n, m, k, \varepsilon)$ *strong 2-source extractor if*

$$\Delta(\mathrm{Ext}(\mathbf{X}, \mathbf{Y}), \mathbf{Y}; \mathcal{U}_m, \mathbf{Y}) \leq \varepsilon\,,$$

*and*

$$\Delta(\mathrm{Ext}(\mathbf{X}, \mathbf{Y}), \mathbf{X}; \mathcal{U}_m, \mathbf{X}) \leq \varepsilon\,.$$

The following theorem says that every 2-source extractor is a strong 2-source extractor with some loss in error.

**Lemma 3** ([Rao07, **Theorem 5.1**])**.** *If* $\mathrm{Ext} : \{0,1\}^n \times \{0,1\}^n \to \{0,1\}^m$ *is a* $(n, m, k, \varepsilon)$ *2-source extractor then* Ext *is a strong* $(n, m, k', \varepsilon')$ *2-source extractor where* $\varepsilon' \leq (2^{k-k'} + \varepsilon)2^m$.

**Lemma 4 (Vazirani's XOR lemma** [Vaz86]**).** $\mathbf{X} = (\mathbf{X}_1, \ldots, \mathbf{X}_t) \sim \mathbb{F}^t$ *be a random variable. If for every* $a_1, \ldots, a_t \in \mathbb{F}$, *not all zero,* $\Delta(\sum_{i=1}^t a_i \mathbf{X}_i; \mathcal{U}_1) \leq \varepsilon$. *Then,* $\Delta(\mathbf{X}; \mathcal{U}_t) \leq \varepsilon \cdot |\mathbb{F}|^{(t+2)/2}$.

The following is a variant of the XOR lemma that includes side information. For a proof, one can look at [ACLV19, **Lemma 13**].

**Lemma 5.** *Let* $\mathbb{F}$ *be a finite field. Given* $\mathbf{X} = (\mathbf{X}_1, \ldots, \mathbf{X}_t) \sim \mathbb{F}^t$ *and* $\mathbf{Y} \sim Y$ *for some set* $Y$ *be random variables. If for every* $a_1, \ldots, a_t \in \mathbb{F}$, *not all zero,* $\Delta((\sum_{i=1}^t a_i \mathbf{X}_i, \mathbf{Y}); (\mathcal{U}_1, \mathbf{Y})) \leq \varepsilon$, *then,* $\Delta((\mathbf{X}, \mathbf{Y}); (\mathcal{U}_t, \mathbf{Y})) \leq \sqrt{\varepsilon} \cdot |\mathbb{F}|^{(t+2)/2}$.

**Definition 7.** *For a set $A \subseteq \mathbb{F}_2^n$, let $\dim_{\mathbb{F}_2}(A)$ denote the dimension of $\mathrm{Span}_{\mathbb{F}_2}(A)$ over $\mathbb{F}_2$, where*

$$\mathrm{Span}_{\mathbb{F}_2}(A) = \{\sum_{i=1}^{n} x_i a_i : x_i \in \mathbb{F}_2 \, and \, a_i \in A\}.$$

**Definition 8.** *For sets $A, B \subseteq \mathbb{F}_2^n$ we define the duality measure of the sets $A, B$ as*

$$D(A, B) = \left|\mathbb{E}_{a\sim A,\, b\sim B}[(-1)^{\langle a,b\rangle}]\right|.$$

**Definition 9 (Rank of Binary Function).** *Rank of a binary function $E : \mathbb{F}_2^n \times \mathbb{F}_2^n \to \mathbb{F}_2$ is the minimum integer $r$ so that there are functions $h_1, h_2 : \mathbb{F}_2^n \to \mathbb{F}_2^r$ and $E(x, y) = \langle h_1(x), h_2(y)\rangle$.*
*Equivalently rank of the function $E$ is same as rank of the $2^n \times 2^n$ matrix over $\mathbb{F}_2$ whose $(x, y)$th entry is $E(x, y)$.*

Also for $\mathbf{X}, \mathbf{Y} \sim \{0, 1\}^n$, we denote the bias of $\langle \mathbf{X}, \mathbf{Y}\rangle$ as

$$\mathrm{bias}(\mathbf{X}, \mathbf{Y}) = \left| \Pr_{x\sim \mathbf{X},\, y\sim \mathbf{Y}}[\langle x, y\rangle = 1] - \frac{1}{2}\right|.$$

**Theorem 3 (Polynomial Freiman-Ruzsa Theorem** [GGMT25, **Theorem 1.2**]**).** *Suppose $A \subset \mathbb{F}_2^n$ such that $|A + A| \le K|A|$, then $A$ can be covered by atmost $2K^{12}$ translates of a subspace $H$ of $\mathbb{F}_2^n$ of cardinality atmost $|A|$.*

[ZBS11] showed that PFR conjecture (now a theorem as stated above) implies the ADC-exp (Approximate Duality Conjecture-exp) which is now a theorem.

**Theorem 4 (ADC-exp** [ZBS11, **Conjecture 1.2**]**).** *For every pair of constants $0 < \gamma, \beta < 1$ there exists a constant $\zeta > 0$ such that the following holds: Suppose that $A, B \subseteq \mathbb{F}_2^n$ are such that $D(A, B) \ge 2^{-\zeta n}$ and $|A| \ge 2^{\beta n}$, then there exists $A' \subseteq A, B' \subseteq B$ such that $|A'| \ge 2^{-\gamma n}|A|, |B'| \ge 2^{-\gamma n}|B|$, $D(A', B') = 1$.*

In a subsequent work there was another version of ADC has been proved from PFR that says that assuming slightly *larger* duality of given two sets $A, B$, we can find $A', B'$, subsets of $A, B$ respectively so that they are orthogonal and $|A'|/|A|$ and $|B'|/|B|$ is at least $2^{-cn/\log n}$, where $c$ is some constant. Formally it is stated below.

**Theorem 5 (Strong ADC** [BSLRZ14, **Lemma 1.10**]**.** *For every pair of sets $A, B \subseteq \mathbb{F}_2^n$ which satisfy $D(A, B) \ge 2^{-\sqrt{n}}$, there are subsets $A' \subseteq A$ and $B' \subseteq B$ so that $|A'| \ge 2^{-cn/\log n}|A|$ and $|B'| \ge 2^{-cn/\log n}|B|$ for some absolute constant $c$ and $D(A', B') = 1$*

### 2.1 Low Rank Disperser to Extractor

In this section we show that constructing 2-source dispersers are enough to construct 2-source extractors. A key ingredient in constructing 2-source dispersers is the following elementary lemma which we are stating without proof.

**Lemma 6** ([ZBS11, **Lemma 3.1**]). *Let* $A, B \subseteq \{0,1\}^n$ *such that* $\dim(A) + \dim(B) > n+1$, *then* $\langle .,. \rangle : A \times B \to \{0,1\}$ *is a non-constant function.*

The next lemma shows how low-rank dispersers are also 2-source extractors (Lemma 2.15 from [ZBS11]). We will include the result as well as its proof for self containment.

**Lemma 7** ([ZBS11, **Lemma 2.15**]). *For all constants* $\delta, \alpha, t > 0$, *there exists a constant* $\zeta$ *such that, every* $(n, \delta n)$ *2-source disperser* $E : \{0,1\}^n \times \{0,1\}^n \to \{0,1\}$ *of rank* $n/t$ *is also a* $(n, 1, (\delta + \alpha)n, 2^{-\zeta n})$ *2-source extractor.*

The above proof follows from the *weaker* version of ADC. Instead of that if we start from Theorem 5 and follow the proof idea of Lemma 7, we get that every two source disperser for the sources of min-entropy $O(n/\log n)$ is also a two source extractor with error $2^{-\sqrt{n}}$ and the same min-entropy requirement.

**Lemma 8 (Extractor for lower min-entropic sources from strong ADC).** *For any constant* $t > 0$ *and* $\delta > 0$ *(*$\delta$ *may not be a constant) we have: Every function* $E : \{0,1\}^n \times \{0,1\}^n \to \{0,1\}$ *which is a* $(n, \delta n)$ *2-source disperser of rank* $n/t$, *is also a* $\left(n, 1, \delta n + \frac{cn}{\log n}, 2^{-\sqrt{n}}\right)$ *2-source extractor. Here* $c$ *is the absolute constant that we get from Theorem 5.*

Additionally, we will need the following well known fact.

**Fact 6.** *A polynomial of degree at most* $d$ *over a field can be uniquely determined by specifying its values at any* $d+1$ *distinct points. In the case of a finite field GF(*$q$*) with* $q$ *elements (where* $q$ *is a prime power), this fact provides a way to construct a sequence of* $q$ *random variables that are* $(d+1)$*-wise independent. Specifically, if the* $d+1$ *coefficients of the polynomial are chosen independently and uniformly at random from GF(*$q$*), then the polynomial's values at any* $d+1$ *distinct inputs are also uniformly and independently distributed.*

*Throughout the paper we only work with* $\mathbb{F}_2$ *and some finite extension of it. Hence we state the above more formally for some extension of* $\mathbb{F}_2$. *Say* $\mathcal{H}_{t,r} := \{p \in \mathbb{F}_{2^r}[Z] : \deg(p) \le t-1\}$. *Then, for distinct* $x_1, \ldots, x_t$ *and* $y_1, \ldots, y_t$ *from* $\mathbb{F}_{2^r}$,

$$\Pr_{p \leftarrow \mathcal{H}_{t,r}} [p(x_1) = y_1 \wedge \cdots \wedge p(x_t) = y_t] = \frac{1}{|\mathbb{F}_{2^r}|^t} = 2^{-rt}.$$

## 3 Strong Two Source Extractor Construction

In this section, we establish that a *random low-degree polynomial* evaluated over a source with sufficient entropy induces a large span. This result serves as a key component in the construction of a strong two-source extractor based on the inner product. Throughout the section, we use $\{0,1\}^r$ and $\mathbb{F}_2^r$ interchangeably for any $r \in \mathbb{N}$. Additionally, note that the additive group of $\mathbb{F}_2^r$ is homomorphic to $\mathbb{F}_{2^r}$. We will use these notions interchangeably and explicitly clarifying any distinctions when necessary.

Throughout this section, for any set $S \subseteq \mathbb{F}_2^n$ and $u \in \mathbb{N}$ with $u > 1$, we define

$$S^{(u)} := \left\{(0^{(u-1)\cdot n} \circ s) : s \in S\right\}.$$

Now we are ready to formally state the large-span property of a randomly chosen low-degree polynomial over a fixed (sufficiently large entropy) source.

**Lemma 9.** *Let $u > 2$ be an integer and $X \subseteq \mathbb{F}_2^n$, such that $|X| \geq un$. Let $p : \mathbb{F}_{2^{un}} \to \mathbb{F}_{2^{un}}$ be a polynomial of degree $kn$ with all the $(un+1)$-many coefficients chosen uniformly and independently from $\mathbb{F}_{2^{un}}$. Define the set $p(X) := \{p(y) : y \in X^{(u)}\}$. Then, for any $d \leq un$,*

$$\Pr_{p \leftarrow \mathcal{H}_{un,un}}\left[\dim_{\mathbb{F}_2}(p(X^{(u)})) \leq d\right] \leq 2^{un-(un-d)^2}.$$

We now recall the following definitions for a $p \in \mathcal{H}_{10n,10n}$:

$$\begin{aligned}
&\text{Dis}_p : \{0,1\}^n \times \{0,1\}^n \to \{0,1\} \\
&\text{Dis}_p(x,y) \to \langle p(0^{9n} \circ x), p(0^{9n} \circ y)\rangle \\
&\text{Ext}_p : \{0,1\}^n \times \{0,1\}^n \to \{0,1\} \\
&\text{Ext}_p(x,y) \to \langle p(0^{9n} \circ x), p(0^{9n} \circ y)\rangle
\end{aligned}$$

*Remark 1.* Note that for any $p \in \mathcal{H}_{10n,10n}$, $p$ takes elements from $\mathbb{F}_2^n$ to $\mathbb{F}_2^{10n}$. So, by Definition 9, for all $p$, we have rank of $\text{Dis}_p$ and $\text{Ext}_p$ are at most $10n$.

Our claim is that with overwhelming probability over the choice of polynomial $p \in \mathcal{H}_{10n,10n}$, the above object is a 2-source disperser for all logarithmic entropy sources.

**Corollary 1 (Disperser of linear rank for log-entropy sources).** *Consider any $\rho \geq \frac{\log 10n}{n}$.*

$$\Pr_{p \leftarrow \mathcal{H}_{10n,10n}}\left[\text{Dis}_p \textit{ is a } (n, \rho n) \textit{ disperser}\right] \geq 1 - 2^{-5n^2}.$$

Combining Lemma 7 and Corollary 1 gives us a *randomized* construction of 2-source extractors for *all* sources having *linear* entropy. More succinctly,

**Theorem 7 (Strong extractor of exponential error).**

*(i) For any constant $\rho > 0$ there exists a constant $\zeta' > 0$ so that the following holds*

$$\Pr_{p \leftarrow \mathcal{H}_{10n,10n}}\left[\text{Ext}_p \textit{ is a } (n, 1, \rho n, 2^{-\zeta' n}) \textit{ strong 2-source extractor}\right] \geq 1 - 2^{-5n^2}.$$

*(ii) There is an absolute constant $C$ so that,*

$$\Pr_{p \leftarrow \mathcal{H}_{10n,10n}}\left[\text{Ext}_p \textit{ is a } \left(n, 1, \frac{Cn}{\log n}, 2^{-\sqrt{n}/2}\right) \textit{ strong 2-source extractor}\right] \geq 1 - 2^{-5n^2}.$$

*Proof.* Here we will be only proving item (i). The second item can be proved by similar idea, using Lemma 8. From Remark 1 rank of $\text{Ext}_p$ over $\mathbb{F}_2$ is $10n$. By Corollary1 and Lemma 7 with parameters $\delta = 0.1\rho$, which is strictly greater than $\log(10n)/n$ and $\alpha = 0.8\rho$, we get $\zeta > 0$ so that,

$$\Pr_{p \leftarrow \mathcal{H}_{10n,10n}}[\text{Ext}_p \text{ is a } (n, 1, 0.9\rho n, 2^{-\zeta n})\text{ 2-source extractor}] \geq 1 - 2^{-5n^2}.$$

From Lemma 3 we have,

$$\begin{aligned} &\text{Ext}_p \text{ is } (n, 1, 0.9\rho n, 2^{-\zeta n})\text{ 2-source extractor} \\ \implies &\text{Ext}_p \text{ is } (n, 1, \rho n, \varepsilon_1) \text{ strong 2-source extractor.} \end{aligned}$$

for $\varepsilon_1 = (2^{-0.1\rho n} + 2^{-\zeta n}) \times 2$. Hence, $\varepsilon_1 \leq 2^{-\zeta' n}$ for some positive constant $\zeta'$ and this completes the proof. □

*Remark 2.* Note that for any full rank matrix $L \in \mathbb{F}_2^{10n \times 10n}$ we have, $\dim_{\mathbb{F}_2}(p(X^{(10)})) = \dim_{\mathbb{F}_2}(L \cdot p(X^{(10)}))$, for $X \subseteq \mathbb{F}_2^n$. Hence following the line of proof given in Lemma 9 and Corollary 1, we can infer the following,

$$\Pr_{p \leftarrow \mathcal{H}_{10n,10n}}\left[\begin{array}{c}\forall X, Y \subseteq \mathbb{F}_2^n \text{ with size at least } 10n, \\ \langle p(X^{(10)}), L \cdot p(Y^{(10)})\rangle \text{ is non-constant}\end{array}\right] \geq 1 - 2^{-5n^2}.$$

If we define a map,

$$\begin{aligned} E_p : \{0,1\}^n \times \{0,1\}^n &\to \{0,1\} \\ (x, y) &\longmapsto \langle p(0^{9n} \circ x), L \cdot p(0^{9n} \circ y)\rangle \end{aligned}$$

Then from proof of part (i) of Theorem 7 we have, for all $\rho > 0$ there is $\zeta' > 0$ so that

$$\Pr_{p \leftarrow \mathcal{H}_{10n,10n}}[E_p \text{ is } (n, 1, \rho n, 2^{-\zeta' n}) \text{ strong 2-source extractor}] \geq 1 - 2^{-5n^2}.$$

And from proof of part (ii) we have, there is an absolute constant $C$ so that,

$$\Pr_{p \leftarrow \mathcal{H}_{10n,10n}}\left[E_p \text{ is a } \left(n, 1, \frac{Cn}{\log n}, 2^{-\sqrt{n}/2}\right) \text{ strong 2-source extractor}\right] \geq 1 - 2^{-5n^2}.$$

### 3.1 Multi-bit Output Extractors

Previously we have seen a randomized construction of a 2-source extractor with only 1 bit output. In this subsection, we will extend it to the *multi-bit* output extractor, with a *small* increment in the error.

**Definition 10.** *A set of matrices $L_1, \ldots, L_r \in \mathbb{F}_2^{r\times r}$ are called independent if for all $v_1 \ldots, v_r \in \mathbb{F}_2$ not all zero, $\sum_{j=1}^{r} v_j L_j$ is a full rank matrix.*

It turns out that one can efficiently construct such independent matrices.

**Lemma 10 (Constructing independent matrices [ZBS11, Section 6.2]).** *Consider the field $\mathbb{F}_{2^r}$ and let $v_1, \ldots, v_r \in \mathbb{F}_{2^r}$ be the $\mathbb{F}_2$ basis of $\mathbb{F}_{2^r}$ with $e_j : \mathbb{F}_{2^r} \to \mathbb{F}_{2^r}$ denoting the invertible map $e_j(x) = v_j \cdot x$ for all $j \in [r]$. Let $L_i$ denote the matrices representing the linear transformation $e_i$, then the matrices $L_1, \ldots, L_r$ are independent.*

$$E'(x,y) = (\langle f(x), L_1 \cdot g(y)\rangle, \langle f(x), L_2 \cdot g(y)\rangle, \ldots, \langle f(x), L_t g(y)\rangle)$$

is a $(n,t,k,\varepsilon)_\infty$ two source extractor.

We use the above-defined explicit matrices $L_i$ to extend our result in the multi-bit output regime, as follows.

**Theorem 8 (Multi-bit output 2-source Extractor).** *Define a map $E'_p : \{0,1\}^n \times \{0,1\}^n \to \{0,1\}^m$, for $m \le 10n$ as follows,*

$$E'_p(x,y) := (\langle p(0^{9n} \cdot x), L_1 \cdot p(0^{9n} \cdot y)\rangle, \ldots, \langle p(0^{9n} \cdot x), L_m \cdot p(0^{9n} \cdot y)\rangle).$$

*where $L_1, \ldots, L_m \in \mathbb{F}_2^{10n\times 10n}$ are explicit matrices from Lemma 10. Then,*

*(i) For constant $\rho > 0$, say, $\zeta' > 0$ is the constant from Theorem 7. Then there exists constant $\beta > 0$ such that if $m = \zeta' n/8$,*

$$\Pr_{p \leftarrow \mathcal{H}_{10n,10n}} [E'_p \text{ is a } (n,m,\rho n, 2^{-\beta n}) \text{ strong 2-source extractor}] \ge 1 - 2^{-5n^2}.$$

*(ii) There exists a constant $C$ so that if $m = \sqrt{n}/8$, we have,*

$$\Pr_{p \leftarrow \mathcal{H}_{10n,10n}} \left[E'_p \text{ is a } \left(n, m, \frac{Cn}{\log n}, 2^{-\sqrt{n}/8}\right) \text{ strong 2-source extractor}\right] \ge 1 - 2^{-5n^2}.$$

*Proof.* Without loss of generality let us assume that our input sources $\mathbf{X}, \mathbf{Y}$ are flat-$\rho n$ sources with support $X, Y$ respectively. Note that, for any non-empty set $S \subseteq [m]$,

$$\sum_{i\in S} \langle p(X^{(10)}), L_i \cdot p(Y^{(10)})\rangle = \langle p(X^{(10)}), L \cdot p(Y^{(10)})\rangle.$$

where $L \in \mathbb{F}_2^{10n\times 10n}$ is a full-rank matrix. Define $E_p^S(x,y) := \langle p(0^{9n} \circ x), L \cdot p(0^{9n} \circ y)\rangle$.

**Proof of (i).** From Remark 2, we have constant $\zeta' > 0$ such that

$$\Pr_{p \leftarrow \mathcal{H}_{10n,10n}} [E_p^S \text{ is } (n, 1, \rho n, 2^{-\zeta' n}) \text{ strong 2-source extractor}] \geq 1 - 2^{-5n^2}.$$

For any $S \subseteq [m]$, if we have $\Delta\Big( \big( \sum_{i \in S} \langle p(\mathbf{X}^{(10)}), L_i \cdot p(\mathbf{Y}^{(10)}) \rangle, \mathbf{Y}); (\mathcal{U}_1, \mathbf{Y}) \Big) \leq 2^{-\zeta' n}$, by using Lemma 5, we can deduce that

$$\Delta\Big( (\langle p(\mathbf{X}^{(10)}), L_1 \cdot p(\mathbf{Y}^{(10)}) \rangle, \ldots, \langle p(\mathbf{X}^{(10)}), L_m \cdot p(\mathbf{Y}^{(10)}) \rangle, \mathbf{Y}); (\mathcal{U}_m, \mathbf{Y}) \Big)$$
$$\leq \sqrt{2^{-\zeta' n}} \times 2^{(m+2)/2}.$$

Here $\mathbf{X}^{(10)}$ and $\mathbf{Y}^{(10)}$ are uniform distributions over $X^{(10)}$ and $Y^{(10)}$. From the choice of our $m$, $2^{-0.5\zeta' n} \times 2^{(m+2)/2} \leq 2^{-\beta n}$ for some positive constant $\beta$ and we are done.

**Proof of (ii)** follows by similar idea using second statement of Remark 2. □]

## 4 Non-malleable Extractors

For any function $f : \{0,1\}^n \to \{0,1\}^n$, we say that $s \in S$ is a *fixed point* of $f$, if $f(s) = s$. Let $\mathcal{F}_n$ be the set of all functions from $\{0,1\}^n$ to $\{0,1\}^n$ *without* any fixed points. Now we state the definition of Non-malleable strong 2-source extractors, as defined by Cheraghchi and Guruswami in [CG14].

**Definition 11 (Non-malleable strong 2-source extractor [CG14]).** *We say* nmExt : $\{0,1\}^n \times \{0,1\}^n \to \{0,1\}^m$ *is a non-malleable* $(n, m, k, \epsilon)$ *strong 2-source extractor if for all functions* $f, g \in \mathcal{F}_n$ *and for all independent sources* $\mathbf{X}, \mathbf{Y} \sim \{0,1\}^n$, *with* $H_\infty(\mathbf{X}), H_\infty(\mathbf{Y}) \geq k$, *the following three properties hold:*

1. $\text{nmExt}(\mathbf{X}, \mathbf{Y}), \text{nmExt}(f(\mathbf{X}), g(\mathbf{Y})), \mathbf{Y} \approx_\varepsilon \mathcal{U}_m, \text{nmExt}(f(\mathbf{X}), g(\mathbf{Y})), \mathbf{Y}$
2. $\text{nmExt}(\mathbf{X}, \mathbf{Y}), \text{nmExt}(\mathbf{X}, g(\mathbf{Y})), \mathbf{Y} \approx_\varepsilon \mathcal{U}_m, \text{nmExt}(\mathbf{X}, g(\mathbf{Y})), \mathbf{Y}$
3. $\text{nmExt}(\mathbf{X}, \mathbf{Y}), \text{nmExt}(f(\mathbf{X}), \mathbf{Y}), \mathbf{Y} \approx_\varepsilon \mathcal{U}_m, \text{nmExt}(f(\mathbf{X}), \mathbf{Y}), \mathbf{Y}$

Recall the definition of $\mathcal{H}_{t,r}$: it denotes the set of univariate polynomials over the field $\mathbb{F}_{2^r}$ of degree at most $(t-1)$. For a $p \in \mathcal{H}_{30n,10n}$ and $m \leq 10n$, let us define our non-malleable extractor $\text{nmExt}_p^m : \{0,1\}^n \times \{0,1\}^n \to \{0,1\}^m$ in the following way:

$$\text{nmExt}_p^m(x, y) := \Big( \langle p(0^{9n} \circ x), L_1 \cdot p(0^{9n} \circ y) \rangle, \ldots, \langle p(0^{9n} \circ x), L_m \cdot p(0^{9n} y) \rangle \Big).$$

In the above equation, $L_1, \ldots, L_m$ are the explicit independent matrices that can be constructed using Lemma 10.

In this section, we will show that (uniformly) sampling a random polynomial of *linear degree*, over an extension field where the degree of extension is *linear*, would yield a strong non-malleable 2-source extractor for all linear entropy sources. Moreover the function obtained by the uniformly chosen polynomial is a strong non-malleable extractor for the sources of min-entropy $O(n/\log n)$, with a slight loss in error. More formally,

**Theorem 9 (Efficient strong non-malleable two source extractor).**

*(i) For every constant $\rho > 0$, there exist constants $\mu, \gamma > 0$ so that with $m = \mu n$, we have,*

$$\Pr_{p \leftarrow \mathcal{H}_{30n,10n}} \left[ \begin{array}{c} \mathrm{nmExt}_p^m \textit{ is a strong two source} \\ (n, m, \rho n, 2^{-\gamma n}) \textit{ non-malleable extractor} \end{array} \right] \geq 1 - 2^{-2n^2}.$$

*(ii) There are constants $C_0$ and $\sigma, \nu > 0$ so that when $m = \nu\sqrt{n}$,*

$$\Pr_{p \leftarrow \mathcal{H}_{30n,10n}} \left[ \begin{array}{c} \mathrm{nmExt}_p^m \textit{ is a strong two source} \\ \left(n, m, \frac{C_0 n}{\log n}, 2^{-\sigma\sqrt{n}}\right) \textit{ non-malleable extractor} \end{array} \right] \geq 1 - 2^{-2n^2}$$

*Remark 3.* To prove the above, we will only use the fact that $\mathcal{H}_{30n,10n}$ is a family of $30n$-wise independent hash functions. Instead of polynomials if we take any arbitrary $30n$-wise independent hash family $\mathcal{H}$ over $\mathbb{F}_{2^{10n}}$, for an uniformly random $h \leftarrow \mathcal{H}$ we can prove the same.

To show the above theorem, we will prove Lemma 11 (which would prove the first item of Definition 11) and Lemma 12 (which would prove the second and third items of Definition 11). In particular, for the first item, we will prove the following.

**Lemma 11.** *Let $f, g \in \mathcal{F}_n$. Then we have:*

*(i) For any constant $\rho > 0$, there exist constants $\gamma, \mu > 0$ such that with probability at least $1 - 2^{-3n^2}$ over the uniformly random choice of $p \in \mathcal{H}_{30n,10n}$ the following holds: for all independent sources $\mathbf{X}, \mathbf{Y} \sim \{0,1\}^n$, with $H_\infty(\mathbf{X}), H_\infty(\mathbf{Y}) \geq \rho n$, we have*

$$\mathrm{nmExt}_p^{\mu n}(\mathbf{X}, \mathbf{Y}), \mathrm{nmExt}_p^{\mu n}(f(\mathbf{X}), g(\mathbf{Y})), \mathbf{Y} \approx_{2^{-\gamma n}} \mathcal{U}_{\mu n}, \mathrm{nmExt}_p^{\mu n}(f(\mathbf{X}), g(\mathbf{Y})), \mathbf{Y}$$

*(ii) There are constants $C_0$ and $\sigma, \nu > 0$ so that, with probability at least $1 - 2^{-3n^2}$ over the uniformly random choice of $p \in \mathcal{H}_{30n,10n}$ the following holds: for all independent sources $\mathbf{X}, \mathbf{Y} \sim \{0,1\}^n$, with $H_\infty(\mathbf{X}), H_\infty(\mathbf{Y}) \geq \frac{C_0 n}{\log n}$, we have*

$$\mathrm{nmExt}_p^{\nu\sqrt{n}}(\mathbf{X}, \mathbf{Y}), \mathrm{nmExt}_p^{\nu\sqrt{n}}(f(\mathbf{X}), g(\mathbf{Y})), \mathbf{Y} \approx_{2^{-\sigma\sqrt{n}}} \mathcal{U}_{\nu\sqrt{n}}, \mathrm{nmExt}_p^{\nu\sqrt{n}}(f(\mathbf{X}), g(\mathbf{Y})), \mathbf{Y}.$$

For the second and third items (which are symmetric) i.e. when *exactly* one of the two sources is corrupted, we will prove the following.

**Lemma 12.** *Let $f, g \in \mathcal{F}_n$. Then,*

*(i) For any $\rho > 0$, there are constants $\tilde{\mu}, \tilde{\gamma} > 0$ such that with probability at least $1 - 2 \cdot 2^{-4n^2}$ over the uniformly random choice of $p \in \mathcal{H}_{30n,10n}$ the following holds: for all independent sources $\mathbf{X}, \mathbf{Y} \sim \{0,1\}^n$, with $H_\infty(\mathbf{X}), H_\infty(\mathbf{Y}) \geq \rho n$, the following two properties hold.*

*1.* $\text{nmExt}_p^m(\mathbf{X}, \mathbf{Y}), \text{nmExt}_p^m(f(\mathbf{X}), \mathbf{Y}), \mathbf{Y} \approx_\varepsilon \mathcal{U}_m, \text{nmExt}_p^m(f(\mathbf{X}), \mathbf{Y}), \mathbf{Y}$
*2.* $\text{nmExt}_p^m(\mathbf{X}, \mathbf{Y}), \text{nmExt}_p^m(\mathbf{X}, g(\mathbf{Y})), \mathbf{Y} \approx_\varepsilon \mathcal{U}_m, \text{nmExt}_p^m(\mathbf{X}, g(\mathbf{Y})), \mathbf{Y}$

*where $m = \tilde{\mu} n$, and $\varepsilon = 2^{-\tilde{\gamma} n}$.*

*(ii) There are constants $C_0$ and $\tilde{\sigma}, \tilde{\nu} > 0$ so that, with probability at least $1 - 2 \cdot 2^{-4n^2}$ over the uniformly random choice of $p \in \mathcal{H}_{30n,10n}$ the following holds: for all independent sources $\mathbf{X}, \mathbf{Y} \sim \{0,1\}^n$, with $H_\infty(\mathbf{X}), H_\infty(\mathbf{Y}) \geq \frac{C_0 n}{\log n}$, we have*

*(a)* $\text{nmExt}_p^m(\mathbf{X}, \mathbf{Y}), \text{nmExt}_p^m(f(\mathbf{X}), \mathbf{Y}), \mathbf{Y} \approx_\varepsilon \mathcal{U}_m, \text{nmExt}_p^m(f(\mathbf{X}), \mathbf{Y}), \mathbf{Y}$
*(b)* $\text{nmExt}_p^m(\mathbf{X}, \mathbf{Y}), \text{nmExt}_p^m(\mathbf{X}, g(\mathbf{Y})), \mathbf{Y} \approx_\varepsilon \mathcal{U}_m, \text{nmExt}_p^m(\mathbf{X}, g(\mathbf{Y})), \mathbf{Y}$

*where $\varepsilon = 2^{-\tilde{\sigma}\sqrt{n}}$ and $m = \tilde{\nu}\sqrt{n}$*

Throughout the section we only prove that with *high probability* over the uniformly random choice of $p$ from $\mathcal{H}_{30n,10n}$, we have $\text{nmExt}_p^m$ is a $(n, m, \rho n, \varepsilon)$ strong 2-source non-malleable extractor, with $\varepsilon = 2^{-O(n)}$ and $m = O(n)$ when $\rho > 0$ is a constant. The proof for the case when input sources have *sub-linear* entropy also follows by similar idea and we skip its proof.

Also the proof idea for Lemma 12 is exactly similar to the proof of Lemma 11. So from now on, we will only focus on proving Lemma 11, which will be covered in Sect. 4.1-4.3.

**A sneak-peak into the Partition Lemma.** For notational ease, let us denote

$$\mathcal{D}_p^m(\mathbf{X}, \mathbf{Y}) := \mathcal{U}_m, \text{nmExt}_p^m(f(\mathbf{X}), g(\mathbf{Y})), \mathbf{Y}$$
$$\phi_p^m(\mathbf{X}, \mathbf{Y}) := \text{nmExt}_p^m(\mathbf{X}, \mathbf{Y}), \text{nmExt}_p^m(f(\mathbf{X}), g(\mathbf{Y})), \mathbf{Y}\,.$$

For any set $\mathcal{P} \subseteq \mathbb{F}_2^n \times \mathbb{F}_2^n$, we denote by $\phi(\mathbf{X}, \mathbf{Y})|_{\mathcal{P}}$, the distribution obtained by restricting $(\mathbf{X}, \mathbf{Y}) \in \mathcal{P}$. We will prove Lemma 11 by conditioning $\phi_p^m$ on various partitions $\mathcal{P}_1, \ldots, \mathcal{P}_k$ of $\mathcal{P}$, showing that *either* the statistical distance in each case between $\phi_p^m(\mathbf{X}, \mathbf{Y})|_{\mathcal{P}_i}$ and $\mathcal{D}_p^m(\mathbf{X}, \mathbf{Y})|_{\mathcal{P}_i}$ is small, *or* the size of the partition $\mathcal{P}_i$ is small. This is enough to imply that $\phi_p^m(\mathbf{X}, \mathbf{Y})$ is *close* to $\mathcal{D}_p^m(\mathbf{X}, \mathbf{Y})$. A more general statement on the statistical distance between two distributions can be stated as follows.

**Lemma 13 (Partition Lemma** [AHL16, **Lemma 3.3**]**).** *Let $\psi_1$ and $\psi_2$ be two functions from $\{0,1\}^n \times \{0,1\}^n \to \{0,1\}^r$. Further, let $\mathcal{P} \subseteq \mathbb{F}_2^n \times \mathbb{F}_2^n$, and let $\mathbf{A}, \mathbf{B} \sim \{0,1\}^n$ be two distributions such that* Supp$(\mathbf{A}, \mathbf{B}) \subseteq \mathcal{P}$*. Finally, let $\mathcal{P}_1, \ldots, \mathcal{P}_k$ be disjoint partitions of $\mathcal{P}$ such that for all $i \in [k]$:*

$$\Delta(\psi_1(\mathbf{A}, \mathbf{B})|_{(\mathbf{A},\mathbf{B}) \in \mathcal{P}_i}; \psi_2(\mathbf{A}, \mathbf{B})|_{(\mathbf{A},\mathbf{B}) \in \mathcal{P}_i}) \leq \varepsilon_i\,.$$

*Then the following holds:*

$$\Delta(\psi_1(\mathbf{A},\mathbf{B});\psi_2(\mathbf{A},\mathbf{B})) \le \sum_i \varepsilon_i \frac{|\mathcal{P}_i|}{|\mathcal{P}|}.$$

*Proof strategy using Lemma* 13 *over flat sources.* Let us fix $f, g \in \mathcal{F}_n$ for the rest of the subsections. We will argue that for a uniformly chosen polynomial $p$, there exist constants $\mu, \gamma > 0$, such that with high probability the following holds:

$$\Delta(\phi_p^{\mu n}(\mathbf{X},\mathbf{Y});\mathcal{D}_p^{\mu n}(\mathbf{X},\mathbf{Y})) \le 2^{-\gamma n},$$

for all independent $\rho n$-flat sources $\mathbf{X}, \mathbf{Y}$ with supports $X$ and $Y$ respectively, and $\mathcal{P} = X \times Y$. Importantly, from Lemma 1, one would then infer the same for any two independent sources $\mathbf{X}, \mathbf{Y}$, where $H_\infty(\mathbf{X}), H_\infty(\mathbf{Y}) \ge \rho n$.

### 4.1 Inverse Image of the Image Under $f$ (resp. $g$) is Large

In this subsection, we analyze the case when $f(x)$ has a large pre-image (in $X$) under $f$. Formally, define:

$$X_{\text{large}} := \{x \in X : |f^{-1}(f(x)) \cap X| \ge 2^{\rho n/2}\}.$$

In the next lemma, we will prove that the two distributions $\phi_p^m(\mathbf{X},\mathbf{Y})$ and $\mathcal{D}_p^m(\mathbf{X},\mathbf{Y})$, when restricted to $X_{\text{large}} \times Y$, are statistically close.

**Lemma 14.** *Given any $\rho > 0$, there are constants $\beta', \mu' > 0$ such that with probability at least $1 - 2^{-4n^2}$ over the uniformly random choice of $p \in \mathcal{H}_{30n,10n}$, the following holds: for all $\mathbf{X}, \mathbf{Y} \sim \mathbb{F}_2^n$ flat-$\rho n$ sources with supports $X$ and $Y$ respectively, we have*

$$\Delta(\phi_p^m(\mathbf{X},\mathbf{Y})|_{X_{\text{large}}\times Y};\mathcal{D}_p^m(\mathbf{X},\mathbf{Y})|_{X_{\text{large}}\times Y}) \le 2^{-\beta' n},$$

*where $m = \mu' n$.*

To prove the above lemma, we will further partition $X_{\text{large}}$ into *disjoint union* of sets $A_{z_1}, A_{z_2}, \ldots, A_{z_\ell}$, with $|A_{z_i}| \ge 2^{\rho n/2}$, where,

$$A_{z_i} := \{x \in X : f(x) = z_i\} \cap X_{\text{large}}\, \forall i \in [\ell].$$

We will first show that for suitable $m$, with high probability, over uniformly random choice of $p$ from $\mathcal{H}_{30n,10n}$, the distribution $\phi_p^m(\mathbf{X},\mathbf{Y})|_{A_{z_i}\times Y}$ is close to $\mathcal{D}_p^m(\mathbf{X},\mathbf{Y})|_{A_{z_i}\times Y}$.

**Lemma 15.** *Given any $\rho > 0$, and $z \in \{z_1, \ldots, z_\ell\}$, there exist constants $\beta', \mu' > 0$ such that with probability at least $1 - 2^{-5n^2}$ over the uniformly random choice of $p \in \mathcal{H}_{30n,10n}$, the following holds: for all independent flat-$\rho n$ sources $\mathbf{X}, \mathbf{Y} \sim \mathbb{F}_2^n$ with supports $X$ and $Y$ respectively, we have*

$$\Delta(\phi_p^m(\mathbf{X},\mathbf{Y})|_{A_z\times Y};\mathcal{D}_p^m(\mathbf{X},\mathbf{Y})|_{A_z\times Y}) \le 2^{-\beta' n},$$

*where $m = \mu' n$,*

The above lemma can be directly used for the distributions restricted to $X_{\text{large}} \times Y$, to get the desired result of Lemma 14.

*Proof of Lemma* 14. From Lemma 15, we know that for all $i \in [\ell]$, with probability at least $1 - \ell \cdot 2^{-5n^2}$, over uniformly chosen $p$ from $\mathcal{H}_{30n,10n}$, for all independent flat-$\rho n$ sources $\mathbf{X}, \mathbf{Y} \sim \mathbb{F}_2^n$ with supports $X$ and $Y$ respectively the following holds:

$$\Delta(\phi_p^m(\mathbf{X}, \mathbf{Y})|_{A_{z_i} \times Y}; \mathcal{D}_p^m(\mathbf{X}, \mathbf{Y})|_{A_{z_i} \times Y}) \leq 2^{-\beta' n}.$$

Since trivially $\ell < 2^n$, we have $\ell \cdot 2^{-5n^2} \leq 2^{-4n^2}$. Consider $\mathcal{P} = X_{\text{large}} \times Y$ and its partitions $\mathcal{P}_1, \ldots, \mathcal{P}_\ell$ to be $A_{z_1} \times Y, \ldots, A_{z_\ell} \times Y$. Using Lemma 13, our result follows. □

*Remark 4.* Similar to $X_{\text{large}}$, we define $Y_{\text{large}}$ with respect to $g$ as follows:

$$Y_{\text{large}} := \{y \in Y : |g^{-1}(g(y)) \cap Y| \geq 2^{\rho n/2}\}.$$

Let us further partition $Y_{\text{large}}$ as $B_{v_1} \sqcup \cdots \sqcup B_{v_p}$, where $\forall\, i \in [p]$,

$$B_{v_i} := \{y \in Y : g(y) = v_i\} \cap Y_{\text{large}}.$$

For any $v \in \{v_1, \ldots, v_p\}$ and any constants $\rho, \rho' > 0$, there are constants $\alpha', \nu' > 0$ such that taking $m = \nu' n$, with probability at least $1 - 2^{-5n^2}$ over the uniformly random choice of $p \in \mathcal{H}_{30n,10n}$, the following holds:

for all independent flat-$\rho n$ sources $\mathbf{X}, \mathbf{Y}$ with support $X, Y$ respectively, with $X' \subseteq X$ of size at least $2^{\rho' n}$, we have

$$\left(\text{nmExt}_p^m(\mathbf{X}, \mathbf{Y}), \mathbf{Y}\right)|_{X' \times B_v} \approx_{2^{-\alpha' n}} (\mathcal{U}_m, \mathbf{Y})|_{X' \times B_v}.$$

Note that $g(B_v) = \{v\}$, and hence if we leak $\text{nmExt}(f(\mathbf{X}), g(\mathbf{Y}))|_{X' \times B_v}$, with a little loss in the parameter we get,

$$\left(\text{nmExt}_p^m(\mathbf{X}, \mathbf{Y}), \mathbf{Y}\right)|_{X' \times B_v}, \text{nmExt}_p^m(\mathbf{X}, v)|_{X'} \approx_\varepsilon (\mathcal{U}_m, \mathbf{Y})|_{X' \times B_v}, \text{nmExt}(\mathbf{X}, v)|_{X'}$$

for $\varepsilon = 2^{-\alpha n}$ and $m = \beta n$, where $\beta, \alpha$ are positive constants. Therefore we get, for any constant $\rho > 0$ we have positive constants $\alpha, \beta$ such that with $m = \beta n$ the following holds:

For all independent flat-$\rho n$ sources $\mathbf{X}, \mathbf{Y} \sim \mathbb{F}_2^n$, with supports $X$ and $Y$ respectively and $X' \subseteq X$ of size at least $2^{\rho' n}$,

$$\phi_p^m(\mathbf{X}, \mathbf{Y})|_{(X', Y_{\text{large}})} \approx_{2^{-\alpha n}} \mathcal{D}_p^m(\mathbf{X}, \mathbf{Y})|_{(X', Y_{\text{large}})}.$$

## 4.2 Inverse Image of the Image Under $f$ (resp. $g$) is Small

Till now we have taken care of the case when $\phi_p^m(\mathbf{X}, \mathbf{Y})$ and $\mathcal{D}_p^m(\mathbf{X}, \mathbf{Y})$ are restricted to the partition $X_{\text{large}} \times Y$. Now let us focus on the subsets of $X$ and

$Y$ which contain those elements whose images have *small* pre-image under $f$ and $g$ respectively. When $|X| = |Y| = 2^{\rho n}$, define,

$$X_{\text{small}} := \{x \in X : 0 < |f^{-1}(f(x)) \cap X| < 2^{\rho n/2}\} \subseteq X,$$
$$Y_{\text{small}} := \{y \in Y : 0 < |g^{-1}(g(y)) \cap Y| < 2^{\rho n/2}\} \subseteq Y.$$

Here, our main goal is to prove the following:

**Lemma 16.** *Fix $f, g \in \mathcal{F}_n$. For $X, Y \subseteq \mathbb{F}_2^n$ with $|X| = |Y| = 2^{\rho n}$ and $X_{\text{small}}$, $Y_{\text{small}}$, defined as before, consider the following property:*

$$|X_{\text{small}} \times Y_{\text{small}}| \geq 2^{1.7\rho n}, \tag{1}$$

*where $\rho > 0$ is some constant. Then, there are positive constants $\beta'', \mu''$ such that for $m = \mu'' n$, with probability at least $1 - 2^{-4n^2}$ over uniformly random choice of $p$ from $\mathcal{H}_{30n,10n}$ the following holds:*
*For all $\mathbf{X}, \mathbf{Y} \sim \mathbb{F}_2^n$ such that $|X| = |Y| = 2^{\rho n}$ and satisfies property 1,*

$$\Delta\Big(\phi_p^m(\mathbf{X}, \mathbf{Y})|_{X_{\text{small}} \times Y_{\text{small}}}; \mathcal{D}_p^m(\mathbf{X}, \mathbf{Y})|_{X_{\text{small}} \times Y_{\text{small}}}\Big) \leq 2^{-\beta'' n}.$$

In order to prove the above lemma, we start with a small technical claim that will be used later.

**Lemma 17.** *Let $X, Y, X_{\text{small}}, Y_{\text{small}}$ be defined as above with $|X_{\text{small}}|, |Y_{\text{small}}| \geq 2^{0.7\rho n}$. Then, the following two properties hold.*

1. *There exists a subset $X'' \subseteq X_{\text{small}}$, with $|X''| \geq 2^{0.1\rho n}$, such that all elements in $X''$ and $f(y)$, for all $y \in X''$* are distinct. *That is, $f|_{X''}$ is injective, and for any $y \in X''$, $y \notin f(X'')$.*
2. *There exists a subset $Y'' \subseteq Y_{\text{small}}$, with $|Y''| \geq 2^{0.1\rho n}$, such that all elements in $Y''$ and $g(z)$ for all $z \in Y''$* are distinct. *That is, $g|_{Y''}$ is injective, and for any $z \in Y''$, $z \notin f(Y'')$.*

We now follow the proof strategy previously employed in Sect. 3 for the randomized construction of strong 2-source extractors. First, we define the following.

**Definition 12.** *For any set $X \subseteq \mathbb{F}_2^n$, a function $f \in \mathcal{F}_n$ and a positive integer $u \geq 2$, and a polynomial $p \in \mathcal{H}_{3un,un}$, define*

$$p\left(X_f^{(u)}\right) := \{p(0^{(u-1)n}x) \circ p(0^{(u-1)n}f(x)) : x \in X\},$$

*where*

$$X_f^{(u)} := \{(0^{(u-1)n} \circ x) \circ (0^{(u-1)n} \circ f(x)) : x \in X\}.$$

*30-feet above proof overview in two lines.* We will show that $\dim((X'')_f^{(10)})$ and $\dim((Y'')_g^{(10)})$ are large, which in turn will imply that $\dim((X_{\text{small}})_f^{(10)})$ and $\dim((Y_{\text{small}})_g^{(10)})$ are also large. To show this we will prove a more general statement that all the sets which satisfy the property given in Lemma 17, have large dimension. For that we need the following formal definition.

**Property $P_f$.** For a set $A \subseteq \{0,1\}^n$ and $f \in \mathcal{F}_n$, we say $A$ satisfies property $P_f$ if

$$f|_A \text{ is injective and } a \notin f(A)\ \forall\ a \in A. \tag{2}$$

**Theorem 10.** *Let $f \in \mathcal{F}_n$. Let $A \subseteq \mathbb{F}_2^n$, such that $|A| \geq 2un$, for a positive integer $u \geq 2$. Further, assume that $A$ satisfies property $P_f$. Then for any $d \leq 1.4un$, the following holds.*

$$\Pr_{p \leftarrow \mathcal{H}_{3un,un}} [\dim_{\mathbb{F}_2}(p(A_f^{(u)})) \leq d] \leq 2^{2un-(2un-d)^2}\,.$$

We will state a similar statement as above which will be needed for Section 5.

**Lemma 18.** *Let $f \in \mathcal{F}_n$. Let $A \subseteq \mathbb{F}_2^n$, such that $|A| \geq 50n$. Further, assume that $A$ satisfies property $P_f$. Then, the following holds.*

$$\Pr_{p \leftarrow \mathcal{H}_{300n,10n}} [\dim_{\mathbb{F}_2}(p(A_f^{(10)})) \leq 10n] \leq 2^{50n-400n^2}\,.$$

By applying the union bound over all set of size $50n$, we get the following corollary.

**Corollary 2.** *Let $f \in \mathcal{F}_n$. Then, with probability at most $2^{-349n^2}$ over the choice of uniformly random $p$ from $\mathcal{H}_{300n,10n}$ we have,*

$$\exists\, A \subseteq \mathbb{F}_2^n \text{ of size at least } 50n \text{ that satisfies } P_f\,, \dim_{\mathbb{F}_2}(p(A_f^{(10)})) \leq 10n\,.$$

Following the (exact) same line of proof that has been provided for the above, it is easy to see that in fact picking a polynomial of degree $300n$, sampled from a source of min-entropy rate 0.9 *still works*!

]In the next remark, we argue that all the above probability calculations hold if one multiplies the space by a full-rank matrix.

*Remark 5.* Since $\text{Span}_{\mathbb{F}_2}(p(A_f^{(u)})) \subseteq \mathbb{F}_2^{2un}$, for any full-rank matrix $M \in \mathbb{F}_2^{2un \times 2un}$, we have

$$M \cdot \text{Span}_{\mathbb{F}_2}(p(A_f^{(u)})) = \text{Span}_{\mathbb{F}_2}(M \cdot p(A_f^{(u)})) = \text{Span}_{\mathbb{F}_2}(p(A_f^{(u)})).$$

Hence, for given $A, f, c, d$ same as in Theorem 10 and any full-rank matrix $M \in \mathbb{F}_2^{2un \times 2un}$, we also have,

$$\Pr_{p \leftarrow \mathcal{H}_{3un,un}} [\dim_{\mathbb{F}_2}(M \cdot p(A_f^{(u)})) \leq d] \leq 2^{2un-(2un-d)^2}\,.$$

We set the value of $u$ to be 10 in Remark 5. Using Lemma 17 we can have the following lemma:

**Lemma 19.** *Let $f \in \mathcal{F}_n$ and let $\rho > 0$ be any constant. Further let $M$ be any $20n \times 20n$ full-rank matrix over $\mathbb{F}_2$. Then with probability at least $1 - 2^{-5n^2}$ over the uniformly random choice of $p \in \mathcal{H}_{30n,10n}$, the following holds: for all $X \subseteq \mathbb{F}_2^n$ of size $2^{\rho n}$ with $|X_{\text{small}}| \geq 2^{0.7\rho n}$ we have,*

$$\dim_{\mathbb{F}_2}\left(M \cdot p((X_{\text{small}})_f^{(10)})\right) \geq 12n\,.$$

Now we will formally argue that the inner-product of the image of $(X_{\text{small}})_f^{(10)}$ and image of $(Y_{\text{small}})_g^{(10)}$ under $p$ is *non-constant.* From there, we show that a random polynomial can be used to construct a strong extractor on the sources $(X_{\text{small}})_f^{(10)}$ and $(Y_{\text{small}})_f^{(10)}$.

By $(\mathbf{X}_{\text{small}})_f^{(10)}$ and $(\mathbf{Y}_{\text{small}})_g^{(10)}$, we denote uniform distributions over $(X_{\text{small}})_f^{(10)}$ and $(Y_{\text{small}})_g^{(10)}$ respectively.

**Corollary 3.** *Fix any $f, g \in \mathcal{F}_n$. Let $M$ be any $20n \times 20n$ full-rank matrix over $\mathbb{F}_2$. Then for any constant $\rho > 0$, there is another constant $\beta_1 > 0$ such that with probability at least $\geq 1 - 2^{-4.5n^2}$, over uniformly random choice of $p \in \mathcal{H}_{30n,10n}$, the following holds: For $X, Y \subseteq \mathbb{F}_2^n$ such that $|X| = |Y| = 2^{\rho n}$ and $|X_{\text{small}}|, |Y_{\text{small}}| \geq 2^{0.7\rho n}$, we have,*

$$\Delta\Big(\langle p((\mathbf{X}_{\text{small}})_f^{(10)}), M \cdot p(\mathbf{Y}_{\text{small}})_g^{(10)})\rangle, \mathbf{Y}_{\text{small}}\,;\, \mathcal{U}_1, \mathbf{Y}_{\text{small}}\Big) \leq 2^{-\beta_1 n}\,.$$

Now we are ready to prove Lemma 16 (main lemma of this subsection). For completeness, we restate the lemma here.

**Lemma 20.** *Fix $f, g \in \mathcal{F}_n$. For $X, Y \subseteq \mathbb{F}_2^n$ with $|X| = |Y| = 2^{\rho n}$ and $X_{\text{small}}$, $Y_{\text{small}}$ are as defined before, consider the following property,*

$$|X_{\text{small}} \times Y_{\text{small}}| \geq 2^{1.7\rho n}\,, \tag{3}$$

*where $\rho > 0$ is some constant. Then, there are positive constants $\beta'', \mu''$ such that for $m = \mu'' n$, with probability at least $1 - 2^{-4n^2}$ over uniformly random choice of $p$ from $\mathcal{H}_{30n,10n}$ the following holds: For all $\mathbf{X}, \mathbf{Y} \sim \mathbb{F}_2^n$ such that $|X| = |Y| = 2^{\rho n}$ and satisfies Eq. 3,*

$$\Delta\Big(\phi_p^m(\mathbf{X}, \mathbf{Y})|_{X_{\text{small}} \times Y_{\text{small}}}; \mathcal{D}_p^m(\mathbf{X}, \mathbf{Y})|_{X_{\text{small}} \times Y_{\text{small}}}\Big) \leq 2^{-\beta'' n}\,.$$

*Proof.* If for $X, Y \subseteq \mathbb{F}_2^n$, both of size $\rho n$, we have $2^{1.7\rho n} \leq |X_{\text{small}} \times Y_{\text{small}}| \leq |X_{\text{small}}| \times 2^{\rho n}$, we can easily conclude that

$$|X_{\text{small}}| \geq 2^{0.7\rho n},\ \text{and}\ |Y_{\text{small}}| \geq 2^{0.7\rho n}\,.$$

For this proof, we introduce the following notations:

We use $\mathbf{X}_{\text{small}}$ and $(\mathbf{X}_{\text{small}})^{(10)}$ to denote uniform distribution over $X_{\text{small}}$ and $(X_{\text{small}})^{(10)}$ respectively. And similarly, we use notations $\mathbf{Y}_{\text{small}}$ and $(\mathbf{Y}_{\text{small}})^{(10)}$ to denote uniform distribution over $Y_{\text{small}}$ and $(Y_{\text{small}})^{(10)}$ respectively.

We will show a more general statement that there exists a constant $\beta'' > 0$ (see Eq. 4), such that with probability at least $1 - 2^{-4n^2}$, over uniformly random choice of $p \in \mathcal{H}_{30n,10n}$, the following holds:

For all $X, Y \subseteq \mathbb{F}_2^n$ where $|X| = |Y| = 2^{\rho n}$ such that they satisfy Eq. 3, we have

$$\Delta\Big(\phi_p^m(\mathbf{X}, \mathbf{Y})|_{X_{\text{small}} \times \mathbf{Y}_{\text{small}}}; (\mathcal{U}_m, \mathcal{U}_m, \mathbf{Y}_{\text{small}})\Big) \leq 2^{-\beta'' n}. \tag{4}$$

To show the above, we will apply Vazirani's XOR lemma (Lemma 5). We need to show that for any $a_1, \ldots, a_m, b_1, \ldots, b_m \in \mathbb{F}_2$, where not all of them are zero, with probability at least $1 - 2^{-4n^2}$, over the uniformly random choice of $p \in \mathcal{H}_{30n,10n}$, we have:

For all $X, Y \subseteq \mathbb{F}_2^n$ both of size $2^{\rho n}$ satisfying *Equation*3,

$$\Delta\Bigg(\Big(\sum_{i=1}^{m} a_i \langle p((\mathbf{X}_{\text{small}})^{(10)}), L_i \cdot p((\mathbf{Y}_{\text{small}})^{(10)})\rangle$$
$$+ \sum_{i=1}^{m} b_i \langle p((f(\mathbf{X}_{\text{small}}))^{(10)}), L_i \cdot p((g(\mathbf{Y}_{\text{small}}))^{(10)})\rangle, \mathbf{Y}_{\text{small}}\Big); \Big(\mathcal{U}_1, \mathbf{Y}_{\text{small}}\Big)\Bigg)$$
$$\leq 2^{-\beta n},$$

for some $\beta > 0$. Fix arbitrary $a_1, \cdots, a_n, b_1, \cdots, b_n \in \mathbb{F}_2$, where not all of them are zero. Observe that the above distribution of the sum of the output bits of $\text{nmExt}_p^m$ reduces to the following distribution

$$\langle p((\mathbf{X}_{\text{small}})^{(10)}), L' \cdot p((\mathbf{Y}_{\text{small}})^{(10)})\rangle + \langle p((f(\mathbf{X}_{\text{small}}))^{(10)}), L'' \cdot p((g(\mathbf{Y}_{\text{small}}))^{(10)})\rangle,$$

where $L' := \sum_{i \in [m]} a_i L_i$ and $L'' := \sum_{i \in [m]} b_i L_i$.

We will denote the above distribution by $\psi_{L',L''}(\mathbf{X}_{\text{small}}, \mathbf{Y}_{\text{small}})$, for the rest of the subsection.

Since, by assumption, not all of $a_1, \cdots, a_n, b_1, \cdots, b_n$ are zero, and since $L_i$ are independent matrices, we know that *at least* one of $L'$ or $L''$ must be full-rank. In particular, either both are nonzero full-rank matrices, or one is 0, while the other remains a full-rank matrix. We will go over all the 3 cases below.

**Case 1**: Both $L', L''$ are full-rank.

**Proof of Case 1.** In this case, we have $\psi_{L',L''}(\mathbf{X}_{\text{small}}, \mathbf{Y}_{\text{small}})$

$$= \langle p(0^{9n}||\mathbf{X}_{\text{small}}), L' \cdot p(0^{9n}||\mathbf{Y}_{\text{small}})\rangle + \langle p(0^{9n}||f(\mathbf{X}_{\text{small}})), L'' \cdot p(0^{(9n}||g(\mathbf{Y}_{\text{small}}))\rangle$$
$$= \langle p(0^{9n}||\mathbf{X}_{\text{small}}) \circ p(0^{9n}||f(\mathbf{X}_{\text{small}})), M \cdot p(0^{9n}||\mathbf{Y}_{\text{small}}) \circ p(0^{9n}||g(\mathbf{Y}_{\text{small}}))\rangle,$$

where

$$M := \begin{pmatrix} L' & \mathbf{0} \\ \mathbf{0} & L'' \end{pmatrix}_{20n \times 20n}.$$

Note that $M$ is full-rank since both $L'$ and $L''$ are full-rank matrices (by assumption). Therefore from Corollary 3 we can conclude, with probability at least $1 - 2^{-4.5n^2}$ over uniformly random choice of $p$ from $\mathcal{H}_{30n,10n}$, we have the following: For all $X, Y$ such that both of size $\rho n$ and satisfy *Equation*3,

$$\Delta\Big(\psi_{L',L''}(\mathbf{X}_{\text{small}}, \mathbf{Y}_{\text{small}}), \mathbf{Y}_{\text{small}}\,;\, \mathcal{U}_1, \mathbf{Y}_{\text{small}}\Big) \leq 2^{-\beta_1 n}\,.$$

**Case 2:** $L'$ is full-rank and $L'' = \mathbf{0}$.

**Proof of Case 2.** In this case,

$$\psi_{L',L''}(\mathbf{X}_{\text{small}}, \mathbf{Y}_{\text{small}}) = \langle p((\mathbf{X}_{\text{small}})^{(10)}), L' \cdot p((\mathbf{Y}_{\text{small}})^{(10)})\rangle\,.$$

Therefore, if we start with the min-entropy of the input sources $0.7\rho n$, and use Theorem 7, we get a constant $\beta_2 > 0$ such that, with probability at least $1 - 2^{-5n^2}$ over uniformly random choice of $p \in \mathcal{H}_{30n,10n}$, the following holds:

for all $X, Y \subseteq \mathbb{F}_2^n$ such that $|X| = |Y| = 2^{\rho n}$ and satisfy Eq. 3, we have

$$\Delta\Big(\langle p((\mathbf{X}_{\text{small}})^{(10)}), p((\mathbf{Y}_{\text{small}})^{(10)}), \mathbf{Y}_{\text{small}}\,;\, \mathcal{U}_1, \mathbf{Y}_{\text{small}}\Big) \leq 2^{-\beta_2 n}\,,$$

which is what we wanted.

**Case 3:** $L' = \mathbf{0}$ and $L''$ is full-rank.

**Proof of Case 3.** In this case,

$$\psi_{L',L''}(\mathbf{X}_{\text{small}}, \mathbf{Y}_{\text{small}}) = \langle p((f(\mathbf{X}_{\text{small}})^{(10)}), L'' \cdot p((g(\mathbf{Y}_{\text{small}})^{(10)})\rangle\,.$$

We consider our random sources as $f(\mathbf{X}_{\text{small}})$ and $g(\mathbf{Y}_{\text{small}})$. Let $X, Y \subseteq \mathbb{F}_2^n$, each of size $2^{\rho n}$ which satisfy Eq. 3. Using Lemma 17, we get that there exists $X'' \subseteq X_{\text{small}}$, and $Y'' \subseteq Y_{\text{small}}$, each of size at least $2^{0.1\rho n}$, such that both $f|_{X''}$ and $g|_{Y''}$ are injective.

If we replace $A$ by $f(X'')$, and $c = 10$, $d = 6n$ in Lemma 9, we get that for $X''$, the following holds:

$$\Pr_{p \leftarrow \mathcal{H}_{30n,10n}}[\dim_{\mathbb{F}_2}(p((f(X'')^{(10)})) \leq 6n] \leq 2^{-15n^2}\,.$$

Since both $|f(X_{\text{small}})|$ and $|g(Y_{\text{small}})|$ are at least $2^{0.1\rho n}$, from Remark 2, there exist a constant $\beta_3 > 0$ such that, with probability at least $1 - 2^{-4.5n^2}$ over the uniformly random choice of $p \in \mathcal{H}_{30n,10n}$, the following holds:

for all $X, Y \subseteq \mathbb{F}_2^n$ each of size $2^{\rho n}$ and $|X_{\text{small}}|$ and $|Y_{\text{small}}|$ at least $2^{0.7\rho n}$, we have

$$\Delta\Big(\langle p((f(\mathbf{X}_{\text{small}}))^{(10)}), L'' \cdot p((g(\mathbf{Y}_{\text{small}}))^{(10)})\rangle, \mathbf{Y}_{\text{small}}\,;\, \mathcal{U}_1, \mathbf{Y}_{\text{small}}\Big) \leq 2^{-\beta_3 n}\,.$$

This finishes the proof of Case 3.

**Finishing off the Proof.** Therefore, case 1 – 3, combined with XOR lemma (Lemma 5), yields that with probability at least $\geq 1-2^{-4n^2}$, over the uniformly random choice of $p$ from $\mathcal{H}_{30n,10n}$, the following holds:

$$\text{For all } X, Y \subseteq \mathbb{F}_2^n \text{ each of size } 2^{\rho n} \text{ and satisfying 1}$$
$$\Delta_1(\phi_p^m(\mathbf{X},\mathbf{Y}))|_{X_{\text{small}}\times Y_{\text{small}}};(\mathcal{U}_m,\mathcal{U}_m,\mathbf{Y}_{\text{small}})) \leq 2^{-\beta n/2}\cdot 2^m\,,$$

where $\beta'' := \min\{\beta_1,\beta_2,\beta_3\}$ and take $m=\mu'' n=\beta n/4$. This finishes the proof of our lemma. □

### 4.3 Putting It All Together: Proof of Lemma 11

Till now, we have shown that our $\text{nmExt}_p^m$ *works* with overwhelming probability, over the uniformly random choice of $p$, on disjoint partitions $\{\mathcal{P}_i\}_i$ of $X\times Y\subseteq\mathbb{F}_2^n$. That is :

$$\text{for all } i,\ \Delta(\phi_p^m(\mathbf{X},\mathbf{Y})|_{\mathcal{P}_i};\mathcal{D}_p^m(\mathbf{X},\mathbf{Y})|_{\mathcal{P}_i}) \leq 2^{-\gamma' n}\,.$$

Using Lemma 13, we will argue that for any two independent sources $\mathbf{X}$ and $\mathbf{Y}$ each having *sufficiently large* support, our non-malleable extractor still works.

*Proof of Lemma* 13 Recall the definitions of the partition of $X$ and $Y$ with respect to $f,g$ respectively.

$$\begin{aligned} X_{\text{large}} &= \{x\in X: |f^{-1}(f(x))\cap X| \geq 2^{\rho n/2}\}\,,\\ X_{\text{small}} &= \{x\in X: 0<|f^{-1}(f(x))\cap X| < 2^{\rho n/2}\}\,. \end{aligned}$$

Similarly for $Y$, we had defined the following:

$$\begin{aligned} Y_{\text{large}} &= \{y\in Y: |g^{-1}(g(y))\cap Y| \geq 2^{\rho n/2}\}\,,\\ Y_{\text{small}} &= \{y\in Y: 0<|g^{-1}(g(y))\cap Y| < 2^{\rho n/2}\}\,. \end{aligned}$$

Note that, $X = X_{\text{large}}\sqcup X_{\text{small}}$ and $Y = Y_{\text{large}}\sqcup Y_{\text{small}}$.

We consider two cases: (1) when $|X_{\text{small}}| = 2^{\Omega(n)}$, and (2) when $|X_{\text{small}}| = 2^{o(n)}$. We solve both cases one by one.

1. **Case I** $(|X_{\text{small}}|\geq 2^{\rho' n}$ **for** $\rho\geq\rho'>0)$**:** Consider the partition,

$$X\times Y = (X_{\text{large}}\times Y)\sqcup(X_{\text{small}}\times Y_{\text{large}})\sqcup(X_{\text{small}}\times Y_{\text{small}})\,.$$

Since $|X_{\text{small}}|\geq 2^{\rho' n}$ for some constant $\rho'>0$, using Remark 4, we know that there are constants $\nu,\alpha>0$ such that with probability at least $1-2^{-4n^2}$, over uniformly random choice of $p$ from $\mathcal{H}_{30n,10n}$, the following holds:

for all independent flat-$\rho n$ sources $\mathbf{X},\mathbf{Y}\sim\mathbb{F}_2^n$, with supports respectively $X$ and $Y$, and further with, $|X_{\text{small}}|\geq 2^{\rho' n}$, we have

$$\Delta(\phi_p^{\nu n}(\mathbf{X},\mathbf{Y})|_{X_{\text{small}}\times Y_{\text{large}}};\mathcal{D}_p^{\nu n}(\mathbf{X},\mathbf{Y})|_{X_{\text{small}}\times Y_{\text{large}}}) \leq 2^{-\alpha n}\,.$$

We further divide this case into two sub-cases, as follows.

(i) **Sub-case I** $\left(|X_{\text{small}} \times Y_{\text{small}}| \leq 2^{1.7\rho n}\right)$:

For a constant $\rho > 0$, we know there are constants $\beta', \mu' > 0$, from Lemma 14. Further, let $\alpha, \nu$ be the positive constants as mentioned above. Finally, consider $\mu_1 := \min\{\nu, \mu'\}$ and $m := \mu_1 n$.

Using these parameters, along with Lemma 13, we get that with probability at least $1 - 3 \cdot 2^{-4n^2}$, for all independent flat-$\rho n$ sources $\mathbf{X}, \mathbf{Y} \sim \mathbb{F}_2^n$, with support $X$ and $Y$ respectively, where $|X_{\text{small}}| \geq 2^{\rho' n}$ and $|X_{\text{small}} \times Y_{\text{small}}| \leq 2^{1.7\rho n}$, the following holds:

$$\begin{aligned}
&\Delta\left(\phi_p^m(\mathbf{X}, \mathbf{Y}), \mathcal{D}_p^m(\mathbf{X}, \mathbf{Y})\right) \\
&\leq 2^{-\beta' n} \cdot \frac{|X_{\text{large}} \times Y|}{|X \times Y|} + 2^{-\alpha n} \cdot \frac{|X_{\text{small}} \times Y_{\text{large}}|}{|X \times Y|} + \frac{|X_{\text{small}} \times Y_{\text{small}}|}{|X \times Y|} \\
&\leq 2^{-\beta' n} + 2^{-\alpha n} + 2^{-0.3\rho n} \leq 2^{-\hat{\gamma}_1 n},
\end{aligned}$$

where $\hat{\gamma}_1 := \frac{1}{2} \cdot \min\{\beta',\ \alpha,\ 0.3\rho\}$.

(ii) **Sub-case II** $\left(|X_{\text{small}} \times Y_{\text{small}}| \geq 2^{1.7\rho n}\right)$:

For a constant $\rho > 0$, we know there are positive constants $\beta'', \mu'' > 0$, from Lemma 16. Take $\mu_2 := \min\{\mu',\ \mu'',\ \nu\}$ and take $m := \mu_2 n$.

Then, with probability at least $1 - 2^{-4n^2}$ for uniformly random choice of $p$ from $\mathcal{H}_{30n,10n}$, the following holds:

For all independent flat-$\rho n$ sources $\mathbf{X}, \mathbf{Y} \sim \mathbb{F}_2^n$, with support $X$ and $Y$ respectively, where $|X_{\text{small}}| \geq 2^{\rho' n}$ and $|X_{\text{small}} \times Y_{\text{small}}| \geq 2^{1.7\rho n}$, we have

$$\Delta\left(\phi_p^m(\mathbf{X}, \mathbf{Y})|_{X_{\text{small}} \times Y_{\text{small}}}, \mathcal{D}_p^m(\mathbf{X}, \mathbf{Y})|_{X_{\text{small}} \times Y_{\text{small}}}\right) \leq 2^{-\beta'' n}.$$

Hence, with probability at least $1 - 3 \cdot 2^{-4n^2}$ we have,

$$\begin{aligned}
&\Delta\left(\phi_p^m(\mathbf{X}, \mathbf{Y}), \mathcal{D}_p^m(\mathbf{X}, \mathbf{Y})\right) \\
&\leq 2^{-\beta' n} \cdot \frac{|X_{\text{large}} \times Y|}{|X \times Y|} + 2^{-\alpha n} \cdot \frac{|X_{\text{small}} \times Y_{\text{large}}|}{|X \times Y|} + 2^{-\beta'' n} \cdot \frac{|X_{\text{small}} \times Y_{\text{small}}|}{|X \times Y|} \\
&\leq 2^{-\hat{\gamma}_2 n},
\end{aligned}$$

where $\hat{\gamma}_2 := \min\{\beta',\ \beta'',\ \alpha\}$.

2. **Case II** $\left(|X_{\text{small}}| < 2^{\lambda n}\right.$ **for all constant** $\left.\lambda > 0\right)$:
Consider the partition

$$X \times Y = \left(X_{\text{large}} \times Y\right) \sqcup \left(X_{\text{small}} \times Y\right).$$

For a constant $\rho > 0$, we know there are constants $\mu', \beta' > 0$, from Lemma 14. Therefore, with probability at least $1 - 3 \cdot 2^{-4n^2}$, over uniformly random choice of $p$ from $\mathcal{H}_{30n,10n}$, the following holds:

For independent flat-$\rho n$ sources $\mathbf{X}, \mathbf{Y} \sim \mathbb{F}_2^n$, with support $X$ and $Y$ respectively, where $|X_{\text{small}}| < 2^{\lambda n}$ for all constant $\lambda > 0$, we have

$$\begin{aligned}
&\Delta(\phi_p^m(\mathbf{X}, \mathbf{Y}), \mathcal{D}_p^m(\mathbf{X}, \mathbf{Y})) \\
&\leq 2^{-\beta' n} \cdot \frac{|X_{\text{large}} \times Y|}{|X \times Y|} + 2^{-0.5\rho n} \quad \left(\text{since } |X_{\text{small}}| \leq 2^{0.5\rho n}\right) \\
&\leq 2^{-\beta' n} + 2^{-\rho n/2} \leq 2^{-\hat{\gamma}_3 n},
\end{aligned}$$

where $\hat{\gamma}_3 := \frac{1}{2} \cdot \min\{\beta', \frac{\rho}{2}\}$.

This finishes the proof of case II.

**Finishing Off.** From our analysis above, we know that for any constant $\rho > 0$, there exist positive constants $\gamma := \min\{\hat{\gamma}_1, \hat{\gamma}_2, \hat{\gamma}_3\}$, and $\mu := \min\{\mu_1, \mu_2, \mu'\}$, such that taking $m = \mu n$, with probability at least $1 - 2^{-3n^2}$ over the uniformly random choice of $p$ from $\mathcal{H}_{30n,10n}$, the following holds:

For all independent flat-$\rho n$ sources $\mathbf{X}, \mathbf{Y} \sim \mathbb{F}_2^n$, we have

$$\begin{aligned}
&\Delta\Big((\text{nmExt}_p^m(\mathbf{X}, \mathbf{Y}), \text{nmExt}_p^m(f(\mathbf{X}), g(\mathbf{Y})), \mathbf{Y}); (\mathcal{U}_m, \text{nmExt}_p^m(f(\mathbf{X}), g(\mathbf{Y})), \mathbf{Y})\Big) \\
&\leq 2^{-\gamma n}.
\end{aligned}$$

The above statement combined with Lemma 1 yields the desired statement. □

## 5 Selecting Polynomial via Two Party Computation

We have seen that if a uniformly sample a polynomial of degree $O(n)$ and coefficients from a *small* extension of $\mathbb{F}_2$ (degree of extension $O(n)$), with high probability we have: For any constant $\rho > 0$ there are constants $\mu, \gamma > 0$ so that,

$$\text{nmExt}_p^m \text{ is a } (n, m, k, \varepsilon) \text{ strong 2 source non-malleable extractor}.$$

where when $k = \rho n$ for some constant $\rho > 0$, we have $\varepsilon \leq 2^{-\gamma n}$ and $m = \mu n$ for some appropriate constants $\mu, \gamma > 0$. And when $k = C_0 n / \log n$ for some fixed constant $C_0$, we have $\varepsilon \leq 2^{-\sigma n}$ and $m = \nu\sqrt{n}$, for constants $\nu, \sigma > 0$.

In this section we will show that even without access to uniformly random coin tosses, one can come up with a *good* polynomial via two party computation. We will define an explicit two party protocol, that outputs a low degree polynomial $p$ so that even when one of the parties are corrupted, $\text{nmExt}_p$ retains its properties. Recall the definition of $\mathcal{H}_{t,cn}$

$$\mathcal{H}_{t,un} := \{p \in \mathbb{F}_{2^{un}}[Z] : \deg(p) \leq t\}.$$

Let us start by proving a technical claim that tells that instead of choosing the polynomial uniformly if one samples it according to a distribution of min-entropy rate at least 0.9, with high probability it will be a *good* polynomial.

**Lemma 21.** *Let* $\mathbf{X}$ *be any distribution on* $\mathcal{H}_{300n,10n}$ *so that* $\frac{H_\infty(\mathbf{X})}{\log|\mathcal{H}_{300n,10n}|} \geq 0.9$ *(i.e. min entropy rate of* $\mathbf{X}$ *is at least* $0.9$*). Then:*

1. *For all constant* $\rho > 0$*, there exist constants* $\mu, \gamma > 0$ *so that the following holds.*

$$\Pr_{p\sim\mathbf{X}}\left[\begin{array}{c}\mathrm{nmExt}_p^{\mu n} \textit{ is a} \\ (n,\mu n,\rho n,2^{-\gamma n}) \textit{ strong 2-source non-malleable extractor}\end{array}\right] \geq 1-2^{-48n^2}$$

2. *There are constants* $C_0 > 0$ *and* $\nu, \sigma > 0$ *so that,*

$$\Pr_{p\sim\mathbf{X}}\left[\begin{array}{c}\mathrm{nmExt}_p^{\mu n} \textit{ is a} \\ \left(n,\nu\sqrt{n},\frac{C_0 n}{\log n},2^{-\sigma\sqrt{n}}\right) \textit{ strong 2-source non-malleable extractor}\end{array}\right] \geq 1-2^{-48n^2}.$$

Now we are ready to describe the two party protocol.

**Definition 13 (Two party protocol for selecting the polynomial).** *The protocol is as follows:*

*(i)* ***Alice:*** *Uniformly samples a polynomial* $q$ *from* $\mathcal{H}_{300n,10n}$ *and broadcasts.*
*(ii)* ***Bob:*** *Uniformly samples a polynomial* $r$ *from* $\mathcal{H}_{30n,10n}$ *and broadcasts.*
*(iii) Both of them agree on the final polynomial* $p(Z) := q(Z)+r(Z)$ *and output.*

**Lemma 22.** *Say* $\mathbf{Y}$ *is the output distribution of the protocol 13. Even if either Alice or Bob is corrupted: If for* $\rho > 0$ *we have* $\mu, \gamma > 0$ *are the constants from item (i) and* $C_0, \sigma, \nu > 0$ *are the constants from item (ii) of Theorem 9*

1.

$$\Pr_{p\sim\mathbf{X}}\left[\begin{array}{c}\mathrm{nmExt}_p^{\mu n} \textit{ is a } (n,\mu n,\rho n,2^{-\gamma n}) \textit{ strong 2-source} \\ \textit{non-malleable extractor}\end{array}\right] \geq 1-2^{-2n^2}$$

2.

$$\Pr_{p\sim\mathbf{X}}\left[\begin{array}{c}\mathrm{nmExt}_p^{\mu n} \textit{ is a } \left(n,\nu\sqrt{n},\frac{C_0 n}{\log n},2^{-\sigma\sqrt{n}}\right) \textit{ strong 2-source} \\ \textit{non-malleable extractor}\end{array}\right] \geq 1-2^{-2n^2}.$$

*Proof.* Note that from Theorem 9 and Lemma 21 it is enough to prove the item 1.

**When both of Alice and Bob are Honest,** $\mathbf{Y}$ is uniform distribution over $\mathcal{H}_{300n,10n}$. Hence, the lemma follows immediately from Theorem 9.

**When Alice is Honest and Bob is Corrupted,** Alice picks polynomial from uniform distribution over $\mathcal{H}_{300n,10n}$. We denote it as $\mathcal{U}'$. Bob picks a polynomial from some arbitrary distribution $\mathbf{X}'$ over $\mathcal{H}_{30n,10n}$. Note that $\mathcal{U}'$ can be written as $(\mathcal{U}^{(1)}, \mathcal{U}^{(2)})$ where,

- $\mathcal{U}^{(1)}$ denotes the uniform distribution from which coefficients of monomials of degree $\leq 30n+1$ is picked
- $\mathcal{U}^{(2)}$ denotes the uniform distribution from which coefficients of remaining monomials are picked.

Therefore, $\mathbf{Y} = \mathcal{U}' + \mathbf{X}' = (\mathcal{U}^{(1)}, \mathcal{U}^{(2)} + \mathbf{X}')$. As, $H_\infty(\mathcal{U}^{(1)}) \geq 270n^2$, i.e. min-entropy rate of $\mathcal{U}^{(1)}$ is at least 0.9, together Theorem 2 and Lemma 21 imply the lemma.

**When Bob is honest and Alice is corrupted.** As Alice has to start the communication, trivially the final polynomial $p$ will be $30n$-wise independent. From Remark 3 we know that if we pick $p$ uniformly from $30n$-wise independent hash family, $\mathrm{nmExt}_p^{\mu n}$ is a $(n, \mu n, \rho n, 2^{-\gamma n})$ strong 2-source non-malleable extractor with probability at least $1 - 2^{-3n^2}$. Hence, this concludes our proof. □

## References


[ACLV19] Aggarwal, D., Chung, K.-M., Lin, H.-H., Vidick, T.: A quantum-proof non-malleable extractor. In: Ishai, Y., Rijmen, V. (eds.) EUROCRYPT 2019. LNCS, vol. 11477, pp. 442–469. Springer, Cham (2019). https://doi.org/10.1007/978-3-030-17656-3_16

[ACO23] Aggarwal, D., Chung, E., Obremski, M.: Extractors: low entropy requirements colliding with non-malleability. In: Annual International Cryptology Conference, pp. 580–610. Springer (2023). https://doi.org/10.1007/978-3-031-38545-2_19

[ADKO15] Aggarwal, D., Dziembowski, S., Kazana, T., Obremski, M.: Leakage-resilient non-malleable codes. In: Theory of Cryptography Conference, TCC (2015)

[ADL14] Aggarwal, D., Dodis, Y., Lovett, S.: Non-malleable codes from additive combinatorics. In: Proceedings of the 46th annual ACM Symposium on Theory of Computing, STOC (2014)

[ADN+19] Aggarwal, D., et al.: Stronger leakage-resilient and non-malleable secret sharing schemes for general access structures. In: Boldyreva, A., Micciancio, D. (eds.) CRYPTO 2019. LNCS, vol. 11693, pp. 510–539. Springer, Cham (2019). https://doi.org/10.1007/978-3-030-26951-7_18

[AGMR24] Alrabiah, O., Goodman, J., Mosheiff, J., Ribeiro, J.: Low-degree polynomials are good extractors. arXiv preprint arXiv:2405.10297 (2024)

[AGV09] Akavia, A., Goldwasser, S., Vaikuntanathan, V.: Simultaneous hardcore bits and cryptography against memory attacks. In: Theory of Cryptography Conference, TCC (2009)

[AHL16] Aggarwal, D., Hosseini, K., Lovett, S.: Affine-malleable extractors, spectrum doubling, and application to privacy amplification. In: International Symposium on Information Theory, ISIT (2016)

[AKO+22] Aggarwal, D., Kanukurthi, B., Obbattu, S.L.B., Obremski, M., Sekar, S.: Rate one-third non-malleable codes. In: Proceedings of the 54th Annual ACM SIGACT Symposium on Theory of Computing, pp. 1364–1377 (2022)

[AO20] Aggarwal, D., and Maciej Obremski. A constant rate non-malleable code in the split-state model. In: FOCS (2020)

[AOR+22] Aggarwal, D., Obremski, M., Ribeiro, J., Simkin, M., Siniscalchi, L.: Privacy amplification with tamperable memory via nonmalleable two-source extractors. IEEE Trans. Inform. Theory **68**(8), 5475–5495 (2022)

[BADTS17] Ben-Aroya, A., Doron, D., Ta-Shma, A.: An efficient reduction from two-source to non-malleable extractors: achieving near-logarithmic min-entropy. In: Proceedings of the 49th Annual ACM SIGACT Symposium on Theory of Computing, STOC (2017)

[BCC+13] Bernstein, D.J., et al.: Factoring rsa keys from certified smart cards: Coppersmith in the wild. In: Advances in Cryptology-ASIACRYPT 2013 (2013)

[BDK08] Biham, E., Dunkelman, O., Keller, N.: A unified approach to related-key attacks. In: Fast Software Encryption: FSE 2008 (2008)

[BGLZ15] Bhowmick, A., Gabizon, A., Lê, T.H., Zuckerman, D.: Deterministic extractors for additive sources. In: Proceedings of the 2015 Conference on Innovations in Theoretical Computer Science, ITCS (2015)

[BH19] Breitnerm J., Heninger, N.: Biased nonce sense: Lattice attacks against weak ecdsa signatures in cryptocurrencies. In: Financial Cryptography and Data Security: 23rd International Conference, FC (2019)

[Blu86] Blum, M.: Independent unbiased coin flips from a correlated biased source—a finite state markov chain. Combinatorica (1986)

[Bou05] Bourgain, J.: More on the sum-product phenomenon in prime fields and its applications. Inter. J. Number Theory (2005)

[Bou07] Bourgain, J.: On the construction of affine extractors. GAFA Geometric Funct. Analy. **17**(1), 33–57 (2007)

[BS19] Badrinarayanan, S., Srinivasan, A.: Revisiting non-malleable secret sharing. In: Ishai, Y., Rijmen, V. (eds.) EUROCRYPT 2019. LNCS, vol. 11476, pp. 593–622. Springer, Cham (2019). https://doi.org/10.1007/978-3-030-17653-2_20

[BSLRZ14] Ben-Sasson, E., Lovett, S., Ron-Zewi, N.: An additive combinatorics approach relating rank to communication complexity. J. ACM **61**(4) (2014)

[CDH+00] Canetti, R., Dodis, Y., Halevi, S., Kushilevitz, E., Sahai, A.: Exposure-resilient functions and all-or-nothing transforms. In: Advances in Cryptology - EUROCRYPT (2000)

[CG88] Chor, B., Goldreich, O.: Unbiased bits from sources of weak randomness and probabilistic communication complexity. SIAM J. Comput. (1988)

[CG14] Cheraghchi, M., Guruswami, V.: Non-malleable coding against bit-wise and split-state tampering. In: Lindell, Y. (ed.) TCC 2014. LNCS, vol. 8349, pp. 440–464. Springer, Heidelberg (2014). https://doi.org/10.1007/978-3-642-54242-8_19

[CG17] Cheraghchi, M., Guruswami, V.: Non-malleable coding against bit-wise and split-state tampering. J. Cryptol. **30**(1), 191–241 (2017)

[CGGL19] Chattopadhyay, E., Goodman, J., Goyal, V., Li, X.: Extractors for adversarial sources via extremal hypergraphs. In: Proceedings of the 52nd Annual ACM SIGACT Symposium on Theory of Computing, STOC (2019)

[CGL16] Chattopadhyay, E., Goyal, V., Li, X.: Non-malleable extractors and codes, with their many tampered extensions. In: Proceedings of the 34th annual ACM Symposium on Theory of Computing, STOC (2016)

[CKOS19] Chattopadhyay, E., Kanukurthi, B., Obbattu, S.L.B., Sekar, S.: Privacy amplification from non-malleable codes. In: Hao, F., Ruj, S., Sen Gupta, S. (eds.) INDOCRYPT 2019. LNCS, vol. 11898, pp. 318–337. Springer, Cham (2019). https://doi.org/10.1007/978-3-030-35423-7_16

[CL16] Chattopadhyay, E., Li, X.: Explicit non-malleable extractors, multi-source extractors, and almost optimal privacy amplification protocols. In: FOCS (2016)

[Cle86] Cleve, R.: Limits on the security of coin flips when half the processors are faulty. In: Proceedings of the Eighteenth Annual ACM Symposium on Theory of Computing, pp. 364–369. Association for Computing Machinery, New York (1986)

[Coh17] Cohen, G.: Towards optimal two-source extractors and ramsey graphs. In: Proceedings of the 49th Annual ACM SIGACT Symposium on Theory of Computing, STOC (2017)

[CZ19] Chattopadhyay, E., Zuckerman, D.: Explicit two-source extractors and resilient functions. In: Proceedings of the 48th annual ACM Symposium on Theory of Computing, STOC (2019)

[DCLW06] Di Crescenzo, G., Lipton, R., Walfish, S.: Perfectly secure password protocols in the bounded retrieval model. In: Halevi, S., Rabin, T. (eds.) TCC 2006. LNCS, vol. 3876, pp. 225–244. Springer, Heidelberg (2006). https://doi.org/10.1007/11681878_12

[DDV10] Davì, F., Dziembowski, S., Venturi, D.: Leakage-resilient storage. In: Garay, J.A., De Prisco, R. (eds.) SCN 2010. LNCS, vol. 6280, pp. 121–137. Springer, Heidelberg (2010). https://doi.org/10.1007/978-3-642-15317-4_9

[DGW09] Dvir, Z., Gabizon, A., Wigderson, A.: Extractors and rank extractors for polynomial sources. Comput. Complex. **18**, 1–58 (2009)

[DKO13] Dziembowski, S., Kazana, T., Obremski, M.: Non-malleable codes from two-source extractors. In: Canetti, R., Garay, J.A. (eds.) CRYPTO 2013. LNCS, vol. 8043, pp. 239–257. Springer, Heidelberg (2013). https://doi.org/10.1007/978-3-642-40084-1_14

[DOPS04] Dodis, Y., Ong, S.J., Prabhakaran, M., Sahai, A.: On the (im) possibility of cryptography with imperfect randomness. In: FOCS (2004)

[DPW18] Dziembowski, S., Pietrzak, K., Wichs, D.: Non-malleable codes. J. ACM (JACM) **65**(4), 1–32 (2018)

[DSS01] Dodis, Y., Sahai, A., Smith, A.: On perfect and adaptive security in exposure-resilient cryptography. In: Pfitzmann, B. (ed.) EUROCRYPT 2001. LNCS, vol. 2045, pp. 301–324. Springer, Heidelberg (2001). https://doi.org/10.1007/3-540-44987-6_19

[Dvi12] Dvir, Z.: Extractors for varieties. Comput. Complexity **21**, 515–572 (2012)

[DW09] Dodis, Y., Wichs, D.: Non-malleable extractors and symmetric key cryptography from weak secrets. In: Proceedings of the 31st annual ACM Symposium on Theory of Computing, STOC (2009)

[Dzi06] Dziembowskim S.: Intrusion-resilience via the bounded-storage model. In: Theory of Cryptography Conference, TCC (2006)

[FKOS22] Faust, S., Krämer, J., Orlt, M., Struck, P.: On the related-key attack security of authenticated encryption schemes. In: International Conference on Security and Cryptography for Networks (2022)

[GGMT25] Gowers, W.T., Green, B., Manners, F., Tao, T.: On a conjecture of marton. Annals of Mathematics (2025). To appear

[GK18a] Goyal, V., Kumar, A.: Non-malleable secret sharing. In: Proceedings of the 50th Annual ACM SIGACT Symposium on Theory of Computing, STOC (2018)

[GK18b] Goyal, V., Kumar, A.: Non-malleable secret sharing for general access structures. In: Shacham, H., Boldyreva, A. (eds.) CRYPTO 2018. LNCS, vol. 10991, pp. 501–530. Springer, Cham (2018). https://doi.org/10.1007/978-3-319-96884-1_17

[GKK20] Garg, A., Kalai, Y.T., Khurana, D.: Low error efficient computational extractors in the CRS model. In: Canteaut, A., Ishai, Y. (eds.) EUROCRYPT 2020. LNCS, vol. 12105, pp. 373–402. Springer, Cham (2020). https://doi.org/10.1007/978-3-030-45721-1_14

[GLM+04] Gennaro, R., Lysyanskaya, A., Malkin, T., Micali, S., Rabin, T.: Algorithmic tamper-proof (atp) security: Theoretical foundations for security against hardware tampering. In: TCC (2004)

[GPR16] Goyal, V., Pandey, O., Richelson, S.: Textbook non-malleable commitments. In: Proceedings of the forty-eighth annual ACM symposium on Theory of Computing, pp. 1128–1141 (2016)

[GSZ21] Goyal, V., Srinivasan, A., Zhu, C.: Multi-source non-malleable extractors and applications. In: Canteaut, A., Standaert, F.-X. (eds.) EUROCRYPT 2021. LNCS, vol. 12697, pp. 468–497. Springer, Cham (2021). https://doi.org/10.1007/978-3-030-77886-6_16

[HDWH12] Heninger, N., Durumeric, Z., Wustrow, E., Halderman, J.A.: Mining your ps and qs: Detection of widespread weak keys in network devices. In: 21st USENIX Security Symposium (USENIX Security 12), pp. 205–220 (2012)

[KRVZ06] Kamp, J., Rao, A., Vadhan, S., Zuckerman, D.: Deterministic extractors for small-space sources. In: Proceedings of the 38th annual ACM Symposium on Theory of Computing, STOC (2006)

[Lew19] Lewko, M.: An explicit two-source extractor with min-entropy rate near. Mathematika **65**(4), 950–957 (2019)

[Li16] Li, X.: Improved two-source extractors, and affine extractors for polylogarithmic entropy. In: FOCS (2016)

[Li17] Li, X.: Improved non-malleable extractors, non-malleable codes and independent source extractors. In: Proceedings of the 49th Annual ACM SIGACT Symposium on Theory of Computing, STOC (2017)

[Li19] Li, X.: Non-malleable extractors and non-malleable codes: partially optimal constructions. In: CCC (2019)

[Li23] Li, X.: Two source extractors for asymptotically optimal entropy, and (many) more. In: 2023 IEEE 64th Annual Symposium on Foundations of Computer Science (FOCS), pp. 1271–1281. IEEE (2023)

[MW97] Maurer, U., Wolf, S.: Privacy amplification secure against active adversaries. In: Kaliski, B.S. (ed.) CRYPTO 1997. LNCS, vol. 1294, pp. 307–321. Springer, Heidelberg (1997). https://doi.org/10.1007/BFb0052244

[Rao07] Rao, A.: An exposition of bourgain's 2-source extractor. Electronic Colloquium on Computational Complexity (2007)

[Raz05] Raz, R.: Extractors with weak frandom seeds. In: Proceedings of the 37th annual ACM Symposium on Theory of Computing, STOC (2005)

[SV86] Santha, M., Vazirani, U.V.: Generating quasi-random sequences from semi-random sources. J. Comput. Syst. Sci. (1986)

[TV00] Trevisan, L., Vadhan, S.: Extracting randomness from samplable distributions. In: FOCS (2000)

[Vad12] Vadhan, S.P.: Pseudorandomness. Foundations and Trends®in Theoretical Computer Science (2012)

[Vaz86] Vazirani, U.V.: Randomness, adversaries and computation (random polynomial time). PhD thesis (1986). AAI8718194

[VN51] Von Neumann, J.: Various techniques used in connection with random digits. Applied Math Ser **12**(36-38) (1951)

[ZBS11] Zewi, N., Ben-Sasson, E.: From affine to two-source extractors via approximate duality. In: Proceedings of the 43rd annual ACM Symposium on Theory of Computing, STOC (2011)

# Author Index


**A**
Aggarwal, Divesh 679
Arpin, Sarah 221
Azevedo-Oliveira, Paco 417

**B**
Ball, Marshall 585
Bogdanov, Andrej 203
Bollauf, Maiara F. 321

**C**
Cao, Jinzheng 385
Carrier, Kevin 444
Castryck, Wouter 167
Chen, Qiyuan 3
Cheng, Qingfeng 385
Cogliati, Benoît 417
Couvreur, Alain 253

**D**
Dachman-Soled, Dana 585
Dartois, Pierrick 67
Decru, Thomas 167
den Hollander, Thomas 131
Ducas, Léo 353
Dutta, Pranjal 679

**E**
Engelberts, Lynn 353
Eriksen, Jonathan Komada 67

**F**
Feng, Yansong 3
Fouotsa, Tako Boris 67

**G**
Gärtner, Joel 514
Gay, William 651
Goubin, Louis 417

**H**
He, William 651
Herlédan Le Merdy, Arthur 67
Houben, Marc 100
Hu, Lei 33

**I**
Invernizzi, Riccardo 67

**J**
Jeudy, Corentin 477
Jiang, Haodong 385

**K**
Kleine, Sören 131
Kocurek, Nicholas 651
Kolesnikov, Vladimir 284
Kutas, Péter 167

**L**
Lau, Jun Bo 221
Laval, Abel 167
Levrat, Christophe 253
Lie, Maja 321
Ling, Cong 321
Liu, Yanyi 617
Loyer, Johanna 353
Luo, Hengyi 3

**M**
Mesnard, Antoine 221
Meyer-Hilfiger, Charles 444
Mukherjee, Saswata 679
Mula, Marzio 131

**N**
Nagargoje, Satyajeet 679
Nitaj, Abderrahmane 3

**O**
O'Donnell, Ryan 651
Obremski, Maciej 679




Y. Tauman Kalai and S. F. Kamara (Eds.): CRYPTO 2025, LNCS 16000, pp. 715–716, 2025.
https://doi.org/10.1007/978-3-032-01855-7

**P**
Pan, Yanbin 3
Pass, Rafael 617
Peceny, Stanislav 284
Perlner, Ray 221
Petit, Christophe 167

**R**
Raghuraman, Srinivasan 284
Rindal, Peter 284
Robert, Damien 67
Robinson, Angela 221
Rosen, Alon 203
Rueger, Ryan 67

**S**
Sanders, Olivier 477
Shen, Yixin 444
Slamanig, Daniel 131
Song, Jun 33
Spindler, Sebastian A. 131

**T**
Tan, Kel Zin 203
Tessaro, Stefano 548
Ti, Yan Bo 167
Tillich, Jean-Pierre 221, 444

**V**
Vasseur, Valentin 221
Vercauteren, Frederik 67
Viera, Andersson Calle 417

**W**
Wesolowski, Benjamin 67

**X**
Xu, Jun 33

**Z**
Zhu, Chenzhi 548

GPSR Compliance

*The European Union's (EU) General Product Safety Regulation (GPSR) is a set of rules that requires consumer products to be safe and our obligations to ensure this.*

*If you have any concerns about our products, you can contact us on ProductSafety@springernature.com*

In case Publisher is established outside the EU, the EU authorized representative is:

Springer Nature Customer Service Center GmbH
Europaplatz 3
69115 Heidelberg, Germany

**Batch number: 08813347**

Printed by Printforce, the Netherlands